THIRD ANNUAL EDITION

The Antique Trader

ANTIQUES & COLLECTIBLES PRICE GUIDE

Edited by Catherine Murphy

A comprehensive price guide to the entire field of
antiques and collectibles for 1987 market.

Illustrated

The Babka Publishing Co.

P.O. Box 1050

Dubuque, Iowa 52001

ISBN: 0-930625-02-1

Library of Congress Catalog Card No. 86-072010

Additional copies of this book may be ordered from:

THE BABKA PUBLISHING CO.
P.O. Box 1050
Dubuque, Iowa 52001

$11.95 plus $1.00 postage and handling.

A WORD TO THE READER

The Antique Trader has been publishing a Price Guide for sixteen years. *The Antique Trader Price Guide to Antiques and Collector's Items* has been available by subscription and on newsstands across the country, first as a semi-annual and then as a quarterly publication, and since 1984 it has been published on a bi-monthly basis.

In 1985, in response to numerous requests to combine the material of the bi-monthly issues and provide a large, complete price guide, the first edition of *The Antique Trader Antiques & Collectibles Price Guide* was issued. The book you now hold in your hands is the 1987 guide, our Third Annual Edition.

This book is the most current price listing available. We think it is also the most reliable book for dealers and collectors to turn to for realistic values of antiques and collectibles. Prices listed in this guide have not been unrealistically set at the whim of an editor who has no material at hand to substantiate the listed values. The Antique Trader Price Guide staff has always used a very methodical compilation system that is supported by experts from across the country as we select listings for the various categories. Prices are derived from antique shops, advertisements, auctions, and antique shows, and on-going records are maintained. Items are fully described and listings are carefully examined by experts who discard unreasonable exceptions to bring you the most reliable, well-illustrated and authoritative Price Guide available.

Our format enables us to maintain a wide range of both antique and collectible items in a running tabulation to which we are continually adding information and prices. Items are diligently researched and clearly described. As new avenues of collecting interest are aroused, new categories are added and if a definite market is established, this material becomes a part of the Price Guide. Country Store Collectibles, Cuspidors, DeLongpre Prints, Eye Cups, Flue Covers, Hairwood Pictures, Ice Cream Scoops, Invalid Feeders, Mother-of-Pearl Flatware, Mucha Artwork, Paisley Shawls, Penny Rugs, Salesman's Samples, Seed Boxes, Spelter Wares, Stanhopes, String Holders,

Tinder Boxes and Twelvetrees Artwork are included in the general listings for the first time. Bauer, Catalina, Jugtown and Volkmar potteries are included in the Ceramics section and Leaf Umbrella pattern and Orrefors are making an initial appearance under the heading of Glass.

Six popular areas of collecting are highlighted in well-illustrated "Special Focus" segments which provide background material and tips on collecting. Our 1987 edition focuses on ABC Plates, Carousel Animals, Jacquard Coverlets, Limoges Porcelain, Souvenir Spoons and Tramp Art and readers are certain to gain helpful information about each of these areas of collecting.

This book should be used only as a *guide* to prices and is not intended to set prices. Prices do vary from one section of the country to another and auction prices, which are incorporated into this guide, often have an even wider variation. Though prices have been double-checked and every effort has been made to assure accuracy, neither the compilers, editor or publisher can assume responsibility for any losses that might be incurred as a result of consulting this guide, or of errors, typographical or otherwise.

This guide follows an alphabetical format. All categories are listed in alphabetical order. Under the category of Ceramics, you will find all types of pottery, porcelain, earthenware china, parian and stoneware listed in alphabetical order. All types of glass, including Art, Carnival, Custard, Depression, Pattern and so on, will be found listed alphabetically under the category of Glass. A complete Index and cross-references in the text have also been provided.

We wish to express sincere appreciation to the following authorities who help in selecting material to be used in this guide: Robert T. Matthews, West Friendship, Maryland; Connie Morningstar, Salt Lake City, Utah; Cecil Munsey, Poway, California; J. Michael and Dorothy T. Pearson, Miami Beach, Florida; Bob Rau, Portland, Oregon; Jane Rosenow, Dickeyville, Wisconsin; Ruth Schinestuhl, Absecon, New Jersey and Vera Tiger, Colorado Springs, Colorado.

The authors of our *"Special Focus"* segments deserve special recognition: "ABC Plates" by Mildred Chalala, Willow Street, Pennsylvania; "Carousel Animals" by Tobin Fraley, Oakland, California; "Hawaiian Souvenir Spoons" by Dorothy T. Rainwater, Bowie, Maryland; "Jacquard Coverlets" by John W. Heisey, York, Pennsylvania; "Limoges China" by Mary Frank Gaston, Bryan, Texas and "Tramp Art" by Connie Morningstar, Salt Lake City, Utah. Their diligent research enables us to present reliable reference material to our readers.

Photographers who have contributed to this issue include: E.A. Babka, Dubuque, Iowa; Susan and Al Bagdade, Northbrook, Illinois; Stanley L. Baker, Minneapolis, Minnesota; Dorothy Beckwith, Platteville, Wisconsin; Donna Bruun, Galena, Illinois; Marie Busch, Amsterdam, New York; Carter Photographers, Tulsa, Oklahoma; Joseph P. Chalala, Willow Street, Pennsylvania; J.D. Dalessandro, Cincinnati, Ohio; Gale DePasquale, Leavenworth, Kansas; Bill Freeman, Birmingham, Alabama; Mary Frank Gaston, Bryan, Texas; Jeff Grunewald, Chicago, Illinois; Vicki Harmon, Escondido, California; William Heacock, Columbus, Ohio; Kyle Husfloen, Galena, Illinois; Robert Johnson, Oakland, California; Joan C. LeVine, New York, New York; Mariann Marks, Honesdale, Pennsylvania; Virginia Marshall, St. Louis, Missouri; Sybill McFadden, Lakewood, New York; James Measell, Berkley, Michigan; John Mebane, Mableton, Georgia; Donald Moore, Alameda, California; Gale E. Morningstar, Salt Lake City, Utah and Leslie A. Sorenson, Muskego, Wisconsin.

For other photographs, artwork, data or permission to photograph in their shops, we express sincere appreciation to the following auctioneers, galleries, shops and individuals: Neal Alford Co. Auctioneers & Appraisers, New Orleans, Louisiana; American Graniteware Association, Downers Grove, Illinois; Andover Antiques, Brimfield, Illinois; Arman's Auction Service, Woodstock, Connecticut; Jim Babcock, Madison, Wisconsin; Bellman Promotions, Inc., Washington, D.C.; Bell Tower Antique Mall, Covington, Kentucky; Blue Ribbon Antiques, Des Moines, Iowa; Richard A. Bourne Co. Inc., Hyannis, Massachusetts; Brouwer's Antiques, Cross Plains, Wisconsin; Butterfield & Butterfield, San Francisco, California; Captain's House Antiques, Keosauqua, Iowa; Diana Charles, Hagerstown, Indiana; Sharee Christians, Dubuque, Iowa; Christie's, New York, New York; Mrs. J. Ciparchia, Norwood, New Jersey; Clark's Antiques, St. Louis, Missouri; Collector's Thrift Shop, Salt Lake City, Utah; Country Antiques, Sparta, Wisconsin; Country House Antiques, Salt Lake City, Utah; D. & L. Antiques, North Berwick, Maine; The Doll Shoppe, Salt Lake City, Utah; Doyle's Auction & Appraisal Service, Fishkill, New York; Edith Dragowick, Dubuque, Iowa; Dunning's Auction Service, Inc., Elgin, Illinois; T. Emert, Cincinnati, Ohio; Frasher's Doll Auction Service, Kansas City, Missouri; Garth's Auctions, Delaware, Ohio; Glick's Antiques, Galena, Illinois; Grunewald Antiques, Hillsborough, North Carolina; Gene Harris Auction Center, Marshalltown, Iowa; 1985 International Carnival Glass Convention, Cedar Rapids, Iowa; Alice Jacob's Antiques, Bridgeport, Illinois and Jane's Antiques, Dickeyville, Wisconsin.

Also to Jeanne and Keith's Antiques, Cassville, Wisconsin; The Klinger Collection at Bix, Anamosa, Iowa; Beverly Kubesheski, Dubuque, Iowa; Lenewee Co. Antiques Show, Adrian, Michigan; Lizabeth's, San Diego, California; Ralph Losinno, Montgomery Auction Exchange, Inc., Montgomery, New York; J. Martin, Mount Orab, Ohio; Robert T. Matthews, West Friendship, Maryland; Miller Antiques, Appleton, Wisconsin; Monroe House Antiques, Anamosa, Iowa; Jerry Nichols' Wolcott House Show, Maumee, Ohio; The Nippon Room, Rexford, New York; Ricklef's Antiques, Anamosa, Iowa; Tammy Roth, East Dubuque, Illinois; Sellner Auctions, Scottsdale, Arizona; Robert W. Skinner, Inc., Bolton, Massachusetts; Sotheby's, New York, New York; Doris Spahn, East Dubuque, Illinois; Stein Collectors International, New York, New York; Sybill's Museum of Antique Dolls and Toys, Lakewood, New York; Theriault's, Anapolis, Maryland; Time Was Museum, Mendota, Illinois; Don Treadway Auction Service, Cincinnati, Ohio; Doris Virtue, Galena, Illinois; Marguerite Wade, Peoria, Arizona; Chris Walker Auctions, Potosi, Wisconsin; Wilson House Antiques, Mineral Point, Wisconsin; Woody Auction Service, Douglass, Kansas and Yankee Peddlar, Avoca, Wisconsin.

The staff of *The Antique Trader Antiques & Collectibles Price Guide* welcomes all letters from readers, especially those of constructive critique, and we make every effort to respond personally.

Catherine Murphy, Editor

ABC PLATES

by Mildred L. Chalala

Along with all children's dishes, plates made especially for children are favorites with many collectors and within this category Alphabet or ABC plates are of special interest. These plates have the complete alphabet on the face of the plate---either on the rim, a few inches from the rim, or spread around the surface of the plate---together with a transferred scene. The letters are embossed (raised) or transferred (printed) and the plates are found in soft paste, tin, glass, enamelware (graniteware) and ironstone.

Most of the potteries that manufactured the early china plates were located in the Staffordshire district of England and the earliest of these plates date back to the late 1700's but it appears that the majority were produced between 1800 and 1900. While visiting several potteries and museums in England in 1970, attempting to track down more information on ABC plates, it became apparent that these plates were considered so insignificant at the time of manufacture that few records were kept. When the potteries needed to expand, records about the plates (as far as anyone could determine) disappeared. Although a few alphabet plates still were being made by Adams, their popularity had declined.

The potteries lack of interest in their alphabet plate production is also evidenced by the fact that only a limited number of potteries bothered to mark their wares. The number of signed plates to be found is small when compared to the quantity of alphabet plates manufactured. When marked or signed plates are discovered, their value automatically increases and so does the price. The "B.P. Co." (Brownhills Pottery Co.) is one of the potteries which produced a large number of the better grade plates and many of them were marked.

It should be noted here that Geoffrey A. Godden's book, *Encyclopaedia of British Pottery and Porcelain Marks,* is an excellent source of information for identifying English marks. Besides the Brownhills Pottery Co.

mark, at least eighteen other ABC plate marks have been located in this volume.

Because of the crude manner in which some of these plates were decorated---a splash of green indicating grass or a smear of blue for sky---it seems likely that the children working in the early potteries were assigned the task of coloring the printed scenes. Most of the ABC plates were exported to America or sold at country bazaars for a pittance. While the workmanship on some plates was poorly executed, others show evidence of great attention having been paid to the subject matter, detail and coloring and one can feel the sense of pride the potter was expressing in his product.

Regardless of the workmanship, the early ABC plates are very collectible and are sought out by those who wish to have a charming wall arrangement or by collectors who have become intrigued by finding yet another completely different plate from any they have heard of or seen before.

A score of subjects has been covered on the Staffordshire plates. They portray the style of dress, the games children played and the emphasis on moral values and good behavior typical of the Victorian period. Some plates illustrate religious themes such as the history of Joseph and His Brethren, quotes from the Bible or the Lord's Prayer. The gamut runs from *Aesop's Fables* to *Robinson Crusoe;* from American Civil War Generals to foreign cities and people of foreign countries. Surely this was an excellent way to arouse a child's curiosity and desire to learn.

Verifiable information is hard to come by when researching alphabet plates. Therefore, some guesswork, some logic and even some hearsay contribute to the reasoning that the plates originally were shipped to the New England and the Middle Atlantic States and as people moved westward they took their personal belongings, including the children's ABC plates, with them. This lends credibility to the fact that collectors have found plates in practically every state of the USA.

Germany was another supplier of ABC plates, although they shipped fewer plates than England. German ABC plates are readily distinguished from the earlier Staffordshire plates because of their delicate Dresden china appearance. The alphabet is usually highlighted with gilt and most are marked "Germany" on the underside. Kittens, children and chickens often comprise the center motif.

It would be an oversight not to mention ABC plates made of tin and glass. Old tin, in general, is very popular and when a tin ABC plate is found, it is considered a prize. Information on tin ABC plates is practically non-existent. However, the subject matter on these plates does, at times, give some clues. One such example is the small "General Tom Thumb" plate. P.T. Barnum took the General to London to entertain Queen Victoria in 1844 and it is presumed this plate was made to commemorate the occasion. "Victoria and Albert," "Shakspere" (sic), "The Prince and Princess" and several others are very well made and are probably English. Other embossed tin plates, inferior in workmanship, were possibly manufactured in America and we know many of the printed tin plates were definitely American-made by the Ohio Art Company, Bryan, Ohio.

Pressed glass was America's contribution to this form of collectible plates. Glass making was one of America's first industries and glass was first pressed in this country by Deming Jarves about 1827. Glass alphabet plates date from later in the 19th century and were made by the Boston & Sandwich Glass Company of Sandwich, Massachusetts, Bryce Brothers of Pittsburgh, Pennsylvania and others. While they are fewer in number and variety, they are well designed and attractive. The Smithsonian Institution reproduced some glass ABC plates a few years ago, using a permanent mark to identify each one as a reproduction.

Whether of china, tin or glass, all ABC plates are choice collectibles.

(Editor's Note: *Mildred and Joseph Chalala have collected ABC plates for over forty years and their quest for these plates has been most rewarding in many ways. Culminating this shared adventure with the publication of a fine, well-illustrated book,* A Collector's Guide to ABC Plates, Mugs and Things, *(Pridemark Press, Lancaster, Pa.), the Chalalas now share their collection with us through the book which was designed to be helpful to both the novice collector and the dealer. Over 500 ABC plates are illustrated and all plates in the collection have been categorized by the type of decoration or scene appearing on each.)*

CERAMIC

ABC Plate

5" d., animals & alphabet multicolored transfer border, American, 20th c. (ILLUS.) $45.00

"Animated Conundrums"

5" d., conundrums (or riddles), "Animated Conundrums" (introductory plate to series of riddle plates), embossed alphabet border, unmarked Staffordshire (ILLUS.) 50.00

Staffordshire Plate

5½" d., children's activities & games, black transfer of children w/parrot & dog & verse w/polychrome enameling, embossed alphabet border, unmarked Staffordshire (ILLUS.) 28.00

Girl and Rabbit Hutch Plate

5½" d., children's activities & games, transfer scene of girl beside rabbit hutch highlighted w/polychrome enameling center, Edge Malkin & Co., 1871-1903 (ILLUS.) 55.00

Franklin Maxim Plate

5½" d., Franklin Maxim, "Constant Dropping Wears Away Stone's - And Little Strokes Fell Great Oaks," black transfer scene center highlighted w/red, orange, blue & green enameling, embossed alphabet border, George Jones, Stoke-on-Trent, 1854 (ILLUS.) 55.00

5½" d., religious theme, "Behold Him rising from the grave," etc., religious scene transfer center highlighted w/colorful enameling, embossed alphabet border, J. & G. Meakin, 1851-90 (ILLUS.) 60.00

Religious Theme Plate

5¾" d., "Flowers That Never Fade" series, multicolored transfer scene of boys & girls dancing center, embossed alphabet border, enameled edge, unmarked Staffordshire 75.00

"Robinson Crusoe" ABC Plate

5¾" d., "Robinson Crusoe" series, black transfer scene of Crusoe center, embossed alphabet border, black edge, unmarked Staffordshire (ILLUS.) 55.00

ABC Plate by J. & G. Meakin

6" d., children's activities & games, black transfer scene of girls in flower garden center, embossed alphabet border, J. & G. Meakin, 1851 (ILLUS.) 45.00

Franklin Maxim Plate

6" d., Franklin Maxim, "He That Hath A Trade Hath An Estate," green transfer scene center highlighted w/polychrome enameling, embossed alphabet border, Staffordshire, stains (ILLUS.) 50.00

Village Blacksmith Plate

6" d., occupations, "The Village Blacksmith," black transfer center, embossed alphabet border, unmarked Staffordshire (ILLUS.) 75.00

6" d., religious theme, "I Lay My Body Down To Sleep - Let Angels Guard My Head - And Through the Hours of Darkness Keep - Their Watch Around My Bed," transfer scene of child lying on bed w/angels overhead highlighted w/colorful enameling, em-

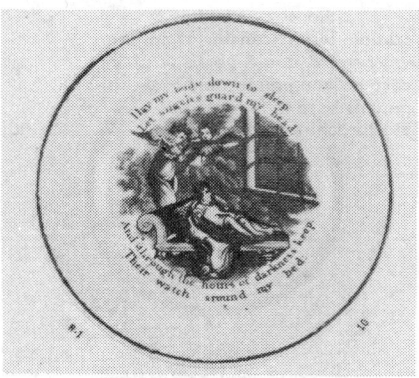

ABC Plate with Angels

bossed alphabet border, J. & G. Meakin, 1851-90 (ILLUS.) 110.00

Franklin Maxim Plate

6 1/8" d., Franklin Maxim, "If You Would Know the Value of Money - Try to Borrow Some - Creditors have Better Memories than Debtors," black transfer scene center highlighted w/polychrome enameling, embossed alphabet border, unmarked Staffordshire (ILLUS.) 110.00

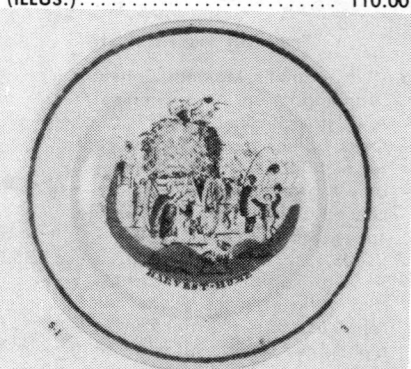

"Harvest Home" Plate

6¼" d., farm scene, "Harvest Home," black transfer scene of bringing home hay highlighted w/red, blue, green & yellow enameling, embossed alphabet border, J. & G. Meakin, 1851-90 (ILLUS.) 95.00

Franklin Maxim Plate

6¼" d., Franklin Maxim, "Not To Oversee Workmen Is To Leave Your Purse Open," black transfer scene of overseer & men working in field highlighted w/red, green, yellow & blue enameling, embossed alphabet border, unmarked Staffordshire (ILLUS.) 110.00

ABC Plate with Indian

6¼" d., Indian series, "Chinonca Watching the Departure of the Cavalcade," grey-green transfer scene center, embossed alphabet border, Chas. Allerton & Sons, 1890 (ILLUS.) 50.00

6½" d., advertising for "N. Currier - Lithographer," black transfer center, printed alphabet border, Adams, England, 1914-40 (ILLUS.) 65.00

Advertising for N. Currier

6½" d., Robinson Crusoe series, "Crusoe Milking," green transfer scene center, printed blue alphabet border 65.00

Franklin Maxim Plate

6½" d., Franklin Maxim, "For Age and Want Save While You May - No Morning Sun Lasts All the Day," pink transfer scene center, embossed alphabet border, pink edge (ILLUS.) . . . . 60.00 to 80.00

"Canary, Bullfinch & Goldfinch" Plate

6¾" d., birds, "Canary, Bullfinch & Goldfinch," black transfer of birds highlighted w/red, white, yellow & green enameling, embossed alphabet border, unmarked Staffordshire (ILLUS.) 60.00

1893 World's Fair Plate

6¾" d., famous places & buildings, "Machinery Building - World's Columbian Exposition," brown transfer scene center, embossed alphabet border, unmarked Staffordshire, ca. 1893 (ILLUS.) . . .   85.00

"The Drive"

7" d., adult activities, "The Drive," black transfer scene of couple in horse-drawn 2-wheel cart highlighted w/polychrome enameling, embossed alphabet border, unmarked Staffordshire (ILLUS.) 65.00

7" d., farm scene, girl tending chickens before barn, pink transfer scene center, embossed alphabet border 75.00

7" d., Teddy Bears at tennis, multicolored transfer scene center, printed alphabet border, American, early 20th c. 100.00

"Baseball" Plate

7" d., "American Sports - Baseball - Out at Third," black transfer, embossed alphabet border, unmarked Staffordshire, 19th c., stains & edge wear (ILLUS.) 35.00

ABC Plate from Germany

7" d., animals, rooster & hens multicolored transfer center, embossed alphabet border, Germany, early 20th c. (ILLUS.) . . .   69.00

"Playing at Lovers"

7" d., children's activities & games, "Playing at Lovers," transfer scene of boy & girl wearing adult's hats & dog looking on at center, embossed alphabet border, unmarked Staffordshire, 19th c. (ILLUS.)...................... 38.00

Nursery Rhyme Plate

7" d., nursery rhyme, "Hey Diddle Diddle" multicolored transfer scene of cow jumping over moon center, printed alphabet border, unmarked, early 20th c. (ILLUS.) .. 32.00

7" d., feeding dish type, "Baby Bunting and Little Dog Bunch," multicolored transfer print scene center, embossed alphabet border, American, 20th c. ....45.00 to 55.00

"The Fox and The Grapes"

7¼" d., Aesop's Fables, "The Fox and The Grapes," multicolored transfer scene center, printed alphabet border, B.P. Co. (Brownhills Pottery Co.), ca. 1875 (ILLUS.)...................... 55.00

7¼" d., American President, brown transfer bust portrait of George Washington center, embossed alphabet border, unmarked Staffordshire, 19th c. (crow's foot & stains) 85.00

7¼" d., hunting scene, green transfer scene of dogs & hunters at the hunt start, embossed alphabet border, unmarked Staffordshire ... 60.00

"Crusoe Rescues Friday"

7¼" d., Robinson Crusoe series, "Crusoe Rescues Friday," brown transfer scene center highlighted w/green & blue, printed alphabet border, B.P. Co., 1887-88 (ILLUS.)...................... 85.00

"A Fishing Elephant"

7¼" d., wild animals, "A Fishing Elephant," pink transfer of elephant fishing beside 2 little girls center, embossed alphabet border, Charles Allerton & Sons, 1890-1912 (ILLUS.) 85.00

7½" d., children's games & activities, blue transfer scene of boys stealing apples & climbing down wall as angry dog barks, embossed alphabet border, unmarked Staffordshire (ILLUS.)..... 62.50

Scene of Boys Stealing Apples

7½" d., clock face & numbers,
brown transfer center, printed
alphabet border, Staffordshire,
19th c. 58.00

Wild Horse Hunt Plate

7½" d., hunting scene, brown transfer scene of wild horse hunt highlighted w/multicolored enameling,
embossed alphabet border, unmarked Staffordshire, 19th c.
(ILLUS.) 67.50

"The Candle Fish"

7½" d., Indian series, "The Candle
Fish," brown transfer of Indians
(2) rowing canoe center, em-
bossed alphabet border, Charles
Allerton & Sons, ca. 1890
(ILLUS.) 55.00

"October" ABC Plate

7½" d., month series, "October,"
brown transfer of youth in classical attire crushing grapes center,
embossed alphabet border, un-
marked Staffordshire (ILLUS.) 68.00

7 5/8" d., hunting scene, black
transfer of hunting dog flushing
game bird highlighted w/poly-
chrome enameling, embossed alphabet border, Staffordshire, late
19th c. 60.00

Sign Language Plate

8" d., Deaf & Dumb sign language
type, green transfer of Mr. and
Mrs. Bunny in Easter finery center, embossed sign language alphabet border, Staffordshire, late
19th c. (ILLUS.) 135.00

ABC Plate with Hunting Scene

8" d., hunting scene, black transfer scene of horses, riders & palm trees & mountainous landscape highlighted w/polychrome enameling, embossed alphabet border, minor stains (ILLUS.) 55.00

"The Dog in the Manger"

8¼" d., Aesop's Fables, "The Dog in the Manger," blue transfer scene center, printed alphabet border, B.P. Co., ca. 1875 (ILLUS.) 85.00

"Little Strokes Fell Great Oaks"

8¼" d., Franklin Maxim, "Little Strokes Fell Great Oaks," black transfer scene highlighted w/polychrome enameling, embossed alphabet border, Staffordshire, late 19th c. (ILLUS.) 80.00

ABC Plate with Organ Grinder

8¼" d., occupations, organ grinder, transfer scene of organ grinder highlighted w/multicolored enameling, embossed alphabet border, Edge Malkin & Co., 1871 (ILLUS.) 68.00

GLASS

4" d., seated dog & numbers center, alphabet border, clear 45.00

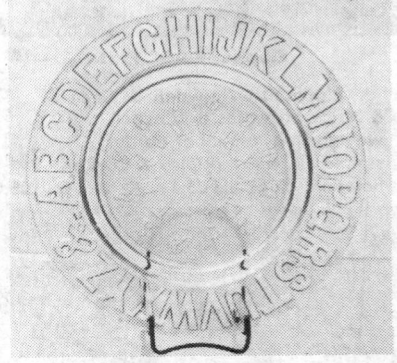

Clock Face ABC Plate

6" d., clock face center w/Arabic & Roman numerals, alphabet border, clear (ILLUS.) 40.00

6" d., deer center, alphabet border, frosted & clear 50.00

6" d., hen & chicks center, alphabet border, clear ....38.00 to 55.00

6" d., rabbit center, frosted & clear 50.00

Duck Family ABC Plate

6" d., duck & ducklings center, alphabet border, clear (ILLUS.) 45.00

Elephant ABC Plate

6" d., elephant w/howdah on back & 3 tiny Brownies in howdah waving flag, alphabet border, signed "R. & C." (Ripley & Co.) on howdah, clear (ILLUS.) 125.00

Emma ABC Plate

6" d., Emma (girl's bust) center, alphabet border, clear (ILLUS.) 50.00
6" d., Garfield bust center, alphabet border, frosted & clear ...55.00 to 110.00

Rover ABC Plate

6" d., Rover (dog) center, alphabet border, clear (ILLUS.) 50.00
6" d., starburst center, alphabet border, scalloped & beaded rim, clear 37.50
6" d., stork center, alphabet border, frosted & clear 50.00

"Christmas Eve" Plate

6¼" d., "Christmas Eve," Santa w/tree & toys descending chimney center, alphabet border, clear (ILLUS.) 165.00
6¼" d., "Christmas Morn," center scene of children w/toys, fireplace w/stockings, Christmas tree & mother & father peeking from behind door, alphabet border, frosted & clear 165.00
6¾" d., Independence Hall center, "1776-1876," clear ....75.00 to 135.00
7" d., American Eagle "Centennial - 1776 - Exhibition - 1876" center, alphabet border, clear....75.00 to 125.00
7" d., clock face center, Roman numerals & alphabet border, amethyst 75.00

Carnival Glass ABC Plate

7½" d., stork center, alphabet & numbers border, marigold Carnival glass (ILLUS.) . . . .　55.00

SILVERPLATE

5½" d., elephant "Jumbo" center, alphabet border, worn plating on brass . . . . 　65.00

6" d., "Hey Diddle Diddle" scene center, alphabet border, Wm. A. Rogers (worn finish) . . . . 　18.00

6" d., Simple Simon scene center, alphabet border, Oneida Silver Co. . . . . 　40.00

Advertising, "Underwood Patent Highchair" center, alphabet border . . . . 　35.00

TIN

"Lava" Soap Plate

4" d., plain center, embossed alphabet border . . . . 　55.00

4¼" d., Victoria & Albert embossed bust portraits center, alphabet border . . . . 　85.00

6" d., bust portrait of George Washington embossed center, alphabet border . . . . 　85.00

6" d., Jack & Jill nursery rhyme lithographed scene & verse center, printed alphabet border, marked "Lava" on inner border, advertising premium for Lava Soap (ILLUS.) . . . . 　55.00

6" d., kitten scene lithographed center, printed alphabet border, Ohio Art Co. .25.00 to 50.00

6" d., plain center, embossed alphabet border . . . . 　40.00

6" d., portrait of Admiral Dewey lithographed center, printed alphabet border . . . . 　60.00

7½" d., Cock Robin bird & verse embossed scene center, alphabet border . . . . .45.00 to 60.00

7¾" d., Peter Rabbit Radio Party lithographed scene center, printed alphabet & animals on clouds border . . . . 　125.00

8" d., "Mary Had a Little Lamb" embossed scene & verse center, alphabet border, dark patina . . . . .60.00 to 85.00

Girl on Swing ABC Plate

8½" d., Girl on Swing lithographed scene center, printed alphabet border (ILLUS.) . . . . 　45.00

9" d., Three Bears & children lithographed scene center, printed alphabet border, Germany . . . . 　35.00

(End of Special Focus)

ADVERTISING CARDS

"Lion Coffee" Trade Card

The Victorian trade card evolved from informal calling cards and hand decorated notes. From the 1850's through the 1890's, the American home was saturated with these black-and-white and chromolithographed advertising cards given away with various products.

Baby food, "Lactated Food," chromolithograph of babies (5) & toys,
8 x 5" $12.00

Baking soda, "Arm & Hammer," Bird
series, set of 30 . . . . 12.00

Bitters, "Hostetter's Bitters," 1908
presidential campaign candidates
Taft & Bryan 8.00

Cigarettes, "Hassan," Lighthouse
series, set of 50 . . . . 35.00

Cigarettes, "Murad," College series,
set of 114 . . . . 350.00

Cigarettes, "Piedmont," Rip Van
Winkle series, 8 x 5", set of 10 . . . 40.00

Cigarettes, "Sweet Caporal," Actress
series, black & white, set of 50 . . . 45.00

Cigarettes, "Tareyton," miniature
pop-up type, London scenes, 1939,
16 in original envelope 12.00

Cigarettes, "Turkish Trophies," 3
cards in triple oval frame, 1902 . . . 35.00

Cigarettes, "Wings," Airplane series, U.S. & foreign planes, set of
200 . . . . 40.00

Cocoa, "Phillips," perpetual
calendar 5.00

Coffee, "Crown Prince Coffees,"
chromolithograph of grandma &
boy 6.00

Coffee, "Lion Coffee," chromolithograph of little boy with Easter

bunny on front, Woolson Spice Co.
Manufacturers of Lion Coffee,
Toledo, Ohio reverse, 7 1/8 x
5 1/8" (ILLUS.) 6.00

Coffee, "Lion Coffee," chromolithograph of robin w/summer
greeting 4.50

Coffee, "Lion Coffee," chromolitho-
graph of birds 4.00

Coffee, various brands, assorted set
of 100 . . . . 115.00

Cologne, "Austin's Forest Flower
Cologne," chromolithograph of
girl holding bouquet 3.00

Cologne, "Hoyt's German Cologne,"
chromolithograph of boy & girl . . . 3.50

Cologne, "Hoyt's German Cologne,"
chromolithograph of boy
painting 3.00

Cologne, "Hoyt's German Cologne,"
chromolithograph of cherubs in
fountain 3.00

Cologne, "Hoyt's German Cologne,"
chromolithograph of girl holding
1889 calendar 5.00

Cologne, "Hoyt's German Cologne,"
chromolithograph of children
dancing around cologne bottle,
1892 calendar reverse 5.00

Condensed milk, "Borden's," babies
pictured, 1887 . . . . 8.00

Dry Goods & Millinery Store

Dry goods store, "T. Lilenfeld Dry
Goods & Millinery, Saginaw City,
Michigan," die-cut chromolithograph bust of little girl w/straw
hat, 6 x 4½" (ILLUS.) 4.00

Food product, "Petijohn's California
Breakfast Food," scene of children
by fireplace 7.00

Gas & electric fixtures, "Casey,"

chromolithograph of Admiral
Dewey, 8½ x 6" 10.00
Graniteware, "Granite Iron Ware,"
chromolithograph of boy & girl,
w/boy tasting food from granite-
ware stew pot 20.00
Grocery store, "A & P" (Atlantic &
Pacific), black mammy holding
white baby beside picket fence ... 15.00
Juke boxes, "Gabel's Automatic En-
tertainer," oak juke box pictured,
"America's Marvel" 8.00
Sewing machines, "Singer,"
Costumes of All Nations series,
Columbian Exposition, 1893, set of
36 .... 75.00

Shoe Polish Advertising Card

Shoe polish, "Frank Miller's Crown
Dressing," chromolithograph of
bootblack at work (ILLUS.) 7.00
Shoe polish, "Frank Miller's Crown
Dressing for Shoes," die-cut shoe
shape, 7" l.................... 10.00

Trade Card with Child

Shoes, "Famous Cash Shoe Store,"
chromolithograph bust portrait of
lovely child, 6 x 4" (ILLUS.) 3.00
Soap, "Soapine," chromolithograph
scene of girl in swing........... 3.50
Soap, various brands, assorted set
of 100 .... 110.00

Stoves, "Garland Stoves & Ranges,"
chromolithograph of baby in high
chair 6.50
Theatre, "Empire Theatre," Carrie
Finnell - the girl w/$100,000 legs
pictured, 1920's 7.00
Thread, "Clark's," No. 1892 of
National Flower series.......... 3.50
Tires, "Good Year Balloon Tires,"
mechanical-type w/tab for moving
facial expressions 10.00
World Fair, "1893 Columbian Exposition," 30,000 lb. chocolate "Ger-
mania Statue" pictured 20.00

"Anchor Brand Wringers"

Wringer, "Anchor Brand," chromolithograph of 6 girls wringing
out skirts of old style bathing
suits (ILLUS.) 8.00
Yeast, "Fleischman," set of 5 .... 42.00

ADVERTISING ITEMS

"Independence Safety Match" Blotter Set

*Thousands of objects made in various
materials, some intended as gifts with pur-
chases, others used for display or given away
for publicity, are now being collected. They
range from ash and drink trays to toys. Also
see ABC PLATES, ADVERTISING
CARDS, ALMANACS, AUTOMOBILE AC-
CESSORIES & LITERATURE, BANKS,
BASEBALL MEMORABILIA, BELLS,
BIG LITTLE BOOKS, BOOKMARKS,
BOTTLE OPENERS, BOTTLES &*

FLASKS, BREWERIANA, BUSTER BROWN, BUFFALO POTTERY, BUTTONS, CALENDAR PLATES, CAMPBELL KID COLLECTIBLES, CANS & CONTAINERS, CARNIVAL GLASS, CIGAR & TOBACCO CUTTERS, COCA-COLA ITEMS, COOKBOOKS, CORKSCREWS, DOULTON & ROYAL DOULTON CHINA, HATPINS, HUMPHREY ARTWORK, JEWEL TEA AUTUMN LEAF WARES, KEWPIE COLLECTIBLES, KITCHENWARES, KNIVES, MAGAZINES, MATCH SAFES & CONTAINERS, MUCHA ARTWORK, OLD SLEEPY EYE POTTERY, PAPER COLLECTIBLES, PAPER DOLLS, PARRISH ARTWORK, POSTCARDS, POSTERS, RADIOS & ACCESSORIES, RED WING POTTERY, SALESMAN'S SAMPLES, SCRAPBOOKS & ALBUMS, SEED BOXES, SIGNS & SIGNBOARDS, SPONGEWARE, SPOOL, DYE & ALLIED CABINETS, STRING HOLDERS, TRAYS, TWELVETREES ARTWORK, WEDGWOOD CALENDAR TILES, WORLD FAIR COLLECTIBLES, WRITING ACCESSORIES, YELLOWWARE and ZEPPELIN COLLECTIBLES.

Ash tray, "Dobbs Hats," black amethyst glass, model of a hat . . . $17.50
Ash tray, "Goodrich Silvertown Tires," rubber tire shape w/green glass insert . . . . .15.00 to 25.00
Ash tray, "Kelly-Springfield Tires," rubber tire shape w/clear glass insert 10.00
Ash tray, "Klamath Machine & Locomotive Works, Klamath Falls, Oregon," Indian head center 30.00
Ash tray, "Pepsin Tutti-Frutti Gum," tin, 4 Victorian ladies, red & beige, made in England for Case Mfg., N.Y., 8" d. 25.00
Ash tray, "Planters Peanuts," ceramic, Mr. Peanut standing by shell . . 57.50
Ash tray, "Roxo Ice Cream, Rockford, Ill.," brass 15.00
Baby's spoon w/long handle, "Gerber's," silverplate . . . . .6.00 to 12.00
Barrel label, "Sleepy Eye Milling Co. 'Chief' Flour," paper, originally glued to top of 196 lb. barrel . . . . .250.00 to 310.00
Beater jar, "Beat it for Hesselschwerdts, Kalona, Iowa," utilitarian crockery, blue stripes & lettering on grey 75.00
Bill hook, "Dorsel's Flour," celluloid, depicts product 22.00
Bill hook, "Oscar Mayer," celluloid, Oscar holding big weiner 15.00
Bill spindle, "National Cash Register Co.," brass 28.00

Blotter, "Indian Motorcycles" 25.00
Blotter, "Kellogg's Corn Flakes," girl pictured, 1907 . . . . 4.00
Blotter, "Pierce Company," roller skates, coaster wagon, dressed doll, etc., pre-1910 . . . . 5.00
Blotter, "Red Goose Shoes," w/red goose 10.00
Blotter, "Tiger Foot Tires," tiger climbing through early car tire, 1920's 9.00
Blotter, "Waterman Pens," w/1915 calendar 5.00
Blotters, "Independence Safety Match," pad of 8 blotters w/multicolored celluloid cover, 8 x 3" (ILLUS.) 8.00
Book, "Kellogg's Cereals," entitled "Funny Jungleland," 1909-32 . . . . . . 23.50
Booklet, "Ben Hur Flour," entitled "Ben Hur Dough Boys," ca. 1903 . . 6.00
Booklet, "Chase & Sanborn," entitled "The History of Our American Flag," lithography by Gray, 1898, 3 x 4", 12 pp. 8.00

"Doe-Wah-Jack" Advertising Booklet

Booklet, "Doe-Wah-Jack (Dowagiac, Michigan) Round Oak Stoves," entitled "How Christmas Came to Windsor," selling Round Oak stove to Queen Victoria, 6" h. (ILLUS.) 15.00
Booklet, "Esmond Mills," entitled "Story of Bunny Cortex," 1922 . . . . 6.00
Booklet, "Old Grist Mill Dog Bread," entitled "The Pug Family Entertains," blue & white lithography by J. Ottmann, 1899, 5 x 3", 12 pp. 8.00
Bowl, cereal, "Cream of Wheat," china, Chef Rastus & Spirit of St. Louis decor 60.00

Bowl, cereal, "Ralston Purina," blue-
glazed ceramic, embossed rabbit,
spoon & checkered cereal box,
"Find The Bottom" & "Um-Um All
Gone," dated 1925, 6" d. 40.00
Bowl, "Royal Granite Steelware,"
grey graniteware, 5" d. 35.00
Breadboard dough scraper, "Sleepy
Eye Flour" on wooden
handle ....375.00 to 450.00
Cake pan, "Swans Down," tin,
square 5.00
Cake tester, "Daniel Webster Flour,"
celluloid, in brass holder 6.00
Calendar, 1892, "Scott's Emulsion,"
child in sailor's suit surrounded by
3 St. Bernard puppies 85.00
Calendar, 1894, "Hood's Sarsaparilla," chromolithograph of little
girls 32.00
Calendar, 1895, "Slade's Spices" 21.00

"Hood's Sarsaparilla" 1900 Calendar

Calendar, 1900, "Hood's Sarsaparil-
la," die-cut of 2 little girls, full
pad w/proverbs, 6" h. (ILLUS.).... 30.00
Calendar, 1902, "Adrience Buckeye
Harvesting Machinery," photo
print "The Young Farmer," 13 x
11" 35.00
Calendar, 1903, "Cascara Quinine,"
die-cut little girl, large 22.00
Calendar, 1904, "Doe-Wah-Jack
(Dowagiac, Michigan) Round Oak
Stoves," w/Indian 290.00
Calendar, 1905, "Hood's Sarsaparilla," full pad & original envelope .. 77.50
Calendar, 1906, "Reliable Tea," fold-
out type, wheelbarrow piled high
w/violets 25.00
Calendar, 1907, "Potlittzer Fruit Co.,
Ft. Wayne," baby black girl & boy
sitting on watermelon, kissing,
entitled "Honeyed Lips" 350.00

"Hello Papa" Calendar

Calendar, 1907, "C. H. Mounton's
Drugs, Winnebago, Minnesota,"
scene of little boy on telephone,
glass pane cemented on wooden
board w/paper calendar pad, 7½
x 3¾" (ILLUS.) 15.00
Calendar, 1910, "Comfort Talcum,"
child & kitten 28.00
Calendar, 1917, "Pompeian Soap,"
Mary Pickford pictured, 7 x 28" ... 37.50
Calendar, 1918, "DeLaval Cream
Separators," girl w/horse pictured, 15 x 27" framed 135.00
Calendar, 1920, "Baldwin Locomotive Works," various models
pictured 100.00
Calendar, 1923, "Carey Bros. &
Meyer, Morris, Ill.," baby & dog,
entitled "Playmate Guardian" 20.00
Calendar, 1930, "Van Dyke Coffee,"
girl w/doll 15.00
Calendar, 1938, "Goodrich Tires,"
hunter & dog 15.00
Calendar, 1948, "Pontiac Automo-
biles," Indian scene, original
envelope 22.00
Calendar, 1951, "Royal Crown Cola,"
Loretta Young pictured, w/full
pad 40.00
Calendar, 1953, "Orange Crush" 40.00
Canister, "Redimade Hot Chocolate,"
milk white glass, 8" d., 12" h. 85.00
Catalogue holder, wall-type, "Sears
& Roebuck," metal 40.00
Cash box w/hinged lid, "Tutti Frutti
Gum" 20.00
Chart, "Arm & Hammer," entitled
"Useful Birds of America," by
M.E. Eaton, ca. 1915, 45 x 30" 140.00
Cheese keeper, "Maytag Dairy
Farms - Newton, Iowa," clear
glass 40.00

Cigar Box

Cigar box, "Standard Cigar Co.,"
book-shaped, paper-covered
wood, colorful picture & "Merry
Christmas & Happy New Year,"
1901 tax stamp (ILLUS.) 30.00
Cigarette case, "Lucky Strike
Cigarettes," celluloid, Art Deco
style 22.00
Clock, alarm-type, "Peters' Shoes,"
New Haven Clock Co. 50.00
Clock, wall regulator, "Hoffman's
Old Time Coffee - 30 cents,"
Ingraham Clock Co., Bristol,
Connecticut 1,100.00
Clock, wall regulator, "Johnson &
Burke Jewelers & Opticians,"
Waterbury Clock Co., Waterbury,
Connecticut 465.00

Wall Clock with Tobacco Advertising

Clock, wall regulator, "Jolly Tar,
Pastime, Old Honesty" & other
tobacco, pressed wood case
w/embossed advertising around
face & "Compliments of John
Finzer & Bros" about pendulum
housing, by Edward P. Baird Co.,
Plattsburg, New York & Seth
Thomas Clock Co., Thomaston,
Connecticut, ca. 1890, 31" h.
(ILLUS.) 1,695.00
Clock, wall regulator, "Sauer's Ex-
tract," oak case, New Haven
Clock Co., New Haven,
Connecticut 975.00
Clock, wall regulator, "Stronghold
Plug Tobacco," oak case, 8-day
key wind movement
w/pendulum 1,300.00
Coffee bin, "A & P," wooden, floor
model, original paint & decal..... 250.00
Coffee bin, "Woolson Spice Coffee,"
wooden floor model w/slant top,
original paint, 50-lb............. 400.00
Coloring book, "Ceresota Flour,"
1912 .... 35.00
Coloring book, "Planters Peanuts,"
w/United States Presidents -
Washington to Johnson, 1963..... 10.00
Comb, pocket-type, "Follett's
Cigars," aluminum, carpenter's
saw shape, 4" l. 10.00
Cookbook, "Sleepy Eye Flour Mills,"
shaped as a cut slice of bread,
w/portrait of Old Sleepy
Eye ....125.00 to 155.00
Cookie cutter, "Davis Baking Powder," tin, model of a cat or rabbit,
each 12.00
Cookie jar, "Borden's Dairy,"
ceramic, figural Elsie the Cow 60.00
Corkscrew, "C.D. Kenny Coffee, Tea
& Sugar," w/original guard, dated
1910 .... 20.00
Corkscrew-bottle opener combination, "Green River Whiskey,"
folding-type 18.00
Counter display, "Beechnut Gum,"
tin, diecut of girl holding pack-
age, fits into base.............. 275.00
Counter display, "Cour Vosier Cognac," bronze finish metal bust of
Napoleon, 8½" w. at base,
7" h.......................... 30.00
Counter display, "Crystal White
Soap," heavy paperboard, small
highway billboard w/latticework
bottom & large 3-dimensional box
of "Crystal White" soap w/goat on
front, ca. 1920 .... 165.00
Counter display jar, "Colcans Taffy-
Tolu," clear glass 65.00
Counter display jar, "Planters
Peanuts," blown clear glass jar

w/peanuts at corners & original
glass lid w/peanut finial 300.00

Counter display jar, "Planters
Peanuts," clear glass barrel-
shaped jar & original glass lid
w/peanut finial ....185.00 to 250.00

Counter display jar, "Planters
Peanuts," clear glass "clipper" jar
& metal lid 45.00

Counter display jar, "Planters
Peanuts," clear glass fish bowl
w/original Planters decal & glass
lid w/peanut finial large
size.....................65.00 to 100.00

Counter display jar, "Planters
Peanuts," clear glass "football" &
original glass lid w/peanut
finial........................ 165.00

Counter display jar, "Planters
Peanuts," clear glass hexagonal
jar & original glass lid w/peanut
finial, 10" h. 77.50

Counter display jar, "Planters
Peanuts," clear glass "leap year"
jar & lid, 10" h. ....50.00 to 100.00

Counter display jar, "Planters
Peanuts," clear glass octagonal
jar & original glass lid w/peanut
finial...................85.00 to 120.00

Counter display jar, "Planters
Peanuts," clear glass rectangular
jar w/red, white & blue decal &
metal lid 75.00

Counter display jar, "Planters
Peanuts," clear glass square jar
w/embossed "Peanuts" on all
sides & glass lid w/peanut finial.. 65.00

Counter display jar, "Planters
Peanuts," clear glass slant-front
"streamline" jar & metal lid 60.00

Counter display jar, "Ramon's Quality Medicine," clear glass w/blue
enameled "Little Doctor" on sides,
tin lid ....50.00 to 70.00

Counter display jar, "Squirrel Brand
Salted Peanuts," clear glass jar &
lithographed tin lid picturing
squirrel, 8½" h.................. 100.00

Crumb set, "Fuller Brush," celluloid
tray & brush, 2 pcs. 12.00

Nestle Co. Glass Cup

Cup, "Nestle Chocolate Co.," glass,
clear w/frosted world map decor,
"Nestle Co." on bottom, 3" d.,
3" h. (ILLUS.) 5.00

Dish, "Old Rose Distilling, Chicago,"
pressed glass w/embossing,
11" w. 95.00

Door push plate, "Fleischmann's
Yeast," graniteware 40.00

Door push plate, "Mayo's Cut Plug
Tobacco," graniteware, rooster,
plugs & tags, extra large size 225.00

Door push plate, "Red Rose Tea,"
graniteware 100.00

Door push plate, "Sunbeam Bread,"
tin w/picture of little Miss
Sunbeam 65.00

Door push plate, "Sweet Heart
Flour," graniteware 45.00

Doughnut cutter, "Rumford Baking
Powder," tin 7.50

Fan, "Hufnagle's Ice Cream," cardboard, color picture of little girl &
grandfather in ice cream parlor .. 30.00

Fan, "Moxie," cardboard, color portrait of Frances Pritchard, 1916 ... 55.00

Fan, "Ritz Restaurant - Paris," cardboard, color picture of men in
Harlequin costumes on ladder
chasing cat on roof 30.00

Fan, "Royal Crown Cola," cardboard,
color picture of Shirley Temple &
"Buy More War Bonds," 1940's.... 25.00

Fan, "Sleepy Eye Milling Co.," die-
cut cardboard bust portrait of
Sleepy Eye, w/tassels of wheat in
headband, advertising on back ... 150.00

"Snap," "Crackle" & "Pop" Figures

Figures, "Kellogg Cereals," plastic
figures of "Snap," "Crackle" &
"Pop," blue, red, white & yellow,
7½" h., set of 3 (ILLUS.) 27.50

Flour sack, "Blair's Certified Flour,"
cloth, w/pattern for toy stuffed
pig one side 12.50

Flour sack, "Ceresota Flour," cloth,
little boy pictured 37.50

Flour sifter, "Shaker Brand," tin,
  ca. 1885 . . . .   20.00
Flour sifter, "Wolf's Flour - Elling-
  wood, Kansas," tin 10.00
Gasoline pump top globe, "Sinclair,"
  milk white glass w/"Dino" the
  dinosaur, 1-pc. 650.00
Horseshoe, "Simmons Liver Extract,"
  iron, full size 35.00
Ice pick, "Robert Leidecker Ice &
  Coal," wooden handle 10.00
Jigsaw puzzle, "Between the Acts
  Little Cigars," lithographed paper
  on wood, entitled "Apache Indian
  Domestic Scene," in cardboard
  box 22.50
Jigsaw puzzle, "Chase & Sanborn's"
  entitled "Native Tea Pickers" 10.00
Jigsaw puzzle, "CoCo Malt," world
  map, 1932 radio premium of "Fly-
  ing Family of the Air" 20.00
Jigsaw puzzle, "Prophylactic Tooth-
  brushes," Uncle Sam, battleship,
  etc., 1908, original box, 8" sq. 70.00
Juice reamer, "Sunkist," transparent
  pink glass 40.00
Key chain, "Newark Shoes for Men
  & Women," w/chrome model of a
  shoe 10.00
Knife, "Spring Bank Cherry Phos-
  phate - Louisville, Ky.," w/cigar
  cutter & corkscrew 45.00
Lamp, "Mobilgas," wooden base,
  glass ball-shaped shade w/flying
  red horse symbol 35.00
Lapel pin, "Heinz," model of a dill
  pickle, 1939, 1" l. . . . . .5.50 to 8.00
Lapel stud, "Smith & Wesson Model
  36," silver finish metal pistol,
  screw-back type. 12.50
Lard pail, "A Merry Christmas & A
  Happy New Year, T. Kitchler
  Bros., Sandusky, Ohio," tin, red
  w/stenciled label, 2 7/8" h. 50.00
Letter opener, "Atlas Bronze Smelt-
  ing Works, Philadelphia," bronze,
  claw-shaped handle 32.50
Letter opener, "Belmont Candy,"
  bronze 18.00
Letter opener, "Detroit Stove
  Works," chrome, "Jewel Stoves" . .   24.00
Letter opener, "Sleepy Eye Milling
  Co.," bronze, Indian head on
  handle . . . . .875.00 to 950.00
Mannikin, "Hanes Pajamas," compo-
  sition, "Merrichild" wearing sleep-
  ers, dog on base, 21" h. 125.00
Marbles, "Planters Peanuts," 14
  agate glass marbles in original
  cloth bag w/Mr. Peanut
  emblem 35.00
Match holder, table model, "Dutch
  Boy Paint," chalkware, figural
  Dutch boy 110.00

Match holder, wall-type, "Diamond
  Match Co.," tin 20.00
Match holder, wall-type, "Juicy Fruit
  Gum," tin 45.00
Match holder, wall-type, "RMS
  Olympic White Star Line," tin 20.00
Match safe, pocket-type, "DeWars -
  The Whiskey of His Forefathers,"
  embossed metal 60.00
Measuring cup, "Calumet Baking
  Powder," tin, 2-cup 12.50
Measuring cup, "Planters Peanuts,"
  tin, 2 5/8" h.   40.00
Measuring cup, "Rumford Baking
  Powder," tin, 1-cup. 15.00
Measuring spoon, "Dr. Price's Bak-
  ing Powder," tin 8.00

"Planters Peanuts" Measuring Spoon

Measuring spoon, "Planters
  Peanuts," red plastic, ½ teaspoon
  to 1 tablespoon, 4" l. (ILLUS.) 8.50
Mechanical pencil, "Ford," "V6" &
  "V8" emblems on side 12.00
Menu-chalkboard, "Dixi-Cola," tin,
  vivid colors, 17½ x 26½" 50.00
Menu holder, "Tasty Ice Cream,"
  celluloid. 18.00
Mirror, hand-type, "Angelus Marsh-
  mallows," 2 cherubs, "Mirror Free
  with Angelus Marshmallows or
  send three 2c Stamps" 45.00
Mirror, hand-type, "Black Hawk
  Bank, Waterloo" 15.00
Mirror, pocket-type, "Aetna Insur-
  ance," 3½" d. 15.00
Mirror, pocket-type, "Alpha Flour,"
  celluloid, pretty girl, oval 35.00
Mirror, pocket-type, "Angelus
  Marshmallows," single cherub on
  green ground, oval . . . . .30.00 to 40.00
Mirror, pocket-type, "Angelus
  Marshmallows," 2 cherubs 60.00
Mirror, pocket-type, "Berry Brothers
  Toy Wagon," 4 children, wagon &
  dog, Whitehead & Hoag, 2"d 120.00
Mirror, pocket-type, "Big Jo
  Flour" 25.00
Mirror, pocket-type, "Colby's Cloth-
  ing House, Taunton, Maine,"
  1876 . . . .   35.00
Mirror, pocket-type, "Compliments
  of Indianapolis WK (Willys Knight)
  Dealers" 50.00
Mirror, pocket-type, "Copper Clad
  Ranges" 19.00

Advertising Pocket Mirror

Mirror, pocket-type, "Garland
   Stoves & Ranges," factory scene,
   early 20th c. (ILLUS.) 35.00
Mirror, pocket-type, "Hires Root
   Beer," w/Hires Kid 50.00
Mirror, pocket-type, "Hoffmann
   Whiskey - The Barkeeper's
   Friend," celluloid, full figure
   nude 225.00
Mirror, pocket-type, "Old Reliable
   Coffee," Dutch man & boats by
   sea ....30.00 to 45.00
Mirror, pocket-type, "Red Cross
   Stoves"........................ 25.00
Mirror, pocket-type, "Worth Hats,"
   nude baby wearing large hat..... 40.00
Money clip, "Hudson Auto Sales-
   man's Award," metal 35.00
Muffin pan, "George Urban Milling
   Co.," tin, 6-cup 15.00

"Doe-Wah-Jack" Mug

Mug, "Doe-Wah-Jack (Dowagiac,
   Michigan) Round Oak Stoves,"
   china, full figure Indian portrait
   on deep green shaded to ochre,
   "The estate of P.D. Beckwith,
   Dowagiac, Mich." on base
   (ILLUS.)...................... 165.00
Napkin ring, "Garland Stoves,"
   metal 21.50
Note pad, "Angostura Bitters,"
   celluloid...................... 25.00
Note pad, "Atlantic Refining Co.,"
   celluloid, 1904 .... 45.00
Pail, "Anchor Brand Peanut Butter,"
   wooden, stave construction,
   stenciled label, varnish
   finish, 6" h.................... 55.00

"Doe-Wah-Jack" Stoves

Pamphlet, "Doe-Wah-Jack (Dowagi-
   ac, Michigan) Round Oak Stoves,"
   entitled "Signals," illustrations of
   Indians (ILLUS.) 55.00
Pamphlet, "Pillsbury's Best," entitled
   "Nations of the Earth," chro-
   molithograph of Uncle Sam by
   Forbes, 6 x 3½" 8.00
Paper clip, "Ghirardelli Chocolates,"
   celluloid...................... 15.00
Paperweight, "Brookville Glove Co.,
   Brookville, Pa.," glass sulphide
   w/glove 40.00
Paperweight, "Fairbanks Scales,"
   nickel-plated brass, model of a
   scale pan on base, "1830-1930" ... 35.00
Paperweight, "Kool Cigarettes,"
   "snow-type," penguin inside...... 40.00
Paperweight, "Morgan Casket Co.,"
   metal, model of a crouching lion,
   6 x 3"........................ 35.00
Paste jar w/lid & bail handle, "Sanford Ink," stoneware pottery 210.00
Pencil clip, "Morton's Salt" 4.50
Pencil clip, "Pontiac Big Six" 17.50

Pencil Sharpener with Advertising

Pencil sharpener, pocket-type,
   "Felix F. Daus Duplicator Co.,"
   celluloid cover, abrasive backside,
   "Whitehead & Hoag Co.," 2¼" d.
   (ILLUS.)........................ 15.00

Perfume bottle, "Lydia E. Pinkham,"
silver finish metal purse-type
flask, embossed "L.E.P." one side
& 3 remedies reverse 55.00

Picture, "Illinois Watch Co.," chromolithograph on canvas, bust portrait of Abraham Lincoln
w/company logo & "The Lincoln
Watch" in lower right corner,
framed, 10 x 7" . . . . 150.00 to 165.00

Pinback button, "Buster Brown
Bread," 1¼" d. 16.00

Pinback button, "Dead Shot Gun
Powder" 45.00

Pinback button, "Deering Harves-
tor," horse pulling thresher,
1 1/8" d. 30.00

Pinback button, "Dr. Le Gear Stock
Remedies," horse, 1¼" d. 10.00

Pinback button, "Flexible Flyer
Sleds," w/Charles Lindbergh 25.00

Pinback button, "Nabisco,"
w/"Uneeda Biscuit" boy in yellow
slicker, 1¼" d. 10.00

Pitcher, "H.N. Oshea, General Mer-
chandise, Graettinger, Iowa,"
utilitarian crockery, Cherry Band
patt., blue & grey 125.00

Plate, "Baker's Chocolate," china,
175th anniversary, 1941, Vernon
Kilns 28.50

Plate, "Waltham Watch Factory,"
china, blue transfer factory scene
on white, Wedgwood, England,
1904, 5¼" d. 40.00

"Munsingwear" Playing Cards

Playing cards, "Munsingwear," original 2-pc. cardboard slipcase
(ILLUS.) 20.00

Pot scraper, "Henkel's Flour" 60.00

Print, "Atlantic & Pacific (A & P)
Stores," chromolithograph scene
of child carrying straw hat filled
w/eggs, 12 x 28" 150.00

Print, "Cream of Wheat," entitled
"Where the Mail Goes, Cream of
Wheat Goes," after Wyeth, 1907,
10 x 15" 35.00

Print, "Woolson Spice," entitled
"Five O'Clock Tea," scene of pup-

pies, kittens, chicks & ducklings
eating on farmhouse steps, by
Trood, dated 1902, original frame,
10 x 18" 50.00

Prints, "Hercules Powder Co.,"
depicting: young man leaving for
war in 1917; sending home German soldiers in 1918; happy return of 1919; all framed under
glass, set of 3 . . . . 395.00

Printer's measure, "Philadelphia
Bulletin," brass, agate & inch
measurements, "In Philadelphia,
Everybody Reads the Bulletin,"
6" l. 22.00

Razor blade holder, "Gem," metal,
"Avoid 5 O'Clock Shadow," man
w/stubble 20.00

Recipe file box, "Gold Medal Flour,"
oak . . . . 16.00 to 22.50

Recipe file box, "Sperry Flour Co.,"
oak w/dovetail construction,
w/Sperry recipes, set 55.00

Record album, "Victor Talking
Machine Co.," hard cover
w/Nipper emblem on front,
1918, w/ten records 40.00

Ruler, "Tums - Nature's Remedy" &
Dallas druggist, wooden, 12" l. . . .   5.50

Seed box, "Rice's Seeds," wooden,
dovetail construction, sweet child
on label 48.00

Shaving mug, "Golden Knight Soap,"
glass 23.50

Shipping crate, "Mason's Shoe Blacking," wooden, dovetail construction, colorful inside label,
stenciled "Challenge Blacking,
Original & Genuine, Mfg. by
Mason, 138 N. Front St., Phila.,"
ca. 1880 . . . .   60.00

Shoe horn, "Sears & Roebuck,"
metal 8.00

Skillet, "Ballard Pancake Flour,
Louisville," cast iron, embossed
flour box 65.00

"Buckeye Root Beer" Dispensers

Soda fountain syrup dispenser, "Buckeye Root Beer," china, brown or tan-glazed log, each (ILLUS. of pr.)...........550.00 to 750.00

Soda fountain syrup dispenser, "Liberty Root Beer," 13½" h.................400.00 to 500.00

String holder, "Compliments of Van Vleet Co., Memphis," glass, patented 1874................... 45.00

String holder, "SSS For The Blood," cast iron, original gold paint, w/closure 115.00

Sugar sack, "C & H," cloth, 10-lb. 5.00

Sugar sack, "Domino," cloth, 10-lb. 5.00

Table, child's, "Calumet," granite-ware top w/ABC's & Calumet Kid, wooden apron & legs 150.00

Tablespoon, "Banner Buggies," silverplate, etched buggy in bowl ... 25.00

Tape measure, "Allied Mills, Wayne Feeds," enameled metal egg w/chick's head as pull 15.00

Tape measure, "Cawston Ostrich Farm, South Pasadena, Calif.," ostrich & child each side 18.50

Tape measure, "Stromberg Carburetors," celluloid, 1919.......... 20.00

Teaspoon, "Doe-Wah-Jack Round Oak Stoves," silverplate, figural Indian handle, stove in bowl...................75.00 to 100.00

Thermometer, "Arbuckles Coffee," tin, depicts package 175.00

Thermometer, "Carter's Ink," graniteware, black & white w/red lettering, 27 x 7".........75.00 to 100.00

Thermometer, "Dr. Pepper," tin w/round glass dial, "Serve Hot or Cold," 16 x 6½" 35.00

Thermometer, "Fatima Cigarettes," graniteware, w/veiled lady ....120.00 to 165.00

Thermometer, "Monarch Paint," graniteware, hand w/paint brush on orange ground 95.00

Thermometer, "None Such New England Mince Meat Pie," pie-shaped, "Like Mother Used to Make," dated 1888 .... 145.00

Thermometer, "Prestone Anti-Freeze," graniteware, "You're Set, Safe, Sure" 45.00

Thermometer, "Stethenson Union Suits," graniteware, man in long johns & another holding up a shirt, 1916 .... 245.00

Thimble, "Daniel Webster Flour," metal 4.00

Thimble, "DeLaval Cream Separators," aluminum, w/logo & "Save $10 a Cow each year" 6.00

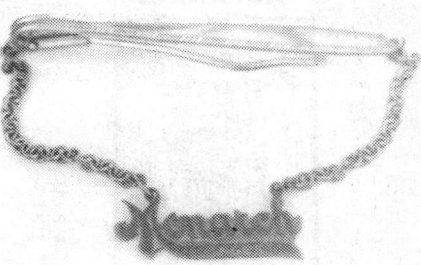

"Monarch Ranges" Tie Bar

Tie bar, "Monarch Ranges," brass, w/chain & emblem (ILLUS.)....... 12.50

Tie clip, "Lima Steam Shovel" 20.00

Tire pressure gauge, "Ajax Tires," brass 8.00

Token, "Palmolive Soap"........... 5.00

Toy car, "Ford," 1964 Mustang 2-door hardtop model 50.00

Toy car, "Ford," 1965 Fairlane model....................... 35.00

Toy clicker, "Buster Brown Shoes," tin, shoe-shaped 14.00

Toy clicker, "Butternut Bread," tin 5.00

Toy clicker, "Endicott Johnson Shoes," tin 6.00

"Weatherbird Shoes" Toy Clicker

Toy clicker, "Weatherbird Shoes," tin, rooster weathervane, red, yellow & black, 2" l. (ILLUS.) 6.00

Toy doll, "Ceresota Flour," uncut cloth boy................70.00 to 110.00

Toy doll, "Old Dutch Cleanser," composition head w/googlie eyes, cloth body, original wooden shoes 75.00

Toy figure, "Cracker Jack," die-cut tin Herbie, stand-up type 10.00

Toy top, "Pluto Water," spinning-type, celluloid 22.50

Toy whistle, "Endicott Johnson Children's Shoes," tin, airplane-shaped, early 1930's 55.00

Trade card, "American Can Co.," tin 65.00

Whet stone, "Lily White Flour"...... 4.50

Yardstick, "Glenwood Ranges," wooden 9.00

ALMANACS

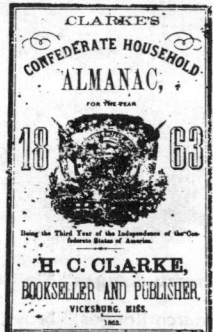

Clarke's Confederate Household Almanac

Almanacs have been published for decades. Commonplace ones are available at $4 to $12; those representing early printings or scarce ones are higher.

Ayer's American Almanac, 1895	$7.00
Ayer's American Almanac, 1902, 1905 or 1907, each	1.50
Burdock Blood Bitters Almanacs, 1890 through 1899, children pictured on covers, set of 8	115.00
DeLaval Almanac, 1948	18.00
Dr. Kilmer's Swamp Root Almanac, 1934 or 1936, each	3.00
Farmer's Almanack, 1828, Robert B. Thomas, 26 pp.	10.00
G.G. Green Almanac of 1890, illustrated by Palmer Cox, 9 x 7"	22.00
The Herbalist Almanac, 1947, Indian pictured on cover	4.00
Hostetter's United States Almanac, 1851	6.00
Hostetter's United States Almanac, 1871	8.00
Mandrake Bitters Almanac, 1885....	15.00
North American Almanac, 1931	5.00
Peruna Almanac, 1912	10.00
Peter Rabbit's Almanac for 1929, illustrated by Beatrix Potter	60.00
Pittsburgh Steel Co. Almanac, 1912	10.00
Rawleigh's Almanac, 1936	15.00
Veedol Almanac, 1926-27, 32 pp. ...	6.50
Vinegar Bitters Almanac, 1874, 48 pp.	11.50

ART DECO

Interest in Art Deco, a name given an art movement stemming from the Paris International Exhibition of 1925, is at an all-time high and continues to grow. This style flowered in the 1930's and actually continued into the 1940's. A mood of flippancy is found in its varied characteristics–zigzag lines resembling the lightning bolt, sometimes steppes, often the use of sharply contrasting colors such as black and white and others. Look for Art Deco prices to continue to rise. Also see BEADED & MESH BAGS, BOOKENDS, CAT COLLECTIBLES, CIGAR & CIGARETTE CASES & LIGHTERS, FURNITURE, GOUDA POTTERY and NORITAKE CHINA.

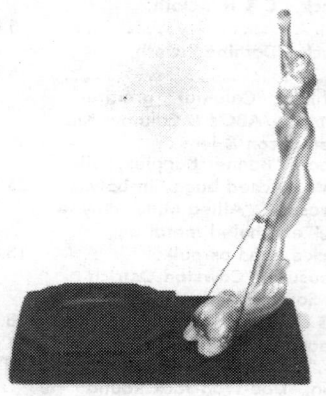

Art Deco Ash Tray

Ash tray, ceramic, club-shaped, black Ace of Clubs decor on orange ground, 2¾" w..........	$18.00
Ash tray, white metal, pearlized figure of nude riding dolphins on black finish base, 8¼ x 4½" base, 9½" h. (ILLUS.)	50.00
Box, cov., black enamel on brass, w/green celluloid lid, 7½" l.	35.00

Bottle Corker

Bottle stopper, porcelain man's head w/tall top hat on cork, impressed "Germany 6327," 4" l. (ILLUS.) 40.00

Art Deco Bracelet by Georg Jensen

Bracelet, sterling silver, raised designs, marked "925.S Georg Jensen Denmark," in original box
(ILLUS.)........................ 325.00

Art Deco Bridge Set

Bridge set: "Congress" playing
cards, score card & tally cards;
profile designs in black, silver &
red, set (ILLUS.) 30.00
Calling card tray, bronze w/inlaid
sterling silver birds decor 45.00
Clock, blue mirrored glass round
face w/chrome balls indicating
hours 55.00
Cocktail shaker, silverplate, penguin
form, "Napier," 13" h........... 450.00
Cordial set, chrome tray & 6 cordials
w/multicolored glass bowls on
chrome stems, 7 pcs. 85.00
Desk set: 4¼" w. pyramid-shaped
inkwell w/hinged lid & milk glass
insert, letter rack, rocker blotter,
tray & sponge holder; silverplate
& brass, signed Bradley & Hubbard, 5 pcs. 95.00
Dresser dish, cov., porcelain, figural
Art Deco lady in short blue skirt &
clown-type blue hat w/yellow
trim, 3 5/8" d., 9½" h. 170.00
Dresser set: brush, hand mirror &
comb; Art Deco style w/mono-
gram, "Webster," 3 pcs. 101.00
Dresser set: 11¾" l. sterling silver
hand mirror & cut glass hair
receiver & powder box w/sterling
silver lids; engraved florals &

leaves on 10-sided bases, mono-
grams on silver lids, 3 pcs........ 175.00
Dresser set: hand mirror, comb, hair
brush & clothes brush; bakelite &
sterling silver, 4 pcs. 125.00
Flask w/hinged cap, nickel silver,
vertical lines decor, curving body,
4" w., 6½" h.................... 38.00
Hair comb, sterling silver 14.00
Lamp, bronze figure of harlequin,
on marble base, holding millefiori
glass globe, overall 8½" h. 375.00
Lamp, frosted green glass figure of
semi-nude woman on rock holding
a white torch 125.00
Perfume bottle, amber glass w/cel-
luloid stopper 30.00
Pin, Bakelite, butterscotch-colored
horse's head w/inset glass eyes &
overlaid metal bridle straps 85.00
Pin, sterling silver, running gazelle
silhouette within foliate
framework 32.00
Pin, tortoise shell, heart-shaped
w/palm trees decor ....:. 35.00
Powder box, cov., green opaque
glass, triangular, 7 x 4½"........ 45.00
Powder box & cover w/flapper head
finial, frosted green glass, Art
Deco nude females on sides...... 35.00
Powder box, cov., pink alabaster
w/ornate brass finial & filigree
trim, figural brass birds w/ivory
beaks form feet................. 135.00

Art Deco Powder Jar

Powder jar, cov., china, figural Art
Deco lady w/comb in hair, 6¾" h.
(ILLUS.)....................... 37.50
Powder jar w/pierced metal cover,
figural hourglass shape w/sundial
top inscribed "My Face Marks the
Sunny Hours" 40.00
Ring, sterling silver, Medussa head
w/hair of writhing snakes 65.00
Telephone dialer, black Bakelite
w/sterling silver trim 18.00

Tumblers, footed, orange & black
glass w/sterling silver overlay,
set of 6 .... 90.00
Vanity purse, chrome w/red
enameling & chain handle,
"Elgin," 55.00

Triple Bud Vase

Vase, ceramic, triple flower holder
w/Art Deco dancing couple
center, ivory vases, black &
orange clothing on figures,
marked Germany, 5" h.
(ILLUS.)....................... 32.00
Vase, mercury glass, paneled ball
shape, mint green, 5½ x 6" 55.00
Vase, art pottery, cream w/yellow
band & enameled typical abstract
flowers, black vertical lines &
dots, signed "Boch Freres,"
9½" h. 58.00
Vase, enameled copper, bullet-
shaped, raised enamel florals in
pink, mauve, turquoise, lime
green & gold on bright magenta
ground, signed "C. Faure',
Limoges, France," 5" w.,
10" h. 3,900.00

Art Deco Vase

Vase, enameled copper, swollen
cylinder w/stepped neck, geometric design of enameled cream triangles alternating w/copper
triangles, by Sarlandie, ca. 1930,
11" h. (ILLUS.) 1,045.00
Whiskey flask, pocket-type, sterling
silver, engine-turned Art Deco
designs, International Silver Co.,
half-pint....................... 155.00

ART NOUVEAU

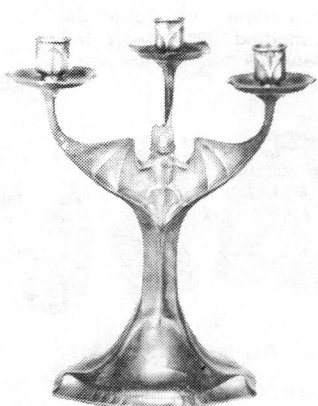

Candelabrum by Kayserzinn

Art Nouveau's primary thrust was between
1890 and 1905 but commercial Art Nouveau
productions continued until about World War
I. This style was a rebellion against historic
tradition in art. Using natural forms as inspi-
ration, it is primarily characterized by undulating or wave-like lines. Many objects
were made in materials ranging from glass
to metals. While interest in Art Nouveau still
remains high, especially for jewelry in the
Nouveau taste, prices appear to be leveling
off. Also see CIGAR & CIGARETTE
CASES, FURNITURE, GOUDA & MET-
TLACH POTTERY, METALS, MUCHA
ARTWORK, NORITAKE CHINA, ROZEN-
BURG DEN HAAG and TEPLITZ
POTTERY.

Bowl, copper, enameled flower-form
& branch handles, signed
"Nekrasoff".................... $65.00
Bowl, sterling silver, undulating
fuchsias in relief, 9½" d. 385.00
Candelabra, 3-light, pewter, shaped
triangular base w/leaves in low
relief, paneled standard continuing to bat-forms w/extended

wings supporting shaped candle cups & drip pans cast w/vines, "Kayserzinn," Germany, ca. 1900, 12" h., pr. (ILLUS. of one) 3,025.00

Cigarette box w/hinged lid, copper, low relief profile of woman's head blowing smoke in cloud formation framed w/leaves & vine, 5 x 4¼", 2½" h. 50.00

Cigarette box w/hinged lid, sterling silver, cover inset w/enameled panel of harem interior & w/border of cabochon stones, Tiffany & Co., New York, 8" l. 880.00

Clothes brush, silverplate, Art Nouveau lady in relief 25.00

Cuff links, sterling silver, Art Nouveau lady's head, pr. 20.00

Desk set: desk box w/calendar, caddy & 10" l. ink stand w/double wells; mottled silver finish, signed "Silvercrest Sterling on Bronze," 3 pcs. 155.00

Dish, silverplate, large florals in relief, Derby Silver Co. 35.00

Dish, sterling silver, Art Nouveau lady's face, berries & leaves in relief interior, 4½" d. 145.00

Dog whistle, sterling silver, bust of Art Nouveau lady 125.00

Dresser set, silverplate, Art Nouveau woman's face in relief, Derby Silver Co., 11 pcs. 450.00

Figure of an Art Nouveau woman wearing long clinging gown & chignon hair-style, playing "Blind Man's Buff," bronze, rectangular base, signed "Burger," 5¼" h. . . . 375.00

Figure of a boy, bronze, signed "E. Illiand," ca. 1890, 14" h. 250.00

Fireplace Fender

Fireplace fender, patinated copper, cast w/iris blossoms & twisting leafage & supporting 2 shaped shelves, possibly England, ca. 1905, 51" w., 29½" h. (ILLUS.) . . . 1,705.00

Gravy boat on attached leaf-shaped tray, pewter, stem-form handle w/locust, "Kayserzinn," 9¾" l. . . . 60.00

Hair brush, silverplate, Art Nouveau lady on handle 35.00

Hair crimper, sterling silver hollow handle embossed w/Art Nouveau lady's head & flowers on each side, 7½" l. 75.00

Hair receiver, silverplate, Art Nouveau lady in relief on cover . . 45.00

Inkwell w/pen holder, bronze, bust of Art Nouveau lady w/flowing hair, signed & dated 1904 . . . . 285.00

Knife, pocket-type, brass, 2-blade w/corkscrew, embossed scene of figures drinking one side & nude lady & grapes opposite, marked "Gostahl" 55.00

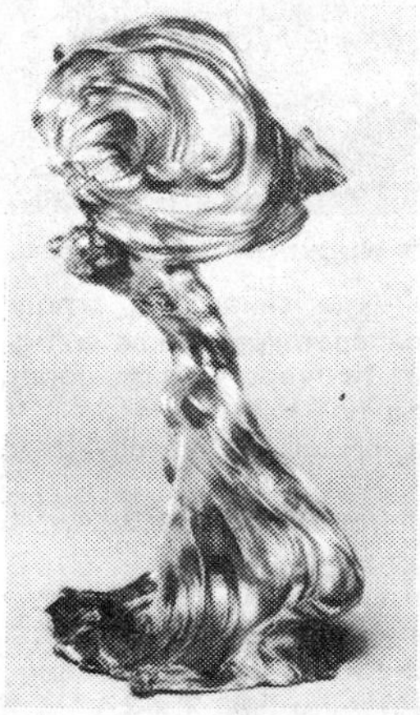

Loie Fuller Lamp after Raoul Larche

Lamp, gilt-bronze, figure of Loie Fuller, her dress swirling about her body, tossing her veils up overhead to conceal the light bulbs, signed "Raoul Larche" & numbered, Paris, France, ca. 1900, 13" h. (ILLUS.) 6,600.00

Locket, brass, embossed head of lovely Art Nouveau lady, florals, etc., scrolling top & bottom, 1 5/8" d. locket w/woven chain . . 65.00

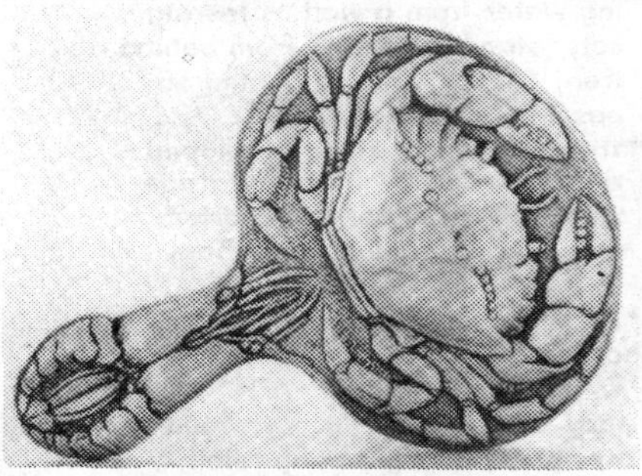

Art Nouveau Hand Mirror

Mirror, hand-type, sterling silver, "repousse" crab on back & twin lobsters on handle, overall 9" l. (ILLUS.) 605.00

Art Nouveau Wall Mirror

Mirror, wall-type, silverplate, ornate
   curvilinear openwork frame w/fig-
   ure of Art Nouveau woman standing to one side below orchid,
   unsigned, probably Germany,
   ca. 1910, 24" h. (ILLUS.) 2,860.00
Nail file, silverplate handle w/Art
   Nouveau lady in relief 15.00
Pendant, brass, full figure Art
   Nouveau lady w/butterfly wings,
   set w/ruby red beads, connecting
   to chain at wing tips, 2 x 2½"
   pendant 60.00
Pin tray, brass, cast w/Art Nouveau
   maiden w/flaring skirt, 7 x 6" 58.00
Pitcher, water, sterling silver, scroll
   handle, lobed lower section
   chased & "repousse" w/nude female astride dolphin clutching a
   bow-knotted laurel garland in outstretched right arm, Tiffany & Co.,
   New York, 19th c., 8" h. 1,760.00
Plaque, bronze, cast w/full figure
   nude female w/flowing hair drawing water from a well as leering
   satyr stands watching from behind
   tree, 4 x 2½", now mounted on
   easel-type wooden frame 225.00
Platter, parcel-gilt silver, scalloped
   rim embossed & chased w/grape-
   vine, reeded edge, gilt interior
   engraved w/monogram, Tiffany
   & Co., New York, ca. 1890,
   17 3/8" oval...................1,210.00
Shoe horn, sterling silver handle
   w/full figure nude
   lady ....60.00 to 75.00
Vase, bronze, w/gilt deep releif
   maiden's head & hand amidst
   floral arrangement on front & gilt
   florals reverse, signed "C.H. Kor-
   schann, Paris," flaring 6" w. base,
   3½" h. 400.00

Mephistopheles Vase

Vase, ceramic, face of
   Mephistopheles in full relief,
   green lustre glaze, signed "R.
   Leon Jeffery," 8" h. (ILLUS.) 80.00
Vase, sterling silver, elongated inverted pear shape, wavy rim,
   body & foot embossed & chased
   w/poppies & undulating tendrils,
   George W. Shiebler & Co., New
   York, retailed by Dowell & Hubbard Co., ca. 1900, 20" h. 1,980.00

AUDUBON PRINTS

Brasilian Caracara Eagle

*John James Audubon, American ornithol-
ogist and artist, is considered the finest nature artist in history. About 1820 he conceived the idea of having a full color book published portraying every known species of*

American bird in its natural habitat. He spent years in the wilderness capturing the beauty in vivid color only to have great difficulty finding a publisher. In 1826 he visited England, received immediate acclaim, and selected Robert Havell as his engraver. "Birds of America," when completed, consisted of four volumes of 435 individual plates, double-elephant folio size, which are a combination of aquatint, etching and line engraving. W.H. Lizars of Edinburgh engraved the first ten plates of this four volume series. These were later retouched by Havell who produced the complete set between 1827 and early 1839. In the early 1840's, another definitive work, "Viviparous Quadrupeds of North America," containing 150 plates, was published in America. Prices for Audubon's original double-elephant folio size prints are very high and beyond the means of the average collector. Subsequent editions of "Birds of America," especially the chromolithographs done by Julius Bien in New York (1859-60) and the smaller octavo (7 x 10½") edition of prints done by J.T. Bowen of Philadelphia in the 1840's are those that are most frequently offered for sale.

American Robin - Plate CCCX (310), hand-colored engraving & aquatint plate from "The Birds of America," printed by Robert Havell, Jr., London, 1832, 16 x 19"...........$320.00

Blue Yellow Back Warbler - Plate XV (15), hand-colored engraving & aquatint plate from "The Birds of America," printed by Robert Havell, Jr., London, 1827, 12½ x 12¼" 1,760.00

Brasilian Caracara Eagle - Plate CLXI (161), hand-colored engraving & aquatint plate from "The Birds of America," printed by Robert Havell, Jr., London, 1833, 38¼ x 25¼" (ILLUS.) 3,300.00

Brown Pelican (Young) - Plate CDXXI (421), Amsterdam Edition (exact facsimile of the Havell Edition, printed in 1971 on rag paper & limited to 250), 26½ x 39½"........................1,400.00

Canada Goose - Plate CCI (201), Amsterdam Edition, 1971, 26½ x 39½"........................1,100.00

Cedar Bird - Plate XLIII (43), hand-colored engraving & aquatint plate from "The Birds of America," printed by Robert Havell, Jr., London, 1828, 19½ x 12¼" ..3,520.00

Columbia Jay - Plate XCVI (96), hand-colored engraving & aquatint plate from "The Birds of America," printed by Robert Havell, Jr., London, 1830, 37 x 25¾" 7,700.00

Fish Crow - Plate CXLVI (146), hand-colored engraving & aquatint plate from "The Birds of America," printed by Robert Havell, Jr., London, 1832, 38 x 25¼"..........1,200.00 to 2,530.00

Great-Horned Owl

Great-Horned Owl - Plate LXI (61), hand-colored engraving & aquatint plate from "The Birds of America," printed by Robert Havell, Jr., London, 1829, 36 7/8 x 25 5/8" (ILLUS.) 6,600.00

Key-West Dove - Plate CCXXVIII (228), hand-colored engraving & aquatint plate from "The Birds of America," printed by Robert Havell, Jr., London, 1833, 19½ x 12¾" 360.00

Le Petit Caporal - Plate LXXV (75), hand-colored engraving & aquatint plate from "The Birds of America," printed by Robert Havell, Jr., London, 1829, 19½ x 12¼" ..2,310.00

Louisiana Heron - Plate CCXVII (217), hand-colored engraving & aquatint plate from "The Birds of America," printed by Robert Havell, Jr., London, 1834, 20 5/8 x 26" 15,400.00

Louisiana Heron - Plate CCXVII (217), Amsterdam Edition, 1971, 26½ x 39½" 1,600.00

Marsh Wren - Plate XCVIII (98), hand-colored engraving & aquatint plate from "The Birds of America," printed by Robert Havell, Jr., London, 1830, 19½ x 12¼"....... 990.00

Mottled Owl - Plate XCVII (97), hand-colored engraving & aquatint plate from "The Birds of America," printed by Robert Havell, Jr., London, 1830, 25¾ x 20¾" ..6,875.00

Norway Rat - Plate LIV (54), from the "Viviparous Quadrupeds of North America," printed & colored by J.T. Bowen of Philadelphia, 1843, 22 x 28" 325.00

Orchard Oriole - Plate XLII (42), hand-colored engraving & aquatint plate from "The Birds of America," engraved, printed & colored by Robert Havell, Jr., London, 1827-38, 26 x 20¾"...3,630.00 to 4,290.00

Painted Bunting - Plate LIII (53), hand-colored engraving & aquatint plate from "The Birds of America," engraved, printed & colored by Robert Havell, Jr., London, 1827-38, 19½ x 12¼" ....2,860.00 to 3,080.00

Pileated Woodpecker - Plate CXI (III), Amsterdam Edition (exact facsimile of the Havell Edition, print. 4 in 1971 on rag paper & limite. to 250), 26½ x 39½" 900.00

Prairie Warbler - Plate XIV (14), hand-colored-engraving & aquatint plate from "The Birds of America," engraved, printed & colored by Robert Havell, Jr., London, 1827-38, 19½ x 12¼" ..990.00 to 1,320.00

Red Headed Woodpecker - Plate XXVII (27), hand-colored engraving & aquatint plate from "The Birds of America," engraved, printed & colored by Robert Havell, Jr., London, 1827-38, 25 3/8 x 21½" ....3,080.00 to 3,410.00

Red-Shouldered Hawk

Red-Shouldered Hawk - Plate LVI (56), hand-colored engraving & aquatint plate from "The Birds of America," engraved, printed & colored by Robert Havell, Jr., London, 1827-38, 38 x 25 3/8" (ILLUS.) 5,500.00

Red-Winged Starling - Plate LXVII (67), hand-colored engraving &

aquatint plate from "The Birds of America," engraved, printed & colored by Robert Havell, Jr., London, 1827-38, 25 7/8 x 20¾" ....1,760.00 to 3,300.00

Republican or Cliff Swallow - Plate LXVII (68), hand-colored engraving & aquatint plate from "The Birds of America," engraved, printed & colored by Robert Havell, Jr., London, 1827-38, 19½ x 12 3/8" ....1,100.00 to 1,650.00

Rocky Mountain Neotoma - Plate IXXX (29), from the "Viviparous Quadrupeds of North America," printed & colored by J.T. Bowen of Phildelphia, 1843, 22 x 28" 325.00

Says Least Shrew - Plate LXX (70), from the "Viviparous Quadrupeds of North America," printed & colored by J.T. Bowen of Philadelphia, 1845, 22 x 28" 325.00

Sea-Side Finch - Plate XCIII (93), hand-colored engraving & aquatint plate from "The Birds of America," engraved, printed & colored by Robert Havell, Jr., London, 1827-38, 19½ x 12¼" ....2,200.00 to 2,475.00

Sharp-Tailed Grouse - Plate CCCLXXXII (382), hand-colored engraving & aquatint plate from "The Birds of America," engraved, printed & colored by Robert Havell, Jr., London, 1827-38, 21½ x 29 1/8" 3,630.00

Swallow-Tailed Hawk

Swallow-Tailed Hawk - Plate LXXII (72), hand-colored engraving & aquatint plate from "The Birds of America," engraved, printed & colored by Robert Havell, Jr., London, 1827-38, 20½ x 27 3/8" (ILLUS.) 3,960.00

Trumpeter Swan - Plate CCCCVI (406), hand-colored engraving & aquatint plate from "The Birds of America," engraved, printed & colored by Robert Havell, Jr., London, 1827-38, 25½ x 38 1/8"....27,500.00

Whip-Poor-Will - Plate LXXXII (82),

hand-colored engraving & aquatint plate from "The Birds of America," engraved, printed & colored by Robert Havell, Jr., London, 1827-38, 25¾ x 20¾" ....3,300.00 to 6,050.00

Yellow Throated Warbler - Plate LXXXV (85), hand-colored engraving & aquatint from "The Birds of America," engraved, printed & colored by Robert Havell, Jr., London, 1827-38, 19 3/8 x 12¼".....1,045.00

AUTOGRAPHS

Values of autographs and autograph letters depend on such factors as content, scarcity and the fame of the writer. Values of good autograph material continue to rise. A.L.S. stands for "autographed letter signed"; L.S. for "letter signed."

Beatles (The), British musical group, black & white press photograph signed by John Lennon, Paul McCartney, George Harrison & Ringo Starr, framed, 14 x 11" $660.00

Brynner, Yul, American actor, photograph signed, 1951 .... 22.00

Byrd, Richard E., (1888-1957) Admiral, United States Navy, typed L.S., 1956, to Dr. Paul Dudley White, w/miniature American flag presented to Dr. White, 2 pcs..... 99.00

Chaplin, Charlie, (1889-1978) movie actor, producer & director, photograph signed, ca. 1917, 10 x 8"... 275.00

Coolidge, Calvin, (1872-1933) 30th President of the United States, document signed, May 1, 1926, appointment of postmaster at Carroll County, Missouri, countersigned by Postmaster General 200.00

Defoe, Daniel, (1660-1731) English novelist, 2 A.L.S., March 9, 1708 (w/integral address leaf) & March 14, 1708, to Thomas Bowrey, each 1 p., 2 pcs. 5,775.00

Dempsey, William Harrison - "Jack," (1895-1984) American heavyweight boxing champion, photograph signed 20.00

Dix, Dorothea L., (1802-87) Superintendent of Union Army women war nurses, L.S., Washington, May 1864.................... 60.00

Edison, Thomas A., (1847-1931) American inventor, photograph signed, "Friend Murray - in 1879 I invented the incandescent lamp,

Thos. A. Edison," w/letter dated October 31, 1931, authenticating photograph, 2 pcs. 250.00

Hitchcock, Alfred, (1899-1981) movie director, caricature signed 55.00

Hoover, Herbert C., (1874-1964) 31st President of the United States, document signed, May 2, 1930, reappointment of postmaster at Carroll County, Missouri 150.00

Kennedy, John F., (1917-63) 35th President of the United States, typed L.S., April 1, 1954, as Senator from the State of Massachusetts, to a constituent in Marlboro regarding tax legislation & revenues, on United States Senate stationery 302.50

Lincoln, Abraham, (1809-65) 16th President of the United States, document signed, Washington, 1864, unconditional pardon for A.W.O.L. Navy man, countersigned by William H. Seward, together w/military pass issued to same sailor & another authorizing passage within the lines & dated 1861, 3 pcs. 1,100.00

Lincoln, Abraham, (1809-65) 16th President of the United States, parchment document signed, August 1, 1865, Second Lieutenant's commission in the Veteran Reserve Corps, countersigned by Secretary of War Edwin Stanton, framed, overall 23 x 19" (severe water damage) 990.00

Mann, Thomas, (1875-1955) German novelist, typed L.S., Beverly Hills Hotel, April 14, 1938, to Mr. Shimkin, regretting that changes in his life make it impossible for him to contribute to his essay volume "Living Philosophies," 1¼ pp......................... 192.00

Multiple: surviving crew members of the British White Star Line steamer "Titanic," L.S. 7,500.00

Robeson, Paul, (1898-1976) American baritone, concert program signed, 1946 .... 50.00

Roosevelt, Franklin D., (1882-1945) 32nd President of the United States, typed L.S., April 12, 1918, as Assistant Secretary of the Navy, to Mrs. A.J. Connor, on Navy Department stationery, together w/sepia photograph of Roosevelt by Bachrach, 2 pcs. 187.00

Shaw, George Bernard, (1856-1950) English dramatist, critic & novelist, autograph note signed on card printed "With Bernard Shaw's compliments," London, November

29, 1927, together w/photograph
of Shaw & Lady Astor in Berlin, 2
pcs. 137.00
Truman, Bess Wallace, (1885-1983)
wife of President Harry S. Truman, L.S., undated, to Mrs. Wil-
liam Smith in appreciation 85.00
Wilson, Woodrow, (1856-1924) 28th
President of the United States,
photograph signed (also signed
by other gentleman in photograph), paper impressed "David R.
Edmonton - Washington, D.C.,"
framed, overall 13 x 9½" 275.00

AUTOMOBILE ACCESSORIES

Assorted Radiator Emblems

Chauffeur's badge, Illinois, 1919 . . . . $30.00
Chauffeur's badge, Illinois, 1926 . . . . 10.00
Chauffeur's badge, Michigan, 1934 . . 11.00
Chauffeur's badge, Michigan, 1937 . . 12.00
Clock, "Maxwell" 45.00
Clock, Waltham, 8-day, w/second
hand 110.00
Duster, lady's, linen . . . . .25.00 to 45.00
Duster, man's, natural linen, Mar-
shall Field & Co. 75.00
Gear shift knob, marbleized blue &
white glass 25.00
Gear shift knob, marbleized caramel
& white glass, large 15.00
Gear shift knob, marbleized red &
white glass 25.00
Gear shift knob, swirled green, pur-
ple, brown, blue & white glass . . . 17.00

Head lamp, "Cadillac," brass, Gray
& Davis, 12 x 9" 40.00
Headlights, "Ford," brass, 1905-10,
pr. 125.00
Hood ornament, "Dodge," ram
w/horns 15.00
Hood ornament, "Nash" 25.00
Hood ornament, "Packard," Goddess
of Speed 50.00
Hood ornament, "Pontiac," Indian
head, 1950's, in original box 48.00
Hood ornament, girl in standing position, bronzed metal,
1930's . . . . .15.00 to 20.00

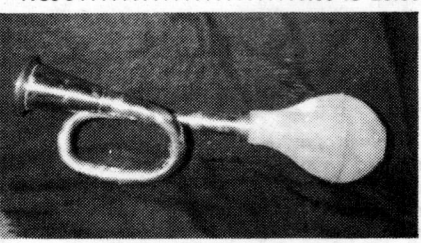

Brass Horn

Horn, brass w/original (worn) rub-
ber squeeze bulb (ILLUS.) 95.00
Ignition switch & ampere panel,
"Ford" 42.50
Jack, "Ford Model T" 25.00
License plate, 1911, Minnesota 225.00
License plate, 1912, Michigan,
graniteware 65.00
License plates, 1913, Pennsylvania,
pr. 20.00
License plate, 1914, California,
graniteware 50.00
License plate, 1914, Missouri,
graniteware 110.00
License plates, 1914, Pennsylvania,
pr. 25.00
License plate, 1915, California 55.00
License plate, 1915, Connecticut,
graniteware 40.00
License plates, 1915, Iowa, pr. 45.00
License plate, 1915, Maine,
graniteware 45.00
License plate, 1915, Massachusetts
dealer, graniteware 30.00
License plates, 1915, Pennsylvania,
pr. 20.00
License plate, 1921, Ohio 20.00
License plates, 1933, Iowa, w/origi-
nal wrappers, pr. 20.00
License plates, 1936, Michigan, pr. . . . 7.00
License plates, 1941, Alabama, pr. . . . 25.00
Luggage rack, "Ford Model T" 35.00
Luggage racks, running board type,
"Wahl Red Cap," ca. 1925, set of 4 150.00
Manifold heater, "Ford Model A,"
cast iron 45.00
Oil can, "Ford" in script,
copper . . . . .15.00 to 25.00

Piston rings, "Plymouth," 1941, original box, set 10.00

Radiator emblem plate, "Chevrolet," oval, blue, 1930's 18.00

Radiator gauge, "Ideal" 9.00

Side light, "Dietz Dainty," brass, 1906 .... 40.00

Side light, "Neverout," brass 150.00

Speedometer, measures speed to 60 m.p.h., "A.C. Spark Plug Co." 47.50

Tail light switch assembly & bracket, "Ford Model T Roadster," 1915-25 .... 32.50

Tire pressure gauge, "Ford Model A" 25.00

Tire pressure gauge, "Schrader," brass, 1928 .... 8.00

Tire pump, "Ford" in script, brass .... 22.00 to 27.00

Tire pump, "Holstein," brass, double barrel 25.00

Tire repair kit, "Super All State," in original tin box 32.00

Vase, clear glass w/etched floral design 25.00

Vase, vaseline glass, w/original wire bracket 45.00

Wheel cover, "Kaiser," chrome 25.00

Wheel cover, "Packard," 1930's 35.00

Wheel lock, heavy steel, pointed, lettered "One Hundred Dollars For Arrest & Conviction of Persons Tampering - Security Auto Theft Signal System" 125.00

Whistle, "Aeromore," exhaust-type, cast iron w/four brass tubes, 1912 patent (connected to manifold or tailpipe) .... 110.00 to 135.00

Wrench, open end, "Cadillac" 5.00

"Ford" Wrenches

Wrenches, "Ford" in script, cast iron, each (ILLUS.) .... 7.00 to 12.50

Wrench, open end, "Maxwell" 5.00

AUTOMOBILE LITERATURE

American Cyclopedia of the Automobile, 1909, illustrated, 336 pp. $15.00

Auto Blue Book, 1919 .... 16.00

Auto Trade Journal, December 1915, new car reviews, illustrated, 356 pp. 29.00

Buick catalog, 1928, illustrated, 12 x 8", 23 pp. 25.00

Cadillac owner's manual, 1923 ...... 30.00

Chevrolet owner's manual, 1923 .... 25.00

Chevrolet truck bodies catalog, 1929-30 .... 75.00

Cole Aero-8 brochure, 1920 .... 25.00

Dodge showroom brochure, 1936 ... 20.00

Dykes Automobile Encyclopedia, 1919 .... 25.00

Edsel catalog, 1960 .... 14.00

Ford Model A instruction manual, 1928, illustrated 22.00

Ford Model T instruction manual, 1919 .... 29.50

Ford Model T sales brochure, 1912, 32 pp. 38.50

Ford owner's manual, 1946 .... 10.00

Ford sales brochure, 1930, 7½ x 5½", 12 pp. 20.00

Ford sales brochure, 1938, 11 color-illustrated models, 16 pp. 14.00

Hudson owner's manual, 1947 ...... 18.00

Hudson sales brochure, 1936 .... 20.00

Hudson sales brochure, 1939 .... 25.00

Kaiser owner's manual, 1948 .... 10.00

Maxwell sales brochure, 1920, 4 pp. 15.00

Mercedes sales brochure, 1923 ..... 65.00

Nash owner's manual, "Advanced Six," 1925, original mail-in warranty cards 30.00

Oakland "Model 34-B" instruction book, price list, 1919 inspection report & owner's booklet, 136 pp. 35.00

Oldsmobile instruction book, 1917 .. 18.00

Oldsmobile owner's manual, 1948 .. 10.00

Oldsmobile sales brochure, 1941, color-illustrated models 16.00

Oldsmobile sales brochure, 1946, color-illustrated models, 24 pp. 12.00

Overland catalogue, 1924 .... 30.00

Packard "Six" owner's manual, 1937 .... 16.00

Packard "Standard 8" sales brochure, 1930, color-illustrated models 25.00

Packard sales brochure, 1936 .... 35.00

Packard shop manual, 1937 .... 39.50

Plymouth service manual, 1936-42 models, illustrated, 216 pp. 20.00

Pontiac owner's manual, 1933 ...... 25.00

Pontiac owner's manual, 1936 ...... 20.00

Pontiac owner's manual, 1957 ...... 25.00

Stevens-Duryea catalog, 1903 .... 40.00

Studebaker "Light Six" brochure, 1922, 11½ x 8", 14 pp. 15.00

AUTOMOBILES

1927 Buick Sedan

Buick, 1927 Standard Six 2-door
sedan (ILLUS.) $9,000.00
Buick, 1953 Estate Wagon, wooden
body 23,000.00
Buick, 1965 Skylark 2-door sports
convertible sedan, red & white
interior, original papers &
stickers 4,700.00
Chevrolet 1954 Bel Air 4-door sedan,
black & white, original chrome. . .2,800.00
Chrysler, 1950 Royal 4-door sedan,
45,000 actual miles 3,300.00
Dodge, 1919 Touring Car, original
leather 8,500.00
Ford, 1925 Model T touring car, all
original except seat covers (top
needs repair) 6,800.00
Ford, 1930 Model A coupe, restor-
able condition 2,500.00
Ford, 1935 standard coupe, 75%
restored 7,000.00
Ford, 1951 2-door sedan, restorable
condition 800.00
Ford, 1960 Galaxie Starliner 2-door
hardtop coupe 4,500.00
Ford, 1964½-65 Mustang, automatic
transmission, air conditioning,
new tires, 90% restored 3,500.00
Ford, 1965 Thunderbird convertible,
blue 5,000.00
Ford, 1966 Galaxie 500 2-door hard-
top, 289 engine 3,750.00
Franklin, 1927 4-door sedan 8,000.00
Graham Paige, 1929 Model 612,
4-door sedan, 6-cylinder, lacquered blue-black fenders,
wooden spoke wheels, original
drapes & English body paint,
restored 7,500.00
Kaiser, 1951 2-door sedan, restor-
able condition 500.00
Kaiser, 1953 Manhattan 4-door
sedan, 18,000 actual miles 3,000.00
Lincoln, 1955 4-door sedan, turbo
drive transmission, dual heaters,
power steering, power brakes &
radio, less than 40,000 actual
miles 9,995.00
Maxwell 1910 Runabout, w/owner's
manual 9,000.00

Oldsmobile, 1949 Eighty-Eight 4-door
sedan, all original 1,400.00
Packard, 1951 standard business
coupe 1,800.00
Pontiac, 1957 Chieftain 4-door
sedan, blue 1,500.00
Studebaker, 1929 Dictator, original
upholstery, window shades,
green 3,400.00
Studebaker, 1962 Lark 4-door
sedan 2,000.00
Willys 1947 Jeep 4,800.00

AVIATION COLLECTIBLES

Bust of Charles Lindbergh

Recently much interest has been shown in collecting items associated with the early days of the "flying machine." In addition to relics, flying adjuncts and literature relating to the early days of flight, collectors also seek out items that picture the more renowned early pilots, some of whom became folk-heroes in their own lifetime, as well as the early planes themselves.

Admission ticket (or pass) to steps
of Capitol Building, June 11, 1927,
for Lindbergh reception $12.00
Ash tray, brass, embossed Sikorsky
helicopter 35.00
Autograph, "Charles Lindbergh," on
uncanceled 1926 first flight cover,
not flown due to improper
cachet 300.00
Bank, bust of Charles Lindbergh
w/aviator's helmet & goggles up,
cast lead, 1929, 6" h. 65.00
Bank, bust of Charles Lindbergh,
"Lindy Bank," cast aluminum,
1928, 6½" h. 125.00
Book, "A Boy's Story of
Lindbergh" 12.00

Book, "All the World's Aircraft Engines & Specifications," illustrated & w/fold-out plates, 1921, 547 pp. 40.00

Book, "Fighting Planes of the World," Law, 1940, 59 color illustrations, 66 pp. 22.00

Book, "We," by Charles Lindbergh, 1927 .... 5.00

Bookends, bronze, Lindbergh "Our Aviator," pr. .... 65.00 to 90.00

Bust of Charles Lindbergh, bronze finish, by B. Arnold, Oregon, Illinois, 6" h. (ILLUS.) 80.00

Catalogue, Aircraft Annual, 1944, 288 pp. 22.00

Cigarette lighter, stainless steel, model of an airplane, 6" l. 45.00

Helmet, khaki-colored cloth w/rubber earphone retainers & chamois lining, early 1940's 30.00

Helmet, lady's, white cloth, 1930's .. 75.00

Lapel pin, advertising "Spirit of Youth Clothing," metal, embossed Lindbergh plane, 11/16" l. 15.00

Lapel pin, "Spirit of St. Louis" airplane, brass 20.00

Photograph, Amelia Earhart wearing uniform, autographed 19.00

Photograph, Amelia Earhart & Mayor of Vermont town standing before airplane, 5½ x 4¼" 85.00

Pinback button, "Welcome Home Lindbergh" 7.00

Pinback button, celluloid, Lindbergh & "Spirit of St. Louis" plane 15.00

Pocket watch & fob, "New York to Paris," Ingraham 175.00

Postcard-invitation, "99 Club," to lecture by Wiley Post & Jimmy Doolittle, 1935 .... 20.00

Poster, "Wright Au Camp D'Auvors," chromolithograph of Wright flying above a tree-lined field, E. Montaut, Paris, copyright 1908, 35 x 17" (some yellowing) 137.50

Sheet music, "Aviator's Two-Step," photograph of Lindbergh 9.00

Sheet music, "Going Up," pictures early airplane & girls 10.00

Sheet music, "Lone Eagle March," photograph of Lindbergh 9.00

Toy, airplane, "Spirit of St. Louis," celluloid, 6 x 5½" 50.00

Trinket box, brown-painted metal over wood, w/sepia-colored photograph of Colonel Lindbergh beside his aircraft on lid, ca. 1927, 7¼ x 3¾ x 2¾" 55.00

World globe on stand, tin, indicating flight path of 1927, 6" h. 55.00

BABY MEMENTOES

Nursery Rhyme Silver by Tiffany

Everyone dotes on the new baby and through many generations some exquisite and unique gifts have been carefully selected with a special infant in mind. Collectors now seek items from a varied assortment of baby mementoes, once tokens of affection to the newborn babe. Also see ADVERTISING ITEMS, BUFFALO POTTERY, CAMPBELL KID COLLECTIBLES, CANS & CONTAINERS, CHILDREN'S MUGS, FURNITURE, GREENAWAY ITEMS, HUMPHREY ARTWORK, INDIAN RELICS, KEWPIE COLLECTIBLES, NURSING BOTTLES, QUILTS under Textiles, ROSEVILLE POTTERY JUVENILE LINE, ROYAL RUDOLSTADT CHINA, SCALES, SUNBONNET BABY COLLECTIBLES, WELLER POTTERY ZONA LINE and the "Special Focus" on ABC PLATES.

Baby's record book, color illustrations by C.M. Burd, soft covers ... $35.00

Baby's record book, illustrated by Fanny Y. Cory, published by Brown & Bigelow, 1920, 6 x 4½", 16 pp. 20.00

Bathtub, graniteware, colorful animals & Teddy Bear decor on yellow ground 85.00

Bib clips, sterling silver, figural rabbits on chain. 35.00

Bonnet, lace & net w/ribbon trim, off-white 20.00

Bowl, white earthenware china, Baby Bunting, Dog Bunch & ABC's decor, D.E. McNicol Pottery, East Liverpool, Ohio, 1892-1910 .... 42.50

Brush & comb, sterling silver, ornate, original box, 2 pcs. 54.00

Cap, crocheted cotton, white, small 12.00

Cap, cotton batiste, tiny tucks & lace trim, white 15.00

Carriage cover, embroidered pique,
white on white 38.00
Christening gown, white cotton,
w/tiny tucks at yoke & bottom
band of European lace, 48" l. 75.00
Christening gown, white cotton,
rows of tiny tucks & lace,
w/matching slip, 39" l. 80.00
Coat & bonnet, pastel silk, 1920's,
w/original hanger 18.00
Feeding dish, earthenware china,
"Baby Bunting lifts his hat" decal
transfer decor, Homer Laughlin,
East Liverpool, Ohio 45.00
Feeding dish, earthenware china,
rolled edge, Baby Bunting decor,
D.E. McNicol Pottery 45.00
Feeding dish, earthenware china,
rolled edge, cats decor, D.E.
McNicol Pottery 36.00
Feeding dish, earthenware china,
rolled edge, Dutch children decor,
D.E. McNicol Pottery 40.00
Feeding dish, earthenware china,
Gingham Dog & Calico Cat decal
transfer decor, in original box 40.00
Feeding dish, earthenware china,
rolled edge, Sunbonnet Kids
decor, D.E. McNicol Pottery 55.00
Feeding dish, heavy earthenware
pottery, "Changing Guard,"
English palace scene decor,
oval 50.00
Feeding dish w/tin hot water compartment underside, Staffordshire
pottery, nursery rhyme decor
w/Little Boy Blue, Jack Horner,
etc., 8" d., 2" h. 75.00
Feeding spoon, silverplate, "Teddy"
on handle w/bear & alphabet on
reverse 12.50
Feeding spoon, sterling silver, stork
& babe on handle, holly & "December" in bowl, Wallace 45.00
Feeding spoon, sterling silver, Etruscan patt., Gorham 13.00
Feeding spoon, sterling silver,
figural winged angel handle, dog
in bowl....................... 37.50
Flatware set, sterling silver, w/nurs-
ery rhyme figure in full relief on
handles: Red Riding Hood on
knife; Bo Peep on fork; Jack & Jill
w/pail of water on spoon; made
by Tiffany & Co. for English outlet,
1892-1902, 3 pcs. (ILLUS. of
part) 1,075.00
Food pusher, sterling silver, Tiffany
& Co. 55.00
Food pusher & spoon, sterling silver,
Man in the Moon patt., original
box, 2 pcs. 165.00
Fork, silverplate, "Puss 'n Boots"
patt., 1881 Rogers, 4¼" l......... 20.00

Fork, sterling silver, "Mary Had A
Little Lamb" 35.00
Fork & spoon, celluloid figural Teddy
Bear handles, Athoware U.S.A.,
4½" l., pr. 35.00
Fork & spoon, sterling silver, Art
Deco style, Georg Jensen, pr. 110.00
Knife & fork, wooden handles,
dated 1870, pr. 22.50
Mug, coin silver, W. McGrew, Cin-
cinnati, Ohio................... 195.00
Mug, coin silver, Medallion patt.,
A. Coles, N.Y.C. 235.00
Pillowcase, sheer linen w/embroid-
ery & tatted edge 18.00
Plate, pressed clear glass, "Hey Did-
dle Diddle," scene of cat & fiddle
& cow jumping over moon center,
Dutch boys & girls dancing border,
5½" d........................ 27.50

Push Sled for Baby

Push sled for baby, bentwood back,
sides & seat (swiveling to enable
child to face front or rear), original iron-tipped runners, varnished
wood w/black trim & green striping & original seashell-printed
moss green upholstery, 49" l.
(ILLUS.)...................... 625.00
Push sled for baby, bentwood back,
sides & seat w/upholstery, bentwood runners w/iron braces &
bentwood push handle, now
painted green w/red upholstery &
runners 350.00
Rattle, celluloid, figural girl holding
doll 48.00
Rattle, celluloid, model of a stork,
6" h. 18.00
Rattle, celluloid, roly poly baby
face 18.00
Rattle, sterling silver, dumbbell-
shaped, engraved "Lullaby,"
ca. 1900 .... 42.50
Rattle, sterling silver, bear in high
chair 52.00
Rattle, sterling silver w/mother-of-
pearl teething ring handle 25.00
Rattles, English silver w/coral handle, baluster form chased

w/scrolls & foliage & hunt w/four
bells, hallmarked Birmingham-
1898 & Chester-1897, pr.
(1 broken) 352.00
Rattle, wooden, puzzle-type,
19th c. 185.00

English Silver Rattle-Whistle

Rattle-whistle, English silver,
baluster form w/borders chased
w/leaftips & ribbonwork, w/coral
teether-handle & hung w/bells,
England, early 19th c. (ILLUS.) 450.00
Rattle-whistle, tin, whistle in handle, drum-shaped head embossed
w/eagle & "For A Good Child,"
5½" l. ....40.00 to 55.00
Shoes, high button style, leather,
black w/white top, pr............ 20.00
Slippers, blue satin, pr. 3.00
Teething ring, ivory, w/sterling
silver bell 75.00
Teething ring, mother-of-pearl,
w/sterling silver bell 45.00

BANKS

*Original early mechanical and cast iron still
banks are in great demand with collectors and
their scarcity has caused numerous reproductions of both types and the novice collector
is urged to exercise caution. The early
mechanical banks are especially scarce and
some versions are seldom offered for sale but,
rather, are traded with fellow collectors attempting to upgrade an existing collection.
Prices for all bank toys continue to rise as interest expands to more collectors. Numbers
before mechanical banks refer to those in
John Meyer's* Handbook of Old Mechanical
Banks. *In past years, our standard reference
for cast iron still banks was Hubert B. Whiting's book,* Old Iron Still Banks, *but because*

*this work is out of print and a beautiful new
book,* The Penny Bank Book - Collecting Still
Banks, *by Andy and Susan Moore pictures
and describes numerous additional banks, we
will use the Moore numbers as a reference
preceding each listing and indicate the Whiting reference in parenthesis at the end. The
still banks listed are old and in good original
condition with good paint and no repairs unless otherwise noted. An asterisk (*) indicates
this bank has been reproduced at some time.
Also see AVIATION COLLECTIBLES,
BASEBALL MEMORABILIA, CANDY
CONTAINERS, CHARACTER COLLECT-
IBLES, COCA-COLA ITEMS, DISNEY
COLLECTIBLES, HULL POTTERY, OC-
CUPIED JAPAN ITEMS, ROSEVILLE &
SHAWNEE POTTERY and ZEPPELIN
COLLECTIBLES.*

MECHANICAL

Bad Accident Mechanical Bank

6   Artillery - Square Block
       House ....\$500.00 to 1,300.00
7   Artillery - 8-sided Block
       House, no soldier.........3,200.00
9   Bad Accident (ILLUS.) 1,320.00
16 Bird on Roof 715.00

Buffalo Bucking Mechanical Bank

26 Buffalo - Bucking
       (ILLUS.) ....2,200.00 to 3,000.00
33 Cabin ....225.00 to 450.00
39 Cat & Mouse 2,200.00
53 Creedmore - Soldier aims rifle
       at target in tree
       trunk............345.00 to 450.00

54 Creedmore - New (Tryolese
      Bank) . . . . .385.00 to 600.00
56 Darktown Battery 1,500.00
58 Dinah . . . . .250.00 to 400.00
69 Dog Speaking . . . . . . .695.00 to 850.00
71 Dog - Trick . . . . .250.00 to 650.00
75 Eagle & Eaglets . . . . .385.00 to 750.00
99 Frogs - Two . . . . .750.00 to 950.00
102 Frog on Round Lattice Base 350.00
118 Hall's Excelsior 275.00

Setting Hen Mechanical Bank

121 Hen - Setting
      (ILLUS.) . . . . . . .1,700.00 to 3,000.00
127 Humpty Dumpty . . . . .275.00 to 480.00

Indian Shooting Bear Mechanical Bank

129 Indian Shooting Bear
      (ILLUS.) 1,500.00
134 Jolly Nigger with Butterfly
      Tie 150.00
136 Jolly Nigger with Straw
      Hat 150.00
137 Jolly Nigger - Starkie Patent,
      red coat, white collar, blue
      tie (aluminum) . . . .225.00 to 255.00
138 Jonah and the Whale 800.00
146 Lilliput - Hall's 325.00
147 Lion and Monkeys 450.00
148 Lion Hunter 3,600.00
155 Mammy & Child, fair con-
      dition (ILLUS.) 2,300.00
160 Minstrel, tin 400.00
163 Monkey & Coconut 2,100.00
165 Monkey & Parrot 265.00
169 Mule Entering Barn . .450.00 to 895.00
177 Organ Bank - with Monkey,
      Cat & Dog . . . . .375.00 to 500.00
180 Organ - Tiny 550.00

Mammy Mechanical Bank

182 Owl - Turns Head . . .200.00 to 325.00
183 Owl with Book - Slot in
      Head 225.00
185 Paddy & His Pig 1,000.00
196 Pony - Trick . . . . .450.00 to 625.00
      Popeye Knockout Bank 400.00
201 Professor Pugfrog 5,600.00
203 Punch & Judy . . . . . .650.00 to 1,100.00
206 Rabbit in Cabbage, worn
      paint .315.00
214 Santa Claus at
      Chimney . . . . .750.00 to 895.00
      Southern Comfort - Soldier
      Shoots Coin into
      Bottle . . . . .70.00 to 85.00
222 Stump Speaker 1,000.00
224 Tammany 365.00
226 Teddy & the Bear in Tree 1,000.00
231 Uncle Sam with Satchel 900.00
237 William Tell . . . . . . .375.00 to 595.00
245 Zoo 825.00

STILL

195 Amish Boy with Pig on Bale
      of Straw, white metal, key
      locked trap, 4¾ x 3½" 65.00
806 Apollo Rocket Ship, cast iron,
      John Wright, 1968, 3" d.,
      4¼" h. 35.00
882 "Arabian Safe" on front,
      desert scenes on sides, cast
      iron, w/key, Kyser & Rex,
      1882, 4" sq., 4½" h.
      (W. 346) 78.00
168 Aunt Jemima (Mammy) with
      Spoon, cast iron, 5¾" h.
      (W. 17) * . . . . .75.00 to 90.00
1486 Automobile - 4 Passengers &
      Large Wheels, cast iron,
      A.C. Williams, 1910,
      5½"l. (W. 159) 750.00
909 Barrel, cast iron, Judd, 1873,
      2¼" d., 2¾" h. (W. 283) . . .   85.00
20 Baseball Player, cast iron,

A.C. Williams, ca. 1909,
5¾" h. (W. 10) 90.00

1440 Battleship "Maine" - small,
cast iron, Grey Iron Casting Co., 1897-1903, 4½" l.
(W. 142) 250.00

951 Bean Pot - w/nickle register
& bail handle, cast iron,
3 7/8" d., 3" h. 125.00

715 Bear - Begging, cast iron,
A.C. Williams & Arcade,
1910-30, 5½" h.
(W. 330) * 45.00

693 Bear Stealing Pig, cast iron,
5½" h. (W. 246) * 720.00

714 Bear Seated on Log, cast iron,
7" h. (W. 328) 585.00

1308 Bear Stealing Honey from
Beehive, cast iron, England,
1908, 7" h. (W. 169) * 200.00

717 Bear with Honey Pot, cast
iron, Hubley, 1936, 6½" h.
(W. 327) * 75.00

681 Beehive ("Dime") Register -
opens at $10.00 total, cast
iron, 1891, 6½" w.,
5½" h. 165.00

74 "Billiken" on base, cast iron,
A.C. Williams, 1909,
2¼" w., 4¼" h.
(W. 50) ....55.00 to 70.00

73 Billiken on Throne, cast iron,
A.C. Williams, 1909-12,
3 1/8" w., 6½" h. 100.00

15 Billy Bounce - "Give Billy a
Penny" on chest, cast iron,
Hubley, ca. 1906,
4 11/16" h. (W. 22) 337.50

79 "Billy Can" on bottom of feet
& base of Funny Man, cast
iron, ca. 1910, 5 1/8" h.
(W. 51) 810.00

984 Blackpool Tower, cast iron,
England, 1908, 4 3/8 x
2 7/8", 7 3/8" h. 115.00

46 Boy Scout - "Made in Canada"
on backpack, cast iron,
5 11/16" h. 365.00

45 Boy Scout, cast iron, A.C.
Williams, 1910, 6" h.
(W. 14) * 85.00

556 Buffalo - "Amherst Stoves" on
side, cast iron, 1930's, 8" l.
(W. 207) 247.50

542 Bull with Long Horns, cast
iron, 4" h., 5" l. (W. 189) ...120.00

555 Bull - "Aberdeen Angus"
embossed inside, alumi-
num, 7¼" l. (W. 190) * 135.00

999 Bungalow (Cottage) with
Porch, cast iron, Grey Iron
Casting Co., 1918-28, 3 x
3¼", 3¾" h. (W. 377) 135.00

Buster Brown & Tige Still Bank

241 Buster Brown & Tige, cast
iron, A.C. Williams,
1910-32, 5½" h.,
W. 2 * (ILLUS.)........... 125.00

768 Camel - small, cast iron,
Hubley & A.C. Williams,
1920-30's, 4¾" h.
(W. 202) 115.00

767 Camel - large, cast iron, A.C.
Williams, 1920's, 6¼" l.,
7¼" h. (W. 201) ..195.00 to 275.00

163 Campbell Kids, cast iron, A.C.
Williams, 1910-20's, 3¼" h.
(W. 45) 150.00

38 Captain Kidd - with shovel
beside tree, cast iron, ca.
1910, 5½" h. (W. 38) 195.00

358 Cat on Tub, cast iron, A.C.
Williams, 1920-34, 4 1/8" h.
(W. 53) 95.00

352 Cat with Ball, cast iron, A.C.
Williams, 1905-19, 5½" l.
(W. 247).........130.00 to 175.00

370 Cat with Blue Bow - seated,
lead, Germany, 4 1/8" h. 45.00

364 Cat with Bow (Tie) - seated,
cast iron, Grey Iron Casting
Co., 1922, 4½" h.
(W. 244) * 65.00

366 Cat with Soft Hair - seated,
cast iron, Arcade, 1910-29,
4¼" h. (W. 248) 77.50

298 Charlie Chaplin beside Ash
Barrel, cast iron & glass
(candy container conver-
sion), Borgfeldt & Co.,
1920's, 3" w., 3¾" h.
(W. 393) 125.00

593 "Chicken Feed" Bag, cast
iron, Knerr, 1973,
4 5/8" h. 55.00

1546 Clock - "Time is Money" on
      face, cast iron, A.C. Wil-
      liams, 1909-31, 3½" h.
      (W. 225) * 65.00

Clown Still Bank

211   Clown - standing, cast iron,
      A.C. Williams, 1908,
      6¼" h., W. 29 * (ILLUS.) . . .   75.00
783   Columbia Savings Bank
      (Globe with Eagle atop),
      cast iron, wood & paper-
      board, 1889, 3" d. globe,
      5½" h. (W. 240) 185.00
1317 Coronation (Elizabeth II)
      Crown, cast iron, England,
      1953, 3" d., 3 3/16" h. 35.00
1645 Cow - reclining, cast iron,
      4" l.   90.00
544   Cow - Holstein, standing,
      small, cast iron, Arcade,
      1910-20, 2½" h., 4½" l.
      (W. 188) 105.00
553   Cow - standing, cast iron,
      A.C. Williams, 1920,
      3¼" h., 5¼" l.
      (W. 200) * 105.00
1146 Cupola Bank (Bank Building) -
      large, cast iron, J.E.
      Stevens, 1872, 3½ x 2¾",
      4¼" h. (W. 306) 50.00
173   Darkie (Sharecropper), cast
      iron, A.C. Williams, ca.
      1901, 5½" h. (W. 18) 85.00
1081 "Deposit Bank" - large print,
      cast iron, Columbia Grey
      Casting Co., 1897, 3 x 2½",
      4¼" h. 52.50
359   Dog on Tub, cast iron, A.C.
      Williams, 1920-34, 4" h.
      (W. 54) 57.50
421   Dog - Boston Bull Terrier -
      standing, cast iron, Vindex
      Toys, 1931, 5¾ x 5¼"
      (W. 112) 95.00
357   Dog - Boxer Bulldog - seated,

      cast iron, A.C. Williams &
      Hubley, 1912-28, 4½" h.
      (W. 105) * . . . . .40.00 to 55.00
443   Dog -"Fido" on Pillow (Dog on
      Cushion), cast iron, Hubley,
      1920's, 7½" w. base,
      5¾" h. (W. 336) 170.00
416   Dog - Puppo (Puppy Dog with
      Bee), cast iron, Hubley,
      1920-30's, 4 7/8" h.
      (W. 338) 85.00
437   Dog - St. Bernard with Pack,
      large, A.C. Williams,
      1901-30's, 7¾" l.
      (W. 113) * 85.00
419   Dog - Scottie, seated, cast
      iron, Hubley, 1930-40, 5" h.
      (W. 110) . . . . .70.00 to 110.00
427   Dogs - Scotties (6) in Basket,
      white metal, worn paint,
      1930's, 4½" h. * 60.00
409   Dog - Spitz, cast iron, Grey
      Iron Casting Co., ca. 1928,
      4½" h., 4¼" l. 247.50
412   Dog - Labrador Retriever, cast
      iron, 4½" l. (W. 104) 225.00
499   Donkey - with saddle, small,
      cast iron, Arcade & A.C.
      Williams, 1910-30's, 4½" l.,
      4½" h. (W. 198) 60.00
500   Donkey with Saddle, cast iron,
      A.C. Williams, 1920's,
      6¼" l. (W. 197) 145.00
48   Doughboy (World War I Sol-
      dier), cast iron, Grey Iron
      Casting Co., 1919, 7" h.
      (W. 40) * 300.00
624   Duck on Grassy Mound, cast
      iron, key-locked trap in
      base, Hubley, 1930's,
      4¾" h. (W. 322) 225.00
616   Duck on Tub - "Save for a
      Rainy Day" on tub, cast
      iron, Hubley, 1930-36,
      5¼" h. (W. 323) 155.00
180   Dutch Boy on Barrel, cast
      iron, Hubley, 1930's,
      5 5/8" h. (W. 36) 67.50
181   Dutch Girl holding Flowers,
      cast iron, Hubley, 1930's,
      5¼" h. (W. 35) . . . . . .65.00 to 90.00
455   Elephant - swivel trunk,
      small, cast iron, 3½" l.
      (W. 70) 202.50
461   Elephant Seated & Trumpet-
      ing - raised trunk touching
      forehead, white metal, key-
      locked trap, Vanio, ca.
      1936, 5¼" h. 30.00
11   Football Player, cast iron,
      A.C. Williams, 1910-31,
      gold repaint, 5¾" h.
      (W. 12) 225.00

12 Frowning Face (hanging-type),
cast iron, 5 5/8" h. 990.00

133 General Eisenhower Bust,
white metal, key-locked
trip, Banthrico, ca. 1945,
5½" h. 25.00

86 Golliwog, aluminum, John
Harper Ltd., England, 6" h.
(W. 52) * 50.00

85 Golliwog, cast iron, John
Harper Ltd., England,
1910-25, 6¼" h.
(W. 3) * . . . . 200.00 to 315.00

531 Horse - "My Pet," cast iron,
Arcade, 1920's, 5" l., 4" h.
(W. 85) 130.00

510 Horse on Tub, cast iron, undecorated, silver finish,
A.C. Williams, 1920's,
5 5/16" h. 126.00

13 "King Midas" - holding bag of
"Gold," cast iron, Hubley,
ca. 1930, 4½" h. (W. 47) . . 1,395.00

176 Mammy with Hands on Hips,
cast iron, Hubley, 1914-46,
5¼" h. (W. 20) * 80.00

282 Man in Barrel (Barrel with
Arms), cast iron, J. & E.
Stevens, late 19th c.,
3 5/8" h. (W. 151) 472.50

26 Mariner at Wheel (sailor at
ship's wheel), lead, key-
locked trap, Germany,
ca. 1905 . . . . 35.00

Mutt & Jeff Still Bank

157 Mutt & Jeff, cast iron, colorful
old paint, A.C. Williams,
1912-31, 4¼" h., W. 13
(ILLUS.) 125.00

8 Officer Cadet (soldier), cast
iron, Hubley, 1905-15,
5½" h. (W. 7) * 247.50

676 Old Abe (Eagle) with Shield,
cast iron, ca. 1880,
3 7/8" h. (W. 255) 650.00

216 Organ Grinder (conversion),
cast iron, Hubley,
6¼" h. 112.50

573 Oscar the Goat - standing,
cast iron, 7¾" h., 9¼" l.
(modern door stop conver-
sion) . . . . 55.00 to 67.50

629 Pig - "I Made Chicago
Famous" embossed on side,
small, cast iron, J.M.
Harper, 1902, 2¼" h.,
4 1/8" l. (W. 177) 126.00

578 Pig Standing - well-fed
porker, cast iron, Shimer
Toy Co., ca. 1899, 5¼" l.
(W. 183) 70.00

631 Pig - "I Made Chicago
Famous'" embossed on
side, large, cast iron, J.M.
Harper, 1902, 2 5/8" h.,
5 5/16" l. 445.50

620 Pig (biggest pig of all), cast
iron, 7¼" l. 85.50

Pistol Packing Pirate

341 Pistol Packing Pirate, white
metal, key-locked trap,
ca. 1940, 6¼" h. (ILLUS.) 45.00

716 Polar Bear Standing, cast
iron, Arcade, ca. 1920,
5¼" h. * 95.00

264 Porky Pig (dressed as boy) -
"Porky" on base, cast iron,
Hubley, ca. 1930, 5¾" h.
(W. 27) 247.50

265 Porky Pig by Barrel, white
metal, Metal Moss Mfg.
Co., late 1930's, 4 7/16 x
5¾" 45.00

561 Possum, cast iron, Arcade,
1910-13, 4½" l., 2 3/8" h.
(W. 205) 350.00

514 Prancing Horse on Oval Base
("Beauty"), cast iron, 4¾ x
4 7/8" 337.50

506 Prancing Horse with Belly

Band, cast iron, 4½ x 5"
(no paint) 225.00

442 Puppo on Pillow (Dog on
Cushion), cast iron, Hubley,
1920's, little paint, 5 5/8 x
6" (W. 336) * 112.50

569 Rabbit on Base - "Bank" one
side, "1884" other, cast
iron, 2¼" h. (W. 97).......900.00

568 Rabbit - seated, small, cast
iron, Arcade, 1910-20,
3½" h. (W. 96) * 80.00

610 "Red Goose Shoes," cast iron,
Arcade, 1920's, 3¾" h. 135.00

736 Reindeer (Elk) with Antlers -
small, cast iron, A.C.
Williams, 1910-35 & Arcade,
1913-32, 6¼" h., 6" l.
(W. 195) 70.00

737 Reindeer (Elk) with Antlers -
large, cast iron, A.C.
Williams, 1910-35,
9½" l.............120.00 to 150.00

Rooster Still Bank

547 Rooster, cast iron, Arcade,
1910-25, 4 5/8" h., W. 187
(ILLUS.)....................85.50

541 Rooster - Polish Rooster,
black w/red topknot, yel-
low legs, cast iron, 5½" h.
(W. 186) * 1,500.00

27 Sailor - small, cast iron,
Hubley, 5¼" h. 157.50

29 Sailor - large, cast iron,
Hubley, 1905-15, 5 5/8" h.
(W. 16) 115.00

103 Santa Sleeping, white metal,
Banthrico, 1950's, 5 7/8" h....80.00

61 Santa with Tree, cast iron,
Hubley, 1914-30, 5 7/8" h.
(W. 32) * 495.00

60 Santa - "Save & Smile"
(hanging-type), cast iron,
England, 7¼" h. (excellent
repaint) 585.00

Save & Smile Money Box

24 Save and Smile Money Box,
cast iron, Sydenham &
McOustra or Chamberlain
& Hill, England, 4" w., 4" h.
W. 46 * (ILLUS.) 355.50

535 "Tally Ho" - fox hunt theme,
cast iron, England, 4¼" h.
(W. 168) 110.00

107 Transvaal Money Box, cast
iron, John Harper Ltd.,
England, ca. 1885, 6 3/16 x
4¼" 720.00

154 "The Trust Bank" - figure of
old banker w/lettering on
vest, cast iron, J. & E.
Stevens Co., late 19th c.,
7¼" h. (W. 317) 1,350.00

585 Turkey - large, cast iron, A.C.
Williams, 1905-12, 4¼" h.
(W. 194)..................415.00

Two-Faced Woman

83 Two-Faced Black Boy (Two-
Faced Woman) - large, cast
iron, A.C. Williams,
1901-19, 4 1/8" h., W. 43
(ILLUS.)...................140.00

594 Two Kids - two goats lock
horns over stump, cast
iron, 4" w., 4½" h.
(W. 262) 1,305.00

307 Wisconsin Beggar Boy - "Help
the Crippled Children of

Wisconsin" on base, cast
iron, 6 7/8" h. 315.00

527 Work Horse with Flynet
(Horse with Flynet), cast
iron, possibly Arcade, ca.
1910, 4 5/8" l., 4" h.
(W. 80) 450.00

533 Work Horse - standing, cast
iron, Arcade, ca. 1910,
5" l., 4" h. (W. 81) * 45.00

GLASS

"Lucky Joe" Mustard Container Bank

Brick house, milk white
w/worn brown paint,
mustard container w/origi-
nal paper labels on bottom,
4" h. 35.00

Clock, advertising "Nash's
Mustard," clear, 4" h. 11.50

Clown, container for
"Grapette" drink, clear 15.00

Elephant standing, container
for "Grapette" drink,
clear 12.50

Fruit jar, advertising "Atlas
E-Z Seal," clear replica
w/embossed lettering 20.00

Glass block, advertising
"Pittsburg Paint," clear 22.50

302 Happifats on Drum, clear,
Borgfeldt & Co., U.S.A.,
1913-21, 4½" h. . . .160.00 to 175.00

House, advertising "Pittsburgh
Paints," clear, 2¼ x 3¼ x
2½" h. 20.00

Liberty Bell, clear, tin
closure 21.50

Log cabin, clear 20.00

"Lucky Joe," Nash's mustard
container, clear (ILLUS.). . . . 17.50

World globe, clear, 4" h. 20.00

POTTERY

Acorn, white clay pottery
w/mottled brown Rocking-
ham glaze, 2¾" h. 60.00

Apple, earthenware pottery,
realistic glaze, Roseville
Pottery Co., 4" d., 3" h. . . . 95.00

Buffalo reclining, earthenware pottery, attributed to
Roseville Pottery Co., 6" l .
(underneath chip) 75.00

Bust of cat, yellowware pottery w/mottled brown &
yellow glaze, attributed to
Roseville Pottery, 4" h. 125.00

Bust of smiling boy w/tooled
hair & prominent ears,
sewer tile pottery,
5¼" h. 130.00

Dog, Spaniel seated, yellowware pottery w/brown-
splashed translucent glaze,
green base trim,
5¼" h. 195.00

Duke of Wellington Toby-type
figure standing, Stafford-
shire pottery, late 19th c. . . 110.00

Elephant standing, white clay
pottery, 2½" h. 27.50

Frog standing w/hands on
tummy, earthenware pot-
tery, shaded green glaze,
6" h. 50.00

House, white clay pottery,
clear glaze w/brown roof,
windows, doors & corners
outlined in blue, 3¼" h.
(minor edge & coin slot
chips) 175.00

Jug, stoneware pottery, grey
w/blue slip-quilled wreath
lettered "Bank" in center,
4¾" h. 150.00

Jug, white clay pottery
w/black lettering "The First
State Bank - Norton, Ks."
on sides & base
w/"Macomb Stoneware
Co.," ½ pt. 150.00

Majolica Owl Bank

Owl standing on stump,
majolica, mottled brown,
6" h. (ILLUS.) 50.00
Pig standing, white clay pottery, 2-tone brown over
white running glaze,
4 7/8" l.................. 25.00
Pig standing, mottled brown
& rust Rockingham-glazed
pottery, 5" l., 2" h. 225.00
Pig standing, yellowware pottery, amber & clear glaze,
5" l. .... 50.00 to 75.00
Turtle, brown-glazed pottery,
Arthur Wood, England,
large, ca. 1935 .... 20.00

TIN

Chein Clown Head Bank

Advertising, "Bokar (A & P)
Coffee," coffee can replica,
black ground 8.00
Advertising, "Boscul Coffee,"
coffee can replica 20.00
Advertising, "Calumet Baking
Powder," baking powder
can replica, 3" h. 15.00
Advertising, "Carnation Con-
densed Milk," milk can
replica 35.00
1538 Advertising, "Dodge," barrel-
shaped, "Economy Barrel
Save 6 (55 gals.) Barrels of
Gas a Year with Dodge -
Bank the Difference,"
J. Chein & Co., 1920's 35.00
Advertising, "Eight O'Clock (A
& P) Coffee," coffee can
replica, red ground 12.00
Advertising, "Gulf Oil," oil
tanker replica............. 15.00
Advertising, "Havoline Motor
Oil," oil can replica 25.00
160 Advertising, "Peters Weather-
bird Shoes," tin & card-
board cylinder, F.L. Rand
Co., 2¼" d., 2" h......... 32.50

Advertising, "Sinclair Gaso-
line," gas pump replica 17.50
Barrel, "Happy Days," J.
Chein & Co. ....8.00 to 15.00
Cash register, J. Chein
& Co. ....10.00 to 20.00
Church, "Day by Day - a
Penny a Meal," J. Chein &
Co., 6½" l. 32.50
Clown head, lever-operated
semi-mechanical, multi-
colored, J. Chein & Co.,
5" h. (ILLUS.) 35.00
Drum, Civil War type, J.
Chein & Co. 7.50
1353 Fireplace, Burnett Ltd.,
England, 4 5/8" w., 5" h. .. 55.00
338 Humpty Dumpty, J. Chein &
Co., ca. 1935, 5¼" h...... 145.00
Jackie Robinson dime
register, square w/cut
corners, "Save & Win" &
portrait of Jackie,
2 5/8" sq. ....50.00 to 75.00
Oval cylinder w/color-printed
squirrel & owl on sides,
3" h..................... 55.00
Pail, "Prosperity Bank,"
w/handle, J. Chein & Co. .. 18.00
Post Office canister w/Mickey
& Minnie Mouse & Pluto on
sides, 1930's, large size,
7" h..................... 125.00
1593 Rocking Horse, cylinder
w/printed picture of Rocking Horse, Still Bank Collectors Club, 1977, inscribed
to noted bank collector,
Bert Whiting, 3" h. 325.00
1383 Uncle Sam hat, J. Chein &
Co., 1941, 3¼" d. 40.00
798 World "Globe Bank," J. Chein
& Co., 1934-77,
4 3/8" h. ....9.50 to 16.00
798-A World "Globe Bank,"
w/Chevrolet advertising,
J. Chein & Co., 1934-77,
4 3/8" h. 12.50
World globe, Ohio Art Co.,
3½" d. 15.00

BASEBALL MEMORABILIA

*Baseball was named by Abner Doubleday
as he laid out a diamond-shaped field with
four bases at Copperstown, New York, in
1839. A popular game from its inception, by
1869 it was able to supports its first all-
professional team, the Cincinnati Red Stock-*

ings. *The National League was organized in 1876 and though the American League was first formed in 1900, it was not officially recognized until 1903. Today, the "national pastime" has millions of fans and collecting baseball memorabilia has become a major hobby with enthusiastic collectors seeking out items associated with players such as Babe Ruth, Lou Gehrig, and others, who became legends in their own lifetimes. Though baseball cards, issued as advertising premiums for bubble gum and other products, seem to dominate the field there are numerous other items available. Also see BANKS and COCA-COLA ITEMS.*

Roy Campanella Baseball Card

Bank, glass, "Yank Bank," w/signatures & silhouettes of Lou Gehrig & Bill Dickey $40.00
Baseball, autographed by Don Larsen 55.00
Baseball, autographed by Mickey Mantle, Johnny Padres, Hank Bauer, Lew Burdette, Warren Spahn, Duke Snider, Ken Boyer & Stan Musial 250.00
Baseball card, 1950, Bowman Gum, Leo Durocher (No. 220) 6.25
Baseball card, 1950, Bowman Gum, Bob Feller (No. 6) 22.00
Baseball card, 1950, Bowman Gum, Gil Hodges (No. 112) 11.50
Baseball card, 1950, Bowman Gum, Bob Lemon (No. 40) 9.50
Baseball card, 1950, Bowman Gum, Pee Wee Reese (No. 21) 15.50
Baseball card, 1950, Bowman Gum, Casey Stengel (No. 217) 20.00
Baseball card, 1950, Bowman Gum, Ted Williams (No. 98) 52.00

Baseball card, 1951, Bowman Gum, Roy Campanella (No. 31) 25.50
Baseball card, 1951, Bowman Gum, Preacher Roe 5.00
Baseball card, 1952, Bowman Gum, Mickey Mantle 125.00
Baseball card, 1952, Red Man Tobacco, Richie Ashburn 6.00
Baseball card, 1952, Red Man Tobacco, Murray Dickson 5.00
Baseball card, 1952, Topps Gum, Warren Spahn (No. 33) 14.50
Baseball card, 1953, Topps Gum, Enos Slaughter (No. 41) 5.25
Baseball card, 1954, Topps Gum, Al Kaline (No. 201)................ 54.50
Baseball card, 1954, Topps Gum, Jackie Robinson (No. 10) 9.50
Baseball card, 1955, Topps Gum, Hank Aaron 40.00
Baseball card, 1955, Topps Gum, Roberto Clemente (No. 164) 99.50
Baseball card, 1955, Topps Gum, Sandy Koufax (No. 123) 49.50
Baseball card, 1956, Topps Gum, Hank Aaron (No. 31) 20.00
Baseball card, 1957, Topps Gum, Roy Campanella, No. 210 (ILLUS.)...................6.00 to 10.00
Baseball card, 1957, Topps Gum, Pee Wee Reese (No. 30) 11.50
Baseball card, 1958, Topps Gum, Willie Mays..................... 11.50
Baseball card, 1959, Topps Gum, Stan Musial (No. 150)............ 9.75
Baseball card, 1960, Topps Gum, Willie McCovey (No. 316) 21.50
Baseball card, 1961, Topps Gum, Harmon Killebrew 4.00
Baseball card, 1964, Topps Gum, Roger Maris (No. 225) 2.00
Baseball card, 1965, Topps Gum, Tug McGraw (No. 533) 3.50
Baseball card, 1965, Topps Gum, Red Schoendienst (No. 556) 1.00
Baseball card, 1966, Topps Gum, Willie McCovey 29.00
Baseball card, 1967, Topps Gum, Don Drysdale (No. 55) 2.00
Baseball card, 1968, Topps Gum, Tom Seaver (No. 45)............. 14.50
Baseball card, 1969, Topps Gum, Gil Hodges (No. 564)................ 2.50
Baseball card, 1969, Topps Gum, Willie Stargel (No. 545) 2.50
Baseball card, 1970, Topps Gum, Willie Mays (No. 600)............ 9.50
Baseball card, 1971, Topps Gum, Pete Rose 22.00
Book, "Babe Ruth's Big Book of Baseball," illustrated, Quaker Oil premium, 1935, 68 pp. 60.00
Book, "Spalding's Official Baseball Guide," 1908.................. 30.00

Figure of the "Cleveland Indian,"
Stanford Pottery, early 1950's,
8" h. 65.00
Figure of Hank Aaron, Hartland 250.00
Magazine, "Time," April 19, 1937,
Bob Feller on cover 35.00
Nodding figure, Mickey Mantle,
composition 50.00
Pencil, mechanical, model of Louis-
ville Slugger baseball bat, "Joe
DiMaggio" 26.00
Pennant, "Mickey Mantle Day," 1968   8.00
Pennant, "New York Yankees,"
1964, w/color photo of team 45.00
Pinback button, Honus Wagner 50.00
Poster, "Red Sox - Champions 1912,"
team photograph below a red
pennant, players listed, 13¾ x
21½" (water damage lower
edge) 440.00
Program, 1928 World Series, St.
Louis Cardinals vs. New York
Yankees (no cover) 150.00
Program, 1943 World Series, St.
Louis Cardinals vs. New York
Yankees 95.00
Program, 1949 World Series, Brook-
lyn Dodgers vs. New York
Yankees 125.00
Program, 1951 All-Star Game at
Briggs Stadium 90.00
Scorecard, 1941, New York Yankees
vs. Cleveland Indians 12.00

Silver Baseball Trophy

Trophy, silver, slightly bombe
w/everted rim, base fluted below
band of scrolling foliage, matching C-scroll handles, acid-etched
one side w/inscription "The
Spaulding Trophy Amateur Baseball League Championship.
Presented by A. G. Spaulding
Bro's. Won by S.I.A.C. (Staten Island Athletic Club) 1888," reverse
w/scene of baseball game, Whiting Mfg. Co., New York, 8¼" h.
(ILLUS.)........................ 770.00

Wrist watch, Babe Ruth, original
band, 1933-35 .... 500.00
Yearbook, 1958 Milwaukee Braves .. 22.00
Yearbook, 1959 New York
Yankees....................... 15.00

BASKETS

Assorted American Indian Baskets

*The American Indians were the first basket
weavers on this continent, and, of necessity,
the early Colonial settlers and their descen-
dents pursued this artistic handicraft to provide essential containers for berries, eggs and
endless other items to be carried or stored.
Rye straw, split willow and reeds are but a
few of the wide variety of materials used. The
Nantucket baskets, plainly and sturdily constructed, along with the baskets woven by
American Indians and at the Shaker settlements, would seem to draw the greatest attention in an area of collecting where interest
has stabilized because of the wide availability of fine baskets by contemporary basket-
weavers for art and craft shows across the
country.*

American Indian basket w/lid,
woven sweetgrass w/openwork
designs, ca. 1915 .... $50.00
American Indian basket, Klamath,
woven coilwork construction,
woven arrowpoint design, 1930's,
3" d. 65.00
American Indian basket, Klamath,
woven coilwork construction, Wild
Geese patt., 8" d. 135.00
American Indian basket, Woodland
tribes, woven natural & faded red
splint, w/two swinging bentwood
handles, 11½ x 9¼", 5¾" h. plus
handles 90.00
American Indian basket-tray,
Macah, woven coilwork construction, natural & shaded blue stripe
patt., dark bottom, 8" d., 5" h. 185.00
American Indian basket-tray, Popa-
go, woven coilwork construction
w/deer (4) & eagle (4) designs
around top, 16" d. 125.00
American Indian burden basket,
Apache, woven coilwork construc-

tion w/red cloth decorations & w/leather patch covering bottom, cotton carrying strap, ca. 1900, 14" d., 11" h. 175.00

American Indian hat-shaped basket, Klamath, woven coilwork construction, 7" w. 126.00

American Indian "strawberry" basket, cov., Chippewa, woven black ash splint in curlique technique, 4" h. (faded colors & minor wear) 20.00

American Indian winnowing basket, Salish, woven willow 168.00

Berry basket, vertical oak splint slats w/nailed rim & base bandings, painted apple green, 2-qt. ... 150.00

"Buttocks" basket, 12-rib construction, woven oak splint, 4½" d., 4" h. plus bentwood handle 105.00

"Buttocks" basket, 18-rib construction, woven ash splint, 6¼ x 5½", 3¾" h. plus bentwood handle 145.00

"Buttocks" basket, 26-rib construction w/pronounced "gizzard" shape, 8 x 7", 4" h. plus bentwood handle.................... 195.00

"Buttocks" basket, 10-rib construction, woven hickory splint, 11 x 9½", 5½" h. plus bentwood handle 50.00

"Buttocks" basket w/double hinged lids, 20-rib construction, woven ash splint, 16 x 12", 8½" h. plus bentwood handle................ 95.00

Cat carrying basket, cov., 28-rib construction, woven splint, hinged woven flap over half of top & the other half w/permanent woven closure, rounded ends, 27 x 13" oval, 10" h. plus handle (minor breaks in splint) 440.00

Cheese basket, woven oak splint, 7" d.......................... 140.00

Shaker Cheese Basket

Cheese basket, Shaker, woven splint, 18 x 19" warped d. (ILLUS.)....................... 475.00

Feather basket w/lid, woven oak splint, painted white, 26½" h..... 350.00

Field (or gathering) basket, woven oak splint, 11" sq., 3" h. plus bentwood handle............... 135.00

Flower or herb gathering basket, machine-cut oak splint, factory-made, early 20th c., large flat square 65.00

Fishing creel basket w/hinged slant lid, woven reed, w/leather & canvas strap, 20th c., 13" w. 25.00

Herb drying basket, woven ash splint, double-wrapped rim & splint-wrapped side handles, 21 x 12", 1¼" deep 275.00

Laundry basket, woven splint, bentwood rim w/handles, 27¾ x 19", 12" h....................... 85.00

Market (or utility) basket, miniature, woven splint, 4" d., 3½" h. plus bentwood handle................ 85.00

Market (or utility) basket, tightly woven splint & cane, 9½" d., 6½" h. plus carved bentwood handle 75.00

Market (or utility) basket, woven splint, 10½" d., 5¾" h., w/swinging bentood handle.............. 175.00

Basket with Swinging Handle

Market (or utility) basket, woven oak split wood, square bottom, round top, 11" top d., 8" h., w/swinging handle (ILLUS.) 95.00

Market (or utility) basket, woven oak splint, stained brown against natural design, 13 x 11½" oblong, 6" h. plus bentwood handle 95.00

Market (or utility) basket, woven split wood, square bottom, round rim, 13½" top d., 8" h. plus carved bentwood handle (minor wear) 115.00

Market (or utility) basket w/double-hinged lid, woven split wood, interior w/green & natural checkerboard design that has completely faded from the exterior, 15 x 7¾" oblong, 6" h. plus bentwood handle ....

Woven Willow Basket

Market (or utility) basket, woven
willow, 13½" d., 10" h. plus
willow-wrapped handle (ILLUS.)...   75.00
Market (or utility) basket, woven
splint, 16½ x 8½" elongated oval,
10½" h. plus bentwood handle
(minor wear & few breaks).......   130.00
Market (or utility) basket, woven
splint w/ribs radiating from handle, 21 x 16" oval, 8½" h. plus
bentwood handle...............   135.00
Melon basket, miniature, 10-rib construction, woven hickory splint,
5" d., 2¾" h. plus bentwood
handle................130.00 to 185.00

Melon Basket

Melon basket, 18-rib construction,
11 x 9½" oval rim opening, 14½"
across widest point, 6" h.
(ILLUS.)........................   145.00
Melon basket, 18-rib construction,
woven hickory splint, old red
paint, 14" d., 8" h. plus bentwood
handle 250.00
Picnic (or storage) basket, woven
oak split wood, hinged lid, swing
handles, 21 x 10", 12" h.........   28.00

Picnic basket or hamper w/hinged
lid, woven willow, 22 x 15 x 8"...   40.00
Picnic basket or hamper, 4-section
hinged lid, w/handles, woven
cane, England, ca. 1910..........   75.00
Rye straw (bread) basket, ovoid,
woven coilwork construction,
9" d., 10" h....................   40.00
Rye straw (bread) basket, coilwork
construction, 12" d., 4½" h. 32.00
Rye straw (bread) basket, coilwork
construction, flaring rim, 12" l. 65.00

Rye Straw Bread Basket

Rye straw (bread) basket, coilwork
construction, flaring rim w/end
handles, Pennsylvania, 15" l.
(ILLUS.)........................   105.00
Sewing basket, cov., woven reed,
w/Chinese coins & silk tassels attached to lid, 7½" d. 15.00
Sewing basket, cov., woven sweetgrass, 8½" d. 20.00
Sewing basket w/hinged lid, woven
split wood, ca. 1920, 11" d.,
3¾" h. 22.00
Shaker bushel basket, woven splint,
kick-up bottom, wrapped rim,
carved side handles 165.00
Shaker basket, woven splint, grey
weathered finish, 5½" d. minia-
ture, 4" h. plus wooden handles ..   125.00
Shaker market basket, woven splint,
7 x 7¾" oval, 4 3/8" h. plus bentwood handle....................   135.00
Storage basket, open, woven split
wood, w/handles at rim, 8¼" d.,
3¼" h. 160.00
Storage basket, open, woven willow, 10½" d. 35.00
Storage basket, open, tightly woven
ash splint, well-shaped bentwood
rim handles each side, 12½" d.,
7" h............................   135.00
Storage basket, open, footed,
woven splint, open handles at
rim, 4 wooden feet, 16 x 12½"
oblong, overall 8" h. 75.00
Winnowing basket, half-round,
woven hickory splint & arched
hickory handles w/rosehead nails,
46" d...................265.00 to 285.00

BEADED & MESH BAGS

Carnival Glass Beaded Bag

Beaded and mesh bags, popular earlier in this century, are now in great demand. Ladies have found them to be the perfect accessory to the casual long gowns now so fashionable. Sterling silver bags and those set with precious stones bring high prices, but the average glass beaded bag is much lower.

Beaded, dark blue iridescent Carnival glass beading on mesh fabric, brass frame & chain handle, 3" w. at top flaring to 7" (ILLUS.) $45.00

Beaded, crystal & white beading, drawstring-type w/long beaded fringe, 1920's 45.00

Beaded, grey iridescent beading, drawstring-type, w/beaded tassels, 1920's 45.00

Beaded, ivory beading, Art Deco style agate clasp, gold chain handle 30.00

Beaded, multicolored beading forming floral basket design, scalloped base w/beaded fringe, marked "El Sah," Whiting-Davis, 8 x 7" 95.00

Beaded, multicolored beading forming floral design w/shaded green leaves accented w/silver beading, metal frame w/twist clasp, black beaded handle, 8¼ x 6" 55.00

Beaded, red beading, diamond-shaped w/red beaded fringe, brass frame & chain handle 50.00

Beaded, red & blue beading forming an overall rose blossom & twining morning glory design on white beaded ground, w/beaded fringe, ornate silverplate frame & double chain handle, 6" w., 10" l. 45.00

Beaded, red, blue & green beading forming floral design on grey beaded ground, drawstring-type .. 37.50

Beaded, red-orange beading forming a rose blossom design on black & gold beaded ground,

w/fringe, original red velvet lining, metal frame & chain handle, 11 x 6¼" 55.00

Beaded, shaded blue beading, brass frame w/chain handle 65.00

Beaded, shaded rusty peach beading forming a design of small half-circles each w/a seed pearl center, ormolu hinged frame applied w/three oval enameled portraits of beautiful women, each oval within lacy ormolu frame encircled w/seed pearls, signed Marabito, Paris, 7¾" w., 7" l..... 375.00

Beaded, shell pink bugle beads, clutch-type w/snap closure, w/interior mirror 20.00

Enameled mesh, orange & green design 40.00

Enameled mesh, pink rose on grey ground, Whiting-Davis 35.00

German silver mesh, w/belt hook clasp.................... 40.00 to 65.00

Gold finish mesh, expandable-type, w/chain, Whiting-Davis, 4 x 3½" 47.50

Gold finish mesh, loop handle, Whiting-Davis, 2¼ x 7" 58.00

Silver finish mesh, w/chain handle, original mirror inside, Whiting-Davis 40.00

Sterling silver mesh, silver frame & chain link handle, 4 x 4½" .... 77.50 to 85.00

Sterling silver mesh, Tiffany & Co., ca. 1900 .... 850.00

Sterling silver mesh, embossed design on frame w/small blue stone in clasp on handle 195.00

BELLS

Russian Silver Sanctuary Bell

Altar sanctuary bell, bronze, sides cast w/openwork scrolls & Evangelists & inscribed "Matthew, Mark, Luke & John" on solid banding, 3½" d., 6 3/8" h. $95.00

Altar sanctuary bell, Russian silver, sides cast & chased w/four reserves of saints, bulbous finial surmounted by cross, borders chased & engraved w/florals, foliage & geometric designs, St. Petersburg, ca. 1855 (lacks clapper), 6¾" h. (ILLUS.) 880.00

Altar sanctuary bell, brass, sides cast w/twelve Apostles, St. Peter's triple crown handle, 4" d., 8" h. 140.00

Animal bell, cow, brass, "Chiantel Fondeur, 1878, Saignegier," 4" d. 65.00

Animal bell, cow, brass w/iron clapper, 7" h. 18.00

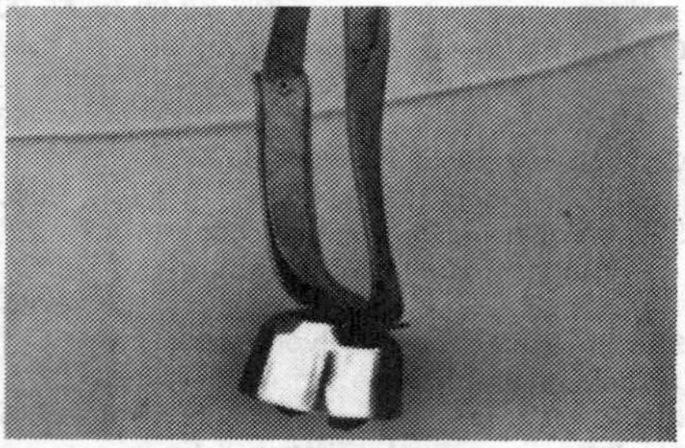

Cow Bell from Shaft Chime

Animal bell, cow, brass shaft chime w/three clappers on iron strap converted to fit leather strap, burnished (ILLUS.) 30.00

Animal bell, cow, sheet iron w/iron clapper 12.00

Animal bell, sheep, brass, elongated form, w/leather neck strap . . . . 25.00 to 40.00

Boxing ring bell, bell metal, ca. 1890, large 75.00

China bell, figural Dutch doll wearing full regalia w/hat, apron & long skirt, marked "Germany" & numbered, 3¾" h. 175.00

China bell, blue Delft-type decor, Germany 42.00

Figural bell, brass, golf ball form bell w/figural golf caddy boy handle, 1¾" d., 3¾" h. 135.00

Figural bell, brass, Elizabethan lady w/legs & feet forming clapper, 2 7/8" d., 5 1/8" h. 85.00

Figural bell, brass, Dutch woman w/basket, 3¼" d., 5¾" h. 95.00

Figural bell, brass, Colonial lady w/tiered skirt & shawl, 3¼" d., 6½" h. 90.00

Silver Figural Bells

Figural bells, Continental silver, 3 women & single man, together w/figural woman silverplate bell, late 19th c., 3 1/8" to 5" h., set of 5 (ILLUS.) 1,045.00

Glass bell, clear cut glass, attributed to Dorflinger, large 375.00

Glass bell, clear cut glass, Straus' Drape patt. 250.00

Glass bell, cranberry, cut handle, 9½" h. 200.00

Glass bell, cranberry Swirl patt., applied opaque white base rim & clear handle, 5 3/8" d., 13½" h. . . 175.00

Glass bell, lime green transparent squared bell, applied enameled metal rooster handle, metal claw & egg clapper, 1¾" d., 4¾" h. . . . 125.00

Glass bell, Nailsea-type, blue w/opalescent loopings, applied clear swirl handle, 5 7/8" d., 12" h. 205.00

Hand bell, brass, figural Roman soldier handle, 2½" d., 5¾" h. . . . 55.00

Hand bell, brass, figural French peasant girl w/jug handle, 3¼" d., 6¼" h. 79.00

Hand bell, brass, figural Napoleon handle, sides cast w/scenes of Battle of Waterloo, 3" d., 6¼" h. . . . . 80.00 to 135.00

English Silver Hand Bell

Hand bell, silver, flat-chased florals & foliage, molded borders, green-stained ivory handle, London, 1836, 5¼" h. (ILLUS.) 330.00

Hand bell, silverplate, ornately chased, ivory handle, Gorham Co., small 95.00

Locomotive bell, brass, "D. & GR. R.R.," 12" d., 10" h., w/iron yoke & cradle, overall 18½ x 19½" 600.00

Locomotive bell, brass, "New York Central R.R.," 15" d., w/yoke & cradle.................695.00 to 750.00

Police (or "Paddy") wagon bell, nickel-plated, embossed "Chicago Police Dept.," ca. 1910, 16" 400.00

Schoolhouse tower bell, cast iron, stamped "Fecit I. Sheridan, Dublin, 1846," Ireland, 16" h. 265.00

Schoolhouse tower bell, cast iron, ca. 1870, w/yoke, overall 21" h. .. 95.00

School teacher's hand bell, brass, turned fruitwood handle, 6" h. ... 70.00

School teacher's hand bell, brass, turned wood handle, 9½" h. 65.00

School teacher's hand bell, bell metal, turned wood handle painted red w/brass finial, 6" d., 11" h. 85.00

Sleigh bell, brass No. 12 size crotal-type (single) 12.00

Sleigh bells, 9 brass graduated crotal-type bells on original leather strap................... 90.00

Sleigh bells, 12 brass graduated crotal-type bells on original leather strap................... 125.00

Sleigh bells, 22 brass graduated small crotal-type bells on original leather strap ....225.00 to 250.00

Sleigh bells, 30 brass graduated small crotal-type bells on leather strap w/cotter keys .....300.00 to 400.00

Sleigh cutter shaft bells, set of 3 brass chimes w/triple clappers on metal shaft 57.50

BIG LITTLE BOOKS

The "Big Little Books" series of small format was originated by the Whitman Publishing Company, Racine, Wisconsin, in 1933. These books covered a wide variety of subjects ranging from adventure stories to tales based on comic strip characters, movie and radio stars. After Whitman's initial success, others including World Syndicate and Saalfield publishing companies, also issued series of small format books. The publisher original-ly assigned a serial number to each book and unless otherwise specified, Whitman's books are listed below.

Ace Drummond, 1935 .... $14.00

Black Silver & His Pirate Crew, 1937 .... 15.00

Blaze Brandon with the Foreign Legion, 1938 .... 10.00

Buck Rogers in Ride 'Em Cowboy, 1937 .... 15.00

Buck Rogers in the City Below the Sea, 1934...................... 37.50

Buck Rogers in the City of Floating Globes, 1935, Cocomalt premium ....75.00 to 110.00

Bugs Bunny & the Giant Brothers, 1949 .... 10.00

Captain Midnight & the Secret Squadron Vs. the Terror of the Orient, 1942 .... 15.00

Chester Gump in the Pole to Pole Flight, 1937 .... 24.00

Dan Dunn & the Dope Ring, 1940 ... 12.00

Danger Trails in Africa, 1935 .... 12.50

David Copperfield, 1934............ 15.00

Dippy the Goof, Walt Disney 1066 Series, 1938 .... 30.00

Doctor Doom & the Ghost Submarine, Foreign Spies, 1939......... 13.50

Donald Duck Sees Stars, "movie flip" page corners, 1941 .... 23.00

Donald Forgets to Duck, 1939 ...... 18.00

Farmyard Symphony, Walt Disney 1058 Series, 1938............... 30.00

Flash Gordon Big Little Books

Flash Gordon and the Tournaments of Mongo, 1935 (ILLUS. left) 46.00

Flash Gordon and the Tyrant of Mongo, "movie-flip" page corners, 1941 (ILLUS. right) 40.00

Flash Gordon in the Water World of Mongo, 1937 (ILLUS. center) 20.00

Flint Roper & the Six-Gun Showdown, 1941 .... 14.00

Gene Autry and the Raiders of the Range, 1946 .... 12.00

Inspector Wade Solves the Mystery of the Red Aces, 1937 .... 8.00

Jane Withers in This is the Life, 1937 .... 9.00

Jimmie Allen in the Airmail Rob-
bery, 1936 .... 10.00
John Carter of Mars, 1940 .... 75.00
Jungle Jim, 1936 .... 42.00
Laughing Dragon of Oz, 1934 (spine
taped) 30.00
Little Miss Muffet, 1936 .... 8.50
Little Orphan Annie in the Movies,
1937 .... 19.00
Little Orphan Annie in the Thieves'
Den, 1948 .... 10.00
Lone Ranger & the Red Renegades,
1939 .... 14.50
Lone Ranger & the Secret Weapon,
1943 .... 15.00
Lone Star Martin of the Texas
Rangers, 1939 .... 14.00
Lost Patrol, 1934 .... 10.00
Mac of the Marines in Africa,
1936 ....12.00 to 18.00
Mary Lee & the Mystery of the Indi-
an Beads, 1937 .... 14.00
Mickey Mouse, 1933 ....80.00 to 95.00
Mickey Mouse & the 'Lectro Box,
1946 .... 27.00
Mickey Mouse & the Sacred Jewel,
1936 .... 30.00
Moon Mullins & Kayo, 1933 .... 12.00
My Life and Times - Shirley Temple,
Saalfield, 1936 .... 20.00
Peggy Brown and the Runaway Auto
Trailer, No. 1491, 1937 .....4.00 to 10.00
Perry Winkle and the Rinkeydinks,
No. 1487, 1936 .... 11.00
Popeye Ghost Ship to Treasure Is-
land, No. 2008, 1967 .... 8.00
Popeye in Puddleburg, Saalfield,
No. 1088, 1934 .... 35.00
Prairie Bill and the Covered Wagon,
No. 758, 1934 .... 6.00
Radio Patrol Trailing the Safe-
blowers, No. 1173, 1937 .... 8.00
Reg'lar Fellers, 1933, Cocomalt
advertising 15.00

Tarzan Big Little Books

Return of Tarzan, 1967 (ILLUS.
center) 5.00
Robinson Crusoe, No. 719, 1933 .... 18.00
Roy Rogers and the Dwarf Cattle
Ranch, No. 1421, 1947 .... 8.00
Roy Rogers and the Mystery of the
Howling Mesa, No. 1448, 1948.... 13.00

Roy Rogers, King of the Cowboys,
No. 1460, 1943 .... 17.00
Shadow and the Ghost Makers,
No. 1495, 1942 .... 25.00
The Silver Streak, No. 1155, 1935 ... 9.00
Skeezix on His Own in the Big City,
No. 1419, 1941 .... 12.00
Skyroads with Hurricane Hawk,
No. 1127, 1936 ....8.50 to 12.00
Story of Charlie McCarthy & Edgar
Bergen, No. 1456, 1938 .....7.50 to 15.00
Tailspin Tommy in the Famous Pay-
roll Mystery, No. 747, 1933....... 16.00
Tailspin Tommy in Great Air Mys-
tery, No. 1184, 1936 ....7.00 to 10.00
Tarzan and the Golden Lion,
No. 1448, 1943 (ILLUS. left) 12.00
Tarzan of the Apes, No. 744, 1933 .. 40.00
Tarzan the Fearless, No. 769, 1934 .. 45.00
Tarzan's Revenge, No. 1488, 1938
(ILLUS. right) 12.00
Tarzan Twins, No. 770, 1934 .... 35.00
Terry and the Pirates, No. 1156,
1935 .... 12.00
Terry and the Pirates and the
Giant's Vengeance, No. 1446,
1939 .... 12.00
Terry and War in the Jungle,
No. 1420, 1946 ....15.00 to 23.00
The Texas Kid, No. 1429, 1937 ..... 8.00
Thumper & the Seven Dwarfs, Walt
Disney, No. 1409, 1944 ....15.00 to 30.00
Tim McCoy and the Sandy Gulch
Stampede, No. 1490, 1939 (miss-
ing 2 pages) 6.50
Tim McCoy on the Tomahawk Trail,
No. 1436, 1937 .... 12.50
Tim Tyler's Luck and the Plot of the
Exiled King, No. 1479, 1939 ...... 17.00
Tiny Tim (The Adventures of),
No. 767, 1935 ....12.00 to 22.00
Tom Beatty - Ace of the Service,
No. 723, 1934 .... 13.00
Tom Mix and His Circus on the Bar-
bary Coast, No. 1482, 1940 ...... 15.00
Tom Mix and the Hoard of Montezu-
ma, No. 1462, 1937 .... 30.00
Tom Mix and the Stranger from the
South, No. 1183, 1935 .... 15.00
Tom Mix & Tony Jr. in Terror Trail,
No. 762, 1935 ....16.00 to 30.00
Tom Mix in the Range War,
No. 1166, 1937 .... 12.00
Tom Mix Plays a Lone Hand,
No. 1173, 1935 .... 22.00
Tom Swift and His Magnetic
Silencer, No. 1437, 1941 .... 35.00
Wash Tubbs in Pandemonia,
No. 751, 1934 ....12.00 to 15.00
Zip Saunders - King of Speedway,
No. 1465, 1939 ....9.00 to 12.00

BOOKENDS

Cast Iron Art Deco Bookends

*Also see AVIATION & CAT COLLECTI-
BLES, LENOX PORCELAIN, MARBLE-
HEAD & McCOY POTTERY, METALS,
NORTH DAKOTA, ROOKWOOD, ROSE-
VILLE, TECO & VAN BRIGGLE POT-
TERY, ROYCROFT ITEMS and SPELTER.*

Art pottery, figure of a cupid w/rab-
bit, American Encaustic Tiling Co.,
Zanesville, Ohio, pr. $40.00
Brass, model of stylized Art Deco
owl, marked Art Brass Co., N.Y.,
4" h., pr. 55.00
Bronze, bust of Robert Burns, 5" h.,
pr. 70.00
Bronze, columns & vignette of wom-
an reading at a desk, Bradley &
Hubbard, 5 x 5 x 2", pr. 50.00
Bronze, figure of golfer wearing
knickers, pr. 85.00
Bronze, figure of nude boy w/Grey-
hound dog, pr. 130.00
Bronze, figure of nude woman in
kneeling position, horseshoe-
shaped stepped base, impressed
"Tinos" & marked Aegte Bronze,
Denmark, 7½" h., pr. 155.00
Bronze, model of Scottie dogs in
various poses, on tiered base,
signed E. B. Parsons, Gorham
Foundries, 7 x 5 x 2½", pr. 450.00
Bronze-finish pot metal, model of
peacock, pr. 38.00
Cast iron, Art Deco style abstract
design in red, green & gold on
grey ground, marked Bradley &
Hubbard, pr. 60.00
Cast iron, full figure nude woman
kneeling w/leg extending forward
as she performs a backbend,
w/her hand at end of drooping
hair, bronze finish, pr. (ILLUS.) ... 75.00
Cast iron, "Girl at Fountain," pr. ... 20.00
Cast iron, girls (2) wearing sunhats
seated back-to-back reading,
original paint, 5" h., pr. 75.00
Cast iron, model of lion on rocks,
original paint, pr. 20.00
Cast iron, model of parrot, 5" h.,
pr. 30.00
Ceramic, model of stylized turkey,

cream & silver crackled glaze, impressed C. H., France, 6¾" h.,
pr. 150.00
Gun metal, model of abstract Art
Deco penguin w/silvery white
front, standing before brushed finish angled disc, pr. 57.00
Pot metal, figure of old man in arm
chair w/book, greenish-gold &
white finish, signed J. Ruhl, pr. ... 70.00
Pressed glass, marked Alacite by
Aladdin, 1939-52, pr. 125.00
Pressed glass, model of sea lion,
clear, pr. 50.00
Wooden, carved teakwood model of
elephant w/ivory eyes, tusks &
toenails, pr. 125.00

BOOKMARKS

Celluloid Bookmark

*Also see COCA-COLA ITEMS and
WORLD FAIR COLLECTIBLES.*

Advertising, "Beich's Chocolates,"
celluloid $25.00
Advertising, "Briggs Piano," celluloid, heart-shaped 15.00
Advertising, "Carnation Milk," celluloid, 1915 .... 25.00
Advertising, "Cracker Jack," tin,
die-cut & color-printed Spaniel
dog 20.00
Advertising, "Crown Piano,"
celluloid 15.00
Advertising, "Denver Dry Goods,"
celluloid 15.00
Advertising, "Dr. Reed Shoes,"
celluloid 15.00
Advertising, "Libby Foods," cel-
luloid, Omaha Fair, 1898 .... 25.00
Brass, Chicago World's Fair, 1934 .. 3.50
Celluloid, "By This Sign Conquer" &
"Rally Day," red, white & blue silk
cord page marker w/tassel
(ILLUS.) 6.50

Celluloid, girl on rocking horse 35.00
Celluloid, model of a bear 15.00
Plique-a-jour enamel & silver-gilt,
   shaped cloisonne & plique-a-jour
   top enameled w/double-headed
   eagle, stem engraved w/scrolling
   foliage, A. Kasakov, Moscow, late
   19th c., 4½" l. 242.00
Sterling silver, embossed ship 29.00
Sterling silver, plain 12.00
Sterling silver, reticulated, engraved
   design 22.00
Woven silk, "Star Spangled Banner,"
   flag pictured, framed 38.00

BOOTJACKS

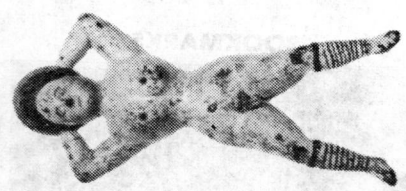

"Naughty Nellie" Bootjack

Cast iron, figural "Naughty Nellie,"
   original paint (ILLUS.) . . .$75.00 to 125.00
Cast iron, model of a mule's
   head 38.00
Cast iron, folding-type, cast in the
   form of a revolver, "The American
   Bulldog Bootjack," 8" l . . . . .65.00 to 75.00
Wooden, tiger stripe maple, folding-
   type 30.00
Wooden, pierced w/three hearts & 5
   circles, 3½" w., 15" l. 535.00
Wooden, lady's, folding-type
   w/hinges, footed 30.00

BOTTLE OPENERS

Corkscrews were actually the first bottle openers and these may date back to the mid-18th century, but bottle openers, as we know them today, are strictly a 20th century item and come into use only after Michael J. Owens invented the automatic bottle machine in 1903. Avid collectors have spurred this relatively new area of collector interest that requires only a modest investment. Our listing, by type of metal, encompasses the four basic types sought by collectors: advertising openers; full figure

openers which stand alone or hang on the wall; flat figural openers such as the lady's leg shape; and openers with embossed engraved or chased handles. Also see BREWERIANA and CORKSCREWS.

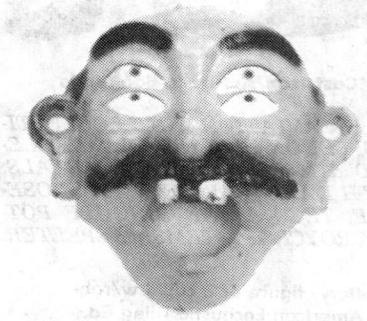

Four-eyed Man Bottle Opener

Advertising, "An Opener for Friend-
   ship, Potosi Brewing Co.," original
   envelope $6.00
Advertising, "Iroquis Brewery,"
   w/Indian 30.00
Advertising, "Jax," counter-type 25.00
Advertising, "S. & H. Green
   Stamps," w/corkscrew 10.00
Advertising, "Schlitz Beer," wooden
   bottle-shaped handle 10.00
Aluminum, full figure cowboy
   w/guitar, John Wright Co. 10.00
Brass, full figure fish w/corkscrew
   in tail, black enamel, marked
   "Germany" 33.50
Brass, full figure sea horse, John
   Wright Co. 35.00
Brass, full figure shark w/corkscrew
   in tail 35.00
Brass, wall-type, full figure cobra
   head 15.00
Brass w/abalone shell inlay, full
   figure fish 35.00
Bronze, full figure camel 35.00
Bronze, full figure nude lady,
   marked "Korbel" 85.00
Cast iron, full figure alligator, John
   Wright Co. 40.00
Cast iron, full figure billy goat, worn
   original paint, John Wright Co.,
   4 3/8" h. 85.00
Cast iron, full figure cockatoo, origi-
   nal paint, John Wright Co. 87.50
Cast iron, full figure crab 15.00
Cast iron, full figure seated
   elephant w/trunk raised,
   3 1/8" h. 185.00
Cast iron, full figure golfer in knick-
   ers & sweater 19.00

Cast iron, full figure goose 45.00
Cast iron, full figure
　　lobster . . . . 17.00 to 25.00
Cast iron, full figure parrot w/long
　　legs, worn original paint, 5" h. . . . 35.00
Cast iron, full figure ram, original
　　paint 35.00
Cast iron, wall-type, four-eyed bald
　　headed man w/mustache, original
　　paint, Wilton Products, 3½ x 3¼"
　　(ILLUS.) 35.00
Cast iron, wall-type, laughing black
　　man, 4½" . . . . 50.00 to 65.00
Chrome-plated metal, full figure
　　pelican 15.00
Stag's horn handle w/sterling silver
　　ferrule 28.00
Sterling silver handle, Windham
　　patt., Tiffany & Co. 45.00

BOTTLES & FLASKS

Glass bottles and flasks have been made since ancient times and the first attempt to manufacture glass in the new world took place at the Jamestown, Virginia settlement, probably between 1609 and 1617. Over one-hundred years passed before another glass factory could survive more than a decade. Caspar Wistar and subsequently his son, operated a glasshouse, from 1739 to 1779, in New Jersey where bottles and other utilitarian wares were produced from ordinary window glass and green, or bottle, glass. Henry William Stiegel, whose glass factory opened in Manheim, Pennsylvania in 1763, produced a fine quality glass in the European tradition by employing German, Venetian and English glass blowers. The quality of Stiegel's glass was so fine that today it is difficult to distinguish from the Continental glasswares produced during the same time span. Today, almost all early glass made in colonial America is categorized as being either Jersey-type or Stiegel-type though few pieces can be positively identified.

Bottles and flasks were either free-blown or pattern-molded and expanded. Stiegel bottles are typically pattern-molded. The Pitkin glasshouse, near Hartford, Connecticut produced bottles of all kinds, but "pitkin" has become a generic term for a flask that is fine-ribbed vertically or spirally, or possibly in a combination of both. A "chestnut" bottle is a globular or ovoid bottle with a tapered neck, somewhat resembling the American chestnut and can be free-blown or pattern-molded and expanded.

"Ludlow," a term often applied to chestnut
bottles, is derived from the fact that early bottle collectors assumed all chestnut-form bottles were made at a glassworks that operated at Ludlow, Massachusetts about 1815. Carboys are large bottles that usually held corrosive liquids and often were encased in wooden crates, while demijohns are usually large narrow-necked wine bottles often originally encased in wicker.

"Bitters" were merely a means of evading a tax on gin imposed by George II of England. Gin merchants added herbs to the gin and sold it for medicinal purposes, evading the tax levy and retaining their margin of profit. For the same reason, Bitters became popular in colonial America. Case bottles are square-bodied bottles that are sometimes tapered. Case gin bottles and other early bottles before the mid-19th century will have pontil scars and applied lips. Sometimes gin and wine bottles have an applied "seal," a glob of molten glass applied to the shoulder or body that is subsequently stamped with a seal. These are referred to as "seal" bottles.

Historical flasks have national themes with portraits of national heroes, prominent people and presidents or patriotic themes. Historical and pictorial flasks constitute a well-researched area of bottle collecting. Figural, ink and nursing bottles represent still other aspects of the overall bottle collecting hobby.

J. Michael Owens patented his automatic bottle making machine in 1891 and, by the very early 1900's, hand blowing of bottles gave way to this automated procedure. Bottles do not have to be hand-blown to be collectible and many of the beer, soda and whiskey bottles that are avidly collected today are those made by machine. A good reference for the beginning bottle collector is Cecil Munsey's "The Illustrated Guide to Collectible Bottles." Collectors of historical flasks will find invaluable material in George and Helen McKearin's comprehensive work, "American Glass."

BARBER

Amber, embossed "T. Noonan and
　　Co. Barber Supplies - Boston,
　　Mass.," frosted finish, original
　　stopper $125.00
Amethyst, enameled daisies decor,
　　pr. (no stoppers) 125.00
Amethyst, enameled designs around
　　shoulder, original stopper 77.50
Blue opalescent, Hobb's Hobnail
　　patt., original stopper 135.00
Camphor, lettered "Witch Hazel,"
　　original stopper 60.00
Chartreuse, enameled gold
　　chrysanthemums, stems & leaves
　　outlined in white (no stopper) 85.00
Cobalt blue, onion-shaped, ornate

silver overlay design on shoulder,
open pontil, 7" h. (no stopper) ... 85.00
Cobalt blue, paneled body, original
porcelain stopper 39.00
Cobalt blue, raised enamel decor,
pontil (no stopper) 75.00
Cobalt blue translucent, squat onion
shape, ground pontil, original
pewter stopper 95.00

Barber Bottle with Enameled Florals

Cranberry, enameled florals & band
of raised enamel dots, 7" h.
(ILLUS.) 145.00
Cranberry, Inverted Thumbprint
patt., ring neck, ground pontil (no
stopper) 125.00
Cranberry opalescent, Hobb's Hobnail patt., frosted finish, original
pewter stopper 175.00
Cranberry opalescent, Swirl patt.,
polished pontil (no stopper) 160.00
Emerald green, embossed "N. Wa-
pler, N.Y." on base (no stopper).. 18.00
Emerald green, raised enamel
decor, polished pontil (no
stopper) 75.00
Mary Gregory type, amethyst, white
enameled boy (no stopper)....... 160.00
Mary Gregory type, amethyst, white
enameled figures, pr. 495.00
Mary Gregory type, cobalt blue,
white enameled girl w/tennis
racquet 160.00
Mary Gregory type, green, white
enameled girl in garden 155.00
Milk white, pink roses decor, original stopper, 7" h. 38.50
Peach satin finish, original
stopper 145.00
Pigeon Blood red, Elongated Honeycomb patt., original stopper...... 120.00
Ruby red, paneled body, original
porcelain stopper 39.00

BITTERS

Group of Bitters Bottles

Abbot Aromatic Bitters, round,
amber 19.00
African Stomach, round, amber..... 55.00
Allen's (William) Congress, rectan-
gular, aqua, ¾ qt. 325.00
Angostura Bark, burnt orange 68.00
Atwood's Genuine, round, aqua,
½ pt. 20.00
Baker's Orange Grove, square
w/roped corners, puce, ¾ qt. 255.00
Barber's Indian Vegetable Jaundice,
Oliver Johnson & Co., Providence,
R.I., 12-sided, aqua, 6 1/8" h. 125.00
Bell's (Dr.) Blood Purifying Bitters -
The Great English Remedy, rec-
tangular, amber, 9¾" h. 175.00
Berkshire Bitters, Amann & Co.,
Cincinnati, O., figural pig, amber,
9½" l. ....1,265.00 to 2,000.00
Big Bill's Best, square, orange-
amber, 12 1/8" h. 95.00
Blue Mountain, rectangular, aqua... 32.50
Bourbon Whiskey, barrel-shaped,
puce, 9¼" h. 200.00
Boyer's Stomach, Cincinnati, round,
clear, 11" h. 42.50
Brown's Celebrated Indian Herb,
Patented Feb. 11, 1868, figural
Indian Queen, amber, 12¼" h.
(ILLUS. center) 400.00
Brown's Celebrated Indian Herb,
Patented 1867, figural Indian
Queen, amber ....265.00 to 325.00
Brown's Iron, square, applied top,
amber, pt....................... 17.50
Bull's (Dr. John) Compound Cedron
Bitters, Louisville, Ky, square, am-
ber, 10" h. 240.00
Burdock Blood, Buffalo, N.Y.,
amethyst 22.50
Caldwell's (The Great Dr.) Herb
Tonic, triangular, amber,
12¾" h. 150.00
Clarke's Compound Mandrake, oval,
aqua, 7 5/8" h. 55.00

Clark's Giant Bitters, Philada., Pa.,
rectangular, aqua, 6¾" h. 32.50
Cole Brothers Vegetable, aqua 47.50
Colleton, rectangular, aqua, 6¼" h.
(slight haze) 120.00
Columbo Peptic, L.E. Jung, New
Orleans, square, amber, 9" h. 30.00
Curtis & Perkins Wild Cherry, pontil,
aqua, original label . . . . . . 82.50 to 95.00
Damaiana, Baja California, round,
aqua, 11¾" h. 32.50
Dandelion (XXX), rectangular strap
flask, clear, 7¼" h. 60.00
Devil-Cert Stomach, round, clear . . . 42.50
DeWitt's Stomach, oval, strap-sided,
amber, 7½" h. 40.00
Digestine, P.J. Bowlin & Sons, rec-
tangular, amber, 8" h. 425.00
Doyle's Hop, 1872, square, amber,
9 5/8" h. 28.00
Drake's Plantation, cabin-shaped,
4-log, amber . . . . 55.00 to 100.00
Drake's Plantation, cabin-shaped,
4-log, dark puce 115.00
Drake's Plantation, cabin-shaped,
6-log, amber (ILLUS. left) 75.00
Drake's Plantation, cabin-shaped,
6-log, lemon amber 75.00
Drake's Plantation, cabin-shaped,
6-log, puce 115.00
Eagle Angostura Bark, globe-
shaped, amber (stained) 35.00
Electric Brand, H.E. Bucklen & Co.,
square, amber 35.00
Fisch's (Dr.), W.H. Ware Patented
1866, figural fish, golden yellow,
11¾" h. 280.00
Fish (The), W.H. Ware Patented
1866, figural fish, amber, 11½" h.
(ILLUS. right) 165.00
Fish (The), W.H. Ware Patented
1866, figural fish, clear, 11 3/8" h.
(potstone) 585.00
Flint's (Dr.) Quaker, Providence,
R.I., rectangular, aqua, ¾ qt. 20.00
Garry Owen Strengthening,
amber 90.00
Genuine Black Walnut Bitters, A.
Graf & Co., St. Louis, Mo. Sole
Proprietors, square, clear,
7¾" h. 125.00
German Hop, square w/roofed
shoulders, amber, ¾ qt. 67.50
Globe (The) Tonic, square, amber,
w/labels 65.00
Greeley's Bourbon, barrel-shaped
w/ten hoops above & below
center band, amber 170.00
Greeley's Bourbon, barrel-shaped
w/ten hoops above & below
center band, light chocolate 300.00
Greeley's Bourbon, barrel w/ten
hoops above & below center
band, orange-amber, ¾ qt. 300.00

Griel's Herb, Lancaster, Pa., round,
aqua . . . . 85.00 to 100.00
Hagan's, triangular, brilliant yellow,
9 7/8" h. 1,250.00
Hall's (E.E.), New Haven, estab-
lished 1842, barrel-shaped, am-
ber . . . . 95.00 to 130.00
Hall's (E.E.), barrel-shaped, yellow-
amber 135.00
Hansard's Genuine Hop, pottery,
cream & brown w/black
lettering 50.00
Hardy's (Dr. Manly) Genuine Jaun-
dice, rectangular, aqua 85.00
Harter's (Dr.) Wild Cherry, rectangu-
lar, amber 30.00
Hartwig's Kantorowicz, 8-sided, milk
white, miniature, 4 1/8" h. 52.50
Hartwig Kantorowicz, Posen, Ham-
burg, Germany, clear 60.00
Henley's (Dr.) Wild Grape IXL, aqua,
9½" h. 60.00
Herb (H.P.) Wild Cherry, cabin-
shaped, amber 22.00
Holtzerman's Patent Stomach, cabin-
shaped, amber . . . . 125.00 to 175.00
Home, square, amber 70.00
Hoofland's (Dr.) German, aqua,
pt. 50.00
Hostetter's (Dr.) Stomach, square,
amber, 9½" h. 15.00
Hostetter's (Dr. J.) Stomach, square,
black amethyst . . . . 85.00 to 100.00
Hostetter's (Dr. J.) Stomach, square,
citron 40.00
Hostetter's (Dr.) Stomach, square,
olive green, ¾ qt. 80.00
Jewett's (Dr. Stephen) Celebrated
Health Restoring, rectangular,
pontil, aqua . . . . 95.00 to 115.00
Kaiser Wilhelm Bitters Co., San-
dusky, Ohio, round, clear,
10 1/8" h. 40.00
Kelly's Old Cabin, cabin-shaped, am-
ber . . . . 485.00 to 600.00
Keystone, barrel-shaped, amber,
¾ qt. . . . . 195.00 to 295.00
Kimball's Jaundice, olive
amber . . . . 235.00 to 275.00
King Solomon's, rectangular,
amber 90.00
Koehler's Stomach Bitters Co., New
York, square, dark amber,
10" h. 100.00
Lacour's, round, golden amber,
9" h. 495.00
Langley's (Dr.) Root & Herb, 99
Union St., Boston, pontil, aqua,
¾ qt. 42.50
Langley's (Dr.) Root & Herb, 76 Un-
ion St., Boston, round, aqua 36.00
Lashs Liver, Nature's Tonic Laxative,
square, amber, 9 3/8" h. 13.50

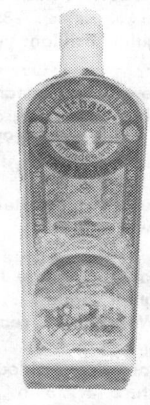

Litthauer Stomach Bitters Bottle

Litthauer Stomach, Hartwig Kantoro-
wicz, Posen, Berlin, Hamburg,
Germany, square case gin shape,
milk white, 9½" h. (ILLUS.) 150.00
Kimball's Jaundice, golden amber .. 250.00
Lash's Bitters Co., N.Y.-Chicago,
S.F., round, amber 55.00
Lash's Kidney & Liver, square,
amber, w/label, 9½" h. 22.50
Lashs Liver, Nature's Tonic Laxative,
square, amber, 9 3/8" h. 12.50
Mampe's Medicinal, olive green 80.00
Marshall's - The Best Laxative and
Blood Purifier, square, amber,
8 5/8" h. 45.00
Mishler's Herb, square, golden
amber, 9" h.................... 36.00

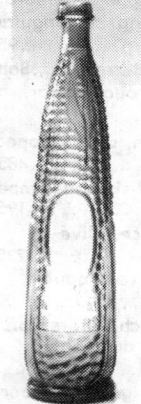

National Bitters Bottle

National, figural ear of corn, amber,
¾ qt. (ILLUS.)................... 215.00
National, figural ear of corn, puce,
¾ qt. 600.00
National, figural ear of corn, light
yellow w/green tint 320.00

National, Patent 1867, figural ear of
corn, amber, 12 5/8" h........... 230.00
National, Patent 1867, figural ear of
corn, dark puce, 12 5/8" h. 600.00
National Tonic, square, roped corners, aqua, 9½" h.............. 400.00
New York Hop Bitters Co., em-
bossed flag 150.00
Old Carolina Bitters, Goodrich Wine-
man Co., amber 300.00
Old Continental, rectangular
w/roofed shoulders, amber,
9 7/8" h. 285.00
Old Hickory Celebrated Stomach, J.
Grossman, New Orleans, square,
amber, 8¾" h................... 75.00
Old Homestead Wild Cherry, cabin-
shaped, amber, 9 7/8" h. 185.00
Old Homestead Wild Cherry, cabin-
shaped, olive amber 190.00
Old Sachem Bitters & Wigwam
Tonic, barrel-shaped, amber 175.00
Old Sachem Bitters & Wigwam
Tonic, barrel-shaped, amethyst ... 485.00
Old Sachem Bitters & Wigwam
Tonic, barrel-shaped, claret red . 265.00
Old Sachem Bitters & Wigwam
Tonic, barrel-shaped, puce 200.00
Oxygenated for Dyspepsia, Asthma
& General Debility, rectangular,
aqua, ½ pt., 7 5/8" h........... 60.00
Parker's Celebrated Stomach,
amber 42.50
Pepsin Calisaya, Dr. Russell Med.
Co., rectangular, green, pt.,
7 7/8" h. ....67.50 to 100.00
Peruvian, square, smooth base,
amber 46.50
Peruvian Tonic, rectangular w/roped
corners, light golden amber 155.00
Phoenix, John Moffat, New York,
rectangular w/wide beveled cor-
ners, aqua, ½ pt............... 52.50
Phoenix, Price 1 Dollar, John
Moffat, New York, rectangular
w/wide beveled corners, olive
green, ½ pt. ....200.00 to 255.00
Pierce's (Dr.) Indian Restorative, rec-
tangular, pontil, aqua 55.00
Polo Club Stomach, Trade Mark F &
M, square, amber, 9 1/8" h. 130.00
Pond's Kidney & Liver, square,
amber, 9½" h.................. 32.50
Poor Man's Family, rectangular,
aqua, ½ pt. 25.00
Prickley Ash, square, amber,
¾ qt.......................... 22.50
Quaker (Old Dr. Warren's), rectan-
gular, aqua, 9¾" h. 45.00
Ramsey's Trinidad, dark olive
amber 27.50
Rex Kidney & Liver, amber 26.50
Rex Kidney & Liver, The Best Laxa-
tive and Blood Purifier, square,

amber, w/50% of label,
9 5/8" h. 55.00
Rose's (E.J.) Magador, amber 60.00
Royal Pepsin Stomach, amber,
8¾" h. 97.50
Rush's, amber.................... 32.50
Sazarac Aromatic, lady's leg shape,
light amber, 10 1/8" h. 400.00

Siegert Angostura Bitters

Siegert (Dr. J.G.B.) Angostura, olive
green, 4½" h. (ILLUS.) 7.50
Soule's (Dr.) Hop, cabin-shaped,
amber 40.00
Stanley's (Dr.) South American
Indian, square, smooth base, yel-
low amber..................... 125.00
Taylor's Hop Bitters, round, tan pot-
tery, 6¾" h. 25.00
Taylor's Trade Mark Perfection,
Manchester, w/monogram,
green 85.00

Tippecanoe Bitters

Tippecanoe, H.H. Warner Co., tree
bark design w/canoe, golden
amber, ¾ qt. (ILLUS.) 65.00

Tippecanoe, H.H. Warner Co., tree
bark design w/canoe, olive
amber, ¾ qt. 93.50
Tonola, Trade Mark, Philadelphia,
w/eagle, square, aqua, 8¼" h.... 160.00
Trinidad Orange Bitters, round,
aqua, 9" h. 75.00
Vermo Stomach, Tonic and Appetiz-
er, square, clear, 9½" h. 95.00
Von Hopf's (Dr.) Curacoa, Chamberlain & Co., Des Moines, Iowa, rectangular, amber, 70% label,
½ pt., 7½" h. ....50.00 to 85.00
Wait's Kidney & Liver, square,
amber, 8¾" h. ....40.00 to 65.00
Warner's Safe Tonic, oval, amber,
7 3/8" h. 300.00
Webb's Improved Stomach, square,
amber, 9" h. 170.00
West India Stomach, square, amber,
8½" h. 50.00
Wheat, rectangular, amber,
9½" h. 70.00
Whitcomb's (Faith) Nerve, rectangular, aqua, pt. 40.00
Whitcomb's (Faith), Boston, Mass.,
U.S.A., rectangular, aqua,
9½" h. 135.00
Yerba Buena, flask-shaped, amber,
8½" h. 50.00
Yochim Bros. Celebrated Stomach,
square, red-amber 85.00
Zingari, amber.................. 175.00

DRUG STORE BOTTLES & JARS

Show Window Bottle

Aqua mold-blown glass bottle, em-
bossed "B.O. Wilson's Botanic
Druggists," 6½" h. 57.50
Aqua mold-blown glass bottle, em-

bossed "J.F. Hancock Manufacturing Pharmacist, Baltimore," cylindrical, original ground glass stopper 20.00

Clear mold-blown glass apothecary jar, bulbous body, pedestal base, w/label "Warner, Sept. 18, 1875" under glass, original ground glass stopper, 10" h. 35.00

Clear mold-blown glass apothecary jar, bulbous body, pedestal base, ball-shaped ground glass stopper, 20" h. 137.50

Clear pressed glass bottle, embossed "H.M. Parchen & Co., Helena, Mt.," corker-type, small 20.00

Clear pressed glass bottle, embossed "Welsh & Bolt Druggists, Boone, Iowa," corker-type 10.00

Cobalt blue mold-blown glass bottle, embossed "Owl Drug Co.," w/owl perched on mortar trademark, 3" h. 38.00

Cobalt blue mold-blown glass bottle, embossed "Brooks Pharmacy, Baton Rouge, 1869" 225.00

Cobalt blue mold-blown glass bottle, embossed "J. & C. Maguire Druggist, St. Louis," double collar 45.00

Emerald green mold-blown glass bottle, embossed "From the Laboratory of G.W. Merchant, Chemist, Lockport, N.Y.," rectangular, applied sloping flanged collar, smooth base, 2-part mold, 2½" w., 5¾" h. 50.00

Milk white pressed glass bottle, embossed "Owl Drug Co.," w/owl on mortar trademark, 5" h. 24.00

Milk white pressed glass bottle, embossed "Jno. Sullivan, Pharmacist, Boston," w/monogram 35.00

Show window bottle, hanging-type, clear blown glass globe (designed to be filled with colored water) fitted w/harness & hanging chains, overall 34" l. 300.00

Show window bottle, clear blown glass, 2-part: footed ovoid bottle fitted w/bottle-form stopper fitted w/ground glass ball-shaped stopper (ILLUS.) 500.00

Show window bottle, clear blown glass, 3-part: footed ovoid bottle fitted w/bottle-form stopper also fitted w/smaller bottle-form stopper & finial-stopper, engraved designs, very large 975.00

FIGURAL

Banana, clear glass w/traces of yellow paint, original screw-on cap .. 75.00

Bear, Kummel-type, black-amber glass 50.00

Bear, Kummel-type, black opaque glass, 11" h. ....70.00 to 90.00

Bear, Kummel-type, dark olive green 45.00

Billy club, green glass, open pontil 125.00

Carrie Nation, clear glass 45.00

Child's boot w/side laces, mottled brown-glazed earthenware pottery, 7" l. 125.00

Figural Bottles

Cigar, amber glass, 5¼" l. (ILLUS.)..................45.00 to 75.00

Coachman, "Van Dunck's Genever," puce glass 285.00

Cucumber, green glass, 4½" l. 55.00

Dog, "Shampoodle," cobalt blue glass, 8" 14.00

Dolphin, clear glass, w/solid glass stopper, 15 3/8" h. 35.00

Ear of corn, green or marigold carnival glass, 5" h., each 225.00

Ear of corn, "National" (bitters), amber (ILLUS.) 225.00

Fish, clear glass w/applied green glass eyes, "Dobson's Shad-Ro-Branco Wine," Portugal, 1969 ..... 15.00

Fish, amber glass, Eli Lily Co. Cod Liver Oil bottle 1970 reproduction by Imperial Glass Co., 6¼" h. (ILLUS.)........................ 17.50

Fish, mottled brown Rockingham-glazed earthenware pottery, 11" h. (small lip chips) 250.00

Grape cluster, clear glass, 6" l. 25.00

Grape cluster, blue glass (ILLUS.)........................ 45.00

John Bull, amber glass 195.00

Liberty Bell, 22 karat gold finish, "1776-1976 Bicentennial," limited edition 25.00

Log Cabin, "Smokine" on roof, "Imported & Bottled by Alfred Andresen & Co., The Western Importers, Minneapolis & Winnipeg, Man.," amber glass, 5 x 3 1/8" base, 6½" h., qt. 190.00

Pig, stoneware pottery, stopper on
 back, 6" l. 135.00
Pig, amber glass, embossed "Good
 Old Bourbon in a Hog" 225.00
Pineapple, amber glass, 9" h.
 (ILLUS.). 200.00
Portly gentleman, amber glass,
 12" h. (minor sickness in base,
 chip on lip) 27.50
Pretzel, Rockingham-glazed pottery
 w/applied pebbles of "salt,"
 3½" h. (ILLUS.) 48.00
Sailor standing at attention along-
 side large shell casing by rope-
 entwined bollard, clear glass,
 13" h. 15.00
Santa Claus standing, clear glass,
 12" h. (some interior sickness) . . . 35.00
Satchel, brown-glazed earthenware
 pottery, "John Turner," cork stop-
 per, 5 7/8" h. 95.00
Statue of Liberty base, milk white
 glass, w/metal figure of Statue of
 Liberty on cover, 1880-90,
 15" h. 310.00
Violin, amber glass, 6¼" h. 15.00
Violin, w/side tab at neck, aqua
 glass (ILLUS.) 30.00
Violin, cobalt blue glass,
 9½" h. 15.00
Washington Monument, clear glass,
 6 5/8" h. 50.00

FLASKS

Chestnut Flask with Vertical Ribs

*(Numbers used below refer to those used in
the McKearin's "American Glass.")*

All-Seeing Eye of God w/lashes on
 upper lid on 6-pointed star (Star
 of David) w/"AD" below - 6-Point
 Star w/arm bent at elbow, fore-
 arm raised vertically, compass in
 hand, unidentified emblem on
 bottom point of star & "GRJA" below, plain lip, vertical medial rib,
 yellow-amber, pt. (GIV-43) 128.00

American Flag w/nine stripes & 13
 stars - "New Granite Glass
 Works" in semicircle enclosing
 "Stoddard" in an arc & beneath
 "N.H.," plain lip, smooth w/heavy
 vertical medial rib, pontil, amber,
 pt. (GX-27) .2,750.00
American Eagle - American Flag
 w/thirteen stars & "For Our Coun-
 try" below, plain lip, vertically
 ribbed edges, pontil, aqua, pt.
 (GII-52) 350.00
American Eagle - American Flag
 w/twenty stars & "For Our Coun-
 try" below, plain lip, vertically
 ribbed edges, pontil, aqua, pt.
 (GII-54) 100.00
American Eagle - Cornucopia with
 Produce, plain lip, vertically
 ribbed edges, amber, pt.
 (GII-73) 110.00
American Eagle - Cornucopia with
 Produce, plain lip, smooth edges,
 pontil, emerald green, pt.
 (GII-74) 385.00
American Eagle - Cornucopia with
 Produce, plain lip, vertically
 ribbed edges, pontil, olive amber,
 pt. (GII-72) . . . . .55.00 to 65.00
American Eagle on laurel wreath &
 "LIBERTY" above - "Willington
 Glass Co., West Willington,
 Conn.," plain lip, smooth edges,
 red-amber, qt. (GII-61) 60.00
American Eagle w/head turned to
 left & shield on breast, thunder-
 bolt in right talons, olive branch
 in left & thirteen 5-pointed stars
 above - Bunch of Grapes
 w/smaller cluster at right, plain
 lip, vertically ribbed edges, pontil,
 light aqua, qt. (GII-55) 100.00
American Eagle w/wings raised -
 Morning Glory & Vine, plain lip,
 heavy vertical medial rib, pontil,
 shaded aqua, qt. (GII-19) 550.00
Anchor & fork-ended pennants
 w/"Baltimore" on one & "Glass
 Works" on other - Phoenix rising
 from flames & "RESURGAM" in
 rectangular panel below, plain lip,
 smooth edges, golden amber, pt.
 (GXIII-53) 350.00
"Baltimore" Monument - "Corn For
 The World" above ear of corn,
 smooth edges, golden amber, qt.
 (GVI-4) 325.00
"Benjamin Franklin" above bust -
 "T.W. Dyott, M.D." above bust,
 plain lip, vertically ribbed edges,
 "Eripuit Coelo Fulmen. Sceptrum-
 que Tryannis" & "Kensington
 Glass Works, Philadelphia" on
 edges, pontil, aqua, qt. (GI-96) . . . 265.00

Chestnut, 28 ribs swirled to the right, flanged lip, pontil, medium sapphire blue, 1½" w. at base, 3¾" h. 250.00

Chestnut, 24 ribs swirled to the left, sheared mouth, pontil, red-amber, Zanesville, Ohio, 2" w. at base, 5 1/8" h. 325.00

Chestnut, 24 vertical ribs, sheared mouth, pontil, red-amber, Zanesville, Ohio, 2¼" w. at base, 5 1/8" h. (ILLUS.)............... 325.00

Chestnut, 24 ribs swirled to the left, pontil, puce..................... 375.00

Double American Eagle w/pennant & oblong frame below, smooth edges, aqua, ½ pt. (GII-125) 75.00

Double American Eagle perched on stick resting on top of laurel wreath, smooth edges, aqua, ½ pt. (GII-126). 125.00

Double American Eagle on oval frame, plain lip, horizontally corrugated edges, pontil, yellow-green, pt. (GII-24) 500.00

Double American Eagle w/head to the left, standing on arrows & pennant to left above large frame, smooth edges, yellow-green, qt. (GII-91) 150.00

Double Elliptical Sunburst w/twenty-four rounded rays, plain lip, horizontally corrugated edges, pontil, yellow-amber, pt. (GVIII-3) 375.00

Double Scroll, plain lip, vertical medial rib, amber, pt. (GIX-10) ... 290.00

Double Scroll, plain lip, vertical medial rib, pontil, green, pt. (GIX-14) 350.00

Double Scroll, plain lip, vertical medial rib, pontil, brilliant cobalt blue, qt. (GIX-2) 1,600.00

Double "Success to the Railroad," plain lip, vertically ribbed edges, pontil, golden amber, pt. (GV-1) .. 125.00

Double Sunburst, plain lip, vertically ribbed edges, pontil, aqua, ½ pt. (GVIII-24)...............150.00 to 200.00

Double Sunburst w/twenty-one rays, plain lip, horizontally corrugated edges, pontil, light olive amber, ½ pt. (GVIII-16) 185.00

"For Pike's Peak" above prospector standing on frame "Old Rye" - American Eagle w/pennant above frame "Pittsburgh PA.," aqua, ½ pt. (GXI-10) 75.00

"Genl Taylor Never Surrenders" around cannon - "A Little More Grape Capt Bragg," plain lip, smooth edges, pontil, aqua, ½ pt. (GX-6) 200.00

"General Washington" above bust -

American Eagle on oval frame, plain lip, horizontal beading w/vertical medial rib, pontil, aqua, pt. (GI-2) ....175.00 to 250.00

"General Washington" above bust - American Eagle on oval frame, plain lip, horizontal beading w/vertical medial rib, pontil, light green, pt. (GI-2) 395.00

"General Washington" above bust - American Eagle w/shield on oval frame w/inner band of 28 small pearls & "T.W.D.," "E Pluribus Unum" in semicircle above sun-rays, plain lip, vertically ribbed edges w/inscription, pontil, emerald green, pt. (GI-14) 1,200.00

"Genl. Taylor" above bust - "Corn For The World" in semicircle above cornstalk, plain lip, vertically ribbed edges, pontil, yellowish olive green, pt. (GI-73) 325.00

"Good Game" below stag w/antlers - Weeping Willow Tree, plain lip, vertically ribbed edges, pontil, aqua, pt. (GX-1) 295.00

Log Cabin w/rail fence - American flag w/semicircle of 9 stars above & "Hard Cider" & cider barrel below, plain lip, horizontally beaded edges w/vertical medial rib, pontil, aqua, pt. (GX-22)............3,400.00

Masonic Emblems - American Eagle w/plain ribbon above & "KCCNC" in oval frame below, plain lip, smooth edges w/single vertical rib, amber, pt. (GIV-19).......... 115.00

Masonic Flask

Masonic Emblems - American Eagle, "Janesville, Ohio" & "J. Shepard (backwards S) & Co.," plain lip, vertically ribbed edges, pontil, light blue-green, pt., GIV-32 (ILLUS.)........................ 245.00

Masonic Emblems - American Eagle, "Janesville, Ohio" & "J. Shepard (backwards S) & Co.," plain lip, vertically ribbed edges, pontil, red-amber, pt. (GIV-32) 550.00

Masonic Emblems w/Clasped Hands & "Union" - American Eagle on shield & "H. & S.," flat collar, smooth edges, pontil, aqua, pt. (GIV-40) ....50.00 to 65.00

Pitkin, blown half-post method, 36 ribs in broken swirl to right, sheared mouth, pontil, light green, 5" h. 100.00

Pitkin, blown half-post method, 21 vertical ribs, sheared mouth, pontil, clear, 5¼" h. 150.00

Pitkin, 36 ribs in broken swirl to the right, overly large neck & sheared mouth, pontil, olive green, 5 3/8" h. 240.00

Pitkin, 36 ribs swirled to the right, sheared neck, pontil, olive green, 5½" h. 110.00

Pitkin, 16 very wide ribs in broken swirl to right, sheared mouth, pontil, light yellow-green, 5 7/8" h. ....150.00 to 200.00

Pitkin, broken swirls, olive green 150.00

Prospector w/tools & cane - American Eagle w/shield, "Arsenal Glass Works Pitts. Pa." in oval frame, applied mouth, smooth base, bright green, pt. (GXI-15) .. 525.00

Shield w/clasped hands - American Eagle on shield & round-ended oblong frame below, smooth edges, aqua, ½ pt. (GXII-31) 75.00

Shield w/clasped hands & "Union" above - frame within open-top laurel wreath, smooth edges, aqua, ½ pt. (GXII-36) 75.00

Shield w/clasped hands, "Union" - American Eagle w/pennants above frame "E. Wormser C" ("o" of Co. just outside frame) above "Pittsburgh" & "PA.," collared mouth, smooth base, brilliant medium bluish green, qt. (GXII-15) 1,550.00

Soldier, "Balt. Md." - Ballet dancer, "Chapman," plain lip, smooth edges, pontil, medium burgundy, pt. (GXIII-13) 2,000.00

Sunburst w/twenty-nine rays & "KEEN" reading from top to bottom of oval - Sunburst w/twenty-nine rays & "P & W" in oval, plain lip, horizontally corrugated edges, pontil, aqua, ½ pt. (GVIII-9) 1,250.00

Sunburst w/twenty-nine rays & "KEEN" reading from top to bottom of oval - Sunburst w/twenty-

nine rays & "P & W" in oval, plain lip, horizontally corrugated edges, pontil, golden amber, ½ pt. (GVIII-9) 240.00

Sunburst w/twenty-nine rays & "KEEN" reading from top to bottom of oval - Sunburst w/twenty-nine rays & "P & W" in oval, plain lip, horizontally corrugated edges, pontil, olive amber, ½ pt. (GVIII-9) 345.00

Sunburst w/twenty-eight rays & "KEEN" in oval - Sunburst w/twenty-eight rays & "P & W" in oval, plain lip, horizontally corrugated edges, pontil, clear forest green, pt. (GVIII-8) 375.00

INKS

Early Ink Bottles

Barrel-shaped, aqua mold-blown glass keg-shaped bottle embossed "Opdyke Bros. Ink" on one side, 2¼" l. 95.00

Blown-three-mold glass, olive amber, Keene, N.H. (ILLUS. left)..... 150.00

Blown-three-mold glass, geometric, olive amber, 2 3/8" d. (McKearin No. GII-2) 85.00

Blown-three-mold glass, medium olive green, Keene, N.H., 2 3/5" d., 1 7/8" h. (McKearin No. GIII-25) 120.00

Cabin-shaped, clear glass mold-blown log cabin replica, embossed "Harrison" one side & "Tippecanoe" reverse, 1840 political campaign item for William H. Harrison & John Tyler, attributed to Whitney Bros., Glassboro, New Jersey, 1 3/8 x 3", 4" h. 6,000.00

Cone-shaped, emerald green mold-blown glass, embossed "Carter's 1897 - Made in U.S.A." on base, 2 3/8" d., 2½" h. 15.00

Cone-shaped, moss green mold-blown glass, open pontil 105.00

Cone-shaped, teal green mold-blown glass...................... 18.00

Cylindrical, aqua mold-blown glass w/applied lip, embossed "Bixby" on base, 2 7/16" d., 2¾" h. 15.00

Domed w/offset neck, aqua mold-blown glass, 2½" d., 1 7/8" h. (ILLUS. right)................... 65.00

Figural "Ma" Carter, porcelain,
marked "Carter's Inx" on base ... 35.00
Figural "Ma" & "Pa" Carter, porcelain, marked "Carter's Inx" on
base, pr. . . . . .90.00 to 150.00
Master size, aqua mold-blown glass,
embossed "S.M. Bixby & Co.,
N.Y.," qt. 65.00
Master size, clear mold-blown glass
cylinder, embossed "Barnards
Universal, St. Louis, Mo.," pillars
& globe 45.00
Master size, emerald green mold-
blown glass, embossed "Design
Patd Feb. 16, 1886" on base &
paper label of "Thaddeus Davids
Co., New York," pt. 11.00
Master size, automatic bottle
machine-made amber glass, embossed "Sanfords Ink One Pint,"
7" h. 15.00
Master size, automatic bottle
machine-made cobalt blue glass,
"Carter's" cathedral w/Gothic
arch "windows," half pint,
2 7/16" h. . . . . .50.00 to 95.00
Master size, automatic bottle
machine-made cobalt blue glass
cylinder, embossed "S. Stafford
Inc. Made in U.S.A." on base, half
pint 20.00
Master size, automatic bottle
machine-made cobalt blue glass,
"Carter's" cathedral w/Gothic
arch "windows," pt., 7 7/8" h. 30.00
Master size, automatic bottle
machine-made cobalt blue glass,
"Carter's" cathedral w/Gothic
arch "windows," qt.,
9¾" h. . . . . .58.00 to 85.00
Octagonal, aqua mold-blown glass,
embossed "Harrison's Columbian
Ink" on sides, 2 1/8" d.,
2 1/16" h. 45.00
Pitkin-type, olive green glass blown
half-post method w/thirty-six ribs
swirled to right, sheared mouth,
pontil, 2 1/8" d., 2" h. 300.00
Square, aqua mold-blown glass, em-
bossed "Caw's Ink New York" on
side, 1 7/8" sq. . . . . .8.00 to 15.00
Square, cobalt blue mold-blown
glass, 2½" h. 7.50
Teakettle-type fountain inkwell
w/neck extending up at angle
from base, amethyst mold-blown
glass 400.00
Teakettle-type fountain inkwell
w/neck extending up at angle
from base, cobalt blue mold-
blown glass, 8-panel body, hinged
cap on spout 240.00
Umbrella-type (8-panel cone shape),
golden amber w/tones of olive

green mold-blown glass, tooled
lip, pontil, 2½" h. (ILLUS.
center) 145.00
Umbrella-type (8-panel cone shape),
teal green mold-blown glass, embossed "Hoover, Philadelphia" on
side, 2¼" octagon, 2 3/8" h. 135.00
Umbrella-type (12-panel cone
shape), aqua mold-blown glass,
open pontil 25.00
Umbrella-type (12-panel cone shape)
aqua mold-blown glass, embossed
"Butler's Ink, Cincinnati" 175.00

MEDICINES

Cod Liver Oil Bottle

Aker's English Remedy For All
Throat & Lung Diseases, rectangu-
lar, cobalt blue, 5¾" h. 8.00
Alexander's Liver & Kidney Tonic
Sure Cure for Malaria, amber 35.00
Allen's (Mrs.) World Hair Balsam,
paneled, open pontil, aqua,
7" h. 40.00
Arabian Tonic Blood Purifier, Stuart
Howell, New York, aqua 25.00
Baker's (Dr.) Pain Panacea, rectan-
gular, pontil, aqua, 5" h. 30.00
Baker's Vegetable Blood & Liver
Cure, Lookout Mountain, Green-
ville, Tenn., orange-amber 210.00
Bell's (Dr.) Pine Tar Honey For
Coughs & Colds on front panel,
Dr. Bell one side, Pine Tar Honey
on other, pale green, 5 5/8" h. 18.50
Blackman's (Dr.) Genuine Healing
Balsam, 8-sided, clear 38.50
Bogle's Hyperion Fluid 32.50
Bonpland's Fever & Ague Remedy,
rectangular, pontil, aqua,
5 1/8" h. 40.00
Brant's Indian Pulmonary Balsam,
8-sided, aqua, 7" h. 55.00
Brinckerhoff's Health Restorative,

New York, rectangular, pontil,
olive green, 7" h. 240.00
Brown's (N.K.) Essence Jamaica
Ginger, oval, aqua, 5¾" h. 22.50
Brush's Elixir Prophylactic For
Prevention of Sea Sickness, rec-
tangular, amber, 5¾" h. 125.00
Bull's (J.W.) Cough Syrup, rectangu-
lar, aqua, 5¾" h. 20.00
Bull's (John) Extract of Sarsaparilla,
Louisville, Ky., iron pontil, blue-
aqua, qt. 195.00
Bull's (John) Extract of Sarsaparilla,
Louisville, Ky., iron pontil, light
blue, qt. 195.00
Burk's Iron Tonic, amber 15.00
Checker's Medicine Co., Winston-
Salem, N.C., Makes People New
All Over, amber, 11" h. 75.00
Clewley's Miraculous Rheumatism
Cure, embossed nun, aqua 115.00
Cod Liver Oil, square, embossed
fish & scales, machine-made
w/threaded lip for cap, amber,
9" h. (ILLUS.) 12.50
Conner's Blood Remedy, Chattanoo-
ga, Tenn., amber, 7½" h. 25.00
Covert's Balm of Life, rectangular
w/beveled corners, pontil, olive
green, 5 7/8" h. 495.00
Dale's Remedy for Epilepsy, aqua,
5¼" h. 20.00
Davis (G.W.) Inflammatory Extir-
pator & Cleanser, aqua 32.00
Davis' (Perry) Pain Killer, rectangular, pontil, aqua, 4 5/8" h. 17.50
Denxon (B.) Healing Balsam,
8-sided, open pontil 45.00
Donnell's Rheumatic Liniment, rectangular, aqua, 5¾" h. 32.50
Farrell's (H.G.) Arabian Liniment,
round, aqua 50.00
Fitzgerald's (Dr.) Clairvoyant Discovery, Dexter, Maine, square, aqua,
5½" h. 8.00
Flower's (Dr. R.C.) Scientific Remedies, amber, 9½" h. 25.00
Folger's (Dr. Robert B.) Olosaonian,
rectangular w/deeply beveled
corners, open pontil, aqua, 90%
label, 6" h. 45.00
Foord's (Dr. A.) Pectoral Syrup, rectangular, aqua, 5½" h. 80.00
Gardner's (Mrs. M.N.) Indian Balsam
of Liverwort, round, pontil,
5 1/8" h. 67.50
Gombault's Caustic Balsam, rectangular, aqua, 6½" h. 10.50
Guysotts (Dr.) Yellow Dock & Sarsaparilla, John D. Park, Cincinnati, O., oval, iron pontil,
10" h. 375.00
Harter's (Dr.) Iron Tonic, rectangular, amber, 9¼" h. (90% label) ... 15.00

Hatch's Universal Cough Syrup - No
Cure - No Pay, paneled, aqua,
paper label, pontil, 6" h. 20.00

Kickapoo Indian Sagwa Bottle

Healy & Bigelow's Kickapoo Indian
Sagwa, rectangular, embossed In-
dian, aqua, original label, 7½" h.
(ILLUS.) 50.00
Holcomb's Blood Purifier, bimal,
deep aqua, 9" h. (nick in
mouth) 65.00
Houck's Patent Panacea, Baltimore,
open pontil, aqua, 6¼" h. 150.00
Ingham's (Dr. H.A.) Nervine Pain
Extractor, rectangular, aqua,
4½" h. 28.00
Jacksons (T.H.) Common Sense Colic
Cure, aqua, 5½" h. 40.00
James' (Dr.) Cherry Tar Syrup, rec-
tangular, ice blue 6.00
Jayne's (Dr. D.) Carminative Balsam,
round, aqua, 5¼" h. 12.50
Jayne's (Dr. D.) Expectorant, rectan-
gular, open pontil, aqua, 5" h. ... 26.50
Johnson's Anodyne Liniment, open
pontil, aqua 25.00
Jones (Dr.) Sangvin A Blood & Nerve
Remedy, Albany, N.Y., aqua,
7½" h. 25.00
Jones' Red Clover Tonic 38.00
Keeler's (Dr. J.N.) Vegetable
Panacea, Philadelphia, wide
beveled edges, aqua, 7" h. 200.00
Kellinger's (Dr.) Magic Fluid, New
York, open pontil, aqua 80.00
Kennedy's (Dr.) Prairie Weed, rec-
tangular, aqua, 8 1/8" h. 11.00
Kilmer's (Dr.) Autumn-Leaf Extract
for Uterine Injection, rectangular,
aqua, 4¼" h. 45.00
Kilmer's (Dr.) Female Remedy, Bing-
hamton, N.Y., rectangular, aqua,
8 3/8" h. 18.00

Kilmer's Swamp Root Medicine Bottle

Kilmer's (Dr.) Swamp-Root Kidney,
Liver & Bladder Remedy, aqua,
8" h. (ILLUS.) 14.00

Larookah's (Dr.) Indian Vegetable
Pulmonic Syrup, deep aqua,
w/complete label, 8½" h. 45.00

Mackenzie's Tonic Febrifuge (dug &
lip repair) 95.00

McLane's (Dr.) American Worm
Specific, round, aqua, 3 7/8" h. .. 22.50

Merchant's (G.W.) Gargling Oil, rectangular, open pontil, green,
5" h. 75.00

Mixer's Cancer & Scrofula Syrup,
aqua 22.00

Montgomery's Hair Restorer, light
amber 20.00

Munyons Inhaler Cure, emerald
green 20.00

Mystic Cure, rectangular, clear,
6½" h. (some light etching) 12.00

Nerve & Bone Liniment, round,
aqua, 4" h. 20.00

Oregon Blood Purifier, baby's face
trademark, amber 40.00

Paine's Celery Compound Bottle

Paine's Celery Compound, square,
amber, 9¾" h. (ILLUS.) 12.50

Parker's Best Tonic, Baltimore, Md.,
aqua 10.00

Peruvian Strengthening Elixir,
amber 15.00

Peruvian Syrup, N.L. Clark & Co.,
rectangular, aqua, 10" 30.00

Pierce's (Dr. R.V.) Compound Extract
of Smart-Weed, rectangular,
aqua, 7" h. 18.00

Pierce's (Dr. R.V.) Golden Medical
Discovery, rectangular, aqua,
8¾" h. 16.00

Pinkham's (Lydia) Emmenagogue,
whittled, pontil, aqua .....60.00 to 75.00

Piso's Cure, Hazeltine & Co., rectangular, green, 5¼" h. 5.00

Primley's Iron & Wahoo Tonic,
square, amber, 9½" h. 20.00

Radam's Microbe Killer, embossed
stoneware pottery jug 60.00

Red Cherry Cough Cure for Con-
sumption, aqua 15.00

Rhode's (Prof.) Fever & Ague Cure,
rectangular, aqua, full label,
8¼" h. 135.00

Risley's Philotoken - Prevents Mis-
carriage, Nervous Antidote, Pain-
ful Menstruation, aqua (stained) .. 22.00

Roback's (Dr. C.W.) Scandinavian
Blood Purifier, rectangular, iron
pontil, aqua, 7¼" h. 85.00

Robert's (M.B.) Vegetable Embroca-
tion, round, pontil, sea green,
5" h. 40.00

Rohrer's Expectoral, Lancaster, Pa.,
amber ....100.00 to 150.00

St. Andrew's Wine of Life Root,
amber, 9" h. 30.00

Sawen's (Dr.) Celebrated Oil Liniment, rectangular, aqua,
5¾" h. 20.00

Sawen's (Dr.) Magic Balm, rectangular, aqua, 5" h. 25.00

Schneck's Pulmonic Syrup, 8-sided,
bluish aqua 30.00

Shaker Digestive Cordial, A.J.
White, New York, rectangular,
aqua, 5¾" h. 72.50

Shaker Syrup No. 1, Canterbury,
N.H., rectangular, aqua, 7¼" h. ... 70.00

Sines (Charles) Celebrated Compound Syrup of Tar, Wild Cherry &
Hoarhound, Phila., Pa., clear 25.00

Sines (Charles) Celebrated Compound Syrup of Tar, Wild Cherry &
Hoarhound, Phila., Pa., pale
aqua 40.00

Sloan's Anti-Colic, square, clear,
4¾" h. 6.00

Smith's Green Mountain Renovator,
E. Georgia, Vt., rectangular,
aqua 40.00

Smolanders Preparations, embossed
lion, aqua (crude) 8.00

Southworth's (Dr.) Blood & Kidney
Remedy, rectangular, aqua,
8¾" h. 18.00

Swain's Vermifuge, Dysentary, Chol-
era, Morbus, Dyspepsia & CC,
oval, pontil, aqua, 5 3/8" h. 42.50

Thomas' (Dr.) Eclectic Oil, rectangular, aqua, 4¼" h. 20.00

Thompson's (Dr.) Eye Water, New
London, Conn., round, aqua,
3¾" h. (neck hazy) 15.00

Tobias' Venetian Liniment, aqua,
8 1/8" h. 155.00

Victor Liver Syrup, Victor Remedies
Co., Frederick, Md., oval, aqua,
8" h. 15.00

Warner's Safe Cure, London, emerald green, ½ pt. 55.00

Warner's Safe Cure, London, amber,
pt. 30.00

Warner's Safe Cure, w/four cities,
amber, pt. 40.00

Warner's Safe Nervine, square collar, slug plate, small 20.00

Warner's Safe Tonic 225.00

Webb's A. No. 1 Cathartic Tonic,
amber ....30.00 to 45.00

Webster's Wonderful Pain Destroy-
ing Liniment, Sprains, Cuts, etc.,
Binghamton, N.Y. 25.00

Wheatley's (J.B.) Compound Syrup,
Dallasburgh, Ky., open pontil,
aqua ....7.00 to 15.00

Winslow's (Mrs.) Soothing Syrup,
round, aqua, 5 1/8" h. 10.00

Wishart's (Dr. L.Q.C.) Pine Tree Tar
Cordial, square, amber, w/label .. 57.50

Woods (Professor) Hair Restorative,
blue-green (dug) 40.00

Wynkoop's (Dr. Robert D.) Iceland
Pectoral, rectangular, aqua,
5 1/8" h. 110.00

MILK

"Baby-Face" Milk Bottle

Amber, embossed "Nob Hill Milk,"
soldier w/rifle & duffle bag & "For
Victory Buy United States Savings
Bonds & Stamps - Colorado
Springs, Colorado," qt. (small in-
side lip chip) 15.00

Amber, embossed "Premium
Quality," qt. 5.00

Amber, orange pyroglaze "Mesaba
Dairy, Golden Guernsey Trademark, Pasteurized, Homogenized,
Dairy Products, Chisholm, Minn.,"
square, qt. 29.00

Clear, "baby-face" top, embossed
"Murphy's Dairy, Neenah," ½ pt.
(ILLUS.) 30.00

Clear, "baby-face" top, embossed
"Dairy Lee," pt. 20.00

Clear, "baby-face" top, embossed
"Woods Dairy - It Whips - For
Mothers Who Care!," pt. 22.50

Clear, "baby-face" top, embossed
"Brookfield Baby Top," qt. 23.00

Clear, "baby-face" top, embossed
"Lemke's Deluxe, Wausau, Wis.,"
qt. 24.00

Clear, cream-top, qt., w/spoon 19.00

Clear, cream-top, embossed
"Anthony's Dairy, Strausstown,
Pa.," qt. 20.00

Clear, cream-top, embossed "Rose-
dale" & "It Whips" 9.00

Clear, embossed "Lone Oak Farm,"
2 oz. miniature 7.00

Clear, embossed "Meadow Gold,"
square, 2 oz. miniature .....6.00 to 7.50

Clear, embossed "All Star," ½ pt. ... 4.50

Clear, embossed "Ditch Brothers,"
½ pt. 8.00

Clear, embossed "Frink Dairy, Denver," & eagle, ½ pt. 5.00

Clear, embossed "Speedwell
Farms," cow's head & "Sealed
Watertown (Mass.) 1909,"
w/Lightning closure, ½ pt. 20.00

Clear, embossed "Sun Beam Dairy,
Perry, Iowa," ½ pt. 3.00

Clear, embossed "Abbott's Alderney
Dairies," odd-shaped tall, pt. 25.00

Clear, embossed "Chestnut Farms
Dairy - Chestnut Farm, Washington, D.C.," cow, fruit & tree,
round, pt. 7.00

Clear, embossed "Jersey Dairy,
Spencer, Iowa," pt. 8.50

Clear, embossed "Turner & West-
cott" & housewife baking cake in
kitchen, pt. 15.00

Clear, embossed "All Star," square,
qt. 5.00

Clear, embossed "Dairy Products -
Spencer, Iowa," square, qt. 6.50

Clear, embossed "Golden Guernsey,
Billings," qt. 7.50

Clear, embossed, "Grafenstein, Brooklyn," tin top, qt. 15.00

Clear, embossed "Liberty Milk Co., Buffalo, N.Y." & Statue of Liberty, round, qt. 13.00

Clear, embossed "Mountain Lily Dairy," qt. 7.00

Clear, embossed "Peter Nagner Dairy, Buffalo, N.Y." & cow in circle, round, qt. 10.00

Clear, embossed "Pure Milk Dairy," qt. 5.75

Clear, embossed "Shamrock Dairy," square, qt. 6.50

Clear, embossed "Sunshine Dairy," square, qt. 16.00

Clear, embossed "Washington, D.C." & scene w/cow, qt. 20.00

Clear, embossed "Andrews Bros. Pure Milk & Cream, Syracuse, N.Y.," ½ gal. 50.00

Green, embossed "Steer Dairy, Meadville, Pa." & bush w/seven blooms, "The State Flower - Pennsylvania Mountain Laurel - Adopted May 5, 1933," round, ½ pt. ... 15.00

Ruby red, embossed "Valley Dairy Ph. 367 - Yerington, Nevada - Drink Milk for Health & Energy," round, ½ pt. 15.00

MINERAL WATERS

Congress Spring Co. Bottle

Artesian Spring Lithia Mineral Water, emerald green, pt. 35.00

Bear Lithia Water, aqua, half gal. 50.00

Betz (Wm.) Mineral Water, Salem, Ohio, 10-sided, iron pontil, blue-aqua 40.00

Castalian Cal. Nat. Min Water in band around shoulder, cylindrical, amber, pt. 18.50

Clark & Co., New York, olive amber, pt. 40.00

Clark & White, olive green, qt. 15.00

Clark & White, "C," olive green 35.00

Congress & Empire Spring Co., Hotchkiss & Sons, Saratoga, green, pt. 30.00

Congress & Empire Spring Co., Hotchkiss & Sons, Saratoga, yellow-green, pt. 65.00

Congress & Empire Spring Co., deep emerald green, qt. 45.00

Congress Spring Co., Saratoga, N.Y., green, pt. 32.00

Congress Spring Co., Saratoga, N.Y., dark green, qt. (ILLUS.) 40.00

Ebberwein (G) Mineral Water, amber 35.00

Empire Spring Co. Bottle

Empire Spring Co., Saratoga, N.Y., emerald green, pt. (ILLUS.) 45.00

Geyser Spring, Saratoga Springs, State of New York, The Saratoga Spouting Spring, aqua, 7¾" h. ... 55.00

Geyser Springs, Avery N. Lord, 66 Broad Street, Utica, N.Y., aqua, qt. 35.00

Guilford Mineral Spring Water, Guilford, Vt., w/monogram, emerald green, qt. 42.50

Guilford Mineral Spring Water, Guilford, Vt., w/monogram, light green, qt. 30.00

Guilford Mineral Spring Water, Guilford, Vt., w/monogram, olive green, qt. 45.00

Hathorn Spring, Saratoga, N.Y., amber, pt. 22.00

Hathorn Spring, Saratoga, N.Y., emerald green, pt. 25.00

Hathorn Spring, Saratoga, N.Y.,
　　amber, qt. 28.00
Hathorn Spring, Saratoga, N.Y.,
　　emerald green, qt. 30.00
Herdmans Excelsior Mineral Water,
　　F.W.H. reverse, green 30.00
John Ryan Excelsior Mineral Water
　　1859, Savannah, Ga., cobalt
　　blue 49.00
Kernan & Co. Mineral Water,
　　clear 14.00
Kohl & Beans Mineral Water,
　　Easton, Pa., light green 75.00
Lansing Mineral & Magnetic Well at
　　the Capital of Michigan, Saratoga-
　　type, cylindrical w/short neck,
　　light amber, 9¾" h. 450.00
Middletown Spring Co., Nature's
　　Remedy, green, qt. 130.00
Missisquoi Spring, w/papoose,
　　yellow-green 185.00
Moses Poland Water, cylinder,
　　green, w/label 15.00
Pablo (J.) & Co., New Orleans, La.,
　　man & dog in canoe, Hutchinson
　　stopper, aqua frosted (lip
　　chips) 85.00
Pablo (S.), New Orleans, La.,
　　embossed eagle, medium teal
　　blue frosted 65.00
Pacific Congress Water Springs
　　Saratoga California, embossed
　　running deer, Pacific Congress
　　Springs reverse, emerald green,
　　pt. 150.00
Penno's Mineral Water, Providence,
　　R.I., light green 55.00
Salvator Mineral Spring, Green Bay,
　　Wis., blob top, amber, qt. (dug) .. 15.00
Schultz (Carl H.) Mineral Springs,
　　N.Y., whittled, emerald green 45.00
Vermont Spring, Saxe & Co., olive
　　green, qt. 60.00
Witter Spring Water, W.M.S. Co.,
　　San Francisco, cylinder, amber ... 35.00

NURSING

"Happy Baby" Nurser

Aqua, pressed glass oval, embossed
　　"Medallion Nursing Bottle" &
　　cartoon-type head w/two concen-
　　tric circles one side & "A. S. Burr
　　Co., Proprietors, Boston, Mass."
　　reverse, square molded lip,
　　smooth base 7.00
Clear, mold-blown glass, cork clo-
　　sure w/central glass tube 45.00
Clear, mold-blown glass, standard
　　oval shape, embossed "McCully
　　Glass, Pittsburgh," 8 oz. 49.50
Clear, mold-blown glass, turtle-
　　shaped, embossed "Acme Nursing
　　Bottle" & monogram within 8-point
　　star, oval, 6" l. ....18.00 to 25.00
Clear, mold-blown glass, turtle-
　　shaped 25.00
Clear, pressed glass, embossed
　　"Baby Bunting" & rabbit, 8 oz. 6.75
Clear, pressed glass, embossed
　　"Betsy Brown Sterilizer" 24.00
Clear, pressed glass, embossed
　　"Happy Baby" & baby each side,
　　8 oz. (ILLUS.) ....10.00 to 15.00
Light aqua, blown glass, chestnut-
　　shaped, long sloping shoulders,
　　mushroom-shaped neck w/tooled
　　nipple mouth, pontil, 7 3/8" h. ... 55.00
Staffordshire pottery, turtle-shaped,
　　blue transfer on white, 19th c. ... 300.00

PICKLE BOTTLES
Amber, embossed "Sanburn Parker
　　& Co., Union Brand Boston Pick-
　　les," embossed star & shield 95.00
Amethyst-tinged clear, hand-made
　　brass lid, 14" h. (small rim
　　chips) 35.00
Aqua, cathedral-type, w/Gothic arch
　　windows, 6-sided, 13" h. 65.00
Aqua, cathedral-type w/Gothic arch
　　windows, embossed "R. & F.
　　Atmore" 250.00
Aqua, embossed "W.D.S./N.Y.,"
　　rolled lip, open pontil, 2¼" w.,
　　7 5/8" h. 110.00
Blue-aqua, cathedral-type w/Gothic
　　arches, roll-over collar, pontil,
　　9" h. 275.00
Emerald green, barrel-shaped,
　　large 27.50
Light green, cathedral-type
　　w/Gothic arch windows, partial
　　label "K. Lewis, Gerkins, 93 Broad
　　St., Boston," roll-over collar,
　　smooth base, 11 5/8" h. 70.00
Yellow (pale), embossed "Bunker
　　Hill Pickle," 7½" h. 45.00

POISONS
Amber, triangular, ribbed body em-
　　bossed "Poison" on 2 sides,
　　ca. 1890, 10¼" h. 70.00

Amber, triangular, rounded back, 2
panels embossed "Poison" 4.00
Clear, triangular, embossed "Cran-
dall Pharmacal Co., Brooklyn,
N.Y.," 3" h..................... 20.00
Clear, square, embossed "Poison -
The Oriental Embalming Fluid Poi-
son - The Egyptian Chemical Co.,
Boston, Mass.," 9" h............ 40.00

Cobalt Blue Poison Bottles

Cobalt blue, ribbed body embossed
"Poison" on 2 sides, ½ oz.,
2¾" h. (ILLUS. right) 25.00
Cobalt blue, 2 panels embossed
"Poison," 3" h.................. 6.00
Cobalt blue, ribbed body embossed
"Poison" on 2 sides, 1 oz., 3½" h.
(ILLUS. center right) 15.00
Cobalt blue, ribbed body embossed
"Poison" on 2 sides, 4 oz., 5" h.
(ILLUS. center left) 10.00
Cobalt blue, ribbed body embossed
"Poison" on 2 sides, 6 oz., 5½" h.
(ILLUS. left) 8.00
Cobalt blue, diamond-quilted body,
embossed "Poison," qt. 55.00
Cobalt blue, embossed skull &
crossbones 40.00
Yellow-amber, ribbed corners, em-
bossed "Dr. Detwiler, Ph.C. Drug-
gist" below neck 20.00

SNUFF BOTTLES

Amber, embossed "P. Lorillard Co.,"
qt............................ 15.00
Amber, embossed "Horseshoe," sol-
id tin lid ....30.00 to 40.00
Amber, sheared lip, pontil 40.00
Aqua, embossed "Doct. Marshall's,"
pontil, 3¾" h. 25.00
Olive amber, octagonal, embossed
"E. Roome, Troy, New York,"
sheared slightly flared lip, pontil,
4¼" h.................95.00 to 125.00
Olive amber, flared lip, embossed
"W" on base, w/seed bubbles 23.00
Olive amber, rectangular, pontil 29.50
Olive green, square w/chamfered
corners, sheared flaring lip, pon-
til, 2 7/8" w., 4¾" h............ 55.00

Yellow-amber, pontil 30.00
Yellow-green, sheared flaring lip ... 30.00
Yellow-green, embossed "E. Roome,
Troy, New York," pontil, 4" h. 95.00

SODAS & SARSAPARILLAS

Early Coca-Cola Bottle

Anchor Bottling Works, Cincinnati,
Ohio, soda, embossed anchor,
paneled base, Hutchinson stopper,
aqua 10.00
Battelle (M.M), Brooklyn, N.Y.,
soda, blob top, iron pontil, teal
blue 85.00
Beldings (Dr.) Sarsaparilla, clear.... 22.00
Belfast Soda Water Gingerale Co.,
San Francisco, Cal., blob top,
blue-aqua 45.00
Bells Sarsaparilla, clear 15.00
Betterley (J.W.), J.W.B. Ravena,
N.Y., soda, Hutchinson stopper,
aqua 9.00
Bristols Sarsaparilla, clear 17.00
Buffum's Sarsaparilla & Lemon
Mineral Water, Pittsburgh,
10-sided, iron pontil, deep cobalt
blue 425.00
Bulls Sarsaparilla, clear 30.00
Cape Argo Soda Works, Marshfield,
Oregon, Hutchinson stopper,
aqua 40.00
C.B. Co., Concord, N.H., soda,
Hutchinson stopper, aqua 16.00
Chas. Grove Cola, Pa., soda, iron
pontil, aqua 30.00
Chocolate Creme, Crystal Springs
Bottling Co., Barnet, Vermont,
soda, Hutchinson stopper, paper
label 65.00
Coca-Cola, straight sides, amber
(ILLUS.)...................... 10.00
Coca-Cola, Portland, Oregon,
amber, 1907 .... 45.00
Coca-Cola, 1915 .... 10.00

Coca-Cola, Nov. 8, 1923 .... 11.00
Coca-Cola, "Big Chief," 1928 .... 8.00
Coca-Cola, Memphis, Tenn.,
   amber 30.00
Coca-Cola, Texarkana, Ark. & Tex.,
   straight sides 20.00
Codd marble-stoppered soda,
   clear 16.50
Conant (F.A.), 252 Girod St., N.O.,
   soda, blob top, iron pontil, forest
   green (dug) 55.00
Foleys Sarsaparilla, amber 25.50
Gold Medal Sarsaparilla, amber 45.00
Henry Gardner, soda, green 15.00
John Graf, Milwaukee, soda,
   8-sided, blob top, amber 18.00
John Ryan 1852 Excelsior Gingerale, Savannah, blob top,
   citron .... 150.00 to 175.00
John Ryan 1859 Savannah, GA, blob
   top, cobalt blue 100.00
John Ryan, Savannah, Georgia,
   1866, soda, blob top, cobalt
   blue 27.50
Kohl & Beans, Easton, Pa., soda,
   squat, name embossed within
   square, medium green 85.00
Lord Baltimore Bottling Co., Baltimore, Maryland, soda, paneled,
   aqua 6.00
Luke Beard, soda, ten-pin shape,
   green 190.00
Magic Cola Bottling Works, Baltimore, Maryland in slug plate,
   soda 6.00
Marlow (J.), Philadelphia, soda, slug
   plate, iron pontil, dark green 30.00
McCormack's (M.) Ginger Ale, Nashville, Tenn., cobalt blue 175.00
McLeans Sarsaparilla, aqua, 9" h.... 42.50
Miles (A.S.), Baltimore, soda, eagle,
   Hutchinson stopper, aqua 10.00

Moxie Bottle

Moxie, paper label, Boston, Massachusetts, 7 oz. (ILLUS.) 17.50
Moxie, Lowell, Mass., aqua 30.00
Mutchler & Weiser, Cherryvale, Kansas, soda, Hutchinson stopper,
   aqua 40.00
Nu-Grape, soda, corset-shaped 4.00

Orange Crush Bottle

Orange Crush, soda, clear, ribbed,
   pat. July 20, ca. 1920
   (ILLUS.) .... 16.00 to 20.00
Owen Casey, Eagle Soda Works, Sac
   City, medium blue streaked
   w/amber swirls 40.00
Owens (J.R.), Parkesburg, Pa.,
   soda, squat, iron pontil, deep
   green 42.00
Pacific Soda Works, Portland, Ore-
   gon, Hutchinson stopper 12.00
Palliser (D.) Mobile, Alabama, soda,
   Hutchinson stopper, aqua 8.00
Parker, soda, squat, blob top, iron
   pontil, sapphire blue 75.00
Pearson (N.R.), Pittsfield, Mass.,
   soda, graphite pontil, light cobalt
   blue (2 minor dings) 85.00
Pepsi Cola, Exmore, Va. 7.50
Pepsi Cola Bottling Co., Pensacola,
   Fla., Hutchinson stopper 395.00
Philip Young & Co., Savannah, Ga.,
   soda, embossed eagle, green 150.00
Pioneer Soda Works, San Francisco,
   soda, monogram variant, aqua ... 150.00
Primleys Sarsaparilla, clear 20.00
Queen City Bottling Works, Parsons,
   Kansas, soda, Hutchinson stopper,
   aqua 20.00
RC Cola 6.00
Reichert Bottling Works, Red Wing,
   Minnesota, embossed, 6¼ fluid
   oz............................... 6.00

Riddle (R.), Philadelphia, soda, blob
top, smooth base, teal blue (dug,
base bruise) 35.00
Rober (T. & H.), soda, iron pontil,
green 150.00
Robinson, Wilson & Legallee, 102
Sudbury St., Boston, soda, squat,
iron pontil, deep blue-green 65.00
Roussel (E.), Philada., soda, blob
top, pontil, emerald green 50.00
Schmidtmann (H.), 413 E. 24th St.,
N. York, reverse w/large H.S.M.,
soda, blob top, blue-aqua 15.00
Seitz Bros., soda, squat, blue-
green 50.00
Seitz Bros., Easton, Pa., soda, olive
green .... 28.00 to 45.00
Southwick & Tupper, N.Y., soda,
8-sided, green 90.00
Spencer (D.H.), Omaha, Nebraska,
soda, Hutchinson stopper, aqua .. 15.00
Star Bottling Co., Oskaloosa, Iowa,
soda, Hutchinson stopper, aqua .. 18.00
Star Ice & Soda Co., Hawaii, applied
color label, 1930's 7.50
Sutton, Cincinnati, soda, iron pontil,
cobalt blue 175.00
To-Ko Bottling Co., Baltimore, Mary-
land in slug plate, soda 6.00
Union Bottle Works, Pittsburgh, Pa.,
soda, Hutchinson stopper,
8½" h. 30.00
Waimea Water Co., Ltd., soda,
Hutchinson stopper 25.00
Whipples Sarsaparilla, clear 24.00
Wild Cherry, Cyrstal Springs Bottling
Co., Barnet, Vermont, soda,
Hutchinson stopper 65.00
Yager's Sarsaparilla, indented front
panel, amber 25.00
Yager's Sarsaparilla, indented front
panel, aqua, 8½" h. 20.00

WHISKEY & OTHER SPIRITS

Beer, "A.B.C.M. Co. 2, Belleville,
Ill.," blob top, cobalt blue 60.00
Beer, "Almadene Est. 1852,"
stoneware 23.00
Beer, "Conrad Seipp Br'g. Co.,
Chicago," amber, miniature 25.00
Beer, "Globe Brewery, Baltimore,"
blob top, amber................ 9.00
Beer, "Honolulu Brewing Co.,
Honolulu, T.H.," blob top, aqua,
qt. 38.00
Beer, "John Fauser, San Francisco,"
amber, 1890's 50.00
Beer, "John Rapp & Son," amber,
pt. 20.00
Beer, "Manhattan Brewing Co.,
Litchfield, Ill.," blob top,
aqua.......................... 18.00
Beer, "Oriental Brewing Co., Balti-
more," blob top, aqua 9.00

Beer, "Pittsburgh Beer, Chas. C.
Stix, 4th Ave." 45.00
Beer, "Progress," amber 6.00
Beer, "Red Wing Brewing Co., Red
Wing, Minn." embossed in circle,
blob top, light amber, picnic size
(½ gal.)....................... 105.00
Beer, "Schlitz," royal ruby,
12 oz. 12.00
Beer, "Schlitz," royal ruby,
16 oz. 30.00
Beer, "Seal Rock Bottling Co., John
Kroger, San Francisco, Cal.,"
amber 20.00
Beer, "E. Shouler Bottling Works,
English Brewed Ginger Beer,
Akron, Ohio," stoneware, "Light-
ning" stopper 25.00
Beer, "Standard Brewery, Chicago,
Ill.," embossed eagle & flag,
aqua, metal stopper, 1880's 15.00
Beer, various midwest breweries,
amber, picnic size (½ gal.)....... 45.00
Beer, various breweries, stoneware,
grey w/cobalt blue swash over
impressed lettering at sides 40.00
Case gin, "E. Kiderlen," tapered,
dark olive green, whittled,
9¼" h......................... 32.50
Case gin, "L D B," free-blown, applied seal, wide flanged lip,
smooth concave base, olive
green, 11 5/8" h. 55.00
Case gin, "A. Van Hoboken, Rotter-
dam," olive green, 9" h. 15.00
Gin, "Elbart Dry Gin," cork-top,
aqua 5.00
Schnapps, "Udolpho Wolfe's," pontil,
olive green 65.00

"Africander Rye" Back Bar Bottle

Whiskey, "Africander Rye," back bar
bottle, clear w/enameled label
(ILLUS.)....................... 108.00

Whiskey, "A.M. Bininger & Co., 38 Broadway, N.Y., Old Kentucky Bourbon," barrel-shaped w/rings above marked center band, golden amber, 8" h.....150.00 to 175.00

Whiskey, "Bininger's Regulator" around clock face, "19 Broad St., New York" on edge, pontil, amber w/olive tone 225.00

"Casper's Whiskey"

Whiskey, "Casper's Whiskey - Made by Honest North Carolina People," cobalt blue, qt. (ILLUS.) 345.00

Whiskey, "Chapin & Gore Sour Mash, 1867," barrel-shaped, amber 75.00

Whiskey, "Chestnut Grove," ewer form w/applied handle, amber ....125.00 to 150.00

Whiskey, "Clarke & Walker, Denver," cylinder, globby top, "One Quart You Bet" at base, yellow-amber, qt..................... 600.00

"J.H. Cutter Old Bourbon"

Whiskey, "J.H. Cutter Old Bourbon," blob top, light amber (ILLUS.) 45.00

Whiskey, "R.B. Cutter's Pure Bourbon," handled jug, pontil, amber 225.00

Whiskey, "Dickel & Co., Nashville, Tenn., Cascade Distillery Co., Tullahoma, Tenn.," stoneware jug, gal.. .... 75.00

Whiskey, "Elk's Pride, Carlisle, Pa.," stoneware jug, brown & tan glaze, miniature 88.00

Whiskey, "Gold Standard Whiskey," 1896 McKinley & Hobart political campaign, gold coins & flags on label, pt. 35.00

Whiskey, "Golden Wedding," marigold Carnival glass, pt. ....15.00 to 20.00

Whiskey, "Griesel Bros., Wines, Whiskey & Cordials, East 3rd St., Winona, Minn.," stoneware jug, gal.. .... 85.00

Whiskey, "The Hayner Distilling Co., Dayton, St. Louis, Atlanta, St. Paul Distillers," clear, qt. 7.50

Whiskey, "J.T. & Co., 341 Walnut St., Philadelphia" seal bottle, squat, glob top, yellow-amber (dug).. .... 20.00

Whiskey, "John P. Gagens Happy Hollow Whiskey, Lafayette, Ind.," stoneware jug w/bail handle, white slip glaze, qt. 65.00

Whiskey, "Kellogg's Nelson County Extra Kentucky Bourbon, W.L. Co. Sole Agents," lip w/inside screw threads & original stopper, amber 35.00

Whiskey, "Kricks Whiskey," back bar decanter, 9 panels swirled to right, clear 20.00

Whiskey, "Lillenthal & Co., San Francisco," applied blob top, amber 175.00

Whiskey, "W. McCully & Co., Pittsburgh, Pa." on base, mold-blown, blob top, golden amber shaded to reddish amber at base.......... 32.00

Whiskey, "E.P. Middleton & Bro. Wheat Whiskey, 1825, Philada.," deep olive amber ....145.00 to 160.00

Whiskey, "Mohawk," figural Indian warrior, rolled lip, yellow-amber, 12½" h....................... 645.00

Whiskey, "Old Methusalem Whiskey," cylinder, dark orange-amber 65.00

Whiskey, "Old Quaker," flask w/cork & label, clear, 1935 ...... 17.50

Whiskey, "W.C. Peacock, Honolulu, H.I.," amber, qt. 60.00

Whiskey, "H. Pharazyn," figural Indian warrior, rolled lip, yellow-amber 695.00

Whiskey, "Ricketts," pontil, black,
qt. 30.00
Whiskey, figural stoneware pig, incised railroad map w/names of
cities from Mounds to Chicago,
map of Mississippi River one side
& incised "St. Louis-The Future
Capitol-Railroad & River Guide
with a Little Fine Old Bourbon"
reverse, Anna (Illinois) Pottery ... 1,950.00
Whiskey, "Thos. Taylor & Co., Sole
Agents For P. Vollmers Old Bourbon, Louisville, Kt" in slug plate,
blob top, deep amber 250.00
Whiskey, "Upper Blue Lick Water,
Stanton & Pierle, Proprietors,
Maysville, Ky.," oval, cornflower
blue, qt. 550.00
Whiskey, "J.C. Wheeler, Groceries &
Liquors, 158 Forest Street, Balti-
more," grey stoneware jug, semi-
ovoid w/strap handle, 7¾" h. 70.00
Whiskey, "Woodland Sour Mash
Whiskey, Crigler & Crigler,
Covington, Kentucky," vertical rib-
bing, brilliant green 150.00
Whiskey, wicker-covered clear flask
w/pewter top 40.00
Wine, "Revd. N.O. Moore 1819" seal
bottle, black, 11½" h. (flake off
inside lip) 335.00

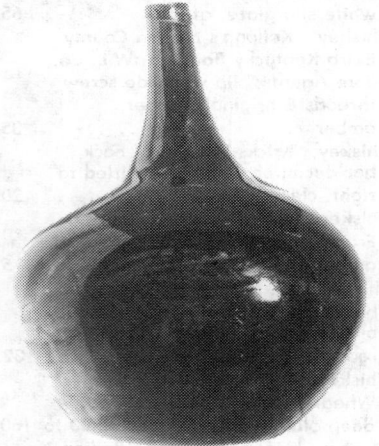

Wine Demijohn

Wine demijohn, kidney-shaped,
green, 17" h. (ILLUS.) 130.00
Wine demijohn, free-blown cylinder,
deep red-amber, 18" h. 90.00
Wine demijohn, free-blown cylinder,
green, 26" h. 75.00

(End of Bottle Section)

BOY SCOUT ITEMS

Boy Scout Handkerchief

*Boy Scout rules and regulations, hand-
books and accouterments have changed with
the times. Early items associated with this
movement are now being collected. A sampling follows.*

Axe, hand-type, "Collins," Boy Scout
model 1507, 1925-33 .... $52.00
Book, "Boy Scouts to the Rescue,"
by George Durstan, published by
Saalfield, 1921 .... 15.00
Book, "Golden Anniversary Book of
Scouting," cover by Norman Rock-
well, published by Golden Press,
1959 .... 25.00
Book, "Matching Mountains with the
Boy Scout Uniform," by Edward F.
Reimer, published by E. P. Dutton,
1929, w/dust jacket 20.00
Bugle, "Rexcraft," w/red tassel, in
felt-lined case 85.00
Calendar, 1949, Norman Rockwell il-
lustration entitled "Friend in
Need," Cub Scout, Boy Scout & in-
jured dog, 16 x 33" 60.00
Camera, folding-type, Kodak, green
leather case, 1927 .... 27.00
First Aid kit w/contents, oval box
w/belt loop, "Bauer & Black,"
1932 .... 40.00
Flint & steel set, 1940's 6.50
Handbook, 1910, by Ernest Thomp-
son Seton, green & white soft
cover 300.00
Handbook, 1914, red leatherette
cover 90.00
Handbook, 1933 .... 25.00
Handkerchief, cotton, orange &
blue, 1930's, 16 x 16" (ILLUS.) 12.00
Jacket patch, "1969 National Jam-
boree Idaho" 15.00
Jigsaw puzzle, World War II Boy
Scout, 375 pcs. 8.00
Knife, pocket-type, Remington No.
RS 333, 1932-35 .... 75.00

Knife, pocket-type, Ulster Knife
Company, model 1036, 1970-76 ... 22.50
Magazine, "Boy's Life," 1916,
February, Norman Rockwell
illustrations 30.00
Magazine, "Scouting," 1917,
March 7.50
Match safe, nickel-plated brass 25.00
Membership card, 1920 .... 10.00
Neckerchief, "1935 Jamboree,"
blue 80.00
Pamphlet, Merit Badge series,
"Horsemanship," 1930 .... 7.00
Pamphlet, Merit Badge series,
"Pioneering," 1920 .... 25.00
Photocard views, Boy Scout camp
scenes & activities, 1920's, lot of
43 .... 28.00
Picture frame, bronze 35.00
Sheet music, "Boy Scouts Parade
March," by Johnson, 1917 .... 20.00
Signals: radio, blinker & telegraph;
battery-operated, Ryan & Co.,
1932, original box 33.00
Telescope, aluminum, 6x lens 10.00
Uniform, complete, 1930's 60.00
Whistle, brass ....12.00 to 18.00
Yearbook for 1922 .... 15.00

BREWERIANA

"Schlitz" Bottle Opener

Beer is still popular in this country but the number of breweries has greatly diminished. More than 1,900 breweries were in operation in the 1870's but we find fewer than 40 supplying the demands of the country a century later. The small local brewery has either been absorbed by a larger company or forced to close, unable to meet the competiton. Advertising items used to promote the various breweries, especially those issued prior to prohibition, now attract an ever growing number of collectors. The breweriana items listed are a sampling of the many items available. Also see BOTTLE OPENERS, BOTTLES, CORKSCREWS and TRAYS.

Ash tray, "Glueck's Beer," blue
glass $12.00
Ash tray, "Pure Springs Brewery,"
cast iron 30.00
Beer glass, "Dick's," w/red circle
logo 10.00

Beer glass, "Grain Belt Beer," clear
glass w/enameled lettering 5.00
Beer glass, "Kuebeler-Stang," clear
glass w/frosted shield 55.00
Beer glass, "Lone Star," clear glass,
cowboy pictured 20.00
Blotter, "Tivoli-Union Brew. Co.,
Denver, Colorado" 6.00
Book, "W. J. Lemp Brewing Co.,"
"Toasts," 1904, 40 pp. 30.00
Bottle opener, "Honorary Budweiser
Brewmaster" & "This calls for
Bud," gold-colored metal, key-
shaped, 1950's, 7" l., original
bag 25.00
Bottle opener, "Pabst," tin, bottle-
shaped 6.00
Bottle opener, "Schlitz," wooden,
bottle-shaped w/multicolored
lithographed label, 4½" h.
(ILLUS.)...................... 10.00
Calendar, 1904, "Blatz Brewery,"
Victorian lady seated w/glass of
beer pictured, published by S.S.
Paterson, Dillon, Montana, oak
frame, 24 x 32" 295.00
Calendar, 1905, "Rainier Beer,"
showgirl pictured, framed,
22 x 30" 275.00
Calendar, 1930, "Goetz Beer," Kan-
sas City Blues, giant baseball &
beer bottles pictured 85.00
Can, cone-top, "Bub's," 12 oz. 45.00
Can, cone-top, "Cook's," steamboat
pictured, 12 oz. 95.00
Can, cone-top, "Hudepohl," 12 oz. ... 15.00
Can, cone-top, "Old Style Lager,"
12 oz........................ 10.00
Can, flat-top, "Atlas Prager Beer,"
12 oz........................ 20.00
Can, flat-top, "Goebel," 8 oz. 10.00
Can, flat-top, "Stegmaier," 12 oz.... 12.00
Coaster, "Crockery City" 30.00
Coaster, "Hanley's Ale,"
aluminum 5.00
Coaster, "Oertel's," bride pictured .. 20.00
Corkscrew, "Pabst," wooden
handle 17.00
Counter display, "Fehr's Beer,"
chalkware model of a bear 125.00
Counter display, "Miller High Life
Beer," chalkware figure of a
young woman, 15" h............ 69.00
Counter display, "Pabst Beer," card-
board, die-cut figure of a
newsboy 85.00
Door push plate, "Senate Beer,"
tin 35.00
Foam scraper, "Ballantine" 10.00
Foam scraper, "Columbia Brewery,
Shenandoah, Pennsylvania," cel-
luloid, paddle-shaped 40.00
Foam scraper, "Harvard Brewing,"
black 20.00

Foam scraper, "Pabst Andeker,"
 black & red 24.00
Foam scraper, "Peerless Beer,"
 celluloid 7.00
Foam scraper, "Stanton Ale" 30.00
Lamp, "Miller High Life," brass &
 tin, glass shade w/girl on cres-
 cent moon 65.00
Match holder, "American Brewing
 Co.," stoneware, eagle pictured .. 110.00
Match safe, "Rochester Brewing
 Co.," w/diamond logo 47.00
Match safe, "Voigt Brewery Co.,
 Detroit," German silver, pre-
 prohibition 65.00
Mirror, pocket-type, "Yuengling's" .. 90.00
Mug, "Bartholomay's, Rochester,
 New York," tan, Mettlach 135.00
Mug, "Dick's Beer," embossed bird,
 11" h. 185.00
Mug, "Miller's High Life Beer,"
 McCoy pottery 15.00
Mug, "Rochester Brew. Co.," salt
 glazed stoneware 95.00
Mug, "Fred Sehring Brewing Co.,
 Joliet," Blue Onion patt., sponged
 cobalt blue handle w/gold leaf
 overlay, front w/transfer of over-
 flowing stein of beer within a
 shield, sprigs of barley & hops,
 dated 1907, 5" 110.00
Mug, "South Bend Brewing Assoc.,"
 factory scene, Mettlach 125.00
Notebook, "Louis Bergdoll Brewing
 Co., Philadelphia," celluloid,
 1905 .... 30.00
Pinback button, "Hagerstown Brewing," factory pictured 30.00
Plate, "Fred Krug Brewing Co. - 50th
 Anniversary, 1859-1909," buildings
 pictured, 10" d. 145.00
Pocket knife, "Anheuser-Busch,"
 sterling silver 195.00
Pocket knife-corkscrew combination,
 folding-type, "Adolphus Busch" ... 38.00
Postcard, "Pabst," comic, 1906 ...... 10.00
Print, "Budweiser," "Fight for the
 Overland Mail," Indians attacking
 stagecoach, 1910, framed, large .. 400.00

"Gluek's Beer" Salt & Pepper Shakers

Salt & pepper shakers, "Gluek's
 Beer," amber glass bottles
 w/paper labels & metal caps,
 4" h., pr. (ILLUS.) 12.50
Salt & pepper shakers, "Miller High
 Life," small glass bottles, 3" h.,
 pr. 15.00
Sign, "Aurora Brewing Co.," self-
 framed tin, small girl wearing
 big hat & holding roses, 1904,
 20 x 13" 390.00
Sign, "Ballantine Beer, Newark,
 New Jersey," self-framed tin,
 Cavalier drinking from Ballantine
 mug, dated 1909, 34 x 22" 2,200.00
Sign, "Barbarossa Beer," self-framed
 tin, old bottles pictured, oval 1,200.00
Sign, "Budweiser," reverse painting
 on glass, girl in red dress, ca.
 1910, 31 x 17" 1,350.00
Sign, "Champagne Velvet Beer,"
 lithographed tin, Colonial scene
 w/cherubs pouring beer, 24" d. .. 1,000.00
Sign, "Deppen Brewing Co., Read-
 ing, Pa.," reverse painting on
 glass, corner-type, stag's head
 above bottle, 25 x 14", original
 box 1,150.00
Sign, "Griesedieck Beer," cardboard, fisherman measuring trout,
 framed, 1930's, 28 x 24" 75.00
Sign, "Hohenadel Beer," self-framed
 tin, John L. Sullivan in boxing
 stance in ring, wearing black,
 green & white boxing garb 1,250.00
Sign, "Krueger Beer," self-framed
 tin, 2 bottles on table w/Pilsener
 glass & cheese, pre-prohibition,
 14" d. 275.00

"Schlitz" Tin Sign

Sign, "Schlitz," tin, automotive
 scene, "Ah! Isn't Schlitz Always
 Good," ca. 1915, 24" d. (ILLUS.) .. 412.50
Sign, "Shaw's Pure Malt," self-
 framed tin, maid serving drink to

tired mother, child on floor
w/toys, 1910, 23 x 16" 375.00
Sign, "Velvet Beer - Terre Haute
Brewing," cherubs pouring beer,
24" 500.00
Tap knob, "A.B.E. Co., Reingold,"
metal 10.00
Tap knob, "Dick's," 1940's 32.00
Tap knob, "Miller High Life,"
wooden 12.00
Thermometer, "Spoetzl Brewery,
Shiner, Texas," brewery
pictured 35.00
Thermometer, "Yuengling," 12" d. . . 35.00

Equestrian Figure after Isidore Bonheur

a fence, on naturalistic base, late
19th c., 27¼" l. (ILLUS.) 6,050.00
Bonheur, Isidore-Jules, equestrian
group of a race horse & jockey
walking on naturalistic ground,
dark brown patina, 19th c.,
30½" l., 24 5/8" h. 11,000.00
Bonheur, Isidore-Jules, group of bull
dog, hound pulling the ear of
the bull in direction desired,
black patina, oval base
w/detailed terrain, early
20th c., 25" l. 1,540.00
Bouraine, Marcel, figure of the God-
dess Diana w/flowing hair, poised
to shoot her arrow, 2 fawns
prancing along beside her, green
patina, ca. 1925, 27½" h. 3,850.00

BRONZES

Lion & Tiger after Barye

*Small bronzes, used as decorative adjuncts
in today's homes, continue to attract interest.
Particularly appealing to collectors today are
"les animaliers" of the 19th century French
school of sculptors who turned to animals for
their subject-matter. These, together with
figures in the Art Deco and Art Nouveau
taste, are very popular with collectors and
available in a wide price range. Also see ART
NOUVEAU.*

Barye, Antoine-Louis, figure group
of Theseus slaying the Centaur,
Theseus atop the beast with a
club in his right hand & holding
the Centaur by the neck w/his left
arm, drapery falling from the
back of the Centaur to the rocky
base, brownish black patina, late
19th c., 14" h. $3,575.00
Barye, Antoine-Louis, group of a
lion w/his right paw on a coiling
serpent, green-brown patina, late
19th c., 13" l. 715.00
Barye, Antoine-Louis, model of
a lion, dark patina, cast by
Barbedienne, 10" l. (ILLUS.
front) 935.00
Barye, Antoine-Louis, model of
a tiger, dark patina, cast by
Barbedienne, 11" l. (ILLUS.
rear) 550.00
Bonheur, Isidore-Jules, equestrian
figure, steeple chase rider taking

Trained Seal after Bouraine

Bouraine, Marcel, model of trained
seal (missing ball), parcel-
silvered, impressed Goldscheider
"La Stele" foundry seal, 18¾" h.
(ILLUS.) 990.00
Carrier-Belleuse, Albert-Ernest,
figure of "Graziella" standing,
w/ivory face & hands, elaborately
dressed in silver & gilt trimmed
medieval costume, holding in her

left hand a threader, on bronze
circular base on a marble socle,
ca. 1890, 29¼" h. 2,750.00

Chiparus, Demetre, figure group,
Russian dancers dressed in
elaborate "Ballet Russes" costumes & holding cymbals above
their heads, polychromed, silvered & gilt-bronze, marble base
ca. 1925, 23½" h. 13,200.00

Claude-Michel (called Clodion),
figure of a seated satyr rubbing
his teary eyes, weathered brown
patina, late 19th c., 25" h. 825.00

Colinet, Claire Jeanne Roberte, bust
of a woman w/solemn face & long
braided hair, looking downward,
her head & body covered
w/drapery, weathered green
patina, early 20th c., 33" h. 2,475.00

Descomps, Joe, figure of a dancer
in Near-Eastern dress, holding a
mask, gilt-bronze, marble stand,
ca. 1900, 25¼" h. 2,200.00

Fratin, Christophe, group of a lion
on his 2 back feet attacking a
rearing horse, brown patina, late
19th c., 8½" h. 660.00

Hannaux, Emmanuel, figure group,
mermaid caressing the locks of a
young man as he wrests a lyre
from her, both perched on a rocky
outcrop amidst lapping waves,
golden brown patina, ca. 1900,
22" h. 1,650.00

Parrots after Kelety

Kelety, Alexandre, group of 2 parrots on perch, damascened &
cold-painted bronze, (replaced)
green marble plinth, early 20th c.,
21¼" h. birds (ILLUS.). 7,150.00

Liberich, Nicholas I., model of a
bear standing on his hind legs,
shaped rock crystal base, late
19th c., 20½" h. 3,300.00

Mene, Pierre-Jules, group of a mare
& foal, standing on naturalistic
ground, rich brown patina, late
19th c., 23 5/8" l., 17¼" h. 5,500.00

Ple', Henri-Honore, figure of an
Arab, bearded man in tunic &
cloak standing w/spear in his
right hand & sword in his left
hand tucked within his sash which
holds other weapons, dark brown
patina, square bronze plinth,
ca. 1885, 4' 7½" h. 11,550.00

Preiss, Ferdinand, figure of a chorus
girl, "Con Brio," cold-painted
bronze & ivory, hexagonal striped
black & green onyx plinth, overall
14 7/8" h. .9,900.00

Riche, Louis, model of a German
shepherd dog reclining, ears
pricked up, golden brown patina,
early 20th c., 24" l. 605.00

Villanis, Emanuelle, bust of an Eastern woman w/medallion headdress, brown & mustard patina,
on a veined marble socle,
ca. 1900, 24¾" h. 1,210.00

Zach, Bruno, figure of a dancer,
young girl wearing a short full-
skirted costume, her left leg kick-
ing high in the air, brown patina,
ca. 1925, 16½" h. 2,530.00

BROWNIE COLLECTIBLES

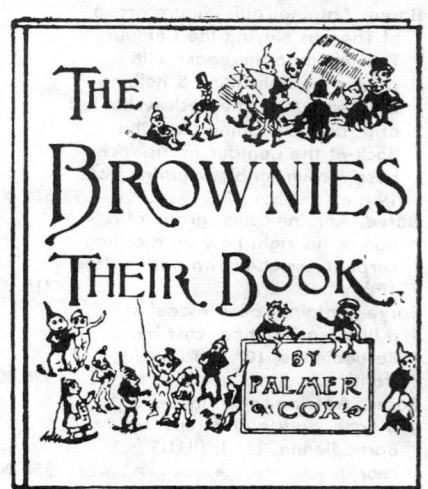

Palmer Cox Book

The Brownies were creatures of fantasy created by Palmer Cox, artist-author, in 1887. Early in this century, numerous articles with depictions of or in the shape of Brownies appeared.

Book, "The Brownies - Their Book,"
by Palmer Cox, 1887 (ILLUS.) $95.00
Book, "The Brownies Through the
Union," by Palmer Cox, 1895 . . . . . 75.00
Book, "Queerie Queers," by Palmer
Cox, 1880's 25.00
Book, "Queer People," by Palmer
Cox, 1888 . . . . 50.00
Candlestick, majolica, Brownie
Uncle Sam 175.00
Card game, Brownies decor 35.00
Cup, porcelain, Brownies decor 40.00
Cup, silverplate, skating Brownies
decor, engraved w/name &
date 75.00
Cup & saucer, china, Brownies play-
ing various games, Paragon 65.00
Demitasse spoon, sterling silver,
twisted handle w/figural Brownie
terminal 35.00
Game, "Jack Straws," lithographed
Brownies decor on container 35.00
Game, "Kick-In Top," lithographed
tin w/wooden top & balls, original
box 25.00
Knife, fork & teaspoon, silverplate,
Brownies decor, 3 pcs. in original
box 35.00
Pinback button, celluloid, figural
Brownies, 2" h. 35.00
Plate, silverplate, scalloped rim
w/relief scrolls & floral border,
engraved center scene
w/Brownies (11) at various pursuits, Homan Silver Plate Co.,
ca. 1900, 7½" d. 68.00
Printing set, rubber stamps
w/Brownies, marked Palmer Cox,
set of 12 in original box 125.00
Puzzle, tracing-type, Brownies
decor, German 60.00
Salt & pepper shakers w/original
tops, white opaline glass, egg-
shaped, w/Brownie Indian, Sailor
& other Brownie characters, Mt.
Washington, pr. 175.00
Soda bottle, embossed Brownies
decor 50.00
Stickpin, Brownie Policeman 20.00

BUCKLES

When it was the height of popularity between 1650 and 1800, the lowly buckle was considered a fashionable status symbol denoting the wearer's wealth by the material from which it was made. Gold, silver, pewter, iron and tin buckles were made in a variety of forms. Though buckle collectors strive to acquire at least a few 18th century examples, they also seek out later buckles in desirable forms that are more affordable. Listed by type as well as material, the following buckles sold within recent months.

Lady's Mother-of-Pearl Belt Buckles

Belt buckle, lady's, cloisonne $125.00
Belt buckle, lady's, green bakelite,
2-part, carved design, w/six
matching buttons, 8 pcs. 32.00
Belt buckle, lady's, gutta percha,
2-part, relief classical ladies'
heads, acorn & leaf border,
3½ x 2½" 30.00
Belt buckle, lady's, mother-of-pearl
shell, 1920's, 1¼ x 7/8" (ILLUS.
right) 5.00
Belt buckle, lady's, mother-of-pearl
shell, 1920's, 1½ x 1" (ILLUS.
left) 7.00
Belt buckle, lady's, mother-of-pearl
shell, 1920's, 2" sq. (ILLUS.
center) 10.00
Belt buckle, lady's, royal blue glass,
2-part, geometric design,
Czechoslovakia 35.00
Belt buckle, lady's, Satsuma-type
china 38.00
Belt buckle, lady's, silver, swans &
cupids decor, hallmarked 75.00
Belt buckle, lady's, silver,
hallmarked for 1899-1900 . . . . 45.00
Belt buckle, lady's, sterling silver,
simple Art Nouveau style design,
Geo. E. Homer, Boston,
ca. 1900 . . . . 25.00
Belt buckle, lady's, sterling silver,
Gorham, 3" oval 28.00
Belt buckle, man's, silver, Masonic
emblems 19.00
Belt buckle, man's, silver, marked
"800," Holland, 3½" d. 150.00
Shoe buckles, copper-colored bead-
ing on cloth, hand-sewn, pr. 8.00
Shoe buckles, steel set w/rhine-
stones, worn original leatherized
cardboard case, pr. 30.00

BUSTER BROWN COLLECTIBLES

Buster Brown & Mary Jane Creamer

Buster Brown was a comic strip created by Richard Outcault in the New York Herald in 1902. It was subsequently syndicated and numerous objects depicting Buster (and often his dog, Tige) were produced. Also see BANKS.

Bill hook, celluloid insert w/Buster
  Brown & Tige $15.00
Book, "Buster Brown Dictionary,"
  1923 . . . . 38.00
Book, "Buster Brown - My Resolu-
  tions," by Richard F. Outcault,
  1906, published by Frederick A.
  Stokes Co., 68 pp . . . . 45.00 to 55.00
Bowl, china, Buster Brown decor 75.00
Coloring book, 1916 . . . . 15.00 to 25.00
Compact, silverplate, advertising
  "Buster Brown Shoes" 12.50
Creamer, china, Buster Brown &
  Mary Jane at tea decor (ILLUS.) . . 52.00
Cup & saucer, china, Buster Brown
  decor, marked "Germany" 35.00
Fan, Buster Brown & Tige decor,
  framed 62.50
Figure, Buster Brown in cart pulled
  by Tige, cast iron, 1900 . . . . 350.00
Fork, silverplate, Buster & Tige
  decor 14.00
Fork & spoon, sterling silver,
  2 pcs. 55.00
Paper doll, w/Army & Navy uni-
  forms, 2 suits & 2 hats, 12" h.,
  7 pcs. 190.00
Pinback button, advertising "Buster
  Brown Shoes," w/Buster & Tige . . . 11.50
Pitcher, china, Buster Brown decor,
  3¼" h. 40.00
Pitcher, china, figural Buster Brown,
  Germany 65.00
Plate, china, Buster Brown & Tige
  decor, 6" d. 50.00
Pocket watch, w/strap & fob 145.00
Postcard, leather, Buster Brown &
  Tige 8.00
Rug, bust portraits of Buster Brown

& Tige, red, blue & yellow,
  machine-made, 53" d. 440.00
Shoe trees, celluloid, w/Buster
  Brown & Tige, pr. . . . . 28.00 to 35.00
Store manikin of Buster Brown, wax
  head, ca. 1910, 38" h. 600.00
Teaspoon, silverplate, Buster Brown
  & Tige handle 15.00
Toy, roly poly figure 175.00
Toy, yo-yo, lithographed tin . . 16.50 to 20.00
Valentine card, signed Richard F.
  Outcault, published by Raphael
  Tuck 8.00

BUTTER MOLDS & STAMPS

Wooden Butter Mold

While they are sometimes found made of other materials, it is primarily the two-piece wooden butter mold and one-piece butter stamp that attracts collectors. The molds are found in two basic styles, rounded cup form and rectangular box form. Butter stamps are usually round with a protruding knob handle on the back. Many are factory made items with the print design made by forcing a metal die into the wood under great pressure, while others have the design chiseled out by hand.

Acorn mold, wooden, hand-carved . . $54.00
Acorn stamp, wooden, hand-carved,
  small 42.00
Big horn sheep mold, wooden, die-
  stamped design 45.00
Cow mold, wooden, hand-carved,
  w/hinged frame & side handle,
  11¾ x 4½" (age cracks) 135.00
Eagle w/heart-shaped shield body
  stamp, wooden, hand-carved,
  4" d. 320.00
Eagle & star stamp, wooden, hand-
  carved, w/turned wood handle,
  3½" d. 225.00

Fish mold, wooden, hand-carved,
18th c. 395.00
Flower & leaves mold, wooden,
hand-carved, round, miniature ... 49.00
Flower stamp, wooden, hand-
carved 38.00
Flower & foliage stamp, wooden,
hand-carved, w/turned wood handle, 4½" d. (age cracks) 85.00

Butter Crock Stamp

Heart flower & leaves half-circle
stamp (made to stamp half the
top of 5 lb. crock), wooden, hand-
carved w/deep sawtooth cuttings,
7 x 3½" (ILLUS.) 310.00
Leaf stamp, wooden, hand-carved,
concave almond shape w/carved
wood handle, 9 x 3¾" 55.00
Pineapple stamp, wooden, hand-
carved diamond-hatched leaves &
fruit, turned wood handle,
ca. 1820, round 85.00
Pinwheel swirl "lollypop" stamp on
handle of butter paddle, wooden,
hand-carved design on handle
end 195.00
Rectangular mold, wooden, carved
"Ridgefarm's Dairy," w/brass
handle 245.00
Rising sun "lollypop" stamp,
wooden, hand-carved, 6¼" l. (age
crack in handle)................ 325.00
Rooster mold, wooden, die-stamped
design 55.00
Rose mold, wooden, hand-carved ... 95.00
Sheaf of wheat mold, pine, hand-
carved 50.00
Sheaf of wheat stamp, walnut,
hand-carved, 4 1/8" d........... 65.00
Starflower stamp w/stylized foliate
design reverse, wooden, deeply
hand-carved, 5¼" d. (edges worn
& minor edge cracks) 415.00
Strawberry mold, wooden, hand-
carved ....75.00 to 85.00
Sunflower stamp, pine, hand-
carved 40.00
Swan mold, pine, hand-carved 125.00
Tulip stamp, wooden, deeply hand-
carved stylized blossoms, chip-
carved edge, turned wood handle,
4 1/8" d. 210.00

BUTTON HOOKS

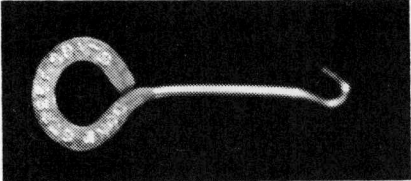

Advertising Button Hook

*From the 1860's through the early years of
the 20th century, people buttoned up their
shoes, along with many layers of garments
and gloves and the button hook was an in-
dispensable part of everyday life. Produced
in a variety of forms and materials, this once
useful gadget is now a popular collector's
item.*

Advertising, "Bond Street Spats,"
metal (ILLUS.)............$5.00 to 8.00
Advertising, "Fair Dept. Store,
Muskegon, Michigan," metal 8.00
Advertising, "Walkover Shoes,"
metal ....5.00 to 8.00
Celluloid handle, plain............ 4.00
Celluloid handle, modelled as a
lady's leg...................... 16.00
Gold-filled handle, ornate design
w/beaded trim, slender chain attached to shield-shaped booklet
w/ivory pages, cover applied
w/three-color gold decor & white
sapphire, 2¼" l. handle 38.00
Mother-of-pearl handle 24.00
Silver handle, engraved decor,
hallmarked, 6" l................ 26.00
Silverplate handle, 9¾" l.......... 15.00
Souvenir, Capitol Building, Washington, D.C. pictured 12.00
Sterling silver handle, embossed
scrolling, 5" l. 12.00
Sterling silver handle, floral engraving, Gorham, 8" l. 22.00
Sterling silver handle, Art Nouveau
style 58.00
Sterling silver handle, Lily of the
Valley patt., Whiting, ca. 1885.... 45.00

BUTTONS

Brass, cupid design, ornate, set of 6
on card $18.00
Brass, Geisha girl in high relief,
early 1900's, 1½" d. 25.00
Brass, embossed Pierrot (French
clown), 1½" d.................. 7.00
Brass, engraved w/full figure Gibson Girl w/gilt golf club, wreath,

crossed clubs & balls, 7/8" d., set
of 6 .... 40.00
Celluloid, "tortoise shell," set
of 12 .... 7.50

Satsuma Button

China, Satsuma, mask, dark blue
background w/gold detail & bor-
der, ca. 1925, 1 1/8" d. (ILLUS.)... 18.00
China, Satsuma, mother & child,
heavy gold trim & borders,
ca. 1920, ¾" d., set of 5 .... 100.00
China, Satsuma, pheasant, wisteria
blossoms & foliage, heavy gold
trim & borders, ca. 1910, ¾" d.,
set of 6 .... 125.00
China, Satsuma, Arhats (elderly
male disciples of Buddha, usually
w/haloes aobut head), set of 6 in
original box 85.00
China, Satsuma, 7 Gods of Fortune,
set of 7 in original box 85.00
China, transfer-printed w/circus
decor, 5/8" 5.00
Gilt metal, cupid in forest w/bow &
arrow, beaded rim, large 5.00
Glass, paperweight-type, rose centered on blue ground w/gold mica
flecks, ½" d. 25.00
Glass, blown, pink & cranberry
swirl, set of 8 .... 17.00
Milk white glass, h.p. floral decor,
ca. 1920, set of 8 .... 10.00
Rhinestone, sterling silver mounting,
1" d. 14.00
Silver, man playing mandolin w/two
ladies, Birmingham hallmark for
1900, set of 6 .... 225.00
Tortoise shell, inlaid silver bird in
flight center, inlaid mother-of-
pearl shell border, large 5.00

CALENDAR PLATES

*Calendar plates have been produced in this
country since the turn of the century, primarily of porcelain and earthenwares but also of
glass and tin. They were made earlier in
England. The majority were issued after 1909,
largely intended as advertising items.*

1907, wildflowers center, calendar
months border $45.00
1908, pink roses center, calendar
months border 32.50
1909, fruit center, Ohio advertising,
8" d. 22.00
1909, New York State Capitol building green transfer center, calendar months border, 9¼" d. 22.50
1909, lilies center, Nebraska advertising, 9½" d. 25.00
1909, holly wreath center, calendar
months border 26.00
1909, beautiful woman center, South
Dakota advertising 35.00
1909, small pink roses wreath
center, calendar months border .. 25.00
1910, holly wreath center, gold rim,
Kansas advertising, 7½" d. 20.00
1910, hunting scene center,
7½" d. 25.00
1910, garlands of flowers & cherubs
ringing in New Year center,
calendar months border, 8" d. 35.00
1910, Gibson Girl portrait center,
9½" d. 45.00
1910, beautiful woman center,
calendar months border 28.00
1910, fruit center, Wisconsin
advertising 22.00
1910, lighthouse scene center 27.50
1911, lady in red riding habit on
horse jumping over calendar
months center, brown floral border, Florida advertising, 8" d. 18.00
1911, cherries & floral center,
Nebraska advertising 14.00
1911, clocks w/time around the
world center, florals & calendar
months border 28.00
1911, ducks in flight center........ 32.50
1911, Sunbonnet Babies decor 125.00

1912 Calendar Plate

1912, owl on open book w/calendar
months on pages, New York advertising, 7½" d. (ILLUS.) 24.00

1912, fruit & floral center, calendar
months within floral horseshoe,
scalloped rim w/ornate gold trim,
Pennsylvania advertising,
8¼" d. 22.00
1912, "White River Tavern" center,
Vermont advertising, 8¼" d. 32.00
1912, Masonic emblem on building
center, calendar months within
fruit border, Illinois advertising,
9½" d. 25.00
1912, cherubs within wreath of pink
roses center 37.50
1914, Liberty Bell & "Philadelphia"
center, calendar months border .. 39.50
1920, "Victory & Peace" center,
calendar months border, Colorado
advertising 25.00
1921, Battleship "Flusser" within
bluebird wreath center 37.50
1922, American flag center, calendar months border, Wisconsin
advertising 40.00
1924, New Year greeting within
floral horseshoe center, calendar
months border 55.00
1928, white herons on blue ground
center, calendar months border,
9" d. 65.00
1933, oriental scene on blue ground
center, calendar months border,
8½" sq. 65.00

CAMPBELL KID COLLECTIBLES

Campbell Kids Rag-Stuffed Dolls

*The Campbell Kids were created by Grace
Weiderseim (Drayton) at the turn of this century and their first use is said to have been
on street car cards. They have been used for
years by the Campbell Soup Company in its*

*advertisements and various objects were
produced graced with illustrations of them.*

Doll, composition, Campbell boy or
girl, 1940's, each $140.00
Dolls, rag-stuffed, Campbell boy &
girl, 12" h., pr. (ILLUS.) 25.00
Dolls, rubber, Campbell boy & girl,
by Ruth Newton, Sun Rubber Co.,
8½" h., pr. 75.00
Feeding dish, pottery, Campbell Kids
decor, "Baby" in gold on rolled
edge, signed Grace Drayton 45.00
Feeding dish, pottery, Campbell Kids
decor, signed Drayton, Buffalo
Pottery 85.00
Fork, silverplate, figural Campbell
boy handle 10.00
Postcard, No. 3, advertising series,
Campbell Kids pictured, 1910 ..... 20.00
Potholder plaque, 1950's 20.00
Print, "September Morn," by Dray-
ton, Campbell premium 95.00
Soup spoon, silverplate, figural
Campbell girl handle 10.00
Teaspoons, silverplate, figural
Campbell Kid handles,
pr. .... 18.00 to 25.00

CANDLESTICKS & CANDLEHOLDERS

Bronze Candelabra

*Also see LIGHTING DEVICES and
SANDWICH GLASS.*

Candelabrum, bronze & Favrile
glass, 6-branch, central freeform
handle enclosing a snuffer recep-
tacle & flanked by 6 slender candle holders, each w/detachable
bobeche & blown glass insert, impressed Tiffany Studios, New
York, 15 7/8" h. (snuffer
missing) $3,300.00
Candelabrum, silver, 5-light, Corinthian column rising to 4 detachable leaf-capped scrolling branches
w/knopped stem continuing to

central socket, engraved w/mono-
gram, London, Edwardian, 1903,
20" h. 385.00

Candelabra, bronze, 3-light, flattened standard cast as a kneeling
nude woman w/light drapery
flowing from one shoulder,
beneath a blossoming arbor set
w/three candle prongs, green
patina, after Emory P. Seidel,
impressed Roman Bronze Works,
N.Y., ca. 1925, 11 5/8" h., pr.
(ILLUS.) 1,760.00

Candelabra, silver, 3-light, spreading circular foot, knopped stem
supporting 2 detachable branches,
upper section of stem terminating
in urn-shaped socket, 14" h.,
pr. 770.00

Candle holder, silver, chamberstick-
type, circular saucer base,
gadroon border w/shells & leaves
alternating w/anthemia, fluted
stem w/detachable gadrooned
nozzle, leaf-capped flying scroll
handle, conical snuffer, engraved
w/armorials, Paul Storr, London,
George III period, 1815,
6½" d. 2,860.00

Candle holder, tin, hand-seamed
candle socket w/hinged shield
folding to conceal candle beneath
domed top when closed, 2½" h. ... 165.00

Candle holder, wrought iron,
miner's "Sticking Tommy,"
10¼" l. 80.00

Candlestick, brass, hexagonal
stepped base, baluster stem,
7" h. (single) 150.00

Candlestick, bronze, 3-leaved base,
detachable bobeche within a
holder designed as a flower w/sil-
vered pistils & 6 extending petals,
impressed Tiffany Studios, New
York, 18" h. (single) 2,860.00

Candlestick, glass & bronze, flat circular base, tripod support ending
in spade feet, elongated pierced
candlecup enclosing lime green
glass, w/bobeche & snuffer, impressed Tiffany Studios, New
York, 1900-20, 17 1/8" h.
(single) 1,760.00

Candlestick, wrought iron spiral
w/pushup & hanging lip on turned
wooden base, 9¼" h. (single) 230.00

Candlesticks, bell metal, domed
square base, baluster stem, urn-
shaped candle cup w/flared
bobeche, w/pushup, mid to late
19th c., 11" h., pr. 176.00

Candlesticks, brass, "capstan," bell
form base, mid-stem drip pan,
tulip-shaped candle cup w/flared

17th Century "Capstan" Candlesticks

bobeche, Dutch, 17th c., 4½" h.,
pr. (ILLUS.) 1,540.00

Candlesticks, brass, notched octagonal foot, baluster stem, vasi-
form candle holder w/flaring
cylindrical bobeche, George II
period, mid to late 18th c.,
6¾" h., pr. 385.00

Candlesticks, brass, scalloped base,
baluster- & ring-turned stem, plain
candle nozzle, Queen Anne peri-
od, mid-18th c., 7¼" h., pr. 900.00

Candlesticks, brass, square petal
form base, turned stem, petal
form bobeche, English, signed
Geo. Grove, 18th c., 8" h.,
pr. 2,640.00

Candlesticks, brass, domed square
base, tapering cylindrical stem,
urn-shaped candle cup w/attached
bobeche, w/pushup, English,
1815-25, 9½" h., pr. 220.00

Candlesticks, brass, Beehive & Diamond patt., Victorian, 10" h.,
pr. 190.00

Candlesticks, brass, stepped base,
baluster- & ring-turned stem,
removable bobeche, 10 7/8" h.,
pr. 175.00

Candlesticks, brass, King of Diamonds patt., 12½" h., pr. 175.00

Candlesticks, pewter, marked C.W.
Woodward, Taunton, Mass.,
3¾" h., pr. 75.00

Candlesticks, silver, bell-shaped
base w/border chased w/acan-
thus leaves & raised on horseshoe
form support, stem & nozzle
w/beaded borders, workmaster
Stephen Wakeva, Faberge, St.
Petersburg, ca. 1900, 6 5/8" h.,
pr. 4,125.00

Candlesticks, silver, shaped square
base, vase-shaped stem, urn socket lightly chased w/foliate panels,
Reed & Barton, 10" h., pr. 352.00

Candlesticks, silver, George II,
shaped circular base w/scrolls &
beads, knuckled dome center,
baluster stem w/scrolls & flutes &
w/shells as the shoulder, matching campana-shaped sconce, con-

forming detachable nozzle, base
w/traces of a crest, John Cafe,
London, 1753, 10 1/8" h., pr. 2,475.00

English Silver Candlesticks

Candlesticks, silver, square stepped
base w/ovolo border, lobed &
fluted column stem w/Corinthian
capital, detachable nozzle engraved w/crest & matching rim,
London, George III period,
1766-67, 13" h., set of 4
(ILLUS.) 3,300.00
Candlesticks, tin, beaded base,
"hogscraper" w/pushup, 4 5/8" h.,
pr................................. 130.00
Candlesticks, wooden, barley twist
stems, pr...................... 15.00

CANDY CONTAINERS (Glass)

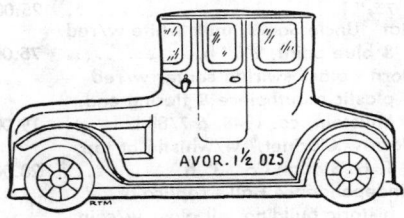

Coupe with Long Hood

*Indicates the container might not have
held candy originally. +Indicates this container might also be found as a reproduction.
‡Indicates this container was also made as
a bank. All containers are clear glass unless
otherwise indicated. Any candy container
that retains the original paint is very desirable and readers should follow descriptions
carefully realizing that an identical candy container that lacks the original paint will be less
valuable.*

Airplane - "Army Bomber 15-P-7,"
J.H. Millstein, 1940's
4 1/8" l.................$20.00 to 27.50
Airplane - "Spirit of Goodwill,"
w/screw cap & propeller, Victory
Glass Co., ca. 1930,
4 5/8" l...................65.00 to 95.00
Amos & Andy in Open Air Taxi -
painted figures, marked "Victory
Glass Co., etc.," w/tin closure,
1928-30, 4½" l.........325.00 to 375.00
Automobile - streamlined touring
car, cork closure, 3 7/8" l........ 30.00
Automobile - streamlined touring
car, w/screw-on cap closure,
3 7/8" l......................... 25.00
Automobile - "Westmoreland
Specialty Co. Limousine," w/tin
wheels, 4" l. ....125.00 to 140.00
Automobile - Hearse No. 1, slanted
hood, tassels at windows, w/tin
closure, 4¼" l.................. 200.00
+Automobile - "Station Wagon,"
w/cardboard closure, 4 7/8" l. ... 23.00
*Automobile - "Trinket" (dish), 5" l.
(flake) 30.00
Automobile - coupe w/long hood,
marked "U.S.A.," w//tin closure
on bottom, ca. 1918, 5¼" l.
(ILLUS.)..................75.00 to 98.00
Baby Chick - standing, painted yellow, w/tin closure, no markings,
ca. 1930, 3 3/8" h. 85.00
‡Barney Google beside bank, painted figure, 3 1/16" h. .....325.00 to 360.00
Barney Google & Ball - painted,
3¾" h. ....195.00 to 225.00
Bear (standing on hind legs) on Circus Tub - w/tin spinning disc & tin
closure, early, 4¼" h. 215.00
Bell - "Liberty Bell" w/glass hanger,
clear, w/tin screw closure on
base, 3 3/8" h. ....35.00 to 45.00
Bell - Liberty Bell w/hanger, green,
w/old closure, 3 3/8" h. ...50.00 to 65.00
Bell - Liberty Bell marked "1776 -
Centennial Exposition - 1876" front
& "Proclaim Liberty Throughout All
the Land" reverse, w/pewter
screw-on cap closure & straps,
3 3/8" h. 100.00
*Bell - "1776 Liberty," blue, 4"
base d., 4 1/8" h. 46.00
*Bird Cage on Stand - Westmoreland
Specialty Co., "Pat Apld For," 2½"
widest d., 4½" h. 65.00
*Boat - U.S.N. Dreadnaught, 5¾" l.,
3 5/8" h. 90.00
Boat - model cruiser, w/cardboard
closure, 4½" l. 24.00
Boat - miniature battleship, w/origi-
nal metal closure, 5½" l. 30.00
Boot - Santa Claus', original label,
3¼" h. 20.00

Bureau - w/real mirror above, original paint, w/tin closure, ca. 1913, 3 7/8" h. 155.00

Bus - marked "Jitney Bus" on tin top unit on glass body, marked "West Bros. Co., etc." on glass body, ca. 1912, 4¼" l. 250.00

+Camera on Tripod - w/wire legs, cord & wooden bulb hanging from lens w/tin closure on back of glass camera, ca. 1915, 5½" h. ....95.00 to 185.00

Cap - military style, amber, 3" top d. (no closure) 24.00

Carpet Sweeper - marked "Baby Sweeper," w/movable twisted wire handle, 2¾ x 2 1/8", ¾" h. w/7" l. wire handle 250.00

Carpet Sweeper - marked "Dolly Sweeper," w/wire handle, tin wheels 295.00

Charlie Chaplin beside Barrel - figure beside barrel marked "Geo. Borgfeldt & Co." on base & w/tin closure on barrel slotted for use as bank, ca. 1915, 3 7/8" h. figure w/some paint .....85.00 to 120.00

Chicken in "Shell" Auto - some paint on chick & shell, marked "V.G." & "U.S.A.," w/tin closure, 1920's, 4¼" l. 175.00

Chicken on Oblong Basket - painted, w/closure, 3" h. 75.00

"Chicken on the Nest" - marked on cardboard closure, J. H. Millstein, 4 5/8" h. 25.00

Clock - round-top shelf model, milk white glass, no paint, 2½ x 1¾" base, 3¼" h. 95.00

Clock - shelf model with octagon-top case, original paper dial inside face, some painted decoration, tin cap closure behind clock face, slotted for use as bank, early 1900's, 3 7/8" h. 140.00

Dirigible - "Los Angeles" marked on side, painted silver, Victory Glass Co., aluminum screw-on cap closure, ca. 1929, 5¾" l. 130.00

*Dog - Hound Pup, open base, 3" h. 10.00

Dog - "Scotty Dog," cardboard closure, head up, 3¼" h. ..18.50 to 24.00

Dog - Bulldog on oblong base, w/closure, 3¾" h. 40.00

Dog - Bulldog w/gilt collar, on round base, painted, marked "U.S.A.," w/metal screw closure, 4¼"h. ....65.00 to 85.00

+Fat Boy on Drum - painted, w/tin closure on base slotted for use as bank, ca. 1915, 4 3/8" h. ....170.00 to 250.00

"Felix" beside Barrel - painted

character, marked on base "Copyright 1922-24 - By Pat Sullivan, etc.," w/tin closure on top of barrel slotted for use as bank, 3 3/8" h. figure ....285.00 to 300.00

Fire Engine - Little Boiler No. 1, 4¾" l., 3" h. 75.00

+Fire Engine - miniature w/solid glass boiler & hose roll on back, 5" l. 20.00

Gas Pump - marked "Gas" on globe & "23 cents Today" on pump, painted, w/tin screw-on cap closure, ca. 1925, 4¼" h. 136.00

Gun - Stough's Whistling Jim, straight-type grip, w/tin whistle, 3 3/8" l. 25.00

Gun - Stough's "Three Dot," w/whistle closure, 3½" l. 20.00

*Gun - small revolver No. 1, 4½" l. 22.00

*Gun - small revolver No. 2, 4½" l. 22.00

Gun - revolver, marked "West Bros. Co., etc.," w/metal clamp-on closure, ca. 1914, 5 3/8" l. 40.00

Gun - plastic automatic pistol w/glass insert in grip, 5 5/8" l.... 25.00

*Gun - revolver No. 1, amber, 7" l. 37.50

*Gun - revolver w/square butt, 7 1/8" l. 23.00

Gun - large revolver No. 1, w/metal screw cap, 7½" l. 27.00

*Gun - revolver No. 2 w/round butt, 7 5/8" l. (no closure) 26.00

Gun, amber, marked "C.P.R. CO." over "Pat'd App. For" on butt end, 7¾" l. 34.50

*Gun, revolver, diamond grip, 7¾" l. 25.00

Hat - Uncle Sam's, milk white w/red & blue paint, 2½" h. 75.00

Horn - glass swirled center w/red plastic mouthpiece & flaring end, Millstein, ca. 1948, 6 7/8" l. 19.00

Horn - "Clarinet," w/whistle at top, T. H. Stough Co., 3" h. 28.00

‡Independence Hall - replica of historic building, all glass w/coin slot in roof, marked "Bank of Independence" & "1776-1876," tin slide on base, 7 3/16" h. 225.00

Jack O'Lantern - painted pumpkin yellow, w/closure, 4" d., 3¾" h. 120.00

Jeep - with driver, w/cardboard closure, 4 3/8" l. 30.00

Kiddie Kar - horse head above wheel, embossed dog on seat, 1910-15, 4½" l. 125.00

Lantern - ribbed glass base, metal closure at top, T. H. Stough, 3" h. 20.00

Lantern - "Beaded No. 2," beaded ribs painted in red, w/screw-on metal closure & long bail handle, 3¼" h. 35.00

Lantern - long-waisted globe w/metal screw-on cap & bail handle, 3 5/8" h. 18.50

Lantern Candy Container

Lantern - square w/beveled panels, w/tin slide closure on top, 4 1/8" h. (ILLUS.) 85.00

*Lantern - "Perko Wonder Junior Kerosene Lantern," 3" d., 6¾" h. 35.00

Locomotive - "Cloetta" on boiler, rare, 2¼" l., 2" h. 150.00

Locomotive - with lithographed tin closure No. 3, 4 3/16" l. 95.00

*"Midget Washer" - scrubboard, 6" w., 8¾" l., 5/8" thick 25.00

Milk Bottle - "Dolly's Milk" & "VG" monogram, 3" h. 32.00

*Moon Mullins - w/black plastic perforated derby hat, painted, 2 7/8" h. 25.00

Mug - "Drum Mug," 2¼" h. 28.00

Naked Child - marked "V.G. Co Jnet, Pa.," w/tin closure on base, 1920's, 3 5/8" h. 60.00

"Nursing Bottle"

Nursing Bottle - flat oval w/red rubber nipple & original paper label, T. H. Stough Co., 1940's, 2¾" h. (ILLUS.)........................ 35.00

Opera Glasses - plain panels, painted decoration, w/screw-on cap closures on large ends, ca. 1908, 2 7/8" h. 125.00

Opera Glasses - plain panels, milk white, painted decoration, w/screw-on cap closures on large ends, ca. 1908, 2 7/8" h. 145.00

Opera Glasses - swirled ribs, w/brass screw-on cap closures, ca. 1904, 4¼" w., 3 3/8" h. 90.00

Owl - traces of paint, unmarked, w/tin cap closure, 1920's 80.00

Phonograph - w/glass record & gilt tin horn, w/tin closure on base, early 1920's, 2 7/8" w., 1¾" h. plus tin horn 185.00

*Pipe - with ornate bowl, swirl stem at base, 4¼" h. 65.00

*Policeman's night stick - amber, 10½" l. 75.00

+Rabbit with Wheelbarrow - originally painted, unmarked, w/tin closure, 1920's, 3¾" l. ....125.00 to 165.00

Rabbit - pushing chick in shell cart, original paint & closure, 4" l., 3 7/8" h. 225.00

Rabbit - running on log, some paint, 4¼" l. 125.00

Rabbit with Basket on Arm - Victory Glass Co., Jeannette, Pa., painted 95.00

Rabbit with Feet Together - square nose, 2 1/8" base d., 5¼" h. 65.00

Rabbit - "Peter Rabbit," by Millstein, 6½" h. ....30.00 to 37.50

Radio - old-time model w/speaker horn on top of cabinet, marked "Tune In" on cabinet & marked "V.G.," etc., w/tin closure, ca. 1925 .... 125.00

Rocking Horse - no paint, heavy glass w/fine details, probably Cambridge Glass, w/tin closure inside base, early, 4½" l. 275.00

Rocking Horse with Clown Rider - some parts painted, w/tin closure, 1920's, 4¼" l. 255.00

Rolling Pin - glass center, metal cap ends w/turned wood handles, marked "V.G. Co. Jnet Pa ¾ oz," 7" l. 115.00

Santa Claus - banded coat, w/closure, 5¼" h. 140.00

Santa Claus - with double cuffs, original paint, w/closure, 4 3/8" h. 125.00

Santa Claus - beside square chimney, 3 5/8" h. 155.00

Santa Claus - descending brick chimney, marked "V.G." monogram on side, Santa originally painted, ca. 1927, 5" h. 80.00

Santa Claus - descending chimney, marked "USA" on chimney, no paint, 5" h. 90.00

Santa with Plastic Head

Santa Claus with Plastic Head - marked "J.H. Millstein Co." etc. inside plastic head, parts of Santa airbrush-painted, 1940's, 5 5/8" h. (ILLUS.) 85.00

"Spark Plug"

"Spark Plug" - marked on side of horse wrapped in blanket, painted, marked "King Feature Syndicate, Inc." on base, w/tin closure, 1923, 3" h. (ILLUS.) 150.00

Stop & Go - clear glass base w/painted green post, red "butterfly" shape signal & blue handle, 4¼" h. 200.00

Suitcase - clear, w/tin closure, 3 5/8" l., 2½" h. ....25.00 to 39.00

Suitcase - milk white, w/painted decal-type decoration, w/tin slide closure, ca. 1908, 2½" h. 130.00

Telephone - Crosetti's desk-type, 1½" base d., 1¾" h. 19.00

Telephone - candlestick-type w/flat-topped hinge, wooden receiver & attached cord, marked "V.G.

Co.," w/tin closure, 1920's, 4 3/8" h. 37.50

Telephone - Lynne-type w/raised dial, wooden receiver & attached cord, 4 3/8" h. 35.00

Telephone - Lynne-type w/sunken dial, wooden receiver & attached cord, 4 5/8" h. 47.50

Telephone - Millstein's "Tot," desk-type, w/cardboard closure, 2 3/8" h. 40.00

Trunk with Round Top - clear, 3" l., 2½" h. (no closure) 95.00

‡Uncle Sam by Barrel - painted figure, w/closure, 3¾" h. 325.00

Wagon - Western-type stagecoach, milk white, original tin top w/seat, 3 3/8" l. 150.00

Windmill - Dutch-type, heavy 6-sided tower w/tin arms, cardboard closure marked "Pla-Toy Co.," 1940's, 4 7/8" h. 60.00

Zeppelin - "Los Angeles" embossed each side, "V.G. Co.," aluminum screw cap closure, 1¾" h., 5¾" l. ....140.00 to 175.00

CANES & WALKING STICKS

Carved Wooden Cane

Canes have been used for thousands of years and probably collected for hundreds of years. Seventeenth and eighteenth century court "dandies" often owned numerous canes, coordinating their use to various costumes and occasions. Today's collector looks for canes made of unique materials or in a unique form. Gadget canes, such as those that convert into a weapon or conceal a whiskey flask in the handle, are probably the most elusive type for the collector to acquire.

Bone-handled cane, carved w/eagle & shield, ebony shaft, 35" l. $55.00

Civil War walking stick, ivory handle carved in the form of a hand clutching a snake, w/inscription on ferrule "Lt. W.S. Bailey, Shiloh, May 6th & 7th, 1867," 39" l. 440.00

Curly maple walking stick, tapered octagonal shat, 35¾" l. 45.00

Ebony walking stick, gold-plated embossed knob handle, 35" l. 85.00

Glass cane, amber, twisted, 36¼" l. 50.00

Glass cane, aqua, bird handle, 4-rib shaft w/twisted tip, 38" l. (chipped tip) 305.00

Glass cane, aqua, square w/twisted handle & tip, 54" l. 47.50

Glass cane, clear, twisted crook handle & tip, square & twisted shaft, 42" l. 135.00

Glass cane, clear w/interior red, white & blue spirals, 41" l. 165.00

Glass cane, clear w/vertical blue & yellow stripes, applied rose on handle, 41" l. 195.00

Glass cane, clear, swirled shaft w/interior gold flecks, 52" l. 235.00

Glass cane, clear, twisted shaft w/interior swirled milk glass ribbon, crook handle, 53" l. 135.00

Glass cane, cobalt blue, signed Libbey 135.00

Glass cane, ice blue, square shaft, 30" l. 95.00

Glass cane, light green, ribbed shaft w/twisted handle & tip, 40" l. 135.00

Glass walking stick, clear w/interior red & white swirls, 33" l. 90.00

Glass walking stick, clear w/red, yellow & pink ribbing, swirled knob head & tip, 49¾" l. 230.00

Gold-handled "Presentation" walking stick, ornate scrolled knob engraved "F. & M. to Dr. J. Gibbs, 1838-1888," 36½" l. 135.00

Gold-handled "Presentation" walking stick, pistol grip handle engraved "Dr. S.S. Robie - presented by Div. 61B of LE, Sept. 14, 1890," ebony shaft, Simon Bros. Co., Philadelphia, Pennsylvania 125.00

Horn-handled cane, turned shaft, so-called "Quaker fighting cane," 35½" l. 65.00

Ivory-handled cane, carved Viking's head & arm................... 155.00

Lady's flask cane, pewter flask top w/screw-on cap, plain, ca. 1890 .. 30.00

Silver-handled walking stick, handle in the form of an eagle's head, monogram on ferrule, vertical silver bands inscribed "Col. Robert Crouse 1774" & "Fort Plain, N.Y.," black painted wooden shaft w/metal tip, 18th c., 36" l. 550.00

Silver-handled walking stick, swirled knob handle w/English hallmark, 37" l. 55.00

Sterling silver handled cane, Victorian 85.00

Sword walking stick, ebony w/ivory head & short stiletto sword, 25½" l. (minor cracks in ivory) ... 110.00

Walrus ivory handled cane, carved as a lion's head 125.00

Whalebone & whale ivory walking stick, bulbous whale ivory knob, whalebone shaft w/metal tip, 31¼" l. 220.00

Wooden cane, carved snake handle, chip-carved shaft w/inscription, 39" l. 75.00

Wooden cane, incised carving, sterling silver band (ILLUS.) 50.00

Wooden cane, carved Masonic emblem & folk art designs, mid-19th c. 77.50

Wooden walking stick, carved entwining snake, painted black w/red knob handle, 34½" l. 185.00

Wooden walking stick, carved man's clenched fist handle w/silver metal band at wrist, 37" l. 250.00

CANS & CONTAINERS

Hygieia Chalk Box

The collecting of tin containers has become quite popular within the past several years. Air-tight tins were at first produced by hand to keep foods fresh, and after the invention of the tin-printing machine in the 1870's, containers were manufactured in a wide variety of shapes and sizes with colorful designs.

Chalk, Hygieia Dustless box (ILLUS.)....................... $5.00

Crackers, McMahon's Paradise Soda store bin 39.00

Flea powder, Hartz Mountain container, little girl powdering dog, 1940's 10.00

Floor wax, Johnson's round container, couple dancing 25.00

Flour, Mother Hubbard 5-lb. container 9.00

Gum, Adams California Fruit bin ... 150.00

Teaberry Gum & Ink Eraser Boxes

Gum, Clark Co. Teaberry Pepsin
Chewing Gum & Carter's "Inky
Racer" boxes, pr. (ILLUS.) 120.00
Gum, Huyler's Pepsin box 6.00
Gun oil, 'Ol Sarge can, Army
sergeant 15.00
Gun powder, Dead Shot drum, fall-
ing duck 110.00
Gun powder, DuPont drum, green,
9" d., 11" h. 30.00
Gun powder, DuPont drum,
w/Indian 85.00
Gun powder, DuPont Superfine FFF
drum 48.00
Gun powder, Hercules Red Dog
Shotgun 2-gal. drum 30.00
Gun powder, New Schultze drum ... 75.00
Gun powder, Robin Hood drum 80.00
Ice cream, Runkel's Pistachio Shreds
5-lb. can 38.00
Ink eradicator, Sanford box, com-
plete w/glass bottles 13.00
Lard, Fort Pitt 50-lb. drum 20.00
Lard, Pheasant Pure container,
colorful, 12" d., 13" h. 125.00
Malted milk, Thompson's store
canister 85.00
Oysters, Baltimore 1-gal. pail 12.00
Oysters, Chaney's pail 15.00
Patent medicine, Bickmore's Fall
Salve flat round box 11.00
Patent medicine, Dr. LeGear's Gall
Remedy 2-oz. container, black &
red 6.50
Patent medicine, Dr. Ramon's Laxa-
tive, Little Doctor 10.00
Patent medicine, Fritch's Salve flat
round box, green & black 4.00
Patent medicine, Jayne's Asthma
Powder container 35.00

Kickapoo Salve Round Tin

Patent medicine, Kickapoo Salve flat
round box, 2" d. (ILLUS.) 20.00
Patent medicine, Watkins Petro-
Carbo Salve 3-oz. flat round box,
red & black 5.00
Peanut butter, Armour's Veribest
1-lb. pail, Mother Goose scenes .. 75.00

Peanut butter, Buffalo 1-lb. pail 55.00
Peanut butter, Hormel 1-lb. pail 22.00
Peanut butter, Jumbo 1-lb. pail 100.00
Peanut butter, Monadnock pail 45.00
Peanut butter, Ontario 1-lb. pail 42.50
Peanut butter, Peter Pan free sam-
ple size 42.50
Peanut butter, Peter Pan 25-lb.
container 50.00
Peanut butter, School Boy 1-lb. pail,
child's face 65.00
Peanut butter, School Boy 2-lb. pail,
child's face 200.00
Peanut butter, Shedd's 5-lb. pail,
elves 15.00
Peanut butter, Sultana 1-lb. pail,
children 25.00
Peanut butter, Sultana pail, blue ... 48.00
Peanut butter, Swift's 5-lb. pail,
Wizard of Oz 45.00
Peanut butter, Teddie pail 60.00
Peanut butter, Toyland 1-lb. pail 90.00
Peanut butter, Yankee pail 25.00
Peanuts, Adams 2-lb. pail 85.00
Peanuts, Brownie 10-lb. container .. 85.00
Peanuts, Buffalo Brand 1-lb.
container 55.00
Peanuts, Buffalo Brand 10-lb.
container 148.00
Peanuts, Golden Vine 10-lb. con-
tainer, brown & yellow 95.00
Peanuts, Grant 10-lb. container 45.00
Peanuts, Mammoth 10-lb. con-
tainer 100.00
Peanuts, Old Reliable 10-lb.
container 150.00
Phonograph needles, Best Talking
Machine box, phonograph
w/horn 10.00
Phonograph needles, RCA Victor
box, dog & phonograph 19.00
Phonograph needles, Songster box,
bird, 1 x 1 x ¼" 25.00
Popcorn, Dickerson's Little Buster
pail 65.00
Popcorn, Jolly Time pail, 1927 ...... 23.00
Popcorn, Jumbo 10-lb. container 35.00
Potato chips, Humpty Dumpty
canister 35.00
Potato chips, Morton's 2-lb. contain-
er, 12" h. 32.00
Pretzels, Mills container 20.00
Pretzels, Sturgis container 25.00
Shoe polish, Parrot Polishine can ... 10.00
Soap, Packer's Tar box 10.00
Spice, A. & P. Great American
"Ginger" box, cockatoo 15.00
Spice, Austex "Chili Powder" box,
devil & firepot 65.00
Spice, Watkins "Black Pepper,"
yellow 22.50
Syrup, Towle's Log Cabin, cabin-
shaped, bear in doorway, mother
flapping pancakes 65.00

Syrup, Towle's Log Cabin, cabin-shaped, "Frontier Inn" 100.00

Syrup, Towle's Log Cabin, cabin-shaped, "Frontier Jail" 55.00

Talcum powder, Air Float container 20.00

Talcum powder, California Perfume Co. container, 2 nude babies playing w/rose, round 90.00

Talcum powder, Colgates shaker can, baby holding talc, brass top, 6" h. 20.00

Talcum powder, Florient sample size 20.00

Talcum powder, Humpty Dumpty shaker can, 8" h. 62.50

Talcum powder, Jap Rose container 18.00

Talcum powder, Jergen's Oriental container, Oriental woman 10.00

Talcum powder, Langlois container, buff w/maroon top 17.50

Talcum powder, Larkin's Modjeska container 25.00

Talcum powder, Massatta container, Oriental woman & child 20.00

Talcum powder, Mennen's sample size 10.00

Talcum powder, Natoma Rose triangular container 150.00

Talcum powder, Nysis container 18.00

Talcum powder, Oakley's Corylopsis container 25.00

Talcum powder, Orange Blossom sample size 15.00

Talcum powder, Peter Rabbit shaker can 90.00

Talcum powder, Rachelle Apple Blossom shaker can, 6" h. 10.00

Talcum powder, Rawleigh's Good Health shaker can, Mother Goose characters 35.00

Talcum powder, Rawleigh's Talcum & Baby Powder shaker can, baby 30.00

Sweet Orchid Talcum Shaker

Talcum powder, Richard Hudnut Sweet Orchid shaker can, 1912 patent, 5½" h. (ILLUS.) 30.00

Talcum powder, Satin Silk shaker can, lady 20.00

Talcum powder, Vogue Royal shaker can 50.00

Talcum powder, Watkins Egyptian container, embossed Egyptian scenes 16.50

Tea, Jack Sprat box 15.00

Tea, Lipton 3-lb. box, East Indian plantation scene w/natives picking tea & water buffaloes, 8 x 5" 65.00

Tea, Lock Brand box, embossed building each side 28.00

Tea, Richelieu Midas box 25.00

Tea, Ridgways box, "Safe Tea First - Established 1836" 25.00

Tea, Royal Shield box 20.00

Tea, Tetley's box, elephant, small .. 22.00

Tea, Tetley 1-lb. box, sunflowers on red 42.50

Tea, Wylie Simpson box, stenciled letters on green................. 32.00

Tire patches, Dutch Girl box, rosy-cheeked girl & "Forever Tight - Never Loosens," w/contents 8.00

Tobacco, American pocket tin 85.00

Tobacco, Bagdad pocket tin, Turk in fez............................ 70.00

Tobacco, Bagley's Burley Boy pocket tin, little boxer boy, "The White Man's Hope"...........425.00 to 600.00

Tobacco, Bagley's Old Colony Mixture pocket tin 70.00

Tobacco, Bagley's Red Belt pocket tin 25.00

Tobacco, Bagley's Wild Fruit lunch box 70.00

Tobacco, Big Ben canister 20.00

Tobacco, Blue Boar Cut Plug canister, fierce Indian Chief 42.50

Tobacco, Bond Street pocket tin 10.00

Tobacco, Bond Street 1-lb. canister.. 12.00

Tobacco, Bootjack Plug pocket tin... 35.00

Tobacco, Bowl of Roses canister, man before fireplace, bowl of roses on table 65.00

Tobacco, Bowl of Roses pocket tin, man before fireplace, bowl of roses on table 185.00

Tobacco, Brandon Mixture box 60.00

Tobacco, Brigg's canister 17.50

Tobacco, Brindley's Mixture canister 15.00

Tobacco, Buckingham Cut Plug canister, orange & multicolors, 4" d., 4¼" h. 42.50

Tobacco, Buckingham Cut Plug pocket tin 42.50

Tobacco, Buckingham sample size pocket tin, "Trial Package" 95.00

Tobacco, Bugler canister 18.00
Tobacco, Bulldog pocket tin,
    bulldog. 95.00
Tobacco, Bulwark Cut Plug pocket
    tin 18.00
Tobacco, Carlton Club pocket tin. . . . 50.00
Tobacco, Central Union Cut Plug
    box, 6" l., 3¼" h. 42.50
Tobacco, Central Union canister
    w/small top 200.00
Tobacco, Central Union lunch pail. . . 30.00
Tobacco, Century pocket safe, opens
    w/combination lock 200.00
Tobacco, Cinco lunch pail 40.00
Tobacco, Climax pocket tin. 10.00
Tobacco, Columbia Mixture small
    box 25.00
Tobacco, Continental Cubes pocket
    tin 200.00
Tobacco, Critic small box 40.00
Tobacco, Cuban Star pail. 35.00
Tobacco, Culture pocket tin 75.00

Dan Patch Cut Plug Box

Tobacco, Dan Patch Cut Plug box,
    6 x 4" (ILLUS.) 55.00
Tobacco, Dill's Best pocket tin 16.50
Tobacco, Dixie Kid Cut Plug lunch
    pail, black baby boy 275.00
Tobacco, Dixie Kid lunch box, white
    boy 195.00
Tobacco, Dixie Queen canister, blue
    knob top 300.00
Tobacco, Dixie Queen canister,
    green 75.00

Dixie Queen Plug Cut Lunch Box

Tobacco, Dixie Queen lunch box,
    7¾ x 5¼", 4¼" h. (ILLUS.). 90.00
Tobacco, Dixie Queen lunch pail. . . . 57.50
Tobacco, Ducco canister 30.00
Tobacco, Edgeworth canister, blue . . 27.50
Tobacco, Edgeworth pocket tin 9.50
Tobacco, Eight Brothers Long Cut
    pail, 5" d., 6½" h. 30.00
Tobacco, Eve pocket tin 190.00

Fashion Cut Plug Lunch Box

Tobacco, Fashion Cut Plug lunch
    box, fashionable couple & early
    automobile (ILLUS.) 100.00
Tobacco, Forest & Stream canister,
    fisherman 50.00
Tobacco, Forest & Stream pocket tin,
    fisherman . . . . 90.00 to 160.00
Tobacco, Forest & Stream pocket tin,
    mallard duck 35.00
Tobacco, Fountain canister, early
    fountain w/figures 300.00
Tobacco, Full Dress pocket tin, man
    in tuxedo. 90.00
Tobacco, Gail & Ax Navy canister
    w/round lift-off lid 250.00
Tobacco, Gold Bond pocket tin 125.00
Tobacco, Grain Cut Plug pocket
    tin 95.00
Tobacco, Granger canister 16.50
Tobacco, Granulated 54 sample size
    pocket tin . . . . 55.00 to 75.00
Tobacco, Great West Cut Plug lunch
    box 26.00
Tobacco, Hand Made pocket tin 125.00
Tobacco, Hiawatha box, 5 x 3 x 2". . 45.00
Tobacco, Hiawatha round box,
    8½" d., 2" h. 75.00
Tobacco, Hickory pocket tin 47.50
Tobacco, Hi-Plane pocket tin, twin
    engine plane 42.50
Tobacco, H-O 1-lb. round box 28.00
Tobacco, Holiday pocket tin 16.00
Tobacco, Honest Labor pocket tin . . . 27.50
Tobacco, Honest Scrap counter bin,
    dog & cat. 695.00
Tobacco, Honeymoon pocket tin,
    man resting on crescent moon,
    w/woman's face in clouds 42.50

Tobacco, Honeymoon pocket tin,
man & woman seated on crescent
moon 400.00
Tobacco, Idle Hour pocket tin, hourglass pictured.................. 45.00
Tobacco, Jewel of Virginia canister
w/square corners 45.00

Just Suits Tobacco Lunch Box

Tobacco, Just Suits lunch box
(ILLUS.)....................... 55.00
Tobacco, Just Suits store canister ... 85.00
Tobacco, Kentucky Club canister 8.00
Tobacco, Kentucky Club pocket tin .. 11.50
Tobacco, Kimbo pocket tin, portrait
of girl, 1910 stamp 110.00
Tobacco, King Koal lunch box, "KK"
in oval, 7¾ x 3½ x 4¾"........ 110.00
Tobacco, Lucky Strike Roll-Cut 1-lb.
box 15.00
Tobacco, Lucky Strike Roll-Cut
pocket tin 32.50
Tobacco, Lucky Strike sample size
pocket tin 40.00
Tobacco, Mail Pouch store bin 120.00
Tobacco, Main Brace lunch box,
basketweave, 7 x 4½ x 4¼" 65.00
Tobacco, Maryland Club pocket tin,
clubhouse 255.00
Tobacco, Mayo's Cut Plug lunch
box 32.50
Tobacco, Mayo's lunch box,
telescoping-type 130.00
Tobacco, Mayo's Roly Poly
Dutchman ....350.00 to 450.00
Tobacco, Mayo's Roly Poly Satisfied
Customer..................... 425.00
Tobacco, Mayo's Roly Poly Singing
Waiter ....350.00 to 450.00
Tobacco, Miners & Puddlers pail,
5½" d., 6½" h. 125.00
Tobacco, Model pocket tin, bust
portrait of man w/outsized
moustache.................... 20.00
Tobacco, New Factory pail, mytho-
logical figure on horse slaying
dragon 125.00
Tobacco, North Pole lunch box,
6 x 4 x 6" 325.00
Tobacco, North Star container
w/square corners 350.00
Tobacco, Oceanic box, 6 x 4" 75.00
Tobacco, Ojibwa pail 135.00
Tobacco, Old English pocket tin,
curved, 4 x 3½" 14.00

Tobacco, Old English store bin...... 200.00
Tobacco, Rex pocket tin, bust portrait of Roman in toga & laurel
wreath flanked by torches 82.50
Tobacco, Richamon Mixture box
w/square corners, pre-1901 ..... 22.50
Tobacco, Scissors oval pocket tin,
scissors each side, ca. 1902 (some
wear) 700.00
Tobacco, Sensible lunch box........ 40.00
Tobacco, Sir Walter Raleigh canister
w/knobbed lid 20.00
Tobacco, Sir Walter Raleigh Christmas canister.................. 22.50
Tobacco, Sir Walter Raleigh pocket
tin ....4.50 to 10.00
Tobacco, Sphinx Mixture box,
4½ x 3¼ x 1¼" 30.00
Tobacco, Stag canister, square
w/round lift-off lid, 4 x 5 x 6".... 65.00

Stag Pocket Tin

Tobacco, Stag pocket tin (ILLUS.).... 35.00
Tobacco, Sure Shot store bin 275.00
Tobacco, Sweet Burley Dark store
canister, 12".................. 135.00
Tobacco, Sweet Cuba 1-lb. canister,
green 50.00
Tobacco, Sweet Cuba store bin, yel-
low, 8 x 10 x 8" ....125.00 to 140.00

Sweet Cuba "Light" Tobacco

Tobacco, Sweet Cuba Light canister
w/square hinged lid, 8" d., 10" h.
(ILLUS.) 110.00
Tobacco, Sweet Mist wedge-shaped
box 100.00
Tobacco, Sweet Tips pocket tin 65.00
Tobacco, Taxi pocket tin, driver in
taxi 950.00
Tobacco, Three Feathers pocket
tin 150.00
Tobacco, Three States (Kentucky,
Virginia & Louisiana) oblong
box 40.00
Tobacco, Tiger 5-lb. canister, red . . .   120.00
Tobacco, Tiger lunch box, red,
10 x 7¾" 45.00
Tobacco, Times Square canister,
New York night scene 42.50
Tobacco, Times Square pocket tin . . .   195.00
Tobacco, Torpedo pocket tin,
"Destroyer" 700.00
Tobacco, Trout Line pocket tin,
fisherman w/creel, rod & reel in
central roundel 750.00
Tobacco, True Blue pail 35.00
Tobacco, Tuckett's Abbey pocket
tin 80.00
Tobacco, Tuxedo pocket tin . . .7.00 to 16.50
Tobacco, Tuxedo sample size 75.00
Tobacco, Twin Oaks casket 65.00
Tobacco, Twin Oaks pocket
tin . . . . .30.00 to 65.00
Tobacco, Union Leader canister
w/lift-off top 125.00
Tobacco, Union Leader lunch box,
basketweave, 7 x 4 x 5" . . .25.00 to 40.00
Tobacco, Union Leader pocket tin,
w/eagle 8.00
Tobacco, Union Leader pocket tin,
w/Uncle Sam . . . . .32.00 to 50.00
Tobacco, U.S. Marine lunch
box .165.00 to 230.00
Tobacco, U.S. Marine lunch
box, basketweave,
7¾ x 5 x 4" . . . . .20.00 to 35.00
Tobacco, U.S. Marine pocket tin 120.00
Tobacco, Van Bibber pocket tin 45.00
Tobacco, Velvet Tobacco, w/pipe &
cigarette . . . . .3.50 to 10.00
Tobacco, Velvet pocket tin, w/pipe's
smoke spelling "Velvet" . . .15.00 to 22.00
Tobacco, Warnick & Brown lunch
box 62.50
Tobacco, Whip pocket tin 280.00
Tobacco, White Manor pocket tin . . .   115.00
Tobacco, Willoughby Taylor pocket
tin 22.50
Tooth powder, Pisso's container 10.00
Tooth powder, Sozodont 35.00
Veterinary medicine, Dr. LeGear's
Gall Remedy, red & black, 5" d. . .   7.50

CARD CASES

Mother-of-Pearl Card Case

*In a more leisurely and sociable era, ladies
made a ritual of "calling" on new neighbors
and friends. Calling card cases held the small
cards engraved or lettered with the owner's
name and sometimes additionally decorated.
The cases were turned out in a wide variety
of styles and material which included gold,
silver, ivory, tortoise shell and leather. A sampling of collectible calling card cases is listed below.*

Brass, Egyptian decor, Bradley &
Hubbard $20.00
Coin silver, A. Coles, New York
City, New York, ca. 1860 . . . .   225.00
Coin silver, engraved w/birds &
scrolling devices, vacant cartouche for monogram, original
box 125.00
Mother-of-pearl shell, Diamond
patt., 4 x 2¾" (ILLUS.) 35.00
Silver, scalloped rim, engraved bee-
hives decor, w/monogram, Bir-
mingham hallmark for 1851 . . . . . .   165.00
Silver, scenic decor against engine-
turned ground, hallmarked 85.00

CARPET BALLS

*Glazed china spheres, about 3½" in di-
ameter, are commonly called "carpet balls"
by collectors who seek them out. Originally
made for a popular 19th century game called
"bowls," these balls were rolled at a smaller
ball called a "jack." Because the game could
be played indoors on the carpet or taken out
to the lawn, the ceramic balls were fired two*

or more times after the design was applied to ensure their durability.

Plaid Carpet Ball

China, blue & white concentric
  circles $40.00
China, blue & white concentric
  circles, Leeds, pr. 140.00
China, green & rose sponge daubing
  on white, 3 5/16" d. 85.00
China, pink & white sponge daubing
  decor 95.00
China, pink dots surrounded by
  frilled white circles on pink
  ground, 3¼" d. 70.00
China, plaid in black & white 55.00
China, plaid in green & white,
  3¼" d. 65.00
China, red & white stick spatter star
  design, 3½" d. 65.00
China, white 95.00
China, white w/"Harold A. Wilson
  Co., Toronot" logo, 2 9/16" d.
  (slight discoloration) 70.00

CASH REGISTERS

"National" Floor Model Cash Register

James Ritty of Dayton, Ohio, is credited with inventing the first cash register. In 1882, he sold the business to a Cincinnati salesman, Jacob H. Eckert, who subsequently invited others into the business by selling stock. One of the purchasers of an early cash register, John J. Patterson, was so impressed with the savings his model brought to this company, he bought 25 shares of stock and became a director of the company in 1884, eventually buying a controlling interest in the National Manufacturing Company. Patterson thoroughly organized the company, conducted sales classes, prepared sales manuals and established salesman's territories. The success of the National Cash Register Company is due as much to these well organized origins as to the efficiency of its machines. Early "National" cash registers, as well as other models, are deemed highly collectible today.

Brass, "National," Model 3, detail
  adder, records single sales
  only $525.00
Brass, "National," Model 5, scrolling
  designs 850.00
Brass, "National," Model 6, extend-
  ed base, original "Amount Pur-
  chased" marquee 1,400.00
Brass, "National,"
  Model 7 . . . . 500.00 to 650.00
Brass, "National," Model 35, flat
  scroll design, hinged front cover,
  ca. 1896 . . . . 500.00
Brass, "National," Model 35, original
  "Amount Purchased" marquee,
  ca. 1897 . . . . 600.00
Brass, "National," Model 130 . . . . 675.00
Brass, "National," Model 313, barber
  shop model, 10" w. 575.00
Brass, "National," Model 313, candy
  store model, registers from 5
  cents to $1.00, 10" w. . . . 525.00 to 600.00
Brass, "National," Model 323 . . . . 750.00
Brass, "National," Model 332,
  14" w. 265.00
Brass, "National," Model 349, dated
  1912 . . . . 675.00
Brass, "National," Model 421 . . . . 350.00
Brass, "National," Model 522-2, side-
  by-side drawers (manual or elec-
  tric) 850.00
Brass, "National," Model 542-C,
  floor model on oak 10-drawer
  "bombe" base (ILLUS.) 1,250.00
Brass & cast iron, "National," Model
  60, w/rosettes on drawer face . . . 350.00
Cast iron, "Murdock & Corbin," ornate, candy store model 590.00
Cast iron, "National," Model 147,
  original "Amount Purchased"
  marquee 600.00
Cast iron, "Premier,"
  Model 1 . . . . 400.00 to 450.00
Mahogany, "National," burled wood
  w/carved floral decor, original
  "Amount Purchased" marquee,
  1885 serial number, restored 3,800.00

Nickel-plated brass, "National,"
  crank-style, floor model on oak
  base, ca. 1902 . . . . .2,500.00
Oak, "National," Model 202, w/em-
  bossed brass trim 185.00
Oak, "National," Model 442, crank-
  style, name in brass script on
  cash drawer 500.00

CASTORS & CASTOR SETS

Five Bottle Castor Set

*Castor bottles were made to hold condi-
ments for table use. Some were produced in
sets of several bottles housed in silverplated
frames. The word also is sometimes spelled
"Caster."*

Castor set, 3-bottle, blue opaque
  glass Bale patt. bottles, silverplate stand w/bail handle $110.00
Castor set, 3-bottle, cranberry glass
  square bottles w/cut & polished
  decor, open salt dip in center, silverplate stand 160.00
Castor set, 4-bottle, blown clear
  glass bottles w/narrow vertical
  ribbed columns, pewter frame,
  Pittsburgh Glass Co. 175.00
Castor set, 4-bottle, Rubina Crystal
  glass Venecia patt. bottles, silverplate stand w/ornate glass
  handle 245.00
Castor set, 5-bottle, blue glass Daisy
  & Button patt. bottles, silverplate
  stand 225.00
Castor set, 5-bottle, clear glass bot-
  tles w/cut & etched decor, revolving silverplate stand (ILLUS.) 240.00
Castor set, 5-bottle, clear glass
  Gothic patt. bottles, silverplate
  stand 70.00

Castor set, 5-bottle, vaseline glass
  bottles w/engraved fern decor,
  silverplate stand w/center handle,
  marked Meriden 265.00
Castor set, 6-bottle, clear glass bot-
  tles w/etched decor, ornate silverplate stand w/embossed Old
  Man Winter on feet & rose
  garlands on bail handle, 22" h. . . . 465.00
Castor set, 6-bottle, vaseline glass
  Daisy & Button patt. bottles,
  revolving silverplate stand w/en-
  graved skirt & ornate bail handle,
  18" h. 460.00
Pickle castor, amber glass insert,
  figural cherubs on footed silverplate frame w/sliding cover,
  dated 1868 . . . . 185.00
Pickle castor, amber glass Daisy &
  Button patt. insert, silverplate
  frame, cover & tongs engraved
  w/birds & florals, marked Hart-
  ford Silver Co. 275.00
Pickle castor, blue glass Inverted
  Thumbprint patt. insert w/enam-
  eled florals, ornate silverplate
  frame, cover & tongs 230.00
Pickle castor, blue shaded to white
  Satin glass insert w/enameled
  florals, footed silverplate frame
  engraved w/florals, fluted rim . . . 135.00
Pickle castor, canary yellow glass
  insert, silverplate frame, cover &
  tongs 185.00

Block Pattern Pickle Castor

Pickle castor, clear glass Block patt.
  insert, silverplate frame, cover &
  tongs, marked Simpson Hall Miller
  (ILLUS.) 145.00
Pickle castor, clear glass Cane &
  Fan insert, footed silverplate
  frame w/pierced rim & tongs,
  marked Meriden 95.00

Pickle castor, clear glass Daisy &
   Button patt. insert, silverplate
   frame & fork 125.00
Pickle castor, clear glass Netted
   Apple Blossom patt. insert, ornate
   footed silverplate frame 265.00
Pickle castor, coral Satin glass insert
   w/white enameled florals, silverplate frame & cover 235.00
Pickle castor, cornflower blue glass
   barrel-shaped insert w/four embossed gold rings around top &
   enameled white beading, scrolls &
   flowers, silverplate frame, cover
   & tongs, marked Webster 255.00
Pickle castor, cranberry glass insert
   w/white enameled band of florals
   & leaves & gold trim, silverplate
   frame, cover & tongs, 10 1/8" h. . . 255.00
Pickle castor, cranberry glass Diamond Quilted patt. insert w/blue
   enameled forget-me-nots, ornate
   footed silverplate frame 235.00
Pickle castor, cranberry glass Invert-
   ed Thumbprint patt. insert, footed
   silverplate frame w/gothic arch
   bail & gallery around oval platform base, w/tongs, marked
   Meriden 275.00
Pickle castor, Rubina Crystal glass
   Inverted Thumbprint patt. insert
   w/enameled florals, silverplate
   frame, cover & tongs 235.00
Pickle castor, ruby glass Optic patt.
   insert, footed silverplate frame
   w/looped bail handle, marked
   Pairpoint, ca. 1894 . . . . 350.00
Pickle castor, sapphire blue glass
   Daisy & Button patt. insert, silver-
   plate frame & tongs, marked
   Rogers 250.00

CAT COLLECTIBLES

Japanese Imari Recumbent Cat

   *Cats—love them or hate them—you have to
respect the fact that today cats are pets in
almost one-fourth of all households in the
United States. Proud, aloof and indifferent,
their haughty poses have been recaptured in
artwork in a variety of materials through the
years, Other representatives catch the inquisi-
tive, cuddly and playful mood of the domestic cat. Both have brought a delightful area
of collecting to cat lovers across the country.
Also see BANKS and BASKETS.*

Andirons, cast iron, model of black
   cat w/marble eyes, 18" h.,
   pr. $95.00
Book, "Who Said Cats?", by Louis
   Wain, 15" 250.00
Bookends, black pot metal, Art
   Deco style Siamese cats, pr. 65.00
Doll, wood-jointed Puss 'n Boots-
   type cat 75.00
Door knocker, brass, model of cat's
   head 55.00
Match holder, bisque, model of a
   black cat yowling, attributed to
   Shafer & Vater, 3½" d., 4¾" h. . . 65.00
Model of a cat wearing clothes,
   bisque, pink shirt, black pants
   w/straps over shoulder, im-
   pressed "Japan," 3" h. 35.00
Model of a Siamese cat in seated
   position, Royal Copenhagen porcelain, No. 3281, 7½" h. 200.00
Model of a cat in recumbent posi-
   tion, Imari china, iron-red spots,
   blue & gilt bow at neck, Japan,
   8½" l. (ILLUS.) 770.00
Model of a cat holding a ball of
   yarn, majolica, black w/inset
   green glass eyes, 10¼" l. 265.00

Oil Painting of "Von Mouser" Cat

Painting, oil on panel, "His Royal
   Highness 'Von Mouser' - 1893,"
   American or English School, dated
   1893, 18½ x 23" (ILLUS.) 3,630.00
Paperweight, bronze model of a cat
   sleeping, on marble base, artist-
   signed 150.00
Pitcher, milk, china, yellow body
   w/molded black & white cat-form
   handle, Japan, 7½" h. 37.50
Plate, pressed glass, Stippled
   Forget-Me-Not patt., 2-handled,
   kitten center, large . . . . . . .45.00 to 75.00

Print, grey & white fluffy kitten sitting atop heap of pillows, pastel shades, signed Gladys Emerson Cook (artist for Barnum & Bailey Circus), matted, 15 x 13" 25.00

Print Angora kittens (2), signed Gladys Emerson Cook, 16 x 12" .. 10.00

Print, "My Little White Kitties Learning Their ABC's," Currier & Ives, small folio, framed, 16 x 12" ....75.00 to 125.00

Print, close-up of recumbent yellow cat w/turned head, signed, Gladys Emerson Cook, matted, 22½ x 16" 40.00

Salt & pepper shakers, figural cats, yellow & ruby cased glass, metal heads w/glass eyes, pr. 50.00

Tape measure, celluloid, figural cat 20.00

Teapot, cov., china, figural black cat w/green eyes 20.00

Toy, printed cloth "Tabby Cat," w/label, 13" h. (unstuffed) 60.00

CELLULOID

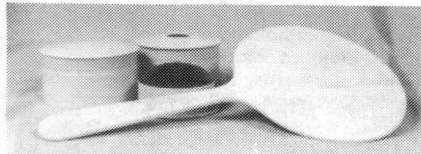

Celluloid Dresser Accessories

Celluloid was our first commercial plastic and early examples are now "antique" in their own right, having been produced as early as 1868 after the perfection of celluloid by John Wesley Hyatt. Also see ADVERTISING ITEMS, BOOKMARKS, BREWERIANA and BUTTONS.

Box, cov., creamy ivory, w/portrait on lid, large $38.00

Bracelet, bangle-type, creamy ivory, carved roses decor 12.00

Dresser set: hand mirror, cov. powder box, shoe horn & large comb; creamy ivory w/green trim, 4 pcs. 35.00

Dresser set: hair brush, hand mirror, cov. hair receiver, cov. jewelry box, shoe horn, button hook, picture frame & glass-covered tray; creamy ivory set w/green rhinestones in an Art Nouveau style design, 8 pcs. 225.00

Dresser set, marbleized ivory, original case w/deep blue satin brocade lining & lock, 13 pcs. 80.00

Dresser set, pearlized green, Art Deco style decor, 14 pcs. 50.00

Fan, folding-type, in original box w/glass lid 20.00

Glove box w/hinged lid & cupids riding glove as finial, creamy ivory, w/glove stretcher, 2 pcs.... 26.00

Hair comb, creamy ivory, lacy openwork top, 8¾" w., 9½" l......... 45.00

Hair receiver, cov., creamy ivory (ILLUS. center) 11.00

Letter opener, creamy ivory, model of a fish...................... 25.00

Manicure set, 7 pcs. on stand, pearlized green 55.00

Mirror, hand-type, creamy ivory w/portrait of lady, Germany, 4" .. 18.00

Mirror, hand-type, w/beveled mirror plate, creamy ivory (ILLUS. right) 20.00

Mirror, pocket-type w/handle, beveled mirror plate, creamy ivory, florals in relief on back 26.00

Model of an airplane, "Spirit of St. Louis" 50.00

Nail file, creamy ivory, Art Deco style handle 10.00

Necktie box, cov., creamy ivory, ornate, Victorian 55.00

Picture frame, creamy ivory, curving sides, 8" h. 22.00

Pinback button, "United Confederate Veterans Reunion, May, 1899, Charleston," Winnie Davis (1864-98) pictured, 1½" d. 20.00

Pinback button w/ribbon, "Wisconsin" & attached 2¼" lithographed tin 3-dimensional football 12.00

Pin cushion box w/removable plush-covered lid, creamy ivory, 3¾" d. (ILLUS. center) 7.50

Powder box, cov., creamy ivory, w/satin puff (ILLUS. left) 12.00

Ring box, cov., creamy ivory 5.00

Rouge container, cov., creamy ivory 3.50

Tatting shuttle, creamy ivory 6.00

CERAMICS

ADAMS

The Adams family has been potters in England since 1650. Three William Adamses made pottery all of it collectible. Most Adams pottery easily accessible today was made in the 19th century and is impressed or marked variously ADAMS, W. ADAMS, ADAMS TUNSTALL, W. ADAMS &

SONS, and W. ADAMS & CO. with the word
"England" or the phrase "made in England"
added after 1891. Wm. Adams & Son, Ltd.,
continues in operation today. Also see FLOW
BLUE, HISTORICAL & COMMEMO-
RATIVE and JASPER WARE.

"Cries of London" Wares

Bowl, 8" d., Cries of London series
   (ILLUS. right) $65.00
Bowl, 10" d., 5" h., footed,
   Shakespeare series (Merchant of-
   Venice), "Portia Pleads with Shy-
   lock," orange lustre border at
   base, interior & exterior rim, red
   scene on cream ground 100.00
Butter pat, Kenoa patt., light blue
   transfer, 4" d. 22.00
Creamer, Jeddo patt., mulberry
   transfer 110.00
Cup & saucer, farmer size, Cries of
   London series (ILLUS. left) 60.00
Pitcher, 4½" h., "Dr. Syntax Setting
   Out," green trim 110.00
Pitcher, 7" h., Cries of London series
   (ILLUS. center) 82.50
Plate, 8" d., Andalusia patt., pink
   transfer 30.00
Plates, 8" octagon, Dickensware ser-
   ies, "Mr. Micawber" & "Christmas
   at Mr. Wardles," black & white,
   pr. 35.00
Plate, 8¼" d., Cries of London
   series 35.00
Plate, 8½" d., Caledonia patt., red
   & green transfer (minor stains) ... 30.00

Palestine Pattern Plate

Plate, 8½" d., Palestine patt., pink
   transfer (ILLUS.) 45.00
Plate, 8¾" d., "Dr. Syntax Tied To
   Tree by Highwaymen" 75.00
Plate, 8¾" d., English country
   scenery w/cows, dark blue transfer (edge wear) 55.00
Plate, 9" d., "Dr. Syntax in Search
   of the Picturesque" 110.00
Plate, 9" d., Villa Regent patt., deep
   blue transfer 85.00
Plate, 9½" d., Caledonia patt.
   w/elk & hunter, black transfer ... 35.00
Plate, 10" d., Cries of London
   series - "Primroses," lady &
   children, green border 30.00
Platter, 12½ x 9½", Abbey patt.,
   deep mulberry transfer,
   ca. 1900 .... 95.00
Platter, 14" l., "View of Regent
   Street," deep blue transfer 275.00
Soup plate w/flange rim, Blenheim
   patt., light blue transfer, 10" d. .. 70.00
Urn & cover w/dog finial, Cries of
   London series, 14½" h. 148.00

AUSTRIAN - MISCELLANEOUS

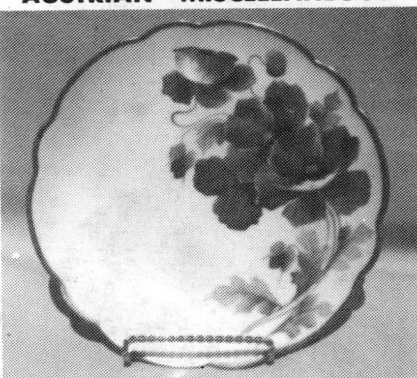

Artist-Signed Austrian China Plate

Numerous potteries in Austria produced
good-quality ceramic wares over many
years. Some factories were established by
American entrepreneurs, particularly in the
Carlsbad area, and other factories made
china under special brand names for American importers. Marks on various pieces are
indicated in many listings. Also see KAUFF-
MANN (Angelique) and ROYAL VIENNA
PORCELAIN.

Cake plate, pierced handles on 4
   sides, Bluebird patt., 9" sq. (Victoria, Carlsbad) $35.00
Cheese & cracker dish, h.p. realistic
   oranges 45.00
Chocolate pot, h.p. poppies in relief

each side on shaded satin ground, heavy gold trim, 10" h. 75.00

Chocolate set: cov. chocolate pot & 4 c/s; roses decal on green ground, 9 pcs. (Victoria, Carlsbad)....................... 110.00

Creamer, Dutch girls (2) chasing goose decal 30.00

Cup & saucer, h.p. geometric decor exterior, gold interior 58.00

Dresser set: cov. powder dish, hair receiver, pin dish & dresser tray; h.p. blue & purple violets, gold trim, 4 pcs. (Carlsbad) 95.00

Ewer, h.p. florals outlined in gold on cream shaded to pink ground, 6" h. (Victoria, Carlsbad) 75.00

Fish set: platter & 6 plates; various fish species decor, 7 pcs. 200.00

Lemonade set: pitcher, 4 tumblers & 4 plates; Art Nouveau decor, artist-signed, 9 pcs. 175.00

Pitcher, 9" h., gold scroll handle, h.p. brown branches, leaves & yellow florals w/raised enamel centers on cream ground (Carls-bad) 75.00

Plate, 8¼" d., scalloped rim, realis-tic poppies on rainbow pastel ground, gold edge, artist-signed (ILLUS.)........................ 35.00

Plate, 8¼" l., handled leaf shape w/irregular rim, decal portrait of pretty brunette lady on shaded green ground, gold trim 45.00

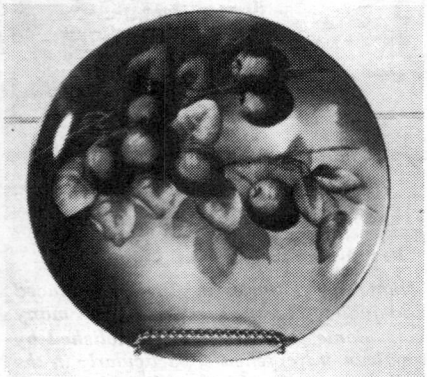

Fruit Plate

Plate, 8½" d., lush dark blue plums & foliage on shaded blue to pur-ple ground, gold rim, artist-signed (ILLUS.)....................... 45.00

Plate, 9" d., floral decal center, pastel border (Carlsbad) 12.50

Plate, 9" d., h.p. portrait of "Amicitia," cherry red border w/gold tracery (pseudo beehive mark)..................95.00 to 125.00

Plate, 9" sq., reticulated rim, Blue-bird patt. (Victoria)............. 35.00

Plate, 9½" d., decal bust portrait of Shakespeare's Beatrice center 75.00

Plate, 10½" d., h.p. floral decor (Victoria, Carlsbad)............. 65.00

Powder box, cov., h.p. red roses & green foliage on turquoise shaded to white ground, heavy gold trim, 5" d. 55.00

Powder box, cov., cupid scene decal on cobalt blue shaded to white, gold trim 45.00

Tea set: cov. teapot, creamer & sugar bowl; h.p. pink florals on light blue shaded to cream ground, 3 pcs. 175.00

Tray, 2-handled, portrait of beautiful woman center, gold trim, 14" l. (pseudo beehive mark) 145.00

Urn, 2-handled, h.p. rose bouquet on shaded ivory ground, 14½" h....................... 145.00

Unique Austrian China Vase

Vase, 5¾" h., applied "antler" form handles at sides, embossed deer's head medallion front (ILLUS.)..... 25.00

Vase, 7 x 4", disc-shaped, h.p. deep orange & yellow nasturtiums 55.00

Vase, 11" h., h.p. portrait reserved on maroon ground w/heavy gold trim (pseudo beehive mark & numbered) 425.00

Vase, 11¾" h., h.p. pink, purple & yellow florals on blue ground 195.00

BAUER POTTERY

The Bauer Pottery was moved to Los An-geles, California from Paducah, Kentucky, in 1909, in the hope that the climate would prove beneficial to the principal organizer, John Andrew Bauer, who suffered from severe asthma. Flower pots, made of California adobe clay, were the first production at the new location but soon they were able to resume production of stoneware crocks and jugs, the mainstay of the Kentucky operation. In the early 1930's, Bauer's colorfully glazed earthen dinnerwares, especially the popular Ring-Ware pattern, became an immediate success. Sometimes confused with its imitator, Fiesta Ware (first registered by Homer Laughlin in 1937), Bauer Pottery is collectible in its own right and is especially popular with West coast collectors. Bauer Pottery ceased operation in 1962.

Bauer Pottery Butter Churn

Bowl, cereal, Ring-Ware patt.,
orange $10.00
Butter churn w/original dasher,
stoneware w/stenciled orange
label, 2-gal., 13" h. (ILLUS.) 100.00
Butter dish, cov., Monterey Moderne
patt., red 45.00
Butter dish, cov., Ring-Ware patt.,
yellow 26.00
Carafe, cov., Ring-Ware patt.
w/wooden handle, orange, red or
turquoise, each 35.00
Carafe, cov., Ring-Ware patt.,
w/raffia-wrapped metal handle,
orange 30.00
Cookie jar, cov., Ring-Ware patt.,
green 20.00
Creamer, Ring-Ware patt., orange .. 10.00
Cup & saucer, Ring-Ware patt.,
orange 15.00
Jar, stacking-type, Ring-Ware patt.,
orange 12.50
Mixing bowl, Ring-Ware patt., red,
5" d. 10.00
Mixing bowl, Ring-Ware patt., blue,
7½" d. 12.50

Mixing bowl, Ring-Ware patt.,
green, 9½" d. 18.00
Mixing bowl, green, 10½" d. 29.00
Mixing bowl, red, 10½" d. 49.00
Pitcher, Monterey Moderne patt.,
green, 2-qt. 15.00
Pitcher, Ring-Ware patt., red,
2-qt. 26.50
Pitcher w/ice lip, Glossy Pastel
Kitchenware patt., light brown ... 28.00
Plate, 6" d., Ring-Ware patt.,
orange 6.00
Plate, 7" d., Ring-Ware patt.,
orange 8.00
Plate, 10½" d., Ring-Ware patt.,
red 10.50
Plate, 10½" d., white 19.00
Platter, squared oblong, Contempo
patt., yellow 25.00
Sauce dish, Ring-Ware patt.,
orange 8.00
Sugar bowl, cov., Ring-Ware patt.,
blue 30.00
Sugar bowl, cov., Ring-Ware patt.,
red 10.00
Tumbler, Ring-Ware patt., black,
6-oz. 30.00
Tumbler w/wooden handle, Ring-
Ware patt., orange 14.00
Vase, 8½" h., swirled design,
white 12.00
Vase (or jardiniere), Mission patt.,
bisque finish, large 65.00

BAVARIAN

Bavarian China Cup & Saucer

Ceramics have been produced by various potteries in Bavaria for many years. Those appearing for sale in greatest frequency today having been produced in the 19th and early 20th centuries. Also see CHILDREN'S DISHES, HUTSCHENREUTHER, KOCH, NYMPHENBURG, PICTORIAL SOUVENIRS, ROSENTHAL and ROYAL BAYREUTH.

Basket w/overhead handle, blue
forget-me-nots decal, h.p. gold
trim, Z.S. & Co. (Zeh, Scherzer &
Co.) $28.00

Bowl, 9" d., scalloped rim, pink floral sprays on pink ground, artist-signed 135.00

Bowl, 10" d., white roses on satin ground, heavy gold trim (Royal) .. 65.00

Bowl, master berry or fruit, ornately scalloped rim w/gold trim, snowballs decal center (Royal Crown).. 45.00

Cake plate, 2-handled, center decal of birds (2) nesting in tree, yellow & gold border, 10¼" d. 35.00

Cake plate, 2-handled, h.p. lavender florals on pearlized ground, 10½" d. 75.00

Cake plate, cabbage roses decor, gold handles, artist-signed & dated 30.00

Cake set: master cake plate & 6 individual plates; shaded pink cabbage roses & ornate gold stenciling decor, 7 pcs. 80.00

Chocolate pot, cov., h.p. pink florals on green ground 80.00

Creamer & cov. sugar bowl, hexagonal form, pink & yellow roses decor, gold trim, pr., Z.S. & Co. (Zeh, Scherzer & Co.) 42.50

Cup, child's, lettered "Remember Me" 30.00

Cup & saucer, demitasse, carnations decal, gold trim, Royal (ILLUS.) ... 20.00

Game plate, grouse center, wide gold border, dusty rose edge (beehive & shield mark) 75.00

Hatpin holder, h.p. pink roses decor 65.00

Marmalade jar, cover & underplate, 2-handled, h.p. pink roses on cream ground, black & gold trim, 6" h., 2 pcs. 98.00

Mug, Blue Onion patt. 35.00

Plaque, pierced to hang, scalloped rim, branch of realistic apples decal center, 12½" d. (Z.S. & Co.) .. 45.00

Plate, 6" d., grape cluster decal 10.00

Plate, 6¾" d., h.p. holly berries & leaves decor (J.C. Louise) 30.00

Plate, 7½" d., h.p. blue & gold border 16.00

Plate, 7½" d., yellow florals decal & pastel border on white 6.50

Plate, 8" d., pink & red roses decor, artist-signed 35.00

Plate, 8¼" d., poppies decal center (Z.S. & Co.) 7.50

Plate, 8½" d., h.p. violets & large pansy-type leaves decor, gold edge 35.00

Plate, 8½" d., h.p. peaches on shaded green ground 37.50

Plate, 8½" d., h.p. pink wild roses decor (pseudo Sevres mark) 35.00

Plate, 9" d., scalloped & embossed rim w/gold edge, h.p. cherry tree

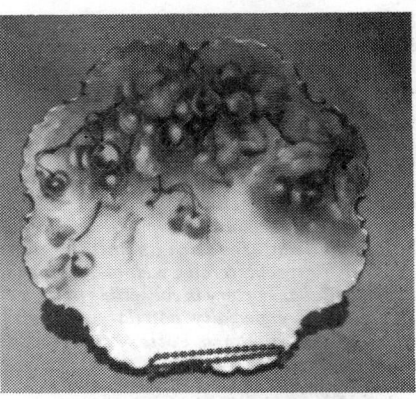

Bavarian China Fruit Plate

branch on shaded yellow to peach ground (ILLUS.)................. 45.00

Syrup pitcher, creamy ivory roses decal on pale green ground 35.00

Teapot, cov., hexagonal, pink & yellow roses decal, gold trim (Z.S. & Co.)............................ 45.00

Tea set: cov. teapot, creamer & sugar bowl; iridescent lustre finish, gold trim, 3 pcs. (Z.S & Co.) .. 95.00

Vase, 5¾" h., mug-shaped, orange lustre dragon-form handle, h.p. yellow & russet corn & husk decor 40.00

Vase, 10¾" h., ovoid w/elongated neck & open handles at sides, reserve portrait of lady w/peacock on dark ground, heavy gold trim........................... 189.00

BECK, R.K.

Game Platter with Deer

Items that are signed R.K. Beck are sought by a group of specialized collectors. Beck was a noteworthy wildlife painter and his original art works have been reproduced in decal form and applied to plates, platters and the like, under the glaze. Though these items are signed R.K. Beck, it should not be construed that these pieces were hand-painted by Beck since they are merely derived from his original art work. Also see BUFFALO POTTERY.

Fish set: platter & 6 plates; various
  species of game fish depicted,
  Buffalo Pottery, 7 pcs. . . .$250.00 to 300.00
Game plate, scene of Buck & Doe at
  lake, gold trim, 9" d. 32.50
Game plate, Bird, Duck, or Prairie
  Chicken decor, each 47.00
Game set: platter & 4 plates; platter
  w/scene of Buck & Doe in forest
  glen & plates w/various deer on
  shaded ground, 5 pcs. (ILLUS. of
  platter) 300.00
Plate, 9" d., ears of corn decor 35.00
Plate, 9" d., fruit decor 40.00
Plate, 10" d., ears of corn
  decor 45.00

BELLEEK

Belleek china has been made in Ireland's County Fermanagh for many years. It is exceedingly thin porcelain. Several marks were used, including a hound and harp (1865-1880), and a hound, harp and castle (1863-1891). A printed hound, harp and castle with the words "Co. Fermanagh Ireland" constitutes the mark from 1891. Belleek-type china also was made in the United States last century by several firms, including Ceramic Art China Works, Columbian Art Pottery, Lenox Inc., Ott & Brewer and Willets Manufacturing Co. Also see COMMEMORATIVE PLATES and LOTUS WARE.

AMERICAN

Lenox Coffee Pot

Bouillon cup & saucer, twig handles,
  gold paste decor on creamy lustre
  ground (Willets) $95.00

Bowl, 6" d., 3½" h., 2-handled, ruffled rim, h.p. violets & enameled
  gold rim & handles (Willets) 175.00
Chocolate pot, cov., dragon handle,
  gold paste florals on cream
  ground (Willets) 395.00
Cider set: cider pitcher & 4 mugs;
  h.p. grape clusters decor, 5 pcs.
  (Lenox) 275.00
Coffee pot, cov., gooseneck spout,
  sterling silver overlay decor,
  6½" h. (Lenox) 195.00
Coffee pot, cov., square pedestal
  base, urn finial, stylized Art Deco
  tulips decor, Lenox, 10½" h.
  (ILLUS.) 125.00
Creamer, gold paste leaves & ber-
  ries on pink ground, gold handle
  & rim, 3" h. (Ceramic Art Com-
  pany) 95.00
Creamer, gold handle, overall pan-
  sies & leaves decor, 3¼" h. (Ott &
  Brewer) 175.00
Creamer & cov. sugar bowl,
  pedestal base, factory-decorated
  gold paste swags & baskets of
  pink roses, pr. (Willets) 150.00

Lenox Creamer & Sugar Bowl

Creamer & cov. sugar bowl, ribbed
  shell form, gold paste floral
  sprays & painted shadow flowers,
  gold trim, Lenox, 4¾" w., pr.
  (ILLUS.) 200.00
Cup & saucer, demitasse, Cactus
  patt. w/gold twig handle
  (Willets) 65.00
Cup & saucer, demitasse, shell-
  molded, ornate decor & gold trim
  (Willets) 85.00
Cup & saucer, demitasse, Victoria
  patt. (Morgan Belleek China Com-
  pany, 1924-29) 85.00
Cup & saucer, heart-shaped
  (Willets) 50.00
Cup & saucer, Tridacna patt., gold-
  trimmed handle & rims, pearlized
  yellow interior (Ott & Brewer) 95.00
Dresser set: tray, powder box & hair
  receiver; blue forget-me-nots
  decor, 3 pcs. (Lenox) 145.00
Ewer, reticulated handle, h.p. lilacs
  decor, 10½" h. (Ott & Brewer) . . . 675.00
Ewer, bulbous, melon-ribbed, gold

paste thistles decor (Ott &
Brewer) 895.00
Fish plates, h.p. fish decor
(Lenox)......................... 100.00
Humidor, cover & insert, h.p. corn
decor (Ceramic Art Company) 225.00

Portrait Jug

Jug, 3-sided, portrait of cavalier on
brown glaze ground, Lenox,
6½" h. (ILLUS.) 450.00
Mug, wide top band w/gold-
trimmed h.p. poppies decor,
5½" h. (Willets) 135.00
Mug, tankard, fraternal, "B.P.O.E."
& h.p. elk, dated 1909, 7" h.
(Lenox)........................ 95.00
Mug, left-handed type, h.p. portrait
of German girl (Willets) 150.00
Mug, h.p. bust portrait of Indian
chief wearing full headdress
(Ceramic Art Company) 155.00
Mug, portrait of Teddy Roosevelt,
artist-signed (Lenox) 650.00
Mug, h.p. gooseberries decor
(Ceramic Art Company) 95.00
Mug, h.p. lemons decor (Willets) ... 135.00
Pitcher, 5" h., bamboo-molded
"Cane" patt., gold handle & gold-
sponged trim (Willets) 150.00
Pitcher, cider, 5¾" h., field enclosed by fence, gold trim, artist-
signed (Lenox) 120.00
Pitcher, cider, 6" h., overall h.p.
multicolored gooseberries on
tinted ground (Lenox)........... 250.00
Pitcher, cov., 10" h., molded spider
web lid & embossed cherries &
leaves on body in heavy gold
(Ceramic Art Company) 500.00
Pitcher, tankard, 13" h., scene of
monk filling wine bottle, artist-
signed (Willets) 400.00
Pitcher, tankard, 15" h., h.p. green,
burgundy & russet grape clusters
on shaded ground, violet rim &
handle, Lenox (ILLUS.) 385.00

Lenox Belleek

Pitcher, tankard, 15" h., gilt dragon
handle, purple & green grapes
decor on shaded cream to blue
ground, artist-signed & dated
(Willets)...................... 325.00
Plate, 9½" d., Tridacna patt., h.p.
gold florals & leaves decor (Ott &
Brewer) 250.00
Salt dip, model of a swan, gold &
soft green trim (Willets) 48.00
Salt dip, ruffled rim, pink roses
decor (Lenox) 20.00
Tobacco jar, cov., h.p. owl & pine
cones, 7½" h. (Lenox) 150.00
Tumbler, h.p. berries decor, 5¾" h.
(Lenox)....................... 85.00
Tumbler, gold & blue edge, pink
lining (Ott & Brewer) 175.00
Tumbler, souvenir, "David's Society,
New York" lettered in black &
red, dated 1899 (Columbian Art
Pottery - Morris & Wilmore) 225.00

Willets Belleek Vase

Vase, 7" h., ornate handles, h.p. gold paste florals & trim, Willets (ILLUS.) 400.00

Vase, 8" h., Worcester-type decor, h.p. gold paste florals on rosy beige ground (Lenox) 235.00

Vase, 8½" h., h.p. pink & yellow tulips on shaded green ground (Willets) 115.00

Vase, 10" h., cylindrical, h.p. country scene w/little girl & ducklings on green ground (Willets) 475.00

Vase, 10" h., cylindrical, h.p. peacocks, lettered "Don't Sleep Here" (Willets) 295.00

Vase, 10" h., h.p. yellow pansies decor (Ott & Brewer) 695.00

Vase, 10½" h., tapering cylinder, colorful pansies decor on shaded brown ground, artist-signed (Lenox)......................... 375.00

Vase, 12½" h., h.p. lion decor (Willets) 425.00

Vase, 15" h., gold handles, h.p. red & white roses on butterscotch ground (Lenox)................. 375.00

Vase, 15" h., chrysanthemums decor, artist-signed (Willets) 395.00

Vase, 15½" h., h.p. blue, green & yellow birds on branches overall decor (Lenox) 300.00

Vase, 16" h., 5" d., cylindrical, yellow roses on tinted ground, artist-signed (Willets) 295.00

IRISH

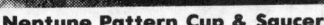

Limpet Pattern Creamer

Basket-dish, Basket Ware, 3-strand, bird's nest form, applied florettes at rim, impressed mark, 4 x 4" ... 850.00

Basket-dish, Basket Ware, 4-strand, heart-shaped w/applied florals at rim, 4 x 4½", 2¼" h. ...200.00 to 250.00

Basket-dish, Basket Ware, 3-strand, Henshall patt., applied roses & florals at rim, medium size 1,650.00

Bread plate, Tridacna patt., pink & gold trim, 11" d., 1st black mark......................... 210.00

Cake plate, Limpet patt., 11" w. across handles, 3rd black mark ... 125.00

Cake server, Basket Ware, 3-strand, 10¼" d. 1,750.00

Centerpiece, "Hippiritus Centre," tall center shell & 3 side shell forms on shell-mounded base, 11½" h., 1st impressed mark 1,475.00

Centerpiece, clam shell on shell-mounded base, 5" h., 1st black mark......................... 470.00

Creamer, Lily patt., pink trim, 2nd black mark 50.00

Creamer, Limpet patt., 2nd black mark (ILLUS.) 80.00

Creamer, Neptune patt., pink trim, 2nd black mark 65.00

Creamer, Shamrock-Basketweave patt., 1st black mark 65.00

Creamer, Toy Shell patt., green trim, 2nd black mark 45.00

Creamer, & open sugar bowl, Echinus patt., pink trim, 2nd black mark, pr...................... 325.00

Creamer & open sugar bowl, Hexagon patt., pink trim, 2nd black mark, pr........................ 142.00

Creamer & cov. sugar bowl, Mask patt., 3rd black mark, pr......... 125.00

Creamer & open sugar bowl, Shamrock-Basketweave patt., 2nd black mark, pr. 125.00

Cup & saucer, demitasse, Limpet patt., 3rd black mark 60.00

Cup & saucer, demitasse, Shamrock-Basketweave patt., 3rd black mark......................... 70.00

Cup & saucer, demitasse, Tridacna patt., green trim, 2nd black mark......................... 95.00

Cup & saucer, Aberdeen patt. 75.00

Cup & saucer, Cone patt., rust & gilt trim, 2nd black mark 155.00

Cup & saucer, Grass patt., 1st black mark......................... 115.00

Cup & saucer, Hexagon patt., pink trim, 2nd black mark 85.00

Cup & saucer, Institute patt., deep pink & gilt trim & monogram, 1st black mark 150.00

Cup & saucer, Limpet patt., 3rd black mark 65.00

Neptune Pattern Cup & Saucer

Cup & saucer, Neptune patt., green
trim, 2nd black mark (ILLUS.) 75.00

Cup & saucer, Thistle patt., 1st black
mark . . . . 175.00 to 225.00

Cup & saucer, farmer size, Grass
patt., 1st black mark 225.00

Cup & saucer, farmer size, Tridacna
patt., green trim, 2nd black
mark 115.00

Demitasse set: demitasse pot,
creamer, open sugar bowl, 2 c/s
& tray; Echinus patt., 1st black
mark, 8 pcs. 2,800.00

Demitasse set: demitasse pot,
creamer, open sugar bowl, 2 c/s
& tray; Hexagon patt., green trim,
2nd black mark, 8 pcs. 2,400.00

Demitasse set: demitasse pot,
creamer, open sugar bowl, 2 c/s
& tray; Neptune patt., pink trim,
2nd black mark, 8 pcs. 2,250.00

Figurine, "Girl Basket Bearer,"
9" h., 3rd green mark 225.00

Flower pot (or jardiniere), Finner
patt., coral handles, applied
roses, daisies & mums, 9" d.,
7" h., 2nd black mark 1,100.00

Irish Belleek Ice Bucket

Ice bucket, cov., parian, cylindrical
body w/continuous molded frieze
of playful frolicking putti in relief
supported on 3-mermaid base,
cover w/central figure of putto
(repaired) seated on dolphin's
back surrounded by 3 seahorses
emerging from choppy sea, 1st
black mark, 1863-91, 18¼" h.
(ILLUS.) 1,320.00

Menu holder, Shell patt., 2nd black
mark 80.00

Model of a Greyhound dog seated,
square base, 6" h., 3rd black
mark 615.00

Irish Belleek Pig

Model of a pig, medium size, 2nd
black mark (ILLUS.) 300.00

Model of a swan, 6 x 3½", 4¾" h.,
2nd black mark 145.00

Pitcher, 7" h., Harp patt., 1st black
mark 300.00

Plate, 5" d., Grass patt., 1st black
mark 55.00

Plate, 5½" d., Ivy patt., gold trim,
2nd black mark 57.00

Plate, 6" d., Aberdeen patt., 2nd
black mark 35.00

Plate, 6" d., Blarney patt., pink &
gold trim, 2nd black mark 90.00

Plate, 6" d., Celtic patt., blue,
green, red & yellow trim, 3rd
black mark 55.00

Plate, 6" d., Hexagon patt., green
trim, 2nd black mark 25.00

Plate, 6" d., Mask patt., 1st black
mark 40.00

Plate, 6" d., Tridacna patt., pink
trim, 2nd black mark 40.00

Plate, 6¼" d., Artichoke patt., gold
trim, 1st black mark 75.00

Plate, 6½" d., Limpet patt., gold
trim, 3rd black mark 40.00

Plate, 7" d., Echinus patt., pink &
gold trim, 1st black mark 85.00

Plate, 7" d., Neptune patt., blue
trim, 3rd black mark 45.00

Plate, 7¼" d., Institute patt., deep
pink & gold trim & monogram, 1st
black mark 135.00

Plate, 8" d., Grass patt., 1st black
mark 80.00

Plate, 8" d., Tridacna patt., pink
trim, 3rd black mark 44.00

Plate, 10" d., Neptune patt., blue
trim, 3rd black mark 80.00

Plate, Sycamore Leaf patt., 1st
green mark 35.00

Salt dip, Diamond patt., 3rd black
mark 25.00

Salt dip, Fluted Star patt., 3rd black
mark 30.00

Salt dip, Harp-Shamrock patt., 3rd
black mark 30.00

Salt dip, Limpet patt., 2nd black
mark 72.50

Salt dip, shamrock-shaped, green
   trim, 2nd black mark 60.00
Soup plate, earthenware, transfer-
   printed & h.p. in green, orange &
   brown, 10½" d., 1st black mark &
   impressed harp & crown 75.00
Spillholder, Cleary patt., 4" h., 1st
   black mark 290.00
Spillholder, upright fish on base,
   7" h., 1st black mark 365.00
Spillholder, Hippiritus patt., pink
   trim, 7" h., 1st black mark & impressed "Belleek Co. Ferm." 350.00
Spillholder, Shamrock Tree Stump
   patt., 2nd black mark 45.00
Tea kettle, cov., Echnius patt., pink
   & gold trim, 1st black mark 585.00

Irish Belleek Tea Kettle

Tea kettle, cov., Grass patt., purple
   trim, 1st black mark (ILLUS.) 675.00
Tea kettle, cov., Hawthorne patt.,
   1st black mark 485.00
Tea kettle, cov., Tridacna patt.,
   green trim, 6" d., 5½" h., 2nd
   black mark 395.00
Teapot, cov., Bamboo patt., yellow
   trim, small size, 2nd black mark . .   350.00
Teapot, cov., Cone patt., rust & gilt
   trim, 2nd black mark 495.00
Teapot, cov., Grass patt., 1st black
   mark . . . . .350.00 to 450.00
Teapot, cov., Hexagon patt., green
   trim, 2nd black mark . . . .225.00 to 250.00
Teapot, cov., Hexagon patt., pink
   trim, 2nd black mark 315.00
Teapot, cov., Limpet patt., medium
   size, 3rd black mark 235.00
Teapot, cov., Neptune patt., green
   trim, medium size, 2nd black
   mark 238.00
Teapot, cov., Neptune patt., pink
   trim, medium size, 2nd black
   mark 350.00
Teapot, cov., Neptune patt., yellow
   trim, medium size, 2nd black
   mark 325.00
Teapot, cov., New Shell patt., green
   & gold trim, 2nd black mark 325.00
Teapot, cov., Tridacna patt., pink

trim, medium size, 2nd black
   mark . . . . .300.00 to 325.00
Teapot, cov., Tridacna patt., green
   trim, large size, 2nd black mark . .   425.00
Tea set: cov. teapot, creamer, cov.
   sugar bowl, tray & 2 c/s; Hexagon
   patt., green trim, 2nd black mark,
   8 pcs. 1,400.00
Tea tray, Thorn patt., pale yellow
   cob on raised thorn, burnt orange
   webbing, 14½" sq., 1st black
   mark 1,250.00
Tea tray, Echinus patt., 15½ x
   12½", 1st black mark 245.00
Tea tray, Tridacna patt., pink trim,
   16" l., 2nd black mark 300.00
Tea urn, Chinese patt., dragon
   spout, paw feet, vivid brown,
   purple lustre & gold trim, 1st
   black mark 3,500.00
Tumbler, octagonal w/fluted sides,
   gold trim, 2nd black mark 125.00
Vase, 9" h., Aberdeen patt., applied
   florals, 2nd black mark . .500.00 to 750.00
Vase, 16" h., Triple Fishes patt.,
   1st black mark 1,775.00

BENNINGTON

Bennington Candlestick

   *Bennington wares, which ranged from
stonewares to parian and porcelain, were
made in Bennington, Vt., primarily in two
potteries, one in which Captain John Norton
and his descendants were principals, and the
other in which Christopher Webber Fenton
(also once associated with the Nortons) was
a principal. Various marks are found on the
wares made in the two major potteries, including J. & E. Norton, E. & L. P. Norton,
L. Norton & Co., Norton & Fenton, Edward
Norton, Lyman Fenton & Co., Fenton's
Works, United States Pottery Co., U.S.P. and
others.*

Baker, oval, mottled brown
Rockingham glaze, 11 3/8 x
8 7/8" . . . .$145.00 to 195.00
Bed pan, mottled brown Rockingham
glaze . . . . .60.00 to 95.00
Book flask, "Departed Spirits," Flint
Enamel glaze 495.00
Box, cov., parian, full figure
sleeping child reclining on
lid, 5¾ x 4¼", 3¾" h. . . . .68.00 to 90.00
Candlestick, slightly domed base,
cylindrical stem w/rings, mottled
brown Flint Enamel glaze
w/streaks of blue, 1849-58
(ILLUS.). 350.00
Coachman (or Toby) bottle, figural
coachman, mottled brown Rockingham glaze, 10¾" h. . .195.00 to 375.00
Coffee pot, helmet cover, paneled
pear-shaped body, gooseneck
spout, mottled brown Flint Enamel
glaze w/traces of green,
12¼" h. 425.00
Crock, straight sides, earred han-
dles, stoneware, cobalt blue slip-
quilled floral on grey, impressed
"E. & L.P. Norton, Bennington,
Vt.," 1861-81, 8" d., 7" h. 260.00
Crock, straight sides, earred han-
dles, stoneware, cobalt blue slip-
quilled floral spray on grey, impressed "J. Norton & Co., Ben-
nington, Vt.," 1859-61, 2-gal. 650.00
Crock, stoneware, cobalt blue slip-
quilled florals on grey, impressed
"E. Norton & Co., Bennington,
Vt.," 1883-94, 4-gal. 210.00
Crock, stoneware, cobalt blue swirls
on grey, impressed "E. Norton &
Co., Bennington, Vt.," 1883-94,
5-gal. 110.00
Cuspidor, Diamond patt., mottled
brown Rockingham glaze, 7¾" d.,
3 5/8" h. 225.00
Foot warmer, Flint Enamel glaze,
9" h. 275.00
Fruit jar, wax sealer, stoneware,
Albany Slip interior, qt. 95.00
Jar, cov., parian, molded acanthus
leaves on base & fruit on lid,
5" d., 6¼" h. 45.00
Jug, straight sides, applied handle,
stoneware, cobalt blue slip-quilled
floral on grey, impressed "E. &
L.P. Norton, Bennington, Vt.,"
1861-81, 10¾" h. (hairline in
neck) 170.00
Jug, ovoid w/strap handle, stone-
ware, brushed brown-ochre floral
& leaf on grey, impressed "L. Norton & Son, Bennington, Vt.,"
1833-40, 11" h. . . . . .500.00 to 675.00
Jug, straight sides, strap handle,
stoneware, brushed cobalt blue

leaf on grey, impressed "E. & L.P.
Norton, Bennington, Vt.," 11½" h.
(crinkled finish glaze above
shoulder) 125.00
Jug, straight sides, applied handle,
stoneware, slip-quilled cobalt blue
floral design on grey, impressed
"J. & E. Norton, Bennington, Vt.,"
1850-59, 1½ gal., 12¾" h. (chip &
minor hairline along base) 235.00
Jug, semi-ovoid, applied handle,
stoneware, brushed cobalt blue
stylized foliage on grey, impressed "J. Norton & Co., Bennington, Vt. 2," 1859-61, 2-gal.,
14" h. 275.00
Jug, straight sides, strap handle,
stoneware, slip-quilled cobalt blue
floral design on grey, impressed
"E. & L. P. Norton, Bennington,
Vt.," 1861-81, 3-gal., 15¼" h. 270.00
Jug, semi-ovoid, stoneware, cobalt
blue slip-quilled standing dog
w/polka dot coat & long tail on
grey, impressed "J. & E. Norton,
Bennington, Vt.," 1850-59, 4-gal.,
16¾" h. 6,100.00
Jug, ovoid, strap handle, stoneware,
cobalt blue slip-quilled compote of
flowers on grey, impressed "J.
Norton & Co., Bennington, Vt.,"
1859-61, 6-gal. 4,200.00
Mixing bowl, mottled brown Rock-
ingham glaze, 1849-59, 8" d. 90.00
Mixing bowl, mottled brown Rockingham glaze, 10" d., 5½" h. 85.00
Model of chick & shell, parian,
marked "Just Out" on base,
4" h. 95.00
Mug, applied ridged handle, mottled
dark brown Rockingham glaze,
4 1/8" h. . . . . .85.00 to 115.00

Bennington Pie Plate

Pie plate, mottled brown Rockingham glaze, 7 7/8" d. (ILLUS.) . . 95.00
Pie plate, mottled brown Rock-
ingham glaze, 9¾" d. 75.00
Pie plate, mottled brown Rock-
ingham glaze, 10½" d. 115.00
Pitcher, 6½" h., Tulip & Heart patt.,

mottled brown Rockingham
glaze 185.00
Pitcher, 9" h., mask spout, mottled
brown Flint Enamel glaze
w/traces of green (blisters &
chips) 275.00
Pitcher, 11¼" h., Diamond patt.,
Flint Enamel glaze, impressed
"1849" mark (flakes on bottom &
kiln adhesion) 225.00
Platter, 14" l., mottled brown Rockingham glaze 200.00
Serving dish, fluted corners forming
scallops, mottled brown, yellow &
black, 9 x 8½" sq. 130.00
Syrup pitcher, parian, Palm Tree
patt., "U.S.P." ribbon (or banner)
mark (never had lid) 175.00
Tobacco jar, cov., octagonal, mottled brown Rockingham glaze 350.00

Standard Toby

Toby pitcher, standard-type, mottled
brown Rockingham glaze, 6" h.
(ILLUS.)...................... 250.00
Wash basin, Flint Enamel glaze,
"1849" mark, 13¾" d., 4½" h. ... 525.00
Wash basin, Scalloped Rib patt.,
mottled brown Flint Enamel glaze
w/traces of green, "1849" mark,
15" d. 525.00

BERLIN (KPM)

The mark, KPM, was used at Meissen from 1723 to 1725, and was later adopted by the Royal Factory, Konigliche Porzellan Manufaktur, in Berlin. At various periods it has been incorporated with the Brandenburg sceptre, the Prussian eagle or the crowned globe. The same letters were also adopted by other factories in Germany in the late 19th and 20th centuries. With the end of the Ger-

man monarchy in 1918, the name of the firm was changed to Staatliche Porzellan Manufaktur and though production was halted during World War II, the factory was rebuilt and is still in business. The exquisite paintings on porcelain produced at the close of the 19th century are eagerly sought by collectors today.

Cup, cov., h.p. portrait reserved on
cobalt blue ground overlaid
w/heavy gold $350.00
Cup & saucer, lion paw feet, ornate
gold decor on cobalt blue ground,
1930 ...." 75.00
Figures, court lady & gentleman
in Empire period attire, 8 5/8" h.,
pr........................... 485.00
Painting on porcelain, beautiful
long-haired maiden, velvet-backed
ormolu frame w/ring at top to
hang, 4½ x 2 7/8" oval 165.00
Painting on porcelain, girl holding
candle, framed, 5¼ x 3¾"....... 250.00
Painting on porcelain, "Blessed Virgin Mary," ormolu frame, early
20th c., 8 x 5¾" 330.00

"La Belle Chocolatiere"

Painting on porcelain, "La Belle
Chocolatiere" (the Chocolate Lady
used as trademark for Baker's
Cocoa), "Adapted from La Belle
Chocolatiere by Jean-Etienne
Liotard (1702-89) in the Dresden
Gallery" written on reverse, early
20th c., 8¾ x 6" (ILLUS.) 1,540.00
Painting on porcelain, 2 orphaned
girls wearing tattered clothing &
standing in a stone doorway, each
w/pensive expression & 1 w/out-
stretched palm, late 19th c., 9¼ x
6 1/8" 2,200.00

Painting on porcelain, handsome musician wearing a claret-colored vest & scarf, colorful sash, white shirt & black knee-length breeches, leaning against a stone ledge & gazing towards the sky as he strums his mandolin, artist-signed, 9 3/8 x 6½" 605.00

"The Finding of Moses"

Painting on porcelain, "The Finding of Moses," infant floating in reed basket while his mother peers at him from screen of bullrushes, artist-signed, late 19th c., 9½ x 6 3/8" (ILLUS.) 1,980.00

Scene of Diana at Bath

Painting on porcelain, scene of Diana at Bath, after Boucher, w/the huntress Diana & her attendant depicted nude on the banks of a river, their colorful garments spread about them & w/dead fowl & hunting dogs nearby, 3rd quarter 19th c., 10 x7½" (ILLUS.) 2,310.00
Painting on porcelain, fashionably dressed woman surrounded by her 7 children, her husband at the doorway, 3rd quarter 19th c., 11 x 8¾" 2,970.00

Painting on porcelain, allegorical representation of woman, w/partially draped maiden holding distaff, hips swathed in diaphanous pink fabric, flanked by matron in red & white drapery w/flowers & crouching elderly woman w/shears, late 19th c., gilt frame, overall 11¾ x 9½" . . . 1,760.00
Painting on porcelain, scene of maiden wearing a white drapery standing on tiptoe on large leaf & admiring the fragrance of a convolvulus, against red-orange sky, 3rd quarter 19th c., 12 x 9¾" 2,090.00
Painting on porcelain, "The Waves' Kiss," delirious shipwrecked sailor caressing a nymph, emerging from the stormy sea, wearing only a strand of long white pearls, signed Wagner, ca. 1910, 12¾ x 10½" 3,300.00
Painting on porcelain, the banished Hagar & Ishmael leaving the house of Abraham & Sarah, 3rd quarter 19th c., 15 1/8 x 12 1/8" 3,300.00
Painting on porcelain, mother holding her infant near an open window within a well-appointed room, late 19th c., 16½ x 12 3/8" 5,775.00
Painting on porcelain, pious nun in a pensive mood, gazing heavenward from her window, 3rd quarter 19th c., 20¾ x 14½" . . . 10,725.00
Plate, 6" d., h.p. blue leaves w/ornate gold trim 37.00
Plates, 9" d., h.p. fruit center, reticulated gold rims, set of 4 . . . . 125.00

Berlin Oval Tray

Tray, 2-handled shaped oval, h.p. stag scene center w/insects in outer edges, shell & scroll-molded handles highlighted in puce & gilt (w/small chip repair to one handle), ca. 1775, 14½" l. (ILLUS.) . . . 660.00

BILOXI (George Ohr) POTTERY

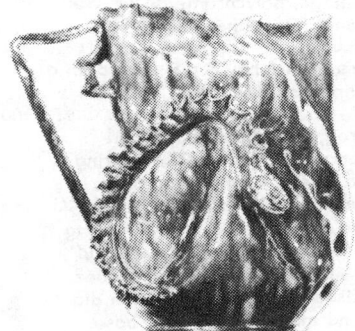

George Ohr Abstract Form Pitcher

George Ohr, the eccentric potter of Biloxi, Mississippi, worked from about 1883 to 1906. Some think him to be one of the most expert throwers the craft will ever see. The majority of his works were hand thrown, exceedingly thin-walled items, some of which have a crushed or folded appearance. He considered himself the foremost potter in the world and declined to sell much of his production, instead accumulated a great horde to leave as a legacy to his children. In 1972, this collection was purchased for resale by an antique dealer.

Bowl, 10½" d., 2½" h., 3 openings
  in sides, clay red, unglazed,
  signed $145.00
Cup, "Here's to your good health
  and your Family's and may they
  all live long and prosper," olive
  green exterior glaze, metallic
  blue glaze interior, dated 1896 &
  signed, 3 x 3" 245.00
Pitcher, 7" h., abstract form, 2
  applied serpents, mottled green
  exterior glaze, brown interior
  (ILLUS.) 12,750.00
Planter, black iridescent glaze,
  3" h. 150.00
Puzzle mug, glossy green glaze,
  signed, 4" h.................... 190.00
Vase, 3½" h., bulbous, crimped &
  folded top, glossy glaze 350.00
Vase, 10" h., cylindrical body
  w/crumpled lip, elongated folded
  handles, gunmetal grey over mottled blue-purple glaze, ca. 1900
  (repair to handles).............3,740.00

BISQUE

Bisque is biscuit china, fired a single time but not glazed. Some bisque is decorated with colors. Most abundant from the Victorian era are figurines and groups, but other pieces from busts to vases were made by numerous potteries in the U.S. and abroad. Also see FAIRY LAMPS.

German Bisque Cigarette Holder

Bust of Abraham Lincoln, signed
  "Isaac Broome," dated 1914,
  10½" h. $925.00
Cigarette & match holder, figure of
  a little boy perched between containers, Germany, 8" h. (ILLUS.) .. 125.00
Figure of a bathing beauty, wearing
  pebbled bisque suit & hat, Germany, 3¼" h.................... 125.00
Figure of little girl holding doll
  (designed to sit on edge of shelf),
  wearing brown dress, blue apron,
  hat & shoes, overall 3½" h. 65.00
Figure of a young girl seated &
  removing her grey stockings,
  wearing large orange bonnet &
  white dress w/blue polka dots,
  Heubach, 3" d., 4¼" h. 125.00
Figure of Dutch girl seated, blonde
  hair, dressed in green, orange &
  white, Heubach, 3½" d., 6" h. ... 98.00
Figure of a young black boy on a
  swing, wearing white shirt & plaid
  pants, 2 7/8" d., 6¼" h. 130.00
Figure of a man seated on a bench
  playing the concertina, dressed in
  lavender blouse, grey pants, long
  tan coat, black boots & cap, on
  circular grass mound base,
  marked "Gardner," Russian,
  4¾" d., 6¾" h. 450.00
Figure of a peasant girl carrying a
  basket, wearing green skirt,
  white blouse & white apron
  w/green & red trim, Heubach,
  5¾" d., 8½" h. 195.00
Figure of a girl dancing, blonde
  hair, wearing blue & white dress,
  Heubach, 11" h................. 325.00

easant girl standing
uaretoot & leaning against a hoe,
Heubach sunburst mark, 11" h. 185.00
Figure of a girl dancing, wearing
rose ribbon in blonde hair, "sanded" aqua dress w/white & gold
trim, Heubach, 11½" h. 240.00
Figure of a boy standing, wearing
sailor suit, pastel coloring, numbered & impressed mark on base,
12½" h. 125.00
Figure of a girl holding a parrot,
blue "sanded" skirt & pink "sand-
ed" vest, Heubach, 13" h. 295.00
Figure of a boy w/cigar, seated on
a wicker chair & wearing glasses
& pastel clothing, Heubach,
14½" h. 380.00
Figure of a lady standing w/a flow-
ing stole over her head, her bare
feet showing from beneath the
hem of her graceful soft blue
gown, Robinson & Leadbeater,
5¼" d., 15 3/8" h. 335.00
Figures, girls seated, dressed in
large ruffled sunbonnets & white
gowns w/pink & aqua trim, 5" h.,
pr. 325.00
Figures, Dutch boy & girl seated,
blonde hair, dressed in green,
orange & grey, Heubach, 3½" d.,
7" h., pr. 225.00
Figures, boy & girl playing musical
instruments, dressed in teal blue
& white w/"sanded" pink trim,
Heubach, 4½ x 3", 10" h., pr. 225.00
Figures, man & woman carrying
baskets, dressed in pastel blue,
lavender, green, pink & yellow
garments, France, 10" d.,
17½" h., pr. 1,135.00

German Bisque Figures

Figures, woman dressed in Roman
influenced garment & dapper gen-

tleman offering a rose, w/minor
damage, polychrome decor, Germany, late 19th c., 20¾" h., pr.
(ILLUS.) 302.50
Figure group, boy & girl seated on a
swing, tan & white, 3 x 2",
5½" h. 100.00
Figure group, Dutch boy & girl
standing back to back, wearing
red, green & white garments,
Heubach, 4¾" base d., 7¼" h. . . . 145.00
Figure group, boy & 2 girls leaning
on fence & watching pr. playful
kittens in basket, pastel shades,
incised number & "R" within diamond mark, 10¼ x 7¼" base,
9" h. 290.00
Figure group, boy & girl standing,
each holding a grey cat, 5¾ x 4",
11½" h. 245.00
Match holder, little boy seated on
stone wall, wicker basket holder
below, Germany, 4 x 3½" 55.00
Model of a cat reclining, white coat
w/black spots, green eyes, pink
bow at neck, 8¾" l. 115.00
Model of dog standing on hind legs,
wearing red, white & blue jacket,
blue & white striped trousers &
ornate hat w/plume, numbered
on base, 10¼" h. 175.00
Model of bulldog standing, tawny
brindle-colored coat, wearing
studded collar, 11 x 11½" 450.00
Nodding figure, seated Oriental lady
wearing comb in elaborate hairdo
& holding an open fan, 8 x 7" 350.00
Piano baby, girl seated w/arms
crossed & resting in lap, wearing
flowing nightgown & huge floppy
hat, Heubach, 5½" h. 310.00
Piano baby, girl seated holding left
hand out & w/right hand resting
on knee, wearing flowing nightgown & cap, Heubach, 5½" h. 135.00
Piano baby, girl seated & feeding
cat from dish, wearing flowing
nightgown, 8½" h. 175.00
Piano baby, seated & pulling off
pink stocking, wearing white
gown w/pink trim & ruffled bonnet, Heubach sunburst mark,
7¾" h. 350.00
Planter, bust of an Indian, black
braided hair & tan & black feathered headdress, brown shirt
w/yellow & green beading,
3¼" d., 6½" h. 175.00
Snow baby, seated, Germany,
1¾" 45.00
Snow babies (4) playing musical
instruments 360.00
Snow baby, sitting in red airplane,
marked Germany & numbered . . . 160.00

BLUE WILLOW

Blue Willow Bread & Butter Plates

This pseudo-Chinese pattern has been used by numerous firms throughout the years. The original design is attributed to Thomas Minton about 1780 and Thomas Turner is believed to have first produced the ware during his tenure at the Caughley works. The blue underglaze transfer print pattern has never been out of production since that time. An oriental landscape incorporating a bridge, pagoda, trees, figures and birds, supposedly tells the story of lovers fleeing a cruel father who wished to prevent their marriage. The gods, having pity on them, changed them into birds enabling them to fly away and seek their happiness together. Also see BUFFALO POTTERY and CHILDREN'S DISHES.

Batter pitcher, cov., Japan, 8" h. ...	$68.00
Bowl, 4½" d., Ridgway	8.00
Bowl, 5½" d., Maastricht	16.00
Bowl, berry, 8¼" d., Minton, 1891-1902	69.00
Butter dish, cover & drain insert, W. Adams & Sons, 1819-64	75.00
Butter pat, England .... 9.00 to	12.00
Cake stand, Barker Bros., 1876-1900, 12¼" d., 2½" h.	185.00
Coffee pot, cov., gold trim, Burleigh	85.00
Compote, octagonal, Job Meigh, 1805-34	225.00
Creamer, large, Buffalo Pottery, 1911	30.00
Creamer, Japan	5.00
Creamer & sugar bowl, child's, Japan, pr.	50.00
Creamer & cov. sugar bowl, Buffalo Pottery, 1911, 5¾", pr.	90.00
Cup & saucer, demitasse, Buffalo Pottery, 1911	27.00
Cup & saucer, Buffalo Pottery, 1914	37.50
Cup & saucer, Johnson Bros.	9.50
Egg cup, Allertons	15.00
Egg cup, Burleigh	7.50
Foot warmer, Booths, 8¼"	98.00
Ginger jar, Sadler, 5" h.	40.00
Gravy boat, child's, Occupied Japan	35.00
Gravy boat w/attached underplate, Allertons	52.00
Gravy boat w/attached underplate, handled, Wood & Sons	36.00
Marmalade jar, cov., Ridgway	25.00
Mug, 2½" h.	38.00
Mug, Japan, 3½" h.	13.00
Mustard jar, cov.	65.00
Pitcher, 4½" h., bulbous, Ridgway ..	37.00
Pitcher, 5¼" h., Allertons	58.00
Pitcher, milk, Allertons	137.00
Pitcher, milk, Japan	45.00
Plates, bread & butter, 5¾" d., Allertons, pr. (ILLUS.)	15.00
Plate, 6" d., Buffalo Pottery, 1911 ...	10.00
Plate, 7" d., Booths, ca. 1912	15.00
Plates, 7" d., Royal Worcester, ca. 1882, set of 8	100.00
Plate, 8" d., Johnson Bros.	10.00
Plate, 8" d., Booths, ca. 1912	20.00
Plate, 9" d., England	12.50
Plate, 9" d., Made in Japan	5.00
Plate, 10" d., Booths, ca. 1912	25.00
Plate, 10½" d., Mason's	55.00
Platter, 8" oval, Johnson Bros.	18.00
Platter, 9" l., Wedgwood	48.00
Platter, 11½" l., Homer Laughlin ...	13.00

Buffalo Pottery Blue Willow Platter

Platter, 12 x 9½", Buffalo Pottery, 1908 (ILLUS.)	40.00
Platter, 13" l., Shenango Pottery	17.50
Platter, 15¼ x 12", Allertons	58.00
Platter w/well & tree center, 17½ x 13", on 3" h. horseshoe-shaped foot, Adams & Prince, late 18th-early 19th c.	250.00
Salt & pepper shakers, large, Japan, pr.	20.00
Sauce dish, Meakin	10.00
Sauce dish, Shenango Pottery, 5" d.	7.50
Sauce tureen, Wedgwood	75.00
Soup ladle, Ridgway	95.00
Soup plate w/flange rim, England ..	15.00
Soup plate w/flange rim, Homer Laughlin	7.00
Sugar bowl, cov., Shenango Pottery	15.00
Sugar bowl, cov., Wood & Sons	35.00
Teacup, handleless, Buffalo Pottery	20.00

barrel-shaped, John-
..., 40-oz., 6½" h. 55.00
teapot, cov., made for Lawleys,
1925-40...................... 85.00

Child's Teapot

Tea set, child's: cov. teapot, cov.
sugar bowl, creamer & 6 c/s;
Japan, 15 pcs. (ILLUS. of
teapot) 120.00
Tea set: cov. teapot, creamer &
sugar bowl; individual size,
Sadler, 3 pcs. 35.00
Tea set: cov. teapot, creamer, cov.
sugar bowl, 4 c/s & 4 plates;
Occupied Japan, 15 pcs. 105.00
Tea tile, Allertons, 6½" d. 33.00
Toast rack 75.00
Toothpick holder, Japan 24.00
Tureen, Ridgway, 12½ x 8" 325.00
Vegetable dish, cov., 2-handled,
Buffalo Pottery, 1911, 9" d....... 50.00
Vegetable dish, cov., Wood & Sons,
9" sq., 5¾" h. 55.00
Vegetable dish, cov., Ridgway,
9½" d. 75.00
Vegetable dish, cov., divided,
England 110.00
Vegetable dish, open, Allertons,
9" oval 30.00

BOCH FRERES

Boch Freres Vases

*This Belgium firm, founded in 1841 and still
in production, first produced stoneware art
pottery of mediocre quality, attempting to upgrade their wares through the years. In 1907,
Charles Catteau became the art director of the
pottery and slowly the influence of his work
was absorbed by the artisans surrounding
him. All through the 1920's, wares were decorated in a distinctive Art Deco motif that is
now eagerly sought along with the hand-
thrown gourd form vessels coated with earth-
tone glazes that were produced during the
same time. Almost all Boch Freres pottery
is marked, but the finest wares also carry the
signature of Charles Catteau in addition to
the pottery mark.*

Vase, 8 3/8" h., modeled as 3 upright square columns on base, abstract geometric orange & black
designs on white ground, ca. 1925
(ILLUS. back right).............$660.00
Vase, 8¾" h., 7¼" d., overall Art
Deco blue florals w/gilt & green
accents & yellow berries decor,
glossy finish 225.00
Vases, 9" h., bulbous, brown & yellow flowerheads amidst blue
leaves on cream-crackled ground,
pr............................ 330.00
Vase, 9" h., cylindrical center section surrounded by curved upright
compartments on circular base,
incised & glazed vivid yellow &
black geometric designs resembling buildings & balloons decor
on white-crackled ground, ca.
1925, signed (ILLUS. back
left)......................... 880.00
Vase, 9½" h., ovoid, blue, turquoise
& black abstract design on vivid
yellow-crackled ground, signed ... 220.00
Vase, 9¾" h., ovoid, peach & tan
florals amidst dark brown & green
leaves on turquoise ground 110.00
Vase, 10" h., tiered cylinder, frieze
of stylized turquoise, navy & black
falcons on white-crackled band ... 308.00
Vase, 10½" h., ovoid, navy blue,
aquamarine, yellow & ochre stylized florals on blue ground....... 220.00
Vases, 11" & 7" h., ovoid, incised &
glazed turquoise & lapis blue,
mustard yellow & black geometric
devices on white-crackled ground,
ca. 1925, signed, pr. (ILLUS. center front & left) 440.00
Vase, 12" h., baluster-shaped, 7
columns of yellow semi-circles
bordered in turquoise & black on
white-crackled ground 220.00
Vase, 12" h., bulbous, gunmetal-
glazed flowerheads & leaves
w/green accents on white 165.00

Vases, 12" h., ovoid, blue-crackled
  glaze, pr........................ 150.00
Vase, 13½" h., 8-sided cylinder
  w/stepped neck, black, white &
  yellow 176.00

BOEHM PORCELAINS

Fledgling Great Horned Owl

*Although not antique, Boehm porcelain
sculptures have attracted much interest, Edward Marshall Boehm excelled in hard porcelain sculptures. His finest creations,
inspired by the beauties of nature, are in the
forms of birds and flowers. Since his death
in 1969, his work has been carried on by his
wife at the Boehm Studios in Trenton, New
Jersey. In 1971, an additional studio was
opened in Malvern, England, where bone porcelain sculptures are produced. We list both
limited and non-limited editions of the Boehm
Studios.*

Boxer, 1950, 9 x 8½" $450.00
Chick, 1954 .... 175.00
Dalmation "Mike," Anheuser-Busch
  mascot, glazed, 1955-59, 3 x 1".... 350.00
Fawn, ca. 1954, 4 x 3" 150.00
Fledgling Bluebird, 1958 .... 220.00
Fledgling Blue Jay, 1957 ...200.00 to 265.00
Fledgling Cedar Waxwing, 1957-73 .. 205.00
Fledgling Chickadee,
  1962-72 ....165.00 to 185.00
Fledgling Goldfinch, 1959-72........ 150.00
Fledgling Great Horned Owl,
  1965-70, 7 x 5" (ILLUS.) 1,500.00
Fledgling Kingfisher, 1960..200.00 to 240.00
Fledgling Magpie, 1964-72.......... 225.00
Fledgling Robin, 1957 .... 240.00
Fledgling Western Bluebirds, 1968-73
  (ILLUS.)......................... 475.00
Fledgling Woodthrush, 1958 .... 240.00
Indigo Bunting, 1957.......410.00 to 450.00
Jaguar, 1981-82, 18" w., 7" d.,
  9¼" h. 2,900.00

Fledgling Western Bluebirds

Lesser Prairie Chickens, 1962-74,
  10" h., pr........................ 950.00
Meadowlark, 1957-64, 8½ x 7½" ... 835.00
Mourning Doves, 1981-82, 13" w.,
  11" d., 17" h. 2,200.00
Nancy Reagan Camellia, 1981-82,
  7½" w., 5¾" d., 3½" h......... 650.00
Northern Baltimore Oriole, 1981-82,
  8½" w., 5" d., 12¾" h. 1,750.00
Otter, 1976 .... 975.00
Prince Charles Rose & Lady Diana
  Rose Floral, 1981-82, 5½" w.,
  4½" d., 6¼" h. 750.00
Prothonotary Warbler,
  1958 ....500.00 to 600.00
Red-Breasted Grosbeaks, 1952,
  pr...........................1,000.00
Red Fox, 1951..................... 300.00
Streptocalyx Poeppigii, 1973,
  19 x 12" 4,600.00
Young and Spirited 1976, 2 fledgling
  American Bald Eagles, 1975-76,
  10½ x 9½".................... 900.00

BOW

Blue-and-White Bow Dish

*The Bow China Works was established in
London about 1747 by Thomas Frye and was
in operation for approximately three decades.*

...uin was produced but attri-
...fficult.

...s ot flowers, each modeled as
a brown-striated yellow "wicker"
basket w/openwork sides formed
of interlocking circlets, filled
w/bouquet of rose, yellow, blue,
iron-red & white blossoms &
green leaves, 4 5/8" & 4 3/8" h.,
pr............................$770.00
Dishes, octagonal, painted oriental-
style decor of pagodas in an extensive river landscape w/figure
in boat center, stylized flowering
lotus & chrysanthemum border,
blue & white, ca. 1750, 10½" l.,
pr. (ILLUS. of one).............. 770.00

Quail Pattern Dish

Dish, octagonal, painted iron-red,
blue, green & gilt oriental-style
Quail patt., iron-red & gilt flowerhead border, ca. 1755, 12½" l.
(ILLUS.)........................ 880.00
Figures of a shepherd & shepherdess: he playing the flute & wearing a flowered jacket & breeches,
w/dog by his side; she wearing a
green bodice & flowered skirt, her
apron filled w/flowers, w/lamb by
her side; on pierced scroll-molded
bases enriched in gilding & applied w/flowerheads, ca. 1755,
7" h., pr. (some repairs &
chips) 880.00
Model of a South American parrot,
predominantly green plumage
delineated in grey & heightened
in purple, blue & yellow, black
eyes, tan beak, head & feet,
clasping an iron-red berry in claw
& perched on a chartreuse-
heightened tree stump applied
w/blue, yellow & puce florettes &
green leaves above a puce-edged
scrolling tripod base, 1758-60,
6 5/8" h.......................7,425.00
Plate, 9¼" d., painted figure & boat
in river landscape center, shaped

panels enclosing floral sprays &
oriental-style river landscapes
border, powder blue ground,
ca. 1755 .... 242.00
Spoon tray, shaped oval, enameled
"famille rose" scene of birds in
flight among flowering chrysanthemum issuing from rockwork,
brown rim, ca. 1755, 6¾" w...... 495.00
Sweetmeat dish & cover w/conch
shell finial, 3 shells supported on
rockwork & applied w/crustacean,
ca. 1755, 7¾" d. (small chips to
shell edges & repaired finial)..... 550.00

BUFFALO POTTERY

*Buffalo Pottery was established in 1902 in
Buffalo, N.Y., to supply pottery for the Larkin Company. Most desirable today is Deldare Ware, introduced in 1908 in two
patterns, "The Fallowfield Hunt" and "Ye
Olden Times," which featured central
English scenes and a continuous border.
Emerald Deldare, introduced in 1911, was
banded with stylized flowers & geometric designs and had varied central scenes, the most
popular being from "The Tours of Dr. Syntax." Reorganized in 1940, the company now
specializes in hotel china. Also see BECK and
BLUE WILLOW under Ceramics.*

DELDARE

Deldare Tankard Pitcher & Candlestick

Bowl, cereal, 6½" d., Ye Olden
Days $195.00
Bowl, fruit, 9" d., 3¾" h., The Fal-
lowfield Hunt - The Death........ 550.00
Bowl, fruit, 9" d., Ye Village
Tavern ....325.00 to 425.00
Bowl, 9" d., Ye Village Street 250.00
Cake plate w/pierced handles, Ye
Village Gossips, 10" d. 200.00

Candlestick, Ye Olden Times,
8¾" h. (ILLUS. right) ....275.00 to 350.00
Candlesticks, Village Scenes,
9½" h., pr...................... 695.00
Card tray, The Fallowfield Hunt -
The Return, 7¾" d. .....280.00 to 375.00
Card tray, Ye Olden Days, artist-
signed, 6½ x 3¾" 235.00
Creamer & cov. sugar bowl, The Fal-
lowfield Hunt - Breaking Cover,
pr............................ 425.00
Cup & saucer, The Fallowfield Hunt -
The Return 200.00
Cup & saucer, Ye Olden
Days...................150.00 to 190.00
Dresser tray, Dancing Ye Minuet,
12 x 9"........................ 500.00
Humidor, cov., octagonal, Ye Lion
Inn, 7" h. 595.00
Mug, The Fallowfield Hunt - Break-
ing Cover, 3½" h............... 270.00
Mug, Ye Lion Inn, 3½" h. 250.00
Mug, The Fallowfield Hunt - The
Death, 4½" h. 270.00
Nut bowl, Ye Lion Inn, 1909, 8" d.,
3¼" h. 380.00
Pitcher, 6" h., octagonal, The Fal-
lowfield Hunt, artist-signed 360.00
Pitcher, 6" h., octagonal, "Their
Manner of Telling Stories - Which
he Returned with a Curtsy," artist-
signed 400.00
Pitcher, 7" h., octagonal, "To Spare
an Old Broken Soldier" one side,
"To Advise Me in a Whisper" re-
verse, dated 1923 .... 475.00
Pitcher, 10" h., octagonal, Ye Olde
English Village 510.00
Pitcher, tankard, 12½" h., "All You
Have To Do Is Teach the Dutch-
man English" one side, "The
Great Controversy" reverse
(ILLUS. left) 875.00
Plaque, Ye Lion Inn, 1909,
12" d. 435.00
Plaque, "Thursday" - Monks fishing
or "Friday" - Monks dining on fish
caught the day before, 12" d.,
each 1,200.00
Plate, 7½" d., The Fallowfield
Hunt - Breaking Cover 160.00
Plate, 8½" d., The Fallowfield
Hunt - The Start 180.00
Plate, 8½" d., The Fallowfield
Hunt - The Death, 1909 .... 195.00
Plate, 8½" d., Ye Town
Crier..................135.00 to 175.00
Plate, 9½" d., The Fallowfield
Hunt - The Start, artist-signed 195.00
Plate, chop, 14" d., An Evening at
Ye Lion Inn, pierced to hang,
artist-signed...........475.00 to 550.00
Plate, chop, 14" d., The Fallowfield
Hunt - The Start........500.00 to 575.00

Punch bowl, The Fallowfield Hunt,
14½" d..............4,275.00 to 5,000.00

Fallowfield Hunt Soup Plate

Soup plate w/flange rim, The Fal-
lowfield Hunt - Breaking Cover,
9" d. (ILLUS.) ....160.00 to 225.00
Teapot, cov., Scenes of Village Life
in Ye Olden Days, 5¾" h. 300.00
Tea tile, The Fallowfield Hunt -
Breaking Cover, artist-signed,
6" d.......................... 225.00
Tea tile, Traveling in Ye Olden
Days, 6" d. ....195.00 to 250.00

Heirlooms Tea Tray

Tea tray, Heirlooms, 13¾ x 10¼"
(ILLUS.)...................... 550.00
Vase, 9" h., hourglass shape, Ye
Olden Village Scenes 325.00

EMERALD DELDARE
Cup & saucer, Dr. Syntax
scenes 350.00
Inkwell, Art Nouveau geometric
decor (top missing) 210.00
Mug, Dr. Syntax scenes, "I give to
the law that are owing, etc.,"
2¼" h........................ 275.00
Pin tray, Dr. Syntax Received by the
Maid 650.00

Plate, 7¼" d., Dr. Syntax
Soliloquising 425.00
Plate, 8¼" d., Art Nouveau florals &
geometric 325.00
Plate, 8½" d., Misfortune at Tulip
Hall 425.00
Plate, chop, 13½" d., Dr. Syntax
sells Grizzle 875.00
Salt shaker, Art Nouveau geometric
& florals, 3" h. (single) 235.00

MISCELLANEOUS

Bluebird Pattern Buffalo China

Bowl, 6" d., Abino Ware 425.00
Butter pat, Blue Willow patt. 20.00
Butter pat, multicolored Art Deco
border, dated 1927 . . . . 10.00
Christmas plate, 1950 . . . . 35.00
Christmas plate, 1951 . . . . 42.00
Christmas plate, 1955 . . . . 35.00
Christmas plate, 1956 . . . . 45.00
Christmas plate, 1957 . . . . 35.00
Christmas plate, 1959 . . . . 32.50
Cup, Blue Willow patt., farmer
size . . . . 25.00 to 40.00
Cup & saucer, Bluebird patt.
(ILLUS.) 7.50
Cup & saucer, Blue Willow patt.,
regular size 18.50

"ABC" Feeding Dish

Feeding dish, ABC border & Dolly
Dingles & Sammy center, signed
Grace Drayton (ILLUS.) 57.50
Fish set: large platter & six 9" d.
plates; various species of game
fish depicted, signed R.K. Beck,
7 pcs. 235.00
Game plate, American Herring Gull,
9" d. 45.00
Gravy boat, Blue Willow patt.,
small 15.00
Jug, Cinderella, 6" h. . . . . . . 325.00 to 400.00
Jug, Rip Van Winkle, dated 1906,
6½" h. . . . . 435.00 to 475.00
Jug, George Washington, blue
decor, gold trim,
7½" h. . . . . 400.00 to 500.00
Jug, Robin Hood, 8¼" h. . . 325.00 to 400.00
Mug, advertising, "Bing & Nathan,"
monk reverse 75.00
Mug, commemorative, "Souvenir of
Calumet Club, Buffalo, N.Y., April
24, 1911" 60.00
Pitcher, 7" h., Chrysanthemum patt.,
blue & white 40.00
Pitcher, 9¼" h., Gloriana 365.00
Pitcher, 9¼" h., Sailor 550.00
Plate, 6½" d., Bluebird patt. (ILLUS.
w/cup & saucer) 6.00
Plate, 7½" d., commemorative,
Generals Wolfe & Montcalm,
w/portraits & monuments, Canadi-
an provinces border, 1908 . . . . 100.00
Plate, 7½" d., commemorative, The
White House, green border 50.00
Plate, 8½" d., Blue Willow
patt. 15.00
Plate, 9¼" d., Blue Willow
patt. 18.00
Plate, 10" d., "Erie Canal" decor 100.00
Plate, 10" d., historical series, The
Capitol Building, Washington,
D.C., blue-green 35.00
Plate, 10" d., historical series,
Faneuil Hall, Boston, Cradle of
Liberty, blue-green on
white 30.00
Plate, 10" d., historical series, Inde-
pendence Hall in Philadelphia,
blue-green on white 30.00
Plate, 10" d., historical series, The
White House, Washington, blue-
green on white 35.00
Plate, 10½" d., Abino Ware, Fishing
Boats scene, artist-signed 302.50
Plate, 10½" d., commemorative,
New Bedford, Massachusetts, bor-
der of whaling & sea scenes, blue
on white, 1908 . . . . 77.50
Platter, 10½ x 8½", Blue Willow
patt. 30.00
Platter, 12 x 9½", Blue Willow patt.,
1916 . . . . 38.00

Platter, 14½" l., Blue Willow
  patt. 45.00
Platter, 16 x 13", Blue Willow
  patt. 75.00
Relish dish, shell-shaped,
  1915 . . . . 40.00
Sauce dish, Blue Willow patt.,
  5" d. 3.00
Shaving mug, scuttle-type, "Wild
  Root" 125.00
Teapot, cov., w/attached metal tea-
  ball, Argyle patt. . . . . . . 125.00 to 150.00
Vegetable dish, cov., Blue Willow
  patt., 11½ x 9" 35.00
Vegetable dish, commercial ware,
  "Biltmore Hotel," green band
  w/pink flowers interior &
  exterior 32.00

CALIFORNIA FAIENCE

Chauncey R. Thomas and William V. Brag-
don organized what was to become Califor-
nia Faience pottery in 1916, in Berkeley,
California. Originally named after its owners,
it later became The Tile Shop, finally adopt-
ing the California Faience name about 1924.
Always a small operation whose output was
a simple style of art pottery, most of which
has a matte glaze that was designed for the
florist shop trade, it also made colorfully deco-
rated tiles. During the mid-1920's, California
Porcelain was produced by this firm for the
West Coast Porcelain Manufacturers of Mill-
brae, California. The great Depression halt-
ed art pottery production and none was
produced after 1930 although some tiles were
made for the Chicago World's Fair about
1932. Collectors now seek out these somewhat
scarce pieces that always bear the incised
mark of California Faience. Also see TILES.

Bowl, 6" d., 2" h., scalloped rim,
  blue interior, black matte finish
  exterior $85.00
Candlesticks, mauve to purple high
  glaze, 7" h., pr. 195.00
Candlesticks, glossy blue glaze,
  pr. 95.00
Console bowl & figure flower
  holder, blue-glazed shell form
  bowl & Chinese laundry woman 6-
  color figure, artist-signed, 15"
  bowl & 6½" h. flower frog,
  2 pcs. 375.00
Potpourri jar, cov., yellow matte
  finish 225.00
Vase, 5½" h., bulbous, ribbed,
  glossy purple glaze 165.00
Vase, 10" h., tan drip over salmon
  pink glaze 195.00

CANTON

Canton Figural Candle Holders

This ware has been produced for nearly two
centuries in potteries near Canton, China. In-
tended for export sale, much of it was origi-
nally inexpensive blue-and-white hand
decorated ware. Late 18th and early 19th cen-
tury pieces are superior to later ones and fetch
higher prices

Candle holders, figural elephants
  w/flaring candle nozzles atop saddles, "famille-rose" decor, each
  w/gilt-striated coral-red hide &
  wearing gilt-ground blanket
  w/pattern of pink-flowered green
  vines, saddles suspending back
  panels painted w/songbirds
  amongst prunus, one holder base
  & one tail restored, 19th c.,
  8¾" w., pr. (ILLUS.) $6,600.00
Dish, enameled "famille-rose" decor
  heightened in gilding w/a cricket,
  butterflies & beetles amidst a
  large cluster of flowers & fruit,
  w/border of butterflies amidst a
  profusion of flowers & fruit, gilt-
  edged rim, mid-19th c., 14¾" d. . . . 440.00
Garden seats, pierced top & sides,
  "famille-rose" decor, painted
  overall w/butterflies amidst
  clusters of flowers & fruit, 2 large
  panels of Mandarin figures at various pursuits reserved between
  rows of gilt-heightened bosses
  w/smaller panels of figures or
  birds above & below, top w/four
  melon-shaped panels of figures on
  gilt ground embellished w/pink-
  flowered green vines, 19th c.,
  19¼" h., pr. 9,350.00
Hot water dish, Inclined Pines patt.,
  figure crossing a bridge in river
  landscape w/paagodas, trellis diapered design at cavetto & rim, exterior w/six floral sprays,
  blue-and-white, Nanking,
  1790-1810, 15½" oval 715.00
Plate, 10" d., bright yellow ground
  painted in shades of pink, purple,

green & blue w/butterfly hovering above peonies & other flowers, pink scrolling vine at cavetto, border w/lavender cell diapered ground reserved w/four yellow panels of fruit & flowers, underside painted on a yellow ground w/crane within a millefleurs border, pale green & black scrolling vine at cavetto, rim w/lush flowering vine interrupted by pink bats, 19th c. 3,850.00

Platter, 12¾ x 10½", blue-and-white, 19th c................... 325.00

Teapot & cover w/berry finial, blue-and-white, ca. 1790 .... 340.00

Vases, 8¾" h., cylindrical, "famille-rose" decor, front & reverse w/panel of Mandarin figures within a gilt Greek key border surrounded by smaller figural panels, clusters of precious objects & sprigs of flowers & fruit, everted rim (each w/restored chip) w/gilt-ground floral border, late 19th c., pr........................... 275.00

Vegetable dish & cover w/knob finial, slit handles, landscape scene, blue-and-white, 8½" d., 4¾" h........................ 255.00

CAPO DI MONTE

Capo-di-Monte Figures

Production of porcelain and faience began in 1736 at the Capo-di-Monte factory in Naples. In 1743 King Charles of Naples established a factory there that made wares with relief decoration. In 1759 the factory was moved to Buen Retiro near Madrid, operating until 1808. Another Naples pottery was opened in 1771 and operated until 1806 when its molds were acquired by the Doccia factory of Florence, which has since made reproductions of original Capo-di-Monte pieces with the "N" mark beneath a crown.

Some very early pieces are valued in the thousands of dollars but the subsequent productions are considerably lower.

Box, cov., enameled relief-molded romantic scene on cover, side panels w/cherubs in various pursuits, gold interior, gilt bronze fittings, 3 1/8" d. \$410.00

Dresser box w/hinged lid, enameled relief-molded scene of children seated in garden on lid, gold interior, ca. 1830 .... 225.00

Figure of a man playing a trumpet, 6" h.......................... 125.00

Figure of "Il Dottore," wearing brimmed floppy hat, flowing coat, breeches & a sash as belt, his right hand held to his face, on shaped rockwork base, all white, 1743-56, 8½" h. (repairs & damage to fingers, hands & sash) 550.00

Figures of soldiers, each modelled as Napoleon or one of his officers & wearing colorful military attire, on square base w/title in gilding, 9" to 9 7/8" h., set of 12 (ILLUS. of part).......................1,100.00

Figures of cherubs in various playful poses, small, set of 6........... 500.00

Figure group, cherubs (3) w/floral garlands, 6" w., 7" h. 250.00

Jewel box, cov., enameled relief-molded scene of hunter & bear on cover, side panels w/various animals, gold trim, velvet-lined interior, gilt bronze fittings, ca. 1820, 5½ x 2½", 3" h. 750.00

Urn, cov., 2-handled, relief-molded cherubs, 8½" h. 225.00

CATALINA ISLAND POTTERY

The Clay Products Division of the Santa Catalina Island Co. produced a variety of wares during their brief ten-year operation. The brainchild of chewing-gum magnate, William Wrigley, Jr., owner of Catalina Island at the time, and his business associate D.M. Retton, the plant was established at Pebbly Beach, near Avalon in 1927. Its two-fold goal was to provide year-round work for the island's residents and building material for Wrigley's ongoing development of a major tourist attraction at Avalon. Early production consisted of brick, roof and patio tiles. Later, art pottery, including vases, flower bowls, lamps and home accessories, were made from a local brown-based clay and, about 1930, tablewares were introduced. These early wares carried vivid glazes but had a tendency to chip readily and a white-bodied, more chip-resistant clay, imported from the mainland was used after 1932. The costs associated with importing clay eventually caused the Catalina pottery to be sold to a California mainland competitor in 1937. These wares were molded and are not hand-thrown but some pieces have handpainted decoration.

Catalina Pottery Planter

Ash tray, model of a cowboy hat,
  blue glaze $15.00
Ash tray, Siesta patt., white glaze,
  h.p. scene 125.00
Candlestick, 2-handled, cobalt blue
  glaze (single) 29.00
Console set: 17" l. console bowl &
  pr. lilypad form candle holders;
  green matte finish, 3 pcs. 150.00
Cruet, gourd-shaped, green glaze .. 36.00
Figure of a mermaid on a shell, turquoise blue & brown glaze, dated
  1937 .... 95.00
Flower frog, Art Deco form, beige
  glaze 12.00
Jardiniere w/lid, h.p. florals on
  medium blue matte finish,
  3½" h. 42.00
Jardiniere w/lid, h.p. sailboat scene
  on blue matte finish, 7" h. 60.00
Mug, early brown clay body, green
  matte finish 42.50
Planter, bust of a girl, matte terra
  cotta skin tones, high glaze turquoise bandana (ILLUS.) 35.00
Plaque, pierced to hang, h.p. scene
  of San Luis Mission 150.00
Plate, 7" d., h.p. scene of Avalon
  Bay 18.00
Tray, scalloped edge, green exteri-
  or, pink interior, 14" oval 15.00
Vase, 6" h., white clay, pink glaze .. 12.00
Vase, 6½" h., matte green finish ... 17.50
Vase, 7" h., ovoid, cactus blossoms
  in low relief, ivory glaze 25.00
Vase, 8" h., blue glaze, pink
  lining 30.00
Vase, 8" h., green drip glaze....... 30.00

Vase, 8" h., ringed body, "Descan-
  so" green matte glaze 40.00
Vase, 8½" h., Toyan red
  glaze .... 60.00 to 75.00
Vase, 9" h., white clay body, turquoise glaze 18.00
Vase, 9½" h., flared lip, Toyan red
  glaze 75.00
Wall pocket, molded basketweave,
  orange glaze 65.00

CAULDON, LTD.

Cauldon Chamber Set

The Staffordshire pottery at Cauldon Place, Shelton, was a direct descendant of the famed Ridgway potteries. After John Ridgway dissolved his partnership with his brother, William, in 1830, he operated the Cauldon Place works independently, selling out to T.C. Brown-Westhead, Moore & Co. in 1855. He remained active in the firm several years. Brown-Westhead, Moore & Co. became Cauldon, Ltd. in 1905 and continued in operation until acquired by Pountney & Co. Ltd. of Bristol in 1962.

Chamber set: wash basin, pitcher,
  cov. slop jar, cov. chamber pot,
  toothbrush holder & (repaired)
  cov. soap dish; colorful rhododen-
  dron decor on creamy ivory
  ground, Brown-Westhead, Moore
  & Co., ca. 1870, 6 pcs. (ILLUS.) ...$220.00
Charger, Poppies patt., 11½" d. 95.00
Fish plates, varying species of fish
  on each, soft peach border
  w/heavy gold tracery, artist-
  signed, set of 10 .... 750.00
Jar, cov., h.p. cattle scene on cream
  ground w/gold trim, artist-signed,
  1905-20, 3 5/8" d., 6" h. 150.00
Plates, 8" d., Indian Tree patt., set
  of 5 .... 55.00
Plates, 10½" d., h.p. floral spray
  center, inner wide gold mosaic
  band & wide cobalt blue border
  w/gold trim, set of 12 .... 350.00
Plate, large h.p. roses overall highlighted w/gold & turquoise
  enameling 450.00
Tea set: cov. teapot, creamer &
  sugar bowl; white w/heavy gold
  trim, 3 pcs. 125.00

CELADON

Celadon Bowl

Celadon is the name given a highly-fired Oriental porcelain featuring a glaze that ranges from olive through tones of green, blue-green and greys. These wares have been made for centuries in China, Korea and Japan. Fine early Celadon wares are costly, later pieces are far less expensive.

Bowl, 6" d., 3" h., China, Ming
Dynasty, 14-15th c. $350.00
Bowl, 12 5/16" d., incised central
floral ornament & line borders,
green, China, possibly Yuan
Dynasty, 1260-1368 (ILLUS.) 1,210.00
Candle holders, model of a Kylin in
recumbent position, its head
slightly turned to one side &
holder rising from middle of back,
China, Ch'ing Dynasty, early
19th c., 5½" l., pr. 1,100.00
Cup & saucer, Rose Mandarin patt.,
large size, China, Ch'ing Dynasty,
ca. 1850 . . . . 90.00
Dish, impressed center peony
medallion & incised wave band interior, carved petal flutes exteri-
or, deep olive green glaze, early
15th c., 12¾" d. 495.00
Garden seat, overall florals & birds
in relief on green celadon ground,
China, Ch'ing Dynasty, ca. 1775,
large. 500.00
Garden seat, barrel form, molded
w/four lion mask & mock ring
handles, top carved w/floral
motifs, China, Ming Dynasty
1368-1643, 17" h. 2,090.00

Jar, relief-carved chrysanthemum
petals below shoulders, under-
glaze-red 3-toed dragon decor &
carved billowing clouds above,

Chinese Celadon Jar

China, K'ang Hsi reign, 1662-1722,
10½" d. (ILLUS.) 1,320.00
Plate, 7¼" d., China, Ch'ing
Dynasty, early 20th c. 48.00
Plate, 9½" d., Thousand Butterflies
decor 135.00
Rice bowl, aqua-green, China,
Ch'ing Dynasty, 19th c., 6" d. 75.00
Teacup & saucer, "famille rose"
decor, China, Ch'ing Dynasty,
ca. 1750 . . . . 90.00
Vase, 14½" h., carved in sinuous
low relief w/full-blown tree peony
branches above band of overlapping leaves, shoulder w/spiralling
petals below short cogwheel-
decorated neck, crackled water-
green glaze, China, Ming Dynasty,
15th c.. . . . . .3,300.00

CHELSEA

Chelsea Leaf-Molded Dish

This ware was made in London from 1754 to 1770 in England's second porcelain facto-ry. From 1770 to 1783 it was operated as a branch of the Derby Factory. Its equipment was then moved to Derby. It has been reproduced and ceramics made elsewhere are often erroneously called Chelsea.

Bowl, 6 3/8" d., exterior naturalistically molded w/overlapping cabbage leaves shading from
emerald green to yellow &
w/puce midribs rising from puce
to yellow footrim, interior painted
in shades of rose, blue, yellow,
iron-red, mauve & green w/floral
bouquet, 3 sprigs & a leaf spray,
red anchor period, ca. 1755.....$4,510.00
Dishes, fig leaf shape, h.p. center
floral spray on puce veining, serrated rim shaded spring green to
yellow, olive brown twig handle,
red anchor period, ca. 1755, 8" l.,
pr. 1,210.00
Dish, modeled as a sunflower & 2
leaves, yellow petals & purple-
brown center, leaves & handle enriched in green, red anchor period, ca. 1755, 9¼" w. (small chip
repairs to petals) 3,850.00
Dish, relief-molded w/various
leaves enriched in tones of green,
yellow, puce & turquoise on
basketwork ground, rim w/brown-
line edge, red anchor period,
ca. 1760, 10" d. (ILLUS.) 2,200.00
Dishes, modeled as a leaf w/puce
veining & green edges resting on
a pierced basket, interior painted
w/tulip sprays, gilt rim, red anchor period, ca. 1760, 10¾" w.,
pr. (one w/footrim chip) 2,090.00

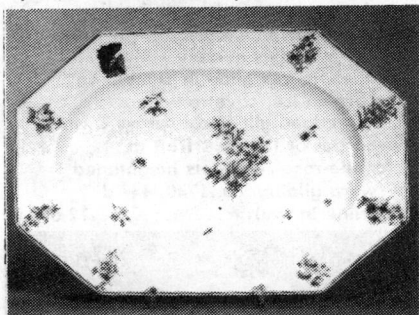

Chelsea Octagonal Oblong Dish

Dishes, octagonal, painted bouquets
& scattered florals sprays center,
trellis-molded border enclosing
oval cartouches of painted butterflies, insects & floral sprays,
brown-line rim, red anchor period, ca. 1750, 12½" l., pr. (ILLUS.
of one) 1,760.00
Needle case, modeled as an aspara-
gus spear, enriched in pale yellow
& green, gilt-metal hinge, ca.
1775, 4¾" l. (repaired) 1,100.00
Plates, 9" d., painted bouquets &
scattered floral sprays center,

feather-molded rim enriched in
green & iron-red, red anchor
period, ca. 1755, pr. (small rim
chip on one) 770.00
Plate, 9 1/8" d., "Hans Sloane,"
large painted spray of yellow &
red apples, green & yellow leaves
& blue blossoms issuing from a
brown branch w/mauve floral
sprigs, 2 leaf sprigs, ladybird & 2
shaded insects to the left, rim
edged in dark brown, late red-
early gold anchor period,
ca. 1758 . . . . .7,700.00
Plate, 9¼" d., painted exotic bird
perched on rockwork center,
borders w/two further birds
perched on foliage branches,
scroll-molded rim enriched in gilt
& blue, red anchor period,
ca. 1775 . . . . .1,760.00
Plate, 9¼" d., painted fruit & foli-
age center, shaped scroll-molded
rim w/five lappet-shaped reserve
panels painted w/moths & highlighted w/gilt & blue, turquoise
& gilt edge, red anchor period,
ca. 1763 . . . . .2,640.00
Plate, 9¼" d., "Hans Sloane," large
painted spray of puce & yellow
flowers w/iron-red, turquoise &
black centers, blue buds & shaded
green & yellow leaves, w/a purple, blue & iron-red dragonfly, a
ladybird, yellow berry sprig &
brown beetle to the left, rim
edged in dark brown, late red
anchor period, ca. 1758 . . . . .11,000.00
Plates, 9¼" d., each painted w/bril-
liant palette exotic birds perched
on rockwork, borders w/two lesser birds among foliage branches,
rims molded w/scrolls & foliage
enriched in blue & gilt, gilt anchor
period, ca. 1765, pr. 2,850.00

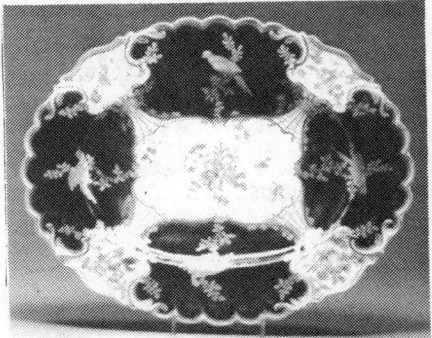

"Mazarine Blue" Oval Platter

Platter, 12 3/8" l., center reserve
painted w/rose, iron-red, puce,

green & mustard yellow floral
cluster & sprigs within gilt scroll &
trelliswork, molded cartouches on
rim painted w/similar floral
clusters rserved between blue
ground decorated in tooled gilding
w/birds perched on leafy
branches, scalloped rim edge
w/feathered gilding, gold anchor
period, 1760-65 (ILLUS.) 770.00
Scent bottle w/stopper, naturalis-
tically modeled as a pale yellow to
puce peach, surmounted by 3
grey-veined green leaves & a
green bud issuing from a mauve
stem, stopper formed as a cluster
of green buds mounted in gilt-
metal at neck, red anchor period,
ca. 1755, 2¼" h. (chips) 1,100.00

CHELSEA LUSTRE WARE

Chelsea Sprig Lustre Pattern

*The name for this ware is misleading since
the design is thought to have originated at
the Coalport, Shropshire, England porcelain
factory during the 1880's, long after the closing of the Chelsea factory. In this attractive
pattern, small grape clusters or sprigs are
raised in relief and colored in blue or purple
lustre on a white ground. It was a popular
pattern from the earliest Victorian years and
is often referred to as "Grandmother's Ware."*

Bowl, 6" d., 3½" h.	$28.00
Cake plate, 10" d.	40.00
Cup & saucer	22.50
Pitcher, milk	50.00
Plate, 9" d.	28.00
Sugar bowl, cov.	48.00
Teapot, cov. (ILLUS.)	135.00

CHINESE EXPORT

*Large quantities of porcelain have been
made in China for export to America from the
1780's, much of it shipped from the ports of
Canton and Nanking. A major source of this*
*porcelain was Ching-te-Chen in the Kiangsi
province but the wares were also made elsewhere. The largest quantities were blue and
white. Prices fluctuate considerably depending on age, condition, decoration, etc. Also see
CANTON and ROSE MEDALLION.*

Barber's Bowl

Barber's bowl, "famille-rose" decor,
painted rose, blue, green, yellow,
turquoise & iron-red flowering
peony branches & vase of flowers
center & 3 floral sprays at rim
(w/repaired chips), ca. 1750,
10½" d. (ILLUS.) $605.00
Charger, "Skating Lesson," painted
center scene of Dutchman holding
long pick on which his student companion steadies herself while 5
smaller figures glide or tumble on
the brown ice, cavetto w/four
brown-edged gilt floral sprays & rim
w/border of florals & fruit in
"famille-rose" enamels heightened
w/worn gilding, ca. 1740, 14" d.
(hairline in rim) 12,650.00

Cider or Ale Jug

Cider (or ale) jug & cover, painted
w/Toby Philpot wearing black hat &

shoes, green coat, white waist &
yellow breeches & seated on iron-
red chair holding page from "Tris-
tram Shandy" on front & w/spread
table reverse, entwined reeded
strap handle (w/hair crack one end)
w/salmon & gilt floral terminals &
cover w/gilt-heightened crouching
beast knop, 1790-1800, 10 1/8" h.
(ILLUS.) 8,525.00
Cup & saucer, "famille-rose" decor,
petal-molded cup enameled w/lo-
tus & applied w/three openwork
lotus sprays curling under to form
foot & saucer molded & decorated
w/peony, dogwood & chrysanthemum sprays enclosing a
medallion 770.00
Custard cup, cov., orange Fitzhugh
patt., w/motto, ca. 1810,
3¼" h......................... 990.00
Ecuelle, cover & stand, each painted
in shades of underglaze-blue w/two
ladies conversing before a garden
fence; ecuelle w/fan-shaped handles pierced w/three hearts; cover
w/green-leafed gold fruit sprig
knop; stand w/central blue floral
sprig within molded ring, ca. 1700,
8 1/8" d. stand 1,760.00

"Lotus" Bowl, Cover & Stand

"Lotus" bowl, cover & stand: the
bowl modeled as a realistic flower
w/partially opened petals & enameled in shaded pink & lime green;
"seeded" cover in pale turquoise
w/iron-red & gilt bud finial; wavy
rim stand centered w/realistic lotus
enclosed by blossoming puce floral
sprays; minor damage, early 19th
c., 6½" d. bowl (ILLUS.) 2,750.00
Model of an owl, brown plumage,
black & yellow eyes, black beak &
black-dashed feet, perched on a
black, turquoise & blue mottled &
pierced rockwork base, late 18th-
early 19th c., 10¼" h............7,150.00
Mug, cylindrical body, painted iron-
red, turquoise-green, black, gold,
blue & terra cotta version of "La

Dame au Parasol" (after Cornelis
Pronk), w/continuous scene of
Chinese lady holding a parasol
above small boy walking toward
water birds beneath bats, iron-red
scroll border at flaring foot, 1740-50,
5½" h. 1,210.00
Pitcher, 9" h., figural fish w/tail
forming handle, flowing blue
cloud mounds near base, "orange
peel" glaze 235.00
Plate, 8 7/8" d., "famille-rose"
decor, enameled scene of lady
wearing black & shaded yellow
costume, holding a fly whisk &
watching another lady, wearing a
rose robe, seated at a marble
table in a garden setting w/two
cranes nearby, cavetto w/blue
foliate scroll border, oxidized
silver-ground rim reserved w/four
black fan-shaped panels of gilt
peony sprigs alternating w/four
iron-red cartouches of gilt scrolling foliage, 1735-40 ....1,760.00
Plate, 9" d., "Judgment of Paris,"
enameled center mythological
scene w/Paris seated & awarding
a gilt apple to Aphrodite flanked
by Hera & Athena holding a
spear, w/a spotted dog & young
attendant at their feet, everted
rim w/puce scrolling shell & leaf
band, ca. 1780 .... 660.00
Plates, 9 5/8" d., Bengal Tiger patt.,
painted center rose-red chrysanthemum blossoms surrounded by 4
panels of blue, iron-red, yellow,
rose, green & gold beasts on pla-
teaux or vases of flowers on
tables reserved within iron-red
borders against grey-stippled
green ground beneath iron-red
demilune devices & within border
of iron-red & green cell diaperwork interrupted by floral panels
on the gilt-edged rim, 1805-15,
pr. (tiny hair cracks in one)......1,760.00
Plate, 9¾" d., brown Fitzhugh patt.
w/monogram, ca. 1810 .... 770.00
Plate, 10¼" d., painted center
scene after sketch by Cornelis
Pronk w/Chinese lady wearing
gilt-heightened blue & lavender
costume beside another wearing a
gilt-patterned blue robe & holding
a flower within a topiary arbor,
w/a young boy to the right, 3
children to the left & 3 ducks in a
pond at the foreground, gilt-
edged rim w/patterned turquoise
ground reserved w/panels of colorful fruit, florals or insects alternating w/iron-red shell &

Painted after Cornelis Pronk Sketch

palmette motifs & iron-red lappet
& aubergine tassel border, ca.
1740, repaired chip on underside
(ILLUS) 7,975.00

Pseudo Tobacco Leaf Pattern Platter

Platter, 16¾" oval, Pseudo Tobacco
Leaf patt., painted iron-red, chartreuse, yellow, rose, salmon &
brown design heightened w/gilt
"mons," iron-red-edged gilt band
border, 1765-75, repaired rim chip
(ILLUS.) 2,090.00

Platter with Motto

Platter, 20" oval, center enameled
in color w/scene of courtier holding an archaic vessel aloft & surrounded by his companions on
steps of pavilion, rim w/wide continuous band of sailing vessels in
river landscape interrupted by an
"en grisaille" eagle's wing crest
above banner inscribed w/motto
"Veritas Vincit Omnia," ca. 1805
(ILLUS.) 2,420.00
Punch bowl, "famille-rose" &
"grisaille" decor w/gold, scene
of Oriental figures & animals on
bank of river w/European sailing
ships & other vessels reserved in
large oblong panel on front &
back within underglaze-blue blossom & foliate scrollwork border
flanked by square panels at sides
painted w/birds in flight or
perched on branches within conforming borders, interior w/large
central spray of florals & fruit
below an underglaze-blue cell
diaper border at rim, ca. 1770,
16" d. 4,730.00
Sauce tureen, cover w/gilt flower
finial & stand, entwined berried
branch handles, brown Fitzhugh
patt., early 19th c., 8" oval 1,430.00
Soup plates, "famille-rose" decor,
painted w/species of blossoming
peonies sprouting from rockwork
in shaded colors & gilt, ca. 1750,
pr. (rim frit on one) 825.00
Tea bowls & saucers, Rockefeller
patt., exterior w/two large oval
panels of ladies at their leisure on
fenced terraces in river landscapes, divided by small shaped
brown & sepia landscape panels
reserved on a gilt scrolling foliage
ground, interior w/band of alternating quatrefoil panels of
"grisaille" birds perched on
branches on a brown trellis
ground, ca. 1770, pr. 660.00
Teapot, cov., globular, "famille-
rose" decor, molded & applied
each side w/pierced hanging
flower basket holding enameled
colorful stems w/raised blossoming flowers between narrow
brown bands of gilt foliage, scalloped domed cover w/high openwork blossoming peony finial,
ca. 1750, 6½" w. 715.00
Tureen & cover w/lotus bud knop,
painted "famille-rose" & "grisaille" decor w/flowering peonies
growing from stylized rockwork,
semi-circular handles (repaired
chips) w/iron-red & gold demi-

Chinese Export Tureen

chrysanthemum blossoms edged in
iron-red, ca. 1760, 12¾" l.
(ILLUS.) 1,320.00
Tureen, cover w/bud finial & stand,
pale iron-red & gilt intertwining
branch handles, green Fitzhugh
patt., w/crest surrounded by motto
"Laus Virtutis Acito," ca. 1820,
14½" oval 3,520.00
Vase, 18" h., ovoid w/short neck,
"famille-rose" decor, enameled
multicolored phoenix birds, cranes,
cockerels & ravens amidst peonies
& plums beneath a magnolia tree,
late 19th c. 1,430.00

CLARICE CLIFF DESIGNS

"Bizarre" Tea Set

Clarice Cliff was a designer for A.J. Wilkinson, Ltd., Royal Staffordshire Pottery, Burslem, England when they acquired the adjoining Newport Pottery Company whose warehouses were filled with undecorated bowls and vases. About 1925, her flair with the Art Deco style was incorporated into designs appropriately named "Bizarre" and "Fantasque" and the warehouse stockpile was decorated in vivid colors. These hand-painted earthenwares, all bearing the signature of designer Clarice Cliff, were produced until World War II and are now finding enormous favor with collectors.

Ash tray, Tonquin patt. $16.00
Basket w/overhead handle, "Bizarre," multicolored Art Deco
   decor, 13" h. 475.00
Bowl, 8" d., "Bizarre," Crocus
   patt. 65.00
Bowl, 9" d., "Bizarre," Gay Day
   patt., vivid florals on cream
   ground, silverplate rim 125.00
Cookie jar, cov., "Bizarre," My
   Garden patt., 6¼" d., 7¼" h. 150.00
Creamer, Pineapple patt., 3¾" h. .. 39.00
Flower frog, mottled green & cream
   stylized pile of rocks w/dark
   brown base, 3 5/8" d., 3¾" h. ... 72.00
Honey pot, cov., "Fantasque," vivid
   orange, blue, green, brown &
   cream decor 65.00
Ivy ring, "Bizarre," green stripes &
   stylized trees decor 135.00
Pitcher, 7¾" h., Autumn Crocus
   patt. 450.00
Pitcher, 8" h., "Fantasque," Land-
   scape patt. 150.00
Pitcher, 10¼" h., 6" d., jug-type,
   Celtic Harvest patt., multicolored
   fruits & florals on cream & gold
   ground 171.00
Plate, 6" sq., "Bizarre," Crocus
   patt. 12.00
Plate, 9" oblong, "Bizarre," Viscaria
   patt. 25.00
Plate, 9¾" d., tan trees w/aqua
   foliage on light grey ground, aqua
   rim 90.00
Platter, 11" l., Tonquin patt........ 30.00
Sauce dish, "Bizarre," Gay Day
   patt. 45.00
Sugar shaker w/metal top, Gay Day
   patt. 50.00
Teapot, cov., Celtic Harvest patt.,
   6" h. 215.00
Tea set: cov. teapot, creamer, sugar
   bowl & 6 c/s; "Bizarre," green,
   orange, black & blue Art Deco
   heart motif on cream ground, 1
   saucer & sugar bowl restored,
   hairline in teapot, 15 pcs. (ILLUS.
   of part) 660.00
Tureen, "Bizarre," Islands Moderne
   patt. 65.00
Tureen, "Fantasque," Canterbury
   Bells patt. 120.00
Vase, 7¼" h., 4 1/8" d., Art Deco
   orange, green & gold florals
   w/rust leaves & tan branches in
   relief on light grey shaded to
   green ground 75.00
Vase, 8" h., 5 5/8" d., brown &
   green branch feet extending up
   sides, Art Deco orange & yellow
   florals w/blue leaves in relief on
   light grey ground, mint green
   interior...................... 110.00

CLEWELL WARES

Clewell Vase

Though Charles W. Clewell of Canton, Ohio, didn't operate a pottery, he is responsible for a category of fine art pottery through his development of a unique metal coating placed on pottery blanks obtained from Owens, Weller and others. By encasing objects in a thin metal shell, he produced copper and bronze finish ceramics. Later experiments led him to chemically treat the metal coating to attain the blue-green patinated effect associated with copper and bronze. Although he produced metal-coated pottery from 1902 until the mid-1950's, Clewell production was quite limited for he felt no one else could competently re-create his artwork and, therefore, operated a small shop with little help.

Box, cov., round, copper-covered
  w/patinated finish & riveted
  seams........................$260.00
Mug, copper-covered w/patinated
  finish & riveted seams...100.00 to 125.00
Planter, bulbous, copper-covered
  w/patinated finish, 6" d..........180.00
Vase, 5" h., copper-covered
  w/green patinated finish.........150.00
Vase, 5½" h., copper-covered
  w/green patinated finish.........150.00
Vase, 5¾" h., copper-covered
  w/patinated finish..............150.00
Vase, 9" h., cylindrical, copper-
  covered w/patinated finish.......176.00
Vase, bud, 10" h., copper-covered
  w/patinated finish..............180.00
Vase, 10¼" h., elongated handles,
  incised decor, copper-covered
  w/patinated finish (ILLUS.).......350.00

CLEWS, J. & R.

James and Ralph Clews established this pottery in Cobridge, England in 1814 and operated it until 1836 when it was taken over by Wood & Brownfield. Some of the wares have been reproduced. Also see CUP PLATES and HISTORICAL & COMMEMORATIVE CHINA.

Cup & saucer, Rebecca at the
  Well $140.00
Cup & saucer, Wilkie series, blue
  transfer "Christmas Eve" 150.00
Plate, 7½" d., Don Quixote series,
  dark blue transfer "Sancho, the
  Priest and the Barber"...........160.00
Plate, 9" d., Wilkie series, dark blue
  transfer "Christmas Eve" (minor
  edge wear) 155.00
Plate, 10" d., Dr. Syntax series,
  dark blue transfer "Dr. Syntax
  Taking Possession of His Living" ..95.00

Dr. Syntax Plate

Plate, 10½" d., Dr. Syntax series,
  blue transfer "Dr. Syntax Bound to
  a Tree by Highwaymen" (ILLUS.) ..125.00
Plate, 10½" d., Dr. Syntax series,
  blue transfer "Dr. Syntax Drawing
  After Nature" 125.00
Plate, 10½" d., dark blue transfer
  of an oriental pagoda by a river ..80.00
Platter, 16½" l., Don Quixote
  series, dark blue transfer "The
  Knight of the Wood Conquered" ..475.00

Clews Platter

Platters, 9 5/8", 12½" & 15 3/8" l.,

Dr. Syntax series dark blue trans-
fer "Dr. Syntax Setting Out on His
Second Tour," "Dr. Syntax Sells
Grizzle" & Wilkie series dark blue
transfer "The Valentine," 3 pcs.
(ILLUS. of one) 1,430.00
Soup plate w/flange rim, Tinturn
Abbey patt..................... 100.00

CLIFTON ART POTTERY

CLIFTON *Clifton*

Clifton Art Pottery Marks

William A. Long, an organizer of the Lon-
huda Pottery, and Fred Tschirner, a chemist,
established the Clifton Art Pottery in New-
ark, New Jersey, in 1905. The first art pottery
produced was designated the Crystal Patina
line and was decorated with a subdued pale
green crystalline glaze which was later also
made in shades of yellow and tan. Indian
Ware, introduced in 1906, was patterned af-
ter the pottery made by the American Indi-
ans. These two lines are the most notable in
the pottery's production though Tirrube and
Robin's-egg Blue lines were also produced.
After 1911, production shifted to floor and
wall tiles and by 1914 the pottery's name was
changed to Clifton Porcelain Tile Company
to better reflect this production.

Flower pot, Indian Ware, dark red
clay w/black & cream geometric
designs, 3½" h................. $50.00
Pedestal, Indian Ware, 10" w. base,
5¼" w. top, 10½" h. 80.00
Pitcher, bulbous, Indian Ware, dark
red clay w/black & cream geometric designs, artist-signed 50.00
Pot, Indian Ware, 3" h. 40.00
Teapot, cov., Indian Ware, small ... 55.00
Vase, 4¾" h., bulbous, Crystal
Patina line, green crystalline
glaze, 1903 .... 100.00

COALPORT

Coalport Porcelain Works operated at Coal-
port, Shropshire, England, from about 1795
to 1926 and has operated at Stoke-on-Trent
as Coalport China, Ltd., making bone china
since then.

Basket, h.p. bouquet of flowers
within pink & gilt floral garland
border on pink ground, shaped
rim enriched in pink & gilt enclosing peach-colored panels, entwined strap handle w/gilding,
ca. 1830, 11½" w...............$245.00
Dessert service: pr. 2-handled
square & 2-handled oval dishes,
pr. leaf-shaped dishes & 18 plates;
h.p. garden flower bouquets within gilt foliage, scroll & shell motifs, apple green borders enriched
w/gilt fruiting vines, ca. 1820,
24 pcs. 2,310.00

Coalport Fruit Cooler

Fruit coolers, covers & liners, overall pattern of blue & gilt flowering
chrysanthemums & foliage, gilt
handles & finial, ca. 1800 (repair
to one), 10¾" h. (ILLUS. of
one)..........................1,320.00
Jardinieres & stands, tapering cylinder molded w/ring handles on
sides, each front reserved w/lake-
land landscape panel w/figures
painted in shades of green,
brown, purple, blue & yellow
within gilt-edged border surrounded by purple drapery continuing to the reverse & then
swagged above basket of fruit
or roses on the capital of a
truncated column, rims & stands
w/patterned gilt borders, 1800-05,
7" & 6 7/8" h., pr. 1,100.00
Plates, dessert, 8¾" d., h.p. floral
bouquet center, rim w/three floral
clusters within gilt-edged panels
reserved on mint green ground
patterned w/gilt & reticulated
diamond-shaped zones, ca. 1850,
set of 16 .... 935.00
Plate, 9" d., pink roses & vivid
green garlands decor, heavy gold
trim, artist-signed, made for Davis
Collamore, New York............ 85.00
Platter, 16½" l., Japan patt., painted underglaze blue, iron-red,

Japan Pattern Platter

peach & gilt w/stylized large floral spray center & gilt-edged rim
w/panels of birds & florals, ca.
1805 (ILLUS.) 350.00
Tea set: cov. teapot w/stand, cov.
sugar bowl, milk jug, 2 cake
plates, 8 teacups, 8 coffee cups &
8 saucers; trailing iron-red foliage
between stylized gilt lappets, ca.
1820, 29 pcs.................... 330.00

COPELAND & SPODE

Spode Basket & Stand

*W.T. Copeland & Sons, Ltd., have operat-
ed the Spode works at Stoke, England, from
1847 to the present. The name Spode was
used on some of its productions. Its predeces-
sor, Spode, was founded by Josiah Spode
about 1784 and became Copeland & Garrett
in 1843, continuing under that name until
1847. Listings dated prior to 1843 should be
attributed to Spode. Also see COM-
MEMORATIVE PLATES and TOBY
MUGS & JUGS.*

Baskets, exteriors molded as scallop
shells enriched in puce, blue &
yellow, interior painted w/formal
scrolling foliage, base & handles
enriched in brown, green & yellow, 4 ball feet, Spode, ca. 1820,
7" l., pr. (1 handle repaired) $770.00
Baskets & stands, creamware, ob-

long 2-handled basketware molded basket w/pierced borders &
shell & scroll motifs & matching
stand, painted green & brown
flowerhead motifs, impressed
Spode mark, ca. 1810, w/repairs
to feet, 10½" l. baskets, 4 pcs.
(ILLUS. of 2) 935.00
Cheese dish, cov., Spode's Tower
patt., blue transfer 135.00
Compote, 9½" d., 2¾" h., open latticework rim, enameled turquoise
dogs & florals on white ground,
gold trim 200.00
Compote, Spode's Net patt., blue
transfer, ca. 1810 .... 295.00
Creamer, Spode's Tower patt., blue
transfer 45.00
Cup & saucer, Italian patt., blue
transfer, large 55.00
Cup & saucer, Spode's Tower patt.,
"We'll Take a Cup O' Kindness
Yet," red transfer 45.00
Dessert set: oval compote, 2 shaped
oval dishes & 14 plates; decorated
"en grisaille" on pale yellow
ground w/birds in landscape cartouches & floral sprays, scroll &
foliate molded rim enriched
w/gilding, Spode, ca. 1820,
17 pcs. 660.00
Dishes, pr. kidney-shaped dishes
transfer-printed in blue w/flower-
ing plants divided by panels of
gilt foliage on grey ground &
w/gilt basket of flowers center &
2-handled dish w/gilt foliage on
mushroom-colored ground, each
w/scroll-molded handles enriched
in gilding, ca. 1800, 11½" d.,
3 pcs. 198.00
Fish platter, h.p. Imari-style florals
& scrolls in cobalt blue, rust, pink
& green, 1847-67 mark,
14½ x 10" 250.00
Flower center, parian, pedestal
base, lacy gilt decor, ca. 1850 .... 185.00
Pitcher, 6½" h., Spode's Fortuna
patt., white horse, rider & dog on
greyish green ground 135.00
Pitcher, 8" h., parian, scene of
Chicago Fire around top, body
w/three medallions of Indians,
Frontiersmen & Miss Liberty
w/eagle & 8 small cameo reliefs
of Mrs. O'Leary's cow, Fort
Dearborn, etc., blue & white,
designed by Frank E. Burley for
Burley & Co., Chicago, limited
edition .... 250.00 to 400.00
Pitcher, water, 8½" h., 8" w., blue
Willow patt., 1847-67 .... 150.00
Plate, 7" d., Trophies patt. 15.00
Plates, 8 3/8" d., gilt roundel of

hatchwork & stylized floral & foliate motifs center, double border
of gilt C-scrolls & dots forming 4
panels, each painted w/a cluster
of fruit & leaves, an exotic bird or
an arrangement of feathers &
shells at cavetto, cobalt blue &
gilt zigzag border w/scalloped
gilt-edged rim, ca. 1820, pr...... 385.00
Platter, 12½"l., Spode's Camelia
patt., blue transfer 75.00
Platter, 19 x 14", Spode's Net patt.,
blue transfer, ca. 1810 .... 350.00
Vase, 7½" h., floral arrangement
reserved on pale green ground
heightened w/heavy gilt scrolling,
Copeland & Garrett, ca. 1850..... 225.00
Vegetable dish, cov., Spode's Net
patt., blue transfer, ca. 1810 ..... 250.00
Vegetable dish, Italian patt., blue
transfer, 11¾ x 7½" 50.00
Vegetable dish, oval, Spode's Tower
patt., pink transfer 45.00

Spode Nautilus Shell Wall Pockets

Wall pockets, modeled as a Nautilus
shell, mottled pink & orange
Moonlight Lustre, one w/major
repair, Spode, ca. 1815, 10½" &
11" l., pr. (ILLUS.) 467.00
Warming plate, Spode's Net patt.,
blue transfer, ca. 1810.......... 195.00

CORDEY

Founded by Boleslaw Cybis in Trenton, New Jersey, the Cordey China Company was the forerunner of the Cybis Studio, renowned for its fine porcelain sculptures. A native of Poland, Boleslaw Cybis was commissioned by his government to paint "el fresco" murals for the 1939 New York World's Fair. Already a renowned sculptor and painter, he elected to remain and become a citizen of this coun-
try. In 1942, under his guidance, Cordey China Company began producing appealing busts and figurines, some decorated by applying real lace dipped in liquid clay prior to firing in the kiln. Cordey figures were assigned numbers that were printed or pressed on the base. The Cordey line was eventually phased out of production during the 1950's as the porcelain sculptures of the Cybis Studios became widely acclaimed. Also see CYBIS.

Bust of a lady, on blue scroll-molded
base, No. 1013, 6½" h.......... $85.00
Bust of a lady wearing a veil,
No. 5026, 7" h. 52.50
Bust of a lady, Queen Elizabeth-type
woman, grey garments, No. 5060,
9½" h....................67.50 to 95.00
Bust of a Russian peasant, No. 103,
15" h......................... 195.00
Busts: lady (No. 3006) & gentleman
(No. 3007); finely molded, each
6" h., pr...................... 110.00
Figure of a gentleman, Colonial
attire, No. 4050, 10¾" h. 78.00
Figure of a gentleman, wearing
frock coat, lace collar, cuffs &
fringed vest, No. 4074, 12" h. 110.00
Figure of a gentleman, Colonial
aristocrat, garments w/porcelain
lace trim, No. 4087-D, 16" h. 115.00
Figure of a girl, Sophisticated
series, No. 5059, 10¾" h......... 75.00
Figure of a girl, Junior Miss series,
No. 5030 .... 62.50
Figure of a grape harvester (lady),
w/fruit in her skirt, No. 304,
16" h......................... 85.00
Figure of a grape harvester (man),
No. 305, 16" h. 55.00

Cordey Half Figure

Figure of a lady, wearing hat
w/pink roses, grey & blue dress
w/lace trim, No. 5036, 9" h.
(ILLUS.)...................... 95.00

Figure of a lady, frilly dress
w/flowers & lace, No. 4062,
10¾" h. 80.00
Figure of a lady, Victorian Godey-
type dress w/ruffles, pleats &
lace, wearing a hat, No. 5062,
13½" h. 135.00
Figure of a lady, wearing lavender
dress, long coat & tall hat, lace &
roses trim, No. 5066, 14" h. 165.00
Figure of a lady, "Madame
DuBarry," No. 5061, 14" h. 185.00
Figure of a lady, wasp-waisted Victorian dress w/bustle & lace,
No. 5584, 16" h. 155.00
Model of bluebird on tree stump,
No. 6004 .... 75.00
Models of black & yellow bird on
tree stump, one facing left &
other right, No. 6023, pr. 140.00
Model of a shoe, No. 1039, 7" h. ... 40.00
Wall pocket, Victorian lady's face in
full relief, ringlets in hair, roses &
lacy wrap at throat, No. 902,
10¼" h. 165.00

COWAN

COWAN

COWAN

Cowan Pottery Mark

*R. Guy Cowan first opened a studio pottery
in 1913 in Cleveland, Ohio. The pottery continued to operate almost continuously, at various locations in the Cleveland area, until it
was forced to close in 1931, due to financial
problems. This fine art pottery, which was
gradually expanded into a full line of commercial productions, is now sought out by collectors.*

Ash tray, gazelle decor, flame
orange & brown glaze $60.00

Cowan Lustre Finish Bowl

Bowl, 7½" d., 2½" h., blue lustre
finish (ILLUS.) 35.00
Bowl, 7½" d., low, blue lustre
finish 16.50
Bowl, 10½" hexagon, pedestal
base, blue lustre finish 25.00
Candle holder, 3-light, branch form,
ivory glaze (single) 65.00
Candle holders, blue lustre finish,
4" h., pr. 21.00
Candle holders, model of a seahorse, 4" h., pr. 20.00
Candlesticks, green matte finish,
4" d., 4" h., pr. 25.00
Candlesticks, handled, white glaze,
4" d., 5" h., pr. 32.00
Figure of a nude lady, ivory glaze,
8" h. 110.00
Figures, Spanish Dancers, ivory
glaze, designed by Alexander
Blazys, pr. 650.00
Flower frog, figural dancing nude
lady w/scarf, 6½" h. 165.00
Flower frog, figural nude lady
w/arms raised, ivory glaze,
6½" h. ....115.00 to 145.00
Matchbook holder, seahorse base,
ivory glaze, 3½" h. 22.00
Trivet, scalloped rim, bust of young
girl framed by flowers, 6½" d. ... 250.00
Vase, 4" h., flowing rust glaze over
green 45.00
Vase, 5" h., horizontally ribbed,
pink glaze 50.00
Vase, 5½" h., matte rose shaded to
bright green finish 60.00
Vase, bud, 6½" h., green
glaze 45.00
Vase, 6½" h., teal blue & maroon
glaze 75.00
Vase, 7" h., aqua & gold glaze 65.00
Vase, 9" h., dragonfly & cattails
decor 88.00
Vase, 9½" h., trumpet-shaped,
flowing iridescent lavender glaze
over beige..................... 90.00
Vase, 12" h., 12" widest d.,
2-handled, oriental red glaze 175.00

CUP PLATES (Staffordshire)

*Like their glass counterparts, these small
plates were designed to hold a cup while the
tea or coffee was allowed to cool in a saucer
before it was sipped from the saucer, a practice that would now be considered in poor
taste. The forerunner of the glass cup plates,
those listed below were produced in various
Staffordshire potteries in England. Their
popularity waned after the introduction of the*

*glass cup plate in the 1820's. Also see CUP
PLATES under Glass and FLOW BLUE
CHINA.*

Adams (W.) & Sons, scene of man
    fishing, black transfer, 4 1/8" d... $25.00
Clews, scene of lady seated in
    wheelbarrow & poem, 1818-34,
    4½" d. 60.00
Ironstone china, Huron shape, all
    white, W. Adams, 4 7/8" d. 12.50
Unmarked Staffordshire, Baronial
    Hall scene, purple transfer 30.00
Unmarked Staffordshire, Chinese
    garden scene w/two women &
    flowers, lustred rim, impressed
    numerals underside, 5" d. 32.50
Unmarked Staffordshire, Corinthian
    patt., blue transfer 32.00
Unmarked Staffordshire, Gothic
    Ruins scene, red transfer 30.00
Unmarked Staffordshire, Marcella
    patt., purple transfer 30.00

Elephant "Alexander,"
    7½ x 6½"............... 225.00 to 275.00
Elizabeth Ann, 5" 200.00
Eros (Cupid) Head on stand, 10" h... 295.00
Eskimo Child Head "Snow Bunting,"
    10½" 325.00
Gretel, 7" 325.00
Hansel, 9" 325.00
Jessica, 9¼" 225.00
Lidded Heart "Thinking of You,"
    4½ x 4", 3" h. 95.00
Madonna "Queen of Angels,"
    11" .... 175.00 to 195.00
Melissa, 10" 450.00
Pandora, 5".......................... 250.00
Peter Pan, 7½" (ILLUS.) 300.00
Pollyanna, 7" 225.00
Priscilla, 14" 950.00
Raccoon "Raffles," 7½ x 9" 250.00
Rose, 5" 265.00
Seal "Sebastian," 5½" 45.00
Unicorns "Gambol & Frolic,"
    8 x 12½" 650.00
Wendy, 6½"............... 150.00 to 215.00
Windflower, 8".................... 250.00
Yankee Doodle Dandy, 9".......... 325.00

CYBIS

Peter Pan

*Though not antique, fine Cybis porcelain
figures are included here because of the great
collector interest. They are produced in both
limited edition and non-numbered series and
thus there can be a wide price range available
to the collector. Also see CORDEY.*

Ballerina "Little Princes," 10" $450.00
Child Clown Head "Funny Face,"
    10½" 325.00
Cybele, 11 x 9½" 575.00
Deer Mouse "In Clover," 3½" 200.00
Desdemona, No. 90 .... 1,500.00

DAVENPORT

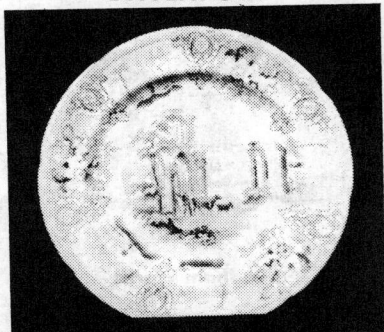

Davenport Plate with Castle Ruins Scene

*The Davenport factory operated under various names at Longport, England, from about
1794 to 1887. Various marks were used, including an anchor. Also see FLOW BLUE,
INVALID FEEDERS and IRONSTONE.*

Compote, 8½" d., 2½" h., relief-
    molded florals at turquoise & gilt
    border, center w/scene of man
    fishing & cows at edge of lake,
    ca. 1860 .... $85.00
Cups & saucers, bone china, florals
    & leaves decor, set of 6 .... 350.00
Pitcher, 7½" h., jug-type, rural
    scenery transfer................. 96.00
Plate, 7 1/8" d., "Legend of Mont-
    rose" transfer, 1850-70 .... 30.00 to 45.00

Plate, 7½" d., Castle Ruins, light
blue transfer (ILLUS.) 68.00

Plate, 7½" d., Grecian urns &
florals on portico, lavender transfer, 1854 English Registry mark ... 25.00

Plate, 9 3/8" d., Cyprus patt.,
mulberry-sepia transfer,
ca. 1850 .... 40.00

Platter, 13¾ x 10 3/8" oblong w/cut
corners, mulberry transfer 95.00

Platter, 18 x 15", Chinoiserie-
Bridgeless patt., blue transfer,
ca. 1810 .... 450.00

Punch bowl, interior w/iron-red,
blue & gilt flowering chrysanthemum issuing from rockwork
within an iron-red trellis pattern
border, rim w/flowering foliage
on a blue ground, exterior
w/band of gilt seaweed on pale
blue ground between bands of
dark blue foliage, ca. 1830,
14" d. 2,200.00

Toothbrush holder, Cyprus patt.,
mulberry-sepia transfer, ca. 1850,
8 x 3½"..................... 125.00

Creamer, Magnolia 100.00
Creamer & open sugar bowl,
Elephant, pr.................. 550.00
Cup & saucer, Elephant (ILLUS.
center) 440.00
Dish, 5-sided, Rabbit, 7¾" w. 330.00
Egg cup, single, Elephant,
2½" h..................300.00 to 385.00
Pitcher, Azalea 325.00
Planter, green circular mirror de-
sign, 6 x 3¼", 3¼" h......... 200.00
Planter, green zig-zag decor, 8¼ x
5¾", 3¾" h................. 450.00
Planter, ruffled, green blocked mir-
ror, 8¾ x 5¼", 3¾" h. 350.00
Plate, 6" d., Elephant 275.00
Plate, 6" d., Grape 95.00
Plate, 6" d., Horse Chestnut........ 65.00
Plate, 8½" d., Duck 105.00
Plate, 8½" d., Grape......100.00 to 140.00
Plate, 8½" d., Horse Chestnut...... 155.00
Plate, 8½" d., Lobster (ILLUS.
right) 440.00
Plate, 8½" d., Paired Turtle (ILLUS.
left)...................... 660.00
Plate, 8½" d., Rabbit......90.00 to 145.00
Plate, 10" d., Mushroom 250.00
Plate, 10" d., Turkey ......265.00 to 330.00
Plate, 12" d., Rabbit 225.00
Platter, 12½" l., Rabbit 220.00
Salt shaker, Rabbit (single)........ 135.00
Tea cup, Snowtree, 4" d., 2¼" h... 95.00
Vase, 6" h., "volcanic" green glaze
w/highlights 200.00

DEDHAM

Dedham Wares

*This pottery was organized in 1866 by Alex-
ander W. Robertson in Chelsea, Mass., and
became A. W. & H. Robertson in 1868. In
1872, the name was changed to Chelsea Keramic Art Works and in 1891 to Chelsea Pottery, U.S.A. About 1895, the pottery was
moved to Dedham, Mass., and was renamed
Dedham Pottery. Production ceased in 1943.
High-fired colored wares and crackle ware
were specialities. The rabbit is said to have
been the most popular decoration on crackle
ware in blue.*

Basin, shallow w/flared lip, Rabbit,
12" d., (some minor glaze flaw) ..$220.00
Bowl, cov., 9" d., Rabbit (some sand
damage) 275.00
Bowl, 6" d., rolled rim, Elephant.... 275.00
Bowl, 7¼" d., Elephant 660.00
Bowl, 7½" d., deep, Rabbit 150.00
Bowl, 10½" d., 2½" h., Rabbit 375.00

Dedham Crackleware Vase

Vase, 7" h., swollen cylinder
w/short neck, butterfly decor on
crackle ground (ILLUS.) 425.00
Vase, 8" h., red, orange & black
"volcanic" glaze 1,000.00
Vase, 8¼" h., baluster-shaped,
green "volcanic" glaze mottled
w/blue & maroon 308.00
Vase, 8½" h., baluster-shaped,
deep oxblood glaze (unsigned) ... 825.00

Vase, 9" h., 6½" d., bulbous
w/short neck & wide mouth,
glossy olive green experimental
glaze 247.50

DELFT

Delft "Adam & Eve" Charger

Delft, a tin-glazed pottery, is of a type that originated in Belgium and Italy centuries ago. Because Dutch traders made the city of Delft the center of their world-wide trade on these items, the term "delft" became synonymous with "tin-glazed pottery." The use of delft to indicate only blue and white is in error since all potters worked in polychrome as well. Delft, faience, and majolica are all tin-glazed pottery.

Apothecary jar, blue & white, Dutch,
18th c., 7½" h. $165.00
Charger, "Adam & Eve," poly-
chrome, painted blue figures
standing on turquoise ground beneath blue-sponged trees bearing
russet-heightened yellow apples &
w/serpent entwined around the
trunk, rim w/blue & yellow bands
within blue-dashed edge, lead-
glazed underside, Bristol, 1700-10,
11¾" d. 1,430.00
Charger, "Adam & Eve," poly-
chrome, painted blue figures
w/manganese hair holding
yellow-ribbed green fig leaves &
walking amidst green & blue-
sponged shrubbery beneath apple
tree w/iron-red-striped yellow
serpent entwined around the
trunk, blue-dashed rim, Bristol,
ca. 1720, 13 5/8" d. (ILLUS.) 1,650.00
Charger, blue & white, painted
Wanli style, center w/jardiniere

filled w/flowers, leaves & scroll
placed on stand in fenced garden
within an octagonal panel, floral
& patterned panel border on scalloped rim, underside w/dotted circles & X's, Dutch, early 18th c.
(restored rim chips) 550.00
Dish, fluted, polychrome, painted
iron-red, salmon, blue & gold
w/central basket of flowers within
lambrequin-bordered roundel,
fluted rim w/conforming border,
Dutch, De Grieksche A, ca. 1710,
"PAK" momogram for Pieter
Adriaensz Kocks, 6 1/8" d. 1,650.00
Dish, deep, polychrome, painted
blue, green, orange & yellow
crane & 2 insects in flight above
pr. pheasants & flowering plants
near a garden fence w/unfurled
scroll of floral vines to right, underside w/pale blue band border,
Dutch, De Drye Clocken Factory,
mid-18th c., 13½" d. 687.00
Drug jar w/domed brass cover,
painted elaborate scroll & foliage
cartouche supporting vase of flowers enclosing the drug name
"SPAANSE," blue & white, Dutch,
ca. 1760, 10½" h. 1,430.00
Garniture set: pr. beaker-shaped
vases & three 10½" h. baluster-
shaped vases w/domed covers;
painted overall blue flowerheads
& foliage on brown ground,
Dutch, ca. 1760, 5 pcs. 990.00
Models of seated spaniels, each
looking straight ahead, on oblong
bases w/canted corners, white
coats enriched w/blue, Dutch,
ca. 1740, 7¼" h., pr. (glaze
repair to one & minor glaze
chips) 2,640.00

Dutch Delft Wall Plaque

Plaques, pierced to hang, painted
manganese bouquets of flowers

within shaped rims & shell motifs,
Dutch, late 18th-early 19th c.,
w/repairs, 14¾" w., pr. (ILLUS. of
one) 1,045.00
Plaque, pierced to hang, painted
portrait of lovely lady center, blue
& white, Dutch, 19th c., 16½" d. . . 395.00
Plates, 8¼" d., polychrome, painted
manganese, green, blue & yellow
bird perched on flowering tree by
building center, border w/stylized
flowerheads, Bristol, ca. 1750,
pr. 385.00
Plate, 9" d., blue w/yellow trim,
Dutch, 18th c. 150.00
Plate, 13½" d., polychrome, painted
blue, iron-red, yellow & green
scene of Chinaman beneath tree
in a fenced garden w/hills in the
distance, rim w/border of flower
swags & sprigs, London, 1750 . . . . 880.00
Plate, 13 5/8" d., polychrome, painted blue, iron-red, green & yellow
bird perched on flowering shrubbery & watching an insect in
flight, rim w/border of petal-
shaped panels of floral sprigs
within stylized flowerhead & leaf-
scroll edge, Dutch, mid-18th c. . . . 330.00
Puzzle jug, pear-shaped body painted w/birds on rocks amidst shrubbery within 3 panels separated by
smaller floral panels above "ruyi-
head" & scroll border, the neck
pierced around floral sprigs &
leafage w/three-spout rim &
pierced gallery, blue & white,
Dutch, De Drye Porceleyne
Flesschen, ca. 1710, 8" h. 1,430.00
Tea caddy, oblong form w/cylindri-
cal neck, blue & white, front & reverse w/slightly raised panel
painted w/two birds amidst oriental shrubbery within herringbone
& trefoil border, the sides
w/"cracked ice" & lotus sprig
ground reserved w/leaf-shaped
panel of perched bird, shoulders
w/scroll-patterned ground reserved w/floral quatrefoils, Dutch,
De Grieksche, ca. 1700, "AD"
monogram for Adriaensz Kocks,
6¼" h. (restored neck) 990.00
Teapot, cov., ball-shaped w/flat
lid & straight spout, brown-ground
body painted w/yellow floral sprigs,
Dutch, Het Jonge Moriaenshooft,
ca. 1700, 2 7/8" h. (rim chip) 1,320.00
Tile picture, 6-tile, manganese, depicting the Prince of Orange on a
horse in a landscape, inscribed
"Prins van Oranje" above, Dutch,
18th c., overall 15¼ x 10¼"
(some repair) 1,326.00

Tile Picture

Tile picture, 6-tile, polychrome, depicting man wearing manganese
top hat, blue jacket, yellow waistcoat & green trousers, holding the
crimson reins of manganese horse
& walking before a manganese &
green tree within a yellow &
manganese border, 19th c.,
w/repairs & hairline cracks to 2
tiles, in wooden frame, 15 7/8 x
10 5/8" (ILLUS.) 1,100.00
Tobacco jar w/brass cover, blue
& white, painted w/pipe-smoking
Indian seated beside cargo including jar labeled "Violet" & parcel
monogrammed "VOC," w/two Dutch
ships in distance, Dutch, De Vergulde
Bloempot, mid-18th c., 13" h. over-
all (restored neck) 1,430.00

Delft Vase & Cover

Vase, cov., 25 1/8" h., octagonal, blue & white, painted continuous scene of chinoiserie figures at various pursuits in garden setting between wide foliate borders on shoulder & foot & w/design repeated on rim & cover, De Vergulde Astonnekens, 1700-05, repaired chips (ILLUS.) 2,310.00

Whimsey, model of a slipper, painted dancing pigs, fiddler & overall clover, blue & white, Dutch, early 20th c. 75.00

DERBY & ROYAL CROWN DERBY

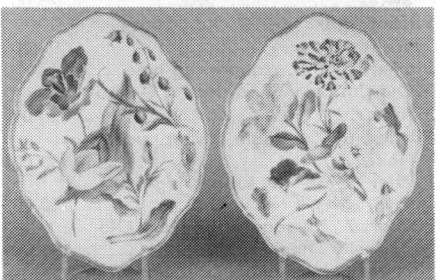

Derby Oval Botanical Dishes

William Duesbury, in partnership with John and Christopher Heath, established the Derby Porcelain Works in Derby, England, about 1750. Duesbury soon bought out his partners and in 1770 purchased the Chelsea factory and six years later, the Bow works. Duesbury was succeeded by his son and grandson. Robert Bloor purchased the business about 1814 and managed successfully until illness in 1828 left him unable to exercise control. The "Bloor" Period, however, extends from 1814 until 1848, when the factory closed. Former Derby workmen then resumed porcelain manufacture in another factory and this nucleus eventually united with a new and distinct venture, Derby Crown Porcelain, Ltd., 1890.

Butter dishes w/covers & stands, blue, iron-red & gilt bands of flowering scrolling foliage, ca. 1800, 7" d. stands, pr. $242.00

Creamer, painted cobalt blue, orange & white floral decor, miniature size, 1 x 1½", 1 1/8" h. 115.00

Cup & saucer, cobalt blue, rust & gold floral decor within cobalt blue & cream panels, ca. 1840 .... 140.00

Dishes, oval, painted w/different botanical specimens named at the reverse: one w/"Annual Lavatera,

Large Flowered St. John's Wort & Scarlet Bizzare Carnation" & other w/"Tulip Oculus Solus, Campanula Coronatos & Evergreen Claucum"; each w/shaped gilt rim, 1811-15, 10½" l., pr. (ILLUS.) 4,620.00

Figure of Shakespeare standing beside pedestal holding books, 1790-1820, 10" h. 650.00

Mansion House Dwarfs

Figures, "Mansion House Dwarfs," one in wide-brimmed floppy hat & other in tall pointed hat, each wearing colorful costume & on circular grassy mound base, Bloor period, ca. 1825, both w/repair to legs & one w/repair to hat & minor chips, 6¾" h., pr. (ILLUS.) 990.00

Pitcher, 6¼" h., jug-type, double scroll handle & spout enriched w/gilding, cylindrical neck w/gilt foliage, body w/puce & gilt flowering foliate scrolls, ca. 1840 .... 286.00

Plate, 8½" d., painted fruiting vine & black currants within a gilt band & foliage surround, spirally molded border w/flowering foliate scrolls, shaped gilt rim, ca. 1795 .... 286.00

Imari Pattern Plate

Plates, 10¼" d., Imari patt., painted
iron-red, blue & gilt w/central
flower spray in the oriental style
& w/border panels of gilt trellis
pattern on blue ground enclosing
lappets w/birds on branches,
ca. 1820, set of 19 (ILLUS.
of one) 2,090.00
Soup plates, King's patt., iron-red,
blue & gilt, marks for 1800 &
1860, set of 15 .... 880.00
Teacup & saucer, Imari patt.,
tall 69.00
Vase, 7" h., gold & brown decoration on blue ground, 1898 .... 250.00

DOULTON & ROYAL DOULTON

*Doulton & Co., Ltd., was founded in Lam-
beth, London, about 1858. It was operated
there till 1956 and often incorporated the
words "Doulton" and "Lambeth" in its
marks. Pinder Bourne & Co., Burslem, was
purchased by the Doultons in 1878 and in
1882 became Doulton & Co., Ltd. It added
porcelain to its earthenware production in
1884. The "Royal Doulton" mark has been
used by this factory, which is still in production. Character jugs and figurines are com-
manding great attention from collectors at
the present time. Also see FLOW BLUE,
GIBSON GIRL PLATES and TOBY MUGS
& JUGS.*

DICKENSWARE

Bowl with Oliver Twist

Ash tray, Mr. Pickwick, "A" mark .. $110.00
Bowl, 6½ x 5", Poor Jo 45.00
Bowl, 7½" d., deep, Dick
Swiveller ....115.00 to 135.00
Bowl, 7½" d., shallow, Oliver
(ILLUS.)....................... 65.00

Bowl, 7¾" d., 4" h., Dickens
characters (3) 145.00
Bowl, 8" d., Sir Roger de Coverly ... 110.00
Bust of Mr. Micawber, small 85.00
Bust of Sgt. Buz Fuz, small 80.00
Bust of Tony Weller, miniature 80.00
Condiment set: mustard pot, salt dip
& pepper shaker; Bill Sykes & Mr.
Pickwick, 3 pcs.................. 170.00
Cup & saucer, Sam Weller 39.50
Ewer, cov., Trotty Veck, 8" h. 100.00
Mug, 2-handled, Cap'n Cuttle,
4¼" h........................ 150.00
Mug, 2-handled, Sairey Gamp,
4 1/8" h. 125.00
Pin tray, Artful Dodger 25.00
Pitcher, 2 3/8" h., 1¼" d., Bill
Sykes 75.00
Pitcher, 2 3/8" h., 1½" d., Sam
Weller 92.00
Pitcher, 5½" h., square jug-type,
Old Curiosity Shop, Nell & Grand-
father, "A" mark 150.00
Pitcher, 6½" h., Sam Weller, signed
Noke 60.00
Pitcher, 6 7/8" h., square jug-type,
Dick Swiveller 105.00
Pitcher, 7" h., square jug-type, Old
Curiosity Shop 130.00
Pitcher, 7" h., square jug-type, Pick-
wick Papers 140.00
Pitcher, 7" h., Sam Weller, signed
Noke 85.00
Plate, 7½" d., Sam Weller, signed
Noke 35.00
Vase, 2¾" h., 2 1/8" d., Fagin 90.00
Vase, 3½" h., 1 7/8" d., Bill
Sykes 75.00
Vase, 5¼" h., 4 1/8" d., 2-handled,
Alfred Jingle................... 88.00
Vase, 7¾" h., 5 3/8" d., 2-handled,
Alfred Jingle................... 155.00
Vase, 8½" h., 4¼" sq., 2-handled,
Uriah Heep 164.00
Vase, 9½" h., 3" d., 2-handled,
Alfred Jingle................... 165.00
Vase, 9½" h., 7¾" d., Cap'n
Cuttle 195.00
Vase, 9½" h., 7¾" d., flared top,
Old Peggoty 192.00
Vase, 9¾" h., 4" d., Fat Boy 160.00

MISCELLANEOUS

Ash tray w/striker & cigar-size
rests, "Hotel Knickerbocker" 75.00
Bowl, fruit, 11¾" d., 7" h., Briar
Rose patt., cobalt blue & white
w/roses decor interior &
exterior 225.00
Bowl, square, "Cotswold Shepherd,"
shepherd, dog & sheep,
w/monogram 125.00
Box, cov., h.p. florals &
beetles decor on matte ground,

Doulton-Burslem, ca. 1888,
3¼ x 3¼ x 2" 135.00
Box, cov., Silicon Ware, blue leaf
border on flowing beige ground,
Doulton-Lambeth, 5 x 5" 125.00
Candlestick, Gleaners series,
4¾" d., 6 5/8" h. (single) 88.00
Figurine, "A Gypsy Dance,"
HN 2157, purple & white dress,
1955-57 .... 300.00
Figurine, "A Gypsy Dance,"
HN 2230, purple & white dress ... 230.00
Figurine, "A La Mode," HN 2544 .... 157.50
Figurine, "A Stitch in Time,"
HN 2352 .... 115.00
Figurine, "A Yeoman of the Guard,"
HN 688, red uniform 595.00
Figurine, "Abdullah," HN 2104, yel-
low chair, orange turban 510.00
Figurine, "Alchemist," HN 1282,
mottled robe, red hat 1,550.00
Figurine, "Alexandra,"
HN 2398 ....145.00 to 195.00
Figurine, "All Aboard," HN 2940,
blue shirt, tan pants, black boots
& cap 150.00
Figurine, "Anna," HN 2802 .... 75.00
Figurine, "Annette," HN 1472, green
dress 300.00
Figurine, "Anthea," HN 1527, purple
dress, red umbrella 485.00
Figurine, "Antoinette," HN 1850, red
& white dress 650.00
Figurine, "Antoinette," HN 2326,
white dress 135.00
Figurine, "Apple Maid" (The),
HN 2160, 1957-62 .... 310.00
Figurine, "At Ease," HN 2473 .... 170.00
Figurine, "Autumn," HN 2087, red
dress 425.00

"Autumn Breezes"

Figurine, "Autumn Breezes,"
HN 1911, peach dress, green
jacket, 1939-76 (ILLUS.) 155.00
Figurine, "Autumn Breezes,"
HN 2147, white dress, black
jacket 310.00
Figurine, "Barbara," HN 1421,
flowered skirt ....525.00 to 675.00
Figurine, "Basket Weaver" (The),
HN 2245 .... 515.00
Figurine, "Bell-O'-the Ball,"
HN 1997 .... 200.00
Figurine, "Bess," HN 2002, red
cloak 220.00
Figurine, "Betsy," HN 2111,
1953-59 .... 270.00
Figurine, "Biddy," HN 1445, green-
yellow dress, blue shawl 195.00
Figurine, "Biddy Penny Farthing,"
HN 1843 .... 125.00
Figurine, "Blithe Morning," HN 2021,
blue & pink dress 165.00
Figurine, "Blithe Morning," HN 2065,
red dress 172.50

"Bonnie Lassie"

Figurine, "Bonnie Lassie," HN 1626
(ILLUS.) 255.00
Figurine, "Bo Peep," HN 1810, blue
dress ....100.00 to 125.00
Figurine, "Breton Dancer," HN 2383,
purple dress, white apron & hat .. 400.00
Figurine, "Bride" (The), HN 1762,
cream dress 425.00
Figurine, "Bridesmaid," M 12, mul-
ticolor gown 210.00
Figurine, "Bridesmaid," M 30, red &
lavender gown 165.00
Figurine, "Bridesmaid," HN 2196,
white dress, pink trim 97.50
Figurine, "Bunny," HN 2214 .... 110.00
Figurine, "Butterfly," HN 720, black
& red costume 655.00
Figurine, "Calumet," HN 1689, green
costume, blue pot 550.00

Figurine, "Calumet," HN 2068,
1950-53 . . . . 610.00
Figurine, "Camellia," HN 2222 . . . . . . 210.00
Figurine, "Captain" (The), HN 2260 . . 185.00
Figurine, "Captain McHeath,"
HN 464, red jacket 475.00
Figurine, "Carmen," HN 1300, light
dress, green shoes 230.00
Figurine, "Carmen," HN 2545, white
blouse, blue skirt 160.00
Figurine, "Carpet Vendor," HN 76,
blue costume, green hat, orange
patterned carpet 1,950.00
Figurine, "Cassim," HN 1231, blue
hat & pants 450.00
Figurine, "Celeste,"
HN 2237 . . . . .195.00 to 225.00
Figurine, "Celia," HN 1727, green
dress 700.00
Figurine, "Cellist" (The), HN 2226 . . . 395.00
Figurine, "Cerise," HN 1607 . . . . 190.00
Figurine, "Chelsea Pair" (female),
HN 577, white flowered dress 585.00
Figurine, "Cherie," HN 2341, blue-
grey dress 115.00
Figurine, "Child Study," HN 604B,
primroses on base 225.00
Figurine, "Chinese Dancer,"
HN 2840, red, green & purple
costume 385.00
Figurine, "Chitarrone," HN 2700,
Lady Musicians series, blue
overdress 550.00
Figurine, "Chloe," HN 1470, yellow
dress, Potted by Doulton 220.00

"Christmas Morn"

Figurine, "Christmas Morn," HN 1992
(ILLUS.) 225.00
Figurine, "Claribel," HN 1950, blue
dress 300.00
Figurine, "Collinette," HN 1999, red
robe 365.00
Figurine, "Columbine," HN 1296,

purple line border on orange &
purple dress 550.00
Figurine, "Columbine," HN 1439, red
multicolored dress 385.00
Figurine, "Coralie," HN 2307, yellow
dress .80.00 to 125.00
Figurine, "Country Lass," HN 1991 . . 120.00
Figurine, "Covent Garden,"
HN 1339, green dress, lavender
apron 795.00
Figurine, "Curly Locks," HN 2049 . . . . 235.00
Figurine, "Cynthia," HN 1686, blue &
red dress 360.00
Figurine, "Daffy Down Dilly," HN
1712, green dress &
hat .200.00 to 250.00
Figurine, "Dainty May," HN 1639,
red dress, green underskirt 260.00
Figurine, "Dancing Years," HN 2235,
1965-71 . . . . 250.00
Figurine, "Daphne," HN 2268 . . . . 135.00
Figurine, "Dawn," HN 1858, green
drape headdress 825.00
Figurine, "Daydreams," HN 1732,
light blue dress, pink trim 250.00
Figurine, "Debutante," HN 2210 . . . . 350.00
Figurine, "Delicia," HN 1681, green
& purple dress 500.00
Figurine, "Denise," HN 2273 . . . . 260.00
Figurine, "Despair," HN 596, mottled
blue 900.00

"Dorcas"

Figurine, "Dorcas," HN 1558, red
dress (ILLUS.) 245.00
Figurine, "Dulcimer," HN 2798, Lady
Musicians series, pink overdress . . 550.00
Figurine, "Dulcinea," HN 1343, red &
black dress, black shoes, Potted
by Doulton 800.00
Figurine, "Fair Lady," HN 2832, red
gown, green sleeves, dark hair,
7¾" h. 115.00
Figurine, "Favorite" (The),
HN 2249 . . . . .85.00 to 160.00

Figurine, "Fiddler" (The), HN 2171 .. 875.00

Figurine, "Fiona," HN 2694, red & white dress 115.00

Figurine, "Flora," HN 2349 ....225.00 to 325.00

Figurine, "Flower Seller's Children" (The), HN 525, boy in green, girl in blue costume 235.00

Figurine, "Foaming Quart," HN 2162, orange & brown costume 135.00

Figurine, "Folly," HN 1750, brown hat, white muff, dark dress, 9½ h. (earthenware) 800.00

Figurine, "French Peasant," HN 2075 ....470.00 to 525.00

Figurine, "Gillian," HN 1670, dark pink dress, 1934-49 .... 350.00

Figurine, "Giselle," HN 2139, blue dress, 1954-69 .... 285.00

Figurine, "Goody Two Shoes," M 81, pink skirt, shaded blue & red overdress, 1939-49 .... 400.00

Figurine, "Gossips," HN 1429, red dress, white dress, 1930-49 ...... 375.00

"Granny's Heritage"

Figurine, "Granny's Heritage," HN 2031, green skirt, light multicolored shawl, 1949-69 (ILLUS.) 335.00

Figurine, "Greta," HN 1485, off-white dress, red shawl, 1931-53 .... 160.00

Figurine, "Grossmith's Tsang Ihang" (Tibetan Lady), HN 582, yellow & blue multicolored costume ....340.00 to 400.00

Figurine, "Guy Fawkes," HN 98, red cloak, 1918-49 .... 795.00

Figurine, "Gwynneth," HN 1980, red dress, 1945-52 .... 200.00

Figurine, "Harlequinade," HN 635, gold costume, 1924-38 ....1,250.00

Figurine, "Harlequinade," HN 780, pink dress, blue, black & orange markings, 1926-38 .... 600.00

Figurine, "Harlequinade Masked,"

HN 769, blue, red & yellow costume, 1925-38 ....1,250.00

Figurine, "Harp," HN 2482, Lady Musicians series, brown dress, 1973-78 .... 750.00

Figurine, "Highwayman," HN 527, red costume, dark coat, 1921-49 .... 415.00

Figurine, "Hornpipe" (The), HN 2161, blue jacket, blue & white striped trousers, 1955-62 .... 600.00

Figurine, "Hurdy Gurdy," HN 2796, Lady Musicians series, blue overdress, 1975-78 .... 575.00

Figurine, "In Grandma's Days," HN 362, blue patterned dress, 1919-38 .... 495.00

Figurine, "In the Stocks," HN 2163, rust jacket, 1955-59 .....465.00 to 575.00

Figurine, "Irene," HN 1621, pale yellow dress, 1934-51 .... 300.00

Figurine, "Janet," M 75, white skirt, shaded rose overdress, 1936-49 ... 280.00

Figurine, "Jean," HN 1878, green dress, red shawl, 1938-49 .... 250.00

Figurine, "Jean," HN 2032, green dress, red cloak, 1949-59 .... 225.00

Figurine, "Judith," HN 2089, rose dress, lilac bodice, 1952-59 ...... 235.00

Figurine, "June," HN 2027, 1949-52.. 310.00

Figurine, "Karen," HN 1994, red dress, 1947-55 .... 310.00

Figurine, "Kurdish Dancer," HN 2867, Dancers of the World series, blue & purple costume 530.00

Figurine, "Lady Anne Nevill," HN 2006, purple dress, ermine trim, 1948-53 .... 750.00

Figurine, "Lady Fayre," HN 1265, purple & red dress, 1928-38 ...... 350.00

Figurine, "Leisure Hour" (The), HN 2055, mottled green & peach dress, 1950-65 ....325.00 to 400.00

"Long John Silver"

Figurine, "Long John Silver,"
HN 2204, dark uniform, 1957-65
(ILLUS.)........................ 400.00

Figurine, "Loretta," HN 2337, rose-
red dress, yellow shawl,
1966-80........................ 110.00

Figurine, "Love Letter," HN 2149,
pink & white dress, blue dress,
1958-76........................ 210.00

Figurine, "Lucy Lockett," HN 524,
yellow dress, 1921-49........... 410.00

Figurine, "Lute," HN 2431, Lady
Musicians series, blue & white
dress, 1972-78 .... 775.00

Figurine, "Madonna of the Square,"
HN 594, green skirt, brown patterned shawl, 1924-38 .... 795.00

Figurine, "Madonna of the Square,"
HN 2034, light green-blue costume, 1949-51 ....450.00 to 600.00

Figurine, "Maisie," HN 1619, pink
dress, 1934-49 .... 300.00

Figurine, "Mam'selle," HN 659, purple & red dress, 1924-38 .... 890.00

Figurine, "Mantilla," HN 2712, Haute
Ensemble series, red dress, black
lace mantilla, 1974-78 .... 285.00

Figurine, "Marigold," HN 1447,
white & purple dress, 1931-49 .... 250.00

Figurine, "Masquerade" (female),
HN 600, pink dress, 1924-49 ..... 350.00

Figurine, "Master Sweep," HN 2205,
green skirt, 1957-62 .... 495.00

Figurine, "Maureen," HN 1771, lilac
dress, 1936-49 ....300.00 to 450.00

Figurine, "Maytime," HN 2113, rose-
pink dress, 1953-67 .... 235.00

Figurine, "Mephistopheles & Marguerite," HN 755, two-sided, lady
w/orange dress & purple cloak
one side, man w/red outfit & red
cloak other side, 1925-49 ....1,950.00

Figurine, "Mirabel," M 74, blue
dress, red cloak, 1936-49 .... 240.00

Figurine, "Mirabel," HN 1744, pink
dress, 1935-49 .... 620.00

Figurine, "Miss Demure," HN 1463,
green dress, 1931-49 .... 249.00

Figurine, "Miss Muffet," HN 1937,
green coat, 1940-52 .... 185.00

Figurine, "Miss 1926," HN 1205,
ermine-trimmed coat, 1926-38....1,650.00

Figurine, "Monica," M 66, shaded
pink skirt, blue blouse, 1935-49... 425.00

Figurine, "Mr. Micawber," HN 557,
brown jacket, black trousers,
1923-39........................ 200.00

Figurine, "Nadine," HN 1886, orange
dress, blue trim, purple ribbon,
1938-49........................ 525.00

Figurine, "Newsboy," HN 2244, dark
jacket, plaid hat, 1959-65 .... 470.00

Figurine, "Old King Cole," HN 2217,
ermine-lined robe, 1963-67 .... 565.00

Figurine, "Old Meg," HN 2494, blue
dress, purple shawl, 1974-76 ..... 225.00

Figurine, "Old Mother Hubbard,"
HN 2314, green dress, polka dot
apron, 1964-75 .... 235.00

Figurine, "Once Upon a Time,"
HN 2047, pink dotted dress,
1949-55........................ 235.00

Figurine, "One of the Forty"
(Thieves), HN 665, yellow patterned robes, 1924-38........... 900.00

Figurine, "One of the Forty"
(Thieves), HN 677, orange, green
& red striped robes, 1924-38...... 725.00

Figurine, "One That Got Away"
(The), HN 2153, brown slicker,
1955-59........................ 275.00

Figurine, "Orange Lady" (The),
HN 1759, pink skirt, 1936-75...... 178.00

Figurine, "Orange Lady" (The),
HN 1953, yellow dress, green
shawl, 1940-75 .... 175.00

Figurine, "Orange Vendor,"
HN 1966, black cloak, red robe,
1941-49........................ 750.00

Figurine, "Organ Grinder" (The),
HN 2173, green jacket, 1956-65 ... 575.00

Figurine, "Owd Willum," HN 2042,
brown jacket, 1949-73 .... 215.00

Figurine, "Paisley Shawl," M 3, blue
dress, lavender shawl, 1932-38 ... 205.00

Figurine, "Paisley Shawl," M 4,
yellow-green dress, rose colored
shawl, 1932-45 ....210.00 to 300.00

Figurine, "Paisley Shawl," HN 1988,
cream & yellow skirt, red hat,
1946-75 ....115.00 to 185.00

Figurine, "Pamela," HN 1469, yellow
dress, 1931-38 .... 460.00

Figurine, "Pantalettes," M 15,
shaded blue dress, red hat,
1932-45 ....155.00 to 200.00

Figurine, "Pantalettes," HN 1362,
green skirt, red tie on hat,
1929-38........................ 280.00

Figurine, "Pantalettes," HN 1412,
pink skirt, green tie on hat,
1930-49........................ 325.00

Figurine, "Pantalettes," HN 1507,
yellow dress, 1932-49 .... 210.00

Figurine, "Past Glory," HN 2484, red
uniform, 1973-78 .... 158.00

Figurine, "Patchwork Quilt" (The),
HN 1984, green dress, 1945-59.... 275.00

Figurine, "Patricia," M 28, blue top,
pink & blue skirt, 1932-45 .... 210.00

Figurine, "Patricia," HN 1414, yellow
dress, 1930-49 .... 365.00

Figurine, "Patricia," HN 1431, pink &
blue dress, 1930-49............. 310.00

Figurine, "Pearly Boy," HN 1547,
green coat, purple pants,
1933-49........................ 365.00

Figurines, "Pearly Boy" & "Pearly

Girl," HN 2035 & HN 2036, red
jackets, 1949-59, pr......295.00 to 355.00
Figurine, "Pecksniff," HN 2098, black
jacket, brown trousers, 1952-67... 260.00
Figurine, "Penelope," HN 1901, red
dress, 1939-75 .... 255.00
Figurine, "Pensive Moments,"
HN 2704, blue dress,
1975-81...................... 150.00
Figurine, "Phyllis," HN 1420,
flowered overskirt & shawl,
1930-49 ....350.00 to 500.00
Figurine, "Phyllis," HN 1486, blue
shawl, pink skirt, 1931-49 .... 515.00
Figurine, "Pierrette," HN 643, black
& red dress, 1924-38 .... 625.00
Figurine, "Pillow Fight," HN 2270,
pink nightgown, 1965-69 .... 160.00
Figurine, "Pirouette," HN 2216,
white dress, 1959-67 .... 210.00
Figurine, "Poke Bonnet," HN 612,
yellow skirt, green plaid shawl,
1924-38....................... 855.00
Figurine, "Polka" (The), HN 2156,
pale pink dress,
1955-69 ....190.00 to 265.00
Figurine, "Polly Peachum," HN 463,
white dress, 1921-49 ....350.00 to 400.00
Figurine, "Polly Peachum," HN 489,
green dress, 1921-38 .... 275.00
Figurine, "Polly Peachum," HN 549,
red dress, deep curtsey, 1922-49.. 240.00
Figurine, "Polly Peachum," HN 550,
red dress, 1922-49 .... 350.00
Figurine, "Polly Peachum," HN 589,
pink dress, yellow underskirt,
1924-49....................... 350.00
Figurine, "Pretty Lady," HN 70, pale
blue dress, 1916-38 .... 595.00
Figurine, "Priscilla," M 14, blue
ruffled dress, 1932-45 .... 250.00
Figurine, "Priscilla," HN 1340, red
dress, purple collar, 1929-49 ..... 215.00
Figurine, "Priscilla," HN 1501, yellow
dress, 1932-38 .... 350.00
Figurine, "Priscilla," HN 1559, pink &
yellow skirt, 1933-49............ 450.00
Figurine, "Proposal" (male),
HN 1209, blue coat, pink waist-
coat, 1926-38 .... 750.00
Figurine, "Prudence," HN 1884, pink
dress, 1938-49 .... 500.00
Figurine, "Prue," HN 1996, red
dress, black bodice, 1947-55 ..... 275.00
Figurine, "Puppetmaker" (The),
HN 2253, green vest, brown
trousers, 1962-73 .... 385.00
Figurine, "Queen Mother," HN 2882,
pink dress 995.00
Figurine, "Queen of Sheba,"
HN 2328, Femmes Fatales series,
purple robe, tiger 995.00
Figurine, "Reverie," HN 2306, peach
dress, 1964-81 .... 210.00

Figurine, "Rhapsody," HN 2267,
green dress, 1961-73 .... 175.00
Figurine, "Rita," HN 1450, blue
dress, 1931-38 ....450.00 to 600.00
Figurine, "River Boy," HN 2128, blue
trousers, white shirt, 1962-75 ..... 140.00
Figurine, "Robin," M 39, blue shirt,
green pants, 1933-45 .... 265.00
Figurine, "Romance," HN 2430,
apricot dress, 1972-80 .... 125.00
Figurine, "Rosamund," M 32, yellow
dress tinged w/blue, 1932-45 ..... 315.00
Figurine, "Rosamund," M 33, shaded
red dress, 1932-45 .... 305.00
Figurine, "Roseanna," HN 1921,
green dress, 1940-49 .... 250.00
Figurine, "Roseanna," HN 1926, red
dress, 1940-59 .... 270.00
Figurine, "Rosebud," HN 1581, light
dress, flower sprays, 1933-38 .... 475.00
Figurine, "Sabbath Morn," HN 1982,
red dress, green-yellow shawl,
1945-59...................... 250.00
Figurine, "Sailor's Holiday,"
HN 2442, apricot jacket,
1972-78 ....135.00 to 165.00

"St. George"

Figurine, "St. George," HN 2067,
purple, red & orange blanket,
1950-76 (ILLUS.)................2,200.00
Figurine, "Sairey Gamp," HN 1896,
1938-52...................... 280.00
Figurine, "Scotties," HN 1349, light
multicolored dress, white scotties,
1929-49...................... 700.00
Figurine, "Scribe," HN 305, olive
green robe, 1918-36 .... 850.00
Figurine, "Seafarer" (The), HN 2455,
beige sweater, 1972-76 ..150.00 to 200.00
Figurine, "Shepherd" (The),
HN 1975, orange smock,
1945-75 .... 175.00
Figurine, "Shore Leave," HN 2254,
dark uniform, 1965-78 ...135.00 to 175.00
Figurine, "Simone," HN 2378, olive
green dress, 1971-81 .....85.00 to 135.00
Figurine, "Skater," HN 2117, red &
white dress, 1953-71 .... 325.00

Figurine, "Spring Morning,"
HN 1922, green coat,
1940-73 . . . . .180.00 to 235.00

Figurine, "Springtime," HN 1971,
blue dress, pink coat, green hat,
1941-49. . . . . 165.00

Figurine, "Summer, The Seasons,"
HN 313, pale green dress,
1918-38. . . . . 595.00

Figurine, "Sunday Morning,"
HN 2184, rose-red dress,
1963-69. . . . . 265.00

Figurine, "Suzette," HN 1487, pink
dress, 1931-50 . . . . .250.00 to 325.00

"Suzette"

Figurine, "Suzette," HN 2026,
1949-59 (ILLUS.) 280.00

Figurine, "Sweet April," HN 2215,
pink dress, 1965-69 . . . . . .285.00 to 335.00

Figurine, "Tailor" (The), HN 2174,
orange vest, 1956-59 . . . . 625.00

Figurine, "Thanksgiving," HN 2446,
blue overalls, 1972-76 . . . . 180.00

Figurine, "Top O' the Hill," HN 1833,
green dress, 1937-71 . . . . 160.00

Figurine, "Uriah Heep," HN 2101,
black jacket, green trousers,
1952-67. . . . . 275.00

Figurine, "Vanessa," HN 1836,
purple bodice, green skirt,
1938-49 . . . . 675.00

Figurine, "Veneta," HN 2722,
olive green overdress,
1974-80 . . . . .95.00 to 135.00

Figurine, "Veronica," HN 1915, red
& white dress, blue hat, 1939-49 . . 300.00

Figurine, "Victorian Lady," M 1, red-
tinged dress, light green shawl,
1932-45. . . . . 295.00

Figurine, "Victorian Lady," M 25, red
ruffled skirt, blue shawl,
1932-45. . . . . 220.00

Figurine, "Victorian Lady," HN 727,

yellow skirt, red shawl,
1925-38 . . . . .200.00 to 295.00

Figurine, "Violin," HN 2432, Lady
Musicians series, brown over-
dress, 1972-78 . . . . 600.00

Figurine, "Virginia," HN 1693, yel-
low dress, 1935-49 . . . . 450.00

Figurine, "Wee Willie Winkie,"
HN 2050, blue nightshirt,
1949-53 . . . . 235.00

Figurine, "Young Miss Nightingale"
(The), HN 2010, green dress, red
surcoat, 1948-53 . . . . 535.00

Ginger jar, cov., squat, veined Sung
"flambe" glaze, 1920's, 10" h. 375.00

Humidor, cov., free form, Chang
Ware, crackled deep red, yellow
& white over deep cobalt blue,
signed Noke, ca. 1920, 5¾" h. . . .1,870.00

Jardiniere, Foliage Ware, 7" d.,
7½" h. 150.00

Jardiniere, Shakespeare series -
Ophelia one side, Hamlet other,
10" d., 8 5/8" h. 325.00

Loving cup, 3-handled, stoneware,
incised deer & hunting dogs
decor, signed Hannah Barlow,
1872-77, 7½ x 10" 495.00

Match holder w/striker, stoneware,
advertising "DeWar's Whiskey,"
tan & brown, 5 5/8" d.,
2 3/8" h. 60.00

Model of a salamander, stoneware,
signed George Tinworth 175.00

Mug, porcelain, 2-handled, Dutch
People series, 3 men on front,
lady & child on back, 1½" d.,
1 3/8" h. . . . . .50.00 to 60.00

Mug, hunting scene w/man on
horse, dogs & fox in relief,
1910-25, 5" w., 4¼" h. 120.00

Mug, Shakespeare series - Sir
Andrew Aguecheek, 4½" d.,
5 5/8" h. 90.00

Mug, stoneware, 3 tan reserve
medallions w/off-white figures of
Victorian woman riding bicycle,
soldier beside bicycle & man riding bicycle on blue ground, brown
handle & border bands, 4¾" d.,
6" h. 300.00

Mug, 3-handled, stoneware, incised
continuous stag & hound scene,
signed Hannah Barlow, 8" h. 250.00

Mug, tankard, Robin Hood series -
"Under the Greenwood Tree" 165.00

Pitcher, 4½" h., 3½" d., Welsh
Ladies series, 3 ladies walking
down path. 140.00

Pitcher, 4¾" h., Moorish Gate
series, 2 Arabs sitting by gate,
yellow w/brown bands & handle. . 85.00

Pitcher, 5" h., 5½" w., Shakespeare
series - Rosalind . . . . .85.00 to 110.00

Pitcher, 5¼" h. Gallant Fishers
series, ca. 1906 .... 110.00
Pitcher, 5½" h., jug-type, flow blue
Eglinton Tournament series,
knights riding horses decor 100.00
Pitcher, tankard, 6½" h., yellow
poppies & green foliage decor.... 100.00
Pitcher, 6 7/8" h., Toasting Mottoes
series, blue transfer on white
w/over-painted red jacket on
toaster, "Here's To A Man," etc.,
gold trim 180.00
Pitcher, 7" h., stoneware, gold
Egyptian figures in relief on black
matte finish ground, silver rim ... 145.00
Pitcher, 7½" h., Coaching Days
series, multicolored coach, men
& horses on cream
ground ....135.00 to 150.00
Pitcher, 8¼" h., 6" d., Leather
Ware, simulated brown leather
lettered "Fill What You Will and
Drink What You Fill" on front,
silverplate rim 135.00
Pitcher, tankard, 8¾" h., Silicon
Ware, colorful bands, dated
1884 .... 118.00
Pitcher, 9¼" h., coronation commemorative, "Queen Victoria
1837-98," Doulton-Lambeth 240.00
Pitcher, 9¼" h., stoneware, incised
white grazing cows on tan, brown
& green glossy borders, signed
Hannah Barlow 675.00
Pitcher, 9½" h., Morrisian Ware,
handle w/stylized grapes &
leaves, Art Nouveau ladies &
rose-covered latticework fence
decor, 1900-24 .... 175.00
Pitcher, tankard, 9½" h., stoneware, 3 reserved medallions w/in-
cised goats decor, brown & green
glossy borders, signed Hannah
Barlow & dated 1880 .... 575.00
Pitcher, Silicon Ware, simulated copper w/embossed bands & nail-
heads, Doulton-Lambeth, pt. 125.00
Plaque, pierced to hang, terra cotta,
"Death of Pheidippides," signed
George Tinworth, 7½" d. 125.00
Plaque, pierced to hang, flow blue
Babes in Woods series, girl in
hooded cape carrying basket, gold
trim, 9½ x 7¾" oval 295.00
Plaque, pierced to hang, "Dr. John-
son Eats the Cheshire Cheese,"
13" d. 145.00
Plate, 8¾" d., flow blue Babes in
Woods series, 2 small girls wear-
ing bonnets & talking to pixie,
gold trim, 1914................. 195.00
Plate, 10" d., Automobile series - "A
Nerve Tonic" or "Room for One,"
1906-07, each 180.00

"Gallant Fishers"

Plate, 10" d., Gallant Fishers series,
fishermen & quote (ILLUS.) 70.00
Plate, 10½" d., scalloped rim, flow
blue Babes in Woods series, scene
of three little girls looking at fire-
fly in forest, scalloped edge...... 232.00
Plate, 13½" d., Jackdaw of Rheims
series - "Bishop and Abbot & Prior
were There" 125.00
Teapot, cov., Robin Hood series -
Robin Hood, Little John & Friar
Tuck decor, 4¼" d., 5½" h. 195.00
Tobacco jar, King's Ware, man
smoking pipe decor on front, silverplate lid, 4" h. 165.00
Tobacco jar, cov., stoneware,
barrel-shaped, dark green monkey sitting w/pipe in low relief on
tan ground, brown bands &
"Tobacco" reverse, 3 7/8" d.,
5¼" h. 75.00
Toothpick holder, 2-handled, Welsh
Ladies series, 2½" h............ 135.00
Tyg (3-handled mug), stoneware, in-
cised dogs decor, silver rim,
signed Hannah Barlow, 7" h. 290.00
Tyg, stoneware, incised stags &
hounds decor, signed Hannah
Barlow, 8" h. 230.00
Vase, 1¾" h., 2 1/8" d., Welsh
Ladies series, group of ladies sit-
ting, small green handles 90.00
Vase, 2½" h., 2¼" d., The All Black
Cricket Team series - black boy
w/cricket paddle - "Out for a
Duck" 135.00
Vase, 5½" h., 3 7/8" w., square
flattened shape, Robin Hood
series - "Robin Hood Slays Guy of
Gisborne" 98.00
Vase, 5¾" h., 3½" d., 2-handled,
flow blue Babes in Woods series,
2 girls talking to small pixie, gold
trim............................ 210.00
Vase, 7" h., 3 3/8" d., barrel-
shaped, Welsh Ladies series, 3
ladies & child walking down
path 175.00
Vase, 7 3/8" h., 3½" d., 2-handled,

flow blue Babes in Woods series,
2 small girls talking to pixie, gold
trim . . . . .250.00 to 275.00
Vase, 8½" h., peacock & thrush
decor, veined Sung "flambe"
glaze, signed Noke & A. Eaton . . . 850.00
Vase, 12" h., stoneware, incised
horses & sheep decor, signed
Hannah Barlow 335.00

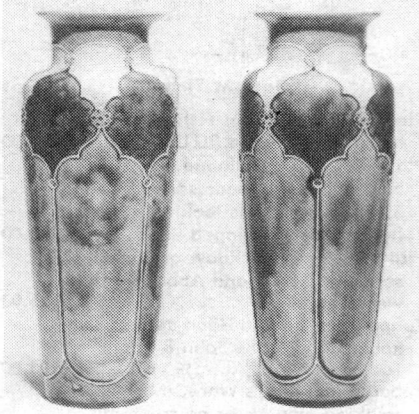

Royal Doulton Stoneware Vases

Vases, 13" h., stoneware, Art Nouveau inspired panels in pale
green, blue & ochre glaze, neck
interior w/streaky blue, green &
ochre glaze, ca. 1910, pr.
(ILLUS.) 440.00
Whiskey jug, King's Ware, "Sporting
Squire" 225.00

DRESDEN

Dresden Covered Vases

*Dresden porcelain has been produced since
the type now termed Dresden was made at
the nearby Meissen Porcelain Works early in
the 18th century. "Dresden" and "Meissen"*

*are often used interchangeably for later
wares. "Dresden" has become a generic name
for the kind of porcelains produced in Dresden and certain other areas of Germany but
perhaps should be confined to the wares made
in the city of Dresden. Also see MEISSEN
and MUSTACHE CUPS & SAUCERS.*

Compote, 9½" d., embossed floral
decor, pedestal base w/two
figures $120.00
Cookie jar, cov., paneled body,
roses decor w/gold trim 80.00
Figure of a child in seated position,
white "lace" dress, 2½" h. 65.00
Figure of a Cancan dancer seated,
wearing soft green costume & hat
& black stockings, 4½" h. 165.00
Figure of a ballerina, blue "lace"
costume w/applied florettes,
6¼" h. 100.00
Figure of a Colonial lady holding
flower basket, soft blue & white
"lace" dress w/florettes, 8" h. 125.00
Figure of a lady seated w/puppy
playing at her feet, pink "lace"
dress w/hoop skirt, applied gold
florettes, gold trim, 8" h. 325.00
Figure of a lady holding small dog
in her arms, attired in 18th c.
style garments, 9½" h. 750.00
Figure group, lady & gentleman in
Colonial style clothing, lady in
ivory "lace" gown w/pink ruffles
& applied florettes, dancing
w/arms outstretched, gentleman
in brown coat w/"lace" cuffs & as-
cot, 7" h. 130.00
Figure group, man seated at piano,
lady wearing "lace" dress & play-
ing the cello, 14 x 9" 400.00
Plates, 6½" d., h.p. portrait center,
ornate gold rim, set of 12 . . . . 550.00
Plate, 6¾" d., reticulated rim,
florals & foliage decor 25.00
Plate, 8½" d., scroll molded border,
floral decor 40.00
Vase, 8½" h., bust portrait of beau-
tiful woman reserved on cobalt
blue ground enriched w/gilt
scrollwork, artist-signed 360.00
Vases, 15" h., conical w/flaring
foot, gold loop side handles, each
w/scene of beautiful woman in a
garden setting, reserved on violet
ground heightened w/gilt foliate
motifs, pr. .1,320.00
Vase, 19" h., bust portrait of lovely
maiden, artist-signed 700.00
Vases, cov., 21 1/8" h., bulbous,
each side w/panel of lovers at
various pursuits between panels
of full-blown summer flowers,
reserved on claret-colored

ground, panels bordered by gilt
bands of scrolling devices, neck
decorated in gilding w/"oeil-de-
perdrix," ca. 1900, pr. (ILLUS.) 990.00
Whimsey, lady's pump w/applied
rose & bow, ruffled "lace" edge . . 175.00

FAIRINGS, GOSS & CREST

"Last One Into Bed"

*Fairings are brightly-colored small por-
celain objects, largely groups and boxes, that
were made in molds in Germany and Bohemia and painted in the late 19th and early
20th centuries. Most related to courtship and
marriage, family life, children, animals and
the like and bore captions. They were originally sold at fairs and bazaars and as souvenir
pieces. In much the same category were the
Goss and Crest miniature pieces, made by
W.H. Goss at Stoke-on-Trent, England, and
other factories, and many bearing crests. All
are now widely sought.*

Bust of Charles Dickens, Goss,
5" h. $55.00
Bust of Shakespeare, Goss 25.00
Figure of a black boy emerging from
china egg w/crest of Felixstowe
on front, Goss, 2" d., 2 1/8" h.
(crest) 68.00
Figure of a black boy sitting up in
china bed w/spider crawling up
side, w/crest of Shanklin on blanket, Goss, 2¾ x 1½", 2½" h.
(crest) 85.00
"Last One Into Bed - Put Out the
Light," fairing, 3¼ x 3 x 2"
(ILLUS.) 72.50
Match holder, figure of black boy
w/red & gold cap, gold pants &
cigarette in mouth standing by
container lettered "Matches" &
w/crest of Chester, Goss, 1½" d.,
3¾" h. (crest) 85.00

Model of Manx Cottage, Goss
(crest) 115.00
Model of Shakespeare's House,
Goss (crest) 100.00
Model of a skull, "Alas Poor
Yorick," Goss (crest) 150.00
"Returning at One O'clock in the
Morning" (fairing) 68.00
"Three O'Clock in the Morning"
(fairing) 185.00
Trinket box, cov., crest-shaped,
w/Norwegian coat-of-arms decal,
Goss 18.00
Trinket box, cov., modeled as a girl
w/her dog seated on chair
(fairing) 110.00
Urn, w/crest of Weymouth &
Melcombe-Recis, Goss, 2¾" h. . . .   24.50
Vase, 2 7/8" h., w/crest of Mass of
Rock, Goss 22.50

FIESTA WARE

Fiesta Ware Carafe

*Fiesta dinnerware was made by the Hom-
er Laughlin China Company of Newell, West
Virginia, from the 1930's until the early
1970's. The brilliant colors of this inexpensive
pottery have attracted numerous collectors
and though it is not even out of production
for a decade, it merits inclusion in our price
guide. On February 28, 1986, Laughlin rein-
troduced the popular Fiesta line with minor
changes in the shapes of a few pieces and a
contemporary color range. The effect of this
new production on the Fiesta collecting market is yet to be determined.*

Ash tray, chartreuse, red or rose,
each $40.00
Ash tray, cobalt blue, grey, medium
green or yellow, each . . . . .28.00 to 35.00
Bowl, fruit, 4¾" to 5½" d., cobalt

blue, grey, ivory, light green, turquoise or yellow, each .....8.00 to 14.00
Bowl, fruit, 4¾" to 5½" d., medium green 18.00
Bowl, individual salad, 7½" d., medium green, turquoise or yellow, each ....32.00 to 40.00
Bowl, nappy, 8½" d., chartreuse, cobalt blue, forest green, grey or yellow, each.............13.00 to 18.00
Bowl, nappy, 9½" d., cobalt blue, ivory, light green or red, each ... 18.00
Bowl, salad, 9½" d., yellow........ 43.00
Bowl, fruit, 11¾" d., medium green or turquoise, each.............. 75.00
Bowl, cream soup, chartreuse, grey, red or rose, each ....22.00 to 30.00
Cake plate, red, 10" d. 45.00
Candle holders, bulb-type, cobalt blue, light green, turquoise or yellow, each pr. 30.00
Candle holders, tripod-type, light green, pr. 185.00
Carafe, cov., red 95.00
Carafe, cov., yellow (ILLUS.) 68.00
Casserole, cov., ivory, light green or turquoise, each 45.00
Casserole, cov., rose 95.00
Coffee pot, cov., demitasse, stick handle, red 135.00
Coffee pot, cov., chartreuse, forest green, grey or red, each......... 95.00

Fiesta Ware Coffee Pot

Coffee pot, cov., rose (ILLUS.) 62.50
Comport, 12" d., low foot, chartreuse, red or yellow, each 45.00
Comport, sweetmeat, high stand, red 80.00
Creamer, stick handle, cobalt blue, ivory or light green, each ..12.00 to 18.00
Creamer, cobalt blue, forest green, grey or light green, each ...8.00 to 12.00
Creamer & cov. sugar bowl, ivory or rose, each pr. 25.00

Cup & saucer, demitasse, stick handle, ivory, cobalt blue or yellow, each 25.00
Cup & saucer, demitasse, stick handle, rose 75.00
Cup & saucer, ring handle, chartreuse, cobalt blue, forest green, ivory, light green or yellow, each 17.00
Cup & saucer, ring handle, red, rose or turquoise, each ....18.00 to 24.00
Demitasse set: stick-handled cov. pot & 4 c/s; cobalt blue, 9 pcs. 275.00
Egg cup, turquoise or yellow, each ....20.00 to 26.00
Gravy boat, cobalt blue, forest green or medium green, each 20.00
Gravy boat, grey 40.00
Marmalade jar, cov., light green, red or turquoise, each .....75.00 to 85.00
Mixing bowl, nest-type, yellow, size No. 1 .... 39.00
Mixing bowl, nest-type, forest green, size No. 2 .... 22.00
Mixing bowl, nest-type, light green or turquoise, size No. 3, each ....22.50 to 27.00
Mixing bowl, nest-type, cobalt blue or red, size No. 4, each 40.00
Mixing bowl, nest-type, cobalt blue, red or turquoise, size No. 5, each 50.00
Mixing bowl, nest-type, medium green, size No. 6 .... 45.00
Mixing bowl, nest-type, forest green or yellow, size No. 7, each....... 90.00
Mug, chartreuse, grey or ivory, each ....30.00 to 35.00
Mug, light green or turquoise, each ....23.00 to 30.00
Mustard jar, cov., ivory or turquoise, each..............45.00 to 50.00
Mustard jar, cov., red 85.00
Onion soup bowl, cov., cobalt blue or light green, each 160.00
Pitcher, jug-type, chartreuse, cobalt blue or turquoise, qt., each 35.00

Fiesta Ware Pitcher

Pitcher, jug-type, forest green, qt. (ILLUS.)........................ 30.00

Pitcher, juice, disc-type, medium
green or yellow, 30 oz., each 25.00
Pitcher, juice, disc-type, red,
30 oz. 115.00
Pitcher w/ice lip, globular, cobalt
blue or yellow, 2-qt., each 55.00
Pitcher w/ice lip, light green or
medium green, 2-qt., each 35.00
Pitcher, water, disc-type, grey 56.00
Pitcher, water, disc-type, rose 75.00
Plate, 6" d., cobalt blue, ivory, for-
est green or turquoise, each 4.50
Plate, 7" d., forest green or grey,
each ....9.00 to 10.00
Plate, 9" d., grey or rose, each..... 14.00
Plate, 10" d., cobalt blue, ivory,
turquoise or yellow, each ..10.00 to 14.00
Plate, grill, 10½" d., light green,
rose or turquoise, each ....17.00 to 20.00
Plate, chop, 13" d., grey, rose, tur-
quoise or yellow, each ....16.00 to 20.00
Plate, chop, 15" d., forest green,
medium green or red, each 27.50
Platter, 13" oval, chartreuse, cobalt
blue, grey or rose, each ...16.00 to 20.00
Relish tray, w/five inserts, cobalt
blue, red or turquoise, each...... 85.00
Salt & pepper shakers, chartreuse,
medium green or turquoise, each
pr............................. 13.00
Sauce dish, chartreuse, forest
green, grey, red, turquoise or
yellow, 4¾" d., each ......10.00 to 13.00
Syrup pitcher w/original lid, turquoise or yellow, each 85.00
Teapot, cov., ivory, medium green
or turquoise, medium,
each ....35.00 to 45.00
Teapot, cov., cobalt blue, red or
turquoise, large, each 65.00
Tumbler, juice, cobalt blue, ivory,
light green, red or turquoise,
5 oz., each 15.00
Tumbler, water, cobalt blue, ivory,
light green, turquoise or yellow,
10 oz., each ....18.00 to 25.00
Utility tray, red 25.00
Vase, bud, 6½" h., yellow 25.00
Vase, 8" h., ivory, medium green,
turquoise or yellow,
each ....160.00 to 195.00

FLOW BLUE

Flowing Blue wares, usually shortened to Flow Blue, were made at numerous potteries in Staffordshire, England, and elsewhere. They are decorated with a blue that smudged lightly or ran in the firing. The same type of color flow is also found on certain wares decorated in green, purple and sepia. Patterns were given specific names, which accompany listings here. The standard reference for collectors of this ware is Flow Blue China, *a series of three books by Petra Williams.*

ABBEY (George Jones & Sons, ca. 1900)
Bowl, 8" to 9" d., footed..$150.00 to 165.00
Bowl, fruit, 13" d. 175.00
Butter tub, cov. 85.00
Cake plate, 9½" d............... 48.00
Chocolate pot, cov., 6" h. ....75.00 to 95.00
Creamer, 3" h. 46.00
Cup, handleless, 3½" h. 40.00
Cup & saucer, twig or ring handle .. 40.00
Dish, 8½" sq.................... 110.00
Marmalade jar, cov. 65.00
Plate, 7½" to 8½" d. ....20.00 to 32.00
Preserve dish, cov., 4½" to
5½" d. ....75.00 to 95.00
Sugar bowl, open 25.00
Teapot, cov. 69.00
Toothbrush holder, 4½" h. 40.00
Trivet, 5" 45.00
Wash basin & pitcher 395.00
Waste bowl...................... 25.00

ALASKA (W. H. Grindley, ca. 1891)
Butter pat 20.00
Egg cup 50.00
Gravy boat w/underplate 85.00
Pitcher, milk.................... 78.00
Plate, 7" to 8" d.............15.00 to 23.00
Platter, 16" l................... 125.00
Soup plate w/flange rim 42.50
Vegetable bowl, cov., oval 125.00

ALTON (W. H. Grindley, ca. 1891)
Creamer & cov. sugar bowl, 5½" h.,
pr............................. 235.00
Gravy boat 55.00
Plate, 7" d. 38.00
Plate, 10" d. 58.00
Platter, 18" 165.00

AMOY (Davenport, dated 1844)

Amoy Plate

Cup & saucer, handleless 77.50
Cup plate......................... 65.00
Honey dish, 5" d. 55.00
Plate, 7½" to 8½" d.
  (ILLUS.)..................65.00 to 78.00
Plate, 10" to 11" d.........95.00 to 125.00
Soup plate w/flange rim, 10½" d. .. 120.00
Sugar bowl, cov. 160.00
Teapot, cov. (professional repair to
  finial) 395.00

ARABESQUE (T. J. & J. Mayer, ca. 1845)
Cup & saucer 75.00
Gravy boat 115.00
Plate, 9½" d..................... 55.00

ARCADIA (Arthur Wilkinson, ca. 1907)
Bowl, cream soup 35.00
Cake stand, 9" d., 4" h. 150.00
Plate, 10" d..................... 35.00
Platter, 16" l. 85.00
Soup plate w/flange rim, 9" d. 45.00

ARGYLE (W. H. Grindley, ca. 1896)

Argyle Platter

Gravy boat w/attached under-
  plate......................... 75.00
Plate, 9" d. 35.00
Platter, 17 x 11" (ILLUS.) ...130.00 to 150.00
Vegetable bowl, cov., oval 185.00
Waste bowl..................... 45.00

ARGYLE (Wood & Son, ca. 1900)
Creamer 40.00
Platter, 12½ x 9½" 100.00
Vegetable tureen, cov., oval 130.00

ASTORIA (Johnson Bros., ca. 1900)

Astoria Platter

Platter, 14" oval (ILLUS.) 165.00
Saucer, 6" d. 15.00
Vegetable bowl, cov. 110.00

BALTIC (W. H. Grindley, ca. 1891)
Bowl, 6½" d. 30.00
Bowl, 12" d. 98.00
Plate, 10" d. 40.00
Platter, 16 x 12" 135.00
Soup plate w/flange rim, 9" d. 35.00

BEAUFORT (W. H. Grindley, ca. 1903)
Butter pat 22.00
Creamer 80.00
Cup & saucer 40.00
Gravy boat 45.00
Plate, 10" d. 50.00

BURLEIGH (Burgess & Leigh, ca. 1903)
Bowl, 10" d. 35.00
Cup & saucer 35.00
Plate, 7½" to 8½" d........15.00 to 20.00
Sauce dish, 5" d................. 14.00

CAMBRIDGE (Alfred Meakin, ca. 1891)
Cup & saucer 65.00
Relish dish..................... 75.00
Sauce dish..................... 20.00

CAMBRIDGE (New Wharf Pottery, ca. 1891)
Creamer 40.00
Sugar bowl, cov. 60.00
Teapot, cov. 150.00
Vegetable bowl, open, oval 65.00

CANTON (James Edwards, ca. 1845)
Bowl, 10" d. 155.00
Butter dish, cov. 180.00
Plates, 8" d., set of 10............ 400.00
Plate, 10½" d. 72.50

CARLTON (Samuel Alcock, 1850)
Dish, closed scroll handles,
  9½" d. 60.00
Gravy boat 150.00
Plate, 8" d. 38.00
Plate, 9½" d. 60.00
Platter, 13½" l. 85.00

**CASHMERE (Ridgway & Morley, G. L. Ash-
worth, et. al., 1840's on)**
Plate, 10½" d. 60.00
Platter, 17" l. 350.00
Sugar bowl, cov. 295.00

CHAPOO (John Wedge Wood, ca. 1850)
Bowl, 7½" d. 165.00
Cup & saucer, handleless 110.00
Honey dish, 4" d. 55.00
Plate, 6½" d. 60.00
Plate, 8" to 9" d.............65.00 to 85.00
Sauce dish, 5" d................. 55.00
Soup plate w/flange rim, 10½" d. ... 105.00

Soup tureen, cov., 12 x 8" oblong,
  10" h. (faint hairline in lid) 1,500.00
Teapot, cov. 425.00

CHEN-SI (John Meir, ca. 1835)
Cup plate 125.00
Plate, 7" to 8" d............65.00 to 75.00
Plate, 9" d...................... 85.00
Soup plate w/flange rim, 10½" d. ... 62.50
Sugar bowl, cov................. 245.00

CHINESE (Thomas Dimmock, ca. 1845)
Cup, demitasse 29.00
Egg cup 40.00
Plate, 8" to 9" d............50.00 to 65.00
Soup tureen underplate, handled,
  14½" d. 250.00

CHUSAN (J. Clementson, ca. 1840)
Honey dish, 5" d. 45.00
Plate, 7" d...................... 70.00
Plate, 9" d...................... 90.00
Vegetable bowl, open, 8½"
  octagon 100.00

CLAREMONT (Johnson Bros., ca. 1891)
Butter pat, 3" d. 20.00
Cup & saucer 42.50
Platter, 18½ x 12½" 50.00
Waste bowl...................... 75.00

CLARENCE (W. H. Grindley, ca. 1900)

Clarence Pattern

Plate, 6" d...................... 25.00
Saucer, 6" d. 16.00
Sauce tureen w/ladle............. 285.00
Soup plate w/flange rim, 9" d. 35.00

CLAYTON (Johnson Bros., ca. 1902)
Dinner service for eight, 56 pcs. ...2,375.00
Platter, 14½ x 10½" 100.00
Sauce dish...................... 16.00

CLIFTON (W. H. Grindley, ca. 1891)
Cup & saucer 25.00
Pitcher, water 205.00
Plate, 6½" d.................... 15.00
Plate, 8½" d.................... 37.00

CLOVER (W. H. Grindley, ca. 1910)
Cup............................. 65.00

Plate, 10" d..................... 22.50
Soup plate w/flange rim, 8" d. 20.00

CLYTIE (Wedgwood & Co., Ltd., ca. 1908)
Plate, 9" d...................... 75.00
Platter, 17 x 13" 210.00

COBURG (John Edwards, ca. 1860)
Creamer 145.00
Plate, 7" d...................... 40.00
Plate, 8½" d.................... 48.00
Plate, 10" d..................... 65.00
Saucer 25.00
Sugar bowl 145.00
Syllabub cup (pedestal base &
  handle) 75.00
Vegetable bowl, cov., 10 x 7"
  oblong 395.00

COLONIAL (J. & G. Meakin, ca. 1891)
Butter dish w/cover & drain insert .. 90.00
Plate, 9" d...................... 37.00
Sugar bowl, cov................. 75.00
Vegetable bowl, cov............. 140.00

COLUMBIA (Clementson & Young, ca. 1846)
Creamer, 5¾" h................. 115.00
Plate, 7½" d.................... 36.00

CONWAY (New Wharf Pottery, ca. 1891)
Bowl, 8" to 9" d............45.00 to 50.00
Plate, 9" to 10" d............35.00 to 50.00
Platter, 10 x 8" 76.00
Platter, 11" l................... 88.00
Saucer, 6" d. 16.00
Soup plate w/flange rim 35.00
Vegetable bowl, open, 9" d. 55.00
Wash basin & pitcher, 2 pcs. 325.00

CORAL (Johnson Bros., ca. 1900)
Plate, 10" d..................... 30.00
Platter 45.00
Relish dish...................... 45.00
Vegetable tureen, cov., handled,
  oval 130.00

DAHLIA (Maker unknown, brush-painted)
Cup, demitasse 65.00
Mug 85.00
Plate, 8½" d.................... 65.00
Vegetable bowl, cov............. 285.00

DAINTY (John Maddock & Son, ca. 1896)
Bone dish 45.00
Cake plate w/shaped handles, 10".. 85.00
Cups & saucers, demitasse, set
  of 8.......................... 475.00
Platter, 10½" l................. 55.00
Vegetable bowl, cov., oval or
  round 195.00

DAISY (Burgess & Leigh, ca. 1897)
Bowl, soup 24.50
Cake stand 195.00

Creamer & cov. sugar bowl, pr. 190.00
Cup, demitasse 45.00
Cup & saucer 42.00
Plate, 9" d....................... 27.50

DALIAH (Edward Challinor, ca. 1850)
Cup & saucer, handleless (rim
   flake) 75.00
Plate, 8½" d. (tiny back hairline) ... 45.00
Sugar bowl, cov. 75.00

DAVENPORT (Wood & Sons, ca. 1907)
Gravy boat 80.00
Soup plate w/flange rim, 9" d. 25.00
Vegetable bowl, cov.......130.00 to 150.00

DELFT (Mintons, ca. 1871)
Gravy boat 75.00
Ladle, 10" l. 65.00
Platter, 13½ x 10" 75.00

DELPH (Wood & Sons, ca. 1907)
Bowl, 10½" d. 75.00
Platter, 14 x 11" 52.00
Platter, 16 x 12½" 75.00
Vegetable bowl, oval 45.00

DOROTHY (Johnson Bros., ca. 1900)

Dorothy Pattern Plate

Bone dish 35.00
Gravy boat w/undertray 86.00
Plate, 8" d. (ILLUS.) 55.00

DRESDEN (Villeroy & Boch, ca. 1900)
Butter pats, set of 6 .... 75.00
Plate, 7" d....................... 20.00
Sauce tureen, cover & underplate,
   3 pcs. 155.00

DUCHESS (W. H. Grindley, ca. 1891)
Bowl, 9½" d. 60.00
Gravy boat w/underplate 100.00
Plate, 9½" d..................... 24.00
Sugar bowl 88.00
Vegetable bowl, open, 9¾" oval ... 50.00

DUNDEE (Ridgways, ca. 1910)
Bone dish ....25.00 to 30.00
Creamer 105.00
Cup & saucer, demitasse 65.00
Cup & saucer 55.00
Platter, 15 x 10" 55.00

EBOR (Ridgways, ca. 1910)
Creamer 125.00
Platter, 12½ x 8½" 62.00
Sauce dish...................... 15.00

FAIRY VILLAS - 3 styles (W. Adams, ca. 1891)

Fairy Villas III Plate

Bowl, 10" d. 77.50
Bowl, cereal 35.00
Butter pat 24.00
Creamer 75.00
Cup & saucer 62.00
Plate, 8" d...................... 30.00
Plate, 9" to 10" d...........45.00 to 65.00
Plate, 12½" d. (ILLUS.) .....95.00 to 125.00
Soup plate w/flange rim,
   9" d....................40.00 to 52.00
Vegetable bowl, cov. 185.00
Vegetable bowl, open 65.00

FLORA (Thomas Walker, ca. 1845)
Creamer 165.00
Pitcher, 2-qt..................... 225.00
Plate, 6" d...................... 45.00
Plate, 7½" d..................... 55.00
Plate, 9½" d..................... 85.00
Sugar bowl, cov. 175.00

FLORAL (Thomas Hughes & Son, ca. 1895)
Butter pat 18.00
Cheese dish, cov. 195.00
Chocolate pot, cov., w/silver lustre,
   12½" h........................ 225.00
Compote 175.00

FORMOSA (Thos., John & Joseph Mayer, ca. 1850)
Plate, 9½" d..................... 80.00

Platter, 16 x 12" 275.00
Saucer, 6" d. 40.00
Vegetable bowl, open, 13 x 10" 185.00

GIRONDE (W. H. Grindley, ca. 1891)

Gironde Pattern Cup & Saucer

Bone dish .... 25.00 to 30.00
Butter pat 19.00
Cup & saucer (ILLUS.) .... 40.00 to 50.00
Dinner service for 4 w/cov. vegeta-
    ble bowl, open vegetable bowl,
    gravy boat, platter & waste bowl,
    25 pcs. 775.00
Pitcher, milk, 8¾" h. 150.00
Platter, 19 x 13½" 150.00
Soup plate w/flange rim 35.00

GOTHIC (Jacob Furnival, ca. 1850)
Pitcher, 6½" h. 125.00
Plate, 7" d. .... 25.00 to 35.00
Soup plate w/flange rim, 10½" d. .. 95.00

GRACE (W. H. Grindley, ca. 1897)
Cup & saucer, demitasse 60.00
Pitcher, milk, 7" h. 135.00
Sugar bowl, cov., helmet-shaped,
    ornate scroll handles .... 165.00 to 185.00

GRENADA (Henry Alcock & Co., ca. 1891)
Creamer .... 85.00 to 100.00
Dinner service for 6 w/cov. butter
    dish, gravy boat, 2 cov. vegetable
    bowls, 2 open vegetable bowls &
    2 platters, 32 pcs. 1,250.00
Pitcher, milk 75.00
Sugar bowl, cov. 100.00

HADDON (W. H. Grindley, ca. 1891)
Butter pat 18.00
Cup & saucer .... 45.00 to 58.00
Gravy boat w/underplate 115.00
Plate, 9" d. 40.00
Platter, 14" l. 135.00
Sauce dish........................ 10.00
Tureen, cov. 365.00

HINDUSTAN (John Maddock, ca. 1855)
Plate, 10" d. 48.00
Platter, 13½" .... 80.00 to 85.00
Platter, 16 x 12" 225.00
Syllabub cup (pedestal base &
    handle) 75.00

HOFBURG, THE (W. H. Grindley, ca. 1891)
Butter pat .... 11.00 to 16.00
Celery tray 48.00
Cup & saucer 35.00
Gravy boat 35.00
Pitcher, 6" h. 70.00
Plate, 7" d. 15.00
Plate, 8½" d. 27.50
Plate, 10" d. 35.00
Platter, 12" l. 45.00
Sauce dish, 5" oval .... 20.00 to 25.00
Sugar bowl, cov. 82.50
Vegetable bowl, cov., round 125.00

HOLLAND, THE (Alfred Meakin, ca. 1891)
Bone dish 34.00
Bowl, nappy 30.00
Gravy boat w/underplate 95.00
Plate, 6" d. 20.00
Plate, 10" d. 42.00
Platter, 12½ x 8¾" 100.00
Sugar bowl, cov. 105.00

HOLLAND (Johnson Bros., ca. 1891)
Butter pat 17.50
Plate, 6½" d. 15.00
Plate, 9" d. 30.00
Plate, 10" d. 38.00
Platter, 8" l. 24.00
Platter, 12½ x 9½" 50.00
Sugar bowl, cov. .... 90.00 to 115.00

HONG KONG (Charles Meigh, ca. 1845)
Cup plate, 4" d. 65.00
Honey dish, 5" d. 75.00
Plate, 9" d. (small flake) 70.00
Plate, 10" d. 125.00
Platter, 20" l. 365.00
Relish dish....................... 125.00
Sugar bowl, cov. 260.00
Teapot, cov. (professional repair) ... 225.00

IDRIS (W. H. Grindley, ca. 1910)
Bouillon cup & saucer............. 36.00
Cup & saucer 40.00
Plate, 9" d. 16.00
Plate, 10" d. .... 20.00 to 28.00

INDIAN (possibly F. & R. Pratt, ca. 1840)
Cake plate 175.00
Honey dish, 4" d. 75.00
Plate, 9½" d. 80.00
Plate, 10½" d. 95.00
Platter, 13½ x 10½" 185.00
Platter, 17" l. 295.00
Soap dish w/cover & drain insert
    (repaired chips on cover) 125.00

Soup plate w/flange rim, 10¾" d. . . . 85.00
Vegetable bowl, cov. 105.00

INDIAN JAR (Jacob & Thos. Furnival, ca. 1843)
Cup, handleless 60.00
Cup & saucer 70.00
Cup plate 75.00
Gravy boat 95.00
Honey dish, 5" d. 65.00
Pitcher, milk 225.00
Plate, 7½" d. 38.00
Plate, 9½" d. 65.00
Plate, 10½" d. 80.00
Platter, 10½" l. 150.00
Platter, 18 x 14" 295.00

IRIS (Arthur Wilkinson - Royal Staffordshire Potteries, ca. 1907)
Celery 150.00
Custard cup 25.00
Plate, 5" d. 65.00
Plate, 9" d. 140.00

ITALIA (W. & E. Corn, ca. 1891)
Cup & saucer 60.00
Plate, 8½" d. 55.00

IVY (Myott, Son & Company, ca. 1900)
Bowl, 10" to 11" d. . . . . 45.00 to 50.00
Cup & saucer, handleless 30.00
Pitcher, 7½" h. 195.00

JENNY LIND (Arthur Wilkinson Ltd. Royal Staffordshire Pottery, ca. 1895)
Bowl, 8" d. 130.00
Butter tub 75.00

JEWEL (Johnson Bros., ca. 1900)
Butter dish, cov. 85.00
Cup & saucer 45.00
Plate, 7" d. 35.00
Platter, 14" l. 85.00

KAOLIN (Podmore & Walker, ca. 1850)
Platter, 13 x 10½" 165.00
Sugar bowl, cov. 100.00

KEELE (W. H. Grindley, ca. 1891)
Bowl, 6" d. 20.00
Bowl, 10" d. 40.00
Butter dish, cov. 115.00
Vegetable bowl, cov., oval 75.00

KELVIN (Alfred Meakin, ca. 1891)
Bone dish 25.00
Bowl, 7" d. 48.00
Creamer 85.00
Plate, 9½" d. 40.00
Platter, small 65.00
Vegetable bowl, cov., oval 165.00

KENWORTH (Johnson Bros., ca. 1900)
Butter dish, cov. 100.00

Butter pat 25.00
Cup & saucer . . . . 45.00 to 60.00
Pitcher, milk, 7½" h. (rim chip
  professionally repaired) 95.00
Posset cup 75.00
Relish tray, 8" l. 52.00
Vegetable bowl, open, 9" oval 48.00

KESWICK (Wood & Sons, ca. 1891)
Bowl, 12 x 9½", shallow . . . . . 45.00 to 60.00
Platter, 12" l. 60.00
Vegetable bowl, open, 12" oblong . . 55.00

KYBER (John Meir & Son, ca. 1870; W. Adams & Son, ca. 1891)

Kyber Pattern Plate

Cup & saucer, handleless (Meir) 125.00
Plate, 7" to 8" d. (Adams) . . . 30.00 to 35.00
Plate, 7" to 8" d. (Meir) . . . . . 38.00 to 50.00
Plate, 9" d. (Adams) 50.00
Plate, 10" d., Adams (ILLUS.) 70.00
Platter, 10 x 7½" (Adams) . . 95.00 to 120.00
Platter, 17" l. (Adams) . . . . . 265.00 to 295.00
Saucer, 6" d. (Adams) 22.50
Saucer (Meir) 38.00
Soup plate w/flange rim, 9" d.
  (Adams) 50.00
Vegetable bowl, open, 10½ x 7¾"
  oblong (Adams) 165.00
Waste bowl, 6¼" (Adams) 95.00

LA BELLE (Wheeling Pottery, ca. 1900)
Bon bon dish, 7½" 50.00
Bone dish 40.00
Bowl, 9½" d., 2½" h. 75.00
Bowl, fruit, 11" d. 135.00
Bowl, 11½" d., loop
  handle . . . . 175.00 to 195.00
Cake plate, 10" d. 45.00
Celery tray 75.00
Centerpiece bowl, 4-footed,
  13 x 10" 325.00
Cup & saucer 60.00
Mint dish, tab handles, 5½" 55.00
Pitcher, milk 185.00
Plate, 9" to 10" d. . . . . 45.00 to 68.00

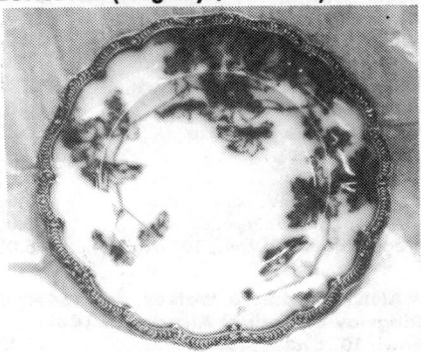

La Belle Chop Plate

Plate, chop, 13" d. (ILLUS.) . . .70.00 to 80.00
Platter, 13" l. 85.00
Saucer 20.00
Soup plate w/flange rim, 7" d. 45.00
Sugar bowl, cov. 95.00
Vegetable bowl, cov., 7¾" d. 145.00
Waste bowl. 60.00

LANCASTER (New Wharf Pottery, ca. 1891)
Butter dish, cov. 40.00
Cup & saucer . . . . .45.00 to 55.00
Gravy boat 65.00
Plate, 9" to 10" d. . . . . .35.00 to 45.00
Saucer 17.00
Soup plate w/flange rim 38.00

LEICESTER (Sampson Hancock, ca. 1906)
Gravy boat w/underplate . . . .72.00 to 85.00
Plate, 7½" d. 38.00
Plate, 10½" d. 47.00
Soup plate w/flange rim 30.00
Vegetable bowl, cov. . . . . . .150.00 to 185.00
Vegetable bowl, open, 10" 45.00

LE PAVOT (W. H. Grindley, ca. 1896)
Platter, 8½ x 4" 28.00
Platter, 12½" to 14½"
  oval . . . . .65.00 to 80.00
Sauce dish, 4¾" d. 25.00
Vegetable bowl, cov., round 75.00

LINDA (John Maddock & Sons Ltd., ca. 1896)
Bowl, 9" d. 45.00
Butter pat 16.00
Creamer & cov. sugar bowl, pr. 195.00
Cup & saucer, demitasse 48.00
Gravy boat w/underplate 86.00
Plate, 9" d. 42.00
Platters, 10" to 14" l., set of 4 . . . . . . 275.00
Teapot, cov. 150.00
Vegetable bowl, cov., 10" oval 135.00

LOBELIA (G. Phillips, dated June 19, 1845)
Coffee pot, cov. 265.00
Pitcher, milk (hairline) 135.00
Sugar bowl, cov. 150.00
Teapot, cov. 200.00

Lonsdale Pattern Plate

Plate, 8" d. 20.00
Plate, 10" d. (ILLUS.) 55.00
Platter, 13½ x 11" 105.00
Platter, 15" l. 77.50
Sauce dishes, set of 6 . . . . 75.00
Sugar bowl, cov. 95.00

LORNE (W. H. Grindley, ca. 1900)
Bowl, soup, 8" d. 18.00
Creamer . . . . .75.00 to 85.00
Gravy boat . . . . .50.00 to 60.00
Plate, 9" to 10" d. . . . . .45.00 to 55.00
Platter, 14" l. 85.00
Platter, 16 x 11½" 95.00
Relish dish. 70.00
Sauce dish, 5½" d. 25.00
Sauce tureen w/cover &
  underplate 185.00

LOUISE (New Wharf Pottery, ca. 1891)
Cup & saucer 35.00
Pitcher, milk 275.00
Vegetable bowl, cov. 125.00

LOZERE (Edward Challinor, ca. 1850)
Creamer . . . . .65.00 to 75.00
Vegetable bowl, 10 x 8" 150.00

LUSTRE BAND (Elsmore and Forster, ca. 1860, brush-painted)
Cup & saucer 50.00
Plate. 38.00
Sauce dish. 20.00

MADRAS (Samuel Alcock & Co., ca. 1845)
Plate, 9" d. 35.00
Platter, 13½" l. 150.00

MADRAS (Doulton & Co., ca. 1900)
Creamer, 5½" h. . . . . .75.00 to 85.00
Cup & saucer 60.00
Pitcher, milk, 7" h. . . . . .135.00 to 180.00
Plate, 8½" to 9½" d. . . . . . . .35.00 to 50.00
Platter, 16" l. 130.00
Relish dish, handled 65.00

Sugar bowl, cov. 125.00
Vegetable bowl, cov., oval 260.00
Waste bowl, 7" d., 3" h. 50.00

MANHATTAN (Henry Alcock, ca. 1900)
Butter pat, 3 3/8" d. 20.00
Creamer, individual size 60.00
Plate, 7" to 8" d. . . . . 32.00 to 42.00
Platter, 10" l. 40.00
Sugar bowl, cov. 75.00
Teapot, cov. 225.00
Vegetable bowl, cov., 10" oval 145.00

MANILA (Podmore Walker, ca. 1845; J. Ridgway or Samuel Alcock, ca. 1845)
Bowl, 10" oval 45.00
Creamer (Podmore Walker) 275.00
Cup & saucer, handleless (Podmore
   Walker) 128.00
Plate, 9" to 10" d. . . . . 80.00 to 90.00
Platter, 15½" l. (Podmore Walker) . . 195.00
Soup plate w/flange rim, 10½" d. . . . 125.00
Teapot, cov. 235.00
Vegetable dish, cov. (Podmore
   Walker) . . . . 375.00 to 450.00

MARECHAL NIEL (W. H. Grindley, ca. 1895)
Butter pat 22.00
Cup & saucer . . . . 28.00 to 35.00
Plate, 9" d. 36.00
Plate, 10" d. 45.00
Sugar bowl, cov. 110.00
Teapot, cov. 265.00

MARGUERITE (W. H. Grindley, ca. 1891)
Butter pat 14.00
Creamer & cov. sugar bowl, pr. 145.00
Plate, 9" d. 34.00
Sauce ladle 60.00
Soup tureen, cov., 12" d. 310.00

MARIE (W. H. Grindley, ca. 1891)
Compote 150.00
Plate, 10" d. 45.00
Platter, 14½" l. 85.00
Platter, 16 x 11" 130.00
Soup plate w/flange rim, 9" d. 34.00

MELBOURNE (W. H. Grindley, ca. 1900)
Bowl, 5½" d. 30.00
Bowl, cov., 8¼" d. 145.00
Bowl, 9" oval 70.00
Butter pat, 3¼" d. 26.00
Creamer, large 145.00
Gravy boat 85.00
Plate, 6" d. 25.00
Plate, 8" d. 35.00
Platter, 10" to 11" l. 65.00
Platter, 16½ x 12½" 150.00
Sauce dish 18.00
Soup plate w/flange rim, 7¾" d. . . . 25.00
Sugar bowl, cov. 95.00
Vegetable bowl, cov., 10" d. 115.00

MESSINA (Alfred Meakin, ca. 1891)
Bowl, soup, 7¼" d. 18.00
Plate, 10" d. 58.00
Soup tureen, cov. 120.00

MONGOLIA (Johnson Bros., ca. 1900)
Creamer 70.00
Cup 20.00
Plate, 9¼" d. 47.50
Sugar bowl 75.00

MORNING GLORY (Maker unknown, probably English, ca. 1860)
Bowl 150.00
Plate, 9¼" d. 55.00
Waste bowl 125.00

NEOPOLITAN (Johnson Bros., ca. 1900)
Bone dish 15.00
Butter pat, 3" d. 18.00
Plate, 9" d. 26.00

NON PAREIL (Burgess & Leigh, ca. 1891)

Non Pareil Pattern Plate

Bowl, soup 55.00
Charger, 12" d. 135.00
Cup & saucer, demitasse 85.00
Cup & saucer 50.00
Plate, 6" d. 30.00
Plate, 8½" d. 45.00
Plate, 9½" d. (ILLUS.) . . . . 47.00 to 55.00
Vegetable tureen, cov. . . . . 185.00 to 250.00

NORMANDY (Johnson Bros., ca. 1900)
Bowl, cereal 55.00
Butter pat 30.00
Cup & saucer 55.00
Plate, 9" to 10" d. . . . . 35.00 to 45.00
Platter, 12½" l. 50.00
Sauce dish 12.00
Sugar bowl, cov. 140.00

OREGON (Johnson Bros., ca. 1900)
Bowl, cereal, 7½" d. 38.00
Plate, 9" d. 52.00
Platter, 12" l. 55.00

OREGON (T. J. & J. Mayer, ca. 1845)

Oregon Pattern Sauce Tureen

Cup & saucer, handleless 60.00
Pitcher, water, 13" h............... 395.00
Plate, 7½" to 8½" d........45.00 to 68.00
Platter, 13½" l..................... 225.00
Sauce tureen, cover, underplate &
   ladle, 6" l., 3 pcs. (ILLUS.) 415.00

ORIENTAL (Ridgways, ca. 1891)

Bowl, 9" d........................ 45.00
Butter pat, 3¼" d................. 20.00
Pitcher, 6" h..................... 125.00
Plate, 6" d....................... 30.00
Plate, 8" d....................... 48.00
Plate, 9¾" d...................... 85.00
Sauce dish........................ 16.00
Soup plate w/flange rim, 9" d. 27.00

ORMONDE (Alfred Meakin, ca. 1891)

Bone dish 23.00
Butter pat 18.00
Plate, 6¾" d...................... 26.00
Platter, 18 x 15" 160.00
Soup plate w/flange rim 60.00

OSBORNE (W. H. Grindley, ca. 1900)

Plate, 6" d....................... 18.00
Plate, 10" d...................... 36.00
Platter, 16 x 11¾" 148.00
Sauce dish, 5½" d................. 14.00
Saucer 10.00

OSBORNE (Ridgways, ca. 1905)

Butter pat 20.00
Gravy boat w/attached
   underplate 95.00
Soup plate w/flange rim, 8¾" d. ... 38.00
Vegetable bowl, cov., cloverleaf-
   shaped................175.00 to 195.00

PARIS (New Wharf Pottery and Stanley Pottery Co., 1890's)

Bowl, 9" d........................ 35.00
Butter pat 18.50
Cup & saucer 55.00
Plate, 9" d....................... 32.00
Platter, 14" l.................... 85.00

PEACH or PEACH ROYAL (Johnson Bros., ca. 1891)

Bone dish 35.00
Gravy boat 85.00
Plate, 7" d....................... 22.00
Plate, 9" d....................... 45.00
Plate, 10" d...................... 55.00
Soup plate w/flange rim 45.00
Spooner 75.00

PELEW (E. Challinor, ca. 1840)

Cup & saucer, handleless 100.00
Plate, 9" to 10" d...........65.00 to 85.00
Platter, 13 x 10" 190.00
Sauce dish........................ 40.00
Soup plate w/flange rim, 10½" d. ... 125.00

PERSIAN MOSS (Utzschneider & Co., ca. 1891)

Bowl, cereal, 6" d. 30.00
Bowl, 8½" d. 40.00
Cup & saucer ....30.00 to 37.00
Vegetable bowl, open, 8" d. 35.00

POPPY (New Wharf Pottery, ca. 1891)

Bowl, cereal 30.00
Chamber pot...................... 74.00
Cup & saucer 45.00
Plate, 8" to 9" d...........30.00 to 40.00

PORTMAN (W. H. Grindley, ca. 1891)

Bowl, footed, small............... 40.00
Bowl, berry...................... 15.00
Butter pat 17.50
Cup & saucer 75.00
Plate, 9" d....................... 25.00
Relish dish, 8¾" 35.00
Soup plate w/flange rim, 8" d. 23.00

PRINCETON (Johnson Bros., ca. 1900)

Butter pat 15.00
Cup & saucer 40.00
Gravy boat 55.00
Pitcher, milk, 9" h............... 155.00
Plate, 9" d....................... 35.00
Sauce dishes, set of 6 .... 100.00
Sauce ladle 85.00
Vegetable bowl, open, oval 90.00

PROGRESS (W. H. Grindley, ca. 1894)

Plate, 9" d....................... 27.00
Plate, 10" d...................... 38.00
Platter, 12" l.................... 65.00
Sauce tureen, cover & underplate... 125.00
Soup plate w/flange rim, 8" d. 24.00

REGENT (Alfred Meakin, Ltd., ca. 1897)

Cup & saucer 75.00
Sugar bowl, cov. 97.00
Platter, 12 x 9¼" 65.00

REGOUT'S FLOWER (Petrus Regout, ca. 1900, brush-painted)

Cup & saucer 45.00

Saucer	20.00
Soup plate w/flange rim, 9" d.	68.00

RICHMOND (Johnson Bros., ca. 1900)

Bowl, 7½" d.	25.00
Creamer	65.00
Plate, 6½" to 7½" d. ....15.00 to 22.00	
Plate, dinner.....................	45.00
Platter, 12½" l.	35.00

ROMEO (Wedgwood Co., ca. 1908)

Bone dish, kidney-shaped,	
6¼ x 3"	30.00
Gravy boat	36.00
Vegetable bowl, cov........90.00 to 110.00	

ROSE (W. H. Grindley, ca. 1893)

Bowl, 7¼" d., 1¼" h.	47.00
Cup & saucer	30.00
Gravy boat w/underplate	75.00
Plate, 6½" d.	13.00
Plate, 7½" to 8½" d. ....25.00 to 32.00	
Platter, 10 x 7¼"	38.00
Platter, 12" l.	40.00
Sauce dish.......................	12.00
Soup plate w/flange rim	35.00
Vegetable bowl, cov.	75.00

ROSEVILLE (John Maddocks, ca. 1891)

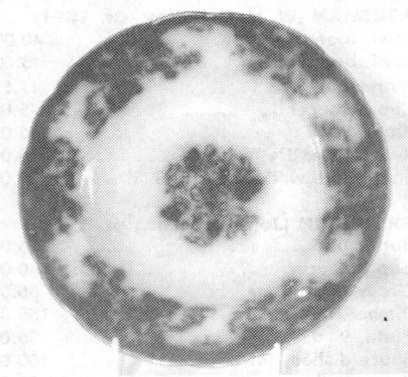

Roseville Soup Plate

Bowl, berry......................	16.00
Cup & saucer	35.00
Plate, 9" d. ....25.00 to 30.00	
Platter, 10" l. ....45.00 to 60.00	
Platter, 16 x 11½"	115.00
Sauce dish.......................	15.00
Soup plate w/flange rim, 8½" d.	
(ILLUS.)........................	40.00
Soup tureen, cov., 14 x 9"	295.00
Sugar bowl, cov.	49.00
Vegetable bowl, open, oval ..45.00 to 55.00	

SABRAON (Maker unknown, probably English, ca. 1845)

Creamer	195.00
Gravy boat ....165.00 to 185.00	

Plate, 8" d.	60.00
Soup plate w/flange rim	75.00

ST. LOUIS (Johnson Bros., ca. 1900)

St. Louis Sugar Bowl

Bone dish	32.50
Butter pat	15.00
Plate, 7" d.	38.00
Plate, 10" d.	62.00
Platter, large	60.00
Sugar bowl, cov. (ILLUS.)..........	60.00

SAVOY (Johnson Bros., ca. 1900)

Savoy Plate

Gravy boat	42.00
Plate, 10" d. (ILLUS.)	40.00
Platter, 14½ x 10½" .....110.00 to 125.00	
Soup plate w/flange rim	36.00

SCINDE (J. & G. Alcock, ca. 1840 and Thomas Walker, ca. 1847)

Cup & saucer, handleless ...85.00 to 100.00	
Cup plate ....65.00 to 75.00	
Gravy boat, cov.	175.00
Honey dish, 5" d.	75.00
Pitcher, milk.....................	135.00
Plate, 8" d.	60.00
Plate, 9" d. (ILLUS.)	66.00
Plate, 10½" d.	85.00
Platter, 11 x 8½" ....155.00 to 170.00	

Scinde Plate

Platter, 13" l. 285.00
Platter, 16 x 12½" 250.00
Relish dish, shell-shaped 85.00
Sauce dish 42.00
Sauce tureen, cover & underplate ... 375.00
Soup plate w/flange rim 75.00
Soup tureen, cov. 450.00
Sugar bowl 175.00
Vegetable bowl, cov., 11 x 9" 350.00
Waste bowl, 6" d. (hairlines) 125.00

SEVILLE (New Wharf Pottery, ca. 1891 and Wood & Son)
Bowl, 6 " d. 20.00
Gravy boat 45.00
Plate, 9" d. 52.00
Platter, 12½ x 9" 125.00
Vegetable bowl, cov. ......195.00 to 215.00

SHANGHAE (J. Furnival, ca. 1860)
Cup & saucer 55.00
Plate, 9" d. 63.00
Plate, 10" d. 95.00
Platter, 13½" l. 165.00
Platter, 15½ x 12" ....135.00 to 145.00
Sauce dish, 5" d. 28.00
Vegetable bowl, cov. 195.00

SHANGHAI (W. & E. Corn, ca. 1900)

Shanghai Plate

Cup & saucer 32.00
Plate, 8½" d. 50.00
Plate, 10" d. (ILLUS.) 60.00

SHANGHAI (W. H. Grindley, ca. 1891)
Bowl, 8" d. 23.00
Plate, 5¾" d. 30.00
Plate, 8" d. 40.00
Sauce dish 50.00
Vegetable bowl, open, 9" oval 60.00

SHAPOO (T. & R. Boote, ca. 1842)
Cup 75.00
Cup & saucer ....95.00 to 110.00
Plate, 7½" d. 50.00
Plate, 8½" d. 70.00
Plate, 9½" to 10½" d. ....80.00 to 90.00
Platter, 12" l. 175.00
Soup plate w/flange rim,
   9½" d. ....95.00 to 120.00

SOBRAON (Maker unknown, English, ca. 1850)
Cup 60.00
Gravy boat 175.00
Honey dish, scalloped rim, 4" d. 65.00
Plate, 6½" d. 46.00
Plate, 8" d. 50.00
Plate, 9½" d. 65.00
Platter, 12" l., scalloped
   corners 170.00
Saucer 35.00
Vegetable bowl, cov. 375.00
Vegetable bowl, open, 10½" d. 120.00

SPINACH (Libertas, ca. 1900, brush-painted)

Spinach Pattern Bowl

Bowl, 8" d. (ILLUS.) 45.00
Creamer, small (crow's foot in
   base) 45.00
Cup & saucer, demitasse 55.00
Cup & saucer ....60.00 to 70.00
Oyster bowl 70.00
Plate, 6" d. 35.00
Vegetable bowl, 10" d. 55.00

SYLVAN (Brown-Westhead, Moore & Co., ca. 1900)
Compote 100.00
Plate, 8" d. 30.00
Soup plate w/flange rim 50.00

TEMPLE, THE (Podmore Walker, ca. 1850)
Creamer 250.00
Cup & saucer, handleless ....65.00 to 75.00
Cup & saucer 95.00
Ladle 75.00
Pitcher, 6" h. 265.00
Plate, 7" d. 55.00
Plate, 9" d. ....65.00 to 75.00
Plate, 10" d. ....85.00 to 95.00
Platter, 13" l. 150.00
Platter, 16 x 12", cut corners 285.00
Waste bowl....................... 165.00

TILLENBERG (J. Clementson, ca. 1845)
Plate, 10" d. 80.00
Platter, 14 x 10½" 130.00

TIMOR (Petrus Regout, ca. 1875 and Luneville, France)
Pitcher & bowl, child's, 4" h.
  pitcher 75.00
Plate, 7" d. 30.00
Plate, 8" d. 36.00
Waste bowl....................... 50.00

TOGO (F. Winkle, ca. 1900)

Togo Pattern Plate

Bowl, 10" d. 45.00
Cup & saucer 35.00
Plate, 7" d. 30.00
Plate, 9" d. 37.00
Plate, 10" d. (ILLUS.) 45.00
Soup plate w/flange rim 30.00
Soup tureen, round................ 125.00
Wash basin & pitcher 325.00

TONQUIN (W. Adams & Son, ca. 1845)
Creamer 275.00
Plate, 6" d. 45.00
Plate, 7½" d. 52.00

Plate, 8½" d. 65.00
Sauce dish........................ 50.00
Soup plate w/flange rim, 10½" d. ... 125.00
Toddy plate, 5" d. 75.00

TOURAINE (Henry Alcock, ca. 1898 and Stanley Pottery Co., ca. 1898)
Bone dish 45.00
Bowl, 5" d. 35.00
Bowl, 9" to 10" d., tab
  handles ....95.00 to 110.00
Butter pat ....27.00 to 35.00
Cake plate, tab handles, square 145.00
Creamer, 3½" h.................. 135.00
Creamer, 4½" h.................. 150.00
Cup & saucer, demitasse.....55.00 to 65.00
Cup & saucer ....55.00 to 70.00
Dinner service for eight w/demi-
  tasse & coffee size cups & sau-
  cers, cov. teapot, creamer, sugar
  bowl, waste bowl, gravy boat
  w/underplate, cake plate, vegeta-
  ble bowls & platters, 92 pcs......5,500.00
Gravy boat w/underplate 140.00
Pitcher, 6" h. 145.00
Pitcher, water, 8" h.............. 400.00
Pitcher, 3-pt. 360.00
Pitcher, milk.................... 250.00
Plate, 6½" d. 25.00
Plate, 7½" to 8½" d.........35.00 to 45.00
Plate, 9" to 10" d. ....40.00 to 58.00
Platter, 10" l. 75.00
Platter, 12" l. 105.00
Platter, 15" l. 135.00
Sauce dish, 4½" d. 18.00
Soup plate w/flange rim, 9" d. 45.00
Sugar bowl, open 80.00
Teapot, cov. 475.00
Vegetable bowl, cov., 9" oval 250.00
Vegetable bowl, open, tab handles,
  9" oval 90.00
Vegetable dish, individual size,
  6 x 4¼" oval 40.00

TURIN (Johnson Bros., date unknown)
Butter pat, 3" d. 18.00
Plates, 7" d., set of 6............. 60.00
Plate, 10" d. 40.00

VERONA (Ford & Sons, Ltd., ca. 1908)
Egg cup 40.00
Gravy boat w/underplate 95.00
Plate, 7" d. 25.00
Plate, 9" to 10" d...........35.00 to 45.00
Platter, 13" l..................... 75.00
Platter, 15" l..................... 110.00
Vegetable bowl, cov. 135.00

VERSAILLES (Furnival, ca. 1894)
Bowl, soup 45.00
Cup & saucer 80.00
Platter, 12" l. 85.00
Soup plate w/flange rim, 9" d. 45.00
Vegetable bowl, cov., oval 110.00

VIRGINIA (John Maddock & Sons, ca. 1891)

Dinner service for six w/cov. sugar bowl, creamer, cov. vegetable bowl & platter, 42 pcs.	1,100.00
Gravy boat	45.00
Platter, 12½" l.	90.00
Platter, 17" l.	125.00
Vegetable bowl, cov., 11½" oval	145.00

WALDORF (New Wharf Pottery, ca. 1892)

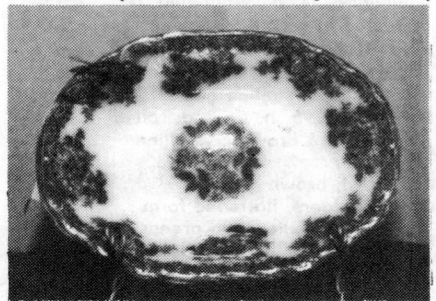

Waldorf Vegetable Bowl

Bowl, 9" d.	70.00
Bowl, soup	45.00
Cup & saucer	50.00
Plate, 8" d.	43.00
Plate, 9" to 10" d.	45.00 to 60.00
Platter, 10" l.	50.00
Sauce dish	30.00
Soup plate w/flange rim	38.00
Vegetable bowl, cov., oval	285.00
Vegetable bowl, open, 9" oval (ILLUS.)	85.00
Waste bowl	50.00

WARWICK (Warwick China Co., ca. 1900)

Celery dish	65.00
Syrup pitcher w/pewter top, 4" h.	125.00
Tea set, cov. teapot, cov. sugar bowl, creamer & 14" d. tray, 4 pcs.	525.00

WATTEAU (Doulton, ca. 1900)

Bowl, 8¾" d., footed	150.00
Plate, 7" d.	30.00
Plate, 8" d.	45.00
Plate, 10" d.	70.00
Platter, 17 x 14"	265.00
Platter w/well & tree	395.00
Sauce tureen, cover, underplate & ladle	325.00
Soup tureen, cover, underplate & ladle	775.00
Teapot, cov.	145.00
Vegetable bowl, cov.	225.00

WATTEAU (New Wharf Pottery, ca. 1891)

Pitcher, milk	85.00
Vegetable bowl, open, 10 x 7" oval	75.00

FRANKOMA POTTERY

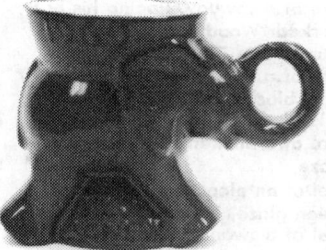

1969 "Nixon - Agnew" Mug

John Frank began producing and selling pottery on a part-time basis during the summer of 1933 while he was still teaching art and pottery classes at the University of Oklahoma. In 1934, Frankoma Pottery became an incorporated business that was successful enough to allow him to leave his teaching position, in 1936, and devote full time to its growth. The pottery was moved to Sapulpa, Oklahoma in 1938 and a full range of art pottery and dinner wares were eventually offered. Since John Frank's death in 1973, the pottery has been directed by his daughter, Joniece. The early wares and limited editions are becoming increasingly popular with collectors today. Also see COMMEMORATIVE PLATES.

Ash tray, arrowhead-shaped, turquoise & brown glaze	$3.00
Bookend, model of charger horse, Ada clay, desert gold glaze, No. 420, 1934-60 (single)	52.50
Bookend, seated figure, ivory glaze, incised leopard mark, 1936-38 (single)	150.00
Bookends, model of a bucking bronco, green glaze, pr.	135.00
Bookends, model of Irish Setter dog, Ada clay, black glaze, pr.	95.00 to 110.00
Bowl, 8" d., green glaze, marked "Frank Potteries," 1933-34	95.00
Candle holder, 2-light, seashell form, tan & green glaze (single)	50.00
Candle holder, figural "Flower Girl," No. 700 (single)	65.00
Casserole, cov., Wagon Wheel patt., horseshoe handles, green glaze, 7½" d.	22.00
Christmas card, 1960, fish tray	50.00
Christmas card, 1961, Aztec tray	25.00
Christmas card, 1966, free-form leaf tray	42.00
Christmas card, 1977, 1979 or 1980, each	13.00
Creamer, Wagon Wheel patt., brown & green glaze, 2½" h.	5.00

Dish, leaf-shaped, marked "Grace-
tone," 9" l. 19.00
Figure of a cowboy, tipping his hat,
marked "Woodward, Okla." on
round base, 7¾" h. 75.00
Figure of a fan dancer, Ada clay,
onyx black glaze, 1935-69,
13½" l., 8½" h................. 185.00
Figure of a Billiken, prairie green
glaze 110.00
Model of an elephant, walking,
green glaze, 1¾" l. 35.00
Model of a swan, closed back, onyx
black glaze, No. 168, 1936-57,
3" h. ....30.00 to 50.00
Mug, brown & green glaze,
6½" h.......................... 7.00
Mug, 1968 (Republican) elephant,
white glaze, 1st edition 70.00
Mug, 1969 elephant, "Nixon - Agnew," flame glaze (ILLUS.) 55.00
Mug, 1970 elephant, blue glaze..... 42.50
Mug, 1971 elephant, black glaze.... 42.50
Mug, 1973 elephant, "Nixon - Ag-
new," coffee glaze 32.50
Mug, 1975 (Democratic) donkey,
autumn yellow glaze 10.00
Mug, 1976 elephant, centennial red
glaze 25.00
Mug, 1978 donkey, woodland moss
glaze 8.50
Pitcher, 2" h., snail-shaped, Ada
clay, mint green glaze 20.00
Pitcher, water, 7½" h., Wagon
Wheel patt., green glaze 12.50
Planter, model of a swan, green
glaze, 9" l. 20.00
Planter, model of a Dutch shoe,
green glaze, No. 913 .... 8.00
Plaque, pierced to hang, bust por-
trait of Will Rogers in relief,
borderless, 1934-35,
4¾ x 4"..................90.00 to 125.00
Plate, dinner, Wagon Wheel patt.,
green glaze...................... 12.00
Salt & pepper shakers, Wagon
Wheel patt., green glaze, pr...... 7.00
Sugar bowl, cov., Mayan Aztec
patt., white glaze 7.00
Vase, 8" h., ram's head, tan &
green glaze..................... 60.00
Wall pocket, model of an acorn,
lavender glaze 12.00

FULPER

*The Fulper Pottery was founded in
Flemington, N.J., in 1805 and operated until 1935, although operations were curtailed
in 1929 when its main plant was destroyed
by fire. The name was changed in 1929 to*
*Stangl Pottery, which continued in operation
until July of 1978, when Pfaltzgraff, a division of Susquehanna Broadcasting Company
of York, Pennsylvania, purchased the assets
of the Stangl Pottery, including the name.*

Bookends, figure of a primitive
man, matte blue glaze, pr.......$150.00
Bowl, 7" d., 3" h., footed, blue
"flambe" glaze on ivory 100.00
Bowl, 7" d., 4" h., 2-handled, red
shaded to purple glaze 50.00
Bowl, 10½" d., 3" h., footed, scalloped rim, glossy blue over tobacco green crystalline glaze 150.00
Bowl, 11" d., 8" h., footed, rolled
rim, blue & brown crystalline
glaze 160.00
Bulb bowl, brown glaze, 8½" d. 85.00
Candle holders, flattened form
w/three handles, sea green
"leopard skin" glaze, original
label & price tag, 6" d., pr. 125.00
Candlesticks, rope-twist stem, maroon & ivory glaze, 11¼" h., pr... 145.00
Chamberstick, turquoise over olive
green crystalline glaze........... 45.00
Compote, matte blue glaze, large .. 65.00
Console bowl, mustard yellow
"flambe" glaze, 10" d. 95.00

"Effigy" Flower Bowl

"Effigy" bowl, shallow circular bowl
supported by 3 seated figures
raised on tiered circular platform,
navy-speckled matte blue glaze,
7½" h. (ILLUS.) 1,320.00
Flower bowl & lily pad flower frog,
aqua glaze, paper label, 9" d.,
2 pcs. 80.00
Flower frog, figural white nude
seated on green base w/yellow
florals, 5½" h.................. 85.00
Flower frog, model of a lily pad,
black-tinged green glazed........ 14.00
Flower pot, rolled rim, blue glaze,
5½" 55.00
Flower pot, brown & blue "flambe"
glaze, 6" 125.00

Jardiniere, 3-handled, black "mirror" and caramel glaze, 4" 75.00

Jug, 2-handled, horizontal ribbing, mottled brown glaze 235.00

Lamp base, green crystalline glaze, unmarked, 10½" 160.00

Mugs, cucumber green glaze, pr. 80.00

Perfume lamp, figural canary birds......................... 425.00

Pitcher, 4" h., green glaze, 125th Anniversary paper label 80.00

Pitcher, 5½" h., gunmetal grey & green glaze.................... 40.00

Powder jar, figural lady w/fan cover, shaded lavender glaze 185.00

Urn, lion's head handles at sides, wisteria blue crystalline glaze, 6" h.......................... 95.00

Vase, 3½" h., brown shaded to mustard "flambe" glaze.......... 60.00

Vase, 4" h., black drip glaze over green 40.00

Vase, 5" h., 3-footed, brown-black Mission matte glaze 90.00

Vase, 6½" h., beehive-shaped, blue-green drip on copper dust glaze 265.00

Vase, 7" h., 2-handled, bulbous, rose glaze 225.00

Fulper 5-Handled Vase

Vase, 10½" h., ball-shaped w/five free-standing ring handles, shaded blue & sky blue glaze, partial paper label (ILLUS.) 5,500.00

Vase, 11" h., hexagonal, mottled Chinese blue & olive green glaze 275.00

Vase, 12" h., 6" d., "leopard skin" glaze 600.00

Fulper Vase

Vase, 8¼" h., black-streaked "cafe au lait" glaze above olive matte glaze w/green crystalline highlights (ILLUS.) 1,980.00

Vase, bud, 8½" h., square base, aqua crystalline glaze 45.00

Vase, 9" h., 2-handled, gunmetal grey & green "flambe" glaze 150.00

Vases, 8¼" h., ovoid w/incurvate shoulder & circular rim, streaked glaze w/mirror finish, taupe shading to steel grey & to green & ochre crystalline glaze in the lower body, ca. 1900, pr. 660.00

Fulper Vase

Vase, 16¼" h., textured black-mottled cucumber green glaze (ILLUS.) 1,760.00

Vase, 17½" h., ribbed ovoid, 2-handled, mottled brown, gold, cream & green glaze, ca. 1915 ... 990.00

GALLE' POTTERY

Fine pottery was made by Emile Galle', the multi-talented French designer and artisan, who is also famous for his glass and furniture.

*The pottery is relatively scarce. Also see the
FURNITURE section for Art Nouveau style
pieces designed by Emile Galle' and GLASS
- Galle'.*

Ewer, broad spout, circular handle
w/openwork details, h.p. vignette
of man on barrel playing a bagpipe & 2 seated peasants front,
gold & brown high glaze, signed,
10" h. $352.00
Ewer, Art Nouveau style, pinched-in
sides, green, gold, beige & rust
poppies in indentations w/gold
vines connecting to green bell-
shaped florals at front on overall
chocolate brown glaze highlighted
w/iridescent gold, 11½" h. 750.00
Model of a duck, Imari-type blue,
white & rusty orange decor,
signed, 15½" l., 7" h. 950.00

Galle' Falcons

Models of horned falcons, one
detailed in white & blue & other in
tan & purple, on square plinths,
signed, 9½" h., pr. (ILLUS.) 1,980.00
Model of a dog seated, fierce expression w/his mouth detailed in
pink & inset glass eyes, indigo
blue & white hearts & dots decor
against lemon yellow ground, ca.
1890, 12½" h. 660.00
Vase, 6" h., h.p. figures (2) on front
panel & bird in cage reverse, blue
& red w/gold, signed 350.00
Vase, 12¼" h., 3 tiers of graduated
ball shapes molded w/blue
florettes & pierced w/irregular
flower holes, each ball w/h.p. river landscape cartouche & the
whole conjoined w/molded
branches & leafage, ca. 1880 . . . . . 770.00
Wall pocket, fan-shaped w/protrud-
ing bow at side, butterflies &
bows decor, sky blue w/touches
of gold & black, 14" h. 395.00
Watch holder, h.p. country scene,
branches, leaves & typical Galle'
insects decor, 10 x 6". 595.00

GAUDY DUTCH

Gaudy Dutch Carnation Pattern

*This name is applied to English soft paste
and ironstone wares with designs copied from
Oriental patterns. Production began in the
18th century. These copies flooded into this
country in the early 19th century. The incor-
poration of the word "Dutch" derives from
the fact that it was the Dutch who first
brought these Oriental wares into Europe.
The ware was not, as often erroneously report-
ed, made specifically for the Pennsylvania
Dutch.*

Coffee pot, cov., Carnation
patt. $1,500.00
Plate, 7" d., War Bonnet patt. 575.00
Plate, 7¼" d., Urn patt. 205.00
Plate, 8" d., Grape patt. . . .250.00 to 350.00
Plate, 8½" d., Oyster patt., Ridgway
border 675.00
Plate, 9¾" d., Carnation patt.
(ILLUS.) 450.00
Plate, 10" d., Double Rose patt. 325.00
Plate, 10" d., Grape patt. 550.00
Tea bowl & saucer, Double Rose
patt. 395.00
Tea bowl & saucer, Grape patt. 350.00
Tea bowl & saucer, Oyster
patt. . . . . .395.00 to 450.00
Tea bowl & saucer, Single Rose
patt. 350.00
Tea bowl & saucer, War Bonnet
patt. 475.00
Waste bowl, Double Rose patt.,
5 3/8" d., 2¾" h. 325.00

GAUDY WELSH

*This is a name for wares made in England
for the American market about 1830 to 1845.
Decorated with Imari-style flower patterns,
often highlighted with copper lustre, it should*

not be confused with Gaudy Dutch wares whose colors differ somewhat.

Gaudy Welsh Pitcher

Bowl, 5" d., Oyster patt., blue, rust
  & copper lustre $58.00
Bowl, 9½" d., 4" h., footed, bold
  pattern (small edge chips) 75.00
Bowl, Morning Glory patt. 75.00
Cake plate, Tulip patt., 10" d. 75.00
Creamer, pedestal foot, flower &
  sprigs in medallions, rust, yellow,
  green & copper lustre, 4 3/8" h. ... 60.00
Creamer, Gwent patt. variant, rust
  flowers in blue panels, 4½" h. 95.00
Creamer, Morning Glory patt. 75.00
Creamer, Oyster patt. 75.00
Cup & saucer, Daisy patt., pink
  flowers on royal blue ground,
  copper lustre trim 37.50
Cup & saucer, Morning Glory patt... 50.00
Cup & saucer, Oyster patt. 60.00
Cup & saucer, flaring cup w/wish-
  bone handle, Tulip patt. ...65.00 to 75.00
Cup & saucer, straight-sided cup,
  Tulip patt. ....30.00 to 45.00
Cup & saucer, Wagon Wheel patt. .. 50.00
Hot water pitcher, Grape IV patt.
  variant 95.00
Mug, child's, Grape II patt.
  variant 58.00
Pitcher, 7¾" h., Deiniolen patt. 210.00
Pitcher, water, Grape-type patt.,
  pink lustre trim, 1830-45
  (ILLUS.) ....250.00 to 285.00
Plate, 7¼" w., scalloped rim, Tulip
  patt. 55.00
Plate, 7½" d., Wagon Wheel
  patt. ....42.50 to 58.00
Sauce tureen & cover w/cornucopia-
  form finial, bulbous body w/ram's
  head handles at sides, Grape
  patt. variant, overall 11½" h.
  (minor hairlines in lid & base) 225.00
Sugar bowl, cov., Morning Glory
  patt. 95.00

GEISHA GIRL WARES

Cookie Jar with Geisha Girls

The beautiful geisha, a Japanese girl specifically trained to entertain with singing or dancing, is the featured decoration on this Japanese china which was cheaply made and mass-produced for export. Now finding favor with collectors across the United States, the ware varies in quality. The geisha pattern is not uniform—Butterfly, Paper Lantern, Parasol, Sedan Chair and other variations are found in this pattern that is usually colored in shades of red through orange but is also found in blue and green tones. Collectors try to garner the same design in approximately the same color tones.

Berry set: master berry bowl & 6
  sauce dishes; blue trim, 7 pcs. ... $40.00
Bowl, 8" d., red trim 23.00
Bowl, 10" d., petal rim, orange trim
  w/gold 60.00
Chocolate pot, cov., ornate double
  handle, girls in garden, red trim
  w/gold, 10" h. 65.00
Chocolate pot, cov., blue trim
  (repaired lid) 45.00
Chocolate pot, cov., Paper Lantern
  patt., red-orange trim 60.00
Chocolate set: cov. chocolate pot &
  4 c/s; red trim, 9 pcs. 100.00
Chocolate set: cov. chocolate pot &
  5 c/s; blue trim, 11 pcs. 70.00
Cookie jar, cov., blue trim 65.00
Cookie jar, cov., melon-ribbed, red
  trim & enameled white beading,
  Oriental seal mark (ILLUS.)....... 65.00
Creamer, green trim 12.00
Creamer & cov. sugar bowl, blue
  trim w/gold, pr. 35.00
Cup & saucer, green trim 8.00
Cup & saucer, red trim ....6.50 to 10.00
Egg cup 6.00
Hatpin holder, orange trim, 4" h. ... 30.00
Match holder w/striker, wall-type,
  orange trim, 3¼" 22.50
Mug, small 14.00

Pitcher, 4" h., blue trim w/gold	85.00
Pitcher, 4" h., green trim	6.50
Pitcher, 7" h., blue trim...........	40.00
Plate, 6" d., red-orange trim	4.50
Plate, 7" d., 5-fluted rim, rust trim..	75.00
Plate, 7¼" d., scalloped edge, blue trim...........................	6.50
Plate, 7½" d., red-orange trim	10.00
Powder jar, cov., red trim	15.00
Powder jar & hair receiver, blue trim, oversized, pr..............	45.00
Powder jar & hair receiver, red trim, pr.............................	38.00
Salt & pepper shakers w/pierced tops, blue trim, ca. 1900, 2½" h., pr.............................	15.00
Sauce dishes, blue trim, 5" d., set of 6	32.00
Sugar bowl, cov., bulbous, red trim, 4½"	8.50
Teapot, cov., blue trim	23.50
Tea set: cov. teapot & 4 c/s; red trim, 9 pcs.....................	139.00
Toothpick holder, red trim	18.00

GIBSON GIRL PLATES

Doulton Gibson Girl Plate

The artist Charles Dana Gibson produced a series of 24 drawings entitled "The Widow and Her Friends," and these were reproduced on plates by the Royal Doulton works at Lambeth, England. The plates were copyrighted by Life Publishing Company in 1900 and 1901. The majority of these plates usually sell within a price range of $70.00 to $85.00 today.

A Message from the Outside World (No. 1)	$70.00
And Here Winning New Friends (No. 2)	82.50
A Quiet Dinner with Dr. Bottles (No. 3)	85.00

Failing to Find Rest and Quiet in the Country She Decides to Return Home (No. 4)	70.00
Miss Babbles Brings a Copy of the Morning Paper (No. 5)	75.00
Miss Babbles, the Authoress, Calls and Reads Aloud (No. 6)	82.50
Mrs. Diggs is Alarmed at Discovering...(No. 7)	72.50
Mr. Waddles Arrives Late and Finds Her Card Filled, No. 8 (ILLUS.)....	100.00
She Becomes a Trained Nurse (No. 9)	76.50
She Contemplates the Cloister (No. 10)	77.50
She Decides to Die in Spite of Dr. Bottles (No. 11)	80.00
She Finds Some Consolation in Her Mirror (No. 12).................	87.50
She Finds That Exercise Does Not Improve Her Spirits (No. 13)......	76.00
She Goes into Colors (No. 14)	67.50
She Goes to the Fancy Dress Ball as "Juliet" (No. 15).................	68.00
She is Disturbed by a Vision (No. 16)	75.00
She is Subject to More Hostile Criticism (No. 17)	72.50
She Longs for Seclusion (No. 18)	85.00
She Looks for Relief Among Some of the Old Ones (No. 19)	72.50
Some Think that She has Remained in Retirement Too Long (No. 20) ..	77.50
The Day After Arriving at Her Journey's End (No. 21)	77.50
They All Go Skating (No. 22)	75.00
They All Go Fishing (No. 23)	76.00
They Take a Morning Run (No. 24)..	68.50

GOLDSCHEIDER

The Goldscheider firm manufactured porcelain and faience in Austria between 1885 and 1953. Founded by Friedrich Goldscheider and carried on by his widow, the firm came under the control of his sons, Walter and Marcell, in 1920. Fleeing their native Austria at the time of World War II, the Goldscheiders set up an operation in the United States. They were listed in the Trenton, New Jersey, City Directory from 1943 through 1950 and their main production seems to have been art pottery figurines.

Bust of an Arab, 12" h.	$285.00
Busts of an Indian Prince & Princess, wearing colorful turbans, 8" h., pr............................	75.00
Busts of an Oriental boy & girl, 8" h., pr.	115.00
Figure of "Southern Lady," 7½" h. ..	50.00

Figure of "Lorenzl," blue lace dress,
marked "Austria," 8" h. 175.00

Figure of a lady, wearing cream &
rose dress & plumed hat & carrying a fur muff, marked "U.S.A.,"
8½" h. 65.00

Figure of a gentleman, holding a
violin, 9½" h. 45.00

Figure of an Oriental girl, 10" h. ... 65.00

Figure of a lady, holding a parasol,
marked "U.S.A.," 11" h. 125.00

Figure of a lady, wearing pastel
dress w/windblown skirts,
11" h. 135.00

Figure of a lady, wearing a grey
cape w/spider web design ornamented w/blue, tan, green &
fuchsia butterflies & insects,
18" h. (base restored) 1,540.00

Figures of a Chinese actor & actress,
12" h., pr. 130.00

Model of a German Shepherd dog,
10" h. 65.00

Model of baby giraffe,
11" h. 45.00

Model of a zebra 45.00

GOUDA

Gouda Vase

While tin-enameled earthenware has been made in Gouda, Holland, since the early 1600's, the productions of modern factories are attracting increasing collector attention. The art pottery of Gouda is easily recognized by its brightly colored peasant-style decoration with some types having achieved a "cloisonne" effect. Pottery workshops located in, or near, Gouda include Regina, Zenith, Plazuid, Schoonhoven, Arnhem and others. Their wide range of production included utilitarian wares, as well as vases, miniatures and large outdoor garden ornaments.

Candlestick, orange, blue & green
decor, lottea mark, 4½" base d.,
4½" h. (single) $69.00

Chamberstick, gold panels & white
florals w/blue & green on black
matte finish, house mark,
5 3/8" d., 3" h. 75.00

Chamberstick, shield-back type,
colorful decor 125.00

Clock, mantel-type w/chimes, painted florals on dial, Art Nouveau
shape case w/flowing wisteria &
tendrils on cream ground, Zuid
mark 600.00

Ewer, cobalt blue, rust & yellow
decor, Metz Royal Zuid mark,
6½" h. 115.00

Humidor w/brass cover, sepia
reserve panels decor,
Goedewaajen-Gouda mark 125.00

Lamp base, abstract floral decor,
Ivora mark, 11½" h. 120.00

Match box holder, colorful decor,
Ivora mark, 2¾" l. 39.00

Pencil tray, advertising, h.p. wind-
mills & boats decor, inscribed
"Compls. of the Holland-America
Line," 10" l. 75.00

Pitcher, 5" h., gold decor on black
ground 55.00

Pitcher, 5½" h., bulbous, maroon,
gold & deep blue florals on glossy
mottled grey ground, green interi-
or, Areo-Royal mark 35.00

Planter, bowl-shaped, autumn
shades, 5½" d. 60.00

Plaque, pierced to hang, Art Deco
style, gold, black, green & orange
decor on white, 12¼" d. 157.00

Plaque, pierced to hang, commemorative-type, inscribed "Koningen
Wilhelmina 1893-1923" & w/color-
ful coat of arms decor, high glaze,
12¾" d. 345.00

Vase, 2" h., 1" d., brown, gold &
green designs, house mark 48.00

Vase, 3" h., squat form, floral
decor 35.00

Vase, 4" h., 3¼" w., straight-sided
hexagon, h.p. florals on black
matte finish, Daua-Holland
mark 60.00

Vase, 5½" h., 6" d., dark high
glaze, Maasserma mark 125.00

Vase, 6½" h., beaker-shaped, h.p.
green borders & blue, rust &
white decor on yellow ground,
Lapac mark 85.00

Vase, 7" h., blue geometric decor
w/touch of red on dark green
matte finish, Massa house mark .. 90.00

Vase, 7 1/8" h., 5" rim d., 2-
handled, h.p. blue, rust, yellow &
black geometric designs, Damascus Holland mark (ILLUS.) 75.00

Vase, 7¾" h., 8½" d., bulbous
w/flaring neck, arched handles,

h.p. stylized yellow, green & purple Art Nouveau florals on blue
ground, early 20th c. 110.00
Vase, 8 1/8" h., 4¾" d., h.p. royal
blue, black, gold, red, green &
brown Art Deco designs, house
mark 90.00
Vase, 8¼" h., 4¾" d., ewer form,
Art Deco style, lavender, mauve &
green florals & thorns on shaded
glossy green ground, house
mark 115.00

Gouda Portrait Vase

Vase, 11½" h., oviform, portrait of
Art Nouveau woman w/flowing
hair on cross-hatched green
ground within violet floral medallion one side & violet irises on
cross-hatched yellow & tan ground
within green leaves, Zuid mark
(ILLUS.) 2,520.00
Wall pocket, h.p. vivid stylized
designs, 11½" h. 145.00
Whimsey, model of a Dutch shoe,
h.p. vivid florals on glossy green
shaded to beige ground, Tresco
house mark & Royal Zuid paper
label, 6½" l.   95.00

GRUEBY

*Some fine art pottery was produced by the
Grueby Faience and Tile Company, established in Boston in 1891. Choice pieces were
created with molded designs on a semi-
porcelain body. The ware is marked and often
bears the initials of the decorators. The pottery closed in 1907. Also see TILES.*

Bowl, 4" d., thick matte greenish
blue glaze exterior, glossy lime

green interior, impressed circle &
lotus mark $160.00
Bowl, 5¼" d., 1¼" h., rolled rim,
matte green glaze 175.00

Table Lamp with Grueby Base

Lamp w/leaded glass shade, bulbous green-glazed base molded
w/upright lotus leafage, domical
shade w/radiating bands of glass
tiles in shades of violet, magenta,
aqua & green, ca. 1900 (ILLUS.) . .2,200.00
Paperweight, model of a scarab, impressed circle & lotus Faience
mark, 2¾ x 2" 250.00
Vase, 3" h., 6¼" d., cucumber
green glaze 225.00
Vase, 6" h., molded leaves in low
relief, cucumber green glaze,
artist-signed 430.00
Vase, 6 1/8" h., 3¼" d., squat bul-
bous body, molded design at
shoulders, rolled rim, matte green
glaze, impressed circle & lotus
mark 250.00
Vase, 7" h., bottle-shaped, green
glaze 175.00

Grueby Chalice Form Vase

Vase, 7" h., chalice form, molded
w/upright lotus leaves in low
relief, thick pooling green glaze
w/patches of cream, artist-signed,
1894-99 (ILLUS.) 550.00
Vase, 10¾" h., ovoid, thick textured
blue glaze 440.00

HAMPSHIRE POTTERY

J.S.T. & C.Co.
KEENE, N.H.

Early Hampshire Pottery Mark

*Hampshire Pottery was made in Keene,
N.H., where several potteries operated as far
back as the late 18th century. The pottery
now known as Hampshire Pottery was established by J.S. Taft shortly after 1870. Various types of wares, including Art Pottery,
were produced through the years. Taft's
brother-in-law, Cadmon Robertson, joined the
firm in 1904 and was responsible for developing over 900 glaze formulas while in charge
of all manufacturing. His death in 1914 created problems for the firm and Taft sold out to
George Morton in 1916. Closed during part
of World War I, the pottery was later reopened by Morton for a short time and
manufactured white hotel china. From 1919
to 1921, mosaic floor tiles became the main
production. All production ceased in 1923.
Also see MAJOLICA.*

Bowl, 4½" d., underglaze relief-
molded dark foliage, brown high
glaze $65.00
Candle holder, green matte finish
(single)....................... 45.00
Chocolate pot, cov., ivory Royal
Worcester-type finish 65.00
Cookie jar, cov., bamboo-molded,
ivory Royal Worcester-type
finish 58.00
Ewer, Arts & Crafts style w/low
relief decor, matte green finish ... 180.00
Jug, matte green finish, 6" h. 45.00
Pitcher, 8" h., melon-molded lower
section w/leaf-molded throat &
lip, stalk handle, ivory Royal
Worcester-type finish w/gilt
veined leaves 115.00
Shaving mug, scuttle-type, relief-
molded designs highlighted in gilt
on glossy blue ground 75.00
Vase, 6" h., 4½" d., mottled blue
matte finish 70.00
Vase, 7" h., blue matte experimental glaze 95.00

Hampshire Pottery Vase

Vase, 8" h., ovoid, leaves in low
relief at shoulder, grey matte finish (ILLUS.) 180.00
Vase, 9½" h., relief-molded lily
pads, green matte finish 135.00

HAVILAND

Haviland Cake Plate

*Haviland porcelain was originated by
Americans in Limoges, France, shortly before
mid-19th century and continues in produc-
tion. Some Haviland was made by Theodore
Haviland in the United States during the last
World War. Numerous other factories also
made china in Limoges. Also see INVALID
FEEDERS and MUSTACHE CUPS &
SAUCERS.*

Bouillon cup & saucer, Princess
patt., Silver blank, Haviland &
Co. $25.00
Bouillon cup, cover & saucer, Prin-
cess patt., Silver blank, Haviland
& Co. 135.00
Bowl, coupe salad, Silver Anniver-

sary patt., Silver blank, Haviland
& Co. 8.00

Bowl, cream soup, Varenne patt.,
St. Germain blank, Theodore
Haviland, Limoges 32.00

Butter dish, cover & drain insert,
Wedding Band patt., Haviland &
Co., 4¾" sq. 80.00

Butter dish, cover & drain insert, tab
handles, floral, leaves & shell decor, sponged gold trim, Theodore
Haviland, Limoges, 8" across
handles 45.00

Butter pat, Princess patt. 9.50

Butter pat, Silver blank, gold trim .. 15.00

Butter pat, Lambelle blank, scalloped gold-sponged rim, blue
carnation-type flower clusters,
green leaves & yellow-green
shadow flowers, Theodore
Haviland, Limoges 6.00

Cake plate, footed, Moss Rose patt.,
Haviland & Co. 70.00

Cake plate, handled, Princess
patt. 40.00

Cake set: 3 footed cake plates & 19
serving plates; h.p. animals, fruit
or floral sprays center, cobalt
blue borders w/elaborate gold
scroll to one side only, Haviland &
Co., late 19th c., 22 pcs. (ILLUS. of
part) 715.00

Chamberstick by Haviland & Co.

Chamberstick, scalloped edges, ring
handle, brushed gold feathering
at edges, Haviland & Co.
(ILLUS.). 75.00

Charger, Star blank, rose garlands
decor, Haviland & Co. 1893 mark,
12½" d. 60.00

Chocolate pot, cov., blue floral &
gold decor, Haviland & Co.,
Limoges, 8¾" h. 95.00

Chocolate pot, cov., Fantaisie blank,
undecorated, Theodore Haviland,
Limoges 60.00

Chocolate pot, cov., Ranson blank,
h.p. purple & red berries & green
& rust leaves decor, Haviland &
Co., 10" h. 175.00

Chocolate pot, cov., Ranson blank,
ribbon handle, roses decor, artist-
signed, Haviland & Co. 150.00

Chocolate pot, cov., Ranson blank,
ribbon handle, blue florals &
winding vines transfer, Haviland &
Co. 95.00

Chocolate set: cov. chocolate pot &
6 c/s; pink roses decor, gold trim,
Charles Field Haviland, 13 pcs. ... 525.00

Coffee pot, cov., Moss Rose patt.,
gold trim, Haviland & Co. ..75.00 to 95.00

Compote, 6½" d., 11" h., Moss Rose
patt., Haviland & Co. 125.00

Cookie jar, cover & 7½" d. underplate, gold scroll handle on cover
& underplate, h.p. pink & white
floral decor & relief-molded scrolls
highlighted in gold, dated 1894,
Charles Field Haviland, GDM
mark, 8" h. 160.00

Creamer, Princess patt. 30.00

Creamer & cov. sugar bowl, Autumn
Leaf patt., Haviland & Co., pr. 42.00

Creamer & cov. sugar bowl, Old
Carnation patt., Diana blank,
Haviland & Co., ca. 1880, pr. 65.00

Cup & saucer, Apple Blossom patt.,
Plain blank, Theodore Haviland,
America 25.00

Cup & saucer, Autumn Leaf patt.,
Haviland & Co. ....17.00 to 25.00

Cup & saucer, Morris Dancers patt.,
Theodore Haviland (ILLUS.) 35.00

Cup & saucer, Nosegay patt.,
Pilgrim blank, Theodore Haviland,
Limoges 18.00

Cup & saucer, Ranson patt., gold
trim, Haviland & Co. 25.00

Cup & saucer, Silver Anniversary
patt., Silver blank, gold trim,
Haviland & Co. 27.50

Cup & saucer, master size, Silver
Anniversary patt., gold trim 75.00

Cup & saucer, Varenne patt. 30.00

Dinner service for eight: 8 each of
dinner plates, luncheon plates,
bread & butter plates, cups & saucers, 10" d. cov.
vegetable dish & 12" platter;
Autumn Leaf patt., Haviland &
Co., 50 pcs. 650.00

Dinner service for eight: 8 each of
dinner plates, salad plates, bread
& butter plates, cups, saucers &
sauce dishes & one creamer, cov.
sugar bowl, gravy boat, 9" d.
vegetable dish, oval cov. vegetable dish & 14" l. platter; Silver
Anniversary patt., Haviland & Co.,
54 pcs. 625.00

Dinner service for twelve: 12 each
of dinner plates, luncheon plates,
bread & butter plates, sauce dish-

es, cups & saucers & ten serving
pieces; Ranson patt., Haviland &
Co., 82 pcs. 1,100.00

Dish, h.p. bluebirds, pond & irises,
Charles Field Haviland, Limoges,
7" sq. 65.00

Dish, 6-sided, pink florals
w/gold painted handle, 8½" w.,
1½" deep 38.00

Dresser tray, overall pink roses
decor, gold trim, 10½ x 8½"
oval 38.00

Dresser tray, single rose spray &
gold trim on creamy white
ground, 12" l. 45.00

Ewer, h.p. grapes & leaves decor,
tones of brown shaded to orange,
9" h. 850.00

Fish platter, fish & seaweed decor,
Charles Field Haviland, 19 x 8" . . . 70.00

Fish set: 21" l. platter & twelve
9" d. plates; various sea life species & pink coral decor, 13 pcs. . . . 350.00

Game set: 22" l. platter & 8 plates;
h.p. shore birds, gold & blue
borders, 9 pcs. 425.00

Gravy boat w/attached underplate,
pink floral decor, gold trim, Theodore Haviland, Limoges 40.00

Gravy boat w/attached underplate,
Varenne patt., Theodore
Haviland, Limoges 45.00

Mustard jar w/spoon, model of a
duck, signed "Sandoz," Theodore
Haviland, Limoges 275.00

Mustard jar w/attached underplate,
Ranson blank, tiny florals interior
& exterior, clear, gold trim,
Haviland & Co. 65.00

Pitcher, 8¼" h., 6" d., rose, green &
gold handle, pink floral blossoms
on pink shaded to green ground,
artist-signed 116.00

Plate, 7½" d., Coromandel patt.,
Pilgrim blank, Theodore Haviland,
Limoges 15.00

Plate, 7½" d., gold fleur-de-lis on
maroon band decor, Theodore
Haviland, New York 4.50

Plate, 7½" d., Ranson blank, undecorated, Haviland
& Co. . . . . 10.00 to 12.00

Plate, 7½" d., Ranson blank, blue
florals & green leaves decor,
Haviland & Co. 15.00

Plate, 8" d., daisies & red clover
decor, gold trim, Charles Field
Haviland 35.00

Plate, 8" d., Field Flowers patt.,
Cannele blank, Haviland & Co. . . . 40.00

Plate, 8½" d., Ranson blank,
undecorated 14.00

Plate, 9½" d., Autumn Leaf patt.,
Plain blank, Haviland & Co. 18.00

Morris Dancers Pattern

Plate, 9½" d., Morris Dancers patt.,
Plain blank, Theodore Haviland
(ILLUS.) 35.00

Plate, 9½" d., Ranson blank, undecorated, Haviland & Co. 23.00

Plate, 9½" d., Silver Anniversary
patt., Silver blank, Haviland
& Co. 12.00

Plate, 9½" d., Varenne patt., St.
Germain blank, Theodore
Haviland, Limoges 21.50

Plate, chop, 12¾" d., h.p. purple
grapes & green leaves on soft
pink shaded to blue ground 95.00

Platter, 12" l., Princess patt., Silver
blank, Haviland & Co. 35.00

Platter, 20½ x 14½", variegated
pink poppies, shaded pods &
green leaves decor, pink & blue
scroll border interspersed w/gold
relief, Theodore Haviland,
Limoges 75.00

Sauce dish, Princess patt. 10.00

Sauce dish, Ranson blank, undeco-
rated, Haviland & Co. 5.00

Sauce dish, Silver Anniversary patt.,
Silver blank, Haviland & Co. 6.00

Sauce dish, Varenne patt., St. Germain blank, Theodore Haviland . . . 12.00

Soup plate w/flange rim, Princess
patt. 17.50

Soup plate w/flange rim, Ranson
blank, undecorated 12.00

HISTORICAL & COMMEMORATIVE

*Numerous potteries, especially in England
and the United States, made various porcelain and earthenware pieces to commemorate persons, places and events. Scarce
English historical wares with American
views command high prices. Objects listed
here are alphabetically by title of views.*

Baltimore Hospital cup & saucer, flowers & leaves border w/rings forming chain along edge, dark blue $1,600.00

Baltimore & Ohio Railroad (Level) cup & saucer, shell border, dark blue (Enoch Wood & Sons) 165.00

Battle Monument, Baltimore plate, long-stemmed roses border, purple, 9" d. (Jackson) 95.00

Battle of Bunker Hill plate, fruits & flowers border, dark blue, 10" d. (Rowland & Marsellus) 35.00

Boston Massacre plate, fruits & flowers border, dark blue, 10" d. (Rowland & Marsellus) 35.00

Boston State House bowl, flowers & leaves border, dark blue, 9½" d. (Rogers) 145.00

Buffalo, New York plate, rolled edge, vignettes border, dark blue, 10½" d. (Rowland & Marsellus) ... 35.00

City Hall, New York plate, flowers within medallions border, dark blue, 10" d. (Ridgway) 155.00

Commodore MacDonnough's Victory plate, shell border, dark blue, 8" d. (Enoch Wood) 137.00

Dam & Waterworks, Philadelphia

The Dam and Waterworks, Philadelphia (sidewheel steamboat) soup plate, fruits, flowers & leaves border, blue, 9" d., Henshall, Williamson & Co. (ILLUS.) 210.00

Delaware Water Gap plate, fruits & flowers border, dark blue (Rowland & Marsellus) 40.00

Elm at Cambridge, Mass. plate, fruits & flowers border, dark blue, 10" d. (Rowland & Marsellus) 35.00

Gilpin's Mills on the Brandywine Creek plate, shell border, dark blue, 9" d. (Enoch Wood & Sons) .. 195.00

Hendrick Hudson plate, rolled edge, vignettes border, dark blue, 10½" d. (Rowland & Marsellus) ... 45.00

Highlands, Hudson River Platter

Highlands, Hudson River platter, shell border, dark blue, 12½" l., Wood (ILLUS.) 1,100.00

Hospital, Boston plate, entwined vine border, dark blue, 9" d. (Stevenson) 225.00

John and Priscilla . . . Speak For Yourself, John plate, fruit & flower border, dark blue, 10" d. (Rowland & Marsellus) 35.00

Lafayette at Franklin's Tomb teapot & (mismatched) cover, floral border, dark blue, 7½" h. (Enoch Wood & Sons) 750.00

Lafayette & Washington cup plate, raised design border, carmine transfer, 3¾" d. (Wood) 275.00

Landing of the Fathers at Plymouth, Dec. 22, 1620, plate, pairs of birds & scrolls & 4 medallions w/ships & inscriptions border, blue, 10" d. (Enoch Wood) .... 145.00 to 225.00

Landing of General Lafayette at Castle Garden, New York, 16 August, 1824, plate, floral & vine border, dark blue, 6½" d. (Clews) 185.00

Landing of General Lafayette at Castle Garden, New York, 16 August, 1824, plate, floral & vine border, dark blue, 10" d. (Clews) 225.00

Landing of General Lafayette at Castle Garden, New York, 16 August, 1824, plate, floral & vine border, medium blue, 10" d. (Clews) 135.00

Landing of the Pilgrims plate, fruits & flowers border, dark blue, 10" d. (Rowland & Marsellus) 35.00

University of Pennsylvania plate, w/outside reserves, blue, 10" d. (Rowland & Marsellus) 40.00

Washington At Prayer, Valley Forge plate, fruits & flowers border, dark blue, 10"d . (Rowland & Marsellus) 70.00

Welcome Lafayette the Nation's Guest and Our Country's Glory cup plate, narrow band border, dark blue, minor damage (Clews)........................ 475.00

Welcome Lafayette Pitcher

Welcome Lafayette the Nation's Guest and Our Country's Glory pitcher, flowers & scrolls border, dark blue, Clews (ILLUS.).......1,600.00
Woodlands, Near Philadelphia cup plate, part border, dark blue, 3¼" d. (Stubbs) 325.00

Woodlands Near Philadelphia Tray

Woodlands, Near Philadelphia tray w/openwork border, dark blue, Stubbs (ILLUS.) 1,100.00

HULL

Bow Knot Pattern Cornucopia-Vase

This pottery was made by the Hull Pottery Company, Crooksville, O., beginning in 1905. Art Pottery was made until 1950 when the company was converted to utilitarian wares.

Ash tray, Serenade patt., pink matte finish, 13 x 10½".......... $22.00
Bank, Corky Pig, pastel yellow, blue & rose, 5" 25.00
Basket, square, interior handle, Blossom Flite patt., 10" h......... 35.00
Basket, Bow Knot patt., blue handle w/pink bow shading to white then to turquoise base, 6½" h......... 55.00
Basket, Iris patt., shaded blue to rose matte finish, 7" h......... 65.00
Basket, scalloped edge, Magnolia Gloss patt., pink flowers on pink ground, 10½" h. 32.50
Basket, Open Rose patt., pink matte finish, 8" h...................... 50.00
Basket, Tokay patt., deep green glossy grapes & leaves on white ground, 8" h. 20.00
Basket, Wildflower patt., rose shaded to yellow matte finish, 7" h.... 60.00
Bowl, 8" d., Calla Lily patt., green shaded to pink matte finish 60.00
Candle holders, Butterfly patt., ivory w/turquoise interior, pr. 25.00
Candle holders, model of pouter pigeon, Open Rose patt., green shaded to pink, 6½" h., pr. 45.00
Canister, tea, cov., Little Red Riding Hood patt...................... 230.00
Console bowl, handled, Magnolia Matte patt., pink shaded to blue matte finish, 12" l. 29.00
Console set: console bowl & pr. candle holders; Parchment & Pine patt., 3 pcs. 45.00
Cornucopia-vase, double, Bow Knot patt., pink shaded to white then aqua base, 13" l., 8" h. (ILLUS.) .. 47.50
Cornucopia-vase, twig handle, Water Lily patt., pink shaded to white, 6½" h. 32.00
Creamer, Little Red Riding Hood patt. 52.00
Ewer, Blossom Flite patt., black on glossy pink ground, 13½" h. 65.00
Ewer, Granada patt., pink shaded to ivory, 10" h. 30.00
Ewer, Magnolia patt., yellow shaded to pink matte finish, 13½" h. 65.00
Ewer, Orchid patt., shaded blue matte finish, 13" h............... 125.00
Figures, Swing Band: leader, drummer, accordionist, flutist & tuba player; h.p. features, ivory finish w/gold trim, 5 pcs.............. 175.00
Flower pot w/saucer, Bow Knot patt., pink shading to white then to blue 45.00

Flower pot w/saucer, Water Lily
patt., pink shaded to turquoise ... 32.00
Honey jug, Blossom Flite patt., black
on glossy pink ground 12.00
Jardiniere, Poppy patt., pink shaded
to blue, 3½" d. 30.00
Jardiniere, Sueno Tulip patt.,
shaded blue, 7" d. 70.00
Match holder, Little Red Riding Hood
patt. 385.00
Pitcher, milk, 8" h., Little Red Riding
Hood patt. .... 100.00 to 125.00
Pitcher, 8" h., Tulip patt., pink
shaded to blue 35.00
Planter, figure of a girl beside a
basket, off-white gown w/red
trim & red hat, 8" h. 20.00
Planter, model of a Dachshund dog,
glossy dark brown, 14 x 6"....... 22.00
Rose bowl, Open Rose patt., white
matte finish, 7" 25.00
Salt & pepper shakers, Little Red
Riding Hood patt., 5½" h., pr..... 32.00
Sugar bowl, cov., Little Red Riding
Hood patt. 135.00
Teapot, cov., Dogwood patt., peach
shaded to turquoise blue,
6½" h. 75.00

Red Riding Hood Pattern

Teapot, cov., Little Red Riding Hood
patt., 8" h. (ILLUS.) ...... 100.00 to 125.00
Tea set: cov. teapot, creamer &
sugar bowl; Bow Knot patt., blue
shading to white then to turquoise
blue, 3 pcs. 195.00
Tea set: cov. teapot, creamer &
sugar bowl; Ebb Tide patt., pink
shaded to turquoise blue, 3 pcs. ... 65.00
Vase, 4" h., Open Rose patt., pink
matte finish 15.00
Vase, 4¾" h., pillow-shaped, Orchid
patt., pink shaded to blue matte
finish 28.00
Vase, 5½" h., Sunglow patt.,
yellow 11.00
Vase, 6" h.., Calla Lily patt., ivory
matte finish 33.00

Water Lily Pattern Vase

Vase, 6½" h., Water Lily patt.,
green shaded to pink (ILLUS.) 18.00
Vase, 8½" h., handled, Bow Knot
patt., pink top shading to white
then to turquoise base 43.00
Vase, 10½" h., Magnolia Matte
patt., shaded pink matte finish ... 35.00
Vase, 12½" h., Wildflower patt.,
pink shaded to blue matte
finish 45.00
Vase, 14" h., Ebb Tide patt., maroon
shaded to green 35.00
Vase, 14" h., Serenade patt., yellow
matte finish 55.00
Wall pocket, Little Red Riding Hood
patt. 150.00
Wall pocket, Woodland patt., glossy
finish, 7½" h. 29.00

HUMMEL FIGURINES

Crown & Full Bee Marks

The Goebel Company of Oeslau, Germany, first produced these porcelain figurines in 1934 having obtained the rights to adapt the beautiful pastel sketches of children by Sister Maria Innocentia (Berta) Hummel. Every design by the Goebel artisans was approved by the nun until her death in 1946. Though not antique, these figurines, with the "M.I. Hummel" signature, especially those bearing the Goebel Company factory mark used from 1934 and into the early 1940's, are being sought by collectors though interest may have peaked about 1980.

"Accordion Boy," full bee mark,
1940-57, 5" h. $125.00
"Accordion Boy," crown mark,
1934-49, 5" h. 225.00
"Adoration," stylized bee mark,
1956-68, 6¼" h. 162.50
"Adoration," 1940-57, 6¼" h. 226.00
"Angel Serenade," 1940-57,
5½" h. 250.00
"Angel with Trumpet," three line
mark, 1963-71, 2" h. 30.00
"Apple Tree Boy," last bee mark
used, 1972-79, 6" h. 85.00
"Apple Tree Girl," 1972-79, 10" h. . . 349.00
"Apple Tree Boy & Girl" lamp bases,
7½" h., pr. 1,450.00

"Auf Wiedersehen"

"Auf Wiedersehen," 1956-68, 7" h.
(ILLUS.). 175.00
"Baker," 1972-79, 4¾" h. 52.50
"Baker," 1956-68, 4¾" h. 82.50
"Baker," 1940-57, 4¾" h. 125.00
"Barnyard Hero," 1963-71, 4" h. 80.00
"Barnyard Hero," 1956-68, 4" h. 95.00
"Begging His Share," 1940-57,
5½" h. . . . . 295.00 to 325.00
"Be Patient," 1940-57, 4¼" h. 117.00
"Be Patient," 1972-79, 6¼" h. 80.00
"Be Patient," 1963-71, 6¼" h. 112.50
"Be Patient," 1956-68, 6¼" h. 165.00
"Be Patient," 1940-57,
6¼" h. . . . . 140.00 to 170.00
"Be Patient," 1934-49, 6¼" h. 400.00
"Bird Duet," 1956-68, 4" h. 85.00
"Bird Duet," 1940-57, 4" h. 130.00
"Birthday Serenade," reverse mold,
1972-79, 5¼" h. 87.00
"Blessed Event," 1972-79, 5½" h. . . . 135.00
"Book Worm," 1972-79, 5½" h. 100.00
"Book Worm," 1956-68, 5½" h. 135.00
"Book Worm," 1972-79, 8" h. 350.00
"Book Worm" bookends, 1972-79,
5½" h., pr. 148.00

"Boots," 1972-79, 5½" h. 57.50
"Boy with Horse," 1972-79, 3½" h. . . . 20.00
"Boy with Toothache," 1963-71,
5½" h. 72.00
"Boy with Toothache," 1956-68,
5½" h. 95.00
"Boy with Toothache," 1940-57,
5½" h. 150.00
"Boy with Toothache," 1934-49,
5½" h. 255.00
"Builder," 1963-71, 5½" h. 92.50
"Carnival," 1963-71, 5¾" h. 115.00
"Celestial Musician," 1940-57,
7" h. 350.00
"Chef, Hello," 1972-79, 7" h. 85.00
"Chick Girl," 1972-79, 3½" h. 52.50
"Chick Girl," 1940-57, 3½" h. 132.00
"Chick Girl," 1956-68, 4¼" h. 120.00
"Chimney Sweep," 1956-68, 4" h. 45.00
"Close Harmony," 1972-79, 5½" h. . . . 98.00
"Congratulations" (no socks),
1940-57, 6" h. 165.00
"Culprits," 1934-49, 6¼" h. 350.00
"Doll Mother," 1972-79, 4¾" h. 75.00
"Farewell," 1934-49, 4¾" h. 275.00
"Farm Boy," 1972-79, 5" h. 70.00
"Feeding Time," 1940-57, 4¼" h. 155.00
"Flower Madonna," white, 1956-68,
8¼" h. 100.00
"Flower Madonna," white, 1940-57,
9" h. 165.00
"Flower Madonna," w/color,
1956-68, 11½" h. 300.00
"Forest Shrine," 1972-79, 9" h. 215.00
"For Father," 1940-57, 5½" h. 165.00
"For Mother," 1963-71, 5" h. 67.50
"For Mother," 1956-68, 5" h. 60.00
"Friends," 1963-71, 5" h. 105.00
"Friends," 1940-57, 5" h. . . . 135.00 to 150.00
"Friends," 1972-79, 10¾" h. 315.00
"Friends," 1940-57, 10¾" h. 525.00
"Girl with Nosegay," 1956-68,
3½" h. 36.00
"Girl with Trumpet," 1963-71,
2¼" h. 40.00
"Globe Trotter," 1940-57, 5" h. 135.00
"Going to Grandma's," 1940-57,
square base, 4¾" h. 150.00
"Going to Grandma's," 1972-79,
square base, 6" h. 240.00
"Going to Grandma's," 1956-68, rec-
tangular base, 6" h. 500.00
"Good Shepherd," 1934-49, 6¼" h. . . . 250.00
"Goose Girl," 1940-57,
4" h. . . . . 90.00 to 130.00
"Goose Girl," 1934-49, 4¾" h. 275.00
"Goose Girl," 1972-79, 7½" h. 192.50
"Happy Birthday," 1956-68, 5½" h. . . . 97.00
"Happy Days," 1934-49, 6¼" h. 500.00
"Happy Traveler," 1972-79, 5" h. 47.50
"Happy Traveler," 1972-79, 7½" h. . . . 182.00
"Happy Traveler," 1940-57, 7½" h. . . . 300.00
"Hear Ye, Hear Ye," 1972-79,
5" h. 65.00

"Hear Ye, Hear Ye," 1972-79,
7" h.......................... 135.00
"Hear Ye, Hear Ye," 1956-68,
7" h.......................... 175.00
"Heavenly Angel," 1972-79,
4¾" h.......................... 45.00
"Heavenly Angel," 1972-79,
6¾" h.......................... 57.00
"Heavenly Protection," 1972-79,
9" h.......................... 180.00
"Heavenly Protection," 1940-57,
9" h.......................... 410.00
"Holy Child," 1956-68, 6¾" h. 100.00

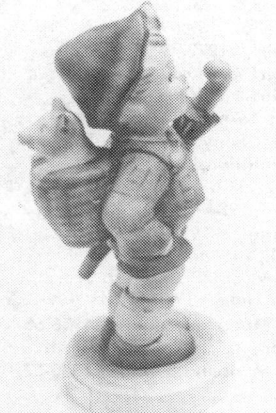

"Home From Market"

"Home From Market," 1956-68,
4¼" h. (ILLUS.) 105.00
"Home From Market," 1972-79,
5½" h.......................... 60.00
"Infant of Krumbad," 1940-57,
5¼" h.......................... 75.00
"Joyful," 1972-79, 4" h. 40.00
"Joyful," 1940-57, 4" h. 110.00
"Just Resting," 1934-49, 5" h........ 250.00
"Kiss Me," w/socks, 1956-68,
6" h.......................... 350.00
"Knitting Lesson," 1963-71, 7½" h. ... 195.00
"Knitting Lesson," 1956-68, 7½" h. ... 200.00
"Let's Sing," 1972-79, 3" h. 35.00
"Let's Sing," 1956-68,
4" h....................140.00 to 175.00
"Little Bookkeeper," 1972-79,
4¾" h.......................... 92.50
"Little Cellist," 1940-57, 6" h........ 195.00
"Little Cellist," 1934-49, 6" h....... 350.00
"Little Drummer," 1956-68, 4¼" h. ... 57.50
"Little Fiddler," 1972-79, 10¾" h. ... 340.00
"Little Gabriel," 1972-79, 5" h....... 50.00
"Little Gabriel," 1956-68, 5" h....... 72.50
"Little Gabriel," 1940-57, 5" h....... 110.00
"Little Gardener," 1972-79, 4" h..... 45.00
"Little Gardener," 1956-68,
4" h....................60.00 to 80.00
"Little Goat Herder," 1972-79,
4¾" h.......................... 60.00

"Little Goat Herder," 1956-68,
4¾" h.......................... 92.50
"Little Goat Herder," 1940-57,
4¾" h.......................... 225.00
"Little Goat Herder," 1956-68,
5½" h...................100.00 to 150.00
"Little Goat Herder," 1940-57,
5½" h.......................... 280.00
"Little Guardian," 1956-68,
4" h....................50.00 to 85.00
"Little Guardian," 1934-49, 4" h. 175.00
"Little Helper," 1940-57, 4" h. 125.00
"Little Hiker," 1940-57, 4½" h...... 72.50
"Little Hiker," 1972-79, 6" h........ 60.00
"Little Hiker," 1956-68, 6" h........ 80.00
"Little Hiker," 1940-57, 6" h........ 150.00
"Little Hiker," 1934-49, 6" h........ 350.00
"Little Pharmacist," 1963-71,
6" h.......................... 110.00
"Little Scholar," 1972-79, 5½" h..... 57.50
"Little Scholar," 1956-68, 5½" h. ... 80.00
"Little Shopper," 1956-68, 4¾" h. ... 55.00
"Little Shopper," 1940-57, 4¾" h. ... 110.00
"Little Shopper," 1934-49, 4¾" h. ... 145.00
"Little Sweeper," 1972-79, 4¼" h.... 45.00
"Little Tailor," 1972-79, 5½" h. 72.50
"Little Thrifty," 1972-79, 5" h........ 50.00
"Lost Sheep," 1940-57, 6¼" h. 280.00
"Lullaby," 1972-79, 3½ x 5" 65.00
"Lullaby," 1956-68, 3½ x 5" 95.00
"Lullaby," 1940-57, 3½ x 5" 155.00
"Lullaby," 1972-79, 6 x 8" 175.00
"The Mail is Here," 1972-79,
4¼ x 6"...................... 205.00
"The Mail is Here," 1963-71,
4¼ x 6"................240.00 to 300.00
"The Mail is Here," 1940-57,
4¼ x 6"...................... 450.00
"March Winds," 1972-79, 5½" h. ... 45.00
"March Winds," 1934-49, 5½" h. 135.00
"Max & Moritz," 1956-68, 5" h. 80.00
"Max & Moritz," 1940-57, 5" h. 145.00
"Meditation," 1972-79, 5½" h. 57.50
"Meditation," 1956-68, 5½" h. 95.00
"Meditation," 1940-57, 5½" h. 135.00

"Meditation"

"Meditation," 1972-79, 7" h.
(ILLUS.) ....125.00 to 148.00
"Meditation," 1972-79, 13¾" h. 750.00
"Merry Wanderer," 1956-68,
4¼" h. 72.50
"Merry Wanderer," 1940-57,
4¼" h. ....80.00 to 130.00
"Merry Wanderer," 1972-79,
4¾" h. 57.50
"Merry Wanderer," 1956-68,
4¾" h. 77.50
"Merry Wanderer," 1934-49,
4¾" h. 310.00
"Merry Wanderer," 1956-68,
6¼" h. ....85.00 to 105.00
"Merry Wanderer," 1940-57,
6¼" h. 215.00
"Merry Wanderer," 1956-68, 7" h. 195.00
"Merry Wanderer," 1972-79,
9½" h. 385.00
"Merry Wanderer," 1972-79,
11¼" h. 350.00
"Mother's Darling," 1972-79,
5½" h. 70.00
"Mother's Darling," 1956-68,
5½" h. 115.00
"Mother's Helper," 1972-79, 5" h. ... 70.00
"Mother's Helper," 1956-68, 5" h. ... 100.00
"Mountaineer," 1972-79,
5" h. ....65.00 to 80.00
"Mountaineer," 1963-71, 5" h. 95.00
"Not For You," 1972-79, 6" h. 70.00
"Not For You," 1956-68, 6" h. 235.00
"On Secret Path," 1972-79, 5¼" h. .. 90.00
"Out of Danger," 1972-79, 6¼" h. .. 80.00
"Out of Danger," 1956-68, 6¼" h. .. 99.00
"Out of Danger," 1940-57, 6¼" h. .. 185.00
"Photographer," 1972-79,
5¼" h. ....85.00 to 95.00
"Photographer," 1963-71, 5½" h. ... 125.00
"Photographer," 1956-68, 5¼" h. ... 150.00
"Photographer," 1940-57, 5¼" h. ... 220.00
"Playmates," 1972-79, 4" h. 65.00
"Playmates," 1956-68, 4" h. 75.00
"Playmates," 1940-57, 4" h. 125.00
"Playmates," 1934-49, 4" h. 265.00
"Playmates," 1956-68, 4¼" h. 120.00
"Postman," 1972-79, 5" h. 65.00
"Postman," 1956-68, 5" h. 115.00
"Postman," 1940-57, 5" h. 185.00
"Prayer Before Battle," 1972-79,
4¼" h. 65.00
"Prayer Before Battle," 1956-68,
4¼" h. ....85.00 to 100.00
"Prayer Before Battle," 1934-49,
4¼" h. 250.00
"Puppy Love," 1972-79, 5" h. 62.50
"Puppy Love," 1940-57, 5" h. 150.00
"Puppy Love," 1934-49, 5" h. 175.00
"Retreat to Safety," 1972-79, 4" h. .. 68.00
"Retreat to Safety," 1963-71, 4" h. .. 75.00
"Retreat to Safety," 1956-68, 4" h. .. 80.00
"Retreat to Safety," 1940-57, 4" h. .. 115.00

"Retreat to Safety," 1963-71,
5½" h. 130.00
"Retreat to Safety," 1956-68,
5½" h. 170.00
"Retreat to Safety," 1940-57,
5½" h. 200.00
"Ride into Christmas," 1972-79,
5¾" h. 200.00
"Ride into Christmas," 1963-71,
5¾" h. 1,750.00
"Ring Around the Rosie," 1972-79,
6¾" h. 1,000.00
"Ring Around the Rosie," 1956-68,
6¾" h. 1,250.00
"St. George," 1972-79, 6¾" h. 110.00
"School Boy," 1972-79, 4" h. 45.00
"School Boy," 1956-68, 4" h. 65.00
"School Boy," 1940-57, 4" h. 100.00
"School Boy," 1972-79, 5" h. 52.50
"School Boy," 1956-68, 5" h. 90.00
"School Boy," 1940-57, 5" h. 120.00
"School Boy," 1934-49, 5" h. 200.00
"School Boy," 1972-79, 7½" h. 150.00
"Schoolboys," 1972-79, 7½" h. 375.00
"Schoolboys," 1963-71, 7½" h. 500.00
"Schoolboys," 1956-68, 10¼" h. 1,350.00
"Schoolboys," 1940-57, 10¼" h. 1,515.00
"School Girl," 1972-79, 4¼" h. 45.00
"School Girl," 1956-68, 4¼" h. 60.00
"School Girl," 1940-57, 4¼" h. 95.00

"School Girl"

"School Girl," 1956-68, 5" h.
(ILLUS.) 100.00
"School Girl," 1940-57, 5" h. 145.00
"Schoolgirls," 1963-71, 7½" h. 500.00
"Schoolgirls," 1956-68, 9½" h. 1,400.00
"Schoolgirls," 1940-57, 9½" h. 1,500.00
"Sensitive Hunter," 1972-79,
4¾" h. 60.00
"Sensitive Hunter," 1956-68,
4¾" h. 110.00
"Sensitive Hunter," 1940-57,
4¾" h. 160.00

"Sensitive Hunter," 1934-49,
4¾" h. 260.00
"Sensitive Hunter," 1956-68,
5½" h. 92.50
"Sensitive Hunter," 1972-79,
7½" h. 120.00
"Sensitive Hunter," 1956-68,
7½" h. 130.00
"Serenade," 1956-68, 4¾" h. 75.00
"Serenade," 1940-57, 4¾" h. 115.00
"Serenade," 1934-49, 4¾" h. 200.00
"Serenade," 1972-79, 7½" h. 120.00
"Serenade," 1956-68, 7½" h. 130.00
"Serenade," 1940-57, 7½" h. 450.00
"She Loves Me," 1972-79, 4¼" h. . . . 56.00
"She Loves Me," 1963-71, 4¼" h. . . . 86.00
"She Loves Me," 1940-57, 4¼" h. . . . 175.00
"Shepherd's Boy," 1972-79, 5½" h. . . 67.50
"Shepherd's Boy," 1940-57, 6½" h. . . 250.00
"Signs of Spring," 1972-79, 4" h. . . . 50.00
"Signs of Spring," 1963-71, 4" h. . . . 70.00
"Signs of Spring," 1956-68, 4" h. . . . 75.00
"Signs of Spring," 1940-57, 4" h. . . . 270.00
"Signs of Spring," 1972-79, 5½" h. . . 70.00
"Signs of Spring," 1963-71, 5½" h. . . 105.00
"Silent Night," 1972-79, 5½ × 4¾" . . 75.00
"Silent Night," 1940-57,
5½ × 4¾" . . . . 170.00 to 195.00
"Singing Lesson," 1956-68, 2¾" h. . . 70.00
"Singing Lesson," 1940-57, 2¾" h. . . 110.00
"Singing Lesson," 1934-49, 2¾" h. . . 225.00
"Sister," 1972-79, 4¾" h. 50.00
"Sister," 1956-68, 5½" h. 80.00
"Sister," 1940-57, 5½" h. 105.00
"Sister," 1934-49, 5½" h. 250.00
"Skier," 1956-68, 5" h. 105.00
"Smart Little Sister," 1972-79,
4¾" h. 72.50
"Smart Little Sister," 1963-71,
4¾" h. 87.50
"Smart Little Sister," 1956-68,
4¾" h. 100.00

"Spring Dance"

"Spring Dance," 1963-71, 6¾" h.
(ILLUS.). 275.00
"Stormy Weather," 1956-68,
6¼" h. 245.00
"Stormy Weather," 1934-49,
6¼" h. 425.00
"Street Singer," 1972-79, 5" h. 50.00
"Street Singer," 1940-57, 5" h. 125.00
"Strolling Along," 1972-79, 4¾" h. . . 55.00
"Strolling Along," 1956-68, 4¾" h. . . 82.50
"Strolling Along," 1940-57, 4¾" h. . . 130.00
"Surprise," 1972-79, 4" h. 58.00
"Surprise," 1956-68, 4" h. 78.00
"Surprise," 1940-57, 4" h. 125.00
"Surprise," 1956-68, 5½" h. 92.50
"Surprise," 1940-57, 5½" h. 235.00
"Surprise," 1934-49, 5½" h. 335.00
"Sweet Music," 1956-68, 5¼" h. 85.00
"Sweet Music," 1972-79, 7" h. 65.00
"Sweet Music," 1956-68, 7" h. 97.00
"Sweet Music," 1940-57, 7" h. 127.50
"Telling Her Secret," 1972-79,
5" h. 95.00
"Telling Her Secret," 1956-68,
5" h. 140.00
"Telling Her Secret," 1940-57,
5" h. 225.00
"Telling Her Secret," 1963-71,
6½" h. 225.00
"Telling Her Secret," 1940-57,
6½" h. 550.00
"To Market," 1972-79, 4" h. 57.50
"Umbrella Boy," 1972-79, 4¾" h. . . . 210.00
"Umbrella Boy," 1963-71, 4¾" h. . . . 255.00
"Umbrella Boy," 1956-68, 4¾" h. . . . 300.00
"Umbrella Boy," 1972-79, 8" h. 510.00
"Umbrella Girl," 1972-79, 4¾" h. . . . 215.00
"Village Boy," 1956-68, 4" h. 42.50
"Village Boy," 1972-79, 5" h. 42.50
"Village Boy," 1963-71, 5" h. 50.00
"Village Boy," 1956-68, 5" h. 65.00
"Village Boy," 1956-68, 6" h. 125.00
"Village Boy," 1940-57, 6" h. 135.00
"Village Boy," 1934-49, 6" h. 245.00
"Village Boy," 1972-79, 7¼" h. 72.50
"Visiting an Invalid," 1972-79,
5" h. 67.50
"Volunteers," 1972-79, 5" h. 80.00
"Volunteers," 1972-79, 5½" h. 87.50
"Volunteers," 1956-68, 5½" h. 185.00
"Volunteers," 1940-57, 5½" h. 260.00
"Volunteers," 1956-68, 6½" h. 250.00
"Waiter," 1956-68, 6" h. 105.00
"Waiter," 1940-57, 6" h. 130.00
"Waiter," 1972-79, 7" h. 90.00
"Wash Day," 1972-79, 6" h. 77.50
"Wayside Devotion," 1956-68,
7½" h. 195.00
"Wayside Devotion," 1940-57,
7½" h. 315.00
"Wayside Devotion," 1934-49,
7½" h. 475.00
"Wayside Devotion," 1940-57,
8¾" h. 295.00

"Wayside Harmony," 1963-71, 4" h.	55.00
"Wayside Harmony," 1956-68, 4" h.	77.50
"Wayside Harmony," 1940-57, 4" h.	125.00
"Wayside Harmony," 1972-79, 5" h.	65.00
"Wayside Harmony," 1963-71, 5" h.	95.00
"Wayside Harmony," 1956-68, 5" h.	105.00
"Wayside Harmony," 1940-57, 5" h.	158.00
"Wayside Harmony," 1934-49, 5" h.	325.00
"We Congratulate," 1972-79, 4" h.	52.50
"We Congratulate," 1963-71, 4" h.	70.00
"We Congratulate," 1940-57, 4" h.	125.00
"Weary Wanderer," 1972-79, 6" h.	70.00
"Weary Wanderer," 1963-71, 6" h.	90.00
"Weary Wanderer," 1956-68, 6" h.	105.00
"Weary Wanderer," 1940-57, 6" h.	175.00
"Which Hand," 1972-79, 5½" h.	47.50
"Which Hand," 1963-71, 5½" h.	72.50
"Whitsuntide," 1972-79, 7" h.	100.00

"Whitsuntide"

"Whitsuntide," 1940-57, 7" h. (ILLUS.)	635.00 to 750.00
"Worship," 1934-49, 5" h.	300.00

IMARI

This is a multicolor ware that originated in China but was imitated and made famous by the Japanese and subsequently copied by English and European potteries. It was decorated in overglaze enamel. It was made in the Hizen and Arita areas of Japan and much of it was exported through the port of Imari.

Arita Imari often has brocade patterns. Imitative wares made elsewhere are now usually lumped together under the generic term Imari. It is currently being reproduced.

Barber's bowl, center w/underglaze-blue, iron-red & gold mons issuing 4 floral sprays, gilt-edged notched rim w/mons at top flanked by 4 floral sprays alternating w/panels at sides painted w/pagodas amidst flowering shrubbery, underside w/two iron-red flowering branches, 1710-25, 11 1/8" d.	$1,320.00
Bowl, 6¾" d., interior w/iron-red, green, deep turquoise, black, grey & gold sprays of chrysanthemums tied w/tasseled gilt ribbon, exterior molded around base w/border of incised petals heightened in gold at the tops, rim edged in (worn) gilding, 18th c.	1,100.00
Bowl, 9½" d., scalloped rim, underglaze-blue decor	122.00

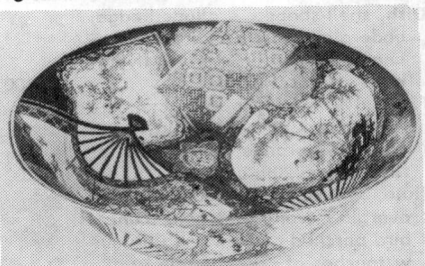

Large Imari Bowl

Bowl, 22" d., slightly everted rim, enameled, gilded & lacquered large scattered fans variously decorated w/flowers & animals, lacquer insects scattered throughout, 1868-1912 (ILLUS.)	4,400.00
Bowl, 24" d., painted & gilded w/shaped reserves containing samurai & bijin, landscapes & animals on a ground scattered w/flowers & scrolling, exterior reserved w/landscapes & birds amidst flowers, mid-19th c.	3,850.00
Charger, underglaze-blue & iron-red, green & yellow overglaze enameling w/gilt trim, 19th c., 15" d.	400.00
Charger, underglaze-blue decor, 16" d.	175.00
Charger, underglaze-blue & iron-red overglaze peacocks in a rocky landscape & smaller birds by a waterfall, gilt trim, underside w/foliate scrolling decor, 1868-1912, 24" d.	770.00

Arita Imari Dish

Dish, underglaze-blue central roundel w/monogram, exotic bird in
flight & perched bird amidst flowers & fruit, rim w/six panels,
Arita, 1660-80, 8 3/8" d.
(ILLUS.) 2,650.00
Dish, shell-shaped, scalloped edge,
underglaze-blue & overglaze
enameled garden scene & flying
birds, 19th c., 10" w. 250.00
Plate, 8½" d., scalloped edge,
underglaze-blue & overglaze
enameled orange florals & butterflies decor, 20th c. 50.00
Plate, 8¾" d., underglaze-blue &
overglaze iron-red & gold scene of
bird perched on flowering prunus
w/touches of green within iron-
red & gilt diaperwork & flowering
foliate scroll ground, 1720-30 (rim
chip) 330.00
Platter, 12½" l., underglaze-blue &
multicolored overglaze enameled
birds & foliage, early 20th c. 110.00
Platter, 15" oval, underglaze-blue &
overglaze iron-red lotus, garden
w/bonsai trees, butterflies &
cranes decor, ca. 1800 .... 395.00
Saki bottle, rectangular body,
underglaze-blue decor w/pine
trees on 2 sides & stylized landscape w/three pavilions on 2
sides, square top w/leaf & cloud
device & w/square spout from
one corner, late 17th c., 7¼" h. ... 660.00
Teabowl & saucer, center of saucer
& exterior of teabowl
w/underglaze-blue, iron-red &
gold vase of flowers between
smaller potted plants on a ter-
race, center of teabowl w/modi-
fied version, each w/blue & gold
demi-mons border, underside of
saucer w/two flowering prunus
branches, 1690-1715 .... 412.00

Temple jar, underglaze-blue & overglaze enameled decor w/Japa-
nese figures, 1930's, 20" h........ 450.00
Vase, 12" h., swollen cylinder
w/flaring rim, underglaze-blue &
typical colored overglaze
enamels, late 19th c. 220.00

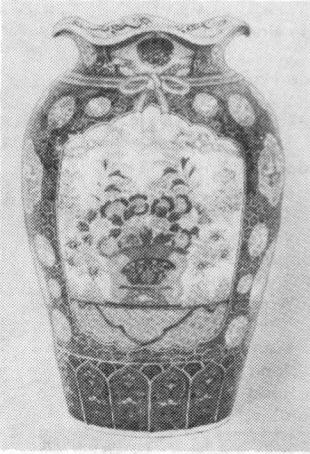

Imari Vase

Vase, 23½" h., baluster-shaped,
ruffled rim, molded bow-tied cord
at neck, underglaze-blue & overglaze enameling in typical colors
w/floral motifs in roundels & reserves on diapered ground (base
crack), 19th c. (ILLUS.) 1,320.00
Vase, 31" h., panels of ho-o birds
amidst peonies & shaped floral
medallions, underglaze-blue &
typical colored overglaze enamels
w/gilt highlighting, 1868-1912 ....1,650.00
Vase, 46"h., underglaze-blue continuous landscape w/peafowl
amidst peony blossoms, hillocks
& waterfalls, base & shoulder
w/lappet & linen-fold formal borders embellished w/animal medallions, neck w/phoenix flying in
clouds, 1868-1912 ....1,650.00

IRONSTONE

*The first successful ironstone was patent-
ed in 1813 by C.J. Mason in England. The
body contains iron slag incorporated with the
clay. Other potters imitated Mason's ware
and today much hard, thick ware is lumped
under the term ironstone. Earlier it was called
by various names, including graniteware.
Both plain white and decorated wares were*

made throughout the 19th century. Tea Leaf Lustre ironstone was made by several firms and is included at the end of this listing. Also see CUP PLATES under Ceramics, FOOD MOLDS and INVALID FEEDERS.

GENERAL

Japan Pattern Ironstone

Bowl, 9" sq., deep, Vista patt., mulberry transfer, Mason's $39.50

Chamber pot, cov., Asia shape, all white, Wooliscroft, 1851-64 . . . . . . 90.00

Chamber pot, all white, Maddock & Co. Royal Stone China, ca. 1906 . . 15.00

Charger, "gaudy," underglaze-blue & overglaze enameled florals, 14¾" d. 350.00

Coffee pot, cov., octagonal, gooseneck spout, "gaudy" decor, copper lustre trim, 10 3/8" h. 115.00

Coffee pot, cov., octagonal, copper lustre scroll decor, 12" h. 60.00

Coffee pot, cov., Wheat patt., all white, Elsmore & Foster, 1853-71 . . . . 195.00

Coffee pot, cov., Wheat patt., lustre finish, Elsmore & Foster, 1853-71 . . 295.00

Compote, 10 5/8" d., 7 7/8" h., scalloped rim & base, T. & R. Boote & Co., 1842-1906 . . . . 80.00

Compote, fluted, all white, miniature, Edwards, 1842-82 . . . . 75.00

Creamer, Gothic shape, all white, Alcock, 4½" h. 35.00

Creamer, "gaudy," Morning Glory patt., underglaze-blue & copper lustre, 5" h. 45.00

Creamer, Sydenham shape, all white, T. & R. Boote, 1853 . . . . 70.00

Creamer, Wheat & Blackberry patt., all white, Thomas Hughes, 1860-94 . . . . 65.00

Cup & saucer, handleless, Ceres shape, all white, Elsmore & Foster, 1853-71 . . . . 40.00

Cup & saucer, handleless, Ceres shape, all white, J. & G. Meakin 55.00

Cup & saucer, handleless, Etruscan shape, multicolored transfer on lavender ground, Wooliscroft, 1851-53 . . . . 50.00

Cup & saucer, handleless, "gaudy," underglaze-blue floral decor w/red & green enameling & copper lustre trim 35.00

Cup & saucer, handleless, "gaudy," underglaze-blue floral decor w/red enameling & purple lustre trim 45.00

Cup & saucer, handleless, "gaudy," Morning Glory w/Strawberry patt., underglaze-blue w/red & green enameling & lustre trim 47.50

Cup & saucer, handleless, Lily-of-the-Valley patt., all white . . 75.00 to 95.00

Dinner service (comprising dinner, dessert & salad plates for 9, pr. sauce tureens, soup plate, & several damaged plates in various sizes): Japan patt., underglaze-blue & iron-red, salmon, rose, blue, brown, green & gilt decor, attributed to Ridgway, Morley, Wear & Co., 1835-42, 50 pcs. (ILLUS. of part) 1,540.00

Dish, octagonal, "gaudy," Morning Glory patt., underglaze-blue w/enameled red & green strawberries & copper lustre trim, 8 5/8" l. 40.00

Dish, shell-shaped, "gaudy," Morning Glory patt., underglaze-blue w/traces of lustre trim (short rim hairlines) 40.00

Egg cup, all white, Meakin 17.00

Memnon Shape by John Meir & Son

Gravy boat, footed, Memnon shape, all white, John Meir & Son, 1857 (ILLUS.) 28.00

Gravy boat, footed, Wheat patt., Anthony Shaw 18.00

Gravy boat & underplate, all white, Jas. Edwards & Son, 1851-82, 2 pcs. 45.00

Mug, "gaudy," Wheel patt., 3" h. 100.00

Pickle dish, Moss Rose patt.,
Meakin, 8½" l. 15.00
Pitcher, 6½" h., octagonal, Vista
patt., pink transfer, Mason's 45.00
Pitcher, 7" h., bulbous, pastoral
scene decor, blue transfer on
white, Mason's. 60.00
Pitcher, 8" h., birds, bamboo &
floral decor, brown transfer,
Brownfield, 1850-91. . . . . 95.00

Mason's "Gaudy" Ironstone

Plate, 6" d., "gaudy," Mason's
Patent (ILLUS.) 60.00
Plate, 7" d., Wheat & Clover patt.,
all white 15.00
Plate, 7½" d., Full Ribbed shape, all
white, J. W. Pankhurst & Co.,
1850-82. . . . . 20.00

Mason's American Marine Pattern

Plates, 8" d., American Marine
patt., Mason's Patent, pr.
(ILLUS.). 80.00
Plate, 8" d., 12-sided, "gaudy,"
Strawberry patt., underglaze-blue
& overglaze enameled strawber-
ries & leaves 75.00
Plate, 8 3/8" d., "gaudy," vintage
decor in underglaze-blue, copper
lustre, orange, yellow & green
enameling. . . . . 20.00 to 30.00
Plate, 8½" d., "gaudy," floral decor
in underglaze-blue, overglaze red,
green & yellow enameling & copper lustre, impressed "Pearl
White" 25.00
Plate, 9 1/8" d., "gaudy," Morning
Glory patt., dark underglaze-blue,
copper lustre trim . . . . 45.00 to 65.00

Plate, 9 1/8" d., Wheat & Clover
patt., all white. 25.00
Plate, 9¼" d., "gaudy," scalloped
rim w/alternating floral medallions, center w/floral & foliage
decor, Lion & Unicorn mark 50.00
Plate, 9½" d., California shape,
multicolored transfer decor, F.M.
& Co. (Francis Morley), 1845-58 . . . 30.00
Plate, 9 5/8" d., Sydenham shape,
all white, Meakin 18.00
Plate, 9¾" d., Persian patt., brown
transfer, Meakin 10.00
Plate, 9 7/8" d., "gaudy," vintage
decor in underglaze-blue, copper
lustre & red & green enameling . . 35.00
Plate, 10" d., Aurora shape, multicolored & black transfer 28.00
Plate, 10" d., Baltic shape, all white,
Wolliscroft, 1851-64. . . . . 20.00
Plate, 10" d., Ceres shape, all
white, Elsmore & Forster, Reg'd
1859 . . . . 18.00
Plate, 10" d., Gothic shape, all
white, Alcock 95.00
Plates, 10" d., printed & painted
w/central flower vase by a fence,
border w/scrolling chrysanthemum divided by shaped panels,
Mason's, ca. 1830, set of 12 . . . . . . 880.00
Plate, 10 1/8" d., "gaudy," underglaze blue & multicolored floral
decor w/gilt trim, Davenport
Stone China 85.00
Plate, 10½" d., Wheat & Clover
patt., all white. 30.00
Platter, 10½ x 8¾", Hybla patt.,
multicolored transfer on green
ground, Broughton & Mayer,
1853-55. . . . . 35.00
Platter, 12" oval, Ceres shape, all
white 20.00
Platter, 20 x 15", Columbia shape,
all white 125.00
Platter, 20 3/8 x 15 3/8", Wheat
patt., all white, Meakin. 50.00
Platter, Ribbed Raspberry with
Bloom patt., all white, Meakin,
1860's 21.00
Platter & 5 plates, President shape,
all white, J. Edwards, 1856,
6 pcs. 135.00
Punch bowl w/handles, berry cluster
decor, all white 125.00
Punch bowl & lid, Lily-of-the-Valley
patt., all white, Anthony Shaw . . . 195.00
Relish dish, Vineyard patt., Daven-
port, 1856 . . . . 42.00
Sauce tureen & cover, Boote's 1851
Octagon patt., all white, 2 pcs.. . . . 75.00
Sauce tureen & cover, Corn & Oats
patt., all white, Davenport,
2 pcs. 75.00
Sauce tureen & cover, Laurel Wreath

patt., all white, Elsmore & Forster, 2 pcs. 175.00

Sauce tureen & cover, Ribbed Raspberry with Bloom patt., all white, Meakin, 2 pcs. 53.00

Sauce tureen, cover & ladle, Baltic shape, all white, Hulme, 3 pcs.... 95.00

Sauce tureen, cover & ladle, Columbia shape, all white, E. & C. Challinor, 3 pcs. 135.00

Sauce tureen, cover & undertray, Memnon shape, all white, John Meir & Son, 1857, 3 pcs. 88.00

Sauce tureen, cover & underplate, Ribbed Chain patt., all white, J. W. Pankhurst, 3 pcs. 105.00

Sauce tureen w/attached undertray, cover & ladle, Sydenham shape, all white, T. & R. Boote, 3 pcs. ... 145.00

Sauce tureen, cover & ladle, Wheat patt., all white, Turner & Goddard, 1867-74, 3 pcs. 115.00

Sauce tureen, cover, undertray & ladle, Berlin Swirl patt., all white, Mayer & Elliot, 1858-61, 4 pcs.... 125.00

Sauce tureen, cover, undertray & ladle, Praire shape, all white, J. Clementson, 4 pcs. 105.00

Sharon Arch Pattern by Davenport

Sauce tureen, cover, underplate & ladle, Sharon Arch patt., all white, Davenport, 4 pcs. (ILLUS.) 150.00

Soap dish, cover & drain insert, octagonal, Grape patt., all white, 3 pcs. 68.00

Soup plate w/flange rim, "gaudy," cobalt blue borders enhanced w/copper lustre chrysanthemums 90.00

Soup plate w/flange rim, Niagara shape, all white, Edward Walley .. 20.00

Soup plate w/flange rim, Wheat patt., all white, Boote 18.00

Soup plate w/flange rim, Wheat & Clover patt., all white, 9" d. 25.00

Soup tureen, cover & ladle, Paris shape, all white, Alcock, 3 pcs. .. 255.00

Sugar bowl, cov., Budded Vine patt., all white, Meakin.......... 65.00

Sugar bowl, cov., Ceres shape, all white, Elsmore & Forster 90.00

Sugar bowl, cov., Double Sydenham shape, white w/copper lustre trim, Livesley-Powell 55.00

Sugar bowl, cov., Wheat & Clover patt., all white 100.00

Syllabub bowl, all white, plain, J. & G. Meakin, 9" d., 6" h. 145.00

Syllabub cups, Trumpet & Vine patt., all white, Edwards, set of 4 ...... 80.00

Moss Rose Pattern Syrup Pitcher

Syrup pitcher w/original pewter top, Moss Rose patt., Knowles, Taylor & Knowles, Pat. 1872, 8¼" h. (ILLUS.)........................ 125.00

Vegetable dish, cov., Atlantic shape, all white, T. & R. Boote ... 85.00

Vegetable dish, cov., Berlin Swirl patt., all white, Mayer & Elliot, 1858-61 .... 115.00

Vegetable dish, cov., Fuchsia patt., all white, Meakin 45.00

Vegetable dish, cov., Gothic shape, Cameo patt., white w/copper lustre trim 75.00

Vegetable dish, cov., Ivy Wreath patt., all white, John Meir, Tunstall, dated May 1860 .... 80.00

Vegetable dish, cov., Leaf & Crossed Ribbon patt., all white, Livesley & Powell, 1851-66 .... 45.00

Vegetable dish, cov., President shape, all white, J. Edwards, 1856 .... 120.00

Vegetable dish, cov., Rosalind patt., brown transfer, Meakin, 11½" l. 165.00

Vegetable dish, cov., Wheat & Blackberry patt., all white, Meakin....................... 80.00

TEA LEAF LUSTRE

Tea Leaf Lustre Butter Dish

Bacon rasher, Henry Burgess,
1864-92 . . . . 40.00
Bowl, 8" sq., Alfred Meakin, from
1875 on 43.00
Bread tray, open handles, Anthony
Shaw, 1850-1900 . . . . 60.00
Butter dish, cov., Bamboo shape,
Alfred Meakin (ILLUS.) . . . .75.00 to 100.00
Butter dish, cov., square, ribbed,
Enoch Wedgwood Ltd., from 1860
on .90.00 to 120.00
Butter pat, Mellor, Taylor & Co.,
1880-1904 . . . . 12.00
Cake plate, Fish Hook shape,
Alfred Meakin 40.00
Chamber pot, cov., Fish Hook
shape, Alfred Meakin 150.00
Chamber pot, cov., Powell & Bishop,
1876-91 . . . . 60.00
Coffee pot, cov., Wilkinson &
Hulme, 1879-85 . . . . 125.00
Compote, footed, Anthony Shaw 250.00
Creamer, Cable shape, Anthony
Shaw, 5¼" h. 45.00
Creamer, embossed "rooster head"
design at handle, Thomas
Furnival, from 1844 on, 6¼" h. 175.00
Creamer, Feather shape, John
Edwards, 1847-1900 . . . . 110.00
Cup & saucer, Thomas Furnival 43.00
Cups & saucers, handleless, Lily-of-
the-Valley patt., Anthony Shaw,
set of 4 . . . . 395.00
Gravy boat w/underplate, Bishop &
Stonier, 1891-1936 . . . . 35.00
Mug, Arthur J. Wilkinson, from 1879
on 75.00
Pitcher, 8 3/8" h., Henry Alcock &
Co., 1891-1910 . . . . 125.00
Pitcher, 12" h., Bishop & Stonier 60.00
Plates, 6½" d., Davenport, 1794-
1887, set of 10 . . . . 200.00
Plates, 7¾" d., Chinese shape,
Anthony Shaw, set of 6 . . . . 80.00
Plates, 8¼" d., W. H. Grindley &
Co., from 1880 on, set of 4 . . . . 75.00
Plate, 8½" d., Niagara shape,
Edward Walley, 1845-56 . . . . 25.00

Platter, 12¼ x 9" oval, Mellor,
Taylor & Co. 45.00
Platter, 15¼ x 10½" oval, Thomas
Furnival 45.00
Sauce dishes, J. & E. Mayer, from
1881 on, set of 5 . . . . 75.00
Sauce tureen & cover, Fish Hook
shape, Alfred Meakin 165.00
Sauce tureen, cover, ladle & under-
tray, W. H. Grindley & Co.,
3 pcs. 350.00
Shaving mug, Chinese shape,
Anthony Shaw 110.00
Soap dish, cover & drain insert,
Bamboo shape, Alfred Meakin . . . 115.00
Soup tureen, Henry Burgess,
13½ x 9" 295.00
Soup tureen, cov., Fish Hook shape,
Alfred Meakin 450.00
Spooner, Fish Hook shape, Alfred
Meakin 170.00
Sugar bowl, cov., Elsmore & Forster,
1853-87 . . . . 100.00
Teapot, cov., Bamboo shape, Alfred
Meakin, 8¾" h. 150.00
Teapot, cov., Cable shape, Henry
Burgess 175.00
Toothbrush holder, Bamboo shape,
Alfred Meakin 125.00
Vegetable dish, cov., Enoch Wedg-
wood Ltd. 125.00
Vegetable dish, open, Henry
Burgess, 10 x 7¾" oblong 50.00
Wash basin, Alfred Meakin,
15" d. 85.00

JASPER WARE

*Jasper ware is fine-grained exceedingly
hard stoneware made by including barium
sulphate in the clay and was first devised by
Josiah Wedgwood, who utilized it for the
body of many of his fine cameo blue-and-white
and green-and-white pieces. It was subsequently produced by other potters, notably
William Adams & Sons, and is in production
at the present. Also see KEWPIE COL-
LECTIBLES.*

WEDGWOOD

Bowl, 7" d., 3 3/8" h., white relief
"Dancing Hours" figures & leaf
bands on black, marked Wedg-
wood only $252.00
Bowl, 10" d., white relief "Dancing
Hours" figures on black, marked
Wedgwood England 550.00
Box, cov., drum-shaped, white relief
classical figures & lion masks on
sage green, marked Wedgwood
only, 3½" 185.00

Box, cov., white relief classical
figures on lid & cherubs around
sides on crimson red, marked
Wedgwood, 1920's, 3 7/8" d.,
1¾" h. 503.00
Box, cov., drum-shaped, white relief
classical figures & lion masks on
light blue, marked Wedgwood
only, 1869, 4¼ x4¼" 195.00
Butter tub, cov., white relief classical ladies on deep blue, silverplate cover, marked Wedgwood
England, 4 5/8" d., 3" h. 105.00
Candle holder, chamberstick-type,
white relief decor on deep blue,
ca. 1840, 4" h. 90.00
Clock case, white relief classical
figures, leaves & florettes on
deep blue, marked Wedgwood
England, 5¼" d., 6¼" h. 225.00
Cookie jar, white relief mythological
classical figures & garlands on
lavender center band, sage green
top & bottom bands, silverplate
cover, rim & handle, marked
Wedgwood only, 4¾" d., 6" h. . . . 750.00
Cookie jar, white relief classical
figures on sage green, silverplate
cover, rim & handle, marked
Wedgwood only, 5" d., 6½" h. . . . 225.00

Wedgwood Jasper Cookie Jar

Cookie jar, white relief hunt scene
on deep blue, silverplate cover,
rim & handle, marked Wedgwood
England, 6½" h. (ILLUS.) 375.00
Cookie jar, black relief garlands of
grapes & leaves w/lion masks &
classical ladies on gold, silverplate cover, rim & handle, marked
Wedgwood only, 5½" d.,
6¾" h. 398.00
Cookie jar, cov., white relief classi-
cal ladies on deep blue, cover
w/acorn finial & white relief
acorns & oak leaves, marked

Wedgwood only, 5 3/8" d.,
7" h. 230.00
Creamer, white relief classical
figures & garlands on deep blue,
3¾" d., 4" h. 105.00
Cup & saucer, white relief classical
figures on deep blue, rope-twist
handle, early 19th c., marked
Wedgwood only 150.00
Dresser tray, white relief classical
ladies on deep blue w/oak leaves
& acorns border, marked Wedg-
wood only, 10½ x 7¾" 150.00
Flower pots & stands, pots w/white
relief vertical ferns & flowerheads
& stands w/border of foliage on
blue, ca. 1810, 4 3/8" h., pr. 495.00

Jasper Ware Flower Pot

Flower pots w/pierced covers, white
relief classical figures depicting
the dipping of Achilles, a sacrifice
subject, lady playing the lyre &
another reading a book, flanked
by tall flower sprays on blue,
bands of stiff leaves at foot & half
paterae at arched top (with
repairs), impressed mark, ca.
1885, 6" h., pr. (ILLUS.
of one) 1,760.00

Jasper Ware Jardiniere

Jardiniere, white relief trailing fruiting vine below scrolling vine
border on blue, handles (repaired)

issuing from flowerhead motifs,
ca. 1785, 7" oval (ILLUS.) 880.00
Mug, white relief classical ladies
on deep blue, hallmarked silver
rim, marked Wedgwood only,
3 7/8" d., 5" h. 135.00
Pitcher, 4 5/8" h., white relief classical figures, flowers & trees on
deep blue, marked Wedgwood
only 110.00
Pitcher, tankard, 6¼" h., 3 7/8" d.,
white relief grapevine & classical
figures on deep blue, marked
Wedgwood only 145.00
Pitcher, 8" h., 3½" d., silverplate
hinged top, white relief garlands
& classical figures on sage green,
marked Wedgwood only 231.00
Plaques, pierced to hang, white relief Goddesses Diana & Ceres on
one, the other w/seated woman
pleading w/young couple on sage
green, 5 7/8" d., pr............. 300.00
Portland vase replica, white relief
continuous frieze of classical
figures said to represent the myth
of Pelius & Thetis on black,
1820-40, 10½" h. 3,400.00
Salt dip, master size, white relief
classical figures on blue, marked
Wedgwood England 98.00
Spill vase, white relief classical
figures & pillars on deep blue,
marked Wedgwood only, ca. 1861,
4" h. 155.00
Spill vase, white relief "Dancing
Hours" figures on black, silver
rim, marked Wedgwood only,
8½" h. 550.00
Sweetmeat jar, cov., white relief
hunting scene on deep blue,
marked Wedgwood only,
3¼" h. 175.00
Teapot, cov., white relief classical
ladies on deep blue, marked
Wedgwood only, 4 5/8" d.,
4" h. 171.00
Urn, 2-handled, white relief "Dancing Hours" figures on light blue,
bolted pedestal base, marked
Wedgwood only, ca. 1800,
6¼" h. 495.00
Vase, 4¾" h., 3½" h., white relief
classical ladies on deep blue,
marked Wedgwood only 130.00
Vase, 6½" h., white relief florals on
black, bolted pedestal base,
marked Wedgwood only 325.00
Vase, cov., 8¾" h., ovoid, white relief band of flowering foliate
scrolls below band of ribbon-
entwined foliage & above band of
stylized anthemion & scrolls on
black, domed cover w/band of

similar foliage, square foot
w/band of stylized foliage, cover
w/finial in the form of cupid leaning on a quiver of arrows, early
19th c. 990.00
Vase, 10 1/8" h., 4½" d., 2-handled,
white relief classical figures on
black, pedestal base w/floral &
foliate band, marked Wedgwood
only 487.00

ADAMS & OTHERS

Bust Portrait of Lord Byron

Cookie jar, cov., white relief hunting scene on blue, Adams 120.00
Hatpin holder, white relief classical
figures on deep blue, Adams,
3¼" h. 165.00
Hatpin holder, white relief bust of
Art Nouveau lady w/flowing hair
on lavender, gold trim, 5¼" h. 125.00
Pitcher, 6" h., white relief classical
figures on blue 75.00
Plaque, pierced to hang, white relief woman & butterfly on green,
Germany, 4¾" d. 35.00
Plaque, pierced to hang, white
relief deer on green, Germany,
5½ x 4½" 45.00
Plaque, pierced to hang, white
relief bust portrait of Lord
Byron within berried foliate &
scroll border on green,
6½ x 5¼" (ILLUS.) 45.00
Plaque, pierced to hang, white relief woman & cherubs on green,
Germany, 8 x 6½" oval.......... 75.00
Powder box, cov., white relief
woman & child on blue,
Schafer-Vater 52.00
Powder dish, white relief classical
lady & cupids on soft green,
4½" d., 2" h. 75.00
Salt dip, white relief classical
figures on blue, silverplate rim &

handle, numbered only, 2 5/8" d.,
1½" h. 60.00
Sugar shaker w/silver lustre pierced
top, white relief classical figures
on deep blue, 7" h. 135.00
Vase, 8" h., white relief figures on
blue, silverplate rim, ca. 1850 .... 40.00

JEWEL TEA AUTUMN LEAF PATTERN

Autumn Leaf Pattern Pie Baker

Though not antique, this ware has a devoted following. The Hall China Company of East Liverpool, Ohio, made the first pieces of Autumn Leaf pattern ware to be given as premiums by the Jewel Tea Company in 1933. The premiums were an immediate success and thousands of new customers, all eager to acquire a piece of the durable Autumn Leaf pattern ware, began purchasing Jewel Tea products. Though the pattern was eventually used to decorate linens, glasswares and tinwares, we include only the Hall China Company items in our listing.

Baking dish, swirl form, 7½" d. $14.50
Bowl, cereal, 6" d. 7.00
Bowl, 7½" d. 15.00
Bowl, cream soup 14.00
Bowls, stacking-type, 18 oz., 24 oz.
& 34 oz. bowls (3) & single cover,
set 57.00
Butter dish, cov., 1 lb. 180.00
Cake plate, 9½" d. 10.00
Casserole, cov., oval, 2-qt. 33.00
Coffee perculator, electric, 8-cup ... 260.00
Coffee pot, cov., drip-type, w/china
insert, 5-cup 45.00
Coffee pot (or casserole) warmer,
oval 130.00
Coffee server, cov., 8½" h. 30.00
Cookie jar, cov., large earred
handles 95.00
Creamer, pre-1940 .... 23.00
Creamer & cov. sugar bowl, 1940,
pr. 15.00
Cup & saucer .... 6.00 to 9.00
Cup & saucer, St. Denis 32.00
Custard cup 4.50
Dinner service for six w/salad bowl,
oval vegetable bowl, 13" l. platter, gravy boat, cov. casserole,
creamer & cov. sugar bowl,
49 pcs. 260.00

Irish coffee mug 65.00
Marmalade jar, cov., w/underplate,
2 pcs. 48.00
Mixing bowl, 7" d. 12.00
Mixing bowls, nested set of 3 ..... 37.00
Pickle dish, 9" oval 18.50
Pie baker, 9½" d. (ILLUS.) 13.00
Pitcher, utility, 2½ pt. 12.00
Pitcher, water, jug-type w/ice lip,
5½ pt. ....16.00 to 25.00
Plate, 6" d. 3.50
Plate, 7" d. 6.00
Plate, 8" d. 7.00
Plate, 9" d. 6.00

Autumn Leaf Pattern Dinner Plate

Plate, 10" d. (ILLUS.) 12.00
Platter, 11½" oval 12.50
Platter, 13½" oval 15.00
Salt & pepper shakers, large (range)
size, pr. 17.00
Sauce dish 3.00

Autumn Leaf Souffle-Casserole

Souffle-casserole, 10 oz. individual
size (ILLUS.) 20.00
Soup coupe, 8¼" d. 10.00
Soup plate w/flange rim 9.50
Teapot, cov., Aladdin lamp shape
w/long spout 45.00
Teapot, cov., square Newport
shape 125.00
Vase, bud 210.00
Vegetable bowl, open, 9" d. 53.00
Vegetable bowl, open, 10½" oval .. 15.00

JUGTOWN POTTERY

Jugtown Creamer

This pottery was established by Jacques and Juliana Busbee in Jugtown, North Carolina, in the early 1920's in an attempt to revive the skills of the diminishing North Carolina potter's art as Prohibition ended the need for locally crafted stoneware whiskey jugs. During the early years, Juliana Busbee opened a shop in Greenwich Village in New York City to promote the North Carolina wares that her husband, Jacques, was designing and a local youth, Ben Owen, was producing under his direction. Owen continued to work with Busbee from 1922 until Busbee's death in 1947 at which time Juliana took over management of the pottery for the next decade until her illness (or mental fatigue) caused the pottery to be closed in 1958. At that time, Owen opened his own pottery a few miles away, marking his wares "Ben Owen - Master Potter." The pottery begun by the Busbee's was reopened in 1960, under new management, and still operates today using the identical impressed mark of the early Jugtown pottery the Busbee's managed from 1922 until 1958.

Batter bowl w/pouring spout, earred handles, grey stoneware w/cobalt blue, large	$38.00
Bottle, corset-shaped, salt-glazed stoneware w/white drip glaze at neck & shoulder, 6½" h.	45.00
Bowl, 5¼" d., grey stoneware w/cobalt blue trim	65.00
Bowl, 6" d., 2" h., crimped rim, oriental-style heavy white glaze	55.00
Bowl, 8" d., Chinese red & blue glaze	115.00
Bowl, 9½ x 7", green frog's skin glaze	70.00
Chamberstick, redware, orange glaze	30.00 to 45.00
Creamer, brown-speckled glaze, 1930's, 4" h. (ILLUS.)	55.00
Cup & saucer, redware, orange glaze	28.00
Jar, cov., 2-handled, brown glaze, 9" h.	55.00
Jug, applied handle, olive green glaze, 4½" h.	40.00
Model of a hen, redware, orange to red glaze, 7¾" h.	165.00
Mug, brown glaze	25.00
Pitcher, 4" h., grey stoneware, olive green to tan glaze	26.00
Pitcher, 5½" h., bulbous, pinched spout, salt-glazed grey stoneware w/splashes of cobalt blue (water-stained interior)	55.00
Plate, 9" d., redware, clear pumpkin & brown speckled glaze	45.00
Plate, 9" d., redware, orange glaze	32.00
Platter, 11" l., redware, orange glaze	42.50
Rice bowl, white oriental-style glaze, small	50.00
Teapot, cov., greenish glaze	65.00
Vase, 3¾" h., white glaze	80.00
Vase, 4½" h., Chinese blue glaze	75.00
Vase, 6" h., redware, frog's skin glaze	90.00
Vase, 6½" h., Chinese blue & red "flambe" glaze, 1937	185.00

KAUFFMANN, ANGELIQUE

Dresser Box with Kauffmann Scene

Angelica Kauffmann (Marie Angelique Catherine Kauffmann) was an accomplished Swiss artist, who lived from 1741 until 1807. Paintings copied from her original work often embellish porcelain and those signed with her name have attracted collectors.

Bowl, 10½" d., center scene w/two lovely ladies after Kauffmann reserved on blue ground w/gold trim	$255.00
Bowl, master berry or fruit, 4-section scalloped rim, center scene after Kauffmann, Carlsbad, Austria blank	95.00
Cake plate, pierced handles, center scene of 2 women & cherubs after	

Kauffmann, dark green border
w/gold tracery 75.00
Cake plate, pierced handles, center
scene after Kauffmann, pearlized
lavender & blue border 65.00
Cake set: handled cake plate w/six
serving plates; "Kauffmann"
signed center scenes, turquoise
borders w/gold, Bavarian blanks,
7 pcs. 95.00
Dresser box w/hinged lid & brass
collar, typical Kauffmann scene on
lid (ILLUS.) 70.00
Humidor, silverplate cover w/pipe
finial, scene of ladies & cupid after Kauffmann reserved on green
ground, Austrian blank 400.00
Plaque, pierced to hang, center portrait after Kauffmann, Victoria,
Austria blank, 10" d. 125.00
Plate, 6" d., scene of maiden &
cupid after Kauffmann, beehive
mark blank 38.00
Plate, 8" d., scene of 3 beautiful
women after Kauffmann, ornate
gold trim 47.50
Plate, center scene of classical lady,
2 attendants & cherub after Kauffmann, cobalt blue border w/gilt
latticework, Victoria, Austria
blank 80.00
Tea set: cov. teapot, creamer, cov.
sugar bowl & 4 plates; Kauffmann
scenes decor, Royal Vienna
blanks, 7 pcs. 225.00
Urn, 2-handled, 2 different Kauff-
mann scenes reserved on dark
ground w/embossed designs highlighted in gold, Royal Vienna
blank, 12" h. 200.00
Vase, 8" h., scene after Kauffmann
reserved on teal blue highlighted
w/gold, Royal Vienna blank 55.00
Vase, 12" h., 2-handled, classical
scene after Kauffmann reserved
on cobalt blue ground 195.00
Vase, 19" h., Kauffmann-type por-
trait reserved on cobalt blue
ground 285.00

KOCH

*Joseph Anton Koch was an Austrian paint-
er and etcher (1768-1839) whose work has often been copied on porcelain. These
reproductions appear on the ceramics of various factories and all carry the artist's signature leading some collectors to lump them
together as "Koch" porcelain.*

Berry set: master bowl & 6 sauce
dishes; grapes decor, 7 pcs. $100.00

Cake plate, pierced handles, grapes
decor, scalloped gold edge, J. C.
Louise, Bavaria blank, 11" d. 47.00
Cake plate, pierced handles, plums
& grapes decor 48.00
Chocolate cup & saucer, apples
decor 30.00
Plate, 6" d., scalloped rim, apples &
cherries decor, J. C. Louise,
Bavaria blank 20.00
Plate, 7½" d., grapes decor 18.00
Plate, 8" d., grapes decor, J. C.
Louise, Bavaria blank 32.00
Plate, 8" d., peaches decor 17.00

Plate with Apples

Plate, 8½" d., apples decor
(ILLUS.) 35.00
Plate, 9" d., strawberries decor 45.00
Plate, 9" d., grapes decor, Bavaria
blank 35.00

LEEDS

Leeds Tea Caddy

The Leeds Pottery in Yorkshire, England, began production about 1758. It made, among other things, creamware that was highly competitive with Wedgwood's. In the 1780's it began production of reticulated and punched wares. Little of its production was marked. Most readily available Leeds ware is that of the 19th century during which time the pottery was operated by several firms.

Bowl, cov., 4¼" d., 4½" h., pearlware, painted dark blue handles & mushroom-shaped cover knop, body w/dark blue, orange & green floral spray, 1780-1800 . . . . . $180.00

Bowl, 10½" d., 4½" h., pearlware, fluted sides, feather-edged rim & footrim, ca. 1750 (minor rim chips) 660.00

Mug, creamware, applied handle, blue river & pagoda scene & cross-hatched diamond border, 6" h. 300.00

Plates, 7¾" octagon, creamware, transfer-printed in black & enriched in colors w/scenes of the "Prodigal Son" & so inscribed within borders of trailing florals, foliage & husks, ca. 1770, set of 6 (w/hairline cracks in 2) 1,430.00

Platter, 10½" oval, reticulated rim, Blue Willow patt. variant 265.00

Tea caddy, cov., square w/cylindrical neck, relief-molded putti holding garlands & birds enriched in blue & black, inscribed "Ann Colridge" one side & w/date "1797" opposite, flat shoulder applied w/four figural cherubs at corners & cover w/seated lion finial, w/repair to one cherub & cover, 6" h. (ILLUS.) 1,540.00

Leeds Teapot

Teapot, cov., creamware, painted w/colorful scene of Aurora & her chariot drawn by winged horses among clouds one side & w/cherubs watching the rising sun reverse, the shoulder & cover enriched in iron-red, puce, green & yellow w/flowering foliage, ca. 1780, minor repair to top of spout, 8¼" w. (ILLUS.) 1,320.00

Toddy plate, 5-color scene of peafowl in tree, green feather edge, 5½" d. (small hairline & edge wear) 265.00

LENOX

Lenox China with Silver Overlay

The Ceramic Art Company was established at Trenton, New Jersey, in 1889 by Jonathan Coxon and Walter Scott Lenox. In addition to true porcelain, it also made a Belleek-type ware. Re-named Lenox Company in 1906, it is still in operation today. Also see BELLEEK-AMERICAN and TOBY MUGS & JUGS.

Bone dish, pink roses decor (Ceramic Art Company mark, 1894-1906) $50.00

Bookends, Art Deco woman's torso, black, pr. 150.00

Box & cover, black w/gold butterfly highlighted w/blue enameled dots on lid 85.00

Bust of young girl, mask-type sculpture, white glaze, 9" h. . . 185.00 to 225.00

Busts of Art Deco woman, glossy cream glaze, 8½" h., pr. 350.00

Candy dish & cover w/long-tailed bird finial, coral pink & white 115.00

Coaster, cobalt blue w/gold-washed sterling silver overlay decor, 3" d. 55.00

Coffee pot, cov., demitasse, cobalt blue w/sterling silver overlay decor 175.00

Coffee set: cov. coffee pot, creamer & open sugar bowl; cobalt blue w/sterling silver overlay, 3 pcs. (ILLUS.) 350.00

Cornucopia-vase, pink-tinged beige, 4½" h. 35.00

Creamer & sugar bowl, bi-centennial commemorative of George Washington's birth, 1932, pr. 95.00

Cup & saucer, white w/sterling silver overlay Art Nouveau florals .. 95.00

Cups & saucers, black & white historical scenes, gold rims, marked "Lenox Historical China - Painted by Minga Pope Polchin 1933," set of 6 .... 200.00

Cups & saucers, Ming patt., set of 8 .... 195.00

Cups & saucers, demitasse, Ming patt., set of 10 .... 225.00

Cups, demitasse, yellow-tinged inserts in sterling silver holders, set of 6 .... 225.00

Decanters & stoppers, chocolate brown shaded to green w/sterling silver overlay on stoppers & bottles w/"Scotch" & "Rye," pr. (Ceramic Art Co. mark) 225.00

Desk set: inkwell w/insert & cover, pen tray & sponge holder; small girl w/pink roses decor, signed & numbered, 4 pcs. 295.00

Dish, shell-shaped, 9½" l. 45.00

Fish plate, "Brook Trout" or "Weak Fish," artist-signed, 9" d., each ... 60.00

Gravy boat w/attached undertray, Mayfair patt., ivory w/gold decor, large 55.00

Letter rack 175.00

Marmalade jar & cover, creamy ivory w/sterling silver overlay (Ceramic Art Co. mark) 75.00

Mayonnaise dish, scalloped edge, red & blue floral decor, sterling silver trim 55.00

Mug with Silver Overlay

Mug, cobalt blue w/sterling silver overlay decor, 6" h. (ILLUS.) 180.00

Mug, 3-handled, enameled blue dots & gold paste decor (Ceramic Art Co. mark, dated 1896) 135.00

Night light, bust of angel, metal base, 5" h. 185.00

Pen holder, green w/white ruffled edge, marked "Custom Made for Shaeffer," 4" d., w/gold finish pen 95.00

Pitcher, 7" h., mask spout, pebbled surface, pink-tinged creamy beige 130.00

Decorated by Witte

Pitcher, tankard, 14¼" h., painted scene of two boys fighting over football, embossed & painted handle & base border, signed "Witte," 1897-1905 green wreath mark (ILLUS.) 650.00

Pitcher, Indian head handle, pink-tinged white glaze 175.00

Plate, 7" d., Ming patt. 16.00

Plate, 8½" d., Ming patt. 22.50

Plate, 9" d., Washington-Wakefield patt. 18.00

Platter, 16½ x 12", scalloped gold rim, draped handles, creamy beige 60.00

Platter, Ming patt., large 100.00

Salt dip, model of a swan 24.00

Salt dip, shell-shaped, coral pink ... 14.00

Salt shaker & pepper mill, flying geese decor, pr. 40.00

Sugar bowl, cov., Ming patt. 45.00

Tea set: cov. teapot w/attached porcelain infuser, creamer & cov. sugar bowl; chocolate brown glaze w/sterling silver overlay decor marked "Mauser," 3 pcs. 375.00

Urn-vase, 2-handled, ivory w/coral handles, 7" h. 55.00

Vase, bud, 4" h., Art Deco style 30.00

Vases, 6" h., orchids decor, signed Morley & numbered, pr. 95.00

Vase, 10" h., creamy beige cone-shaped ribbed sides w/florals molded in relief at front & reverse, pink-tinted base 75.00

Vase, 10" h., swan handles, cream & coral-pink decor, gold trim 80.00

Vase, 12" h., 9" d., Ming patt. 175.00

LIMOGES PORCELAIN

by Mary Frank Gaston

"T&V," "D&C," "JP," "CA," "MR," "WG&C," "AL," (and the list could go on and on) are not simply a lot of random initials! Those letters identify just a few of the many porcelain factories which operated in and around the city of Limoges, France, during the latter part of the 19th century. Today a large variety of china marked with such initials comprises an extensive portion of the collectible porcelain market. In addition to seeking exquisitely decorated and unusual items made by Limoges potteries during the late Victorian era, collectors discover that interpreting the many diverse marks and searching for rare and even undocumented marks are other interesting pursuits which make the "thrill of the chase" for Limoges porcelain so fascinating and challenging!

The Limoges porcelain industry traces its beginnings to 1768 when kaolin, the special type of natural clay required for making true porcelain, was discovered in the village of St. Yrieix, near Limoges. A few years later, a Limoges faience pottery was successful in making true (or hard paste) porcelain, characterized by a translucent and vitreous body.

That factory soon gained the support of the Comte d'Artois, brother of King Louis XVI. In 1784, the factory was sold to the king, and thereafter it functioned as a subsidiary to Sevres, the royal porcelain manufacturer. The Limoges pottery remained under royal ownership until the end of the French Revolution in 1796 when it was sold to a few of its former employees.

After the Revolution, the development of a large-scale porcelain industry was encouraged because of an absence of royal control and an abundant supply of local natural resources required for porcelain production. During the first quarter of the 19th century, the number of persons employed in making china in Limoges increased from a few hundred to several thousand. Limoges soon became the center of the French porcelain industry.

The "golden age" for Limoges, however, did not arrive until after the 1840's. Prior to that time, porcelain was owned only by royalty and the very wealthy. In Limoges, as manufacturing and decorating techniques were perfected, greater production became possible. The growing number of factories and increased technology generated competition. Consequently, prices became less expensive. Those conditions, plus the arrival on the scene in 1840 of David Haviland (a New York City importer of china table wares), set a chain of events in motion which were the key to the future prosperity of the industry.

As an importer of table wares, David Haviland realized that his customers were becoming tired of the English earthenwares which were basically the only type of dishes available and affordable for the majority of middle class Americans. In the late 1830's, Haviland imported some French porcelain. Although his first attempts to promote French porcelain were not successful, Haviland was quick to put his finger on just why the new French china did not sell well. It was not that the dishes were made of porcelain; the problem was that the shapes and decoration were too "foreign." Because he knew that porcelain was indeed superior to earthenware, especially for table china, Haviland was convinced a market existed for porcelain dinner services if the china could be fashioned and decorated to suit American tastes. To solve the problem, Haviland moved to France in 1841 and settled in Limoges in 1842.

Often it is erroneously implied that David Haviland immediately began making porcelain when he arrived in Limoges. He did not, however, produce his own porcelain until 1865. During those intervening years, Haviland commissioned china from other Limoges factories to be made according to his specifications. He then exported the china to New York through his importing firm of Haviland Bros. Between 1847 and 1865, Haviland also operated a decorating studio where he hired artists to decorate the white ware made by the other Limoges factories. During those years, Haviland gained world renown for his porcelain designs and decorations.

History proves that David Haviland was correct in his belief that Americans would prefer porcelain dinner ware once it was designed to meet their needs and pocketbooks. From the mid-1800's through the 1920's, huge amounts of Limoges porcelain were exported to the United States since Limoges factories were eager to take advantage of the big North American market opened up by Haviland. By the last quarter of the 19th century, most Limoges factories were making porcelain almost totally for export. Other Americans and Europeans became interested in gaining a corner of the lucrative market. Many followed Haviland's pattern by first setting up exporting businesses in Limoges, later establishing decorating studios, and eventually building factories to both produce and decorate the china.

It is not surprising that the Haviland company became the best known of all the Limoges factories. Haviland provided an enormous market for the other factories' production and for some years was able to maintain almost a virtual monopoly over the exporting end of the industry. Once Haviland began manufacturing china, his company also became the largest. Moreover, prior to 1876, Limoges china was rarely marked. Thus, American consumers did not know (and probably did not really care) which factory actually made a particular piece of china.

Lack of proper factory attribution for Limoges porcelain ceased, however, after 1876 when the Haviland Company implemented a rather precise printed marking system. A simple initial mark was applied in green underglaze to identify the company. Another mark incorporating the full name of the factory was applied overglaze in some other color when the china was decorated at the factory. Most of the other Limoges factories quickly followed suit, using the same method for marking their production.

Today collectors can be grateful for the institution of this marking procedure. Not only can the work of specific factories be properly identified, but whether or not a piece was factory-decorated can also be determined by the presence or absence of the overglaze mark.

The marking system coincided with the American china painting passion of the late 1800's. Almost all of the Limoges factories, including Haviland, made and exported undecorated china in response to the demands of that special market for these wares. A large supply of both French-decorated Limoges and American-decorated Limoges from that period has survived the toll of time. The differentiation between the two is a very important part of collecting and evaluating Limoges.

Although the part played by David Haviland and his company in the development of the Limoges porcelain industry should by no means be minimized, serious Limoges collectors are keenly aware that the Havialnd Company was but one of the many which made fine quality porcelain. There is also a definite contrast between the types of products and decorations used by the Haviland Company and other Limoges factories.

While beautifully decorated artistic and exhibit pieces were made by Haviland, the bulk of the firm's production was geared to dinner services decorated with pastel floral transfer designs. Other Limoges factories made similar sets, but most produced a larger line of decorative items ranging from dresser sets, desk sets, candlesticks, and trinket boxes to large vases, urns, and jardinieres. Decoration themes were not confined to flowers but included fruit, birds, animals, and figures. Vivid colors and rich gold accents were other distinguishing traits.

Such examples which represent creative workmanship and beautiful decoration are eagerly sought by collectors. Because of the vast amounts of china produced and exported by the numerous Limoges factories from the late 1800's through the 1920's, a wide and varied assortment is available. Lovely pieces can be found on the shelves of antique shops, or displayed under brilliant lights at antique shows, or mixed in with sundry other items at estate auctions and flea market stalls. Prices range from moderate to expensive. Limoges definitely provides tremendous collecting opportunities.

In addition to the china made by Haviland & Co., some of the most visible Limoges manufacturers' products include those whose initials introduced this article: Tressemann & Vogt (T&V); R. Delinieres & Co. (D&C); J. Pouyat (JP); Charles Ahrenfeldt (CA); M. Redon (MR); Wm. Gurein & Co. (WG&C); and A. Lanternier (AL).

(Editor's Note: *Mary Frank Gaston is a prolific author, delving into the histories of numerous types of collectible chinawares and writing with authority on the subject. She is the author of* Collector's Encyclopedia of Limoges Porcelain, *a well-illustrated book, published by Collector Books, Paducah, Kentucky, which identifies the marks of the various Limoges porcelain manufacturers. She also wrote an article, "Limoges Porcelain, French and American Decoration" for the July 3, 1985 issue of* THE ANTIQUE TRADER WEEKLY *newspaper.)*

* * * * *

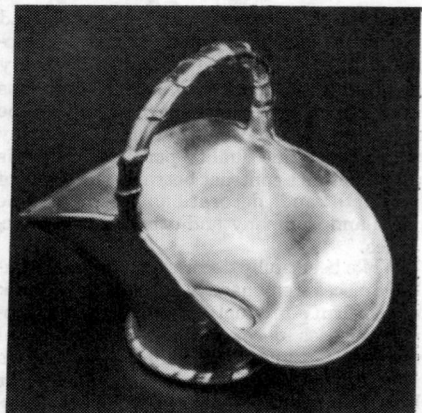

Limoges Basket decorated in America

Basket, h.p. gold surface by Stouffer
   Studio, H. Balleroy blank
   (ILLUS.) $125.00

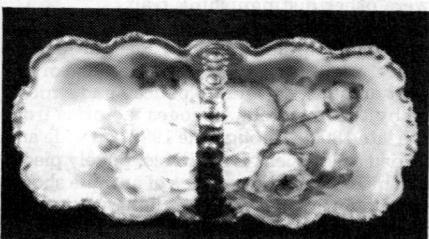

Limoges Basket with Roses

Basket, irregular rim, floral-molded
   gilt handle, multicolored roses
   decor, artist-signed "Duvall," Jean
   Pouyat, 9¼ x 4½" (ILLUS.) 150.00
Bouillon cup & saucer, white w/gold
   trim (Tressemann & Vogt) 9.00
Bowl & cover w/shell finial, 7" d.,
   underwater decor w/shells & seaweed in soft shades of green,
   coral & lavender, artist-signed &
   dated 1898 (Jean Pouyat) 59.00
Bowl, 9¼" w., 2¼" h., 6-sided, scalloped rim, large h.p. pink roses
   on green ground (Tressemann &
   Vogt) 85.00
Bowl, 9½" d., scalloped rim, h.p.
   pink overall w/coin gold overlay
   (Jean Pouyat) 70.00
Bowl, 10" d., scalloped rim, overall
   floral decor, ornate gold interior
   & exterior trim, Coronet (George
   Borgfeldt) 70.00
Bowl, 10 x 12", shell-shaped
   w/ribbed, scalloped & gilt edge,
   h.p. yellow & brown ducklings
   decor (Jean Pouyat) 95.00
Cache pot, cylindrical w/pseudo ring
   handles at sides, ball feet, h.p.

overall forest scene w/fox chasing
   rabbit, 12" h. (William Guerin) . . . 375.00
Cake plate, pierced handles, pink
   roses & gold decor, artist-signed,
   11" d. (Tressemann & Vogt) 40.00
Candle holder, chamberstick-type
   w/ring handle, pink roses decor,
   gold trim (G.D.A. - Gerard,
   Dufraisseix & Abbot) 45.00

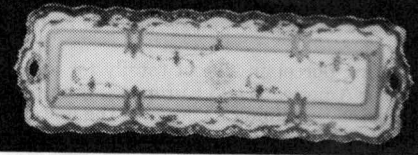

Limoges Card Tray

Card tray, pierced handles, scalloped rim, gold-beaded inner
   border & raised gold floral sprays,
   Blakeman & Henderson (ILLUS.) . . . 150.00

Charger by the Emile Coiffe Firm

Charger, fluted rim, pink roses
   decor on shaded green inner
   border, wide gold rim, 12" d.,
   Emile Coiffe (ILLUS.) 165.00

Charger by J. Granger Company

Charger, ornately molded irregular
   rim, enameled decor & gold trim,
   12½" d., J. Granger (ILLUS.) 175.00

Limoges Chocolate Pot

Chocolate pot, cov., raised gold
   florals & foliage decor on white,
   9" h., Emile Coiffe blank w/Bawo
   & Dotter decoration (ILLUS.) 165.00
Chocolate pot, cov., h.p. lavender
   thistles on pale green ground
   (Jean Pouyat) 125.00
Cookie jar & cover w/twig finial,
   pink florals & green leaves decor,
   gold trim, artist-signed (Tressemann & Vogt)................. 75.00

Covered Cookie Jar & Underplate

Cookie jar, cover & underplate, multicolored roses decor, gold trim,
   5" h. jar & 8½" d. underplate,
   pr., Tressemann & Vogt (ILLUS.) .. 225.00
Creamer & cov. sugar bowl, cream-
   er w/dragon handle & puffy
   square form sugar bowl, h.p.
   shaded pink cabbage roses on
   light blue ground, gold trim, pr.
   (Tressemann & Vogt) 110.00

Limoges Creamer & Sugar Bowl

Creamer & cov. sugar bowl, ornately molded handles, enameled
   heavy gold decor & trim, Vignaud
   blanks w/decoration by B & T
   (French) Studio, pr. (ILLUS.) 145.00
Creamer & open basket-form sugar
   bowl, embossed scrollwork & scalloped rims, h.p. purple florals &
   raised gold scrollwork decor, pr.
   (Tressemann & Vogt) 125.00
Cup & saucer, demitasse, h.p.
   florals & ornate gold trim on
   white (Charles Ahrenfeldt - made
   for Charles Reizenstein Co., Al-
   legheny, Pa.) 60.00

T & V Cup & Saucer

Cup & saucer, double ring handle,
   floral & leaf decor, gold trim,
   Tressemann & Vogt (ILLUS.) 70.00

E. Coiffe Cup & Saucer

Cup & saucer, scalloped border, enameled ornate gold scrollwork, Emile Coiffe (ILLUS.) 60.00

Leaf-Shaped Dish

Dish, leaf-shaped, gold branches & trim, 5½" l., Wm. Guerin & Co. blank w/American decoration (ILLUS.) 40.00

Dish, palette-shaped, h.p. pinecone decor, 8½" l. (GDA) 32.00

Dish, 3-compartment, scalloped edges, gold handles joined at center, coin gold florals & leaves decor on lush cobalt blue ground, 12" d. 165.00

T & V Dresser Tray

Dresser tray, ornately molded rim, pink & white roses decor, gold trim, artist-signed "Vogt," 13 x 8½", Tressemann & Vogt (ILLUS.) 165.00

Dresser tray, ornately molded rim, h.p. large roses, gold trim, 13¼ x 9" (Blakeman & Henderson) 65.00

Dresser tray, irregular shape, red currant berries decor, gold trim (Tressemann & Vogt) 75.00

Fish plate, h.p. fish, 9" d., L. S. & S. (L. Strauss exporter) 75.00

Fish plate, scalloped rim w/heavy

gold trim, underwater scene w/fish, reeds & florals, artist-signed "Roche," 9½" d. 95.00

Fish Platter

Fish platter, scalloped rim, underwater scene w/fish & seaplants, gold accents, 18" l., decorated by Lazeyras, Rosenfeld & Lehman (ILLUS.) 450.00

Fish set: 21" l. platter & eleven 8½" d. plates; 6 varied species of fish, artist-signed, 12 pcs. 350.00

Game plaques, pierced to hang, pheasant on one & quail on other, each on pastel ground w/floral & coin gold trim, artist-signed, 13½" d., pr. 485.00

Game plate, scalloped gold rococo border, duck decor, artist-signed "Max," 10" d. (Coronet) 85.00

Game plate, scalloped gold rococo border, h.p. pheasant decor, 13¼" d. (Coronet) 245.00

Game set: 18 x 12" platter & six 9" d. plates; each w/h.p. varied bird species, 7 pcs. (L D & C) 295.00

Hair receiver, dainty florals & birds decor on off-white ground, gold trim at scalloped base (Jean Pouyat) 65.00

Limoges Hatpin Holder

Hatpin holder, dainty pastel floral decor, gold trim, 4" h., Emile Coiffe (ILLUS.) 65.00

Humidor, cov., pinecone decor on shaded green to gold ground (Jean Pouyat) 72.00

T & V Humidor

Humidor, cov., vivid red-orange
    florals & insect decor, gold-
    sponged trim, 6½" h., Tres-
    semann & Vogt (ILLUS.) 225.00

Ice Cream Serving Tray

Ice cream serving tray, pink floral
    decor, gold trim, artist-signed &
    dated 1913, 16½ x 8½", Parou-
    taud Freres blank w/American
    decoration (ILLUS.) 125.00
Ice cream set: 16 x 10½" ice cream
    serving tray & eight 6½" d. in-
    dividual plates; scalloped gold
    rim, roses & lilacs decor, each
    piece artist-signed "Felix," 9 pcs.
    (L D & C) 175.00

Jardiniere with Violets Decor

Jardiniere, h.p. violets decor,
    6½" h., R. Delinieres & Co. blank
    w/American decoration (ILLUS.) . . 225.00

Jardiniere with Swan Handles

Jardiniere, footed, swan's neck han-
    dles, gold encrusted florals & gold
    trim, pearlized interior, 11" d.,
    7½" h., Paroutaud Freres blank
    w/American decoration (ILLUS.) . . 275.00
Loving cup, h.p. cupids decor & let-
    tered initials & dates "1853-1903"
    in gold, 5½" d., 6" h. (Jean
    Pouyat) 72.00

Mayonnaise Bowl with Undertray

Mayonnaise bowl w/attached under-
    tray, chain of florals decor, wide
    gold borders, Emile Coiffe blank
    w/decoration by B. & H. (French)
    Studio (ILLUS.) 45.00
Mug, portrait of smiling monk read-
    ing fashion pages, 5¼" h. (Jean
    Pouyat) 79.00
Mug, acorn decor in autumn colors,
    5½" h. (Jean Pouyat) 45.00
Mug, portrait of brown & white Ter-
    rier dog against shaded brown to
    yellow ground, 6" h. (Wm. Guerin
    for M. Henderson, Chicago) 85.00

Limoges Pen Tray

Pen tray, footed, yellow floral
decor, gold accents, 6" l., Gerard,
Dufraisseix & Morel (ILLUS.) 65.00

Ornate Picture Frame

Picture frame, easel-type, floral
decor w/gold accents, 6½" w.,
9" h., Bawo & Dotter Elite Works
(ILLUS.) 200.00
Pitcher, cider, 5" h., 8" d., ribbed
handle, h.p. pink & white florals
on dark green ground (Jean
Pouyat) 150.00
Pitcher, cider, 5½" h., 8" d., crab
apples decor (Jean Pouyat) 60.00
Pitcher, 7" h., thistles decor (Tressemann & Vogt) 65.00
Pitcher, tankard, 11" h., h.p. currants & leaves on multicolored
ground, dated 1908 (Jean
Pouyat) 130.00
Pitcher, tankard, 11" h., h.p. multicolored grapes decor (Tressemann & Vogt) 215.00
Pitcher, tankard, 11½" h., coin gold
handle, pink roses & gold latticework & scrolls on peach ground
(Kittel & Klingenberg) 110.00
Pitcher, tankard, 13" h., red cherries on purple ground, artist-
signed (R. Delinieres) 145.00
Pitcher, tankard, 13½" h., h.p.
colorful portrait of cavalier (decorated by B. & H. Studio,
Limoges) 450.00
Pitcher, tankard, 15" h., h.p. floral
decor (Jean Pouyat) 215.00
Pitcher, tankard, 15" h., green &
pink chrysanthemums decor,
artist-signed "Laurent" (Tressemann & Vogt) 250.00
Pitcher, tankard, 15½" h., serpentine handle, h.p. grape clusters
on shaded pastel ground (Jean
Pouyat) 170.00

Plaque with American Decoration

Plaque, h.p. river scene, 8½" w.,
11½" h., R. Delinieres & Co.
blank w/American decoration
(ILLUS.) 250.00
Plate, 6" d., miniature-type portrait
of gentleman & lady center, blue
border, gold trim (Wm. Guerin) .. 85.00
Plates, 6" d., green holly leaves &
red berries border decor, gold-
trimmed scalloped edge, set of 8
(Tressemann & Vogt) 180.00
Plate, 6¾" d., h.p. lavender orchid
& lily-of-the-valley decor, gold
trim (Tressemann & Vogt) 20.00

Plate decorated by Ahrenfeldt

Plate, 8" d., cupids decor center,
gold trim, Laviolette blank
w/decoration by C. Ahrenfeldt
(ILLUS.) 90.00
Plate, 8½" d., h.p. florals & leaves
decor, ornate gold embossed
border (Tressemann & Vogt) 45.00
Plate, 8½" d., purple flowers

w/green & gold leaves decor, artist-signed (Tressemann & Vogt) 28.00

Plate, 8¾" d., grapes & leaves decor, gold edge, artist-signed (Coronet) 45.00

Plate, 10" d., h.p. boat scene (Coronet) 95.00

Plate with Cupids

Plate, 10" d., ornately molded rim, h.p. scene of cupids center, enameled gold florals & gold trim, J. Granger (ILLUS.) 275.00

Plate, 10" d., h.p. portrait of peasant girl standing against wall (Coronet) 75.00

Plate, 10" d., rabbits (2) & dish of carrots before fence on yellow shaded to green ground, artist-signed (Coronet) 65.00

Punch bowl, h.p. pink & yellow florals on dark green ground, 9½" d. (Tressemann & Vogt) 200.00

Ring tree, model of a hand, blossoms decor (Tressemann & Vogt) 40.00

Tea set: cov. teapot, creamer, cov. sugar bowl & tea tile; roses decor, gilt trim, 4 pcs. (Wm. Guerin) 165.00

Limoges Toothbrush Holder

Toothbrush holder, h.p. floral border, gold top, 4" h., Emile Coiffe blank w/American decoration (ILLUS.)....................... 35.00

Limoges Vase with American Decoration

Vase, 7½" h., ornate gilt handles, h.p. florals on shaded ground, R. Delinieres & Co. blank w/American decoration (ILLUS.) 125.00

Vase with Portrait Decoration

Vase, 8" h., h.p. portrait reserve front, M. Redon blank w/American decoration (ILLUS.) 175.00

Vase, 9" h., gold handles & gold legs, h.p. mums decor (M. Redon) 125.00

Vase, 12" h., cylindrical, h.p. pink & yellow roses overall decor (Tressemann & Vogt)................. 125.00

Vase, 12½" h., elaborately entwined handles, roses decor near base, Latrille Freres blank w/Bawo & Dotter decoration 600.00

Vase with American Decoration

Vase, 14½" h., swollen cylinder
w/collared neck, h.p. roses overall, Bernardaud & Co. blank
w/American decoration (ILLUS.) .. 250.00

(End of Special Focus)

LOTUS WARE

Lotus Ware Rose Bowl

Avidly sought by many collectors are these exquisite bone china wares made by Knowles, Taylor & Knowles, of East Liverpool, Ohio, in the last decade of the 19th century and into the 20th. The firm also produced ironstone and hotel china.

Bowl, 6 x 4¼" oval, beaded rim,
reticulated ends, all white,
signed $525.00
Dish, shell-shaped w/coral shell
feet, all white, signed, 6" l. 125.00
Creamer, h.p. green & gold roses,
4¼" h. 155.00
Rose bowl, scalloped & crimped rim
w/beaded edge, h.p. violets one
side & cupids riding in chariot
pulled by doves opposite, artist-
signed (ILLUS.) 395.00
Tea set: cov. teapot & creamer; gold

paste florals in relief on white,
2 pcs. 550.00
Tea set: cov. teapot, creamer &
sugar bowl; all white, 3 pcs.
(mend on bottom of teapot) 500.00
Vase, 9" h., 2-handled, h.p. pastel
pink & blue floral sprays, 1893
form 550.00

LUSTRE WARES

Lustred wares in imitation of copper, gold, silver and other colors were produced in England in the early 19th century and onward. Gold, copper or platinum oxides were painted on glazed objects which were then fired, giving them a lustred effect. Various forms of lustre wares include plain lustre- with the entire object coated to obtain a metallic effect, bands of lustre decoration and painted lustre designs. Particularly appealing is the pink or purple "splash lustre" sometimes referred to as "Sunderland" lustre in the mistaken belief it was confined to the production of Sunderland area potteries. Objects decorated in silver lustre by the "resist" process, wherein parts of the objects to be left free from lustre decoration were treated with wax, are referred to as "silver resist."

COPPER

Copper Lustre Vase & Pitcher

Creamer, copper lustre body
w/wide blue band w/embossed
house, 3 3/8" h. $38.00
Creamer, copper lustre body w/yel-
low band decor, 1810-30,
3½" h. 70.00
Goblet, copper lustre body w/white
band highlighted w/polychrome &
copper lustre floral decor,
4 1/8" h. (pinpoint rim flakes) 55.00
Goblet, copper lustre body w/dou-
ble white bands w/pink lustre
spots, 4½" h. 40.00
Match holder, copper lustre body
w/cream "sanded" band 35.00
Mug, copper lustre body w/wide
white band highlighted w/poly-
chrome & lustre florals, ribbed
base, 3 5/8" h. 50.00

Pitcher, 5" h., copper lustre body
w/yellow band of copper lustre
leaves 40.00
Pitcher, 5¼" h., copper lustre body
w/blue band of embossed
figures 90.00
Pitcher, 5¼" h., copper lustre body
w/white reserves transfer-printed
in purple w/scenes of "Charity"
highlighted w/(worn) enameling . .   95.00
Pitcher, 5½" h., copper lustre body
w/tan band decor 75.00
Pitcher, 5½" h., copper lustre body
w/enameled pink florals 82.50
Pitcher, 5½" h., copper lustre body
w/yellow band decor 60.00
Pitcher, 6¾" h., copper lustre body
w/canary yellow band w/white
reserve transfer-printed in red &
highlighted w/polychrome
enameling w/scene of classical
woman & child 165.00
Pitcher, 7" h., copper lustre body
w/blue band decor 90.00

"Hero of New Orleans" Pitcher

Pitcher, 8¼" h., copper lustre body
w/embossed beading at rim &
wide yellow center band transfer-
printed in black w/bust portrait of
"General Jackson - The Hero of
New Orleans" on each side & enriched w/enameled foliage, ca.
1830 (ILLUS.) 462.00
Pitcher, copper lustre body w/pink
oyster shell decor 115.00
Pitchers & vase: pr. pitchers (6" &
6½" h.) w/copper lustre bodies
reserved w/yellow bands & oval
reserves transfer-printed &
enameled w/pastoral scenes;
6½" h. 2-handled vase w/copper
lustre body & yellow band reserved w/oval transfer-printed in
puce w/scenes of sheep, England,
early 19th c., 3 pcs. (ILLUS. of
pitcher & vase) 330.00

SILVER & SILVER RESIST

Leeds Dessert Service

Dessert set: pr. shaped & pr. square
dishes, shell-shaped dish, 2-
handled oval compote & 6 plates
(1 plate repaired); iron-red & silver lustre flowering plants separated by silver lustre fruiting vine
panels on canary yellow ground,
Leeds, ca. 1810, 12 pcs. (ILLUS. of
part) 2,420.00
Mug, "silver resist" florals & foliage
on purple lustre ground w/copper
lustre trim, 3 3/8" h. (pinpoint
flakes on base) 55.00
Pitcher, 4 3/8" h., "silver resist,"
w/reserve transfer-printed in
black & enameled in iron-red,
blue, yellow, black, brown &
green w/plump robin perched on
oak branch on silver resist
ground, ca. 1815 . . . .   385.00

Silver Lustre Pitchers

Pitchers, 5½" & 3½" h., larger
transfer-printed in blue w/hunting
scene after Morland & other
w/scene of woman grinding corn
on silver lustre ground, ca. 1810
(ILLUS.) 770.00
Pitcher, 5¾" h., silver lustre, "The
Farmers Creed" inscription,
1810-30 . . . .   495.00
Pitcher, 8¼" h., "silver resist" lustre
body w/oval reserve transfer-
printed in iron-red & enameled
yellow, blue, mauve & green on
each side w/scene of farmer, his
wife & domestic animals & inscribed "Trust in God" & "The
Husbandman's Diligence Provides
Bread" & w/heart-shaped panel
w/further inscription below spout,
ca. 1815 . . . .   412.00

SUNDERLAND PINK & OTHERS

Staffordshire Pink Lustre Pitchers

Bowl, 8½" d., 4" h., transfer-printed in black w/"Mariner Arms" & "A West View of the Cast Iron Bridge" on pink splash lustre ground 125.00

Creamer, copper lustre handle, transfer-printed in black w/portrait of Commodore Bainbridge & w/red stars around rim on pink splash lustre ground, 3" h. 95.00

Creamer & open sugar bowl, pink & purple lustre decor, Gray's Pottery, Stoke, Staffordshire, 1934-61, pr. 55.00

Mug, pink lustre, House patt., 2" h. 95.00

Mug, pink lustre lily-of-the-valley & gold trim on white, 3" h. 55.00

Mug & saucer, child's, pink splash lustre w/copper lustre trim 55.00

Pancake dish w/handled perforated cover, interior & exterior decor w/enameled gold fern fronds on pink lustre bands, 1830's, 8½" d. underplate 50.00

Pepper pot, pink splash lustre, 4½" h. 85.00

Pitchers, 5¼" h., one w/oval reserve transfer-printed in puce w/English manor scene on pink lustre ground enriched w/foliage & other w/flowering foliage overall on pink lustre ground, ca. 1820, pr. (ILLUS.) 275.00

Bust Portrait of Perry

Pitchers, 7 5/8" & 5½" h., each transfer-printed in black w/bust portraits of American military heroes on pink splash lustre ground, w/discoloration on larger pitcher, ca. 1815, pr. (ILLUS. of one) 1,320.00

Pitcher, 9" h., transfer-printed in black w/verse "A Frigate in Full Sail," scene of sailor & maid & joined French & English coats of arms w/"Crimea," highlighted w/polychrome enameling on pink splash lustre ground (crow's foot in side & some wear) 175.00

Plaque, pierced to hang, transfer-printed in black w/"The Gauntlet Clipper Ship" center, pink splash lustre borders, ca. 1820, 8¾ × 7¾" 160.00

Plaque, pierced to hang, "God is Love" center, pink splash lustre borders, Staffordshire, 9" l. 148.00

Plate, 6¾" d., scalloped rim, Pratt-type w/polychrome bas relief border & pink splash lustre center, Staffordshire 50.00

Punch bowl, pink lustre hunting scenes (4) decor, 1800-10, 12" d., 5" h. (small chip on base) 660.00

Salt dip, footed, pink splash lustre, 3" d., 2" h. 65.00

Tea bowl & handleless cup, pink lustre florals, leaves & trim on white, 2 pcs. 65.00

Tea set: eight 7" d. plates & 8 c/s; pink lustre floral decor, ca. 1840, 24 pcs. 175.00

MAASTRICHT

Maastricht Sauce Dish

This ware was made in Holland during the 19th century and much of it was exported to this country. The pottery, named De Sphinx, produced ironstone services with transfer prints.

Bowl, 10" d., Blue Willow
  patt. $25.00
Bowl, fruit, Timor patt. 50.00
Charger, scene of Dutch windmills,
  men in boat fishing, farm buildings & cattle, blue transfer,
  pierced to hang, 15¾" d. 75.00
Compote, 8½" d., 4½" h., wide
  gold lustre border, Pa Jong patt.,
  Oriental scene 55.00
Game plate, decal bird center on
  white ground, shaded rust border,
  9½" d. 28.00
Hot plate, Ionian patt., blue
  transfer 45.00
Plaque, pierced to hang, decal clus-
  ter of realistic pears, shaded rust
  border 30.00
Sauce dish, Chinoiserie decor, blue
  transfer, 4" d. (ILLUS.) 10.00
Vegetable tureen, cov., Pink Willow
  patt. 70.00

MAJOLICA

*Majolica, a tin-enameled-glazed pottery, has
been produced for centuries. It originally took
its name from the island of Majorca, a source
of figuline (potter's clay). Subsequently it was
widely produced in England, Europe and the
United States. Etruscan majolica, now avidly sought, was made by Griffen, Smith & Hill,
Phoenixville, Pa., in the last quarter of the
19th century. Most majolica advertised today
is 19th or 20th century. Once scorned by most
collectors, interest in this colorful ware so
popular during the Victorian era has now revived and prices have risen dramatically in
the past two years. Also see MINTON, MUS-
TACHE CUPS & SAUCERS, OYSTER
PLATES and WEDGWOOD.*

ETRUSCAN

Etruscan Bamboo Pattern Creamer

Bowl, master berry, Shell & Sea-
  weed patt. $120.00

Butter pat, Begonia Leaf patt. 25.00
Butter pat, Geranium patt. 25.00
Cake stand, pedestal base, Maple
  Leaf patt. . . . . .125.00 to 145.00
Cake tray, 2-handled, pink gerani-
  ums & green leaves on yellow
  ground, 12" across handles 90.00
Cake tray, Shell & Seaweed patt. . . . 715.00
Cigar humidor & cover w/two ap-
  plied shells, Albino Shell & Sea-
  weed patt. 2,310.00
Compote, 9" d., 5" h., Daisy
  patt. . . . . .140.00 to 200.00
Compote, 9¼" d., Grape Leaf
  patt. 150.00
Compote, Maple Leaves patt. 145.00
Creamer, Bamboo patt., lavender
  lining, 4½" h. (ILLUS.) 100.00
Creamer, Coral patt. 275.00
Creamer, Shell & Seaweed patt. 125.00
Creamer & open sugar bowl, Water
  Lily patt., pr. 125.00
Creamer & open sugar bowl, Wild
  Rose patt., pr. 110.00
Cup & saucer, Bamboo patt. 100.00

Shell & Seaweed Cup & Saucer

Cup & saucer, Shell & Seaweed patt.
  (ILLUS.) . . . . .175.00 to 195.00
Mug, Pineapple patt.,
  3½" h. . . . . .55.00 to 100.00
Pitcher, 4½" h., Butterfly patt. 70.00
Pitcher, 5¼" h., Hawthorne patt.,
  cobalt blue 75.00
Pitcher w/pewter lid, 6" h., Corn (or
  Maize) patt. 150.00
Pitcher, milk, 6" h., Shell & Sea-
  weed patt. 245.00
Pitcher, 8¼" h., Fern patt. 150.00
Pitcher, cider, Shell & Seaweed
  patt. 375.00
Plate, 8" d., Bamboo patt. 65.00
Plate, 8" d., Classical Series patt.,
  low relief mythological figures in
  green center, yellow border 45.00
Plate, 8½" d., Albino Shell & Sea-
  weed patt. 80.00
Plate, 8¾" d., Leaf on Plate patt.,
  green leaf on closely woven yel-
  low basketweave ground 70.00
Plate, 9" d., Grape Leaf patt., pink
  edge 55.00
Plate, 9" d., Maple Leaves patt., 3
  small green & brown maple leaf

branches on white ground, yellow
edge........................... 95.00
Plate, 9" d., Strawberry (or blackberry) & Basketweave patt., berries & leaves on blue
ground..................70.00 to 110.00
Spooner, Shell & Seaweed patt. 418.00
Syrup pitcher w/pewter lid, Bamboo
patt.......................... 375.00
Syrup pitcher w/pewter lid, Sun-
lower patt., realistic sunflower
on cobalt blue pebbled
ground..................220.00 to 275.00
Teacup & saucer, Shell & Seaweed
patt........................... 195.00
Teapot, cov., Albino Shell & Seaweed patt. 250.00
Teapot, cov., Shell & Seaweed
patt.......................... 385.00
Tea set: cov. teapot, creamer &
cov. sugar bowl; Bamboo patt.,
3 pcs......................... 360.00

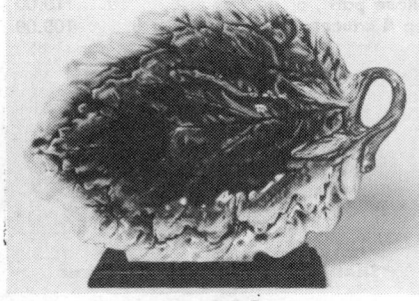

Etruscan Leaf Tray

Tray, Leaf patt., 12" l. (ILLUS.)...... 90.00
Tray, Oak Leaf patt., 12" l. 100.00

GENERAL
Ash tray, full figure Dutch boy seated on green leaf tray,
5 x 4 x 3"..................... 48.00
Asparagus serving set, footed
cradle-type pierced bowl molded
as realistic bunch of asparagus,
on underplate, 2 pcs. 295.00
Bowl, 9½" d., 4¾" h., twig handles,
flared foot, incised squares overlaid in center w/pink flowers &
green leaves, brown trim 115.00

Majolica Bowl

Bowl, 10" d., 4" h., footed, sunflower & leaves on white basketweave
ground, pink band at foot, lavender lining (ILLUS.) 115.00
Bread tray, Pineapple patt.,
11" oval 65.00
Bread tray, Bamboo & Fern patt.,
cobalt blue oval center, green
fern leaves on brown bamboo
border, Wardle & Co., Hanley,
England, 14 x 10½" 195.00
Butter dish, cov., Shell, Seaweed &
Waves patt. 175.00

Majolica Butter Dish

Butter dish, cov., yellow basketweave w/pink floral finial, lavender lining, 7" d. (ILLUS.) 150.00
Butter pat, Begonia Leaf on Basketweave patt. 20.00
Cake set: 11¼" d. master cake
plate & six 7¼" d. serving plates;
branch w/green leaves outlined in
pink on cream ground, Germany,
7 pcs......................... 95.00
Compote, 12½" d., 12¼" h., scalloped pedestal foot, intricate
openwork handles & rim, pale
blue interior, red cherry clusters
on green & brown shading to
cream exterior, numbered on
base 130.00
Creamer, pink florals on yellow &
blue ground, English Registry
mark, 4" h..................... 28.00
Creamer, Pineapple patt. ....65.00 to 80.00
Creamer & sugar bowl, stylized yellow water lily blossoms on turquoise shaded to green pads,
numbered on base, pr. 130.00
Cup & saucer, Bird & Fan patt.,
Wardle & Co., England.......... 65.00
Cup & saucer, Open Rose patt. 125.00
Cup & saucer, Shell & Seaweed
patt., England................. 125.00
Cuspidor, cobalt blue rim, green lily
pads on brown bamboo ground... 100.00
Ewer, swan spout & handle, sides &
base applied w/realistically
colored reeds & cattails, early
20th c., 17½" h. 410.00

Minton Majolica Garden Seat Base

Garden seat base, figural young
  blackamoor sitting on tasseled
  cushion & supporting a seat on his
  shoulders w/one arm, Minton,
  1871, 18" h. (ILLUS.) 1,320.00
Match holder, figural elf-like character holding apple & seated between 2 containers, striker at
  side, 5½ x 4½" 85.00
Mug, Bamboo & Floral patt., English
  registry mark 95.00
Mustache cup & saucer, Bird & Fan
  patt. 250.00

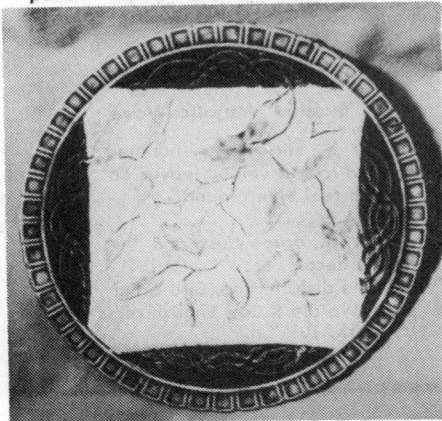

Napkin Plate

"Napkin" plate, napkin on cobalt
  blue ground, 9" d. (ILLUS.) 80.00
Pitcher, 5¼" h., Bent Tree Trunk
  patt., caramel ground, pink lining,
  Wardle & Co., Hanley, England ... 40.00
Pitcher, 5½" h., Fan & Scroll with
  Insect patt., cream ground 135.00
Pitcher, 6" h., Begonia Leaf patt.,
  dark brown 65.00

Pitcher, 6" h., figural dragon han-
  dle, floral decor on cobalt blue
  ground 85.00
Pitcher, 7" h., Fan, Pond Lily &
  Dragonfly patt.................. 110.00
Pitcher, 7" h., twig handle, Robin on
  Branch patt., pink lining 70.00
Pitcher, 7¼" h., Blackberry & Picket
  Fence patt. 75.00

Majolica Corn Pattern Pitcher

Pitcher, 7½" h., Corn (or Maize)
  patt., English registry mark
  (ILLUS.)...................... 110.00
Pitcher, tankard, 7½" h., hex-
  agonal, mustard yellow handle,
  roses decor on olive ground, pink
  lining, marked "776 Frie Onnang,
  Made in France" 125.00
Pitcher, 8" h., Bamboo patt., yellow,
  Wardle & Co., Hanley, England ... 135.00
Pitcher, 8" h., figural tan pig
  w/laurel wreath & red sash, car-
  rying a ham, marked "755 Frie
  Onnang, Made in France"........ 125.00
Pitcher, 8" h., Little Girl & Dog
  patt., kneeling child looking up at
  seated large dog 125.00
Pitcher, 8½" h., Basketweave &
  Bamboo patt., Banks & Thorley ... 100.00
Pitcher, 8½" h., figural owl, marked
  "Morley & Co., Majollica, Wells-
  ville, O." 183.00
Pitcher, 10½" h., figural Pug dog
  w/open mouth, seated & wearing
  collar 250.00
Pitcher, 11" h., figural rooster,
  marked "St. Clements, France" ... 95.00
Pitcher, 16" h., figural fish forms
  top, white stork w/green rushes &
  yellow flowers on cobalt blue
  ground at base 260.00
Plaque, pierced to hang, green &
  red pears w/green leaves &
  brown branch on blended brown
  & cream ground, 10 1/8" d. 105.00
Plate, 6¾" d., Pineapple patt....... 55.00

Plate, 7¾" d., Fern & Bamboo patt.,
English registry mark 75.00
Plate, 8" d., Bird & Fan patt.,
English registry mark 55.00
Plate, 8" d., Fern & Bow patt.,
Banks & Thorley, English registry
mark 65.00
Plate, 8" d., Napkin patt., marked
"Morley & Co., Majollica, Wells-
ville, O." 80.00
Plate, 8" d., Pond Lily patt. by J.
Holdcroft, white lilies & buds on
deep green pads 45.00
Plate, 8½" d., New England Astor
patt., attributed to James Taft,
Hampshire Pottery, Keene, New
Hampshire 55.00
Plate, 8¾" d., Overlapping Begonia
Leaves patt. 45.00
Platter, 10½ x 6¾", 2 brown
baskets w/yellow florals & leaves
on pale green ground, lavender
border 60.00
Platter, 11" l., cherries & butterflies
on turquoise ground, Germany . . . 65.00
Platter, 11" l., twig handles, rustic
fence decor w/pink blossoms on
blended green & turquoise
ground 85.00
Teapot, cov., Bamboo patt., James
Taft, Hampshire Pottery, Keene,
New Hampshire 145.00
Teapot, cov., Butterfly & Bird patt.,
blue, yellow & tan, England 135.00

Bird & Fan Tea Set

Tea set: cov. teapot, cov. sugar
bowl & creamer; Bird & Fan patt.
on stippled white ground, 3 pcs.
(ILLUS.) 175.00
Toothpick holder, Pineapple patt. 65.00
Toothpick holder, florals & leaves in
relief on shaded deep to light
green at scalloped rim 58.00
Toothpick holder, pink & green
starflowers & green leaves
decor 65.00
Tray, Maple Leaf patt., green
w/browns, 7½" l. 15.00
Tray, Begonia Leaf patt.,
12" l. . . . . 95.00 to 145.00

Tray, 2-handled, Fan & Scroll patt.,
blue bow-form handles, colorful
fan & scroll on white stippled
ground, brown double gadroon
edge, Fielding & English registry
marks, 14" l. 95.00
Umbrella stand, blue, yellow, pink,
red & green florals in high relief
decor, late 19th-early 20th c.,
19" h. 175.00
Umbrella stand, scalloped base &
rim, swirls of amethyst & light &
dark green, 11" d., 22" h. 385.00
Vase, 6½" h., 8½" d., yellow
daisies w/green & brown leaves
on sanded ground, red lining &
handles 95.00
Vase, 7" h., magenta leaves on
cream ground, Avalon Pottery 65.00
Vase, 7" h., green leaves on cream
ground, marked "Avalon
Faience," Chesapeake Pottery,
Baltimore 65.00

"Sanded" Majolica Vase

Vase, 10" h., stick-type, 2-handled,
applied rose & veined leaves on
sanded teal blue ground
(ILLUS.) 90.00
Vase, 12" h., grape clusters &
leaves decor 85.00
Vegetable dish, footed, Bird & Fan
patt., Wardle & Co., English regis-
try mark, 10¾" d. 135.00

MARBLEHEAD POTTERY

*This pottery was organized in 1904 by Dr.
Herbert J. Hall as a therapeutic aid to pa-
tients in a sanitarium he ran in Marblehead,
Massachusetts. It was later separated from
the sanitarium and directed by Arthur E.
Baggs, a fine artist and designer, who bought
out the factory in 1916 and operated it until
its closing in 1936. Most wares were hand-*

thrown and decorated and carry the company mark of a stylized sailing vessel flanked by the letters "M" and "P." Also see TILES.

Marblehead Pottery Mark

Bookends, model of owl, tobacco
   brown, pr. (small chip) $135.00
Bowl, squat bulbous shape, matte
   grey glaze. 65.00
Candlestick, blue-grey glaze, 3" h.
   (single). 40.00
Vase, 2¾" h., greenish blue glaze. . 25.00
Vase, 3½" h., mottled red & brown
   glaze 100.00
Vase, 3½" h., blended wisteria
   (lavender) & powder blue glaze . . 115.00
Vases, 3½" & 7" h.: one w/sloping
   sides & green, ochre & yellow
   leafage on pale grey matte
   ground; second of bulging cylindrical form w/stylized charcoal
   grey leafy trees on matte grey-
   blue ground, ca. 1910, pr. 1,320.00
Vase, 5" h., mottled plum & medium
   blue glaze 145.00

Marblehead Vases

Vase, 5¼" h., cobalt blue matte
   glaze (ILLUS. right) 70.00
Vase, 5½" h., funnel-shaped, blue
   glaze 90.00
Vase, 6" h., expanding cylinder,
   blue glaze 110.00
Vase, 6" h., cylindrical, pink glaze. . 65.00
Vase, 6¾" h., blue glaze 85.00
Vase, 9½" h., blue matte glaze
   (ILLUS. left) 180.00
Wall pocket, fine-ribbed horizontal
   lines, blue glaze, 5" h. 88.00

Wall pocket, blue glaze, 6" h. 55.00
Wall pocket, cobalt blue matte
   glaze 80.00

MARTIN BROTHERS POTTERY

Martin Brothers Bird Jar

Martinware, the term used for this pottery, dates from 1873 and is the product of the Martin brothers—Robert, Wallace, Edwin, Walter and Charles Martin, often considered the first British studio potters. From first to final stages, their hand-thrown pottery was completely the work of the team. The early wares may be simple and conventional, but the Martin brothers built up their reputation by producing ornately engraved, incised or carved designs on their wares. The amusing face-jugs are considered some of their finest work. After 1910, the work of the pottery declined and can be considered finished by 1915, though some attempts were made to fire pottery as late as the 1920's.

Character jug, double-faced, 5" h. . .$450.00
Humidor, cov., incised birds decor,
   1880 . . . . 215.00
Inkwell, birds decor 225.00
Model of a grotesque bird w/remov-
   able head, supporting himself on
   webbed feet, mottled pale blue,
   inky blue, beige & ochre glaze, on
   wooden base, overall 13" h.
   (ILLUS.) 3,300.00
Pitcher, 5" h., snake handle,
   ca. 1910 . . . . 100.00
Pitcher, 11" h., incised peacock
   decor 350.00
Vase, 6" h., gourd-shaped, streaked
   red & brown "flambe" glaze 150.00
Vase, 10" h., incised palmettes
   decor 175.00

Vase, 11" h., incised cranes decor .. 200.00
Vase, 13" h., 4-necked grotesque
   form, claw feet 550.00
Vase, incised ivy leaves decor,
   miniature size 40.00

MASSIER (Clement) POTTERY

Clement Massier was a French artist potter who worked in the late 19th and early 20th centuries creating exquisite earthenware items with lustre decoration.

Chamberstick, saucer base, ring
   handle, brown drip on iridescent
   turquoise glaze $135.00
Ewer, iridescent lavender, pink &
   green swirled glaze, miniature ... 110.00
Ewer, iridescent pink, copper &
   green swirled glaze, miniature ... 190.00
Plaque, sculpted w/large standing
   woman wearing a sinuously flowing gown, iridescent scarlet, gold,
   green & violet glaze, 1900,
   19¼" d. 3,080.00
Toothpick holder, iridescent glaze,
   signed 125.00
Vase, 2¾" h., bees (4) decor on
   iridescent ground 135.00

MAYER (T.J. & J.)

Thomas, John & Joseph Mayer, operated the Furlong Works and Dale Hall pottery in Burslem, England, from 1843 to 1855, making various types of ceramics. Also see FLOW BLUE and PARIAN.

Bowl, 10" d., Canova patt., flowing
   blue transfer................... $32.00
Pitcher, 9½" h., 6-sided, Florentine
   patt., brown transfer 165.00
Plate, 8" d., Canova patt. 45.00
Plate, 9½" d., Garden Scenery
   patt., light blue transfer 55.00
Soup plate w/flange rim, Canova
   patt., blue transfer, 10" d. 25.00

MC COY

Collectors are now beginning to seek the art wares of two McCoy potteries. One was founded in Roseville, O., in the late 19th century as the J.W. McCoy Pottery, subsequently becoming Brush-McCoy Pottery Co., later Brush Pottery. The other was founded also

in Roseville in 1910 as Nelson McCoy Sanitary Stoneware Co., later becoming Nelson McCoy Pottery. In 1967 the pottery was sold to D.T. Chase of the Mount Clemens Pottery Co., who sold his interest to the Lancaster Colony Corp. in 1974. Productions of this company are still marked McCoy and Nelson McCoy, Jr. is President of the company known yet as the Nelson McCoy Pottery Co.

Basket, Pinecone patt., small $20.00
Bookends, model of a lily, white
   blossoms edged in deep pink
   w/green foliage, 1948, pr. 18.00
Bowl, 6" d., Zuniart, Brush-McCoy .. 45.00
Coffee set: cov. coffee pot & 4
   mugs; El Rancho Bar-B-Que,
   5 pcs. 70.00
Cookie jar, Antique Touring Car,
   1962-64 .... 32.00
Cookie jar, Barnum's Animals,
   1972-74 .... 42.50
Cookie jar, Bear, toes inward,
   1943-45 .... 57.50
Cookie jar, Chef's Head w/"Cook-
   ies" on hat band, 1962-64 .... 37.00
Cookie jar, Chipmunk, 1959-62 ..... 40.00
Cookie jar, Circus Horse with
   Monkey, 1962 .... 65.00
Cookie jar, Dog on Basketweave,
   1956-57 .... 30.00
Cookie jar, Early American Chest or
   Chiffonier, 1967 .... 34.00
Cookie jar, Hen on Nest, 1959 ...... 50.00
Cookie jar, Little Clown, 1945 ...... 30.00
Cookie jar, Mother Goose,
   1947-51 .... 58.00
Cookie jar, Pelican, yellow,
   1940-43 .... 50.00
Cookie jar, Puppy, 1961-62 .... 33.00
Cookie jar, Rocking Chair, w/dal-
   mations, 1972 .... 85.00
Cookie jar, Rooster, 1955-57 ...... 35.00
Cookie jar, Snoopy, 1970.......... 50.00
Cookie jar, Spaceship, Friendship,
   1962-63 .... 40.00
Cookie jar, W.C. Fields, 1972-74 .... 57.00
Cookie jar, Wedding Jar, 1961 ...... 30.00
Cookie jar, Windmill, 1961 .... 28.00
Cookie jar, Yosemite Sam, 1971-72.. 30.00

McCoy Dog Feeding Dish

Dog dish, embossed "To Man's Best
Friend - His Dog," green glaze,
7½" d., 2¼" h. (ILLUS.) . . . .　15.00

Jardiniere, Springwood patt., pink,
1961, 8" d. . . . .　25.00

Jardiniere, underglaze slip-painted
chrysanthemums, brown glaze,
marked Loy-Nel-Art, 13" h. . . . . . .　90.00

Juice reamer, figural clown, orange,
small . . . .　40.00

Mixing bowls, Nurock line, mottled
yellow & brown Rockingham-type
glaze, 4" to 8" d., 1916, set of 5 . .　150.00

Mugs, El Rancho Bar-B-Que line,
1960, pr. . . . .　20.00

Pitcher, 6½" h., duck's neck handle,
relief-molded florals & foliage,
brown, 1935 . . . .　50.00

Pitcher, blue iris decor on yellow
ground . . . .　95.00

Fawn Planter

Planter, fawns (3) before a forest
scene, 1954, 11½ x 8" (ILLUS.) . . .　45.00

Pretzel jar, cov., dark green, 1926 . .　150.00

Tea set: cov. teapot, creamer &
sugar bowl; Ivy patt., 1950,
3 pcs. . . . . .30.00 to 40.00

Tea set, Pinecone patt., 1946,
3 pcs. . . . .　35.00

Vase, 4" h, 5" d., globular, underglaze slip-painted florals, brown
glaze, marked Loy-Nel-Art . . . .　65.00

Vase, 6" h., Zuniart line, Brush-
McCoy, 1923 . . . .　80.00

Vase, 13" h., underglaze slip-
painted florals, brown glaze,
marked Loy-Nel-Art . . . .　225.00

Vase, hand holding cornucopia,
white, 1942 . . . .　28.00

Wall pocket, model of a lily, 1940 . .　65.00

Wall pocket, conical, embossed figure of a Mexican man w/serape,
blue-green, 1941 . . . .　15.00

Wall pocket, Sunburst Gold patt.,
1957 . . . .　15.00

Wall pocket, blue bird atop pink &
blue flower, 1948, 2½ x 5¼ x
6½" . . . .　11.00

Water sprinkler, model of a turtle,
green, 1950 . . . .　15.00

MEISSEN

Meissen Coffee Pot

*The secret of true hard-paste porcelain,
known long before to the Chinese, was "discovered" accidentally in Meissen, Germany,
by J.F. Bottger, an alchemist, working with
E.W. Tschirnhausen, and the first European
true porcelain was made in the Meissen Porcelain Works organized about 1709. Meissen
marks have been widely copied by other factories. Some pieces listed here are recent. Also
see INVALID FEEDERS.*

Bowl, 10" l., leaf-molded, pink
w/gold highlighting, ca. 1920 . . . . .$160.00

Candelabra, 4-light, modeled w/put-
ti emblematic of the "Four Seasons," the first w/"Autumn"
offering "Winter" a cup of wine;
the second w/"Summer" admiring
"Spring" & her flowers, below a
central socket fitted w/three
scrolling branch arms applied
w/floral & fruiting vines, heightened w/pale green enamel & gild-
ing, 19¼" h., pr. 1,320.00

Chocolate pot & cover w/rose finial,
dark pink, orange, yellow & blue
floral bouquets & green foliage
each side, ca. 1923, 12" h. . . . .　215.00

Coffee pot, cov., pear-shaped, each
side w/nude children in landscape
vignettes below a foliate border,
cover painted w/landscapes, blue
& white, ca. 1765, 9½" h.
(ILLUS.) . . . .　462.00

Compote, 7¾" d., 8¼" h., molded
as a pineapple w/foliage rising
from base & details outlined in
gold w/floral & butterfly
interior . . . .　325.00

Cup & saucer, demitasse, Blue
Onion patt. . . . .　35.00

Cup & saucer, demitasse, portrait
decor on cobalt blue ground . . . . .　100.00

Meissen Cup & Saucer

Cup & saucer, quatrefoil, painted in
a Kakiemon palette w/flowering
plants enriched in gilding alternating w/iron-red panels enclosing
scrolls, minor foot rim chip to cup,
ca. 1730 (ILLUS.) 660.00
Cutting board, Blue Onion patt.,
10 x 6" 135.00
Dish, leaf-shaped, Blue Onion
patt. 75.00

Meissen Peony Dish

Dishes, modeled as an open peony
blossom w/yellow center, shaded
rose petals & green leaves w/stem
& bud handle (one repaired), Dot
period, ca. 1765, pr. in fitted box
(ILLUS. of one) 2,640.00
Figure of the frightened Harlequin,
wearing an iron-red, turquoise,
yellow, blue, puce & black
diamond-checkered jacket & blue
& white breeches, cowering
w/one hand raised to protect his
face, 6½" h................... 385.00
Figure of a maiden asleep in a chair
w/a love note tucked in her
"lace" bodice, pale blue slippers
cast aside, 7 3/8" h............. 412.00
Figure of a lady of "The Order of
Pug Dogs" (representing a member of this society---a disguised
form of the Freemason movement
in 18th century Germany prohibit-
ed in the Catholic regions), holding a pug dog under one arm

while another peeps out from her
flower-sprigged white skirt, waisted oblong base w/h.p. scenes &
details picked out in gold, late
19th c., 11¼" h................1,430.00
Figure group, 4 putti emblematic of
"Summer," 1 holding a scythe,
another w/sheaf of wheat over
his shoulder, scroll-molded base
w/details picked out in gilding,
6" h............................ 770.00
Figure group, Juno & 3 cupids, the
goddess wearing a pale pink
drapery falling about her knees, 2
gold arm bands, a string of pearls
& a tiara, seated on a cloudy
perch w/her peacock at her side
& attended by 3 cupids, 1 holding
a mirror for her, another offering
an additional pearl necklace & the
last w/large flower-filled cornucopia, scroll-molded base w/floral
sprays, late 19th c., 8¾" h.
(miniscule chips) 935.00
Figure group, the goddess Venus in
diaphanous drapery holding a
bow & arrow on her lap & riding
in a chariot drawn by a team of
swans driven by cupid, on a
cloud-molded base, late 19th c.,
15 3/8" l. 1,870.00
Fruit coolers, covers & liners,
enameled each side w/colorful
birds perched in tree, cover
w/pierced gallery reserving 2
small panels painted w/bird on
leafy branch, purple fruit knop
w/three green leaves, supported
on 3 bun feet, whole w/gilt details, 7¾ & 7 7/8" h., pr. 825.00
Gravy boat w/underplate, floral
decor, 19th c................... 125.00
Model of a frog, enriched in green,
black, yellow & flesh tones,
3" l. 605.00
Model of a Husky dog, brown &
black eyes, black nose &
whiskers, muzzle & ears heightened in pale iron-red enamel,
standing on an oval cobblestone
base, late 19th c., 9 1/8" h.
(minor chips) 550.00

Meissen Leopards

Models of leopards in recumbent
position, white coats spotted in

black & lightly shaded in salmon, grey muzzles & paws, russet-edged green & black eyes, repairs to some limbs & tail tips, ca. 1745, 5 7/8" & 6 7/8" l., pr. (ILLUS.)....................22,000.00

Models of swans, incised plumage, looking to the left & right respectively w/black faces & feet & iron-red beaks, circular grass mound bases applied w/reeds enriched in turquoise, 8¾" h., pr. 880.00

Napkin ring, Blue Onion patt. 48.00

Nodding figure, jolly, rotund Chinese woman seated in a cross-legged position wearing a colorful flowered kimono, head, tongue & hands weighted for movement, late 19th c., 7" h.................1,650.00

Plates, 9"d., Capo-di-Monte style, center w/two cupids floating on billowy clouds, each within a lightly molded border of classical figures between urns or trees, rim edged w/band of stiff leaves w/gilt details, late 19th c., set of 6............................ 715.00

Plates, dinner, 9¾" d., bouquets of "deutsche Blumen," Dulong patt. border painted in colors w/cartouches enclosing birds on branches, within gilt scrolls, ca. 1750, set of 12 ....2,860.00

Plate, 10" d., Blue Onion patt. 75.00

Platter, 15 3/8" oval, insects surrounding a large yellow bird & 3 smaller birds perched in a tree above a flowering purple thistle & an iron-red chrysanthemum, gilt rim, 1760-70 .... 880.00

Rolling pin, Blue Onion patt. 150.00

Salt box, Blue Onion patt. 135.00

Salt dips, oval, h.p. bouquets of "deutsche Blumen" & scattered flower sprays, ca. 1750, 3½" l., set of 4 .... 385.00

Scent bottle w/gold stopper, rococo cartouche-shaped body painted front w/fashionable lady standing in a garden scene, reverse w/seated youth playing a guitar, each within a conforming panel surrounded by brown- & gilt-edged molded S-scrolls & separated at sides by narrow panels of gold foliate scrollwork repeated around oval foot, neck & footrim mounted in gold, ca. 1745, 5 1/8" h........................2,860.00

Soup plate w/flange rim, Blue Onion patt., 9¼" d................ 35.00

Soup tureen, cov., bombe body & cover colorfully painted w/sprays & sprigs of "deutsche Blumen" &

molded on an Alt-ozier border, green twig handles w/colorful floral terminals, brown-edged cover w/pale puce rose sprig knop, 1755-65, 14 5/8" oval (flowers w/small chips) 2,310.00

Spooner, Blue Onion patt. 65.00

Teacup & saucer, Blue Onion patt. ... 65.00

patt. 65.00

Teapot, cov., bullet-shaped, flat cover reserved either side w/brown-edged cartouche painted w/"Holzschnittblumen," one side w/brown-spotted iron-red tulips & green leaves, other w/purple-centered white ranunculus & green leaves, cover w/yellow marigold & blue forget-me-nots, brown-edged faceted spout, wishbone handle & knop w/gilt scrollwork or dots, yellow ground, ca. 1740, 2 7/8" h. 1,120.00

Tureen, naturalistically modeled as a partridge, w/plumage delineated in tones of grey, brown & iron-red, on a basket-molded nest, ca. 1745, 6½" l..........1,540.00 to 1,760.00

Meissen Covered Tureen

Tureen, naturalistically modeled as a swan w/plumage delineated in touches of grey, brown & black eyes, salmon & black beak & black feet, after J. J. Kaendler, late 19th c., 14½" h. (ILLUS.) 1,760.00

Vase, cov., 53" h., ovoid, each side w/shaped panel of courting couples playing musical instruments or relaxing at a garden party beneath a sculpture, within elaborate floral encrusted borders & applied w/birds, cover surmounted by figure of Ceres holding a cornucopia & wearing a flowing purple garment, whole heightened by pastel enamels & gilt details, late 19th c. 5,500.00

METTLACH

Winter Scene Mettlach Plaque

Ceramics with the name Mettlach were produced by Villeroy & Boch and other potteries in the Mettlach area of Germany. Villeroy and Boch's finest years of production are thought to be from about 1890 to 1910. Also see STEINS.

Beaker, printed under glaze boy
  playing flute, No. 1024 .... $65.00
Beaker, printed under glaze cavalier
  pouring wine, No. 1096, ¼ liter .. 95.00
Creamer & cov. sugar bowl, etched
  Art Nouveau decor, blue & tan,
  No. 2947 & No. 2948, pr......... 175.00
Loving cup, 3-handled, printed under
  glaze scenes of musicians,
  No. 993, 7" h. 310.00
Mug, advertising "Minneapolis
  Brewing 1897," printed under
  glaze 85.00
Pitcher, 7" h., etched florals,
  No. 2947 .... 195.00
Pitcher, 9" h., deep blue & gold Art
  Nouveau trees on ivory ground,
  No. 2947 .... 175.00
Pitcher, 16" h., "phanolith" etched
  cameo relief scene of musicians &
  dancers, No. 7022 .... 900.00
Plaques, pierced to hang, etched
  barefoot girl carrying basket,
  No. 1607 & No. 1652, 11" d., pr. ... 895.00
Plaque, pierced to hang, cameo
  relief birds by water, No. 1677,
  14¾" d. 900.00
Plaque, pierced to hang, etched
  Dragoons (4) on horseback,
  No. 2079, 15" d. 1,175.00
Plaques, pierced to hang, etched
  knight trying to kiss maiden on
  one & knight being kissed by
  maiden after returning from battle
  on other, No. 2322 & No. 2323,
  15" d., pr. 1,400.00

Plaques, pierced to hang, etched
  gnome in tree w/two bottles on
  one & gnome in tree drinking
  from mug on other, No. 2112 &
  No. 2113, 16" d., pr. 3,000.00
Plaque, pierced to hang, etched
  young girl in snow-covered field,
  Winter, No. 2998, 18" d.
  (ILLUS.) 2,550.00
Plaques, pierced to hang, etched
  night scene w/angel on one &
  day scene w/angel on other,
  No. 2769 & No. 2770, 18½" d.,
  pr. 7,000.00
Plaque, pierced to hang, cameo relief Trojan lady & her servants on
  blue-grey ground, No. 2443,
  19" d. 935.00
Vase, 9" h., cameo relief multicolored geometric design,
  No. 1829 .... 195.00
Vase, 9½" h., 6" d., etched orange
  & blue florals w/green & gold
  foliage on grey ground, shell
  pink interior, No. 1844 .... 375.00
Vase, 11½" h., dragon handles,
  mosaic geometric design,
  No. 1409 .... 295.00

Mettlach Art Nouveau Vase

Vase, 13" h., etched Art Nouveau
  florals, No. 2422 (ILLUS.) 625.00
Vases, 13¾" h., 6" d., 4 panels
  etched w/children at various
  pursuits depicting the Four
  Seasons, No. 1591, pr............ 785.00
Vase, 15¾" h., etched w/two
  scenes of lovers, No. 2207 .... 700.00
Vase, 14" h., pedestal base, ovoid
  body, collared throat & flaring
  rim, etched w/four panels of
  cherubs representing the Four
  Seasons, pink lining, No. 1537 .... 350.00

MINTON

Minton Majolica Jardiniere

The Minton factory in England was established by Thomas Minton in 1793. The factory made earthenware, especially the blue-printed variety and Thomas Minon is sometimes credited with invention of the blue "Willow" pattern. For a time majolica and tiles were also an important part of production, but bone china soon became the principal ware. Mintons, Ltd., continues in operation today. Also see MAJOLICA, OYSTER PLATES and TILES.

Barber's bowl, blue transfer decor, 1878 . . . . $125.00

Bust of Evangeline, majolica, 16" h. 600.00

Candlestick, majolica, group of 3 monkeys, mustard yellow & green glaze, 9" h. (single) 225.00

Dresser tray, h.p. large red roses decor, 12 x 9" 95.00

Figure of Ariadne on panther, parian, 1864, 16" l. 300.00

Fish plates, each w/different fish amidst aquatic background, gilt scrolled borders, ca. 1890, set of 8 . . . . 605.00

Game pie dish & cover, majolica, modeled as a brown straw basket, sides w/green oak leaves, cover colorfully glazed & molded w/dead game including a hare, mallard & bird, all resting on a bed of ferns & oak leaves, bright blue interior glaze, 1868-88, 12 1/8" l. . . . . 1,760.00 to 2,310.00

Garden seat, majolica, hexagonal baluster form, scalloped circular top w/central pierced flowerhead within a border of rosettes alternating w/panels of scrolling foliage, sides molded in low

relief w/panels of foliate scrolls centering a floral patera, streaky turquoise glaze, dated 1896, 20¾" h. 550.00

Jardiniere, majolica, modeled as a large white conch shell w/details picked out in brown & ochre w/turquoise interior, atop a cluster of deep red coral on a rockwork base w/seaweed, the whole above a streaky brown & green base, dated 1876, 26" h. (ILLUS.) 1,100.00

Jardinieres & stands, majolica, quatrefoil shape, modeled w/two Triton figure handles, rim w/egg & dart motif incorporating fruiting vines, base molded w/four faun masks w/band of egg & dart on acanthus-capped scroll feet, naturalistic polychrome glaze, 1856, 23" h., pr. . . 5,827.00

Jug, majolica, cylindrical, molded to simulate stone walls of a medieval castle, decorated in relief w/continuous frieze of dancing figures wearing colorful rustic costumes between molded branch borders entwined by ivy, shell-molded cover w/court jester's head finial, dated 1870, 13" h. (finial repaired) 880.00

Minton Pate-Sur-Pate Plate

Plates, 10¼" d., pate-sur-pate, playful nymphs, cupids & flowering plants on a blue ground divided by flowerheads & foliage within gilt scroll surrounds on an ivory ground, 1913-50, set of 12 (ILLUS. of one) 1,980.00

Plates, luncheon, wide gold border, pink rose buds highlighted w/blue enameling, set of 6 . . . . 210.00

Stilton cheese stand, majolica, buff-colored high dome lid modeled in the form of a beehive decorated

in relief w/climbing purple blackberries amidst green brambles,
handles & plinth formed as brown
branches, interior w/bright blue
glaze, dated 1862, 13¼" h. (base
w/haircracks & restorations to
feet) 2,750.00

Sugar shaker, Art Deco style florals
in shades of yellow, green &
orange, 2½" d., 5" h. 52.00

Tazza, h.p. red rose center surrounded by yellow & white buds
on blue-green ground, 1877,
9½" d., 3" h. 75.00

Tea & coffee set: cov. oblong teapot
& stand, cov. sugar bowl, cream
jug, lemon juice jug, waste bowl,
two 7½" d. plates, two 9" d. cake
plates, 12 coffee cans, 11 teacups
& 24 saucers; h.p. multicolored
garden flowers reserved on gilt
ground, ca. 1820 & later,
56 pcs. 6,600.00

Tea caddy, cov., blue, green, pink &
yellow stylized florals on ivory
ground 75.00

Teapot, cov., flowing pink decor on
white ground w/ornate gold
trim......................... 150.00

Bowl, 4¾ x 2¾", Earthworm patt. in
blue, brown & white on
yellowware 300.00

Chamber pot, exterior w/white slip
band w/blue feathering seaplants
& brown striping on yellowware,
2" h. miniature 60.00

Mug, embossed rim w/green stripe,
brown feathering seaplants &
black striping, 2 5/8" h. (stains &
small base flakes)............... 190.00

Mug, white slip band w/blue
feathering seaplants & brown
striping on yellowware, 2¾" h.... 95.00

Mug, wide mocha band w/dark
brown-black feathering seaplants
& blue striping on yellowware,
4 1/8" d., 6 3/8" h.............. 93.00

Pepper pot, pierced chocolate brown
dome top, pear-shaped body
w/white, brown & yellow-ochre
striping, 4 3/8" h. 135.00

Pepper pot, brown band w/black
twig-like designs & black & green
striping, ca. 1820, 4½" h. 225.00

Pepper pot, Cat's Eye patt., in
white, tan & black w/orange-tan,
white & black striping on blue
band (w/flakes on dome & top
flange), 4½" h. (ILLUS. left) 600.00

Pitcher, 5¾" h., barrel-shaped,
black feathering seaplants on tan
w/blue & embossed green striping, w/flakes on spout & short
hairlines, (ILLUS. right) 450.00

MOCHA

Mocha Pepper Pot and Pitcher

Mocha decoration is found on basically utilitarian creamware or yellowware articles and is achieved by a simple chemical reaction. A color pigment of brown, blue, green or black is given an acid nature by infusion of tobacco or hops. When this acid nature colorant is applied in blobs to an alkaline ground color, it reacts by spreading in feathery seaplant designs. This type of decoration is usually accompanied by horizontal bands of light color slip. Produced in numerous Staffordshire potteries from the late 18th until the late 19th centuries, its name is derived from the similar markings found on mocha quartz.

Bowl, 4½" d., rust-brown band
w/dark brown feathering
seaplants & green striping $345.00

MOORCROFT

Moorcroft-Macintyre Vases

This ware is made in a pottery established at Cobridge, England, in 1913, by William Moorcroft and now headed by his son Walter. Several marks have been used through the years. Earlier pieces bring the higher prices.

Bowl, 4" d., Florian Ware, stylized
blue florals outlined in white slip
on white ground $90.00
Bowl, 9" d., Pomegranate line 90.00
Bowl, 10" d., crimson florals on blue
& green ground, Moorcroft-
Macintyre, ca. 1913 .... 175.00
Butter pat, floral decor 25.00
Cigarette box, cov., floral decor on
pale green ground, 1930-45 mark
& original paper label,
4½ x 3¼" 125.00
Compote, 7½" d., 5½" h., red,
orange & purple cornflowers on
mottled green ground, 1922-28
mark, made for "W.W. Furse,
Fracombe" 495.00
Creamer & sugar bowl, large colorful flowers front & reverse on
cobalt blue shaded to green
ground, 1913-28 mark, pr. 130.00
Goblet, yellow & green lilacs within
blue panels & lilacs w/gold trim
on white ground, painted interior
top band, Moorcroft-Macintyre,
1897-1913, made for "Stonier &
Co., Liverpool," 3¾" w., 5¾" h. ... 525.00
Marmalade jar w/attached undertray & silverplate lid, blue pansies
decor, Moorcroft-Macintyre,
1897-1913 .... 150.00
Paperweight, portrait of gentleman
in khaki & Rudyard Kipling poem,
Moorcroft-Macintyre, dated 1897 .. 125.00
Pitcher, 5" h., squat form, orchids
decor on cobalt blue ground,
1930-45 mark 165.00
Pitcher w/pewter lid, 6" h., blue
floral decor, Moorcroft-Macintyre,
1897-1913 .... 185.00
Pitcher w/pewter lid, 7" h., Gesso
Faience line w/slip-trailed decor,
Moorcroft-Macintyre, 1897-1913 ... 250.00
Plate, Flamminian line, lustre
glaze 70.00
Tea set: cov. teapot, creamer &
sugar bowl; pink floral decor on
cobalt blue ground, 1930-46 mark,
3 pcs. 225.00
Teapot stand, poppies decor,
Moorcroft-Macintyre, 1897-1913 ... 125.00
Vase, 3" h., squat form, Columbine
patt., "flambe" glaze 65.00
Vase, 4" h., wide ruffled neck, Florian ware, green & blue stylized
florals outlined in white slip on
white ground 165.00
Vase, 4 1/8" h., 3 1/8" d., Pomegranate line, rich colors 115.00
Vase, 5½" h., Florian ware, stylized
blue & green florals outlined
w/white slip & gilt trim on white
ground, Moorcroft-Macintyre,
1897-1913 .... 200.00

Vase, 6¼" h., 5¾" d., band of triangular beading bisecting center
on shaded cobalt to light blue &
yellow ground, shaded cobalt blue
interior, 1930-45 mark 275.00
Vase, 6½" h., Hazledene line,
moonlight landscape w/trees,
blue, ca. 1914 .... 375.00
Vases, 9½" h., slender baluster
shape, gilt & blue florals on olive
green ground, Moorcroft-
Macintyre, pr. (ILLUS.) 770.00
Vase, 11" h., Hazledene line, landscape w/trees, blue & olive
green, 1916-21 mark 600.00
Vase, 12" h., bottle-shaped, grapes
& leaves decor, "flambe" glaze ... 175.00

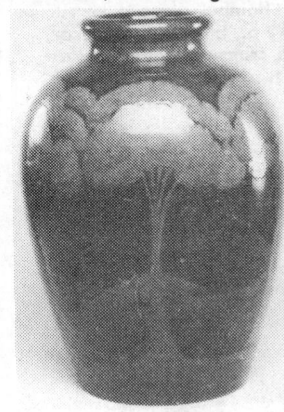

Hazledene Vase

Vase, 16½" h., ovoid w/rolled neck,
Hazledene line, hilly landscape
w/trees in shades of blue-grey,
heather green & midnight blue,
ca. 1920 (ILLUS.) 1,045.00

MOORE (Bernard)

*Bernard Moore, associated with Moore
Bros. St. Mary's Works until this Staffordshire pottery was sold in 1905, established his
own firm at Wolfe St., Stoke-on-Trent the
same year. He specialized in fine glaze-effects
on the wares produced until 1915.*

Bowl, 10¼" d., footed, hemispherical, red & silver lustre stylized
gladioli decor, 1907 .... $242.00
Dish, shell-shaped, "flambe" glaze,
4½" 39.00
Figure of an Oriental man, "flambe"
glaze, 4" h. 200.00
Ginger jar, cov., "flambe" glaze,
7" h. 175.00

Model of an elephant, "flambe"
   glaze, 2" h. 80.00
Model of a monkey, "flambe" glaze,
   2" h. 135.00
Model of a rabbit, "flambe" glaze,
   1½" h. 80.00
Vase, 2¾" h., "sang de boeuf"
   glaze 85.00
Vase, 4" h., red "flambe" glaze 65.00
Vase, 4¼" h., bulbous tapering
   body w/short neck, red, orange &
   pewter grey "flambe" glaze,
   ca. 1915 . . . .   120.00
Vase, 4½" h., dragon decor,
   "flambe" glaze 195.00
Vase, 5½" h., bulbous w/narrow
   neck, red & black exotic fish
   decor, "flambe" glaze 575.00
Vase, 5¾" h., blue dragon decor,
   beige & crimson "flambe" glaze . .   152.00
Vase, 7" h., beige & tan "flambe"
   glaze 180.00

Bernard Moore Vase

Vase, 19½" h., slightly waisted
   w/cylindrical neck, red "flambe"
   winged fire-breathing dragon
   above a flaming sea on muted
   green ground, ca. 1905
   (ILLUS.) 1,100.00

NEWCOMB COLLEGE POTTERY

*This pottery was established in the art
department of Newcomb College, New
Orleans, La., in 1897. Each piece was hand
thrown and bore the pottery's mark and decorator's monogram on the base. It was always
a studio business and never operated as a factory and its pieces are therefore scarce, with
the early wares being eagerly sought. The pottery closed in 1940.*

Newcomb College Scenic Plaque

Bowl, 4½" d., incised florals on
   matte blue ground $500.00
Plaque, pierced to hang, relief-
   molded scene of cottage within
   grove of tall trees, blue, grey-
   green & pink glaze, 9¾ x 5½"
   (ILLUS.) 2,200.00
Vase, 3 5/8" h., pale pink & green
   design at rim, blue ground,
   signed Anna Frances Simpson 345.00
Vase, 4" h., bulbous, floral rim, royal blue matte glaze, signed Sadie
   Irvine 245.00
Vase, 4" h., 5" widest d., moss-
   laden tree scene, shaded blue
   matte glaze, signed Anna Frances
   Simpson 675.00
Vase, 4½" h., stylized tulips on
   blue-green matte glaze ground,
   artist-signed 425.00
Vase, 5" h., floral decor on soft
   blue-grey ground, artist-signed . . .   225.00
Vase, 5" h., moon shining through
   moss-laden trees scene, artist-
   signed 725.00
Vase, 6" h., white floral decor on
   matte blue ground, artist-signed . .   360.00
Vase, 8½" h., iris decor, artist-
   signed 625.00

NEW HALL

*The New Hall porcelain factory, located in
Staffordshire, England, operated from 1781
until 1835. The early production was hard-
paste porcelain in imitation of Chinese export
wares but about 1811 they switched to bone
china production. Tea wares and tea sets
formed the bulk of their production.*

Cup & saucer, grey transfer w/scene
   of soldiers on horses on cup &

country homes on saucer, 1812-35
mark........................... $55.00
Cup & saucer, handleless, purple
lustre, ca. 1810 .... 80.00
Tea & coffee service: cov. teapot,
waste bowl, milk jug, 6 teabowls,
8 coffee cans, 6 saucers & 2
saucer dishes; transfer-printed in
black & painted in iron-red, blue,
green & puce w/three chinoiserie
figures & a butterfly in a garden
setting, 1795-1805, 25 pcs. 400.00

New Hall Tea Service

Tea & coffee service: cov. teapot
w/stand, cream jug, waste bowl,
9 teabowls (1 chipped), 10 coffee
cans (2 cracked) & 7 saucers;
painted iron-red in the Oriental
style w/chinoiserie figures on terraces, ca. 1815, 30 pcs. (ILLUS. of
part)........................... 715.00
Tea set: cov. teapot w/underplate,
sugar bowl, creamer & c/s;
chinoiserie decor, 6 pcs. 1,250.00
Tea set: cov. teaopt, cream jug, 2
plates (1 repaired), waste bowl &
10 c/s; transfer-printed in black
w/portrait of Queen Caroline &
inscribed "Long Live Queen Caroline" below, borders w/pink lustre
bands, formed pieces w/royal
arms to the reverse, ca. 1820,
25 pcs. 1,210.00

NILOAK

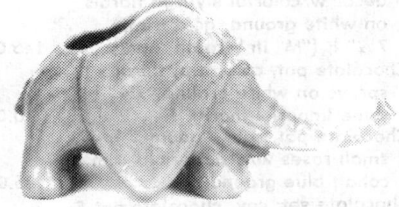

Elephant Planter

*This pottery was made in Benton, Arkan-
sas, and featured hand-thrown vari-colored
swirled clay decoration in objects of classic
forms. Designated Mission Ware, this line is*

*the most desirable of Niloak's production
which was begun early in this century. Less
expensive to produce, the cast Hywood line,
finished with either high gloss or semi-matte
glazes, was introduced during the economic
depression of the 1930's. The pottery ceased
operation about 1946.*

Bowl, 6½" d., Mission Ware, brown
& cream marbleized swirls $55.00
Candle holder, saucer base, brown,
cream, turquoise blue & rouge
marbleized swirls, w/paper label
(single) 50.00
Candlestick, Mission Ware, marbleized swirls, 6" h. (single)...... 52.50
Candlestick, Mission Ware, marbleized swirls, 9" h. (single)..... 130.00
Cornucopia-vase, Hywood line, blue
glaze, 7" h...................... 6.00
Ewer, Hywood line, blue glaze,
16" h........................... 30.00
Mug, Hywood line, geometric flowers on pink ground, 3½" h. 7.00
Pitcher, 2½" h., Mission Ware,
cream, turquoise blue & brown
marbleized swirls 25.00
Pitcher, 3¼" h., Hywood line, yellow glaze....................... 20.00
Pitcher, 6" h., Hywood line, geometric design in relief, blue glaze 32.00
Planter, Hywood line, model of a
deer, blue glaze, 9 x 6" 10.00
Planter, Hywood line, model of an
elephant, shaded blue glaze
(ILLUS.)........................ 20.00
Planter, Hywood line, model of a
squirrel ....12.50 to 20.00
Planter, Hywood line, model of a
swan, blue or yellow, each 12.50
Vase, 3" h., Mission Ware, marbleized swirls 27.00
Vase, 4½" h., Mission Ware, brown,
blue & beige marbleized
swirls ....38.00 to 45.00
Vase, 5" h., Hywood line, blue
matte glaze..................... 20.00
Vase, 6½" h., hourglass shape, Mission Ware, marbleized swirls 42.50
Vase, 7" h., Mission Ware, mar-
bleized swirls 65.00
Vase, bud, 7" h., Mission Ware,
marbleized swirls 60.00
Vase, 7½" h., pear-shaped, Mission
Ware, earth tone marbleized
swirls 78.00
Vase, 7¾" h., Mission Ware, mar-
bleized swirls 85.00
Vase, 8" h., Hywood line, mottled
blue glaze, original label 20.00
Vase, 8" h., Mission Ware, mar-
bleized swirls 77.50
Vase, 9" h., cylindrical, Mission
Ware, marbleized swirls 155.00

Niloak Mission Ware Vase

Vase, 9" h., Mission Ware, cream,
terra cotta & blue marbleized
swirls (ILLUS.)................... 100.00

Vase, 10" h., gourd-shaped, Mission
Ware, marbleized swirls ..95.00 to 110.00

Vase, 10½" h., bulbous, Mission
Ware, marbleized swirls 125.00

Vase, 14" h., Mission Ware, marbleized swirls 300.00

Vase, Hywood line, 4 open tulips on
grey shaded to pink ground 32.00

NIPPON

Nippon Ewer

*This colorful porcelain was produced by
numerous factories in Japan late last century and until about 1921. There are numerous
marks on this ware, identifying the producers
or decorating studios. The hand-painted
pieces of good quality have shown a dramatic price increase within the past three years.
Also see CHILDREN'S DISHES & MUGS
and MUSTACHE CUPS & SAUCERS.*

Ash tray, triangular w/three cigarette rests, "moriage" dragon
decor on grey ground, 5½" w.
(green "M" in Wreath mark) $150.00

Basket, ruffled rim, h.p. yellow &
lavender violets, gold beading &
trim, 4" h....................... 45.00

Berry set: 10½" d. master bowl & 5
sauce dishes; h.p. lake scene
w/swans, 6 pcs. 125.00

Bouillon cups & saucers, h.p. large
butterflies & light blue florals, set
of 6 .... 150.00

Bowl, 7½" d., 2-handled, h.p. Indian
in canoe decor 110.00

Bowl, 9¼" d., footed, h.p. lilacs &
foliage w/lavish gold trim on pale
green ground (Maple Leaf
mark) 110.00

Bowl, 10" w., octagonal, cobalt blue
border w/lavish gold florals, h.p.
orchids decor interior (green "M"
in Wreath mark) 200.00

Cake set: master cake plate & 4
serving plates; "moriage" dragon
decor, 5 pcs.................... 125.00

Cake set: master cake plate & 6
serving plates; h.p. bluebirds &
florals w/gold trim on white
ground, 7 pcs. 110.00

Candle holder, chamberstick-type,
ring handle, heart-shaped medallions w/pink & white roses decor,
ornate gold trim 125.00

Candlesticks, hexagonal base &
stem, h.p. Art Deco style floral
decor, 8¼" h., pr. (green "M" in
Wreath mark)................... 285.00

Celery set: 13½" l. celery tray & 5
individual salt dips; h.p. celery
stalk decor, gold trim, 6 pcs.
(green "M" in Wreath mark) 95.00

Celery tray, gold pierced handles,
Art Deco decor, 11" l. 25.00

Celery tray, pierced handles, h.p.
pink roses decor, blue border
w/gold trim, 11" l. 30.00

Cheese dish w/slant lid, Gouda-type
decor w/colorful stylized florals
on white ground, gold trim,
7½" l. ("M" in Wreath mark) 145.00

Chocolate pot, cov., h.p. floral
sprays on white ground, 9¾" h.
(blue Imperial mark) 110.00

Chocolate pot, cov., "gaudy," h.p.
small roses w/ornate gold trim on
cobalt blue ground 185.00

Chocolate set: cov. chocolate pot &
4 c/s; ornate gold beading on
white ground, 9 pcs. 105.00

Chocolate set: cov. chocolate pot &
5 c/s; pink roses & green foliage
on creamy ivory ground, 11 pcs. ... 295.00

Chocolate set: cov. chocolate pot &

6 c/s; h.p. lake scene w/snow-capped mountain in distance on pale blue ground, 13 pcs. 300.00

Condensed milk can holder, cover & underplate, h.p. pink florals on shaded green ground, gold trim . . 125.00

Cookie jar, cov., large handles, white florals w/lavish gold trim & jeweled centers, swirling bands of enameled beading, 7" h. (blue Maple Leaf mark) 200.00

Cookie jar, cov., footed, melon-ribbed, "gaudy," h.p. red & pink florals w/ornate gold trim on cobalt blue ground, 7¾" h. (blue Maple Leaf mark) 350.00

Cookie jar, cov., hexagonal, 2-handled, h.p. scenic decor w/ornate gold outlining (blue Maple Leaf mark) 325.00

Creamer, child's, h.p. lake & cottage scene on green ground (Rising Sun mark) 35.00

Creamer & cov. sugar bowl, ornate gold trim on handles, rims & base, h.p. pink & yellow florals w/aqua leaves outlined in heavy gold on white ground, pr. (Maple Leaf mark) 145.00

Creamer & cov. sugar bowl, h.p. gold dragons on cobalt blue ground, pr. (SNB Nagoya mark) . . 185.00

Cruet w/original stopper, h.p. river scene w/palm trees 265.00

Cup & saucer, Azalea patt. 16.00

Dish, 3-footed, h.p. lake scene w/swans, lavish gold trim, 6¾" d., 2¾" h. (blue Maple Leaf mark) 85.00

Dresser set: tray, cov. jewel box & hatpin holder; h.p. multicolored daisies on green ground, 3 pcs. . . 90.00

Dresser set: tray, hatpin holder, cov. footed hair receiver, footed trinket box & footed dish; "mori-age" dragon decor on grey ground, 5 pcs. (green "M" in Wreath mark) 225.00

Ewer, "moriage" grape clusters & leaves, beaded trim (ILLUS.) 121.00

Nippon Ferner

Ferner, quadrilobed, gold feet & handles, h.p. desert scene w/Arab on camel in an oasis setting, 10¾" w. across handles, 5¾" h. (ILLUS.) 200.00

Fish set: 23 x 9" oval platter & six 8½" d. plates; h.p. fish in underwater scene, wide green borders w/lavish gold trim & beading, 7 pcs. 595.00

Game plates, h.p. birds in naturalistic setting, ornate floral medallion borders w/ornate gold trim, pr. ("M" in Wreath mark) 350.00

Humidor, cov., h.p. playing cards decor w/"moriage" trim, 5" h. (green "M" in Wreath mark) 410.00

Nippon Humidor

Humidor, cov., h.p. horse-drawn carriage w/driver scene, 5½" h., green "M" in Wreath mark (ILLUS.) 295.00

Humidor, cov., h.p. windmill scene, 6" h. (green "M" in Wreath mark) 245.00

Humidor, cov., hexagonal, h.p. owl on a leafy branch, blue shaded to creamy ivory ground, 6¾" h. (green "M" in Wreath mark) 365.00

Humidor, cov., relief-molded & h.p. horses heads decor, 7½" h. (green "M" in Wreath mark) 720.00

Lemonade set: pitcher & 6 mugs; h.p. orange poppies w/gold trim, 7 pcs. 225.00

Letter holder, h.p. sailboat scene w/palm trees on shore, 3" h. (green "M" in Wreath mark) 125.00

Marmalade jar, cover & underplate, h.p. purple grapes decor, gold trim, 2 pcs. 55.00

Matchbox holder & ash tray combination, h.p. bird on branch & floral decor, 3½" h. (blue "M" in Wreath mark) 150.00

Mayonnaise bowl, underplate & ladle, h.p. violets decor, gold trim, 3 pcs. 130.00

Mug, relief-molded & h.p. child's face, 3" h. (Rising Sun mark) 55.00

Mug, h.p. playing cards & dice decor, 5" h. (green "M" in Wreath mark) 245.00

Mug, h.p. Dutch windmill on river shore scene, 5½" h. (green "M" in Wreath mark) 215.00

Napkin ring, h.p. river, trees & house scene (green "M" in Wreath mark) 64.00

Nut bowl, relief-molded & h.p. hazel nuts decor, 7" sq. 95.00

Nut bowl, pentagonal, 3 ball feet, relief-molded & h.p. nuts & foliage w/"moriage" slip trim on shaded orange to brown ground, 9½" w. (green "M" in Wreath mark) 150.00

Nut set, 5¾" d. footed master nut bowl & 5 individual nut cups; green & gold floral decor, scalloped rim w/lavish gold beading, 6 pcs. 145.00

Pancake dish & dome cover, h.p. cobalt blue florals, ornate gold trim 175.00

Pitcher, milk, 6¾" h., 7" w., hexagonal, pink florals & green foliage on white ground, ornate gold trim & pink jeweling around base & top (green "M" in Wreath mark) 175.00

Pitcher, tankard, 11" h., gold handle & rim, h.p. yellow & purple grapes against autumn-colored foliate ground 195.00

Plaque, pierced to hang, h.p. bust portrait on an Indian in full headdress within border of enameled blue flowers w/red jeweled centers & "moriage" beading, 7¾" d. 145.00

Plaque, pierced to hang, h.p. sailboats on water scene in shades of green & orange, 9" d. (Maple Leaf mark) 185.00

Plaque, pierced to hang, relief-molded & h.p. squirrel eating nuts, 9" d. (green "M" in Wreath mark) 395.00

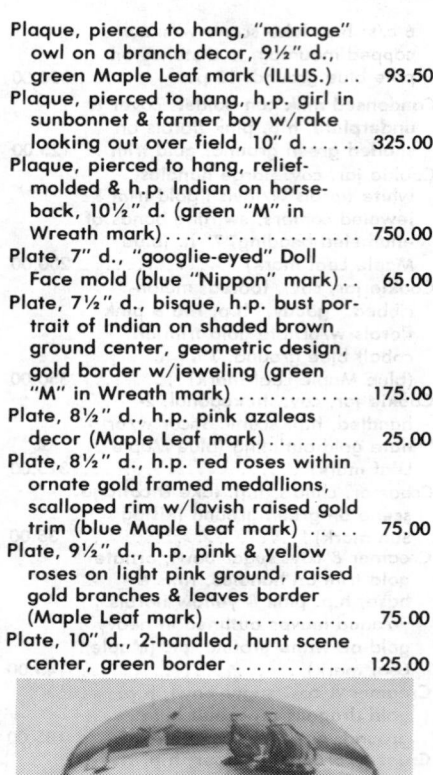

Nippon Plaque

Plaque, pierced to hang, "moriage" owl on a branch decor, 9½" d., green Maple Leaf mark (ILLUS.) .. 93.50

Plaque, pierced to hang, h.p. girl in sunbonnet & farmer boy w/rake looking out over field, 10" d...... 325.00

Plaque, pierced to hang, relief-molded & h.p. Indian on horseback, 10½" d. (green "M" in Wreath mark).................... 750.00

Plate, 7" d., "googlie-eyed" Doll Face mold (blue "Nippon" mark).. 65.00

Plate, 7½" d., bisque, h.p. bust portrait of Indian on shaded brown ground center, geometric design, gold border w/jeweling (green "M" in Wreath mark) 175.00

Plate, 8½" d., h.p. pink azaleas decor (Maple Leaf mark) 25.00

Plate, 8½" d., h.p. red roses within ornate gold framed medallions, scalloped rim w/lavish raised gold trim (blue Maple Leaf mark) 75.00

Plate, 9½" d., h.p. pink & yellow roses on light pink ground, raised gold branches & leaves border (Maple Leaf mark) 75.00

Plate, 10" d., 2-handled, hunt scene center, green border 125.00

Nippon Powder Box

Powder box, cov., h.p. sailboat scene, heavy gold beading & trim, 5½" d. (ILLUS.) 98.00

Punch bowl & base, h.p. roses decor on cobalt blue ground, cobalt blue border w/lavish gold trim, gold handles, 2 pcs.................... 375.00

Punch set: bowl, base & 4 cups; h.p. lake scene w/swans, ornate black & gold trim, 6 pcs. (green "M" in Wreath mark) ....500.00 to 600.00

Relish, pierced handles, h.p. pink & red roses decor on gold ground, overall heavy enameled beading (Royal Kinran Crown mark) 65.00

Rose bowl, relief-molded & h.p. purple grape clusters w/orange & yellow foliage on brown shading to yellow ground, 3½" h. (green "M" in Wreath mark) 235.00

Salt dip, h.p. Art Nouveau florals
w/gold trim 18.00

Salt & pepper shakers, h.p. pink
roses decor on gold ground, overall enameled turquoise beading,
pr............................. 125.00

Sardine dish, cover w/gold sardine
finial & underplate, h.p. scenic
decor, 2 pcs. (green "M" in
Wreath mark).................. 90.00

Spoon tray, h.p. Dutch windmill on
river shore scene 60.00

Stein, h.p. landscape scene
w/flowering trees & house, 7" h.
(green "M" in Wreath mark) 375.00

Stein, h.p. house scene w/two
figures in a garden, 7" h. (green
"M" in Wreath mark) 410.00

Sugar shaker, hexagonal, gold handles, Art Deco decor, 5" h. (blue
Maple Leaf mark) 90.00

Sugar shaker, gold handle, pleated
body, h.p. pale green florals
w/white "moriage" beading, 5" h.
(green "M" in Wreath mark) 125.00

Teapot, cov., 4-footed, h.p. pink &
red roses w/gold tracery on cobalt blue ground, ornate gold
beading 150.00

Tea set: cov. teapot, creamer & cov.
sugar bowl; child's, relief-molded
& h.p. "googlie-eyed" Doll Face
mold, 3 pcs. (blue "Nippon"
mark) 95.00

Tea set: cov. teapot, creamer, cov.
sugar bowl & tray; octagonal,
gold Greek Key patt. on cobalt
blue band decor, ornate gold
trim, 4 pcs. 350.00

Nippon Tea Strainer

Tea strainer, h.p. red & pink florals,
gold trim (ILLUS.)............... 80.00

Tea tile, pink & white floral decor,
10" d......................... 40.00

Toothpick holder, 3-handled, h.p.
white daisies on mint green
ground 45.00

Tray, bisque, h.p. scenic decor center, enameled multicolored border
w/ornate gold trim, 12 x 9" 150.00

Tray, h.p. sailboat scene w/palm
trees in foreground, 14 x 6"...... 70.00

Urn, cov., large red, pink & orange
roses on gold ground within or-

nate gold beaded medallion center, overall red, pink & orange
roses on cobalt blue ground
w/gold tracery, ornate gold trim,
14" h......................... 480.00

Vase, 4¼" h., bulbous, 2-handled,
h.p. woodland scene 195.00

Vase, 5" h., 2-handled, pale violet
flowers on matte finish w/gold
trim.......................... 75.00

Vase, 5½" h., h.p. yellow & red
roses on dark green ground...... 105.00

Vase, 6" h., squatty, 2-handled, h.p.
forest scene against "tapestry"
textured ground................ 365.00

Vase, 6¼" h., 2-handled, h.p. desert scene w/Arab on camel, gold
trim.......................... 345.00

Nippon Vase

Vase, 7" h., h.p. pink roses reserved on gold ground w/overall
heavily enameled turquoise blue
beading (ILLUS.)................ 300.00

Vase, 7" h., bulbous w/slender flaring neck, relief-molded & h.p.
acorns & foliage decor (blue
Maple Leaf mark) 430.00

Vase, 7½" h., 2-handled, Wedgwood jasper-type decor w/white
butterflies & floral relief on blue
(green "M" in Wreath mark) 285.00

Vase, 8" h., h.p. iris blossoms &
trailing foliage, ornate gold trim &
jeweling at base & neck 150.00

Vase, 8½" h., 2-handled, cobalt
blue ground reserved w/colorful
h.p. scene of ostriches in a desert
setting w/palm trees & pyramid,
lavish gold trim (green "M" in
Wreath mark).................. 425.00

Vase, 8½" h., 9" w., twig handles,
h.p. pink & white floral decor on
green shaded to blue ground, ornate gold trim 125.00

Vase, 9" h., h.p. Art Nouveau style
orange peonies decor 190.00
Wall pocket, "moriage" coiling drag-
on decor on grey ground,
6¾" h. 65.00
Whiskey jug, square, h.p. scenic
decor, 8" h. (blue Maple Leaf
mark) 425.00

NORITAKE

Noritake Humidor

Noritake china, still in production in Japan, has been exported in large quantities to this country since early in this century. Though the Noritake Company first registered in 1904, it did not use "Noritake" as part of their backstamp until 1918. Interest in Noritake has escalated as collectors now seek out pieces made between the "Nippon" era and World War II (1921-41). The Azalea pattern is also popular with collectors. Also see CHILDREN'S DISHES and PHOENIX BIRD CHINA.

Ash tray, trefoil w/figural yellow
bird, 3½" w. $50.00
Ash tray, relief-molded horseheads
decor, 4½" w. 185.00
Basket, Tree in Meadow patt., 4 3/8
x 2½", overall 4" h. 30.00
Bowl, 6½" d., floral basket & birds
on ivory ground 35.00
Bowl, 7½" w., 3" h., gold handles &
gold Greek Key border, panels of
stylized "moriage" florals w/bead-
ing exterior, orange & white poppies w/green foliage interior 60.00
Butter dish, cov., Azalea patt. 85.00
Cake plate, triangular w/three open
handles, large butterfly & floral
band decor on orange lustre
ground, 9¼" w. (red "M" in
Wreath mark) 45.00
Candlesticks, Indian-type designs in
bright red on white ground,
3¾" h., pr. 85.00

Candlesticks, square fluted base,
floral decor w/lavish gold trim,
9" h., pr. 150.00
Celery set: 12½" l. celery tray
w/pierced handles & 6 individual
salt dips; sunset on lake scene,
7 pcs. (red "M" in Wreath
mark) 65.00
Cheese dish & slant lid w/bird finial,
gold lustre, 7¾" l. (red "M" in
Wreath mark) 95.00
Chocolate set: cov. chocolate pot &
5 c/s; water scene w/sailboats &
trees, ornate gold trim, 11 pcs. . . . 225.00
Cigarette holder, bell-shaped, bird
finial, blue lustre finish 85.00
Creamer & sugar bowl, Roseara
patt., pr. 22.00
Demitasse set: cov. coffee pot & 6
c/s; Azalea patt., 13 pcs. 975.00
Dish w/figural Griffin center handle,
hexagonal, wide orange border,
lustre finish, 1930's 32.00
Fruit set: 12½ x 7½" tray & 6 han-
dled sauce dishes; strawberries,
cherries & lemons on blue lustre
ground, gold trim, 7 pcs. 125.00
Humidor, cov., 2-handled, relief-
molded fox decor, 6¼" h., green
"M" in Wreath mark (ILLUS.) 600.00

Noritake Art Deco Inkwell

Inkwell, model of an owl, Art Deco
style, 3½" h. (ILLUS.) 225.00
Lemon dish, ring handle, Tree in
Meadow patt., 5½" d. 11.00
Marmalade jar & ladle, Azalea
patt. 100.00
Match holder w/striker, beehive-
shaped, tan lustre finish (green
"M" in Wreath mark) 45.00
Mustard jar & cover w/rose finial,
Art Deco lady decor 38.00
Napkin ring, h.p. full-blown roses &
foliage, 2¼" w. (green "M" in
Wreath mark) 25.00
Napkin rings, Art Deco style, h.p.
bust portrait of lady in red coat &

hat w/white fur trim on one &
gentleman w/grey top hat &
checkered collar on other,
2¼" w., pr. (red "M" in Wreath
mark) 70.00

Nappy, handled, Azalea patt. 27.50

Nappy, handled, irregular scalloped
rim, h.p. lake scene w/swans,
6½" w. ("M" in Wreath mark) 38.00

Night light, figural owl on branch,
7½" h................600.00 to 800.00

Nut bowl, relief-molded squirrel eating nut decor, 6½" l. (green "M"
in Wreath mark) 200.00

Plaque, pierced to hang, h.p. Art
Deco style lady in ball gown
against orange lustre ground,
7¾" d. (red "M" in Wreath
mark) 125.00

Plaque, pierced to hang, relief-
molded & h.p. bust profiles of
Indians (2) in full headdress,
10½" d. (green "M" in Wreath
mark) 550.00

Plate, 6" d., h.p. beautiful green-
eyed blonde lady w/fuchsia hat
center.......................... 85.00

Plate, 6½" to 7½" d., Azalea
patt.....................5.00 to 8.50

Plate, 6½" d., Tree in Meadow
patt............................ 8.50

Plate, 10" d., Azalea patt. 16.00

Plate, 10" d., Tree in Meadow
patt............................ 90.00

Relish, 2-handled, 4-compartment,
Azalea patt., 10" d. 95.00

Sauceboat w/attached underplate &
ladle, h.p. underwater scene
w/fish & reeds, ornate gold trim,
2 pcs. 65.00

Spooner, 2-handled, Azalea patt.,
8" l. 65.00

Teapot, cov., Tree in Meadow
patt. 75.00

Tea set: cov. teapot, creamer, sugar
bowl, 6 cake plates & 6 c/s; swan
in lake decor, black borders
w/lavish gold trim, 21 pcs........ 375.00

Toothpick holder, Azalea patt. 80.00

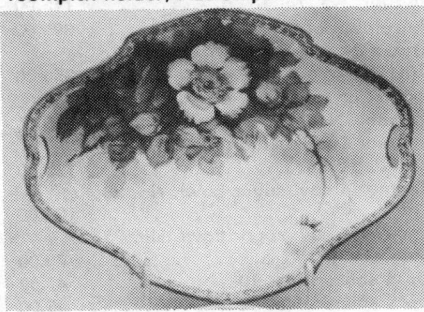

Noritake Tray

Tray, pierced handles, h.p. florals
on shaded green, yellow & ochre
ground, enameled gold scrolled
rim w/blue jeweling, 8" l.
(ILLUS.)....................... 28.00

Vase, 5¾" h., fan-shaped, Tree in
Meadow patt................... 115.00

Noritake Vase

Vase, 5¾" h., scalloped base, floral
decor, silver rim (ILLUS.) 25.00

Vases, 12" h., urn-shaped, gold
handles, scenic decor, pr........ 250.00

Vegetable bowl, cov., Azalea patt.,
10¼" d. 55.00

Wall pocket, multicolored floral
decor on tan lustre ground,
applied bee & butterfly, 5" h. 38.00

Wall pocket, flaring mouth, wide
band w/lake scene, blue lustre
finish, 8¼" h................... 55.00

NORTH DAKOTA SCHOOL OF MINES POTTERY

Indian Head Medallion

*All pottery produced at the University of
North Dakota School of Mines was made
from North Dakota clay. In 1910, the Univer-*

sity hired Margaret Kelly Cable to teach pottery making and she remained at the school until her retirement. Julia Mattson and Margaret Pachl were other instructors between 1923 and 1970. Designs and glazes varied through the years ranging from the Art Nouveau to modern styles. Pieces were marked "University of North Dakota - Grand Forks, N.D. - Made at School of Mines, N.D." within a circle and also signed by the students until 1963. Since that time, the pieces bear only the students' signatures. Items signed "Huck" are by the artist Flora Huckfield and were made between 1923 and 1949. We list only those pieces made prior to 1963.

Bowl, 6" d., incised crocus decor, signed Cable (Margaret Kelly Cable) $125.00
Bowl, 8" d., deep, turquoise glaze, artist-signed 70.00
Bowl, embossed florals on blue ground, signed Cable (Margaret Kelly Cable) 50.00
Bookend-bowl combination, ivy design on green streaked w/black ground, signed Cable, 5½ x 3½" (single) 250.00
Candlesticks, maroon glaze, tall, pr. 135.00
Figure of cowboy, signed Julia Mattson 110.00
Medallion, pierced for thong, bust portrait of Indian head in low relief, tan to reddish brown matte glaze, 2" d. (ILLUS.) 100.00
Paperweight, "Parents Day," deep blue, 1938, 3½" d. 65.00
Tile, scenic decor, 6 colors, 1928, signed Mattson 450.00
Tray, single stylized fish on glossy black ground, 3" w., 7" l....... 65.00
Vase, 2½" h., squat, mottled green, artist-signed 48.00
Vase, 3¾" h., flaring rim, sea green glaze, artist-signed 45.00
Vase, 4" h., 5½" w., concentric rings around top, turquoise glaze, artist-signed 90.00
Vase, 4½" h., incised decor, pink glaze, dated Dec. 1937 .... 135.00
Vase, 5½" h., incised daffodils decor, signed Mattson 250.00
Vase, 6" h., cobalt blue decor, signed "Huck" (Flora Huckfield)... 110.00
Vase, 6" h., cobalt blue, signed J. Mattson 95.00
Vase, 6½" h., green glaze, signed Cable 95.00
Vase, bud, 8½" h., green semi-gloss glaze, signed Cable 65.00
Vase, bowl-shaped, Prairie Rose patt., signed "Huck" (Flora Huckfield) 150.00

OLD IVORY

Old Ivory Pattern No. 16

Old Ivory china was produced in a great diversity of table pieces, most of which bear pattern stock numbers.

Berry set: master bowl & 5 sauce dishes; No. 7, 6 pcs............. $135.00
Berry set: master bowl & 6 sauce dishes; No. 11, 7 pcs............. 225.00
Bowl, cereal, 6½" d., No. 15 .... 40.00
Bowl, soup, 8" d., No. 84 .... 45.00
Bowl, 9½" d., handled, No. 10 ..... 85.00
Bowl, 9½" d., No. 28 .... 95.00
Bowl, 9½" d., No. 82 .... 75.00
Bowl, 10" d., No. 11 .... 70.00
Cake plate, pierced handles, No. 28, 10" d. 65.00
Cake plate, pierced handles, No. 122, 10" d. 90.00
Cake plate, pierced handles, No. 75, 11½" d. 125.00
Cake plate, pierced handles, No. 10 .... 100.00
Cake set: master plate w/pierced handles & 6 serving plates; No. 200, 7 pcs.................... 265.00
Celery tray, No. 90, 8½" oval 70.00
Celery tray, No. 84, 11" l........... 77.50
Celery tray, No. 11, 11¾" l........ 47.50
Charger, No. 73, 13" d. 145.00
Chocolate pot, cov., No. 11 .... 395.00
Cookie jar, cov., No. 16 (ILLUS.) .... 250.00 to 350.00
Cookie jar, cov., No. 60 .... 150.00
Creamer, No. 8 .... 65.00
Creamer & cov. sugar bowl, No. 10, pr........................... 135.00
Creamer & cov. sugar bowl, No. 28, pr........................... 100.00
Creamer & cov. sugar bowl, No. 75, pr........................... 75.00
Cup & saucer, No. 10 .... 47.50
Cup & saucer, No. 22 .... 45.00
Cup & saucer, No. 166 .... 25.00

Dresser tray, No. 84, 12 x 7" 145.00
Mustard pot, cov., No. 16 .... 200.00

Old Ivory Mustard Pot

Mustard pot, cov. (ILLUS.) 65.00
Nappy, handled, No. 16 .... 75.00
Pickle dish, No. 11, 8½" oval 25.00
Pickle dish, No. 200, 8¼ x 4¾" 40.00
Plate, 6" d., No. 15 .... 25.00
Plate, 6" d., No. 16 .... 23.00
Plate, 6" d., No. 75 .... 22.50
Plate, 6" d., No. 84 .... 30.00
Plate, 6" d., No. 200 .... 19.00
Plate, 7" d., No. 16 .... 24.00
Plate, 7" d., No. 22 .... 55.00
Plate, 7½" d., No. 7 .... 25.00
Plate, 7½" d., No. 10 .... 27.50
Plate, 7½" d., No. 17 .... 30.00
Plate, 8" d., No. 10 .... 35.00
Plate, 8" d., No. 41 .... 35.00
Plate, 8½" d., No. 28 .... 35.00
Plate, 8½" d., No. 32 .... 60.00
Plate, 9½" d., No. 6 .... 95.00
Plate, 9½" d., No. 7 .... 25.00
Plate, 9½" d., No. 84 .... 95.00
Plate, 13" d., No. 16 .... 150.00
Plate, 13" d., No. 78 .... 80.00
Relish tray, No. 84, 6¼ x 4½" 50.00
Relish tray, No. 84, 8½ x 5" 60.00
Relish tray, No. 200, 8½ x 5" 57.50
Salt & pepper shakers, No. 15,
　pr. 92.50
Salt & pepper shakers, No. 16, pr. ... 95.00
Salt & pepper shakers, No. 28,
　pr. 105.00
Sauce dish, No. 16 .... 14.00
Soup plate w/flange rim, No. 84,
　9½" d. 100.00
Sugar shaker, No. 84 .... 190.00
Tea cup & saucer, No. 16 .... 45.00
Tea cup & saucer, No. 84 .... 45.00
Teapot, cov., hexagonal, No. 16 .... 290.00
Teapot, cov., hexagonal, No. 84 .... 275.00
Toothpick holder, No. 10 .... 135.00
Tray, No. 16, 11½" l. 55.00
Tray, No. 200, 11½" l. 57.50
Vegetable dish, cov., No. 7 .... 39.00
Vegetable dish, open, No. 7 .... 30.00
Waste bowl, No. 16 .... 115.00
Waste bowl, No. 84 .... 95.00

OLD SLEEPY EYE

Old Sleepy Eye Items

Sleepy Eye, Minn., was named after an Indian Chief. The Sleepy Eye Milling Co. had stoneware and pottery premiums made at the turn of the century first by the Weir Pottery Company and subsequently by Western Stoneware Co., Monmouth, Ill. On these items the trademark Indian head was signed beneath "Old Sleepy Eye." The colors were Flemish blue on grey. Later pieces by Western Stoneware to 1937 were not made for Sleepy Eye Milling Co. but for other businesses. They bear the same Indian head but "Old Sleepy Eye" does not appear below. They have a reverse design of teepees and trees and may or may not be marked Western Stoneware on the base. These items are usually found in cobalt blue on cream and are rarer in other colors.

Bowl (salt bowl), 6½" d., 4" h.,
　Flemish blue on grey stoneware,
　Weir Pottery, 1903 .... $400.00
Butter jar, Flemish blue on grey
　stoneware, Weir Pottery, 1903 .... 410.00
Mug, cobalt blue on grey, small Indian head on handle, Western
　Stoneware Co., World War I era,
　1914-18, 4¼" h. .... 350.00 to 400.00
Mug, cobalt blue on white, small Indian head on handle, Western
　Stoneware Co., 1906-37 ..140.00 to 170.00
Pitcher, 4" h., cobalt blue on white,
　w/small Indian head on handle,
　Western Stoneware Co., 1906-37
　(half-pint) 142.50
Pitcher, 5¼" h., cobalt blue on
　grey, w/small Indian head on
　handle, Western Stoneware Co.,
　World War I era, 1914-18 (pint) ... 155.00
Pitcher, 6¼" h., cobalt blue on
　white, w/small Indian head on
　handle, Western Stoneware Co.,
　1906-37 (quart) 177.50
Pitcher, 7¾" h., cobalt blue on
　white, w/small Indian head on
　handle, Western Stoneware Co.,
　1906-37 (half-gallon) .....175.00 to 245.00
Pitcher, 8½" h., cobalt blue on
　white, w/small Indian head on
　handle, Western Stoneware Co.,
　1906-37 (gallon) 225.00

Pitcher, "Standing Indian," Flemish
blue on grey stoneware 1,095.00
Pitchers, set of 5 . . . . .1,200.00
Stein, all blue, Western Stoneware
Co., 7¾" h. 750.00
Stein, blue on white, Western Stone-
ware Co., 1906-37, 7¾" h. 485.00
Stein, brown on white, Western
Stoneware Co., 7¾" h. 795.00
Stein, brown on yellow, Western
Stoneware Co., 7¾" h. 715.00
Stein, chestnut brown, 1952, 22 oz.
size . . . . .350.00 to 375.00
Sugar bowl, cobalt blue on white,
Western Stoneware Co., 1906-37,
4" h. . . . . .350.00 to 425.00
Vase, 9" h., Flemish blue on grey
stoneware, Indian head signed,
dragonfly, frog & bullrushes
reverse, Weir Pottery Co., 1903. . . 250.00
Vase, 9" h., grey stoneware, molded w/cattails & dragonfly each
side . . . . .135.00 to 185.00

OWENS

Utopian Mug

Owens pottery is the product of the J.B. Owens Pottery Company, which operated in Ohio from 1890 to 1929. In 1891 it located in Zanesville and produced art pottery from 1896, introducing "Utopian" wares as its first art pottery. The company switched to tile after 1907. Efforts to rebuild after the factory burned in 1928 failed and the company closed in 1929.

Honey jug, handled, Utopian, underglaze slip-painted Indian portrait,
standard brown glaze, artist-
signed, 7" h. $525.00
Humidor, cov., Utopian, underglaze
slip-painted pipe, cigar &
matches, standard brown glaze,
artist-signed 195.00
Lamp, Soudanese line, gold decor
on glossy black ground 295.00
Mug, underglaze slip-painted cher-
ries, standard brown glaze,
4½" h. 115.00
Mug, Utopian, underglaze slip-
painted pansies, standard brown
glaze (ILLUS.) 130.00
Pitcher, 4" h., Utopian, ruffled rim,
underglaze slip-painted florals,
green shaded to tan ground,
artist-signed 145.00
Pitcher, 12" h., left-handed, under-
glaze slip-painted florals, standard brown glaze, artist-signed . . . 300.00
Pitcher, cider, Henry Deux line, portrait of Art Nouveau lady w/flow-
ing hair 85.00
Vases, 3¾" h., Soudanese line, in-
laid pink florals on ebony black
glossy ground, pr. 220.00
Vase, 3¾" h., Utopian, twisted
form, underglaze slip-painted berries, standard brown glaze 80.00
Vase, 4" h., 6" widest d., 2-handled,
Utopian, underglaze slip-painted
yellow florals, copper brown
ground 135.00
Vase, 5" h., 4" top d., 3-handled,
Henry Deux line, lizards on foliate
branches, matte green ground . . . 75.00
Vase, 6½" h., Henri Deux line, incised bust of Art Nouveau woman
w/flowing hair 250.00

Owens Utopian Vase

Vase, 11" h., Utopian, underglaze
slip-painted floral decor, standard
brown glaze, artist-signed
(ILLUS.) 200.00
Vase, 12½" h., Lotus line, under-
glaze slip-painted bird in flight on
shaded light ground 250.00
Vase, 13" h., Opalesce Inlaid line,
inlaid floral decor & overglaze
wavy olive green lines over cop-
per on light ground 435.00
Vase, 13" h., gourd-shaped, Matt
Utopian, underglaze slip-painted
florals, light brown matte finish . . 165.00

Vase, Aborigine line, American
Indian designs, matte finish,
ca. 1907 . . . . 95.00
Water set: pitcher & 6 tumblers;
green matte glaze, 7 pcs. 200.00

OYSTER PLATES

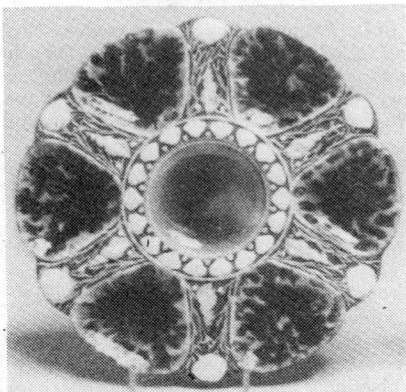

Oyster Plate by Minton

Oyster plates intrigue a few collectors. Oysters were shucked and the meat served in wells of these attractive plates specifically designed to serve oysters. During the late 19th Century, they were made of fine china and majolica. Some plates were decorated in the realistic "trompe l'oeil" technique while others simply matched the pattern of a dinner service. Following is a random sampling of oyster plates that were sold in the past eighteen months.

Dresden porcelain, multicolored
floral clusters, set of 4 . . . . $115.00
German porcelain, h.p. in shades of
pink, unusual shape, set of 6 . . . . . 350.00
Haviland china, bright yellow &
brown decor, gold trim, marked
"Haviland & Co.," 8¾" d 50.00
Haviland china, gold flowers &
green leaves on white ground
w/gold trim, marked "Haviland &
Co.," 8¾" d 50.00
Haviland china, brushed gold rim,
pink floral decor on white ground,
marked "Theodore Haviland" 50.00
Haviland china, 5 wells, pink floral
decor w/gold trim 37.00
Haviland china, seaweed decor, set
of 12 . . . . 450.00
Limoges china, realistic shell-shaped
wells, marked "Lanternier,
Limoges," dated 1899, 8" d 35.00
Limoges china, 6 wells, white
w/gold trim, 9¼" d 49.00

Majolica, turquoise shell-molded
wells & green seaweed, brown
center well on yellow basketweave ground, marked "Minton,"
9" oblong 150.00
Majolica, green or blue, marked
"Minton" . . . . 90.00 to 120.00
Majolica, Shell & Seaweed
patt. 75.00
Majolica, brown & blue wells sepa-
rated by reversed shells, marked
"Minton," mid-19th c., 9" d., set
of 7 . . . . 385.00
Majolica, 6 shell-molded wells
around a central circular well,
green & brown streaked tortoise
shell glaze, between borders
molded w/shells & seaweed in
shades of tan, ochre, brown,
green & pink, impressed "Minton"
marks for 1873 & 1876, 9" d. 1,100.00
assembled set of 12 . . . . 1,100.00
Union Porcelain Works, Brooklyn,
New York, china, "trompe l'oeil"
technique w/realistic clam form
wells separated by molded shell-
fish & seaweed, 9" d 115.00

PARIAN

Parian Pitcher

Parian is unglazed porcelain in the biscuit stage, and takes its name from its resemblance to Parian marble used for statuary. Parian wares were made in this country and abroad through much of the last century and continue to be made.

Bust of Milton, Bridgwood & Clarke,
ca. 1860, 7½" h. $70.00
Bust of Ophelia, by W.C. Marshall,
Copeland for Crystal Palace Art
Union, 11" h. 225.00

Figure of a Colonial boy seated on rock & holding bird above his head, Retriever dog seated by his side, 9½" h. 135.00

Figure of a woman w/fishing net, "The Net Mender," 4¼" d., 11½" h. 152.00

Figure of Ruth, oval base, 13" h. ... 175.00

Figure of a nude woman w/drapery over her left arm & a turtle at her right foot, circular base, un-marked, 16" h................... 160.00

Jug, branch handle, relief-molded white lilies & leaves on lavender ground, ca. 1850, 5¼" d., 7½" h. 135.00

Jug, lavender handle, relief-molded lavender figures of Naomi & Ruth on white ground, Alcock, 1847 English registry mark, 4¼" d., 9" h. 185.00

Jug w/hinged pewter lid, relief-molded white figures depicting "Commerce," "Music," "Art" & "Science," deep blue trim, 1862 English registry mark, 5" d., 9¾" h. 165.00

Loving cup, 2-handled, relief-molded white Bacchanalian scene w/grapes & vines on blue ground, base inscribed "The Society of Fine Arts Medal Presented to Charles Meigh For The Best Model of a Mug Ornamented in Relief," ca. 1840, 8 3/8" d., 6 7/8" h. 300.00

Model of owls (2) sitting on branch, "Match Making," 1871 English registry mark, 5½ x 4½", 7" h. .. 270.00

Pitcher, 6¾" h., branch handle, relief-molded figure of boy climbing tree to bird's nest one side & boy seated in tree holding nest of birds reverse, blue & white, Mayer's Longport, ca. 1850........... 225.00

Pitcher, 7" h., twig handle, relief-molded Arabian scenes, all white 175.00

Pitcher, 7¾" h., wheat & stylized leafage in relief, all white, English registry mark (ILLUS.)....... 80.00

Pitcher, 8" h., mask handle, relief-molded mythological figures on lavender ground, Alcock, 1830-59....................... 118.00

Pitcher, 9" h., relief-molded scenes of children at various games on lavender ground, Alcock 285.00

Spillholder, babes in woods scene in relief on sage green ground, T.J. & J. Mayer, 1850's 85.00

Vases, 7½" h., applied grapes & leaves, pr.................. 70.00

Vase, 8" h., model of a hand, white 75.00

PARIS & OLD PARIS

Old Paris Cups & Saucers

China known by the generic name of Paris and Old Paris was made by several Parisian factories from the 18th through the 19th century; some of it is marked and some is not. Much of it was handsomely decorated.

Cups & saucers, swan form cups w/arched neck forming handles, plumage-molded exterior smear-glazed in white, eyes & beaks picked out in gilding, cups & saucers w/gilt interiors & oval saucer rims w/molded band of feathers smear-glazed in white, ca. 1810, set of 10 (ILLUS. of part) $9,350.00

Dessert set: fruit cooler w/gilt pineapple finial, compote & 12 plates; cream borders w/wreaths of hydrangea, sweet pea, primrose, forget-me-nots, morning glory & other flowers, centering EB monogram w/crown, gilt rims, ca. 1815, 14 pcs. (repair to cooler liner) 687.50

Monkey band figure, wearing top hat, playing cymbals while riding a huge poodle dog, 7 x 6" 255.00

Plates, 9 1/8" d., gold berry vine roundel center surrounded by 10 flowerheads, gilt-edged lilac-ground rim w/grey grasses & black-edged yellow petal-shaped panels, ca. 1810, set of 18 (3 w/chips) 2,200.00

Tea set, cobalt blue w/lavish gold trim, 33 pcs. 1,000.00

Old Paris Tray

Tray, center finely painted in sepia "camaieu" w/bacchic procession within a gilt oval, scalloped & barbed rim (hairline) w/a gilt floral swag pendant from foliate scrolls beneath a foliate vine border, ca. 1800, 13 3/8" sq. (ILLUS.)........................ 440.00

Vases, 9 3/8" h., campana-shaped w/loop handles, each reserved front & reverse w/oval panels painted in sepia "camaieu" w/cupid amidst clouds holding a dove, torch, arrow or laurel branch & wreath, trumpet-shaped neck decorated in gilding w/single figures amidst foliate scrolls, gilt egg-and-dart rims & circular foot, mounted on square grey marble plinth, 1785-95, pr. (now mounted as table lamps)................1,540.00

Vases, 12" h., blended blue border w/gold trim, scenic decor, pr..... 295.00

Vases, 28" h., ovoid w/trumpet-shaped neck, each reserved on front w/a rectangular panel naturalistically painted w/an inscribed Italianate view of "Villa." or "Isola Bella" above molded gilt palmettes & acanthus, beadwork & tongue-and-dart gadrooning on lower section, ankle & circular foot, repeated on rim & shoulder, neck w/claret ground decorated w/palmettes, scrolls, swags, military emblems & other neoclassical devices, sides w/winged caryatid handles terminating in long palmettes, Nast Factory, ca. 1820, pr. 26,400.00

PAUL REVERE POTTERY

Barbara's Pitcher

This pottery was established in Boston, Mass., in 1906, by a group of philanthropists seeking to establish better conditions for underprivileged young girls of the area. Edith Brown served as supervisor of the small "Saturday Evening Girls Club" pottery operation which was moved, in 1912, to a house

close to the Old North Church where Paul Revere's signal lanterns had been placed. The wares were mostly hand decorated in mineral colors and both sgraffito and molded decorations were employed. Although it became popular, it was never a profitable operation and always depended on financial contributions to operate. After the death of Edith Brown in 1932, the pottery foundered and finally closed in 1942.

Bowl, 6" d., 1½" h., 3 chicks in colorful landscape scene on white w/blue band, artist-signed & dated 1936 ....$410.00

Bowl, 10" d., blue, marked "S.E.G." (Saturday Evening Girls) & dated 1922 .... 40.00

Bowl & flower frog, blue, marked "S.E.G." 60.00

Bowl inscribed "Eleanor - Her Bowl" & underplate, marked "S.E.G.," 2 pcs. 260.00

Calendar holder, marked "S.E.G." & artist-signed, 3¾" h. 115.00

Creamer, shaded blue w/white band at neck lettered "Barbara - Her Pitcher" in black & enriched w/small flowers, 4¼" h., hairline (ILLUS.)......................... 150.00

Egg cup, chick decor 55.00

Jar, cov., cobalt blue, purple & gun metal grey, 5" h................ 110.00

Paperweight, octagonal, geese decor, marked "S.E.G." 95.00

Plate, ochre, marked "S.E.G." 35.00

Salt dip, yellow w/black rim, marked "S.E.G.," 1¾" d. 45.00

Tea tile, trees decor on creamy ivory ground, marked "S.E.G.," 2½" w. octagon................. 125.00

Tea tile, 5½" d................... 85.00

Vase, 4½" h., tapered cylinder, turquoise drip on mustard yellow glaze, marked "S.E.G." & w/paper label 80.00

Vase, 4½ x 3½", matte yellow glaze, artist-signed 60.00

Vase, 5½ x 4½", textured pink glaze, w/label & dated 1927...... 55.00

Vase, 6" h., apothecary jar form, deep blue glossy glaze, marked "S.E.G." & dated 1922 .... 110.00

Vase, 10" h., semi-glossy Prussian blue glaze, marked "S.E.G." 90.00

Wall pocket, dark green glaze...... 79.00

PETERS & REED

In 1897, John D. Peters and Adam Reed formed a partnership to produce flower pots in Zanesville, Ohio. Formally incorporated as Peters and Reed in 1901, this type of production was the mainstay until after 1907 when they gradually expanded into the art pottery field. Frank Ferrell, a former designer at the Weller Pottery, developed the "Moss Aztec" line while associated with Peters and Reed and other art lines followed. Though unmarked, attribution is not difficult once familiar with the various lines. In 1921, Peters and Reed became Zane Pottery which continued in production until 1941.

Bowl, 6" d., low, Moss Aztec line,
  dragonfly decor $25.00
Bowl, 8" d., 3" h., vines & berries in
  high relief, green w/brown
  highlights 35.00
Flower frog, model of a turtle 45.00
Jardiniere, Moss Aztec line, grape &
  vine border, signed Ferrell,
  8" d. 50.00
Jug, single handle, sprigged on ear
  of corn decor front & reverse,
  glossy brown glaze, 5½" d.,
  5½" h. ....,...... 95.00
Jug, single handle, sprigged on
  grape garlands & lion's head,
  standard glossy brown glaze,
  5½" h. 65.00

Peters & Reed Jug

Jug, single handle, S-scroll molded
  body, sprigged on cavalier's head,
  standard glossy brown glaze
  (ILLUS.) 105.00
Pitcher, 4½" h., sprigged on wreath
  decor, standard glossy brown
  glaze 40.00
Pitcher, tankard, 17" h., sprigged on
  grape clusters w/leaves decor,
  standard glossy brown glaze 155.00
Powder box, cov., Landsun line,
  blended colorful glaze, round 30.00
Vase, 6½" h., Landsun line, blended
  glaze 35.00
Vase, 8" h., Chromal line, scenic
  decor 180.00

Chromal Ware Vase

Vase, 9" h., 7" d., Chromal ware,
  scenic landscape decor w/road,
  trees & fence (ILLUS.) 210.00
Vase, 9½" h., Shadow ware, brown
  & blue drip glaze on blue 58.50
Vase, 9½" h., hexagonal, mottled
  black, brown & green glaze 85.00
Vase, 11" h., Landsun line, blended
  glaze 78.00
Vase, 12" h., Montene ware, iridescent copper-bronze glaze 225.00
Wall pocket, Pereco line, profile of
  Egyptian Pharaoh wearing headdress w/asp, green matte finish,
  8" h. ....40.00 to 50.00

PEWABIC POTTERY

Mary Chase Perry (Stratton) and Horace J. Caulkins were partners in this Detroit, Michigan pottery. Established in 1903, Pewabic Pottery evolved from their Revelation Pottery — "Pewabic" meaning "clay with copper color" in the language of Michigan's Chippewa Indians. Caulkins attended to the clay formulas and Mary Perry Stratton was the artistic creator of forms and glaze formulas, eventually developing a wide range of colors for her finely textured glazes. The pottery's reputation for quality wares and architectural tiles enabled it to survive the depression years of the 1930's. After Caulkins died in 1923, Mrs. Stratton continued to be active in the pottery until her death, at age ninety-four, in 1961. Her contributions to the art pottery field are numerous. Also see TILES.

Ash tray, grape cluster decor,
  iridescent green glaze, 3½" l. $95.00
Ash tray, iridescent glaze, 4" sq. ... 65.00

Bowl, 4½" d., pinwheel design,
iridescent glaze 110.00
Bowl-vase, 6¾" d., 5" h., flowing
plum to blue iridescent glaze 475.00
Vase, 4" h., cylindrical, mottled
iridescent pink glaze w/red &
blue lustre highlights 150.00
Vase, 4½" h., gourd-shaped, irides-
cent gold w/flowing blue glaze . . . 175.00
Vase, 5½" h., bulbous w/short
neck, wide angled shoulder,
iridescent purple-grey glaze, early
20th c. 410.00

PHOENIX BIRD or FLYING TURKEY

Phoenix Bird Sugar Bowl

*The phoenix bird, a symbol of immortal-
ity and spiritual rebirth, has been handed
down through Egyptian mythology as a bird
that consumed itself by fire after 500 years
and then rose again, renewed from its ashes.
This bird has been used to decorate Japanese
porcelain, designed for export, for more than
100 years. The pattern incorporates a blue design of the bird, variously known as the "Flying Phoenix," the "Flying Turkey" or the
"Ho-o," stamped on a white ground. It became popular with collectors because there
was an abundant supply since the ware was
produced for a long period of time. Pieces can
be found marked with Japanese characters,
with a "Nippon" mark, or a "Made in Japan"
or "Occupied Japan" mark. Though there are
several variations to the pattern and border,
we have lumped them together since values
seem to be quite comparable. A word of caution to collectors, Phoenix Bird pattern is still
being produced.*

Bowl, 5" oval, Flying Turkey $10.00
Bowl, soup, 7¼" d., Flying Turkey . . 60.00
Bowl, 9" d., Phoenix Bird 26.00
Butter pat, Phoenix Bird 8.50
Celery tray, Phoenix Bird, marked
"Made in Japan" 20.00
Chamberstick w/ring handle,
Phoenix Bird 150.00

Chocolate pot, cov., Phoenix Bird,
marked "Japan" 120.00
Coffee pot, cov., loop handle,
Phoenix Bird, marked "Japan,"
7"h. 65.00
Creamer, Phoenix Bird, marked
"Made in Japan," 2½" h. 11.00
Creamer, Flying Turkey, marked
"Japan" 14.00
Cup & saucer, demitasse, Phoenix
Bird 13.00
Cup & saucer, Phoenix Bird, marked
"Occupied Japan" 15.00
Custard cup, Phoenix Bird, marked
"Made in Japan" 8.00
Egg cup, Phoenix Bird, large 13.00
Ginger jar, cov., Phoenix Bird,
5" h. 30.00
Ladle, Phoenix Bird, marked
"Noritake" 35.00
Pitcher, buttermilk, 6" h., Phoenix
Bird, marked "Japan" 45.00
Plate, 8½" d., Flying Turkey,
marked "Noritake" 20.00
Plate, dinner, 9¼" d., Phoenix Bird,
marked "Made in Japan" 30.00
Rice bowl, cov., Phoenix Bird,
marked "Nippon," 6" h. 90.00
Salt shaker, Phoenix Bird, marked
"Made in Japan" 10.00
Salt & pepper shakers, Flying
Turkey, pr. 25.00
Soup plate w/flange rim, Phoenix
Bird 10.00
Sugar bowl, cov., Phoenix Bird,
3½" h. (ILLUS.) 20.00

Phoenix Bird Teapot

Teapot, cov., Phoenix Bird, marked
"Japan," 4½" h. (ILLUS.) 45.00
Teapot, cov., Phoenix Bird, marked
"Noritake" 65.00
Tea tile, Flying Turkey 20.00
Vegetable bowl, open, Phoenix Bird,
marked "Japan," 10" oval 30.00

PICKARD

*Pickard, Inc., making fine hand-decorated
china today in Antioch, Ill., was founded in*

Chicago in 1894 by Wilder A. Pickard. The company now makes its own blanks but once bought them from other potteries, primarily from the Havilands and others in Limoges, France. Also see COMMEMORATIVE PLATES.

Bowl, 7½" d., ornate gold rim, h.p. oranges decor, Bavarian blank, 1894-1904 . . . . $250.00

Bowl, cov., 9" d., fruit decor, ornate gold trim, artist-signed 350.00

Bowl, 9" d., roses & fleur-de-lis decor, Haviland blank 95.00

Bowl, 9" d., h.p. strawberries on shaded ground, ornate gold trim, 1898 . . . . 225.00

Bowl, 10" d., h.p. large red Art Nouveau style poppies on gold ground 160.00

Bowl, 10" d., center reserve w/"still life" fruit on gold ground, black border w/enameled florals, signed Yeschek 255.00

Pickard Fruit Bowl

Bowl, fruit, 12½" w. across handles, 4½" h., gold w/wide cobalt blue borders filled w/purple grapes, fruits & flowers, artist-signed, 1912-19 mark (ILLUS.) 425.00

Cake plate, open handles, peacock decor, heavy gold trim, artist-signed 150.00

Candy dish, handled, 2-part, overall gold-etched florals, 6¼" l. 45.00

Creamer & open sugar bowl, Aura Argenta Linear patt., artist-signed, pr. 85.00

Creamer & open sugar bowl, gold handles & rims, colorful florals, foliage & trailing ivy decor, Limoges blank, 1905, pr. 65.00

Demitasse pot, cov., poinsettias & ornate gold trim on pearlized ground, artist-signed & dated 1905, 7½" h. 245.00

Dish, pierced handles, green center w/gold floral tracery & 4 floral sprays, profuse gold edge, artist-signed, 13½" l. 95.00

Ewer, tri-pour spout, bulbous body, deep sea green matte ground w/heavy gold at spout, handle &

neck & gold blueberries & leaves on body, artist-signed, 6½" h. 325.00

Marmalade jar & cover w/gilt ribbon finial, ornate gilt handles & scalloped gilt rim, orange water lilies & green lily pads outlined in gold on cream ground, artist-signed, 1898 mark 165.00

Mustard jar, cover & attached underplate, oval, h.p. Art Nouveau gold, black & green design, Nippon blank 85.00

Pitcher, 7¼" h., 6" widest d., h.p. orange & gold grapes & green & brown leaves on cream ground shading to yellow & green, heavy gold trim, artist-signed, 1905-10 . . 195.00

Pitcher, 8" h., Aura Argenta Linear patt., artist-signed 295.00

Pitcher, 9½" h., bulbous, wide gold border & handle, red currants & green leaves decor, artist-signed 245.00

Pitcher, cider, cherry clusters & heavy gold decor, artist-signed . . . 395.00

Pitcher, cider, Italian Garden patt., signed E. Challinor 425.00

Pitcher, cider, orange & gold stylized tulips w/green & gold leaves, turquoise, yellow & gold trim, artist-signed 265.00

Plate, 8½" d., h.p. birds (3) w/encrusted gold decor 60.00

Plate, 8½" d., h.p. orange poppies 65.00

Plate, 8½" d., Italian Garden patt., signed E. Challinor, 1912 . . . . 135.00

Plate, 8½" d., nuts decor, heavy gold border, artist-signed, 1905-10 . . . . 65.00

Plate, 8¾" d., scalloped gold rim, h.p. violets 65.00

Plate, 9" d., gold scalloped rim, h.p. gooseberries on tinted ground, 1895 mark 140.00

Plate, 10" d., scenic decor, gold-etched border, signed Marker 150.00

Punch set: punch bowl & 10 matching cups; currants, shaded leaves & wide gold borders interior & exterior decor, signed M. Rosti Leroy, 11 pcs. 1,250.00

Rum jug w/original stopper, h.p. Indian corn decor, 7½" h. 265.00

Sugar bowl, cov., 2-handled, gold-etched overall 27.50

Sugar shaker, long-stemmed violets decor, coin gold top, artist-signed, 1910 . . . . 195.00

Tea set: cov. teapot, creamer & sugar bowl; h.p. gold & silver Art Nouveau style decor on creamy ivory ground, Limoges blank, 3 pcs. 285.00

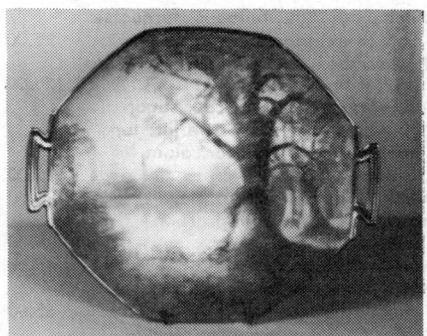

Tray by E. Challinor

Tray, octagonal, angular gold handles, lake scene w/lone tree in
foreground, signed E. Challinor,
14" w. (ILLUS.) 385.00

Vase, 4½" h., lavender dogwood-
type blossoms on cream ground,
heavy gold trim, artist-signed,
1905 .... 110.00

Vase, 5¼" h., lake scene w/two tall
trees, Nippon blank, signed E.
Challinor 345.00

Vase, 6" h., Art Deco violets on
gold, green & black ground 55.00

Vase, 7" h., band of red roses on
gold "brocade" ground, signed E.
Challinor, 1919-22 .... 295.00

Vase, 8" h., scene of sailboats on a
brilliant blue sea against the setting sun within a border of pink &
red roses, artist-signed,
1898-1904 .... 295.00

Vase, 8" h., peacock overlooking
lake scene, Nippon blank, signed
E. Challinor 450.00

Vase, 10" h., baluster-shaped, gold-
etched overall, 1920 .... 75.00

Vase, 10½" h., palm trees & water
scene, signed E. Challinor, 1912-19
mark 300.00

Vase, 12" h., 4½" w., peacock in a
lush garden scene, signed E. Challinor, Limoges blank 495.00

Vase, 13" h., roses decor, heavy
gold trim, artist-signed 285.00

PICTORIAL SOUVENIRS

*These small ceramic wares, expressly made
to be sold as a souvenir of a town or resort,
are decorated with a pictorial scene which is
usually titled. Made in profusion in Germany, Austria, Bavaria, and England, they were
distributed by several American firms including C.E. Wheelock & Co., John H. Roth (Jonroth), Jones, McDuffee & Co., Stratton Co.,
and others. Because people seldom traveled
in the early years of this century, a small souvenir tray or dish, picturing the resort or a
town scene, afforded an excellent, inexpensive
gift for family or friends when returning from
a vacation trip. Seldom used and carefully
packed away later, there is an abundant supply of these small wares available today at
moderate prices. Their values are likely to
rise.*

Ash tray, "South Station, Boston,
Massachusetts" scene, crimped
edges $25.00

Celery tray, "Capitol Building,
Washington, D.C." scene, marked
"Nippon" 50.00

Creamer, "Brooklyn, New York"
scene on pink lustre ground, gold
lettering, marked "Germany" 15.00

Creamer, "Courthouse, Winner,
South Dakota" scene, 3" h....... 12.50

Creamer, "Freeport, Illinois" scene
on pearlized ground, pink handle
& shell feet, marked "Germany" .. 29.00

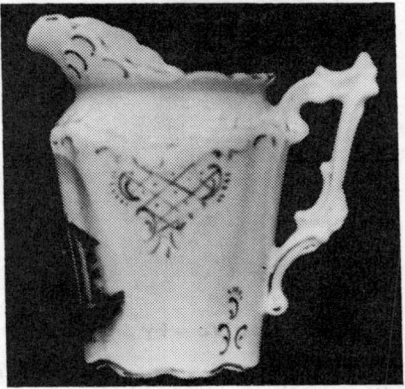

Pictorial Souvenir Creamer

Creamer, "Public School, Savanna,
Ill." scene & gilt highlights on
white, marked "Wheelock - Made
in Germany for H.E. Sipes, Savanna, Ill. - Dresden" on bottom,
4" h. (ILLUS.) 30.00

Cup & saucer, "Iowa State Capitol"
scene on white, gold trim 19.00

Mug, "Public Library, Cedar Rapids,
Iowa" scene, cobalt blue ground,
marked "Germany," 2½" h....... 22.00

Mug, "Coles County Court House,
Charleston, Illinois" scene,
marked "Wheelock" 14.00

Mug, "Watch Works, Elgin, Illinois"
scene on white, gold trim 15.00

Pitcher, 7" h., "Erie Canal" scene,
cobalt blue ground ......100.00 to 125.00

Plate, 8" d., "Courthouse, Spokane,
Washington" scene, marked
"Made in Germany" 25.00
Plate, 8" d., "Monroe St. Bridge,
Spokane, Washington" scene,
marked "Made in Germany" 25.00
Plate, "Arlington Hotel, Hot Springs,
Arkansas" scene, flow blue trans-
fer, marked "Wheelock" 20.00
Plate, "Williamsburg, Virginia"
vignette, floral border, marked
"Jonroth" 25.00
Plate, "St. Mary's Academy, Nau-
voo, Illinois" scene, marked
"Wheelock" 16.00
Whimsey, model of a lady's shoe,
"Courthouse, Freeport, Illinois"
scene, marked "Germany" 15.00

PISGAH FOREST

Pisgah Forest Vase by Stephen

Walter Stephen experimented with making pottery shortly after 1900 with his parents in Tennessee. After their deaths, in 1910, he eventually moved to the foot of Mt. Pisgah in North Carolina where he became a partner of C. P. Ryman. Together they built a kiln and a shop but this partnership was dissolved in 1916. During 1920, Stephen again began to experiment with pottery and, by 1926, had his own pottery and equipment. Pieces are usually marked and may also be signed "W. Stephen" and dated. Walter Stephen died in 1961 but work at the pottery still continued, although on a part-time basis.

Bowl-vase, turquoise glaze, signed
"Stephen - 1937," 4½" h. $36.00
Creamer, amethyst crackle glaze ... 27.50
Creamer & sugar bowl, maroon
glaze, pr...................... 40.00
Pitcher, 4" h., blue glaze, dated
1931 .... 35.00

Pitcher, 8½" h., bulbous, turquoise
glaze exterior, pink interior 25.00
Powder box, cov., cameo-like white
relief on sky blue 150.00
Tea set: cov. teapot, cov. sugar
bowl, creamer & waste jar; turquoise glaze exterior, plum
interior, 4 pcs. 125.00
Vase, 3¼" h., maroon glaze 22.00
Vase, 5½" h., mottled green
glaze 28.00
Vase, 6" h., 2-handled, blue glaze .. 45.00
Vase, 6" h., 2-handled, turquoise
shaded to deep plum glaze 65.00
Vase, 6¼" h., turquoise crackle
glaze exterior, pink interior,
signed "Stephen - 1940" 125.00
Vase, 6½" h., rich wine glaze,
signed "Stephen - 1937" (ILLUS.) .. 70.00
Vase, 6½" h., green glaze exterior,
rose interior, dated 1938 .... 24.50
Vase, 9" h., turquoise glaze, dated
1940 .... 60.00

PRATT WARES

Pratt Jug

The earliest ware now classified as Pratt wares was made by Felix Pratt at his pottery in Fenton, England from about 1810. He made earthenware with bright glazes, relief sporting jugs, toby mugs and commercial pots and jars whose lids bore multicolored transfer prints. The F. & R. Pratt mark is mid-19th century. The name Pratt ware is also applied today to mid and late 19th century English ware of the same general type as that made by Felix Pratt.

Character jug, 2-sided, bust of Bacchus, ca. 1790, 9" h............$225.00
Compote, 9½" d., 5¼" h., gold
borders, color-printed "Spanish
Dancers" scene on glossy
ground 245.00

Figure of "Hope," ca. 1800, 7" h. ... 115.00

Figure of the "Woman of Samaria,"
1850, 7" h. 110.00

Figure of the "Widow of Zarapeth,"
1810, 10" h. 115.00

Figure group, Napoleon III, Princess
Eugenie & the Prince, 1856,
8" h. 135.00

Figure group, Prince & Princess of
Wales, 8" h. 125.00

Mug, 2 color-printed scenes
reserved on maroon ground,
4¼" h. 135.00

Mug, color-printed "Fury" railroad
scene, ca. 1850 .... 115.00

Pitcher, 7¾" h., jug-type, relief-
molded oval panels of peacocks in
landscapes enriched in blue,
brown, green & ochre, vine border above & acanthus-leaf & bell-
flowers below, ca. 1790 (ILLUS.) .. 550.00

Pitcher, 7¾" h., jug-type, relief-
molded & h.p. peacock reserved
in roundel, vine border above &
acanthus-leaf border below,
ca. 1790 .... 250.00

Pitcher, 8" h., relief-molded & painted w/two boys playing cards on
sides, ca. 1820 .... 125.00

Plaque, relief-molded w/bird
perched on cherry tree branch
highlighted w/brown, ochre &
green, ca. 1775, 5¾" d. 528.00

Plate, 7" d., color-printed center
scene of 18th century gentleman
reading newspaper captioned
"The Times," typical gold, black &
plum border 95.00

Plate, 9" d., color-printed scene of
"Haddon Hall" center, green,
brown & gold gadroon
border ....65.00 to 95.00

Plate, color-printed center scene of
2 inebriated souls toasting, "The
Queen - God Bless Her," typical
border 65.00

QUIMPER

*This French earthenware pottery has been
made in France since the end of the 17th century and is still in production today. Because
the colorful decoration on this ware, predomi-
nently of Breton peasant figures, is all hand
painted and each piece is unique, it has become increasingly popular with collectors in
recent years. Most pieces offered today date
from about the mid-19th century to the
present. Modern potteries continue to operate today and contemporary examples are
available in gift shops.*

Ash tray, Breton peasant man
decor, Henriot Quimper, after
1922 .... $35.00

Barber's bowl, rooster decor, H. B.
Quimper, 12 x 8" 375.00

Bowl, 9½" d., peasant man decor,
H. B. Quimper 110.00

Butter pot & cover w/rooster on lid,
latticework, crosshatching & circle
designs, Henriot Quimper, after
1922, 4" h. 175.00

Cheese dish, cov., H.B.
Quimper ....165.00 to 185.00

Chocolate pot, cov., double-ring
handle, straight short spout, fleur-
de-lis decor, H.B. Quimper, early
20th c. 160.00

Christmas plate, 1981, Breton peasant couple beside Christmas tree,
"Noel" at top, 9" d. ....35.00 to 40.00

Henriot Quimper Cup Plate

Cup plate, peasant woman decor,
Henriot Quimper, after 1922, 4" d.
(ILLUS.)....................... 22.00

Cups & saucers, bulbous cups
w/thick handles, peasant boy on
one & peasant girl other, florals
on saucer, pink clay shows
through glaze, Henriot Quimper,
pr.......................... 125.00

Custard cup, peasant man decor,
H.B. Quimper 25.00

Dish, red & yellow-orange floral decor on deep muted green, Henriot
Quimper, 5½" d............... 45.00

Figure of a fisherman w/net on
shoulders, 4½" h.............. 155.00

Figure of small child seated, signed
"Savigny," H.B. Quimper 225.00

Figure of Ste. Vierge w/Infant, H.B.
Quimper 175.00

Figure group, dancing peasant couple, signed "Micheau Vernez,"
Henriot Quimper, 13" h. 190.00

Inkwell, cov., square, peasant man
playing horn, blue dashes at margins, Henriot Quimper (ILLUS.) ... 175.00

Quimper Inkwell

Knife rest, peasant decor, H.B.
  Quimper 37.50
Pitcher, 6½" h., peasant man lean-
  ing on fence decor, 19th c........ 550.00
Pitcher, 7½" h., crimped spout,
  peasant woman decor, Henriot
  Quimper 185.00

Figural Pitcher

Pitcher, figural old woman w/hands
  in apron pockets, coif forms spout
  & ribbons form handle, predomi-
  nently maroon & blue, C. Maillard
  (ILLUS.)....................... 250.00
Planter, corner hanging-type,
  w/liner, coat-of-arms decor,
  Porquier-Beau, 1872-1913, 16" h... 775.00
Plaque, bagpipe form, peasant man
  decor, Henriot Quimper.......... 135.00
Plaques, scalloped rims, peasant
  man on one & peasant woman on
  other, w/ring on top to hang,
  Henriot Quimper, 4½" d., pr. 125.00
Plate, 6" d., floral decor, Henriot
  Quimper 20.00
Plate, 7" d., pale orange & blue
  florals & rings of orange & blue,
  Henriot Quimper 45.00

Plate, 9" d., peasant man decor,
  signed "H.B. Quimper" on front
  only 75.00
Plate, 9½" d., peasant woman
  decor on celadon green ground,
  "a la touche" border, H. B.
  Quimper 48.00
Plate, 9¾" d., yellow & blue concentric bands at border, peasant
  woman decor center, Henriot
  Quimper 95.00
Plate, 10" d., bird decor, Henriot
  Quimper 125.00
Powder jar, cov., Breton peasant
  man decor, H. R. Quimper 210.00
Relish, fluted rim, peasant girl decor, yellow ground, H.B. Quimper,
  9¾" l. 110.00
Salt dip, double, model of Dutch
  wooden shoes, Henriot Quimper.. 55.00
Salt dip, double, peasant man &
  woman decor, H. B. Quimper,
  1883-1910..................... 60.00
Vase, 8" h., corset-shaped, Breton
  peasant woman decor, H. R.
  Quimper 295.00
Wall pocket, peasant woman w/dis-
  taff, 4" d., 10½" h.............. 225.00

REDWARE

Redware Jar

Red earthenware pottery was made in the
American colonies from the late 1600's.
Bowls, crocks and all types of utilitarian
wares were turned out in great abundance to
supplement the pewter and handmade treenware. The ready availability of the clay, the
same used in making bricks and roof tiles, ac-
counted for the vast production. The lead-
glazed redware retained its reddish color,
though a variety of colors could be obtained
by adding various metals to the glaze. Interesting effects occurred accidentally
through unsuspected impurities in the clay
or uneven temperatures in the firing kiln

which sometimes resulted in streaks or mottled splotches. Also see FOOD MOLDS and SLIPWARE.

Apple butter jar, semi-ovoid w/handle, clear glaze w/brown splotches, 5 7/8" h. (minor rim glaze chips)....................$235.00

Bowl, 8¼" d., 3" h., clear interior glaze w/brown splotches around sides & in center 185.00

Creamer & cover w/knob finial, bulbous bottom, applied strap handle, running brown glaze w/yellow & white splotches, 4" h. plus lid (minor chips & edge wear) 100.00

Cup, ridged band, mottled yellow & brown glaze, early 19th c. 85.00

Cuspidor, lady's, handled, scrolls in relief, clear lead glaze 125.00

Flask, rust glaze w/manganese splotches, 18th cent............. 240.00

Flower pot w/attached saucer, scalloped top, brown speckling & splotches on rust & cream glaze, 5¾" d., 7" h. 175.00

Jar, semi-ovoid w/shaped rim, green glaze w/orange splotches, 7¼" h. (ILLUS.) 205.00

Jar, ovoid, earred handles, incised straight & wavy lines at shoulder, green glaze w/orange splotches, 9½" h. (old chips & short hairlines)...................... 425.00

Jug, ovoid, applied large strap handle, greenish glaze, 5 5/8" h. (flake on edge of base) 220.00

Jug, ovoid, applied well-shaped loop handle, black-speckled metallic glaze, 6 3/8" h. 110.00

Match holder, wall-type, model of an acorn w/striker, original paint, 4½" d. 130.00

Model of a lion in recumbent position on rectangular base, tooled details, inscribed "L.E. Sr. 8-16-52," unglazed, 8½" l. (small edge flakes) 170.00

Model of a rooster on square base w/canted sides, white slip w/amber glaze, painted red comb, 5" h. (paint flaking on comb) 210.00

Pitcher, 2¼" h., clear glaze (rim chips) 95.00

Pitcher, 9" h., ovoid body w/high flaring lip, applied mask below spout, incised American eagle w/shield & banner inscribed "E. Pluribus Unum" each side, deep green running glaze, attributed to Virginia (kiln adhesions on base & lip) 650.00

Pitcher, 9" h., ovoid body w/flared mouth, applied strap handle, clear

lead glaze w/splotches of brown & green & splashes of yellow slip (small edge chips)............... 475.00

Preserving jar, 2 bands of incised line decoration, mottled greenish glaze w/yellow slip & brown designs, Pennsylvania, 7" h. (some wear & chips).................. 305.00

Preserving jar, straight sides, collared neck, greenish glaze w/orange spots & brown stripes, 7¾" h. (old edge chips).......... 215.00

Preserving jar, ovoid, tooled lines at base & neck, deep green glaze, 10" h. (old base chip)........... 175.00

RED WING

Red Wing Spongeware Bowl

Various potteries operated in Red Wing, Minnesota, from 1868, the most successful being the Red Wing Stoneware Co., organized in 1878. Merged with other local potteries through the years, it became known as Red Wing Union Stoneware Co. in 1894, and was one of the largest producers of utilitarian stoneware items in the United States. After a decline in the popularity of stoneware products, an art pottery line was introduced to compensate the loss and this was reflected in a new name for the company, Red Wing Potteries, Inc., in 1930. Stoneware production ceased entirely in 1947, but vases, planters, cookie jars and dinnerwares of art pottery quality continued in production until 1967 when the pottery ceased operations altogether.

Applesauce (self-sealing fruit) jar, stoneware, w/Weir patent "ball" lever lock closure for lid & wire bail handle w/wooden grip, 3-gal. $137.50

Ash tray, wing-shaped, signed "Red Wing Pottery - 75th - 1878-53" on bottom, red glaze 22.00

Basket, art pottery line, green glaze interior, white exterior, 10" l. 35.00

Batter bowl w/pouring lip at rim & wire bail handle w/wooden grip,

Grey Line stoneware w/Sponge-
band decor 300.00

Beater jar, grey stoneware w/cobalt
blue "Eggs, Cream, Salad Dressing" on front & advertising
reverse 85.00

Beater jar, Grey Line stoneware
w/Spongeband decor 98.00

Bowl, 5½" d., turned-in rim,
Brushed Ware, designs in relief,
green stain on tan stoneware 40.00

Bowl, 6" d., paneled sides, spongeware, blue & rust daubing on grey
stoneware 52.50

Bowl, 7½" d., Saffronware, blue &
rust daubing on yellow 55.00

Bowl, 8" d., Greek Key patt., stoneware, dull blue fading to grey,
w/advertising center ...... 65.00 to 85.00

Bowl, 8" d., Grey Line stoneware
w/Spongeband decor 75.00

Bowl, 8" d., spongeware, blue &
rust daubing on grey stoneware,
w/Minnesota advertising center .. 75.00

Bowl, 9" d., paneled sides, spongeware, blue & rust daubing on grey
stoneware (ILLUS.) .... 60.00 to 80.00

Bowl, 10" d., Grape Lattice patt.,
Saffronware 70.00

Bowl, 10" d., Greek Key patt.,
stoneware, light blue around top
fading to grey 55.00

Bowl, 12" d., stoneware, white
w/two blue pinstripes at rim 45.00

Box, cov., art pottery line, green
glaze, 6½ x 4" 47.50

Butter churn, white glaze stoneware, large (4") red wing decal
signature, complete w/lid,
5-gal. .... 150.00 to 175.00

Butter churn, semi-ovoid, earred
handles, salt-glazed stoneware,
cobalt blue slip-quilled leaf & "6,"
impressed "Red Wing Stoneware
Co." signature, complete w/lid,
6-gal. 575.00

Butter crock, cov., "North Star" Pottery signature on base, 2-lb. 275.00

Butter crock & cover w/flat knob,
rolled rim, spongeware, blue &
rust daubing on tan stoneware ... 395.00

"Cap" bowl w/lid, spongeware, blue
& rust daubing on grey stoneware, 7" d. 85.00

Casserole, cov., Grey Line
w/Spongeband decor, 1½ qt. 140.00

Console set: large bowl & pr. candlesticks; art pottery line, mauve
& tan glaze, 3 pcs. 32.50

Cookie jar, cov., barrel-shaped,
Grey Line w/Spongeband decor .. 125.00

Cookie jar, cov., Saffronware,
"Cookies" on front, 9¼" d.,
8½" h. 75.00

French Chef Cookie Jar

Cookie jar, cov., art pottery line,
figural French Chef, blue glaze
(ILLUS.) 38.00

Cookie jar, cov., art pottery line,
figural Katrina (Dutch Girl), yellow glaze 32.50

Cookie jar, cov., art pottery line,
figural Monk, "Thou Shalt Not
Steal" 32.50

Crock, straight sides, salt-glazed
stoneware, cobalt blue slip-quilled
"Double P" & "2," embossed "Minnesota Stoneware Co." on base,
2-gal. 52.50

Crock, straight sides, stoneware,
large (4") red wing decal signature, 2-gal. 40.00

Crock, straight sides, salt-glazed
stoneware, cobalt blue slip-quilled
birch leaf & "2," 2-gal. 55.00

Crock, straight sides, salt-glazed
stoneware, cobalt blue slip-quilled
"Lazy 8" & "4," impress "Red Wing
Union Stoneware" on bottom, 4-
gal. 175.00

Crock, straight sides, salt-glazed
stoneware, cobalt blue slip-quilled
"butterfly" & "20," impressed "Red
Wing Stoneware Co." on side,
20-gal. 300.00

Fruit jar w/screw-on zinc lid, "Stone
Mason Fruit Jar, Union Stoneware
Co., Red Wing, Minn." printed in
black on stoneware, qt. 85.00

Fruit jar w/screw-on zinc lid, "Stone
Mason Fruit Jar, Union Stoneware
Co., Red Wing, Minn." printed
in black on stoneware,
half-gal. .... 100.00 to 125.00

Hot water bottle w/stopper, triangular, brown glaze, 1920's 70.00

Jug, standard shoulder, white-glaze
stoneware, signed "Minnesota
Stoneware Co." on bottom, short,
1 qt. 120.00

Jug, beehive shape, brown glaze,
signed "Minnesota Stoneware
Co." on bottom, half-gal. 45.00

Red Wing Liquor Jug

Jug, standard shoulder, white-
glazed stoneware, advertising
"John Baum, Wholesale Liquors,
Stillings, Mo.," half-gal. (ILLUS.) . . 100.00
Jug, standard shoulder, white-
glazed stoneware, signed "Minnesota Stoneware Co." on bottom,
1-gal. . . . . .35.00 to 40.00
Jug, wide mouth, brown glaze,
signed "Minnesota Stoneware
Co." on bottom, 1-gal. 60.00
Jug, brown-glazed standard shoul-
der, red "wing" decal on grey bot-
tom, 2-gal.   285.00
Jug, beehive shape, white glaze,
red "wing" decal & oval "Red
Wing Union Stoneware Co." mark,
3-gal. 165.00
Jug, standard shoulder, white glaze,
large red "wing" & oval "Red
Wing Union Stoneware Co." mark,
5-gal. 45.00
Jug, beehive shape, white glaze,
large red "wing" decal & oval
"Red Wing Union Stoneware Co."
mark, 5-gal. 165.00
Juice reamer, Grey Line stoneware
w/spongeband decor 425.00
"Koverwate" (crock cover-weight
designed to hold pickles under
brine), 5-gal. (crock) size 95.00
"Koverwate" (crock cover-weight
designed to hold pickles under
brine), 10-gal. (crock)
size. . . . . .85.00 to 100.00
Milk pan, Albany slip glaze, "North
Star" on bottom 50.00
Mixing bowls, spongeware, blue &
russet red daubing on tan, 6", 8"
& 10" d., set of 3. . . . .   255.00
Model of a badger on football,
stump base, signed "Red Wing
Potteries" & dated 1939 . . . .   100.00

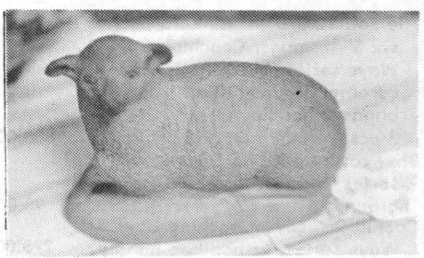

Red Wing "lunch hour" Piece

Model of a sheep, lunch hour piece
(ILLUS.). 165.00
Mug, brushed ware, green stain on
tan, "Red Wing Union Stoneware
Co." 27.50
Pantry jar w/original lid, Grey Line
stoneware w/blue stripes & red
"wing" decal, 1-lb. . . . . . .125.00 to 160.00
Pitcher, 8" h., Grey Line stoneware
w/spongeband decor, w/Iowa
advertising 145.00
Pitcher, 8" h., Saffron ware, w/Min-
nesota advertising . . . . .75.00 to 90.00
Pitcher (so-called Russian milk pitch-
er without pouring spout), brown
glaze, 1-gal. 65.00
Poultry feeder (or waterer),
stoneware, "KoRec Feeder,"
half-gal. . . . . .45.00 to 50.00
Toothpick holder, model of a gopher
on a log, signed "Red Wing Pot-
teries" & dated . . . . .100.00 to 125.00
Vase, 11" h. lion in low relief, tan
shaded to grey. 95.00
Vase, 12" h., brushed ware, flamin-
goes & cattails in low relief,
green stain on tan, Red Wing Un-
ion Stoneware Co. 55.00
Water cooler, cov., white glaze
stoneware, blue bands & "Water
Cooler" w/red "wing" decal, origi-
nal spigot, 5-gal. . . . . .200.00 to 250.00

RIDGWAY

*There were numerous Ridgways among
English potters. The firm J. & W. Ridgway
operated in Shelton from 1814 to 1930 and
produced many pieces with scenes of historical interest. William Ridgway operated in
Shelton from 1830 to 1865. Most wares
marked Ridgway that have been offered in
this country were made by one of these two
firms, or by Ridgway Potteries, Ltd., still in
operation. Also see FLOW BLUE and
HISTORICAL & COMMEMORATIVE
CHINA.*

Ale set: 12 3/8" h. tankard pitcher &
six 5" h. mugs; Coaching Days &
Ways series, black transfer on
caramel ground, silver lustre top
bands & handles,
7 pcs. . . . . $275.00 to 300.00

Box, cov., Coaching Days & Ways
series, black transfer on caramel
ground, 5½ x 4¼", 2¼" h. 95.00

Cookie jar, cov., Coaching Days &
Ways series, w/bamboo handle . . . 225.00

Cup & saucer, Coaching Days &
Ways series - "Walking up the
Hill," black transfer of stagecoach
on caramel 45.00

Dessert set: 13½" w. 2-handled
compote, two 2-handled square
dishes & 2 leaf-shaped dishes;
each painted & printed in colors
w/floral specimens within foliate-
molded borders enriched in turquoise & pale yellow & outlined in
gilding, ca. 1810, 5 pcs. 495.00

Mug, Coaching Days & Ways series -
"Pony Express," black transfer of
2 horses & rider on caramel, sil-
ver lustre rim, 5" h. 55.00

Pitcher, tankard, 9¼" h., Coaching
Days & Ways series, black transfer on caramel ground, silver lus-
tre handle 110.00

Pitcher, tankard, 12½" h., Coaching
Days & Ways series, silver lustre
handle & rim, ca. 1900 . . . . 160.00

Plaque, pierced to hang, Coaching
Days & Ways series - "Taking up
the Mails," black transfer on yellow ground, silver lustre edge,
12" d. 100.00

Plate, 7¾" d., Coaching Days &
Ways series - "Charles Recognized," black transfer on caramel,
silver lustre rim 45.00

Plate, 9" d., Coaching Days & Ways
series - "Paying the Toll," silver
lustre border 27.00

Plate, chop, 13½" d., Coaching Days
& Ways series - "In A Snow Drift,"
black transfer on brown, dated
Nov. 1905 . . . . 125.00

Tea caddy, Coaching Days & Ways
series, square w/round cover,
black transfer scenes on all sides,
4" sq., 5¾" h. 150.00

Teapot, cov., Coaching Days & Ways
series, black transfer on caramel
ground, silver lustre trim, 5" d.,
5¼" h. 95.00

Tray, Coaching Days & Ways series -
"A Christmas Visitor," black transfer on caramel ground, scalloped
silver lustre rim, 12½" d. 100.00

Tumbler, Coaching Days & Ways se-
ries, silver lustre trim, 4" h. 27.50

ROCKINGHAM

Rockingham "Butterfly" Box

*An earthenware pottery was first estab-
lished on the estate of the Marquis of Rockingham in England's Yorkshire district about
1745 and occupied by a succession of potters.
The famous Rockingham glaze of mottled
brown, somewhat resembling tortoise shell,
was introduced about 1788 by the Brameld
Brothers, and was well received. During the
1820's, porcelain manufacture was added to
the production and fine quality china was
turned out until the pottery closed in 1842.
The popular Rockingham glaze was subsequently produced elsewhere, including Bennington, Vt., and at numerous other U.S.
potteries. We list herein not only wares
produced at the Rockingham potteries in
England, but also items from other potteries
with the Rockingham glaze. Also see TOBY
MUGS & JUGS.*

Bean pot, cov., ribbed, mottled
brown glaze, 7" d. $85.00

Bedpan, mottled brown
glaze . . . . 45.00 to 60.00

Bowl, 5¼" d., 2 5/8" h., canted
sides, flaring rim, mottled brown
glaze 50.00

Bowl, 5¾" d., 3¼" h., canted sides
w/panels, mottled brown glaze . . . 80.00

Bowl, 8" d., 2" h., canted sides,
mottled brown glaze 55.00

Box, cov., butterfly-shaped, porcelain, painted iron-red, beige,
yellow, blue & brown & enriched
in gilding, ca. 1820, 2½" w.
(ILLUS.) 1,760.00

Creamer, paneled sides, mottled
brown glaze, 5" h. 40.00

Cuspidor, mottled brown glaze 65.00

Cuspidor, shell-molded top, mottled
brown glaze 125.00

Dish, fluted sides, mottled brown
glaze, 5" d. 40.00

Dish, deeply ribbed sides, mottled
brown glaze, 8" d. 265.00

Dish, scalloped edge, mottled brown
glaze, 11 x 9" oblong (some sur-
face wear) 115.00

Mixing bowl, mottled brown & yellow glaze, 10" d.,
5½" h. . . . . 70.00 to 110.00

Model of a dog in seated position, well-detailed tooling on feet & tail, free-standing front legs, high base, mottled brown glaze, 10" h. (minor base chips from kiln adhesion) 175.00

Mug, strap handle, paneled sides, mottled brown glaze, 4" h........ 65.00

Pie plate, mottled brown glaze, 9" d.....................85.00 to 105.00

Pie plate, mottled brown glaze, 10½" d., 1¼" h. ....80.00 to 95.00

Pie plate, mottled brown glaze, 11¾" d., 1 3/8" h. 125.00

Pitcher, 5½" h., bulbous base, mottled brown glaze 75.00

Pitcher, 7" h., tulips in relief at sides, mottled brown glaze 150.00

Pitcher, tankard, 12 3/8" h., embossed floral beneath spout, mottled brown glaze 400.00

Pitcher, water, birds in swamp in relief at sides, mottled brown glaze 90.00

Rockingham Porcelain Plate

Plates, 9¼" d., porcelain, center w/h.p. royal arms & Order of St. George crest within gilt zig-zag & clover, thistle, rose & leek bands, pale blue border w/gilt honeycomb, acorn & oak leaf branches, printed puce griffin mark w/"Rockingham Works Brameld, Manufacturers to the King, Queen & Royal Family" & date 1832, set of 12 w/damage to three (ILLLUS. of one)................30,800.00

Platter, 14¾" octagon, mottled brown glaze 185.00

Pot, cov., w/side handle, embossed leaf on lid, mottled brown glaze, 6" d. 65.00

Salt box, cov., wall-type, half-round w/hanging tab in crest of back, embossed peacock & palm tree

design, mottled brown glaze, 6½" h. 135.00

Soap dish, pierced top & drain hole at side, mottled brown glaze, 7½ x 5½" oblong 65.00

Teapot, cov., Rebecca at Well patt., mottled brown glaze, 6½" h...... 45.00

Rebecca at Well Teapot

Teapot, cov., Rebecca at Well patt., mottled brown glaze, 8" h. (ILLUS.)..................... 125.00

Toby "barrel" bottle, end of barrel marked "2," mottled brown glaze, 9½" h. (small flake on base from kiln adhesion) 125.00

ROOKWOOD

Rookwood Bowl by Sara Sax

Considered America's foremost art pottery, the Rookwood Pottery Company was established in Cincinnati, Ohio in 1880, by Mrs. Maria Longworth Storer. To accurately record its development, each piece carried the Rookwood insignia, or mark, was dated, and, if individually decorated, was usually signed by the artist. The pottery remained in Cincinnati until 1959 when it was sold to Herschede Hall Clock Company and moved to Starkville, Mississippi, where it continued in operation until 1967. Also see TILES.

Ash tray, figure of a clown, 1929,
Sara Alice (Sallie) Toohey $95.00

Ash tray, figure of nude lady, maroon glaze, 1950 .... 75.00

Ash tray, fish-shaped, green matte
finish, 1937 .... 60.00

Bookends, figure of an Oriental lady
seated cross-legged, glossy turquoise glaze, ca. 1922, William
Purcell McDonald, 9" h., pr...... 357.50

Bookends, model of a panther,
green high glaze, 1951, pr........ 170.00

Bookends, model of a rook, green,
1922, pr. 185.00

Bowl, 4" h., black florals on burgundy ground interior, glossy black
exterior, 1920, Sara Sax
(ILLUS.)........................ 290.00

Bowl, 5" d., 3" h., deeply incised
floral decor, blue shaded to burgundy ground, 1908, Cecil A.
Duell........................... 135.00

Bowl, 5½" d., large pink blossoms
decor, yellow matte finish, 1928,
Margaret Helen McDonald 295.00

Bowl, 7" d., 3½" h., incised cerise
poppies & green leaves decor,
brown matte finish, 1905, Rose
Fechheimer 180.00

Bowl, 7" widest d., 5" h., bulbous,
pink, red & green floral decor,
Wax Matte glaze, 1927, Sara
Elizabeth (Sallie) Coyne 70.00

Bowl, 13 x 3½", deep cobalt blue
exterior, cobalt blue & green crystalline interior, high glaze, 1921 .. 110.00

Box, cov., bust of Art Deco style
lady & florals within medallion on
lid, lions & floral decor around
sides, 1927, 4 x 2¾" 195.00

Bust of an Art Deco lady, glossy
white glaze, 1921, 7½" w.,
8" h............................ 225.00

Candle holder, 3-light, white dogwood blossoms & green leaves
decor on cream ground, Vellum
glaze, Edith Noonan (1904-10),
8" h. (single) 210.00

Candle holder, curved handle, underglaze slip-painted floral decor,
standard glaze, 1892 (single) 250.00

Candlesticks, Grecian ladies (2) on
each side, glossy turquoise glaze,
1916, 10" h., pr. 150.00

Chocolate pot, cov., cylindrical
w/elongated spout, underglaze
slip-painted yellow florals, shaded
black-brown to yellow standard
glaze, 1891, Amelia Browne
Sprague 247.50

Chocolate pot, cov., underglaze slip-
painted berries & foliage decor,
standard glaze, 1890, Anna Marie
Valentien....................... 750.00

Creamer, pinched neck, incised holly berries & leaves decor, 1898,
Rose Fechheimer, 3" h. 340.00

Creamer, bulbous w/elongated
spout & loop handle, underglaze
slip-painted apple blossoms decor,
standard glaze, 1892, Kate C.
Matchette, 3¼" h. 192.50

Creamer & open sugar bowl, sailing
ships decor, 1886, pr............. 185.00

Ewer, underglaze slip-painted blue,
black & yellow flowers, standard
glaze, 1902, Marianne Mitchell,
7" h............................ 375.00

Ewer, trefoil top, underglaze slip-
painted clustered leaves & berries, standard glaze, 1900,
Elizabeth Neave Lincoln, 9¼" h. .. 465.00

Figure of Pan seated on turtle, turquoise glaze, 1921, 7 x 5"........ 125.00

Flower holder, model of a frog,
green glaze, 1927 .... 70.00

Rookwood Flower Holder

Flower holder, model of a Rook
above pierced tubes, shaded turquoise blue, 1928 (ILLUS.) 95.00

Flower pot, tulips in relief decor,
blue glaze, 1932 .... 35.00

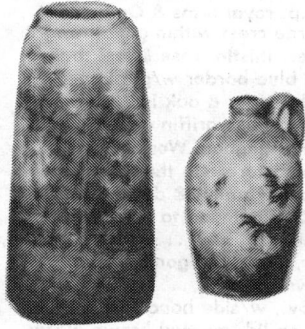

Rookwood Vase & Honey Jug

Honey jug, green feathering reeds &
butterfly decor, 1883, Albert

Robert Valentien, 4" h. (ILLUS. right) 300.00

Humidor, cov., olive green crystalline glaze, 6½" h............... 125.00

Mug, baluster-shaped, underglaze slip-painted portrait of Indian "Geronimo," standard glaze, 1899, Elizabeth Weldon Brain, 5¼" h. . .1,210.00

Mug, diagonally looped handle, underglaze slip-painted purple grapes decor, standard glaze, 1907, Caroline Steinle, 6" h....... 192.50

Paperweight, incised potter at the wheel, green matte finish, 1935, 3½" d........................... 170.00

Paperweight, figure of a nude lady, seated, white glaze, 1931, Louise Abel 225.00

Paperweight, model of an elephant, blue matte glaze, 1941 .... 75.00

Paperweight, model of an elephant & 2 clowns, blue glaze, 1922 ..... 125.00

Paperweight, model of an open book w/Harvard University logo, 1905 .... 95.00

Paperweight, model of a rooster, 5-color glaze, 1930, William Purcell McDonald, 5".......... 180.00

Pen tray, oblong, incised oak leaves, blue glaze, 1922 .... 45.00

Pitcher, 4¾" h., tri-corner spout, underglaze slip-painted golden leaves & blue berries, shaded green & brown standard glaze, 1896, Cora Crofton 365.00

Pitcher, water, 7" h., incised Arts & Crafts style designs, green matte finish, 1904 .... 195.00

Pitcher, 9" h., barrel-shaped, molded scene of boys drinking from mugs, "Cincinnati Cooperage Co.," blue glaze, raised Ribbon mark (1881-82) 500.00

Plaque, "Birches at Twilight," by Charles Schmidt (1896-1927), 8 × 5" tile w/original frame, backing & labels 1,650.00

Rookwood Scenic Plaque

Plaque, underglaze slip-painted scene of country stream & trees in deeply shaded blues & greens w/shaded pink sky, 1916, Elizabeth McDermott, 8¼ × 6¼" (ILLUS.) 1,100.00

Plaque, "Early Shadows," Vellum glaze, Frederick Rothenbusch (1896-1931), 14½ × 9¼" 2,800.00

Potpourri (rose petal) jar, cov., red clay body incised w/butterflies & foliage, tan to reddish brown glaze w/swirls of white, gold-flecked lid, 1885, Matthew Andrew Daly, 6¾" h. 650.00

Rose bowl, molded berry sprays decor, Vellum glaze, 1930, 2¾" top d., 6½" h. 70.00

Vase, 5" h., 2-handled, underglaze slip-painted florals, standard brown glaze, 1890, Artus Van Briggle 675.00

Vase, 5" h., ovoid, floral & foliate swag around shoulder, Vellum glaze, 1922, Lenore Asbury 150.00

Vase, 5" h., pentagonal, blurred floral decor in shades of blue & green, Wax Matte glaze, 1930, Lorinda Epply 115.00

Vase, 5" h., purplish matte glaze w/multicolored swirls at top, 1918, Elizabeth Neave Lincoln 190.00

Vase, 5" h., underglaze slip-painted florals, standard brown glaze, 1905, Edith Noonan.............. 195.00

Vase, 5¼" h., underglaze slip-painted daisies decor, standard brown glaze, 1900, Edward T. Hurley 295.00

Vase, 5½" h., fat straight-sided cylinder, pink band of yellow-centered white daisies & green leaves at shoulder, Vellum glaze, 1915, Mary G. Denzler 1,650.00

Vase, 6" h., expanding cylinder, underglaze slip-painted stylized blue, green & yellow florals, brown over yellow Wax Matte glaze, 1931, Jens Jensen......... 115.00

Vase, 6" h., cylindrical, blue w/border of 4 waterlilies, Vellum glaze, 1913, Carrie Steinle 176.00

Vase, 6" h., 6¾" d., underglaze slip-painted florals, standard brown glaze, 1903, Elizabeth Neave Lincoln................... 385.00

Vase, 6¾" h., expanding cylinder w/collared neck, underglaze slip-painted scenic band w/blue trees against pink sky, Vellum glaze, 1916, Lenore Asbury 4,180.00

Vase, 7" h., incised blue floral decor, Wax Matte glaze, 1921, Louise Abel.................... 170.00

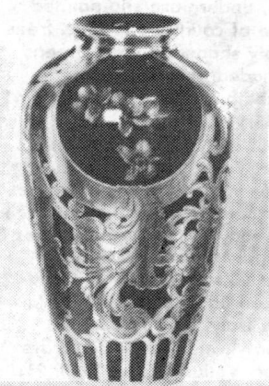

Rookwood Vase with Silver Overlay

Vase, 8" h., underglaze slip-painted florals, standard glaze, w/detailed sterling silver overlay, 1893, Louise Abel, silver by Gorham (ILLUS.) 4,000.00

Vase, 8" h., early autumn scene of trees in a meadow, Vellum glaze, 1916, Edward George Diers (ILLUS. with honey jug) 800.00

Vase, 9" h., underglaze slip-painted holly decor around shoulder, mauve shaded to green ground, Iris glaze, 1903, Olga Geneva Reed 725.00

Vase, 9" h., underglaze slip-painted monkey's arm reaching out from behind green foliage to grasp at red & orange currants, standard glaze, 1891, Kataro Shiraya-madani 1,200.00

Vase, 9¼" h., ovoid, underglaze slip-painted grey-blue, pink, blue-black & white winter scene of snow-covered fields & a winding river, Vellum glaze, 1918, Sara Elizabeth (Sallie) Coyne 880.00

Vase, 9¾" h., baluster-shaped, barren dark blue & olive green trees on the rocky banks of a river w/white rapids, Vellum glaze, 1913, Lenore Asbury 7,700.00

Vase, 10¾" h., baluster-shaped, slender birch trees in green field, Vellum glaze, 1914, Lorinda Epply 825.00

Vase, 12¾" h., squat oviform, molded lavender & blue dogwood blossoms & branches on blue ground, 1912, Charles Stewart Todd 6,050.00

Vase, 14¼" h., slender ovoid, deep lavender wisteria blossoms pendant from mustard & green vines & leaves on shaded green ground, 1900, Albert Robert Valentien 770.00

Early Rookwood Vase

Vase, 24" h., footed spherical body w/conical neck, brown, navy blue & white swallows flying beneath blossoming white wisteria on a gilded blue ground, 1883 (ILLUS.) 880.00

ROSEMEADE

Peacock Bud Vase

Laura Taylor was a ceramic artist who supervised Federal Works Projects in her native North Dakota during the Depression era and later demonstrated at the potter's wheel during the 1939 New York World's Fair. In 1940, Laura Taylor and Robert J. Hughes opened the Rosemeade-Wahpeton Pottery, naming it after the county and town of Wahpeton where it was located. Rosemeade Pottery was made on a small scale for only about twelve years with Laura Taylor designing the items and perfecting colors. Wildlife animals and birds are popular among collectors. Hughes and Taylor married in 1943 and the pottery did a thriving business until her death in 1959. The pottery closed in 1961 but stock was sold from the factory salesroom until 1964.

Ash tray w/figure of bear at side . . .	$16.00
Candlesticks, square form, purple glaze, pr.	7.50
Flower bowl w/figural leaping fawn flower frog	30.00
Model of a bear	25.00
Model of a bird on stump	15.00
Model of a Greyhound dog, bronze lustre finish	65.00
Model of an elephant, pink glaze, 3" h.	22.00
Model of a pheasant, w/original paper label, 7 x 13"	155.00
Pie bird, figural elephant seated, pink glaze, 4" h.	45.00
Planter, model of a koala bear, matte finish	38.00
Planter, model of a squirrel	15.00
Planter, model of a swan, beige finish	7.50
Plaque, wall-type, gopher decor	20.00
Salt & pepper shakers, figural buffalo, pr.	15.00
Salt & pepper shakers, figural cat, pr.	15.00
Salt & pepper shakers, figural cow, pr.	15.00
Vase, bud, 8" h., model of a peacock, orange, green & blue glaze (ILLUS.)	25.00
Whimsey, model of a boot, black glaze, 7½" h.	45.00

ROSE MEDALLION - ROSE CANTON

Rose Medallion Punch Bowl

This Chinese ware, made through last century and in the present one, features alternating panels of people and of flowers, birds or insects. Most pieces have four to six medallions, and colors utilized are appealing. The ware is called Rose Canton if flowers fill all the panels. Unless otherwise noted, our listing is for Rose Medallion wares.

Basket & underplate, reticulated sides & plate, late 19th c., 12" d.	$450.00
Bouillon cup & saucer	45.00
Bowl, 7½" d.	85.00
Bowl, 7¾" d., 3¾" h., lobed rim . . .	95.00
Bowl, 8" d., w/wooden stand	175.00
Bowl, cov., Rose Canton, ca. 1800 . .	135.00
Box w/domed lid, octagonal, Rose Canton, ca. 1800, 13" w.	250.00
Butter pat, Rose Canton	35.00
Candlesticks, 1820-40, 8" h., pr.	690.00
Creamer, marked "Made in China," 4" h.	85.00
Cup & saucer, hexagonal	30.00
Cup & saucer, octagonal	60.00
Cup & saucer, scalloped rim	75.00
Dish, 5¼" l.	25.00
Garden seat, barrel-shaped, top & sides pieced w/cash medallions, 18" h.	1,650.00
Mug, 5¾" h.	165.00
Plate, 6" d., ca. 1850	25.00
Plate, 7¼" d., Rose Canton, marked "China"	40.00
Plates, 7½" sq. w/cut corners, set of 8	325.00
Plate, 8" d.	98.00
Plate, 8½" d., Rose Canton	52.00
Plate, 9½" d.	65.00
Plates, 10" d., set of 6	325.00
Platter, 9¾" oval	95.00
Platter, 18" l.	175.00
Punch bowl, ca. 1870, 13" d., 6" h.	600.00
Punch bowl, mid-19th c., 16" d.	1,980.00
Punch bowl, 1850-90, 23" d., 10" h., w/carved wooden stand, 2 pcs. (ILLUS.)	6,875.00
Rice bowl	40.00
Sauce dish	50.00
Soap dish w/insert, 5½" l.	155.00
Tea cup & saucer, marked "China"	30.00
Teapot, cov., globular w/gooseneck spout, individual size, 3" h.	135.00
Teapot, cov., cylindrical, white spout, woven reed handle, 5" h. . .	150.00
Teapot, cov., cylindrical, woven reed handle, Rose Canton	100.00
Teapot, cov., twisted side handle, Rose Canton	285.00
Tea set: cov. teapot, creamer & cov. sugar bowl; bulbous, 3 pcs.	195.00
Tea set: cov. teapot, creamer & cov. sugar bowl; Rose Canton, 3 pcs. . . .	335.00
Tea set, cov. teapot & 2 cups in fitted wicker basket, 4 pcs.	175.00

Tureen, cov., w/stand, ca. 1800,
   large........................... 400.00
Vases, 7" h., ca. 1900, pr. 125.00
Vases, 8" h., applied foo dog handles & salamander decor, pr...... 350.00
Vases, 12" h., cylindrical w/slender
   collared neck, pr. 300.00

Rose Medallion Vases

Vases, 14" & 13 7/8" h., baluster-
   shaped, shoulders applied w/iron-
   red-heightened gilt dragons, sides
   of neck w/gilt kylins pouncing on
   iron-red balls, minor imperfec-
   tions, ca. 1875, pr. (ILLUS.) 1,540.00
Vases, 16" h., pr. 850.00
Vases, 24" h., slender ovoid
   w/puckered sides, ribbon & bow
   at neck to simulate cloth bag, applied foo dog handles, 19th c.,
   pr............................. 990.00
Wine pot, marked "China" 240.00

ROSENTHAL

*The Rosenthal porcelain manufactory has
been in operation since 1880 when it was established by P. Rosenthal in Selb, Bavaria.
Tablewares and figure groups are among its
specialties.*

Cake plate, bust portrait of Rembrandt on pale blue shaded to
   dark blue ground, 11" d......... $55.00
Cup & saucer, Dresden-type,
   multicolored floral garlands decor,
   gold trim & handle 60.00
Dish, diamond-shaped, model of a
   pelican perched on rim, h.p.
   waterlilies decor, 8 x 3½" 100.00
Dresser set: 12 x 8½" tray, pin tray
   & cov. powder box; overall h.p.
   lavender floral decor, 3 pcs. 75.00
Figure of a snake charmer wearing

green-dotted blue skirt w/gilt
   highlights & leaning over a shaded brown & blue coiled cobra,
   artist-signed, 7½" h. 308.00
Figure of a ballerina, artist-signed,
   12" h......................... 550.00

Rosenthal Figure of a Dancer

Figure of a dancer in a stylized
   pose, colorful exotic costume, beside a seated buddha figure on an
   oval base heightened w/gilding,
   artist-signed, ca. 1920, 16¾" h.
   (ILLUS.)....................... 605.00
Fruit set: 10" d. master bowl & six
   8" d. serving plates; pink roses on
   tinted blue, green, yellow & pink
   ground, gold trim, 7 pcs......... 385.00
Model of a Bulldog, white w/black
   spots, 6 x 4".................... 175.00
Model of a butterfly, 4 x 2¼" 48.00
Model of a horse, grey & white,
   artist-signed, 10¼ x 9¾" 260.00
Model of a rabbit w/"laughing"
   mouth, white, 5¼" h. 60.00
Mug, red cherries w/green leaves &
   trailing vines on shaded green
   ground, artist-signed, 4¾" h. 57.50
Plaque, pierced to hang, Delft-type
   canal scene, 9 5/8" d. 65.00
Plaque, pierced to hang, St. Jerome
   w/flowing white beard, supporting his head against one hand as
   he reads the Scriptures, whole in
   darkened landscape near the en-
   trace to a cave, ca. 1900,
   9 7/8 x 7 7/8" 550.00
Plaque, pierced to hang, 2 squirrels,
   artist-signed, 10 x 8" 400.00
Plate, 9" d., peaches decor 35.00
Urn, cov., h.p. scene of a woman in
   a garden setting, 10½" h. 230.00
Vase, 6½" h., "pate-sur-pate" white

Angel fish & stork under a pale
blue clouded sky, dark green cattails around base, artist-signed ... 250.00
Vase, 7½" h., grape clusters
w/trailing vines on blue shaded to
green ground 100.00
Vases, cov., 7¾" h., ovoid, h.p.
scene of semi-nude women wearing red, blue & violet skirts
frolicking in a forest setting,
ca. 1931, pr. 1,650.00
Vase, 10" h., portrait of a beautiful
woman reserved on iridescent red
ground, lavish gold trim, artist-
signed 400.00

ROSEVILLE

*Roseville Pottery Company operated in
Zanesville, O., from 1898 to 1954 after having been in business for six years prior to that
in Muskingum County, Ohio. Art wares similar to those of the Owens and Weller Potteries were produced. Items listed here are by
patterns or lines.*

APPLE BLOSSOM (1948)

Apple Blossom Cornucopia-Vase

Basket w/overhead branch handle,
apple blossoms in relief on blue,
green or rose, 10" h., each $55.00
Bowl, 8" d., apple blossoms in relief
on green 28.00
Candlesticks, apple blossoms in
relief on green or rose, 4" h.,
each pr....................... 37.00
Cornucopia-vase, apple blossoms in
relief on green, 6" h. (ILLUS.) 25.00
Creamer, apple blossoms in relief
on blue 18.00
Ewer, apple blossoms in relief on
blue or rose, 15" h., each........ 125.00
Flower pot w/saucer, apple blossoms in relief on green, 5" h. 58.00
Jardiniere & pedestal base, apple
blossoms in relief on blue, overall
24½" h., 2 pcs. 450.00

Planter, apple blossoms in relief on
rose, 8" l. 35.00
Tea set: cov. teapot, creamer &
sugar bowl; branch handles, apple
blossoms in relief on blue, green
or rose, 3 pcs., each
set .... 105.00 to 130.00
Vase, 7" h., 2-handled, appled blossoms in relief on blue or green,
each 37.50

AZTEC (1916)

Vase, 9½" h., bottle-shaped w/long
neck, white slip geometric design
at shoulder on grey 200.00
Vase, 10" h., blue & white slip geometric designs on beige 225.00
Vase, 11" h., multicolored slip geometric designs on blue 295.00

BANEDA (1933)

Baneda Vase

Bowl, 8" d., 3" h., band of embossed pods, blossoms & leaves
on raspberry pink 35.00
Console bowl, hexagonal, band of
embossed pods, blossoms &
leaves on green, 11" w., 3" h..... 110.00
Urn, band of embossed pods, blossoms & leaves on raspberry pink,
7" h. 75.00
Vase., 4" h., tab handles, band of
embossed pods, blossoms &
leaves on raspberry pink
(ILLUS.)...................... 30.00
Vase, 6" h., ovoid, band of embossed pods, blossoms & leaves
on green or raspberry pink,
each .... 55.00 to 70.00
Vase, 8" h., base handles, band of
embossed pods, blossoms &
leaves on green................ 67.50
Vase, 8½" h., band of embossed
pods, blossoms & leaves on raspberry pink 130.00
Wall pocket, band of embossed
pods, blossoms & leaves on raspberry pink, 8" h. 400.00

BANKS & BOTTLES (early 1900's)

Bank, bust of Uncle Sam, 4" h. 135.00
Bank, model of an apple, 4 x 3" 125.00
Bank, model of a beehive, 2½" h. . . 225.00
Bank, model of a buffalo, 6 x 3" . . . 200.00
Bank, model of a cat's head, 4" h. . . 225.00
Bank, model of a dog's head,
　4" h. 200.00
Bank, model of a lion's head,
　2½" h. 175.00
Bank, model of a pig, 5 x 2½" 150.00
Bank, model of a pig,
　5½ x 4" . . . . 150.00 to 175.00
Bottle, model of a monkey 200.00
Jug, "Ye Olden Time," 4" h. 150.00

BITTERSWEET (1940)

Basket, overhead branch handle,
　orange bittersweet pods & green
　leaves on green bark-textured
　ground, 10" h. 56.00
Cornucopia-vase, orange bittersweet
　pods & green leaves on yellow
　bark-textured ground, 8" h. 33.00
Vase, 5" h., orange bittersweet
　pods & green leaves on yellow
　bark-textured ground 16.00
Vase, 6" h., high-low handles,
　orange bittersweet pods & green
　leaves on green bark-textured
　ground 30.00
Vase, 10" h., 2-handled, orange bit-
　tersweet pods & green leaves on
　yellow bark-textured ground 47.50

BLACKBERRY (1933)

Basket w/semi-circular handle, band
　of blackberries & leaves in relief
　on green textured ground, 7" h. . . 250.00
Bowl, 8" d., band of blackberries &
　leaves in relief on green textured
　ground 95.00
Console bowl, 2-handled, band of
　blackberries & leaves in relief on
　green textured ground, 13" w. . . . 155.00
Jardiniere, band of blackberries &
　leaves in relief on green textured
　ground, 4" h. 90.00
Jardiniere, band of blackberries &
　leaves in relief on green tex-
　tured ground, 6" to 7" h.,
　each . . . . 120.00 to 150.00
Vase, 4" h., globular, band of black-
　berries & leaves in relief on green
　textured ground 110.00
Vase, 5" to 6" h., band of blackber-
　ries & leaves in relief on green
　textured ground, each . . . 100.00 to 125.00
Vase, 9" h., 2-handled, band of
　blackberries & leaves in relief on
　green textured ground 148.00

BLEEDING HEART (1938)

Basket, hanging-type, pink blossoms

& green leaves on shaded pink,
　8" w. 85.00
Bookends, pink blossoms & green
　leaves on shaded blue, pr. 87.00
Ewer, pink blossoms & green leaves
　on shaded blue, green or pink,
　6" h., each 45.00
Flower pot w/saucer, pink blossoms
　& green leaves on shaded
　green 75.00
Pitcher, water, asymmetrical w/high
　arched handle, pink blossoms &
　green leaves on shaded green . . . 85.00
Plate, 10½" hexagon, border of
　pink blossoms & green leaves on
　shaded blue 62.50
Rose bowl, pink blossoms & green
　leaves on shaded green, 4" to
　6" h., each . . . . 40.00 to 58.00

Bleeding Heart Vase

Vase, 8" h., pink blossoms & green
　leaves on shaded green (ILLUS.) . . 50.00

BURMESE (1950's)

Candle holder-bookends, figural
　bust of Burmese man, black
　glaze, pr. 225.00
Candle holder-bookends, figural
　bust of Burmese woman, green
　glaze, pr. . . . . 125.00 to 150.00
Console set: 10" l. planter & pr. low
　candle holders; black glaze,
　3 pcs. 105.00
Planter, green glaze, 14½ x 5",
　4" h. 46.00
Plaques, pierced to hang, figural
　busts of Burmese man & woman,
　black glaze, pr. . . . . 200.00 to 250.00

BUSHBERRY (1948)

Basket w/angular overhead handle,
　berries & leaves on green bark-
　textured ground, 6½" h. 47.50
Basket w/overhead branch handle,
　pedestal base, berries & leaves
　on blue, green or russet bark-
　textured ground, 12" h., each 100.00

Bowl, 6" d., berries & leaves on
green bark-textured ground 35.00
Candle holders, berries & leaves on
blue bark-textured ground, pr. . . .   25.00
Cornucopia-vase, double, berries &
leaves on green bark-textured
ground, 8" h. 42.50
Mug, berries & leaves on green
bark-textured ground, 3½" h. 42.50
Rose bowl, berries & leaves on
green bark-textured ground,
4" d. 30.00
Teapot, cov., berries & leaves on
green bark-textured ground 90.00

Bushberry Vase

Vase, 4" h., berries & leaves on
blue or green bark-textured
ground, each (ILLUS.) 25.00
Vase, 6" h., high-low handles, ber-
ries & leaves on russet bark-
textured ground 30.00

CAPRI (late line)
Ash tray, mottled pink, large 25.00
Basket, relief-molded leaf design,
yellow, 10" h. 75.00
Bowl, 7" d., quadrilobed, maroon . . .   20.00
Dish, boat-shaped, deep red,
7" l. 30.00
Dish, leaf-shaped, white, 14" l. 20.00
Pitcher, 5" h., bulbous, tan 12.00
Vase, 9" h., tan 30.00

CARNELIAN I (1910-15)
Candle holder, antique gold drip
glaze on green (single) 30.00
Flower holder, fan-shaped, dark
blue drip glaze on light blue,
6" h. 30.00
Jardiniere, antique gold drip glaze
on green, 7" d., 5" h. 27.50
Vase, 6" h., antique gold drip glaze
on green 22.50
Vase, 8" h., 5" w., 2-handled, fan-
shaped, turquoise blue drip glaze
on aqua blue 32.00
Wall pocket, medium blue drip
glaze on light blue, 8" h.
(ILLUS.) 55.00

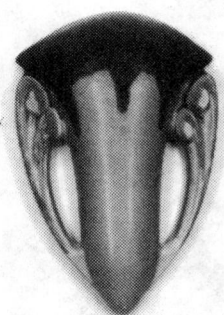

Carnelian I Wall Pocket

CARNELIAN II (1915)
Console bowl, intermingled shades
of raspberry, 14" d. 55.00
Ewer, intermingled shades of rasp-
berry, 12½" h. 95.00
Urn, intermingled shades of blue &
green glaze, 5" h. 30.00
Vase, 6" h., intermingled shades of
rose & ivory glaze 45.00
Vase, 10" h., intermingled shades of
green & pink glaze 60.00
Wall pocket, intermingled shades of
blue & lilac glaze, 8" h. 65.00

CHERRY BLOSSOM (1933)
Basket, hanging-type, cherry blossoms & ivory fencework against
brown combed ground, 8" 230.00
Console bowl, cherry blossoms &
pink fencework against blue
combed ground 155.00
Jardiniere, cherry blossoms & ivory
fencework against brown combed
ground, 4" h. 105.00
Lamp, cherry blossoms & pink fence-
work against blue combed
ground, 9" h. 450.00
Vase, 5" h., cherry blossoms & ivory
fencework against brown combed
ground 100.00
Vase, 5" h., cherry blossoms & pink
fencework against blue combed
ground 95.00

CLEMANA (1934)
Vase, 6½" h., stylized blossoms &
embossed latticework on blue or
green ground, each 80.00
Vase, 8" h., stylized blossoms & em-
bossed latticework on brown
ground 165.00
Vase, 9" h., bulbous base & wide
straight neck, stylized blossoms &
embossed latticework on blue
ground 90.00

CLEMATIS (1944)

Clematis Cornucopia-Vase

Basket w/double circular handle,
clematis blossoms on brown tex-
tured ground, 7" h. 35.00
Candle holders, clematis blossoms
on green textured ground,
4½" h., pr. 38.00
Console bowl, clematis blossoms on
brown textured ground,
8" d. 40.00
Cornucopia-vase, clematis blossoms
on brown or green textured
ground, 6" h., each (ILLUS.) 32.00
Ewer, clematis blossoms on brown
or green textured ground, 10" h.,
each 58.00
Flower pot w/saucer, clematis blos-
soms on blue textured ground 35.00
Jardiniere & pedestal base,
clematis blossoms on green
textured ground, overall
25" h. . . . . 325.00 to 400.00
Teapot, cov., clematis blossoms on
brown textured ground 47.50
Vase, double bud, 5" h., clematis
blossoms on blue textured
ground 40.00
Vase, 9" h., clematis blossoms on
brown textured ground 60.00

COLONIAL (early 1900's)

Shaving mug, blue sponge-daubed
decor . . . . 45.00 to 55.00
Soap dish w/cover & drain insert,
multicolored sponge-daubed
decor, 4" 72.00
Toothbrush holder, handled, multi-
colored sponge-daubed decor,
5" h. 65.00
Wash basin & pitcher, blue sponge-
daubed decor, 16" d. basin &
11" h. pitcher, 2 pcs. 275.00

COLUMBINE (1940's)

Basket, columbine blossoms in relief
on shaded blue ground, 10" h. . . . 95.00

Bowl, 5" d., 2-handled, columbine
blossoms in relief on shaded pink
ground 45.00
Console set: 11" d. bowl, flower
frog & pr. 3" h. candle holders;
columbine blossoms in relief on
shaded tan ground, 4 pcs. 85.00
Ewer, columbine blossoms in relief
on shaded blue ground, 7" h. 50.00
Rose bowl, columbine blossoms in
relief on shaded blue ground,
7" widest d., 4½" h. 25.00

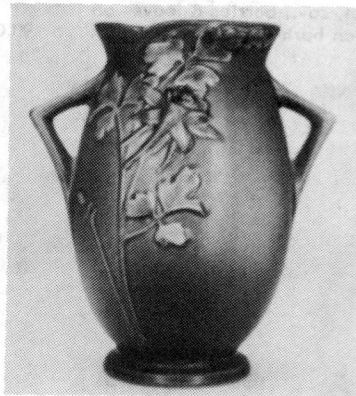

Columbine Vase

Vase, 6" h., 2-handled, columbine
blossoms in relief on shaded blue
ground (ILLUS.) 37.50
Vase, 10" h., columbine blossoms in
relief on shaded tan ground 65.00

CORINTHIAN (1923)

Corinthian Vase

Ash tray, fluted body w/embossed
fruit & floral band at rim, green &
ivory 50.00
Bowl, 9" d., fluted body w/em-
bossed fruit & floral band, green
& ivory 45.00

Flower pot w/saucer, fluted body
w/embossed fruit & floral band,
green & ivory . . . . .75.00 to 85.00
Jardiniere, fluted body w/embossed
fruit & floral band at shoulder,
10" h. 110.00
Vase, 7" h., bulbous, fluted body
w/embossed fruit & floral band at
neck (ILLUS.) 45.00
Wall pocket, fluted body w/narrow
embossed fruit & floral band at
rim, 8" h. 53.00

CORNELIAN (early 1900's)
Pitcher, 5½" h., yellow & brown
sponge-daubed decor, gold
trim 65.00
Pitcher, 6" h., embossed ear of
corn, high gloss cobalt blue
glaze . . . . .45.00 to 55.00
Toothbrush holder, brown & blue
sponge-daubed decor on light
blue ground, 5" h. 60.00

COSMOS (1940)

Cosmos Vase

Basket, overhead handle, realistic
cosmos blossoms in relief on ivory
band, shaded blue ground,
10" h. 75.00
Basket, hanging-type, realistic cos-
mos blossoms in relief on green
band, shaded tan ground, 7" 125.00
Bowl, 4" d., realistic cosmos blossoms in relief on blue band, shad-
ed green or tan ground, each 55.00
Vase, 4" h., ring handles at midsec-
tion, realistic cosmos blossoms in
relief on blue band, shaded green
or tan ground, each . . . . . . .22.00 to 27.00
Vase, 8" h., realistic cosmos blossoms in relief on ivory band,
shaded blue ground 45.00
Vase, 12½" h., realistic cosmos
blossoms in relief on ivory band,
shaded blue ground (ILLUS.) 110.00

Wall pocket, realistic cosmos blossoms in relief on blue band, shad-
ed tan ground, 6½" h. 65.00

CREMONA (1927)
Bowl, 6" sq., relief-molded floral
cluster & arrowhead leaves, mot-
tled green 26.00
Urn, relief-molded small floral
cluster & arrowhead leaves, mot-
tled light blue & green, 4" h. 38.00
Vase, 10½" h., angular handles at
shoulder, relief-molded small
floral cluster & arrowhead leaves,
mottled green 70.00

DAHLROSE (1924-28)

Dahlrose Vase

Basket, hanging-type, ivory blossoms in relief on mottled tan
shaded to green . . . . .60.00 to 75.00
Bowl, 10½" oval, angular rim han-
dles, ivory blossoms in relief on
mottled tan shaded to green 40.00
Jardiniere & pedestal base, ivory
blossoms in relief on mottled tan
shaded to green, overall 30½" h.,
2 pcs. . . . . .425.00 to 550.00
Vase, 6" h., square, ivory blossoms
in relief on mottled tan shaded to
green 43.00
Vase, 6" h., 2-handled (ILLUS.) 45.00
Vase, 10" to 11" h., each . . . .65.00 to 85.00
Wall pocket, angular rim handles,
9" h. 65.00

DOGWOOD I (1916-18)
Bowl, 7" d., dogwood blossoms on
textured green ground 35.00
Sand jar, dogwood blossoms on tex-
tured green ground, 10" h. 125.00
Umbrella stand, dogwood blossoms
on textured green ground 300.00
Vase, 8" h., bulbous, dogwood blossoms on textured green ground . . 55.00
Vase, 12" h., dogwood blossoms on
textured green ground 85.00

DOGWOOD II (1928)

Dogwood II Basket

Basket, dogwood blossoms on matte
  green ground, 6" h. (ILLUS.) 55.00
Vase, 7" h., dogwood blossoms on
  matte green ground 55.00
Vase, double bud, 8" h., dogwood
  blossoms on matte green
  ground 38.00
Wall pocket, elongated branch han-
  dles, dogwood blossoms on matte
  green ground 85.00

DONATELLO (1915)

Donatello Jardiniere & Pedestal

Basket, cherubs in light relief on tan
  band, green & ivory fluted body,
  overall 8" h.   50.00
Bowl, 5" d., cherubs in light relief
  on tan band, green & ivory fluted
  body 30.00
Candlesticks, flaring base & top,
  8" h., pr. 100.00
Flower frog, ivory & green fluted
  sides, ivory top . . . . 25.00 to 35.00
Flower pot w/saucer, 4" to 5" h.,
  2 pcs., each set . . . . 65.00 to 85.00

Jardiniere & pedestal base, overall
  28" h., 2 pcs. (ILLUS.) . . . . 475.00 to 500.00
Pitcher, 6½" h., bulbous . . . 140.00 to 165.00
Plate, 6" to 8" d., each . . . . 200.00 to 250.00
Powder jar, cov. 350.00
Vase, 6" h. 55.00
Vase, 8½" h., cylindrical 55.00
Vase, 12" h., footed 110.00
Wall pocket, 11½" h. 85.00

DUTCH (pre-1916)

Ale set: tankard pitcher & 2 mugs;
  creamware w/varied Dutch
  decals, 3 pcs. 235.00
Humidor, cov., creamware w/Dutch
  decals 225.00
Mug, creamware w/decal of Dutch
  children, 4" h. 45.00
Pitcher, 8" h. 140.00
Water set: tankard pitcher & 6 tum-
  blers; creamware w/decals of
  Dutch children, 7 pcs. . . . 375.00 to 450.00

FALLINE (1933)

Candle holder, ring handles, impressed triangles & peapod decor
  on base, blue shaded to green &
  tan, 4" h. (single) 95.00
Vase, 6" h., 2-handled, globular
  body w/short neck, impressed triangles at shoulder, peapod
  shapes on body, blue shaded to
  green & tan . . . . 125.00 to 150.00
Vase, 8" h., expanding cylinder, impressed triangles & peapod decor,
  browns shaded to tan 145.00

FERRELLA (1930)

Console bowl w/attached flower
  frog, reticulated low footed base
  w/molded shells, pierced rim,
  mottled brown 215.00
Flower frog, mottled red &
  turquoise 22.00
Vase, 5" h., 2-handled, reticulated
  base w/molded shells & pierced
  rim, mottled red & turquoise 150.00

FLORENTINE (1924-28)

Florentine Double Bud Vase

Bowl, 5" d., bark-textured panels alternating w/embossed garlands of

cascading fruit & florals, dark
brown tones 30.00

Candlestick, flaring base, bark-
textured panels alternating w/em-
bossed pendant garlands of fruit
& florals, brown tones, 8½" h.
(single)........................ 40.00

Jardiniere, handled, bark-textured
panels alternating w/garlands of
cascading florals & fruit, brown
tones, 8" to 9" h., each..125.00 to 175.00

Umbrella stand, bark-textured
panels alternating w/berries &
foliage, ivory, tan & green,
18½" h................175.00 to 195.00

Vase, double bud, 4½" h., 9" w., 2
cylindrical bark-textured columns
joined by gate, brown tones
(ILLUS.)....................... 40.00

Vase, 8" h., flaring base, bark-
textured panels alternating
w/pendant garlands of fruit &
florals........................ 45.00

Vase, 12" h., bark-textured panels
alternating w/cascading garlands
of florals & fruit, brown tones 75.00

Wall pocket, central bark-textured
panel flanked by pendant floral
garlands, brown tones,
12½" h..................70.00 to 85.00

FOXGLOVE (1940's)

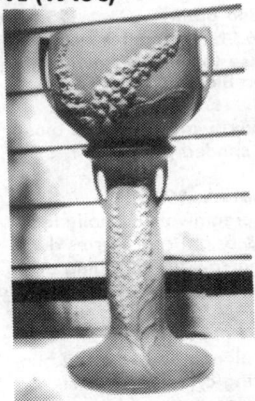

Foxglove Jardiniere & Pedestal

Basket w/overhead handle, white
foxglove spray on shaded green
ground, 10" h. 80.00

Bookends, white foxglove spray on
shaded blue or green ground,
each pr....................... 75.00

Console bowl, white foxglove spray
on shaded pink ground, 10" d. ... 35.00

Cornucopia-vase, white foxglove
spray on shaded green ground,
8" h. 40.00

Ewer, white foxglove spray on
shaded pink ground, 15" h. 175.00

Jardiniere & pedestal base, white
foxglove spray on shaded blue
ground, overall 30½" h., 2 pcs.
(ILLUS.)....................... 725.00

Tray, open handles, white foxglove
spray on shaded green ground,
11" l. ....38.00 to 45.00

Vase, 9½" h., 2-handled, white foxglove spray on shaded blue
ground 50.00

Vase, 18" h., white foxglove spray
on shaded blue ground ..195.00 to 250.00

Wall pocket, white foxglove spray
on shaded pink ground, 8" h. 77.00

FREESIA (1945)

Freesia Ewer

Basket w/overhead handle, white
blossoms & green leaves in relief
on shaded brown or green tex-
tured ground, 8" h., each ..45.00 to 55.00

Bowl, 10" d., 2-handled, white to
yellow blossoms in relief on shaded tangerine textured ground 48.00

Candlesticks, angular handles above
flat circular base, white blossoms
& green leaves in relief on shaded
blue or tangerine textured
ground, 4½" h., each
pr.......................35.00 to 48.00

Cornucopia-vase, white to yellow
blossoms & green leaves on shaded blue or tangerine textured
ground, 6" h., each 27.00

Ewer, white blossoms & green
leaves on shaded blue textured
ground, 6" h. (ILLUS.)............ 45.00

Tea set: cov. teapot, creamer &
sugar bowl: white blossoms &
green leaves in relief on shaded
green textured ground, 3 pcs. 145.00

Vase, bud, 7" h., angular handles
rising from bulbous base, slender
flaring neck, white blossoms &

green leaves in relief on shaded
blue textured ground 32.50
Vase, 10½" h., angular base han-
dles, white blossoms & green
leaves in relief on shaded green
textured ground. 65.00
Vase, 18" h., white to yellow blos-
soms & green leaves on shaded
brown textured ground 275.00

FUCHSIA (1939)

Fuchsia Candle Holders

Bowl, 10" d., pendant fuchsia blossoms on brown w/cream
highlights 43.00
Bowl-vase, pendant fuchsia blos-
soms on brown or green w/cream
highlights, 3" h., each . . . . .30.00 to 35.00
Candle holders, pendant fuchsia
blossoms on blue w/cream high-
lights, 2½" h., pr. (ILLUS.) 45.00
Console bowl, pendant fuchsia blos-
soms on green w/tan highlights,
14" l. 85.00
Vase, 6" h., pendant fuchsia blos-
soms on blue w/cream high-
lights 47.50
Vase, 8" h., 2 handles rising from
base to mid-section, pendant fuchsia blossoms on blue or brown
w/cream highlights,
each . . . . .55.00 to 65.00
Vase, 15" h., pendant fuchsia blos-
soms on brown w/cream
highlights 155.00

FUTURA (1928)

Basket, hanging-type w/original
chains, cone-shaped w/angular
shoulder, round collared neck,
mottled terra cotta glaze 190.00
Candlestick, cone-shaped base
w/angular handles, globular candle nozzle w/flaring rim, blended
tan & green glaze, 4" h. (single) . . 85.00
Jardiniere, 2-handled, sharply canted sides, relief-molded foliage on
blended tan & green glaze, 15"
widest d., 10" h. 275.00
Vase, 6" h., octagonal, low foot,
canted sides, metallic crystalline
decor on blue ground 135.00
Vase, 10" h., cylindrical w/short
wide canted neck, yellow & pur-
ple glaze 290.00

GARDENIA (1940's)

Gardenia Bookends

Basket w/overhead handle, overlapping leaf form rim, white gardenia blossom on shaded green,
12" h. 92.50
Basket, hanging-type w/chains, 2-
handled, white gardenia blossom
on shaded tan 70.00
Bookends, white gardenia blossom
on shaded grey, 5 x 4½ x 5", pr.
(ILLUS.) 55.00
Candlesticks, white gardenia blos-
som on shaded grey, 4½" h.,
pr. . . . . .30.00 to 45.00
Ewer, globular w/long slender neck,
white gardenia blossom on shad-
ed grey, 6" h. 45.00
Jardiniere, straight sides, white
gardenia blossom on shaded
green, 4" d. 22.50
Pedestal, white gardenia blossom
on shaded green . . . . .125.00 to 175.00
Vase, 10½" h., 2 handles rising
from base to shoulder, white
gardenia blossom on shaded
green 55.00
Window box, white gardenia blos-
som on shaded green, 8" l. 35.00

HOLLY (before 1916)

Creamer, creamware w/holly leaf
cluster & bright red berries decal
decor, narrow green piping at rim
& handle . . . . .350.00 to 385.00

IMPERIAL I (1916)

Basket w/elongated overhead handle, flaring cylinder, pretzel-
twisted vine & grape leaves in relief on green & brown textured
ground, 13" h. . . . . .85.00 to 110.00
Console bowl, pierced handles,
pretzel-twisted vine & grape
leaves in relief on green & brown
textured ground, 8" d., 2½" h. 30.00
Jardiniere, pretzel-twisted vine
& grape leaves in relief on green
& brown textured ground,
11½ x 10" 185.00
Umbrella stand, pretzel-twisted vine
& grape leaves in relief on green
& brown textured ground 250.00

Vase, 8½" h., pierced handles,
   globular w/collared neck, pretzel-
   twisted vine & grape leaves in relief on green & brown textured
   ground 75.00
Vase, bud, 12" h., cylindrical w/flar-
   ing base, pretzel-twisted vine &
   grape leaves in relief on green &
   brown textured ground 72.50
Wall pocket, 2-prong, pretzel-
   twisted vine & grape leaves on
   green & brown textured ground,
   10" h. 100.00

IMPERIAL II (1924)
Candle holder, saucer base, orange
   & green mottled glaze, 2" h.
   (single) 75.00
Flower pot, expanding cylinder,
   splotched orange & green matte
   glaze, 5½" h. 135.00
Vase, 4½" h., mottled turquoise
   blue glaze 45.00
Vase, 7" h., semi-ovoid, turquoise
   blue textured matte glaze, creamy
   white relief floral decor around
   neck 125.00
Vase, 9" h., expanding cylinder,
   splotched blue, yellow & cream
   glaze 135.00
Wall pocket, globular, mottled red &
   grey glaze, 6½" h. ......195.00 to 225.00

IRIS (1938)

Iris Vase

Basket, hanging-type, iris & leaves
   on shaded blue ground, 5" 130.00
Bowl-vase, iris & leaves on shaded
   blue ground, 3" h. 25.00
Console bowl, 2-handled, iris &
   leaves on shaded pink ground,
   12" l., 3½" h. 60.00
Flower frog, iris & leaves on shaded
   blue ground, 6 x 3" 22.50
Vase, 5" h., iris & leaves on shaded
   blue ground (ILLUS.) 35.00

Vase, bud, 7" h., iris & leaves on
   shaded pink ground 40.00
Wall shelf, iris & leaves on shaded
   blue ground, 8" h. 135.00

IXIA (1930's)

Ixia Centerpiece

Bowl, 7" d., lavender floral cluster
   on shaded green 45.00
Candle holders, white floral cluster
   on shaded pink, 2" h., pr. 15.00
Centerpiece, 1-piece console set
   w/candle holders attached to center bowl, lavender floral cluster
   on shaded green, 13" l.
   (ILLUS.) ....85.00 to 100.00
Flower pot w/saucer, white floral
   cluster on shaded pink, 5" h. 45.00
Vase, 10½" h., pointed closed handles at shoulder, lavender floral
   cluster on shaded green 50.00
Vase, 15" h., lavender floral cluster
   on shaded green 85.00

JONQUIL (1931)
Basket w/overhead handle, jonquil
   blossoms & leaves in relief
   against textured tan ground,
   10" h. 150.00
Bowl, 6" d., 3" h., 2-handled, jonquil
   blossoms & leaves in relief
   against textured tan ground 70.00
Console bowl w/flower frog, shallow w/wide rim, jonquil blossoms
   & leaves in relief against textured
   tan ground, 2 pcs. 130.00
Flower pot w/interior flower frog
   attached, jonquil blossoms &
   leaves in relief against textured
   tan ground, 5½" h. ....80.00 to 95.00
Jardiniere, jonquil blossoms &
   leaves in relief against textured
   tan ground, 7" to 8" h.,
   each ....85.00 to 100.00
Vase, 6" h., bulbous, jonquil blossoms & leaves in relief against
   textured tan ground 85.00
Vase, bud, 7" h., jonquil blossoms &
   leaves in relief against textured
   tan ground 40.00
Vase, 12" h., jonquil blossoms &
   leaves in relief against textured
   tan ground 275.00

JUVENILE (1916 on)

Juvenile Pitcher & Cereal Bowl

Bowl, cereal, 6" d., seated dog
  decor (ILLUS. right) 45.00
Bowl, cereal, chicks decor . . .45.00 to 60.00
Cup, duck w/hat decor 40.00
Cup & saucer, chicks decor 80.00
Egg cup, chicks decor 75.00
Feeding dish w/rolled edge, rabbits
  decor, 7" d. 42.00
Feeding dish w/rolled edge, nursery
  rhyme "Little Jack Horner,"
  8" d. 38.00
Feeding dish w/rolled edge, nursery
  rhyme "Tom, the Piper's Son,"
  8" d. 45.00
Feeding dish w/rolled edge, Sun-
  bonnet Girl decor, 8" d. 85.00
Mug, duck w/hat decor, 3" h. 42.00
Mug, chicks decor 50.00
Pitcher, 3" h., chicks decor 48.00
Pitcher, 3½" h., seated dog decor
  (ILLUS. left) . . . . 55.00 to 65.00
Pitcher, 4" h., standing rabbits
  decor 40.00
Pitcher, ducks decor 25.00
Pitcher, Sunbonnet Girl decor 62.00
Plate, 7" d., standing rabbits
  decor 42.50
Plate, 8" d., duck w/hat decor 40.00

LA ROSE (1924)
Bowl, 6½" d., 3" h., draped green
  leaves & red roses on creamy
  ivory 40.00
Candlesticks, draped leaves & red
  roses on creamy ivory, 4" h. 45.00
Flower pot & saucer, draped green
  leaves & red roses on creamy
  ivory 75.00
Vase, 9½" h., draped green leaves
  & red roses on creamy ivory 45.00
Vase, double bud, gate-form,
  draped green leaves & red roses
  on creamy ivory 48.00
Wall pocket, draped leaves & red
  roses on creamy ivory, 9" h. 47.50

LAUREL (1934)
Candlesticks, laurel branch & berries
  in low relief, reeded panels at
  sides, green, 4" h., pr. 45.00

Urn-vase, laurel branch & berries in
  low relief, reeded panels at sides,
  brown, 6½" h. 50.00
Vase, 8" h., expanding cylinder
  w/pierced angular handles at
  mid-section, laurel branch & berries in low relief, reeded panels
  at sides, brown or deep yellow,
  each . . . . .75.00 to 82.50
Vase, 10" h., laurel branch & berries
  in low relief, reeded panels at
  sides, brown or green,
  each . . . . .85.00 to 100.00

LOTUS (1952)
Candle holders, footed, stylized
  lotus petals in relief, burgundy &
  yellow high-gloss finish, 2½" h.,
  pr. 45.00
Planter, stylized lotus petals in
  relief, burgundy & yellow high-
  gloss finish, 10½" l. . . . . . . .72.00 to 85.00
Vase, 10" h., cylindrical, stylized
  lotus petals in relief, blue & white
  high-gloss finish 130.00
Vase, 10" h., stylized lotus petals
  in relief, tan & green or tan &
  yellow high-gloss finish,
  each .95.00 to 125.00

LUFFA (1934)
Candle holders, high domed base,
  angular handles, relief-molded ivy
  leaves & blossoms on shaded
  green wavy horizontal ridges,
  5" h., pr. 125.00
Console bowl w/flower frog, relief-
  molded ivy leaves & blossoms on
  shaded brown & green wavy
  horizontal ridges, 9 x 6", 2 pcs. . . 70.00
Jardiniere & pedestal base, relief-
  molded ivy leaves & blossoms on
  shaded brown & green wavy
  horizontal ridges, overall 24½" h.,
  2 pcs. . . . . .500.00 to 600.00
Vase, 8½" h., cylindrical, relief-
  molded ivy leaves & blossoms on
  shaded green wavy horizontal
  ridges 50.00
Vase, 13" h., conical, relief-molded
  ivy leaves & blossoms on shaded
  brown & green wavy horizontal
  ridges 150.00
Vase, 24½" h., relief-molded ivy
  leaves & blossoms on shaded
  green wavy horizontal ridges 325.00
Wall pocket, relief-molded ivy
  leaves & blossoms on shaded
  green wavy horizontal ridges,
  8½" h. 205.00

MAGNOLIA (1943)
Basket w/overhead handle, magnolia blossoms on textured blue,

green or tan ground, 7" h.,
each ....40.00 to 55.00
Bookends, magnolia blossoms on
textured green ground, pr....... 62.00
Bowl, 5" d., 3" h., 2-handled, magnolia blossoms on textured blue
or green ground, each 33.00
Bowl, 10" d., magnolia blossoms on
textured blue or tan ground,
each ....55.00 to 65.00
Candlesticks, angular handles rising
from flared base, magnolia blossoms on textured blue ground,
5" h., pr...................... 52.00
Cornucopia-vase, magnolia blossoms
on textured green ground, 6" h... 30.00
Creamer & sugar bowl, magnolia
blossoms on textured green or
tan ground, each pr. ......27.00 to 33.00
Ewer, magnolia blossoms on textured tan ground, 10" h. 58.00
Mug, magnolia blossoms on textured blue or tan ground, 3" h.,
each 35.00
Pitcher, cider, magnolia blossoms on
textured blue or green ground,
each 80.00
Planter, shell form, angular base
handles, magnolia blossoms on
textured blue or green ground,
6", each 35.00
Teapot, cov., magnolia blossoms on
textured blue ground .....65.00 to 80.00
Vase, double bud, 4" h., 2 columns
joined by gate applied w/magno-
lia blossoms, textured blue
ground 35.00

Magnolia Vase

Vase, 5" h., 7" w., single handle, 3-
tier, magnolia blossoms on textured green ground (ILLUS.) 45.00
Vase, 14" to 16" h., magnolia blossoms on textured tan ground,
each ....125.00 to 175.00

MAYFAIR (late 1940's)
Bowl, 10" d., buff glaze............ 18.00
Flower pot, green glaze, 6" h....... 27.00
Pitcher, 5" h., green glaze 22.50

Planter, brown glaze, 10" l........ 40.00
Vase, 12" h., brown glaze 40.00

MING TREE (1949)
Basket w/overhead branch handle,
oriental branches in relief on
blue, green or white ground,
8" h., each ....65.00 to 80.00
Bowl, 11½ x 4", oriental branches
in relief on green or white
ground, each ....55.00 to 75.00
Candle holders, branch handles, bulbous, oriental branches in relief
on white ground, pr. ......25.00 to 32.00
Creamer & sugar bowl, oriental
branches in relief on white
ground, pr. 50.00
Vase, 8" h., asymmetrical branch
handles, oriental branches in
relief on white ground.......... 55.00
Vase, 12" h., oriental branches in
relief on white ground.......... 95.00

MOCK ORANGE (1950)

Mock Orange Planter

Basket, footed, white blossoms &
green leaves on green or pink
ground, 8" h., each 70.00
Basket, hanging-type, white blossoms & green leaves on pink
ground 125.00
Planter, oblong base, cluster of
white blossoms & green leaves at
base of handle, green body, 7" l.,
4" h. (ILLUS.) 35.00
Vase, 8½" h., curved handle rising
from base to rim, white blossoms
& green leaves on yellow
ground 38.00
Vase, 10" h., fan-shaped, white
blossoms & green leaves on pink
ground 35.00
Vase, 18" h., white blossoms &
green leaves on yellow ground ... 295.00

MODERNE (1930's)
Candle holders, white w/rose highlights, pr. 40.00
Console bowl, medium blue w/white
highlights, 12" d., 7" h.......... 85.00

Rose bowl, turquoise blue w/deep
gold highlights, 6½" h. 40.00

Moderne Vase

Vase, 6" h., low foot, cone-shaped
w/base handles, white w/rose
highlights (ILLUS.) . . . . .35.00 to 48.00
Vase, 12" h., white w/rose
highlights 88.00

MONGOL (1904)
Vase, 7" h., cylindrical, "Sang de
Boeuf" high-gloss finish 345.00
Vase, 10½" h., cylindrical, "Sang de
Boeuf" high-gloss finish 450.00
Vase, 14" h., flaring cylinder
w/short neck & wide mouth,
"Sang de Boeuf" high-gloss
finish 600.00

MONTACELLO (1931)
Basket, pointed overhead handle,
white stylized trumpet flowers
w/black accents on band, mottled
blue & tan ground, 6½" h. 160.00
Candlesticks, white stylized trumpet
flowers w/black accents on band,
mottled turquoise shaded to tan
ground, 4½" h., pr. 100.00
Vase, 5" h., conical, white stylized
trumpet flowers w/black accents
on band, mottled tan ground 40.00
Vase, 10½" h., pierced handles at
base, white stylized trumpet flowers w/black accents on band,
mottled blue & tan ground 165.00

MORNING GLORY (1935)
Basket w/angular overhead handle,
globular, stylized pastel morning
glories in low relief on green
ground, 10½" h. 475.00
Console bowl, 2-handled, stylized
pastel morning glories in low
relief on white ground,
11½ x 4½" 175.00
Planter, stylized pastel morning
glories in low relief on green
ground, 7¼ x 4¼" 150.00

Vase, 7" h., angular base handles,
pillow-shaped, stylized pastel
morning glories in low relief on
green ground . . . . .165.00 to 185.00
Vase, 10½" h., angular side han-
dles, bulbous base, stylized pastel
morning glories in low relief on
white ground 400.00
Vase, 15" h., 2-handled, expanding
cylinder, stylized pastel morning
glories in low relief on white
ground . . . . .575.00 to 625.00

MOSS (1930's)
Candle holders, pendant moss on
pink shaded to green ground,
2" h., pr. 35.00
Console blue w/flower frog, pen-
dant moss on pink shaded to blue
ground, 14" 60.00
Ewer, pendant moss on pink shaded
to green ground, 6" h. 57.50
Jardiniere, pendant moss on pink
shaded to blue ground, 4" d. 35.00
Vase, 9" h., pendant moss on pink
shaded to blue ground 62.00
Vase, 12" h., pendant moss on pink
shaded to green ground 140.00

MOSTIQUE (1915)

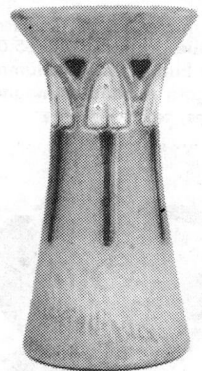

Mostique Vase

Bowl, 5½" d., glossy stylized iris
blossom designs on pebbled grey
ground 24.00
Console bowl w/flower frog, glossy
designs on pebbled tan ground . . . 40.00
Umbrella stand, glossy stylized
floral designs on pebbled tan
ground, 20" h. 235.00
Vase, 8" h., glossy pink & green
stylized floral design on pebbled
brown ground. 55.00
Vase, 10" h., glossy yellow, green &
blue arrowhead motif on pebbled
grey ground, glossy green interior
(ILLUS.) 22.50

Wall pocket, glossy geometric
design on pebbled brown ground,
12" h. 75.00

NORMANDY (1924)

Normandy Jardiniere & Pedestal

Jardiniere, ribbed body & band of
grapevines & clusters, green &
ivory w/brown ground band,
10" d., 7½" h. 175.00
Jardiniere, ribbed body & band of
grapevines & clusters, green &
ivory w/brown ground band,
8½" h. 300.00
Jardiniere & pedestal base, ribbed
body & band of grapevines &
clusters, green & ivory w/brown
ground band, overall 28" h.,
2 pcs. (ILLUS.) . . . . 675.00 to 750.00
Umbrella stand, ribbed body & band
of grapevines & clusters, green &
ivory w/brown ground band,
20" h. . . . . 375.00 to 450.00

ORIAN (1935)

Orian Vase

Bowl, 6" widest d., elongated side
handles, glossy burgundy w/tur-
quoise lining 105.00
Vase, 7½" h., glossy pale brown
w/green lining & handles
(ILLUS.) 65.00
Vase, 10½" h., glossy burgundy
w/turquoise lining 95.00

PANEL (1920)

Bowl, 4" d., panel of florals on deep
green ground 32.00
Bulb bowl, panel of florals on
brown-black ground, 8" d. 65.00
Candle holders, flat base, panel of
florals on brown-black ground,
2¼" h., pr. 25.00
Candlesticks, square flaring base,
panel of florals on brown-black
ground, 8½" h., pr. 95.00
Vase, 7" h., panel of naturalistic
leaves on dark green ground 75.00
Vase, 11" h., panel w/nude lady on
brown-black ground 225.00
Wall pocket, panel w/nude lady on
brown-black ground, 7" h. 225.00

PAULEO (1914)

Vase, 9½ x 6½", ovoid w/short
slender neck, h.p. floral decor . . . 600.00
Vase, 16½" h., baluster form, mottled deep blue-grey & cream 750.00
Vase, 19" h., swollen cylinder
w/short neck, matte finish 350.00

PEONY (1930's)

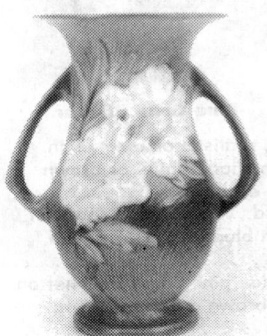

Peony Vase

Basket w/overhead handle, peony
blossoms in relief against textured pink shaded to green
ground, 10" h. 70.00
Bowl, 4" d., peony blossoms in
relief against textured green
ground 27.50
Console set: bowl & pr. candle
holders; peony blossoms in relief

against textured gold ground,
3 pcs. 75.00

Cornucopia-vase, peony blossoms in
relief against textured gold
ground, 6" h. 37.00

Creamer & sugar bowl, peony blossoms against textured green
ground, pr. 50.00

Ewer, peony blossoms against textured gold or pink ground, 10" h.,
each 75.00

Mug, peony blossoms against textured pink or green ground,
3½" h., each 35.00

Teapot, cov., peony blossoms
against textured pink ground 65.00

Vase, 10" h., peony blossoms
against textured green ground
(ILLUS.) 45.00

Vase, 13" h., peony blossoms
against textured pink shaded to
green ground 75.00

PINE CONE (1931)

Pine Cone Pitcher

Bookends, realistic pine cones in
relief on shaded blue or brown
ground, each pr. 160.00

Bowl, 12" d., footed, pine cones in
relief on blue or green ground,
each 55.00

Candlesticks, pine cones in relief on
blue or brown ground, 4½" h.,
each pr. 80.00

Cider set: pitcher & 4 mugs; pine
cones in relief on blue ground,
5 pcs. 395.00

Cornucopia-vase, pine cones in
relief on blue ground, 8" h. 75.00

Ewer, pine cones in relief on blue
ground, 10" h. 145.00

Jardiniere & pedestal base, pine
cones in relief on green ground,
overall 30" h., 2 pcs. . . . . 600.00 to 800.00

Pitcher, 10" h., pine cones in relief
on brown ground (ILLUS.) 135.00

Planter, base handle, pine cones in
relief on blue ground, 6" 40.00

Plate, 7½" d., pine cones in relief
on brown ground 245.00

Tray, double, center handle, pine
cones in relief on green ground,
13" 75.00

Vase, bud, 7" h., single handle rising from base to mid-section, pine
cones in relief on brown or green
ground, each . . . . 40.00 to 50.00

Vase, 12" h., pine cones in relief on
green ground 110.00

Vase, 18" h., urn-shaped, pine
cones in relief on blue ground 700.00

Window box, pine cones on blue,
brown or green ground, 15" l.,
each 95.00

POPPY (1930's)

Poppy Bowl

Basket w/pointed overhead handle,
poppies on shaded pink ground,
12½" h. 95.00

Bowl, 4" h., poppies on shaded pink
ground (ILLUS.) 37.50

Ewer, poppies on shaded turquoise
blue or pink ground, 18" h.,
each . . . . 175.00 to 200.00

Jardiniere, yellow poppies on turquoise blue shaded to white
ground, 8" d. 175.00

Vase, 8" h., 2-handled, pink poppies
on yellow shaded to pink
ground 40.00

Vase, 10½" h., 2-handled, yellow
poppies on turquoise blue shaded
to white ground 68.00

PRIMROSE (1932)

Basket, hanging-type, cluster of
long-stemmed blossoms & pad-
like leaves in relief on pink
ground 125.00

Candlesticks, cluster of long-
stemmed blossoms & pad-like
leaves in relief on pink ground,
4½" h., pr. 125.00

Cornucopia-vase, cluster of long-
stemmed blossoms & pad-like
leaves in relief on tan ground,
6" h. 28.00

Vase, 4" h., 2-handled, long-stemmed blossoms & pad-like leaves on blue ground 37.50

Vase, 8" h., pillow-shaped, 2-handled, long-stemmed blossoms & pad-like leaves on blue or pink ground, each 40.00

Wall pocket, long-stemmed blossoms & pad-like leaves on tan ground, 8½" h. 250.00

RAYMOR (1952)

Bowl, 8" d., sloping sides, dull tan finish 58.00

Butter dish, cov., dull green finish 40.00

Casserole, cov., dull green finish, 11" d. 31.00

Coffee pot, cov., w/stand, swinging-type, dull black finish 120.00

Cup & saucer, dull grey finish 20.00

Pitcher, water, 10" h., dull brown or white finish, each ....40.00 to 52.00

Plate, dinner, dull green or white finish, each ....9.00 to 14.00

Salt & pepper shakers, dull white finish, pr. 14.00

ROSECRAFT (1916-19)

Bowl, 6" d., glossy black 32.00

Candlesticks, glossy lavender, 8" h., pr. 48.00

Ginger jar, cov., glossy black, 8" h. ....170.00 to 200.00

Vase, 5½" h., 2-handled, glossy black 65.00

Vase, bud, 8" h., 1½" d., glossy cobalt blue or yellow, each ..50.00 to 65.00

ROSECRAFT VINTAGE (1924)

Rosecraft Vintage Vase

Bowl, 6" d., 4" h., curving band of brown & yellow grapevine w/fruit & foliage at shoulder, dark brown matte ground 50.00

Jardiniere, curving band of brown & yellow grapevine w/fruit & foliage at shoulder, dark brown matte ground, 11 x 10" 175.00

Pedestal base, curving band of brown & yellow grapevine w/fruit & foliage at flaring base, dark brown matte ground............ 300.00

Vase, 5" h., band of brown & yellow grapevine w/fruit & foliage at shoulder, dark brown matte ground (ILLUS.).................. 42.00

Wall pocket, band of brown & yellow grapevine w/fruit & foliage, dark brown matte ground, 9" h.....................90.00 to 110.00

Window box, band of brown & yellow grapevine w/fruit & foliage, dark brown matte ground, 11½ x 6" 185.00

ROZANE (1917)

Basket w/tall overhead handle, cluster of delicately tinted pink, lavender & yellow roses w/green leaves against stippled ivory ground, 11" h. 115.00

Basket, hanging-type, cluster of delicately tinted pink, lavender & yellow roses w/green leaves against stippled pink ground, 9 x 6" 110.00

Bowl, 8½" d., 4½" h., cluster of pink, lavender & yellow roses w/green leaves against stippled ivory ground.................... 55.00

Candlesticks, cluster of pink, lavender & yellow roses w/green leaves against stippled ivory ground, 8" h., pr. 105.00

Cuspidor, cluster of pink, lavender & yellow roses & green leaves against stippled ivory ground..... 120.00

Jardiniere & pedestal base, clusters of pink, lavender & yellow roses w/green leaves against stippled ivory ground, overall 28½" h., 2 pcs. ....300.00 to 400.00

Umbrella stand, cluster of pink, lavender & yellow roses w/green leaves against stippled ivory ground, 19½" h. 350.00

Vase, 8" to 10" h., cluster of pink, lavender & yellow roses & green leaves against stippled ivory ground, each ....55.00 to 70.00

Wall pocket, cluster of pink, lavender & yellow roses & green leaves against stippled mint green ground, 7½" h. 85.00

ROZANE ROYAL, LIGHT (1904)

Bowl, 5" d., ring handles at shoulder, slip-painted pale pink roses on cream shaded to grey ground 140.00

Pitcher, tankard, 13½" h., slip-
painted plums & foliage on shad-
ed grey ground 265.00
Vase, 6" h., twisted square form,
slip-painted pink & purple clover
on cream shaded to grey-green
ground, signed Josephine Imlay . . 310.00
Vase, 8½" h., slip-painted lily-of-
the-valley decor, signed Hester
Pillsbury. 165.00
Vase, 10½" h., slip-painted clusters
of blueberries & foliage decor,
signed Mae Timberlake 475.00
Vase, 13" h., slender cylinder
w/narrow neck, slip-painted
sweetpea blossoms in delicate
shades of lavender & pale pink on
cream shaded to pale grey
ground, artist-signed 395.00

RUSSCO (1930's)
Bowl, 8" d., 5" h., octagonal rim,
narrow vertical ribbon panels,
blue matte lustre glaze 50.00
Candle holders, octagonal base,
narrow vertical ribbon panels,
rust matte lustre glaze, 4½" h.,
pr. 35.00
Vase, 5" to 7" h., octagonal rim,
narrow vertical ribbon panels, terra cotta matte lustre glaze,
each .45.00 to 55.00
Vase, bud, 8" h., trumpet-shaped,
base handles, octagonal rim,
green matte glaze w/crystalline
overlay. 95.00
Vase, 10" h., octagonal rim, gold
matte glaze w/crystalline
overlay. 50.00

SAVONA (1924-28)
Vase, 7" to 8" h., fluted body, stylized floral beading at rim, blue,
each .100.00 to 140.00
Vase, 12½" h., fluted body w/grape
garlands at shoulder, lime
green 210.00
Wall pocket, angular rim handles,
fluted body, stylized floral bead-
ing at rim, blue, 8" h. 250.00

SILHOUETTE (1940's)
Basket w/overhead handle rising
from base to opposite mid-
section, silhouette floral panel,
shaded rust or white w/turquoise,
10" h., each 60.00
Bowl, 6" d., 3¼" h., silhouette floral
panel, shaded turquoise 35.00
Planter, silhouette floral panel,
shaded rust, 9" l. 25.00
Vase, 8" h., urn-shaped, silhouette
panel of a nude, shaded rust 135.00

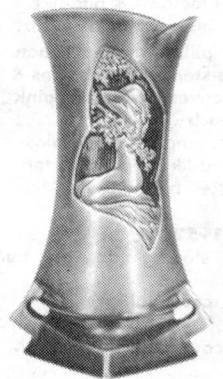

Silhouette Vase

Vase, 10" h., waisted cylinder on
square base, silhouette panel of a
nude, shaded turquoise (ILLUS.) . . 140.00

SNOWBERRY (1946)

Snowberry Ewer

Ash tray, shallow, snowberry branch
in relief on shaded rose ground . . 35.00
Basket w/overhead handle rising
from mid-section to top of shaped
rim, snowberry branch in relief on
shaded blue, green or rose
ground, 8" h., each . . . . . . .45.00 to 60.00
Bowl, 11" l., footed, 2-handled,
snowberry branch in relief on
shaded green ground 45.00
Creamer & sugar bowl, angular han-
dles, snowberry branch in relief
on shaded green ground, pr. 25.00
Ewer, snowberry branch in relief on
shaded green ground, 6" h.
(ILLUS.). 45.00
Flower pot w/attached saucer,
snowberry branch in relief on
shaded blue ground, 5½" h. 45.00

Teapot, cov., snowberry branch in
relief on shaded blue ground . . . . .　60.00
Vase, 7" h., angular handles, snowberry branch in relief on shaded
blue, green or rose ground,
each .45.00 to 55.00
Vase, 18" h., snowberry branch in
relief on shaded blue or green
ground, each 195.00

STEIN SETS (before 1916)
Ale set: tankard pitcher & 2 mugs;
Benevolent & Protective Order of
Elks (B.P.O.E.), creamware
w/brown elk & clock decal em-
blems, 3 pcs. . . . .　225.00
Ale set: tankard pitcher & 4 mugs;
Fraternal Order of Eagles (F.O.E.),
creamware w/brown spread-
winged eagle & rock decal decor,
5 pcs. . . . .　295.00
Ale set: tankard pitcher & 6 mugs;
Loyal Order of Moose, creamware
w/brown moose head & "Howdy
Pap" decal decor, 7 pcs. . . . .　740.00
Mug, creamware w/decal scene of
young woman kissing dog while
man looks on, "Try it on the
Dog," 5" h. . . . .　195.00
Mug, B.P.O.E., creamware w/brown
elk & clock decal emblems . . . .　80.00
Mug, F.O.E., creamware w/brown
spread-winged eagle & rock decal
decor, 5" h. . . . .　60.00
Mug, Knights of Pythias, creamware
w/colorful decal of heroic scene,
5" h. . . . .　175.00
Mug, Knights Templar, creamware
w/"Englewood Commandery, No.
59...," emblematic shield decal
reverse, 5" h. . . . .　120.00
Mug, Shrine, creamware w/"Kosair -
Louisville, 1934-1935" & emblem
decal, 6" h. . . . .　68.00
Pitcher, tankard, 11½" h., B.P.O.E.,
creamware w/brown elk & clock
decal emblems . . . .　125.00
Pitcher, tankard, 11½" h., Loyal
Order of Moose, creamware
w/brown moose head & "Howdy
Pap" decal decor . . . .　175.00

SUNFLOWER (1930)
Bowl, 4" d., chrysanthemum-type
yellow sunflowers on mottled
green ground . . . .　55.00
Candlesticks, chrysanthemum-type
sunflowers on mottled green
ground, 10" h., pr. . . . .　140.00
Console bowl, diamond-shaped, 2-
handled, chrysanthemum-type
sunflowers on mottled green
ground, 12½" l., 3" h. . . . .　95.00

Sunflower Vase

Vase, 4" h., 2-handled, chrysanthemum-type sunflowers on mot-
tled green ground (ILLUS.) . . . .　45.00
Vase, 8" h., bulbous bottom,
chrysanthemum-type sunflowers
on mottled green ground . . . .　135.00

TEASEL (1936)
Basket w/low overhead handle,
cylindrical w/flaring dentil rim,
footed, embossed teasel spray,
shaded blue or tan, 10" h.,
each . . . .　130.00
Bowl, 4" d., flattened sphere, closed
handles, embossed teasel spray,
glossy blue . . . .　20.00
Candle holders, flat base, embossed
teasel spray, pink shaded to rose,
low, pr. . . . .　25.00
Console set: bowl, flower frog & pr.
candle holders; embossed teasel
spray, shaded blue, 4 pcs. . . . .　90.00
Vase, 4" h., embossed teasel spray,
shaded blue . . . .　28.00
Vase, 9" h., embossed teasel spray,
beige shaded to tan . . . .　60.00
Vase, 15" h., 2-handled, embossed
teasel spray, shaded blue . . . .　125.00

THORN APPLE (1930's)
Bookends, trumpet-like flower one
side & prickly burr reverse on
shaded pink ground, pr. . . . .　125.00
Candlesticks, trumpet-like flower &
prickly burr on shaded blue
ground, 4½" h., pr. . . . .　85.00
Flower pot, trumpet-like flower one
side & prickly burr reverse on
pink shading to green ground,
5" h. . . . .　22.00
Vase, 4" h., squatty, 2-handled,
trumpet-like flower one side &
prickly burr reverse on shaded
pink ground . . . .　33.00
Vase, 12" h., trumpet-like flower
one side & prickly burr reverse on
shaded blue ground . . . .　135.00
Wall pocket, triple, trumpet-like
flower & prickly burr on shaded
pink ground, 8" h. . . . .　110.00

TOPEO (1934)

Console bowl, shaped rim, 4 areas of relief-molded beading, glossy deep red glaze, 13" l., 4" h....... 225.00

Vase, 6" h., spherical w/wide mouth, 4 areas of relief-molded beading, glossy deep red glaze... 145.00

Vase, 6½" h., ovoid w/waisted neck, 4 areas of relief-molded beading, green shaded to blue glaze 65.00

Vase, 7" to 8" h., 4 areas of relief-molded beading, glossy deep red glaze, each.............110.00 to 135.00

TOURIST (before 1916)

Bowl, 5¾" d., 3" h., transfer-printed & painted scene of early touring car & roadway on creamware 300.00

Bowl, 7" d., 3½" h., transfer-printed & painted scene of early touring car & roadway on creamware 850.00

Jardiniere, transfer-printed & painted scene of early touring car & roadway on creamware, 12 x 10" 750.00

Vase, 9½" h., transfer-printed & painted scene of early touring car & roadway on creamware 350.00

TUSCANY (1924-28)

Bowl, 6¼" d., 2½" h., open handles terminating in embossed clusters of blue grapes & green leaves, mottled grey.................... 20.00

Candle holders, flared base w/open handles rising from clusters of grapes & leaves to candle nozzle, mottled pink, 3" h., pr.......... 25.00

Console set: 10" d. footed bowl, flower frog & pr. candle holders; handles terminating in clusters of grapes & leaves, mottled pink, 4 pcs.......................... 75.00

Vase, 4" to 6" h., open handles terminating in clusters of grapes & leaves, mottled grey, each.................30.00 to 40.00

Vase, 8" h., handles terminating in clusters of grapes & leaves, mottled pink 35.00

Wall pocket, open handles terminating in clusters of grapes & leaves, mottled grey or pink, 7" h., each ....50.00 to 65.00

VELMOSS SCROLL (1916)

Bowl, 9" d., 2½" h., incised stylized red roses & green leaves, creamy ivory matt glaze 30.00

Candlesticks, incised stylized red roses & green leaves, creamy ivory matt glaze, 8" h., pr........ 115.00

Jardiniere, incised stylized red roses

& green leaves, creamy ivory matt glaze, 11 x 9"................... 200.00

Vase, 5" h., globular, incised stylized red roses & green leaves, creamy ivory matt glaze 38.00

Vase, 10" h., expanding cylinder, footed, incised stylized red roses & green leaves, creamy ivory matt glaze 85.00

Wall pocket, incised stylized red roses & green leaves, creamy ivory matt glaze, 11" h.......... 155.00

VISTA (1920's)

Basket w/overhead handle, embossed green coconut palm trees & lavender-blue pool against grey ground, 6½" h. 95.00

Jardiniere, embossed green coconut palm trees & lavender-blue pool against grey ground, 7¼ x 6½" .. 95.00

Urn, 2-handled, embossed green coconut palm trees & lavender-blue pool against grey ground, 8" d., 8½" h. 80.00

Vase, 15" h., tapering cylinder, embossed green coconut palm trees & lavender-blue pool against grey ground 175.00

Window box w/liner, embossed coconut palm trees & lavender-blue pool against grey ground.... 250.00

VOLPATO (1918)

Bowl, 8" d., w/flower frog, garlands of vines & roses in relief above fluted body, glossy ivory, 2 pcs. ... 100.00

Console set: 14" oval bowl & pr. 4" h. candle holders; garlands of vines & roses in relief, glossy ivory, 3 pcs. 135.00

Flower pot w/saucer, garlands of vines & roses in relief, glossy ivory, 6" d., 6" h. 85.00

Urn, cov., garlands of vines & roses in relief above fluted body, fluted cover, glossy ivory, 8" h. 175.00

Vase, 6" h., 2-handled, garlands of vines & roses in relief above fluted body, glossy ivory 58.00

Vase, 10" h., garlands of vines & roses in relief above fluted body, glossy ivory.................... 70.00

WATER LILY (1940's)

Basket w/pointed overhead handle, water lilies in relief on textured blue, brown or pink shaded to green ground, 8" h., each ....50.00 to 60.00

Basket, hanging-type w/original chains, water lilies in relief on textured blue or pink shaded to green ground, 9", each 50.00

Bookends, water lilies in relief on textured pink shaded to green ground, pr. 75.00

Candle holders, angular side handles, water lilies in relief on textured brown ground, 2" h., pr. . . . 30.00

Water Lily Cookie Jar

Cookie jar, cov., 2-handled, water lilies in relief on textured blue ground (ILLUS.). 125.00

Cornucopia-vase, water lilies in relief on textured pink shaded to green ground, 8" h. 40.00

Ewer, water lilies in relief on textured pink shaded to green ground, 6" h. 35.00

Model of a conch shell, water lilies in relief on textured brown ground, 6" to 8" h., each . .35.00 to 55.00

Vase, 4" h., water lilies in relief on textured blue ground 25.00

Vase, 9" h., pedestal base, water lilies in relief on textured blue, brown or pink shaded to green ground, each . . . . .45.00 to 60.00

WHITE ROSE (1940's)

White Rose Ewer

Basket w/circular handle, white roses in relief on blue or pink shaded to green ground, 8" h., each 65.00

Bookends, white roses in relief on blue ground, pr. 70.00

Console set: bowl, flower frog & pr. candlesticks; white roses in relief on pink shaded to green ground, 4 pcs. 100.00

Ewer, white roses in relief on blue ground, 15" h. (ILLUS.) 75.00

Pitcher, white roses in relief on pink shaded to green ground 65.00

Teapot, cov., white roses in relief on blue ground 85.00

Vase, 4" h., white roses in relief on blue or brown ground, each. 20.00

Vase, 6" h., white roses in relief on blue or pink shaded to green ground, each . . . . .27.00 to 35.00

Vase, 9" h., fan-shaped, 2-handled, white roses in relief on brown or pink shaded to green ground, each 50.00

WINCRAFT (1948)

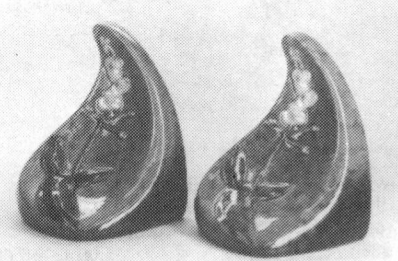

Wincraft Bookends

Basket w/overhead handle, shaped rim, berries & foliage in relief on glossy blue, tan or green ground, 12" h., each . . . . .55.00 to 65.00

Bookends, florals in relief on glossy dark brown ground, 5½" h., pr. (ILLUS.). 55.00

Console bowl, footed, florals in relief on glossy lime green ground, 12" l., 4" h. 55.00

Creamer & sugar bowl, florals in relief on glossy shaded blue ground, pr. 28.00

Cup & saucer, florals in relief on glossy lime green ground 95.00

Teapot, cov., florals in relief on glossy lime green ground 50.00

Vase, 10" h., cylindrical, tab handles, black panther & green palm trees in relief on glossy shaded lime green or tan ground, each 155.00

Wall pocket, square, ivy vine in

relief on glossy lime green or
turquoise blue ground, 8½" h.,
each . . . . .75.00 to 95.00

WINDSOR (1931)
Basket w/overhead handle, fan-
shaped, footed, mottled terra cotta & orange shading to brown
matt glaze, 4½" h. 150.00
Vase, 5" h., stylized ferns against
mottled blue ground 90.00
Vase, 8½" h., 2-handled, bulbous
base, stylized ferns against mottled terra cotta ground . .165.00 to 185.00

WISTERIA (1933)

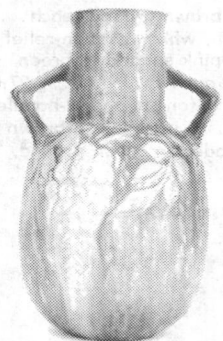

Wisteria Vase

Bowl, 6" to 8" d., angular rim handles, lavender wisteria & vines on
textured blue to brown ground,
each .45.00 to 65.00
Console set: 12" l. bowl & pr. 4" h.
candle holders; lavender wisteria
& vines on textured blue to brown
ground, 3 pcs. . . . . .165.00 to 195.00
Jardiniere, lavender wisteria & vines
on textured brown ground,
8" d. 175.00
Vase, 5" h., wisteria & vines on tex-
tured blue to brown ground 75.00
Vase, 9½" h., angular handles,
wisteria & vines on textured
blue to brown ground (ILLUS.) 115.00

ZEPHYR LILY (1940's)
Basket w/overhead handle, cylindrical w/flaring shaped rim, white &
yellow lilies on blue ground w/im-
pressed oval swirls, 10" h. 60.00
Basket, hanging-type w/original
chains, rose & yellow lilies on
green ground w/impressed oval
swirls, 7½" d. 65.00
Bowl, 6" d., yellow lilies on brown
shaded to green ground w/im-
pressed oval swirls 30.00

Candlesticks, rose & yellow lilies on
green ground, 4½" h., pr. 45.00
Cookie jar, cov., white & yellow
lilies on blue ground, 10" h. 110.00
Creamer & sugar bowl, yellow lilies
on brown shaded to green
ground, pr. 58.00
Ewer, white & yellow lilies on blue
ground, 10" h. 70.00
Flower pot w/saucer, white & yel-
low lilies on blue ground, 5" h. 45.00
Jardiniere & pedestal base, yellow
lilies on brown shaded to green
ground, overall 24½" h.,
2 pcs. . . . . .350.00 to 495.00
Tray, leaf shape, white & yellow
lilies on blue ground, 14½" l. 40.00
Vase, 6" h., urn-shaped, white &
yellow lilies on blue ground 40.00
Vases, 18" h., white & yellow lilies
on blue ground, pr. 475.00

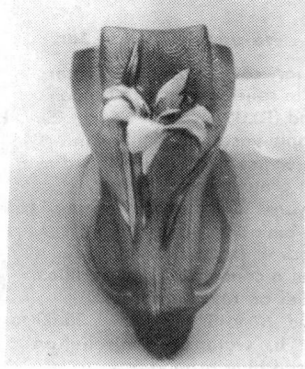

Zephyr Lily Wall Pocket

Wall pocket, base handles, yellow
lily on green ground, 8" h.
(ILLUS.) 60.00

ROYAL BAYREUTH

*Good china in numerous patterns and de-
signs has been made at the Royal Bayreuth
factory in Tettau, Germany, since 1794. Listings below are by the company's lines, plus
miscellaneous pieces. Interest in this china
remains at a peak and prices continue to rise.
Pieces listed carry the company's blue mark
except where noted otherwise.*

CORINTHIAN
Candlestick, saucer base, tall stem,
flaring candle cup joined to base
w/elongated handle, white Etruscan figure & Greek Key borders
on black ground, tangerine lining,
6" h. (single) $95.00

Creamer, pinched spout, white classical ladies on black ground, yel-
low lining, 4" h. 60.00
Creamer, bulbous, green ground,
5" h. 90.00
Inkwell, black ground, 3 x 2½" 45.00
Loving cup, 3-handled, white classi-
cal figures on black ground 45.00
Smoker's set: cigarette jar & ash
tray; black ground, 2 pcs. 45.00
Tobacco jar, cov. 150.00
Vase, 3½" h., Etruscan figures on
tangerine ground 40.00

DEVIL & CARDS

Devil & Cards Saucer

Ash tray 125.00
Candlestick, low (single) 290.00
Candy dish . . . . .175.00 to 250.00
Creamer, figural red devil
handle . . . . .115.00 to 150.00
Dresser tray 475.00
Humidor & cover w/figural red devil
finial 525.00
Match holder 175.00
Mug, figural red devil handle,
4¾" h. . . . . .150.00 to 200.00
Pitcher, 7½" h. 350.00
Pitcher, 8½" h. . . . . .325.00 to 400.00
Plate, 6½" d.   87.50
Saucer (ILLUS.) 85.00
Sugar bowl, cov. . . . . .175.00 to 300.00

DEVIL & DICE

Devil & Dice Demitasse Cup

Cup, demitasse (ILLUS.) 150.00
Cup & saucer, demitasse 250.00
Match holder, figural red devil at
one corner 95.00

MOTHER-OF-PEARL FINISH

Poppy Creamer

Bowl, 9½ x 6", oak leaf
molded . . . . .295.00 to 345.00
Bowl, 10" d., Murex Shell patt. 170.00
Box, cov., Murex Shell patt. 170.00
Chamberstick, Murex Shell patt. 130.00
Cookie jar, cov., Murex Shell
patt. . . . . .295.00 to 365.00
Cookie jar, cov., oak leaf molded . . 535.00
Creamer, Murex Shell patt. w/coral
handle 75.00
Creamer, oak leaf molded 125.00
Creamer, poppy-molded, pearlized
w/gold center (ILLUS.) 110.00
Match holder, wall-type, Murex
Shell patt. 75.00
Mustard jar, cov., grape cluster
mold, pearlized w/pink high-
lights 95.00
Mustard jar, cover & ladle, Murex
Shell patt., set 55.00
Mustard jar, cov., poppy-molded,
pink-tinged 90.00
Pitcher, milk, Murex Shell
patt. 135.00
Pitcher, water, grape cluster
mold . . . . .375.00 to 425.00
Pitcher, water, poppy-molded 435.00
Powder box, cov., Oyster & Pearl
patt. 125.00
Salt & pepper shakers, grape cluster
mold, lavender-tinged, pr. 125.00
Wall pocket, grape cluster mold 185.00

ROSE TAPESTRY

Basket, 3-color roses, 8 x 4",
3½" h. 185.00
Basket, 3-color roses, 4¾" w.,
4¾" h. 310.00
Basket, 3-color roses,
6¾" h. . . . . .325.00 to 395.00
Bowl, 10½" d., 3-color roses 700.00

Bowl, yellow & pink roses,
small 275.00
Cake plate, pierced handles, 3-color
roses, 10½" d.................. 425.00
Chocolate pot, cov., pink roses 1,050.00

Rose Tapestry Creamer

Creamer, pinched spout, 3-color
roses, 3½" h. (ILLUS.) ...150.00 to 185.00
Creamer, pink roses, 3½" h........ 165.00
Creamer, corset-waisted, 3-color
roses, 4" h..................... 185.00
Creamer & open sugar bowl, 3-color
roses, pr. ....225.00 to 325.00
Cup & saucer, pink & white
roses 175.00
Cup & saucer, 3-color roses 300.00
Dish, cloverleaf form w/handle, 3-
color roses, 5 x 4½" 120.00
Dresser set: dresser tray, hair receiver & cov. powder box; 3-color
roses, 3 pcs.................... 600.00
Dresser tray, 3-color roses,
11 5/8 x 8¼" ....250.00 to 325.00
Hair receiver, pink roses,
4½" d..................145.00 to 200.00
Hair receiver, pink & yellow
roses ....175.00 to 195.00
Hair receiver, 3-color
roses ....135.00 to 195.00
Hatpin holder, 3-color
roses ....275.00 to 350.00
Match holder, wall-type, pink &
yellow roses, gold trim,
4½ x 3½"..............195.00 to 225.00
Pin box, cov., pink roses........... 165.00
Pin dish, 3-color roses, 3 3/8" d..... 80.00
Pitcher, 6" h., corset-waisted, pink
roses 210.00
Planter, 2 gilt handles at base, flut-
ed rim, pink roses, 2¾" h. (no in-
sert) 150.00
Plate, 7½" d., 3-color roses 195.00
Powder box, cov., 3-footed, 3-color
roses, 4" d.................... 175.00
Powder box, cov., 3-footed, pink &
white roses, 4½" d............. 225.00
Salt & pepper shakers, 3-color
roses, pr...................... 425.00
Toothpick holder, footed, 3-color
roses 175.00
Vase, 5" h., 3-color roses ..165.00 to 180.00

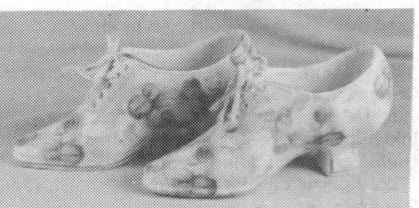

Rose Tapestry Lady's Shoes

Whimsies, lady's shoes w/silk laces,
3-color roses, 5½" l., pr.
(ILLUS.)........................ 800.00

SAND BABIES

Sand Babies Creamer

Creamer (ILLUS.) ....100.00 to 125.00
Cup & saucer, demitasse
(unmarked) 50.00
Match holder, wall-type............ 195.00
Planter, small.................... 75.00

SNOW BABIES
Box, cov., arrowhead form......... 80.00
Chamberstick, saucer
base ....125.00 to 175.00
Chocolate pot, cov., 7" h...150.00 to 175.00
Dish, 4" sq....................... 45.00
Feeding dish.............110.00 to 125.00
Flower pot (no liner) 60.00
Mug, 3" h........................ 75.00
Nappy, babies on sled 70.00
Pitcher, 6" h. 185.00
Tea tile, 6" d................60.00 to 85.00
Wall pocket...................... 135.00

SUNBONNET BABIES
Ash tray, diamond-shaped, babies
mending, 5¼" l................. 98.00
Bowl, cereal, babies sweeping 150.00
Box, cov., oval, babies sweeping ... 190.00
Cake plate w/pierced
handles, babies washing,
10½" d................195.00 to 250.00
Compote, 4" d., 2½" h., babies
cleaning...................... 345.00
Creamer, pinched spout, babies
fishing ....145.00 to 165.00
Cup & saucer, babies sweeping..... 165.00

Feeding dish, babies fishing,
7½" d. 165.00

Sunbonnet Babies Hair Receiver

Hair receiver, ruffled rim, babies
washing, 2¾" h. (ILLUS.) 295.00
Mug, babies ironing, 3¼" h. 150.00
Plate, 6" d., babies
cleaning. . . . . .95.00 to 125.00
Plate, 7½" d., babies washing &
ironing 140.00
Rose bowl, babies washing &
ironing, 3" h. 190.00
Salt & pepper shakers, babies
mending & babies washing, pr. . . . 190.00
Sugar bowl, cov., babies
fishing . . . . .135.00 to 150.00
Tray, babies washing, 10 x 7" 300.00
Waste bowl, babies fishing. 125.00

TOMATO ITEMS

Tomato Sugar Bowl & Creamer

Tomato berry set, master bowl & 6
sauce dishes, 7 pcs. 125.00
Tomato cookie jar, cov. 125.00
Tomato creamer & cov. sugar bowl,
pr. (ILLUS.) 80.00
Tomato cup & saucer, demitasse. . . . 45.00
Tomato mustard pot, cov. 45.00
Tomato pitcher, milk 155.00
Tomato salt & pepper shakers, pr. . . . 45.00
Tomato tea set, cov. teapot, cream-
er & sugar bowl, 3 pcs. 170.00

MISCELLANEOUS

Ash tray, spade-shaped, musicians
decor 45.00
Bowl, 9½" d., scenic decor w/cattle

grazing amidst trees on shaded
green ground 85.00
Cake plate, pierced handles, scenic
decor w/boy seated on a log & 3
donkeys on green shaded to
brown ground, 10½" d. 150.00
Candlesticks, penguin decor on yel-
low ground, pr. 135.00

Hunt Scene Chamberstick

Chamberstick, shield-back type, fox
hunt scene decor, 4" h. (ILLUS.) . . 245.00
Chocolate set: chocolate pot & 4
cups; scenic decor w/boy & 3
donkeys, 5 pcs. 275.00
Compote, 6" w., 2¾" h., sheep
decor 40.00
Creamer, wide mouth, scenic decor
w/Brittany girl at seashore, sailboat & seagull in distance,
3 3/8" h. 55.00
Creamer, pinched spout, "tapestry,"
pastoral scene of man tending
turkeys, 3½" h. 145.00
Creamer, pinched spout, "tapestry,"
portrait of woman & horse resting
beneath tree, 3½" h. 175.00
Creamer, bulbous base, straight
neck, beaded handle, pastoral
scene w/cows & trees on green
ground, 3¾" h. 60.00
Creamer, cavaliers (2) decor,
3¾" h. 55.00
Creamer, desert scene w/Arab on
horse decor on blue & gold
ground, 4" h. 95.00
Creamer, hunting scene w/fox &
hounds, 4" h. 75.00
Creamer, pinched spout, pastoral
scene w/sheep, 4" h. 110.00
Creamer, roses & ivy & gold trim on
pale green shaded to white
ground, 4" h. 52.00
Creamer, girl w/water jug decor . . . 225.00
Creamer, "tapestry," castle scene . . 200.00
Creamer, figural alligator 160.00
Creamer, figural apple 65.00

Creamer, figural bellringer 225.00
Creamer, figural bull, black or
  brown, each 170.00
Creamer, figural cat, black 110.00
Creamer, figural clown, red 155.00
Creamer, figural cockatoo 175.00
Creamer, figural crow, black 85.00
Creamer, figural Dachshund dog 125.00

Eagle Creamer

Creamer, figural eagle, 3½" h.
  (ILLUS.) 145.00
Creamer, figural elk . . . . 75.00 to 100.00
Creamer, figural fish head 110.00
Creamer, figural flounder 160.00

Grape Cluster Creamer

Creamer, figural grape cluster
  (ILLUS.) 135.00
Creamer, figural "Man of the Moun-
  tain" .80.00 to 110.00
Creamer, figural milk maid 250.00
Creamer, figural oak
  leaf . . . . .85.00 to 125.00
Creamer, figural orange,
  4" h. .60.00 to 80.00
Creamer, figural owl 165.00
Creamer, figural pansy, blue or pur-
  ple, each . . . . .100.00 to 135.00
Creamer, figural parakeet 145.00
Creamer, figural pear 125.00
Creamer, figural perch 142.50
Creamer, figural poodle,
  grey . . . . .135.00 to 170.00
Creamer, figural poppy, red 100.00
Creamer, figural rooster 180.00
Creamer, figural rose 165.00
Creamer, figural St. Bernard dog . . . 137.50

Creamer, figural Santa Claus 485.00
Creamer, figural seal, shaded grey
  to pink 200.00
Creamer, figural snake 700.00
Creamer, figural water-
  melon . . . . .135.00 to 165.00
Creamer & cov. sugar bowl, Little
  Miss Muffet & Jack & Beanstalk
  decor, pr. 85.00
Creamer & cov. sugar bowl, figural
  strawberry, pr. 135.00
Dresser tray, "tapestry," scenic
  decor w/castle on mountain,
  waterfall & village under moonlit
  clouded sky, 11 x 8" 350.00
Match holder, hanging-type, "tapes-
  try," tavern scene, gold trim 225.00
Mustard jar, cov., figural apple 50.00
Mustard jar, cov., figural poppy,
  red 65.00
Pitcher, 7" h., musicians decor 140.00
Pitcher, tankard, 8" h., Arab horse-
  man & palm tree decor 150.00
Pitcher, lemonade, figural lemon . . . 265.00
Plaque, pieced to hang, "tapestry,"
  gold scalloped rim, hunting scene
  decor, 9" d. 235.00
Powder jar, cov., figural pansy,
  yellow 225.00
Salt dip, footed, sheep decor 60.00
Salt & pepper shakers, figural grape
  cluster, purple, pr. 65.00
String holder, figural
  rooster . . . . .150.00 to 200.00
Teapot, cov., figural grape cluster,
  green 275.00
Tea set: cov. teapot, creamer &
  sugar bowl; fox hunt scene,
  3 pcs. 350.00
Toothpick holder, 2-handled, footed,
  girl & dog decor 90.00
Vase, 3¼" h., "tapestry," castle
  scene decor 138.00
Vase, 4" h., "tapestry," village
  scene w/mountains & trees on
  shaded blue, green & brown
  ground 225.00
Vase, 4¼" h., 2½" d., scene of
  Dutch boy flying kite & running
  dog on grey shaded to brown
  ground 55.00
Vase, 4¾" h., 5" d., pastoral scene
  w/white long-haired goats (3) on
  green shading to tan ground, gold
  trim 92.50
Vase, 5" h., bottle-shaped, "tapes-
  try," scene of court lady 295.00
Vase, 6" h., portrait of beautiful girl
  w/long brunette hair wearing
  large hat & ruffled dress 125.00
Vase, 7" h., desert scene w/Arabs &
  camels 150.00
Vase, 10"h., bust portrait of beauti-
  ful woman reserved on blue 210.00

"Tapestry" Vase

Vase, "tapestry," portrait of beautiful girl beside pony (ILLUS.) 425.00
Wall pocket, model of a grape cluster, pink 175.00
Whimsey, model of a man's high-top
shoe, black 75.00
Whimsey, model of a lady's high
button shoe, 2-tone brown, w/silk
laces 110.00

ROYAL BONN & BONN

*Bonn and subsequently Royal Bonn china
were produced in Bonn, Germany, in a
manufactory established in 1755. Later wares
made there are often marked Mehlem or bear
the initials FM or a castle mark. Most wares
were of the hand-painted type. Clock cases
were also made in Bonn.*

Bowl, 9" d., 4" h., collared foot,
blue floral decor $45.00
Cheese dish w/slant lid, roses decor
w/gold trim, marked Mehlem 125.00
Cookie jar, lavender, rose & yellow
florals on shaded blue ground, silverplate cover, rim & handle,
4 3/8" sq., 7¼" h. 85.00
Ewer, h.p. parrot in tree decor,
12" h. 85.00
Jardiniere, h.p. multicolored floral
decor, 15" d., 12" h. 365.00
Plate, 9" d., floral decor w/gilt
tracery 55.00
Urn, cov., gold handled, gold
footed, "The Cries of London"
reserved on deep red ground
w/ornate gilt detailing,
32" h. 1,900.00
Vase, 4" h., bulbous, overall pink &
yellow roses on soft green
ground 85.00

Vase, 6" h., portrait of lovely woman reserved on cranberry red
ground within Art Nouveau style
gilt border, artist-signed 195.00
Vase, 8" h., 5" d., gold & orange
floral decor on brown shaded to
yellow ground 90.00
Vase, 8½" h., double-handled, blue,
pink & magenta florals on pale
blue ground w/gold trim, crown
mark 125.00
Vase, 10" h., gold ram's head handles, scene of a young lady in a
garden setting, artist-signed 125.00
Vase, 11" h., 2-handled, scalloped
rim, soft pink & white orchids on
blue ground w/gilding 145.00
Vase, 12¼" h., 5" widest d., green
handles, neck & square base
w/gilt trim, oval panel w/scene of
cattle & farmhouse on white
ground enriched w/gilding, artist-
signed 195.00

ROYAL COPENHAGEN

1929 Royal Copenhagen Mark

*This porcelain has been made in Copenha-
gen, Denmark, since 1715. The ware is hard-
paste. Also see COMMEMORATIVE
PLATES and INVALID FEEDERS.*

Bouillon cups & saucers, Flora Danica patt., botanical specimen
within border heightened w/pink
enamel & gilding, set of 12 .....$6,875.00
Figure of Balinese Dancer, by
Malinowski 225.00
Figure of Goose Girl, No. 527,
9½" h................175.00 to 235.00
Figurine of Pan, seated & playing
pipes, artist-signed, 5½" h. 285.00
Fruit basket & stand, reticulated
sides applied w/pastel-colored
floral encrustations, Flora Danica
patt., botanical specimen within
border heightened w/pink enamel
& gilding, 9" oval basket & 10½"
oval stand, pr. 1,320.00
Model of a bunny, seated, white,
3 x 3¼" 110.00
Pickle dishes, leaf-shaped, Flora
Danica patt., botanical specimen
within border heightened w/pink
enamel & gilding, twig-form handle terminating in pastel-colored
flowers, 7 1/8" & 8¼" l., 2 pr. ... 825.00

Plate, 7" d., commemorative, Frederick IX - 1947-72, blue & white 45.00

Plates, dinner, 10¼" d., Flora Danica patt., botanical specimen within border heightened w/pink enamel & gilding, set of 12 ....3,300.00 to 4,750.00

Soup plates, Flora Danica patt., botanical specimen within border heightened w/pink enamel & gilding, 8 5/8" d., set of 12 ....3,850.00

Soup tureen, cov., Flora Danica patt., botanical specimen within border heightened w/pink enamel & gilding, 13¼" oval ....2,200.00 to 2,640.00

Vase, 15" h., bulbous, floral bouquet on blue ground, artist-signed, 1925 .... 330.00

ROYAL DUX

Royal Dux Polar Bear

These wares were made in Bohemia and many were imported to the United States around the turn of the century. Although numerous pieces were originally inexpensive, collectors have taken a fancy to the ware and the prices of the better pieces continue to rise.

Card tray, model of a frog standing on a shell & playing an accordion, beige matte finish, pink triangle mark, 6 x 5" $95.00

Centerpiece compote, three 12" h. figures of dancing ladies wearing cobalt blue gowns surround standard, variegated cobalt blue florals & overall gold scrolling in relief in bowl, pink triangle mark, stamped "Czechoslovakia" & dated 1924, overall 20" h......... 550.00

Figure of lady w/water jug at shell-shaped lily pond, earth tones, 9½ x 9½" 330.00

Figure of a semi-nude Art Deco dancer, 9¾" h. 375.00

Figure of peasant woman holding a basket, 10¾" h. 350.00

Figure of a barefoot woman kneel-

ing over a reflecting pool, beige, brown & gold tones, 11" h....... 395.00

Figure of a maiden w/tambourine, 14" h. 180.00

Figure of lady w/water jug & cup, 18" h. 300.00

Figures, peasant boy & peasant girl, pink, green & gold garments & satin finish flesh tones, pink triangle mark & "Bohemia," 11½" h., pr................................ 550.00

Figure group, shepherdess & goats, she wearing rose toga, beige sheepskin robe & green turban, white & tan goats, semi-glossy finish, 4½" d., 14¾" h. 595.00

Figure group, mother & 2 boys, pink, green & gold w/flesh tones, matte finish, 16¼" h............. 650.00

Figure group, 2 Art Nouveau style semi-nude ladies sitting atop shell, gold, green & cream 475.00

Model of a fawn in cautious stance, oak foliage on base, 11½" l., 8" h............................ 110.00

Model of a white polar bear w/black nose, 20" l. (ILLUS.) 418.00

Vase, 5" h., 2-handled, applied florals & fruit on dusty rose ground 85.00

Vase, 9" h., relief-molded Art Nouveau lady's head & flowing hair forming handles, green-swirled body, pink triangle mark 225.00

Vase, 10" h., 2-handled, Art Nouveau stylized floral decor 114.00

Vase, 17" h., Art Nouveau "Siren of the Waves" in relief 300.00

ROYAL RUDOLSTADT

Royal Rudolstadt Match Holder

This factory's wares came from Thuringia, Germany, where a faience factory was established in 1720. E. Bohne, made hard paste porcelain here from 1854, and most wares found today date from the late 19th century.

Bowl, 8 3/8" d., footed, h.p. poppies decor $65.00

Child's set: plate, cup & saucer; Happy Fats decor, 3 pcs. 185.00

Chocolate set: cov. chocolate pot & 4 c/s; roses & ferns decor, gold trim, 9 pcs. 98.00

Cup & saucer, yellow & green roses decor 30.00

Dresser set: hatpin holder, hair receiver & cov. powder jar; large poppies on shaded green to white ground, 3 pcs. 100.00

Ewer, green serpentine spout, brown handle, h.p. bird, butterfly, ferns & grasses w/gold trim on ivory ground, 11¾" h. 150.00

Match holder, figure of little girl standing beside basket on mound base, overall 6" h. (ILLUS.) 50.00

Mayonnaise bowl, underplate & ladle, pink & purple floral decor, 3 pcs. 125.00

Pitcher, feather scroll handle, reverse twist mold body, bird & fern decor 80.00

Plate, 6" d., roses decor, artist-signed 20.00

Plate, 8¼" d., winter scene w/ice man & sleigh decor 60.00

Relish, overall bluebirds decor, 13" l. 37.00

Sugar bowl, cov., 2-handled, blue-bird decor 35.00

Tray, double-pierced handles, Day Lilies decor, 12 x 8½" 67.50

Vase, 12" h., baluster-shaped, large h.p. pink roses on pastel ground, ornate gold trim 75.00

Whimsey, lady's shoe, reticulated... 65.00

ROYAL VIENNA

Framed Charger

The second factory in Europe to make hard-paste porcelain was established in Vienna in 1719 by Claud Innocentius de Paquier. The factory underwent various changes of administration through the years and finally closed in 1865. Since then, however, the porcelain has been reproduced by various factories in Austria and Germany, many of which have reproduced also the early beehive mark. Early pieces, naturally, bring far higher prices than the later ones or the reproductions.

Centerpiece bowl w/cover & stand, each piece painted either side w/oval panel depicting various allegorical figures including parting lovers within gilt borders, reserved on a claret-colored ground w/purple panels between claret ovals, each outlined w/pale blue band & heightened in gilding, late 19th c., 16¼" h. $935.00

Chargers, one emblematic of "Night" w/angel holding a child & floating in a moonlit sky, painted after Kaulbach, the other a self-portrait of the artist & his wife, painted after Rembrandt, each signed Ferstl, late 19th c., 14 5/8" d., framed, pr. (ILLUS. of one) 2,420.00

Charger, "The Return of Columbus, 1494," Columbus standing on a wharf & unloading cargo, including exotic birds & tobacco leaves, assisted by Indians wearing colorful feather costumes, while noblemen, peasants, children & others look on, within deep claret border heightened w/gilt details, late 19th c., 20 1/8" d. 1,100.00

Compote, 9½" d., 2-handled, portrait decor on cobalt blue ground, gold trim 145.00

Cup & saucer, portrait of beautiful girl, overall blue jeweling........ 295.00

Cup & saucer, scene w/warriors & girl on cup, saucer w/purple center & pink & blue scenes w/gold at border, overall gold & white relief details 390.00

Plate, 8¼" d., mythological scene on gold ground center, cobalt blue border 250.00

Plates, 9½" d.: portraits of Autumn as a fair-haired maiden wearing a pale yellow gown within a lustrous blue-grey border; Cecelia seated at a spinet in her chambers within lustrous pale green border; Ruth standing in wheat field within cobalt blue border w/gilt details; Marie Antoinette within pale green border reserved

w/apple green panels alternating
w/small floral panels within
smaller pale pink borders; first
3 signed Wagner, ca. 1900,
set of 4 . . . . .2,200.00

Plates, 9 5/8" d., portrait of Marie
Antoinette (after Vigee LeBrun) on
one & portrait of Desdemona on
other, each within gilt bands & a
luminous turquoise border heightened in gilding w/various Neoclassical devices within white-
beaded borders, artist-signed,
late 19th c., pr. 990.00

Plate, 9¾" d., center scene of
Daphne & Apollo 390.00

Plate, center scene entitled "Hectors
Abschied," purple, pink & blue
border w/heavy gold relief 600.00

Tea caddy, cov., scene of lady & 2
children at waterfall, artist-
signed 729.00

Vienna Tete-a-Tete

Tete-a-tete: cov. coffee pot, hot
water pot (missing cover), cov.
sugar bowl, pr. coffee cans &
saucers & circular tray; each piece
reserved w/vivid mythological
scenes within gilt-bordered rectangles on ground filled w/wide
blue borders w/gold foliate &
diamond motifs & narrow pink,
cream & patterned gold borders,
19th c., w/minor chips & other
repairs, 14 1/8" d. tray (ILLUS.) . .1,100.00

Vase, 10" h., oval reserve w/bust
portrait of a lovely lady w/pink
flowers in her dark hair on olive
green ground w/gilt details,
ca. 1910 . . . . 302.00

Vases, cov., 21 5/8" h., continuous
frieze w/"The Entrance of Charles
V into Antwerp" & "The Crowning
of Marie de' Medici," reserved between cobalt blue borders heightened in gilding, on stands, 1
artist-signed, ca. 1900, pr. 1,650.00

ROYAL WORCESTER

Royal Worcester Shell Dish

*This porcelain has been made by the Roy-
al Worcester Porcelain Co. at Worcester,
England, from 1862 to the present. For earlier porcelain made in Worcester, see WOR-
CESTER. Royal Worcester is distinguished
from those wares made at Worcester between
1751 and 1862 that are referred to as only
Worcester by collectors.*

Basket, double branch-form side
handle, 3 stubby feet, bark-
textured base, embossed florals
on pale green ground, ca. 1875,
6½" d., 6" h. $350.00

Candlesticks, trefoil base, stem
w/three sphinx caryatids supporting deep candle cup molded w/lo-
tus leaves, satin finish w/gold
highlights, ca. 1868, 7½" h., pr. . . . 400.00

Cup & saucer, demitasse, cattle in
highland scene, artist-signed 185.00

Dish, shell form on 3 shell feet, h.p.
florals & gold trim on blue-tinged
ivory ground, ca. 1897, 7½" w.,
7" l. (ILLUS.) 195.00

Ewer, burnished gold salamander
handle, dull heavy Roman gold &
silver florals & foliage w/heron in
flight on gold-spattered glossy
cream ground, 1880, 5½" d.,
11½" h. 505.00

Ewer, folded back rim, elaborate
scrolled acanthus leaf handle, bas
relief floral & acanthus leaf detail
on shoulder & turned base, turquoise rim & body w/deep cream
shoulder, handle & base accented
w/gold, gold & white daisy sprays
decor, 20th c., 15½" h. 735.00

Figure, "Wind," 1916, 6" h. 125.00

Figure of Kate Greenaway type girl
carrying basket, off-white glossy
finish w/gold trim & flesh tones,
1882, 6¾" h. 410.00

Figure of classical lady holding a
bird, beige & burnished gold, satin finish, 2 5/8" d., 10¼" h...... 400.00

Figures, gentleman & lady standing
before tree trunk, each wearing
green hat & holding basket,
cream & beige w/green details &
gold trim, 10½" h., pr. 850.00

Jug, basket-shaped, center handle
w/spout at each end, embossed
bust of gentleman one side & lady
the other, cream & beige w/tan &
green details & burnished gold
trim, satin finish, 11 x 4 7/8",
6½" h. 595.00

Mug, holly decor, dated 1892,
3¼" h. 75.00

Pitcher, 4½" h., winged griffin handle, elongated spout, overall burnished gold design on glossy
cream ground, 1886 .... 125.00

Pitcher, 6¼" h., ornate handle, gold
chrysanthemums outlined in red
w/burnished gold trim on cream
body, 1888. .... 145.00

Pitcher, 7" h., gold mask spout &
handle, floral decor w/burnished
gold tracery on ivory ground,
numbered & dated 1889 .... 225.00

Royal Worcester "Tusk" Pitcher

Pitcher, 8" h., tusk form, molded
stag's horn handle, h.p. pink
honeysuckle w/yellow centers &
green & deep rust gold-veined
leaves, heavy gold trim (ILLUS.) .. 155.00

Pitcher, 15¼" h., bulbous, beaded
florals w/gold overlay on off-
white ground, artist-signed....... 295.00

Plate, 8" d., sprays of apple blossoms, fruit & foliage against overall burnished gold large circles
design, 1876 .... 70.00

Plate, 9½" d., lily pad form, lavender florals on beige matte finish,
ca. 1889 .... 75.00

Spillholder vases, embossed full figure of a girl w/sunflowers & cattails, dated 1908, pr. 460.00

Tea caddy, shaded peach to cream
w/gold trim, 4½" h............. 85.00

Teapot, cov., h.p. red, yellow &
green florals on beige matte finish ground.................... 250.00

Toothpick holder, 3-handled, h.p.
floral decor................... 95.00

Vase, 3½" h., rectangular w/canted
sides, white textured body w/ap-
plied frog & ivy vine............ 265.00

Vase, 5¾" h., 2-handled, cattle in
highland scene, artist-signed,
1906 .... 275.00

Vase, 8½" h., footed, pink florals
on blue wicker-textured ground,
1873 .... 450.00

Vase, 10½" h., cylindrical, gilt
bronze filigree base, h.p. florals
w/burnished gold trim on glossy
cream ground.................. 295.00

Vase, cov., 11¼" h., 5 cows grazing
in a misty landscape, whole reserved on an ivory ground between lightly molded borders
w/pale peach & yellow details &
enriched by gilding, artist-signed
& dated 1902 .... 660.00

Vase, 13" h., flaring stick-type,
reticulated gold rim, bird on
flowering branch & bird flying
amidst gold-tinged clouds w/gold
setting sun, cluster of gold florals
reverse, artist-signed & dated
1885 .... 495.00

Wall pockets, white, circular,
cherubs beside grape-laden basket decor, artist-signed, ca. 1862,
pr............................ 550.00

ROZENBURG DEN HAAG

*This Dutch earthenware and porcelain fac-
tory was established in 1885 at The Hague.
It is noted for the exceptionally thin earthenware made in the late 19th and early 20th
centuries. Subtle shapes and fine enameled
decoration combine to make it an exquisite
production greatly influenced by the Art Nouveau movement. The ware was marked
Rozenburg den Haag with a stork and crown.*

Cups & saucers, demitasse, one
w/lavender poppies & other
w/brown & rust pansies, 1903,
pr............................$357.00

Cups & saucers, demitasse, paneled
cups & hexagonal saucers, soft
yellow, brick red & soft green

wildflowers or birds on snow
white ground, ca. 1913, set of 12
in satin-lined fitted case........8,250.00
Tray, blue & lavender hummingbird
amidst elaborately scrolling vines
& blossoms on pale green shaded
to cream ground, ca. 1904,
15" oval 525.00
Vase, bud, 5½" h., bottle-shaped,
pr. parrots amidst scrolling green,
lavender & brown florals,
ca. 1902....................... 330.00
Vase, 6¾" h., bulbous, 2-handled,
multicolored florals, artist-
signed 400.00
Vase, 8½" h., multicolored florals,
parrots & Art Nouveau designs
decor 425.00

Rozenburg Vase

Vase, 11½" h., baluster-shaped,
2-handled, green, brown, yellow &
olive green birds amidst olive &
deep green thorny branches
w/brown & yellow floral clusters
on white ground, ca. 1900
(ILLUS.) 2,970.00

SALTGLAZED WARES

*This whitish ware has a pitted surface tex-
ture, which resembles an orange skin as a result of salt being thrown into the hot kiln to
produce the glaze. Much of this ware was sold
in the undecorated state, but some pieces
were decorated. Produced during the last century in England, the United States and elsewhere, most pieces are unmarked.*

Basket, scalloped flared rim, loop
handles, sides pierced & molded
w/florals, Staffordshire, ca. 1760,
9½" oval $440.00

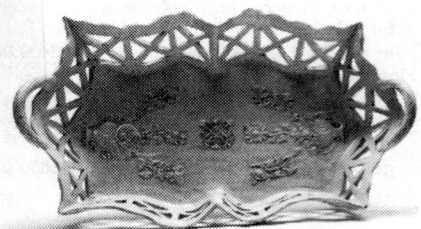

Saltglaze Basket

Basket, shaped & pierced latticework rim, rope twist handles,
center w/relief-molded musical
trophy flanked by vases of flowers, Staffordshire, ca. 1755, small
hairline, 12¾" l. (ILLUS.) 2,860.00
Pitcher, 7¼" h., 4¼" d., relief-
molded soldiers (3) & large
hawk-like birds around base,
Ridgway & Abington, Hanley,
dated August 1, 1856 .... 130.00
Pitcher, 8½" h., jug-type, Apostle
patt., Charles Meigh, registered
Mar. 17, 1843 .... 490.00
Pitcher, 8½" h., jug-type, twisted
branch handle, relief-molded
grape clusters & leaves over interlaced bamboo body, grey &
green, w/pewter lid, ca. 1849 .... 175.00
Pitcher, 8¾" h., bulbous, relief-
molded scene from Grimm's Fairy
Tales of grandmother teaching girl
to spin, white.................. 155.00
Pitcher, 9" h., relief-molded classical
figures on orchid ground, Samuel
Alcock, ca. 1850 .... 175.00
Pitcher, 10" h., relief-molded beehive, flowers & bees, impressed
Dudson, ca. 1898............... 185.00
Tea caddy, square body, flat shoulders, cylindrical neck, sides relief-
molded w/flowering trees & birds
enriched in brown, Staffordshire,
ca. 1755, 6¼" h. (minor rim
repair) 880.00

Saltglaze Teapot

Teapot, cov., globular, enameled
florals below trellis patt. band en-

riched in green interrupted by
flowerheads, faceted spout
w/iron-red trim, minor chips at
rim, Staffordshire, ca. 1765, 7" d.
(ILLUS.) 550.00
Wall pocket, cornucopia-form, relief-
molded w/portrait of Flora holding a cornucopia of flowering
plants center within a scroll-
molded cartouche, pierced scrolling rim w/shell motif, lower part
w/flowering foliage, attributed to
William Greatbach for Whieldon
or Wedgwood, Staffordshire,
ca. 1760, 10" l 550.00

SAN ILDEFONSO (Maria) POTTERY

Bowl signed "Marie"

*Created by a Pueblo Indian woman,
Maria Montoya Martinez, and her husband,
Julian, this glossy and matte glaze black pottery was always fired in a primitive manner.
After 1923, Maria began to sign items,
"Marie," "Maria," or "Marie and Julian."
San Ildefonso pottery items also might
carry the signatures of other village potters
of that era, "Rosalia," "Tonita," and others.
Popovi Da was Maria's son who worked with
her after 1956 until his death and items signed
"Maria and Popovi Da" can be so dated. Considered a true artistic achievement, early
items signed by Maria, or her contemporaries,
command good prices.*

Bowl, 2½" top d., 4" widest d.,
glossy & matte black on black
bird decor, signed Blue Corn $400.00
Bowl, 4½" d., 3" h., glossy & matte
black on black, signed Vigil,
1970's 175.00
Bowl, 5½" d., glossy & matte black
on black, signed Marie, ca. 1920
(ILLUS.) 600.00
Bowl, 5½" d., 4" h., glossy & matte
black on black, signed Marie &
Julian, 1934-43 . . . . 425.00
Jar, bulbous, signed Desideria, 4½"
top d., 8" widest d., 6" h. 250.00

Planter, glossy & matte black on
black, signed Lupita Martinez 125.00
Plate, glossy & matte black on
black, signed Maria, ca. 1931 . . . . 950.00

SARREGUEMINES

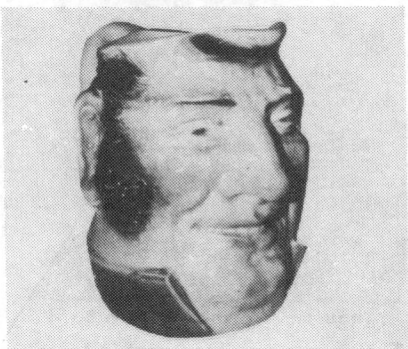

Sarreguemines Character Jug

*This factory was established in Lorraine,
France, about 1770. Subsequently, Wedg-
wood-type pieces were produced as was
Mocha ware. In the 19th century, the factory turned to pottery and stoneware.*

Bowl, 2-handled, embossed toma-
toes on basketweave ground $28.00
Character jug, majolica, beige &
brown flesh tones w/ruddy cheeks
& nose, robin's egg blue interior,
3 5/8" d., 5¼" h. 65.00
Character jug, majolica, flesh tones
w/rosy cheeks & dark hair,
7½" h. (ILLUS.) . . . . 85.00 to 125.00
Character jug, "The Scotsman," teal
blue interior, 8" h. . . . . 68.00 to 85.00
Jardiniere, bulbous w/slightly
crimped scalloped edge, applied
satyr's mask handles, molded at
mid-section w/continuous grapevine above a wavy band, details
picked out in gilding, on white
marble stand w/black veining surrounded by a gilt-bronze collar
molded w/palmette devices, late
19th c., 18" w. 550.00
Pitcher, 12¾" h., majolica, figural
parrot 85.00
Pitcher, embossed scene of children
playing amidst trees 85.00
Plate, 7½" d., majolica, apples &
leaves decor 30.00
Plate, 7¾" d., majolica, straw-
berries decor 22.00
Plate, 8" d., "music plate," transfer
print 24.00

Plates, 8" d., various Napoleonic
   battle scenes, set of 6 . . . . 165.00
Vase, 9" h., "sang de boeuf"
   glaze 125.00
Wall shelf, majolica, bearded Norse
   god in relief, cobalt blue, brown &
   green, 17" w. 850.00

SATSUMA

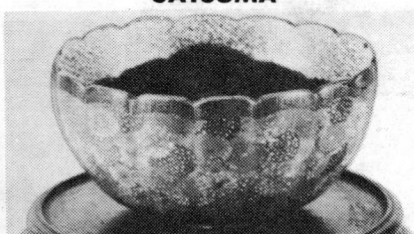

Thousand Flowers Pattern Bowl

*These wares have been made in Japan for
centuries, and the early pieces are scarce and
high-priced. But mass-produced Satsuma-
type ware is plentiful and has been turned out
for the past century and a quarter. The so-
called "Thousand Faces" design is considered
desirable by collectors and all Satsuma prices
have escalated in the last decade. Also see
BUTTONS.*

Beaker, Thousand Flowers patt.,
   multicolored florals & gold on
   blue ground, Taisho period
   (1912-26) $185.00
Bowl, 5½" d., temple scene decor,
   Meiji period, 1880's 575.00
Bowl, 6" d., scalloped rim, lobed
   body, Thousand Flowers patt.,
   Meiji period, ca. 1900 (ILLUS.) 550.00
Bowl, 9" d., fluted & scalloped rim,
   Thousand Faces patt. w/three
   poets, women, demons & ornate
   gold interior, dragons & crests
   exterior, Showa period (after
   1926) 175.00
Box w/dome lid, multicolored fans
   decor, silver trim, Meiji period
   (1868-1912), 5½" d. 365.00
Cookie jar, cov., diapered borders,
   Samurai warriors, florals & butterflies decor w/ornate gold on blue
   ground, Showa period 135.00
Creamer, bamboo-molded handle,
   florals & insects outlined in gold,
   Meiji period, late 19th c.,
   4¼" h. 90.00
Cup & saucer, dragon handle, ha-
   loed Arhats (disciples of Buddha),
   Kwannon (diety of Mercy) & dragon decor, Showa period, ca. 1930
   (ILLUS.) 45.00

Satsuma Cup & Saucer

Jardiniere & cover w/"kara-shi shi"
   (lion-dog) finial, upright handles,
   footed, chrysanthemums decor,
   Meiji period, late 19th c.,
   13½" h. 265.00
Koro (incense burner) w/pierced lid,
   rounded shoulders, concave sides,
   tripod base, dragon decor, Meiji
   period, late 19th c., 2 3/8" h. 275.00
Koro w/pierced lid, Samurai warri-
   ors decor, Showa period, 5" w. . . . 135.00
Plaque, pierced to hang, water fowl
   w/mate on pond, peonies,
   chrysanthemums & hanging
   wisteria w/ornate gold decor,
   Meiji Period, ca. 1900, 9¾" d. 255.00
Plate, 9" d., lady & children in a
   garden setting center, butterflies
   & floral border 290.00
Plate, 10" d., cobalt blue underside
   extending to front w/encrusted
   Greek Key border w/florals &
   scrolling, 7 Arhats (elderly male
   disciples of Buddha, usually w/ha-
   loes about head) without haloes
   wearing gosu blue, red & black
   garments amidst bamboo trees
   decor, gilt speckles & encrusted
   gold trim, Edo period, ca. 1860 . . . 775.00
Rice bowl, hexagonal, haloed
   Arhats & Kwannon figures decor,
   some gold trim, Showa period,
   4" w. 100.00
Salt dip, Samurai warriors in bowl,
   Showa period 45.00
Teapot & cover w/multicolored floral
   decor, spout w/diapering, body
   w/enameled scene of children
   playing ball in a garden, 4¼" w.,
   3" h. 585.00
Teapot, cov., overall colorful
   enameled florals against gold
   scalloped reserves depicting
   family life obverse & reverse,
   Kinkozan, Meiji period, ca. 1900,
   4½" across spout to handle,
   3½" h. 270.00
Tea set: cov. teapot, creamer, cov.
   sugar bowl & c/s; flying cranes

decor, bamboo handles, Kinkozan,
5 pcs. 200.00
Tea set: cov. teapot, cov. creamer,
cov. sugar bowl, 6 plates & 6 c/s;
lavender wisteria on cream
ground w/ornate gold trim, ca.
1920, 21 pcs. 275.00
Toothpick holder, cylindrical, black
border w/ornate gold scrollwork
at base & top, scene of children
at school within panels of colorful
"nishikide" diapering, late Edo
period, ca. 1868, 7/8" d.,
2¼" h. 250.00
Urn, cov., footed, multicolored
florals in relief, ornate gold trim,
17" h. 250.00
Vase, 2¾" h., bulbous shoulders,
rectangular base & top, h.p. hanging wisteria w/gold tracery 80.00
Vase, 4 5/8" h., double gourd
shape, h.p. Geisha in an interior
scene front & Samurai warriors
reverse, ca. 1900 . . . . 247.50
Vase, 6" h., Thousand Butterflies
patt. 360.00
Vase, 7½" h., elongated bulbous
form, tapering neck w/poly-
chrome & gilt lappet borders,
bird, butterfly & floral reserves on
diapered ground, late 19th c. 357.50
Vase, 8" h., geese in flight decor,
1880 . . . . 70.00
Vase, 10" h., War Lords decor 145.00
Vase, 12" h., elephant head han-
dles, overall scene of Arhats &
white elephant, encrusted gold
trim, 1920's 275.00

19th Century Satsuma Vase

Vase, 15¼" h., baluster form, landscape scene w/group of ladies &
children one side, group of
Samurai on other, base & shoulder w/diapered pattern, 19th c.
(ILLUS.) 1,000.00

Vase, 24" h., Samurai warriors, at-
tendants & children at play decor,
Meiji period, ca. 1880 . . . . 950.00
Vase, 44" h., Samurai warrior & War
Lords decor 2,300.00

SCHLEGELMILCH

*Handpainted china marked "RS Germany"
and "RS Prussia" continues to grow in
popularity. According to Clifford J. Schlegelmilch in his book "Handbook of Erdmann
and Reinhold Schlegelmilch—Prussia—
Germany and Oscar Schlegelmilch—Germany," Erdmann Schlegelmilch established
a porcelain factory in the Germanic provinces
at Suhl, in 1861. Reinhold, his younger
brother, worked with him until 1869 when he
established another porcelain factory in Tillowitz, upper Silesia. China bearing the name
of this town is credited to Reinhold Schlegelmilch. It customarily bears also the phrase
"RS Germany." Now collectors seek additional marks including E.S. Germany, R.S.
Poland and R.S. Suhl. Prices are high and collectors should beware the forgeries that sometimes find their way to the market. Also see
MUSTACHE CUPS & SAUCERS.*

R.S. GERMANY

R.S. Germany Marks

Berry set: master berry bowl & 4
sauce dishes; red roses on pale
green ground, gold trim, 5 pcs. $135.00
Bowl, 7½" d., footed, poppies
decor, satin finish 45.00
Bowl, 9½" d., white rose sprays on
shaded tan ground, gold edge 35.00
Bowl, 10" d., iris mold, floral
decor 65.00
Bowl, 10" d., fluted rim, orange
floral decor 65.00
Bowl, 11" d., carnation mold, pink
rose clusters on white satin
finish 195.00
Bowl, 13 x 8¼" oblong, footed,
pierced handles, iris mold, Sum-
mer Season portrait, satin finish . . 495.00
Cake plate, pierced handles, daisies
decor, gold edge & wheat spikes,
9¾" d. 45.00
Cake plate, pierced handles, white
hydrangea puffs on cream to light
brown ground, 9¾" d. 45.00

Cake plate, icicle mold, narcissus
decor, 10½" d. 75.00
Cake plate, pierced handles, snowball blossoms decor, 11" d. 35.00
Candle holder, lily-of-the-valley
decor on green ground (single) ... 68.00
Candy dish, pedestal base, relief-
molded pastel buds & lush iridescent turquoise floral decor 57.00
Celery tray, pink roses w/green
leaves on cream shaded to light
grey ground, 5 3/8" w., 12¼" l. ... 50.00
Cheese & cracker dish, 2-tier, white
lilies on green ground 48.00
Chocolate cup & saucer, white &
pink florals, green leaves & gold
tracery on cream shaded to blue
ground 25.00
Chocolate pot, cov., black & white
photo-type portrait of woman on
blue lustre ground, gold trim 200.00
Chocolate pot, cov., paneled mold
w/flat scalloped base, white wild
roses on white ground shaded to
soft green at edges 210.00
Chocolate set: cov. chocolate pot &
2 c/s; floral decor on green
ground, gold rims, 5 pcs. 195.00
Chocolate set: 10" h. cov. chocolate
pot & 5 c/s; irregular leaf-molded
dark green rims, variegated roses
on shaded yellow to green
ground, 11 pcs. 275.00
Chocolate set: cov. oval chocolate
pot & 6 tall c/s; purple grape
clusters & green leaves outlined
in gold on white ground, 13 pcs... 425.00
Creamer, Cottage scene decor 45.00
Ferner, 4 curved legs, 2-handled,
roses decor on green ground,
3½" w., 4" h.................... 85.00
Hair receiver, cov., lavender & yellow pansies decor 40.00
Hatpin holder, paneled sides, white
roses decor, 4½" h. 50.00
Mustard pot, cover & ladle, roses
decor 35.00
Nappy, triangular w/single handle,
groups of white hydrangeas on
shaded light green ground, gold
trim........................... 35.00
Nut set: footed master nut bowl & 4
individual nut bowls; white
daffodils decor, 5 pcs. 85.00
Pin box, cov., diamond-shaped,
deeply scalloped lid w/turned-up
points, pink wild roses decor 75.00
Pitcher, lemonade, lily decor 120.00
Plate, 6" d., calla lilies & deep
green foliage on green-tinted
pearlized lustre finish 22.00
Plate, 6¼" d., tulips decor on cream
shaded to brown ground
(ILLUS.)....................... 17.50

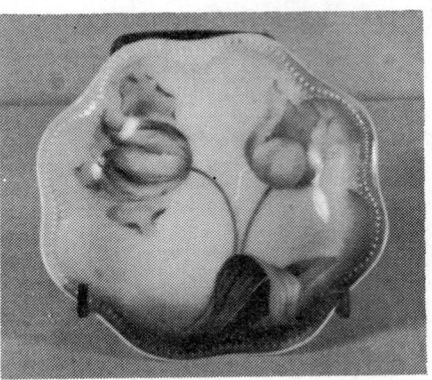

R.S. Germany Plate

Plates, 6½" d., Cotton Plant patt.,
set of 6 .... 65.00
Plate, 8" d., white roses w/gold
highlights on green ground 35.00
Plate, 8¼" d., pheasants & landscape w/house & tower decor 55.00
Plate, 8¼" d., Sheepherder scene .. 125.00
Plate, 8½" d., large pink & white
roses on brown shaded to pink
ground 40.00
Plate, 8½" d., large white poppies
on shaded green satin finish 45.00
Ramekin, pink roses on white satin
finish 30.00
Relish dish, pierced handles, pink &
white floral decor 35.00
Relish tray, Bird of Paradise patt.,
8" l.......................... 75.00
Relish tray, daisies on shaded green
ground, 12" l.................. 40.00
Relish tray, iris decor.............. 47.00
Sauce bowl w/underplate, deep purple violets on shaded pale green
ground 48.00
Sauce dish, pink floral decor 12.00
Shaving mug, floral decor 60.00
Syrup pitcher, cover & underplate,
hydrangeas decor 60.00
Teapot, pink roses on green
ground 195.00
Tea set: cov. teapot, creamer & cov.
sugar bowl; white florals on shaded green ground, gold trim,
3 pcs. 125.00
Tea tile, white & pink florals
w/green leaves & gold tracery on
cream shaded to blue ground,
6¼" d. 34.00
Toothbrush holder, hanging-type,
red roses on shaded blue
ground 65.00
Tray, pierced handles, Farmhouse
scene, 10½ x 5" 92.00
Vase, 3" h., bulbous, acorns on
shaded tan ground 50.00
Vase, 4" h., Cottage scene 42.00

Vase, 8" h., pr. of parrots in black
medallion reserved on pale blue
ground 145.00
Wall pocket, parrot perched on
floral-laden branch in full relief,
all white 85.00

R.S. PRUSSIA

R.S. Prussia Berry Set

Berry set: 9" d. master bowl & 4
sauce dishes; ruffled & scalloped
rims, Stag scene on shaded
green, 5 pcs. 1,800.00
Berry set: 10½" d. master bowl & 6
sauce dishes; large red roses &
green shadow flowers decor, gold
trim, 7 pcs. 325.00
Berry set: master bowl & 6 sauce
dishes; medallion mold, Madame
Lebrun portraits in medallions,
cobalt blue border, 7 pcs. (ILLUS.
of part) 2,900.00
Bowl, 5¼" d., scalloped rim, cream
& yellow lilies decor 65.00
Bowl, 5½" d., Old Man in the
Mountain scene 175.00
Bowl, 5½" d., 2 1/8" h., 3-footed,
iris mold w/yellow accent on
petals, pink & yellow roses decor,
gold trim 115.00
Bowl, 6 x 5½", shell mold, floral
decor on shaded blue satin
finish 115.00
Bowl, 6¼" d., 2" h., pastel
lavender, blue & green lilacs on
shaded yellow satin finish 140.00
Bowl, 8¾" d., iris mold, poppies
decor 145.00
Bowl, 9" d., cabbage mold, mauve
exterior w/gold sheaves of
wheat, white interior w/deep red
roses, satin finish 650.00
Bowl, 9" d., pink roses decor, satin
finish 275.00
Bowl, 10" d., iris mold, roses on
shaded green ground . . . .175.00 to 235.00
Bowl, 10" d., 12-point rim w/fleur-
de-lis, lily-of-the-valley decor on
shaded white to soft green 220.00
Bowl, 10" d., iris mold, Summer
Season portrait 750.00

Bowl, 10" d., jewel mold, Melon
Boys "keyhole" portrait, green
tones 1,200.00
Bowl, 10" d., scalloped rim, Victor-
ian Couple Vignette decor 650.00
Bowl, 10¼" d., violet mold, Mill
scene on shaded dark to light
green 750.00

R.S. Prussia Bowl

Bowl, 10½" d., cloverleaf mold, As-
sorted Florals (pond lilies, hydran-
geas & ruffled tulips) decor
(ILLUS.) 225.00
Bowl, 10½" d., 12-point mold
w/florals in alternate points,
Swallows (bluebirds) & shadow
flowers on white shaded to blue . . 425.00
Bowl, 10½" d., medallion mold, Old
Man in the Mountain scene 575.00
Bowl, 10½" d., Sheepherder
scene. 1,200.00
Bowl, 10½" d., Winter Season
portrait 750.00
Bowl, 11" d., Masted Schooner
scene, brown to white pearlized
finish 650.00
Bowl, 11 x 8½" oval, Old Man in
the Mountain scene 650.00
Bowl, 13 x 8½" oval, 4-medallion
mold, Old Man in the Mountain
scene, shaded blue-green
ground 595.00
Bread tray, pierced handles, roses
decor, satin finish, 12½" l. 98.00
Bread tray, pierced handles,
4-medallion mold, Pheasant
scene, yellow, orchid, green,
orange & blue ground, 13¾" l. . . . 475.00
Bread tray, plume mold, pink floral
decor 125.00
Butter pat, scalloped edge, pink
rose sprays decor 45.00
Cake plate, Melon Eaters scene,
10" d. 645.00

Cake plate, pierced handles, ripple
mold rim w/gold border, floral
decor, 11" d. 225.00
Cake plate, pierced handles, Swans
w/Gazebo scene, 11¼" d. 545.00
Cake plate, Sheepherder scene
w/Swallows (13), satin finish 400.00

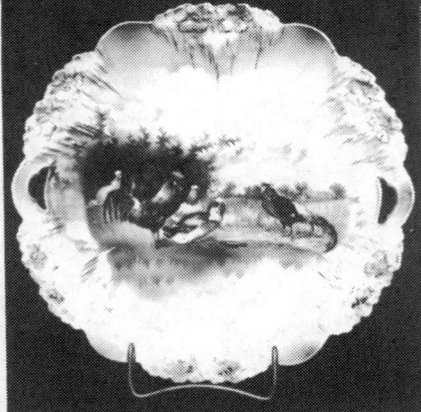

Barnyard Scene Cake Plate

Cake plate, pierced handles, icicle
mold, Barnyard scene (ILLUS.) 750.00
Celery tray, pierced handles, cabbage roses on white satin finish,
11½" l. 180.00
Celery tray, pierced handles, icicle
mold, Swan scene, 12" l. 375.00
Celery tray, lily-of-the-valley & leaf
mold, shaded green to white,
12" l. 135.00
Celery tray, stippled floral mold,
roses decor, dark cream shaded
to green ground, 12" l. 175.00
Celery tray, swag & tassel mold,
Sheepherder scene,
12" l. .... 340.00 to 525.00
Celery tray, red poinsettias on pink
ground, 12" l. (unmarked) 145.00
Celery tray, scalloped mold, pierced
handles, snowball decor, satin finish, 12¼" l. 150.00
Celery tray, carnation mold,
lavender & pink carnations decor,
satin finish 185.00
Celery tray, cloverleaf mold, roses &
daisies decor .... 195.00 to 285.00
Chocolate pot, cov., scalloped rim,
daisy mold, pink roses & white
daisies reflected in water decor,
gold trim, 9" h. 396.00
Chocolate pot, cov., ball-footed
mold, yellow & violet florals
w/dark pink shading on yellow &
ivory ground, gold trim,
9¼" h. 375.00
Chocolate pot, cov., point & clover

mold, pink roses & white hydrangeas outlined in gold, 10¼" h. ... 395.00
Chocolate pot, cov., Mill scene..... 1,350.00
Chocolate pot, cov., footed, roses
decor & gold beading on white ... 275.00
Chocolate pot, cov., pink & yellow
violets decor w/yellow & ivory
beading & gold trim on shaded
pink ground 325.00
Chocolate pot, cov., paneled mold,
white roses on white shaded to
green & tan satin finish 250.00
Chocolate pot, cov., 4-sided w/bulg-
ing scroll-molded upper section &
ring finial on lid, white floral
cluster on green shaded to white
ground 245.00

R.S. Prussia Chocolate Set

Chocolate set: cov. chocolate pot &
6 footed c/s; Assorted Florals on
shaded ground, set (ILLUS.)...... 2,150.00
Dresser tray, carnation mold, roses
decor, satin finish, 11½" l. 550.00
Dresser tray, icicle mold, Swan
scene, 11¾" l. 920.00
Dresser tray, iris mold, Spring
Season portrait 525.00
Ewer, Summer Season portrait,
9" h. 1,365.00
Ferner, footed, jeweled, pink florals
on green ground, 7½ x 3½" 395.00
Ferner, Castle scene............... 375.00
Hair receiver, cov., icicle mold rim,
square, Swan scene 185.00
Hair receiver, cov., Mill scene 175.00
Hatpin holder, snowball decor 225.00
Humidor, cov., hexagonal, roses &
snowballs decor................. 750.00
Ice cream set: 11" d. master bowl &
five 6" d. bowls; icicle mold rims,
Snowbirds scene, 6 pcs.......... 4,000.00
Lemonade pitcher, 9" h., carnation
mold, light & dark pink roses on
lavender & tan ground, satin
finish 700.00
Marmalade jar, cover & underplate,
2-handled, Castle scene......... 600.00
Mustache cup, floral mold, Madame

Lebrun portrait, Tiffany-type
iridescent finish 500.00
Mustard jar & cover w/flower finial,
drape mold, pink roses decor,
satin finish 130.00
Mustard jar, cov., floral mold, portrait of girl w/ribbon in her hair,
red iridescent Tiffany-type finish .. 150.00
Pin box, footed, jeweled, Old Man
in the Mountain scene, soft grey
shaded to green ground, 3¾ x
1½" 100.00
Pin tray, icicle mold, Old Man in the
Mountain scene, green shaded to
brown ground, 5½ x 3¼"........ 120.00
Pitcher, tankard, 10½" h., leaf base
& ball mold, Mill scene on shaded
brown ground, lavish gold
trim 1,450.00
Pitcher, tankard, 11½" h., carnation
mold, pink & yellow roses on dark
green shaded to white ground.... 650.00
Pitcher, tankard, 13" h., stippled
floral mold, lilies decor on blue
shaded to white ground 975.00

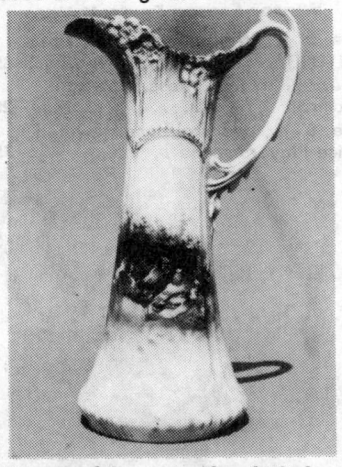

Barnyard Scene Tankard Pitcher

Pitcher, tankard, 14" h., icicle mold,
Barnyard scene (ILLUS.) 2,050.00
Pitcher, tankard, 15" h., elongated
scalloped border w/relief florals,
Madame Recamier portrait on
dark green shaded to cream
ground, gold handle, Tiffany-type
iridescent border 850.00
Plate, 6" d., scalloped rim, white
narcissus trimmed in gold on
pearlized finish 60.00
Plate, 7½" d., icicle mold, Old Man
in the Mountain scene, white
shaded to green ground 120.00
Plates, 8" d., keyhole mold, Spring,
Summer, Autumn & Winter por-
traits, set of 4..................3,800.00

Plate, 8" d., scalloped rim, Swans
(3) on Lake scene 300.00
Plate, 8½" d., 6-point & clover
mold, pink, white & lavender
floral arrangement in a bowl,
shaded dark pink ground 135.00
Plate, 8½" d., icicle mold, Swans (3)
on Lake scene, shaded light blue
ground 400.00
Plate, 8½" d., elongated scalloped
border, rope edge, Melon Boys
scene ....525.00 to 625.00
Plate, 8¾" d., fleur-de-lis mold,
shadow flowers, multicolored poppies & scrolling, Nile green shaded to turquoise blue & light green
ground 150.00

Spring Season Portrait Plate

Plate, 8¾" d., Spring Season portrait (ILLUS.) 975.00
Plate, 10" d., pierced handles,
rounded scalloped border,
peaches decor on white ground .. 150.00
Plate, 10¼" d., pierced handles,
fleur-de-lis mold, Summer Season
portrait, satin finish 825.00
Plate, 11" d., pierced handles,
pointed border mold, Barnyard
scene, pale lavender shaded to
beige ground 625.00
Powder box, cov., floral decor on
shaded green ground, gold trim,
5" sq. 175.00
Powder box, cov., stippled floral
mold, Madame Recamier portrait,
satin finish 595.00
Relish tray, icicle mold, Swan on
Lake w/Temple & Pine Trees
scene, 8" l. 145.00
Relish tray, pearlized white florals
on green ground, 9½" l.......... 65.00
Salt dip, scalloped, white floral
decor on soft green ground 95.00
Sauce dish, Peacock & Bluebirds
scene, 5½" d. 125.00

Sauce dish, ribbon & jewel mold,
Spring Season portrait, cobalt blue
trim, 5½" d. 250.00
Shaving mug, Madame Lebrun por-
trait, Tiffany-type finish 474.00
Shaving mug, pink roses decor 295.00
Sugar shaker, pale pink dogwood
blossoms on creamy white
ground 60.00
Sugar shaker, roses decor 135.00
Sugar shaker, Victorian Couple
Vignette decor, heavy gold trim . . 225.00
Syrup pitcher, cover & matching
underplate, point & clover mold,
pink & white roses on ivory
ground, leaf finial, gold trim 225.00
Syrup pitcher, cover & matching
underplate, scalloped rim, floral
decor, satin finish 150.00
Talcum shaker, base handles, roses
decor, 5" h. 225.00
Tea cup & saucer, double dome
mold, scalloped base, pink roses
on lustre ground 75.00
Teapot, cov., iris mold, poppies
w/green foliage on pastel yellow
ground 135.00

(Tea set illustration)

R.S. Prussia Tea Set

Tea set: cov. teapot, creamer & cov.
sugar bowl; footed, floral decor,
gold trim, 3 pcs. (ILLUS.) 187.00
Tea set: cov. teapot, creamer & cov.
sugar bowl; Melon Eaters scene,
3 pcs. 1,800.00
Tea set: cov. teapot, creamer & cov.
sugar bowl; molded leaves on
scalloped base, large snowballs &
green leaves decor, satin finish,
3 pcs. 350.00
Tea set: 6" h. cov. teapot, creamer
& cov. sguar bowl; scalloped
beaded bases, Swan on Lake
scene, satin finish, 3 pcs. 800.00
Toothpick holder, 2-handled, roses &
snowballs decor. 100.00
Toothpick holder, 3-handled, floral
decor w/gold accents 135.00
Tray w/pierced handles, scalloped
rim, white & rose florals on satin
finish, 11½ x 7¼" 130.00
Tray, iris mold, Fall Season vertical
portrait on lavender & yellow
ground, 12 x 6" 850.00
Tray, icicle mold, Sheepherder
scene, 12 x 7½" 395.00

Tray, pierced handles, beaded
medallion mold, pheasant decor,
14 x 7" oval 500.00
Urn, cov., jewel mold, Mill scene,
green ground, 6½" h. 600.00
Vase, 4¼" h., Castle scene on
green ground 295.00

Winter Season Portrait Vase

Vase, 5" h., Winter Season portrait
(ILLUS.). 350.00
Vase, 6¼" h., Countess Potocka
portrait 200.00
Vase, 8" h., pedestal base, jeweled,
Dice Players scene 550.00

Melon Boys Scene Vase

Vase, 9" h., loving cup form,
jeweled, Melon Boys scene
(ILLUS.) 1,150.00
Vase, 10½" h., ornate open handles
at sides, leaf-molded rim, pink
roses on shaded blue to yellow &
tan ground 290.00
Vase, 11¾" h., waisted cylinder
w/bulging upper portion, openwork C-scroll handles, Hanging
Flower Basket decor on shaded
satin finish ground 395.00

OTHER MARKS

Suhl.

Other Schlegelmilch Marks

Berry set: master bowl & 4 sauce
dishes; shell-shaped, satin finish,
5 pcs. (R.S. Poland) 325.00
Bon bon, pierced handles, poppies
decor, 7¼ x 6¼" (R.S. Tillowitz) .. 42.00
Bowl, 9½" d., fox hunt scene
w/horse & dogs in a forest setting
(E.S. Prov. Saxe) 75.00
Bowl, 9½" d., 2½" h., Art Nouveau
lady in lavender gown on soft
green lustre ground, gold border
(E.S. Prov. Saxe) 232.00
Cake plate, Indian Chief portrait on
red-orange ground, 9¾" d. (E.S.
Prove Saxe) 400.00
Candlestick, violets decor, pearlized
finish, single (R.S. Poland) 110.00
Clock, boudoir, blue forget-me-nots
& green vines on white ground,
gold trim, 4½ x 4" (E.S. Prussia).. 135.00
Creamer & cov. sugar bowl, pink
roses decor, pr. (R.S. Tillowitz) ... 60.00
Ewer, green & gold chrysanthemums
decor, ornate handle, 13½" h.
(R.S. Suhl) 275.00
Hair receiver, cov., violets decor,
pearlized finish (R.S. Poland) 100.00
Hatpin holder, pink rosebuds on
shaded rust ground (R.S.
Poland) 85.00
Match holder, Victorian woman portrait decor on iridescent green
ground (E.S. Prov. Saxe) 185.00
Pitcher, cider, magnolia blossoms
decor, gold trim, satin finish (R.S.
Tillowitz) 125.00
Plate, 6½" d., ladies (3) & cherub
decor, border of bands of green &
deep pink outlined in gold, ornate
gold rim (E.S. Prov. Saxe) 42.00
Powder box, footed, geese decor on
cobalt blue ground (E.S. Prov.
Saxe) 55.00
Ring tree, violets decor, pearlized
finish (R.S. Poland) 100.00
Vase, 4½" h., ornate open handles,
Barnyard scene (R.S. Poland) 145.00
Vase, 6½" h., "Night Watch" scene
after Rembrandt (R.S. Suhl) 210.00
Vase, 11¼" h., portrait of beautiful
woman on iridescent ground
w/raised turquoise beading (E.S.
Prov. Saxe) 245.00

SEVRES

Sevres Centerpiece Bowl

*Some of the most desirable porcelain ever
produced was made at the Sevres factory,
originally established at Vincennes, France,
and transferred through permission of Madame de Pompadour, to Sevres as the Royal
Manufactory about the middle of the 18th
century. King Louis XV took sole respon-
sibilty for the works in 1759 when production
of hard paste began. Between 1850 and 1900,
many biscuit and soft-paste porcelains were
again made. Fine early pieces are scarce and
high-priced. Many of those available today
are late productions. The various Sevres
marks have been copied.*

Box, cov., h.p. pastoral scene on
cover, "bleu-du-roi" (cobalt blue)
sides, 5" w., 2½" h.............$395.00
Busts of Bacchantes, bisque, he
w/beard & laughing expression &
an animal skin strapped to his
shoulder, his companion similarly
modeled, both w/fruiting vines in
their hair, heads tilted to the left
& right respectively, each on a
flaring "bleu-du-roi" pedestal enriched w/gilt scrolling, gilt-bronze
mounts, 19th c., 10½" h., pr. 385.00
Casket w/hinged lid, reserved
w/panel of ladies & gentleman at
various leisurely pursuits in a garden w/trio of musicians entertain-
ing them on lid & w/landscape
vignettes on sides within scrolling
gilt borders reserving colorful floral blossoms, interior w/sprays of
summer flowers, gilt-bronze
mounts, attributed to Sevres, late
19th c., 13¾" w. 1,540.00
Centerpiece bowl, bulbous, painted
w/sprays of full-blown colorful
flowers between scrolling gilt
borders & reserved on white
ground, gilt-bronze mounts
w/pierced collar & 4 scrolling

feet, late 19th c., 14¼" h.
(ILLUS.) 1,540.00

Coffee can & saucer, reserved
w/gilt-edged roundel colorfully
painted w/a floral bouquet on a
purple marbleized ledge against
shaded tan ground, cup w/bird's
nest & cluster of fruit on ledge,
"bleu-du-roi" ground, gilt dentil
rims w/tooled gilt foliate scroll
border & base of cup w/gilt "oeil-
de-perdrix" diapered band,
1782........................1,045.00

Cup & saucer, exotic birds among
flowering foliage in landscapes
within gilt band surrounds reserved on blue ground, gilt dentil
rims, 1767 & 1773 .... 770.00

Ewer, baluster-shaped w/flared rim
w/chased gilt, chased gilt borders
on green ground reserving continuous battlefield scene w/Napo-
leon & retinue, molded gilt
handle, artist-signed, 1804-14,
11" h......................... 897.00

Pedestals, bisque, continuous frieze
of dancing maidens playing flutes
or tambourines & men w/wine
vessels between "bleu-du-roi"
(cobalt blue) borders & white
palmette-molded bands enriched
by gilding, gilt-bronze mounts,
late 19th c., 41¼" h., pr.......22,550.00

Plates, 9¼" d., pink & green scattered rose sprays, border w/band
of berried foliage, gilt dentil
rim, artist-signed, 1790, set
of 12 ....2,640.00

18th Century Sevres Plate

Plate, 9¾" d., bleu Starhemberg
patt., center w/sprigs of shaded
pink roses & green leaves, bright
blue ground rim patterned w/gold-
dotted circlets, colorfully painted

w/floral sprays & bordered in
lightly molded foliate C-scrolls
heightened in gilding & alternating w/gilt fan devices, artist-
signed, dated 1771 (ILLUS.) 1,210.00

Plate, 9¾" d., center scene of Napoleon at the Battle of Austerlitz,
"bleu-du-roi" border enriched
w/enameled gold eagles & other
devices, artist-signed 295.00

Sevres Solitare Set

Solitare set: sugar bowl & cover
w/gilt flowerhead finial, cov.
chocolate pot (handle missing),
c/s & diamond-shaped tray on 4
ball feet; painted in colors & gilt
w/flowerheads & shell motifs entwined w/puce ribbons & foliate
garlands suspending foliate swags,
borders w/blue panels enriched
w/gilt net patt., artist-signed,
1763, 5 pcs. (ILLUS.)............3,960.00

Tea set: cov. teapot, sugar bowl,
creamer, fruit bowl, 2 cake plates
& 15 c/s; reserved w/gilt-edged
medallions colorfully painted
w/various birds on "Bleu Celeste"
(sky blue) ground, ornate gold
trim, 36 pcs. 5,785.00

Urns, reserved w/oval panel of lady
w/mandolin & gentleman seated
in a tree-filled landscape on pale
pink ground, gilt-bronze mounts
w/tassel handles, artist-signed,
14" h., pr...................... 950.00

Vase, 10" h., ovoid w/cylindrical
neck, glossy blue & violet flambe'
glaze, 1 side mounted w/silver
bearded iris blossoms & leaves
in high relief, neck & foot each
w/simple band at edge, ca.
1900........................2,090.00

Vases, cov., 17 5/6" h., reserved
w/scene of a lady & gentleman in
an elegant interior on front &
landscape scene reverse within
scrolling gilt borders on "bleu-
du-roi" ground, gilt-bronze mounts,
artist-signed, late 19th c., pr 1,760.00

Vases, cov., 28½" h., elongated oviform, obverse w/two black wom-
en wearing dark lavender &
yellow-streaked gowns & holding
a garland of magenta flowers,
reverse w/two nude black men
playing a flute & panpipe amongst
exotic foliage & birds, ca. 1925,
pr. 18,700.00
Vase, cov., 29 7/8" h., classical
maiden seated beside a brook
offering a putto water from the
shell she holds aloft, while another
soars above placing a flower in
her hair, reverse w/pastoral landscape, each within gilt borders
heightened w/lustrous pastel-
colored panels, whole reserved on
pale pink ground, gilt-bronze
mounts, late 19th c. 2,640.00
Vases, cov., 38" h., oval panel
w/Bacchic celebration on the
banks of a stream, first w/scantily
clad nymph pouring wine for Bacchus while 2 putti soar overhead
bearing grapes, second w/drunk-
en god fast asleep while his
companions comfort him, further
painted on reverse w/landscape
panels & reserved on "bleu-du-roi"
ground w/gilt details, artist-
signed, late 19th c., pr. 7,150.00

SHAWNEE

Shawnee "Corn King" Line

*The Shawnee Pottery operated in Zanes-
ville, Ohio, from 1937 until 1961. Much of the
early production was sold to chain stores and
mail order houses including Sears Roebuck,
Woolworth and others. Planters, cookie jars
and vases, along with the popular "Corn
King" oven ware line, are among the collectible items which are pentiful and still reasonably priced.*

Bank-cookie jar combination, figural
    Smiley Pig, brown or salmon $125.00
Bowl, 6½" oval, "Corn King"
    line 16.00
Butter dish, cov., "Corn King"
    line 26.00
Casserole, cov., "Corn King" line,
    1½ qt. 28.00

Cookie jar, Fruit Basket........... 30.00
Cookie jar, jug-shaped w/heart &
    tulips decor.................... 67.50
Cookie jar, figural Dutch Boy,
    marked "Great Northern"....... 100.00
Cookie jar, figural Dutch Girl, tulip
    & floral decor, gold trim 115.00
Cookie jar, figural Farmer Pig, blue
    or green scarf ....35.00 to 45.00
Cookie jar, figural Mugsey dog 45.00
Cookie jar, figural Puss 'n Boots 35.00
Cookie jar, figural Smiley Pig, floral
    decor & green scarf, gold trim.... 125.00
Cookie jar, figural Winnie Pig, blue
    or green collar................. 60.00
Creamer & cov. sugar bowl, "Corn
    King" line, pr. (ILLUS.
    right) 30.00
Creamer & cov. sugar bowl, figural
    Puss 'n Boots, gold trim, pr....... 125.00
Mixing bowls, "Corn King" line,
    nesting-type, set of 3 .... 60.00
Pitcher, milk, 8" h., figural Bo Peep,
    lavender bonnet 57.50
Pitcher, figural Chanticleer
    Rooster 26.00
Pitcher, figural Smiley Pig.......... 30.00
Planter, figural clown............. 8.00
Planter, figural man w/push cart,
    gold trim 20.00
Planter, figural seated Oriental
    couple 25.00
Planter, model of a deer........... 11.00
Planter, model of an elephant,
    black 25.00
Planter, model of a fawn, yellow ... 12.00
Planter, model of a pup on a shoe,
    blue 15.00
Plate, salad, 8" oval, "Corn King"
    line 16.00
Platter, 12" oval, "Corn King" line .. 27.50
Relish dish, "Corn King" line 13.50
Salt & pepper shakers, "Corn King"
    line, 3¼" h., pr. 7.00
Salt & pepper shakers, "Corn King"
    line, 5½" h., pr. 9.50
Salt & pepper shakers, yellow daisy
    decor, large, pr. 14.00
Salt & pepper shakers, figural Bo
    Peep, small, pr.................. 17.00
Salt & pepper shakers, figural Dutch
    Boy & Dutch Girl, gold trim,
    pr............................. 27.50
Salt & pepper shakers, figural Puss
    'n Boots, small, pr. 11.50
Salt & pepper shakers, figural Sailor
    Boy, small, pr. 13.50
Salt & pepper shakers, model of a
    flower pot, pr.................. 8.00
Salt & pepper shakers, model of a
    milk can, pr.................... 15.00
Teapot, cov., Cookie House 83.00
Teapot, cov., "Corn King" line,
    30 oz. (ILLUS. left) 30.00

Teapot, cov., "Corn King" line, in-
dividual size 60.00

Teapot, cov., heart & tulips decor,
2-cup size 38.00

Vase, model of a doe in
shadowbox 14.00

Wall pocket, model of a clock 16.00

SLIP WARE

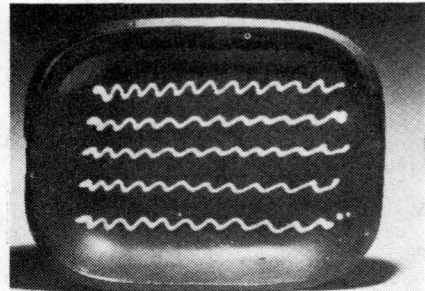

Slip Ware Dish

*This term refers to ceramics, primarily red-
ware, decorated by the application of slip, or
semi-liquid paste made of clay. Such wares
were made for decades in England and Germany and elsewhere on the Continent, and in
the Pennsylvania Dutch country and elsewhere in the United States. Today, contemporary copies of early Slip Ware items are
featured in numerous decorator magazines
and offered for sale in gift catalogues. These
reproductions hurt dealers who handle au-
thentic old pieces of Slip Ware.*

Charger, coggled edge, yellow slip
criss-crossed wavy lines & dots on
redware, clear glaze, 12¼" d.,
2¼"h. (hairlines) $275.00

Dish, 5 rows of yellow slip zig-zags
on redware, probably Pennsylvania, late 19th c., 16 x 12"
(ILLUS.) 500.00

Dish, coggled edge, yellow slip 4-
line bands of irregular stripes,
dogs & broken line segments on
redware, early 19th c., 18 x
11½", 3" deep (rim chips) 880.00

Pie plate, coggled edge, yellow slip
3-line designs on redware,
8¼" d. 195.00

Pie plate, coggled edge, brown slip
dots, initials & date "1873" on red-
ware, 8 3/8" d. 195.00

Pie plate, coggled edge, yellow slip
4-line crow's foot design on red-
ware, 9" d. 510.00

Pie plate, coggled edge, yellow slip
polka dots on redware, impressed
"Johnsonville, Pa.," 9" d. 125.00

Pie plate, coggled edge, yellow slip
3-line crow's foot & wavy line designs on redware, 9 3/8" d. (rim
hairline) 400.00

Pie plate, coggled edge, 3-line yellow slip crow's foot, dot & wavy
line design on redware, 9¾" d.
(hairlines) 350.00

Pie plate, coggled edge, yellow slip
4-line crow's foot design & dots on
redware, 9¾" d. 375.00

Pie plate, coggled edge, yellow slip
3-line crow's foot & dot design on
redware, 10¼" d. (edge chips) . . . 275.00

Pie plate, coggled edge, yellow slip
3-line bold double "S" curve on
redware, 10 5/8" d. (rim
hairline) 425.00

SPATTERWARE

Spatterware Cups & Saucers

*This ceramic wares takes its name from the
"spattering" of designs on it in color with rustic decor and flowers, houses and eagles and
the like. Much of that now available in this
country was imported from potteries in
England last century.*

Beaker, blue, brown & yellow rain-
bow spatter, 2½" h. $275.00

Creamer, Peafowl patt., free-hand
blue, green, yellow & black peafowl on red spatter ground,
4 1/8" h. (chips on side of
spout) 300.00

Creamer, Rose patt., free-hand red,
green & black rose on blue & pur-
ple spatter ground, 3¾" h. 325.00

Creamer, Thistle patt., free-hand
red & green thistle, red & yellow
spatter panels, 3 7/8" h. (short
hairline in bottom) 525.00

Cup, handleless, Beehive patt., free-
hand green, yellow & black beehive on blue spatter ground, blue
spatter border (professional
repair) 300.00

Cup & saucer, handleless, Acorn &
Oak Leaf patt., free-hand black,
brown & green acorns, purple
spatter borders 375.00

Cup & saucer, handleless, Cornflower patt., free-hand blue, green & black cornflowers, red & yellow rainbow spatter borders 675.00

Cup & saucer, handleless, purple spatter, miniature size 85.00

Cup & saucer, handleless, Fort patt., free-hand black, red, green & yellow-ochre fort, blue spatter borders, miniature size (pinpoint edge flakes) 450.00

Cup & saucer, handleless, Tree patt., free-hand black & green tree, blue spatter borders, miniature size 450.00

Cup & saucer, handleless, Tulip patt., free-hand blue, red, green, black & yellow-ochre tulip, red spatter borders, miniature size ... 400.00

Cups & saucers, Peafowl patt., free-hand blue, green, ochre & black peafowl, pale blue spatter, pr. (ILLUS.)........................ 575.00

Dish, red & blue striped rainbow spatter border & center cross, 7½ x 5 3/8" oblong w/cut corners (minor edge wear & glaze flakes) 650.00

Mug, blue spatter, 3 7/8" h. (edge wear & small hairline at base of handle) 150.00

Mug, blue & brown rainbow spatter, 4¾" h. (pinpoint rim flakes & minor crazing in bottom)........ 225.00

Pitcher, 9¾" h., paneled, free-hand red, blue, green & black four-petal flower, red & blue spatter rim border, impressed "Davenport" (stains & small chip on foot) 350.00

Plate, 7" d., red, blue & green rainbow spatter, impressed "Adams" 190.00

Plate, 7" d., Thistle patt., free-hand colorful thistle center, shaded green to black & green border ...1,430.00

Plate, 7½" d., Peafowl patt., free-hand red, yellow, green & black peafowl on blue spatter ground .. 300.00

Plate, 8 3/8" d., Acorn patt., free-hand brown, black & green acorns & oak leaves center, blue spatter border (minor stains & wear) 375.00

Plate, 8½" d., Star patt., free-hand red, blue & green star, blue spatter border, impressed "Stone China" 300.00

Plate, 9¼" d., Peafowl patt., 14-sided, blue spatter border, impressed "Adams" mark 300.00

Plate, 9½" d., Bull's Eye patt., olive green & red spattered bull's eye center, rainbow spatter borders .. 205.00

Plate, 9½" d., Dahlia patt., free-hand, red, blue & green dahlia, blue spatter border............. 270.00

Plate, 9½" d., Fort patt., free-hand black, red & green fort, blue spatter border (small edge flake)..... 345.00

Plate, 9¾" d., Rose patt., free-hand red, green & black rose center, blue spatter border (minor wear) 215.00

Plate, 9¾" d., Tulip patt., free-hand blue, green, red, black & yellow tulip, blue spatter border (pinpoint rim flakes) 285.00

Sauce dish, Peafowl patt., free-hand red, blue, green & black peafowl center, red spatter border, 5" d. (stains & minor glaze flakes) 245.00

Soup plate, Peafowl patt., free-hand, blue, green, red & black peafowl, blue spatter border, impressed "Adams," 8 5/8" d. 500.00

Peafowl Pattern Sugar Bowl

Sugar bowl, cov., Peafowl patt., blue spatter (ILLUS.) 400.00

Sugar bowl, cov., Rose patt., free-hand rose on blue spatter ground (rim chip)...................... 302.50

Sugar shaker, bulbous base & dome top, blue & purple rainbow spatter on white, 5" h. (small chips around rim & dome) 410.00

Teapot, cov., Peafowl patt., free-hand green, yellow, blue & black peafowl on red spatter ground, 7¼" h........................ 750.00

Toddy plate, Acorn patt., free-hand green, yellow & black acorns & oak leaves center, purple spatter border, 5 1/8" d. (glaze flakes) ... 375.00

Toddy plate, Dahlia patt., free-hand red, blue, green & black dahlia, red spatter border, 5¼" d........ 325.00

Toddy plate, Tulip patt., free-hand red, blue, green & black tulip, blue spatter border, 5¼" d....... 350.00

Waste bowl, Fort patt., free-hand black, red, green & yellow fort, blue spatter border, 4½" d., 2 3/8" h. 475.00

SPONGEWARE

Spongeware Bowl

Spongeware's designs were spattered or daubed on in colors, sometimes with a piece of cloth. Blue and blue-and-white ware predominated. Some collectors lump Spatterware and Spongeware into a single category, but dealers offer them as separate wares. Also see RED WING POTTERY.

Batter bowl, blue daubing on white, large $275.00

Bean pot, cov., blue daubing on white 295.00

Bowl, 4" d., 1 5/8" h., brown & green daubing on yellowware 35.00

Bowl, 6" d., blue & rust daubing on tan 37.50

Bowl, 6" d., paneled sides, blue & rust daubing on tan 42.50

Bowl, 6½" d., canted sides, blue daubing on white 65.00

Bowl, 7" d., 2" h., blue daubing on white 80.00

Bowl, 7¼" d., paneled sides, blue & rust daubing on tan (ILLUS.) 52.50

Bowl, 8½" d., paneled sides, blue & rust daubing on tan, w/black transfer advertising center 50.00

Bowl, 8½" d., 2½" h., canted sides, brown daubing on yellowware ... 38.00

Bowl, 9" d., 6¼" h., blue daubing on white 165.00

Bowl, 9¼" d., 4¼" h., green daubing on white 75.00

Bowl, 9 3/8" d., 4¼" h., brown & green daubing on yellowware ...... 50.00 to 67.50

Bowl, 12" d., 5" h., molded arch-panel sides, blue daubing on white 185.00

Bread plate, pierced handles, blue daubing on white, 10" d. 95.00

Butter crock, cov., molded Greek Key band, blue daubing on white, 7½" d. 180.00

Butter crock, blue daubing on white, stenciled "Butter" in blue, 6" d., 3¾" h. (no lid) 225.00

Casserole, cov., blue & rust daubing on tan, 8 5/8" d. 110.00

Casseroles, individual size, brown daubing on yellowware, 5 x 2", set of 6 .... 140.00

Chamber pot, blue daubing on yellowware, miniature size, 1 5/8" h. 32.50

Chamber pot, blue daubing on white ....75.00 to 90.00

Coffee pot, cov., blue daubing on white, 19th c. 225.00

Coffee pot, cov., blue daubing on yellowware 245.00

Crock w/lid, blue daubing on white, 9" d., 6" h. 185.00

Cup plate, blue daubing on white, 3 1/8" d. (rim chip) 60.00

Cuspidor, green daubing on cream, 7½" d., 5" h. 100.00

Cuspidor, lady's, blue daubing on grey 90.00

Custard cup, blue daubing on white, 2 3/8" h. (hairline) 30.00

Custard cup, brown daubing on yellowware 25.00

Dish, blue daubing on white, 6¼" d., 2" h. 145.00

Flower pot w/attached saucer, blue daubing on white, 8¼" h. (minor chip on saucer rim) 225.00

Spongeware Hot Water Pitcher

Hot water pitcher, blue daubing on white, 9½" h. (ILLUS.) 250.00

Hot water pitcher, bulbous w/flaring mouth, blue daubing on white, 11½" h. (small lip chips) 250.00

Grease jar, cov., green & rust daubing on cream 38.00

Jardiniere, bulbous, blue daubing on white, brown rim edge, 11" d., 9½" h. 140.00

Mixing bowl, rust & blue daubing on tan, 5" d. 40.00

Mixing bowl, blue & brown daubing on cream, w/Iowa advertising, 7" d., 5" h. 45.00

Mixing bowl, green daubing & brown bands on cream, 10¼" d., 5¼" h. 100.00

Mixing bowl, green daubing on cream, 10½" d. 130.00

Mixing bowl, paneled sides, blue & rust daubing on tan, 11" d. 110.00

Mug, blue daubing on white,
3½" h. 155.00
Mug, blue daubing on cream, gilt
rim, 3 5/8" h. 85.00
Mug, red, blue & green daubing on
white, 3 7/8" h. 225.00
Mug, brown daubing on yellowware,
4½" h. 65.00
Pitcher, 4½" h., brown & green
daubing on yellowware (minor
stains) 75.00
Pitcher, tankard, 6" h., brown &
green daubing on tan 55.00
Pitcher, 6½" h., bulbous w/straight
neck, blue daubing on white
(hairline in handle) 90.00
Pitcher, 6½" h., square handle,
green daubing on white 95.00
Pitcher, 7½" h., embossed staves &
bands in brown & green daubing
on cream 45.00
Pitcher, tankard, 8¾" h., blue daubing on white .... 165.00 to 195.00
Pitcher, tankard, 8 7/8" h., blue
daubing on white 275.00
Pitcher, 9" h., dark blue daubing on
cream 300.00
Pitcher, poinsettia-molded, blue
daubing on white 185.00
Plate, 7½" d., blue daubing on
white 75.00
Plate, 8¼" d., blue daubing on
white 90.00
Plate, 8¼" d., light blue rim & light
blue daubing on white 90.00

Spongeware Plate

Plate, 9½" d., blue daubing on
white (ILLUS.) 155.00
Platter, 13½ x 10" oblong, cobalt
blue rim & blue daubing on
white 155.00
Platter, 14½" oblong, blue daubing
on white 195.00
Salt box, hanging-type, relief-
molded peacock design, brown
daubing on yellowware, w/lid 150.00
Soap dish, blue daubing on white... 125.00
Toothbrush holder, blue daubing on
cream stoneware................ 65.00

STAFFORDSHIRE FIGURES

Elephant Spillholder Vase

Small figures and groups, made of pottery
were produced by the majority of the
Staffordshire, England, potters in the 19th
century and were used as mantel decorations
or "chimney ornaments," as they were sometimes called. Pairs of dogs were favorites and
were turned out by the carloads, and 19th century pieces are still available. Well-painted
reproductions also abound and collectors are
urged to exercise caution before investing.

Dog, Pug in seated position, white
coat w/apricot spots, brown head,
feet & tail, 4½" h. $85.00
Dog, Spaniel, white coat w/black
spots, 5½" h. 165.00
Dog, Whippet seated on pillow,
3½" h. 60.00
Donkeys, 8½" l., 9" h., pr......... 150.00
Elephant w/yellow & green back
cloth suspending tassels standing
before a tree trunk spillholder
vase, oval base, ca. 1850, 6¾" h.
(ILLUS.) 330.00
Equestrian figure, Prince Royal on
horseback, w/drum, 1845, 8" 150.00
Equestrian figure, Princess Royal on
horseback, w/flag, 1845, 8" 150.00
Equestrian figure, Duke of Can-
naught on horse, 1850, 13" h. 110.00
Equestrian figure, Lord Wolseley on
horseback, ca. 1885, 13" h. 110.00
Figure of Brittania seated, wearing
plumed helmet & holding shield
w/British lion, 5¾" h. 310.00
Figures, milk seller & his wife,
wearing colorful peasant clothing,
on circular grass mound bases enriched w/gilding, ca. 1850, 7" h.,
pr............................... 528.00
Figure of "Charlotte at the Tomb of
Werther," ca. 1800, 9" h. 160.00

Figure of Jenny Lind as Alice in "Robert the Devil," blue bodice, tartan skirt, oval base w/title inscribed in gilt script, 9¾" h. 635.00

Figure of Iphigenia holding fruit, 1800, 10" h. 200.00

Figure of actor John Philip Kemble as "Hamlet," holding a skull, 10¾" h. 226.00

Figure of King John at Runnymede, 1850, 13" h. 220.00

Figure of Scottish Highlander w/pipes, ca. 1850, 14" h. 90.00

Figure group, Isaac Van Amburgh wearing a Roman gladiator costume, standing w/a leopard, lion & lioness, 5¾" h. 5,233.00

Figure group, Elephant of Siam, elephant on a stage reaching up to a figure in a clock tower, shaped oval base applied w/grasses, enriched in green, iron-red, blue & grey, ca. 1840, 6" w. 495.00

Staffordshire Figure Group

Figure group, Uncle Tom & Eva, Uncle Tom seated on rockwork holding a book in his left hand, Eva seated on his knee, oval base applied w/yellow hat & inscribed "Uncle Tom & Eva" in gilt, Eva's right foot missing, ca. 1852, 8¼" h. (ILLUS.) 418.00

Figure group, Topsy & Eva seated arm in arm, oval scroll-molded base, 8¼" h. 225.00

Figure group, Princess Royal seated on the back of a St. Bernard dog, 1845, 9" h. 275.00

Figure group, Androcles & the lion, oval gilt-lined base, 9¾" h. 183.00

Figure group, Edward Morgan &

Jenny Jones by a milepost, "Langollen. 1 mile," man in blue jacket, yellow waistcoat, girl in Welsh costume, oval gilt-lined base, 11" h. 395.00

Figure group, 2 archers & dog w/spillholder vase, 1850, 13" h. ... 145.00

Figure group, "Politos Menagerie," 6 figures, elephant, lions & monkeys, Obadiah Sheratt, 6-footed rectangular base, 13¼" h. 9,172.00

"The Death of Monrow"

Figure group, 'The Death of Monrow," black-striped yellow tiger w/eyes, teeth (1 repaired) & tongue heightened in iron-red, gnawing the head of the rigid lieutenant wearing a rose-sashed red hunting jacket w/yellow epaulets & breeches, on a green rectangular base w/black-marbleized apron w/title inscribed in black in 2 molded ovals above an iron-red, blue & green molded floral vine & raised on 6 bracket feet (3 w/repaired chips), Obadiah Sherratt, ca. 1830, 13 5/8" l. (ILLUS.) 7,975.00

Giraffe & palm trees, 5½" h. 130.00

Horses, one w/manganese-sponged coat, the other w/large manganese spots, each w/iron-red mouth, modelled rearing above an iron-red globe on green & blue square plinth above rounded rectangular base, the first base w/green top, blue-banded iron-red, green & manganese vine border & manganese footrim, the other marbleized in blue & green, ca. 1830, 6¾" & 6 5/8" h. respectively, pr. (restored) 3,250.00

Lions, standing, glass-eyes, 13" l., 10" h., pr. 325.00

Rabbit in crouched position w/ears down, on grassy mound base, 3¼" l. 220.00

Staffordshire Rabbits Circa 1850

Rabbits nibbling on lettuce leaves, splashed in black, both w/repair to 1 ear, ca. 1850, 10" l., pr. (ILLUS.) 1,540.00

Watch holder, sailor & lass flanking arbor, 1850, 7" h. 135.00

Watch holder, man & woman flanking tree trunk, cobalt blue & pink, ca. 1840, 10½" h. 135.00

STANGL POTTERY BIRDS

Stangl Cockatoo

Johann Martin Stangl, who first came to work for the Fulper Pottery in 1910 as a ceramic chemist and plant superintendent, acquired a financial interest and became president of the company in 1926. The name of the firm was changed to Stangl Pottery in 1929 and at this time much of the production was devoted to a high grade dinnerware to enable the company to survive the depression years. Around 1940 a very limited edition of porcelain birds, patterned after the illustrations in John James Audubon's "Birds of America," were issued. Stangl subsequently began production of less expensive ceramic birds and these proved to be popular during the war years, 1940-46. Each bird was hand-painted and each was well marked with impressed, painted or stamped numerals which indicated the species and the size. Collectors are now seeking these ceramic birds which we list below.

Allen Hummingbird, No. 3634, 3½" h. $45.00

Bird of Paradise, No. 3408, 5½" h. 70.00

Bluebird (Double), No. 3276-D, 8½" h. 130.00

Blue Jay, No. 3715, 10¼" 445.00

Blue Jay, No. 3716, 10¼" 445.00

Bobolink, No. 3595, 4¾" h. 97.00

Brewer's Blackbird, No. 3591, 3½" h. 75.00

Canary facing left - Blue Flower, No. 3747, 6¼" h. 110.00

Canary facing right - Rose Flower, No. 3746, 6¼" h. 80.00

Cardinal, No. 3444, 6½" h.......... 80.00

Cockatoo, No. 3405, 6" h.......... 37.50

Cockatoo, No. 3484, 11 3/8" h. (ILLUS.) ....160.00 to 185.00

Cock Pheasant, No. 3492, 6¼ x 11" 145.00

Flying Duck, No. 3443, 9" h........ 230.00

Group of Chickadees, No. 3581, 5½ x 8½" 125.00

Group of Goldfinches, No. 3635, 4 x 11½" 145.00

Hen, No. 3446, 7" h............... 95.00

Hen Pheasant, No. 3491, 6¼ x 11".. 115.00

Indigo Bunting, No. 3589, 3¼" h. ... 40.00

Kentucky Warbler, No. 3598, 3" h. ... 36.00

Key West Quail Dove, No. 3454, 9" h...................... 210.00

King Fisher, No. 3406, 3½" h. 50.00

Kingfisher, No. 3406-S, 3½" h. 57.50

Love Bird, No. 3400, 4" h.......... 40.00

Magpie-Jay, No. 3758............. 650.00

Oriole, No. 3402, 3¼" h. 35.00

Oriole, No. 3402-S, 3¼" h.......... 40.00

Pair of Blue Jays, No. 3717, 12½" .. 250.00

Pair of Hummingbirds, No. 3599, 8 x 10½" 215.00

Pair of Kingfishers, No., 3406-D, 5" h........................ 85.00

Pair of Parakeets, No. 3582, 7" h. ... 135.00

Pair of Wrens, No. 3401-D, 8" h..... 86.00

Penguin, No. 3274, 5½" h. 290.00

Quacking Duck, No. 3250-F, 2¼" h...................... 35.00

Red-Headed Woodpecker, No. 3751-S, 6¼" h. 60.00

Red-Headed Woodpecker (Double), No. 3752-D, 7¾" h. 350.00

Rooster, grey, No. 3445, 9" h. 95.00

Scarlet Tanager (Double), No. 3750-D, 8" h. 350.00

Scissor-Tailed Flycatcher, No. 3757, 11" h........................ 410.00

Swallow, No. 3852 .... 55.00

Titmouse, No. 3592, 2½" h. 40.00

Turkey, No. 3275, 3½" h. 250.00

Western Blue Bird, No. 3815........ 110.00
White Headed Pigeon, No. 3518,
  12½" l., 7½" h.................. 495.00
Wilson Warbler, No. 3597, 3½" h. .. 40.00
Wren, No. 3401, 3½" h. 42.00
Yellow Warbler, No. 3447, 5" h. 45.00

STONEWARE

Stoneware Butter Churn

  Stoneware is essentially a vitreous pottery, impervious to water even in its unglazed state, that has been produced by potteries all over the world for centuries. Utilitarian wares such as crocks, jugs, churns and the like, were the most common productions in the numerous potteries that sprang into existence in the United States during the 19th century. These items were often enhanced by the application of a cobalt blue oxide decoration. In addition to the coarse, primarily salt-glazed stonewares, there are other categories of stoneware known by such special names as basaltes, jasper and others. Also see ADVERTISING ITEMS, BENNINGTON & RED WING POTTERY and KITCHENWARES.

Butter churn, slightly ovoid, earred
  handles, slip-quilled cobalt blue
  scalloped design, flower w/stem
  & date "1840" on grey, unmarked
  except for impressed "2," attributed to the New York area, 2-gal.,
  13½" h., complete w/wooden lid
  & dasher (ILLUS.) $572.00
Butter churn, slightly ovoid, molded
  rim, earred handles, slip-quilled

cobalt blue floral spray on grey,
  impressed "New York Stoneware
  Co. (Satterlee & Mory), Fort Edward, N.Y.," 1861-65, 3-gal...... 198.00
Butter churn, semi-ovoid, molded
  rim, earred handles, slip-quilled
  cobalt blue lion on grey, impressed
  "J. Burger, Jr., Rochester, N.Y.,"
  ca. 1860, 8-gal.................4,000.00
Crock, stenciled cobalt blue florals,
  leaves & label "Hamilton & Jones,
  Greensboro, Pa." on gun metal
  grey, half-gal. 145.00
Crock, straight sides, earred handles, slip-quilled cobalt blue
  single flower & leaves on grey,
  impressed "White's Utica" (Noah
  White, Utica, New York), 1865-77,
  7½" h. 130.00
Crock, straight sides, earred handles, slip-quilled cobalt blue thistle on grey, impressed "J. Burger
  Jr., Rochester," 1878-90, 2-gal. ... 128.00

Whittemore Crock with Fish

Crock, straight sides, earred handles, slip-quilled cobalt blue fish
  on grey, impressed "R.O. Whittemore, Havanna, N.Y.," 1860-80,
  8¼" d., 7½" h. (ILLUS.) 1,430.00
Crock, straight sides, earred handles, slip-quilled cobalt blue stylized half-length figure of a man
  sprouting flowers from his shoulders on grey, impressed "M.
  Woodruff & Co., Cortland, New
  York," 1849-85, 9¾" d., 9¼" h. ..1,980.00
Crock, straight sides, earred handles, slip-quilled cobalt blue lyre-
  type design on grey, impressed
  "Whites, Utica, N.Y.," 1865-77,
  3-gal., 10½" h. 150.00
Crock, slightly ovoid, earred handles, slip-quilled stylized florals
  on grey, impressed "Ithaca, N.Y.,"
  3-gal., 11½" h. 225.00
Crock, stenciled cobalt blue "A.
  Conrad, New Geneva, Pa." & dots
  on grey, 9" d., 12" h. (ILLUS.) 75.00

"New Geneva" Crock

Crock, slightly ovoid, earred handles, stenciled cobalt blue label "James Hamilton & Co., Greensboro, Pa.," floral swags & "3" on dark grey, 1850-80, 3-gal., 13½" h. (chips on one handle) ... 215.00

Crock, slightly ovoid, earred handles, stenciled cobalt blue & brushed label "Williams & Reppert, Greensboro, Pa." & "3" on dark grey, ca. 1870, 3-gal., 14¾" h. 175.00

Crock, straight sides, earred handles, slip-quilled cobalt blue polka dot bird on grey, impressed "4," unmarked, 4-gal., 11½" h. 250.00

Crock, straight sides, earred handles, slip-quilled cobalt blue wildflowers on grey, impressed "Whites, Utica, N.Y.," 1865-77, 4-gal., 11½" h. 285.00

Crock, straight sides, earred handles, slip-quilled cobalt blue double flowers on grey, impressed "Woodruff, Cortland," 1849-90, 5-gal. 265.00

19th Century Crocks

Crocks, slip-quilled or brushed cobalt blue decor on grey & impressed variously (left to right): "S. D. Kellogg, Whately"; unmarked; "O.L. & A.K. Ballard, Burlington, Vt."; "F.B. Norton & Co., Worcester, Mass."; 19th c., from 7½" to 12½" h., group of 4 (ILLUS.) 1,210.00

Cuspidor, brushed cobalt blue feather strokes on grey, impressed "1," 9" d. (hairline) 97.50

Jug, stenciled cobalt blue leaf signature on grey, Western Stoneware Co., Monmouth, Illinois, 1906 to present, 1-gal. 30.00

Jug, ovoid, strap handle, brownish amber glaze on grey, impressed "Swan & States, Stonington," 1823-35, 10" h. (old base chips) ... 85.00

Jug, semi-ovoid, strap handle, slip-quilled cobalt blue stylized flower & leaves on grey, impressed "S. Hart" (Fulton, N.Y.), 1840-76, 10¼" h. 155.00

Jug, straight sides, brushed cobalt blue initials on grey, impressed "J. Fisher, Lyons, N.Y.," 1882-1902, 10½" h. 50.00

Jug, semi-ovoid, strap handle, slip-quilled cobalt blue label "John H. Donley, 45 Washington St., Binghamton, N.Y.," impressed "Geddes, N.Y.," 1883-87, 11½" h. 155.00

Jug, slightly ovoid, strap handle, stenciled deep blue label "Jas. Hamilton & Co., Greensboro, Pa." & 4 large stars on dark grey & brushed w/feathering, 1850-80, 11½" h. 80.00

Jug, semi-ovoid, strap handle, slip-quilled cobalt blue stylized florals on grey, impressed "Ottman Bros. & Co., Fort Edward, N.Y.," 1872-92, 11½" h. (minor lip & base flakes) 125.00

Jug, ovoid, strap handle, brushed cobalt blue oval on grey, impressed "Lyons," New York, ca. 1855, 11¾" h. 130.00

Jug, semi-ovoid, strap handle, slip-quilled cobalt blue 3-sprigged fern-like plant on grey, impressed "S.W. Braun, Buffalo, N.Y.," 1856-96, 13½" h. 135.00

Jug, semi-ovoid, strap handle, slip-quilled cobalt blue figure w/head & horns of stag & wings on grey, impressed "O.L. & A.K. Ballard, Burlington, Vt.," 1856-67, 2-gal., 13½" h. 1,100.00

Jug, semi-ovoid, strap handle, brushed cobalt blue bird w/topknot on grey, impressed "Haxton & Co., Fort Edward, N.Y.," 1857-82, 2-gal., 14" h. (hairlines & lip chip) 325.00

Jug, slightly ovoid, strap handle, slip-quilled cobalt blue single flower & stem w/leaves on grey, impressed (indistinctly "Seymour Brothers," Hartford, Connecticut, 1867-71, 2-gal., 14" h. 105.00

Jug, slightly ovoid, strap handle, brushed cobalt blue floral spray on grey, impressed "N. Clark, Jr.,

Athens, N.Y.," 1843-91, 2-gal.,
   14" h. 175.00
Jug, straight sides, strap handle,
   brushed cobalt blue single flower
   on grey, impressed "West Troy
   Pottery," 1870-80, 2-gal.,
   14¼" h. 95.00
Jug, straight sides, strap handle,
   brushed cobalt blue floral on
   grey, impressed "A.K. Ballard,
   Burlington, Vt.," 1867-72, 2-gal.,
   14½" h. (minor flakes) 95.00
Jug w/unusual pouring spout, strap
   handle, slip-quilled cobalt blue
   floral spray on grey, impressed
   "New York Stoneware Co., Fort
   Edward, N.Y.," 1861-85, 2-gal.,
   15" h. 140.00
Jug, semi-ovoid, slip-quilled cobalt
   blue stylized foliage on grey, impressed "Somerset Potters Works"
   (Somerset, New Jersey), 1847-
   1909, 2-gal., 14" h. 145.00
Jug, ovoid, applied double loop han-
   dles, brushed bold cobalt blue floral design & "4" on grey,
   unmarked, 4-gal., 16¾" h. 235.00
Jug, semi-ovoid, applied handle,
   slip-quilled cobalt blue grape cluster on grey, impressed "Cowden &
   Wilcox, Harrisburg, Pa.," 1870-81,
   4-gal. 595.00
Pitcher, 10¼" h., slip-quilled cobalt
   blue line at top of handle, large
   flower on body & bud beneath lip
   on grey, impressed "Cowden &
   Wilcox, Harrisburg, Pa.," 1870-90,
   1-gal. (few inside rim flakes) 800.00
Pitcher, 11¼" h., ovoid, cobalt blue
   daub at handle on grey, impressed label "C. Crolius Manufacturer, Manhattan Wells, New
   York," 1825-40 . . . . 1,700.00
Preserving jar, collared neck,
   brushed cobalt blue primitive figure of a man wearing a cap &
   wide band at rim & base on grey,
   unmarked, 8" h. 850.00
Preserving jar, collared neck, sten-
   ciled cobalt blue label "A.P.
   Donaghho, Parkersburg, W. Va."
   on grey, 1866-1908, 8" h. 55.00
Preserving jar, stenciled cobalt blue
   label "Hamilton & Jones, Greensboro, Pa." on dark grey, 1880-
   1915, 9¾" h. 105.00
Preserving jar, straight sides, col-
   lared neck, brushed cobalt blue
   swatches w/running drips on
   grey, unmarked, probably Pennsylvania, 1880's, 8¾" h. (ILLUS.
   right) 75.00
Preserving jar, slightly ovoid,
   brushed cobalt blue spray on

Preserving Jars

grey, impressed "1," 1-gal.,
   9 3/8" h. (ILLUS. left) 85.00
Water cooler, keg-shaped, em-
   bossed cobalt blue bands &
   brushed & slip-quilled cobalt blue
   stylized floral & foliage on grey,
   unmarked, 4-gal., 13" h. 775.00
Water cooler, earred handles, col-
   lared neck, stenciled cobalt blue
   label "R.T. Williams, Manufacturer, New Geneva, Pa." &
   brushed cobalt blue stripes &
   wavy lines on grey, w/turned
   wooden plug, 4-gal., 15" h. 145.00

TECO POTTERY

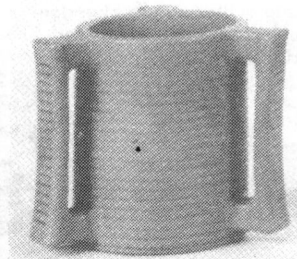

Teco Pottery Loving Cup

   *Teco Pottery was actually the line of art
pottery introduced by the American Terra
Cotta and Ceramic Company of Terra Cotta
(Crystal Lake), Illinois in 1902. Founded by
William D. Gates in 1881, American Terra
Cotta originally produced only bricks and
drain tile. Because of superior facilities for ex-
perimentation, including a chemical laboratory, the company was able to develop an art
pottery line, favoring a matte green glaze in
the earlier years but eventually achieving a
wide range of colors including a metallic lus-*

tre glaze and a crystalline glaze. Though some hand-thrown pottery was made, Gates favored a molded ware because it was less expensive to produce. By 1923, Teco Pottery was no longer being made and in 1930 American Terra Cotta and Ceramic Company was sold.

Bookend, "Rebecca at Well," shades of tan, light brown & blue high gloss glaze, 7 x 5" (single) $475.00
Bowl, 9½" d., shallow, leaves & berries in relief, matte green finish 120.00
Candlestick, trumpet-shaped, foot & top w/chased silver overlay of tulips & sinuous leaves, matte green finish, 16¼" h. (single) 825.00
Loving cup, 3-handled, horizontal ribbing, matte green finish, 6¼" h. (ILLUS.) 330.00
Pitcher, 4" h., ovoid w/flared undulating rim, C-shaped handle, silvery green glaze 5,280.00
Pitcher, 8½" h., flowing double handles, silvery green glaze 250.00
Urn, elephant ear handles, dark green glaze, 8½" d., 5½" h. 225.00
Vase, 3" h., bulbous, pinched sides, matte green finish 45.00
Vase, 4½" h., baluster form, streaked matte green finish 100.00
Vase, 4¾" h., ovoid, matte green finish 110.00
Vase, 5¼" h., dark green glaze 95.00
Vase, bud, 6" h., matte green finish. . . . . .65.00 to 75.00
Vase, 6½" h., buttress sides, matte rose finish 75.00
Vase, 7¼" h., wide mouth, tapering form centered by 4 square full-length vertical handles, brown glaze, ca. 1905 . . . . 550.00

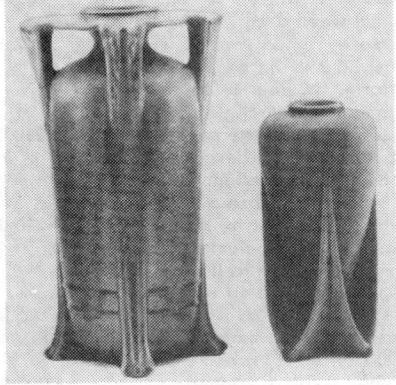

Teco Pottery Vases

Vase, 8½" h., bullet form on 4 elongated "V" feet, matte green finish, ca. 1909 (ILLUS. right) 880.00

Vase, 8½" h., ovoid w/collared neck, silvery green glaze 175.00
Vase, 11¼" h., shaped square "shelf" centering mouth on 4 raised handles w/floral detail, cylindrical body on 4 fluted feet w/ring detail, matte green finish, ca. 1905 (ILLUS. left) 1,540.00
Vase, 12½" h., jack-in-pulpit form, deep green glaze 400.00
Wall pocket, matte green finish, 15 x 7" 180.00

TEPLITZ

Teplitz Centerpiece

This ware was produced in numerous potteries in the vicinity of Teplitz in the Bohemian area of what is now Czechoslovakia during the late 19th and early 20th centuries. Vases and figures, of varying quality, were the primary productions and most were hand decorated. These items originally retailed in gift shops at prices from 25 cents to around $2. Now collectors are searching out these marked items and prices for finer examples are soaring.

Centerpiece, loving cup shape, gold scalloped rim & foot, gold double-twisted branch handles & reticulated outer wall, body & base decorated in the Tiffany manner w/turquoise, amber, opal & cobalt blue jeweling, 15" w., 9¾" h. $325.00
Centerpiece, Art Nouveau maiden in diaphanous drapery reclining amidst water lilies (ILLUS.) 800.00
Compote, 6", Art Nouveau women & florals in high relief, marked "Amphora-Teplitz". 400.00
Dish, 2-handled, lady & gentleman seated on bench decor, 7½" d. . . . 165.00
Ewer, gold double twig handle ter-

minating in cluster of relief-
molded florals, reticulated soft
pink neck, h.p. pink florals outlined in gold on pale green
ground, marked "Turn-Teplitz,"
6½" h. 125.00
Ewer, ornate handle, narrow white
neck, applied white florals on
cobalt blue ground, lavish gold
trim, 10" h. 135.00
Vase, 5¾" h., molded floral handles, blue, yellow & pink blossoms & buds on creamy ivory
ground, gold accents, artist-
signed 125.00
Vase, 7½" h., pink iris w/cobalt
blue centers & long slender green
leaves in relief on light green
ground, marked "Depose Turn
Wien" in crown 125.00
Vase, 8" h., pear-shaped, bust portrait of beautiful lady w/long
blonde hair wearing jewels,
marked "Turn-Teplitz-Bohemia" &
"Amphora, Austria, RStK" 450.00
Vase, 9½" h., 15½" w. across twisted handles, pedestal base, overall
multicolored jeweling, marked
"Amphora-Teplitz" 325.00
Vase, 9½" h., 2-handled, maroon
enameled gladiator decor, matte
finish, artist-signed, marked
"Amphora-Teplitz" 105.00
Vase, 10½" h., 2-handled, h.p.
roses w/gold tracery on mottled
soft yellow & green ground,
marked "Stellmacher-Teplitz" 175.00
Vase, 13" h., 14" widest d., bulbous,
stylized bird & florals in relief,
cobalt blue trim, marked
"Amphora-Czechoslovakia" &
dated 1922 .... 165.00
Vase, 16" h., 2-handled, florals &
foliage on shaded tan ground,
gold trim, ca. 1880 .... 450.00
Vase, 18½" h., lavender poppies &
green leaves on creamy ivory
ground, gold trim, crown mark ... 195.00
Vase, 18¾" h., 6¾" w., footed
ovoid w/long slender neck applied w/figure of mermaid, flesh-
toned maiden, white florals & lavish gold on wide glossy brown
body band shading to green satin
foot 595.00

TIFFANY POTTERY

*In 1902 Louis C. Tiffany expanded Tif-
fany Studios to include ceramics, enamels,
gold, silver and gemstones. Tiffany pottery*
*was usually molded rather than wheel-
thrown, but it is of the craftsman-type carefully finished by hand. A limited amount was
produced until about 1914. It is scarce.*

Tiffany Pottery Vase

Vase, 4¾" h., spherical, molded
fruiting tomato plants pendant
from incurved rim, beige ground
heightened w/dark green & black
overglaze, signed $880.00
Vase, 5½" h., cylindrical, molded
band of interlacing circular bird
medallions beneath leaf panels on
shoulder, tan-over-white glaze,
signed 385.00
Vase, 6" h., ribbed urn form, molded band of tapering leaves, tan
drip glaze heightened at shoulder
w/green, signed 660.00
Vase, 6 1/8" h., ovoid, molded band
of 3 leaves intercepted by 3 openwork handles, yellow-orange
glaze, signed 462.00
Vase, 6¼" h., cylindrical, molded
milkweed decor, glossy yellow
glaze, signed 412.50
Vase, 6 3/8" h., shaped spherical
form, shoulder & foot w/incised
bands, caramel glaze w/pendant
brown drip patterns, signed 330.00
Vase, 6 3/8" h., floriform, molded
as pierced overlapping leaves,
brown drip glaze over a high
gloss black glaze, signed 1,320.00
Vase, 7¼" h., baluster-shaped,
molded grape trellis highlighted in
green enamel on white ground,
signed 605.00
Vase, 12½" h., molded corn &
stalks, glossy green glaze heightened w/black, signed 990.00
Vase, 20" h., swollen cylinder tapering towards base, ringed neck,
pale yellow glaze, signed
(ILLUS.) 825.00

TILES

Low Art Tile by Arthur Osborn

Tiles have been made by potteries in the United States and abroad for many years. Apart from small tea tiles used on tables, there are also decorative tiles for fireplace, floors and walls and this is where present collector interest lies, especially in the late 19th century American-made art pottery tiles. Also see DELFT and PHOENIX BIRD.

American Encaustic Tiling Co., Zanesville, Ohio, William McKinley, blue-glazed intaglio bust portrait, 1896 campaign item w/candidate's biography pasted on reverse, 3 x 3" $95.00

American Encaustic Tiling Co., Zanesville, Ohio, dedication portrait, April 19, 1892, green glaze, 4 x 4" (corner flake) 75.00

American Encaustic Tiling Co., Zanesville, Ohio, stylized oriental junk w/pagoda-type buildings in background, 4 x 4" 25.00

American Encaustic Tiling Co., Zanesville, Ohio, portrait of President Harding, blue, 4 x 4" 55.00

American Encaustic Tiling Co., Zanesville, Ohio, stylized floral, iridescent green glaze, 6 x 6" 16.00

American Encaustic Tiling Co., Zanesville, Ohio, multicolored scene, crystalline glaze, 6 x 6" ... 48.00

American Encaustic Tiling Co., Zanesville, Ohio, silver deer on black, 6 x 6" 30.00

American Encaustic Tiling Co., Zanesville, Ohio, Simple Simon scene, 6 x 6" 80.00

American Encaustic Tiling Co., Zanesville, Ohio, pot of flowers in low relief, glossy olive green glaze, 24 x 6" (fireplace panel) ... 150.00

Batchelder Tile Co., California, incised medieval hunter w/spear & dog, 4 x 4" 67.00

California Faience Company, Berkeley, California, glossy blue, 4 x 4" 95.00

Cambridge Art Tile Company, Covington, Kentucky, "Night" and "Morning," classical female figures in sheer drapery after Ferdinand Mersman, 18 x 6", pr. 475.00

Grueby Faience & Tile Company, Boston, Massachusetts, 2 swimming water fowl at sunset, ca. 1905, 4 x 4" 467.00

Grueby Faience & Tile Company, Boston, Massachusetts, mottled blue glaze, 6 x 2" (border tile) 40.00

Grueby Faience & Tile Company, Boston, Massachusetts, matte grey cherubs playing cymbals on blue ground, grey matte border, 6 x 6" 60.00

Grueby Faience & Tile Company, Boston, Massachusetts, incised 3-color grapes, 6 x 6" 165.00

Grueby Faience & Tile Company, Boston, Massachusetts, monk decor, 6 x 6" 100.00

Grueby Faience & Tile Company, Boston, Massachusetts, winged youth, 6 x 6" 125.00

Grueby Faience & Tile Company, Boston, Massachusetts, 7-color landscape w/trees, hills & sky, 6 x 6" 700.00

Low (J. & J.G.) Art Tile Works, Chelsea, Massachusetts, geometric design, dark blue & grey glaze, dated 1881, 6 x 6" 20.00

Low (J. & J.G.) Art Tile Works, Chelsea, Massachusetts, nude child astride large flying bird, olive green glaze, 1883, 6 x 6" 145.00

Low (J. & J.G.) Art Tile Works, Chelsea, Massachusetts, portrait of cavalier, green glaze, 8¼ x 8¼" 165.00

Low (J. & J.G.) Art Tile Works, Chelsea, Massachusetts, procession of monks in chapel, signed "A.O." (Arthur Osborn), yellow-green glaze, impressed "Copyright 1881" reverse, original frame, overall 15" w., 20½" h. (ILLUS.) 1,320.00

Marblehead Pottery, Marblehead, Massachusetts, white sailing ship against blue matte ground, 5 x 5" 200.00

Marblehead Pottery, Marblehead, Massachusetts, stylized plant maze, brown glaze, 6 x 6" 25.00

Mintons China Works, Stoke-on-

Trent, Staffordshire, England,
Aesop's Fables, brown transfer
scene of calf, goat, sheep & lion
or scene of King Cram & King Log
on white, 6 x 6", each 95.00

Mintons China Works, Stoke-on-
Trent, Staffordshire, England,
brown transfer scene of Hancock
House on white, 6 x 6" 30.00

Mintons China Works, Stoke-on-
Trent, Staffordshire, England,
brown floral transfer on white,
6 x 6", pr. 80.00

Moravian Pottery & Tile Works,
Doylestown, Pennsylvania,
Aladdin-type lamp decor,
4 x 4" 40.00

Moravian Pottery & Tile Works,
Doylestown, Pennsylvania,
Mayflower ship, terra cotta glaze,
4 x 4" 60.00

Moravian Pottery & Tile Works,
Doylestown, Pennsylvania,
armored knight on horse in relief,
ochre & blue, 7¼ x 4" 40.00

Mosaic Tile Co., Zanesville, Ohio,
General Pershing, white bust on
blue basalt ground, "Zanesville
Post No. 29 American Legion
Building Fund Mfg. by the Mosaic
Tile Co., Zanesville, Ohio"
reverse, 5 x 3½" oval 50.00

Mosaic Tile Co., Zanesville, Ohio,
Walter Crane's depiction of Her-
cules & the Wagoner or of King
Cole, 6 x 6", each 95.00

Mosaic Tile Co., Zanesville, Ohio,
Walter Crane's depiction of Little
Bo Peep, blue, tan & cream,
6 x 6" 95.00

Mosaic Tile Co., Zanesville, Ohio,
German Shepherd decor 110.00

Pardee (C.) Works, Perth Amboy,
New Jersey, Grueby-type matte
scene of brown houses w/green
trees, ca. 1910, 4¼ x 4¼" 247.50

Pardee (C.) Works, Perth Amboy,
New Jersey, sailing ships on blue
ground, 6 x 6" 55.00

Pewabic Pottery, Detroit Michigan,
fish in low relief, 3 x 3" 95.00

Providential Tile Works, Trenton,
Ohio, girl leading flock decor on
grey-green ground, 10 x 16",
framed (slight crazing) 125.00

Rookwood Pottery Co., Cincinnati,
Ohio, underglaze slip-painted
florals, 4 x 4" 45.00

Rookwood Pottery Co., Cincinnati,
Ohio, underglaze slip-painted
apples & foliage on branch,
6" sq. 85.00

Rookwood Pottery Co., Cincinnati,
Ohio, underglaze slip-painted

Dutch seaside scene in shades of
blue & green on white ground,
1929 .... 125.00

Trent Art Tile Co., Trenton, New
Jersey, bust profile portrait of
woman, brown glaze,
4¼ x 4¼" 60.00

Trent Art Tile Co., Trenton, New
Jersey, bust profile portrait of
woman, turquoise blue glaze,
4¼ x 4¼" 70.00

TOBY MUGS & JUGS

"Napoleon" Jug by Evans

*The Toby is a figural jug or mug usually
delineating a robust, genial drinking man.
The name has been used in England since the
mid-18th century. Copies of the English mugs
and jugs were made in America. Also see
BENNINGTON.*

Copeland-Spode "Winston Churchill"
Toby $65.00

Creil Et Montereau "Abbot" Toby,
blue robe, France, 1870's (small
base chip) 155.00

Evans "Napoleon" Toby, ironstone
w/colorful enameling, marked
"Napoleon Jug - Pat. Apl. for,
Alfred E. Evans, Phila. Pa.,"
10¾" h. (ILLUS.) 375.00

Lenox, "William Penn" Toby, coral
pink w/white handle, 7" h. 145.00

Lenox "William Penn" Toby,
w/Indian head handle,
7" h. .... 175.00 to 225.00

Lenox "William Penn" Toby, polychrome .... 200.00 to 275.00

Rockingham glaze Toby, mottled
brown, large................... 120.00

Royal Doulton "Cap'n Cuttle" Toby,
full seated figure, 1948-60,
4½" h. 165.00

Royal Doulton "Cliff Cornell" Toby,
blue, 1956, 5½" h. 275.00

Royal Doulton "Cliff Cornell" Toby,
blue, 1956, 9" h. . . . . . . .225.00 to 275.00
Royal Doulton "Cliff Cornell" Toby,
1956, brown, 9" h. 245.00
Royal Doulton "Cliff Cornell" Toby,
tan, 1956, 9" h. 375.00
Royal Doulton "Double XX" (Man on
a Barrel) Toby (extra strong
stoneware), maroon coat, black
breeches & tricorn hat, 1939-69,
6½" h. 675.00
Royal Doulton "Fat Boy" Toby, full
seated figure, 1948-60 . . . . 120.00
Royal Doulton "Old Charley" Toby,
full seated figure, 1939-60,
8¾" h. . . . . .125.00 to 180.00
Royal Doulton "Sairey Gamp" Toby,
1948-60 . . . . .125.00 to 180.00
Royal Doulton "Sam Weller" Toby,
full seated figure, 1948-60,
4½" h. . . . . .135.00 to 165.00
Royal Doulton "Sir Winston
Churchill" Toby, 1941 to present,
5½" h. 60.00
Royal Doulton "Squire" Toby, full
seated figure, 1950-69,
6" h. . . . . .225.00 to 300.00
Shorter & Son "Beefeater" or
"Coachman" Toby, full seated fig-
ure, ca. 1925, 7½" h., each 60.00
Shorter & Son, "Dick Whittington &
Cat" Toby, 4½" h. 40.00
Shorter & Son "Huntsman" Toby,
1930's 50.00
Shorter & Son "King Neptune" Toby,
w/lobster, seahorse & dolphin 55.00
Shorter & Son "Old King Cole" Toby,
1930's, 5½" h. 60.00
Shorter & Son, "Pensioner" or
"Sailor" Toby, full seated figure,
1930's, each 60.00
Shorter & Son "Scotty" Toby,
1930's 62.50
Staffordshire Toby, seated man
w/green hair, holding mug &
snuff box, cobalt blue w/copper
lustre, 4½" h. 115.00
Staffordshire Toby, printed Blue Wil-
low patt. overall 275.00
Staffordshire "Hearty Good Fellow"
Toby, standing figure, 1875 . . . . . . 135.00
Staffordshire "Policeman" Toby,
1920's, 9" h 90.00
Staffordshire "Punch & Judy" Tobies,
1860's, 11" h., pr. 400.00
Staffordshire copy of "Yorkshire"
Toby, ca. 1900, 10" h. 225.00
Wood (Ralph) Toby, full seated fig-
ure wearing brown tricorn & coat,
ochre-brown treacle-glazed waistcoat, breeches & shoes, w/cham-
fered oblong base colored drab
green, 1770-75, 9½" h. 990.00

VAN BRIGGLE

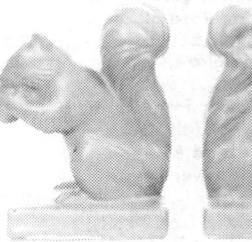

Squirrel Bookends

*The Van Briggle Pottery was established
by Artus Van Briggle, who formerly worked
for Rookwood Pottery, in Colorado Springs,
Colo., at the turn of the century. He died in
1904 but the pottery was carried on by his
widow and others. From 1900 until 1920, the
pottery was dated. It remains in production
today, specializing in Art Pottery.*

Ash tray, figure of an Indian maiden
grinding corn kneeling at side,
blue glaze $85.00
Bookends, model of peacock on
base, Persian Rose (maroon to
blue-green) glaze, 5" h., pr. 95.00
Bookends, model of squirrel, Per-
sian Rose glaze, 7" h., pr.
(ILLUS.) 75.00
Bookends, model of bear climbing
tree trunk, mulberry glaze, pr. . . . 300.00
Bookends, model of puppy dog,
Mountain Craig (green & brown)
glaze, pr. 100.00
Bookends, model of ram, Persian
Rose glaze, pr. 70.00
Bowl, 3½" d., 2½" h., turquoise &
beige glaze 60.00
Bowl, 5" d., 4½" h., footed, brown
glaze 45.00
Bowl, 6" d., relief-molded acorn &
leaf, rose shaded to burgundy
glaze . . . . .30.00 to 45.00
Bowl, 9" d., relief-molded dragon-
flies, shaded mint blue
glaze .38.00 to 45.00
Bowl, dark green glaze, dated
1906 . . . . 200.00
Bowl, maroon glaze, dated 1918 . . . . 75.00
Bowl, Pinecone patt., Persian Rose
glaze, ca. 1920 . . . . 125.00
Bowl-vase, medium green glaze
w/blue highlights, 1907-12 . . . . . . 110.00
Candle holders, 2-light, tulip-form
candle nozzles, Persian Rose
glaze, pr. 68.00
Candlestick, shaded brown glaze,
4¼" h. (single) 15.00
Candlesticks, handled, Persian Rose
glaze, dated 1915, 8" h., pr. 175.00

Conch shell, Turquoise Ming (royal
blue over turquoise) glaze, 9" l. . . . 40.00
Conch shell, Persian Rose glaze,
12½" l. 52.50
Console bowl, blue glaze,
pre-1920. . . . . 38.00
Console bowl & flower frog, "Siren
of the Sea" bowl w/full figure
mermaid on one side &
w/seashell form flower frog,
15" d., 5" h., 2 pcs. 350.00
Console bowl & flower frog, "Lady
of the Lake" bowl w/semi-nude
lady at side & turtle on rock flower frog, Turquoise Ming glaze,
15" d. bowl, pr. 140.00
Console set: bowl, flower frog & pr.
candlesticks; relief-molded oak
leaves & acorns, raspberry on
blue shaded to grey glaze, ca.
1926, 4 pcs. 195.00
Creamer, melon-ribbed, midnight
black glaze 35.00
Cup, pink exterior, white interior,
1907-12. . . . . 95.00
Flower frog, model of 3 frogs,
cobalt blue & plum glaze, dated
1915 . . . . 110.00
Flower frog, model of turtle, Tur-
quoise Ming glaze 30.00
Lamp w/original shade, "Damsel of
Damascus," kneeling girl holding
urn on shoulder, blue glaze 300.00
Lamp w/original shade, model of a
swan, Persian Rose (maroon to
blue-green) glaze 125.00
Letter holder, footed, relief-molded
swan, Persian Rose glaze 45.00
Model of a boot, blue glaze,
2½" h. 25.00
Model of a dog, Turquoise Ming
(royal blue over turquoise) glaze,
2" h. 35.00
Model of a rabbit, Turquoise Ming
glaze, 3" h. 48.00
Mug, green mottled glaze, dated
1902 . . . . 495.00
Pitcher, 3½" h., Persian Rose
glaze 40.00
Plaque, pierced to hang, relief bust
of "Big Buffalo," Persian Rose
glaze 60.00
Vase, 2½" h., relief-molded butter-
flies, Persian Rose glaze, 1919. . . . 75.00
Vase, bud, 4¼" h., squatty w/elon-
gated neck, relief-molded flower
petals & twisted stems, pale blue
glaze, dated 1904 . . . . 522.50
Vase, 5½" h., Turquoise Ming
glaze, dated 1905 . . . . 195.00
Vase, 6" h., hourglass form, relief-
molded spiderwort blossoms &
foliage, Turquoise Ming glaze,
dated 1918 . . . . 170.00

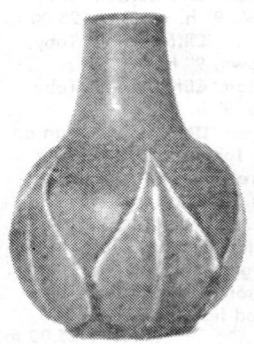

Van Briggle Vase

Vase, 8" h., relief-molded leaves,
green, blue & black glaze
(ILLUS.). 220.00
Vase, 10" h., relief-molded
daffodils, Persian Rose glaze 125.00
Vase, 11" h., "Lorelei," Turquoise
Ming glaze 185.00
Vase, 13" h., 2-handled, Persian
Rose glaze, 1922-29 . . . . 165.00
Vase, 16" h., relief-molded yucca
pods & leaves, Persian Rose
glaze 425.00

VOLKMAR POTTERY

*Baltimore-born Charles Volkmar studied
painting, sculpture and pottery making in
Paris for almost eighteen years before returning to the United States to operate a kiln at
Green Point, Long Island, New York in 1879.
By 1882, he had established his own studio
at Tremont, New York, making hand-thrown
and molded wares enhanced with either applied or underglaze slip decoration. Later he
established and operated potteries at various
New York and New Jersey locations and
these included the Menlo Park Ceramic Company (with J.T. Smith), Volkmar Keramic
Company, Volkmar & Cory (with artist Kate
Cory), and the Crown Point Pottery. In 1902,
Volkmar was joined by his son, Leon, and together they established the Volkmar Kilns at
Metuchen, New Jersey in 1903. It is thought
the last pieces were made about 1911.*

Candlesticks, textured turquoise
crackled glaze, 8¾" h., pr. $125.00
Chamberstick, fluted drip pan,
undulating handle, dark matte
blue glaze, 5" d., 2¾" h. 85.00
Mug, h.p. blue Delft-type clipper
ship decor & "Hudson - Fulton,
1909," 5" h. 185.00

Mug, green-brown semi-volcanic
drip glaze, 7" h. 150.00
Plaque, pierced to hang, blue Delft-
type historical series, "Washington...Mt. Vernon, Va.,"
11¼" d. . . . . .200.00 to 250.00
Vase, 5½" h., hand-thrown, matte
brown drip glaze, ca. 1910 . . . . . . 345.00
Vase, 5½" h., green
glaze . . . . .150.00 to 185.00
Vase, 9¼" h., 5" d., heavy matte
green textured glaze, 1903-11 . . . . 325.00
Vase, bulbous, matte green tex-
tured glaze, 1903-11 . . . . 225.00

WARWICK

Warwick Cider Pitcher

Numerous collectors have turned their
attention to the productions of the Warwick
China Manufacturing Company that operated in Wheeling, West Virginia, from 1887
until 1951. Prime interest would seem to lie
in items produced before 1914 that were decorated with decal portraits of beautiful wom-
en, monks and Indians. Fraternal Order
items, as well as floral and fruit decorated
items are also popular with collectors.

Cookie jar, cov., 2-handled, colorful
poppies decor on shaded brown
ground $95.00
Jug, portrait of monk 45.00
Match holder w/saucer base, white
w/gold trim, 6" d. 35.00
Mug, maiden bidding farewell to
warrior on horseback on brown
ground, 5" h. 50.00
Mug, floral decor on white ground . . 45.00
Mug, portrait of monk holding wine
glass on dark ground 45.00
Pitcher, 6" h., floral decor on white
ground 42.00
Pitcher, 9½" h., poinsettias decor
on deep red ground 125.00
Pitcher, tankard, 13" h., "B.P.O.E."
& Elk decor 145.00

Pitcher, cider, portrait of monk
wearing red on brown ground
(ILLUS.) 135.00
Pitcher, hot water, scalloped rim,
pink floral clusters on white
above dark teal blue flecked
w/gold base, 2-qt. 60.00
Plaque, pierced to hang, monk
portrait, 9½" d. 38.00
Plate, 9½" d., scene of monk smell-
ing flowers 96.00
Tea tile, scene of young couple
pushing wheelbarrow filled
w/flowers, scalloped gold border,
6" d. 36.00
Tray, reddish-brown gooseberries
decor on brown shaded to cream
ground, 9¼ x 6½" 29.00
Tray, floral & fruit decor,
11¼ x 7½" 45.00
Vase, 9" h., elongated neck, roses
decor on brown ground 85.00
Vase, 11½" h., twig handles, portrait of beautiful woman on dark
ground 165.00
Vase, 12" h., urn-shaped, nastur-
tiums decor on brown ground 125.00

WEDGWOOD

Reference here is to the famous pottery es-
tablished by Josiah Wedgwood in 1759 in
England. Numerous types of wares have been
produced through the years to the present.
Also see COMMEMORATIVE PLATES,
FLOW BLUE and JASPER WARE.

BASALTES

Bust of Mercury

Bowl, 7½" d., 3½" h., allegorical
figures decor, ca. 1870 ....$185.00
Bowl, 10" d., "The Dancing Hours,"
figures in relief around sides..... 375.00
Bulb pot, bow-fronted, molded
w/putti supporting a foliate
garland within recessed panel, 4
scroll feet, late 18th c., 8¼" w. .. 440.00
Bust of George Washington, w/his
head slightly turned to the right,
on flaring socle, 20th c.,
13¾" h. 495.00
Bust of Sir Walter Scott, by Wyon,
1870, 14" h. 400.00
Bust of Mercury w/winged helmet,
18" h. (ILLUS.) ....850.00 to 1,500.00
Candlesticks, classical figures &
trees in low relief, flaring foliate
scroll feet, ca. 1850, 4¾" h., pr... 495.00
Figure of Cupid, 19th c., 8" h. 825.00
Figure of Cleopatra, seated nude
figure w/asp on her wrist,
marked Wedgwood only,
9 3/8" h. 650.00
Figure of Aphrodite, seated nude
figure holding shell, on scrolling
wave base, marked Wedgwood
Etruria & impressed "Aphrodite,"
mid-19th c., 10½" h. 265.00
Figure of young Bacchus, scantily
draped in goat skin & w/foliage in
his hair, carrying a branch, on circular tree stump base applied
w/fruiting vine & band of oak
leaves, late 19th c., 11¾" h. 770.00
Figure of Venus, standing,
w/drapery falling from her waist,
square base impressed "Venus
Vitrix" & inscribed "H.O. Rendel"
in gilt, marked Wedgwood & let-
ter "C," late 19th c., 19 7/8" h. 467.00

Basaltes Jardiniere

Jardinieres, applied lion's masks
suspending fruiting vines above
cameos of classical figures &
w/band of fruiting foliage, ca.
1840, 4½" h., pr. (ILLUS. of one).. 440.00
Model of bulldog, inset white glass
eyes w/brown centers, marked
Wedgwood only, 5 x 2", 2¾" h. .. 357.00

Model of cat, inset yellow glass
eyes, marked Wedgwood only,
4½ x 3 3/8", 4¾" h. 325.00
Spill vase, classical figures & trees
decor, dated 1908, 8" h. 100.00
Teapot, cov., enameled white, pink,
yellow & blue florals & green
leaves decor, marked Wedgwood
only, 5 3/8" d., 4½" h. 375.00
Teapot, cov., octagonal, molded
w/Muse one side & w/Apollo
reverse, each flanked by sporting
& musical trophies suspended
from ribbons, shoulder band of
acanthus & lower band of interlaced gothic arches, handle &
straight spout w/husks, ca. 1800,
7¼" w. 550.00
Vase, 6" h., 4½" d., 2-handled, enameled pink & yellow florals &
green leaves decor, marked
Wedgwood only 300.00

CALENDAR TILES

King's Chapel, Boston

1891 Adams Lean-to-House, Quincy,
blue-grey....................... ,70.00
1892 "1744 Mount Vernon - 1892,"
blue-grey 65.00
1896 Trinity Church, Boston,
blue or brown, each 65.00
1897 Old Federal Street Theatre -
Present Site of J. McD & S Co.,
brown.......................... 75.00
1898 King's Chapel, Boston, brown
(ILLUS.)........................ 85.00
1899 Washington Elm, brown 60.00
1911 U.S. Frigate "Constitution" &
U.S. Battleship "Florida," w/five
lines printing under each picture,
brown.......................... 50.00
1914 Pier Head of Commonwealth
Docks, Boston, 4 lines of print,
brown.......................... 50.00
1916 Massachusetts Institute of
Technology, light brown 55.00
1929 House of Seven Gables, Salem,
brown.......................... 50.00

CANEWARE

Bowl, 7" d., footed, enameled blue
   leaf decor, ca. 1830 . . . . 275.00
Game pie dishes, covers & liners,
   oval, fruiting grapevine in relief
   around exterior, interior & liner
   fully glazed, covers w/cauliflower
   sprig knop, dated 1872, 11 7/8" &
   7¼" l., pr. 770.00
Potpourri jar w/acorn-shaped lid, 2-
   handled, blue decor, marked
   Wedgwood only, 8½" d., 10" h. . . 475.00
Teapot, cov., applied in relief
   w/dark brown scene of domestic
   employment, cover w/radiating
   acorns & oak leaves, ca. 1810,
   6¾" w. (repair to tip of spout &
   cover) 550.00
Teapot & cover w/dog finial, foliage
   decor, 1825 . . . . 200.00
Wall pocket, basketweave-molded,
   enameled blue stripe decor,
   ca. 1800, 7" w. 275.00

CREAMWARE

Wedgwood Creamware Oval Dish

Dish, applepickers decor center,
   brown rim, signed Emil Lessore,
   dated 1862, 3½" oval 352.00
Dishes, h.p. clusters of fruit center,
   transfer-printed rim w/green
   scrolling floral branches, gilt trim,
   artist-signed, ca. 1880, 10¼" oval,
   pr. (ILLUS. of one) 275.00
Pitcher w/pewter lid, milk, Fallow
   Deer patt., blue & white, late
   19th c. 155.00
Plate, 8" d., Agricultural series,
   garden tools or spinning wheel
   decor, each 150.00
Sauce tureen w/attached undertray
   & cover, ribbed body w/ram's
   head handles, impressed Wedg-
   wood mark 175.00
Soup tureen & cover w/flowerhead
   finial, 2 foliate-molded handles,
   bands of blue & green flowering
   foliage between black lines,
   ca. 1810, 17" oval 330.00

Stocking warmers, infant-size model
   of foot (to fill w/hot water), 4" l.,
   4" h., pr. 325.00
Teapot, cov., bamboo-molded &
   highlighted w/enamel, ca. 1860 . . 115.00

Tray painted by Emil Lessore

Tray, diamond-shaped, embracing
   cupids amidst clouds center, ochre
   rim, signed Emil Lessore, ca.
   1865, 6¼" w. (ILLUS.) 222.00

DRABWARE

Jug, classical ladies in relief,
   marked Wedgwood England,
   7½" h. 300.00
Pitcher, 4½" h., 4" d., classical
   ladies in relief on glazed grey
   ground, ca. 1820 . . . . 181.00
Sugar bowl, cov., blue & grey 150.00
Teapot & cover w/dog finial, large
   straight spout, florals in relief on
   sides, 7" h. 118.00
Whiskey jug, hunting scenes on
   sides, ca. 1830, 6" h. 150.00

ROSSO ANTICO

Rosso Antico Sugar Bowl

Creamer, redware w/black relief
   decor 375.00
Sugar bowl & cover w/crocodile fini-
   al, tab handles, redware decorated w/Egyptian-style motifs, ca.
   1805 (ILLUS.) 575.00
Sugar bowl & cover w/crocodile fini-
   al, redware decorated in black relief w/Egyptian inspired designs &
   band of stylized key patt., late
   18th c., 6" w. 352.00

Teapot & cover w/crocodile finial, squat redware body decorated in black relief w/Egyptian inspired motifs above band of stylized key patt., ca. 1810, 10" w. 550.00

TERRA COTTA

Terra Cotta Spillholder Vase

Creamer, enameled florals on terra cotta ground, 1800, large 110.00
Figure of a boy sleeping, lying naked on a rectangular draped base w/canted corners, 19th c., 4¾" l. 1,045.00
Spillholder vases, modeled as clusters of 4 bamboo canes on oval rockwork base, ca. 1840, one w/hairline crack to base, 4½" h., pr. (ILLUS. of one) 1,045.00
Sugar bowl, cov., enameled florals on terra cotta ground, large 140.00
Teapot, cov., ribbed pumpkin form, bamboo-molded handle & spout . . 350.00
Tea set: cov. teapot, cov. sugar bowl & creamer; covers w/croco-dile knops, raised black jasper Egyptian motifs on brick red terra cotta, ca. 1800, 3 pcs. 2,950.00
Vase, 5¼" h., Portland vase shape, flaring rim w/band of pensile grass, angular handles applied w/masks, black relief lilies & foli-age, mid-19th c. 264.00

MISCELLANEOUS

Fairyland Lustre Bowl

Bowl, 5" d., footed, Fairyland Lus-tre, gilt & yellow playful goblins on a blue & green ground en-riched in gilt, Portland vase mark, ca. 1920 (ILLUS.) 600.00
Bowl, 7¼" w., 8-sided, Butterfly Lustre, multicolored butterflies outlined in gold on mottled multi-colored iridescent ground 395.00
Bowl, 8" w., 8-sided, Dragon Lustre, flying cranes & dragon breathing flames on pearl lustre interior & dragons on blue lustre exterior, diapered border. 485.00
Bowl, 8" d., 5½" h., Fairyland Lus-tre, scene of "Leaping Faun" in-terior & "Garden of Paradise" exterior, all outlined in gold, on multicolored lustred ground 2,000.00
Bowl, 8" d., Willow patt., blue & shaded red transfer, ornate gold trim. 125.00
Butter tub w/stand, deep blue decor on white, ca. 1850 . . . . 125.00
Cookie jar, majolica, green & mot-tled brown exterior, robin's egg blue lining, silverplate footed base, center band & hinged lid w/Sphinx finial, 7" d., 7½" h. 255.00
Creamer, majolica, grape clusters & leaves on green ground, 3½" d., 5" h. 65.00
Cup & saucer, demitasse, Butterfly Lustre, multicolored butterflies outlined in gold on cobalt blue ground 195.00
Dessert set: platter & 6 bowls; majolica, colorful florals, ribbons & bows decor, 7 pcs. 325.00
Pitcher, 6¾" h., majolica, large leaf & floral spray each side on tex-tured cream ground, blue lining . . 95.00

Pitcher with Pewter Lid

Pitcher w/pewter lid, tankard, 6¾" h., Rockingham ware,

wheel-engraved parrots on branch each side & flowerhead on strap handle, mottled brown glaze, pewter lid engraved w/flower spray, ca. 1880 (ILLUS.) 286.00

Pitcher, 8½" h., majolica, bamboo-molded w/sprig of flowers in relief, marked Wedgwood only ... 150.00

Pitcher, historical series, "Washington Headquarters," blue transfer 85.00

Plaque, Fairyland Lustre, "Picnic by a River" printed in gold & painted w/yellow, blue, red-violet, purple & black scene of elves in green, brown & black landscape w/blue river beneath blue sky within "Roseberry Bead" border w/mother-of-pearl lustre rim, ca. 1921, wooden frame, 10 5/8 x 4¾" 1,650.00

Plate, 7" d., majolica, vines, blossoms & berries on cream ground 60.00

Plate, 8½" d., majolica, Oriental patt. 65.00

Plate, 9" d., commemorative, "Boston Public Library" or "King's Chapel," blue transfer, each 28.00

Plate, 9" d., majolica, Bird & Fan patt. 82.50

Plate, 9" d., majolica, brown nuts & florals on turquoise ground 55.00

Plate, 9¾" d., shell-shaped, Moonlight Lustre, deep mottled pink lustre, marked Wedgwood only ... 180.00

Plate, 9¾" d., Washington Vase patt., mulberry-sepia transfer, ca. 1855 .... 60.00

Plate, 10" d., month series, "December," Kate Greenaway type boy & girl w/mistletoe 125.00

Plate, 10" d., Queen of Spades center, diamonds, hearts, spades & clubs border 75.00

Plate, 10¼" d., Ivanhoe series, "Front de Boeuf Extorting Silver from Isaac the Jew," flow blue transfer 60.00

Plate, 11" d., Butterfly Lustre....... 200.00

Platter, 13 x 10", majolica, bow handles, cobalt blue & white florals on turquoise ground, marked Wedgwood only 125.00

Platter, 15 x 10 7/8", floral border, pastoral scene of farmers, cattle & village, blue transfer, dated 1911 .... 132.00

Platter, 19 x 9", majolica, Seaweed & Shell patt. 200.00

Punch bowl, Butterfly Lustre, printed in gold w/butterflies & small insects, mottled blue exterior stained w/ruby lustre, mother-of-

pearl interior w/central stylized medallion surrounded by 5 butterflies painted in shades of yellow, green & orange, rim w/"Papillon" border, 1914-29, 11" d...........1,540.00

Salt dip, Fairyland Lustre, mottled orange exterior, mottled blue interior w/foo dog decor center, 2¼" d........................ 135.00

Saucer, Washington Vase patt., mulberry-sepia transfer, ca. 1855, 6" d. 30.00

Strawberry set: 13" l. platter & eight 6" d. plates; overall h.p. strawberry blossoms & leaves decor, 9 pcs. 495.00

Teapot, cov., blue Ferrara patt., harbor scene, 6¼" d., 5" h. 106.00

Tea set: cov. teapot, creamer & cov. sugar bowl; bamboo-molded w/terra cotta florals in relief, 3 pcs. 179.00

Tray, majolica, green bamboo-molded border, colorful florals, foliage & bird in flight on cream basketweave ground, 14 x 11½" 350.00

Vase, 4¼" h., 2½" d., Hummingbird Lustre, mottled blue lustre ground w/colorful hummingbirds finely outlined in gold 180.00

Vase, 8¾" h., 4¼" d., Fairyland Lustre "Candlemas" vase, candles w/human heads & holly outlined in gold 1,297.00

Vase, 8¾" h., 5 7/8" d., pedestal base, Dragon Lustre, mottled powder blue lustre exterior w/maroon & gold dragons chasing the sacred pearl, all outlined in gold, mother-of-pearl lustre interior, intricate design at rim........ 485.00

Vase, cov., 9" h., Fairyland Lustre, "Fairy Under the Rainbow" 2,050.00

Vase, 11¾" h., 5¾" d., trumpet-shaped, Hummingbird Lustre, colorful hummingbirds outlined in gold on rich mottled blue lustre exterior, mottled flame lustre inside top rim 465.00

WELLER

Die-Stamped Weller Mark

This pottery was made from 1872 to 1945 at a pottery established originally by Samuel

A. Weller at Fultonham, Ohio, and moved in 1882 to Zanesville. Numerous lines were produced and listings below are by the pattern or lines. Most desirable is the Sicardo line.

ARCOLA (1920's)

Candlesticks, realistically painted roses molded in relief against glossy blended green & cream ground, 12" h., pr. $70.00

Vase, 5½" h., 2-handled, realistically painted cluster of cherries & foliage molded in relief against glossy blended brown & beige ground 55.00

ARDSLEY (1920-28)

Candle holders, water lily form, green matte glaze, 3" h., pr. . . . . .45.00 to 55.00

Console bowl & flower frog, molded cattails & grasses, green matte glaze, 8" d., 4½" h. 55.00

Console set: 16½" d., 3½" h. bowl, 9½" h. Kingfisher flower frog & pr. candlesticks; molded cattails & grasses, green matte glaze, 4 pcs. 325.00

Umbrella stand, molded water lilies at base, cattails & grasses body, green matte glaze, 19" h. 335.00

Vase, 12" h., molded water lily at base, cattails & grasses body, green matte glaze 45.00

BALDIN (1915-20)

Baldin Jardiniere & Pedestal Base

Bowl, 7" d., realistically painted apples & branches molded in low relief against earth tones 65.00

Jardiniere & pedestal base, realistically painted apples & branches molded in low relief against earth tones, overall 34" h. (ILLUS.) . . . . .365.00 to 585.00

Vase, 6" h., realistically painted apples & branches molded in low relief against earth tones 65.00

Vase, 7½" h., semi-ovoid, realistically painted apples & branches molded in low relief against midnight blue 85.00

Vase, 9½" h., cylindrical, w/band of realistically painted apples & branches molded in low relief against earth tones 135.00

Vase, 11" h., conical, w/band of realistically painted apples & branches molded in low relief against midnight blue 165.00

BLUE DRAPERY (1915-20)

Basket, hanging-type, clusters of roses pendant from rim, vertical folded blue matte drapery ground 60.00

Candlestick, double gourd form, clusters of roses pendant from nozzle, vertical folded blue matte drapery ground, 9" h. (single) 35.00

Planter, clusters of roses pendant from rim, vertical folded blue matte drapery ground, 9½" l., 4½" h. 38.00

Vase, 6" h., clusters of roses pendant from rim, vertical folded blue matte drapery ground 30.00

Wall pocket, clusters of roses pendant from rim, vertical folded blue matte drapery ground, 9" h. 52.00

BLUE WARE (pre-1920)

Jardiniere, 3-footed, ivory relief of classical ladies against deep blue ground, 8½" h. 175.00

Vase, 10" h., ivory relief of classical ladies dancing against deep blue ground 125.00

Vase, 13" h., ivory relief of classical lady holding cluster of grapes against deep blue ground . . . . .180.00 to 210.00

BONITO (1927-33)

Bowl, 5" d., h.p. florals & foliage on cream ground 55.00

Bowl, 9½" d., h.p. multicolored floral decor on cream ground 75.00

Vase, 5" h., open handles, h.p. florals & foliage on cream ground 52.00

Vase, 6" h., h.p. blue daisies & green foliage on cream ground . . . 40.00

Vase, 7" h., closed scroll handles at mid-section, colorful flowers on cream ground, artist-signed 65.00

Vase, 9½" h., wildflowers & leaves on cream ground, artist-signed ... 85.00

CACTUS (early 1930's)

Figure of a boy w/bag, blue & green, 5" h. 42.00

Model of a kneeling camel, brown, 4" h. 45.00

Model of a grinning cat, tan, 5½" h. 95.00

Model of an elephant, blue, 4" h. 90.00

Model of a monkey, green, 4" h. ... 32.00

Model of a snail, green, 3½" h. 65.00

CAMEO (1935-39)

Basket, hanging-type w/original chains, white relief florals on matte soft green 42.00

Vase, 6½" to 7½" h., white relief florals on matte coral or soft green, each 24.00

Vases, 14½" h., white relief florals on matte powder blue, pr. 140.00

CHASE (late 1920's)

Vase, 5½" h., bulbous, white relief fox hunt scene on deep blue ....155.00 to 175.00

Vase, 6½" h., globular, white relief fox hunt scene on deep blue 195.00

Vase, 9" h., straight sides, wide mouth, white relief fox hunt scene on deep blue 145.00

CHENGTU (1925-36)

Urn, Chinese red-orange semi-gloss finish, 5½" h. 75.00

Vase, 6½" to 7½" h., Chinese red-orange semi-gloss finish, each ....35.00 to 50.00

Vase, 11" h., expanding squared form, Chinese red-orange semi-gloss finish 85.00

COPPERTONE (late 1920's)

Coppertone Vase

Ash tray w/figural frog seated on rim, blotchy semi-gloss green over brown glaze, 6½" w............. 75.00

Bowl, 10 x 7" oblong, figural frog seated at end, swimming fish in relief on sides, blotchy semi-gloss green over brown glaze 135.00

Candle holders, flower-form, blotchy semi-gloss green over brown glaze, 2" h., pr.................. 35.00

Model of frog, 2" h. 25.00

Model of a frog w/banjo, 7½" h. ... 225.00

Model of a frog on a lily pad, gardenware w/hole for water tube, green body & yellow chest, 15 x 11½" 550.00

Model of a turtle, 5 x 1½" 85.00

Vase, 5" to 6" h., blotchy semi-gloss green over brown glaze, each ....22.00 to 30.00

Vase, 7" h., 2-handled, globular w/flaring rim, blotchy semi-gloss green over brown glaze 55.00

Vase, 8" h., frog handles, lily pads on sides, blotchy semi-gloss green over brown glaze (ILLUS.) 165.00

COPRA (1915)

Basket, h.p. floral decor, shaded brown ground, 8" d., overall 11½" h. 195.00

Bowl, 10¼" d., 5" h., applied closed ring handles at sides, h.p. poppies decor, shaded brown to sand grey ground 115.00

Vase, 8" h., applied closed ring handles at sides, expanding cylinder w/low foot, pink & white poppies & brown leaves, shaded russet to dark brown ground............. 110.00

Vase, 10" h., h.p. pink floral decor, shaded brown ground 180.00

DICKENSWARE 2ND LINE (1900-05)

Dickensware 2nd Line Vase

Mug, sgraffito bust portrait of Indian
in full headdress 435.00
Mug, sgraffito bust portrait of
monk 175.00
Pitcher, tankard, 12" h., sgraffito
portrait of Indian in full head-
dress, artist-signed 925.00
Pitcher, tankard, 12" h., sgraffito
portrait of jester, signed Upjohn . . 950.00
Vase, 5½" h., sgraffito portrait of
Indian in full headdress, green
matte finish 395.00
Vase, 6" h., 3-handled, sgraffito
fish 300.00
Vase, 7½" h., flask-shaped, sgraf-
fito full-length portrait of lady
golfer 375.00
Vase, 9½" h., sgraffito portrait,
"Dombey & Son" 500.00
Vase, 10" h., sgraffito portrait of
jester 750.00
Vase, 14" h., sgraffito bust portrait
of Indian in full headdress, artist-
signed 1,800.00
Vase, 16" h., tapering cylinder
w/wide flaring mouth, sgraffito
scene of classical woman playing
a harp, shaded grey to yellow to
green matte finish, ca. 1900
(ILLUS.) 357.50

EOCEAN (1898-1918)

Eocean Vase

Pitcher, tankard, 10½" h., slip-
painted purple grapes on grey
shaded to white ground 230.00
Vase, 3½" h., slip-painted floral
decor on cream shaded to grey
ground 40.00
Vase, 6½" h., slip-painted red
florals on grey shaded to white
ground 80.00
Vase, 8" h., slip-painted pansy
decor on shaded light to deep
grey ground (ILLUS.) 250.00

Vase, 10½" h., slip-painted red
tulips on grey shaded to white
ground 280.00
Vase, 12" h., slip-painted floral
decor on cream shaded to grey-
green ground 290.00

EOCEAN ROSE (1898-1918)

Mug, slip-painted cherries decor on
pink shaded to grey-green to dark
green ground, artist-signed, 4"
widest d., 5¼" h. 185.00
Vase, 6" h., 5" d., slip-painted lily-
of-the-valley decor on pink
shaded to grey ground 150.00
Vase, 10" h., cylindrical w/indenta-
tions around neck, slip-painted
berries on grey shaded to pink
ground, artist-signed 130.00

ETNA (1906)

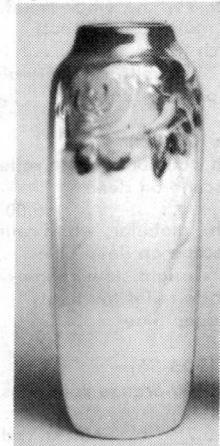

Etna Vase

Jardiniere, relief-molded & painted
realistic yellow nasturtiums on
shaded grey, 9½ x 9" 85.00
Pitcher, 6½" h., relief-molded &
painted realistic pansies on
shaded grey 90.00
Vase, 4½" h., bulbous base
w/tapering cylindrical neck,
relief-molded & painted realistic
lizard on shaded light to dark
grey 190.00
Vase, 6½" h., cylindrical, relief-
molded & painted realistic lilacs
on shaded grey 95.00
Vase, 9" h., 2-handled, globular,
relief-molded & painted realistic
deep pink florals on shaded dark
to light grey 150.00
Vase, 11" h., cylindrical w/flattened
bulbous base, relief-molded &
painted realistic white narcissus

w/yellow centers on light shaded
to dark grey 155.00
Vase, 14¼" h., cylindrical, relief-
molded & painted realistic mauve
& raspberry red roses & olive
green thorny branch on shaded
grey-blue to light grey
(ILLUS.) 275.00

FLEMISH (1915-28)

Flemish Jardiniere & Pedestal

Jardiniere, roses in relief on tan
basketweave ground, 7½" h. 70.00
Jardiniere & pedestal base, pink
florals in relief on tan ground,
overall 26½" h., 2 pcs. 485.00
Jardiniere & pedestal base, grape
clusters & vines in relief on
shaded tan ground, overall 32" h.,
2 pcs. (ILLUS.) . . . . 525.00 to 575.00
Tub, rim handles, roses in relief on
tan basketweave ground, 4" h. . . . 46.00

FLORETTA (1904)

Pitcher, tankard, 11" h., slip-painted
purple grapes in low relief on oat-
meal grey ground 145.00
Vase, 5" h., 2-handled, slip-painted
grapes in low relief, shaded
brown glaze 85.00
Vase, 5" h., slip-painted red straw-
berries in low relief on grey
shaded to white ground 52.50
Vase, 8" h., 8" d., 2-handled, ovoid,
slip-painted cascading purple
grape clusters on shaded oatmeal
grey ground 95.00
Vase, 9" h., slip-painted florals in
low relief on shaded oatmeal grey
ground 110.00

FOREST (1915)

Basket, realistically molded &
colored forest scene, overall
10" h. 145.00

Jardiniere, realistically molded &
painted forest scene, 8½" h. 165.00
Planter, tub-shaped, realistically
molded & painted forest scene,
3¾" h. 42.00
Planter, tub-shaped, realistically
molded & painted forest scene,
6½" h. 55.00
Vase, 8" h., fan-shaped, realistically
molded & painted forest scene . . . 62.50

GLENDALE (1920's)

Candle holders, birds & nest w/eggs
in low relief, shades of russet,
blue & grey, 5½" d. base,
pr. 65.00 to 80.00
Centerpiece & flower frog, shallow
bowl w/sea gulls & waves in low
relief, flower frog in the form of a
bird's nest w/eggs, shades of
sandy beige, tan, russet, grey,
black & white, 15½" d.,
2 pcs. . . . . 225.00 to 265.00
Vase, 4" h., globular, nesting bird in
low relief, shades of deep grey,
tan & yellow 115.00
Vase, 5" h., ovoid, bird standing
amidst dense foliage in low relief,
shades of tan, russet & yellow . . . 110.00

GLORIA (after 1936)

Ewer, bulbous, branch w/black-
berries & white blossoms in relief
on caramel matte finish ground,
9" h. 40.00
Jardiniere, footed, ruffled rim,
yellow flower & green foliage
w/hovering butterfly in relief on
caramel matte finish ground,
5" h. 20.00
Vase, 13" h., white lilies & slender
green leaves in relief on caramel
matte finish ground 45.00

GOLDEN GLOW (late 1920's)

Bowl, 3" h., applied loop feet, molded wavy line decor on mottled tan
ground 45.00
Bowl, 16 x 3½", 2-handled, molded
spray of leaves on mottled tan
ground 45.00
Bowl-vase, applied loop feet, semi-
ovoid, molded branch & spray of
leaves on mottled tan ground,
5½" h. 35.00
Vase, 11" h., double-handled, mold-
ed spray of leaves on mottled tan
ground 60.00

GREORA (early 1930's)

Vase, 5" h., shaded orange to green
splashed glaze 25.00
Vase, 11½" h., cylindrical, shaded
orange to green splashed glaze . . 125.00

HOBART (1920's)

Flower frog, figure of a nude girl w/duck, soft green matte finish, 4½" 135.00

Flower frog, figures of 2 nude ladies rising from the sea, turquoise blue matte finish, 7" 110.00

Flower frog, figure of a nude lady in classical pose on pedestal base pierced for flowers on outside edge, white matte finish, 8½" h......................... 85.00

HUDSON (1920's-1935)

Hudson Line Vases

Bowl, 6" d., 4" h., underglaze slip-painted floral decor, ivory matte glaze 50.00

Bowl, 6¾" d., 2¾" h., underglaze slip-painted clover blossoms & foliage 175.00

Vase, 6" h., cylindrical, underglaze slip-painted bright yellow & green florals, grey shaded to blue matte glaze, signed Claude Leffler 145.00

Vase, 6" h., underglaze slip-painted pansies, blue matte glaze, signed Hester Pillsbury 205.00

Vase, 7" h., 5" d., underglaze slip-painted pale pink- & blue-tinged dogwood blossoms, pastel matte glaze, artist-signed 155.00

Vase, 8" h., underglaze slip-painted spray of wild rose blossoms around top, shaded blue matte glaze 145.00

Vase, 8½" h., 2-handled, globular w/short neck, underglaze slip-painted sailing ships on bright blue-green waves, grey shaded to pink matte glaze, signed Sara Reid McLaughlin.................. 800.00

Vase, 9" h., underglaze slip-painted dogwood blossoms, blue shaded to pink matte glaze (ILLUS. left)..................... 200.00

Vase, 9¼" h., underglaze slip-painted moonlit water scene 450.00

Vase, 9½" h., semi-ovoid, underglaze slip-painted lavender & brown-black chrysanthemums & grey-green foliage, lavender shaded to pink glaze, signed Claude Leffler.................. 695.00

Vase, 9½" h., underglaze slip-painted berries & vine, white matte glaze (ILLUS. right) 60.00

Vase, 9½" h., underglaze slip-painted cherry blossoms, blue matte glaze..................... 150.00

Vase, 10" h., underglaze slip-painted florals, pastel matte glaze, signed Sarah Timberlake .. 875.00

Vase, 13" h., underglaze slip-painted daffodils, tan shaded to beige matte glaze, signed Hester Pillsbury........................ 375.00

Vase, 13½" h., underglaze slip-painted colorful berries & trailing vine, signed Sara Reid McLaughlin 275.00

JAP BIRDIMAL (1904)

Pitcher, tankard, incised & slip-painted Art Nouveau style white florals on blue ground, artist-signed 495.00

Urn, incised & slip-painted blue trees on white ground, 9"........ 300.00

Vase, 4" h., incised & slip-painted geese on lavender ground...............250.00 to 265.00

Vase, 11½" h., incised & slip-painted flying geese............. 275.00

KLYRO WARE (1920's)

Planter, pseudo corner posts & fence-like rim w/cluster of florals & foliage against white ribbed ground ....75.00 to 85.00

Vase, bud, 7" h., tapering hexagon, pendant blossoms & foliage against white ribbed ground 35.00

Vase, 8½" h., square, pseudo corner posts & fence-like rim w/cluster of pink florals & pendant berries against ribbed ground 40.00

Wall pocket, cluster of pink florals & pendant berries against ribbed ground, 7½" h. 50.00

LAMAR (1920-25)

Vase, 9" h., swollen cylinder, black lustre scene on deep raspberry red lustre ground 135.00

Vase, 13" h., black lustre scene on deep rapsberry red lustre ground 150.00

Wall pocket, black lustre scene on deep raspberry red lustre ground, 7½" h........................ 55.00

L'ART NOUVEAU (1903-04)

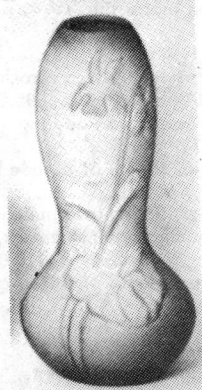

L'Art Nouveau Vase

Pitcher, tankard, 11" h., relief-
    molded grape clusters, shaded
    deep brown glossy finish 100.00
Umbrella stand, relief-molded trail-
    ing floral rim, cobalt blue, green
    & yellow 255.00
Vase, 9" h., shell-shaped, relief-
    molded profile bust of woman,
    reverse w/sea shell, matte
    finish 200.00
Vase, 12" h., relief-molded pink
    florals & trailing green stems,
    green & rose matte finish
    (ILLUS.)...................... 85.00

LA SA (1920-25)

LaSa Vase

Vase, 7½" h., scenic decor, irides-
    cent glaze 285.00
Vase, 8½" h., scenic decor
    w/lakeshore & mountains, irides-
    cent pink & gold glaze 295.00
Vase, 9" h., scenic decor, iridescent
    glaze (ILLUS.) 235.00
Vase, 13½" h., scenic decor w/palm
    trees, iridescent pink & gold
    glaze 400.00

LOUWELSA (1896-1924)

Louwelsa Jardiniere & Pedestal

Candlestick, vase form w/wide flar-
    ing base & long slender neck,
    slip-painted pansies, standard
    brown glaze, 9" h. (single) 95.00
Clock, fan-shaped top, slip-painted
    florals, standard brown glaze,
    7" h.......................... 390.00
Ewer, slip-painted florals, standard
    brown glaze, artist-signed, 3" h... 125.00
Ewer, fluted top, square base w/in-
    dented sides, slip-painted
    standard brown glaze, 6" base d.,
    9½" h. 195.00
Jardiniere, slip-painted carnations,
    standard brown glaze, 9" 190.00
Jardiniere & pedestal base, slip-
    painted yellow florals & green
    leaves, standard brown glaze,
    2 pcs. (ILLUS.).................. 950.00
Lamp, kerosene-type, 3-footed,
    globular, slip-painted jonquils,
    standard brown glaze, artist-
    signed, 12" h.................. 400.00
Mug, slip-painted yellow & green
    ear of corn, standard brown
    glaze, artist-signed 245.00
Pitcher, tankard, 12" h., slip-painted
    grape clusters & vines, standard
    brown glaze, artist-signed 240.00
Stein, slip-painted red cherries &
    green foliage, standard brown
    glaze, w/Art Nouveau style silver
    overlay, 6" h.................. 675.00
Umbrella stand, slip-painted florals,
    standard brown glaze, 22" h...... 280.00
Vase, 2" h., 2-handled, squatty, slip-
    painted golden wheat, standard
    brown glaze 150.00
Vase, 4" h., 6" d., bulbous w/short
    narrow neck, slip-painted yellow
    pansies, standard brown glaze ... 165.00

Vase, 5" h., slip-painted pansies, shaded blue glaze 425.00

Vase, 7¼" h., 4" d., 2-handled, slip-painted brown & green foliage, standard brown glaze, artist-signed 125.00

Vase, bud, 8" h., teardrop shape, slip-painted yellow & orange iris, standard brown glaze 130.00

Vase, 8½" h., 4½" d., slip-painted large white flowers w/brown centers, standard brown shaded to green glaze, artist-signed 150.00

Vase, 9" h., slip-painted carnations, standard brown glaze, artist-signed 250.00

Vase, 9¼" h., slip-painted foliage, standard brown glaze, artist-signed 350.00

Vase, 14" h., cylindrical, slip-painted yellow tulip, standard brown shaded to orange glaze 240.00

MARBLEIZED (1914)

Cuspidor, marbleized butterscotch & dark brown swirls, glossy 95.00

Jardiniere, marbleized grey & lavender swirls, glossy, 11½" d., 9½" h. 185.00

Vase, 6½" h., marbleized black, grey & white swirls, glossy 65.00

Vase, 9½" h., trumpet-shaped, marbleized butterscotch & dark brown swirls, glossy 135.00

MARVO (mid-1920's)

Marvo Jardiniere

Console bowl, molded palm leaves & fronds, tan matte finish, 12" d. 45.00

Jardiniere, molded ferns & fronds, green matte finish, 7" h. (ILLUS.) 48.00

Pitcher, 8" h., molded palm leaves & fronds, green matte finish 95.00

Vase, bud, 9" h., molded ferns & fronds, green matte finish 25.00

Vase, 12" h., low foot, expanding

cylinder, molded palm leaves & fronds, tan matte finish 70.00

MUSKOTA (1920's)

Figure of a boy seated on a rock fishing, 6½" h. ....95.00 to 110.00

Figure of a woman in kneeling position, 7½" h. 280.00

Flower holder, model of a nude boy w/drapery, 6" h. 85.00

Flower holder, figure of a nude woman leaning against a rock, 8" h. ....110.00 to 145.00

Flower holder, model of a frog on a lily pad. 50.00

Model of a fence, 5" h. 120.00

Model of a frog 65.00

Model of a gate w/cats & pots, 7" h. 195.00

OAK LEAF (pre-1936)

Ewer, molded & realistically colored oak leaves on front & acorns reverse, shaded green matte finish, 8½" h. 42.00

Planter, molded & realistically colored oak leaves on front & acorns reverse, shaded blue matte finish, 6" h. 65.00

Wall pocket, molded & realistically colored oak leaves & acorns, shaded tan matte finish, 8½" h. ... 25.00

PANELLA (mid to late 1930's)

Panella Footed Bowl

Bowl, 7" d., 3½" h., footed, pansies in relief within panels, shaded blue matte finish (ILLUS.) 40.00

Cornucopia-vase, pansies in relief within panels, shaded blue matte finish, 5½" h. 20.00

Ginger jar, cov., pansies in relief within panels, shaded blue matte finish 40.00

Vase, 7½" h., pansies in relief within panels, shaded green matte finish 25.00

PARAGON (1920's-30's)

Vase, 4" h., overall incised pattern of stylized florals & leaves, gold semi-gloss finish over tan 30.00

Vase, 7½" h., overall incised pattern of stylized florals & leaves,
deep red semi-gloss finish over
black 60.00
Vase, 9¾" h., overall incised pattern of stylized florals & leaves,
deep red semi-gloss finish over
black 95.00

PATRA (late 1920's-33)
Bowl, 4½" d., footed, stylized
florals at green-bordered rim, tan
stippled body 40.00
Vase, 6½" h., stylized florals at
green-bordered rim, tan stippled
body 55.00
Vase, 10" h., stylized florals at
green-bordered rim, tan stippled
body 65.00

PIERRE (mid 1930's)
Cookie jar, cov., molded basketweave effect, blue-green over
cream semi-matte finish 50.00
Pitcher, 7½" h., molded basketweave effect, blue-green over
cream semi-matte finish 30.00
Teapot, cov., molded basketweave
effect, pink semi-matte finish,
8½" h. 55.00

PUMILA (1920-28)
Bowl, 3½" h., pond lily form, shaded green matte finish w/tan
interior...................... 40.00
Candle holders, pond lily leaf form
base, molded lily cup, shaded
green matte finish w/tan interior,
3" h., pr. 35.00
Vase, 7" h., scalloped rim, panels of
overlapping pond lily leaves,
shaded tan to brown matte
finish 35.00

ROBA (mid to late 1930's)
Bowl, 7" w., tri-cornered, molded
swirls w/floral sprigs in relief,
shaded tan ground 30.00
Cornucopia-vase, molded swirls
w/floral sprigs in relief, shaded
blue ground, 5½" h. 25.00
Vase, 6" h., draped leaf foot, wide
ruffled rim, molded swirls w/flo-
ral sprigs in relief, blue shaded to
white 35.00

ROMA (1914 - late 1920's)
Jardiniere, relief-molded & tinted
red roses & green foliage pendant
from blue swag on ivory ground,
7" d.......................... 38.00
Jardiniere, relief-molded & tinted
red roses & green foliage on ivory
ground, 10¾" d. (ILLUS.) 75.00

Roma Jardiniere

Jardiniere & pedestal base, relief-
molded & tinted red & green floral
band on ivory ground, overall
34½" h., 2 pcs. ....325.00 to 425.00
Vase, 4" h., relief-molded & tinted
red roses on ivory ground........ 20.00
Vase, 8" h., footed, 5-prong flower
holder w/curved band of relief-
molded & tinted red roses on
ivory ground.................... 48.00
Vase, double bud, 8½" h., footed
base, square prongs forming a
"V" w/pierced ovoid near top,
relief-molded & tinted bands of
red roses & green foliage on ivory
ground 45.00
Vase, 10" h., cluster of relief-
molded & tinted deep purple
grapes w/green & tan vine on
ivory ground.................... 55.00
Wall pocket, relief-molded & tinted
red roses & green leaves
w/hovering bee on ivory ground.. 65.00

ROSEMONT (1920's)
Bowl, 10½" d., 2½" h., 3-footed,
rolled rim, stacked effect, stylized
flower & narrow band on glossy
black ground 40.00
Jardiniere, blue & brown bird
perched on flowering branch on
glossy black ground, 7½" h. 260.00
Vase, 7" h., pale blue florals on
glossy black ground 90.00

RUDLOR (1930-36)
Vase, 6" h., asymmetrical closed
handles, low relief pink florals
w/green foliage on ivory matte
spiral striped ground 20.00
Vase, 8" h., pierced & curved handles, tapering cylinder, low relief
white florals w/green foliage &
brown branches on green matte
spiral striped ground 25.00
Vases, 13¼" h., asymmetrical
closed handles, low relief pink

florals w/green leaves & brown
branches on white matte spiral
striped ground, pr. 140.00

SICARDO (1902-07)

Sicardo Vase

Candlestick, iridescent glaze,
signed, 8½" h. (single) 250.00
Vase, 2" h., iridescent glaze,
signed 200.00
Vase, 5" h., berries & vine design in
iridescent green to brown glaze,
signed (ILLUS.) 240.00
Vase, 6½" h., bulbous, iridescent
blue-green to emerald green
glaze 375.00
Vase, 9½" h., iridescent blue-green
to crimson glaze 525.00
Vase, 15" h., cylindrical, iridescent
glaze 700.00

SILVERTONE (1925-29)

Basket w/overhead handle, relief-
molded florals against textured
ground, shaded pastel blue &
grey, 8" h. 85.00
Basket w/overhead branch handle,
fan-shaped, relief-molded grape
cluster & vines against textured
ground, shaded pastel lavender &
blue, 13" h. 145.00
Vase, 6" h., relief-molded florals
against textured ground, shaded
pastel lavender & blue 70.00
Vase, 8" h., 2-handled, bulbous,
relief-molded yellow florals
against textured ground, shaded
pastel lavender & blue 115.00
Vase, 12" h., 2-handled, ruffled rim,
relief-molded butterfly & florals
against textured ground, shaded
pastel lavender & blue 120.00
Vase, 15" h., trumpet-shaped, relief-
molded florals against textured
ground, shaded blue & grey 175.00

STELLAR (1934)

Rose petal jar, cov., white stars on
black matte finish, 6½" h. 120.00

Vase, 6" h., white stars on black
matte finish 165.00

VELVA (1928-33)

Urn, cov., panel of stylized florals &
foliage in relief, shaded tan matte
finish, 8" h. 85.00
Vase, 6" h., panel of stylized florals
& foliage in relief, shaded green
matte finish 40.00
Vase, 9½" h., panel of stylized ber-
ries & leaves in relief, shaded tan
matte finish 55.00
Vase, cov., 11½" h., panel of sty-
lized florals & foliage in relief,
shaded green matte finish 80.00

VOILE (1920-28)

Vase, 5½" h., fan-shaped, apple
trees in relief, realistic coloring
on tan ground 55.00
Vase, 7" h., fan-shaped, apple trees
in relief, realistic coloring on
creamy ivory ground 60.00
Vase, 9" h., expanding cylinder, ruffled rim, apple trees in relief,
realistic coloring on tan ground . . . 60.00

WARWICK (late 1920's)

Basket, pillow-shaped w/branch-
molded overhead handle continuing to molded tree bark ground
w/branch of leaves & florals in
relief, 7" h. 65.00
Ferner, molded tree bark ground
w/branch of green leaves & red
florals in relief, matte finish,
6" d. 95.00
Vase, 5" h., 2-handled, molded tree
bark ground w/branch of green
leaves & red florals in relief 40.00
Vase, bud, 7" h., molded tree bark
ground w/branch of green leaves
& red florals in relief 25.00

WILD ROSE (1930's)

Wild Rose Vase

Basket, open wild rose decor, shaded green matte finish, 6" h. 60.00
Console set: console bowl & pr. candle holders; open wild rose decor, shaded green matte finish, 3 pcs. 85.00
Ewer, open wild rose decor, shaded pink matte finish, 14" h. 60.00
Vase, double bud, 6" h., open wild rose decor, shaded pink matte finish 25.00
Vase, 8" h., open wild rose decor, shaded green or pink matte finish, each 32.00
Vase, 9½" h., open wild rose decor, shaded pink matte finish (ILLUS.). 40.00

WOODCRAFT (1920-33)

Woodcraft Wall Pocket

Ash tray, bark-textured ground w/oak leaves in low relief & figural squirrel at side 100.00
Basket w/overhead branch handle, model of an acorn w/textured rim & smooth body, brown earthtones, 9½" h. 125.00
Bowl, 8" d., 4½" h., bark-textured ground w/three foxes peering from den in low relief 90.00
Pitcher, tankard, 12½" h., bark-textured ground w/three foxes peering from den in low relief, branch handle 490.00
Planter, bark-textured ground w/figural squirrel at rim, 4" d., 4½" h. 95.00
Planter, bark-textured ground w/leaves in low relief & 3 foxes peering from den on side, 5½" h. . . . . .150.00 to 175.00
Vase, double bud, 8" h., 2 tree trunks w/central floral-laden vine . . . . .30.00 to 45.00
Vase, 9" h., chalice-form w/three tree trunks rising from foot to base of bowl, florals & foliage in low relief, brown earthtones 80.00

Vase, bud, 10" h., tree trunk w/open limbs, red fruit & green leaves in low relief. . . . . . . .30.00 to 40.00
Vase, 14" h., tree trunk form w/fruit & foliage in low relief & figural owl perched on branch, brown earthtones 175.00
Wall pocket, cone-shaped tree trunk w/florals & vines in relief & full figure squirrel at bottom, 9" h.. . . . . .95.00 to 135.00
Wall pocket, cone-shaped tree trunk w/owl peering from knothole, 11¾" h. (ILLUS.) 125.00

WOODROSE (pre-1920)

Chamberstick, model of an oaken bucket w/clusters of blueberries, brown matte finish 85.00
Jardiniere, model of an oaken bucket w/pendant red roses & green leaves on brown matte ground, 4¾" h. 45.00
Vase, 8½" h., model of an oaken bucket w/pendant florals 30.00
Wall pocket, expanding cylinder, model of an oaken bucket w/pendant florals, 6½" h. 40.00
Wall pocket, model of an oaken bucket w/pendant florals, 10½" h.. . . . . 65.00

ZONA BABY LINE (1930's)

"Strutting Duck" Feeding Dish

Bowl, cereal, 5½" d., relief-molded rabbit & bird on branch decor 30.00
Creamer, "Strutting Duck" decor, 3½" h.. . . . . .35.00 to 45.00
Feeding dish w/rolled edge, "Strutting Duck" decor, 7" d. (ILLUS.) . . . 45.00
Feeding dish, relief-molded rabbit & bird on branch decor, 7" d.. . . . . .40.00 to 50.00
Mug, relief-molded rabbit & bird on branch decor, 3" h.. . . . . 35.00

WHIELDON-TYPE WARES

The Staffordshire potter, Thomas Whieldon, first established a pottery at Fenton in 1740. Though he made all types of wares generally in production in the 18th century, he is best known for his attractive, warm-colored green, yellow and brown mottled wares molded in the form of vegetables, fruit and leaves. He employed Josiah Spode as an apprentice and was briefly in partnership with Josiah Wedgwood. The term Whieldon ware is, however, a generic one since his wares were unmarked and are virtually indistinguishable from other similar wares produced by other potters during the same period.

Basket, sides pierced w/interlocking circles, folded rim, mottled light brown & manganese tortoise shell glaze, ca. 1750, 10¼" d. $7,700.00

Candle holder, model of a sphinx supporting a candle nozzle on its head, wings incised w/feather markings, chest molded w/ornaments & draped in cloth, oblong base, mottled manganese, blue & green tortoise shell glaze, applied w/mottled manganese & blue flowerheads, ca. 1760, 9¼" h. (repair to neck & 1 flowerhead) . . 3,300.00

Whieldon-Type Oval Dish

Dish, border molded w/entwined branches suspending clusters of fruit & foliage, center molded w/dense circle pattern, pale blue, green & manganese glaze, reverse entirely splashed in grey, Wedgwood, ca. 1760, 9¾" w. (ILLUS.) .1,870.00

Dish, deep, molded w/overlapping cauliflower leaves enriched in green & manganese revealing the creamy white cauliflower, center molded w/C-scrolls & star-shaped motif enriched in yellow, minor rim chips, ca. 1760, 10¾" d. (ILLUS.) 2,090.00

Whieldon-Type Cauliflower Dish

Dish, striated manganese glaze, ca. 1765, 14¼" d. (minor rim chip) . . . 550.00

Model of a cat in seated position w/head turned to the right, mottled manganese tortoise shell glaze, ca. 1760, 3¾" h. 1,100.00

Model of a rabbit, mottled manganese, green & ochre tortoise shell glaze, oblong base, ca. 1755, 2¾" l. (chip repairs to base, glaze repair to body) 935.00

Plate, 8¾" d., lobed, border molded w/entwined foliate branches suspending grapes, apples & hazelnuts against a trellis patt. ground, mottled green, ochre & manganese tortoise shell glaze accented w/manganese dots, ca. 1760 (small rim chips) 1,210.00

Tea caddy, square, each side molded in relief w/"chinoiserie" figures & birds among trees, background incised w/squares & covered in a translucent green glaze, flat shoulder incised w/similar panels & splashed in green, ca. 1760, 4" h. (hairline crack to base) 440.00

Teapot, cov., globular, branch handle, spout & finial, splashed in manganese, green & grey-blue, ca. 1760, 5½" w. 770.00

Tureen, cov., modeled in the form of a melon w/shallow grooves & raised netting, cover w/applied branch finial w/melon blossoms & foliage, mottled green & yellow tortoise shell glaze, ca. 1750, 11¼" w. (minor chips to finial, small repair to interior of rim, small hairline crack) 22,000.00

Vase, 6¾" h., 5 "finger" sections divided by foliage & blue lines, molded leaves enriched in green, blue & ochre, rim enriched in blue, ca. 1760 (minor chips) 935.00

WORCESTER

Worcester Oval Footed Dish

The famed English Worcester factory was established in 1751 and produced porcelains. Earthenwares were made in the 19th century. Its first period is known as the "Dr. Wall" period; that from 1783 to 1792 as the "Flight" period; that from 1792 to 1807 as the "Barr and Flight & Barr" period. The firm became Barr, Flight & Barr from 1807 to 1813; Flight, Barr & Barr from 1813 to 1840; Chamberlain & Co. from 1840 to 1848, and Kerr and Binns from 1852 to 1862. After 1862, the company became the Worcester Royal Porcelain Company, Ltd., known familiarly as Royal Worcester, which see.

Beaker, flaring rim, sepia figures & buildings in an extensive river landscape on yellow ground, rim & lower part w/band of stylized gilt foliage, Barr and Flight & Barr period, ca. 1800, 4" h. $418.00

Chamberstick, scalloped gadroon-edged saucer base w/gilt rim & palmette-scroll handle, pale green ground reserved w/gilt scroll-edged cartouche painted in shades of rose, iron-red, blue, purple & yellow w/an exotic bird in a landscape scene, cylindrical candle nozzle decorated w/gilt "seaweed" below gilt gadrooned rim, Flight, Barr & Barr, 1825-35, 4 1/8" d. 330.00

Cup & saucer, insects & clusters of apples, peaches, cherries & grapes within a gilt scroll border, rims w/rich apple green band, painted by the Spotted Fruit painter, Dr. Wall period, ca. 1760 . . . . .1,100.00

Dish, footed, cluster of fruit within gilt shaped panel outlined w/scrolls, sides pierced w/flower-head motifs & lozenge pattern covered in apple green glaze, feather-molded rim enriched in gilding, painted by the Spotted Fruit painter, Dr. Wall period, ca. 1770, 11¾" oval (ILLUS.) 1,320.00

Fruit coolers, covers & liners, "shanked" cylindrical cooler & waisted cover each painted in blue, yellow, green, maroon & black w/small cornflower sprigs alternating w/gilt leaf sprigs, shoulder & cover rim w/cornflower vine border within gilt bands, shoulder w/further gilt berry vine border, twisted foliate-scroll handles & loop knop heightened in gilding, Chamberlain period, ca. 1840, 11" & 11¼" h., pr. 1,540.00

Jug, bulbous body molded as overlapping cabbage leaves, painted in underglaze-blue w/flowering plants, cylindrical neck w/stylized foliage, loop handle, Dr. Wall period, ca. 1760, 8" h. 605.00

Worcester Dr. Wall Period Mug

Mug, cylindrical, reeded loop handle, transfer-printed in underglaze-blue one side w/trees & flowering plants by a fence, reverse w/a building among trees & rockwork in the Oriental style, Dr. Wall period, ca. 1765, 6" h. (ILLUS.) 350.00

Plate, 9" d., Imari Brocade patt., central chrysanthemum spray surrounded by radiating panels of diaperwork & flowering plants superimposed w/four mons, Dr. Wall period, ca. 1765 . . . . .1,980.00

Platter, 11½" oblong, "chinoiserie" decor, transfer-printed in black & colorfully enameled w/Mandarin gentleman seated at table, holding a teabowl & surrounded by 3 admiring ladies & a child, rim w/iron-red & gold scallop-and-dot border, Dr. Wall period, 1770-75 . . 660.00

Sauce tureen & cover w/bud sprig knop heightened in gilding, Bishop Sumner patt., painted in a famille-verte palette of iron-red, green, blue, yellow, turquoise & purple w/six iron-red-edged panels of

kylins, birds or a deer amidst
shrubbery, shell-shaped handles
heightened in gilding, Dr. Wall
period, 1770-75, 6½" l. 1,650.00
Sugar bowl, cov., 2-handled, exotic
birds in extensive river landscapes on yellow ground, rims
w/bands of stylized gilt foliage,
lower parts w/band of trailing foliage in gilt, cover w/loop finial,
Chamberlain period, ca. 1820,
7¼" w. 440.00
Sweetmeat stand, shell form, mold-
ed as a central finely fluted &
scalloped bowl above 3 similarly
fluted scallop-shell form bowls, all
supported on a triangular pierced
rockwork stand encrusted
w/mosses & a variety of small
shells, Dr. Wall period, ca. 1770,
6¼" h. 880.00
Tea caddy, cov., painted in the
Kakiemon palette w/shaped
panels enclosing flowering plants
outlined in gilding reserved on
blue scale ground, domed cover
w/flowerhead finial, Dr. Wall
period, ca. 1760, 6¼" h. (cover
repaired) 770.00
Tureens & covers, naturalistically
molded as a white cauliflower
w/tightly packed florettes enclosed
by heavily ribbed leaves, Dr.
Wall period, ca. 1760, 4 1/8" &
4" h., pr. 6,050.00
Vegetable tureen & cover w/coronet
finial, entwined strap & foliage
handles, Bengal Tiger patt.,
Chamberlain period, ca. 1840,
9¾" d. 385.00

YELLOWWARE

Yellowware Mug

*Yellowware is a form of utilitarian ware
produced in the United States from the 1850's
onward. Its body texture is less dense and
vitreous (impervious to water) than stoneware. Most, but not all, yellowware is un-*
*marked and its color varies from deep yellow
to pale buff. In the late 19th and early 20th
centuries, bowls in graduated sizes were widely advertised. Still in production, yellowware
is plentiful and still reasonably priced. Also
see FOOD, CANDY & MISC. MOLDS.*

Baking pan, embossed florals on
bottom, 10 x 3" $58.00
Beater jar, brown pin stripes decor
& Iowa advertising 55.00
Bedpan, large. 35.00
Bowl, 4¾" d., white band w/blue
pin stripes decor 13.50
Bowl, 7" d., 2 brown pin stripes
decor 18.00
Bowl, 8" d., 4 white pin
stripes 30.00
Bowl, 9" d., flared, 3 white pin
stripes 20.00
Bowl, 10" d., white bands
decor 37.00
Bowl, 11½" d., 6½" h., embossed
Indian heads & shields, interior
w/white glaze, unglazed exterior
& w/random blue sponging, wire
bail handle w/wooden grip, base
embossed w/eagle & "Pure Food
Cooking Ware, Made in U.S.A." . . 160.00
Butter crock, cov., single white
band 58.00
Casserole, cov., 7½" d. 45.00
Chamber pot, white band decor,
miniature size, 2½" 37.50
Chamber pot w/lid, cobalt blue
band 110.00
Colander, pierced star & circle
design, 12¾" d., 6" h. 145.00
Pickle crock, cov., earred handles at
sides, 9½" h. 90.00
Fruit (or canning) jar w/original lid,
5½" h. (hairline & chips on rim) . . 35.00
Milk cooling basin, 12" d. 55.00
Mixing bowl, brown bands decor,
10" d. 38.00
Mixing bowl, blue band decor,
12" d., 6½" h. 65.00
Mixing bowl, brown pin stripes
decor, 14¼" d., 7½" h. 45.00
Mug, 2 blue bands at top & bottom,
4¾" h. (ILLUS.) . . . . 30.00 to 40.00
Pitcher, 9" h., Basket Weave &
Flower patt. 140.00
Pitcher, milk, plain 55.00
Plate, 8" d., beaded rim 40.00
Rolling pin w/turned wood
handles . . . . 145.00 to 210.00
Salt box, wall-type, blue band
decor 90.00
Salt dip, master size, blue pin stripe
decor, 3" d. 110.00
Water set: large pitcher & 4 mugs;
blue pin stripe decor, marked
"Buckeye 100% Pure," 5 pcs. 190.00

ZSOLNAY

This pottery was made in Pecs, Hungary, in a factory founded in 1855 by Vilmos Zsolnay. Currently Zsolnay pieces are being made in a new factory.

Ewer, bulbous base, narrow neck & reticulated cup-shaped top w/cobalt blue interior glaze, overall colorful birds, florals & insect decor outlined in gold on deep yellow ground, 13¼" h. $295.00
Ewer, 4 large reticulated medallions in relief on body, ornate gold decor 185.00
Pitcher, water, iridescent geometric design on red-brown ground 275.00

Zsolnay Plaque

Plaque, pierced to hang, molded rim, incised Dutch landscape scene w/farmer & horse-drawn cart before windmill in shades of iridescent amber, yellow & green, early 20th c., 15½ x 10¼" (ILLUS.) 990.00
Plate, 10¾" d., red, blue & silver lustre Persian-style decor 275.00
Potpourri (rose petal) jar, cov., double-walled vessel w/overall reticulated outer wall, enameled decor, 11½" h. 225.00
Vase, 3¼" h., reticulated, blue, yellow, white & gold decor 100.00
Vase, bud, 3¾" h., 2¾" bottom d., reticulated outer layer, brown & green glaze, highlighted w/gold . . 155.00
Vase, 6½" h., double-walled reticulated sides, cobalt blue glaze, gold trim 325.00
Vase, 6½" h., double-walled reticulated body, cobalt blue, beige & gold 350.00
Vase, 7" h., bulbous body, waisted neck & flaring scalloped rim, iridescent green glaze 90.00
Vase, 7" h., tapering cylinder w/flaring ruffled rim, vertical ribbed body, iridescent blue glaze (ILLUS.) 110.00

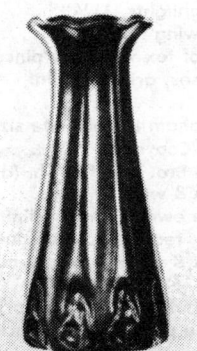

Zsolnay Vase

Vase, 10" h., Pilgrim flask form w/reticulated pedestal base & applied reticulated medallion each side, ornate rigaree-type handles at neck 450.00
Vase, squat melon-ribbed body, narrow neck, ruffled rim, iridescent green glaze 65.00

(End of Ceramics Section)

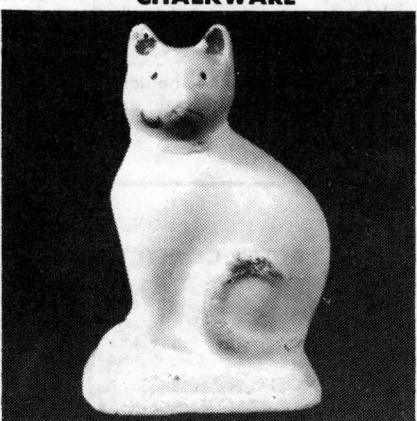

Chalkware Cat

CHALKWARE

So-called chalkware available today is actually made of plaster-of-paris, much of it decorated in color and primarily in the form of busts, figurines and ornaments. It was produced through most of the 19th century and the majority of pieces were quite inexpensive when originally made. Today even early 20th century pieces are collectible. Also see BREWERIANA.

Bank, model of a dove, worn original black & green paint w/red &

yellow highlights, 11¼" h.
(chipped wing tip) $145.00

Bank, bust of fox wearing "pince-
nez" glasses, original paint,
20th c. 50.00

Bust of Abraham Lincoln, life size,
stamped "Copyright 1907 . . .
Caproni & Bro. Inc.," 32" h. (discoloration & wear) 82.50

Group of a ewe & lamb reclining,
oval base, features picked out in
red, black & yellow, w/greenish
gold base, 6" h. 320.00

Model of a bull standing, features &
curly mane picked out in black,
19th c. 550.00

Model of a cat seated, white coat
w/black spots on ears & tail, features picked out in black, 6" h.
(ILLUS.) 176.00

Model of a cat seated, worn old
black repaint, white eyes &
pinkish red ears & mouth, 16" h.
(old chips & hairline in base) 385.00

Model of a dog carrying a basket,
rectangular plinth base, 19th c.,
5" h. 255.00

Model of a dog in standing position,
low oblong base, worn poly-
chrome paint, 7¾" h. 190.00

Model of a rabbit in an egg shell,
worn yellow-ochre & red paint,
6½" h. 115.00

Models of squirrels seated & nibbling on nuts, original paint,
19th c., 6" h., pr. 315.00

Store counter-top sucker holder,
figure of Statue of Liberty, origi-
nal paint 200.00

CHARACTER COLLECTIBLES

Buck Rogers "Strato-Kite"

*Numerous objects made in the likeness of
or named after movie, radio, television, comic*

strip and comic book personalties or charac-
ters abounded from the 1920's through the
1940's. Scores of these are now being eager-
ly collected and prices still vary widely. Also
see BANKS, BIG LITTLE BOOKS,
BROWNIE COLLECTIBLES, BUFFALO
POTTERY, BUSTER BROWN, CAMP-
BELL KIDS, CANDY CONTAINERS,
CHILDREN'S BOOKS, CHRISTMAS
TREE LIGHTS & ORNAMENTS, COMIC
BOOKS, COOKBOOKS, DISNEY COL-
LECTIBLES, DOLLS, GAMES and
KEWPIES.

Adams Family card game $15.00
Amos & Andy figures, chalkware, by
Art Statuary Co., Kansas City,
Mo., 7½" h., pr. 175.00
Amos & Andy game, "Card Party,"
1930 . . . .   50.00
Amos & Andy sheet music, "Check &
Double Check," Pepsodent theme,
1930 . . . .   25.00
Amos & Andy tablet 15.00
Andy Gump "Thrift Bank," square
tin can, Andy & "Save a Little -
Have a Lot," 1920's, 3" h. 400.00
Andy Gump clothes brush, w/mir-
ror, advertising "Walkers Big
Dandy Bread" 24.00
Andy Gump figure, wooden, cut-out
silhouette, 28" h. 55.00
Andy Gump nodding figure, bisque,
Germany, 4" h. 90.00
Andy Gump pinback button, "For
President" 25.00
Andy Gump & Min toothbrush
holder, bisque 65.00
Annie Oakley (Annie Get Your Gun)
hat, 1950 . . . .   18.00
Barney Google mug, china, Barney,
bird & pig decor, Germany 20.00
Batman charm bracelet 35.00
Batman comb, in plastic shield-
case 8.50
Batman hat, dated 1966 . . . .   5.00
Batman lamp 60.00
Batman license plate, tin, 1966 . . . . .   15.00
Batman & Robin "walkie-talkie"
radio 35.00
Beatles book, pop-up type, "Yellow
Submarine," 1968, 9½ x 15" 19.00
Beatles game, "Flip Your Wig,"
1964 . . . .   75.00
Beatles lunch box w/thermos bottle,
"Yellow Submarine," 1968 . . . . 115.00
Beatles toy, "Yellow Submarine," by
Corgi, original box 275.00
Beatles record case, "Disk-Go-
Case," red & white vinyl, holds
45 rpm records 85.00
Beatles talcum powder tin, portraits
front & back, by Margo of May-
fair, 5 x 7" 265.00

Beatles token, wooden nickel from
  1964 tour 6.00
Betty Boop figure, bisque, playing
  drum, original paint 85.00
Betty Boop figure, wood-jointed,
  4¼" h. 80.00
Betty Boop perfume bottle, glass,
  figural, yellow paint 38.00
Betty Boop valentine, mechanical-
  type 18.00
Bimbo (Betty Boop's dog) figure,
  wood-jointed, label on chest reads
  "Bimbo," copyright by Fleischer
  Studios, 7". 325.00
Blondie marionette, Hazelles Air-
  plane Control Marionette Co.,
  1940's 45.00
Blondie & Dagwood doll stroller,
  tin 49.00
Buck Rogers "Solar Scout" manual,
  1936, Cream of Wheat premium . .   50.00
Buck Rogers Map of the Solar Sys-
  tem, Cocomalt premium, 1933 . . . .   265.00
Buck Rogers ring, "Ring of Saturn,"
  plastic, glows in dark 225.00
Buck Rogers toy, "Strato-Kite,"
  w/envelope, 1946-50 (ILLUS.) 30.00
Bugs Bunny wrist watch, seated
  Bugs eating a carrot, carrot
  hands, brown leather band,
  Warner Bros., 1951 . . . .   75.00
Bullwinkle hand puppet 12.00
Captain Marvel bank, dime
  register . . . . .45.00 to 55.00
Captain Marvel coloring book, large
  size, 1943 . . . .   65.00
Captain Midnight decoder, 1942,
  "Photo-matic Code-O-Graph,"
  Ovaltine premium 45.00
Captain Midnight decoder, 1948,
  "Miro-Magic Code-O-Graph,"
  Ovaltine premium 50.00
Captain Midnight decoder, 1949,
  "Key-O-Matic Code-O-Graph,"
  Ovaltine premium 50.00
Captain Midnight decoder manual,
  1948 . . . .   50.00
Captain Midnight membership
  token, brass, 1940 . . . .   20.00

Captain Midnight Mug

Captain Midnight mug, Ovaltine
  premium, red plastic (ILLUS.) 25.00

Captain Midnight "Shake-Up" Mug

Captain Midnight "Shake-Up" mug,
  Ovaltine premium, blue plastic
  w/red lid (ILLUS.) 40.00
Casper the Ghost cookie jar,
  ceramic 400.00
Casper the Ghost pinback button,
  Kellogg's Pep Cereal premium 4.00
Charlie Chaplin coloring book,
  1917 . . . .   30.00
Charlie Chaplin glove box,
  wooden 35.00
Charlie Chaplin marionette, jointed
  celluloid figure dances from
  string, 1930's, 6" h. 77.00
Charlie Chaplin pencil box, tin,
  w/picture, 1920's . . . . .35.00 to 65.00
Charlie Chaplin pencil sharpener,
  made in Germany, 1920's 85.00
Charlie Chaplin squeeze toy, compo-
  sition head, 1920's 225.00
Charlie McCarthy book, "A Day with
  Charlie McCarthy & Edgar Ber-
  gen," 1938 . . . .   10.00
Charlie McCarthy doll, compo-
  sition 60.00
Charlie McCarthy fork, silverplate . .   15.00
Charlie McCarthy knife, silver-
  plate 18.00
Charlie McCarthy lapel pin,
  enameled 28.00
Charlie McCarthy marionette,
  lithographed cardboard, tab in
  back makes eyes & mouth move,
  20" 30.00
Charlie McCarthy perfume bottle,
  glass. 20.00
Charlie McCarthy ventriloquist
  dummy, composition, 1936 . . . .   300.00
Cisco Kid coloring book, Saalfield,
  1954 . . . .   15.00
Crazy Cat pull toy, Crazy Cat

chasing 2 mice, metal platform,
1930's 750.00
Daddy Warbucks pinback button,
Kellogg's Pep Cereal premium 6.50
Daddy Warbucks rubber stamp,
1930 .... 5.00
Daisy (from Dagwood & Blondie)
toy, straw-filled mohair, Knicker-
bocker Toy Co., 1930's 225.00
Dale Evans pinback button, 1953 .... 6.00
Dennis the Menace figure, rubber,
dated 1958, original clothes, 13".. 55.00
Dennis the Menace hooked rug,
Dennis holding toy bear & melting
ice cream cone, mid-1950's,
60 x 36" 75.00
Dick Tracy badge, "Dectective
Club" 16.00
Dick Tracy book, pop-up type, "The
Capture of Boris Arson," 1935 .... 65.00
Dick Tracy booklet, "Vault of
Death," Big Thrill Chewing Gum
No. 3 premium.................. 20.00
Dick Tracy coloring book, ca. 1946 .. 18.00
Dick Tracy Junior Detective kit 37.50
Dick Tracy "siren" pistol, tin, Louis
Marx & Co., 1934, boxed, 7" l. ... 32.50

Dick Tracy Squad Cars

Dick Tracy toy, "Squad Car No. 1,"
friction drive (ILLUS. front) 60.00
Dick Tracy toy, "Squad Car No. 1,"
flashing light & siren, 1940's
(ILLUS. back).................... 75.00
Dick Tracy wallet.................. 8.00
Dick Tracy watch fob, 1934 .... 20.00
Dionne Quintuplets book, "The
Country Doctor," by W. Thornton,
1936, hard cover, 37 black & white
photographs 30.00
Dionne Quintuplets book, "Soon
We'll Be Three Years Old," 1936 .. 16.50
Dionne Quintuplets books, "Story of
the Dionne Quintuplets," "We're
Two Years Old" & "Here We Are
Three," Saalfield, set of 3 .... 45.00
Dionne Quintuplets bridge tally
cards, Quintuplets' home pictured,
1930's, set of 12................ 10.00
Dionne Quintuplets calendar, 1941,
playing dress-up 13.50
Dionne Quintuplets calendar, 1945,
"Harvest Days".................. 18.50

Dionne Quintuplets calendar, 1948 .. 15.00
Dionne Quintuplets scrapbook, 200
pictures & articles 50.00
Don Winslow manual, "Squadron of
Peace," illustrated, 1939, 28 pp. ... 75.00
Ed Wynn Fire Chief siren,
lithographed tin 45.00
Eddie Cantor pin, "Magic Club" 18.00
Ella Cinders pinback button 12.50

Elmer Fudd Metal Figure

Elmer Fudd figure, metal, standing
beside tub, 5 x 3¾" base, 5½" h.
figure (ILLUS.).................. 40.00
Elvis Presley "I.D." bracelet, on
original card dated 1956 .... 12.50
Felix the Cat blotter, rocker-type,
Japan 10.00
Felix the Cat doll, stuffed cloth, Eng-
lish version, 1920's 95.00
Felix the Cat figure, wood-jointed
w/leather ears, marked "Pat Sul-
livan Pat. June 23, 1925," Schoen-
hut, 8" h. ....175.00 to 200.00
Felix the Cat pencil box, 1934-39 ... 28.00
Felix the Cat pen wiper............ 50.00
Felix the Cat pinback button, Kel-
logg's "Pep" Cereal premium 20.00
Flash Gordon game, "Target," tin,
1950's ....65.00 to 80.00
Flash Gordon "signal" pistol, Louis
Marx & Co., 1935 .... 250.00
Flash Gordon water pistol, plastic,
original box, 1950's.............. 85.00
Foxy Grandpa figure, bisque,
5¾" h......................... 125.00
Foxy Grandpa paint book 35.00
Gasoline Alley cookie cutters, origi-
nal box, set 20.00
Gene Autry cap pistol, repeating Jr.
Model, 3-shooter, cast iron,
w/jeweled leather
holster ....25.00 to 40.00
Gene Autry guitar, wooden, by
Hemony, original case, early
1940's 95.00
Gene Autry holster, leather, dated
1949 .... 10.00

Gene Autry ring, "Horseshoe
Nail".......................... 20.00
Gene Autry ring, plastic, eagle..... 45.00
Gene Autry ring, portrait 40.00
Gene Autry slippers, in original
box 25.00
Gene Autry song book, 1932,
64 pp.......................... 20.00
Gene Autry song book, 1938, 88
songs, 95 pp. 15.00
Gene Autry song book, 1942 .... 10.00
Gene Autry spurs, pr. 30.00
Gene Autry wallet 30.00
Gene Autry wrist watch, his gun in-
dicating seconds, back die-bossed
"Always Your Pal, Gene Autry,"
green radium hands, brown leath-
er band, copyright 1948 .... 195.00
Gene Autry & Champ pennant,
"Back in the Saddle Again" 25.00
Green Hornet fork & spoon, metal,
pr............................. 20.00
Green Hornet mug 30.00
Green Hornet jigsaw puzzles, set of
4 .... 40.00
Green Hornet pinback button,
flasher-type, 3" d.............. 6.50
Green Hornet & Kato mask set,
1966 .... 8.00
Happy Hooligan book, "Happy Hooli-
gan Home Again," by F. Opper,
1909, full color, large size....... 50.00
Happy Hooligan book, "Story of
Happy Hooligan," published by
McLoughlin, 1932 .... 30.00
Hopalong Cassidy badge, star-
shaped, "Hopalong Cassidy Bar 20
Ranch," 1950, "Eaco" embossed on
badge, on card 11.00
Hopalong Cassidy bank, bust of
Hoppy, brown plastic, 4½" h. 22.00

Hopalong Cassidy Barette

Hopalong Cassidy barette, brass,
embossed, 2" l. (ILLUS.).......... 20.00
Hopalong Cassidy book, "Hopalong
Cassidy Lends a Helping Hand,"
pop-up type, 1950, published by
Doubleday, hard cover.......... 30.00
Hopalong Cassidy camera w/flash
attachment, Galter Products Co.,
1940, original box 70.00
Hopalong Cassidy cap pistol, Wyan-
dotte, 8" l. 70.00
Hopalong Cassidy cereal bowl,
white china w/picture of Hoppy .. 19.00
Hopalong Cassidy fork, silverplate .. 8.00

Hopalong Cassidy gameboard,
"Stagecoach" game one side &
"Target" reverse, 1950 .... 32.00
Hopalong Cassidy hair bow, 1950,
on original card 12.00
Hopalong Cassidy lamp, "Bar 20
Ranch," light w/revolving color
insert, 1949 .... 115.00
Hopalong Cassidy lamp, wall-type,
gun in holster, Alacite glass,
Aladdin 115.00
Hopalong Cassidy milk jug, glass
w/bail handle, gal. 30.00
Hopalong Cassidy money clip, "Bar
20" 21.00
Hopalong Cassidy mug, opaque
white glass w/color decal
picture .... 8.00 to 12.50
Hopalong Cassidy pencil case, ca.
1950, 5 x 11" 15.00
Hopalong Cassidy pennant, black
felt, w/Hoppy, Topper & other
cowboy symbols, 19" l. ....9.50 to 15.00
Hopalong Cassidy pocket knife, Im-
perial Knife Co., 1950's 28.00
Hopalong Cassidy radio, red or
black metal w/silver foil design
on front, Arvin, 1948 .... 155.00
Hopalong Cassidy ring, signet 15.50
Hopalong Cassidy rug, chenille,
horsehead & fence, 4' x 2' 100.00
Hopalong Cassidy "sparkler" toy 35.00
Hopalong Cassidy teaspoon,
silverplate 10.00
Hopalong Cassidy token, "Lucky
Coin" 9.00
Hopalong Cassidy tumbler, plastic,
yellow 13.50
Hopalong Cassidy wrist watch, pic-
ture of Hoppy on face, black
strap, die-bossed "Good Luck
from Hoppy," U.S. Time,
1950-67 ....55.00 to 75.00
Howdy Doody doll, wood-jointed &
composition 115.00
Howdy Doody handkerchief, signed
Bob Smith, 1950's 17.00
Howdy Doody iced tea spoon,
Crown silverplate 15.00
Howdy Doody key chain, take-apart
type, w/instructions 5.00
Howdy Doody lunch box, tin,
1950's 25.00
Howdy Doody marionette, 16" 82.50
Howdy Doody mug, Ovaltine
premium 23.00
Howdy Doody night light........... 34.00
Howdy Doody phonograph 88.00
Jack Armstrong flashlight, bullet-
shaped 20.00
Jack Armstrong game, "Magic An-
swer Box" 32.50
Jack Armstrong pedometer, "Hike-o-
Meter" 17.00

Jack Armstrong telescope.......... 17.00
Jack Webb (Dragnet) coloring book,
   1957 .... 12.00
Jack Webb (Dragnet) whistle 5.00

Jackie Coogan Pencil Box

Jackie Coogan pencil box, tin,
   7¾ x 2" (ILLUS.) 22.00
Jeff (of Mutt & Jeff) figure, celluloid,
   4" h............................. 45.00
Katzenjammer Kids teaspoon,
   silverplate 22.00
Kayo figure, bisque, 2¼" h......... 45.00
Lil Abner bank, mechanical-type,
   tin, 1953..................... 75.00
Lil Abner paint set, 1951 .... 15.00
Lone Ranger badge, "Safety Club,"
   radio premium, 1933 .... 12.00

Lone Ranger Bandana

Lone Ranger bandana, red, black &
   white linen, ca. 1940, 21 x 23"
   (ILLUS.)........................ 25.00
Lone Ranger book, "Lone Ranger
   and The Mystery Ranch," 1940's,
   published by Grosset & Dunlap,

hard bound, w/dust jacket 12.00
Lone Ranger cowgirl outfit, Esquire
   Novelty Co., 1947, medium size .. 85.00
Lone Ranger guitar, 1940's 100.00
Lone Ranger gun, cast iron, six-
   shooter 44.00
Lone Ranger hair brush, multi-
   colored decal on black wood
   handle, 1938, 8¾" l. 16.00
Lone Ranger paint book, Whitman,
   1940 .... 25.00
Lone Ranger pedometer, 1943, Kix
   Cereal premium................. 17.00
Lone Ranger pocket knife, red
   w/picture, slogans & 3-dimen-
   sional silver bullet 31.50
Lone Ranger ring, "Atom Bomb,"
   w/instructions ....25.00 to 35.00
Lone Ranger ring, "flashlight,"
   w/manual, Cheerios premium,
   mid-1940's 27.00
Lone Ranger ring, "Six-Shooter,"
   Cheerios premium, 1940's 45.00
Lone Ranger scrapbook, w/famous
   cowboy photos, clippings, maga-
   zine stories, arcade cards, etc.,
   ca. 1938 .... 150.00
Lone Ranger toothbrush holder,
   dated 1938 ....20.00 to 35.00
Lord Plushbottom pinback button,
   Kellogg's Pep Cereal premium 5.00
Lucy (from Charlie Brown) wrist
   watch, 1952.................... 50.00

Maggie & Jiggs Figures

Maggie & Jiggs figures, wood-
   jointed bodies & papier mache
   heads, Jiggs w/original "Corned
   Beef & Cabbage" pail & Maggie
   w/rolling pin, Schoenhut,
   copyright 1924, International Fea-
   ture Service, 8" & 9" h., pr.
   (ILLUS.)........................ 825.00
Melvin Purvis badge, "Secret
   Operator" 9.00
Melvin Purvis Secret Operator's
   Manual, 1937, 28 pp. 35.00

Uncle Bim (The Gumps) nodding figure, bisque 125.00
Uncle Remus game, "Zip," marble shooting type, Parker Bros. 20.00
Uncle Walt (Skeezix) nodding figure, bisque, 3" h..................... 75.00
Uncle Walt pinback button, Kellogg's "Pep" Cereal premium 4.00
Wild Bill Hickok coloring book, 1962 .... 10.00
Wild Bill Hickok thermos bottle, 1955 .... 10.00
Wild Bill Hickok & Jingles badge, "Deputy Marshall," star-shaped badge & official identification card, in original leather case 15.00
Wimpy ring, Post Toasties Cereal premium, 1949 .... 12.00
Winnie Winkle cookie cutter, Pillsbury Flour premium 22.50
Winnie Winkle nodding figure, bisque ....75.00 to 100.00
Winnie Winkle pinback button, Kellogg's "Pep" Cereal premium 4.00
Winnie Winkle ring, Post Toasties Cereal premium, 1949 .... 12.00
Woody Woodpecker alarm clock, animated-type 185.00
Yellow Kid cap buster, cast iron, Ives....................85.00 to 150.00
Yellow Kid pinback button No. 6.... 30.00
Yellow Kid pinback button No. 10... 25.00
Yellow Kid pinback button No. 26... 30.00
Zorro wrist watch, original box 45.00

CHILDREN'S BOOKS

Pop-Up Book

The most collectible children's books today tend to be those printed after the 1850's and while age is not completely irrelevant, illustrations play a far more important role in determining the values. While first editions are highly esteemed, it is the beautifully illustrated books that most collectors seek. The following books, all in good to fine condition, were sold within the past twelve months.

Also see BIG LITTLE BOOKS, BROWNIE COLLECTIBLES, BUSTER BROWN, CHARACTER COLLECTIBLES, COMIC BOOKS, DISNEY COLLECTIBLES, GREENAWAY ITEMS and HUMPHREY ARTWORK.

"A Child's Garden of Verses," by Robert Lewis Stevenson, illustrated by Jessie Wilcox Smith, published by Scribner's, 1933 .... $45.00
"Adventures of Bob White," by Thornton Burgess, 1923, w/dust jacket 18.00
"A Gallery of Children," by A.A. Milne, 12 color illustrations by Saida, published by David McKay, 1925, 1st American edition 75.00
"Baby's Doings," published by Saalfield, 1940, linen 20.00
"Billy Whiskers' Pranks," by Frances Montgomery, illustrated by Frances Brundage, published by Saalfield, 1925 .... 25.00
"Book of the Child," illustrated by Jessie Wilcox Smith, published by Stokes, 1903, 1st edition ....250.00 to 300.00
"Doctor Doolittle in the Moon," written & illustrated by Hugh Lofting, 1928 .... 25.00
"The Eclectic Fourth Reader," by William H. McGuffey, 1879 .... 5.00
"Fairy Tales," by Hans Christian Andersen, 100 illustrations by Frances Brundage, published by Saalfield, 1925 .... 10.00
"Father Tuck's Railway ABC," 4 pages color illustrations, published by Raphael Tuck, 1900 .... 20.00
"Freckles Comes Home," by Gene Stratton Porter, New York, 1929, 1st edition 55.00
"Goldilocks & the 3 Bears," pop-up type, 1934 .... 55.00
"Goody Two Shoes," published by McLoughlin, 1897 .... 22.00
"Grimm's Fairy Tales," illustrated by Johnny Gruelle, 1914 .... 35.00
"Henny Penny & Her Friend," published by McLoughlin Bros., 1899, linen 9.00
"Hours in Storyland," published by McLoughlin, 1893, 9½ x 7½" 28.00
"Jack Frost's Painting & Drawing Book," published by Hamming Publishing Co., 1905 .... 12.50
"Johnny Giraffe," by Marjorie Barrows, 1935..................... 15.00
"Katzenjammer Kids Story Book," 1937 .... 12.00
"Royal Little People," by Elizabeth Tucker, 1895 .... 50.00
"Sleeping Beauty," illustrations by

Arthur Rackham, 1920, w/dust
jacket 125.00

"The Tale of Flopsy Bunnies," by
Beatrix Potter, color illustrations,
1909 . . . . 40.00

"The Tar-Baby and Other Rhymes of
Uncle Remus," by Joel Chandler
Harris, illustrated by A.B. Frost &
E.W. Kemble, published by Apple-
ton & Co., 1904 . . . . 75.00

"The Three Bears," pop-up type,
1935 . . . . 35.00

"Tom the Bootblack," by Horatio
Alger, Jr., 1889 . . . . 10.00

"Uncle Remus - His Songs & His Say-
ings," by Joel Chandler Harris,
1881 . . . . 95.00

"Water Babies," by Charles Kings-
ley, 1878 . . . . 85.00

"Wood's Natural History for Chil-
dren," 1908 . . . . 12.00

CHILDREN'S DISHES

Milk White Glass Punch Set

During the reign of Queen Victoria, doll houses and accessories became more popular and as the century progressed, there was greater demand for toys which would subtly train a little girl in the art of homemaking. Also see ABC PLATES, AKRO AGATE GLASS, BABY MEMENTOES, BROWNIE COLLECTIBLES, BUFFALO POTTERY, BUSTER BROWN & CAMPBELL KIDS COLLECTIBLES, CARNIVAL GLASS, CAT COLLECTIBLES, CHARACTER COLLECTIBLES, DEPRESSION GLASS, DISNEY COLLECTIBLES, GREENAWAY ITEMS, KEWPIE COLLECTIBLES, NIPPON CHINA, OCCUPIED JAPAN, PATTERN GLASS, SUNBONNET BABIES and WORLD FAIR COLLECTIBLES.

Berry set: master bowl & 4 sauce
dishes; pressed glass, Flute patt.,
clear, 5 pcs. $45.00

Bowl, china, Simple Simon decor,
marked "Meakin," 6¾" d. 10.00

Butter dish, cov., pressed glass, Arrowhead in Ovals patt., clear 35.00

Butter dish, cov., pressed glass,
Colonial patt., Cambridge Glass
Co., green 45.00

Butter dish, cov., pressed glass,
Fernland patt., Cambridge Glass
Co., cobalt blue 50.00

Butter dish, cov., pressed glass,
Hobnail & Paneled Thumbprint
patt., amber 85.00

Butter dish, cov., pressed glass,
Lion patt., clear 120.00

Butter dish, cov., pressed glass,
Rexford patt., clear 25.00

Butter dish, cov., pressed glass,
Wild Rose patt., milk white 70.00

Cake stand, pressed glass, Ribbon
Candy patt., green 60.00

Castor set, 4-bottle, pressed glass,
American Shield patt., clear bot-
tles, pewter stand 100.00

Chamber set: wash basin & pitcher,
slop jar, cov. soap dish, cov.
toothbrush-comb holder & chamber pot; china, h.p. florals on
white ground, marked "Ger-
many," 6 pcs. 180.00

Creamer, china, Blue Willow patt.,
1½" h. 13.50

Creamer, china, children playing
w/kitten & ball of twine, rabbit &
dog, ca. 1900, marked
"Germany" 35.00

Creamer, graniteware, blue 35.00

Creamer, pressed glass, Amazon
patt., clear 28.00

Creamer, pressed glass, Bucket
patt., clear 29.00

Creamer, pressed glass, Drum patt.,
clear 38.00

Creamer, pressed glass, Lion patt.,
clear 69.00

Creamer, pressed glass, Nursery
Rhymes patt., clear 36.00

Creamer, pressed glass, Tulip &
Honeycomb patt., clear 18.50

Cup & saucer, china, Blue Willow
patt., marked "Japan" . . . . . .5.00 to 10.00

Cup & saucer, china, Golliwogs
decor, marked "Royal
Rudolstadt" 23.00

Pitcher, water, pressed glass, Gallo-
way patt., clear 17.00

Pitcher, water, pressed glass, Oval
Star patt., clear 30.00

Plate, china, 6 colorful mice dressed
as people around center w/cat
pointing to blackboard picturing
cheese while student mice listen,
"The smallest scholar learns with
ease to spell the name of every
cheese," 7" d. 50.00

Punch cup, pressed glass, Tulip & Honeycomb patt., clear 12.00

Punch cup, pressed glass, Whirligig patt., clear 8.00

Punch set: bowl & 6 cups; pressed glass, Flattened Diamond & Sunburst patt., clear, 7 pcs. 55.00

Punch set: bowl & 6 cups; pressed glass, Nursery Rhymes patt., milk white, 7 pcs. (ILLUS.) 300.00

Punch set: bowl & 6 cups; pressed glass, Wild Rose patt., milk white, 7 pcs. .... 165.00 to 200.00

Sauce dish, pressed glass, Patee Cross patt., clear................ 8.00

Spooner, pressed glass, Arrowhead in Ovals patt., clear 19.00

Spooner, pressed glass, Hawaiian Lei patt., clear 10.00

Spooner, pressed glass, Inverted Strawberry patt., Cambridge Glass Co., clear................ 38.00

Spooner, pressed glass, Menagerie patt., fish, blue .... 55.00 to 100.00

Sugar bowl, cov., pressed glass, Arrowhead in Ovals patt., clear 19.00

Sugar bowl, cov., pressed glass, Nursery Rhymes patt., clear...... 67.00

Table set: cov. butter dish, cov. sugar bowl, creamer & spooner; pressed glass, Flattened Diamond & Sunburst patt., 4 pcs. 67.50

Menagerie Pattern Table Set

Table set: cov. butter dish, cov. sugar bowl, creamer & spooner; pressed glass, Menagerie patt., amber, 4 pcs. (ILLUS.) 3,250.00

Table set: cov. butter dish, cov. sugar bowl, creamer & spooner; pressed glass, Sweetheart patt., clear, 4 pcs. 80.00

Table set: cov. butter dish, cov. sugar bowl, creamer & spooner; pressed glass, Tappan patt., clear, 4 pcs. 65.00

Teapot, cov., china, 3 bears decor, marked "Germany"............. 45.00

Teapot, cov., china, small girl feeding teddy bear decor, marked "Germany" 37.00

Teapot, cov., graniteware, curved spout, side handle, blue, 3" h. ... 35.00

Tea set: cov. teapot, creamer & sugar bowl; china, "tapestry,"

French lady & gentleman decor, marked "Royal Bayreuth," 3 pcs... 450.00

Tea set: cov. teapot, 3 plates & 3 c/s; china, white w/gold band decor, marked "Nippon," 10 pcs. 110.00

Tea set: cov. teapot, creamer, sugar bowl & 4 c/s; graniteware, white w/blue & red trim, 11 pcs. 150.00

Tea set: cov. teapot, creamer, sugar bowl, 3 c/s & 4 plates; china, blue lustre w/black trim, marked "Noritake," 13 pcs. 65.00

Tea set: cov. teapot, creamer, sugar bowl & 6 c/s; china, circus decor, lustre trim, marked "Bavaria," 15 pcs. 125.00

Tea set: cov. teapot, creamer, sugar bowl & 6 c/s; china, Greenaway-type girls w/carts on white ground, 15 pcs. 265.00

Tea set: cov. teapot, creamer, sugar bowl, 4 c/s & 4 plates; ironstone china, ribbed, all white, 15 pcs. .. 175.00

Tray, pressed glass, Doyle's 500 patt., blue, 6 5/8" 35.00

Tumbler, pressed glass, Nursery Rhymes patt., clear.............. 17.00

Water set: pitcher & 4 tumblers; pressed glass, Fancy Cut patt., clear, 5 pcs. 80.00

Water set: pitcher & 4 tumblers; pressed glass, Oval Star patt., clear, 5 pcs. 75.00

CHILDREN'S MUGS

Sunderland Lustre Mug

The small size mug used by children first attempting to drink from a cup, appeals to many collectors. Because they were made of china, glass, pottery, graniteware, plated silver and silver, the collector is given the opportunity to assemble a diversified collection or to single out one particular type of decoration, such as Franklin Maxims, or a specific material, such as glass, around which to base

*his collection. Also see CARNIVAL, CUS-
TARD, DEPRESSION and PATTERN
GLASS.*

China, Indian wearing headdress decal, green lustre edge, 2" h. $15.00

China, lion riding bicycle decal, pink
lustre rim, Germany, early
20th c. 12.00

China, "Think of Me" in gilt & pink
lustre trim, Germany, 2¼" h. 29.00

China, h.p. girl w/dog decor,
marked "Nippon" (Japan, 1891-
1921). 60.00

Coin silver, plain, R.W. Wilson,
Philadelphia 95.00

Graniteware, Dutch children decal
on white, Germany. 28.00

Graniteware, "Mary Had A Little
Lamb" scene & verse decal on
blue 35.00

Pressed glass, Birdland patt.,
clear 22.00

Pressed glass, Butterfly patt.,
clear 23.50

Pressed glass, Cats (2) Fighting
patt., clear 25.00

Pressed glass, Dahlia patt., light
amber, 2¾" 40.00

Pressed glass, Dog & Bird patt.,
blue 35.00

Pressed glass, Doyle's No. 500 patt.,
amber 30.00

Pressed glass, Drum patt., clear 27.50

Pressed glass, Elephant patt., blue. . 35.00

Pressed glass, Grape & Festoon
w/Shield patt., clear 15.00

Pressed glass, "H.M.S. Pinafore"
patt., clear 25.00

Pressed glass, Hobnail patt., clear,
2" h. 8.50

Pressed glass, "Humpty Dumpty"
patt., w/"Tom the Piper's Son"
reverse, clear. 45.00

Pressed glass, Little Bo Peep patt.,
clear 25.00

Pressed glass, Little Lamb patt.,
clear 37.50

Pressed glass, Thousand Eye patt.,
amber or blue, 2½" h., each 18.00

Pressed glass, Wee Branches patt.,
blue 32.00

Pressed glass, Wee Branches patt.,
clear 26.50

Silver, engraved continuous scene of
house, trees & lake around sides,
Russia, dated 1891 . . . . 185.00

Staffordshire pottery, underglaze-
blue & overglaze red & green
enameling & lustre trim, 19th c.,
2 3/8" h. 65.00

Staffordshire pottery, "Shuttlecock,"
red transfer of children at play,
Allertons, 19th c., 2½" h. 45.00

Staffordshire pottery, "Convolvulus -
Foxglove," mulberry transfer of
children in period clothing, 19th
c., 2½" h. 55.00

Staffordshire pottery, "Goldfinch,"
brown transfer & worn purple
lustre trim," 2½" h. 45.00

Staffordshire pottery, black transfer
of cat seated by bowl one side &
zebra running reverse, highlighted
in polychrome enameling, 3½" h.
(stains, crow's foot & rim glaze
flakes) 85.00

Staffordshire pottery, cream band
w/black transfer of man in stocks,
"A Wild Cat Banker Secured - A
Public Service" & "Happy New
Year," 3" h. 65.00

Sterling silver, chased band of children's profiles amidst foliage,
styized leaf bracket handle,
w/monogram, Gorham & Co., late
19th c. 154.00

Sunderland lustre pottery, pink-
splashed overall, 2½" h.
(ILLUS.). 65.00

CHRISTMAS TREE LIGHTS

*Along with a host of other Christmas-
related items, early Christmas tree lights are
attracting a growing number of collectors.
Comic characters seem to be the most popular form among the wide variety of figural
lights available, most of which were manufactured between 1920 and World War II in Germany, Japan and the United States. Figural
bulbs listed are painted clear glass unless
otherwise noted.*

BULBS

Angel, milk white w/painted details
& brown hair, 4" h. $27.00

Bell w/embossed reindeer, blue 15.00

Betty Boop. 16.00

Bird, red, white or blue, each 12.00

Bluebird, milk white, 4" h. 12.00

Boy in hip boots 35.00

Candle . . . . 10.00 to 12.50

Candy cane. 50.00

Cardinal. 11.00

Cat, seated 20.00

Child w/ball 13.00

Chinese lantern 19.50

Clown, roly-poly 22.00

Clown, standing on ball, red 25.00

Cow jumping over the moon 40.00

Dirigible, red & black, 2¼" 37.00

Dog w/long ears 40.00

Ear of corn 18.00

Elephant, milk white, 4" h.	25.00
Elephant seated on ball	35.00
Flame, red	12.00
Frog	15.00 to 19.50
Girl w/rose	25.00
Goldfish bowl	20.00
Grape cluster, purple	10.00
Humpty Dumpty seated on brick wall	40.00
King w/blackbirds	45.00
Lady w/handbag, milk white, 3" h.	20.00
Lantern, round, milk white	11.00
Little Boy Blue	35.00
Little Jack Horner	20.00
Old King Cole	45.00
Orphan Annie, milk white, marked "C 1935," 3 1/8" h.	30.00
Parakeet, milk white	18.00
Pelican, milk white	15.00
Pocket watch, blue	25.00
Princess Summer, Winter, Spring & Fall (from Howdy Doody)	110.00
Queen of Hearts	35.00
Rose	14.00
Santa Claus' head, 3-sided	40.00
Santa Claus emerging from chimney	35.00
Santa Claus, house & girl, milk white, flat oval	27.00
Skull & crossbars	35.00
Snowman w/hat, pipe & holly sprig	15.00
Strawberry	19.50
Three Men in a Tub	45.00

STRINGS

Bambi, light holders w/various characters, Mazda, made by British Thomson Houston Co., original box, set of 16 (no plug)	90.00
Cartoon characters: Andy Gump, Betty Boop, Moon Mullins, Kayo, Smitty, Dick Tracy, Orphan Annie & Sandy; figural, original box, set of 8	350.00
Walt Disney characters: 2 each Mickey & Minnie Mouse & 1 each Porky Pig, Pinocchio & Jiminy Cricket; set of 7 in original box	25.00
Walt Disney characters: Mickey Mouse, Minnie Mouse, Jiminy Crickett, Pluto, Donald Duck, Pinocchio, Dwarf & Pig; Paramount, set of 8	120.00
Walt Disney characters, Mickey Mouse & Friends at Christmas, standard-series bulbs, each w/bell-shaped plastic shade decorated w/decal, Noma, 1936, set of 8	85.00 to 150.00

CHRISTMAS TREE ORNAMENTS

Dresden-Type Christmas Tree Ornament

The German blown glass Christmas tree ornaments and other commercially-made ornaments of wax, cardboard and cotton batting, were popular from the time they were first offered for sale in the United States in the 1870's. Prior to that time, Christmas trees had been decorated with homemade ornaments that usually were edible. Now nostalgic collectors who seek out ornaments that sold for pennies in stores across the country in the early years of this century, are willing to pay some rather hefty prices for unusual or early ornaments.

Angel in flight, papier mache	$98.00
Apple, blown glass, red & yellow, 1¾" h.	65.00
Automobile, blown glass, green	85.00
Banana, blown glass, yellow, 4½" l.	80.00
Banana, cotton batting	65.00
Bass fiddle, blown glass, 3½"	30.00
Bear, Dresden-type cardboard, silver	295.00
Bicycle & rider, Dresden-type cardboard, silver, Germany, late 19th c., 2 7/8" h. (minor damage)	495.00
Bird, blown glass, spun glass tail, spring clip	17.00 to 25.00
Boot w/stirrup, Dresden-type cardboard, riding boot w/embossed details, silver w/red silk lining, Germany, late 19th c., 4 1/8" h. (silk deteriorated)	220.00
Bull dog, blown glass, 3"	65.00
Bust of Al Jolson, blown glass, 4"	265.00
Bust of Indian, blown glass	120.00
Candy cane, blown glass	12.00
Carrot, cotton batting	7.00
Champagne carrier, Dresden-type cardboard, 2 silver baskets each holding a bottle, late 19th c., 3¾" h. (ILLUS.)	385.00

Cigar, blown glass, silver w/pink
  stripes, 6¾" l. 8.00
Clown w/mask face on horseback,
  cotton batting, crepe paper
  costume 225.00
Cockatoo, blown glass 20.00

Delivery Tricycle Christmas Ornament

Delivery tricycle, Dresden-type cardboard, silver tricycle w/painted
  driver, red chest mounted behind,
  late 19th c., 3¼" l., 2 5/8" h.
  (ILLUS.) 687.50
Dog, Greyhound, Dresden-type
  cardboard 295.00
Doll's head, blown glass, w/paper-
  weight eyes 75.00
Doll's head, Dresden-type
  cardboard 75.00
Eagle w/glass eyes, Dresden-type
  cardboard 265.00
Ear of corn, blown glass, pink
  w/frosted husks, 3¼" h. . . . 55.00 to 65.00
Elf on mushroom, blown glass,
  spring clip 35.00
Fish, blown glass, silver w/red &
  black, 3¼" l. 25.00
Foxy Grandpa, blown glass 250.00
Frog, Dresden-type cardboard,
  iridescent green w/gilt underside,
  Germany, late 19th c., 2" l. 412.50
Girl in red hood, blown glass,
  3" h. 50.00

Figural Christmas Tree Ornament

Gnome holding fabric money bag
  w/label "Dollar 5000," Dresden-
  type cardboard, late 19th c.,
  3¾" h. (ILLUS.) 330.00
Goldfish, blown glass, large 150.00
Grape cluster, silver, 4 3/8" l. 215.00
Grape cluster, blue, 6¼" l. 285.00
Horn, blown glass 11.50
House, blown glass 10.00
Knight's head, Dresden-type card-
  board, painted face in silver armor w/gilt visor, Germany, late
  19th c., 3" l. 522.50
Kugel (blown glass ball), amber
  glass w/mercury interior, Germa-
  ny, 4" d. 50.00

Blown Glass Christmas Tree Ornament

Owl, blown glass, 3" h. (ILLUS.) 12.00
Owl, blown glass, gold, red &
  white, spun glass tail, spring clip,
  7" h. 50.00
Parasol, blown glass 20.00
Parrot, blown glass 20.00

CIGAR & CIGARETTE CASES, HOLDERS & LIGHTERS

Russian Silver Cigarette Case

Also see ADVERTISING ITEMS.

Cigar case, silverplated brass,
  hinged 3-compartment case w/ap-

plied dragon on cover, reverse
w/butterfly & scrolling decor $90.00
Cigar holder, bakelite w/sterling silver, original case 25.00
Cigar holder, ivory, overall
carving........................ 27.00
Cigar holder, meerschaum, carved
scene of boy teasing girl, original
case, 6" l. 175.00
Cigar holder, meerschaum, carved
w/three dogs, original case 65.00
Cigar holder, meerschaum w/amber
stem, carved w/horse, original
case 85.00
Cigar lighter, butler's, sterling silver, tiny ball font, snuffer w/two-
prong frame on wooden handle,
marked "Whiting" 185.00
Cigar lighter, counter-type, "Hawk-
eye," pat. 1910, automatic 325.00
Cigar lighter, desk or table model,
sterling silver, ornate feet, bulbous body w/snuffer on chain,
wooden handle, Victorian,
4½" w., 3½" h................. 125.00
Cigar lighter, desk or table model,
model of a skull, 10" h.......... 225.00
Cigarette case, chrome, bust profile
portrait of Indian w/full
headdress 15.00
Cigarette case, chrome & black
enamel, Art Deco style design,
"Evans" 15.00
Cigarette case, niello silver, hinged
cover depicting a winter troika
scene within oval frame surrounded by scrolling foliage on stippled
ground, reverse w/similarly niel-
loed scrolls centering an applied
interlaced monogram, maker's
mark NB, Moscow, 1899-1908,
4" l. (ILLUS.) 308.00
Cigarette case, niello silver, hinged
cover w/checkerboard design centering crest, reverse w/checker-
board design centering floral
bouquet, gold-washed interior,
marker's mark K.P., Russian 475.00
Cigarette case, parcel gilt, oblong,
engine-turned case engraved
w/men in a wooded landscape
one side & a putto on reverse,
w/hinged match compartment,
maker's mark IH, St. Petersburg,
ca. 1850, 5½" l................. 264.00
Cigarette case, shagreen (sharkskin)
covered wood, silver hinges,
Austria....................... 175.00
Cigarette case, silver & enamel,
hinged cover enameled w/two
horses on cobalt blue ground..... 180.00
Cigarette case, sterling silver,
w/two gold-washed bands,
marked "Elgin," 4 x 3".......... 110.00

Cigarette case, sterling silver,
hinged cover chased w/an Art
Nouveau female mask & florals .. 155.00

Sterling Silver Cigarette Case

Cigarette case, sterling silver, overall reeding (ILLUS.) 55.00
Cigarette holder, bakelite w/silver
overlay....................9.00 to 15.00
Cigarette holder, ivory w/14k gold
trim.......................... 22.50
Cigarette holder, meerschaum,
carved w/horse 24.00
Cigarette holder, rhinestone-studded
black bakelite, gold band, eject-
ing mechanism, 6¼" l. 38.00
Cigarette holder, sterling silver,
"repousse" & chased decor,
6" l. 55.00
Cigarette lighter, table or desk
model, chrome, Art Deco style
model of an airplane 50.00
Cigarette lighter, table or desk
model, silverplate Queen Anne
patt., "Ronson" 15.00
Cigarette lighter, 14k gold set
w/diamonds & rubies, 1920's,
¾" w., 4 3/8" l. 495.00

CIGAR & TOBACCO CUTTERS

Cast Iron Tobacco Cutter

*Both counter-type and individual cigar and
plug tobacco cutters were in widespread use
last century and earlier in this century. Some*

counter types were made in combination with lighters and vending machines and were used to promote various tobacco packaging companies.

Counter-type, cast iron, advertising, "Brown & Williamson" $85.00

Counter-type, cast iron, advertising, "Charles Denby Cigars," ornate base w/etched glass top 120.00

Counter-type, cast iron, advertising, "Five Bros. Tobacco Works, John Finzer & Bros., Louisville, Ky.," ornate & w/original painted pin-striping 95.00

Counter-type, cast iron, advertising, mechanical, "Hyneman Bros. Cigars, Boston," walnut box below 225.00

Counter-type, cast iron, advertising, "King Alfred 10c Cigar," Waterbury clock on top, ornate, 1901 ... 575.00

Counter-type, cast iron, advertising, "Lorillard's Tin Tag," 1875 patent 48.00

Counter-type, cast iron, advertising, "Spearhead Brand Tobacco, P. J. Sorg & Co." ....115.00 to 135.00

Counter-type, cast iron, embossed "Griswold" ....80.00 to 100.00

Counter-type, cast iron, figural imp thumbing his nose, "Pat. Appl. For" (ILLUS.) ....85.00 to 100.00

Counter-type, cast iron, ornate side plates, "Johnson Co., Quincy, Illinois," 1914 .... 55.00

Counter-type, nickel-plated brass, "Cinco," wind-up, 6½" l. 190.00

Desk model, bronze, model of owl .. 195.00

Desk model, nickel-plated brass w/wooden grips, model of a pistol, cock & fire to cut cigar, break barrel for matches 165.00

Pocket-type, advertising, "Swift's Cleanser," metal 45.00

Pocket-type, 14k gold, dragons decor 95.00

Pocket-type, gold, Birmingham, England hallmark for 1898, blade marked "Sheffield" 95.00

Pocket-type, metal, gentleman's boot, 1870's, 2 x 1½" 164.00

Pocket-type, mother-of-pearl & brass, scissors-type 30.00

Pocket-type, sterling silver, w/tamper & opener, embossed & chased w/grotesque face, florals & scrolling devices, 2¾" l. 55.00

Pocket-type, sterling silver, "repousse" florals, scissors-type .. 40.00

Pocket-type, sterling silver, fob-type 30.00

CLOCKS

Carriage Clock

Also see ADVERTISING ITEMS, ART DECO, AUTOMOBILE ACCESSORIES, CHARACTER COLLECTIBLES, COCA-COLA, CUT GLASS, DISNEY COLLECTIBLES, FABERGE, KEWPIE ITEMS and WORLD FAIR COLLECTIBLES.

Animated, Lux Clock Co., Waterbury, Connecticut, black "Shoeshine Boy" $300.00

Animated, Lux Clock Co., Waterbury, Connecticut, "Windmill" 65.00

Animated electric, United Electric Co., Brooklyn, New York, "F.D.R. - Man of the Hour," 30-hour time & strike movement, white metal figure of F.D. Roosevelt at ship's wheel 80.00

Banjo, Chelsea Clock Co., Chelsea, Massachusetts, drum clock w/white porcelain dial, "eglomise" panel in throat & "eglomise" scene of Perry's Lake Erie Victory in lower door, 31" h. 575.00

Banjo, Simon Willard, Boston, Massachusetts, drum clock w/white-painted dial surmounted by brass ball & eagle finial, cross-banded mahogany case w/"eglomise" panel in throat depicting acanthus leaves flanked by brass fillets & "eglomise" panel in lower door inscribed "A. Willard's Patent," ca. 1810, 34" h. (throat panel restored) 7,150.00

Banjo, attributed to Munro, Concord, Massachusetts, drum clock w/white-painted dial surmounted by brass ball & eagle finial, gilt-wood case w/"eglomise" panel in throat flanked by brass fillets & "eglomise" panel in lower door

depicting a bucolic scene, ca.
1820, 35" h. (throat panel
restored) 1,650.00
Carriage, Waterbury Clock Co.,
Waterbury, Connecticut, 2½" d.
white porcelain dial, brass case
w/beveled glass sides, dated
"Jan. 29, 1901" on door, miniature
size 295.00
Carriage, retailed by Bailey & Co.,
Philadelphia, lever-set time &
strike movement w/alarm, white
enamel dial, engraved brass case
w/beveled glass sides, ca. 1870,
5 3/8" h. (ILLUS.) 605.00
Carriage, Waterbury Clock Co.,
Waterbury, Connecticut, 24-hour
movement w/alarm, nickel-plated
brass case w/beveled glass
sides........................... 195.00
China case, Ansonia Clock Co., Ansonia, Connecticut, time & strike
movement, Royal Bonn china case
w/multicolored florals on white
ground, boudoir size 385.00

Double Dial Calendar Clock

Double dial calendar, Ithaca Calendar Clock Co., Ithaca, New York,
Model No. 4 variant, 30-day time,
strike & calendar movement,
manufactured by E.N. Welch Clock
Co., restored 12" dial, ca. 1866,
29" h. (ILLUS.) 715.00
Double dial calendar, Seth Thomas,
Thomaston, Connecticut, Parlor
Model Calendar No. 8, 8-day
time, strike & calendar movement, 8½" d. dials, walnut case,
27" h. ....795.00 to 875.00
Double dial calendar, Waterbury
Clock Co., Waterbury, Connecticut, 8-day time, strike & calendar movment, oak die-stamped

Eastlake design case, ca. 1890,
29" h. 650.00
Double dial calendar, Seth Thomas,
Thomaston, Connecticut, Office
Model No. 5, double dials w/pat-
ent date of 1876 on lower dial,
8-day time, strike & calendar
movement, oak case, 50" h. 3,900.00
Grandfather, Abel Hutchins, Concord, New Hampshire, white-
painted dial w/"Rocking Ship,"
minute & date registers & inscribed w/maker's name, mahogany hooded case w/pierced
crest centering 3 brass finials &
w/fluted quarter columns flanking
the upper door, waist w/paneled
door flanked by conforming
columns w/brass capitals, line-
inlaid base w/inlaid oval reserve,
bracket feet, 20" w., 92" h.
(restoration to feet & crest).....4,775.00
Grandfather, unknown maker, white-
painted dial w/minute & date
registers, cherrywood hooded
Federal-style case w/arched
crest centering 3 brass ball &
steeple finials & w/colonettes
flanking the upper door, waist
w/inlaid molded door flanked by
brass-fitted quarter columns, line-
inlaid molded base, bracket feet,
Connecticut, ca. 1800, 92" h.
(restoration to crest) 5,775.00
Grandfather, David Williams, Newport, Rhode Island, white-painted
dial inscribed w/maker's name,
minute & date registers, mahogany hooded case w/pierce-carved
cresting centering 3 brass urn &
acanthus finials & w/arched upper
door flanked by brass stop-fluted
columns, waist w/line-inlaid cockbeaded door flanked by conforming columns, line-inlaid base, ogee
bracket feet, 17¾" w., 94" h.
(minor restoration to one
foot) 9,625.00
Grandfather, David Rittenhouse,
Philadelphia, brass dial w/minute
& date registers surmounted by
medallion inscribed w/maker's
name, walnut Chippendale-style
hooded case w/arched upper door
flanked by columns, waist
w/molded & arched door, molded
base, ogee bracket feet, ca. 1780,
17½" w., 94" h. 10,450.00
Grandfather, John Rogers, Newton,
Massachusetts, engraved brass
dial w/maker's name, minute &
date registers, mahogany hooded
case w/pierce-carved cresting
centering 3 brass finials &

w/fluted quarter columns flanking
upper door, waist w/molded &
arched door, molded base, stepped plinth base, ca. 1770,
17" w., 95" h. 6,600.00

Grandfather, unknown maker,
white-painted dial w/floral spandrels, phases of the moon, minute
& date registers, inlaid mahogany
hooded case w/pierced & shaped
crest centering 3 brass finials,
waist w/inlaid door flanked by
fluted quarter columns w/brass
capitals, inlaid base, bracket feet,
New England, ca. 1805, 17¾" w.,
97" h. (some restorations) 5,775.00

Grandfather, John Ferguson,
Philadelphia, engraved brass dial
w/date registers & phases of the
moon signed by maker, walnut
Chippendale-style hooded case
w/swan's neck cresting ending in
carved rosettes & centering 3 urn
on pedestal finials, arched upper
door flanked by fluted quarter
columns, waist w/hinged door
flanked by fluted quarter columns,
base w/shaped panel flanked by
conforming columns, ogee bracket
feet, Philadelphia, ca. 1770,
17½" w., 101½" h. 13,200.00

Kitchen, Gilbert Clock Co., Bristol,
Connecticut, 8-day time & strike
movement, gingerbread-carved
golden oak case 150.00

Kitchen, Ingraham Clock Co., Bristol,
Connecticut, 8-day time & strike
movement, gingerbread-carved
oak case 125.00

Kitchen, Seth Thomas, Thomaston,
Connecticut, Dover model, 8-day
time & strike movement w/alarm,
walnut case 255.00

Kitchen, E.N. Welch Mfg. Co.,
Bristol, Connecticut, time & strike
movement, pendulum w/"Welch"
logo, gingerbread-carved walnut
case . . . . .135.00 to 195.00

Schoolhouse, Waterbury Clock Co.,
Waterbury, Connecticut, round-
top, mahogany case w/cross-
banded inlay & scrolling sides,
short drop, ca. 1900, 28" 200.00

Shelf, or mantel, Case-on-Case,
Daniel Hubbard, Medfield, Massachusetts, white & gold-painted
dial, mahogany & "eglomise"
Federal-style case w/shaped
cresting in upper case centering
urn-and-foliate brass finial over
upper door w/"eglomise" panel
centering dial above panel bearing maker's name, lyre & foliate
motifs; lower case w/"eglomise"

Federal "Case-on-Case" Clock

door centering mill & waterfall
scene within foliate motif border,
molded base, brass ball feet,
ca. 1820, 36" h. (ILLUS.) 41,800.00

Shelf, or mantel, Pillar-and-Scroll
case, Eli Terry, Plymouth, Connecticut, white-painted dial
w/reverse-painted spandrels in
upper part of door & oval reverse-
painted landscape in lower door,
mahogany case w/scrolling crest
centering 3 brass urn finials,
w/original weights, pendulum &
original label "Made & Sold by Eli
& Samuel Terry," 31" h. 2,800.00

Shelf, or mantel, Steeple case,
Waterbury Clock Co., Waterbury,
Connecticut, 30-hour time & strike
movement, rosewood veneer
"Gothic" model case, ca. 1895,
15" h. 165.00

Shelf, or mantel, Steeple case,
Waterbury Clock Co., Waterbury,
Connecticut, 30-hour time, strike
& alarm movement, mahogany
veneer "Gothic" model case
w/reverse transfer of American
Eagle in lower door, ca. 1895,
19¾" h. (some damage to veneer
of case) 125.00

Shelf, or mantel, Triple Decker case,
E.W. Adams, Seneca Falls, New
York, brass 8-day movement,
painted wooden dial, mahogany
veneer case w/molded cornice
above "eglomise" panels w/eagle
& doors w/gilt cornucopiae of
colorful flowers on blue ground
center door & w/red drapery
swags in lower door, all flanked
by turned columns, C-scroll feet,
40" h. (some veneer damage & no
weights) 610.00

Shelf, or mantel, Birge & Fuller,
Bristol, Connecticut, 8-day time &
strike movement, mahogany
veneer ogee-molded case,
33" h. 295.00

Shelf, or mantel, New Haven Clock
Co., New Haven, Connecticut,
8-day time & strike movement,
cast iron case w/marbleized & gilt
trim........................... 175.00

New Haven Mantel Clock

Shelf, or mantel, New Haven Clock
Co., New Haven, Connecticut,
time & strike movment w/open
escapement, brass & J. & G. Low
Art Tile pottery case (ILLUS.) 495.00

Shelf, or mantel, E.N. Welch
Manufacturing Co., Bristol, Connecticut, 30-hour brass movement,
white-painted metal dial, mahogany ogee-molded case w/reverse-
painted tablet in lower door,
ca. 1865, 15¼" w., 25¼" h. 185.00

Cast Iron Clock with Washington

Shelf, or mantel, unknown American
maker, 30-hour time & strike
movement, white-painted dial,
cast iron gilt & polychrome-
decorated case w/portrait of
George Washington & scene of
Mount Vernon, late 19th c., 16" h.
(ILLUS.)......................... 275.00

Ship's, Chelsea Clock Co., Chelsea,
Massachusetts, bronze case,
w/ship's bell.................... 650.00

Civil War Soldier Clock

Statue, carved & giltwood case incorporating figure of Confederate
soldier holding large circular clock
embellished w/oak leaves &
acorns in one hand & grasping
hammer which strikes large bell-
metal bell suspended from American eagle's beak, oval vase,
1850-75, 18¾" h. (ILLUS.)........1,980.00

"Swinging doll" model, Ansonia
Clock Co., Ansonia, Connecticut,
white enameled dial w/Roman
numerals & brass circular case
w/ornate shell crest supported on
brass rod cylinder continuing to
spreading foot & hung w/bisque
child seated in brass wire swing,
ca. 1890, 12" h. ....660.00 to 925.00

Wag-on-Wall, white-painted wooden
dial w/colorful free-hand floral
spandrels, now w/modern brass
works, 12" h. (old works still in
back of case) 200.00

Wall regulator, Gilbert Clock Co.,
Winsted, Connecticut, Model
No. 3, rosewood case w/brass
trim, ca. 1870, 50" h. 1,400.00

Wall regulator, Sessions Clock Co.,
Bristol, Connecticut, 1882 Eclipse
model, die-stamped pattern oak
case 600.00

Wall regulator, Seth Thomas, Thomaston, Connecticut, Office Model No. 2, 8-day time & strike movement, 12" dial, walnut case, overall 26" h. . . . . .875.00 to 925.00

Wall regulator, Seth Thomas, Thomaston, Connecticut, Office Model No. 3, 8-day time & strike movement, walnut case. 325.00

Wall regulator w/calendar, Seth Thomas, Thomaston, Connecticut, Office Model No. 6, 8-day time, strike & calendar movement, 12" dial, walnut case 975.00

Wall regulator, Waltham Clock Co., Waltham, Massachusetts, weight-driven movement, wooden-framed dial, oak case w/trefoil-shaped crest above glazed door & molded pediment, early 20th c., 14¼" w., 40" h. 577.50

Wall regulator, E.N. Welch Mfg. Co., Bristol, Connecticut, Sembrich model, 8-day time & strike movement, walnut case 625.00

CLOISONNE

17th Century Hot Water Bowl

Cloisonne work features enameled designs on a metal ground. There are several types of this work, the best-known utilizing cells of wire on the body of the object into which the enamel is placed. In the plique-a-jour form of cloisonne, the base is removed leaving translucent enamel windows. "Pigeon Blood" cloisonne is a pseudo-cloisonne with foil enclosed within clear glass walls. Cloisonne is said to have been invented by the Chinese and brought to perfection by the Japanese. Also see BUCKLES.

Bowl, pastel cherry blossoms & peaches on turquoise blue ground, 9" d. $250.00

Box, cov., orange florals & pale blue stippled panel on lid, white florals on cobalt blue ground around sides, Japan, early 20th c., 2½ x 2", 1" h. 100.00

Censers, duck-form, each standing

on a lotus pad base decorated in bright blue w/yellow, red & turquoise blue detailing, removable wings pierced on top, Ching Dynasty, 1736-95, 4 3/8", pr. 1,430.00

Flask, "Moonflask," colorful florettes borne on scrolling wire vines all on a black ground between lotus petals, neck & foot w/similar motifs on turquoise blue ground, set w/bossed ruyi-form handles, 18th c., 12¾" h. 17,600.00

Ginger jar, cov., dark blue florals & vines on white ground, Chinese, 6¾" h. 225.00

Hot water bowl, interior & exterior decorated w/an overall pattern of scrolling flowering lotus centered on yellow crossed vajras below a band of red lappets on a deep turquoise blue ground, base w/a white flower surrounding the plug, Ming Dynasty, 17th c., 16" d. (ILLUS.) 880.00

Humidor & cover w/brass Foo dog finial, blue border at top & base, multicolored peonies & chrysanthemums w/two-tone green leaves & double T fret decor on brick red ground, teakwood stand, unmarked, 5 5/8" d., 8" h. 270.00

Cloisonne Incense Burner

Incense burner, lobed form supported on 3 short cylindrical legs, gilt rim set w/curving pierced handles, decorated overall w/three large blue taotie masks each suspending a stiff leaf, reserved on a pale turquoise blue floral cell pattern ground, Ching Dynasty, 1736-95, 7¾" h. (ILLUS.) 1,650.00

Jar, cov., 3-footed, multicolored florals & butterflies on black ground enhanced w/goldstone, Japan, ca. 1890, 4" h. 225.00

Models of mountain goats, each
standing w/head turned slightly to
the side, body w/overall stylized
bird motifs on a turquoise blue
ground, hinged back apparatus,
curled horns & hoofs gilded,
carved wood stands, 19½" h.,
pr. 9,075.00
Plate, colorful border, white cranes,
peonies & foliage w/scenic terrain
on marine blue ground, Japanese,
9¾" d. 295.00
Plique-a-jour bowl, seaweed &
colorful goldfish swimming
against soft green ground, 5" d. . . 695.00
Salt dip, footed, orange florals,
green foliage & scrolling gold decor, Japanese, 2 1/8" d., 1" h. . . . 65.00
Teapot, cov., coiling dragon on
green ground, 4" h. 295.00
Vase, delicate naturalistic spray of
flowers in pastel tones on robin's
egg blue ground, w/foil inclu-
sions, silver rim, 3¾" h. 400.00
Vase, Art Nouveau style, pink &
white flowers w/green & grey
foliage against black ground enhanced w/goldstone, silver mount-
ings, Japanese, 4" d., 7½" h. 2,200.00
Vase, bird perched on a branch
amidst pink & white cherry blossoms & green foliage on shaded
pink ground, Japanese, 7½" w.,
18½" h. 1,650.00

COCA-COLA ITEMS

Wall-type Bottle Opener

*Coca-Cola promotion has been achieved
through the issuance of scores of small objects through the years. These, together with
trays, signs, and other articles bearing the
name of this soft drink, are now sought by
many collectors. Also see BOTTLES.*

Bank, tin, model of cooler,
ca. 1948 . . . . $60.00
Baseball scorekeeper, "Perpetual
Counter," 1906 . . . . 95.00

Billfold, black leather w/embossed
Coca-Cola bottle, 1915 . . . . 35.00
Bingo card, 1930 . . . . 15.00
Blotter, 1916, bottles on marble-top
counter . . . . .14.00 to 20.00
Blotter, 1947, couple skiing 5.00
Blotter, 1953 . . . . 3.00
Blotter, 1957 . . . . 5.00
Book, "Romance of Coca-Cola,"
1916 . . . . 25.00
Book, "When You Entertain," by Ida
B. Allen, 1932, 124 pp. 16.50
Bookcover, 1925. . . . . 35.00
Bookmark, Lillian Nordica, 1903,
2 x 6" 235.00
Bottle opener, wall-type, cast iron,
"Star X," 1925, w/box (ILLUS.) 20.00
Bottle opener, wall-type, "Sprite
Boy" 23.00
Calendar, 1914, Betty, framed 475.00
Calendar, 1929, w/full pad 265.00
Calendar, 1935, boy & dog fishing
from stump, Norman Rockwell
illustration 175.00
Calendar, 1940. . . . . 125.00
Calendar, 1943, w/pads. 45.00
Calendar, 1948. . . . . 45.00
Calendar, 1959, "American Birds,"
6 x 7" 5.00
Cigar band labels, bottle on one &
glass on other, pr. 175.00
Cigarette box, 1936, 50th Anniver-
sary, frosted glass, oblong 210.00
Cigarette lighter, figural plastic
bottle, 1954. 18.00

Coca-Cola Clock

Clock, wall regulator, Gilbert Clock
Co., walnut case, dial inscribed
"Drink Coca-Cola" & "in bottles -
5c" on door tablet, late 19th c.,
30" h. (ILLUS.) 1,000.00
Counter display bottle, Dec. 25,
1923, blue tint, 20" h. 200.00
Counter display jar, clear glass,

front embossed "Coca-Cola Pepsin Gum," reverse embossed "Manufactured by Franklin Mfg. Co., Richmond, Va.," 1908 ...... 325.00

Fan, cardboard, Sprite Boy pictured 18.00

Fan, woven reed & paper, glass pictured & "5c everywhere," 1911 ... 50.00

Game, cribbage board, wooden, w/pegs, 1930's ....38.00 to 50.00

Game, "Dominoes," in original box, 1940's 27.00

Knife, pocket-type, "Coca-Cola 5c" .. 35.00

Match strike plate, porcelain square, "Drink Coca-Cola" over "Strike Matches Here" lower rough surface, pierced to hang, 4½" sq. 85.00

Menu sign, wooden, "Drink Coca-Cola," w/slots for paper strips w/various menus, 1930's, 24¾ x 13½" 95.00

Mirror, pocket-type, 1909, girl at table w/glass of Coca-Cola, "J.B. Carrol Chicago" etc. on rim, oval 240.00

Mirror, pocket-type, 1911, Coca-Cola Girl, "The Whitehead-Hoag Co." etc. on rim, oval 150.00

Mirror, pocket-type, 1916, Garden Girl, "Whitehead & Hoag Co." etc. on rim, oval 195.00

Mirror, pocket-type, 1917, Elaine, 2¾ x 1¾" oval 155.00

Nature Study Cards, "Wild Flowers of America" series, artist-signed, 8 x 2", set of 20 .... 15.00

Neckerchief, Kit Carson, printed cotton, red, white & black, 1950 ....18.00 to 30.00

Note pad, celluloid cover, Hilda Clark at table front, 1902, 5 x 2½" 450.00

Olympic record indicator, "1932 Los Angeles Xth Olympiad," black, red & white on green 97.50

Paperweight, bottle cap in glass, 1960's, 3" d. 22.50

Paperweight, red "controlled bubble" glass lettered "Coke is Coca-Cola" in white, 1950's, 3½" d. 75.00

Pencil box, red leatherette cover w/"Coca-Cola Delicious...Refreshing" in gilt, ca. 1930 .... 40.00

Pencil sharpener, cast iron, figural miniature bottle, ca. 1935 .... 20.00

Perfume bottle w/stopper, miniature ice green glass bottle replica, 1930's 35.00

Ping pong paddles, 1940-50, pr., in original box 70.00

Plate, china, Coca-Cola bottle & glass center, red & yellow lettering "Refresh Yourself - Drink

Coca-Cola" on rim, Knowles China Co., 1930's, 7¼" d. 125.00

Playing cards, 1939, girl holding bottle & glass 25.00

Playing cards, 1951, Cowgirl bust portrait 40.00

Playing cards, 1956, Ice Skating Girl 30.00

Poster, cardboard, girl in colorful clown suit, 1947, 36 x 20" 50.00

Poster, cardboard, colorful scene of bottle of Coca-Cola floating in Arctic waters, 1944, framed 150.00

Poster, cardboard, multicolored ballerina, clown, boy & dog, artwork by Haddon Sundblom, large 650.00

Poster, paper, "Get This Kit Carson Kerchief," 1950's 25.00

Pretzel bowl, aluminum, 3 bottle-shaped legs, 1936, 8¼" d. 65.00

Radio, model of a cooler, red Bakelite case, 1949-53 ....265.00 to 350.00

Ruler, wooden, "Delicious" & "Refreshing," 7" l. 10.00

Sign, graniteware, "Drink Coca-Cola," convex, red, 24" d. 60.00

Sign, tin, "Ice Cold Coca-Cola Sold Here," 5-color, self-framed, 1930's, 19½" d. 265.00

Sign, double-sided sidewalk-type, tin in metal frame, 1930's, 20½" w., 33½" h. 175.00

Soda fountain glass, "Coca-Cola" in white on clear, semi-flared, 1920's ....40.00 to 50.00

Soda fountain glass, "Coca-Cola" in white on clear, shaped top, 1935 .... 35.00

String holder, tin, "Drink Coca-Cola in Bottles," red, yellow & white, 1930's, 16" h. 350.00

Study cards, "America's Fighting Planes in Action" (World War II series), 1943, set of 20 ....30.00 to 48.00

Coca-Cola Thermometer

Thermometer, plastic, red & white, 1970's, 18" d. (ILLUS.) 80.00

Thermometer, tin, bullet-shaped,

w/silhouette portrait of girl drinking from bottle at bottom, 1939, 6½" w., 16" h. 65.00

Thermometer, tin, twin bottles, 1941-42, 7" w., 16" h. . . . . .50.00 to 65.00

Thermometer, tin, bottle-shaped, "Trade Mark Registered Bottle Pat'd Dec. 25, 1923" on bottle, 1930's, 17" h. 80.00

Toy, cardboard cut-outs of athletes, "Olympic Games of 1932," uncut. . 45.00

Toy truck, battery-operated, 1950's, original box, 14" l. 75.00

Toy truck, w/six original glass bottles, Metalcraft, 1930 . . . . 290.00

Tray, glass change receiver, 1901, Hilda Clark, 8¼" d. 1,500.00

Tray, change, 1906, "Relieves Fatique," 6¼ x 4½" oval . . . . .300.00 to 325.00

Tray, change, 1909, Beautiful Girl at table w/glass of Coca-Cola (once called St. Louis World Fair Girl), 6 x 4¼" oval 175.00

Tray, change, 1914, Betty, 6 x 4¼" oval . . . . .75.00 to 90.00

Tray, change, 1917, Elaine, 6 x 4¼" oval 85.00

Tray, change, 1920, Garden Girl, 6 x 4¼" oval 175.00

Tray, 1904, Hilda Clark, 9¾" d. 1,200.00

Tray, 1906, "Relieves Fatique - 5c," medium oval, 13 x 10½" 700.00

Tray, 1914, Betty, 13¼ x 10½" oblong 195.00

Tray, 1914, Betty, 15¼ x 12½" oval 245.00

Tray, 1917, Elaine, 19 x 8½" oblong 210.00

Garden Girl Tray

Tray, 1920, Garden Girl, 13¼ x 10½" oblong (ILLUS.) 400.00

Tray, 1923, Flapper Girl, 13¼ x 10½" oblong. 165.00

Tray, 1925, Girl at Party, 13¼ x 10½" oblong. 160.00

Tray, 1926, Sports Couple, 13¼ x 10½" oblong. 180.00

Tray, 1927, Curb Service, 13¼ x 10½" oblong. 190.00

Tray, 1927, Soda Fountain Clerk, 13¼ x 10½" oblong 140.00

Tray, 1928, Girl with Bobbed Hair, 13¼ x 10½" oblong . . . . .120.00 to 170.00

Tray, 1929, Girl in Swimsuit holding Bottle, 13¼ x 10½" oblong . . . . .135.00 to 200.00

Tray, 1930, Bathing Beauty in Swim Cap, 13¼ x 10½" oblong . . . . .130.00 to 145.00

Tray, 1930, Girl with Telephone, 13¼ x 10½" oblong . . . . . .95.00 to 120.00

Tray, 1931, Farm Boy with Dog (by Norman Rockwell), 13¼ x 10½" oblong 300.00

Tray, 1932, Girl in Yellow Swimsuit, 13¼ x 10½" oblong 275.00

Tray, 1933, Francis Dee, 13¼ x 10½" oblong. 95.00

Tray, 1934, Johnny Weismuller & Maureen O'Sullivan (Tarzan & Jane), 13¼ x 10½" oblong 300.00

Tray, 1935, Madge Evans, 13¼ x 10½" oblong . . . . .75.00 to 135.00

Tray, 1936, Hostess, 13¼ x 10½" oblong 70.00

Tray, 1937, Running Girl, 13¼ x 10½" oblong . . . . .65.00 to 110.00

Tray, 1938, Girl in the Afternoon, 13¼ x 10½" oblong . . . . . . .45.00 to 55.00

Tray, 1939, Springboard Girl, artwork by Haddon Sundblom, 13¼ x 10½" oblong 62.50

Tray, 1940, Sailor Girl, 13¼ x 10½" oblong . . . . .45.00 to 65.00

Tray, 1941, Girl Ice Skater, 13¼ x 10½" oblong. 55.00

Tray, 1942, Two Girls at Car, 13¼ x 10½" oblong. 70.00

Tray, 1948, Girl with Wind in Her Hair, 13¼ x 10½" oblong 45.00

Tray, 1950, Girl with Menu, 13¼ x 10½" oblong . . . . .22.00 to 35.00

Tray, 1961 TV Thanksgiving Scene, 18¾ x 13½". 25.00

Vending machine, Vendo model 33 . . . . 350.00

Vendor's bottle holder, 1940's 125.00

War ration token holder, 1940's 95.00

COFFEE GRINDERS

Most coffee grinders collected are lap or table and wall types used in many homes in the late 19th and early 20th centuries. However, large store-sized grinders have recently been traded.

Tin Coffee Grinder

Lap-type, maple base w/machine dovetailing & drawer, cast iron hopper & handle, "Adams" $110.00

Lap-type, maple base w/machine dovetailing & drawer, pewter hopper, cast iron crank handle 125.00

Lap-type, oak base w/machine dovetailing & drawer, cast iron hopper & handle, "Logan Strobridge" 70.00

Lap-type, tin base w/drawer, cast iron handle w/wooden knob, "Universal No. 109" by Landers, Frary & Clark, w/patent date of 1909 (ILLUS.) 70.00

Lap-type, wooden base w/machine dovetailing & drawer, tin hopper, cast iron handle w/wooden knob 65.00

"Enterprise No. 7"

Store counter model, 2-wheel, cast iron, "Enterprise No. 7," original paint, 17" d. wheels, 21½" h. (ILLUS.) 325.00

Store counter model, 2-wheel, cast iron, "Enterprise No. 9," original paint, w/patent date of 1873, 20" d. wheels, 24" h. 650.00

Store counter model, 2-wheel, cast iron "National Specialty No. 5," original paint & decals, 12½" d. wheels, 18" h. 475.00

Store floor model, 2-wheel, cast iron, "Crescent, Rutland, Vermont," 31" d. wheels, 60" h. 1,200.00

Table model, advertising, "Grand Union Tea Co.," cast iron 225.00

Table model, clamp-on type, cast iron, "Enterprise No. 0," 11½" h. 38.00

Wall-type, brass, "Arcade" 100.00

Wall-type, cast iron, "Adams," mounted on wooden board 40.00

Wall-type, cast iron, "Brighton," mounted on wooden board 65.00

Wall-type, cast iron, "Arcade," w/clear glass jar marked "Crystal," ca. 1910 . . . . 75.00

Wall-type, cast iron w/glass jar, "Arcade No. 3" 85.00

Wall-type, cast iron & wood, "Telephone Mill, Arcade Mfg. Co.," w/1893 patent date, 6½" w., 13" h. 335.00

Wall-type, tin, "Regal," mounted on wooden board 48.00

COMIC BOOKS

Donald Duck Comic Book

Comic books, especially first, or early issues of a series, are avidly collected today. Prices for some of the scarce ones have reached extremely high levels. Prices listed below are for copies in fine to mint condition.

Adventure Comics, No. 103, 1946 . . .	$165.00
All Star, No. 33, 1947	450.00
Annie Oakley & Tagg, Dell No. 4 . . .	9.00
Bambi, No. 2, 1942	40.00
Batman, No. 23, 1944	65.00
Batman, No. 54, 1949	21.00
Big Shot, No. 47, 1944	12.00
Black Arrow (The), Classic Comics No. 1, 1946	40.00
Blackhawk, No. 14	15.00
Brave & the Bold (The), No. 34	22.00
Bringing Up Father, No. 5, 1921	14.00
Buck Jones, Dell No. 460	4.00
Buck Rogers, Famous Funnies No. 2	25.00
Captain Marvel, No. 53, 1946	9.00
Captain Video, No. 1, 1951	30.00
Crime Suspenstories, No. 16, 1953 . .	85.00
Dick Tracy Gets His Man, No. 4, 1938	35.00
Dime Comics, No. 1, 1945	60.00
Donald Duck, first edition, 1935	165.00
Donald Duck in Christmas on Bear Mountain, No. 178	60.00
Donald Duck in No Such Varmit, No. 318 (ILLUS.)	30.00
Famous Funnies, No. 17, 1935	35.00
Flash Comics, No. 10, 1940	100.00
Gene Autry, No. 47, 1944	25.00
Green Lantern, No. 2, 1960	50.00
Green Lantern, No. 4, 1961	30.00
Gumps (The), No. 4	15.00
Hot Dog, No. 1, 1954	8.00
I Love Lucy, Vol. 1, No. 2	5.00
Is This Tomorrow?, 1947	120.00
Joe Palooka, S & K No. 5	30.00
Joe Palooka, S & K No. 10	10.00
Lancer, No. 3, 1969	2.25
Lassie, Dell No. 20, 1955	4.00
Lone Ranger (The), Vol. 1, No. 57 . .	7.50
Looney Tunes, Dell No. 149	35.00
Mad Magazine, No. 25	10.00
Man fron U.N.C.L.E. (The), No. 20 . .	1.50
Marvel Family, No. 8	5.00
Our Gang, No. 14, 1944	20.00
Panic, No. 10	12.50
Pogo Parade, No. 1, 1953	30.00
Popeye, No. 25, 1939	40.00
Popeye & Wimpy, No. 17, 1940	40.00
Popular Comics, No. 132	6.50
Raggedy Ann and Andy, Dell No. 1, 1946	25.00
Red Ryder, Dell No. 14, 1943	20.00
Red Ryder, Dell No. 118, 1953	4.00
Rin Tin Tin, Dell No. 3, 1955	4.00
Roy Rogers & Trigger, Dell No. 3, 1952	4.00
Sergeant Preston, Dell No. 8, 1953 . .	4.00
Skippy's Own Book of Comics, 1934	175.00
Superman, No. 18, 1942	75.00
Superman, No. 57, 1949	17.00
Supermouse, No. 36	10.00
Tally-Ho, 1944	30.00

Tom Mix, No. 50	6.00
Uncle Scrooge in Only a Poor Old Man, No. 386	100.00
Uncle Tom's Cabin, Classics Illustrated No. 15, 1965	5.00
Wagon Train, Dell No. 6, 1960	4.00
Walt Disney's Comics & Stories, Vol. 2, No. 12, 1942	65.00
Whiz, No. 38, 1942	28.00

COMMEMORATIVE PLATES

Limited edition commemorative and collector plates rank high on the list of collectible items. The oldest and best-known of these plates, those of Bing & Grondahl and Royal Copenhagen, retain leadership in the field, but other companies are turning out a variety of designs, some of which have been widely embraced by the growing numbers who have made plate collecting a hobby. Plates listed below are a representative selection of the fine porcelain and glass plates available to collectors.

BAREUTHER

Bareuther 1970 Father's Day

1967 Christmas, Stiftskirche	$144.00
1968 Christmas, Kappelkirche	52.00
1969 Christmas, Christkindlesmarkt	35.00
1970 Christmas, Chapel in Oberndorf	26.00
1971 Christmas, Toys for Sale	42.00
1972 Christmas, Christmas in Munich	47.00
1973 Christmas, Sleigh Ride	31.00
1974 Christmas, Black Forest Church	45.00
1975 Christmas, Snowman	36.50

1976 Christmas, Chapel in the
Hills 25.00
1977 Christmas, Story Time......... 33.50
1978 Christmas, Mittenwald 29.00
1979 Christmas, Winter Day 21.00
1980 Christmas, Mittenberg 24.00
1981 Christmas, Walk in the
Forest........................... 22.00
1982 Christmas, Bad Wimpfen 23.00
1983 Christmas, The Night Before
Christmas 22.50
1984 Christmas, Zeil on the River
Man 22.50
1969 Father's Day, Castle
Neuschwanstein................. 36.50
1970 Father's Day, Castle Pfalz
(ILLUS.)........................ 16.00
1971 Father's Day, Castle
Heidelberg 21.00
1972 Father's Day, Castle
Hohenschwangau 25.00
1973 Father's Day, Castle Katz...... 27.00
1974 Father's Day, Castle
Wurzburg....................... 23.00
1975 Father's Day, Castle
Lichtenstein.................... 25.50
1976 Father's Day, Castle
Hohenzollern 22.00
1977 Father's Day, Castle Eltz 22.00
1978 Father's Day, Castle
Falkenstein..................... 24.50
1979 Father's Day, Castle
Rheinstein 24.00
1980 Father's Day, Castle Cochum .. 24.00
1981 Father's Day, Castle
Gutenfels 24.00
1982 Father's Day, Castle
Zwingenberg 23.50
1983 Father's Day, Castle
Lauenstein..................... 23.50
1984 Father's Day 20.00
1969 Mother's Day, Dancing 29.00
1970 Mother's Day, Mother &
Children........................ 19.50
1971 Mother's Day, Doing the
Laundry 21.50
1972 Mother's Day, Baby's First
Step 22.50
1973 Mother's Day, Mother Kissing
Baby........................... 20.00
1974 Mother's Day, Musical
Children....................... 20.00
1975 Mother's Day, Spring Outing... 23.00
1976 Mother's Day................. 19.00
1977 Mother's Day................. 19.00
1978 Mother's Day................. 18.50
1979 Mother's Day................. 18.50
1980 Mother's Day................. 19.50
1981 Mother's Day................. 19.00
1982 Mother's Day................. 20.00
1983 Mother's Day................. 18.50

BING & GRONDAHL
1895 Christmas (ILLUS.)............2,300.00

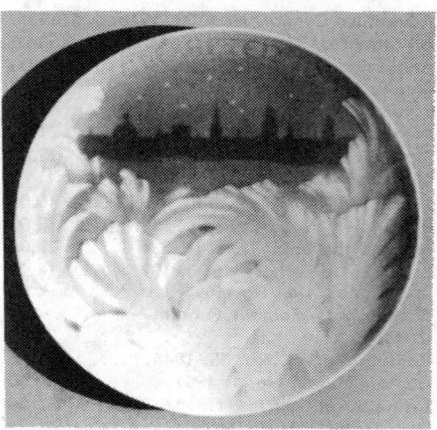

Bing & Grondahl First Issue

Year	Price
1896	1,045.00
1897	620.00
1898	365.00
1899	815.00
1900	565.00
1901	205.00
1902	175.00
1903	155.00
1904	71.00
1905	68.50
1906	40.00
1907	52.50
1908	30.00
1909	35.00
1910	35.00
1911	30.00
1912	30.00
1913	31.00
1914	28.00
1915	55.00
1916	29.00
1917	30.00
1918	30.00
1919	27.50
1920	27.00
1921	28.00
1922	24.00
1923	26.00
1924	24.50
1925	27.00
1926	26.00
1927	33.50
1928	22.00
1929	30.00
1930	36.00
1931	32.00
1932	35.00
1933	27.00
1934	27.50
1935	29.00
1936	26.50
1937	30.00
1938	44.50
1939	62.00

1940	68.00
1941	115.00
1942	71.00
1943	71.00
1944	39.00
1945	50.00
1946	28.00
1947	36.00
1948	23.00
1949	27.00
1950	44.00
1951	35.50
1952	29.00
1953	36.50
1954	35.00
1955	34.50
1956	47.00
1957	53.00
1958	39.00
1959	50.00
1960	83.00
1961	49.00
1962	27.50
1963	51.00
1964	26.00
1965	29.00
1966	23.50
1967	22.00
1968	19.00
1969	14.00
1970	12.00
1971	9.00
1972	8.00
1973	13.00
1974	8.50
1975	8.50
1976	9.00
1977	9.50
1978	10.00
1979	12.50
1980	16.00
1981	16.00
1982	16.00
1983	23.50
1984	25.50
1969 Mother's Day, Dog & Puppies	280.00
1970 Mother's Day, Birds & Chicks	25.50
1971 Mother's Day, Cat & Kitten	7.50
1972 Mother's Day, Mare & Foal	8.00
1973 Mother's Day, Duck & Ducklings	8.00
1974 Mother's Day, Bear & Cubs	13.50
1975 Mother's Day, Doe & Fawn	8.00
1976 Mother's Day, Swan Family	8.00
1977 Mother's Day, Squirrel & Young	7.50
1978 Mother's Day, Heron	9.50
1979 Mother's Day, Fox & Cubs	11.50
1980 Mother's Day, Woodpecker & Young	12.50
1981 Mother's Day, Hare & Young	14.00
1982 Mother's Day, Lioness & Cubs	19.00

1983 Mother's Day, Raccoon & Young	16.00
1984 Mother's Day, Stork & Nestlings	17.50
1960 Jubilee, Kronborg Castle	85.00
1965 Jubilee, Churchgoers	45.00
1970 Jubilee, Amalienborg Castle	12.00
1975 Jubilee, Horses Enjoying Meal	17.50
1980 Jubilee, Yule Tree	18.00

FRANKOMA

1974 Frankoma Christmas Plate

1965 Christmas, Goodwill Towards Men	210.00
1966 Christmas, Bethlehem Shepherds	110.00
1967 Christmas, Gifts for the Christ Child	89.00
1968 Christmas, Flight into Egypt	18.50
1969 Christmas, Laid in a Manger	12.50
1970 Christmas, King of Kings	10.50
1971 Christmas, No Room in the Inn	7.50
1972 Christmas, Seeking the Christ Child	7.00
1973 Christmas, The Annunciation	7.00
1974 Christmas, She Loved & Cared (ILLUS.)	7.00
1975 Christmas	6.50
1976 Christmas	5.50
1977 Christmas	8.00
1978 Christmas	6.50
1979 Christmas	8.00
1980 Christmas	8.00
1981 Christmas	6.50
1982 Christmas	7.50
1983 Christmas	12.00
1984 Christmas	11.50

HUMMEL (Goebel Works)

1971 Christmas	555.00
1972 Christmas	41.50
1973 Christmas	110.00
1974 Christmas	47.00
1975 Christmas	43.50

1976 Christmas.................... 42.50
1977 Christmas.................... 62.50
1978 Christmas.................... 43.00
1979 Christmas.................... 33.00
1980 Christmas.................... 39.00
1981 Christmas.................... 48.00
1982 Christmas.................... 78.00
1983 Christmas................... 100.00
1984 Christmas.................... 66.00
1975 Anniversary................. 127.00
1980 Anniversary.................. 68.50
1975 Mother's Day, Rabbits......... 34.00
1976 Mother's Day, Cats........... 51.00
1977 Mother's Day, Panda.......... 50.00
1978 Mother's Day, Doe & Fawn 50.00
1979 Mother's Day, Long Eared
   Owl................................ 51.00
1980 Mother's Day, Raccoon &
   Baby 51.00
1981 Mother's Day, Ringed Seal..... 51.00
1982 Mother's Day, Swan 58.00
1983 Mother's Day................. 72.00

LALIQUE (Glass)

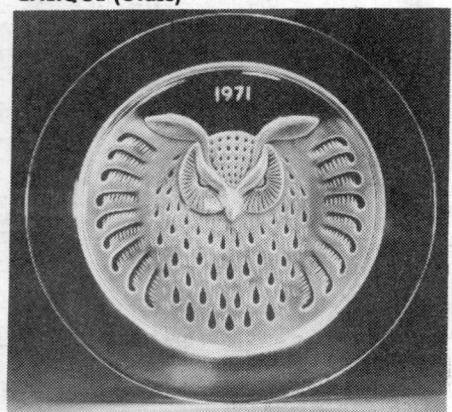

1971 Lalique Annual Plate

1965 Annual 1,170.00
1966 Annual 185.00
1967 Annual 135.00
1968 Annual 74.00
1969 Annual 75.00
1970 Annual 56.00
1971 Annual (ILLUS.)............... 55.00
1972 Annual 47.00
1973 Annual 43.50
1974 Annual 53.50
1975 Annual 55.00
1976 Annual 87.50

LENOX BOEHM

1970 Wood Thrush................. 199.00
1971 Goldfinch.................... 69.00
1972 Mountain Bluebird 55.00
1973 Young American Bald Eagle ... 61.00
1973 Meadowlark 51.00
1973 Mute Swans................. 192.50

1974 Rufous Hummingbirds 60.00
1975 American Redstart............ 47.00
1976 Cardinals 47.00
1977 Robins...................... 38.00
1978 Mockingbirds................. 46.00
1979 Golden-crowned Kinglets...... 51.50
1980 Black-throated Blue Warblers .. 70.00
1981 Eastern Phoebes............. 74.50
1973 Wild Life - Raccoons 65.00
1974 Wild Life - Red Fox 42.50
1975 Wild Life - Rabbits 54.00
1976 Wild Life - Chipmunks......... 57.00
1977 Wild Life - Beaver 57.00
1978 Wild Life - Whitetail Deer 59.00
1979 Wild Life - Squirrels.......... 63.00
1980 Wild Life - Bobcats.......... 72.00
1981 Wild Life - Martens 86.00
1982 Wild Life - Otter.............. 89.00

ORREFORS (Glass)

1970 Annual, Notre Dame
   Cathedral 24.50
1971 Annual, Westminster
   Abbey 24.50
1972 Annual, Basilica Di San
   Marco.......................... 24.50
1973 Annual, Cologne Cathedral 61.00
1974 Annual, Rue De La Victoire.... 42.00
1975 Annual, Basilica Of San Peitro,
   Rome 36.00
1976 Annual, Christ Church,
   Philadelphia 36.00
1977 Annual, Mazjuid-E-Shah 81.00
1978 Annual, Santiago de
   Compostela..................... 56.50
1971 Mother's Day, Flowers For
   Mother 15.50
1972 Mother's Day, Mother with
   Children....................... 16.50
1973 Mother's Day, Mother &
   Child.......................... 15.00
1974 Mother's Day, Mother &
   Child.......................... 15.00
1975 Mother's Day, Child's First
   Steps 45.50
1976 Mother's Day, Children &
   Puppy 17.50
1977 Mother's Day, Child & Dove ... 17.50
1978 Mother's Day, Mother &
   Child.......................... 17.50

PICKARD LOCKHART

1970 Woodcock & Ruffed Grouse.... 295.00
1971 Green-Winged Teal &
   Mallard........................ 200.00
1972 Mockingbird & Cardinal 200.00
1973 Wild Turkey & Pheasant....... 175.00
1974 Bald Eagle 675.00
1975 White-Tailed Deer 110.00
1976 American Buffalo 195.00
1977 Great Horned Owl 115.00
1978 American Panther 195.00
1979 The Red Foxes 87.00
1980 Trumpeter Swan............. 175.00

PORSGRUND

1970 Porsgrund Christmas

1968 Christmas, Church Scene	165.00
1969 Christmas, Three Kings	16.50
1970 Christmas, Road to Bethlehem (ILLUS.)	9.00
1971 Christmas, A Child is Born	9.50
1972 Christmas, Hark the Herald Angels Sing	15.50
1973 Christmas, Promise of the Savior	14.00
1974 Christmas, The Shepherds	33.50
1975 Christmas, Road to Temple	15.50
1976 Christmas, Jesus & the Elders	16.50
1977 Christmas, Draught of the Fish	15.00
1978 Christmas, Guests are Coming	13.00
1979 Christmas, Home for Christmas	14.00
1980 Christmas, Preparing for Christmas	14.50
1981 Christmas, Christmas Skating	17.00
1982 Christmas, White Christmas	19.00
1983 Christmas	19.00
1984 Christmas	23.00
1971 Father's Day, Fishing	4.50
1972 Father's Day, Cookout	4.00
1973 Father's Day, Sledding	4.50
1974 Father's Day, Father & Son with Wheelbarrow	4.50
1975 Father's Day, Skating	4.50
1976 Father's Day, Skiing	4.50
1977 Father's Day, Soccer	5.50
1978 Father's Day, Canoeing	5.50
1979 Father's Day, Father & Daughter	11.00
1980 Father's Day, Sailing	8.50
1981 Father's Day	9.00
1982 Father's Day	10.00
1983 Father's Day	10.00
1984 Father's Day	13.50
1970 Mother's Day, Mare & Foal	4.50
1971 Mother's Day, Boy & Geese	4.50
1972 Mother's Day, Doe & Fawn	4.50
1973 Mother's Day, Cat & Kittens	6.00
1974 Mother's Day, Boy & Goats	6.00
1975 Mother's Day, Dog & Puppies	6.00
1976 Mother's Day, Girl & Calf	6.00
1977 Mother's Day, Boy & Chickens	8.50
1978 Mother's Day, Girl & Pigs	8.50
1979 Mother's Day, Boy & Reindeer	8.50
1980 Mother's Day, Girl & Lambs	8.75
1981 Mother's Day, Boy & Birds	9.00
1982 Mother's Day, Child with Rabbit	9.50
1983 Mother's Day, Mother & Kittens	12.50
1984 Mother's Day	13.50

RED SKELTON PLATES

Freddie the Freeloader

1976 Freddie (ILLUS.)	375.00
1977 W.C. Fields	63.50
1978 Happy	64.00
1979 Freddie in the Bath Tub	190.00
1980 Freddie's Shack	68.50
1981 Freddie on the Green	51.00
1982 Love That Freddie	50.00
1983 70 Years Young	58.00
1984 Torchbearer	43.00

RORSTRAND

1968 Christmas, Bringing Home the Tree	280.00
1969 Christmas, Fisherman Sailing Home	53.00
1970 Christmas, Nils with His Geese	18.50
1971 Christmas, Nils in Lapland (ILLUS.)	18.00
1972 Christmas, Dalecarlian Fiddler	11.00
1973 Christmas, Farm in Smaland	65.50
1974 Christmas, Vadstena	52.00

1971 Rorstrand Christmas

1975 Christmas, Nils in
    Vastmanland 11.50
1976 Christmas, Nils in Uppland 10.00
1977 Christmas, Nils in Varmland ... 10.50
1978 Christmas, Nils in Fjallbacka... 15.00
1979 Christmas, Nils in
    Vaestergoetland 17.00
1980 Christmas, Nils in Holland 20.00
1981 Christmas, Nils in Gotland 17.50
1982 Christmas, Nils at Skansen 26.00
1983 Christmas, Nils in Oland 29.00
1984 Christmas, Angerman Land 30.50

ROYAL COPENHAGEN

1955 Royal Copenhagen Christmas

1908 .... 1,110.00
1909 .... 82.50
1910 .... 60.00
1911 .... 78.00
1912 .... 70.00
1913 .... 63.00
1914 .... 61.00
1915 .... 73.00
1916 .... 43.00

1917 .... 42.00
1918 .... 43.00
1919 .... 42.00
1920 .... 41.50
1921 .... 37.00
1922 .... 36.00
1923 .... 34.00
1924 .... 52.00
1925 .... 40.00
1926 .... 41.00
1927 .... 68.00
1928 .... 40.00
1929 .... 40.00
1930 .... 50.00
1931 .... 50.00
1932 .... 44.50
1933 .... 72.00
1934 .... 59.50
1935 .... 80.00
1936 .... 71.00
1937 .... 77.00
1938 .... 132.00
1939 .... 150.00
1940 .... 210.00
1941 .... 170.00
1942 .... 185.00
1943 .... 250.00
1944 .... 100.00
1945 .... 195.00
1946 .... 81.00
1947 .... 110.00
1948 .... 96.50
1949 .... 98.50
1950 .... 105.00
1951 .... 185.00
1952 .... 67.00
1953 .... 66.50
1954 .... 66.50
1955 (ILLUS.) 100.00
1956 .... 87.50
1957 .... 48.50
1958 .... 63.50
1959 .... 63.50
1960 .... 84.00
1961 .... 82.00
1962 .... 120.00
1963 .... 39.00
1964 .... 35.00
1965 .... 31.50
1966 .... 28.00
1967 .... 26.00
1968 .... 16.50
1969 .... 17.50
1970 .... 19.00
1971 .... 11.50
1972 .... 9.50
1973 .... 9.00
1974 .... 8.00
1975 .... 8.00
1976 .... 16.00
1977 .... 9.50
1978 .... 10.00
1979 .... 32.50
1980 .... 14.50

1981	18.00
1982	19.50
1983	21.00
1984	23.00
1971 Mother's Day, American Mother	11.00
1972 Mother's Day, Oriental Mother	6.00
1973 Mother's Day, Danish Mother	6.50
1974 Mother's Day, Greenland Mother	6.00
1975 Mother's Day, Bird in Nest	7.00
1976 Mother's Day, Mermaids	6.50
1977 Mother's Day, The Twins	8.00
1978 Mother's Day, Mother & Child	8.00
1979 Mother's Day, A Loving Mother	9.00
1980 Mother's Day, An Outing with Mother	8.50
1981 Mother's Day, Reunion	12.00
1982 Mother's Day, Children's Hour	13.00

SCHMID HUMMEL

1971 Christmas, Angel	32.50
1972 Christmas, Angel with Flute	18.50
1973 Christmas, The Nativity	140.00
1974 Christmas, The Guardian Angel	23.00
1975 Christmas, Christmas Child	21.00
1976 Christmas, Sacred Journey	23.50
1977 Christmas, Herald Angel	14.25
1978 Christmas, Heavenly Trio	20.50
1979 Christmas, Starlight Angel	17.00
1980 Christmas, Parade into Toyland	24.50
1981 Christmas, A Time to Remember	25.50
1982 Christmas, Angelic Procession	24.50
1983 Christmas, Angelic Messenger	26.50
1984 Christmas	29.00
1972 Mother's Day, Playing Hooky	16.00
1973 Mother's Day, Little Fisherman	48.50
1974 Mother's Day, Bumblebee	14.50
1975 Mother's Day, Message of Love	12.50
1976 Mother's Day, Devotion for Mother	21.00
1977 Mother's Day, Moonlight Return	24.50
1978 Mother's Day, Afternoon Stroll	16.50
1979 Mother's Day, Cherub's Gift	15.50
1980 Mother's Day, Mother's Little Helpers	23.00
1981 Mother's Day, Playtime	26.00

1982 Mother's Day, The Flower Basket	28.00

SPODE

1970 Christmas, Patridge	46.50
1971 Christmas, Angels Singing	22.50
1972 Christmas, Three Ships A-Sailing	22.50
1973 Christmas, Three Kings of Orient	45.00
1974 Christmas, Deck the Halls	44.00
1975 Christmas, Christbaum	20.00
1976 Christmas, Good King Wenceslas	20.00
1977 Christmas, Holly & Ivy	33.00
1978 Christmas, While Shepherds Watched	20.00
1979 Christmas, Away in a Manger	28.00
1980 Christmas, Bringing in the Boar's Head	22.50
1981 Christmas, Make We Merry	46.00

WEDGWOOD

1969 Christmas, Windsor Castle	190.00
1970 Christmas, Trafalger Square	24.00
1971 Christmas, Picadilly Circus	24.00
1972 Christmas, St. Paul's Cathedral	26.00
1973 Christmas, Tower of London	25.00
1974 Christmas, Houses of Parliament	23.50
1975 Christmas, Tower Bridge	25.00
1976 Christmas, Hampton Court	23.50
1977 Christmas, Westminster Abbey	25.00
1978 Christmas, Horse Guards	30.00
1979 Christmas, Buckingham Palace	32.00
1980 Christmas, St. James Palace	32.50
1981 Christmas, Marble Arch	34.00
1982 Christmas, Lambeth Palace	49.00
1983 Christmas, All Souls, Langham Palace	38.50
1984 Christmas, Constitution Hall	40.00
1971 Mother's Day	13.50
1972 Mother's Day	20.00
1973 Mother's Day	15.50
1974 Mother's Day	19.00
1975 Mother's Day	24.00
1976 Mother's Day	22.00
1977 Mother's Day	24.00
1978 Mother's Day	19.00
1979 Mother's Day	13.50
1980 Mother's Day	22.00
1981 Mother's Day	22.50
1982 Mother's Day	22.00
1983 Mother's Day	23.00
1984 Mother's Day	25.00

(End of Commemorative Plate Section)

COOKBOOKS

1916 Jell-O Cookbook

Cookbook collectors are usually good cooks and will buy important new cookbooks as well as seek out notable older ones. Many early cookbooks were published and given away as advertising premiums for various products used extensively in cooking. While some rare, scarce first edition cookbooks can be very expensive, most collectible cookbooks are reasonably priced.

Advertising, "Angelus Recipe Booklet," 1930's $7.00
Advertising, "Calumet Baking Powder Cookbook," w/Kewpie cover 20.00
Advertising, "Campbell Soup Helps For the Hostess," 1916 .... 15.00
Advertising, "Jell-O," 1916, 18 pp. (ILLUS.)....................... 45.00
Advertising, "Lowney's (Chocolate) Cookbook," 1908 .... 12.00
Advertising, "Royal Baking Powder War Time Recipes," 1917 .... 5.00
Advertising, "Rumford's Baking Powder Cookbook," 1906, girl w/wheat on cover 10.00
Advertising, "Southern Pacific Railroad Rice Cookbook," 1901 .... 10.00
Advertising, "Welch's Howdy Doody Cook Book".................... 19.00
"The American Cookbook," by Gillette, 1889, hardbound 20.00
"Blondie's Cookbook," by Chic Young, 1947 .... 15.00
"Boston Cooking School Cookbook," by Fannie Farmer, published by Little Brown, 1897, hardbound 75.00
"Catering for Two," by Alice L. James, 1898 .... 12.50
"The Congressional Cook Book," 1933, international recipes of Congressmen's wives, 834 pp. 22.00

"Derrydale Cook Book of Fish & Game," 1927, 2 vol. in slipcase ... 150.00
"Fine Old Dixie Recipes," 1939, wooden cover w/illustration of black woman 40.00
"McNess Cookbook," 1896 .... 10.00
"Methodist Church Cookbook, Center, North Dakota," 1930 ..... 12.00
"The Modern Cook Book," by Ida Bailey Allen, 1935 .... 10.00
"New Orleans Recipes," 1938, hand-tinted cover w/illustration of handsome black woman 16.00
"The New York Times Cook Book," published by Harper Row, 1961 ... 10.00
"Prudence Penny's Cookbook," 1930's, 385 pp. 25.00
"200 Years of Charleston Cooking," Woodward, 1930 .... 12.00
"Universal Cookbook," by Jeanie L. Taylor, 1888, 185 pp. 10.50
"The Virginia Housewife Cookbook," 1838 .... 350.00
"White House Cookbook," 1900 ..... 25.00
"WLS Prairie Farmer Cookbook," 1941 .... 12.50

COOKIE CUTTERS

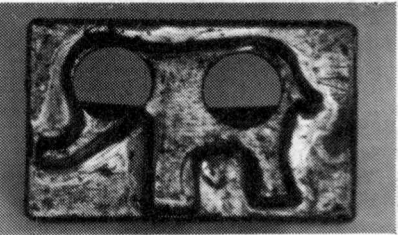

Baby Elephant Cutter

Recently there has been an accelerated interest in old tin cookie cutters. For the most part, these were made by tinsmiths who shaped primitive designs of tin strips and then soldered them to a backplate, pierced to allow air to enter and prevent a suction from holding the rolled cookie dough in the form. Sometimes an additional handle was soldered to the back. Cookie cutters were also manufactured in great quantities in an outline form that could depict animals, birds, star and other forms, including the plain round that sometimes carried embossed advertising for flour or other products on the handle. Aluminum cookie cutters were made after 1920. Only tin cutters are listed below. Also see ADVERTISING ITEMS.

Baby elephant, flat backplate pierced w/two large holes, w/strap handle (ILLUS.) $40.00

Bear walking, flat backplate pierced
w/single hole, 3¾" l. 20.00
Bird standing, flat backplate pierced
w/single hole, w/strap handle . . . 50.00
Bull w/curved horns, flat backplate
pierced w/three holes, 4½" l. 47.50
Cat w/crimped tail & pierced circle
designs, flat backplate pierced
w/single hole, 6" l. 145.00
Chicken, flat backplate pierced w/a
star, 4" h. 22.50
Dog w/short tail, flat backplate
pierced w/single large hole,
6¼" l. 40.00
Dove standing, flat backplate
pierced w/single hole, 4¾" h. 17.50
Eagle w/spread wings, flat back-
plate, 6½" l. 85.00
Ear of corn, flat backplate,
5½" h. 65.00
Fish w/scalloped fins & flowing tail,
flat backplate pierced w/single
large hole, 5" l. . . . . .55.00 to 65.00
Goose, flat backplate pierced
w/single hole, 3¾" h. 15.00
Heart, diamond, spade.& club out-
lines, w/strap handles, 1930's, set
of 4 in original box. 22.00
Horse's head, flat backplate pierced
w/single hole, 3¾" h. 115.00
Lion, flat backplate pierced w/single
hole, 4½" l. 12.50
Man dancing jig, flat backplate
pierced w/two holes, 6¾" w.,
9¼" h. 165.00
Moose w/impressive rack of antlers,
flat backplate pierced w/four
holes, 6" h. 175.00

Old Woman with Cane Cutter

Old woman w/cane, flat backplate
pierced w/large center hole
(ILLUS.). 45.00
Pig standing, flat backplate pierced
w/two small holes, 4½" l. 22.50
Profile bust of man singing, flat

backplate pierced w/two holes,
3¾" h. 100.00
Rabbit standing upright, flat back-
plate pierced w/two holes,
8¼" h. 100.00
Rooster, flat backplate pierced
w/single large hole, 4" h. 25.00
Squirrel seated, flat backplate
pierced w/single hole, 3½" h. 20.00
Star, 6-pointed, flat backplate,
3½" w. 6.00
Turkey, flat backplate pierced
w/two holes, 5½" l. 95.00
Woman wearing crimped skirt
w/pierced circle designs, flat
backplate pierced w/single large
hole, 4½" h. 115.00

CORKSCREWS

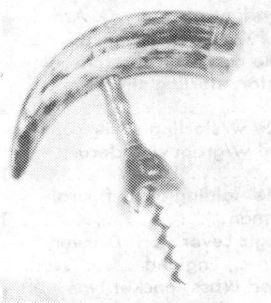

Tusk-Handled Corkscrew

*More corkscrews should be available to col-
lectors in years to come since wine sales in
the United States have shown a profound increase within the past decade. The corkscrew
is virtually an essential adjunct to wine since
the cork closure adheres tightly to the glass
wine bottle and without the pointed spiral
shaft of the corkscrew to remove it, the wine
could remain bottled forever. Today corkscrew collectors seek out those with unique
form, with early patent dates, or with desirable handles that are made from a wide variety of materials. Also see BREWERIANA.*

Advertising, brass, bullet-shaped,
"Drink Lemp," 1897 patent date . . $32.00
Advertising, brass, lever action
type, "Pacific Wine Co.,"
Chicago" 15.00
Advertising, twisted wire, ring-type,
"Listerine," 3½". 6.00
Advertising, wood & metal, "Hen-
nessy Cognac," ca. 1930 . . . . 39.00
Advertising, wood & metal, "Keen
Kutter" 20.00
Boar's tusk handle (ILLUS.) 35.00

Bone handle w/steel spiral worm shaft, 3½" handle 20.00

Bone handle w/embossed brass barrel, Edward Thomason's patent of 1802 .... 350.00

Brass, wing-type, ca. 1910, large ... 25.00

Brass spiral worm shaft & button w/wooden handle & bottle brush, variant of Henshall's 1795 patent, ca. 1840 .... 95.00

Cast iron, bar-mount type, "Yankee No. 7," R. B. Gilchrest's patent of 1913 .... 195.00

Cast iron, figural lady's legs, German 50.00

Cast iron, figural "Old Snifter," caricature of Congressman Andrew Volstead, author of Prohibition legislation, w/bottle opener 70.00

Chrome-plated, figural parrot, w/bottle opener 25.00

Heeley's "Pullezi," concertina mechanism, variant of Henry D. Armstrong's 1902 patent 95.00

Ivory handle carved in the form of an alligator, sterling silver cap, 5" l. 250.00

Ivory handle w/sterling silver cap embossed w/grapevine decor, 6¾" l. 115.00

Ivory handle, folding-type, figural nude woman................... 115.00

Metal, "Magic Lever Cork Drawer," early 20th c., England 65.00

Nickel-plated brass, pocket-type, funnel-shaped w/original leather case, Prohibition-era 22.00

Stag's horn handle w/ornate sterling silver cap, w/bottle opener, Gorham, 5½" l. 110.00

Stag's horn handle, 6" l. 40.00

Whale's tooth handle w/Art Nouveau decor & sterling silver cap, ca. 1900, 9" l................... 195.00

Wooden, carved, figural man, removable head w/corkscrew 45.00

CORONATION ITEMS

Items commemorating the coronation of English monarchs have been produced for many years. The spectacular 1981 Royal Wedding, uniting Charles, the Prince of Wales, and Lady Diana Spencer in matrimony, has created new interest in English Royalty. Listed in chronological order according to reign, the following items have been sold, or offered for sale, in recent months. Also included are items produced at the observance of Queen

Victoria's 50th and 60th Jubilee and at her death.

Victoria (1837-1901) basket, vaseline glass, applied handle $50.00

Victoria bottle w/stopper, glass, relief portrait of Victoria on stopper, 4½" h. 30.00

Victoria bust, bisque, painted, 9" h. 65.00

Victoria cup plate, china, coronation portrait 35.00

Victoria playing cards, Goodall's.... 100.00

Victoria watch fob, metal, embossed portrait of Victoria obverse, "Victoria Regina" reverse 18.00

Victoria (50th Jubliee - 1887) bowl, pressed glass, "Her Crown, 1887, The Queen's Jubilee" in stippled lettering, 3½" d. 32.00

Victoria bowl, china, portrait of Victoria center w/dates of birth & coronation in black, scalloped rim, 9" d. 70.00

Victoria bowl, pressed glass, portrait of Victoria center, "1887" on rim, 9" d. 65.00

Queen Victoria Jubilee Bowl

Victoria bowl, pressed glass, crown center w/"1837" above & "1887" below, within laurel wreath, 10" d. (ILLUS.) ....50.00 to 65.00

Victoria bust, parian, marked "Jubilee 1887, R.S. Morris sculpt., R & L." 325.00

Victoria mug, stoneware, portrait of Victoria front, dates of birth, ascension to the throne, marriage & reign reverse, brown & white decor, 1887, 5" h. 65.00

Victoria plate, china, portrait of Victoria & "Jubilee 1887," sepia transfer on pink ground, 9" d..... 40.00

Victoria plate, pressed glass, "The Queen's Jubilee, 1887," amber, 10" d......................... 75.00

Victoria (60th Jubilee - 1897) basket,

handled, china, turquoise blue decor, 5¾" h. 55.00

Victoria beaker, stoneware, dated 1897, Royal Doulton, 5" h. 85.00

Victoria bowl, glass, gilt portrait of Victoria, 1897, 8½" d. 65.00

Victoria bust, parian, "1897," on black wooden stand, 2 x 1½", overall 6½" h. 75.00

Victoria cup & deep saucer, china, "Jubilee Year," 1897 .... 45.00

Victoria figure, parian, dated 1897, 9" h. 85.00

Victoria jug, stoneware, embossed portrait of Victoria at her coronation & her jubilee, "1837-1897," on tan ground w/olive green trim, Doulton Lambeth, 5½" h. 195.00

Victoria lithograph on silk, portrait of Victoria & "Queen Victoria - Diamond Jubilee," narrow black frame, 8¾ x 6¾" 50.00

Victoria pitcher, stoneware, double cameo portrait of the young & old Victoria, "1837-97" & "She Wrought Her People Lasting Good," thistle & roses border, cobalt blue, olive green & brown glaze, Doulton Lambeth, 7½" h. .. 150.00

Victoria plate, china, h.p. medallion portrait in blue & rust, scalloped edge, 9" d. 85.00

Victoria plate, china, portrait of Victoria center, floral border w/inscription "Diamond Jubilee" 80.00

Victoria tea tile, china, portrait cartouche w/roses, thistle & shamrock, black & white, 6¼" d. 95.00

Victoria tumbler, china, portrait of Victoria within gilt beaded border, pastel decor on white ground, Carlton Ware, W & R, 4" h. 65.00

Victoria wall tile, sepia tones, 1897, 8" square. 200.00

Victoria (1901) cup, porcelain, h.p. portrait of Victoria & "In Memoriam" 85.00

Victoria cup plate, china, portrait of Victoria & inscription commemorating her death, 5" d. 75.00

Victoria match safe, pocket-type, silver, engraved bust of Victoria 85.00

George VI (1936-52) cake plate, china, portraits of George & Elizabeth Bowes-Lyon 22.50

George VI medal, English silver, portrait of George & Elizabeth Bowes-Lyon, Royal Mint issue, 1937, original box 2¼" d. 85.00

George VI mug, china, multicolor decor, dated 1937, Royal Doulton 65.00

George VI newspaper, "London News" w/illustrations of coronation 20.00

George VI Official Coronation Programme 50.00

George VI shaving mug, scuttletype, china, portraits of George & Elizabeth 35.00

George VI tea tile, portraits of George & Elizabeth, 10¼" 35.00

George VI tumbler, china, George & Elizabeth portraits, "Official Design of the British Pottery Manufacturing Federation," 4" h. 20.00

Elizabeth II (1952--) ash tray, jasper ware, white relief portrait of Elizabeth on royal blue ground, 1953 .... 42.50

Elizabeth II bank, cast iron, model of a crown w/"Elizabeth II" & date of coronation inscribed around base 30.00

Elizabeth II box, printed tin, portrait of Elizabeth, 5¾ x 4¼" 20.00

Elizabeth II dessert set: twelve 9½" d. plates & 12 c/s; china, portrait of Elizabeth w/flag surrounds, gold trim, Meakin, 36 pcs. 480.00

Elizabeth II loving cup, china, portraits of Elizabeth I & Elizabeth II w/flags, crests & ships of The Spanish Armada in relief, Royal Doulton, 11" h. 420.00

Elizabeth II pitcher, portraits of Elizabeth I & Elizabeth II w/flags & crests in relief, Windsor Castle reverse, Royal Doulton, 6" h. 125.00

COUNTRY STORE COLLECTIBLES

"Star" Egg Carrier

Country store museums have opened across the country in an effort to recreate those slower-paced days of the late 19th and early 20th centuries when the general store served as the local meeting place for much of rural

America. Here one not only purchased neces-
sary supplies for upcoming weeks, but caught
up on important news events and local gos-
sip. With strong interest in colorful tin cans
during the early 1960's, came the realization
that these stores and neighborhood groceries
were fast disappearing, replaced by the so-
called supermarkets, and collectors began
buying all items associated with these early
stores. Also see ADVERTISING ITEMS,
CASH REGISTERS, SIGNS & SIGN-
BOARDS and STRING HOLDERS.

Bag rack, iron wire, counter-top
  model w/nine graduated sections,
  31 x 14 x 10" $125.00
Bin (for dried beans, etc.), pine,
  hinged slant lid, original finish ... 250.00
Broom rack, ceiling suspension-type,
  bent iron wire circle w/rings for
  24 broom handles, overall
  16½" d. ....65.00 to 85.00
Broom rack, wall-type, bent iron
  wire, 25 x 14", 28" h............. 45.00
Buggy whip rack, hanging-type, cast
  iron circle, 13" d. 55.00
Cabinet, hanging-type, pine, 10 narrow shelves, tambour slide raises
  & lowers at front, 21" w., 23" h... 110.00
Ceiling fan, "Emmerson," wooden
  blades 250.00
Coffee bean dispenser, counter-top
  model, tin, 3-section, porcelain
  knobs, 24" w., 12½" deep, 7" h.
  at front, 8½" h. at back 300.00
Coffee bean dispenser, counter-top
  model, toleware, painted blue,
  brass trim, 10" d., 26" h. 165.00
Combination safe, cast iron, w/com-
  bination, 23 x 27", 30" h. 800.00
Counter, oak, paneled on 3 sides,
  11 drawers at rear, 52" l. 450.00
Counter, pine, paneled on 3 sides,
  21 drawers at rear, 84" l. 350.00
Counter, quarter-sawn oak w/mar-
  ble top, front w/chamfered panels
  & carved pillars, refinished,
  72" l. 650.00
Counter display jars, clear glass jars
  w/etched brass bands marked
  "Fruit Drops," "Jelly Beans" &
  "Gum Balls," set of 3 in fitted
  copper tray 550.00
Counter-top desk, pine, slant lid lifting to compartments in dovetailed
  case w/drawer below, original
  finish, ca. 1830, 24" w., 22" deep,
  12½" h. 500.00
Counter-top display case, walnut
  w/beveled glass lift-lid,
  dovetailed case, applied base
  molding, 34½" w., 22¾" deep,
  6¾" h. 85.00
Customer "credit" account rack,
  oak 50.00

Dry measure, bentwood round,
  1 peck ....50.00 to 65.00
Egg carrier, wooden, w/compart-
  mented interior tray, for 1 dozen
  eggs, lid marked "Star, Mfg. by
  John C. Elb, Rochester, N.Y., Pat.
  1903-1906," 8¼ x 6½", 2¾" h.
  (ILLUS.)........................ 35.00
Handkerchief display box, oak,
  7-drawer 125.00
Ladder on wheels, oak, 10'. 100.00
Lantern, kerosene hanging-type,
  brass font, original burner, glass
  chimney & tin shade (polished,
  lacquered & electrified) ..265.00 to 375.00
Meat & cheese slicer, oak & iron,
  adjustable slicing thickness, pre-
  1891 .... 85.00
Pocket knife display case, oak
  w/beveled glass top & front, mirrored back, drawer at rear,
  31" w., 25" deep, 35" h. 395.00
Ribbon display cabinet, oak, 12
  glass-fronted tilt-out doors & 2
  sliding drawers 475.00
Root beer barrel, wooden, iron claw
  feet & brass spigot 200.00
Shoe fitting stool, wooden seat,
  bent iron wire legs 50.00
Show case, cherrywood frame, glass
  top & front, Queen Anne style
  feet, 96" l. 800.00
Show case, oak frame, beveled
  glass top & front, opens from rear
  w/sliding doors, 96" l. 400.00
Store hook (to remove boxes from
  upper shelves), double-handled,
  marked "Grabal 8/24-20" 75.00
Strawholder jar, pressed glass,
  brass lid...................... 90.00
String holder, cast iron, beehive-
  shaped, ca. 1880 .... 38.00
String holder, emerald green glass,
  bell-shaped 150.00
Tea bin, slant lid, printed tin, lady
  pictured, 16" h. 195.00
Wrapping paper holder & cutter,
  wood & iron, 12" w. 28.00

COW CREAMERS

These silver and earthenware cream jugs
were modeled in the form of that beautiful bo-
vine animal, the original source of their in-
tended contents. The most desirable versions
are the early silver and Dutch Delft faience
creations turned out in the 18th century, as
well as those produced in the Staffordshire
potteries before the mid-19th century. How-

ever, traditional style cow creamers, made in the late 19th or in the 20th centuries, are also deemed collectible. The following group of cow creamers were offered for sale, or sold at auction, within recent months.

Pottery, Jackfield-type, cow in standing position on oval base, black glaze, gold trim, early 20th c. $65.00

Pottery, Staffordshire, cow standing w/tail curled up to form handle & mouth forming spout, sponged in black & puce, w/seated figure of milkmaid at task on oblong octagonal base enriched in green, ca. 1810, 6½" l. (repair to base & lid) 715.00

Staffordshire Cow Creamer

Pottery, Staffordshire, cow standing w/tail curled up to form handle & mouth forming spout, sponged in manganese & yellow, w/seated figure of milkmaid at task on oblong base, ca. 1780, repair to cover, 1 ear & horns, 6¾" l. (ILLUS.)........................ 825.00

Pottery, Whieldon-type, cow standing w/tail curled up to form handle & mouth forming spout, splashed in manganese, w/seated figure of milkmaid on octagonal base enriched in blue, green & manganese, ca. 1760, 6¼" l. (repairs to horns, ears & corner of base) 825.00

Pottery, Whieldon-type, cow standing w/tail curled up to form handle & mouth forming spout, tortoise shell glaze, on waisted oblong base enriched w/green, ca. 1760, 6¾" l. (repair to 1 ear & tail) 1,540.00

Pottery, Whieldon-type, cow standing w/tail curled up to form handle & mouth forming spout, manganese stripe markings, on

shaped oblong base, ca. 1750, 7¼" l., pr. (replaced cover for 1 & other cover missing, repair to tail, ears & horn) 2,090.00

CURRIER & IVES

Across the Continent

This lithographic firm was founded in 1835 by Nathaniel Currier with James M. Ives becoming a partner in 1857. Current events of the day were portrayed in the early days and the prints were hand-colored. Landscapes, vessels, sport, and hunting scenes of the west all became popular subjects. The firm was in existence until 1906. All prints listed are hand-colored unless otherwise noted.

Across the Continent - "Westward the Course of Empire Takes Off," after F.F. Palmer, large folio, complete margins, 1868 (ILLUS.) $12,100.00

American Speckled Brook Trout, after A.F. Tait, large folio, 1864 (slight foxing) 1,430.00

Apples and Plums - First Premium, small folio, 1870 .... 135.00

Barefoot Girl (The), small folio 95.00

Bass Fishing, small folio, margins slightly trimmed, beveled pine frame, overall 17" w., 13¾" h. 285.00

Battle of Cerro Gordo - April 18th, 1847, small folio 135.00

Battle of Fair Oaks, Va., May 31st, 1862, small folio 235.00

Battle of the Wilderness - May 5th & 6th, 1864, small folio 160.00

Beatrice Cenci, small folio 30.00

Beautiful Dreamer (The), small folio 45.00

Bed Time, small folio 45.00

Betrothed (The), small folio, 1848 ... 50.00

Broadway Belle (A), small folio 38.00

Broadway, New York, South from the Park, small folio, framed 440.00

Brook Trout Fishing, small folio, 1872 .... 125.00

Burning of the Clipper Ship "Golden

Light" - Sailed from Boston to San Francisco, Feb. 12, 1853, small folio 975.00

Camping Out - "Some of the Right Sort," large folio, 1856 ....3,250.00

Central Park - The Bridge, small folio ....250.00 to 295.00

Death of Major Ringgold - Of the Flying Artillery - At the Battle of Palo Alto (Texas), May 8th, 1846, small folio 80.00

Elizabeth (half-length), small folio, 1846 .... 45.00

Farmer's Son (The), small folio 55.00

Flower Vase (The), small folio, 1848 ....70.00 to 95.00

Franklin's Experiment, June 1752 - Demonstrating the Identity of Lightning and Electricity - from which he invented the lightning rod, small folio, 1876 (some stains & foxing) 625.00

Fruit Piece (The), grapes, blackberries, pears, etc. in glass dish, small folio, 1867 .... 195.00

Fruits of the Seasons (apples, peaches, grapes, blackberries & cherries), small folio, 1870 .... 80.00

George M. Dallas, small folio, N. Currier, 1846.................... 85.00

German Beauty (The), small folio, molded walnut frame............ 95.00

Going to Pasture - Early Morning, small folio, beveled mahogany veneer frame, overall 16½ x 12¾" 145.00

Grand National Democratic Banner - Polk the young Hickory - Dallas and Victory - The People's Candidates for President and Vice-President, small folio, 1844 ...... 250.00

"Liberty Enlightening The World"

Great Bartholdi Statue - Liberty Enlightening The World, large folio, 1883, few nicks & tears in edges (ILLUS.) 2,420.00

Happy Home (The), small folio, framed, overall 20" w............ 85.00

Home in the Wilderness (A), small folio, 1870, framed (some spots in margins) 350.00

Home of Washington - Mount Vernon, medium folio, 1852 ...... 210.00

Hudson Near Coldspring - Chapel of Our Lady, small folio ....160.00 to 275.00

Hungry Little Kitties, small folio, framed...................... 30.00

Landing of the Pilgrims at Plymouth, 11th Dec. 1620, small folio, curly maple frame, overall 19¾" w., 15¾" h. (small tear in margin) ... 105.00

Life in the Woods - Starting Out, large folio, 1860, framed, overall 34½ x 26¾" (water stains in bottom margin) 2,100.00

Little Brothers, small folio, 1875, framed, overall 16 3/8 x 12 3/8".. 75.00

Little Manly

Little Manly, small folio, 1874, framed (ILLUS.) 80.00

Little Nellie, small folio, original gilt frame, ovearll 11 x 15" 55.00

Little Volunteer (The), small folio, 1861 .... 175.00

New England Home (A), small folio 165.00

New Suspension Bridge, Niagara Falls (The), small folio, framed ... 300.00

Niagara Falls - From the Canada Side, small folio ....125.00 to 150.00

No You Don't, three-quarter length portrait of girl w/rose, small folio 50.00

Noontide A Shady Spot, small folio 135.00

Old Blanford Church, Petersburg, Va., F.F. Palmer, small folio 150.00

Old Homestead (The), F.F. Palmer, medium folio 195.00

Old Oaken Bucket, rural scene, 2 columns & 2 lines of verse, small folio, 1872 .... 150.00

Old Plantation Home (The), small folio, 1872, framed 125.00
On the Owago, small folio 135.00
Pair of Nutcrackers (Squirrels), small folio 125.00
Partridge Shooting, small folio, 1870 .... 285.00
Pet of the Family (The), small folio 50.00
Pilot Boat in a Storm, small folio 350.00
Placid Lake, Adirondacks, small folio 175.00
Queen of Beauty (The), small folio .. 35.00
Rafting on the St. Lawrence, medium folio 335.00
Rally 'Round the Flag, small folio 100.00
Rip Van Winkle's Cottage in the Catskills, small folio 185.00
Rosanna, small folio, N. Currier, 1849 .... 40.00
Ross Castle, Lake of Kilarney, small folio 75.00
Sailor's Adieu & Sailor's Return, small folio, framed, pr. 440.00
Saratoga Lake, small folio 135.00
Saratoga Springs, small folio 215.00
Silver Cascade - White Mountains, small folio 150.00
Sinking of the "Cumberland" by the Iron Clad "Merrimac," small folio, 1862 .... 200.00
Snipe Shooting, small folio 495.00
Soldier's Dream of Home (The), small folio, framed 135.00
Source of the Hudson (The), small folio 275.00
Spendthrift, small folio, 1870 .... 275.00
Spring Flowers, small folio, 1861 .... 245.00
Steamship "President" - The Largest in the World, small folio, N. Currier 265.00

Stella

Stella, small folio, 1872 (ILLUS.) 70.00
Summer Morning, small folio 160.00

Summer Morning, medium folio 185.00
Sunnyside - On The Hudson, small folio 165.00
Sure Thing (A), small folio, 1884 .... 195.00
Surrender of Genl. Joe Johnston Near Greensboro, N.C., April 26th, 1865, small folio 140.00
Surrender of Port Hudson, La., small folio, 1863 .... 125.00
Susie, small folio 45.00
Take Care (girl's head), small folio 45.00
Thatched Cottage (The), small folio 80.00
Tomb of Kosciusko - West Point, small folio 145.00
Tree of Temperance, small folio, N. Currier, original giltwood frame .. 175.00
Trotting Mare - "Nancy Hanks" - Record 2:04, small folio, 1892 .... 225.00
Trying It On, small folio, 1874 ...... 125.00
Turn of the Tune (The), small folio 225.00
Two Little Fraid Cats & My Little White Kittens, small folio, bird's eye maple veneer frames, pr. 170.00
Two Pets (The), small folio, N. Currier, 1848.................... 45.00
Under Cliff - On the Hudson, small folio 175.00
Valkyrie, small folio 150.00
Valley Falls - Virginia, small folio... 175.00
Vase of Flowers (The), small folio, N. Currier, 1847................. 115.00
View from Fort Putnam, N.Y., small folio 250.00
View from Peekskill, Hudson River, N.Y., 1862, medium folio, framed 550.00
View of the Distributing Reservoir on Murray's Hill, City of New York, small folio, N. Currier, 1842 .... 365.00
View of the Park Fountain and City Hall, N.Y., 1846, small folio, N. Currier..............175.00 to 350.00
View on the Hudson from Ruggles House, Newburgh, small folio 275.00
Vigilant, small folio 150.00
Virginia Home in the Olden Time (A), small folio, 1872 .... 225.00
Watkin's Glen, New York, small folio 265.00
Wedding Day (The), small folio, N. Currier, 1846.................... 55.00
Why Don't He Come?, small folio 35.00
Will You Be True?, small folio, oval 45.00
Winter (girl's head), small folio, 1870 .... 55.00
Winter Evening, medium folio, N. Currier, 1854.................... 450.00

Woodcock Shooting, small folio, N.
Currier, 1855. . . . . 375.00
Woodlands in Winter, small
folio 300.00
Wreck of the "Atlantic," small folio,
1873 . . . . 145.00

CUSPIDORS

Ironstone China Cuspidor

*The cuspidor, or spittoon, is a bowl-shaped
vessel into which tobacco chewers could spit.
These containers were a necessity in an era
when much of the male population chewed
tobacco and even some ladies were known to
"take a chew." Made of metal, earthenware
pottery, china and glass, they ranged in size
from the large barroom floor models to small
glass cuspidors designed for the ladies.*

Brass, Dayton Mfg., Dayton, Ohio . . $75.00
Cast iron w/tin insert, mechanical-
type, model of a turtle, step on
head to lift cover, 1891 patent,
14" l. . . . . .140.00 to 225.00
China, flared top, ornate floral
decor, lady's, 3¼" h. 165.00
China, creamy white lilies w/green
& brown foliage w/gilt details on
cerulean blue shaded to white
ground, square top w/ruffled rim,
6" h. 52.00
China, Pine patt., red, green &
beige lustre on white ground,
English registry mark for 1870,
6 7/8" d. 60.00
China, floral decor on orchid
ground, lady's 52.00
Glass, amber, blown, miniature,
2" h. (pinpoint flakes on base) . . . 175.00
Glass, amber, blown, folded over
rim, 7¾" top d., 4½" h. 175.00
Glass, amber, blown, flattened rim,
8¼" top d., 4½" h. 190.00
Glass, Carnival, blue, lady's, signed,
3¼" h. 95.00
Glass, Carnival, marigold, hex-
agonal, 4" h. 38.00

Glass, cased, pink interior w/green
pulled loopings & gold dust, clear
exterior, polished pontil, 9"
widest d., 4¾" h. 105.00
Glass, cased, light blue interior,
white exterior, lady's 85.00
Glass, cobalt blue 60.00
Glass, milk white, hexagonal,
4" h. 49.00
Glass, Rubina Crystal w/enameled
decor, lady's 135.00
Glass, Tortoise Shell, lady's 135.00
Glass, white opalescent, pressed,
Piasa Bird patt., lady's 45.00
Ironstone china, faint Venetian
Diamond-type molding, h.p.
florals (ILLUS.) 45.00
Rockingham glaze pottery, em-
bossed floral decor, mottled
brown. 65.00

DECOYS

Black Duck, Common Duck & Loon Decoys

*Decoys have been utilized for years to lure
flying water fowl into target range. They have
been made of carved and turned wood, papier mache, canvas and metal, and some are
in the category of outstanding folk art and
command high prices.*

Black Duck, carved wood, worn
original paint, by Chauncey
Wheeler, Alexandria Bay, New
York (1862-1937) $3,300.00
Black Duck in preening position,
Down East Decoy Co., Maine
(ILLUS. center), Common Duck,
hollow cedar construction, by
Henry Grant, Barnegat Bay, New
Jersey (ILLUS. left) and Loon, hol-
low construction, original paint,
Maritime Provinces area (ILLUS.
right), set of 3 . . . . 550.00
Bluebill Drake, carved wood, glass
eyes, worn working repaint, bot-
tom initialed "T.F.," 13½" l. 75.00
Bluebill Hen, carved wood, original
paint, by Bill Hollis, Ogensburg,
New York, ca. 1930, 12½" l. 115.00
Bluebill Hen, carved wood, original

paint, small tail chip, by Chauncey
Wheeler, Alexandria Bay, New
York (1862-1937) 990.00

Bluebill Hen & Drake, Mason Detroit
Grade, pr...................... 350.00

Brant Goose, carved wood w/root
head, old working repaint, glass
eyes, Maine area, 15" l. 65.00

Brant Goose, carved wood, Green-
backville, Virginia, ca. 1925 ...... 125.00

Broadbill Drake, carved wood, by
Ward Brothers, Crisfield,
Maryland 2,800.00

Bufflehead Drakes, carved wood, by
Jim Foote, pr..................2,200.00

Canada Geese, flat sheet iron
stick-up type, 1 w/head up & 3
w/heads down, worn original
black & white paint, 29" l.,
set of 4 .... 80.00

Canada Goose in feeding position,
carved wood, old black & white
paint w/traces of brown, 22½" l.
(repairs to neck & age cracks) 245.00

Canada Goose, Herter's Decoy Co.,
balsa wood body w/pine head &
wooden base, original paint...... 99.00

Canada Goose, carved wood, by
George Boyd, Seabrook, New
Hampshire 6,000.00

Canvasback Drake, carved wood,
old worn working repaint, glass
eyes, 14¼" l. (old putty repair at
neck) 60.00

Canvasback Hen, Mason Premier
Grade, carved wood, hollow construction, original paint, glass
eyes, 15½" l. (replaced eye &
minor bill repair) 285.00

Coot, Herter's Decoy Co., balsa
wood 30.00

Crow, Mason Premier Grade 600.00

Fish, "Perch," carved wood w/tin
fins & tack eyes, 7" l. 100.00

Fish, "Pike," carved wood, painted
eyes, original realistically shaded
green paint, 18" l. 145.00

Fish, "Smelt," carved wood, tack
eyes, green & white paint, 7" l. .. 60.00

Fish, "Sucker," carved wood w/cop-
per fins, red & white paint,
10" l. 110.00

Geese, waxed cardboard folding-
type decoys in original canvas bag
marked "One Dozen Complete
Johnson's Folding Goose Decoys.
Large.," 28" l., set of 12 .... 432.00

Goldeneye Hen & Drake, carved
wood, by Ward Brothers, Crisfield,
Maryland, pr. 5,500.00

Golden Merganser, carved wood, by
F. J. Dobbins, Jonesport, Maine .. 145.00

Great Black Back Gull, carved

wood, possibly Massachusetts
Bay area......................4,400.00

Greater Yellowlegs, carved wood... 900.00

Green Wing Teal, carved wood, by
Capt. Harry Jobes, pr. 175.00

Green Wing Teal Hen, Mason
Premier Grade, carved wood 2,200.00

Lesser Yellowlegs, carved cedar
wood w/iron bill, original paint,
Long Island, New York area,
ca. 1870 .... 99.00

Mallard Drake, carved wood, old
worn repaint, glass eyes,
16" l. 85.00

Mallard Hen, carved wood, original
paint, glass eyes, by Kempinger,
Oshkosh, Wisconsin, ca. 1930,
15½" l. 160.00

Mallard Hen, carved wood, by A.
Elmer Crowell, East Harwich,
Massachusetts.................2,900.00

Mallard Hen & Drake, Mason
Challenge Grade, glass eyes,
pr............................. 450.00

Merganser Hen & Drake, Mason
Challenge Grade, carved wood,
pr............................9,900.00

Mute Swan, carved cedar, hollow
construction, original paint, attributed to Captain Chip Alsop,
Barnegat Bay, New Jersey 418.00

Pintail Drake, carved wood, hollow
construction, old worn working
repaint, by Jim Rayker, Fox Lake,
Illinois, 14½" l. 75.00

Pintail Drake, carved wood, by
Charles Perdew, Henry, Illinois ... 850.00

Pintail Duck, carved wood, by Hec
Whittington, Illinois 1,265.00

Pintail Duck, carved wood, original
paint, by August Haas, Peru,
Illinois (1890-1962) 5,225.00

Redbreasted Merganser Hen, carved
wood, by Joe Lincoln, Accord,
Massachusetts.................4,400.00

Redhead Drake, Mason Challenge
Grade, original paint w/old touch-
up, glass eyes, 13¾" l. (shot
scars) 190.00

Redhead Hen, carved wood, hollow
construction, worn original paint,
glass eyes, by Chris Smith,
Algonac, Michigan, ca. 1920,
15" l. 150.00

Redhead Hen, Mason Challenge
Grade.......................... 400.00

Ruddy Duck in courting position
w/tail fanned out, carved wood,
by Charles "Shang" Wheeler,
Stratford, Connecticut 12,100.00

Shorebird, tin folding-type, original
paint w/minor wear, stenciled interior label w/patent date of
1874, 11" h. on wooden base..... 70.00

Swan, carved cedar, hollow construction, weathered original
paint, New Jersey area 900.00
Swan hissing w/crooked neck,
carved cedar, hollow construction,
worn original paint, Barnegat Bay,
New Jersey area 1,210.00
Swan in preening position, carved
cedar, hollow construction, worn
original paint, Barnegat Bay, New
Jersey area 1,100.00

DE LONGPRE (PAUL) PRINTS

Pansies & Lily-of-the-Valley

*Paul de Longpre, born in Lyons, France, to
a Creole mother from Martinique and a
French artist-father, showed a talent for
painting at an early age. He first exhibited
his works in 1876 and was an immediate success, both artistically and financially.
However, his bank failed and he subsequently
immigrated to the United States, settling in
New York City, where he turned his talents
to the painting of flowers exclusively. He later
moved to California. In 1900, prices for his
original floral paintings ranged from $90.00
to $350.00.*

American Beauty roses yard long
picture, framed $75.00
Basket of lilacs print, framed 82.50
Basket of roses print, framed 65.00
Chrysanthemums or violets print,
unframed, 16 x 9", each 18.00
Chrysanthemums yard long picture,
framed 100.00
Pansies & lily-of-the-valley print
(ILLUS.) 20.00
Pink roses yard long picture 45.00
Yellow roses & lavender violets yard
long picture, framed 60.00

DISNEY (Walt) COLLECTIBLES

Bambi Planter

*Scores of objects ranging from watches to
dolls have been created in imitation of Walt
Disney's copyrighted animated cartoon
characters, and an increasing number of collectors are now seeking these, made primarily by licensed manufacturers. Also see
BANKS, BIG LITTLE BOOKS and
CHRISTMAS TREE LIGHTS.*

Alice in Wonderland birthday candle
holders, original box $55.00
Alice in Wonderland figure, ceramic,
Walt Disney Productions, copy-
right 1960 . . . . 35.00
Alice in Wonderland wrist watch,
Bradley 25.00
Bambi celluloid, Bambi approaching
Thumper in the forest, applied to
a watercolor & pastel background,
stamped WDP, 1940, 7½ x 8½" . . 1,045.00
Bambi napkin ring, sterling silver . . . 41.50
Bambi planter, ceramic, tan, pink &
green on beige, glossy, marked
Bambi, Walt Disney Productions
on bottom, 7" l., 7" h. (ILLUS.) 22.50
Big Bad Wolf book, "Who's Afraid of
the Big Bad Wolf," 1st edition,
1933 . . . . 85.00
Cinderella Better Little Book, 1950 . . 15.00
Cinderella bracelet, 1950's 28.00
Cinderella planter, ceramic, pastel
blue, pink, green & yellow, im-
pressed WDP, 6½" l., 6½" h. 17.50
Cinderella & Prince handkerchief,
1940's 3.50
Clarabelle the Cow book, 1938 . . . . . 25.00
Clarabelle the Cow tumbler, glass,
figure in red, 4 3/8" h. 17.00
Disney characters book, "Here They
Are," Mickey, Minnie, Donald,
Pluto, colored pictures by Walt
Disney, Ardra Wavle, 1940 . . . . 16.00
Disney characters book, "School
Days in Disneyville," 1939 . . . . 25.00
Disney characters charm bracelet . . . 33.00

Disney characters cookie jar, bus-shaped, license says "Disneyland U.S.A." 150.00

Disney characters crayon box, tin, 1946 .... 18.00

Disney characters lunch box, school bus w/Disney characters, w/thermos bottle 38.50

Disney characters rug, Mickey & Minnie in airplane, Donald in parachute, label reads "Alexander Smith-Good Housekeeping," 27 x 45" 300.00

Disney characters sand pail, Mickey & Pluto selling cold drinks while Minnie watches & Clarabelle dances, 3" 55.00

Disney characters toy, windup tin "Disneyland Roller Coaster," figure 8 roller coaster w/two passenger cars, J. Chein & Co., 1940's, 10" h. 285.00

Donald Duck book, "Funny Stories About Donald & Mickey," copyright 1945, 128 pp. 24.00

Donald Duck camera, Walt Disney Enterprises, Herbert George Co... 21.50

Donald Duck charm, celluloid, 1" ... 20.00

Donald Duck figure, rubber, Seiberling, 5" h. 95.00

Donald Duck figure, composition, walks, Borgfeldt, 11" h. 550.00

Donald Duck jigsaw puzzle, Donald on picnic 10.00

Donald Duck napkin ring, celluloid .. 30.00

Donald Duck pencil case, W.D.P., Hassenfeld Bros., Inc. 20.00

Donald Duck pitcher, ceramic, figural, marked Donald Duck, Walt Disney, U.S.A., 6 1/8" h. 33.50

Donald Duck planter, pottery, Donald in cowboy suit 40.00

Donald Duck ring, sterling silver, Donald in relief, size 7 .... 55.00

Donald Duck salt & pepper shakers, ceramic, Walt Disney Enterprises, pr. 25.00

Donald Duck sprinkling can, tin, Walt Disney Enterprises, 1938, 3" 45.00

Donald Duck toothbrush holder, bisque 125.00

Donald Duck Toy

Donald Duck toy, Donald & Pluto in car, Sun Rubber Co., 6½" l. (ILLUS.) 31.50

Donald Duck toy, windup tin "Donald Duck Duet," Donald playing drum & Goofy dancing, Louis Marx & Co., 1946, original box ... 390.00

Donald Duck wrist watch, oblong or round, U.S. Time, 1948 .... 110.00

Donald Duck & Joe Carioca "turnabout" cookie jar 62.00

Donald Duck Candy Pail

Donald Duck & nephews Huey, Louie & Dewey candy pail, Overland Candy Co., Chicago, 1949, 3 oz., 3½" h. (ILLUS.) 22.50

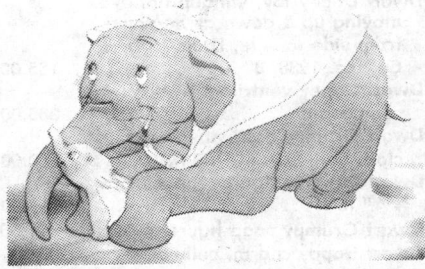

Dumbo the Elephant Celluloid

Dumbo the Elephant celluloid, within the protection of his mother, Courvoiser Galleries, 1941, 8½ x 10½" (ILLUS.) 880.00

Dumbo the Elephant creamer, ceramic, Walt Disney Productions, 6" h. 23.50

Dumbo the Elephant hand puppet ... 8.00

Dumbo the Elephant Little Golden Book, "Dumbo," 1947 .... 5.00

Dumbo the Elephant pitcher, ceramic, 2-qt. 30.00

Dumbo the Elephant wall pocket 24.00

Dwarf Bashful figure, composition .. 125.00

Dwarf Bashful figure, rubber, Seiberling 38.00

Dwarf Doc candy container, glitter-
covered papier mache, Walt Dis-
ney Productions 28.00
Dwarf Doc toothbrush holder, "Doc
Says Brush Your Teeth" 42.50
Dwarf Dopey bank, ceramic 32.50

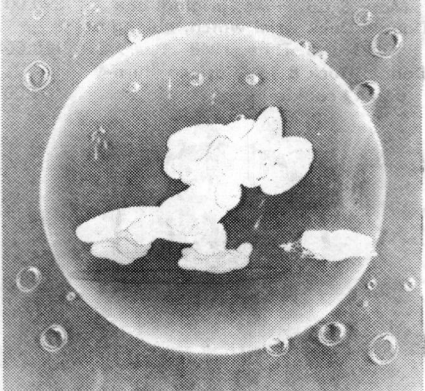

Dwarf Dopey Celluloid

Dwarf Dopey celluloid, Dopey within
a bubble w/bar of soap surrounded by floating bubbles, applied to
airbrushed background, Glosson,
Cincinnati label, 1937, 8½ x 8½"
(ILLUS.) 1,430.00
Dwarf Dopey charm, celluloid,
1930's 20.00
Dwarf Dopey toy, windup tin, eyes
moving up & down as he walks
from side to side, Louis Marx &
Co., ca. 1938, 8" h. 185.00
Dwarf Dopey ventriloquist dummy,
composition 385.00
Dwarf Grumpy doll, vinyl head,
cloth body, Gund, 13" h. 100.00
Dwarf Grumpy figure, rubber,
4¼" h. 15.00
Dwarf Grumpy soap figure, 1930's . . 21.50
Dwarf Happy charm, celluloid,
1930's 20.00
Dwarf Sneezy figure, rubber,
Seiberling 37.50
Dwarf Sneezy soap figure, 1930's . . . 35.00
Dwarfs, Bashful, Doc, Dopey,
Grumpy, Sleepy, Sneezy & Happy
figures, hard rubber, Seiberling,
1938, set of 7 . . . . 220.00
"Fantasia" movie program, 1940 . . . . 25.00
Ferdinand the Bull book, "Ferdinand
the Bull," ca. 1938. . . . . 11.50
Ferdinand the Bull bracelet, marked
Walt Disney Enterprises. 40.00
Ferdinand the Bull figure, bisque,
3" h. 22.50
Ferdinand the Bull figure, rubber,
Seiberling, 1938-40 . . . . 48.00
Ferdinand the Bull soap figure. 25.00

Flower the Skunk (Bambi) salt &
pepper shakers, pr. 35.00
Geppeto soap figure, 1939, 3¾" h.
(chipped foot) 15.00
Goofy figure, bisque, 1930's,
3½" h. 48.00
Horace Horsecollar figure, bisque . . . 56.00
Jiminy Cricket figure, bisque,
3" h. 65.00
Jiminy Cricket figure, wood-jointed,
Ideal, 8" h. . . . . 250.00 to 295.00
Jiminy Cricket mask, paper, Gillette
Blue Blades premium, 1939 . . . . . . 14.00
Joe Carrioca pencil sharpener,
celluloid 15.00
Ludwig Von Drake game, "Tiddly
Winks" 12.00
Ludwig Von Drake pencil box 18.00
Ludwig Von Drake toy, windup tin
Ludwig walking, Linemar, 6" 125.00
Mickey Mouse alarm clock, animat-
ed "wagging head" Mickey,
Bayard Co., France, 1930's to
1969, original box . . . . 65.00 to 85.00
Mickey Mouse alarm clock, full fig-
ure on face, Ingersoll, 1934 . . . . . . 290.00
Mickey Mouse alarm clock, full fig-
ure on face, celluloid case, Inger-
soll, 1947 . . . . 100.00 to 150.00
Mickey Mouse alarm clock, travel-
type, Phinney-Walker, Germany . . 30.00
Mickey Mouse apron, sailcloth,
1935 . . . . 30.00
Mickey Mouse baby spoon, silver-
plate, Wm. Rogers & Son 11.50
Mickey Mouse bank, dime register,
1939 . . . . 68.00
Mickey Mouse bank, book-shaped,
red leather & brass, Zell Products
Co., 1930's 65.00
Mickey Mouse bank, aluminum, fig-
ure of Mickey w/hands on hips,
France, early 1930's, 8" h. 1,200.00
Mickey Mouse bank, treasure chest
shape, souvenir of 1933 Chicago
World Fair, Zell Products Co. 120.00
Mickey Mouse birthday card,
1932 . . . . 20.00
Mickey Mouse book, "Alphabet,"
1936 . . . . 65.00
Mickey Mouse book, "Mickey Mouse
Crusoe," 1938 . . . . 65.00
Mickey Mouse book, "Mickey Mouse
Fire Brigade," 1936, published by
Whitman, hard cover w/original
dust jacket, 10 x 7 x ¾" 80.00
Mickey Mouse book, "Mickey
Mouse's Friends Wait for The
County Fair," 1937 . . . . 21.50
Mickey Mouse book, "Mickey Mouse
Story," Book No. 1, David McKay,
1931 . . . . 75.00 to 100.00
Mickey Mouse book, "Mickey Mouse
Stories," Book No. 2, McKay,

1934, soft cover, 8½ x
6¼ x 3/8" 65.00

Mickey Mouse book, pop-up type,
"King Arthur's Court," 1933 ...... 200.00

Mickey Mouse bubble gum card
album, Vol. No. 1, w/thirty-
three cards 350.00

Mickey Mouse camera (for 126
film) 38.00

Mickey Mouse card game, "Canasta
Junior," 2 sealed decks, plastic
tray & box, 1950, set 25.00

Mickey Mouse card game, "Old
Maid," ca. 1935 .... 42.50

Mickey Mouse card game, "Snap,"
w/box 60.00

Mickey Mouse card games, "Library
of Games," 5 volumes of card
games, 1946 .... 50.00

Mickey Mouse charm, celluloid 16.50

Mickey Mouse crayon box, tin,
Chein 12.50

Mickey Mouse creamer & cov. sugar
bowl, china, Mickey playing banjo
decor, lustre finish, pr. 35.00

Mickey Mouse cuff links, Hickock,
1950, pr. 18.00

Mickey Mouse cup, saucer & dinner
plate, printed tin, Ohio Art Co.,
3 pcs. 75.00

Mickey Mouse doll, stuffed felt,
stamped "Steiff" on bottom of
foot, 6" h. 298.00

Mickey Mouse doll, stuffed cloth,
Ideal, 1930's, 11" h. 200.00

Mickey Mouse doll, stuffed cloth
body, rubber face, felt ears,
Gund, 1940's, 22" h. ......50.00 to 75.00

Mickey Mouse feeding dish, Patriot
china, 7" d. 57.50

Mickey Mouse figure, bisque, long
snout & toothsome grin, Germany,
1¾" h. 150.00

Mickey Mouse figure, celluloid, cowboy w/jointed arms & legs,
4½" h. 250.00

Bisque Mickey Mouse Figure

Mickey Mouse figure, bisque,
marked "Mickey Mouse" on chest
& "Made in Japan" on back, 5" h.
(ILLUS.)...................... 45.00

Mickey Mouse figure, wood-jointed,
Borgfeldt, Pat. 8-17/1926,
5" h. ....150.00 to 225.00

Mickey Mouse figure, bisque,
Mickey playing saxophone,
marked Walt Disney, 3" w. base,
5½" h. 65.00

Mickey Mouse figure, hard rubber,
Seiberling, 1930's, 6" h. 125.00

Mickey Mouse figure, chalkware,
9¾" h. 95.00

Mickey Mouse figure, composition,
Knickerbocker Toy Co., 1930's,
12" h. 425.00

Mickey Mouse game, "Bean Bag" ... 75.00

Mickey Mouse game, "Dominoes,"
original box 68.00

Mickey Mouse game, "Magic Picture," Camay Soap premium,
1930's 115.00

Mickey Mouse game, "Quoits" (ring
toss), lithographed paper on
wood, English, 18½" sq. 80.00

Mickey Mouse game, "Scatter Ball,"
Louis Marx & Co., 1934 .... 250.00

Mickey Mouse handkerchiefs, printed cotton, Days of the Week
series, ca. 1930, set of 7 .... 175.00

Mickey Mouse kaleidoscope,
8¾" l. 22.50

Mickey Mouse key ring, leather 20.00

Mickey Mouse lamp, painted tin,
original parchment shade w/pic-
tures, signed Walt Disney Enterprises, 10½" h. 135.00

Mickey Mouse mug, marked Patriot
China & W.D.E. 45.00

Mickey Mouse napkin ring, celluloid,
ca. 1938 .... 30.00

Mickey Mouse napkin ring, sterling
silver 75.00

Mickey Mouse pencil box w/ruler &
eraser, Dixon, 1925-35 .... 125.00

Mickey Mouse pencil sharpener,
bakelite, ca. 1935 .... 85.00

Mickey Mouse pillow case, embroidered, 1932................... 25.00

Mickey Mouse planter, ceramic,
Mickey as cowboy, multicolored
glossy finish, 4 x 7 x 6½"........ 30.00

Mickey Mouse pocket watch, die-
debossed back, Ingersoll, 1933 ... 350.00

Mickey Mouse popcorn popper,
mechanical figure of Mickey,
1930's 145.00

Mickey Mouse radio, wooden
case w/scenes of Mickey
playing a bass fiddle, a piano,
a tuba & flute, Emerson,
7½" h. ....850.00 to 2,500.00

Mickey Mouse Sterling Silver Ring

Mickey Mouse ring, sterling silver,
Walt Disney Productions, 1930's,
¾" h. figure of Mickey (ILLUS.) . . .   175.00

Mickey Mouse sand shovel, printed
tin 65.00

Mickey Mouse sugar bowl, china,
1930's 22.00

Mickey Mouse tea set: teapot,
creamer, sugar bowl, 2 c/s & 4
plates; china, orange lustre trim,
ca. 1935, 11 pcs. 195.00

Mickey Mouse teaspoon, silverplate,
pie-eyed Mickey, Rogers Bros. 22.00

Mickey Mouse tool chest, tin, 1936 . .   95.00

Mickey Mouse toothbrush holder,
bisque, movable arms,
5" . . . . .195.00 to 250.00

Mickey Mouse toy, battery-operated
Mickey drummer, lighted eyes,
Linemar, 1941 . . . . .195.00 to 375.00

Mickey Mouse toy, battery-operated
"Mickey the Magician," Linemar . .   450.00

Mickey Mouse toy, windup tin
Mickey on bicycle, Linemar 150.00

Mickey Mouse toy, windup tin
Mickey on unicycle, Linemar 425.00

Mickey Mouse toy, windup tin circus
train, Lionel No. 1536, engine,
tender w/Mickey shoveling & 3
lithographed circus scene cars,
ca. 1936 . . . . .1,500.00

Mickey Mouse toy, windup tin "Dip-
sey Car," Linemar 350.00

Mickey Mouse toy, windup tin "Dip-
sey Car," Louix Marx & Co. 300.00

Mickey Mouse toy chest, Odora Co.,
ca. 1932 . . . .   265.00

Mickey Mouse toy top, spinning-
type, Walt Disney Enterprises,
1930's 110.00

Mickey Mouse toy washing machine,
tin, marked Walt Disney Enter-
prises, Ohio Art Co. 95.00

Mickey Mouse umbrella, Mickey
handle, Disney characters screen-
printed on blue silk top 125.00

Mickey Mouse watch fob, original
leather strap, 1930's 75.00

Mickey Mouse "weather house,"
1940's 90.00

Mickey Mouse world globe, metal

w/decals intact, Rand McNally,
1955, 10" h. 98.00

Mickey Mouse wrist watch, round
dial, yellow-gloved minute & hour
hands & 3 Mickey figures on subsidiary seconds dial, metal band
w/Mickey figures, 1933 . .350.00 to 600.00

Mickey Mouse wrist watch, oblong
dial, red band, Ingersoll Deluxe
model, w/Fred Astaire on
box .175.00 to 250.00

Mickey Mouse wrist watch, oblong
dial, red leather band, U.S. Time,
1948-50's . . . . .72.50 to 125.00

Mickey Mouse wrist watch, no figure of Mickey on oblong dial, U.S.
Time, 1960's 25.00

Mickey Mouse Club hat, black
w/plastic ears . . . . .8.50 to 15.00

Mickey Mouse Club lunch pail (no
thermos) 8.50

Mickey Mouse & Donald Duck book,
"Detective Adventures," by Walt
Disney, printed in England by per-
mission WD-MM Ltd., 94 pp. 95.00

Mickey Mouse & Donald Duck cray-
on box, tin, ca. 1940 . . . .   35.00

Mickey Mouse & Donald Duck sand
pail, tin, marked Walt Disney,
England, 1930's . . . . .50.00 to 95.00

Mickey & Minnie Mouse bandana,
Mickey as cowboy & Minnie as
Indian, Walt Disney Productions,
20" sq. 32.00

Mickey & Minnie Mouse coloring
book, Saalfield, 1933-34 . . . .   80.00

Mickey & Minnie Mouse creamer,
china, 2½" 30.00

Mickey & Minnie Mouse cup &
saucer, printed tin 30.00

Mickey & Minnie Mouse dolls,
stuffed cloth, original clothes,
1930's, 14" h., pr. 395.00

Mickey & Minnie Mouse figures,
wooden, w/decals on front, Borg-
feldt, 1934, 3¼" h., pr. . . .125.00 to 195.00

Mickey & Minnie Mouse figures,
bisque, Mickey w/cane & Minnie
w/umbrella & purse, Walt E. Dis-
ney, Japan, 4½" h., pr. 145.00

Mickey & Minnie Mouse figures, cel-
luloid, jointed, w/label on foot
"M.M. Copr. 1928-30 by Walter E.
Disney," 5" h., pr. 385.00

Mickey & Minnie Mouse handker-
chief, cotton 6.00

Mickey & Minnie Mouse masks,
cardboard, pr. 50.00

Mickey & Minnie Mouse paper dolls,
1930's 100.00

Mickey & Minnie Mouse pen & pencil set, Inkograph, Walt Disney
Enterprises 100.00

Mickey & Minnie Mouse pillow top,

stamped for embroidery, Vogue
Needlecraft No. 98, 1931 copyright ....45.00 to 75.00
Mickey & Minnie Mouse pitcher, tin,
Mickey & Minnie at piano 7.50
Mickey & Minnie Mouse plate,
Bavarian china, Mickey playing
piano center & Mickey & Minnie
around border, gold rim edge,
7½" d. 55.00
Mickey & Minnie Mouse sand pail,
tin, Ohio Art Co., 1930's, 3" h. ... 57.50
Mickey & Minnie Mouse tea set:
cov. teapot, creamer, sugar bowl
& 4 c/s; china, Mickey & Minnie at
various pursuits, blue borders,
marked Walt Disney, 11 pcs. 105.00
Mickey & Minnie Mouse tea set:
cov. teapot, creamer, cov. sugar
bowl, 4 c/s, 4 plates & cake serving plate; china, tan lustre trim,
Walt E. Disney & "Made in
Japan," 16 pcs. 140.00

Mickey & Minnie Toothbrush Holder

Mickey & Minnie Mouse toothbrush
holder, bisque, names impressed
on back, 1¾ x 3½ x 4½"
(ILLUS.)...................... 110.00
Mickey Mouse & Pluto ash tray,
china 90.00

Mickey Mouse & Pluto Celluloid

Mickey Mouse & Pluto celluloid,
from "The Pointer," Mickey &
Pluto in fond embrace, applied
to airbrushed background,
10½ x 8½" (ILLUS.) 880.00
Mickey Mouse & Pluto feeding dish,
china, 3-compartment............   50.00
Mickey Mouse & Silly Symphony
song folio, illustrated, 1934 ......   45.00
Minnie Mouse book, "Story of Min-
nie Mouse," hardbound, copy-
right, 1938, 5 x 5½", 92 pp.......   25.00
Minnie Mouse bowl, Salem China
Co., Disney Enterprises,
1934 ....37.00 to 50.00
Minnie Mouse charm, sterling
silver 22.50
Minnie Mouse doll, stuffed cloth,
Knickerbocker Co., 1936,
11" h..................375.00 to 475.00
Minnie Mouse doll, stuffed cloth,
Gund, 1940's, 13" h............. 175.00
Minnie Mouse doll, stuffed vel-
veteen cloth, Steiff tag 195.00
Minnie Mouse figure, bisque, Minnie
w/mandolin, 3½" h..............   35.00
Minnie Mouse figure, wood-jointed,
5½" h..................100.00 to 150.00
Minnie Mouse marionette, composi-
tion, 1940's, 13" h. ....90.00 to 165.00
Minnie Mouse mug, Patriot china,
1930's 47.50
Minnie Mouse plate, Patriot china,
6½" d. 65.00
Minnie Mouse ring, sterling silver ..   60.00
Minnie Mouse toothbrush holder,
bisque, movable arms 225.00
Minnie Mouse toy, windup tin Min-
nie knitting while rocking in chair,
Linemar 250.00
Minnie Mouse toy, windup tin Min-
nie playing xylophone, Linemar .. 285.00
Minnie Mouse wrist watch, Timex,
1968 ....60.00 to 100.00
Peter Pan schoolbag..............   45.00
Pinocchio alarm clock, Bayard 92.50
Pinocchio bank, composition, signed
Disney Enterprises ....85.00 to 100.00
Pinocchio board game, 1939, signed
Walt Disney Enterprises..........   50.00
Pinocchio book, "Pinocchio," Walt
Disney, Cocoa Malt ad back
cover, 1939 ....   18.00
Pinocchio book, "pop-up" type,
1932 ....75.00 to 125.00
Pinocchio card game, 1939 ....   9.00
Pinocchio coloring book, 1939 ......   18.50
Pinocchio cookie jar, ceramic.......   55.00
Pinocchio creamer & sugar bowl,
pr............................   28.00
Pinocchio doll, wood & composition,
jointed, Ideal, 8".........75.00 to 100.00
Pinocchio doll, wood & composition,
jointed, Ideal, 11" 115.00

Pinocchio doll, wood & composition,
Ideal, 19".......................... 315.00
Pinocchio figure, bisque, 3" h....... 22.50
Pinocchio figure, chalkware, marked
WDP, ca. 1940, 4" h. 35.00
Pinocchio knife, fork & spoon, sil-
verplate, Pinocchio & Donkey 40.00
Pinocchio mask, paper, Gillette Blue
Blades advertising premium,
1939 .... 12.00
Pinocchio pencil sharpener 20.00
Pinocchio pinback button, celluloid,
1¼" d............................ 20.00
Pinocchio sheet music, "When You
Wish Upon A Star" 20.00
Pinocchio soap figure 22.50
Pinocchio stamp album, 1940 .... 12.00
Pinocchio teapot, cov., tin 28.00
Pinocchio tea set, tin, Ohio Art Co.,
1939, 15 pcs..................... 57.50
Pinocchio teaspoon, silverplate 12.50
Pinocchio tea tray, tin, 1934 .... 11.00
Pinocchio toy, battery-operated
Pinocchio & xylophone 67.50
Pinocchio toy, windup tin, Linemar,
5½" 130.00
Pinocchio toy, windup tin, Louis
Marx & Co., 1939 .... 43.00
Pinocchio toy, windup tin "Pinocchio
the Acrobat," Louis Marx & Co.,
1939 .... 195.00
Pinocchio toy, windup tin Pinocchio
on trapeze, Louis Marx & Co.,
1939 .... 140.00
Pinocchio valentine, mechanical,
1939 .... 20.00
Pinocchio wrist watch, Ingersoll,
U.S. Time........................ 87.50
Pinocchio xylophone................ 75.00

DOLL FURNITURE & ACCESSORIES

Bathtub, tin, printed scene of children at beach on sides, Germany,
9 x 3"............................. $24.00
Bed, brass, tubular, w/original mesh
spring & mattress, late 19th c., 21
x 16" ....125.00 to 200.00
Bed, mahogany, poster-type
w/canopy top, turned posts w/urn
finials, arched headboard, w/mat-
tress & linens, 20th c. copy of old
style, 22½" l., 22¼" h. posts..... 132.00
Bed, oak, spool-turned spindles in
high back, wire mesh springs, ca.
1890, 25 x 14" (folds for
storage) 90.00
Bed, painted maple or birch, original dark red finish, original horsehair mattress, 19th c., 18" l. 145.00

Victorian Doll Bed

Bed, walnut, Victorian-style w/high
back, 19th c., 24 x 12" (ILLUS.) ... 165.00
Bottle sterilizer & rack, tin, w/six
glass bottles, marked "Amaco" ... 30.00
Buggy, woven wicker, w/"opera"
windows in hood, spoke wheels
w/rubber tires, painted, 1930's,
according to size ....65.00 to 115.00
Carpet sweeper, "Universal," tin ... 24.00
Carriage, metal & canvas, "Kozee
Kar," by Kozee Kar Co., Minneapolis, Minnesota, 1940's 35.00
Carriage, tin & steel, blue paint,
wheels w/rubber tires 45.00
Carriage, wicker, woven ornate C-
scroll details, wooden spoke
wheels w/metal rims, w/parasol,
late Victorian 185.00

19th Century Doll Carriage

Carriage, wooden, original paint &
stenciled decor, wooden spoke
wheels w/metal rims, original
fringed canopy & upholstery,
19th c. (ILLUS.) 475.00

Cedar chest w/hinged lid & interior tray, w/copper finish studded bandings, 1925-35, 18 x 9½", 7½" h. 65.00

Chair, Thonet-type bentwood, overall 16" h. 35.00

Chair, wooden, spindle back, original worn red paint w/yellow striping, 10" h. 24.00

Chest of drawers, American Empire style, grain-painted tiger stripe maple finish, oblong top w/cut corners & scrolling backsplash above 3 drawers, C-scroll front feet, bootjack sides, ca. 1850, 9" w., 9" h. 225.00

Chest of drawers, pine, oblong top set w/silvered tin easel-type mirror above 3 drawers, 15" w., overall 24" h. 85.00

Coffee grinder, wooden w/cast iron hopper & handle, w/paper label "Little Tot," 3¾" h. ....30.00 to 60.00

Cook stove, cast iron, "Eagle," complete w/stove lids & side attachment, 13½ x 11" 145.00

Cradle, die-cast metal, suspended-type swinging on framework, ornate, 6 x 4½" 65.00

Cradle, pine, spindle-sided crib on rockers, pre-1900, 15" l. 50.00

Cradle, walnut, low country-style on rockers, 22" l. 50.00

Cradle, wicker, w/adjustable hood w/side windows, 1940's ....25.00 to 45.00

Cupboard, golden oak, shaped crest above glazed door & single drawer, 6½" w., 12½" h. 75.00

Cupboard, painted pine, 1-piece wire nail construction, open top w/shelves above single cupboard door, bracket feet, old green paint, 20¼" h. 55.00

Bliss-type Doll House

Doll house, Bliss-type, lithographed paper on wood, central dormer & covered front porch, 18" w., 20" h. (ILLUS.) 635.00

Doll house, wooden, Schoenhut, 16 x 16" 275.00

Doll house, wooden, 2-story, 2 sides swing open, white w/blue shutters, 1940's, very large 175.00

Doll house armchair, blue, Renwal .. 7.00

Doll house armchair, metal, Tootsietoy 10.00

Doll house bed, metal, Tootsietoy .. 10.00

Doll house candle sconce, 2-light, gilt metal, w/cut glass prisms & bobeches, ca. 1900, 1" scale 242.00

Dollhouse chaise lounge, metal, Tootsietoy 22.00

Doll house chest of drawers, cast iron, 3 drawers w/ornate filigree fronts, original red, blue & white paint w/yellow striping, 6¼" h. .. 70.00

Doll house crib on wheels, cast iron, 2¼" h. 25.00

Doll house highchair, cast iron, 3¼" h. 25.00

Doll house dining table, round top, metal, Tootsietoy 15.00

Doll house refrigerator, Renwal 5.00

Doll house table lamp, metal, Tootsietoy 10.00

Doll house tea cart, metal, Tootsietoy 25.00

Doll house washing machine, Renwal 9.00

Dutch oven, cov., cast iron, "Griswold, Pat. 1920" 35.00

Egg beater, iron & tin, "Baby Bingo" 10.00

Egg beater, iron & tin, "Betty Taplin" 7.00

Egg beater, wood & tin, red-painted handles 15.00

Fainting couch, hardwood frame w/upholstery, old paint 125.00

Food grinder, cast iron, "Pony" 18.00

Foot stool, walnut, square nail construction, scalloped apron, 4 x 2¼", 2¼" h. (age cracks) 95.00

Highchair, cast iron, "Kilgore" 40.00

Highchair, cast iron & tin 30.00

Highchair, wicker, 19th c. ...165.00 to 225.00

Kettle w/bail handle, copper, impressed "1 cent" 22.00

Kettle, 2-handled, graniteware, blue & white swirls 26.00

Kitchen cabinet, "Hoosier" style, oak, original label, refinished 295.00

Kitchen cabinet, wooden, handmade, 24" h. 65.00

Mirror, hand-type, silverplate, Art Nouveau style, beveled glass, 3½" l. 18.00

Mixing bowl, yellowware, 3½" d. .. 15.00

Muffin pan, tin.................... 6.00

Nursing bottle w/nipple & metal
sterilizer 37.50

Parasol, black silk w/ruffles,
18" d. 42.50

Piano stool, adjustable top, light
natural refinishing, 9" h......... 30.00

Purse, sterling silver mesh, hinged
frame w/clasp & chain, 2½" l. 98.00

Quilt, pieced Bow Tie patt., red &
white cotton, 18" sq. ......22.00 to 35.00

Quilt, pieced Log Cabin patt., colorful velvet & black, 21 x 18" 105.00

Quilt, pieced velvet w/trapunto
flower & leaves in center square,
ca. 1880, 22" sq. 150.00

Quilt, pieced red & white cotton
blocks, overall quilting 85.00

Rocking chair, bentwood, 15" h. 37.00

Roller skates, leather & tin......... 18.00

Rolling pin, turned walnut, 1-piece.. 22.00

Sad iron, "Dazey," w/trivet 35.00

Sad iron, "Dover No. 922," 2-piece .. 35.00

Sad iron, "Pearl" 25.00

Sad iron, "Sensible," 2-piece 65.00

Saucepan, graniteware, green &
white swirls, 2½" d. 16.00

Saucepan, long handle, graniteware, turquoise blue 35.00

Skillet, cast iron, "Wagner Ware,"
4½" d. 15.00

Sofa, "camel-back" style, wooden
frame grained to resemble rosewood, floral brocade upholstery,
early 20th c., 11½" l............. 75.00

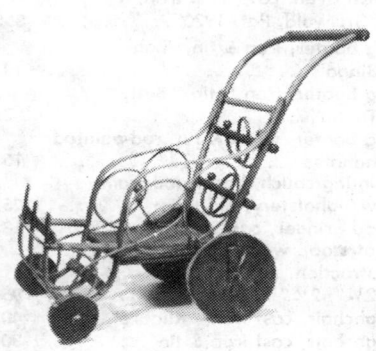

Doll's Stroller

Stroller, bentwood, solid wooden
wheels, 19" h. (ILLUS.).......... 95.00

Stroller, wicker & wood, high
wooden spoke rear wheels,
Victorian 395.00

Table, drop-leaf, mahogany, Turn-
of-the-Century, extra long
leaves 225.00

Table, drop-leaf, pine, early 20th c.,
original paint 145.00

Table, drop-leaf, walnut, oblong top
w/rounded drop leaves, turned
legs, 14 x 13" top plus 7¼" l.
leaves, 15½" h.................. 200.00

Table, golden oak, round top, pedestal base, ca. 1900 .... 135.00

Table, graniteware top w/alphabet
& nursery rhyme scenes, painted
hardwood apron & square legs,
ca. 1930.................98.00 to 150.00

Teakettle, brass, wire bail handle
w/black wooden grip, 4" d.,
2½" h. 85.00

Teakettle, copper, 2¼" d., 2¾" h... 45.00

Toaster, tin 10.00

Trunk, metal over wood, brass trim,
w/inside tray, 10 x 6" 32.50

Doll Size Waffle Iron

Waffle iron, cast iron w/wooden
handles, 4" d. (ILLUS.) 35.00

Wash basin & pitcher, white w/gold
trim, signed "K.T. & K.".......... 95.00

Washboard, "Little Housekeeper,"
6 x 3½" 12.00

Wash boiler, copper, "Don't Wash
on Saturday".................... 90.00

Washing machine, wooden......... 85.00

Wash tub, tin, brown, 7" d.,
2¾" h.......................... 9.00

DOLLS

*Also see CAMPBELL KID, CAT & DIS-
NEY COLLECTIBLES and PAPER & PIN
CUSHION DOLLS.*

Alabama (Indestructible) Baby by
Ella Smith, Roanoke, Alabama,
cloth, oil-painted features & hair,

applied ears, stitched mitten-
shaped hands, stitched toes,
1904-24, dressed, 14" $1,150.00
Alexander (Madame) Baby Genius,
composition head, sleep eyes,
cloth body, 1942, dressed, 20" 115.00

Elise by Madame Alexander

Alexander (Madame) Elise, hard
plastic & vinyl (ILLUS.) 250.00
Alexander (Madame) Jackie, hard
plastic w/vinyl over plastic arms,
1962, dressed, 21" 850.00
Alexander (Madame) Margaret
O'Brien, hard plastic, 1948-56 .... 200.00
Alexander (Madame) McGuffey
Ana, composition, painted side-
glancing eyes, 1935-39, dressed,
9" 295.00
A.M. (Armand Marseille) bisque
head girl marked "Germany 323 A
8/0 M," blue glass "googly" side-
glancing eyes, (new) h.h. (human
hair) wig, composition body,
dressed, 7½" 500.00
A.M. bisque socket head girl
marked "Just Me Germany A310 7
OM," blue side-glancing eyes,
"bee sting" closed mouth, 5-piece
straight-legged composition body,
dressed, 9" 660.00
A.M. bisque head character baby
marked "518," blue sleep eyes,
bent limb body, dressed, 16" 450.00
A.M. bisque head girl marked
"1894," blue eyes, blonde h.h.
wig, ball-jointed composition
body, dressed, 18" 300.00
A.M. bisque head girl marked
"370," brown sleep eyes, open
mouth, kid body, bisque hands,
dressed, 21" 275.00
A.M. bisque head girl marked
"390," blue glass sleep eyes, open
mouth w/upper row of teeth, light
brown h.h. wig, jointed composi-

tion body, jointed wrists, dressed,
26" 585.00
Amosandra, rubber, Sun Rubber
Company, designed by Ruth E.
Newton, 1948, 10" 45.00
Barbie (by Mattel), No. 2, vinyl plastic, movable head, painted eyes
w/white irises, heavy eyeliner,
pointed "Oriental" eyebrows,
rooted brunette saran hair, 1959 .. 250.00
Barbie, hard plastic, bubble cut hair,
1964 .... 120.00
Belton bisque dome head girl
marked "O," blue threaded glass
eyes, closed mouth, wood & composition body, dressed, 9" 550.00
Belton bisque head girl, blue
threaded eyes, closed outlined
mouth w/white space between
lips, straight wrists, dressed,
14½" 1,500.00
Bergmann (C.M.) bisque head girl,
blue sleep eyes, open mouth,
(replaced) h.h. wig, ball-jointed
composition body, dressed,
23½" 395.00
Bisque head Negro girl marked
"DEP," brown stationary set eyes,
open mouth w/upper row of
teeth, pierced ears, brown h.h.
wig, jointed composition body,
straight wrists, dressed, 12" 595.00
Bisque shoulder head girl marked
"F.G." (F. Gaultier), blue paperweight stationary glass eyes,
closed mouth, blonde h.h. wig,
kid leather body, dressed,
13½" 1,260.00

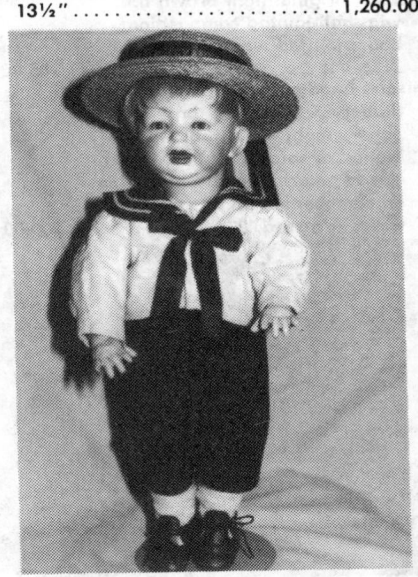

Bisque Head Toddler

Bisque head toddler marked "Hertel & Schwab," dressed, 16" (ILLUS.).. 950.00

Bisque head girl marked "R. D." (Rabery & Delphieu), blue paper-weight eyes, open mouth w/upper teeth, jointed body, dressed, 17" 975.00

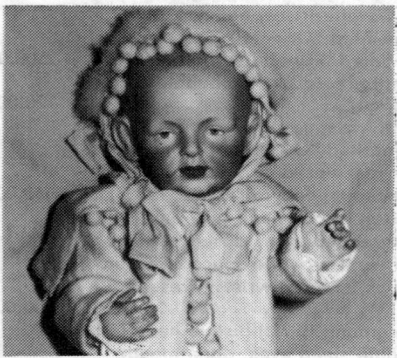

Bisque Head Character Baby

Bisque head character baby marked "F.S. & Co. 1267" (Franz Schmidt), dressed, 19" (ILLUS.) 1,650.00

Bisque head girl marked "G.K." (Gebruder Kraus), brown station-ary glass eyes, open mouth, pierced ears, blonde h.h. curly wig, jointed composition body, jointed wrists, dressed, 21" 575.00

Bisque head girl marked "E 9 D Depose" (E. Denamur), blue sta-tionary eyes, open mouth, pierced ears, original light brown h.h. wig, ball-jointed composition body, jointed wrists, dressed, 21" 1,285.00

Bisque head girl marked "R. 3 D." (Rabery & Delphieu), brown paperweight eyes w/brushed blonde eyebrows, outlined open-closed mouth, pierced ears, joint-ed composition body, straight wrists, dressed, 23" 1,760.00

Bisque Head Girl

Bisque head girl marked "DEP 10," dressed, 24" (ILLUS.)............. 850.00

Bisque head girl marked "A11T," blue paperweight eyes under mauve-shaded lids, closed mouth, pierced ears, (replaced) brown mohair wig, jointed wood & com-position body, fixed wrists, dressed, 25" (small flakes on ears & eyelid, minor body wear).....18,700.00

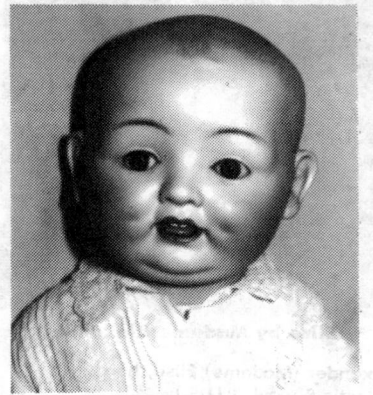

Bisque Head Baby

Bisque head character baby marked "C.P. 208," dressed, 27" (ILLUS.) .. 875.00

Brookglad Poor Pitiful Pearl, vinyl, blue sleep eyes, rooted blonde hair, 1957, dressed, 13".......... 79.00

Bru bisque swivel head girl marked "Bte S.G.D.G.," brown paper-weight eyes w/blushed lids, out-lined open-closed mouth, pierced ears, gusseted kid body, bisque lower arms, original dress, 16"...........................6,050.00

Bru (unmarked) bisque head girl, blue paperweight stationary glass eyes, closed mouth, pierced ears, brown h.h. wig, ball-jointed com-position body, jointed wrists, dressed, 20½" 2,395.00

Bru bisque head girl marked "Jne R," blue paperweight stationary glass eyes, open mouth w/upper row of teeth, brown h.h. wig in long curls, ball-jointed composi-tion body, jointed arms & wrists, dressed, 21½".................3,800.00

Bru bisque head girl marked "Jne R," brown paperweight stationary eyes, closed mouth, pierced ears, original blonde h.h. wig, ball-jointed composition body, jointed wrists, dressed, 23"............8,625.00

Bru bisque head girl marked "Jne R 12," dressed, 27" (ILLUS.) 4,700.00

Bru Bisque Head Girl

Bru bisque head girl marked
"Jne R," blue paperweight
stationary glass eyes, closed
mouth, pierced ears, light brown
h.h. wig, original composition
body, jointed wrists, dressed,
36" 12,000.00
Buddy Lee, trademark doll for H.D.
Lee Co., hard plastic, dressed,
14" 128.00
Bye-lo Baby, bisque head marked
"Grace S. Putnam," blue sleep
eyes, stuffed cloth body, celluloid
hands, dressed, 11" 325.00
Chase (Martha) stockinette boy,
dressed, 16" 550.00
Chase (Martha) stockinette girl,
molded bobbed hair, dressed,
17" 625.00
Chase (Martha) stockinette boy,
dressed, 28" 600.00
China head boy, molded blonde hair
w/exposed ears, pink tint,
Steuber body, dressed, 14"...... 275.00
China head body, molded black hair
w/sausage curls, cloth body,
leather hands & feet, dressed,
16" 237.00
China head lady, molded blonde
hair, jointed kid body, dressed,
16½" 125.00

China Head Lady

China head lady, molded black hair
w/center part, painted blue eyes,
cloth body, china arms & legs,
dressed, 17" (ILLUS.) 165.00
China head lady, molded black hair
looped in front of exposed
pierced ears & w/back in vertical
curls, blue eyes, white line between lips, cloth body, bisque
forearms, ca. 1850, dressed, 21"
(finger tips broken off left
hand) 775.00
China head lady, molded & painted
black "covered wagon" flat-top
hairstyle w/center part & sausage
curls, painted blue eyes & red
eyelines, rosy pink cheeks, original cloth body, china arms & legs,
dressed, 24" .... 300.00 to 495.00

China "Pet Name" Lady

China head pet name lady w/turned
head, molded & painted blonde
common hairstyle & w/name
"Agnes" molded in china shoul-
derplate dress yoke & highlighted
in gilt, painted blue eyes, cloth
body, china arms & legs, dressed,
26" (ILLUS.) 250.00
China head lady, molded & painted
blonde elaborate hairstyle
w/bangs & long curls down neck,
painted blue eyes & red eyelines,
cloth body, china hands & legs,
1860's, redressed, 27" 550.00
China head lady, molded & painted
black "covered wagon" flat-top
hairstyle w/center part & curls at
ears, painted brown eyes & red
eyelines, rosy pink cheeks, cloth
body, china arms & legs,
dressed, 34" 1,100.00
Clown doll, molded muslin face,
cloth body, felt suit, 24" 55.00
Crissy, all vinyl, brown sleep eyes
w/lashes, open mouth w/painted

teeth, rooted black hair w/grow feature w/knob in center of back, Ideal, 1968-69, dressed, 18" 35.00

Dewees Cochran "Laurielike," latex swirl head, painted facial features, h.h. wig, 5-piece latex body, original clothes, 14" 880.00

Effanbee "Ann Shirley," composition, dressed 350.00

Effanbee "Little Lady," composition, dressed, 18" 95.00

Effanbee "Patsy Ann," composition, 1936, dressed, 18" 140.00

Effanbee "Patsy Joan," composition, dressed 195.00

Effanbee "Patsy Jr.," composition, 1931-32, dressed, 11½" 135.00

Effanbee "Patsy Lou," composition, 1922, dressed, 22" 125.00

Effanbee "Patsy Ruth," composition head, cloth body, composition arms & legs, 1935, dressed, 27" .. 700.00

Effanbee "Skippy," composition head, cloth body, composition arms & legs, dressed, 14" 275.00

Effanbee "Suzanne," composition, 1940, dressed, 13½" 135.00

Floradora (Armand Marseille), bisque head, sleep eyes, original blonde h.h. wig, dressed, 18" 265.00

French Fashion, bisque swivel head w/cork pate marked "2," blue threaded glass eyes, outlined, closed mouth, pierced ears, gusseted kid body, individually stitched fingers, dressed, 13½"... 685.00

French Fashion, bisque head, blue paperweight eyes, pierced ears, cloth body, china hands, dressed, 15" 880.00

French Fashion, bisque swivel head w/cork pate, dark blue threaded glass eyes, outlined, closed mouth, pierced ears, kid body, kid-over-wood knee & elbow joints, bisque lower arms, dressed, 15½" 1,760.00

Frozen Charlie, china, painted blue eyes, molded & painted blonde hair, 14½" 247.00

Fulper Pottery shoulder head girl, kid body, dressed, 16" 250.00

Georgene Averill Madame Hendren "baby," composition head, cloth body, 1917, dressed, 11"..85.00 to 125.00

Georgene Averill bisque head "Bonnie Babe," flange neck, brown glass sleep eyes, open mouth w/two lower teeth, molded & painted hair, cloth body jointed at shoulders & hips, rubber arms & legs, ca. 1920, dressed, 18" ....750.00 to 1,200.00

Gerber Baby, vinyl head, blue

"flirty" eyes w/painted lashes, open mouth, molded & painted hair, cloth body, vinyl arms & legs, Atlanta Novelty Co., Atlanta, Georgia, 1979, dressed & in wicker basket, 17" 220.00

Goebel (William) bisque head girl, ball-jointed composition body, 1879-1925, dressed, 25" 375.00

Greiner (Ludwig) papier mache shoulder head girl, painted features, molded hair, cloth body, kid lower arms, patented 1858, original jester-type outfit w/bells, 12" (minor damage) 385.00

Greiner papier mache head lady, original label w/patent date March 28, '58, original clothes, 23" 375.00

Greiner papier mache shoulder head lady, molded wavy black hair w/center part & exposed ears, cloth body, leather arms, w/1858 patent label, dressed, 28" 1,250.00

Handwerck (Heinrich) bisque socket head girl marked "109 7½," brown sleep eyes, ball-jointed composition body, dressed, 18"... 395.00

Handwerck (Heinrich) bisque head girl, brown eyes, open mouth, blonde h.h. (human hair) wig, ball-jointed composition body, dressed, 22" 400.00

Handwerck (Heinrich) bisque head girl, blue set eyes, auburn h.h. wig, chunky body, dressed as a sailor, 31" 825.00

Handwerck (Heinrich) bisque head girl, blue eyes, blonde mohair wig, dressed, 43".............2,000.00

Hebee-Shebee, composition, 11" 350.00

Heubach (Ernst) - Koppelsdorf bisque socket head character boy marked "407," sleep eyes, open mouth w/four teeth, blonde Dutch boy style h.h. wig, jointed composition body, dressed, 9".......... 145.00

Heubach (Ernst) - Koppelsdorf bisque socket head character baby marked "320," blue sleep eyes, 5-piece composition body, dressed, 12" 350.00

Heubach (Ernst) - Koppelsdorf bisque dome head baby marked "339," blue glass sleep eyes, closed mouth, cloth body, celluloid hands, dresseed in christening gown, 15"................. 575.00

Heubach (Ernst) - Koppelsdorf bisque shoulder head girl marked "275," blue sleep eyes, h.h. wig, pink kid body, dressed, 20" 235.00

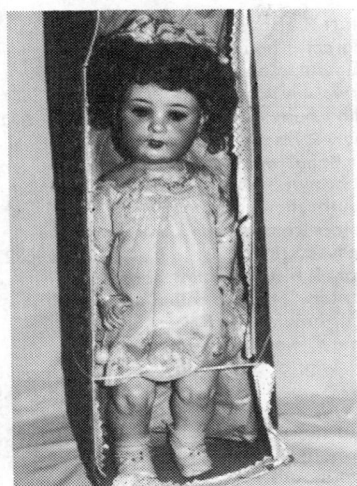

Heubach - Koppelsdorf Girl

Heubach (Ernst) - Koppelsdorf
bisque socket head girl, blue
sleep eyes, open-closed mouth,
composition body, dressed, 22"
(ILLUS.) 750.00
Heubach (Gebruder) bisque head
girl marked "8192 14/0," blue
sleep eyes, open mouth w/teeth,
composition body, dressed, 6½" . . 150.00
Heubach (Gebruder) bisque head
somber-faced character boy, intaglio eyes, closed mouth, compo-
sition body, dressed, 12" 650.00

Heubach & K (star) R Boys

Heubach (Gebruder) bisque head
"whistling" boy, blue intaglio side-
glancing eyes, molded hair, cloth
body, composition arms, dressed,
16" (ILLUS. right) 605.00
Heubach (Gebruder) bisque head
character girl marked "11702,"

sleep eyes, closed mouth, cloth
body, dressed, 20" 1,475.00
Horsman "Ella Cinders," composition
head, painted black hair, cloth
body, composition arms & legs,
1925, dressed, 18" 175.00
Horsman "HeBee-SheBee," composi-
tion, 8¾" 350.00
Horsman "Rosebud," composition
head, blue tin eyes, original h.h.
wig, cloth body, composition arms
& legs, dressed 175.00
Judy Garland as "Dorothy" of the
Wizard of Oz, composition, brown
sleep eyes, open mouth w/six
teeth, glued on h.h. wig, Ideal,
1939, dressed, 18" . . . . . . 725.00 to 850.00
Jumeau bisque head girl marked
"DEP," blue glass sleep eyes,
open mouth w/molded upper row
of teeth, pierced ears, dark
brown h.h. wig in long curls, ball-
jointed composition body, jointed
wrists, dressed, 12" 562.00
Jumeau bisque head girl marked
"Depose Tete Jumeau Bte SGDG
5," brown paperweight eyes, outlined closed mouth, pierced ears,
blonde h.h. wig, ball-jointed composition body, straight wrists,
dressed, 14" 1,540.00
Jumeau bisque head girl marked
"DEP," blue glass sleep eyes,
open mouth w/molded upper row
of teeth, pierced ears, dark
brown h.h. wig in pigtails, ball-
jointed composition body, jointed
wrists, dressed, 15" 707.00

Jumeau Bisque Head Girl

Jumeau bisque head girl marked "Tete 8," blue paperweight eyes, closed mouth, pierced ears, mohair wig, composition body, dressed, 19" (ILLUS.) 1,980.00

Jumeau bisque head girl marked "EJ," blue paperweight eyes, closed mouth, applied pierced ears, original h.h. wig, dressed, 19" 5,500.00

Jumeau bisque socket head girl marked "Depose Tete Jumeau Bte SGDG 9," blue paperweight eyes w/brushed eyelids, outlined closed mouth, pierced ears, blonde mohair wig, ball-jointed composition body, dressed, 20" 6,875.00

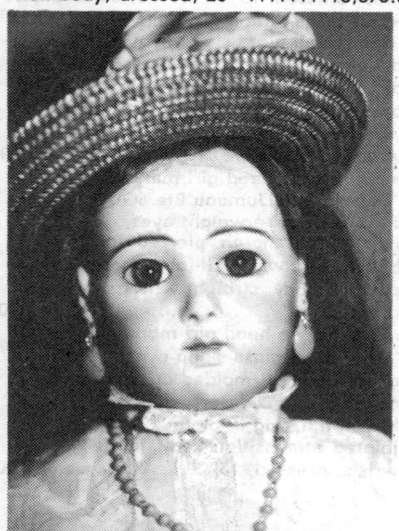

Jumeau Girl

Jumeau bisque head girl w/long face, dressed, 22" (ILLUS.) 8,000.00

Jumeau bisque head girl marked "Tete," blue paperweight stationary eyes, closed mouth, pierced ears, original blonde curly h.h. wig, original ball-jointed composition body, jointed wrists, dressed, 26" 3,750.00

Jumeau bisque head girl marked "1907," brown stationary eyes, open mouth w/molded upper row of teeth, pierced ears, dark blonde h.h. wig in long curls, ball-jointed composition body, jointed wrists, dressed, 28" 1,800.00

K (star) R (Kammer & Reinhardt) bisque socket head "Kaiser Baby" marked "100 28," brown glass eyes, open-closed mouth, 5-piece composition body, dressed, 10½" 330.00

K (star) R bisque socket head character baby marked "126," blue sleep eyes, open mouth w/wobbly tongue, jointed composition body, dressed, 17" 600.00

K (star) R bisque socket head "Kaiser Baby" marked "100 50," painted brown eyes, open-closed mouth, molded & painted hair, 5-piece composition body, dressed, 18" 632.00

K (star) R bisque socket head girl marked "117" (so-called Mein Liebling), brown sleep eyes, closed "pouty" mouth, original blonde h.h. wig, original body, dressed, 18" 4,700.00

K (star) R - Simon & Halbig bisque head character baby marked "26 Germany 42," blue sleep eyes, open mouth w/two teeth & tremble tongue, 5-piece composition body, w/voice box, dressed, 17".. 440.00

K (star) R - Simon & Halbig bisque socket head boy marked "46," brown sleep eyes, open mouth, pierced ears, blonde mohair wig, jointed composition body, dressed, 17" (ILLUS. w/Heubach boy) 462.00

K (star) R - Simon & Halbig bisque socket head character toddler marked "126 50," brown "flirty" sleep eyes, open mouth w/two inset teeth & tremble tongue, ball-jointed wood & composition body, dressed, 22" 660.00

K (star) R - Simon & Halbig bisque socket head baby marked "126," blue sleep eyes, open mouth w/two teeth, jointed composition body, dressed, 25" 800.00

Kathe Kruse Dolls

Kathe Kruse girl (Model No. 1),
molded muslin, painted blue eyes
& brown hair, dressed, 17"
(ILLUS. left) 1,100.00

Kathe Kruse baby (Du Mein Model
VI), molded muslin, painted blue
eyes & brown hair, late 1920's,
dressed, 19½" (ILLUS. right) 3,520.00

Ken, No. 1 (750 stock number), hard
plastic, blue eyes, brunette
flocked crew-cut hair, hollow torso marked "Ken T.M. Pats. Pend.
MCMLX by Mattel, Inc.," 1961,
dressed, 12".............95.00 to 150.00

Ken (750 stock number), hard plastic, blue eyes, painted crew-cut
hair, hollow torso marked "Ken
T.M. Pats. Pend. MCMLX by Mat-
tel, Inc.," 1962, dressed, 12" 20.00

Kestner (J.D.) bisque girl marked
"251," all bisque, open mouth,
original h.h. wig, dressed, 4½" .. 195.00

Kestner (J.D.) bisque boy, all
bisque, painted features, molded
blonde hair, 5-piece chubby body,
painted brown shoes, white socks
w/blue stripe at top, dressed,
9½" 300.00

Kestner (J.D.) bisque socket head
girl marked "A Germany 5 J.D.K.
221," brown "googly" side-
glancing eyes, "watermelon"
smile, ball-jointed composition
body, undressed, 10¾" 1,760.00

Kestner (J.D.) bisque socket head
character boy marked "143," blue
sleep eyes, jointed composition
body, dressed as a sailor, 11" 400.00

J.D.K. 221 GesGesch," blue
"googly" side glancing eyes,
"watermelon" smile, brown h.h.
wig, ball-jointed wood & composition toddler body, dressed, 13"
(ILLUS.) 3,850.00

Kestner (J.D.) bisque socket head
Hilda look-alike marked "257
Made in Germany," blue sleep
eyes, open mouth w/two porcelain teeth, mohair wig, dressed,
14½" 775.00

Kestner (J.D.) bisque head "fat
faced" character baby marked
"210," blue set eyes, open-closed
mouth, jointed kid body, undressed, 15" 400.00

Kestner (J.D.) bisque shoulder head
girl marked "154," blue threaded
sleep eyes, original kid body,
bisque hands, dressed, 17"....... 279.00

Kestner (J.D.) bisque socket head
child marked "Made in 11 Germany 12 129," blue sleep eyes, open
mouth w/teeth, ball-jointed composition body, dressed, 18" 302.00

Kestner (J.D.) bisque socket head
character baby marked "16 245
JDK, jr. Hilda," blue eyes, open
mouth w/two inset teeth &
tongue, (repainted) composition
body, dressed, 19".............2,860.00

Kestner (J.D.) bisque turned shoulder head girl, blue sleep eyes,
open mouth, blonde h.h. wig, kid
body, dressed, 19" 450.00

Kestner (J.D.) bisque socket head
girl marked "13," brown sleep
eyes, open mouth, ball-jointed
composition body, dressed,
20½" 400.00

Kestner Girl

Kestner (J.D.) bisque head girl
marked "G Made in H Germany

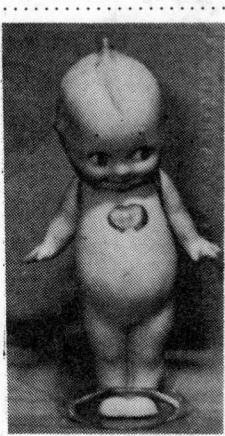

Bisque Kewpie

Kewpie, bisque, moveable arms, 5"
(ILLUS.)........................ 125.00

Kewpie, bisque, moveable arms,
Rose O'Neill label on back, original clothes, 8½" 475.00
Kewpie, celluloid, 2" 35.00
Kewpie, composition, w/moveable
arms, Rose O'Neill heart label,
11" ....75.00 to 145.00
Kewpie, Negro, composition, heart
label, 1930's, dressed, 11" 250.00
Kewpie, composition, jointed arms &
hips, 13" ....165.00 to 195.00
Kley & Hahn bisque head girl
marked "Walkure," brown sleep
eyes, ball-jointed composition
body, dressed, 25" 400.00
Kley & Hahn bisque head girl, blue
sleep eyes, jointed body, dressed,
32" 675.00
Krauss (Gebruder) bisque head boy
marked "44 18" & w/starburst, papier mache body, composition
limbs, painted shoes & socks,
dressed, 9" 135.00
Lenci boy, pressed felt, dressed as
mountain climber w/knapsack,
14" 495.00
Lenci girl, felt, blonde hair
w/braids, holding 3 felt flowers,
dressed, 14½" 231.00
Lenci child, felt, painted brown
eyes, dressed in Scandinavian
costume, 16" 880.00
Lenci child, felt, painted blue eyes,
dressed as a Dutch boy, 17" 440.00

Lenci Girl

Lenci girl, felt, in provincial costume
w/pink felt & white lace headdress, black & purple felt skirt,

top & shoes, embroidered & metal
accents, some moth damage, ca.
1930, 19" (ILLUS.)................ 330.00
Little Red Riding Hood, cloth, Arnold
Printworks, 1890's, 16".......... 250.00
Mae Star phonograph doll, composition head, grey sleep eyes, original h.h. wig, cloth body, composition arms & legs, dressed &
w/six records, 29" 495.00
Mattel "Baby Say 'N See," vinyl
head w/rooted hair, eyes
w/molded rubber lashes, open
mouth, cloth body, vinyl arms &
legs, pull ring on left side, lips
move as she talks, 1967-68,
dressed, 17" 55.00
Mattel "Tiny Chatty Brother," vinyl,
1963-64, dressed 15.00
Mortimer Snerd, composition head,
hands & feet, Ideal, 1939,
dressed, 13" 95.00
Mr. Peanut, cloth 7.00
Musical automaton of a girl playing
a tambourine, Jumeau bisque
head w/blue paperweight eyes,
closed mouth, moving her head &
gesturing as she shakes the tambourine, Decamps (French), early
20th c., 17¼" 3,300.00
Musical automaton of an Oriental
tea server, unmarked bisque head,
open-closed mouth, pierced ears,
original black mohair wig, head
turning & nodding, left hand moving the tray into position while
the right hand raises the pot &
pours, works contained in the
base playing a single tune "Valse
de Bluett" as indicated on original
tune sheet, French, late 19th c.,
19" 3,575.00
Nancy Ann Storybook "Daffy-Down-
Dilly," bisque, mohair wig,
dressed, 5½" 46.50
Nancy Ann Storybook girl, hard
plastic, painted features, original
wig & clothes 25.00
Nippon (all) bisque girl, "googlie"
eyes painted to the side, ca. 1915,
5" 85.00
Nippon bisque socket head girl,
blue sleep eyes, ball-jointed composition body, ca. 1915, 17" 295.00
Norah Wellings Negro boy, cloth,
dressed, 9" 95.00
Norah Wellings Negro girl, cloth,
black hair, glass eyes, undressed
except for black shoes, bangle
bracelets & hoop earrings, 14" ... 135.00
Papier mache girl, molded blonde
hair, painted features, cloth body,
papier mache limbs, dressed,
11½" 65.00

Papier mache shoulder head man, painted features, kid body, wooden hands, dressed as Turkish Lord, 14" 850.00

Papier mache shoulder head girl, insert pupilless black glass eyes, open mouth w/bamboo teeth, pierced nostrils, black-painted brush strokes on pate covered by original h.h. wig, kid body, 1820-25, dressed, 33" 1,050.00

Parian shoulder head girl, painted blue eyes, red eyelines, molded blonde hairstyle w/exposed ears, cloth body, china limbs, dressed, 13" 175.00

Parian shoulder head girl, painted blue eyes, molded blonde hair, kid leather body, dressed, 16".... 550.00

Parian shoulder head lady, molded decorative collar at shoulder plate, painted eyes, molded hair w/braids in back, original cloth body, leather arms & hands, dressed, 22" 474.00

Poncho (from the Cisco Kid), cloth w/highly painted buckram mask face, ca. 1944, dressed, 16" 40.00

Queen Louise (Armand Marseille) bisque socket head girl, brown sleep eyes, open mouth w/four teeth & dimpled chin, ball-jointed composition body, dressed, 26" .... 425.00 to 474.00

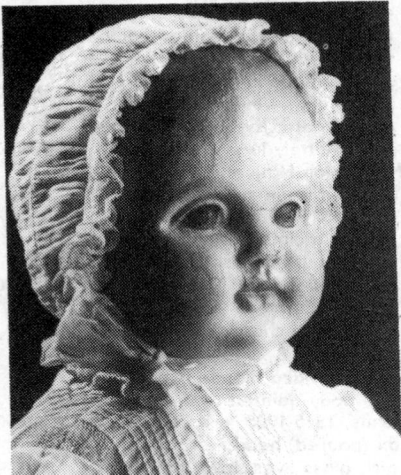

Sheppard Baby

Rag-stuffed (J.B. Sheppard & Co., Philadelphia) baby, pressed hard mask & oil-painted facial features, painted brown eyes w/black pupils & molded eyelids w/tinted arched brows, closed mouth w/rose-shaded lips & cheeks, softly

swirled brown hair, stitched fingers, original clothes, 22" (ILLUS.) 2,300.00

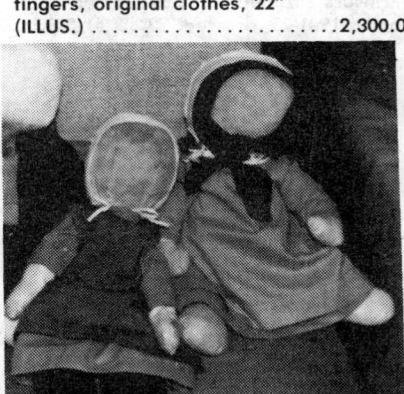

Faceless Amish Girls

Rag-stuffed faceless Amish-type girls, original clothes & caps, ea. (ILLUS.) .... 120.00 to 175.00

Rag-stuffed Missionary Ragbaby type (possibly by Julia Beecher, Elmira, New York, 1893-1910), silk jersey, molded & painted features, wool hair, stitched fingers & toes, dressed, 22" .... 345.00 to 600.00

Rag-stuffed "Topsy-Turvy," stockinette & cloth w/black child one end & white child opposite (full gathered skirt concealing one), ca. 1930, 13"...................... 185.00

Ravca couple, cotton, stuffed silk, nylon faces w/contours created by hand stitching & then h.p., wool hair, dressed, pr. .... 200.00 to 450.00

Rita Hayworth as "Carmen," composition, glued on red mohair wig, Uneeda Doll Company, 1948, dressed, 14" 250.00

Schmidt (Bruno) bisque head character baby, "flirty" eyes, 1900-25, dressed, 29" 1,750.00

Schmidt (Franz & Co.) bisque head girl marked "1267," painted brown eyes, open-closed mouth, w/dimples, 5-piece composition body, dressed, 14" head circumference 2,500.00

Schmitt & Fils bisque head girl, blue threaded stationary eyes, closed mouth, original wig, composition body, dressed, 12"............. 7,500.00

Schoenau & Hoffmeister bisque head girl, blue stationary eyes, open mouth w/upper row of teeth, dark blonde h.h. wig in pigtails, ball-jointed composition body, jointed wrists, dressed, 21" (body repainted) 595.00

Schoenau & Hoffmeister bisque head
Princess Elizabeth, chubby toddler
body, 1901-25, dressed, 23".....2,800.00

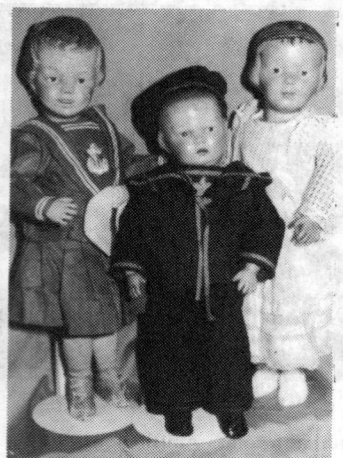

Schoenhut Dolls

Schoenhut girl, wooden, painted
eyes, molded & painted hair,
dressed (ILLUS. left)............1,575.00
Schoenhut boy, wooden, painted
eyes, painted hair, dressed (ILLUS.
center) 575.00
Schoenhut girl, wooden, painted
eyes, molded & painted hair
w/headband, dressed (ILLUS.
right) ....550.00 to 1,250.00
S.F.B.J. (Societe Francaise de Fabri-
cation de Bebes et Jouets) bisque
socket head character girl marked
"237," inset stationary eyes, open
mouth w/four molded teeth,
molded & flocked hair, dressed,
16"..........................1,750.00

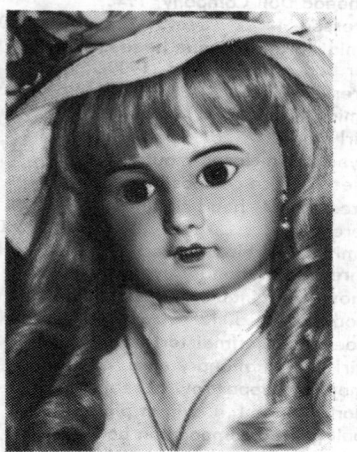

S.F.B.J. Bisque Head Girl

S.F.B.J. bisque socket head girl,
blue glass sleep eyes, open mouth
w/molded upper row of teeth,
pierced ears, blonde h.h. wig,
jointed composition body, dressed,
26" (ILLUS.) 1,150.00
Shirley Temple, composition, Ideal,
1934, dressed, 18".............. 415.00
Simon & Halbig bisque socket head
character baby marked "1294,"
brown sleep eyes, brown h.h.
wig, bent limb body, dressed,
23" 462.00
Simon & Halbig bisque socket head
girl marked "1039," brown sleep
eyes, pierced ears, original mohair wig, original chunky body,
dressed, 26" 1,050.00
Skipper, vinyl, bendable legs, Mattel, 1967, dressed, 9¼"........... 18.00
Springfield, Vermont, Joel Ellis, Co-
operative Manufacturing Co. girl,
wooden, paint worn off face,
15" 600.00
Steiner (Jules) bisque swivel head
girl marked "BTE SGDG Paris A
4," blue stationary eyes, closed
mouth, blonde h.h. wig in long
curls, original body, straight
wrists, dressed, 11½"...........1,800.00
Steiner (Jules) bisque swivel head
girl marked "BTE SGDG Paris A
5," blue paperweight eyes, outlined closed mouth, pierced ears,
dots accenting eye corners & nostrils, jointed composition body,
straight wrists, dressed, 24" 4,070.00
Truly Scrumptious (from Chitty Chitty
Bang Bang), vinyl, painted features, rooted synthetic & painted
hair, Mattel, 1968-69, dressed 225.00
UNIS (Union Nationale Inter Syn-
dicale) bisque swivel head girl
marked "71 France 149 301 R
(within a circle), blue sleep eyes,
open mouth w/inset teeth, jointed
composition body, dressed, 19"... 330.00
Wagner & Zetzsche "haralit" composition head character girl marked
"1 Inge, W & 2," blue intaglio
eyes, molded blonde braids, kido-
line body, jointed composition
arms, 1875-1925, dressed, 12" 286.00
Wax (poured) head Pierotti-type
girl, glass eyes, inset hair, wax
arms & legs, dressed, 17"........ 850.00
Wooden lady, Queen Anne type
w/"tuck" comb, original painted
features, original (frayed) garments, 15" h. 1,650.00

(End of Doll Section)

DOOR KNOCKERS

Also see CAT COLLECTIBLES.

Brass, cat w/arched back	$48.00
Brass, "Imps"	28.00
Brass, pheasants	45.00
Bronze, American eagle	30.00
Bronze, Foo dog, large	100.00
Cast iron, basket of flowers, original paint, indoor model	18.00
Cast iron, basket of flowers	35.00
Cast iron, bird house w/bird, original blue & white paint, 4" h.	27.50
Cast iron, cherub's head	55.00
Cast iron, elf seated on toadstool, horseshoe-shaped backplate w/floral finial, 6 x 4½"	55.00
Cast iron, English hunt scene	35.00
Cast iron, lady's hand	19.50
Cast iron, parrot, indoor model	32.00
Cast iron, red-headed woodpecker on tree trunk, original colorful paint	35.00 to 45.00
Sterling silver, Arabian heads, indoor model, pr.	600.00

DOOR STOPS

Mayflower Ship Door Stop

All door stops listed are flat-back cast iron unless otherwise noted.

Abraham Lincoln	$135.00
Advertising, frog, full figure, "I Croak for the Jackson Wagon," 5½ x 4½ x 3"	425.00
Aunt Jemima, full figure, blue dress, red polka dot bandana, 8½" h.	95.00 to 115.00
Basket of flowers, original polychrome paint, marked "Hubley," 7½" w.	75.00

Basket of poppies & snapdragons, original paint	58.00
Bellhop, original colorful paint, 9" h.	225.00
Boy holding Teddy Bear, marked "Albany Foundry"	240.00
Cat, Angora in reclining position, original white paint, marked "Hubley," 10¾" l., 5½" h.	95.00 to 110.00
Charlie Chaplin, old repaint	275.00
Cornucopia of flowers on oblong base, old green & white repaint, 10¼" h.	40.00
Cottage w/path & garden, original paint, marked "Albany Fdy. Co.," 9" w., 5¾" h.	75.00
Dog, Airedale in seated position, original polychrome paint, 7 3/8" h.	85.00
Dog, Cocker Spaniel, on oval base	95.00
Dog, German Shepherd, full figure, 13" l.	145.00
Dog, Irish Setter (brass)	145.00
Ducks (2), one preening & the other eating, on grassy base, original paint, 8¼" h.	250.00
Dutch milkmaid w/braided hair carrying two pails, full figure, colorful repaint, 9¼" h.	145.00
Fox sleeping w/tail curled around body	135.00
Frog seated on haunches w/head back & mouth open, full figure, traces of old green paint, 9" h.	275.00
Goose w/wings spread, full figure, old black paint, 7" h.	95.00
Horse standing, full figure, worn original chestnut brown paint, 11" h.	65.00 to 85.00
Lady, Art Deco style, standing w/outstretched arms & grasping the hem of her long skirt, full figure, 7" w., 9" h. (bronze)	135.00
Lion standing, full figure, old silver paint, 5 x 7 x 9"	350.00
Little Black Sambo holding open umbrella, full figure, on square base	400.00
Mayflower ship, original paint, 12" h. (ILLUS.)	25.00 to 35.00
Monkey in seated position w/tail curled under his body, 8½" h.	205.00
Napoleon on horseback (brass)	65.00
Owl on stump amidst berries & foliage, bronze finish, Hubley	185.00
Peacock, original colorful paint	75.00 to 95.00
Penguin, full figure, worn original black & white paint, 10½" h.	350.00
Pirate standing w/sword in hands, old colorful paint, 13¾" h.	65.00
Pot of geraniums, original polychrome paint, 7¼" h.	45.00

Rabbit in seated position, black,
10¼" w., 11¾" h. 150.00
Ram in standing position w/head
raised, full figure, old white &
black repaint, 5¾" h. 235.00
Raven, original black paint 75.00
Siamese lady in seated position, full
figure, 16" h. 165.00
Southern Belle, 6½" h. . . . . . .60.00 to 75.00
Sunbonnet Baby, old lavender, blue
& white repaint, 6¼" h. 150.00
Teddy Roosevelt on horseback 130.00
Witch on broomstick (brass) 125.00

ENAMELS

Battersea Enamel Bonbonniere

Enamels have been used to decorate a variety of substances, particularly metals. The best-known small enameled wares such as patch and other small boxes and napkin rings are the Battersea Enamels made by the Battersea Enamel Works in the last half of the 18th century. However, the term is often loosely applied to other English enamels. Russian enamels, usually on a silver or gold base, are famous and expensive. Early 20th century French enamel on copper wares and those items produced in China at the turn of the century in imitation of the early Russian style, are also drawing dealer and collector attention. Also see ART DECO and FABERGE.

Battersea bonbonniere in the form
of a leopard's head, enameled in
tones of brown, yellow, puce &
pale blue, hinged lid w/interior
scene of archers hunting a leop-
ard, ca. 1780, 3" l. (ILLUS.) $2,640.00
Battersea snuff box in the form of a
black & white King Charles spaniel recumbent on a yellow & iron-
red cushion, hinged cover w/in-
terior floral sprays & scrolling,
ca. 1770, 2¼" l. 935.00
Beaker, cylindrical, silver-gilt,

enameled multicolored geometric
motifs & foliage on gilt ground,
Ovchinnikov, Moscow, 1908-17,
2¾" h. 462.00
Bonbonniere w/hinged lid,
enameled bullfinch in realistic
tones on white ground, sides &
base enameled w/various insects,
Birmingham, George III period,
ca. 1770, 2½" d. 715.00
Bonbonniere in the form of a lion's
head, embossed & delicately
enameled to simulate the coat of
a lion, hinged cover w/interior
scene of a Roman warrior in com-
bat w/a lion, Bilston, ca. 1770,
3" l. 3,300.00
Box, cov., copper, enameled spray
of shaded purple & mauve plums
nestled amidst luminescent green
leaves on deep mauve over a
hammered ground, greenish yellow interior, signed Louis C. Tif-
fany, 6¼" d., 4¾" h. 2,200.00
Etui (case for small articles),
enameled w/neo-classical allegorical figures reserved against deep
blue overlaid w/a white diapered
design, gilt-metal mounts, fitted
w/five implements, South
Staffordshire, ca. 1770,
3 7/8" h. 880.00
Kovsh, silver-gilt, enameled mul-
ticolor florals & scrolling foliage
within blue bead borders, Russian, workmaster Maria Semyeno-
va, Moscow, ca. 1900, 3½" l. 440.00
Scent bottle case, slightly tapering
form, enameled w/scenes of
fisherman within gilt scrollwork
borders reserved against sky blue
ground, interior fitted w/scent
bottle, funnel, ivory slide, spoon
& scissors, South Staffordshire,
ca. 1770, 2¾" h. 1,760.00
Snuff box in the form of a pair of
cooing doves, enameled in shades
of blue, green & brown, hinged
cover w/interior scene of nesting
doves on white ground, Bilston,
George III period, ca. 1770 . . . . . . 3,300.00

Russian Enamel Spoons

Spoons, silver, enameled w/vivid
florals & foliage, Russian, set of 6
(ILLUS.) 1,650.00
Sugar bowl, bombe' form w/in-
curved neck & swing handle,
silver-gilt, enameled stylized foliage & geometric forms w/white
bead borders, maker's mark E.C.,
Moscow, ca. 1910, 4½" l. 990.00
Vase, pear-shaped, copper,
enameled band of "repousse" luminescent green & mauve poppies
on slender stems amongst green
& brownish green leaves, hammered purple ground heightened
w/rainbow iridescence, signed
Louis C. Tiffany, 10 7/8" h. 2,750.00

EPERGNES

George III Silver Epergne

*Epergnes were popular as centerpieces on
tables of last century. Many have receptacles
of colored glass for holding sweetmeats or
other edible items or for flowers or fruits.
Early epergnes were made entirely of metal
including silver.*

Amethyst glass, single lily, ruffled
rim, in 10" d. ruffled & pleated
bowl on stand, 15" h. $150.00
Blue opalescent glass, single lily, in
fluted bowl 65.00
Blue opalescent glass, 3-lily, in
10" d. scalloped bowl, 22" h. 395.00
Cased glass, 4-lily, rose pink lilies
cased in white w/ruffled rims &
applied white spiraling rigaree
trim, 16" h. 350.00
Cranberry glass, 3-lily, lilies w/ir-
regular 5-petal tops & applied
clear spiral twist rigaree trim, in
ruffled bowl, 10 1/8" d.,
22¼" h. 325.00

Cranberry glass, 4-lily, lilies w/ap-
plied spiraling rigaree, in fluted
bowl, 19½" h. 500.00
Cranberry glass, 4-lily, center lily &
3 smaller lilies w/fluted rims &
applied spiraling rigaree, in 10" d.
fluted bowl, 21" h. 390.00
Cranberry to clear glass, 3-lily, flut-
ed rims, Stevens & Williams, in
ornate brass holder w/applied
lion masks, 16½" w., 12½" h. . . . 275.00
Pink glass, single lily, ruffled rim,
raised on footed silverplate base,
overall 14½" h. 195.00
Rubina crystal glass, 4-lily, center
lily & 3 smaller lilies, fluted tops,
in 10" d. fluted base w/applied
rigaree trim, overall 21" h. 390.00
Sapphire blue glass, 3-lily, w/ap-
plied spiral twist rigaree, 20" h. . . . 195.00
Silver, central basket w/four circular
& 2 oval smaller baskets, in the
George III style w/Vitruvian
scrolls, bust profiles of Roman
warriors & swags on diapered
ground, raised on 4 paw feet,
Germany, ca. 1900, 19½" h. 4,675.00
Silver, pierced center basket & 4
dishes, central pierced canopy
fluted & decorated w/trailing foliage & beading & w/pineapple finial, supported on slender columns
wrapped w/flowering tendrils, on
4 openwork floral & foliate scroll
feet linked by rococo aprons of
flowers & fruit, George III, Francis
Butty & Nicholas Dumee, London,
1768-69, 23" h. (ILLUS.) 8,800.00
Turquoise blue opalescent glass, sin-
gle lily in bowl w/fluted rim,
17" h. 250.00
White opaque glass, 3-lily, Hobnail-
in-Square patt., in 10½" d.
bowl 100.00
White Satin glass w/applied blue
Satin glass trim, single lily w/ruf-
fled rim rising above 2 ruffled
bowls pierced by a central silverplate post w/ornate footed base,
marked "S. & G.," 27½" h. 1,250.00
Yellow glass, single lily, w/applied
spiral twist rigaree, in ruffled
bowl 260.00

EYE CUPS

*The eye cup was an early means of treat-
ing an injured or infected eye. The oval cup,
filled with a medicated solution, was held
over the open eye. With the advent of eye*

droppers and plastic dropper bottles, the eye
cup became obsolete.

Clambroth Eye Cup

Amber, blown, w/finger grips, 8-
  panel stem, squat $210.00
Amethyst, blown, w/finger grips,
  1½" oval, 1¾" h. 255.00
Aquamarine 37.50
Black 18.50
Clambroth, 8-panel stem & cup
  (ILLUS.) 12.50
Clear, 8-panel, "22" 7.50
Clear, "John Bull," 1917 . . . . . .15.00 to 20.00
Clear, "Woltra," original box 10.00
Clear, w/blue eye in relief on
  base 35.00
Cobalt blue, 8-panel 14.00
Cobalt blue, w/eye in relief,
  "Elder" 25.00
Cobalt blue, fish bowl style 55.00
Cobalt blue, "John Bull," 1917 . . . . . 30.00
Cobalt blue, "Royal," original box . . 8.50
Cobalt blue, "Wyeth" . . . . .5.00 to 9.50
Custard 5.50
Emerald green, "John Bull," 1917 . . . 30.00
Emerald green 40.00
Iridescent blue 18.50
Medium blue, 8-panel stem, em-
  bossed "Glasko" 60.00
Medium green, fish bowl style
  w/wide lip 90.00
Milk white . . . . .10.00 to 17.50
Peacock blue 18.00
Red slag 29.50
Yellow w/red lip trim 23.50

FABERGE

Carl Faberge (1846-1920) was goldsmith and
jeweler to the Russian Imperial Court, and
his creations are recognized as the finest of
their kind. He made a number of enamel fan-
tasies, including Easter eggs, for the Imperial
family and utilized precious metals and jewels
in other work.

Bell push, silver, translucent enamel
  & wood, square w/incurved sides,
  enameled translucent pale blue
  over a "guilloche" ground & applied w/flowerheads at corners,
  red stone cabochon thumbpiece,
  sides applied w/ribbon-tied laurel
  swags, workmaster Johan Viktor
  Aarne, St. Petersburg, ca. 1900,
  2¼" sq. $2,750.00

Faberge Silver Cake Basket & Kovsh

Cake basket, silver, fluted w/scal-
  loped border, spreading base,
  ribbon-tied laurel wreath handles,
  workmaster Alexander Wakeva,
  St. Petersburg, ca. 1910, 7 3/8" d.
  (ILLUS. left) 1,980.00
Card case, mother-of-pearl, gold &
  enamel, upright rectangular shape,
  hinged cover applied w/white
  enamel plaque w/a diamond-set
  foliate spray, lower border set
  w/diamonds, outer borders enameled opaque white, diamond-set
  thumbpiece, workmaster Henrik
  Wigstrom, St. Petersburg, ca. 1900,
  3 3/8" h. 17,600.00
Desk clock, silver & translucent
  enamel, triangular, enameled
  translucent pale purple over a
  sunburst ground, silver border
  w/foliage at corners, white enamel dial w/border of seed pearls,
  workmaster Henrik Wigstrom, St.
  Petersburg, ca. 1900, 4¾" h. . . .13,200.00
Frame, silver & translucent enamel,
  enameled translucent oyster white
  over "guilloche" ground & set
  w/eight cabochon moonstones,
  beaded borders topped by a ribbon bow, workmaster Andrei
  Gorianov, St. Petersburg, ca.
  1910, 5½" h. 11,000.00
Kovsh, silver, shell-shaped, 3 scroll
  feet, everted scalloped border &
  foliate-capped scroll handle, workmaster Julius Rappaport, St.
  Petersburg, ca. 1880, 5½" l.
  (ILLUS. right) 1,540.00

Match case, silver-gilt & translucent
enamel, rectangular w/rounded
corners, enameled translucent
deep blue over "guilloche" ground,
border of hinged cover chased
w/leaf tips, base w/striker,
diamond thumbpiece, workmaster
Michael Perchin, St. Petersburg,
ca. 1900, original fitted wood
case, 1¾" l. 4,620.00

Faberge Model of a Rabbit

Model of a plump rabbit, carved
purpurine (vitreous compound
ranging from bright red to dark
crimson), faceted demantoid garnet eyes w/chip, 1¾" l.
(ILLUS.) 10,450.00
Model of a long-haired Dachshund
dog, agate, carved in an attentive
standing posture looking straight
ahead, w/gold-set red stone eyes,
St. Petersburg, ca. 1900,
3 3/8" l. 4,070.00
Parasol handle, gold & translucent
enamel, bulbous, enameled translucent powder blue over "guilloche" ground & w/a central
diamond, workmaster Michael
Perchin, St. Petersburg, ca. 1900,
1 3/8" h. 1,870.00
Patch box, cover enameled "en
plein" after a painting by Vasnet-
sov depicting Tsarevich Ivan & his
promised consort riding on the
back of a wolf, within shaded
moss green, dark blue & brown
geometric motifs enhanced w/fili-
gree scrolling, sides similarly
decorated, workmaster Fedor
Ruckert, Moscow, ca. 1902,
2" d. 7,700.00
Punch bowl, silver, 4 large ball
feet, 2 upturned ring handles
applied w/beadwork & chased
w/scrolls in the Old Russian style,
lobed upper border set on each
side w/roundel embossed
w/horses' heads flanked by pairs
of silver studs mounted w/green
& yellow hardstone cabochons,
Moscow, ca. 1910, 10½" l. 6,600.00

Vase, bud, silver-mounted ceramic,
globular, cobalt blue ceramic body
w/silver base & neck mounts,
w/pendant swags of laurel, workmaster Anders Nevalainen, St.
Petersburg, ca. 1900, 2½" h. 1,980.00

FAIRY LAMPS

*These are candle burning night lights of the
Victorian era. Best known are the Clarke
Fairy Lamps made in England, but they were
also made by other firms. They were produced
in two sizes, each with a base and a shade.
The Fairy Pyramid Lamps listed below all
have a clear glass base and are approximately 2 7/8" d. and 3¼" h. The Fairy Lamps are
usually at least 4" d. and 5" h. when assembled and these may or may not have an additional saucer or bottom holder to match the
shade in addition to the clear base.*

FAIRY PYRAMID LAMPS

Satin Glass Pyramid Fairy Lamp

Apple green satin glass shade
w/embossed ribs, marked Clarke
clear glass base, 2 7/8" d.,
3½" h. $125.00
Blue & white striped glass shade,
Swirl patt., acid finish, attributed
to Stevens & Williams, marked
Clarke clear glass base, 2½" d.,
4" h. 150.00
Heavenly blue mother-of-pearl satin
glass shade w/white lining, Diamond Quilted patt., marked
Clarke clear glass base, 2¾" d.,
3 5/8" h. (ILLUS.) 150.00
Lemon yellow satin glass shade
w/white lining, enameled bird on
leafy branch decor, marked
Clarke clear glass base, 2 7/8" d.,
3¾" h. 195.00
Orange glass shade, Diamond Quilt-
ed patt., acid finish, marked

Clarke clear glass base, 2 7/8" d.,
4" h. 110.00

Pink satin glass shade w/white lining, marked Clarke clear glass
base, 2 7/8" d., 3 5/8" h. 125.00

Sapphire blue glass shade, Drape
patt., acid finish, marked Clarke
clear glass base, 2 7/8" d.,
3¼" h. 140.00

Spatter glass shade, pink, yellow &
white spatter, white lining,
marked Clarke clear glass base,
2 7/8" d., 3¼" h. 100.00

Verre Moire (Nailsea) glass shade,
frosted chartreuse w/white
opaque loopings, marked Clarke
clear glass base, 2 7/8" d.,
3½" h. 145.00

FAIRY LAMPS

Burmese glass shade & matching
ruffled base, salmon pink shaded
to yellow, acid finish, marked
Clarke clear glass candle cup,
4" d., 5" h. 450.00

Burmese glass shade & matching re-
versible ruffled base, salmon pink
shaded to yellow acid finish, unsigned Webb, marked Clarke
clear glass candle cup, 7" d.,
5 3/8" h. 550.00

Burmese glass shade & matching
ruffled base w/applied leaf to
hold menu, salmon pink shaded
to yellow, acid finish, unsigned
Webb, marked Clarke clear glass
candle cup, 3 7/8" d., 5½" h. 495.00

Burmese glass fairy lamp-epergne,
salmon pink shaded to yellow,
acid finish, 3 lamps on marked
Clarke clear glass bases & pr.
vases in brass holders fastened to
mirrored base, attributed to
Webb, 12 x 5¾", 10" h. 1,510.00

Clear to opalescent crown-shaped
glass shade (made for Queen Victoria's 1887 Jubilee), marked
Clarke clear glass base, 3" d.,
4 3/8" h. 180.00

Heavenly blue mother-of-pearl satin
glass shade w/white lining, Diamond Quilted patt., on cream-
colored Tunnecliffe pottery base
w/light blue bands, pink roses &
green leaves, marked Clarke
clear glass candle cup, 4" d.,
4" h. 275.00

Lemon yellow homogenous satin
glass shade, Swirl patt., marked
Clarke clear glass base, 3 7/8" d.,
4 5/8" h. 165.00

Rose mother-of-pearl satin glass
shade & matching base w/crimped
rim, Diamond Quilted patt.,

marked Clarke clear glass candle
cup, 6¼" d., 5¾" h. 635.00

Spatter glass shade & matching
base, pink & white spatter, applied crystal feet & drippy crystal
sides on base, 3 3/8" d.,
4" h. 231.00

Turquoise satin glass shade &
matching hat-shaped base
w/pleated brim & clear frosted
border, cream lining, marked
Clarke clear glass insert 535.00

Verre Moire (Nailsea) glass shade &
matching ruffled base, cranberry
w/white opaque loopings, marked
Clarke clear glass insert, 6" d.,
5 1/8" h. 425.00

Verre Moire (Nailsea) glass shade &
matching ruffled base, chartreuse
w/opaque white loopings, marked
Clarke clear glass candle cup,
7¾" d., 6½" h. 450.00

FIGURAL FAIRY LAMPS

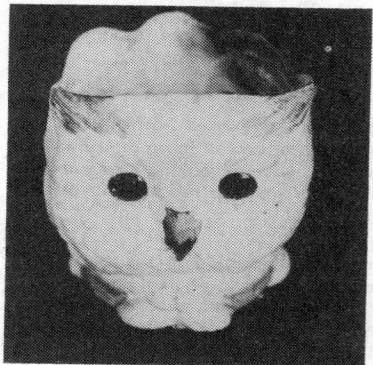

Bisque Three Face Fairy Lamp

Bisque, dog's head, brown glass
eyes, shaded brown & tan coat,
blue ribbon at neck, 3" d.,
3 7/8" h. 150.00

Bisque, owl's head, brown glass
eyes, shaded grey feathers, blue
ribbon at neck, 2 7/8" d.,
3½" h. 150.00

Bisque, three-face, cat, dog & owl
w/glass eyes, triangular, 3" h.
(ILLUS.) 245.00

Glass, double baby face, frosted
emerald green, marked Clarke
clear glass base, 2 5/8" d.,
4½" h. 170.00

Glass, owl, painted eyes, frosted
clear body, marked Clarke clear
glass base, 4¼" h. 225.00

FANS

Needle Lace Fan

Also see ADVERTISING ITEMS and COCA-COLA ITEMS.

Embroidered silk, large colorful dragon, carved ivory sticks, mid-19th c., 12" l. opening to 21" $450.00

Ivory "brise," folding-type, painted & varnished w/central scene of Rebecca at Well flanked by floral & landscape reserves, 7¾" l...... 120.00

Lace, "needle" lace depicting bride flanked by large leaves, flowers & heraldic shield motifs, pierced & gilded mother-of-pearl sticks, late 19th c., 10¾" l. (ILLUS.).......... 522.50

"Mourning Fan" and Case

Mourning fan, black silk, ebony sticks, opening to 18", original case (ILLUS.) 60.00

Ostrich feather, white & purple, 4" tortoise shell center, 14" d. 90.00

Ostrich feather, blue, ivory handle.. 125.00

Painted canvas, folding-type, landscape scene, artist-signed, original box 65.00

Painted paper, "gouache" painting of Louis XVI style scene of an al fresco musical gathering, pierced & carved mother-of-pearl sticks applied w/love trophies, late 19th c., 10½" l., in gilded frame w/scroll & shell foot 402.50

Painted paper, "gouache" painting of picnic scene after Boucher, mother-of-pearl sticks backed w/figural reserve & multicolor foil floral decor, France, 1880's,

12¾" l., in gilded double-sided glass case w/scroll foot 330.00

Painted silk, center w/scene of frolicking cupids, black lace edging, carved ebony sticks w/gold roses, 13½" l., opening to 26" ... 40.00

Painted silk, large Art Nouveau style black, grey & white poppy w/black sequin trim, 13½" l...... 75.00

Painted vellum, folding-type, central scene of St. Paul on the road to Damascus flanked by 2 oval reserves of cherubs, pierced & carved ivory sticks w/gold foil accents, 10¾" l. 120.00

Printed & painted paper, colored woodcut print depicting the storming of the Bastille w/text on one side & patriotic song, "L'Epoque de la Liberte" reverse, wooden sticks, France, 1790's, framed 275.00

Printed & painted paper, multicolored ballooning scene, reverse w/song "Voyage Historique du Globe," wooden sticks, France, 1780's.................. 352.00

French Silk Fan

Silk, "L'oracle," color printed w/questions & numerical "bull's eye," reverse w/one hundred answers, France, probably 19th c., 11" l. (ILLUS.) 175.00

Silver foil w/oval h.p. pastoral scene center, carved ivory sticks w/mirror, 9½" l., opening to 17" 40.00

FARM COLLECTIBLES

Also see BELLS, LANTERNS, METALS, POSTERS, SALESMAN'S SAMPLES, SCALES, SEED BOXES and WOODENWARES.

Barley sickle, long thin curved blade, signed "Long" $35.00

Calf weaner, tin 25.00

Chick feeder, glass, "Sana Fount,"
2-compartment 43.00
Chick feeder, tin, "Moe's Line,"
12" l. 15.00

Wrought Iron Corn Dryer

Corn dryer, wrought iron, 10-prong
(ILLUS.) 9.50
Corn dryer, wrought iron,
24-prong 18.00
Corn planter, wooden w/tin hopper,
original paint, 34" l. 60.00
Corn sheller, small hand-type,
"Black Hawk," 1886 patent date . . 40.00
Cow tag, brass oval w/die-stamped
numeral, 2¼" l. . . . . .2.50 to 5.00

Cranberry Rake

Cranberry rake, pine w/walnut
tines, 16½" w. (ILLUS.) 170.00
Egg crate, wooden slat construction
w/wire bail handle, 2-dozen
size 45.00
Egg crate, wooden slat construction,
"Owosso Mfg. Co., Owosso,
Mich.," 12-dozen size . . . . . .15.00 to 20.00
Egg gathering basket, collapsible
folding-type, iron wire, according
to size & details . . . . .17.00 to 30.00
Grain measure, bentwood round,
original sage green paint, 8½" d.,
6" h. 30.00
Grain scoop, tin . . . . .20.00 to 35.00
Grain scoop, wooden, shovel-
shaped w/short 4½" l. hook han-
dle, overall 15" l. 75.00
Grain shovel, carved from single
block of wood, nice patina,
33½" l. (age cracks in handle) . . . 135.00
Grain shovel, carved from single
block of cherrywood, open "D"
handle, extra large scoop 195.00
Hay fork, wooden, 3-tine, 1-piece,
60" l. 75.00

Hay knife, wooden handle, steel
blade 10.00
Ox yoke, double, pine w/bentwood
neck noose & wrought iron ring,
48" l. 125.00
Plow, walking-type, "John Deere,"
steel blade 30.00
Potato planter, "Acme" 15.00
Sheep shears, wrought iron, "Henry
Nickelson Sons" 35.00
Tractor seat, cast iron, "Oliver
Chilled Plow Works, South Bend,
Ind." 300.00
Tractor wrench, flat, "Oliver,"
large 7.50

FIREARMS

Sharps Breech Loading Pistol

Carbine, U.S. Springfield 1873 Trapdoor model, .45-70 caliber, 22" l.
barrel $475.00
Carbine, Winchester 1873, first mod-
el, w/saddle ring, .44-40 caliber,
20" l. round barrel 550.00
Fowler, full stock, curly maple stock
w/engraved brass butt plate &
trigger guard, lock marked "Henry
Parker Warranted," Bucks County,
Pennsylvania, original finish, ca.
1830, 41½" l. barrel, overall 57".. 400.00
Musket, flintlock, "Whitney Contract
1812" Type II w/comb, made for
Massachusetts, stamped "V" over
"S.F." in diamond over "M.S." &
"P" in oval & "M.S." on barrel
(minor damage at trigger
guard) 1,100.00
Musket, Colt 1861 Special model,
dated 1863 on lock, single-shot,
.58 caliber, 40" l. barrel 425.00
Musket, Harpers Ferry 1827 model,
.69 caliber 215.00
Musket, Remington 1856 model
w/Maynard tape primer conversion, long-range sight, original
ramrod 350.00
Pistol, Sharps breech-loading model,
first type, percussion-type, walnut
grips, 5" l. barrel (ILLUS.) 770.00
Revolver, Colt 1849 pocket model,

.31 caliber, 5" l. octagonal
barrel 400.00
Revolver, Colt 1851 Navy model,
6-shot, .36 caliber, 7" l.
barrel . . . . .250.00 to 365.00
Revolver, Colt 1860 Army model,
percussion-type, 6-shot, .44
caliber 950.00
Revolver, Benjamin F. Joslyn Stan-
dard Army model, percussion-
type, 1861-62, 5-shot, .44 caliber . . 580.00
Revolver, Manhattan Pocket or Navy
model, Series II, 1859 patent date,
5-shot, .36 caliber, 6½" l.
barrel 412.00
Revolver, C. S. Pettingill Navy (or
Belt) model, walnut grips, late
1850's, 6-shot, .34 caliber, 4½" l.
octagonal barrel 500.00
Revolver, Savage Percussion Cap
model, 2-piece walnut grip, ca.
1860, 7 1/8" l. octagonal barrel . . . 660.00
Revolver, Smith & Wesson No. 1,
second issue, nickel-plated brass,
rosewood grips, 1860-68, 7-shot,
.22 caliber, 7" l. 200.00
Revolver, Starr 1858 Army model,
walnut grips, 1856 patent date,
6-shot, .44 caliber, 6" l. barrel . . . 770.00
Revolver, Whitney Navy model, wal-
nut grips, brass guard, ca. 1860,
6-shot, .36 caliber 220.00
Rifle, Cochran Underhammer Revol-
ving Turret model, second type, by
C. B. Allen, Springfield, Massachusetts, 1830's, 9-shot, .40 cali-
ber, octagonal barrel 6,200.00
Rifle, Green breech-loading model,
by A.H. Waters Armory, Millbury,
Massachusetts, 1859-60, .53 cali-
ber, 35" l. round barrel 475.00
Rifle, Kentucky full stock, cherry-
wood stock, percussion lock
marked "---Golcher, Philada," ca.
1830, heavy octagonal barrel,
double set triggers w/brass
mounts (some rust at breech) 375.50
Rifle, Kentucky half-stock,
percussion-type, marked
"Richards, New Orleans, La." 185.00
Rifle, Pennsylvania half-stock, walnut stock w/brass mounts &
patchbox, pewter fore & end
caps, double-set trigger & back
action lock marked "Josh. Golch-
er," octagonal barrel marked
"J.V. Geiger, Towanda, Pa. 271"
on top, 33¾" l. barrel (crack beginning in side plate & needs
cleaning) 330.00
Rifle, Remington Long Range Creed-
more model, walnut stock
w/checkered pistol grip, 1873-90,
.44-100 caliber, 34" l. barrel 990.00

Rifle, Stevens Ideal Rifle No. 44½
model, double set triggers, Ballard action, Stevens-Pope barrel,
w/Lyman 30 power target scope
patented 1861, .22 caliber 1,750.00
Rifle, U.S. Springfield 1873 Trapdoor
model, .45 caliber, 32 5/8" l. barrel, w/ramrod & bayonet 375.00
Rifle, Winchester 1873 model,
nickel-plated lever & forend cap,
.38-40 caliber, 24" l. octagonal
barrel 325.00
Rifle, Winchester 1892 model, .44-40
caliber, 24" l. barrel 500.00

FIRE FIGHTING COLLECTIBLES

Painted Leather Fire Bucket

Badge, "Member, Fire Dept., Floyda-
da, Texas" $35.00
Badge, "Sioux City Fire Dept." 30.00
Badge, shield-shaped top inscribed
"Foreman," attached metal "rib-
bon" w/"Calhoon Fire Dept." 50.00
Book, "Old Fire Laddies, New York
& Brooklyn," 1885 . . . . 125.00
Book, "Our Firemen," New York,
1887 . . . . 150.00
Book, "Sheboygan Fire Department
Rules & Regulations," leather-
bound, 1901 . . . . 70.00
Bucket, leather, "Columbia Eagle
Fire Society," painted w/shield &
spread-winged American eagle,
banner in eagle's beak inscribed
"No. 2," banner below w/name,
branded "J. Fenno, Boston,"
19th c., 13" h. (ILLUS.) 2,640.00
Fire alarm box, "Harrington Signal
Co." 95.00
Fire alarm system, box, registar,
take-up reel & bell, "Gamewell" . . 500.00

Fire cart, American LaFrance 40 gallon chemical-type, w/hose, brass
nozzle & original wooden wheels,
1900-20 . . . . 650.00
Fire engine bell, brass 150.00
Fire house alarm bell, brass & cast
iron, "Gamewell" 140.00
Fireman's helmet, leather, w/brass
eagle crest, labeled "Cairns &
Bros.," ca. 1900 . . . . 200.00
Fireman's parade belt, "Hyde Park,
New York, Volunteer," leather,
19th c. 175.00
Fireman's parade torch w/wooden
handle 55.00

Fireman's Trumpet Horn

Fireman's trumpet horn, presentation piece, silver, beaded rim,
"repousse" florals & applied
Roman warrior's masks at rim,
"repousse" oval reserves
w/presentation inscription, masted sailing ship & "Don't give up
the ship," original strap on
eagle's-head rings, Peter L.
Krider, Philadelphia, ca. 1865,
22½" h. (ILLUS.) 2,970.00
Fireman's trumpet horn, presenta-
tion piece, silverplated brass, engraved inscription, dated "1862" . . 450.00
Fireman's uniform: coat, cap & trousers; labeled "Pettibone & Co.,
Cincinnati, Ohio," 3 pcs. 195.00
Fireman's uniform buttons, silver &
brass (3 sizes), "City of New York
Fire Department," attached to
"Bureau of Uniform Inspection"
card, early 1920's, set of 6 . . . . . . 35.00
Hose nozzle, 2-handled, brass,
24" l. 75.00
Lantern, "Dietz Fire King,"
copper . . . . 60.00 to 90.00

FIREPLACE & HEARTH ACCESSORIES

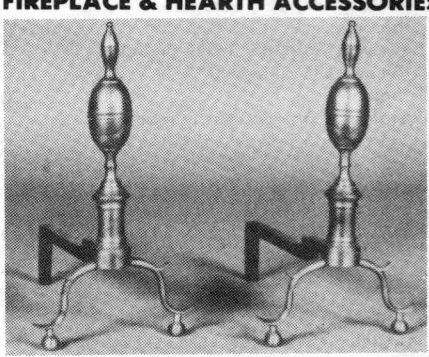

Federal Andirons

Also see KITCHENWARES *and*
METALS.

Andirons, bell metal, Federal,
spherical ring-turned finial, columnar standard, spurred arch cabriole supports, slipper feet, Boston,
early 19th c., 14" h., pr. $285.00
Andirons, brass, Federal (late),
acorn finial, baluster & ring-
turned standard, spurred arch
supports, ball feet, 1825-50,
18" h., pr. 165.00
Andirons, brass, Federal, double
lemon tops, columnar standard,
spurred arch supports, ball feet,
late 18th c., 19" h., pr. 352.00
Andirons, brass, Federal, urn-
shaped finial, columnar standard
on square plinth, spurred arch
supports, penny feet, w/urn-
shaped logstop, New York or
Philadelphia, 1800-10, 27" h.,
pr. 1,430.00
Andirons, brass & wrought iron,
Federal, banded spherical finial,
columnar standard & base,
w/brass gallery & conforming logstops, each stamped "Hunneman,
Boston," 1810-25, 12¼" h., pr. 715.00
Andirons, brass & wrought iron,
Federal, urn finial, shaped hexagonal standard, spurred arch
supports, ball feet, w/pierced gallery & conforming logstops,
stamped "R. Wittingham, New
York," ca. 1810, 23½" h., pr. 990.00
Andirons, bronze, Victorian Egyptian
Revival style, pineapple finial,
reeded columnar standard ending
in female mask w/Egyptian head-
dress, ca. 1890, 37¼" h., pr. 2,310.00
Bellows, painted & decorated pine,
polychrome bird, rose & other
florals on white ground,
releathered sides, brass nozzle,
18¼" l. 90.00

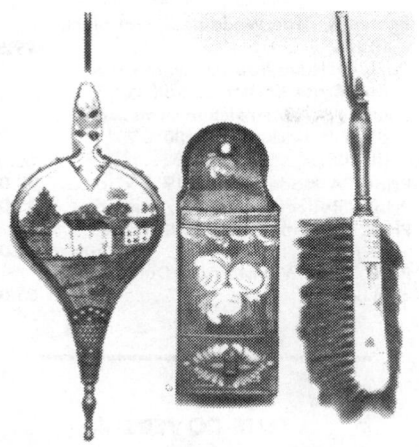

Fireplace Accoutrements

Bellows, painted & decorated pine, free-hand landscape w/houses, trees & mountains in shades of green, white, red, yellow & black front & red & gilt stenciled design on darkened cream ground reverse, releathered sides, original brass nozzle, 17¾" l. (ILLUS. left) 2,100.00

Bellows, maple w/some curl, scratch-carved compass design filled in w/dark brown stain & tan paint, worn leather sides, wrought iron nozzle, 20" l. (age cracks in handles) 235.00

Chestnut roasting pan, copper & brass w/wrought iron handle, 20¼" l. 150.00

Clock-jack, wrought iron & brass, iron frame, wooden pulleys, brass facings, balance wheel & 4 arms w/paddle ends, England, 18th c., 11½" h. (no crank) 440.00

Coal hod, copper, helmet-shaped, tubular bell metal handles & mounts, circular domed foot, 19th c., 14" h. 110.00

Coal hod, iron, helmet-shaped, hinged lid, 3-legged 145.00

Dutch oven, cov., cast iron, footed, w/wrought iron fixed handle w/swivel ring, 13½" d., 7" h. 300.00

Ember tongs, wrought iron, scissors-form w/rattail curls on handles & penny ends, 18th c., 10½" l. 85.00

Ember tongs, wrought iron, scissors-form w/shaped shank & penny ends, ball finial, 18th c., 27" l. 55.00

Fireplace fender, brass, serpentine rail w/acorn finials above wire mesh screen, serpentine base, 18th c., 54" w., 17½" h. 1,650.00

Fireplace fender, wrought iron, alternating twisted & wavy spindles w/cast ball finials, scrolled feet, 41" w., 11" h. 225.00

Hearth broiler, cast iron, rotary-type, radiating spokes, handle marked "Patent," 13½" d., 12" l. handle (old break in outer rim of wheel) 235.00

Hearth broom, birch splint, 36" l. 95.00

Hearth brush, turned wood handle w/original paint & back w/red & black designs highlighted in gold leaf, 15" l. (ILLUS. right) 700.00

Hearth fork, wrought iron, 2-tine, early 19th c. . . . . .45.00 to 95.00

Hearth griddle, cast iron pan w/wrought iron feet, fixed wrought iron handle w/swivel ring, 15" d. 175.00

Hearth skewer, wrought iron, twisted shaft, rattail scroll ends, 18th c., 21" h. 75.00

Hearth skillet, wrought iron, 3-legged, long handle, 7¾" d. 30.00

Hearth toaster, rotary-type, wrought iron, 4 twisted arches, footed, open penny end on handle, 18th c. 325.00

Hearth trivet, wrought iron, 9 bars on squared surface shelf, cabriole legs w/penny feet, handle w/exceptional heart form continuing to flattened end w/ring 595.00

Oven peel, wrought iron, punch-decorated triangles & circles on 6" oval space of handle, overall 54" l. 260.00

Pipe box, tole, original free-hand yellow, green, red & white floral & scroll designs on brown comb-grained japanned finish, 13" h. (ILLUS. center) 4,000.00

Potato rake, wrought iron, well-shaped handle w/hanging ring, 19½" l. 95.00

Reflector oven (for toasting meat before open fire), tin, w/hinged door at front opening to spit & 2 skewers, 19" l., 18" h. (some old damage) 130.00

Reflector oven, tin, made to be used w/clock-jack, 55" h. 275.00

Trammel, wrought iron, sawtooth-type, simple tooling on bottom hook, adjusts up from 48" l. 47.50

Trammel chain, wrought iron links, early 19th c., 80" l. . . . . .50.00 to 65.00

Waffle iron, cast & wrought iron, long handle, 18th c., overall 30" l. . . . . .60.00 to 100.00

FISHER (Harrison) GIRLS

Harrison Fisher's Red Cross Nurse

The Fisher Girl, that chic American girl whose face and figure illustrated numerous magazine covers and books at the turn of the century, was created by Harrison Fisher. A professional artist who had studied in England and was trained by his artist father, he was able to capture an element of refined, cultured elegance in his drawings of beautiful women. They epitomized all that every American girl longed to be and catapulted their creator into the ranks of success. Harrison Fisher, who was born in 1877, worked as a commercial artist full time until his death in 1934. Today collectors seek out magazine covers, prints, books and postcards illustrated with Fisher Girls.

Book, "The Alternative," by George
    Barr McCutcheon, illustrated by
    Harrison Fisher, 1st edition $65.00
Book, "American Beauties," pub-
    lished by Bobbs-Merrill Company,
    1909, first edition 195.00
Book, "The American Girl," 11 color
    illustrations, 1909, 17½ x 12" 250.00
Book, "A Song of Hiawatha," by
    Henry Wadsworth Longfellow, il-
    lustrated by Harrison Fisher,
    1906 ....110.00 to 150.00
Book, "Bachelor Belles," 21 color il-
    lustrations, published by Mead &
    Co., 1908 .... 175.00
Book, "The Harrison Fisher Book,"
    published by Scribners, color &
    black & white illustrations, 1907,
    11 x 8¾" 185.00
Book, "Nedra," by George Barr
    McCutcheon, illustrated by Harri-
    son Fisher, 1905................. 6.00
Postcard, "The Bride" 7.00
Postcard, "The First Evening in Their
    Own Home," oval black frame,
    7½ x 5½" 29.50
Postcard, "The Honeymoon," oval
    black frame, 7½ x 5½"......... 29.50
Postcard, "Their New Love," oval
    black frame, 7½ x 5½"......... 29.50

Postcard, "The Wedding," oval black
    frame, 7½ x 5½" 29.50
Poster, "Have You Answered the
    Red Cross Christmas Roll Call?"
    nurse w/outstretched arms, sol-
    diers in background, 30 x 20"
    (ILLUS.)........................ 50.00
Print, "A Modern Eve," 19½ x 16" .. 40.00
Print, "Reflections," 1908, framed ... 45.00
Print, "Sweetheart," 1909, framed,
    13 x 17".................25.00 to 35.00
Print, "You Will Marry A Dark Man,"
    21 x 17½" 55.00

FLUE COVERS

All flue covers listed are embossed & lithographed tin.

Basket of flowers $22.00
Blue Willow motif 20.00
Cherub against sky blue center,
    gold shading to deep blue outer
    rim, pierced tin border, 7¼" d.... 48.50
Gibson-type girl, square, ornate
    metal frame 22.00
Lake scene with girls (2) in boat &
    swimming swans 39.00
Little girl dressed in red, playing
    w/dog, Germany............... 35.00
Maiden seated beside lake, dark
    blue border, Belgium 28.00
Maidens (4) gathering mushrooms
    w/butterflies hovering above,
    pastel tones 49.00
Maidens (3) reposing in lush garden,
    Germany 59.00
Roman scene w/children, oval...... 25.00
Tiger kitten 30.00
Victorian child wearing bonnet &
    carrying flowers, shaded blue
    ground 40.00
Victorian children w/doll, beaded
    metal frame w/chain hanger,
    Germany, 9¼" d. 35.00

FOOD, CANDY & MISC. MOLDS

Cake, lamb, cast iron, marked
    "Griswold," 2-part, 12" h. $65.00
Cake, Santa Claus, "Hello Kiddies,"
    cast iron, marked "Griswold,"
    12" h..................175.00 to 210.00
Candle, 24 pewter tubes in wooden
    frame 440.00

Chocolate, acorn, tin, 2-part 22.00
Chocolate, football player, tin,
   1900's 38.00
Chocolate, heart, "To My Valen-
   tine," tin, 3-part 72.00
Chocolate, Kewpie, tin, 6" h. 125.00
Chocolate, lamb, tin, large 65.00
Chocolate, Passover plates (6)
   w/Hebrew inscriptions, tin,
   11½ x 11" 40.00
Chocolate, rabbit in seated position,
   tin, 2-part, 6" h. 65.00
Chocolate, rabbit on grassy mound,
   tin, 2-part, marked "Made in
   Germany," 6¼" h. 12.50
Chocolate, rabbit, tin, hinged,
   11" h. 125.00
Chocolate, rabbit standing, tin,
   15¾" h. 65.00
Chocolate, rabbit standing
   w/basket, tin, 18" h. 85.00
Chocolate, rabbits (2) kissing, book-
   shaped, tin, 8 x 7" 30.00
Chocolate, rabbits (45) standing, tin,
   11½ x 11' 30.00
Chocolate, rooster, tin 60.00
Chocolate, Santa Claus, tin,
   2" h. 10.00
Chocolate, Santa Claus w/pack &
   Christmas tree, tin, marked
   "Dresden," 6¼" h. 65.00
Chocolate, Santa Claus, tin,
   10½ x 5½" 150.00
Chocolate, Santa Clauses (4), tin,
   marked "Dresden" & "T.C.
   Weygand, New York," 9¼" l.,
   4½" h. 65.00
Chocolate, snowmen (45), tin,
   11½ x 11" 28.00
Chocolate, swan, tin, 2-part 17.50
Chocolate, turkey, tin 55.00
Food, dolphin, ironstone 29.00
Food, ear of corn, stoneware,
   ca. 1880, 8½ x 6½" 55.00
Food, ear of corn, yellowware,
   6½" oval . . . . 25.00 to 32.00
Food, fish, redware, clear glaze
   w/brown splotches & drips,
   11½" l. (small chips) 350.00

Tin Fish Mold

Food, fish, tin, 8½" l.
   (ILLUS.) 22.00
Food, fish, curved, tin,
   12½" l. 45.00
Food, geometric design center, cop-
   per w/tin lining, 7½ x 5½"
   oval 50.00

Food, grape cluster center,
   yellowware 35.00
Food, leaf center, ironstone,
   G. Jones 54.00
Food, orange & leaves center, fluted
   sides, ironstone, 8½" d., 5" h. . . .   45.00
Food, pear center, copper w/tin
   lining 75.00
Food, pear center, ironstone 50.00
Food, pinwheel center, yellowware,
   small 21.00
Food, rabbit center, fluted sides,
   tin, 3¾" oval 17.50
Food, rose blossom & leaves center,
   paneled sides, copper w/tin lin-
   ing, 6¾" oval 70.00
Food, roses center, ironstone,
   medium 50.00
Food, sheaf of wheat center,
   yellowware, 6" 45.00
Food, 6-pointed star, copper, 4" w.,
   pr. 60.00
Food, turk's turban, copper,
   8¼" d. 50.00
Food, turk's turban, redware, clear
   glaze w/brown splotches, 8¼" d.,
   3" h. 90.00
Food, turk's turban, redware, clear
   glaze w/black daubing at rim,
   8¼" d., 4¼" h. 130.00

Redware Turk's Turban Food Mold

Food, turk's turban, redware,
   creamy amber glaze w/brown
   splotches, 8¾" d. (ILLUS.) 115.00
Food, turk's turban, redware, bright
   green glazed exterior w/yellow
   slip interior, 9" d., 4" h. 175.00
Ice cream, Ace of Spades card,
   pewter 38.00
Ice cream, baby, pewter 45.00
Ice cream, baby shoe, pewter 26.00
Ice cream, baseball player,
   pewter 65.00
Ice cream, basket of flowers, pew-
   ter, 3" h. 30.00
Ice cream, bird, pewter 35.00
Ice cream, bow, pewter, 5¼" w. . . .   20.00
Ice cream, calla lily, 3-part, pewter,
   marked "E & Co., N.Y." 35.00

Ice cream, cauliflower, pewter,
marked "Brevete," 1-qt. 125.00
Ice cream, champagne bucket,
pewter 68.00
Ice cream, cherub, pewter, marked
"E & Co., N.Y.," 5" h. 27.50
Ice cream, chicken, pewter 35.00
Ice cream, Christmas wreath,
pewter 65.00
Ice cream, chrysanthemum,
pewter 37.50
Ice cream, clown, pewter, marked
"S & Co.," 5¼" h. 17.50

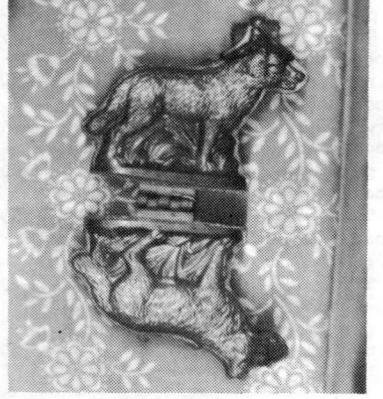

Pewter Dog Ice Cream Mold

Ice cream, dog standing, pewter
(ILLUS.) 65.00
Ice cream, eagle w/shield & crossed
swords, pewter 50.00
Ice cream, eagles (2), pewter 50.00
Ice cream, ear of corn, pewter,
7" h. 32.00
Ice cream, elephant, pewter,
marked "E & Co., N.Y." 40.00
Ice cream, fish, pewter, 5¾" l. 55.00
Ice cream, fleur-de-lis, pewter 35.00
Ice cream, four-leaf clover & heart,
pewter 34.00
Ice cream, fruits & vegetables, pew-
ter, English hallmark, 8" d. 450.00
Ice cream, George Washington,
pewter . . . . 65.00 to 75.00
Ice cream, harp 38.00
Ice cream, heart, pewter, 3¼" h. 45.00
Ice cream, horseless carriage,
pewter 45.00
Ice cream, horseshoe w/"Good
Luck," pewter 32.00
Ice cream, Jack of Diamonds card,
pewter, marked "E & Co.," 4 x
2¾" 17.50
Ice cream, lady's high boot, pewter,
5¾" h. 20.00
Ice cream, log, pewter, 4¼" h. 30.00
Ice cream, morning glories (2),
pewter, miniature 45.00

Ice cream, owl, pewter 56.00
Ice cream, potato, pewter 50.00
Ice cream, pretzel, pewter 30.00
Ice cream, rabbit, pewter, marked
"E & Co., N.Y.," 4½" h. 37.50
Ice cream, ring, pewter, 4¼" d. 17.00
Ice cream, rosebud, double,
pewter 32.00
Ice cream, Santa Claus in long coat,
pewter, 12" h. 325.00
Ice cream, strawberries (2), pewter,
marked "E. & Co., N.Y.,"
2 7/8" h. 27.50
Maple sugar, heart, diamond &
spade, carved wood, ca. 1850,
17 x 4 x 2" 150.00
Maple sugar candy, hearts alternat-
ing w/geometric shapes, carved
wood, 3½" w., 16" l. 220.00
Maple sugar candy, rooster, deeply
carved wood, 8¾" sq., 1½" h. . . . 240.00
Maple sugar candy, rose, carved
wood, 2-part, 2¼ x 1¾" 55.00
Maple sugar candy, stars & hearts,
carved wood, 3½" w., 15" l. 220.00
Pudding, crown, tin, w/center
upright 30.00
Pudding, fruit cluster center, copper
w/tin lining 85.00
Pudding, fruit cluster tops, pewter,
3-part, English registry mark for
1868, 6½", 7" & 8½" h., set
of 3 . . . . 295.00
Pudding, melon-shaped, tin, 2-part,
w/handle, 7¼" 18.00

FOOT & BED WARMERS

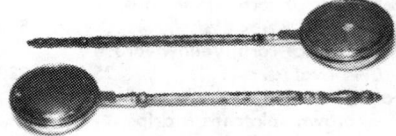

Brass Bed Warmers

Bed warmer, brass pan w/pierced
foliate design on lid, turned wood
handle, 19th c., 42" l. $220.00
Bed warmer, brass pan w/engraved
floral design on lid, turned wood
handle w/original red & yellow
paint w/black dots, 44" l. (repair
to handle) 600.00
Bed warmer, brass pan w/pierced &
engraved peafowl design on lid,
baluster-turned wood handle
w/original grain-painted finish,
19th c., 44" l. 242.00
Bed warmer, brass pan w/floral &

scrolling design on lid, turned wood handle w/worn original grain-painted finish, 44½" l. (ILLUS. top) 300.00

Bed warmer, brass pan w/pierced & engraved floral design on lid, turned wood handle (ILLUS. bottom) 275.00

Bed warmer, brass pan w/pierced geometric design on lid, turned maple handle, 18th c. 220.00

Bed warmer, copper pan w/simple floral engraving on lid, turned wood handle, 41" l. 225.00

Bed warmer, copper pan w/pierced & engraved floral design, turned fruitwood handle, 44" l. 198.00

Bed warmer, copper pan w/pierced & engraved foliate design centering a stylized flower, ring-turned fruitwood handle, 19th c., 45½" l. 275.00

Bed warmer, copper pan w/pierced & engraved sunburst design on brass lid, turned fruitwood handle, 19th c., 45" l. 242.00

Foot warmer, carpet-covered tin w/brass ends, 14 x 8" 37.50

Foot warmer, carpet-covered tin, hot water type, oval w/brass stopper 45.00

Foot warmer, copper, hot water type, dovetail construction 175.00

Foot warmer, pewter, hot water type, w/brass cap & handles, semi-circular 95.00

Foot warmer, pierced tin box w/perforated heart & circle designs, in mortised walnut frame w/turned corner posts, 9 x 7¾", 5¾" h. 150.00

Foot warmer, pierced tin box in mortised frame w/turned corner posts, metal ember pan, early 19th c. ....115.00 to 135.00

Foot warmer, pierced tin box w/soapstone insert on top, original whale oil burner & clamp, 9½ x 4½", 6½" h. 120.00

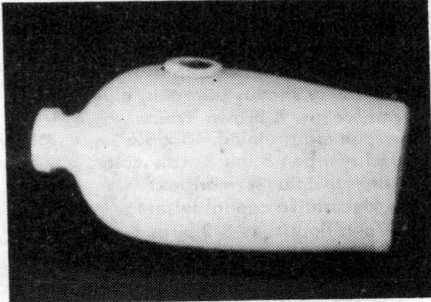

Stoneware Pottery Foot Warmer

Foot warmer, stoneware pottery, bottle-shaped (ILLUS.) .....15.00 to 25.00

Foot warmer, stoneware pottery, model of a pig, marked "Ad-Har-Co., Saranac Lake, N.Y." 90.00

Foot warmer, stoneware pottery, marked "Dorchester Pottery, Boston, Mass., patented Nov. 5, 1912" ....55.00 to 75.00

Foot warmer, stoneware pottery, blue & white, marked "Henderson Foot Warmer" ....130.00 to 180.00

Foot warmer, stoneware pottery, blue & white, marked "Logan".... 250.00

FOOT SCRAPERS

Cast Iron Foot Scraper

Cast iron, flat bar on quatrefoil base, 10¾ x 8¼" $30.00

Cast iron, bar supported on scrollwork frame, 6" w., 4½" h. (ILLUS.)........................ 85.00

Cast iron, full-figure model of a duck supporting scraper bar on back, 14½" l. 355.00

Cast iron, model of a Dachshund dog w/round tail curled over his back, 21" l., 7½" h. ....75.00 to 95.00

Cast iron, model of a Scottie dog ... 65.00

Cast iron, cat silhouette w/open eye & long tail, on rectangular base w/four holes to attach to porch, 17" l. 255.00

Cast iron, pig silhouette w/cut-out eye, 12" l., 8½" h. 195.00

FRACTURS

Fractur paintings are decorative birth and marriage certificates of the 18th and 19th centuries and also include family registers and similar documents. Illuminated family documents, birth and baptismal certificates, religious texts and rewards of merit, in a particular style, are known as "fractur" be-

cause of the the similarity to the 16th century type-face of that name. Gay watercolor borders, frequently incorporating stylized birds, angels, animals or flowers surrounded the hand-lettered documents, which were executed by local ministers, school masters or itinerant penmen. Most are of Pennsylvania Dutch origin.

Fractur Bookplate

Birth record for George Pane, pen & ink & watercolor, vital statistics in ornamental calligraphy in English, dark-haired young man in blue waistcoat w/gold buttons & frilled white stock & tie, holding spray of flowers, flanked by large pink rose blossoms & paired birds, Lycoming County, Pennsylvania, April 14, 1810, The Rev. Henry Young, framed, 10½ x 8½" $1,540.00

Birth record for Berks County, Pennsylvania infant, dated 1794, pen & ink & watercolor, vital statistics in ornamental German calligraphy, w/border of 2 fat angels, stylized tulips & hearts w/rainbow executed in shades of blue, brown, green, brownish red & ochre, in mahogany veneer frame, 17½ x 12½" 2,400.00

Birth record for George Enderlein, pen & ink & watercolor, vital statistics recording birth of 1799 in center roundel, w/painting of man holding bow & arrow flanked by distelfink roundels & w/vases of tulips flanking all, framed 6,600.00

Birth record for Dauphin County, Pennsylvania infant in 1798, printed and hand-colored vital statistics within heart-shaped device

w/two smaller hearts at base & borders of meandering floral vines executed in shades of red, yellow & green, framed, 18¾ x 15¾" 375.00

Bookplate, pen & ink & watercolor, inscribed in ornamental German calligraphy & painted w/bird, heart & flowers, dated 1828, in period frame, 5¾ x 4¼" (ILLUS.) 1,760.00

Bookplate for Sarah Wachter, pen & ink & watercolor, inscribed & dated Mar. 16th, 1825 at bottom, lidded urn in brilliant red, yellow & black, framed, 6¾ x 4" 1,320.00

Bookplate, pen & ink & watercolor, painted birds & flowers, Southeastern Pennsylvania, dated 1814, in period frame painted black, 6 3/8 x 4" 1,760.00

Family record, printed & painted record of marriage of Henrick & Judith Martin in 1811 & the births of their 4 children, w/red & black border & yellow, red & black tulips, framed, 16½ x 11¾" 250.00

Haus Segen (house blessing), printed & hand-colored, printed blessing within heart-shaped device surrounded by further hearts, flowers, birds & leaping deer in shades of red, yellow & olive brown, printed in Ephrata by Samuel Baumann, framed, 22 x 15½" 600.00

Marriage record for Margaret Grove & Messelmiah Reese, pen & ink & watercolor, vital birth & 1857 marriage statistics in ornamental calligraphy above figures of dark-haired lady holding hands w/dark-haired gentleman presenting bouquet of colorful flowers, in shades of red, yellow, blue, green & black, attributed to Henry Young, contemporary frame, 14 7/8 x 10" 3,750.00

Vorschrift (writing specimen) w/German inscription, "Gott Allein die Jhr...," pen & ink & watercolor, ornamental calligraphy encircled w/wreath of florals & birds in shades of green, blue, red, yellow & brown, frame w/painted graining, 10 x 9½" 750.00

Vorschrift, pen & ink & watercolor, Pennsylvania German text w/decorative capital letters w/pen flourishes & 2 birds & vase of flowers in shades of blue, olive green & brownish red, mortised cherrywood frame, 11 5/8 x 9 5/8" 375.00

Vorschrift, pen & ink & watercolor, central text within flower blossoms surround, upper corners w/two birds w/long colorful tails flanked by stylized tulips in shades of red, yellow, green & blue, anonymous, Southeastern Pennsylvania, dated 1823, 16 x 13¼" 522.00

FRAMES

Ornate English Silver Frame

Beaded, Victorian, dated 1912, 8½" w., 5½" h. $20.00
Bird's eye maple, plain, 9" w., 11" h. 45.00
Bird's eye maple, beveled edges, 10½" w., 12½" h. 125.00
Brass, cast w/military flags at top, 1900's, oval, 18" w., 21" h. 37.50
Brass-plated cast iron, easel-type, rococo-style cast w/ornate openwork scrolls, 5" w., 7" h. 45.00
Bronze, ornately cast framework, Gorham, 8" w., 10" h. 225.00
Bronze-finish cast iron, easel-type, full figure maiden each side w/florals & vines in relief in the Art Nouveau taste, 5 x 8" opening, pr. 110.00
Cast iron, easel-type, cast w/various World War I military symbols, dated 1917, 9" w., 6½" h. 48.00
Cast iron, ornate, cast w/crest surmounted by a spread-winged eagle w/blossoms & trailing vines at sides, colorful red, yellow, green & gilt repaint, oval, 9½" w., 12¾" h. 65.00
Celluloid, easel-type, 2½" w., 3½" h. 10.00
Cherrywood w/curly maple turned posts & corner blocks, 14½" w., 17" h. 200.00

Curly maple, 3" w. w/beveled edges, old red finish, 27 3/8" w., 23 3/8" h. 200.00
Oak, hand-carved birds & branches, 1885, 5½" w., 10" h. 18.00
Silver, central circular medallion bordered by ornate "repousse" curvilinear design, on green velvet backing, impressed "JL WD," w/English hallmark for 1900, 7¾" h., pr. (ILLUS.) 605.00
Silver, heart-shaped, "repousse" floral motif, on crimson velvet backing, English, 1900, 8" h. 660.00
Silver, tapering rectangle, ornate "repousse" floral border, impressed "J.D. & S" (James Dixon & Sons), w/English hallmark for 1902, 8" h. 605.00

Early 20th Century Silver Frame

Silver, rectangular center in oval border w/four "repousse" hearts, impressed "M & C," w/English hallmark for 1905, 11¾" h. (ILLUS.) .. 1,430.00
Sterling silver, Tiffany & Co., 7½" w., 10" h. 145.00
Walnut, box-style, ebonized stripes & gilt inner lining, 2" deep, 13 7/8" w., 11¾" h. 45.00
Walnut, cross-bar, applied hearts at corners, chip-carved edges, 19½" w., 16" h. 65.00
Walnut, hand-carved design, ca. 1830, deep oval, 5½" w., 6½" h. 75.00
Walnut, w/gilt inner liner, oval, 8" w., 10" h., pr. 125.00
Walnut, w/original graining & gilt inner liner, oblong w/oval 7½ x 9½" opening, overall 14¼" w., 16" h. 65.00

FRATERNAL ORDER COLLECTIBLES

Masonic Plate

B.P.O.E. (Benevolent & Protective Order of Elks) ash tray, brown elk & clock emblems on orange shaded to brown ground, Western Stoneware $18.00

B.P.O.E. collar box w/drawer, leather, elk & clock emblems 40.00

B.P.O.E. plate, tin, "Grand Lodge Reunion Philadelphia, July 15-20, 1907" .... 50.00 to 60.00

B.P.O.E. shaving mug, china, elk's head, w/name, T. & V., Limoges 75.00

B.P.O.E. watch fob, brass, elk's head in relief & blue enamel clock 25.00

I.O.O.F. (Independent Order of Odd Fellows) cast iron grave marker .. 6.00

I.O.O.F. medal, ornate, dated 1834, on braided purple & white cord... 50.00

Knights of Columbus match safe, 1919, w/marked matches 95.00

Knights Templar dish, Lenox china, 1903, 5¾" d., 2½" h............. 45.00

Knights Templar ceremonial hat, plumed, ca. 1900 .... 45.00

Masonic book, "Masonic Manual," 1855, leather bound 28.00

Masonic plate, china, 23k gold trim, Sanders Mfg. Co., Nashville, Tennessee (ILLUS.) 20.00

Masonic ring, 14k green gold band w/white enamel cross & crown center & motto "In Hoc Signo Vinces," orange & black enamel emblems 172.00

Masonic stick pin, 14k gold w/pearl setting 45.00

O.E.S. (Order of the Eastern Star) plate, china, "75th Anniversary, Indiana Grand Chapter" 10.00

Shrine 1899 goblet, green glass.................. 145.00 to 165.00

Shrine 1900 goblet, clear glass, "Washington, D.C.".............. 120.00

Shrine 1901 tumbler, clear glass, "Syria Temple, Pittsburgh, Pa.," w/grasshoppers 30.00

Shrine 1903 mug, clear glass, "Pittsburgh," w/Indian Chief Saratoga 85.00

Shrine 1904 mug, clear glass, "Atlantic City," fish handle 65.00

Shrine 1906 plate, clear glass, "Los Angeles" & "May" ....45.00 to 55.00

Shrine 1907 goblet, clear glass, "Los Angeles" 70.00

Shrine 1908 mug, ruby-flashed glass, "Pittsburgh" & "St. Paul," 5¼" h. 65.00

Shrine 1909 champagne, clear glass, "Louisville," tobacco leaves at base ....50.00 to 65.00

Shrine 1910 champagne, clear glass, "New Orleans" ....55.00 to 65.00

Shrine 1911 goblet, clear glass, "Rochester," "New York" & "Pittsburgh" 95.00

Shrine stein, china, desert scene w/Arabs & camels in relief, Made in Germany, 9" h. 75.00

Shrine tray, bronze-finish metal, Arabs & camels scene, "Lu Lu Patrol of Philadelphia, Compliments of J.W. Dawson, Rochester, N.Y." in relief, ornate rim, 1911, 6¾ x 5½" 59.00

Shrine watch fob & strap, "Terre Haute, Indiana," 1912............ 15.00

W.O.W. (Woodmen of the World) belt buckle, cast white metal, crossed axe & sledge hammer emblem & W.O.W., w/worn red leather belt..................... 25.00

W.O.W. fraternal symbols (star, plow, scythe, axe, etc.), cast white metal, 7 pcs. in fitted case, 9¾ x 8" 40.00

FRUIT JARS

Acme, w/shield, clear, pt. $3.00

Atlaz E-Z Seal, amber, qt........... 32.00

Atlas Good Luck, w/clover, clear, pt............................. 4.50

Atlas Mason Improved Pat'd, aqua, qt............................. 3.50

Atlas Strong Shoulder Mason, aqua, qt............................. 2.00

Ball Deluxe Jar, clear, qt.......... 5.00

Ball Mason (backwards s), aqua, qt............................. 25.00

Ball Perfect Mason, aqua, ½ pt. 20.00

Ball Perfect Mason

Ball Perfect Mason, citron, pt.
  (ILLUS.). 45.00
Ball Perfect Mason, amber,
  ½ gal. 21.50
Ball Sure Seal, blue, qt. 2.50
Boldt Mason Jar, green, pt. 35.00
Burnham (C.) & Co. arched over
  Manufacturers & Philada., green,
  qt. 400.00
Chambers (A. & D.H.) Union Fruit
  Jar, Pittsburgh, Pa., aqua, qt. 105.00
Columbia, clear, ½ pt. 17.50
Commonwealth Fruit Jar, clear,
  ½ gal. 65.00
Crystal Jar, clear, ½ gal. 50.00
Crystal Jar C G, clear, qt. 30.00
Curtis & Moore Trade Mark, Boston,
  Mass., clear, ½ gal. 17.00
Dandy (The) Trade Mark, clear,
  ½ gal. 25.00
Darling (The) Imperial, w/ADM
  monogram, clear, midget 155.00
Decker's Iowana, clear, qt. 10.00
Eureka, clear, pt. 10.00
Excelsior Improved, aqua, ½ gal. . . . 60.00
Flaccus (E.C.) Co., w/steer's head,
  amber, pt. 250.00
Gem (The), aqua, midget 20.00
Genuine Boyds Mason, aqua,
  ½ gal. 40.00
Genuine Mason, olive green, pt. . . . 28.50
G J Co., aqua, qt. 12.00
Globe, clear, pt. 20.00
Globe, aqua, qt. 14.50
Green Mountain, G.A. Co., clear,
  qt. 15.00
Haines 2 Patent March 1st 1870,
  aqua, ½ gal. 295.00
Hartell's Airtight Glass Cover,
  Patented Oct. 19, 1858, amethyst,
  qt. 1,000.00
Haserot (The) Company Cleveland,
  Mason Patent, aqua, qt. 20.00
Howe (The) Jar, clear, qt. 30.00
Keystone Trade Mark Registered,
  clear, qt. 6.00

Knowlton Vacume Fruit Jar, w/star,
  aqua, ½ gal. 24.00
Leader (The), amber, pt. . . . 200.00 to 225.00
Leader (The), amber, ½ gal. 115.00
Lightning, aqua, qt. 6.00
Lightning, amber, ½ gal. 42.50

Lightning Trade Mark

Lightning Trade Mark, amber, qt.
  (ILLUS.). . . . . .25.00 to 45.00
Lyman (W.W.), Patd Aug 5th, 1862,
  aqua, qt. 39.00
Magic (The) Fruit Jar, w/star,
  amber, ½ gal. 650.00
Marion (The) Jar, Mason's Patent
  Nov. 30th, 1858, aqua, pt. 20.00
Mason's Improved, aqua, midget . . . 13.00
Mason's Improved, clear, qt. 2.75
Mason's Patent Nov. 30th, 1858,
  w/star on base, amber, qt. 95.00
McDonald Perfect Seal, aqua, pt. . . . 10.00
Millville Atmospheric Fruit Jar,
  aqua, qt. 36.00
Moore's Patent Dec. 3d, 1861, aqua,
  qt. 85.00
Potter & Bodines Airtight Fruit Jar,
  Philada., aqua, ½ gal. 395.00
Premium, Coffeyville, Kas.,
  amethyst, pt. 10.00
Royal, green, ½ gal. 90.00
Safety Valve, Patd May 21, 1895,
  w/HG monogram in triangle,
  aqua, ½ gal. 39.00
Sun (in circle) Trade Mark, aqua,
  qt. 55.00
Van Vliet (The) Jar of 1881, aqua,
  pt. 625.00
Wan-eta Cocoa, Boston, amber,
  qt. 20.00
Weir (The), Patented March 1st,
  1892, stoneware, qt. 22.50
Wilcox (B.B.), Patd. March 26, 1867,
  aqua, qt. 65.00
Woodbury, aqua, qt. 25.00

FURNITURE

Furniture made in the United States during the 18th and 19th centuries is coveted by collectors. American antique furniture has a European background, primarily English, since the influence of the Continent usually found its way to America by way of England. If the style did not originate in England, it came to America by way of England. For this reason, some American furniture styles carry the name of an English monarch or an English designer. However, we must realize that, until recently, little research has been conducted and even less published on the Spanish and French influences in the areas of the California missions and New Orleans.

After the American Revolution, cabinetmakers in the United States shunned the prevailing styles in England and chose to bring the French styles of Napoleon's Empire to the United States and we have the uniquely named "American Empire" style of furniture in a country that never had an emperor.

During the Victorian period, quality furniture began to be mass-produced in this country with its rapidly growing population. So much walnut furniture was manufactured, the vast supply of walnut was virtually depleted and it was of necessity that oak furniture became fashionable as the 19th century drew to a close.

For our purposes, the general guidelines for dating furniture will be:

Pilgrim Century - 1620-85
William & Mary - 1685-1720
Queen Anne - 1720-50
Chippendale - 1750-85
Federal - 1785-1820
  Hepplewhite - 1785-1800
  Sheraton - 1800-20
American Empire - 1815-40
Victorian - 1840-1900
  Early Victorian - 1840-50
  Gothic Revival - 1840-90
  Louis XV (rococo) - 1845-70
  Louis XVI - 1865-75
  Eastlake - 1870-95
  Renaissance - 1860-85
  Jacobean & Turkish Revival - 1870-90
Art Nouveau - 1890-1918
Turn-of-the-Century - 1895-1910
Mission (Arts & Crafts movement) - 1900-15
Art Deco - 1925-40

All furniture included in this listing is American unless otherwise noted. Also see MINIATURES (Replicas).

ARMOIRES & WARDROBES

Armoire, Art Nouveau, mahogany & smoked glass, carved crest above central glazed door flanked by smaller doors, on base carved w/clematis blossoms, vines & leaves, attributed to Louis Marjorelle, Nancy, France, ca. 1910, 73½" w., 80½" h. $3,300.00

Armoire, Louis XV Provincial, oak, molded overhanging cornice above pr. fielded paneled doors over short central drawer flanked by longer drawers, shaped apron, short cabriole legs, France, mid-18th c., 62" w., 79½" h. 1,760.00

Louis XV Provincial Armoire

Armoire, Louis XV Provincial, walnut, shaped cornice w/wide overhang, frieze w/inlaid urn & chevron banding above pr. shaped paneled doors, shaped apron w/vine inlay, short cabriole legs, France, late 18th c., 55" w., 92" h. (ILLUS.) . . .4,950.00

Armoire, Louis XV Provincial, oak, molded overhanging cornice above pr. paneled doors, w/scroll-carved cresting & foliate scroll mid banding, flanked by fluted pilasters, short cabriole legs, France, late 18th c., 64" w., 96" h. 3,190.00

Armoire, Louis XV Provincial, cherrywood, molded cornice above pr. paneled doors, shaped apron, short cabriole legs, Louisiana, late 18th c. 4,950.00

Kas (American version of the Netherlands Kast or wardrobe), walnut, 2-part construction: upper part w/projecting molded cornice above pr. elaborately paneled doors within paneled sections; lower section w/arrangement of 3 shallow drawers over deeper

drawers, molded base, large ball
feet, Pennsylvania, 1750-80,
94" w., 78" h. 11,000.00
Schrank (Pennsylvania-German ver-
sion of a massive wardrobe),
painted & decorated walnut, 3-
part construction: upper part
w/removable projecting cornice;
middle section w/pr. tall paneled
doors; base w/pr. short drawers
& applied molding above & below,
large ball feet; painted & decorated w/polychrome urns of tulips on
cornice frieze, door panels & lower drawer fronts on a grain-
painted brown ground, Pennsylvania, 1760-80, 67" w., 78" h. (restoration to painted decoration on
door panels) 3,300.00
Schrank, walnut, 3-part construction:
upper part w/removable molded
cornice; middle section w/pr.
arch-molded double-paneled
doors; base w/pr. thumb-molded
drawers & applied molding, ogee
bracket feet; Pennsylvania, late
18th c., 86" h. 6,825.00

American Empire Gothic Wardrobe

Wardrobe, American Empire in the
Gothic taste, mahogany, projecting
cornice above pr. Gothic-arch
paneled cupboard doors w/original
brass keyhole escutcheons flanked
by free-standing columns with Ionic
capitals, leaf-carved & melon-
reeded legs, signed Joseph Stewart,
Jr., New York, dated 1831, 69" w.,
90" h. (ILLUS.) 3,850.00
Wardrobe, Biedermeier-style,
butternut, American, mid-
19th c. 1,200.00
Wardrobe, Federal - American Em-
pire transitional in the Classical
taste, mahogany, removable bro-

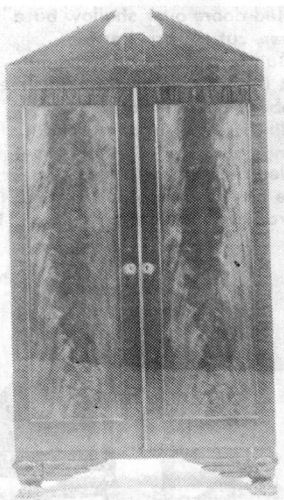

American Classical Wardrobe

ken pediment cornice, plain frieze
above pr. paneled doors opening
to shelves & arrangement of 4
short drawers, eagle-carved hairy
paw feet, ca. 1815, 49" w., 95" h.
(ILLUS.) 3,575.00
Wardrobe, Federal, mahogany,
shaped pediment fitted at center
& 4 corners w/urn finials &
figured mahogany frieze above
pr. tall doors w/figured mahogany
panels outlined w/brass trim
(opening to drawers & linen
slides) flanked by stop-fluted
pilasters, vase- and ring-turned
feet w/brass sabots, attributed
to Honore Lannuier, New York,
1800-15, 55" w., 103" h. 24,200.00
Wardrobe, Federal, mahogany,
projecting cornice w/molded edge
& outset corners over pr. paneled
cupboard doors fitted w/reeded
brass trim (opening to 4 removable bins, 2 drawers, single shelf
& side compartment w/wooden
hooks) flanked by reeded
colonettes, bulb feet w/brass ball
caps, w/paper label of "M. Alli-
son's Cabinet & Furniture Warehouse," New York, ca. 1817 . . . .11,000.00
Wardrobe, Victorian, Gothic Revival
substyle, pine, cove-molded cornice above pr. doors w/Gothic
arch-molded panels over pr. short
drawers in base w/applied molding at lower edge, original finish,
ca. 1840, 50" w., 84" h. 650.00
Wardrobe, Victorian, early country-
style, grain-painted finish, cove-
molded cornice above pr. double-

paneled doors over shallow base
drawer, cut-out bracket feet,
dovetail construction throughout,
red & black flame-grained finish . . 995.00
Wardrobe, Victorian (late), oak,
scrolling crest w/applied scroll
carvings above pr. doors w/inset
beveled oval mirror plates over
single base drawer applied
w/scroll carvings, refinished 1,200.00

BEDS

American Empire Maple Bed

American Empire "cannonball" low
poster bed, painted pine & maple,
boldly scrolling head & footboards
w/"rolling pin" crests flanked by
ring- and baluster-turned posts
w/cannonball finials, original
rope-peg siderails, flattened ball
feet, grain-painted vivid pumpkin
orange & brown, 1825-50 . . . . 1,500.00
American Empire low poster bed,
mahogany & mahogany veneer,
shaped headboard w/carved crest
flanked by turned & ornately
carved posts ending in paw feet,
conforming lower footboard,
46" h. posts (restored) 770.00

American Empire poster bed, maple,
double-paneled headboard
w/carved fruit bowl at crest
flanked by turned tall posts
carved w/acanthus & water leaves
& w/shaped finials, scrolling footboard centering bow-shaped scroll
flanked by conforming posts,
animal paw feet, New York State,
1820-35, restored, 55" w., 77" h.
posts (ILLUS.) 1,760.00
American Empire "sleigh" bed, wal-
nut, double size 900.00
American Empire country-style low
poster bed, poplar w/curly maple
posts, shaped headboard w/scroll-
ing ends & "rolling pin" crest &

blanket-roll foot rails flanked by
bold ring- and baluster-turned
posts w/flaring beaker form finials, refinished, repaired &
w/replaced siderails, 50½ x 70",
54½" h. posts 550.00
American Empire country-style low
poster bed, scrolling headboard
w/"rolling pin" crest flanked by
bold vase- and ring-turned posts
w/bell-shaped finials, original
rope-peg siderails, old dark finish,
three-quarter size 280.00
Brass tester bed, Victorian, tubular
rods in foot centered w/foliate
crest & head centered w/scrolling
crest, corner posts w/baluster-
shaped finials joined by tester
centered w/crown, England, late
19th c., 108" to top of center
crown . . . . 1,500.00 to 1,800.00
Brass bed, tubular, ornate scrolls,
double size 895.00
Brass bed, tubular posts w/brass
ball finials & tall cylindrical corner
posts w/ball finials, late 19th c.,
extra large double size 1,980.00
Brass bed, tubular, rounded head &
footrails above 5 upright rods
headed by solid brass balls, single
size, pr. 600.00
Cast iron & brass bed, half-round
head & footboards w/openwork C-
scroll designs in iron & brass,
original siderails, flaking white
paint on iron, 69½" h. headboard,
double size 1,300.00
Chippendale tall poster bed,
mahogany, shaped headboard
flanked by ring-turned tapering
posts, stop-fluted & spirally-turned
footposts on square legs, Marlboro feet, Newport, Rhode Island,
ca. 1775, 54½" w., 89½" h. posts
(replaced siderails & restoration
to headboard) 5,500.00
Federal tester bed, cherrywood,
shaped headboard flanked by
square tapering posts & reeded
tapering cylindrical footposts,
New England, 1800-30, 57" w.,
89" h. (w/tester of later
date) 1,760.00
Federal tester bed, mahogany,
shaped headboard flanked by
ring-turned tapering posts &
w/plume-carved reeded &
waterleaf-carved urn-shaped footposts w/spade feet, original rope-
peg siderails & tester, 56" w.,
91" h. 4.400.00
Federal tester bed, mahogany, rak-
ing headboard flanked by reeded
urn-shaped posts on square taper-

ing legs, spade feet, original rope-peg siderails & footrails, Massachusetts, 1790-1810, 55" w., 62¾" h. posts, w/tester 5,500.00
Federal tester bed, mahogany, maple & pine, shaped pine headboard flanked by faceted maple headposts, footrail flanked by mahogany reeded & leaf-carved footposts ending in ring-turned tapering cuffed feet, Massachusetts, ca. 1810, 48" w., 70" h. posts, w/tester (restored) 3,520.00

Federal Tester Bed

Federal tester bed, curly maple, shaped headboard flanked by baluster-turned posts w/acorn finials & w/conforming footposts, each post w/gilt-metal cap mounted on tapering legs w/vase-form feet, original red pine tester, Eastern Massachusetts, ca. 1800 (ILLUS.) 8,025.00
Federal tester bed, maple, shaped pine headboard flanked by square tapering posts & w/conforming footposts, square legs, New England, ca. 1825, 54" w., 82" h. posts, w/tester (restored headboard & siderails) 3,575.00
Federal tester bed, maple, shaped paneled headboard & baluster-turned footrail flanked by elaborately ring- and baluster-turned posts, New England, 1800-20, 55½" w., 78" h. posts, w/tester 1,760.00
Federal tall poster bed, mahogany, scrolling headboard flanked by reeded posts, footrail flanked by conforming posts, replaced siderails, double size 950.00
Federal tall poster bed, mahogany &

birch, shaped headboard flanked by square tapering posts, footrail flanked by reeded & waterleaf-carved columns & urn-form base w/swag- and palmette-carved designs on punchwork ground w/stars & w/pointed finials, square feet, attributed to Samuel McIntyre, Salem, Massachusetts, ca. 1815, 56" w., 71" h. posts (altered siderails) 2,200.00
Federal country-style low poster bed, painted finish, shaped headboard w/scrolling ends & conforming footboard flanked by turned posts w/ball finials, original rope-peg siderails, old red paint, first half 19th c., 40" w., 31" h. posts . . 495.00

Federal Country-Style Poster Bed

Federal country-style tall poster bed, maple, paneled scrolling headboard w/"rolling pin" crest ending in "acorn" terminals flanked by baluster- and ring-turned posts above compressed baluster over octagonal plinth on blocked legs & turned feet, early siderails, probably Pennsylvania, now fitted w/modern tester, 61" w., 80" h. posts (ILLUS.) 1,870.00
Federal country-style bed, painted hardwood, raking headboard flanked by low turned posts w/mushroom cap finials, conforming footboard & posts w/tapering feet, original rope-peg siderails, early (but not original) black-painted graining over red, 49½" w., 34" h. posts 275.00
Federal country-style bed, stained pine, shaped headboard flanked by blocked & turned posts

Federal Country-Style Bed

w/shaped finials, red-stained
finish, New England, ca. 1810,
48" w., 33" h. posts (ILLUS.) 1,760.00
Mission-style (Arts & Crafts movement) bed, oak, headboard
w/plain crestrail above 7 flat uprights flanked by square tapering
corner posts & lower conforming
footboard, w/decal of L. & J. G.
Stickley, double size ....176.00 to 330.00

Victorian Eastlake Bed

Victorian bed, Eastlake substyle,
walnut & burl walnut, high-back
w/arched crest above scallop-and-
spindle crestrail above burl-inset
panels flanked by square posts,
conforming footboard, 89" h.
headboard, 58½" w. (ILLUS.) 605.00
Victorian bed, Renaissance Revival
substyle, black walnut, high-back
w/shaped crest, applied oval
medallions & burl-inset panels,
conforming footboard, 1870-80.... 850.00
Victorian bed, Renaissance Revival
substyle, walnut & burl walnut,
typical carvings & burl panel trim,
original finish, 89" h. headboard.. 522.50
Victorian bed, Renaissance Revival
substyle, walnut & burl walnut,

highback w/shaped crest centering applied cartouche & fruit carvings flanked by squared posts
w/urn-turned finials, conforming
footboard, late 19th c., original
finish, 74" h. headboard 385.00
Wicker bed, loom-woven, 1920's,
single size 350.00

BEDROOM SUITES

Victorian Bedroom Furniture

Art Deco: pr. twin beds w/attached
chrome reading lamps, pr. bed-
side tables, chest of drawers,
vanity & upholstered stool & side
chair; enameled ivory & black
metal, design by Norman Bel
Geddes for Simmons Co.,
ca. 1935, 8 pcs................. 3,850.00
Victorian Eastlake substyle: bed,
chest of drawers w/mirror & commode; walnut & burl walnut, typical incised carvings & panels,
3 pcs................1,200.00 to 1,600.00
Victorian Renaissance Revival substyle: bed, drop-front dresser
w/mirror & commode; walnut
w/burl walnut panels, carved
eagle crestings on bed & dresser
& white marble slab tops on commode & dresser, original wooden
pulls on case pieces, ca. 1870,
3 pcs. (ILLUS. of part) 6,700.00
Victorian Renaissance Revival in the
cottage-style: bed, chest of drawers & commode; walnut w/gold-
ochre grain-painted panels &
aplied walnut fruit-carved pulls,
ca. 1885, 3 pcs.................2,500.00
Victorian Rococo substyle: bed,
chest of drawers & commode;
walnut & burl walnut, white marble slab tops & grape cluster-
carved pulls on case pieces,
3 pcs. 2,000.00

BENCHES

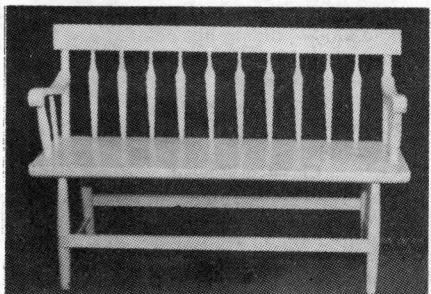

Deacon's Bench

Child's bench, Amish, pine, solid-
board sides w/cut-out feet joined
by plain backrail w/single upright
slat over stayrail attached to
plank seat, refinished 125.00
Child's schoolhouse bench w/folding
seat, birch & cast iron, 2-seat
model 48.00
Church pew, oak, short 90.00
Deacon's bench, painted pine & pop-
lar, plain crestrail above 10
arrow-form spindles, downswept
arms on turned supports, plank
seat, turned legs w/flattened
stretchers, now w/numerous lay-
ers of paint, 45" l. (ILLUS.) 400.00
Deacon's bench, painted pine, plain
crestrail above 18 "arrow" spindles & 3 turned uprights, downswept arms on turned supports,
plank seat, turned legs w/flat-
tened stretchers, w/traces of
original red paint, 72" l. 950.00

Hall Bench

Hall bench, Turn-of-the-Century,
oak, machine-carved, ornate crest
above paneled back w/two panels
of relief-carved cherubs, hinged
seat lifting to storage compart-

ment, animal paw feet, early
20th c. (ILLUS.) 950.00
Kneeling bench, primitive pine,
plank top, plain apron, cut-out
sides forming short legs, worn
brown finish, 55 x 5" top,
5¾" h. 120.00
Mammy's bench, painted & decorat-
ed, plain crestrail above 9-spindle
back, turned arms on spindle supports, plank seat w/original baby
guard, turned legs on rockers,
original paint & stenciled decoration, early 19th c., small size,
31" l. 2,450.00
Mammy's bench, painted finish, sin-
gle crestrail above medial stayrail
& 3 uprights, roll-over plank seat
w/original removable baby guard,
turned legs w/flattened stretchers
on rockers, 71" l. (black repaint
over weathered finish & some age
cracks & repairs) 300.00
Mammy's bench, painted & decorat-
ed, plain crestrail above 12-
spindle back, shaped arms on
turned supports, plank seat
w/original baby guard, turned
legs w/flattened stretchers on
rockers, old paint & stenciling . . .1,350.00
Mammy's bench, painted & decorat-
ed, shaped crestrail above 18-
spindle back, downswept arms
w/scrolling grips, plank seat
w/original baby guard, turned
legs w/flattened stretchers on
rockers, original colorful stenciled
& free-hand decor on dark
ground 2,475.00
Mammy's bench, painted & decorat-
ed, plain crestrail above 2 vase-
form splats & 3 uprights, downswept arms w/shaped grips,
plank seat w/solid board baby
guard, turned legs joined by flattened stretchers on rockers, simulated rosewood-painted finish
w/mustard yellow striping & trim,
1830-40 . . . . .1,450.00
Wagon seat, painted hardwood,
double chairback style w/two
slats between turned uprights,
(replaced) rush seat, turned heavy
legs w/stretchers 425.00
Water bucket bench, painted pine,
sheet zinc-covered oblong top,
plain apron, 1-board sides w/cut-
out feet joined by medial shelf,
original dark red paint, 42 x 16¾"
top, 25" h. (lower shelf is late
addition) 135.00
Water bucket bench, oblong top
w/well for pails, bootjack sides &
back forming feet & enclosing

medial shelf, old dark red stain,
Amish origins 600.00
Water bucket bench, painted pine,
3-tier, mortised construction,
stepped tiers joined to shaped
sides w/cut-out feet, worn original green paint, 62" w.,
46½" h. 675.00
Water bucket bench, painted pine,
5-tier, board-and-batten back &
shaped sides forming superstructure w/hanging cornice above 3
open shelves raised above 2
wider bucket shelves, early red
paint 1,200.00
Window bench, Federal, mahogany,
each side w/chairback ends &
w/paneled crestrail & medial stayrail between shaped stiles, reeded seatrail, upholstered seat,
sabre legs w/carved lion's paw
feet, New York, 1800-20,
52" l. 5,500.00
Federal country-style bench, painted
& decorated, scalloped crestrail
above turned spindles, scrolling
arms, plank seat, turned legs
w/flattened stretchers, painted
dark finish, Pennsylvania, 19th c.,
71" l. 660.00
Federal country-style bench, poplar,
shaped crestrail above half-
spindle back, downswept arms on
turned supports, plank seat,
turned legs w/turned stretchers,
Pennsylvania, ca. 1840, 72" l. 660.00
Mission-style (Arts & Crafts movement) "spindle-back" bench, plain
crestrail above 29-spindle back,
drop-in seat cushion w/springs,
flat arms above spindle sides,
w/red decal label of Gustav Stickley, Model No. 286, ca. 1905,
47½" l. 8,800.00

BOXES

Georgian Knife Boxes

Bible box, painted & decorated,
free-hand & stenciled designs on

red ground, signed & dated 1832,
Norwegian origins 325.00
Candle box w/sliding lid, painted &
decorated, blue w/black striping,
signed & dated 1856 .... 225.00
Candle box, hanging-type, pine,
original blue paint, 22" l., 14" h.
at backplate 165.00
Knife box, Classical Revival, mahogany, reeded cylindrical form &
adjustable lid w/acanthus-carved
pineapple finial, plinth base on
acanthus-carved animal paw feet,
attributed to David Sackriter,
Philadelphia, Pennsylvania, ca.
1815, 12½" d., 27½" h. 7,425.00
Knife boxes, George III, inlaid mahogany, hinged serpentine-fronted
lid inlaid w/oval reserve of conch
shell opening to fitted interior in
conformingly shaped case, w/in-
laid geometric borders throughout, brass hinges & silver drop-
ring handles, England, late
18th c., 13½" to 14½" h., set
of 3 (ILLUS. of part) 2,090.00
Knife boxes, George III, inlaid mahogany, hinged serpentine-fronted
lid opening to fitted interior in
conformingly-shaped case, w/in-
laid tulipwood borders throughout, England, late 18th-early
19th c., 14½" to 16½" h.,
set of 3 .... 1,870.00
Knife boxes, George III, mahogany,
urn-form body w/scrolling acanthus
handles & domed gadrooned cover
w/mushroom finial & leaf-tip
carved edge, turned pedestal
pedestal base, England, late
18th c., 21" h., pr. 3,630.00
Sewing (or work) box w/hinged lid,
painted finish, oblong top
w/molded edge lifting to deep
well, applied molding at base,
original painted bold decor w/ini-
tials & date "1832" 660.00
Storage box & cover, butternut, oblong top w/molded edge, applied
molding at base, worn old green
paint, 23 x 12¼", 12¼" h. 115.00
Storage box w/hinged lid, painted
pine, oblong top w/molded edge
lifting to well in case w/applied
molding at base, sponge-daubed
painted finish, 38 x 17", 17" h. ... 210.00

BUREAUS PLAT

Louis XV bureau plat, kingwood
marquetry w/ormolu mounts,
shaped oblong top w/inset leather
writing surface & ormolu rim,
frieze w/three quarter-veneered &
banded drawers each side, cabri-

Louis XV Bureau Plat

ole legs, fitted w/ormolu foliate
drawer handles, keyhole escutcheons, "chutes" & "sabots," France,
mid-18th c., 58 x 32¼" top, 30" h.
(ILLUS.) 8,800.00
Louis XV style bureau plat, kingwood w/gilt-bronze mounts, oblong top inset w/three leather
writing surfaces, frieze w/three
drawers, semi-cabriole legs,
w/gilt-bronze drawer handles,
"chutes" & "sabots," France,
ca. 1900, 66" l., 31½" h. 3,300.00
Louis XV style bureau plat, kingwood w/ormolu mounts, shaped
top inset w/gilt-tooled brown
leather writing surface w/cross-
banded border & ormolu rim,
shaped frieze w/three working
drawers & 3 false drawers each
side, cabriole legs, w/ormolu foliate drawer handles, shell mounts
on ends & foliate "sabots," signed
H. Nellson, ca. 1910, 78" l.,
31¼" h. 19,800.00
Louis XV-XVI bureau plat, kingwood
& satinwood marquetry w/ormolu
mounts, shaped oblong top w/in-
set leather writing surface & ormolu rim, frieze w/three working
& 3 false drawers all faced
w/"bois satine" quarter veneer,
cabriole legs, w/pierced ormolu
foliate drawer handles & keyhole
escutcheons, acanthus & bellflower "chutes" & pierced leaf-tip
"sabots," France, 1750-75,
69 x 37" top, 31" h. 33,000.00

CABINETS
China cabinet, Mission-style (Arts &
Crafts movement), oak, overhanging top above single glazed cupboard door, square legs raised on
casters, red decal mark of Gustav
Stickley, No. 820, ca. 1907,
36" w., 64" h. 1,540.00
China cabinet, Turn-of-the-Century,

golden oak, molded crest above
glazed bow-fronted cupboard
doors flanked by Corinthian
columns & curved glass sides,
molded base of conforming outline, machine-carved animal paw
feet on casters, ca. 1915, original
finish .... 600.00 to 750.00

Victorian China Cabinet

China cabinet, Victorian cottage-
style, stained maple & pine, ornate galleried top w/spool-turned
spindles & ball finials on turned
uprights above pr. glazed cupboard doors flanked by glazed
canted sides, apron conforming to
gallery, turned legs, flattened ball
feet, 1890's (ILLUS.) 650.00
Corner cabinet, Turn-of-the-Century,
oak w/beveled glass pentagonal
front, 5-sided dentiled cornice
above griffin-carved panels & conforming glazed-panel doors &
sides, labeled "T.G. Buckley &
Co., 690 Dudley St., Boston,
Mass.," 34" w., 24" deep,
80¼" h. 2,400.00
Dental cabinet, oak, 1-piece construction, oblong top above pr.
cupboard doors opening to shallow drawers over 6 long drawers,
26" w., 16" deep, overall 65" h. ... 1,700.00
Dental cabinet, walnut, 2-part construction: upper part w/molded
cornice above pr. cupboard doors
w/frosted glass panels opening to
shelves raised on baluster-turned
supports; lower section w/plain
top above arrangement of 14
shallow drawers & 6 graduated
deeper drawers w/original brass

Dental Cabinet

pulls, scalloped apron, baluster-
turned legs, ball feet (ILLUS.) 1,200.00
Filing cabinet, Turn-of-the-Century,
golden oak, 4-drawer (10 x 12"),
original finish 275.00
Filing cabinet, Turn-of-the-Century,
golden oak, 8-drawer, original
finish ....300.00 to 400.00

Octagonal Bolt Cabinet

Hardware store bolt cabinet, oak,
80-drawer octagonal shape, original white porcelain pulls
(ILLUS.) ....800.00 to 1,200.00
Kitchen cabinet, Turn-of-the-Century
"Hoosier" type cabinet, oak, plain
top above "flour bin" cupboard
door & short cupboard doors over
tambour slide raising to storage
compartment for spices, white
graniteware work surface above
shallow drawer over pr. cupboard doors & 3 graduated

drawers, square legs,
original finish ....250.00 to 450.00

Early 20th Century Kitchen Cupboard

Kitchen cabinet, Turn-of-the-Century,
maple, 2-part construction: upper
part w/plain top above oval mirror inset flanked by glazed cupboard doors above 4 shallow
drawers w/pull-down drawers
each end raised above open work
surface; lower section w/wide
overhang top above case w/three
drawers over pr. cupboard doors
& shallow drawer, paneled sides
(ILLUS.) 800.00
Pool cue cabinet, Victorian Renaissance Revival substyle, shaped
crest w/molded cornice centering
3 urn finials above open cabinet,
w/mirrored back, fitted w/cue
rack, molded base w/pendant
acorn drops at corners 1,200.00
Sewing cabinet, Shaker, pine & butternut, square top above 4 graduated drawers w/original pulls,
plain sides, Mount Lebanon, New
York, ca. 1870, 16" w., 24½" h.
(lacks base) 1,980.00
Side cabinet, Victorian Renaissance
Revival Substyle, ebonized wood
w/gilt-bronze & Sevres' porcelain
mounts, attributed to Alexander
Roux, New York, ca. 1860 ....3,300.00
Store display cabinet, Early 20th c.,
oak, w/glass top, sides & mirrored back, 63" h............... 330.00
Vitrine (glass-doored display) cabinet, Louis XVI style, mahogany
veneer w/ormolu mounts, early
20th c.........................2,200.00
Vitrine cabinet, Louis XV style,

decorated in the "Vernis Martin"
(japanned or oriental lacquer)
style, w/ormolu mounts, early
20th c., 67" h. 3,410.00

CANDLESTANDS

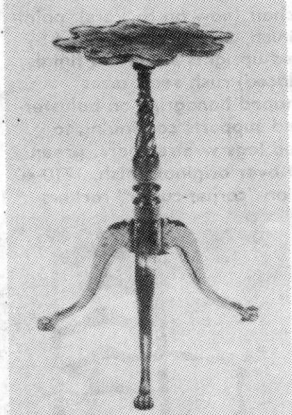

Federal Candlestand

American Empire country-style candlestand, tiger stripe maple,
round top, heavy baluster-turned
standard, (replaced) C-scroll tri-
pod, 15¾" top d., 26½" h. 220.00

Chippendale tilt-top candlestand,
mahogany, round dished top tilting & revolving on birdcage support, turned standard w/com-
pressed ball & ring turnings,
downswept cabriole tripod, shod
slipper feet, Philadelphia,
1760-90, 23½" top d., 29" h.
(repair to standard block & break
in one foot) .4,620.00

Federal tilt-top candlestand,
mahogany, oval top tilting above
urn-turned standard, arched
square tapering tripod, spade
feet, North Shore, Massachusetts,
1790-1810, 25½" oval top,
27½" h. 1,320.00

Federal tilt-top candlestand,
mahogany, oval top w/reeded
edge tilting above tapering column on reeded urn-turned standard, downswept tripod, pad
feet, Massachusetts, 1790-1810,
23" l. top, 29" h. 1,320.00

Federal tilt-top candlestand,
mahogany, cloverleaf-shaped top
tilting above urn-formed standard,
down-curving legs, ball feet, New
York, ca. 1815, 24 x 20" top,
29" h. 1,980.00

Federal tilt-top candlestand, walnut,
circular dished top tilting &

revolving above birdcage support,
urn-turned standard, cabriole
legs, shod pad feet, Pennsylvania,
ca. 1790, 20" top d., 29" h. 3,300.00

Federal candlestand, bird's eye
maple, square top, turned standard w/cup-form base, downswept tripod, snake feet, early
19th c. 1,100.00

Federal candlestand, cherrywood &
birch, round dished top w/deeply
scalloped edge, spiral- and ring-
turned standard, angular cabriole
legs, claw feet, New England,
ca. 1810, 15" top d., 27½" h.
(ILLUS.) 4,675.00

Federal candlestand, mahogany,
square top, baluster-turned standard, arched cabriole legs, slipper
feet, Massachusetts, 1790-1810,
28¾" h. 385.00

Federal candlestand, painted finish,
square top w/invected corners,
urn- and ring-turned standard,
downswept cabriole legs, snake
feet, red & black grain-painted
finish, New England, ca. 1810,
15" sq. top, 26" h. 1,320.00

Federal country-style candlestand,
cherrywood, 1-board square top,
turned standard, downswept tripod w/chip-carved feet, ca. 1835,
15½" sq. top, 27½" h. 425.00

Queen Anne Candlestand

Queen Anne tilt-top candlestand,
walnut, round dished top tilting
above turned standard w/com-
pressed ball, cabriole tripod,
snake feet, Pennsylvania, 1775,
minor old repair to standard,
21¾" d., 28" h. (ILLUS.) 6,600.00

Queen Anne tilt-top candlestand,
walnut, figured walnut round top
tilting above birdcage support,
ring-turned standard, downswept
tripod, pad feet, original finish,
ca. 1740 (top reattached) 2,250.00

Shaker candlestand, birch, round
top, turned tapering standard,
downswept tripod w/elongated
pad feet, 14" top d., 25" h.
(damage to one foot) 1,540.00

William & Mary candlestand, walnut,
round top, ring- and baluster-
turned standard, downswept
cabriole legs, pad feet, England,
early 18th c., 19" top d.,
27½" h. 1,980.00

CHAIRS

Late Victorian "Patented" Highchairs

Child's armchair, Mission-style (Arts
& Crafts movement), oak, "Morris" style w/adjustable back,
original cushions $350.00

Child's highchair, Early American
"slat-back" style, back w/two
horizontal slats between "thumb-
back" uprights, turned arms, rush
seat, splayed turned & tapering
legs w/footrest, painted green,
1st half 19th c. 660.00

Child's highchair, oak, spindle-back,
plank seat, turned legs, 20th c....   45.00

Child's highchair-stroller combination, Victorian patent-type, walnut
or oak, machine-carved details,
cane seat, each (ILLUS. of two
types).................275.00 to 425.00

Child's rocker w/arms, bentwood
w/cane seat & back, "Thonet"
(Austria) label, 1900-20 ...70.00 to 125.00

Child's rocker w/arms, Shaker No. 0
size, 3-slat back w/cushion bar,
woven tape seat, original
finish........................1,320.00

Child's rocker w/arms, Turn-of-the-
Century, golden oak, plain crestrail above flattened spindles, flattened bentwood arms, plank seat,
turned legs w/stretchers on
rockers, refinished 135.00

Child's rocker w/arms, Windsor-
style, plain crestrail above 5

bamboo-turned spindles, shaped
seat, bamboo-turned legs
w/stretchers on rockers,
refinished w/light brown stain ... 135.00

Airondack rocker w/arms,
elaborately bent twig work 245.00

American Colonial "ladder-back"
armchair (now on rockers), painted finish, 3-slat back flanked by
turned uprights w/turned finials,
(replaced) rush seat, arms
w/shaped handgrips on baluster-
turned supports continuing to
turned legs w/stretchers, green
paint over original finish, 1710-40,
now on "carpet-cutter" rockers ..1,450.00

Delaware River Valley Armchair

American Colonial "ladder-back"
armchair, maple, 5-slat back
flanked by turned uprights w/ball-
turned finials, rush seat, shaped
arms on baluster-turned supports
continuing to turned legs ending
in ball feet & joined by bulbous-
turned frontal stretcher, Delaware
River Valley, ca. 1760, w/some
foot restoration (ILLUS.) 3,575.00

American Empire "Classical" Armchair

American Empire "classical" armchair, ebonized mahogany, probably by Duncan Phyfe or Charles H.
Lannuier, New York, ca. 1815
(ILLUS.) 4,400.00
American Empire "cane-seat" side
chairs, tiger stripe maple, "angel
wing" crestrail w/roll-over top
above vase-form splat, cane seat,
sabre legs w/concave flattened
frontal stretcher, 1830-45, set
of 5 .... 880.00
American Empire "slip-seat" side
chairs, rosewood, plain crestrail
above medial stayrail, slip seat,
sabre legs, 1830-45, set
of 4 ....1,000.00
American Empire "slip-seat" side
chairs, mahogany, molded crestrail above acanthus-carved stayrail flanked by molded stiles continuing to seatrails, slip seat,
sabre legs, New York, ca. 1815,
set of 8 (some restoration &
repairs).......................2,750.00

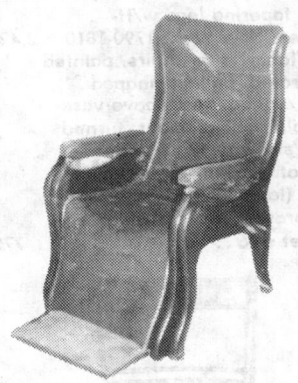

Barber's Chair

Barber's chair, walnut frame, velvet
upholstery, early 20th c. (ILLUS.).. 110.00
Barber's chair, maple frame, velvet
upholstery, "Archer Mfg. Co.,
Rochester, N.Y., 1876 Patent,"
sliding upholstered headrest, oblong back, shaped arms w/swan's
head terminals, squared cabriole
legs, gilt-metal mechanical pedal
(needs refinishing) 400.00
Barber's chair, oak frame, simple
carving, hydraulic base, "Koken,"
early 20th c..................... 500.00
Bentwood rocker w/arms, caned
oval back & rounded seat between open scrolling arms continuing to form elaborately
scrolling sides forming integral
rockers, ca. 1900 (ILLUS.) 825.00

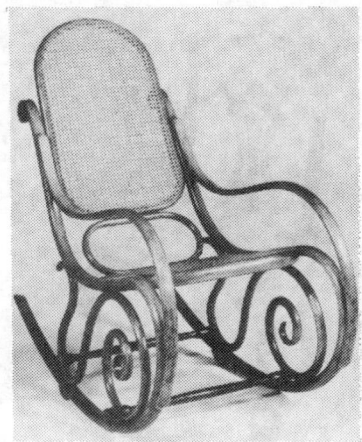

Bentwood Rocker

Bentwood side chair, wooden seat,
Thonet, Austria, late 19th - early
20th c. 30.00
Boston rocker, painted & decorated,
shaped crestrail over vase-form
splat & shaped stiles, scrolling
arms, roll-over seat, turned legs
on rockers, free-hand & stenciled
decor at crest & splat on dark
ground, ca. 1835 .... 440.00
Chippendale open armchair, walnut,
cupid's bow crestrail w/scrolling
ears above Gothic-pierced splat,
serpentine arms w/scrolled terminals, trapezoidal slip seat, plain
seatrail, square Marlborough legs
w/stretchers, Pennsylvania,
1765-85 (repair to crestrail &
pieced feet) 1,210.00
Chippendale wing armchair, mahogany, upholstered back &
shaped crest flanked by ogival
wings, seat w/loose cushion,
square molded legs w/H-
stretcher, Massachusetts, ca. 1785
(patch to rear leg) 7,150.00
Chippendale wing armchair, mahogany, arched crest flanked by
shaped wings & scrolling arms,
acanthus-carved cabriole legs,
claw-and-ball feet, New York, ca.
1770 (no upholstery) 17,050.00
Chippendale side chairs, cherrywood, plain crestrail above 4 vertical splats flanked by molded
uprights, plain seatrail, slip seat,
square legs w/molded corners
joined by H-stretcher, Long Island,
New York, 1780-1800, set
of 4 ....4,950.00
Chippendale side chairs, mahogany,
cupid's bow crestrail w/central
shell carving & scrolled ears

Chippendale Side Chair

above pierced vase-form splat,
slip seat, plain seatrail, shell-
carved cabriole legs, claw-and-
ball feet, New York, ca. 1770, set
of 3 (ILLUS. of one) 7,975.00
Chippendale side chairs, walnut,
cupid's bow crestrail w/carved
scroll & leafage border above
vertically-pierced splat, square
slip seat, molded Marlborough
legs w/H-stretcher, Philadelphia,
1760-90, pr. 1,870.00
Deck chair, folding-type, beech-
wood, slat construction, worn varnish finish, w/"Adirondack Chair
Co." label, early 20th c., overall
61" l. 655.00

Federal "Lolling" Chair

Federal (Martha Washington) "lolling" open armchair, inlaid mahogany, upholstered back
w/shaped crest, shaped arms
w/intersecting-line & bellflower

inlay, serpentine-fronted upholstered seat, line- and bellflower-
inlaid square tapering legs,
signed "J. Wells" (John Wells,
Hartford, Connecticut), ca. 1800
(ILLUS.) 26,400.00
Federal (Martha Washington) "loll-
ing" open armchair, mahogany,
upholstered back w/shaped crest
& seat, downward curving arms,
square tapering legs w/H-
stretcher, Massachusetts, 1775-95
(rear legs splice & patch to left
arm) 3,300.00
Federal wing armchair, cherrywood,
upholstered shaped back w/ser-
pentine crest flanked by ogival
wings & shaped arms, seat
w/loose cushion, square tapering
legs w/stretchers, New England,
ca. 1790 . . . . .3,850.00
Federal wing armchair, mahogany,
upholstered shaped back w/ser-
pentine crest flanked by S-shaped
wings continuing to scrolling
arms, seat w/loose cushion,
square tapering legs w/H-
stretcher, New York, 1790-1810 . .2,420.00
Federal "fancy" side chairs, painted
& decorated, balloon-shaped
back w/yoked crest above vase-
form splat, shaped seat, turned
legs w/stretchers, free-hand
florals at crest on grain-painted
ground (later enhanced w/addi-
tional brown), Pennsylvania, ca.
1810, set of 6 . . . . 770.00

Federal "Fancy" Chair

Federal "fancy" side chairs, painted
& decorated, cage-type crest centered w/scrolled tablet above 3
horizontal spindles flanked by
shaped stiles, balloon-shaped rush
seat, ring-turned splayed legs

w/ball feet joined by box stretchers, New England, early 19th c.,
set of 8 (ILLUS. of one) 3,300.00
Federal "shield-back" side chair,
mahogany, shaped crest above
shield-form back w/three leaf-
carved splats, over-upholstered
seat, square tapering legs, spade
feet, New York, 1790-1810.......1,760.00
Federal side chairs, mahogany, leaf-
carved crestrail above square
back w/pierced urn & swag-
carved splat, over-upholstered
seat, ring-turned tapering legs,
spade feet, Philadelphia, ca. 1800,
set of 4 ....6,875.00
Federal country-style "arrow-back"
rocker w/arms, painted & decorated, plain crestrail above medial
stayrail over 4 arrow-form spindles, turned arms on turned supports, plank seat, turned legs on
rockers, original red paint w/yel-
low striping & traces of original
gilt stenciling at crest 175.00
Hitchcock signed side chairs, painted & decorated, "pillow" crestrail
above pierced slat, rush seat,
turned legs w/stretchers, original
black-over-red ground w/yellow
striping & gilt-stenciled decor, set
of 4 ....1,250.00
Hitchcock-type side chair, curly
maple, roll-over crestrail above
vase-form splat, caned seat, ring-
and baluster-turned tapering legs,
button feet, stripped of paint &
refinished 220.00
Louis XV "bergeres" (armchairs
w/upholstered inward-carving
arms), beechwood, upholstered
back & sides w/serpentine beechwood toprail carved w/flower-
heads, seat w/loose cushion,
cabriole legs w/flowerhead-
carved knees, France,
ca. 1750, pr. 14,300.00
Louis XV "fauteuils" (open armchairs), beechwood, cartouche-
shaped backrest within carved
flowerhead & acanthus-scroll
frame, padded armrests on volut-
ed supports, serpentine-fronted
upholstered seat, cabriole legs
w/flowerhead-carved knees,
signed "I. Lebas," France,
mid-18th c., pr................11,550.00
Mission-style (Arts & Crafts movement) armchair, oak, plain crestrail above vertical splats, flattened arms above 5 vertical slats,
w/leather cushions, attributed to
Gustav Stickley 450.00

Gustav Stickley "Morris" Chair

Mission-style (Arts & Crafts movement) "Morris" armchair, oak, oblong back w/five horizontal slats
adjusting between flattened arms
above multi-spindled sides, loose
upholstered back & seat cushions,
No. 367, red decal mark of
Gustav Stickley, ca. 1910
(ILLUS.) 4,400.00
Mission-style (Arts & Crafts movement) rocker w/arms, oak, oblong
crestrail above beaker-form splat
flanked by straight uprights, flattened open arms, square leather
seat, square legs on rockers,
branded "Roycroft" mark,
ca. 1910 .... 935.00
Mission-style (Arts & Crafts movement) rocker w/arms, oak, V-
back crestrail above 5 vertical
splats, shaped arms, upholstered
seat, square legs w/stretchers on
rockers, red decal mark of Gustav
Stickley, ca. 1910, refinished 275.00
Mission-style (Arts & Crafts movement) rocker w/arms, oak, oblong
crestrail above 3-slat back, flattened arms, square seat, plain
seatrail, square legs on rockers,
L. & G. J. Stickley, early 20th c. .. 357.00
Mission-style (Arts & Crafts movement) rocker w/arms, oak, 4-slat
back, flattened arms on 5 vertical
upright splats, square legs on
rockers, original worn cushions,
1902-13 ....425.00 to 600.00
Mission-style (Arts & Crafts movement) side chairs, oak, oblong
crestrail above 3 horizontal slats,
slip seat, slightly tapering square
legs, w/decal label of Gustav
Stickley, 1905-10, set of 3 .... 220.00

Mission-style (Arts & Crafts movement) side chairs, oak, oblong crestrail above 8 spindles, slip seat, square legs, in the manner of Gustav Stickley, early 20th c., set of 4 .... 385.00

Queen Anne corner armchair, walnut, horseshoe-shaped backrail w/cushion-molded crest above 2 vase-form splats & 3 turned uprights, plain seatrail, cabriole front leg & 3 turned legs, pad feet, Massachusetts, 1740-60 (repair to 3 feet) 1,980.00

Queen Anne open armchair, painted maple, yoked crestrail above vase-form splat in "spooned" back, flaring arms w/scrolled grips, trapezoidal seat, block-and-baluster-turned legs w/bead-and-reel frontal stretcher, Spanish feet, New England, 1730-50 (feet pieced)........................ 935.00

Queen Anne Armchair

Queen Anne open armchair, walnut, serpentine crestrail centering a carved shell w/flared ears above shaped splat, S-curved arms ending in scrolled hand-holds, slip seat, shaped seatrail, cabriole legs, paneled trifid feet, Pennsylvania, 1740-70 (ILLUS.) 22,000.00

Queen Anne wing armchair, mahogany, shaped crestrail above upholstered back & seat flanked by ogival wings & outward scrolling arms, cabriole legs w/blocked & turned H-stretcher, pad feet, Massachusetts, 1740-60.........13,200.00

Queen Anne "balloon-seat" side chairs, walnut, yoked crestrail above vase-form splat in "spooned" back, balloon-shaped slip seat, plain seatrail, cabriole

legs w/block- and ring-turned stretchers, pad feet, Massachusetts, 1740-60, pr. 17,050.00

Queen Anne side chair, cherrywood, yoked crestrail above vase-form splat in "spooned" back, over-upholstered seat, cabriole legs w/H-stretcher, pad feet, Massachusetts, 1740-50 (some restoration) 1,650.00

Queen Anne side chairs, maple, yoked crestrail above vase-form splat flanked by baluster- and ball-turned uprights, rush seat, baluster- and ring-turned legs w/ball-turned frontal stretcher, shod pad feet, New York, 1740-60, pr. 1,320.00

Queen Anne side chair, walnut, yoked crestrail above vase-form splat in "spooned" back, shaped seatrail, cabriole legs w/block-and vase-turned stretchers, pad feet, Newport, Rhode Island, 1740-60 (some restoration).......6,600.00

Queen Anne Side Chairs

Queen Anne side chairs, walnut, shaped crest w/shaped ears above pierced vase-form splat flanked by tapering stiles in "spooned" back, trapezoidal slip seat, plain seatrail, cabriole legs w/shod pad feet, Annapolis, Maryland, 1740-60, pr. (ILLUS.)...................28,600.00

Queen Anne country-style side chair, painted maple, yoked crestrail above vase-form splat & vase-turned stiles, woven rush seat, baluster-turned legs w/bulbous frontal stretcher, shod pad feet, w/black repaint 335.00

Queen Anne country-style side chair, stained maple, yoked crestrail above vase-form splat in "spooned" back, rush seat, block-and baluster-turned legs w/turned stretchers, New England, 1740-60........................ 265.00

Salem rocker, painted & decorated, shaped roll-over crestrail above 7-spindle back, shaped arms on turned supports, shaped plank seat, splayed bamboo-turned legs on rockers, painted black-over-red grained finish w/free-hand florals at crestrail, New England, ca. 1830 ....250.00 to 385.00

Shaker rocker w/arms, No. 6 size, 4-slat back, turned uprights w/flame finials, shaped arms w/mushroom grips, woven tape seat (some damage) 715.00

Shaker side chair, No. 2 size, 3-slat back, turned uprights w/shaped finials, woven tape seat, Watervliet, New York 475.00

Shaker "tilting" side chair, 3-slat back between turned uprights w/shaped finials, woven tape seat, w/"tipping" device on rear legs, Engfield, Connecticut ....1,600.00 to 2,750.00

Turn-of-the-Century dining chairs, golden oak, pressed pattern back crestrail above "rope-twist" spindles, solid board seat, turned legs w/numerous stretchers, refinished, set of 4 .... 600.00

Turn-of-the-Century dining chairs, golden oak, pressed pattern back above flattened spindles & turned uprights, caned seat, turned legs w/numerous stretchers, refinished & recaned, ca. 1910, set of 6 ....1,200.00

Victorian parlor armchair, Eastlake substyle, walnut, machine-carved details in framework, square upholstered back & seat, padded arms, ca. 1885 .... 250.00

Victorian Renaissance Revival Armchair

Victorian parlor armchair, Renaissance Revival substyle, rosewood, shaped crestrail incorporating portrait medallion w/carved drops on ears, tufted upholstery in back & w/arms raised on caryatid supports, trumpet-shaped legs on casters, attributed to John Jelliff, Newark, New Jersey, ca. 1865 (ILLUS.) 1,990.00

Victorian parlor armchair, rococo substyle, finger-molded frame w/carved floral & grape cluster crest, tufted upholstery in back, serpentine seatrail, demi-cabriole legs, original finish & worn upholstery ....300.00 to 375.00

Victorian Rococo Armchair by Belter

Victorian parlor armchair, rococo substyle, pierce-carved laminated rosewood, frame incorporating C-scrolls & cornucopia w/grape clusters & florals, shaped open arms, demi-cabriole legs on casters, John Henry Belter, New York, New York, ca. 1865 (ILLUS.) 8,250.00

Victorian parlor armchair, "Sleepy Hollow" type, walnut, finger-molded crestrail continuing down to roll-over arms, tufted upholstery, refinished 475.00

Victorian parlor side chairs, Eastlake substyle, walnut, velvet upholstery, set of 4 .... 300.00

Victorian parlor side chairs, rococo substyle, rosewood, Hawkins patt., John & Joseph Meeks, New York, New York, pr. 4,300.00

Victorian parlor side chairs, rococo substyle, pierce-carved ebonized rosewood framework, tufted upholstery in balloon back, over-upholstered seat, turned legs, pr. 495.00

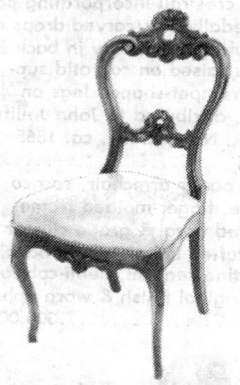

Victorian Parlor Side Chair

Victorian parlor side chairs, rococo
substyle, rosewood, rose & leaf-
carved crestrail over finger-
molded shaped stiles & scroll-
carved stayrail, over-upholstered
seat, semi-cabriole legs, late 19th
c., set of 8 (ILLUS. of one) 825.00

Victorian Patent Rocker by Hunzinger

Victorian rocker, patent-type, walnut, cloth-covered metal back &
seat, ebonized details on stiles &
scrolling arms, stamped "Hunzinger, N.Y., Pat. March 30, 1869
& April 18, 1876" (ILLUS.) 495.00
Wallace Nutting signed Windsor
"brace-back" style side chair,
bowed crestrail over 9-spindle
back, shaped saddle seat, vase-
and ring-turned splayed tapering
legs w/bobbin stretchers,
Framingham, Massachusetts, early
20th c. 450.00
Wicker armchair, woven reed,
rounded back w/roll-over crest
continuing to form arms above
upright spindles w/interlaced

swag supports, cane seat, wicker-
wrapped legs w/C-scrolls & curlicues, painted white.....175.00 to 280.00
Wicker rocker w/arms, woven reed
latticework back enhanced by C-
scrolls, upholstered horsehair
seat, woven latticework apron
joining cabriole legs, w/label
"Wakefield Rattan Co., Boston,
New York & Chicago," ca. 1900 ... 550.00
Wicker rocker w/arms, woven fan-
shaped crestrail enhanced w/C-
scrolls above canework, scrolling
arms on woven cage supports, upholstered "stuffed" round seat,
woven latticework apron joining
"cage" legs, w/label of
"Wakefield Rattan Co., Boston,
New York & Chicago," late
19th c. 825.00

20th Century Wicker Rocker

Wicker rocker w/arms, loom-woven
fibre, upholstered back & loose
cushion, painted gold, 1920's
(ILLUS.)......................... 175.00
Wicker side chair, Victorian-style
w/lacy heart motif in back &
curlicues, cane seat, wicker-
wrapped legs, late 19th c. 250.00
Wicker side chair, Victorian-style
w/lyre-form back w/numerous
curlicues, square cane seat,
wrapped legs w/curlicue brackets
& cross-stretchers, 19th c. 290.00
Windsor "birdcage" side chairs,
bamboo-turned, birdcage crest
above 7-spindle back & turned uprights, shaped seat w/incised
edge, bamboo-turned legs, old
blue repaint, pr. 600.00
Windsor "birdcage" side chairs,
bamboo-turned, birdcage crest
over 7-spindle back & turned uprights, shaped seat w/incised
edge, bamboo-turned legs

w/stretchers, set of 4 (one signed H. Ladd) 1,400.00

Windsor "bow-back" armchair, 7-spindle back, bowed crestrail above turned spindles, arms continuing from medial rail on turned supports, shaped seat, baluster- and ring-turned splayed legs w/"bobbin" stretchers, black paint 450.00

Windsor "bow-back" side chair, bowed crestrail over 7-spindle back, shaped saddle seat, splayed baluster- and ring-turned legs w/"bobbin" stretchers 375.00

Windsor "brace-back" continuous armchair, bowed crestrail w/brace above 9-spindle back continuing to shaped hand-holds, shaped seat w/projecting brace support, vase-turned splayed tapering legs w/"bobbin" stretchers, New York, ca. 1875 .... 3,300.00

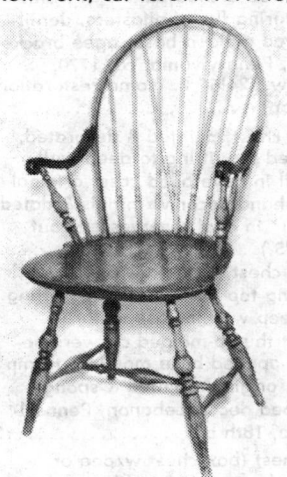

Windsor "Brace-Back" Armchair

Windsor "brace-back" armchair, bowed crestrail w/brace above 7-spindle back, shaped arms, saddle seat, vase- and ring-turned splayed tapering legs w/"bobbin" stretchers (ILLUS.) 2,800.00

Windsor "brace-back" side chair, bowed crestrail w/brace above 7-spindle back, saddle seat w/projecting brace support & incised edge, vase- and baluster-turned splayed legs 900.00

Windsor "comb-back" armchair, 5-spindle comb above bowed 7-spindle back, shaped arms on bamboo-turned uprights, shaped seat, bamboo-turned splayed legs

w/stretchers, Pennsylvania, late 18th c. 1,430.00

Windsor "comb-back" armchair, 5-spindle comb w/shaped crestrail & scrolling ears above 9-spindle back & shaped arms, saddle seat, turned legs w/stretchers, blunt arrow feet, Philadelphia, ca. 1775 .... 4,675.00

Windsor "continuous" armchair, bowed crestrail above 7-spindle back continuing to arms supported on spindles & turned uprights, shaped seat, vase- and ring-turned splayed tapering legs w/H-stretcher, now painted brown over early green, New England, ca. 1780 .... 1,045.00

Windsor "fan-back" armchair, shaped crestrail above 7-spindle back, scrolling arms on turned supports, shaped seat, baluster- and ring-turned splayed legs w/"bobbin" stretchers 1,100.00

Windsor "fan-back" armchair, shaped crestrail w/scrolling ears above 9-spindle back, shaped arms on baluster- and ring-turned supports, saddle seat w/incised edge, vase-and ring-turned splayed legs w/worn-down feet, Philadelphia, ca. 1770 .... 1,250.00

Windsor "fan-back" side chair, shaped crestrail w/scrolling ears above 7-spindle back & turned uprights, shaped saddle seat, vase- and ring-turned splayed legs w/"bobbin" stretchers 900.00

Windsor "low-back" armchair, horseshoe-shaped backrail w/cushion-molded crest & shaped hand-holds above 16 baluster-turned spindles, D-shaped leather-covered seat, turned legs w/bulb feet joined by block-and baluster-turned X-stretchers, painted black, Rhode Island, ca. 1760 .... 8,800.00

Windsor "low-back" armchair, horseshoe-shaped backrail w/cushion-molded crest above baluster-turned spindles, shaped saddle seat, baluster-turned legs w/X-stretcher, worn-down ball feet 1,000.00

Windsor "rod-back" side chair, plain crestrail above 7-spindle back, shaped saddle seat, bamboo-turned splayed legs w/shaped stretchers 400.00

Windsor "writing" armchair w/fan-back, shaped crestrail above 6-spindle back over horseshoe-

shaped rail w/projecting writing
surface at one side fitted w/draw-
er below, shaped seat also fitted
w/drawer below, ring- and vase-
turned splayed tapering legs
w/"bobbin" stretchers, New
England, ca. 1785 . . . . .3,960.00

CHESTS & CHESTS OF DRAWERS

Dower Chest

Apothecary chests, pine, oblong top
over case w/sixteen chamfered
drawers w/porcelain pulls flanked
by fluted stiles, ca. 1880,
57½" w., 11" deep, 39" h., pr. . . . 770.00
Blanket chest, walnut, 6-board construction, oblong top lifting to
deep well w/till in dovetailed
case, shaped apron, dovetailed
bracket feet, worn original red &
black paint, mid-19th c., 30¼ x
15¼", 18" h. 600.00
Blanket chest, painted & decorated
pine, oblong top w/applied molded edge lifting to deep well
w/till, applied base molding,
turned & tapering legs, ball feet,
sponge-painted sides & lid
w/borders, Pennsylvania, early
19th c., 31 x 15¼", 18½" h. 330.00
Blanket chest, poplar, oblong top
w/molded edge lifting to deep
well w/till & drawer beneath in
dovetailed case, applied base
molding, refinished w/traces of
old red remaining, 37 x 17½",
19¾" h. 300.00
Blanket chest, birch, 1-board oblong
top opening to deep well w/till in
case w/single long drawer below,
shaped skirt continuing to bracket
feet, ca. 1840, 42" w., 38" h. 675.00
Blanket chest, painted & decorated,
oblong top lifting to deep well in
dovetailed case, applied base
molding, heavy turned feet, original smoked decoration on yellow
ground, salmon pink feet, 42½ x
18", 32¾" h. 950.00

Blanket chest, painted pine, 6-board
construction, oblong top w/mold-
ed edge lifting to deep well w/till
in dovetailed case, applied base
molding, turned legs, flattened
ball feet, original brown sponge-
daubed decor on pumpkin ground,
early 19th c., 48¾ x 22",
24¾" h. 800.00
Blanket chest, Chippendale, painted
pine & poplar, oblong top
w/molded edge on original
wrought iron rat-tail hinges lifting
to deep well in case w/three
arched panels at front, each
w/traces of original colorful floral
decor, molded base, turned feet
(of later date), Pennsylvania,
1750-1800, 50½ x 23", 23¾" h. . . .1,650.00
Blanket chest, Chippendale, walnut,
oblong top w/molded edge lifting
to deep well w/till in case
w/three arched panels at front
centering fluted pilasters, dentil-
carved molded base, ogee bracket
feet, Pennsylvania, ca. 1770,
52" w., 24½" h. (some restoration
to top) 1,100.00
Dower chest, painted & decorated,
domed top lifting to deep well
w/till in dovetailed case, original
free-hand decor w/initials & dated
"1831" in oval reserves at front
(ILLUS.) 895.00
Dower chest, painted & decorated,
oblong top w/molded edge lifting
to deep well in case w/three
short thumb-molded drawers below, applied base molding, turnip
feet, original painted & sponge-
daubed decor, Lebanon, Pennsyl-
vania, 18th c. 2,875.00
Mule chest (box chest w/one or
more drawers below lift-top storage compartment---forerunner of
chest of drawers), 6-board construction, painted & decorated
pine, oblong top w/molded edge
lifting to deep well above single
long drawer, sides continuing to
form cut-out feet, painted grey-
white w/"smoked" decoration,
New England, ca. 1815, 37" w.,
29" h. 880.00
Mule chest, painted & decorated
pine, oblong top lifting to deep
well above arrangement of two
short drawers over long drawer,
sides continuing to form bootjack
feet, painted yellow w/spiral
sponge-daubed & dotted decor in
red, green & ochre, New England,
ca. 1810, 38" w., 39" h. (ILLUS.) . .8,250.00

Mule Chest

Mule chest, painted & decorated pine, oblong top w/molded edge lifting to deep well above 2 long cockbeaded drawers w/turned wood pulls, scalloped apron continuing to form cut-out feet w/one-board ends, original brushed dark brown flame graining over natural pine (now varnished over), 43" w., 39½" h. 825.00

Sugar Chest

Sugar chest, Federal, mahogany, oblong top w/rounded corners lifting to deep well in case w/one false & 1 cockbeaded working drawer flanked by reeded pilasters, paneled sides, baluster- and ring-turned legs, ball feet, Kentucky, 1810-20, 30½ x 24", 31" h. (ILLUS.) 3,520.00

American Empire "bow-front" chest of drawers, mahogany, oblong top w/outset rounded corners set w/three recessed short drawers & scrolling backsplash above case w/four bow-fronted drawers flanked by ring- and rope-carved columns continuing to baluster-turned legs, original brass drop ring handles, old finish w/minor veneer damage, 41" w., overall 51 7/8" h. 1,250.00

American Empire Chest of Drawers

American Empire chest of drawers, birch w/flame grain mahogany veneer facade, oblong top set w/pr. short recessed drawers & curly birch backsplash above case w/pr. short drawers over 3 slightly recessed cockbeaded long drawers flanked by bold ring-turned & rope-carved columns continuing to bold double ball feet, refinished & w/original brass rosette handles, 43¾" w., overall 56¾" h. (ILLUS.) 625.00

American Empire chest of drawers, cherrywood, oblong top above case w/two long drawers over pr. slightly recessed long drawers flanked by half-round spiral-turned columns, ring- and ball-turned feet, ca. 1835, 43" w., 40" h. 825.00

American Empire chest of drawers, cherrywood, oblong top above case w/ogee-molded deep upper drawer over 3 long graduated drawers w/original Rockingham-glazed "Bennington-type" pulls, ring-turned legs 795.00

American Empire chest of drawers, cherrywood & curly maple, oblong top above 3 short drawers & deep drawer over 3 slightly recessed & graduated long drawers flanked

by free-standing turned columns
continuing to square tapering
feet, signed by maker on back-
boards, ca. 1840 . . . . 675.00
American Empire chest of drawers,
tiger stripe maple & cherrywood,
oblong cherrywood top w/tiger
maple raking backsplash w/pillar
ends above case w/pr. shallow
short drawers over deep long
drawer above 3 slightly recessed
graduated long drawers flanked
by pineapple & acanthus-carved
pilasters, vigorously carved
animal paw feet, signed "Made by
D. Ferguson, No. 2, Feb. 1830,
Nichols," 47½" w., 58" h. (gilt
brass drop handles are late
19th c. replacements) 900.00
Chippendale "bonnet-top" chest-on-
chest, tiger stripe maple, 2-part
construction: upper part w/swan's
neck cresting centering 3 spirally-
turned finials over central fan-
carved short drawer flanked by
shaped drawers above 4 long
graduated thumb-molded drawers;
lower section w/four graduated
thumb-molded long drawers,
molded base centering fan-carved
pendant, short cabriole legs,
claw-and-ball feet, New England,
ca. 1870, 42" w., 91" h. 46,200.00
Chippendale "bonnet-top" chest-on-
chest, walnut, 2-part construction:
upper part w/bonnet top centered
by 3 flame finials above 3 frieze
drawers w/fan-inlaid central
drawer over 4 graduated long
drawers flanked by fluted
pilasters w/cushion-molded capitals; lower section w/four graduated long drawers, molded base,
ogee bracket feet, Massachusetts,
1780-1800, 42½" w., 81¼" h. . . . 30,800.00
Chippendale tall chest of drawers,
cherrywood, oblong top w/applied
molding below, case w/arrange-
ment of 2 short drawers over 6
long thumb-molded drawers, cut-
out bracket feet, Connecticut, ca.
1790, 38" w., 62" h. (restorations
to top moldings & feet) 2,420.00
Chippendale tall chest of drawers,
tiger stripe maple, oblong top
w/applied molding below, case
w/five graduated thumb-molded
long drawers, bracket feet, New
England, 1770-90, 39" w.,
47" h. 3,300.00
Chippendale tall chest of drawers,
tiger stripe maple, oblong top
w/applied molding below, case
w/arrangement of 2 short draw-

ers over 5 long thumb-molded
drawers, shaped bracket feet,
New England, ca. 1790, 39" w.,
61" h. 4,400.00

Chippendale Tall Chest

Chippendale tall chest of drawers,
walnut, oblong top w/applied
molding below, case w/three
short & 5 long graduated
drawers flanked by fluted quarter
columns, molded base, ogee
bracket feet, minor age cracks &
replaced brass drop handles,
45 5/8" w., 68 5/8" h. (ILLUS.) . . . 4,000.00
Chippendale "block-front" chest of
drawers, mahogany, oblong top
w/blocked front & molded edge
above case of conforming outline
w/four graduated long drawers
within cockbeaded surrounds,
molded base, claw-and-ball feet,
Massachusetts, ca. 1760, 37½" w.,
31" h. (feet restored) 17,600.00

Chippendale "Reverse Serpentine" Chest

Chippendale "reverse-serpentine"
chest of drawers, mahogany, oblong top w/reverse serpentine
front & molded edge above case

of conforming outline w/four graduated long drawers within cockbeaded surrounds, ogee bracket feet, Massachusetts, ca. 1780, 39½" w., 31½" h. (ILLUS.) 11,000.00

Chippendale chest of drawers, cherrywood, oblong top w/molded edge above 2 short & 3 long graduated drawers flanked by fluted quarter columns, gadroon skirt continuing to ogee bracket feet, Connecticut, 1790-1810, 43" w., 37½" h. 5,225.00

Chippendale chest of drawers, mahogany, oblong top w/molded edge above case w/four long thumb-molded graduated drawers flanked by fluted quarter columns, ogee bracket feet, Pennsylvania, ca. 1780, 37" w., 34" h. (some restoration to one foot) 8,525.00

Chippendale chest of drawers, tiger stripe maple, oblong top w/molded edge above 4 long graduated drawers within cockbeaded surrounds, shaped bracket feet, New England, ca. 1790, 42" w., 36" h. 2,970.00

Chippendale chest of drawers, tiger stripe maple, oblong top w/molded edge above pr. short drawers over 3 long graduated thumb-molded drawers, shaped apron w/drop pendant, cut-out bracket feet, New England, ca. 1785, 39" w., 39¾" h. (some restoration to underside of top) 6,875.00

Chippendale country-style chest of drawers, cherrywood, oblong top above case w/four graduated & cockbeaded long drawers, bracket base w/cut-out feet, refinished & replaced brass drop handles, 36" w., 33½" h. 1,600.00

Chippendale country-style chest of drawers, maple, oblong top above case w/four thumb-molded drawers, 1-board sides, cut-out bracket base, refinished w/traces of old red showing through, 37½" w., 40½" h. 1,750.00

Federal tall chest of drawers, Hepplewhite style, inlaid cherrywood, projecting molded cornice above case w/three small drawers over 4 graduated long line-inlaid drawers flanked by cross-banded inlaid stiles, flaring French feet, refinished & w/replaced brass oval drop ring handles, early 19th c., 42" w., 52½" h.........2,600.00

Federal "bow-front" chest of drawers, mahogany, oblong top w/bowed front & outset rounded corners set w/two recessed short drawers & backsplash above case w/four bow-fronted drawers w/flame mahogany veneer flanked by baluster- and rope-turned columns continuing to vase- and ring-turned legs, ball feet, 37½" w., 39" h............. 950.00

Federal "bow-front" chest of drawers, inlaid mahogany, oblong top w/bowed front above case of conforming outline w/four cockbeaded drawers faced w/flame-birch & cross-banded border & & center panels, inlaid shaped skirt, tall bracket feet, Portsmouth, New Hampshire, ca. 1810, 40½" w., 38½" h. 19,800.00

Federal "bow-front" chest of drawers, mahogany oblong top w/outset rounded corners set w/two recessed "bow-fronted" short drawers & shaped scrolling backsplash above case w/four graduated & cockbeaded long bow-fronted drawers flanked by baluster-turned & rope-twist columns, shaped apron, ring- and vase-turned legs, ball feet, Massachusetts, 1810-15, 40½" w., 49" h. 715.00

Federal "bow-front" chest of drawers, tiger stripe maple, oblong top w/bowed front & cross-banded edge over case of conforming outline w/four cockbeaded & graduated long drawers, shaped apron, flaring bracket feet, New England, ca. 1800, 42½" w., 39" h. 1,980.00

Serpentine-Front Chest of Drawers

Federal "serpentine-front" chest of drawers, inlaid walnut, oblong top w/serpentine front & line-inlaid edge above case of conforming outline w/four line-inlaid graduated long drawers flanked by canted line-inlaid corners, shaped skirt continuing to splayed bracket feet, Maryland or Virginia, ca. 1800, 38" w., 36" h. (ILLUS.) 25,300.00

Federal chest of drawers, bird's eye maple, oblong top w/outset rounded corners & cross-banded edge above case w/four cross-banded & veneered long drawers flanked by reeded outset rounded columns, shaped skirt, turned legs, Massachusetts, 1800-10, 40½" w., 35" h. 1,320.00

Federal chest of drawers, cherrywood, oblong top above case w/four graduated long drawers w/original brass oval drop ring handles, baluster-turned legs, tapering feet 1,175.00

Federal chest of drawers, cherrywood, oblong top w/outset rounded corners above case w/four graduated cockbeaded long drawers flanked by fluted quarter columns, molded base, cut-out bracket feet. 2,200.00

Federal chest of drawers, maple, oblong top above case w/four cockbeaded & graduated long drawers, shaped skirt, ring-turned legs, ball feet, New England, 1800-20, 44" h. 880.00

Federal chest of drawers, maple & curly maple veneer, oblong top above 4 cockbeaded & reverse graduated long drawers faced w/curly maple, original brass oval drop ring handles, shaped skirt, bracket feet, New England, ca. 1800, 39" w., 37" h. 3,080.00

Hepplewhite Federal Chest of Drawers

Federal chest of drawers, tiger stripe maple, 1-board top above case w/four drawers within cockbeaded surrounds, scalloped apron & 1-board ends continue to form bracket feet, original oval

brass drop ring handles, early refinishing, 40½" w., 40" h. (ILLUS.) 4,250.00

Federal chest of drawers, painted & decorated, oblong top above case w/four long drawers, shaped skirt continuing to bracket feet, shaded brown painted graining w/simulated line-inlay on top & drawer fronts, New England, ca. 1810, 39" w., 40" h. 2,420.00

Federal country-style chest of drawers, birch, oblong top above case w/four graduated thumb-molded drawers w/turned wood pulls, scalloped apron continuing to cut-out bracket feet, 41½" w., 42" h. 950.00

Federal country-style chest of drawers, cherrywood, oblong top above case w/four graduated & cockbeaded long drawers w/original oval brass drop ring handles, scalloped apron continuing to form cut-out bracket feet w/one-board sides, refinished, 45" w., 37" h. 900.00

Federal country-style chest of drawers, curly maple, oblong top above case w/four graduated long drawers w/turned wood pulls, paneled ends, ring-turned legs, ball feet 1,450.00

Federal country-style chest of drawers, maple & walnut veneer, oblong top above case w/four drawers faced w/walnut veneer & w/embossed brass drawer knobs flanked by applied spool-turned columns, reeded legs, ca. 1840, 43" w., 39" h. (restored) 400.00

Federal country-style chest of drawers, painted finish, oblong top w/scrolling backboard above case w/four drawers w/turned wood pulls, ring- and baluster-turned legs, turnip feet, painted red & black graining 895.00

Federal country-style chest of drawers, tiger stripe maple, oblong top above case w/pr. short drawers over 3 long graduated drawers w/original pressed clear flint glass pulls, paneled ends, scalloped apron, ring- and baluster-turned feet .1,700.00

Mission-style (Art & Crafts movement) tall chest of drawers, quarter-sawn oak, oblong top w/plain backboard above case w/two short drawers over 4 long drawers w/original pulls, square legs, attributed to Gustav Stickley 3,300.00

Mission-style (Arts & Crafts movement) chest of drawers, quarter-sawn oak, oblong top w/low back-rail above case w/two short drawers over 3 long drawers, original copper drop handles, square legs, red decal mark of Gustav Stickley, Style No. 901, ca. 1907, 37" w., 42" h. 1,540.00

Gustav Stickley Dresser

Mission-style (Arts & Crafts movement) chest of drawers w/mirror, quarter-sawn oak, oblong top supporting rectangular mirror plate between tapering square uprights above case w/two short drawers over 2 long drawers, arched apron, square legs, red decal mark of Gustav Stickley, Style No. 911, ca. 1906, 48" w., 66" h. (ILLUS.) 1,430.00

Queen Anne "bonnet-top" chest-on-chest, cherrywood, 3-part construction: upper part w/molded swan's neck cresting ending in carved rosettes & centering 3 brass finials above dentil-carved molding over 5 short thumb-molded drawers w/concave fan & punchwork details on central drawer above 4 graduated long thumb-molded drawers flanked by fluted quarter columns; middle section w/three graduated long thumb-molded drawers flanked by conforming quarter columns; base w/shaped skirt, short cabriole legs, pad feet, Connecticut, ca. 1780, 40" w., 88" h. 27,500.00

Queen Anne chest on frame, painted maple, 2-part construction: flat-top chest w/projecting molded cornice above pr. short drawers over 4 graduated long drawers

w/original brass bat's wing handles; frame w/scalloped apron, vase-turned legs, button feet ...10,500.00

Queen Anne Chest-on-Frame

Queen Anne chest-on-frame, walnut, 2-part construction: flat-top chest w/projecting molded cornice above pr. short drawers over 4 graduated long drawers; frame w/scalloped skirt, short cabriole legs, trifid feet, Pennsylvania, 1750-80, minor repairs, 41" w., 69" h. (ILLUS.) 6,600.00

Queen Anne chest-on-frame, walnut, 2-part construction: flat-top chest w/projecting molded cornice w/arrangement of 5 short drawers over 4 long graduated drawers; lower section w/applied molding at top & single long thumb-molded drawer, scalloped apron, cabriole legs, trifid feet, Pennsylvania, 1750-70, 40½" w., 80½" h. 10,450.00

Queen Anne "Block-Front" Chest

Queen Anne "block-front" chest of
drawers, mahogany, oblong top
w/blocked front & molded edge
above case of conforming outline
w/four graduated drawers within
cockbeaded surrounds, skirt
w/shaped pendant continuing to
bracket feet, original brass bat's
wing handles & keyhole escutcheons, Eastern Massachusetts,
ca. 1760, 32½" w., 29¾" h.
(ILLUS.) 45,100.00

Shaker chest of drawers, pine,
square top over 4 thumb-molded
drawers, canted base, Mt. Lebanon, New York, ca. 1830, w/frag-
ment of label on back "No. 9,
2nd House Wagon & Co., Shaker's
Chairs, Columbia County, N.Y.,"
16" w., 15" deep, 34" h. 3,025.00

Shaker chest of drawers, painted
pine, oblong top over case w/five
graduated long drawers w/turned
wood pulls, sides w/vertical moldings at back edge, overall brilliant blue paint, Watervliet, New
York, ca. 1860, 44" w., 49" h. 9,900.00

Shaker chest of drawers, painted
pine, oblong top above case
w/four long drawers w/original
mushroom-turned pulls, cut-out
bracket feet, salmon pink
paint 3,300.00

Turn-of-the-Century "chiffonier"
chest of drawers, golden oak,
w/mirror 325.00

Turn-of-the-Century chest of drawers, golden oak, 5 drawers
w/original brass drop handles,
original darkened finish 300.00

Turn-of-the-Century dresser w/mir-
ror, golden oak, large mirror
plate, w/applied foliate carvings
at crest, swiveling in lyre-form
support above serpentine-fronted
chest w/four drawers, large size,
refinished 1,100.00

Oak Dresser

Turn-of-the-Century dresser w/mir-
ror, golden oak, oval mirror
swiveling in lyre-form support
above serpentine-fronted oblong
top w/small serpentine-fronted
chest recessed to one side over
arrangement of conformingly-
shaped short drawers above long
deep drawer, square legs, ca.
1900 (ILLUS.) 295.00

Victorian Tall Chest of Drawers

Victorian tall chest of drawers, Eastlake substyle, walnut & burl walnut, oblong top w/three quarter
gallery above case w/pr. short
drawers over 5 long drawers,
typical machine-carved incised
lines (ILLUS.) 1,095.00

Princess Dresser

Turn-of-the-Century "Princess" dresser w/large mirror, golden oak,
serpentine-fronted chest w/two
drawers over long drawer, origi-
nal brasses, refinished (ILLUS.) . . . 595.00

Victorian chest of drawers, cottage-style, painted pine, oblong top w/molded edge above 3 long drawers w/pressed wood fruit & foliate pulls & applied moldings, refinished in natural, medium size 400.00

Victorian chest of drawers, Renaissance Revival substyle, walnut w/burl walnut panels, oblong top w/molded edge above case w/six graduated long drawers w/original wood & brass pear-shaped pulls 610.00

COMMODES

Louis XV Commode

French Empire commode, mahogany w/ormolu mounts & dark grey marble top, oblong marble slab top above plain frieze drawer over 3 long drawers fitted w/ormolu wreath-form pulls & flanked by ebonized pilasters w/ormolu capitals & bases, bun feet, France, early 19th c., 50" w., 35" h. 2,200.00

Louis XV commode, kingwood parquetry w/ormolu mounts & rouge marble top, shaped marble slab top above case w/two short & single long drawers w/ormolu handles & keyhole escutcheons, cabriole legs headed by ormolu foliate "chutes" continuing down to ormolu "sabots," signed "A. Criaerd," France, ca. 1730, 46½" w., 33¾" h. 50,600.00

Louis XV commode, fruitwood marquetry w/"breche de'alep" marble top, bombe form, serpentine marble slab top above case w/two long drawers inlaid "sans traverse" w/entertwined floral sprays in various stained fruitwoods within amaranth borders outlined w/pierced foliate ormolu scroll & berried vine borders, slightly flaring tapering legs headed by elaborate ormolu pierced foliate "chutes" ending in ormolu

foliate "sabots," attributed to D. Genty, France, late 18th c., restored, 57" w., 33¼" h. (ILLUS.) 33,000.00

Louis XV Provincial commode, fruitwood w/ormolu mounts, oblong top w/serpentine front & finger-molded edge above case w/three short drawers over 2 long drawers, all fitted w/cartouche-shaped keyhole escutcheons & female mask & foliate scroll handles, France, mid-18th c., 50" w., 35½" h. 3,575.00

Louis XV Provincial commode, walnut, oblong top w/serpentine front & finger-molded edge above case w/three drawers of conforming outline fitted w/applied carvings & ormolu keyhole escutcheons & handles, slightly splayed sides, scalloped skirt centering carved shell, short cabriole legs, scrolled toes, France, mid-18th c., 56" w., 33" h. 6,600.00

Louis XV-XVI transitional commode, kingwood & tulipwood parquetry w/ormolu mounts & marble mottled grey top, shaped oblong marble slab top above case of breakfront outline w/three short & 2 long drawers, each quarter-veneered within crossbanding, w/ormolu wreath & bow keyhole escutcheons & handles & w/ormolu paw "sabots" on short cabriole legs, France, third quarter 18th c., 50" w., 34" h. (rear legs spliced) 4,125.00

Louis XVI Provincial commode, fruitwood w/ormolu mounts, oblong top w/molded edge above 3 long graduated drawers w/ormolu round drop-ring handles & pierced ribbon-tied keyhole escutcheons, circular tapering legs, France, late 18th c., 42½" w., 35" h.........2,970.00

Victorian Commode

Victorian commode, Renaissance
Revival substyle, walnut w/white
marble slab top, oblong marble
slab top w/rounded corners above
single drawer w/applied molding
& fruit-carved pull over pr. cupboard doors w/appalied carvings
& central stylized roundels, plinth
base, on casters (ILLUS.) 575.00

Victorian commode, rococo substyle,
walnut w/white marble slab top,
oblong marble top w/canted corners above single drawer over
single cupboard door w/applied
fruit-carved pulls, canted corners
w/applied scrolling foliate carvings, molded base, ca. 1865,
18½" w., 30" h.................. 440.00

Victorian commode, rococo substyle,
walnut w/white marble slab top,
oblong marble top above single
drawer w/carved grape cluster
pull above pr. cupboard doors,
33" w., 30" h. (needs
refinishing) 275.00

Victorian lift-top commode, cottage-
style, grain-painted finish, hinged
top lifting to storage well above
paneled cupboard door, applied
base molding, flattened ball
feet........................... 450.00

CRADLES

Field Cradle

Country-style low cradle on rockers,
cherrywood, arched head & footboards pierced w/hand-holds,
shaped sides, refinished &
w/replaced rockers, 37½" l. 275.00

Country-style low cradle on rockers,
maple, dovetail construction,
shaped head & footboards, scrolling sides, scalloped rockers, late
18th - early 19th c., 38" l........ 220.00

Country-style low cradle on rockers,
painted maple, arched head &
footboards, canted sides, old red
paint.......................... 105.00

Country-style low cradle on rockers,
painted pine, arched head & footboards, shaped sides, red paint,
late 18th c., 35" l.............. 330.00

Country-style low cradle on rockers,
pine, canted sides joined to
turned posts w/shaped finials,
19th c., 36" l., 27" h. posts....... 155.00

Country-style low cradle on rockers,
redwood, dovetail construction,
canted sides, 1850's, 37½" l 185.00

Country-style low cradle on rockers,
walnut, dovetail construction,
arched head & footboards, shaped
sides pierced w/hand-holds,
traces of old red stain, 37" l...... 175.00

Country-style low cradle on rockers,
walnut, dovetail construction,
scroll-cut headboard pierced
w/heart design, shaped sides
pierced w/hand-holds & applied
w/brass pegs to lace, worn finish,
43½" l. 255.00

Field (or slave) cradle, suspended-
type, bentwood slats in frame
w/sleigh-like runners & cast iron
wheels, Ford-Johnson Co.,
Chicago 450.00

Field (or slave) cradle, suspended-
type, bentwood slats in frame
w/sleigh-like runners, no wheels,
47" l. (ILLUS.) 300.00

Hooded cradle on rockers, Irish oak,
shaped hood, paneled sides
joined to corner posts w/turned
finials at footrail, on "carpet-
cutter" rockers, Dublin, Ireland,
18th c........................1,500.00

Hooded cradle on rockers, painted
pine, shaped hood, canted sides,
old worn red finish, late 18th c. .. 475.00

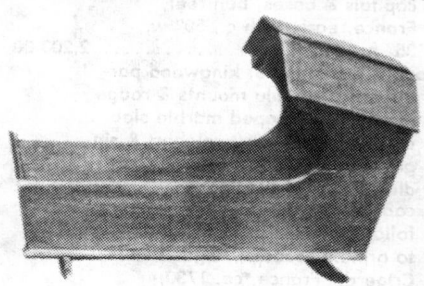

Hooded Cradle

Hooded cradle on rockers, painted
pine & birch, pine hood top, birch
sides, dovetail construction at one
end, old red finish, 29" l.,
26½" h. (ILLUS.) 285.00

Hooded cradle on rockers, wicker,
loom-woven fibre, original red
stain, early 20th c. 475.00

Hooded cradle on rockers, wicker,
woven willow basket w/hood on
rockers, old green paint 250.00

Platform-type cradle, wicker, lattice-

woven sides, trestle platform
w/extension pole one end curling
over to form mosquito netting
hook 595.00
Spindle-sided cradle on rockers,
painted finish, shaped head &
footrails & plain siderails above
arrow-form spindles, turned corner posts w/ball finials, bamboo-
turned legs joined by flat stretchers on rockers, original paint
w/yellow striping 685.00
Suspended-type cradle, Victorian,
Renaissance Revival substyle, mahogany, sides w/shaped panels
centering inlaid star, corner posts
w/acorn finials, trestle base,
original "alligatored" finish,
45" l. 198.00

CUPBOARDS

Hanging Cupboard

Chimney cupboard, primitive pine,
molded cornice above 1-board
door opening to single shelf
w/broom space below, molded
base, original dark brown finish
w/yellow striping, 15¼" w.,
10¾" deep, 68" h. (minor repair
at hinge) 575.00
Chimney cupboard, Shaker, painted
pine, molded cornice over 2 (door-
over-door) raised panel cupboard
doors opening to shelves, cut-out
bracket feet, original red-washed
stain, New Lebanon, New York,
ca. 1800, 35" w., 19½" deep,
72" h. 3,520.00
Corner cupboard, American Empire
country-style, painted & decorated, 2-part construction: upper part
w/molded cornice above 12-pane
glazed cupboard door flanked by
applied half-round baluster- and
ring-turned columns; lower section w/short drawer over double-
paneled cupboard door flanked by
conforming applied half-round
columns, bulbous-turned feet,
remnants of original mustard yel-
low paint, 1820-40 . . . . .3,200.00
Corner cupboard, American Empire
country-stye, cherrywood, 1-piece
construction, flat top above plain
frieze, applied ring- and baluster-
turned half-round moldings above
pr. 8-pane glazed cupboard doors
over short central drawer & pr.
raised panel cupboard doors
flanked by conforming applied
moldings, scalloped apron continuing to cut-out bracket feet,
mid-19th c. .4,500.00
Corner cupboard, Chippendale,
cherrywood, 1-piece construction,
swan's neck crest centering urn-
shaped finial above arched,
glazed & mullioned cupboard door
opening to 3 shaped shelves
w/pr. paneled cupboard doors
below, molded base, ogee bracket
feet, Pennsylvania, ca. 1790,
43" w., 90" h. (repaired) 5,500.00
Corner cupboard, Chippendale-style,
pine, 2-part construction: upper
part w/molded, canted cornice
above pr. 8-pane glazed cupboard
doors opening to shelves; lower
part w/four short drawers over
pr. paneled cupboard doors,
bracket feet, early 19th c. 1,650.00
Corner cupboard, Federal, cherry-
wood, 1-piece construction, molded cornice above pr. 6-pane
glazed doors opening to shelves
above short central drawer over
pr. paneled cupboard doors,
bracket feet, small size (needs
refinishing) 1,000.00
Corner cupboard, Federal, cherry-
wood & poplar, 1-piece construction, molded coved cornice
above single 12-pane glazed cupboard door w/medial molding
above cupboard doors below,
scalloped apron continuing to
cut-out bracket feet, 1790-1810,
38¼" w., 85" h. 2,090.00
Corner cupboard, Federal country-
style, walnut, 1-piece construction, deeply molded cornice above
frieze w/incised sunburst carvings
& pr. 8-pane glazed cupboard
doors above medial molding & pr.
paneled cupboard doors, bracket
feet 1,850.00

Corner cupboard, butternut, 2-part construction: upper part w/shaped cornice above barrel-fronted paneled cupboard door; lower section w/vertical-paneled barrel-fronted cupboard door above conforming base, Norwegian-influenced Minnesota piece, small size 2,495.00

Hanging cupboard, pine, single door w/breadboard ends within cockbeaded surrounds, ca. 1830, refinished, 16" w., 6" deep, 24" h. (ILLUS.)......................... 365.00

Hanging cupboard, butternut, molded cornice above paneled cupboard door over single dovetailed drawer flanked by chamfered corners, molded base, old dark red-brown painted finish, original lock & key, 24¼" w., 27½" h. (one strip of side molding replaced) 625.00

Hanging cupboard, pine, flat projecting cornice over single cupboard door opening to shelves flanked by canted corners, England, 19th c., 20" w., 31" h. 330.00

Hanging cupboard, painted pine, flat top over single double-paneled cupboard door within cockbeaded surrounds & w/applied perimeter (picture frame) moldings, old red finish w/edge wear, 27" w., 8½" deep, 39¾" h. (lock removed) 275.00

Hanging Cupboard with Flame Graining

Hanging corner cupboard, painted pine, molded cornice above raised panel cupboard door over thumb-molded drawer, original worn red-painted flame graining finish, 29" w., 42½" h. (ILLUS.) 400.00

Jelly cupboard, cherrywood, 1-board oblong top above case w/single

4-panel overlapping cupboard door opening to shelves, chamfered corners, peg construction throughout, original red-stained finish 1,850.00

Jelly cupboard, American Empire country-style, curly walnut, oblong top w/molded edge above single paneled cupboard door opening to shelves, molded base, turned short legs, flattened ball feet, ca. 1840, 36½" w., 41" h. 1,200.00

Jelly cupboard, painted pine, oblong top above long drawer & pr. short drawers over pr. recessed cupboard doors, valanced skirt, square feet, old blue-painted finish, New England, early 19th c., 44" w., 58½" h. 465.00

Jelly cupboard, painted walnut, oblong top w/three-quarter shaped gallery above pr. ogee-molded short drawers over pr. paneled cupboard doors, turned feet, original red-painted finish 765.00

Walnut Jelly Cupboard

Jelly cupboard, walnut, oblong top above long drawer w/turned mushroom pulls over pr. paneled cupboard doors, square legs, 19th c., refinished (ILLUS.) 650.00

Linen press, Chippendale, 2-part construction: upper part w/molded cornice above pr. double-arch paneled cupboard doors flanked by applied fluted pilasters; lower section w/band of mid-molding over 3 thumb-molded drawers, molded base, shaped bracket feet, Pennsylvania, 1760-90, 51" w., 79" h. (cornice & 1 pilaster restored) 4,180.00

Linen press, mahogany, 2-part construction: upper part w/coved cornice above pr. paneled cupboard doors opening to drawers; lower section w/two short drawers over

2 long drawers, original brass drop-ring handles, bracket feet, England, 50" w., 77" h. 3,150.00

Linen press, inlaid mahogany, 2-part construction: upper part w/molded cornice above pr. line-inlaid paneled cupboard doors opening to sliding shelves; lower section w/oblong top w/molded edge over pr. short line-inlaid drawers & pr. long cockbeaded drawers, shaped bracket feet, Pennsylvania, 1790-1810, 50" w., 84" h. 3,300.00

Pewter cupboard, primitive pine, 1-piece construction w/open shelves & replaced plate rails above board-and-batten cupboard doors in base, 1-board sides, cut-out bracket feet, old grey repaint worn to expose early red below, 45" w., 71½" h. (ILLUS.) 700.00

Primitive Pine Pewter Cupboard

Pewter cupboard, pine, 2-piece construction: upper part w/plain cornice molding above open shelves w/plate rails; lower section w/oblong top above 3 short drawers over pr. paneled cupboard doors, molded base, restored & refinished w/pleasant brown stain, 54¼" w., 86" h. 2,000.00

Pie safe, poplar, oblong top above long drawer over pr. cupboard doors w/three punched tin panels in each & w/conforming panels in sides. 375.00 to 500.00

Pie safe, walnut, oblong top above pr. short drawers w/turned wood pulls over pr. cupboard doors w/diamond & compass punched

tin panels & w/conforming panels in sides, bracket feet, refinished, 42½" w., 56" h. 900.00

Spice cupboard, hanging-type, oak, coved cornice above raised panel cupboard door opening to arrangement of open compartments flanked by pr. short drawers over 3 short drawers all above single long drawer, w/ring pulls on all drawers, molded base, 19th c., 16" w., 7" deep, 16" h. 975.00

Step-back wall cupboard, American Empire country-style, poplar, 2-part construction: upper part w/flaring cove-molded cornice above pr. double-arch 6-pane glazed cupboard doors & stationary 3-pane arch-top center panel over 5 short drawers & open pie shelf; lower section w/oblong top above short convex central drawer flanked by slightly longer drawers above pr. slightly recessed paneled cupboard doors w/applied half-round columns in center panel & at stiles, turned feet, old dark refinishing, Pennsylvania, 59½" w., 86" h. (replaced bottom board). 2,250.00

Step-back wall cupboard, Chippendale, cherrywood, 2-part construction: upper part w/ogee-molded cornice above 3-pane central glazed panel flanked by 6-pane cupboard doors on rat-tail hinges & chamfered stiles over short thumb-molded drawers & open pie shelf below; lower section w/oblong top over 3 short drawers & pr. double-paneled cupboard doors, molded base, bracket feet, Pennsylvania, 1770-90, 61" w., 83" h. 9,350.00

Step-back wall cupboard, Federal country-style, butternut, 1-piece, coved cornice above pr. paneled cupboard doors & open pie shelf over pr. short drawers above paneled cupboard doors, scalloped apron, cut-out bracket feet, ca. 1835, 49½" w., 79" h. 2,250.00

Step-back wall cupboard, Federal country-style, pine, 2-part construction: upper part w/deeply molded cornice above pr. 6-pane glazed cupboard doors opening to shelves above open pie shelf; lower section w/pr. cockbeaded short drawers above pr. paneled cupboard doors, applied molding at base, cut-out bracket feet, ca. 1840, 45" w., 83" h. 2,420.00

Step-back wall cupboard, Federal country-style, cherrywood, 2-part construction: upper part w/coved cornice above pr. 8-pane glazed cupboard doors opening to shelves & open pie shelf below; lower section w/oblong top above 3 short drawers over pr. paneled cupboard doors, applied molding at base, turned feet, original old red-stained finish 3,750.00

Step-back wall cupboard, Turn-of-the-Century, oak, 2-part construction: upper part w/shaped cornice applied w/machine-carved scrolling foliage above pr. glazed cupboard doors; lower section w/oblong top above pr. short drawers over pr. paneled cupboard doors, square legs on casters 525.00

Step-back wall cupboard, Victorian country-style, grain-painted finish, 2-part construction: upper part w/coved cornice above pr. paneled cupboard doors; lower section w/oblong top over single long drawer above pr. cupboard doors, scalloped bracket feet, ca. 1875 . . . . 1,475.00

Wall Cupboard

Wall cupboard, Federal, painted pine, 2-part construction: upper part w/molded cornice above frieze w/fish-scale details over pr. 6-panel glazed cupboard doors flanked by reeded pilasters & open pie shelf; lower section w/oblong top w/applied molding over three short drawers & pr. paneled cupboard doors flanked by reeded

pilasters, applied base molding & well-shaped ogee-molded feet, old dark finish, 55" w., 83¼" h. (ILLUS.) 4,750.00

Wall cupboard, Federal country-style, painted finish, 1-piece construction, picture frame molding around pr. door-over-door cupboards, molded base, painted green over grey finish, early 19th c. 1,295.00

Wall cupboard, Federal country-style, pine, 2-part construction: upper part w/ogee-molded cornice above pr. raised panel cupboard doors opening to shelves & w/open pie shelf below; lower section w/oblong top above 3 short frieze drawers over pr. raised panel cupboard doors, bracket feet, Pennsylvania, early 19th c., 62" w., 89" h. 3,520.00

Late 19th Century Painted Cupboard

Wall cupboard, Victorian country-style, painted & decorated, 1-piece, molded cornice above pr. paneled cupboard doors opening to shelves over single long drawer w/pr. paneled cupboard doors below, cut-out bracket feet, vigorously painted overall, Indiana origins, ca. 1880 (ILLUS.) 595.00

DESKS

American Empire butler's desk, mahogany veneer on pine, oblong top above deep upper drop-front drawer opening to bird's eye maple interior w/false center drawer flanked by short working drawers over 3 long drawers flanked by bold S-curve heavy flattened stiles continuing to C-scroll feet, original Sandwich glass clear knobs, 45" w., 49½" h. 675.00

Mission-style (Arts & Crafts movement) "chalet" desk, oak, arched crest above shallow serpentine-fronted shelf over paneled drop-front opening to form leather-lined writing surface & paper rack ledges & w/sides continuing to form trestle base joined by shallow shelf-stretcher, attributed to Gustav Stickley, ca. 1902, 24¾" w., 46" h. 715.00

Mission-style (Arts & Crafts movement) lady's writing desk, oak, oblong top above central drawer flanked by short double drawers w/iron handles, paneled sides, square legs, w/red decal mark of Gustav Stickley, Style No. 709, ca. 1904, 42 x 23½" top, 29" h. 412.00

Gustav Stickley Drop-Front Desk

Mission-style (Arts & Crafts movement) drop-front desk, oak, oblong top above pr. cupboard doors on copper strap hinges opening to fitted interior of pigeonholes & small drawers above drop-front writing surface over lower shelf w/long drawer below, original copper hardware throughout, attributed to Gustav Stickley, ca. 1906, minor restoration, 38" w., 56" h. (ILLUS.) 2,650.00

Mission-style (Arts & Crafts movement) fall-front desk, oak, oblong top w/three-quarter mortised & tenon gallery above paneled drop-front on copper strap hinges above 2 open shelves, paneled sides continuing to form feet, attributed to Gustav Stickley, 1902, 25¾" w., 51" h. 1,650.00

Mission-style (Arts & Crafts movement) table-desk, oak, oblong top, apron w/single drawer

w/turned pulls, straight legs w/three vertical slats each side joined by medial stretcher-shelf, ca. 1915, 42 x 26" top, 30" h. 440.00

Queen Anne Desk

Queen Anne slant-front desk, walnut, oblong hinged lid opening to fitted compartment raised on tapering cylindrical legs w/shod pad feet, probably North Carolina or Virginia, 1740-60, 30½" deep, 34½" h. (ILLUS.) 3,300.00

Queen Anne slant-front desk on frame, cherrywood, hinged lid opening to fitted interior w/five pigeonholes over arrangement of fan-carved central drawer flanked by 3 small drawers above case w/three graduated long drawers; frame w/shaped apron, short cabriole legs & shod pad feet, Connecticut, ca. 1760, 32" w., 40" h. (now fitted w/brass drawer pulls & keyhole escutcheons engraved w/florals) 13,750.00

Queen Anne slant-front desk on frame, walnut, hinged lid opening to arrangement of valanced pigeonholes over short drawers & centering a fluted prospect door, w/secret drawer & retractable panel below opening to well, above base w/shaped skirt, turned tapering legs & shod pad feet, Pennsylvania, ca. 1780, 37" w., 43" h. (repairs to lid & restored valances) 11,000.00

Schoolmaster's desk, Hepplewhite country-style, painted pine, low gallery above hinged slant lid opening to pigeonholes, square tapering legs, layers of grey paint, 26" w., 23" deep, 35" to top of gallery. 225.00

Schoolmaster's desk, Sheraton country-style, painted hardwood &

maple, low gallery above slant lid
lifting to well, turned & tapering
legs, worn painted finish, mid-
19th c. 450.00
Shaker sewing desk, butternut & red-
painted hardwood, superstructure
w/paneled central cupboard door
flanked by 3 short drawers above
plain top over slide (or pull-out)
work surface above case w/arrange-
ment of 6 short drawers w/original
turned pulls, turned legs, attributed to Joshua Bussell, Alfred,
Maine 24,750.00

Turn-of-the-Century Drop-Front Desk

Turn-of-the-Century drop-front desk,
oak, shaped crest centering
carved medallion above inset beveled mirror plate flanked by
shelves supported by turned spindles, hinged drop-front w/applied
carvings opening to compartments
& pigeonholes & forming writing
surface above open shelves joined
to sides (ILLUS.) 498.00
Turn-of-the-Century roll-top desk,
quarter-sawn oak, S-roll opening
to 34 compartments, kneehole
flanked by 4 drawers, plinth
base, 50" w. 2,200.00

Turn-of-the-Century Desk

Turn-of-the-Century roll-top desk,
quarter-sawn oak, S-roll opening to
numerous pigeonholes & short drawers, kneehole flanked by drawers,
paneled sides & back, refinished,
60" w. (ILLUS.) 3,250.00
Turn-of-the-Century roll-top desk,
quarter-sawn oak, S-roll opening
to 45 compartments, kneehole
flanked by 4 graduated drawers,
65" w. . . . . .2,500.00 to 4,750.00
Victorian butler's desk, Eastlake
substyle, walnut w/burl walnut
panels, oblong top above false-
fronted drawer folding down to
form writing surface and reveal
inner compartments over 5 long
drawers, all w/burl walnut
panels, flanked by reeded posts
w/incised decoration, late 19th c.,
36 5/8" w., 55½" h. 825.00
Victorian Davenport desk, walnut,
Renaissance substyle, walnut
w/gilt-incised decor, sloping writing surface lifting to well above
columnar supports on plinth base
& w/drawers at side, ca. 1865,
26" w., 40" h. . . . . .360.00 to 880.00
Victorian lady's desk, bamboo-
turned, lacquered slant lid
w/bamboo gallery above lacquered shelf fitted w/inkwell,
pressed wood sides, bamboo-
turned legs w/cross stretcher,
England, ca. 1870, together
w/bamboo chair w/basket-
weave paneled back & seat,
pr. 300.00
Victorian "patent" desk, Wooton
Standard Grade, walnut & bird's
eye maple, hinged doors opening
to cubbyhole sections & drop-front
writing surface . . . . .5,250.00 to 12,500.00
Victorian "patent" desk, Wooton
Rotary Model, walnut, leather-inset
oblong top above 3 frieze drawers
raised on double pier pedestals incorporating various compartments,
60" w., 32" h. . . . . . . .1,650.00 to 2,750.00
Victorian slant-front desk, walnut &
burl walnut, 2-part construction:
upper part w/drawers over slant-
front opening to fitted interior
w/pigeonholes, small drawers &
hidden compartment; lower section
w/graduated drawers, overall
65" h. 1,500.00
Wallace Nutting signed Chippendale-
style "block-front" & "shell-
carved" kneehole desk, mahogany,
oblong top above frieze w/central
concave drawer flanked by convex
shell-carved drawers over kneehole flanked by rows of blocked

drawers, blocked ogee-bracket
feet, 38" w., 34¼" h. 6,600.00
Wicker desk w/oak top, superstruc-
ture w/woven openwork back &
three-quarter gallery above shelf
over woven wicker cupboard door
one end & open shelves opposite;
oblong oak top w/plain woven
apron above kneehole flanked by
open shelves & w/bookshelf raised
on support each side, wicker-
wrapped legs, w/label of Paine
Furniture Co., Boston, Massachu-
setts, 60" w., 39" h. 1,100.00

DINING SUITES

Art Nouveau dining suite: extension
table & 6 chairs; fruitwood, oblong table w/massive legs carved
w/berries & leafage & chairs
w/shaped backrests elaborately
carved w/berries & leaves above
caned seats, attributed to Marjorelle, France, ca. 1900,
7 pcs. 6,050.00
Mission-style (Arts & Crafts move-
ment) dining suite: table, china
cabinet, buffet, server & 6 chairs;
oak, signed Stickley Bros.,
10 pcs. 7,500.00
Turn-of-the-Century (Empire Revival)
dining suite: table & 4 chairs;
golden oak, 42" d. round table
w/pedestal & animal paw feet &
chairs w/cane seats, original
finish, ca. 1900, 5 pcs. 800.00
Turn-of-the-Century (Empire Revival)
dining suite: table w/animal paw
feet (& 4 extension leaves), large
china cabinet, sideboard w/mirror-
backed superstructure & shelves
& 6 side chairs; golden oak,
orignal condition, ca. 1900,
9 pcs. 5,000.00
Twentieth Century Gothic Revival
dining suite: table, sideboard,
hutch-type cabinet & 6 chairs;
oak, 88 x 40" table w/baluster-
turned legs & bun feet,
9 pcs. 2,950.00
Twentieth Century Jacobean Revival
dining suite: table (& 2 extension
leaves), server, sideboard, china
cabinet, pr. host chairs & 6 side
chairs; mahogany, 1900-20,
12 pcs. 4,500.00
Victorian (late) dining suite: round
top table, sideboard & 6 chairs;
oak, animal paw feet on
extension-type table, cabriole-
legged chairs & sideboard w/oval
mirror in superstructure & mirror-
backed side cabinets, late 19th-
early 20th c., 8 pcs. 1,980.00

Primitive Pine Dry Sink

Cherrywood dry sink w/step-back
cupboard superstructure, 2-part
construction: upper part w/plain
crest above pr. double-paneled
cupboard doors; lower section
w/oblong work well above pr.
conforming cupboard doors,
46" w., overall 77" h. 770.00
Painted maple dry sink w/step-back
cupboard superstructure, grain-
painted finish, 1-piece, superstructure w/coved cornice, pr. raised
panel cupboard doors & open
shelf w/three short drawers
below over oblong work well in
case w/pr. raised panel cupboard
doors, molded base, ogee bracket
feet 2,500.00
Painted maple dry sink, open work
well above case w/pr. raised
panel cupboard doors, (worn
down) bracket feet, original
(worn) mustard yellow paint 550.00
Painted pine dry sink w/hinged
work surface top, 1-board hinged
top lifting to reveal work well in
case w/pr. short drawers above
pr. paneled cupboard doors, 1-
board sides, cut-out bracket feet,
original blue-painted interior, old
(but not original) grain-painted
exterior, Pennsylvania, 19th c. . . . 795.00
Painted pine dry sink, zinc-lined oblong work well in case w/single
cupboard door, plain base, short
ring- and vase-turned legs, ball
feet, old blue paint 340.00
Painted pine dry sink, oblong work
well w/work surface & drawer
to right & wide overhang above
case w/pr. paneled cupboard
doors, 1-board sides continuing
to form cut-out feet, original sal-
mon pink paint 1,200.00
Painted pine dry sink, oblong work
well w/work surface to left above
short drawer over case w/pr.
paneled cupboard doors w/origi-
nal iron latches & porcelain
knobs, sides continuing to form

cut-out feet, yellow paint, large
size 1,295.00

Painted walnut dry sink w/step-back
cupboard top, 2-part construction:
superstructure w/molded cornice
above pr. paneled cupboard doors
over open shelf w/small drawers
below at each end; base w/open
work well above pr. paneled cupboard doors, cut-out bracket feet,
early grain-painted finish over
original red, Pennsylvania,
19th c.........................1,500.00

Painted pine & poplar dry sink, oblong work well above case w/pr.
cupboard doors, worn paint shows
several coats of paint beneath,
small size 300.00

Painted poplar dry sink w/shelf
raised above oblong work well
w/galvanized sheet metal lining
in case w/pr. short drawers over
pr. paneled cupboard doors, cut-
out bracket feet, old red repaint,
41" w., 17" deep, 44½" to top of
shelf 550.00

Poplar dry sink w/step-back cupboard superstructure, 1-piece,
superstructure w/coved cornice
above pr. double-paneled cupboard doors w/arrangement of 6
small drawers beneath over case
w/oblong work well & small work
surface above short drawer at
one side above pr. paneled cupboard doors, cut-out bracket feet,
early 19th c., 58" w., 82" h. 2,090.00

Primitive pine dry sink, oblong work
well above pr. cupboard doors & 3
short drawers, sides continuing to
form bootjack feet, probably New
England, 19th c., 27" h. 465.00

Primitive pine dry sink, oblong work
well w/original (worn) zinc lining
above case w/pr. paneled cupboard doors, bracket feet,
stripped & refinished in natural,
52" w. (ILLUS.) 600.00

Primitive pine dry sink, oblong zinc-
lined work well above pr. plain
cupboard doors opening to
shelves, cut-out bracket feet, layers of peeling worn paint 300.00

GARDEN & LAWN FURNITURE (Cast Iron)

Settee, twisted iron wire serpentine-
crested back enhanced w/C-scroll
designs continuing to form arms,
cast open latticework seat &
apron, 19th c., old white paint,
52" w. 500.00

Settee, cast fern design in back &
downswept arms, openwork scroll
design in seat, 76" l. (ILLUS.) 880.00

Garden Settee with Fern Design

Settees, cast Vintage patt. back continuing to form arms, pierced grid
design in seat, entwined grape
cluster legs, painted white, 44" l.,
pr.......................700.00 to 880.00

Garden Settee by Peter Timmes & Son

Settees, cast rectangular back
pierced w/three panels of scrolling foliage, pierced grid design in
seat, signed "Peter Timmes &
Son, Brooklyn, New York,"
1850-75, 33" l., pr. (ILLUS.
of one)..............5,500.00 to 9,900.00

Settee by Lister & Fee

Suite: pr. settees & pr. armchairs;
each cast w/rectangular back
pierced w/panels of scrollwork &
w/grid-pierced seats, part of
group signed "Lister & Fee, Brooklyn, New York," 1850-75, 4 pcs.
(ILLUS. of part) 11,000.00
Table, cast w/pierced lacy scroll top
& foliate scroll legs, painted
green, 41½" d., 27" h. 200.00
Urn, inverted bell shape on square
plinth, painted grey-green,
33½" h. 300.00

HALL RACKS & TREES

Turn-of-the-Century Hall Tree

Hall rack, Thonet-signed bentwood,
framework w/arched back set
w/scrolling hooks above open
space at right w/shelf over bentwood umbrella supports to left,
complete w/umbrella drip pans,
original paper labels, Austria,
ca. 1910, 72" h. 825.00
Hall settle bench, Victorian (late)
Jacobean Revival style, oak, over-
hanging canted cornice
w/machine-carved details & high
paneled back w/recessed panels
of hunting scenes & smaller figure
panels, lift-top seat w/loose cushion flanked by heavy downswept
arms & w/conforming machine-
carved seat-front panels, large
bun feet, late 19th c., 66¾" w.,
74" h. 715.00
Hall tree, Turn-of-the-Century, gold-
en oak, scrolling machine-carved
crest above high back centered
w/beveled glass mirror plate
flanked by brass coat hooks
above lift-lid seat flanked by
scrolling arms, original finish
(ILLUS.). 550.00

Hall tree, Victorian, cast iron, center pole w/hat & coat hooks at
top & fitted w/circular pierced
rack for umbrellas at center &
w/round umbrella pan in base,
painted white................... 550.00

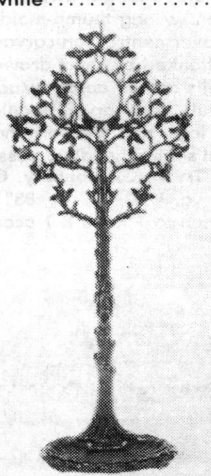

Cast Iron Hall Tree

Hall trees, Victorian, cast iron, in
the form of a tree w/leafy
branches supporting molded
hooks & centering an oval mirror
plate (missing), w/shell-form
insert pan at base of trunk,
"November 16, 1858" patent,
71" h., pr. (ILLUS. of one) 495.00
Hall tree, Victorian, wicker, hand-
woven natural fibre trim on
wrapped pole fitted w/bentwood
hooks, painted white 295.00
Hat rack, Victorian, walnut,
expandable-type w/turned pegs
fitted w/brass rosettes & white
porcelain buttons ....38.00 to 50.00

HIGHBOYS

Chippendale "bonnet-top" highboy,
walnut, 2-part construction: upper
part w/swan's neck cresting centering 3 spirally-turned finials
above central fan-carved drawer
& flanking short drawers over 4
graduated thumb-molded long
drawers; lower section w/long
drawer above central fan-carved
drawer & flanking short drawers,
shaped skirt, angular cabriole
legs, claw-and-ball feet, Massachusetts, ca. 1775, 41" w.,
89" h. (feet reduced) 24,200.00
Queen Anne "bonnet-top" highboy,
cherrywood, 2-part construction:
upper part w/concave-molded

swan's neck cresting terminating in carved rosettes & centering 3 ball-and-steeple finials over fan-carved short drawer flanked by short drawers & 4 graduated thumb-molded long drawers; lower section w/long thumb-molded drawer over central fan-carved drawer flanked by short drawers, fleur-de-lis carved apron w/acorn drop finials, leaf-carved angular cabriole legs, pad feet, original brass bat's wing handles, possibly by Isaac Tryon, Glastonbury, Connecticut, ca. 1760, 41" w., 83" h. (restoration to 1 knee & 1 acorn pendant) 39,600.00

Queen Anne Highboy

Queen Anne "bonnet-top" highboy, mahogany, 2-part construction: upper part w/molded bonnet centering a fluted & scroll-carved plinth w/turned finial above case w/two false drawers over 3 short drawers & 4 graduated long drawers; lower section w/long drawer over 3 short drawers, shaped apron, cabriole legs, curled slipper feet, Rhode Island or Connecticut, ca. 1770, 39" w., 85" h. (ILLUS.) 17,600.00

Queen Anne "bonnet-top" highboy, walnut, 2-part construction: upper part w/shaped bonnet w/molded edge centering a fluted plinth supporting a stop-fluted & spiral-carved flame finial above frieze w/two shaped panels over pr. short & 3 graduated long drawers

above mid-molding; lower section w/single long drawer over short central drawer flanked by deeper short drawers, shaped skirt w/concave-carved shell, cabriole legs, squared knees, shod pad feet, attributed to Townsend or Goddard shops, Newport, Rhode Island, 1740-60, 39¼" w., 87¼" h. 77,000.00

Queen Anne "flat-top" highboy, maple, 2-part construction: upper part w/cove-molded cornice above 4 thumb-molded long drawers; lower section w/applied molding above case w/long drawer over central concave fan-carved drawers & flanking drawers, shaped apron w/pendant acorn drops, cabriole legs, shod pad feet, New Hampshire, 1740-60, 41¼" w., 75" h. (few small chips & repairs) 9,900.00

Queen Anne "flat-top" highboy, cherrywood, 2-part construction: upper part w/projecting molded cornice above pr. short drawers over 4 long thumb-molded graduated long drawers; lower section w/long drawer over 3 short thumb-molded deeper drawers, shaped skirt, cabriole legs, pad feet, Connecticut, ca. 1760, 40" w., 77" h. 9,350.00

William & Mary Highboy

William & Mary "flat-top" highboy, walnut, 2-part construction: upper part w/molded cornice above pr. short drawers over 3 long drawers, all within cockbeaded surrounds; lower section w/short shallow central drawer flanked by deeper drawers, arched skirt, trumpet-turned legs joined by shaped stretcher, ball feet, Massachusetts, 1700-30, 39½" w., 63" h. (ILLUS.) 18,700.00

ICE BOXES

Oak 2-Door Ice Box

Oak ice box, 2-door, original brass hardware, refinished & polished handles & hinges (ILLUS.) 600.00
Oak ice box, 3-door, original brass hardware, refinished & polished handles & hinges 850.00

Oak 4-door Ice Box

Oak ice box, 4-door, "Leonard Cleanable Refrigerator Co., Grand Rapids, Mich.," 42" w., 24" deep, 50" h. (ILLUS.) 750.00
Oak ice box, 5-door store size, ca. 1915, 60" w., 72" h. 625.00
Oak ice box, 8-door store size w/beveled mirror plate centered in front door, 86" h. . . . . .400.00 to 750.00

LOVE SEATS, SOFAS & SETTEES

Louis XVI Canape'

Canape' (French term for sofa or settee), Louis XV, giltwood, serpentine crestrail centering carved shell flanked by flowering vines above upholstered serpentine-fronted seat w/loose cushion, foliate-carved apron, cabriole legs w/flowerhead-carved knees, signed "I. Govrdin," France, mid-18th c. .34,100.00
Canape', Louis XVI, giltwood, molded crestrail continuing downward to padded arms carved w/twisted ribbon, upholstered back, sides & seat w/loose cushion, bowed seatrail carved w/leaf-tips, circular stop-fluted tapering legs, signed "I. Avisse," late 18th c., 50" l. (ILLUS.) 4,400.00
Day bed, Federal country-style, walnut, turned head & footrails raised on ring-turned supports, scalloped siderails, ring-turned feet, now fitted w/upholstered mattress, end bolsters & pillows 650.00

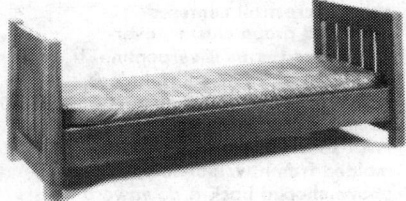

Mission Oak Day Bed

Day bed, Mission-style (Arts & Crafts movement), oak, attributed to Gustav Stickley, Model No. 216, 5 vertical slats each end, unsigned, 80" l. (ILLUS.) 1,100.00
Day bed, Victorian, oak frame, upholstered & button-tufted seat & rolled end, flat-carved legs, late 19th c., 72" l 440.00

Victorian Lounge or Fainting Couch

Lounge, Victorian, Louis XV substyle, walnut, finger-molded &
floral-carved frame, tapestry-type
upholstery (ILLUS.) 700.00

Late Victorian Love Seat

Love seat, Victorian, Eastlake substyle, golden oak frame, plush upholstery (ILLUS.) 225.00
Love seat, Victorian, Louis XV substyle, walnut, medallion-back
w/tufted upholstery beneath serpentine crestrail centered
w/carved grape cluster, over-
upholstered arms & serpentine-
fronted seat, demi-cabriole legs,
original finish & upholstery 685.00
Love seats, Victorian, Rococo Revival substyle, walnut, finger-
molded frame w/leaf-carved crest
above shaped back & downward
curving arms, serpentine seatrail
centering carved shell, demi-
cabriole legs, ca. 1865,
pr. 1,100.00
Racamier (couch similar to the one
in David's celebrated portrait of
Madame Racamier), Victorian,
Rococo Revival substyle, pierce-
carved laminated rosewood frame
in the Rosalie patt., John Henry
Belter, New York, New York,
ca. 1855.............7,500.00 to 9,900.00

Settee, bentwood, designed by Otto
Wagner for Thonet, curving bentwood back & arms w/upholstered
inset, wide upholstered seat,
square legs w/simple stretcher,
w/Thonet label, ca. 1905, 47" l...2,420.00

Art Nouveau Settee

Settee, Art Nouveau, mahogany
with mother-of-pearl inlay, upholstered seat (ILLUS.).............. 302.50
Settee, Federal, mahogany, shaped
crestrail w/cross-banded lower
edge centering an oblong panel
carved w/tied leafage, bow & war
trophies above upholstered back
flanked by downward-curving
reeded arms on baluster-turned
supports, bowed seat above conforming seatrail, reeded tapering
legs on casters, Salem, Massachusetts, ca. 1805, 47¾" l. 55,000.00

Federal Mahogany Settee

Settee, Federal, mahogany, upholstered back & sloping sides continuing to baluster-turned reeded arm
supports, upholstered seat, ring-
turned & reeded baluster-shaped
legs on casters, ca. 1810, 77" l.
(ILLUS.) 1,320.00

Federal Mahogany Settee

Settee, Federal, mahogany, reeded crestrail & sloping downswept sides on baluster-turned reeded arm supports, upholstered bowed seat & conformingly shaped reeded seatrail, reeded tapering legs on casters, ca. 1820 (ILLUS.) 2,800.00

Settee, Federal country-style, painted & decorated, shaped crestrail w/"angel wings" above 3 wide vase-form splats, downward scrolling bold arms on turned supports, roll-over seat, bulbous-turned legs w/flattened frontal stretcher, original free-hand decoration & striping at crest, seatrail & stretchers on light ground 975.00

Settee, Mission-style (Arts & Crafts movement), oak, plain crestrail above 5 vertical splats, single vertical slat on each side below flat armrails, L. & J.G. Stickley label, Model No. 232, 1912, 72" l. 1,100.00

Settee, Mission-style (Arts & Crafts movement), oak, plain crestrail above 5 vertical slats, flattened arms on vertical slat sides, upholstered leather seat, attributed to Gustav Stickley, Model No. 226, 78" l. 660.00

Settee, Queen Anne, oak, solid 5-panel cross-banded back, plank seat w/loose cushion, shaped arms on baluster-turned supports, cabriole legs, pad feet, England, ca. 1730 .... 2,200.00

Settee, Shaker, dark varnish finish, plain slat crestrail above 18-spindle back, shaped plank seat, turned legs 5,500.00

Settee, Victorian, Eastlake substyle, rosewood frame, "tufted" upholstery on back & arms, geometrically-incised & parcel-gilt arm supports, turned tapering feet, ca. 1880 .... 935.00

Settee, Victorian, Renaissance substyle, walnut & burl walnut, shaped crestrail centering carved cartouche ornamentation above upholstered back & seat 715.00

Settee, Windsor, cushion-molded backrail continuing to shaped arms above bamboo turned spindles, shaped arms, bamboo-turned legs w/conforming stretchers, 1775-1810 (restored) 2,650.00

Sofa, American Empire, walnut, rounded crestrail w/rosette-carved scrolling ears continuing to padded arms faced w/spiral-twist cornucopiae, plain seatrail, winged animal paw feet, velvet upholstery & bolsters, ca. 1840, 76" l. 1,500.00

Sofa, American Empire, mahogany, plain crestrail w/scroll-and-leaf carvings at downswept ends, upholstered back & seat, cylindrical "pillow" arms above foliate-carved lyre-form legs on large ball feet, Philadelphia, 1810-35, 72" l. 990.00

Sofa, American Empire, mahogany, rounded crestrail w/rosette-carved scrolling ears continuing to padded arms faced w/spiral-twist cornucopiae facing, plain seatrail, winged animal paw feet, grey velvet upholstery & bolster, ca. 1840, 76" l. 1,500.00

Sofa, American Empire, mahogany, shaped crestrail w/scroll-carved ears, upholstered back & roll-over arms, carved winged animal paw feet, New York, 1825-35, 84" l. 3,000.00

Country Couch

Sofa, American Empire country-style, solid walnut, solid-board back w/roll-over crestrail & solid-board seat continuing to arms in lyre outline, heavy turned tapering legs, ball feet, Southern origins, refinished & w/small repairs, 89½" l. (ILLUS.) 1,400.00

Sofa, Centennial (1876) Queen Anne style, walnut, upholstered double-arched back flanked by curved wings continuing to double-scrolled armrests, trapezoidal seat, carved cabriole legs, claw-and-ball feet 660.00

Sofa, Chippendale, mahogany frame, upholstered serpentine back & roll-over arms, Marlborough legs, Philadelphia, 1760-80 .... 60,500.00

Sofa, Federal, mahogany, shaped crestrail carved w/acanthus-motifs flanked by outward scrolling reeded & flowerhead-carved arm supports, reeded seatrail & downward-curving reeded legs w/brass foliate feet on casters, ca. 1815, 72½" w. (repairs) 3,850.00

Sofa, Federal, mahogany, molded crestrail w/swag-and-tassel & bow-knot carved central reserve, upholstered back & downswept arms on reeded arm supports, reeded tapering legs on brass casters, New York, ca. 1815, 78" l. .... 2,200.00 to 8,800.00

Sofa, Federal, mahogany, arched upholstered back & shaped arms above upholstered serpentine-fronted seat, oval-inlaid dies above square tapering line- and bellflower-inlaid legs (now on brass casters), Baltimore, Maryland, ca. 1795, 78" l. 14,300.00

Sofa, Federal, mahogany, molded crestrail centered w/carved swag-and-tassel motif panel flanked by carved thunderbolts & tied bow-knots above upholstered back & seat, shaped arms above acanthus-carved colonettes, reeded seatrail, ring-turned & reeded tapering legs on brass casters, attributed to Duncan Phyfe, New York, ca. 1805, 80" w. (lacks caster wheels) 16,500.00

Sofa, Mission-style (Arts & Crafts movement), oak, plain crestrail above vertical slats, 3-cushion seat & 3 cushions for back, original finish, "Quaint Furniture" label 600.00

Sofa, Victorian, Renaissance Revival substyle in the manner of J. Jelliff, w/full relief carved bust portrait in crestrail & full relief bust portrait arm terminals, walnut, 3-chairback style, (worn) tufted upholstery 3,300.00

Sofa, Victorian, Rococo Revival substyle, pierce-carved laminated rosewood, serpentine crestrail centered w/ornately-carved urn flanked by full-carved florals above upholstered back, seat & arms, serpentine-fronted seatrail w/floral carvings, John Henry Belter, New York, New York, ca. 1855 .... 24,000.00

Sofa, Victorian, Rococo substyle, pierce-carved laminated rosewood, Rosalie patt., serpentine-carved crest, upholstered back & serpentine-fronted seat, demi-cabriole legs, John Henry Belter, New York, New York, ca. 1855 .... 3,850.00 to 7,700.00

Sofa, Victorian, Rococo Revival substyle, pierce-carved rosewood frame, serpentine crest & serpentine-fronted seat, ca. 1850 (no upholstery) 1,540.00

Sofa, wicker, serpentine crestrail w/three arches above openwork design of panels, caned seat, wrapped legs w/ornate stretchers, openwork apron, ca. 1880 ... 1,200.00

LOWBOYS

Chippendale "Tray-Top" Lowboy

Chippendale "tray-top" lowboy, cherrywood, oblong "tray-top" w/molded edges above arrangement of 4 short thumb-molded drawers w/original brass bat's wing handles, shaped skirt w/C-scrolls on 3 sides, shell- and volute-carved cabriole legs, claw-and-ball feet, Connecticut, ca. 1780, 33" w., 29" h. (ILLUS.) 22,000.00

Chippendale lowboy, walnut, oblong top w/molded edge & notched corners above long thumb-molded drawer & central short shell- and acanthus- and scroll-carved drawer flanked by short drawers, all w/original pierced brass bat's wing handles, acanthus-carved cabriole legs, claw-and-ball feet, Philadelphia, ca. 1770, 35" w., 31" h. 71,500.00

Queen Anne lowboy, cherrywood, oblong top w/molded edge above case w/long drawer over short central drawer flanked by deeper short drawers, scalloped skirt centering concave-carved fan, angular cabriole legs, pad feet, Connecticut, ca. 1770 .... 7,425.00

Queen Anne lowboy, cherrywood, oblong top w/molded edge above long single drawer over concave fan-carved central drawer flanked by short drawers, all w/original brass bat's wing handles, scalloped skirt, cabriole legs, pad feet, Connecticut 45,000.00

Queen Anne lowboy, tiger stripe maple, oblong top w/molded edge & invected corners above case w/two rows of 2 short thumb-molded drawers, scalloped skirt centering shaped pendant w/pierced heart, squared cabriole legs w/molded cuffs, fluted Spanish feet, Delaware Valley, 1750-70, 32½" w., 29¼" h. 93,500.00

Queen Anne lowboy, tiger stripe maple, oblong top w/molded edge above case w/long thumb-molded drawer over 3 short deeper drawers, shaped skirt, angular cabriole legs, shod pad feet, New England, 1760-80, 39" w., 29½" h. 9,350.00

Queen Anne Lowboy

Queen Anne lowboy, walnut, oblong top w/molded edge & rounded corners above case w/two rows of 2 short thumb-molded drawers, shaped skirt, squared cabriole legs w/molded cuffs, fluted Spanish feet, Delaware Valley, 1750-70, knee brackets restored, 34" w., 39" h. (ILLUS.). 27,500.00

Queen Anne style lowboy, painted cherrywood, oblong 2-board top w/thumb-molded edge above case w/single drawer, angular cabriole legs, pad feet, old dark paint, Massachusetts, ca. 1800 . . . . 4,225.00

MIRRORS

American Empire "cheval" mirror, mahogany, oblong mirror plate within framework w/raking crest tilting between blocked & turned columns w/urn finials above trestle base w/carved animal paw feet, ca. 1840 . . . . 1,320.00

American Empire over-mantel mirror, giltwood & gesso, flat-molded cornice w/sprig relief above baluster-turned framework w/blocked corners, 3-section mirror plate w/split-spindle dividers, acanthus leaf & gadroon relief throughout, 1825-35, 47" w., 29¾" h. 605.00

American Empire wall mirror, giltwood & gesso, molded broken cornice hung w/gilt spherules & frieze of florals over oblong mirror plate flanked by baluster-turned columns, 45" h. 285.00

Chippendale wall mirror, mahogany & giltwood, scrolling pierced crest centering applied molded phoenix bird above oblong mirror plate within giltwood molding, conforming scrolled pendant below, mid-18th c., 19" w., 34" h. 935.00

Federal "convex" wall mirror, giltwood, carved spread-winged American eagle crest surmounted on flaring plinth hung w/gilt spherules over elaborate vase of trailing leafage, convex mirror plate within ebonized surround & cove-molded border hung w/gilt spherules, conforming pendant below, early 19th c., 22½" d., overall 53" h. 4,400.00

Federal Wall Mirror

Federal wall mirror, giltwood & gesso, lyre-shaped, lyre-form pediment hung w/olive branch & flanked by American eagle's heads, twist-carved upper section & relief of stars & acanthus on framework (ILLUS.) 5,500.00

Federal 2-part wall mirror, giltwood, broken cornice hung w/gilt spherules above "eglomise" panel depicting a naval battle within Greek Key border above oblong mirror plate flanked by rope-twist columns, labeled "James Todd,

Portland, Maine," ca. 1820,
18¼" w., 33" h. 660.00

Queen Anne wall mirror, walnut veneer, scrolling crest above
cushion-molded frame enclosing
oblong mirror plate, England, ca.
1750, 12" w., 23" h. 770.00

Queen Anne 2-part wall mirror,
divided glass etched w/star motifs
in upper arch-top plate over oblong lower plate within cushion-
molded frame, England, ca. 1700,
24" w., 52½" h. 8,800.00

Turn-of-the-Century wall mirror, tin,
commemorative-type, diamond-
shaped frame w/central mirror
plate flanked by coat hangers &
embossed w/pictures of Admiral
Dewey, Hobson & the Battleship
Maine, ca. 1898 . . . . 95.00

Victorian pier mirror, Renaissance
Revival substyle, walnut w/burl
walnut panels, original finish. 350.00

Victorian pier mirror, rococo substyle, carved giltwood, elaborately carved floral & foliate
framework, ca. 1850, 104" h. 1,650.00

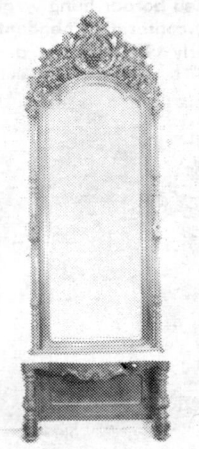

Victorian Pier Mirror

Victorian pier mirror, rococo substyle, pierce-carved foliate & fruit
cresting, shaped oblong mirror
plate within molded framework
flanked by fluted, ring- and
baluster-turned uprights over
white marble slab shelf supported
on ring-turned & acanthus-carved
uprights (ILLUS.) 2,860.00

PARLOR SUITES (Victorian)
Eastlake substyle: settee, armchair
& pr. side chairs; walnut, typical
incised carvings, original finish &
upholstery, 4 pcs. 600.00

Eastlake substyle: pr. love seats,
lady's & gentleman's armchairs,
platform rocker & side chair;
cherrywood, typical carvings,
replaced upholstery, ca. 1885,
6 pcs. 1,995.00

Louis XVI substyle: settee & 6 side
chairs; walnut, shield-shaped
backs below stylized crest, round
upholstered seat, fluted turned
legs on casters, 7 pcs. 3,700.00

Renaissance Revival substyle: sofa
& armchair; walnut & burl walnut,
triple shield-back sofa & shield-
back chair w/cabochon-carved
crests, tapering baluster-turned
legs, original excellent condition,
2 pcs. . . . . .1,800.00 to 3,500.00

Renaissance Revival substyle: sofa &
armchair; gilt-incised rosewood,
shaped crest w/machine-carved
designs centering portrait roundel,
upholstered back, arms & seat,
short trumpet-turned legs on
casters, attributed to Herter Bros.,
2 pcs. 22,000.00

Renaissance Revival substyle: settee,
armchair & pr. side chairs; rosewood, carved in the manner of
John Jelliff w/portrait busts in
relief at crest, teal blue "tufted"
upholstery, 4 pcs. 3,950.00

Renaissance Revival substyle: sofa
& 6 matching side chairs; walnut,
elaborate crestrails centering
porcelain plaques, "tufted" upholstery on chairbacks & unusual
3-seat style sofa, trumpet-turned
legs, 7 pcs. .3,850.00

Rococo substyle: settee & armchair;
carved laminated rosewood, settee
w/triple-arched crestrail centering
carved flowers & fruit flanked by
C-scrolls above upholstered back
& seat, flower-carved demi-cabriole legs & balloon-backed chair of
similar form, John Henry Belter,
New York, New York, ca. 1855,
2 pcs. 7,700.00

Rococo substyle: sofa, gentleman's
armchair & pr. side chairs; elabo-
rately carved rosewood in the
Rosalie pattern, attributed to John
Henry Belter, New York, New
York, ca. 1855, 4 pcs. 10,725.00

Rococo substyle: sofa, lady's & gentleman's armchairs & pr. side
chairs; carved laminated rosewood in the Fountain Elms pattern, attributed to John Henry
Belter, New York, New York,
ca. 1855, upholstered, 5 pcs. 46,200.00

Rococo substyle: sofa, lady's &
gentleman's armchairs & 4 side

chairs; pierce-carved laminated rosewood, attributed to John & Joseph Meeks, New York, 7 pcs. 8,250.00

Victorian Parlor Furniture

Rococo substyle: sofa, pr. armchairs & 6 side chairs; rosewood, finger-molded frames carved w/C-scrolls & S-scrolls, 9 pcs. (ILLUS. of part) 4,675.00
Rococo substyle: pr. sofas, lady's & gentleman's armchairs & 6 side chairs; rosewood, finger-molded frames w/ornately carved floral crests, serpentine seatrails on sofas & balloon backs on chairs, ca. 1865, 10 pcs. 7,500.00
Steer's horn "eclectic" style: settee, rocker & 3 armchairs; steer's horn frames w/upholstery, ca. 1850, 5 pcs. 4,675.00

SCREENS

Victorian Fire Screen

Fire screen, Victorian, rosewood frame w/barley-twist details centered w/needlepoint panel depicting bowl of flowers, English (ILLUS.). 650.00
Folding screen, 2-fold, pierce-carved red cinnabar lacquer panels w/figures mounted against gold

cloth backing, China, 19th c., each panel 24" w., 71" h. 880.00
Folding screen, 3-fold, painted wood, Art Deco city landscape w/luminous evening scene of tall skyscrapers (possibly New York), by J. Banigan Sullivan, signed, ca. 1940, overall 61¾" w., 58½" h. . .3,850.00
Folding screen, 4-fold, Chinese coromandel lacquer, gilt chinoiserie scenes on black front & gilt florals reverse 4,950.00

Folding Screen

Folding screen, 4-fold, painted wood, each panel w/three hand-colored engravings of birds laid down on canvas within painted laurel & berry borders & w/lower border painted "en grisaille" armorials, Continental, 19th c., each panel 17" w., overall 73¼" h. (ILLUS.) 8,250.00
Folding screen, 6-fold, black lacquer w/mother-of-pearl inlay, painted colorful equestrian figures of hunters amidst hills & trees within wide borders w/lozenge-shaped panels of birds in flowering trees, each panel 18½" w., 83½" h. . . .4,950.00
Folding screen, 8-fold, Chinese coromandel lacquer, carved bas relief & decorated in colors on aubergine-brown ground w/Immortals amidst clouds above court ladies & w/wide borders of mythical beasts one side & w/exotic birds amidst rockwork, flowering & fruiting reverse, early 18th c., each panel 16" w., 90½" h. 14,300.00
Pole screen, Queen Anne, cherrywood, 18th c. needlework panel w/vase of flowers adjustable on turned standard w/urn-shaped finial, cabriole legs, pad feet, 1750-1800, 51" h. (ILLUS.) 1,430.00

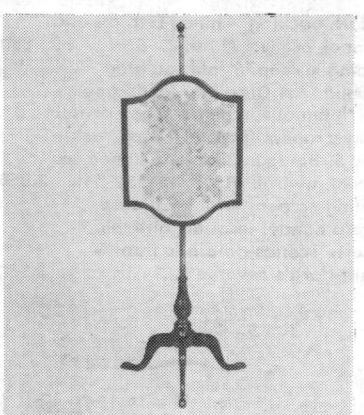

Pole Screen

Pole screen, Queen Anne, mahogany, oblong screen w/flame-stitched embroidery adjustable on turned rod, downswept tripod w/pad feet, late 18th c. 2,500.00

SECRETARIES

American Empire secretary-bookcase, gilt-stenciled mahogany, 2-part construction: upper part w/angular cornice above arched frieze over glazed & mullioned single cupboard door flanked by free-standing columns w/brass capitals; lower section w/veneered drawer above gilt-stenciled paneled cupboard door flanked by conforming columns, leaf-carved ball feet, New York, 1820-30, 42½" w., 88" h. 7,480.00

Biedermeier-style drop-front secretary, tiger stripe maple, 1-piece, oblong top above case w/drop-front opening to form writing surface & reveal scalloped pigeonholes, short drawers & secret compartments above three long drawers w/turned wood pulls flanked by turned columns, paneled sides, turnip-turned feet, American-made in the German taste, 1840's, overall 44½" h. 3,700.00

Chippendale "bonnet-top" secretary-bookcase, walnut, 2-part construction: upper part w/molded swan's neck cresting w/rounded terminals centering an urn finial above frieze w/applied concave-carved shell flanked by grasses over arch-molded cupboard doors opening to shelves, pigeonholes & short drawers above pr. candle slides; lower section w/slant front open-

ing to fitted interior of 4 fan-carved & 4 blocked short drawers centering pilaster-carved document drawers & fan-carved & blocked prospect door opening to reveal 3 short drawers & secret drawers above case w/four cockbeaded long graduated drawers, ogee bracket feet, Philadelphia, ca. 1780, 38" w., 87" h. (some restoration to bonnet top) 25,300.00

Chippendale Secretary-Bookcase

Chippendale secretary-bookcase, cherrywood, 2-part construction: upper part w/molded swan's neck crest centering 3 spiral-turned finials above pr. shaped & paneled cupboard doors flanked by fluted pilasters; lower section w/hinged thumb-molded lid opening to fitted interior over four graduated long drawers above a scrolled and bead-molded skirt on cabriole legs w/ball-and-claw feet, Norwich, Connecticut, 1760-90 (2 replaced finials), 92½" h. (ILLUS.) 17,600.00

Chippendale "bonnet-top" secretary-bookcase, walnut, 2-part construction: upper part w/molded swan's neck crest centering 3 suppressed ball- and flame-carved finials above tympanum (recessed ornamental panel) over pr. paneled cupboard doors opening to adjustable shelves above blocked small drawers & w/candle slides below; lower section w/hinged slant front opening to elaborate stepped interior flanked by valanced pigeonholes over shell-carved drawers & fluted document drawers above case w/four graduated long drawers flanked by fluted quarter columns, ogee bracket feet, Pennsylvania, ca. 1780, 41¾" w., 99½" h. (restored) ...22,000.00

Federal drop-front secretary-bookcase, mahogany & satinwood, 1-piece, removable white marble oblong slab top above baize-lined drop-front writing surface opening to fitted interior w/central prospect section & flanking pigeonholes over arrangement of 6 drawers w/pr. paneled cupboard doors below, molded base, cut-out bracket feet, New York, ca. 1825, 43" w., 61" h. 1,870.00

Federal secretary-bookcase, mahogany veneer, 2-part construction: shaped crest flanked by square plinths w/ball-and-steeple finials & central plinth w/giltwood eagle finial above pr. glazed & mullioned cupboard doors opening to shelves over pr. cupboard doors opening to pigeonholes, drawers & document slots; lower section w/foldout writing flap over 3 graduated long drawers w/original brass pulls flanked by reeded pilasters, reeded tapering legs continuing to tapering feet, Massachusetts, 1800-10, 41¾" w., 92" h. (some restoration to pediment & interior drawers).....................7,700.00

Federal secretary-bookcase, Hepplewhite-style, oak, 2-part construction: upper part w/molded cornice above pr. 4-pane glazed cupboard doors opening to shelves; lower section w/slant-front opening to central document door flanked by short drawers over arch-top pigeonholes above case w/three graduated long drawers within cockbeaded surrounds, shaped apron, bracket feet, ca. 1790, 42" w., 78" h. 4,500.00

Federal secretary-bookcase, mahogany, 3-part construction: upper part w/shaped cornice centering 3 brass finials & oval inlay above pr. geometrically glazed doors opening to shelves; middle section w/fall-front opening to fitted interior w/valanced pigeonholes, small drawers & cupboard doors opening to horizontal document slots; lower section w/four graduated & cockbeaded long drawers w/oval brass drop ring handles, shaped skirt, flaring French feet, New England, ca. 1810, 40½" w., 82" h. 2,860.00

Federal country-style secretary-bookcase, cherrywood, 3-part construction: upper part w/canted cornice above pr. 6-pane glazed cupboard doors opening to shelves; middle section w/slant front opening to simple interior w/drawers & pigeonholes; writing table base w/single drawer on ring- and baluster-turned legs, tapering feet, refinished, ca. 1840, 36¼" w., 77" h. 1,500.00

Federal country-style secretary-bookcase, cherrywood, 3-part construction: upper part w/molded cornice above pr. glazed cupboard doors; middle section w/slant-front folding out to form baize-lined writing surface & expose interior w/small drawers, document slots & compartments; writing table base w/single drawer on turned legs, ca. 1855 (repair to hinges on doors) 1,800.00

Turn-of-the-Century "side-by-side" secretary-bookcase, oak, drop-front desk w/compartmented interior above 3 drawers & surmounted by mirror beside glazed "curio" (or bookcase) cabinet, applied machine carvings to drop-front & drawers, brass hardware, ca. 1910 .... 575.00

Turn-of-the-Century "side-by-side" secretary-bookcase, oak, drop-front desk w/compartmented interior above drawers beside mirror-backed "curio" (or bookcase) cabinet w/bow-fronted (bent) glass door, demi-cabriole legs 1,295.00

Double Side-by-Side

Turn-of-the-Century "double side-by-side" secretary-bookcase, oak, central section w/lion-mask crest over pr. short cupboard doors & mirror-backed shelf over drop-

front writing section opening to
fitted interior above 3 drawers
& flanked by pr. bow-fronted
"curio" (or bookcase) cabinets
w/leaded glass doors opening to
shelves, demi-cabriole legs, paw
feet, 56" w., 74" h. (ILLUS.).......1,320.00
Victorian cylinder-roll secretary-
bookcase, Eastlake substyle, walnut & burl walnut, 2-part construction: upper part w/scalloped crest
& typical incised frieze above pr.
glazed cupboard doors opening to
shelves; lower section w/cylinder
rolling back to fitted interior
w/small drawers & slots above
single long drawer & pr. paneled
cupboard doors, original finish,
ca. 1880, 95" to 99" h.,
each.................880.00 to 1,250.00

Victorian Gothic Revival Secretary

paneled cupboard doors w/applied
quatrefoil designs, bracket feet,
signed J. & J.W. Meeks-Makers,
No. 14 Vesey St., New York, New
York, ca. 1840, 50" w., 94" h.
(ILLUS.) 5,575.00
Victorian cylinder-roll secretary-
bookcase, Renaissance Revival substyle, 2-part construction: upper
part w/molded cornice & ornate
crest above pr. paneled cupboard
doors; lower section w/cylinder
rolling back to fitted interior
above graduated drawers, 1870's,
refinished.....................6,800.00
Victorian cylinder-roll secretary-
bookcase, Renaissance Revival substyle, 2-part construction: upper
part w/molded cornice centered
w/fully-carved female bust over
pr. glazed cupboard doors opening
to shelves; lower section w/cyl-
inder rolling back to numerous
compartments & drawers above 3
drawers, plinth base, ca. 1860,
original finish, 108" h. 4,200.00
Victorian secretary-bookcase, Renaissance Revival substyle, walnut
& burl walnut, 2-part construction:
upper part w/molded cornice above
pr. glazed cupboard doors opening
to shelves; lower section w/slant
front opening to interior w/pigeon-
holes & small drawers above case
w/graduated drawers, ca. 1876,
54" w., 104" to 110" h.,
each ....2,500.00 to 2,750.00
Victorian drop-front secretary, rococo
substyle, rosewood, pierce-carved
cornice above drop-front opening
to form writing surface & reveal
scalloped pigeonholes over shelves

Cylinder-Roll Victorian Secretary

Victorian cylinder-roll secretary-
bookcase, Eastlake substyle, walnut & burl walnut, 2-part construction: upper part w/molded cornice
above frieze inlaid w/burl walnut
above pr. glazed cupboard doors
opening to shelves & flanked by
reeded stiles; lower section
w/cylinder rolling back to fitted
interior above case w/long drawer
over short drawers & cupboard
door, plinth base, refinished
(ILLUS.) 2,850.00
Victorian cylinder-roll secretary-
bookcase, Gothic Revival substyle,
rosewood, 2-part construction:
upper part w/molded over-hanging
cornice above pr. glazed cupboard
doors w/applied rosewood Gothic
arch & quatrefoil details; lower
section w/cylinder rolling back to
reveal pull-out writing flap &
numerous pigeonholes above pr.

Victorian Drop-Front Secretary

& central compartment flanked by
letter rack slots over small drawers, trestle base joined by floral
& C-scroll carved stretcher, ca.
1850 (ILLUS.) 2,200.00

SIDEBOARDS

American Empire "Classical" Sideboard

American Empire "Classical" sideboard, mahogany w/ormolu
mounts (ILLUS.)................3,750.00
Federal sideboard, inlaid mahogany,
shaped oblong top above pr.
slightly bowed drawers over
recessed cupboard doors flanked
by short drawers over bottle
drawers, all w/line-inlaid ovals
& circles & inlaid dies above
square tapering legs w/cross-
banded cuffs, New York, ca. 1790,
70" w., 40" h. 5,225.00
Federal sideboard, inlaid mahogany,
serpentine-fronted oblong top
above case of conforming outline
w/long central drawer w/original
brass oval drop-ring handles over
pr. slightly recessed fan-inlaid
cupboard doors flanked by deep
concave-fronted cupboard doors,
husk-inlaid hexagonal legs w/in-
laid cuffs, w/label of Elbert
Anderson, New York, ca. 1800,
76" l., 41½" h. 10,450.00

Federal sideboard, mahogany, oblong top w/molded edge & outset
rounded corners above case
w/long cockbeaded drawer flanked
by short drawers over pr. cupboard
doors flanked by bottle drawers &
fluted columns continuing to ring-
turned & reeded tapering legs,
Massachusetts, ca. 1815, 48" w.,
41" h. 4,400.00

Federal Sideboard

Federal sideboard, mahogany,
oblong serpentine-fronted top
above case of conforming outline
w/central cockbeaded drawer
flanked by cockbeaded cupboard
doors, square legs, spade feet,
Annapolis, Maryland, 1790-1810,
72" w., 41½" h. (ILLUS.)........11,000.00
Federal country-style hunt board,
oblong top w/shaped backsplash
above case w/two deep drawers
w/original brass drop-ring handles,
square tapering legs, South
Carolina origins 9,300.00

L. & J.G. Stickley Oak Sideboard

Mission-style (Arts & Crafts movement) sideboard, oak, oblong top
w/shaped plate rack at rear over
case w/arrangement of central
cupboard doors flanked by short
drawers over long drawer, arched
apron, square legs, signed "The

Work of L. & J.G. Stickley," Style No. 709, ca. 1910, 53¾" w., 48" h. (ILLUS.) 660.00

Mission-style (Arts & Crafts movement) sideboard, oak, designed by Harvey Ellis & executed by Gustav Stickley, oblong top w/plain backboard above case w/central drawer flanked by short drawers over long deep drawer, tall square legs joined by stretcher-shelf, w/red decal label of Stickley, Model No. 800, ca. 1904, 54" w., 42¾" h. 935.00

Mission-style (Arts & Crafts movement) sideboard, oak, oblong top w/shaped plate rack at rear over 3 central drawers flanked by cupboard doors over long drawer, square straight legs, signed Gustav Stickley, 56" w., 49" h. 880.00

Mission-style (Arts & Crafts movement) sideboard, oak, oblong top w/low backrail w/scrolling ends above case w/two short drawers over pr. cupboard doors, each pierced w/an oval cloverleaf design & closed w/outer swivel latch, hammered copper keyhole escutcheons, hinges & handles, signed Charles Rohlfs & dated 1907, 60" w., 47" h. 6,050.00

Turn-of-the-Century sideboard, golden oak, superstructure & oblong case w/heavy carvings incorporating gargoyles, griffins, etc., 60" w., 66" h. 2,800.00

Turn-of-the-Century Sideboard

Turn-of-the-Century sideboard, golden oak, superstructure w/molded cornice centering carved pediment above mirrored back flanked by shelves on vigorously carved supports & fluted & turned columns, oblong top w/shaped front

above pr. bow-fronted short drawers over long drawer & pr. cupboard doors w/applied carvings within molded framework, carved feet, ca. 1900 (ILLUS.) 1,495.00

Victorian sideboard, cottage-style, painted finish, superstructure w/scalloped crest on high back w/three-quarter gallery enclosing shelf raised above case w/oblong top over 3 short drawers within cockbeaded surrounds & cupboard doors w/applied picture frame moldings, (replaced) turnip feet, worn old brown painted graining, late 19th c., 53½" w., 70½" h. ... 575.00

Victorian sideboard, eclectic-style incorporating both Renaissance & Eastlake substyles, walnut, 2-part construction: superstructure w/pierce-carved cresting above 2-tier shelf arrangement w/mirrored back; base w/oblong top over 3 short drawers & 3 cupboard doors w/applied elaborate carvings & pr. drawers below, plinth base, 61" w., 95" h. 1,650.00

Victorian sideboard, Renaissance Revival substyle, walnut, superstructure w/ornate rounded crest applied w/burl walnut panels & fruit carvings above medial shelf over recessed oval panel on scrolling supports over case w/white marble slab top above pr. short drawers over cupboard doors w/recessed oval panels, plinth base, ca. 1865, 46" w., 80" h. 1,430.00

Victorian sideboard, Renaissance Revival substyle, walnut, superstructure w/ornate rounded crest centering fully-carved deer's head over 2-tier shelf arrangement above case w/pink marble slab top over drawers & cupboard doors hung w/carved pendant fruit & grape clusters, original finish 2,800.00

STANDS

Basin stand, corner-type, mahogany, quarter-round top pierced for basin & receptacles w/shaped gallery fitted w/shelf, scalloped apron, square legs joined by medial shelf w/drawer below, flaring feet joined by shaped stretcher, Massachusetts, ca. 1805, 22" w., 38" h. 1,210.00

Basin stand, Federal country-style, painted & decorated, oblong top pierced for basin & w/shaped backsplash, plain apron, ring- and vase-turned legs joined by medial shelf w/drawer below, tapering

feet, painted yellow w/green
striping 725.00
Basin stand, Federal country-style,
painted & decorated, shaped bow-
fronted top pierced for basin
w/shaped three-quarter gallery
w/scrolled ears & details, shaped
continuous sides joined by medial
shelf w/drawer below, ring- and
baluster-turned feet, original free-
hand florals at gallery & drawer
front & line details in green, black
& purple on mustard yellow
ground, ca. 1850 . . . . 975.00

Federal Basin Stand

Basin stand, Federal, mahogany, oblong top w/shaped three-quarter
gallery fitted w/shelves & pierced
for basin & receptacles, plain
apron, square tapering legs joined
by medial shelf w/drawer below,
flaring feet, Massachusetts,
1800-15, 20 x 16" top, 38½" h.
(ILLUS.) 1,320.00
Crock stand, painted pine, semi-
circular 4-tier step-back style,
painted light green finish, 33" w.,
24" deep, 25" h. 160.00
Dictionary stand, twisted iron wire
frame 50.00
Lamp stand, Victorian, Eastlake sub-
style, walnut, round top inset
w/veined white marble slab,
baluster- and ring-turned standard
on downswept tripod w/incised
details 400.00
Plant stand, Mission-style (Arts &
Crafts movement), oak, square
top, deep apron, splayed legs,
Model No. 660, by Gustav Stickley, ca. 1900, 18" sq. top, 20" h.
(ILLUS.). 990.00

Mission Style Plant Stand

Plant stand, Mission-style (Arts &
Crafts movement), oak, open gallery on square form composed of
single vertical slats centering lower shelf, branded mark of Limbert
Co., ca. 1910, 12" d., 32½" h. 440.00

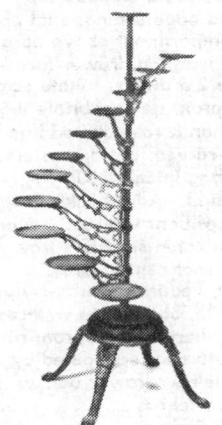

Victorian Plant Stand

Plant stand, Victorian patent-type,
cast iron, 12 graduated swiveling
round platforms on rod standard,
ornate foliate-cast base w/four
legs, late 19th c., 44" h.
(ILLUS.) 5,500.00
Sewing stand, American Empire
(classical revival), crotch mahogany veneer, oblong cruciform top
w/cut-out corners flanked by D-
shaped drop leaves above central
drawer flanked by short recessed
drawers over work bag raised on
columnar supports continuing to
downswept vigorous acanthus-

carved legs & animal paw feet
joined by shaped stretcher, first
half 19th c. 3,630.00

Victorian Sewing Stand

Sewing stand, Victorian, rococo substyle, rosewood, stepped top
w/molded edge & hinged lid opening to compartment above apron
w/single working drawer faced to
resemble 2 drawers, foliate scroll-
carved apron, demi-cabriole legs
w/cabochon & rose-carved knees
& foliate-carved feet on casters,
w/work bag intact (ILLUS.) 1,200.00
Smoking stand, "Adirondak" construction of bent saplings, square
top w/log cabin smoker's tray
w/lift-off roof center, 31¾" h. 85.00
Wash stand, Federal country-style,
curly maple, oblong top w/three-
quarter gallery, plain apron, ring-
and vase-turned legs joined by
medial shelf w/drawer below,
ball-turned feet 525.00
Wash stand, Federal country-style,
pine, dovetailed fold-back top lifting to area pierced for basin & 4
accessories above pr. cupboard
doors over single drawer, turned
tapering legs, ball feet, refinished, 18¾" w., 15¾" deep,
overall 36½" h. 375.00
Wash stand, primitive pine, oblong
top w/shaped backsplash over
single drawer, turned legs joined
by medial shelf, 1850's 325.00
Wash stand, primitive poplar, ob-
long top w/shaped three-quarter
gallery, apron w/single drawer
w/turned wood pull, baluster- and
ring-turned legs joined by scalloped stretcher-shelf, turned feet,

refinished, 22½ x 18½" top,
28½" h. plus gallery 220.00
Wash stand, Shaker, cherrywood &
poplar, square top w/shaped three-
quarter gallery, apron w/single
drawer, square tapering legs
joined by medial shelf, Pleasant
Hill, Kentucky 1,045.00
American Empire 1-drawer stand,
cherrywood, 2-board square top,
apron w/single drawer w/turned
mushroom pull, ring- and
baluster-turned legs, tapering
feet, 23½" w., 28 5/8" h. 175.00
American Empire 2-drawer stand
w/drop-leaves, grain-painted finish, square top flanked by drop
leaves, apron w/two short drawers w/brass pulls, tapering square
standard on quadruped platform
w/C-scroll feet 495.00
American Empire 2-drawer stand,
tiger stripe maple, 1-board square
top, apron w/convex drawer over
plain drawer, each w/turned
wood pull, bulbous-turned legs . . . 375.00
American Empire 2-drawer stand,
tiger stripe maple, oblong top
above 2 convex-fronted drawers
w/original opalescent pressed
glass pulls, baluster-and-ring-
turned legs joined by medial
shelf, turned feet, ca. 1840 . . . . . .1,650.00
American Empire country-style
1-drawer stand, cherrywood &
mahogany, oblong top above
single drawer w/(replaced) glass
pulls, urn-turned standard on
downswept tripod, refinished. 175.00
American Empire country-style
2-drawer stand, curly maple,
1-board square top, apron w/pr.
convex-fronted drawers w/turned
wood pulls, turned legs & feet,
ca. 1845, 20¾" w., 29" h. 450.00

American Empire Country-Style Stand

American Empire country-style
2-drawer stand, walnut, oblong
1-board top, apron w/pr. convex-
fronted drawers w/turned wood
pulls, turned & blocked legs,
tapering turned feet, refinished
(ILLUS.)........................ 300.00

Federal 1-drawer stand, tiger stripe
maple, oblong top, apron w/single
drawer w/original brass knob,
square tapering legs, New England, ca. 1810, 18 x 16" top,
18" h. 1,430.00

Federal 2-drawer stand, walnut,
square top, apron w/pr. drawers,
square tapering legs, Virginia, ca.
1800, 19½" w. top 715.00

Federal country-style 1-drawer
stand, cherrywood, square top,
apron w/single drawer, turned
legs, double baluster-turned
feet.......................... 425.00

Federal country-style 1-drawer
stand, maple, oblong top, apron
w/single drawer, ring-turned
tapering legs, early 19th c.,
20" w. top, 29½" h. 245.00

Federal country-style 1-drawer
stand, painted birch & maple, oblong top, apron w/single drawer
w/turned pull, ring- and vase-
turned legs, turnip feet, old red-
brown paint, ca. 1830 .... 300.00

Federal country-style 1-drawer
stand, walnut, square top, apron
w/single drawer within cockbeaded surround, square tapering
legs, 17" sq. top, 28½" h. 600.00

Federal country-style 2-drawer
stand, birch, oblong 1-board top,
apron w/pr. drawers w/(replaced)
brass pulls, turned & reeded legs,
ball feet, 20¾ x 16¾" top,
28" h. 390.00

Federal country-style 2-drawer
stand, tiger stripe maple, plain
oblong top, apron w/pr. drawers
w/turned wood pulls, ring- and
vase-turned legs, tapering
feet.......................... 650.00

Mission-style (Arts & Crafts movement) 2-drawer stand, quarter-
sawn oak, oblong top, apron
w/pr. drawers w/turned pulls,
square tapering legs, attributed to
Gustav Stickley 467.50

Victorian stand, Renaissance Revival
substyle, walnut w/shaped white
marble top, conforming apron, 4
turned post supports & flattened
curved legs joining medial shelf
w/turned center finial, 21 x 17"
top, 29" h..................... 247.50

Victorian Stand

Victorian stand, Gothic Revival
substyle, rosewood w/round
marble slab top (ILLUS.) 1,100.00

Victorian country-style 1-drawer
stand, maple & tiger stripe maple,
square top, apron w/single drawer w/turned pull, ring- and
baluster-turned legs 345.00

Victorian country-style 2-drawer
stand, walnut, oblong top, apron
w/two short drawers, turned legs,
original finish.................. 210.00

William & Mary 1-drawer stand,
walnut, oblong top w/molded
edge, apron w/single drawer,
ring- and vase-turned legs joined
by baluster- and ring-turned
stretchers, Pennsylvania, 1700-40,
25¼ x 17¾" top, 27" h. (top is
early replacement) 1,870.00

STOOLS

Foot stool, American Empire, mahogany, oblong upholstered top,
double cyma-curved legs joined by
baluster-turned medial stretcher,
Philadelphia or New York, ca.
1820-30, 22 x 18¼" top, 15" h. ... 440.00

Foot stool, Louis XV, giltwood, upholstered oblong top, foliate-
carved serpentine apron, short
cabriole legs carved w/stylized
shells, hoof feet, France, 1725-50,
22" l., 12" h. 4,400.00

Foot stool, Mission-style (Arts &
Crafts movement), oak, leather
top, square legs, low stretchers,
attributed to Gustav Stickley, No.
300, 1907 catalogue, 20 x 16½",
15" h. 357.00

Foot stool, Mission-style, oak,
leather-upholstered top, arched
skirt, square legs, w/decal label

of "L. & J.G. Stickley, Fayetteville, New York," ca. 1908, 19 x 15" top, 16" h. 330.00

Foot stool, painted pine, oblong top, scalloped apron, splayed bootjack ends, mustard yellow paint, 14 x 8" top, 7½" h. 45.00

Foot stool, Shaker, twisted rope hemp cord laced top, round tapering legs w/stretchers, original dark stained finish, 14 x 12½" top, 15" h. 75.00

Foot stool, Victorian, rosewood, upholstered oblong top w/beadwork trim, demi-cabriole legs, mid-19th c., 20" l. 300.00

Foot stool, Victorian, upholstered octagonal top, steer's horn legs, 14" w., 8½" h. 45.00

Foot stool, wicker, basketweave-woven seat w/roll-over sides & beadwork apron, wicker-wrapped legs w/X-stretcher, w/label "Wakefield Reed Chair Co., Wakefield, Mass.," late 19th c. 925.00

Organ stool, stained oak, back w/shaped crest above 6 spindles, round seat swiveling in center post, 4 turned legs w/iron claw & glass ball feet 115.00

Organ stool, walnut, back w/plain crestrail above turned spindles, round seat swiveling in center post, cast iron claw & glass ball feet, original finish 170.00

Piano stool, child size, birth, round seat swiveling on center post, 4 turned splayed legs, 9" h. 30.00

American Empire Classical Piano Stool

Piano stool, American Empire, mahogany, carved & turned backrail joined to dolphin-carved siderails, needlepoint upholsterd seat swiveling on boldly-turned

acanthus-carved standard continuing to acanthus-carved tetrapod base w/hairy animal-paw feet, New York or Philadelphia, ca. 1840 (ILLUS.) 440.00

Federal Mahogany Piano Stool

Piano stool, Federal, mahogany, circular padded seat w/reeded seatrail swiveling on threaded support w/acorn drop center & reeded tapering legs, ball feet, now upholstered w/black horsehair & brass tacks, 1810-20, 13½" seat d., 20½" h. (ILLUS.) 1,100.00

Federal stools, mahogany, oblong needlepoint upholstered slip seats, molded seatrails, curule-form legs joined by baluster- and ring-turned stretchers, oblong disc feet, 1815-25, 18¼ x 16" seats, 17" h., pr. 1,210.00

Federal stool, mahogany, upholstered concave seat w/exposed seatrail, curule-form legs joined by ring-turned stretcher w/roundels, brass paw feet, attributed to Duncan Phyfe, New York, ca. 1820, 20 x 16" seat, 17" h. 6,050.00

Queen Anne Stool

Queen Anne stools, walnut, needlework-upholstered slip seats worked in "petit-point" & "gros point" w/figures in landscapes, plain seatrails, cabriole legs, pad feet, England, early 18th c., pr. (ILLUS. of one) 18,700.00

Turn-of-the-Century stool, oak, round seat, bowed legs joined w/stretcher-shelf, ball feet, 15" seat d., 19" h. 25.00

TABLES

American Empire (Classical Revival) card table, mahogny, hinged oblong top w/canted corners swiveling to reveal open well, frieze w/ebony veneer, carved lyre support, fitted w/brass stringing, on acanthus-carved tetrapod w/brass paw feet on casters, New York, ca. 1810 (losses to veneer & some brass stringing) 3,410.00

American Empire card table, mahogany, oblong top w/canted corners swiveling above conformingly shaped frieze, acanthus-carved dolphin standards & acanthus-carved uprights, shaped plinth base on acanthus-carved & gilt & verte-painted dolphin feet on brass casters, New York, ca. 1820, 37" w., 29½" h. 3,850.00

American Empire card table, mahogany, hinged serpentine top w/outset rounded corners above conformingly shaped frieze joining star- and punch-carved posts continuing to vigorously carved rope-twist legs & turned tapering feet on brass casters, original finish, attributed to Portsmouth, New Hampshire, 37¼ x 19" folded-down top, 39" h. 1,000.00

American Empire card table, mahogany w/brass inlay, hinged D-shaped oblong top w/brass-inlaid rosewood crossbanding swiveling above a well w/marbleized paper lining, frieze w/brass-inlaid ebony band, trestle-form base w/reeded supports joined by fluted & ring-turned stretcher, acanthus-carved downswept legs on acanthus-chased brass feet on casters, probably Boston, ca. 1825, 36" w., 29" h. 1,980.00

American Empire dressing table, mahogany, oblong top set w/framed oblong mirror swiveling in acanthus-carved lyre-form support, case w/two short drawers over long drawer, ring-turned &

acanthus-carved legs, tapering feet 2,800.00

American Empire drop-leaf breakfast table, cherrywood & mahogany, D-shaped top w/single oblong drop leaf, ogee-molded frieze, bulbous ring-turned legs, turned feet, 19th c., top opening to 40 x 40", 29" h. 198.00

American Empire drop-leaf breakfast table, mahogany, oblong top flanked by short drop leaves w/canted rounded corners, plain frieze, spirally-turned legs w/ring-turned & tapering feet on casters, Massachusetts, 1820-30, top opening to 48 x 42," 28¾" h. 265.00

American Empire "Drum" Table

American Empire "drum" table, Classical Revival style, mahogany w/gilt-stenciled decor, round top, conforming apron w/four working & 4 false drawers w/gilt-stenciled foliage, acanthus-carved standard & legs ending in animal paw feet on wooden balls, New York, ca. 1830, 47" d., 31" h. (ILLUS.) 2,200.00

American Empire library table w/drop leaves, mahogany w/brass inlay, oblong top w/D-shaped drop leaves, brass & ebony-inlaid frieze, 4 acanthus-carved scrolling supports rising from circular brass-topped base raised on 4 acanthus-carved legs ending in hairy animal paw feet w/casters, New York, ca. 1820, 40 x 39" top, 30" h. (small repairs to top) 1,980.00

American Empire pier table, stenciled & gilt mahogany w/marble top, oblong veined dark marble top above frieze stenciled w/florals & leaves, stenciled turned heavy columns & gilt pilasters flanking mirrored back & stenciled w/"fleur-de-lis" & lyre device above shaped stretcher-shelf, gilt winged hairy-paw feet, ca. 1815, 36" w., 37" h. (marble top w/crack) 2,420.00

American Empire pier table, mahogany w/white marble top, oblong marble slab top, plain frieze supported by columns w/Corinthian capitals & w/mirror plate behind, shaped plinth on acanthus-carved feet, Philadelphia, 1825-35, 40" w., 37" h. .... 1,000.00 to 2,500.00

Art Nouveau 2-Tier Table

Art Nouveau 2-tier table, fruitwood marquetry, lobed top & undertier inlaid in various fruitwoods w/chrysanthemum blossoms & leafage, cylindrical legs w/flaring feet, signed "Galle" in marquetry, ca. 1900, 35" w., 28¾" h. (ILLUS.) 1,870.00

Art Nouveau 2-tier tea table, inlaid wood w/ormolu mounts, oblong top w/ormolu handles at each end & shaped undertier inlaid w/waterlilies, undulating molded legs, signed "L. Marjorelle" in marquetry, Nancy, France, ca. 1905, 36½ x 24¼" top, 31¼" h. 2,860.00

Art Nouveau 3-tier table, fruitwood marquetry, cartouche-form top inlaid w/dragonfly & poppy blossoms raised on 4 serpentine legs centering a larger lower shelf inlaid w/arrowroot & poppy buds, signed "Galle" in marquetry, France, ca. 1900, 26¾" w., 34" h. (missing lowest shelf) 1,045.00

Biedermeier console table, fruitwood, oblong top, deep apron w/single drawer, scrolling supports centering a wooden backboard, canted base, Germany, 1800-50, 31 x 12½" top, 33" h. 330.00

Biedermeier work table, mahogany & fruitwood marquetry, circular top centered w/artist-signed "gouache" of wedding party in landscape, conforming frieze w/single drawer veneered w/palmettes, columnar supports w/scrolling H-shaped stretcher, Germany, 1825-50, 20½" w., 30½" h. 1,925.00

Billiard table, Brunswick-Balke-Colland Co., "Monarch Cushion" slate-top, leather pockets, w/cue rack & ball rack 450.00

Butcher's cutting block table, round maple slab top, 3 heavy turned legs, 29" d., 26" h. ...... 155.00 to 355.00

Chair-table, painted finish, round top tilting on mortised & pinned chair frame w/one-board seat & sides, shoe feet, scrubbed top, original dark blue paint on base, New York, 1780-1800 .... 3,500.00

Child's work table, painted finish, oblong top w/low three-quarter gallery & wide overhang, apron w/single drawer w/turned wood pull, ring- and baluster-turned legs, tapering feet, early blue paint, Pennsylvania Amish origins 800.00

Chippendale card table, mahogany, oblong hinged top w/molded edge above apron w/single drawer & gadroon-carved edge, cabriole legs, claw-and-ball feet, Philadelphia, ca. 1770, 36" w., 29½" h. 4,950.00

Chippendale drop-leaf dining table, mahogany, oblong top flanked by oblong drop leaves, cyma-curved shaped apron, cabriole legs, claw-and-ball feet, Massachusetts, ca. 1770, top opening to 46½ x 45½", 28" h. (restoration to molding one end) 12,100.00

Chippendale drop-leaf dining table, mahogany, oblong top flanked by oblong drop leaves, plain apron, square legs, Marlboro feet, Pennsylvania, ca. 1770, top opening to 52½ x 42", 28¾" h. 2,530.00

Chippendale tilt-top tea table, cherrywood, scalloped square top tilting & revolving above birdcage support on ring- and flattened ball-turned standard, cabriole tripod, claw-and-ball feet, attributed to Eliphalet Chapin, East Windsor, Connecticut, 28" h. 12,650.00

Chippendale tilt-top tea table, mahogany, round top tilting & revolving above birdcage support on urn-shaped standard, acanthus-

carved downswept tripod, claw-
and-ball feet, New York, ca.
1775, 32" d., 28" h. 3,190.00

Chippendale Tilt-Top Tea Table

Chippendale tilt-top tea table,
mahogany, round top w/piecrust
edge tilting & revolving above
birdcage support on ring- and
flattened ball-turned standard,
acanthus-carved cabriole tripod,
claw-and-ball feet, Philadelphia,
ca. 1770, w/engraved plaque on
underside listing owners, 1741-
1942, 32" d., 28" h. (ILLUS.) 41,250.00
Chippendale tray-top tea table,
mahogany, oblong-top w/molded
edge & cusped corners above
plain apron w/convex-molded
edge, cabriole legs w/shell-carved
knees, claw-and-ball feet, New
York, 1750-80, 32 x 20¼" top,
27" h. (restoration to one foot
& 2 moldings) 49,500.00

Chinese Chippendale Table

Chippendale "Chinese" table, mahogany, oblong top, plain frieze
carved w/crosshatching at lower
edge & pierced brackets joining
stop-fluted square tapering legs
w/Marlboro feet (ILLUS.) 22,000.00

Tortoise Shell Sewing Table

English Regency sewing table, tortoise shell & ivory, hinged lid
opening to tapering body on
square standard w/canted corners
& concave-sided molded base,
veneered overall w/tortoise shell
panels within ivory borders, England, 1800-25, 15¼ x 14" top,
28½" h. (ILLUS.) 3,575.00
English Regency writing table, cala-
mander wood, oblong top
w/shaped corners w/inset tooled
leather writing surface, conforming frieze w/pr. working drawers
front & false drawers reverse,
trestle base w/downswept legs
ending in brass casters, gilt-
bronze circular knop handles on
drawers, England, early 19th c.,
36½ x 23½" top, 29" h. 13,200.00

Federal Banquet Table

Federal 2-part banquet table, cherrywood, shaped D-form top w/deep
oblong drop leaf one side, conforming plain frieze, ring- and
rope-twist turned legs, tapering
feet on casters, top opening to
103 x 47½" (ILLUS.) 1,265.00
Federal card table, inlaid mahog-
any, hinged oblong top w/bowed
front & line-inlaid edge above
conforming apron centering a

flame-birch veneer panel & smaller panels at dies, line-inlaid square tapering legs, Massachusetts, 1790-1810, 36" w., 29½" h. 825.00

Federal card table, inlaid mahogany, hinged oblong top w/serpentine front & outset rounded corners above conforming apron w/three flame-birch inlaid panels & demi-lune band, reeded tapering legs & tapering feet, attributed to the School of John and/or Thomas Seymour, Boston, Massachusetts, 36½" w., 29½" h. (repair to one leg) 6,050.00

Federal card table, inlaid mahogany, hinged oblong top w/bowed front, serpentine sides & crossbanded edges, conforming apron w/inlaid dies centering a checkerband oval reserve, line-inlaid square tapering legs, Massachusetts, ca. 1800, 36" w., 30½" h...3,410.00

Federal console table, mahogany, D-shaped top painted to simulate marble, plain apron w/reeded pilasters, acanthus-carved & reeded tapering legs, tapering cuffed feet, attributed to Henry Connelly, Philadelphia, ca. 1800, 51" w., 34½" h. (replaced painted top simulates original marble top) ..26,400.00

Federal "accordion-action" dining table, mahogany, round top w/accordion-action on 8 fluted legs extending to large oval, Rhode Island, 1810-20 ....9,900.00

Federal drop-leaf dining table, painted & decorated, oblong top w/oblong drop leaves, plain apron, square legs, overall shaded brown painted graining finish, New England, 1800-20, top opening to 41½ x 40", 27" h. 1,430.00

Federal dressing table, mahogany, oblong top w/outset rounded corners supporting oblong framed mirror on S-supports above case w/arrangement of 3 short drawers over long drawer flanked by ring-turned corner columns continuing to ring-turned & reeded legs joined by medial stretcher-shelf & ending in brass ball feet, School of Duncan Phyfe, New York, ca. 1815 ....2,970.00

Federal Pembroke table, cherrywood, oblong top flanked by oblong drop leaves, apron w/single cockbeaded drawer, square tapering legs w/cross-stretcher, 39 x 33" extended top, 27" h. (restoration to stretcher) 660.00

Federal Pembroke table, cherrywood, oblong top w/shaped ends flanked by shaped drop leaves, plain apron, square tapering legs w/X-stretcher, Massachusetts, ca. 1810 ....1,450.00

Federal Pembroke Table

Federal Pembroke table, curly maple, oblong top w/serpentine ends flanked by serpentine oblong drop leaves, apron w/single drawer, molded square tapering legs, New England, ca. 1800, 35½ x 35" extended top, 28¾" h. (ILLUS.).....4,125.00

Federal Pembroke table, inlaid mahogany, oblong top w/rounded ends & line-inlaid edges flanked by D-shaped drop leaves, apron w/single drawer, bookend-inlaid dies & icicle-inlaid square tapering legs, New England, ca. 1800, 39 x 31" extended top, 28" h. 4,950.00

Federal Pembroke table, tiger stripe maple, oblong top flanked by shaped drop leaves, plain apron, square tapering legs, medium size 4,400.00

Federal Serving Table

Federal serving table, mahogany, oblong top w/reeded edge, frieze w/pr. short drawers over long drawer flanked by reeded dies continuing to ring-turned & reeded tapering legs joined by medial shelf, brass ball feet, New York, ca. 1805, some restoration to shelf, 36 x 19½" top, 36" h. (ILLUS.) 4,400.00

Federal work table, inlaid mahogany, oblong top w/outset rounded corners, apron w/two short drawers w/checker-line inlaid borders & w/slide fitted for sewing basket below flanked by ring-turned colonettes continuing to reeded tapering legs & feet, Boston, Massachusetts, ca. 1805, 18½ x 15" top, 30" h. 18,700.00

Federal work table, mahogany, square top w/molded edge, apron w/two cockbeaded short drawers, ring-turned & reeded tapering legs on brass casters, School of Duncan Phyfe, New York, ca. 1810, 18½" w., 30" h. 4,730.00

Federal country-style dressing table, painted finish, oblong top w/shaped three-quarter gallery set w/pr. recessed drawers, apron w/single long drawer, turned legs, worn grey paint 375.00

Federal country-style dressing table, painted & decorated pine, oblong top w/molded edge & scroll-earred splashboard, apron w/single long drawer w/mushroom-turned pulls, turned legs, flattened ball feet, free-hand florals, fruit & foliage on black & red painted graining w/gilt stenciling & yellow pin striping . . . .625.00 to 775.00

Federal country-style drop-leaf dining table, cherrywood, oblong top w/deep drop leaves, plain apron, 6 fluted tapering legs, ca. 1840 . . . 900.00

Federal country-style drop-leaf dining table, curly maple, oblong top w/deep drop leaves, plain apron, 6 turned legs continuing to turned feet. . . . . .600.00 to 800.00

Federal country-style Pembroke table, cherrywood, oblong top w/oblong drop leaves, plain dovetailed apron w/swinging leaf supports, square tapering legs, 41 x 38¾" extended top, 28¼" h. 575.00

Federal country-style work table, butternut, removable 2-board top w/wide overhang, apron w/small central drawer flanked by short drawers, baluster-turned legs, turnip feet, worn finish w/traces of

old red, ca. 1840, 59 x 34" top, 29" h. 525.00

Federal country-style work table, walnut, 2-board top w/wide overhang, plain apron w/single drawer, ring- and baluster-turned legs, turnip feet, on casters, 60 x 38" top 800.00

Harvest table, birch, oblong 1-board top w/drop leaves, ring- and baluster-turned legs, tapering feet, refinished, 108 x 20" top w/9½" l. drop leaves, 29" h. 3,000.00

Harvest table, birch & cherrywood, oblong top flanked by short drop leaves, plain apron, ring- and baluster-turned bulbous legs, turned tapering feet, 108" l. 4,700.00

Hutch Table

Hutch table, maple, round top tilting above well, sides of base w/bootjack ends on chip-carved shoe feet, w/traces of early red stain, 1740-60, 46" d., 27" h. (ILLUS.) 9,350.00

Hutch table, pine, 2-board oblong top pinned to chair base w/lift-lid in seat & sides continuing to form cut-out feet, very worn old brown painted graining, 48 x 33¾" top, 39½" h. 900.00

Hutch table, pine & cherrywood, oval top tilting above oblong seat fitted between scrolling armrests on block- and baluster-turned legs joined by turned stretchers, 51" w. top 1,870.00

Hutch table, pine, 3-board round top pivoting on shoe-foot base w/lift-lid in seat 4,840.00

Louis XVI writing table, mahogany w/ormolu mounts, oblong ormolu-banded hinged top opening to form fabric-lined writing surface over 3 frieze drawers w/ormolu keyhole escutcheons, raised on shaped trestle supports centering ormolu rosettes, on casters,

France, 1750-75, 49½ x 29½" top,
28½" h. 16,500.00

Table by Limbert & Co.

Mission-style (Arts & Crafts movement) center table, oak, oval top,
shaped apron, wide flaring supports w/cut-out sections joined by
oblong lower shelf, Limbert & Co.,
ca. 1910, 45 x 30" oval top, 29" h.
(ILLUS.) 770.00
Mission-style (Arts & Crafts move-
ment) occasional table, oak,
round top, 4-spindle sides joined
by medial shelf to form shoe-foot
base, red decal label of Gustav
Stickley, ca. 1905, 30¾" d.,
29¾" h. 3,520.00
Mission-style (Arts & Crafts move-
ment) serving table, oak, oblong
top w/shaped three-quarter gallery, apron w/two short drawers,
straight legs w/stretcher-shelf,
signed Gustav Stickley, 38½ x 18"
top, 39" h. 990.00

Table by L. & J. G. Stickley

Mission-style (Arts & Crafts movement) trestle base table, oak,
oblong top, side supports joined
by oblong shelf, decal label of
L. & J.G. Stickley, No. 596,
ca. 1910 (ILLUS.) 1,100.00

Queen Anne Card Table

Queen Anne "turret-top" card table,
walnut, folding hinged porringer-
shaped top, apron w/single drawer & shaped drop pendant, cabriole legs w/high slipper feet,
probably Rhode Island, 1720-40,
w/old repair to one rear leg, 34 x
29" top, 28¾" h. (ILLUS.) 33,000.00
Queen Anne card table, walnut,
hinged oblong top above plain
apron w/single cockbeaded drawer, cabriole legs, paneled trifid
feet, Pennsylvania, ca. 1770 . . . . .4,675.00
Queen Anne corner table w/half-
round drop leaf, walnut, triangular top w/hinged half-round
drop leaf, shaped apron, circular
tapering legs, pad feet, Southern,
1750-70, 43" w., 29" h. (top
opening to 39" l.) 7,425.00
Queen Anne drop-leaf breakfast
table, cherrywood, oblong top
flanked by oblong drop leaves,
shaped apron, cabriole legs, pad
feet, New England, ca. 1750,
36 x 35" extended top, 28" h. 9,625.00

Queen Anne Table by Townsend

Queen Anne drop-leaf dining table,
maple & birchwood, oblong top
w/D-shaped drop leaves, cyma-
shaped apron, turned tapering
legs, pad feet, by John Townsend,

Newport, Rhode Island, ca. 1755,
59 x 54" extended top, 27" h.
(ILLUS.) 10,450.00
Queen Anne drop-leaf dining table,
walnut, oblong top w/half-round
drop leaves, scalloped apron,
cabriole legs w/shell-carved
knees, stockinged trifid feet,
Pennsylvania, 1740-70, 48½ x 41"
extended top, 28½" h. 20,900.00
Queen Anne tea table, painted &
decorated, square top tilting
above baluster-turned standard,
cabriole tripod, pad feet, overall red & brown-painted graining,
New England, ca. 1790, 22" sq.
top, 27" h. 1,760.00
Queen Anne tray-top table, cherrywood, oblong top w/molded edge,
shaped apron, cabriole legs, slipper feet (possible restoration to
legs) 26,400.00
Saloon card table, Turn-of-the-
Century, oblong top, plain apron,
turned legs w/wrought iron mug
holders attached to each, 42 x 31"
top 850.00
"Sawbuck" table, pine, 1-board top
w/breadboard ends, X-bar base
w/flattened stretchers made to fit
top, 50½ x 28¼" top, 27¼" h. 395.00
Shaker drop-leaf dining table, birch
w/bird's eye maple drawer front,
oblong top flanked by oblong
drop leaves, apron w/single
drawer w/turned pull at one end,
turned tapering legs, button feet,
Alfred, Maine 1,870.00
Shaker drop-leaf dining table,
cherrywood oblong top w/oblong
drop leaves, maple apron w/draw-
er & turned legs w/bulbous-turned
feet, 1850-1900 ....1,575.00

Shaker Side Table

Shaker side table, maple, square
top, apron w/single drawer,
turned tapering legs w/bulbous
turning above tapering feet, Canterbury, New Hampshire, ca.
1830, refinished w/traces of old
red paint, 20½ x 19" top, 30" h.
(ILLUS.)...................... 935.00
Tavern table, Queen Anne, curly
maple, oval top, shaped apron,
turned legs, pad feet, 1740-60,
39" oval top, 26½" h. 15,400.00
Tavern table, Queen Anne, maple,
oval top, plain apron, turned
tapering legs, pad feet, New England, 1750-80, 39½ x 30½" top,
26" h. 5,775.00

Victorian Renaissance Revival Dining Table

Victorian dining table, Renaissance
Revival substyle, walnut, round
extension top, octagonal pedestal
w/scrolling tetrapod w/applied
roundels on casters, 48" d.
(ILLUS.) ....950.00 to 1,200.00
Victorian parlor center table, rococo
substyle, pierce-carved rosewood
w/white marble turtle-shaped slab
top, apron w/pierce-carved grape
clusters & medallions, cabriole
legs joined by serpentine cross-
stretcher centered w/floral urn,
attributed to John Henry Belter,
New York, New York, ca. 1855,
medium to large size 15,950.00
Victorian parlor center table, Early
Victorian, walnut w/brown-veined
round marble slab top, apron
w/scroll & floral carvings, octagonal pedestal acanthus,
gadroon & flute-carved pedestal
w/animal paw feet, large........ 935.00
Wallace Nutting signed trestle base
table, pine top, maple base, 50 x
30" top, 30½" h. 350.00

(End of Furniture Section)

GAMES

Peter Pan Tiddledy Winks

Airplane Express board game, Milton Bradley, No. 4609 . . . . $25.00

Alee-Oop, wooden playing pieces in cardboard cylinder, Roy-Toy Company, New York, 1939 . . . . 17.50

Anagrams, McLoughlin Bros., pre-1920. . . . . 22.00

Ancient Game of China (Mag Jong), boxed & complete, Milton Bradley, No. 4502 . . . . 45.00

Archie Bunker card game 10.00

Barney Google & Spark Plug game board, original box, Milton Bradley, 1923 (dice cup missing) 55.00

Baseball pinball game, glass top, metal balls 12.00

Billy Whiskers board game, complete w/brass-bound counters, spinners & instruction sheet & box, Saalfield Publishing Co., 1923-26. . . . . 50.00

Calling All Cars board game, complete w/metal cars, spinner, playing pieces & box, Parker Bros., 1938 . . . . 30.00

Chiromagica, magnetic discs at center direct pointer under glass to correct answer around perimeter, McLoughlin Bros., late 19th c., 11¾" sq. . . . . 165.00 to 265.00

Cribbage board, wooden, complete w/pegs & w/gutta percha case, 1860 . . . . 125.00

Dominoes, inlaid ebony tiles, miniature size, ca. 1900 . . . . 25.00

Dominoes, white celluloid tiles w/black dots, original box 45.00

Eddie Cantor's New Game - Tell It To The Judge board game, complete w/playing pieces, dice, cards & original box, Parker Bros., 1936 . . . . 25.00 to 45.00

Fairies Cauldron Tiddledy Winks, snap chips into wooden cauldron hanging from tripod, original box, Parker Bros., ca. 1925 . . . . 37.50

Fan-Tel Fortune Telling, 48 wooden sticks & 2 instruction sheets in cardboard cylinder, Schoenhut, 1937 . . . . 8.00

Frog Who Would A Wooing Go

board game, original box w/chromolithographed frog in 18th c. attire, United Game Co. 95.00

Game of Fish Pond, original box, McLoughlin Bros., 1890's . . . 48.00 to 55.00

Get My Goat wooden puzzle blocks game, original box, 1914 . . . . 32.00

Government Game, complete in original box, Milton Bradley, 1939 15.00

Hearts dice game, 1914 . . . . 10.00

Hop Ching Checker Game, Pressman Toy Corp., 1930's 16.50

Lotto card game, McLoughlin Bros., ca. 1900 . . . . 12.00 to 15.00

Lucky Strike bean bag toss game 85.00

Mah Jong, complete w/celluloid tiles & markers in black wooden box w/gilt chinoiserie decor, 1930's 45.00

Peter Pan Tiddledy Winks, complete w/chips & cup & original box, Whitman Publ. Co., 1930's (ILLUS.). 12.00

Popeye Pipe Toss Game

Popeye Pipe Toss, original box, King Features Syndicate, 1935 (ILLUS.). 35.00

Sergeant Preston Game

Sergeant Preston board game, original box, Milton Bradley (ILLUS.) . . 15.00

GLASS

ACORN

This pattern was made in a limited number of pieces in both opaque and translucent colored glass. Resembling the fruit of the oak tree, after which it is named, this glass is thought to have been first produced at Hobbs Glass Co., Wheeling, West Virginia, about 1890 and was later made by the Beaumont Glass Co., Martins Ferry, Ohio. Collectors are alerted to the fact that the more plentiful salt shakers are sometimes ground down and offered for sale as toothpick holders, somewhat scarcer in this pattern.

Salt shaker w/original top, blue opaque	$50.00
Salt shaker w/original top, chartreuse opaque	55.00
Salt shaker w/original top, white opaque	45.00
Salt & pepper shakers w/original tops, pink shading to white opaque, pr. ....65.00 to	100.00
Sugar shaker w/original top, black amethyst	115.00
Sugar shaker w/original top, blue opaque, w/gold spattered decor	90.00
Sugar shaker w/original top, cranberry	95.00
Sugar shaker w/original top, pink shading to white opaque	125.00
Syrup pitcher w/original top, emerald green translucent	125.00
Syrup pitcher w/original top, pink	160.00
Toothpick holder, pink shading to white opaque	65.00
Toothpick holder, pink shading to white opaque, w/enameled decor	75.00

AGATA

Agata was patented by Joseph Locke of the New England Glass Co., in 1887. The application of a mineral stain left a mottled effect on the surface of the article. It was applied chiefly to the Wild Rose (Peach Blow) line but sometimes was applied as a border on pale opaque green. In production for a short time, it is scarce. Items listed below are of the Wild Rose line unless otherwise noted.

Bowl, 5¼" d., 2½" h., fluted rim	$970.00
Bowl, 8" d., 3 1/8" h., green opaque	1,475.00
Celery vase, 6¼" h.	1,000.00

Cruet w/original stopper, green opaque, 5¾" h.	795.00
Mustard pot w/silverplate top, green opaque, 3" h. ....450.00 to	525.00
Mustard pot w/silverplate top	1,295.00
Punch cup, green opaque	275.00
Toothpick holder	495.00

Agata Tumbler

Tumbler (ILLUS.)	650.00
Tumbler, green opaque ....550.00 to	875.00

AKRO AGATE

Scottie Dog Powder Jar

This marbled ware was made by the Akro Agate Company in Clarksburg, West Va., between 1932 and 1951 and most articles bear on the reverse side the likeness of a crow flying through a capital letter A. The majority of these pieces were small.

Ash tray, oval, marbleized blue swirls in white opaque	$8.00
Cup, child's playtime item, Chiquita patt., lilac opaque	25.00

Cup, child's playtime item, Interior
Panel patt., lemonade &
oxblood 14.00
Cup, child's playtime item, Oc-
tagonal O patt., lemonade &
oxblood 27.00
Cup & saucer, child's playtime item,
marbleized orange swirls in white
opaque 12.00
Plate, 4¼" d., child's playtime item,
Octagonal O patt., lemonade &
oxblood 20.00
Plate, child's playtime item, Interior
Panel patt., lemonade &
oxblood 14.00
Powder jar, Colonial lady cover,
white opaque 38.00
Powder jar, Scottie dog cover, Nile
green opaque (ILLUS.) 55.00
Smoking set: match holder & four 3"
ash trays; marbleized blue swirls
in white opaque, 5 pcs. 24.00
Tea set, child's playtime item: cov.
teapot & 2 c/s; green opaque,
5 pcs. 35.00
Tea set, child's playtime item: cov.
teapot, creamer, sugar bowl & 4
c/s; Chiquita patt., green opaque,
11 pcs. in original box 65.00
Tea set, child's playtime item: cov.
teapot, creamer, cov. sugar bowl,
4 c/s & 4 plates; Concentric patt.,
15 pcs. in assorted
colors . . . . .68.00 to 85.00
Tea set, child's playtime item, Chiq-
uita patt., cobalt blue, 22 pcs. 85.00
Tumblers, child's playtime item, Octagonal patt., 2 lime & 2 white
opaque, set of 4 . . . .   20.00
Water set, child's playtime item:
pitcher & 6 tumblers; Stippled
Band patt., transparent green,
7 pcs. 65.00

ALEXANDRITE

*This glass, shading from a yellowish color
to rose to blue, was produced by Thomas
Webb & Sons and Stevens & Williams of
England. A somewhat similar ware was made
by Moser of Carlsbad.*

Bottle w/matching stopper, ovoid
w/faceted base extending up ⅓
sides to form flat plane,
10½" h. $375.00
Finger bowl & matching underplate,
crimped rims, 5" d. bowl &
6½" d. plate, pr. 945.00
Spooner, cylindrical w/piecrust-
crimped collar, Expanded Dia-

mond patt. interior, Thomas Webb
& Sons, 3" d., 4¼" h. 645.00
Tazza, pedestal foot, Honeycomb
patt., 5½" d., 2" h. 795.00
Vase, 2¾" h., Honeycomb patt.,
Webb 1,250.00
Vase, 3" h., 2½" d., folded over
star-shaped top, Honeycomb patt.,
Webb 595.00
Wine, Honeycomb patt., Webb,
4½" h. 750.00

AMBERINA

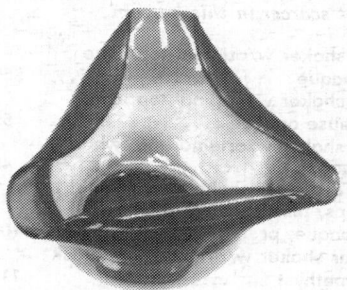

Amberina Bowl

*Amberina was devised by the New
England Glass Company, and pressed
Amberina was made by Hobbs, Brockunier
& Company (under a license from the former) and by other glass factories. A similar
ware called Rose Amber was made by Mt.
Washington Glass Works. The glass shades
from amber to red. Cut and plated Amberina also were made. About the turn of this
century and again in the 1920's, the Libbey
Glass Co. made some Amberina.*

Basket, corset-shaped body w/flar-
ing fan-shaped rim & applied
amber loop handle, signed Libbey,
7½" h. to top of rim $1,400.00
Berry set: master bowl & twelve
5" d. sauce dishes; pressed Daisy
& Button (101) patt., Hobbs,
Brockunier & Co., 13 pcs. 1,000.00
Bowl, 6" w., 3½" h., tricornered
w/folded rim (ILLUS.) 275.00
Bowl, 7" h., 4-footed, melon-
ribbed 325.00
Bowl, 10 x 8½" oblong, pressed
Daisy & Button (101) patt., Hobbs,
Brockunier & Co. 250.00
Castor set, 6 etched bottles in
silverplate frame w/tap bell
top, overall 20" h. 1,950.00
Celery vase, scalloped top, Diamond
Quilted patt., New England Glass
Co., 7" h. 375.00

Cordial, applied clear handles,
enameled floral decor 85.00
Creamer, flattened bulbous bottom,
applied amber handle, Inverted
Thumbprint patt., 2½" h. 165.00
Creamer, applied clear reeded han-
dle, Inverted Thumbprint patt.,
4½" h. 125.00
Cruet w/original amber facet-cut
stopper, applied amber handle,
New England Glass Co., 3" d.,
6¾" h. 250.00
Cruet w/original stopper, Rose
Amber, Mt. Washington Glass
Co. 325.00
Cruet w/faceted stopper, Reverse
Amberina, applied clear ribbon
handle, Diamond Quilted patt. . . . 185.00

Amberina Assortment

Cruet w/original amber facet-cut
stopper, applied amber handle,
Inverted Thumbprint patt. (ILLUS.
right) . . . . 310.00 to 450.00
Curtain tiebacks, pewter shanks, at-
tributed to Boston & Sandwich
Glass Co., 3½" d., pr. 68.00
Cuspidor, hourglass-shaped, ruffled
edge 275.00
Dish, canoe-shaped, pressed Daisy &
Button (101) patt., Hobbs, Brock-
unier & Co., late 19th c., 8" l. 500.00
Finger bowl, Baby Inverted Thumb-
print patt. (ILLUS. left front) 225.00

Hobbs, Brockunier & Co. "101" Pattern

Ice cream dish, pressed Daisy & Button (101) patt., Hobbs, Brockunier
& Co., 6" w. (ILLUS.) 150.00

Jar, cov., Honeycomb patt., Thomas
Webb, 3¾" h. 350.00
Lemonade mug, applied amber
handle, Inverted Thumbprint
patt. .70.00 to 95.00
Model of a pear, 3¾" h. 125.00
Mug, applied amber handle, Dia-
mond Quilted patt., 2¾" h. 110.00
Mugs, applied twisted handles,
Honeycomb patt., set of 6 . . . . 450.00
Mustard jar w/pewter hinged lid
(ILLUS. center front w/assort-
ment) 120.00
Parfait, New England Glass Co.,
3 5/8" h. 135.00
Perfume bottle w/original long-
daubered stopper, bulbous,
signed Libbey & w/original paper
label, 3½" d., 4¾" h. 585.00
Pitcher, 5" h., bulbous, applied
amber reeded handle, Reverse
Amberina, Diamond Quilted
patt. . . . . .200.00 to 225.00
Pitcher, 7½" h., applied amber
reeded handle, square mouth, Inverted Thumbprint patt., New
England Glass Co. (ILLUS. center
rear w/assortment) 275.00
Pitcher, water 9½" h., applied
amber handle, enameled apple
blossom branches, leaves & buds,
Mt. Washington 525.00
Punch cup, applied amber reeded
handle, Expanded Diamond
patt. .75.00 to 90.00
Punch cup, applied amber reeded
handle, Inverted Thumbprint patt.,
2 5/8" . . . . .110.00 to 150.00
Salt & pepper shakers w/original
tops, Inverted Thumbprint patt.,
pr. (mold flaw on salt) 135.00
Shade for hanging kerosene lamp,
Plated Amberina, ruffled top,
14" d. 2,750.00
Spooner, Inverted Thumbprint patt.,
4¾" 200.00
Spooner, pressed Daisy & Button
(101) patt., Hobbs, Brockunier &
Co. . . . . .200.00 to 350.00
Syrup jug w/ornate silverplate top
w/hinged lid & loop handle, Baby
Thumbprint patt., New England
Glass Co., late 19th c., 5½" h. . . . 525.00
Toothpick holder, Baby Inverted
Thumbprint patt., Rose Amber,
Mt. Washington 175.00
Toothpick holder, tricornered, Baby
Inverted Thumbprint patt. 245.00
Toothpick holder, 3-footed, pressed
Daisy & Button (101) patt., Hobbs,
Brockunier & Co. . . . . .175.00 to 195.00
Toothpick holder, square top, Vene-
tian Diamond patt. 175.00

Toothpick holder, tricornered top,
Libbey, 2 1/8" h. 200.00
Tumbler, Expanded Diamond patt. . . 175.00
Tumbler, Inverted Thumbprint
patt. . . . . .85.00 to 100.00
Tumbler, Swirl patt., New England
Glass Co., 2½" d., 3¾" h. 95.00
Tumbler, Plated Amberina 900.00
Tumbler, whiskey, Diamond Quilted
patt., New England Glass Co.,
2 1/8" d., 2 5/8" h. . . . . . .95.00 to 135.00
Tumble-up (water carafe w/tumbler
top), Inverted Thumbprint patt.,
attributed to New England Glass
Co., 6" h. 500.00
Vase, 4" h., ovoid on flat base,
Drape patt. 150.00
Vase, 4" h., bulbous w/square top,
Inverted Thumbprint patt. 125.00
Vase, 4½" h., flared & ruffled rim,
signed Libbey 175.00
Vase, 4¾" h., 5¼" widest d., flori-
form w/five-scallop rim, signed
Libbey, ca. 1917 . . . . 565.00
Vase, 5 7/8" h., 4 1/8" d., egg-
shaped, scalloped top, enameled
pink & white florals & branches
decor 195.00
Vase, 7½" h., lily form, signed
Libbey 400.00
Vase, 7¾" h., Inverted Thumbprint
patt. (ILLUS. left rear w/assort-
ment) 125.00
Vase, 8½" h., 3" d., trumpet-
shaped, scalloped top, in silver-
plate handled stand 110.00
Vase, 9¼" h., lily form, optic-
ribbed 350.00
Vases, 12¾" h., 5½" d., applied
amber feet, ruffled rim, encrusted
dull Roman gold lilies & leaves
decor, pr. 439.00
Vase, 16" h., trumpet-shaped, optic-
ribbed, Rose Amber, Mt. Wash-
ington 1,250.00
Water set: 8¼" h. pitcher w/applied
clear handle & 6 tumblers; Diamond Quilted patt., New England
Glass Co., late 19th c., 7 pcs. 770.00

ANIMALS

*Americans evidently like to collect glass
animals and for the past fifty years, American glass manufacturers have turned out a
wide variety of animals to please the buying
public. Some were produced for long periods
and some were later reproduced by other companies, while others were made for only a
short period of time and are rare. We have not*

*included late reproductions in our listings and
have attempted to date the productions where
possible. Evelyn Zemel's book, "American
Glass Animals A to Z," will be helpful to the
novice collector. Also see STEUBEN.*

Kingfisher Flower Frog

Angel Fish bookends, clear, A. H.
Heisey & Co., 3½ x 2¼" wave
base, 7" h., pr. $169.00
Asiatic Pheasant, clear, A. H.
Heisey & Co., 1944-45, 7¼" l.,
10¼" h. 235.00
Baby Chick, clear, New Martinsville
Glass Mfg. Co., 1" h. 35.00
Bird of Paradise, clear, Duncan &
Miller Glass Co., 13½" l.,
8½" h. 400.00
Bunnies, clear, ears up, ears back
or ears lying down, New Martins-
ville Glass Mfg. Co., 1", each 45.00
Chicks, clear, heads up or heads
down, A. H. Heisey & Co.,
1948-49, 1", each 75.00
Chinese Pheasants, ice blue, Paden
City Glass Mfg. Co., 13¾" l.,
5¾" h., pr. 160.00
Clydesdale Horse, clear, A. H.
Heisey & Co., 1942-48, 8" l.,
8" h. 295.00
Deer standing, blue, Fostoria Glass
Co., 2 x 1" base, 4½" h. 33.00
Donkey standing, clear, A. H.
Heisey & Co., 1944-53, 4¼" l.
base, 6½" h. 215.00
Duckling floating, clear, A. H.
Heisey & Co., 1947-49, 2¼" h. 109.00
Elephant w/trunk up, clear, A. H.
Heisey & Co., 1944-53, large,
6½" l., 4¼" h. 265.00
Elephant bookends, clear, Fostoria
Glass Co., 1938-44, 5¾ x 3" base,
7¾" h., pr. 125.00
Gazelle bookends, clear, New Mar-
tinsville Glass Mfg. Co., 8½" h.,
pr. 135.00

Horse Head bookend, clear, A. H.
Heisey & Co., 1937-55, 4¼ x 2¾"
base, 7¼" h. (single) . . . . .95.00 to 125.00
Horse Head cigarette box & cover
w/horsehead finial, clear, A. H.
Heisey & Co., 4 x 3¼", 3½" h. . . .   55.00
Horse jumping bookends, clear, K.
R. Haley, 1947, 9¼" l., 7¼" h.,
pr. 58.00
Horse rearing bookend, clear,
Fostoria Glass Co., 3 x 5" base,
6" l., 7½" h. (single) 35.00
Horse rearing bookend, clear, New
Martinsville Glass Mfg. Co., 5¼ x
3¼" base, 5¾" l., 8" h. (single) . .   95.00
Horse rearing bookend, clear, L. E.
Smith, 1940's, 3 x 5½" base,
5¾" l., 8" h. (single) 18.00
Horse rearing bookend, dark blue,
L. E. Smith, 1940's, 3 x 5½" base,
5¾" l., 8" h. (single) 50.00
Kingfisher (bird) flower frog pierced
w/ten holes, clear, A. H. Heisey &
Co., 4¾" base d. (ILLUS.) 200.00
Rooster Head cocktail shaker, clear,
A. H. Heisey & Co., 3-piece
w/strainer in first section,
14½" h. . . . . .57.00 to 85.00
Sea Horse handled cigarette jar &
cover w/scallope shell finial,
Waverly patt., clear, A. H. Heisey
& Co., 5½" h. 175.00
Viking Duck ash tray w/slot for
cigarette in head & slot for book
matches in tail, flamingo, A. H.
Heisey & Co., 3¼ x 2¼" base,
overall 4¾" l. 149.00

APPLIQUED

Stevens & Williams Rose Bowl

*Simply stated, this is an art glass form with
applied decoration. Sometimes master glass
craftsmen applied stems or branches to an art
glass object and then added molded glass
flowers or fruit specimens to these branches
or stems. At other times, a button of molten*

*glass was daubed on the object and a tool
pressed over it to form a prunt in the form
of a raspberry, rosette or other shape. Always
the work of a skilled glassmaker, applied
decoration can be found on both cased (2-
layer) and single layer glass. The English firm
of Stevens and Williams is renowned for the
appliqued glass they produced.*

Basket, applied clear twisted thorn
handle, vaseline opalescent Stripe
patt., 3 applied pink flowers on
vaseline branches, 6½" d.,
8¼" h. $225.00
Bowl, 6" d., 2 5/8" h., cranberry
w/applied clear "mat-su-noke"
branches w/clusters of button
flowers, etched English registry
number on base 562.00
Bowl, 10¾ x 7¾", 6¼" h., sapphire
blue w/applied clear dolphins on
sides, clear feet & clear shell trim
around top & floral prunts front &
reverse, White House Glass
Works of Sturbridge, England 325.00
Jam or jelly dish, cased, pink w/ap-
plied vaseline rigaree around center & vaseline ruffled edge, white
interior, w/embossed silverplate
holder, 6" d., 8" h. 125.00
Pitcher, 7½" h., ruffled tricornered
top, applied amber stalk handle,
cased, cream opaque w/applied
pink florals, pink interior, Stevens
& Williams. 525.00
Rose bowl, cased, custard opaque
w/applied amber stem & leaves &
pink, white & rose florals w/ap-
plied amber centers, polished
pontil, Stevens & Williams,
6½" d., 5½" h. (ILLUS.) 300.00
Vase, 6½" h., 2¼" d., footed, shad-
ed white to pale & deeper pink,
applied amber branch, green
leaves & white florals, Stevens &
Williams. 175.00
Vase, 6¾" h., 2¾" d., applied
amber feet, amber branch & leaf
w/applied pink & white spatter
flower w/amber center 110.00
Vase, 7¼" h., 6" d., jack-in-pulpit
type, soft gold w/white inside top
rim & applied amber edging, applied amber leaves & pink & white
florals w/amber centers 135.00
Vase, 10¼" h., 4¾" d., cased,
cream opaque, applied amber
edging at ruffled rim, applied amber stem, rose & green leaves &
pink & white florals, Stevens &
Williams. 265.00
Vase, 13½" h., cased, white opaque
w/applied amber leaves & chest-
nuts, Stevens & Williams 275.00

ART GLASS BASKETS

Art Glass Baskets

Popular in the late Victorian era, these ornate hand-crafted glass baskets were often given as gifts. Sometimes made with unusually tall handles and applied feet, these fragile ornaments usually command a good price when they survive intact. Also see AMBERINA, APPLIQUED, CAMBRIDGE, CRANBERRY, CZECHOSLOVAKIAN, FENTON, FRY, RUBINA VERDE, SATIN, SILVER OVERLAY & DEPOSIT, SPANGLED, SPATTER, STEUBEN AURENE, STEVENS & WILLIAMS and TIFFIN under Glass.

Aqua, Diamond Quilted patt., applied pink petals at rim & applied clear handle, 5¾" h. $195.00
Cased, pink exterior, white interior, applied clear petal feet, ruffled edge & handle, 3¾" d., 8¼" h. (ILLUS. right). 225.00
Cased, pink exterior w/strings of brown spatters, pink interior, dimpled sides, applied clear thorn handle, 5 1/8" d., 6¼" h. 125.00
Cased, white satin exterior, deep rose satin interior, applied camphor edge at rim & camphor double twig handle, 7" h. 225.00
Cranberry, embossed hobnail effect under closely crimped & ruffled rim, applied clear thorn handle, 6 x 5", 5½" h. 195.00
Cranberry, rose bowl shape w/pulled prunts on body & applied clear florals at flattened rim, applied clear feet & thorn handle, 8½" h. 245.00
Creamy opaque, Pointed Hobnail patt., rose lining, applied clear handle, 5½" oval, 5¾" h. (ILLUS. left). 195.00
Green shaded to amber, Swirl patt., applied amber feet, leaves &

twisted thorn handle, 6½" d., 11" h. 225.00
Lemon yellow opaque, Hobnail patt., applied clear edging at ruffled rim & clear thorn handle, 7 3/8 x 5¾", 7¼" h. 175.00
Pink opalescent stripe, embossed hobnail effect at ruffled edge, applied pink twisted handle, 8 x 6½", 7¼" h. 195.00
Sapphire blue, applied clear wafer foot, clear edge around top & clear spun rope handle, 5 x 3½", 3 1/8" h. 275.00
Spangled, pink spatter w/mica flecks, applied clear twisted double handle, 6" h. 96.00
Spatter, maroon, yellow & white, melon-ribbed, white lining, 3¾" d., 6 5/8" h. 135.00
Spatter, pink, brown & blue, ruffled rim, white lining, applied clear handle, 5 x 3", 5" h. 95.00
Vaseline opalescent, Diamond Quilted patt., ruffled rim, applied pink florettes & clear leaves on body & clear twisted thorn handle, 6¾ x 5¾", 7" h. 210.00
Yellow opaque "crackle," swirl-ribbed exterior, ruffled rim, applied clear thorn handle, 5 3/8" d., 6¾" h. 175.00

BACCARAT

Baccarat Rose Tiente Swirl Bottle

Baccarat glass has been made by Cristalleries de Baccarat, France, since 1765. The firm has produced various glasswares of excellent quality and paperweights. Baccarat's Rose Tiente is often referred to as Baccarat's Amberina.

Cologne bottle w/matching stopper, Rose Tiente Pinwheel patt., 2 1/8" d., 5 5/8" h. $70.00

Cologne bottle w/matching stopper,
Rose Tiente Swirl patt., 2½" d.,
6½" h. 65.00

Cologne bottle w/matching stopper,
Rose Tiente Swirl patt., 2 5/8" d.,
7" h. (ILLUS.) 70.00

Cologne bottle w/matching stopper,
Rose Tiente Pinwheel patt.,
2 5/8" d., 7 1/8" h. 75.00

Cologne bottle w/matching stopper,
Rose Tiente Pinwheel patt., 3" d.,
7 7/8" h. 80.00

Cologne bottle w/matching stopper,
Rose Tiente Swirl patt., 3¼" d.,
8" h. 80.00

Decanter w/"trapped air bubble"
stopper, cone-shaped, plain,
clear, signed 90.00

Epergne, Rose Tiente Swirl patt.,
10" d. bowl-base dish, overall
15¼" h. (unscrews into 3 parts) . .   440.00

Fairy lamp on matching saucer
base, Rose Tiente Pinwheel patt.,
5½" d., 4¼" h. 195.00

Finger bowl, Rose Tiente Swirl patt.,
4½" d., 2¼" h. 30.00

Jar, cov., Rose Tiente Swirl patt.,
2¾" d., 4¾" h. 75.00

Perfume atomizer w/original bulb &
pewter fittings, Rose Tiente Pin-
wheel patt., 6" h. 65.00

Perfume bottle w/original stopper,
Rose Tiente Pinwheel patt.,
1½" d., 4 1/8" h. 50.00

full-length portrait of Napoleon in
oval on body 395.00

Plates, 5½" d., Swirl patt., blue, set
of 6 . . . .   65.00

Powder box, cov., Rose Tiente Swirl
patt., 3" d. 60.00

Relish, Rose Tiente Swirl patt.,
9½" l. 95.00

Tazza, low foot, scalloped edge,
Rose Tiente Swirl patt., 5¼" d.,
2¼" h. 75.00

Tumbler, Rose Tiente Swirl patt.,
3½" h. . . . . .40.00 to 55.00

Tumble-up (water carafe w/tumbler
top), peacock blue 165.00

Tumble-up (water carafe w/tumbler
top) & underplate, Rose Tiente
Swirl patt., signed, 3 pcs. 140.00

Vase, 8" h., pinched top, clear to
cranberry, enameled floral decor,
signed 120.00

Vase, 10¼" h., white opaque, h.p.
birds & branch decor 185.00

Vase, 14" h., Rib & Star patt., clear
w/amber 200.00

Vase, 15" h., 6½" d., Rose Tiente
Swirl patt. in ormolu base 225.00

Wine cooler, Brilliant Period cut
crystal, Cane patt., silverplate
mounts, signed, 7¼" d., 9½" h. . . .   675.00

BLOWN THREE MOLD

Blown Three Mold Decanters

This type of glass was entirely or partially blown in a mold from about 1820 in the United States. The object was formed and the decoration impressed upon it by blowing the glass into a metal mold, usually of three but sometimes more sections, hinged together. Mold-blown glass actually dates back to ancient times. Recent research reveals that certain geometric patterns were reproduced in the 1920's and collectors are urged to read all recent information available. McKearin refer-

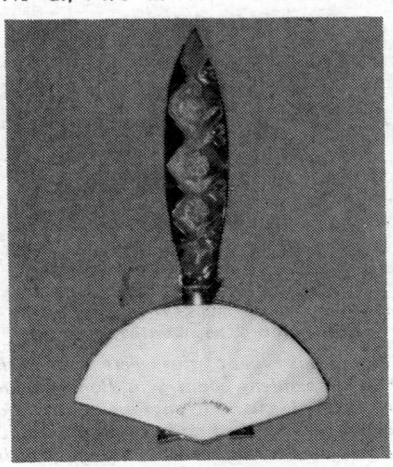

Baccarat Perfume Bottle

Perfume bottle w/original stopper,
white opaque pseudo shell-form
bottle w/gilt-metal collar, clear &
frosted stopper w/sculptured
florals, signed, 7¾" h. (ILLUS.) . . .   80.00

Pitcher, water, tankard, 15" h.,
clear, wide-ribbed base, etched

ence numbers are to George L. and Helen McKearin's book, "American Glass."

Castor bottle w/original brass
  screw-on shaker top, rayed base,
  geometric, clear, 4" h. (GI-7) $35.00
Creamer, wide flaring mouth,
  pinched spout, bold handle, rayed
  base, geometric, clear (GIII-20) . . . 300.00
Cruet (no stopper), geometric, clear,
  4½" h. (GI-24) 45.00
Cruet w/solid "Tam-o-Shanter" stop-
  per, geometric, deep sapphire
  blue, 6¾" h. (GI-7) 220.00
Decanter w/original stopper, rayed
  base, geometric, clear, ½ pt.
  (GIII-6) 210.00
Decanter (no stopper), geometric,
  clear, pt. (GIII-2) 170.00
Decanter (no stopper), barrel-
  shaped w/sloping shoulders,
  rayed base, geometric, olive am-
  ber, pt., GIII-16, each (ILLUS. of
  pair) 400.00
Decanter (no stopper), flanged lip,
  geometric, olive amber, qt.
  (GIII-19) 850.00
Decanter w/original ribbed stopper,
  baroque, sapphire blue, 9½" h.
  (GV-8) 2,300.00
Dish, geometric, clear, 4¼"
  (GIII-23) 195.00
Dish, geometric, clear, 6" (GIII-21) . . 195.00
Flip glass, geometric, clear,
  5 1/8" h. (GII-18) 65.00
Flip glass, geometric, clear, 6" h.
  (GII-22) 110.00
Hat shape, geometric, cobalt blue,
  2¼" h. (GIII-25) 190.00
Inkwell, geometric, dark olive
  green, open pontil, 2" d., 1¾" h.
  (GII-18) 100.00
Inkwell, geometric, light blue-green,
  open pontil, 2 3/16" d., 2" h.
  (GII-15) 700.00
Inkwell, geometric, olive amber,
  open pontil, 2¼" d., 1 3/16" h.
  (GIII-29) 80.00
Tumbler, whiskey, diamond base,
  geometric, deep amber, 2 7/8" d.,
  2 7/8" h. (GII-18) 2,700.00
Tumbler, barrel-shaped, geometric,
  clear, 3½" h. (GII-18) 95.00
Wine, knop stem on flat base,
  geometric, clear, 4" h.
  (GII-19) . . . . .150.00 to 235.00

BLURINA

This is a name collectors have given a Bohemian-type glass shading from blue to a ruby or amber color.

Blurina Tumbler

Rose bowl, ball-shaped, Inverted
  Thumbprint patt., 4" d. $300.00
Sweetmeat jar, h.p. large vivid
  shasta daisies (2), leaves,
  branches & buds decor, silverplate
  cover 265.00
Toothpick holder, hat-shaped
  w/jack-in-pulpit rim 90.00
Tumbler, Inverted Thumbprint patt.
  (ILLUS.) 110.00
Vase, 6¼" h., 5" d., blue shaded to
  deep rose, crimped rim, applied
  green flower, amber stem &
  leaves decor 135.00

BOHEMIAN

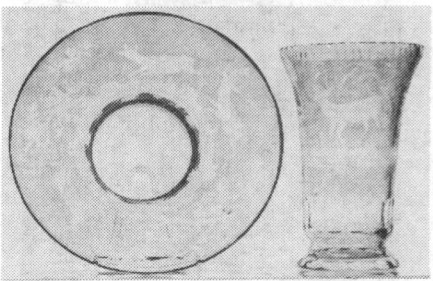

Bohemian Glass Centerpiece Set

Numerous types of glass were made in the once-independent country of Bohemia and fine colored, cut and engraved glass was turned out. Flashed and other inexpensive wares also were made and many of these, including ruby-shaded glass and etched ruby glass, were exported to the United States last century and in the present one. One favorite pattern in the late 19th and early 20th centuries was Deer and Castle. Another was Deer and Pine Tree.

Beaker, engraved florals & drinking
  toast, ruby, frosted & clear, mid-
  19th c., 5½" h. $145.00

Bowl, scalloped rim, cranberry overlay, enameled medallions decor,
large. 375.00
Butter dish, cov., Deer & Castle
patt., ruby, frosted & clear. 100.00
Centerpiece set: 12" d. bowl & pr.
10½" h. vases; Deer in Forest
patt., amber, frosted & clear,
3 pcs. (ILLUS. of part). 300.00
Chalice, clear pedestal base, ruby
cup w/Vintage patt. etching,
8" h. 150.00
Decanter w/original clear stopper,
Vintage patt., ruby, frosted &
clear, 11¾" h. 85.00
Dresser set: pr. dresser bottles &
powder jar; Deer & Pine Tree
patt., ruby, frosted & clear,
3 pcs. 95.00
Finger bowls & underplates, shaped
rims, engraved scrolling foliate
bands on sides, star-cut bases,
ruby, clear & frosted, 9½" d.
underplates, set of 12 . . . . 220.00
Finger bowls & underplates, Coin Dot
patt., purple overlay cut to clear,
set of 12 . . . . 675.00

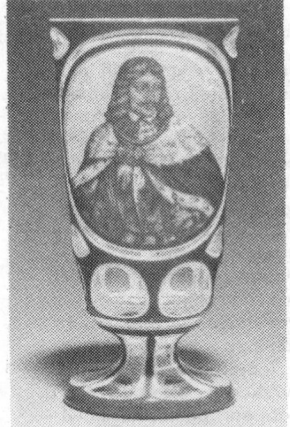

Bohemian Double Overlay Goblet

Goblet, double overlay of blue cut
to white & clear, reserved w/h.p.
portrait of gentleman wearing
ermine-lined cloak & breast plate
& holding sword against acid-
etched ground, ca. 1840, 7" h.
(ILLUS.). 825.00
Goblet, Vintage patt., ruby, frosted
& clear 45.00
Mug, Deer in Forest patt., ruby,
frosted & clear 42.00
Mustard jar, cov., Deer & Castle
patt., ruby, frosted & clear. 48.00
Perfume bottle w/matching stopper,
ruby w/enameled cream & gold
scrolls decor, 1¾" d., 3¾" h. 78.00

Perfume bottle w/original clear
facet-cut "bubble" stopper, alternating clear & amber panels
w/etched florals, 2 1/8" d.,
5" h. 100.00
Sweetmeat jar & cover, footed, Bird
& Castle patt., ruby, frosted &
clear, 10" h. 65.00
Tankard, Deer in Forest patt., ap-
plied amber handle, amber, frosted & clear, w/pewter mounts,
2¾" d., 4¼" h. 188.00
Tankard, clear w/square ruby re-
serve etched w/florals & leaves,
hinged pewter lid w/ruby inset,
3¼" d., 4¼" h. 275.00
Tankard, ruby cut w/clear square
panels enclosing named views alternating w/clear roundels,
hinged pewter lid w/ruby inset &
ball finial thumblift, star-cut base,
ca. 1880, 5" h. 252.00
Toothpick holder, Vintage patt.,
ruby, frosted & clear 45.00
Vase, 7½" h., chalice form, amber
cut to clear checkered diamond &
leaf motifs, Renaissance-style
silver-gilt collar w/three pendant
tassels mounted w/various colored pastes & silver-gilt base supported on 3 paw feet, mid-
19th c. 550.00
Vase, 11½" h., footed cylinder, blue
w/dull gold decor 95.00
Vase, 22¼" h., baluster-shaped,
double overlay, ruby cut to white
& clear w/rococo scrollwork &
leafage heightened w/gilt, reserved
w/oval medallions front & reverse
w/h.p. scene of young maiden in
landscape & young girl pulled in
cart by young boys within tooled
gilt & jeweled borders, ca. 1840. .1,760.00
Wine set: decanter w/stopper & 6
wines; ruby cut to clear, dated
1904, 7 pcs. 450.00

BREAD PLATES & TRAYS

*Scores of special bread plates were pro-
duced last century and early in this one, of
pattern glass and as commemorative pieces.
Also see HISTORICAL & COMMEMORA-
TIVE, IOWA CITY and PATTERN
GLASS.*

American Flag tray, 38-star version
of flag, clear, 11 x 8". $49.00
Arched Leaf patt. plate, clear 20.00
Barred Forget-Me-Not patt. plate,
clear 30.00

Chain & Star patt. plate, clear 22.50
Dewdrop In Points patt. plate,
clear 18.00
Huckle patt. tray, clear 24.00
"It is Pleasant to Labor for Those
Whom We Love" plate, grapevine
center, clear 40.00
Lotus with Serpent plate, clear,
12¾" .38.00 to 45.00
Maple Leaf patt. plate w/portrait of
U.S. Grant, "Let Us Have Peace,"
clear, 9½" d. 42.50
Sheaf of Wheat patt. tray, "Give Us
This Day," clear 35.00
Stippled Fan patt. plate, clear 25.00
Three Presidents patt. tray, clear . . . 59.00

Grant "Patriot and Soldier" Plate

"Ulysses S. Grant - Patriot and Soldier" square plate, clear
(ILLUS.) 45.00

BRIDE'S BASKETS

Mt. Washington Bride's Basket

*These are berry or fruit bowls, once popu-
lar as wedding gifts; hence the name.*

Blue opalescent Lattice patt. bowl
w/fluted edge, silverplate frame
w/ornate handle marked
"Biggins - Rogers Co., Walling-
ford, Conn.," ca. 1890 . . . . $145.00
Burmese bowl, enameled decor, Mt.
Washington, silverplate frame . . .2,500.00

Cased bowl, shaded rose to pale
pink interior, white exterior,
enameled pastel florals & green
leaves interior & exterior decor,
ormolu basket-frame, 7¼ x 5"
bowl, 6 5/8" h. 150.00
Cased bowl, amber to cranberry in-
terior, white exterior, ruffled rim,
enameled trim, 9" d. 130.00
Cased bowl, red shaded to pink in-
terior, white exterior, crimped
rim, silverplate basket-frame,
9¼" d., 11" h. to top of handle. . . 195.00
Cased bowl, cream interior
enameled multicolored scrolls &
garlands, blue exterior, tricornered w/folded-over ruffled edge,
silverplate pedestal base w/three
dolphins in stem, 9¾" d.,
8½" h. 252.00
Cased bowl, blue interior w/ena-
meled scrolls & florals, white exterior, clear edging, metal rim at
base as fitter for silverplate
frame, 7½ x 10" bowl, 9¾" h. . . . 245.00
Cased bowl, yellow-gold interior
w/enameled white florals, pink
foliage & leaves, white exterior,
ruffled rim, silverplate frame,
13½" d., 11½" h. 565.00
Cranberry bowl w/greenish yellow
mottling, ruffled rim, enameled
floral decor, silverplate stand
w/entwined florals at base & 3
winged cupids in stem, 8" h. 375.00
Cranberry bowl, Inverted Thumb-
print patt. w/enameled white
daisies, bluebells, green leaves &
gold trim, attributed to Mt.
Washington, silverplate holder
marked "Pairpoint" 575.00
Cranberry shaded to pink bowl
w/enameled blue, white & gold
decor, footed silverplate frame
cast w/cherries & leaves, 11" d. . . 200.00
Mother-of-pearl pink Satin bowl,
Diamond Quilted patt., enameled
floral, insect & gold spiderweb decor, silverplate frame w/two
detachable birds, elaborate handles & overall embellishments,
marked "Quadruple Plate Warranted Aurora S.P. Mfg.," 10½" d.
bowl, overall 10 3/8" h. 985.00
Mother-of-pearl orange Satin bowl,
Herringbone patt., enameled gold
palm fronds decor, attributed to
Mt. Washington, silverplate frame
mounted w/gold-washed lion at
each side, overall 18" w., 12" h.
(ILLUS.) 2,900.00
Red Satin bowl, ruffled & fluted rim,
enameled decor, silverplate
frame 255.00

Bride's Basket

Rose (shaded light to dark) bowl, heart-shaped w/fluted rim, enameled floral & scroll motifs, embossed footed silverplate holder, w/grape cluster suspended from handle, marked "Forbes Silver Co.," ca. 1900, 9¼ x 8½" bowl (ILLUS.) 450.00

Rubina Verde opalescent bowl, square top, enameled blue, orange & white scrolls decor, silverplate frame w/conforming scrollwork, 10" sq., bowl overall 14½" h. 450.00

BRISTOL

Bristol Cookie Jar

While glass was made in several glasshouses in Bristol, England, the generic name Bristol glass is applied today by collectors to a variety of semi-opaque glasses, frequently decorated by enameling, and made both

abroad and in United States glasshouses in the 19th and 20th centuries.

Box w/hinged lid, ormolu feet, white opaque w/enameled soft blue & creamy white scenes of ladies & a gentleman on lid & sides within lavender floral borders, 3¾" d., 3¾" h. $100.00

Box w/hinged lid, cased, heavenly blue w/white lining, enameled cupids at various pursuits within white & gold scrollwork, 3¼" d., 4 3/8" h. 165.00

Cheese dish, cov., creamy white satin finish w/enameled bands of green, blue & red designs, gold trim, 10" d., 7" h. 165.00

Cookie jar, pink w/enameled yellow, blue & white daisy-like florals & green leaves, white lining, silverplate rim, 4 5/8" d., 6" h. (ILLUS.) . . 165.00

Cookie jar, translucent blue w/enameled yellow, pink, blue & coral florals w/green leaves, silverplate & brass rim, cover & bail handle, 5" d., 6½" h. 105.00

Cruet w/original blue ball-shaped stopper, heavenly blue opaque w/applied blue handle, enameled yellow florals & leaves decor, 2 3/8" d., 6" h. 75.00

Decanter, white opaque w/enameled green & gold trim, 9" h. 65.00

Dresser tray, turquoise blue w/enameled gold florals & foliage, 11 x 7¾" oblong 118.00

Ewer, applied handle, bulbous base, shaded blue w/enameled birds & florals decor 160.00

Mug, applied handle, blue w/white enameled decor & worn gilding, "Remember Me," 4" h. 25.00

Bristol Perfume Atomizer

Perfume atomizer, melon-ribbed,
beige w/enameled daisies &
leaves decor, 6½" h. (ILLUS.)..... 47.50

Perfume bottle w/original stopper,
French blue w/enameled white
blossoms, green leaves & white
beading, 8" h. 75.00

Sweetmeat jar, cov., robin's egg
blue w/enameled parrot & cranes
decor, 4¼" h. 165.00

Vase, 9" h., ruffled & crimped rim,
cased, white w/pink lining, h.p.
floral decor..................... 50.00

Vase, 9½" h., bulbous w/narrow
neck, yellow shading to blue 45.00

Vase, 9½" h., pink w/enameled
white lilies & leaves decor 115.00

Vase, 10" h., crimped rim, "cafe au
lait" w/floral decor & gold trim... 62.50

Vase, 10" h., soft green opaque
w/floral decal 40.00

Vase, 11¾" h., 5½" h., applied
black handles highlighted w/gold,
dove grey w/enameled birds (4),
blue florals & gold & white dots
decor 172.00

Vases, 12½" h., white frosted
w/enameled white florals & green
leaves, pr...................... 95.00

Vases, 13" h., white opaque w/ena-
meled vivid Narcissus, green
leaves, cattails & wine-colored
fronds, pr...................... 135.00

BURMESE

Mt. Washington Pitcher

Burmese is an homogeneous glass that shades from pink to pale yellow and was patented by Frederick S. Shirley and made by the Mt. Washington Glass Co. A license to produce the glass in England was granted to Thomas Webb & Sons, which called its articles Queen's Burmese. Gunderson Burmese was made briefly about the middle of this century. Also see FAIRY LAMPS.

Bowl, 3 7/8" d., 2½" h., ruffled rim,
acid finish, attributed to Webb ...$195.00

Bowl, 4½" w., tricornered, Mt.
Washington Glass Co. 310.00

Bowl, 5¾" d., 2¾" h., ruffled rim .. 365.00

Celery vase, square top, Hobnail
patt., acid finish, Gunderson,
1950's, 7" h. 170.00

Cologne bottle w/sterling silver
screw-on top, enameled prunus
blossoms decor, Thomas Webb &
Sons, 3¾" widest d., 5" h. 585.00

Condiment set: salt & pepper
shakers w/original tops & mustard
jar; ribbed bodies, in silverplate
frame 475.00

Cookie jar, cov., Mt. Washington
Glass Co...................... 650.00

Creamer & open sugar bowl,
enameled acorn decor, attributed
to Thomas Webb & Sons, in silverplate holder, set 800.00

Cruet w/original stopper, melon-
ribbed, satin finish, refired yellow
edge on spout, Mt. Washington
Glass Co., 6½" h........800.00 to 885.00

Cup, applied handle, glossy,
Gunderson 125.00

Cup & saucer 275.00

Marmalade jar, glossy, h.p. floral
band decor, silverplate lid &
spoon, 4" h. 165.00

Mustard pot, cov., ribbed, acid
finish 145.00

Mustard pot, enameled floral
decor 150.00

Pitcher, water, 6¾" h., 6" d., applied yellow handle, acid finish,
signed Thos. Webb & Sons Queens
Burmese Ware 775.00

Pitcher, 8½" h., Gunderson 240.00

Pitcher, tankard, 9" h., glossy, New
England Glass Co............... 450.00

Pitcher, water, 9¾" h., Hobnail
patt., satin finish, Mt. Washington
Glass Co...................... 750.00

Pitcher, water, acid finish, Mt.
Washington Glass Co. (ILLUS.) ...1,050.00

Punch cup, glossy 325.00

Rose bowl, 8-crimp top, acid finish,
attributed to Thomas Webb &
Sons, 2½" d., 2½" h............. 165.00

Rose bowl, 8-crimp top, acid finish,
enameled green leaves & red berries decor, attributed to Thomas
Webb & Sons, 2½" d., 2½" h..... 300.00

Rose bowl, 8-crimp top, acid finish,
enameled lavender 5-petal flowers, green & brown leaves decor,
attributed to Thomas Webb &
Sons, 3½" d., 3¼" h............. 345.00

Rose bowl, acid finish, "Queen's Design" decor, Mt. Washington Glass
Co., 5" d., 2¼" h............... 945.00

Salt shaker w/original top, Ribbed
Pillar patt., glossy, Mt. Washington Glass Co. (single) 200.00
Salt & pepper shakers w/original
tops, Ribbed Pillar patt., acid finish, Mt. Washington Glass Co., in
original silverplate footed holder
chased w/florals & bee on
handle .... 350.00 to 395.00
Scent bottle w/hallmarked gold-
washed silver domed lid,
enameled gold branches, leaves &
berry clusters decor, 3¼" d.,
4¾" h. 795.00

Mt. Washington Sugar Bowl

Sugar bowl, open, applied wishbone
feet, acid finish, Mt. Washington
Glass Co. (ILLUS.) 700.00
Sweetmeat jar, enameled grape
clusters on leafy vine decor, silverplate rim, cover & bail handle,
Thomas Webb & Sons, 6½" h. 685.00
Toothpick holder, curled-in trefoil
top, Diamond Quilted patt., Mt.
Washington Glass Co., 2 1/8" h. .. 310.00
Toothpick holder, bulbous w/col-
lared 6-sided top, acid finish,
undecorated, 2½" d.,
2½" h. .... 225.00 to 300.00
Toothpick holder, bulbous w/col-
lared 6-sided top, acid finish,
enameled green leaves & red berries decor, 2½" d., 2½" h. 275.00
Toothpick holder, bulbous w/col-
lared 6-sided top, acid finish,
enameled lavender 5-petal flowers, green & brown leaves decor,
2½" d., 2½" h. 245.00
Toothpick holder, bulbous base
w/square flaring top, enameled
foliage decor, Thomas Webb &
Sons 350.00
Toothpick holder, round base,
square top, Diamond Quilted
patt., glossy, ca. 1887 .... 360.00
Toothpick holder, round base,
square top, Diamond Quilted
patt., refired yellow rim, Mt.
Washington Glass Co., 2¾" h. ... 335.00

Burmese Toothpick Holder

Toothpick holder, round base,
square top, acid finish, h.p.
florals w/raised enamel beading
(ILLUS.)....................... 425.00
Toothpick holder, hat shape w/ruf-
fled rim, acid finish, enameled
floral bouquets & leaves w/tracer-
ies, Mt. Washington Glass Co..... 525.00
Tumbler, Gunderson, 1950's 115.00

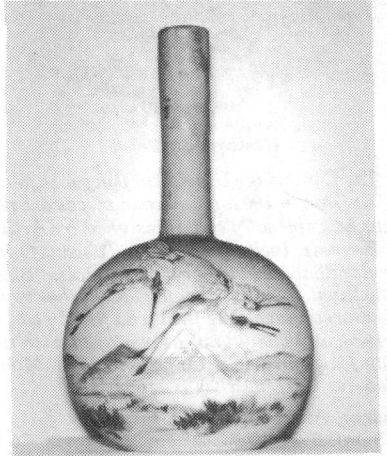

Vase with Egyptian Designs

Vase, bottle-shaped, enameled
Sacred Ibis (2) in flight over a
sunlit desert oasis w/pyramids,
pool of blue water, sand dunes &
Royal Palm in raised gold, Mt.
Washington Glass Co.
(ILLUS.) .... 2,450.00 to 3,000.00
Vase, 3" h., 2½" d., star-shaped
top, acid finish, enameled brown
foliage, white & blue floral decor,
Thomas Webb & Sons 295.00
Vase, 3¼" h., 3 1/8" d., bulbous
w/pinched in sides, acid finish,
enameled green leaves & red ber-
ries decor, attributed to Thomas
Webb & Sons 325.00

Vase, 4 1/8" h., 2 5/8" d., flared
ruffled top, acid finish, enameled
lavender 5-petal flowers, green &
brown leaves decor, paper label
"Queen's Burmese Ware, Thos.
Webb & Sons Patented" 325.00

Vase, 5½" h., 3" d., flower petal
top w/applied frosted edging,
pedestal foot, acid finish,
enameled brown pinecones &
green pine needles decor, signed
Thos. Webb Queen's Burmese
Ware 575.00

Vase, 6" h., lily form, glossy, refired
rim, Mt. Washington Glass Co. ... 400.00

Whimsey, model of a top hat,
glossy, Mt. Washington Glass Co.,
2 15/16" widest d., 1 5/8" h. 425.00

CAMBRIDGE

Heliotrope Bowl

*The Cambridge Glass Company was found-
ed in Ohio in 1901. Numerous pieces are now
sought, especially those designed by Arthur
J. Bennett, including Crown Tuscan. Other
productions included crystal animals, "Black
Amethyst," "blanc opaque," and other types
of colored glass. The firm was finally closed
in 1954, and should not be confused with the
New England Glass Co., Cambridge, Mass.
Also see CHILDREN'S DISHES.*

Basket, Azure Blue (dark opaque
blue), 5½" w. $75.00

Basket, pressed Caprice patt., blue,
4" sq. 35.00

Basket, 2-handled, Decagon patt.,
crystal, 11½" h. 35.00

Basket, Georgian patt., Moonlight
(delicate pastel blue), 7" 60.00

Bowl, 7½" d., 2½" h., Heliotrope,
purple opaque (ILLUS.) 150.00

Bowl, 8" oval, 4-footed, Seashell
patt., Mandarin Gold (very light
golden yellow) 50.00

Bowl, 9" d., footed, Ram's Head
handles, Jade (blue-green
opaque) 95.00

Bowl, 10" d., footed, Honeycomb
patt., Amberina (ruby top delicately blending off to amber),
unsigned 100.00

Bowl, 11" d., Honeycomb patt.,

Rubina (ruby top blending to
blue, then to green) 173.00

Bowl, 11" d., Ribbed Optic patt.,
Rubina 125.00

Bowl, 12" d., 4-toed, etched Rose
Point patt., crystal 55.00

Bowl, 15" oval, 2-handled, scalloped
rim, etched Rose Point patt.,
crystal 65.00

Butter dish, cov., etched Appleblos-
som patt., crystal 100.00

Candlestick, Doric Column, Ivory
(light cream opaque), 9" h.
(single)...................... 67.00

Ebony Candlesticks

Candlesticks, twisted stems, Ebony
(opaque black), 9" h., pr.
(ILLUS.)..................... 100.00

Candlesticks, 2-light, Everglade
patt., amber, pr. 145.00

Candy box, cov., 3-part, etched
Portia patt., crystal 40.00

Candy jar, cov., Honeycomb patt.,
Rubina 135.00

Claret, Heatherbloom (delicate
orchid) 200.00

Cocktail, etched Elaine patt., crystal,
3 oz. 29.00

Cocktail, amethyst bowl, clear Nude
Lady stem, 3 oz. 85.00

Cocktail, Mandarin Gold bowl, clear
Nude Lady stem, 3 oz. 85.00

Cocktail, Pistachio (delicate pastel
green) bowl, clear Nude Lady
stem 130.00

Cocktail shaker, etched Rose Point
patt., crystal, w/chrome lid 195.00

Comport, royal blue top, clear Nude
Lady stem 225.00

Console bowl, rolled edge, Decagon
patt., Ebony, 12" d. 35.00

Console set: 8½" d. Ram's Head
bowl & pr. Doric Column candlesticks, Heliotrope, 3 pcs. 350.00

Creamer & sugar bowl, etched Rose
Point patt., crystal, pr. 45.00

Crown Tuscan ash tray, 3-footed,
Charleton decor, 4" 42.50
Crown Tuscan bowl, 10" d., 3-toed,
Seashell patt. 80.00
Crown Tuscan bowl, 13" d., shallow,
Seashell patt. 48.50
Crown Tuscan cocktail, Nude Lady
stem ....85.00 to 95.00
Crown Tuscan compote, 6" d., 4" h.,
Seashell patt. 30.00
Crown Tuscan compote, 7", Nude
Lady stem 150.00
Crown Tuscan compote, 8", Seashell
patt. 65.00
Crown Tuscan ivy ball, keyhole
stem, 8"..................35.00 to 48.00
Crown Tuscan torte plate, Seashell
patt., 14" d. 65.00
Crown Tuscan vase, pillow-shaped,
etched Diane patt. 125.00
Crown Tuscan wine, Nude Lady
stem 90.00
Cruet set: oil & vinegar cruets on
handled tray; pressed Caprice
patt., blue, 3 pcs. 125.00
Cup & saucer, etched Gloria patt.,
crystal 18.00
Cup & saucer, pressed Caprice patt.,
blue 37.50
Cup & saucer, pressed Caprice patt.,
crystal 14.00
Cup & saucer, pressed Caprice patt.,
La Rosa (delicate pastel pink) 25.00
Decanter w/original stopper, etched
Rose Point patt., crystal 170.00
Figure flower holder, "Bashful Char-
lotte," crystal, 6½" h. 50.00
Figure flower holder, "Bashful Char-
lotte," green, 6½" h. 145.00
Figure flower holder, "Bashful Char-
lotte," pink, 6½" h. 115.00
Figure flower holder, "Bashful Char-
lotte," crystal, 8½" h. 75.00
Figure flower holder, "Bashful Char-
lotte," blue satin finish,
11" h. 625.00
Figure flower holder, "Bashful Char-
lotte," green, 11" h. 225.00
Figure flower holder, "Bashful Char-
lotte," Moonlight, 11" h. 550.00
Figure flower holder, "Bashful Char-
lotte," pink satin finish,
11" h. 165.00
Figure flower holder, "Draped
Lady," pink, 6½" h. 95.00
Figure flower holder, "Draped
Lady," amber, 8½" h. 175.00
Figure flower holder, "Draped
Lady," crystal, 8½" h. 50.00
Figure flower holder, "Draped
Lady," Mocha (delicate pastel
brown), 8½" h. 225.00
Figure flower holder, "Draped
Lady," amber, 13" h. 325.00

Figure flower holder, "Draped
Lady," crystal, 13" h. 150.00
Figure flower holder, "Draped
Lady," frosted, 13" h.....175.00 to 255.00
Figure flower holder, "Rose Lady,"
Dianthis (light transparent pink),
8½" h. ....185.00 to 250.00
Figure flower holder, "Two-Kid,"
amber, 9" h. 225.00
Figure flower holder, "Two-Kid,"
Dianthis, 9" h. ....200.00 to 250.00
Goblet, pressed Caprice patt., blue,
10 oz. ....32.50 to 45.00
Goblet, pressed Caprice patt.,
crystal, 10 oz. 15.00
Goblet, etched Rose Point patt.,
crystal 22.50
Goblet, amethyst bowl, clear Nude
Lady stem 115.00
Goblet, Carmen (clear brilliant ruby
red) bowl, clear Nude Lady
stem 125.00
Night lamp, figural owl, dark pur-
ple, on ebony (black opaque)
base 2,800.00
Night lamp, figural owl, white
opaque, on ebony (black opaque)
base 650.00
Punch set: punch bowl, base & 12
punch cups; crystal, marked "Near
Cut," 15 pcs. 575.00

Cambridge Tomato Glass Vase

Vase, 10" h., trumpet-shaped,
Tomato, yellow-green at top,
blending into red & to yellow-
green at bottom (ILLUS.) 80.00
Wine, Decagon patt., amber 12.00
Wine, etched Rose Point patt.,
crystal 47.00
Wine, cranberry bowl, frosted Nude
Lady stem 50.00
Wine, gold bowl, frosted Nude Lady
stem 50.00
Wine, green bowl, frosted Nude
Lady stem 50.00

CARNIVAL GLASS

Earlier called Taffeta glass, the Carnival glass now being collected was introduced early in this century. Its producers gave it an iridescence that attempted to imitate that of some Tiffany glass. Collectors will find available books by leading authorities Donald E. Moore, Sherman Hand, Marion T. Hartung and Rose M. Presznick.

ACANTHUS (Imperial)

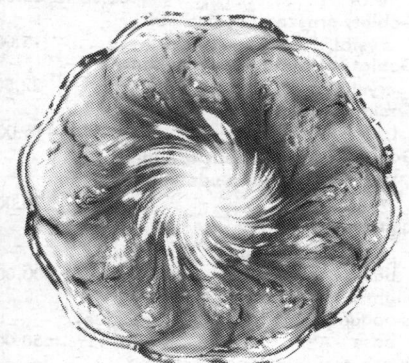

Acanthus Bowl

Bowl, 8" to 9" d., green	$75.00
Bowl, 8" to 9" d., marigold (ILLUS.)	60.00
Bowl, 8" to 9" d., purple	58.00
Bowl, 8" to 9" d., smoky	65.00
Plate, 9" to 10" d., marigold	125.00
Plate, 9" to 10" d., smoky	179.00

ACORN (Fenton)

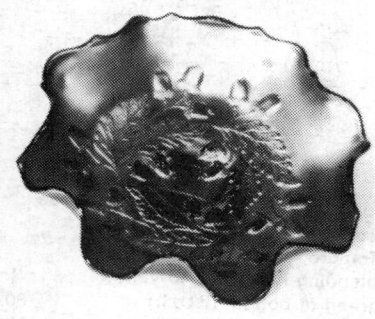

Acorn Bowl

Bowl, 5" d., aqua opalescent	60.00
Bowl, 5" d., blue	25.00
Bowl, 5" d., marigold over milk white	300.00
Bowl, 7" d., aqua opalescent	80.00
Bowl, 7" d., blue	50.00

Bowl, 7" d., green	27.00
Bowl, 7" d., ice blue	150.00
Bowl, 7" d., marigold	25.00 to 30.00
Bowl, 7" d., marigold over milk white	175.00
Bowl, 7" d., red (ILLUS.)	380.00
Bowl, 7½" d., ruffled, vaseline	125.00
Bowl, 8" to 9" d., blue	60.00
Bowl, 8" to 9" d., green	35.00
Bowl, 8" to 9" d., ribbon candy rim, purple	55.00
Bowl, 8" to 9" d., red	475.00
Compote, vaseline (Millersburg)	2,100.00

ACORN BURRS (Northwood)

Acorn Burrs Tumbler & Pitcher

Berry set: master bowl & 2 sauce dishes; purple, 3 pcs.	175.00
Berry set: master bowl & 4 sauce dishes; green, 5 pcs.	260.00
Berry set: master bowl & 6 sauce dishes; marigold, 7 pcs.	225.00
Bowl, master berry, 10" d., marigold	68.00
Bowl, master berry, 10" d., purple	130.00
Butter dish, cov., marigold	140.00
Butter dish, cov., purple	200.00
Creamer, marigold	80.00
Pitcher, water, marigold	375.00
Pitcher, water, purple (ILLUS.)	470.00
Punch bowl, marigold	400.00
Punch bowl base, ice blue	175.00
Punch bowl & base, ice green, 2 pcs.	1,800.00
Punch bowl & base, purple, 2 pcs.	450.00
Punch cup, green	32.50
Punch cup, ice blue	75.00
Punch cup, marigold	20.00
Punch cup, purple	25.00
Punch cup, white	65.00 to 80.00
Punch set: bowl, base & 5 cups; marigold, 7 pcs.	300.00
Punch set: bowl, base & 6 cups; green, 8 pcs.	975.00

Punch set: bowl, base & 6 cups;
marigold, 8 pcs. 375.00
Punch set: bowl, base & 6 cups;
purple, 8 pcs. 650.00
Sauce dish, green 30.00
Sauce dish, marigold . . . . .18.00 to 25.00
Sauce dish, purple 58.00
Spooner, green . . . . .80.00 to 95.00
Spooner, marigold. 67.50
Spooner, purple 100.00
Sugar bowl, cov., marigold. 95.00
Sugar bowl, open, purple 190.00
Table set: cov. sugar bowl, creamer,
spooner & cov. butter dish;
marigold, 4 pcs. 395.00
Table set: cov. sugar bowl, creamer,
spooner & cov. butter dish; pur-
ple, 4 pcs. . . . . .450.00 to 500.00
Tumbler, green 65.00
Tumbler, marigold. 47.50
Tumbler, purple (ILLUS.) 60.00
Water set: pitcher & 6 tumblers;
green, 7 pcs. 900.00
Water set: pitcher & 6 tumblers;
marigold, 7 pcs. 580.00
Water set: pitcher & 6 tumblers;
purple, 7 pcs. 735.00

ADVERTISING & SOUVENIR ITEMS

Brooklyn Bridge Bowl

Bell, souvenir, BPOE Elks, "Atlantic
City, 1911," blue 1,050.00
Bell, souvenir, BPOE Elks, "Parkers
burg, 1914," blue 1,250.00
Bowl, "Central Shoe Store,"
purple 185.00
Bowl, "Horlacher," Butterfly patt.,
purple 125.00
Bowl, "Horlacher," Peacock Tail
patt., purple 60.00
Bowl, "Horlacher," Thistle patt.
purple . . . . .80.00 to 95.00
Bowl, 8½" d., "H. Mayday & Co.,
1910," Wild Blackberry patt.,
purple . . . . .190.00 to 350.00
Bowl, souvenir, BPOE Elks, "Atlantic
City, 1911," blue, 1-eyed Elk 375.00
Bowl, souvenir, BPOE Elks, "Detroit,
1910," purple, 1-eyed Elk 450.00

Bowl, souvenir, BPOE Elks, "Detroit,
1910," purple, 2-eyed Elk (Millers
burg) . . . . .750.00 to 1,025.00
Bowl, souvenir, Brooklyn Bridge, un-
lettered, marigold (ILLUS.) 550.00
Bowl, souvenir, "Millersburg Court-
house," purple 425.00
Bowl, souvenir, Millersburg Court
house, unlettered, purple 1,050.00
Hat, "Miller's Furniture - Harris-
burg," basketweave, marigold. . . . 95.00
Plate, "Ballard, California," purple
(Northwood) 275.00
Plate, "Davidson Chocolate Society,"
6¼" d., purple 195.00
Plate, "Driebus Parfait Sweets,"
6¼" d., purple. 190.00
Plate, "Eagle Furniture Co.," purple . 190.00
Plate, "Fern Brand Chocolates,"
purple 195.00
Plate, "Greengard Furniture Co.,"
purple . . . . .375.00 to 400.00
Plate, "E.A. Hudson Furniture Co.,"
7" d., purple (Northwood). 170.00
Plate, "Morris N. Smith,"
purple 250.00
Plate, "Old Rose Distillery,"
green . . . . .170.00 to 190.00
Plate, "Paradise Soda," purple
(Northwood) 155.00
Plate, "Rhodes Chocolate, Pueblo,"
purple 550.00
Plate, "Spectors Department Store,"
marigold 220.00
Plate, souvenir, BPOE Elks, "Atlantic
City, 1911," blue 600.00
Plate, souvenir, BPOE Elks, "Par-
kersburg, 1914," 7½" d., blue 900.00

AGE HERALD
Bowl, 8" to 9" d., collared base,
straight edge, purple 500.00
Plate, purple .1,500.00

APPLE BLOSSOMS

Apple Blossoms Syrup

Bowl, 7" d., collared base, mari-
gold 30.00
Bowl, 7" d., collared base, peach
opalescent ....75.00 to 110.00
Bowl, 7" d., collared base, purple .. 60.00
Rose bowl, marigold............... 35.00
Syrup pitcher, marigold (ILLUS.) 375.00

APPLE BLOSSOM TWIGS
Banana boat, ruffled, peach
opalescent...................... 175.00
Banana boat, ruffled, purple 60.00
Bowl, 8" to 9" d., marigold......... 30.00
Bowl, 8" to 9" d., peach
opalescent ....90.00 to 115.00
Bowl, 8" to 9" d., purple 100.00
Bowl, 8" to 9" d., white............ 70.00
Plate, 9" d., blue ....125.00 to 140.00
Plate, 9" d., marigold .....100.00 to 120.00
Plate, 9" d., peach opalescent 250.00
Plate, 9" d., purple........160.00 to 190.00
Plate, 9" d., white 75.00
Plate, 9" d., ruffled, smoky 350.00
Plate, 9" d., ruffled, white 100.00

APPLE TREE
Pitcher, water, marigold 130.00
Pitcher, water, white 550.00
Tumbler, blue..................... 40.00
Tumbler, marigold ....25.00 to 37.50
Tumbler, white ....125.00 to 150.00
Water set: pitcher & 6 tumblers;
blue, 7 pcs.................... 460.00
Water set: pitcher & 6 tumblers;
marigold, 7 pcs................. 325.00

AUSTRALIAN
Bowl, 9" to 10" d., Kingfisher,
purple 105.00
Bowl, 9" to 10" d., Kookaburra,
purple 100.00
Bowl, 9" to 10" d., Magpie,
marigold 95.00
Bowl, 9" to 10" d., Magpie, purple .. 125.00
Bowl, 9" to 10" d., Swan,
marigold 80.00
Bowl, 9" to 10" d., Thunderbird,
marigold 70.00
Bowl, 9" to 10" d., Thunderbird,
purple 110.00
Sauce dish, Emu, marigold 75.00
Sauce dish, Kangaroo, purple 70.00
Sauce dish, Kookaburra, purple 42.50
Sauce dish, Magpie, purple 55.00
Sauce dish, Swan, marigold ..35.00 to 50.00
Sauce dish, Swan, purple 50.00
Sauce dish, Thunderbird, purple 45.00

AUTUMN ACORNS (Fenton)
Bowl, 8" to 9" d., amber 65.00
Bowl, 8" to 9" d., blue 45.00
Bowl, 8" to 9" d., green 37.50
Bowl, 8" to 9" d., marigold......... 35.00

Bowl, 8" to 9" d., purple 50.00
Plate, green ....650.00 to 925.00

AZTEC (McKee)
Tumbler, marigold................. 450.00

BASKET (Northwood)

Aqua Opalescent Basket

Aqua opalescent, 4½" d., 4¾" h.
(ILLUS.) ....275.00 to 325.00
Cobalt blue...............90.00 to 115.00
Green........................... 265.00
Ice green...............175.00 to 250.00
Lavender 95.00
Marigold 65.00
Purple 95.00
Smoky 250.00
White 150.00

BASKETWEAVE VARIANT CANDY DISH (Fenton's Hat)
Ice green....................... 70.00
Marigold 45.00
Red 225.00

BEADED CABLE (Northwood)

Beaded Cable Rose Bowl

Bowl, 7" d., ruffled, marigold 30.00
Candy dish, green................. 45.00
Candy dish, marigold 30.00

Candy dish, purple 60.00
Rose bowl, aqua opalescent 250.00
Rose bowl, blue .... 75.00 to 90.00
Rose bowl, green 85.00
Rose bowl, ice blue 1,000.00
Rose bowl, marigold 55.00
Rose bowl, purple (ILLUS.) 70.00
Rose bowl, white .... 475.00 to 600.00

BEADED SHELL (Dugan or Diamond Glass Co.)

Beaded Shell Water Set

Berry set: master bowl & 3 footed
 sauce dishes; purple, 4 pcs. 200.00
Bowl, master berry, marigold 54.00
Butter dish, cov., purple 160.00
Creamer, marigold 60.00
Creamer, purple .... 45.00 to 70.00
Mug, blue .... 65.00 to 85.00
Mug, marigold .... 130.00 to 185.00
Mug, purple 80.00
Mug, white .... 650.00 to 1,225.00
Pitcher, water, marigold 300.00
Pitcher, water, purple 530.00
Rose bowl, green 40.00
Sauce dish, marigold 20.00
Spooner, footed, marigold 40.00
Sugar bowl, open, marigold 45.00
Table set, purple, 4 pcs. 525.00
Tumbler, blue 42.50
Tumbler, marigold .... 50.00 to 65.00
Tumbler, purple 47.50
Water set: pitcher & 6 tumblers;
 marigold, 7 pcs. (ILLUS.) 700.00

BEADS & BELLS

Bowl, 7" d., peach opalescent 37.50
Bowl, 7" d., purple 40.00

BEAUTY BUD VASE

Marigold, 8" h. .... 25.00 to 35.00
Purple, 8" h. 40.00

BIG FISH BOWL (Millersburg)

Green 325.00
Marigold, square 450.00
Purple, ice cream
 shape .... 475.00 to 500.00

Purple, round 267.00
Purple, square 307.00
Vaseline 3,500.00

BIRDS & CHERRIES

Bon bon, blue 60.00
Bon bon, green 75.00
Bon bon, marigold 38.00
Bon bon, purple 49.50
Bowl, 10" d., blue 450.00
Compote, blue 65.00
Compote, green 42.00
Compote, marigold 55.00
Compote, purple .... 50.00 to 65.00

BLACKBERRY (Fenton)

Miniature Blackberry Compotes

Basket, blue 40.00
Basket, red 260.00
Bowl, 5" d., purple 30.00
Bowl, 7" d., red 185.00
Bowl, 10" d., ruffled, green 125.00
Bowl, 10" d., ruffled, purple 125.00
Compote, miniature, blue 72.50
Compote, miniature, green 45.00
Compote, miniature, marigold
 (ILLUS. right) 55.00
Compote, miniature, purple (ILLUS.
 left) 55.00
Compote, miniature, white 375.00
Plate, openwork rim, marigold 220.00
Plate, openwork rim, white 400.00

BLACKBERRY BLOCK (Fenton)

Blackberry Block Pitcher

Pitcher, water, green 1,000.00
Pitcher, water, marigold 285.00
Pitcher, water, purple 900.00
Pitcher, water, vaseline 5,000.00
Pitcher, water, white 900.00
Tumbler, blue..............55.00 to 65.00
Tumbler, green 245.00
Tumbler, marigold................ 52.50
Tumbler, purple 100.00
Water set: pitcher & 4 tumblers;
  purple, 5 pcs. (ILLUS. of
  part) 1,300.00

BLACKBERRY BRAMBLE
Compote, ruffled,
  green ....35.00 to 45.00
Compote, ruffled, purple 37.50

BLACKBERRY SPRAY
Basket, medium, red 230.00
Bon bon, marigold 22.00
Bon bon, red 210.00
Bowl, 7" d., red 245.00
Compote, 5½" d., green 42.00
Hat shape, Amberina............. 200.00
Hat shape, aqua 35.00
Hat shape, aqua opalescent 145.00
Hat shape, blue 32.50
Hat shape, ice green opalescent 275.00
Hat shape, marigold............. 62.50
Hat shape, red................. 265.00
Hat shape, vaseline w/marigold 45.00

BLACKBERRY WREATH (Millersburg)
Bowl, 5" d., blue................ 40.00
Bowl, 5" d., green 40.00
Bowl, 5" d., marigold............. 32.50
Bowl, 5" d., purple 40.00
Bowl, 7" d., blue............... 350.00
Bowl, 7" d., green 42.50
Bowl, 7" d., marigold............. 36.50
Bowl, 7" d., purple 40.00
Bowl, 7" w., tricornered,
  purple 85.00
Bowl, 8" to 9" d., green 67.50
Bowl, 8" to 9" d., marigold......... 42.50
Bowl, 8" to 9" d., purple 62.50
Bowl, 10" d., green 65.00
Bowl, 10" d., marigold 67.50
Bowl, 10" d., purple 145.00
Bowl, ice cream, large, blue 750.00

BLOSSOM TIME
Compote, purple 90.00

BLUEBERRY (Fenton)
Tumbler, blue..............50.00 to 65.00
Tumbler, marigold................ 35.00
Water set: pitcher & 5 tumblers;
  blue, 6 pcs.................... 900.00

BO PEEP
Mug, marigold 150.00
Plate, marigold 350.00

BOUQUET
Pitcher, water, blue 465.00
Pitcher, water, marigold 179.00
Tumbler, blue.................... 40.00
Tumbler, marigold................ 28.00
Water set: pitcher & 5 tumblers;
  marigold, 6 pcs................. 300.00

BROKEN ARCHES (Imperial)

Broken Arches Punch Set

Punch bowl & base, marigold,
  12" d., 2 pcs. 245.00
Punch cup, marigold.............. 15.00
Punch cup, purple 20.00
Punch set: bowl, base & 6 cups;
  marigold, 8 pcs. (ILLUS.) 335.00
Punch set: bowl, base & 6 cups;
  purple, 8 pcs.................. 550.00

BUTTERFLIES

Butterflies Bon Bon

Bon bon, blue ....45.00 to 60.00
Bon bon, green ....35.00 to 45.00
Bon bon, marigold 40.00
Bon bon, purple (ILLUS.) 47.50

BUTTERFLY & BERRY (Fenton)
Berry set: master bowl & 6 sauce
  dishes; blue, 7 pcs.............. 425.00
Berry set: master bowl & 6 sauce
  dishes; marigold, 7 pcs. 165.00
Bowl, 7" d., 3-footed, marigold 48.00
Bowl, 8" to 9" d., footed, blue...... 77.50
Bowl, 8" to 9" d., footed, green 86.00
Bowl, 8" to 9" d., footed,
  marigold 60.00

Bowl, 8" to 9" d., footed,
  purple 95.00
Bowl, master berry or fruit,
  4-footed, blue.................... 128.00
Bowl, master berry or fruit,
  4-footed, green 140.00
Bowl, master berry or fruit,
  4-footed, marigold 62.50
Bowl, master berry or fruit,
  4-footed, purple................. 197.50
Bowl, master berry or fruit,
  4-footed, white 200.00
Butter dish, cov., blue 155.00
Butter dish, cov., marigold 90.00
Creamer, green 145.00
Creamer, marigold 50.00
Hatpin holder, blue................ 475.00
Hatpin holder, marigold 700.00
Nut bowl, blue.................... 725.00
Nut bowl, purple 185.00

Butterfly & Berry Pitcher

Pitcher, water, marigold
  (ILLUS.)......................... 190.00
Sauce dish, blue 32.50
Sauce dish, green 45.00
Sauce dish, marigold 30.00
Spooner, blue..................... 95.00
Spooner, green 95.00
Spooner, marigold................. 55.00
Spooner, purple................... 90.00
Sugar bowl, cov., green 125.00
Sugar bowl, cov., marigold........ 67.50
Table set, marigold, 4 pcs......... 300.00
Tumbler, blue..................... 37.50
Tumbler, green 50.00
Tumbler, marigold................. 25.00
Tumbler, purple................... 125.00
Vase, 7" h., blue 45.00
Vase, 8" h., marigold............. 30.00
Vase, 9" h., purple 55.00
Vase, 10" h., blue................ 46.50
Vase, red 400.00
Water set: pitcher & 6 tumblers;
  green, 7 pcs.................... 665.00
Water set: pitcher & 6 tumblers;
  purple, 7 pcs. 1,300.00

BUTTERFLY & FERN (Fenton)

Pitcher, water, blue ....350.00 to 395.00
Pitcher, water, green 450.00
Pitcher, water, purple 385.00
Tumbler, blue.................... 55.00
Tumbler, green 40.00
Tumbler, marigold................. 37.50
Tumbler, purple................... 40.00
Water set: pitcher & 4 tumblers;
  purple, 5 pcs................... 475.00
Water set: pitcher & 6 tumblers;
  blue, 7 pcs..................... 685.00
Water set: pitcher & 6 tumblers;
  green, 7 pcs.................... 695.00
Water set: pitcher & 6 tumblers;
  marigold, 7 pcs................. 500.00

BUTTERFLY & TULIP

Butterfly & Tulip Bowl

Bowl, 9" w., 5½" h., footed,
  marigold (ILLUS.) 250.00
Bowl, 9" w., footed, purple 700.00
Bowl, 10½" square flat shape,
  footed, marigold 310.00
Bowl, 10½" square flat shape,
  footed, purple ....900.00 to 1,200.00

CAPTIVE ROSE

Captive Rose Bowl

Bon bon, 2-handled, blue,
  7½" d............................ 60.00
Bon bon, 2-handled, purple,
  7½" d............................ 35.00
Bowl, 8" to 9" d., ribbon candy rim,
  blue (ILLUS.) 50.00
Bowl, 8" to 9" d., green 55.00
Bowl, 8" to 9" d., ruffled rim,
  marigold 30.00

Bowl, 8" to 9" d., ribbon candy rim,
  purple 42.50
Plate, 9" d., blue ....130.00 to 145.00
Plate, 9" d., green ....175.00 to 225.00
Plate, 9" d., marigold 120.00
Plate, 9" d., purple 125.00

CAROLINA DOGWOOD
Bowl, 8½" d., blue
  opalescent ....295.00 to 325.00
Bowl, 8½" d., marigold 40.00
Bowl, 8½" d., marigold on milk
  white ....295.00 to 450.00
Bowl, 8½" d., peach
  opalescent...................... 110.00
Plate, 8 5/8" d., peach
  opalescent...................... 300.00

CAROLINE
Basket w/applied handle, peach
  opalescent...................... 335.00
Bowl, 8" to 9" d., peach
  opalescent...................... 50.00
Bowl, 8" to 9" w., tricornered,
  peach opalescent............... 50.00
Bowl, 9" sq., peach opalescent 65.00
Plate, w/handgrip, peach
  opalescent...................... 135.00

CATTAILS & WATER LILY - See Water Lily & Cattails

CHATELAINE
Pitcher, purple 2,000.00
Tumbler, purple 375.00

CHECKERBOARD

Checkerboard Pattern

Goblet, marigold.................. 130.00
Goblet, purple 296.00
Pitcher, water, purple.............1,750.00
Tumbler, marigold................. 550.00

CHERRY (now attributed to Dugan - formerly Northwood)
Bowl, 7" d., 3-footed, crimped rim,
  peach opalescent................ 55.00

Bowl, 8" to 9" d., 3-footed,
  marigold 35.00
Bowl, 8" to 9" d., 3-footed, peach
  opalescent..................... 155.00
Bowl, 8" to 9" d., 3-footed, purple .. 55.00
Plate, ruffled, purple 125.00

CHERRY or CHERRY CIRCLES (Fenton)
Bon bon, 2-handled, blue 55.00
Bon bon, 2-handled, marigold 60.00
Bon bon, 2-handled, purple 50.00
Bon bon, 2-handled, red..........1,300.00
Bowl, 7" d., 3-footed, peach opales-
  cent w/plain interior 41.50
Bowl, 8" to 9" d., white............ 70.00
Plate, 6" d., marigold 42.00

CHERRY or HANGING CHERRIES (Millersburg)

Millersburg Cherry Pitcher & Tumbler

Banana compote (whimsey), green
  or marigold.................... 725.00
Banana compote (whimsey),
  purple 715.00
Bowl, 5" d., ruffled, blue satin 600.00
Bowl, 5" d., piecrust rim, purple.... 35.00
Bowl, 7" d., green 100.00
Bowl, 7" d., marigold 60.00
Bowl, 7" d., purple 115.00
Bowl, 8" to 9" d., dome-footed,
  marigold 75.00
Bowl, ice cream, 10" d., green or
  purple 120.00
Bowl, ice cream, 10" d.,
  marigold ....75.00 to 90.00
Bowl, ruffled, Hobnail exterior,
  marigold, large 485.00
Butter dish, cov., marigold 125.00
Butter dish, cov., purple 180.00
Creamer, green or marigold 62.50
Creamer, purple 77.50
Pitcher, milk, marigold 650.00
Pitcher, water, green (ILLUS.) 700.00
Pitcher, water, purple 545.00

Plate, 7" d., purple 300.00
Spooner, green 48.00
Spooner, marigold................. 66.50
Spooner, purple.............70.00 to 85.00
Sugar bowl, cov., marigold...60.00 to 75.00
Sugar bowl, cov., purple 125.00
Tumbler, green (ILLUS.) 225.00
Tumbler, marigold................. 225.00
Tumbler, purple 320.00

CHERRY CHAIN (Fenton)
Bon bon, 2-handled, marigold 42.50
Bowl, 5" d., blue 55.00
Bowl, 5" d., white 36.50
Bowl, 8" to 9" d., white........... 125.00
Bowl, 10" d., Orange Tree exterior,
  blue 65.00
Bowl, 10" d., Orange Tree exterior,
  marigold 40.00
Plate, 6" to 7" d., marigold 46.50

CHRISTMAS COMPOTE

Christmas Compote

Purple (ILLUS.) ....2,600.00 to 3,900.00

CHRYSANTHEMUM or WINDMILL & MUMS

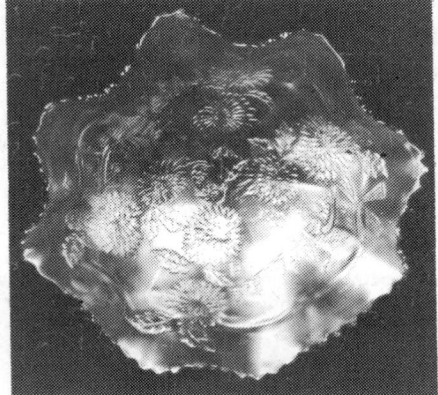

Chrysanthemum Bowl

Bowl, 8" to 9" d., 3-footed,
  blue 100.00

Bowl, 8" to 9" d., 3-footed,
  green 80.00
Bowl, 8" to 9" d., 3-footed,
  marigold 40.00
Bowl, 10" d., 3-footed, blue 75.00
Bowl, 10" d., 3-footed, green...... 150.00
Bowl, 10" d., 3-footed, marigold
  (ILLUS.)...................... 55.00
Bowl, 10" d., 3-footed, purple 65.00
Bowl, 10" d., collared base, red 950.00

CIRCLED SCROLL (Dugan or Diamond Glass Co.)

Circled Scroll Tumbler

Bowl, master berry, purple......... 75.00
Creamer, marigold ....40.00 to 57.50
Creamer, purple 65.00
Pitcher, water, marigold 950.00
Spooner, marigold................. 47.50
Tumbler, marigold (ILLUS.) .300.00 to 345.00
Tumbler, purple 1,050.00

COBBLESTONES BOWL (Imperial)
Green, 9" d...................... 37.50
Purple, 9" d...............50.00 to 60.00

COIN DOT (Northwood)

Coin Dot Bowl

Bowl, 7" d., ribbon candy rim, green
  (ILLUS.)........................ 50.00
Bowl, 7" d., marigold.............. 36.00
Bowl, 7" d., purple 28.00
Bowl, 7" d., red................... 450.00
Bowl, 8" to 9" d., stippled, aqua.... 50.00
Bowl, 8" to 9" d., blue.......40.00 to 55.00
Bowl, 8" to 9" d., green .....25.00 to 30.00
Bowl, 8" to 9" d., marigold......... 27.50
Bowl, 8" to 9" d., peach
  opalescent...................... 195.00
Bowl, 8" to 9" d., purple 37.50
Pitcher, water, marigold 130.00
Plate, purple...................... 55.00
Rose bowl, green ....50.00 to 65.00
Rose bowl, ice green 65.00
Rose bowl, marigold............... 50.00
Rose bowl, purple 70.00
Tumbler, marigold................. 48.00
Water set: pitcher & 6 tumblers;
  marigold, 7 pcs................. 425.00

COIN SPOT

Compote, 7" d., marigold 25.00
Compote, 7" d., fluted, peach
  opalescent...................... 46.00
Plate, 9" d., purple............... 35.00

COMET or RIBBON TIE (Fenton)

Comet Bowl

Bowl, 8" to 9" d., blue (ILLUS.) 67.50
Bowl, 8" to 9" d., green 51.50
Bowl, 8" to 9" d., marigold........ 33.50
Bowl, 8" to 9" d., purple 37.50
Plate, 9" d., ruffled, blue 160.00
Plate, 9" d., ruffled, purple 115.00

CONE & FLUTE

Creamer, marigold 15.00
Pitcher, marigold.................. 110.00

CONSTELLATION

Compote, marigold 65.00
Compote, white 130.00

CORAL (Fenton)

Bowl, 8½" d., collared base,
  green 120.00
Bowl, 9½" d., collared base,
  marigold ....55.00 to 70.00
Plate, 9" d., marigold 700.00

CORN BOTTLE

Corn Bottle

Green........................... 225.00
Marigold 225.00
Smoky (ILLUS.) 210.00

CORN VASE (Northwood)

Corn Vases

Aqua opalescent 2,750.00
Green........................... 350.00
Ice green........................ 280.00
Marigold (ILLUS. center) 385.00
Pastel blue 375.00
Purple (ILLUS. right) 400.00
White (ILLUS. left) 200.00

CORNUCOPIA

Candlestick, white (single) 85.00
Candlesticks, ice blue, pr. 115.00

COSMOS

Bowl, 5" d., green 37.50
Bowl, 9" d., green 60.00
Bowl, 9" d ., marigold 27.50
Bowl, 10" d., marigold............ 45.00

Bowl, ice cream, 10½" d.,
  marigold 88.00
Plate, 9" d., green 62.50
Plate, 9" d., marigold 65.00

Cosmos Plate

Plate, chop, 10½" d., marigold
  (ILLUS.)........................ 115.00

COSMOS & CANE

Cosmos & Cane Butter Dish

Bowl, 8" to 9" d., marigold........ 50.00
Bowl, 10" d., white........120.00 to 135.00
Butter dish, cov., white (ILLUS.)..... 300.00
Compote, marigold 60.00
Compote, white 165.00
Creamer, marigold 95.00
Cuspidor, clambroth 675.00
Cuspidor, white 750.00
Pitcher, white 1,200.00
Rose bowl, Headdress interior,
  marigold 150.00
Spooner, 2-handled, marigold 65.00
Tumbler, amber 125.00
Tumbler, clambroth................ 110.00
Tumbler, marigold................. 75.00
Tumbler, marigold, w/advertising... 120.00
Tumbler, white.................... 175.00

COUNTRY KITCHEN (Millersburg)

Bowl, 5" d., ruffled, marigold 97.50
Spooner, marigold................. 100.00
Sugar bowl, cov., vaseline 550.00

CRAB CLAW (Imperial)

Crab Claw Water Set

Bowl, 8" to 9" d., fluted rim,
  smoky 50.00
Pitcher, marigold.................. 220.00
Sauce dish, smoky 20.00
Tumbler, marigold................. 45.00
Water set: pitcher & 4 tumblers;
  marigold, 5 pcs. (ILLUS.) 350.00

CRACKLE

Candy jar, cov., marigold 50.00
Cuspidor, marigold 50.00
Plate, 9½" d., purple............. 40.00
Water set: cov. pitcher & 5 tum-
  blers; marigold, 6 pcs........... 90.00

CRUCIFIX

Candlesticks, marigold, pr......... 400.00

CUT ARCS

Bowl, 9" d., marigold............. 20.00
Compote, 6½" d., 5" h., green 25.50

DAHLIA (Dugan or Diamond Glass Co.)

Berry set: master bowl & 5 sauce
  dishes; purple, 6 pcs............ 275.00
Berry set: master bowl & 6 sauce
  dishes; white, 7 pcs. 225.00
Bowl, master berry, 10" d., footed,
  white 170.00
Butter dish, cov., marigold 85.00
Creamer, marigold 80.00
Creamer, purple ....75.00 to 125.00
Creamer, white 105.00
Creamer & spooner, purple, pr. 225.00
Pitcher, water, purple 600.00
Pitcher, water, white ......550.00 to 600.00
Sauce dish, purple................ 33.00
Sauce dish, white 36.50
Spooner, marigold................. 60.00
Spooner, purple 75.00

Sugar bowl, cov., purple 100.00
Table set: cov. sugar bowl, cov. but-
ter dish & spooner; marigold,
3 pcs. 200.00
Table set, purple, 4 pcs. . . .825.00 to 850.00
Table set, white, 4 pcs. 650.00
Tumbler, marigold. 82.50
Tumbler, purple. 92.50
Tumbler, white. 175.00
Water set: pitcher & 6 tumblers;
marigold, 7 pcs., ...1,025.00

DAISIES & DRAPE VASE (Northwood)
Aqua opalescent . . . . .350.00 to 400.00
Blue 185.00
Marigold 135.00
Purple 230.00
White . . . . .145.00 to 175.00

DAISY & LATTICE BAND
Pitcher, tankard, marigold . .90.00 to 125.00
Tumbler, blue.   50.00
Tumbler, marigold. 20.00
Water set: pitcher & 6 tumblers;
marigold, 7 pcs. 225.00

DAISY & PLUME

Daisy & Plume Rose Bowl

Bowl, 8" to 9" d., 3-footed,
marigold 45.00
Candy dish, footed, green 48.00
Compote, green 37.50
Compote, marigold 32.50
Compote, purple 45.00
Rose bowl, 3-footed, blue 50.00
Rose bowl, 3-footed, green 60.00
Rose bowl, 3-footed, ice blue. 800.00
Rose bowl, 3-footed, ice green 750.00
Rose bowl, 3-footed, marigold 50.00
Rose bowl, 3-footed, purple
(ILLUS.). 70.00

DAISY BLOCK ROWBOAT
Marigold, 12" l., 4" w.,
3¼" h. . . . . .150.00 to 175.00
Purple 215.00

DAISY WREATH (Westmoreland)
Bowl, 8" to 9" d., blue opalescent . . 400.00
Bowl, 8" to 9" d., milk glass
w/marigold overlay . . . . .150.00 to 200.00
Bowl, 8" to 9" d., peach
opalescent. . . . . .65.00 to 95.00
Plate, 9" d., ruffled, aqua 350.00

DANDELION (Northwood)

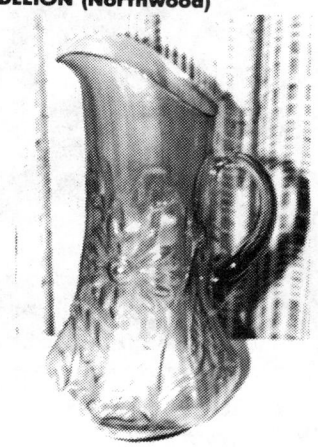

Dandelion Pitcher

Mug, aqua opalescent . . . . .450.00 to 475.00
Mug, blue 425.00
Mug, ice blue. 625.00
Mug, green. . . . . .650.00 to 700.00
Mug, marigold 235.00
Mug, purple 265.00
Mug, Knight's Templar, ice blue. . . .1,000.00
Mug, Knight's Templar, ice green . . . 900.00
Mug, Knight's Templar, marigold . . . 375.00
Pitcher, water, tankard, green 750.00
Pitcher, water, tankard, marigold
(ILLUS.) . . . . .275.00 to 325.00
Pitcher, water, purple 825.00
Pitcher, water, white 2,000.00
Tumbler, green 90.00
Tumbler, ice blue . . . . .150.00 to 185.00
Tumbler, ice green 245.00
Tumbler, marigold. 45.00
Tumbler, purple 52.50
Tumbler, smoky 75.00
Tumbler, white. 120.00
Water set: pitcher & 6 tumblers;
marigold, 7 pcs. 600.00
Water set: pitcher & 6 tumblers;
purple, 7 pcs. 800.00

DANDELION, PANELED (Fenton)
Pitcher, water, blue . . . . . . .325.00 to 375.00
Pitcher, water, green. 325.00
Pitcher, water, marigold 265.00
Pitcher, water, purple 800.00
Tumbler, blue.   35.00
Tumbler, green 40.00

Tumbler, marigold................ 35.00
Tumbler, purple.................... 35.00
Water set: pitcher & 5 tumblers;
blue, 6 pcs...................... 850.00

Paneled Dandelion Pitcher

Water set: pitcher & 6 tumblers;
green, 7 pcs. (ILLUS. of
pitcher) 735.00
Water set: pitcher & 6 tumblers;
marigold, 7 pcs.................. 450.00
Water set: pitcher & 6 tumblers;
purple, 7 pcs. 650.00

DIAMOND (Millersburg)
Pitcher, water, green............. 195.00
Pitcher, water, marigold 185.00
Pitcher, water, purple 175.00
Punch bowl & base, purple, 2 pcs. .. 900.00
Tumbler, green.................... 42.50
Tumbler, marigold................. 40.00
Tumbler, purple.............35.00 to 45.00
Water set: pitcher & 6 tumblers;
green, 7 pcs. 348.00
Water set: pitcher & 6 tumblers;
marigold, 7 pcs.................. 390.00
Water set: pitcher & 6 tumblers;
purple, 7 pcs. 475.00

DIAMOND & RIB VASE
Vase, 8" h., green 22.00
Vase, 10" h., green 30.00
Vase, 10" h., marigold............. 22.00
Vase, 10" h., purple 29.00
Vase, 11" h., ice green 36.00
Vase, 19" h., purple 395.00

DIAMOND & SUNBURST
Decanter w/stopper, marigold...... 60.00
Wine, marigold 25.00
Wine, purple ....50.00 to 60.00
Wine set: decanter w/stopper & 6
wines; marigold, 7 pcs. 325.00
Wine set: decanter w/stopper & 6
wines; purple, 7 pcs. 495.00

DIAMOND CONCAVE
Pitcher w/cover, vaseline 550.00
Tumbler, ice blue 30.00
Tumbler, vaseline 210.00

DIAMOND LACE (Imperial)

Diamond Lace Pitcher & Tumbler

Bowl, 5" d., marigold............. 10.00
Bowl, 5" d., purple 22.00
Bowl, 8" to 9" d., clambroth....... 55.00
Bowl, 8" to 9" d., marigold........ 32.50
Bowl, 8" to 9" d., purple 60.00
Bowl, 10" d., purple 65.00
Pitcher, water, purple (ILLUS.) 235.00
Tumbler, purple (ILLUS.) 45.00
Water set: pitcher & 6 tumblers;
purple, 7 pcs. 440.00

DIAMOND POINT COLUMN

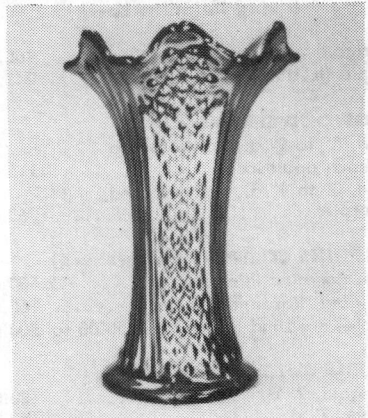

Diamond Point Column Vase

Vase, 8" h., green (ILLUS.) 40.00
Vase, 10" h., white................ 42.50

DIAMOND RING
Bowl, 8" to 9" d., marigold........ 35.00

Diamond Ring Bowl

Bowl, 8" to 9" d., smoky
(ILLUS.)..................30.00 to 40.00

DIVING DOLPHINS FOOTED BOWL

Diving Dolphins Bowl

Marigold 160.00
Purple (ILLUS.) 245.00

DOGWOOD SPRAYS

Bowl, 8" to 9" d., dome-footed,
peach opalescent................ 115.00
Bowl, 8" to 9" d., dome-footed,
purple 65.00

DOLPHINS COMPOTE (Millersburg)

Blue, Rosalind interior 2,500.00
Marigold, Rosalind interior 168.00
Purple, Rosalind interior ...750.00 to 800.00

DOUBLE DUTCH BOWL

Marigold, 7" d. 20.00
Purple, 7" d. 42.00
Marigold, 8" to 9" d., footed 45.00
Purple, 8" to 9" d., footed 80.00

DOUBLE STAR or BUZZ SAW (Cambridge)

Cruet w/stopper, green, large, 6" .. 400.00
Cruet w/stopper, marigold, large,
6" 200.00

Pitcher, water, green......325.00 to 400.00
Pitcher, water, marigold 425.00
Tumbler, green 45.00
Water set: pitcher & 6 tumblers;
green, 7 pcs. 500.00

DOUBLE STEM ROSE

Bowl, 8" to 9" d., dome-footed,
marigold 26.00
Bowl, 8" to 9" d., dome-footed,
peach opalescent................ 100.00
Bowl, 8" to 9" d., dome-footed,
purple 47.50
Bowl, 8" to 9" d., dome-footed,
white 77.50
Plate, dome-footed,
white ....135.00 to 185.00

DRAGON & LOTUS (Fenton)

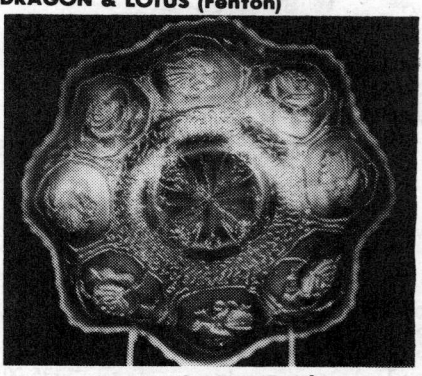

Dragon & Lotus Bowl

Bowl, 7" d., 3-footed, blue 50.00
Bowl, 7" d., 3-footed, green........ 50.00
Bowl, 7" d., 3-footed, purple 50.00
Bowl, 8" to 9" d., amber 80.00
Bowl, 8" to 9" d., collared base,
aqua opalescent (ILLUS.) 650.00
Bowl, 8" to 9" d., 3-footed, blue 65.00
Bowl, 8" to 9" d., 3-footed, green... 57.50
Bowl, 8" to 9" d., collared base,
lime green opalescent 485.00
Bowl, 8" to 9" d., 3-footed,
marigold 37.50
Bowl, 8" to 9" d., 3-footed, peach
opalescent.................... 435.00
Bowl, 8" to 9" d., 3-footed,
purple ....50.00 to 85.00
Bowl, 8" to 9" d., red .....525.00 to 625.00
Bowl, ice cream shape, 10" d.,
amber 175.00
Bowl, ice cream shape, 10" d.,
blue 60.00
Bowl, ice cream shape, 10" d.,
red 625.00
Plate, collared base, blue 700.00
Plate, collared base, ruffled,
marigold 350.00
Plate, spatula footed, marigold 650.00

DRAGON & STRAWBERRY BOWL (Fenton)
Bowl, 9" d., blue 435.00
Bowl, 9" d., green 400.00
Bowl, 9" d., marigold 300.00

DRAPERY (Northwood)
Candy dish, tricornered, ice blue ... 95.00
Candy dish, tricornered, purple 120.00
Candy dish, tricornered, white 90.00
Rose bowl, aqua opalescent 265.00
Rose bowl, blue 350.00
Rose bowl, ice blue 475.00
Rose bowl, marigold 345.00
Rose bowl, purple 160.00
Rose bowl, white 360.00
Vase, 7" h., aqua opalescent 150.00
Vase, 7" h., blue 60.00
Vase, 8" h., ice green 100.00
Vase, 8" h., white 52.50

EMBROIDERED MUMS (Northwood)
Bowl, 8" to 9" d., amber 125.00
Bowl, 8" to 9" d., blue 125.00
Bowl, 8" to 9" d., ice blue 365.00
Bowl, 8" to 9" d., ice green 265.00
Bowl, 8" to 9" d., marigold 52.00
Bowl, 8" to 9" d., purple 85.00
Plate, ice green ....775.00 to 875.00

ESTATE
Creamer, marigold opalescent 45.00
Creamer, peach opalescent 75.00
Creamer & sugar bowl, aqua
   opalescent, pr.................. 275.00
Mug, marigold 72.50

FANCIFUL (Dugan)
Bowl, 8" to 9" d., blue 82.50
Bowl, 8" to 9" d., peach
   opalescent..................... 150.00
Bowl, 8" to 9" d., purple 65.00
Bowl, 8" to 9" d., ruffled, white 110.00
Plate, 9" d., blue 180.00
Plate, 9" d., marigold 90.00
Plate, 9" d., peach opalescent 300.00
Plate, 9" d., purple ....175.00 to 225.00
Plate, 9" d., white ....150.00 to 175.00

FANTAIL
Bowl, 9" d., footed, blue 72.50
Bowl, 9" d., shallow, footed, w/But-
   terfly & Berry exterior, blue 95.00
Bowl, 9" d., footed, green 80.00
Bowl, 9" d., footed, marigold 50.00

FARMYARD (Dugan)
Bowl, ribbon candy rim,
   purple ....1,900.00 to 2,500.00
Bowl, square, purple (ILLUS.) 2,900.00

Farmyard Bowl

Plate, 10" d., purple 8,125.00

FASHION (Imperial)
Bowl, 9" d., clambroth 25.00
Bowl, 9" d., marigold 20.00
Bowl, 9" d., ruffled, smoky 45.00
Compote, smoky 150.00
Creamer, marigold 22.50
Creamer, purple 30.00
Creamer, smoky 50.00
Creamer & sugar bowl, marigold,
   pr............................. 60.00
Pitcher, water, marigold ...100.00 to 115.00
Pitcher, water, purple .....825.00 to 900.00
Pitcher, water, smoky 335.00
Punch bowl & base, marigold,
   12" d., 2 pcs. 72.50
Punch cup, marigold 12.50
Punch cup, smoky 30.00

Fashion Punch Set

Punch set: 12" d. bowl, base &
   6 cups; marigold, 8 pcs.
   (ILLUS.) ....185.00 to 245.00
Rose bowl, marigold, 7" d. 65.00
Sugar bowl, marigold 20.00
Sugar bowl, smoky 90.00
Tumbler, marigold................. 22.50
Tumbler, smoky 65.00
Water set: pitcher & 6 tumblers;
   marigold, 7 pcs. ....225.00 to 275.00

FEATHER & HEART
Pitcher, water, marigold 350.00

Heart & Feather Pitcher

Pitcher, water, green (ILLUS.) 550.00
Pitcher, water, purple 475.00
Tumbler, green 150.00
Tumbler, marigold................ 55.00
Tumbler, purple...........70.00 to 115.00

FEATHER STITCH BOWL
Blue 55.00
Marigold 42.50

FEATHERED SERPENT
Berry set: master bowl & 6 sauce
  dishes; green, 7 pcs. 140.00
Berry set: master bowl & 6 sauce
  dishes; marigold, 7 pcs. 195.00
Bowl, 8" to 9" d., green 70.00
Bowl, 8" to 9" d., marigold........ 48.00
Bowl, 8" to 9" d., purple 47.50
Bowl, 10" d., ruffled, blue 63.50
Bowl, 10" d., fluted, green 45.00
Bowl, 10" d., flared, purple 62.50
Sauce dish, green 20.00
Sauce dish, marigold 16.50

FENTON'S (OPEN EDGE) BASKET
Black 365.00
Blue 65.00
Ice blue, w/three rows of lace 125.00
Ice green....................... 90.00
Marigold ....18.00 to 25.00
Purple 50.00
Red....................210.00 to 250.00
Vaseline ....40.00 to 58.00
White, square................... 70.00

FENTON'S FLOWERS
Rose bowl, blue................. 75.00
Rose bowl, green 56.50
Rose bowl, ice green opalescent.... 650.00
Rose bowl, marigold.............. 65.00
Rose bowl, white................. 275.00

FENTONIA
Butter dish, cov., footed, blue 150.00
Butter dish, cov., footed, marigold.. 120.00
Creamer, blue 50.00

Creamer, marigold 65.00
Pitcher, water, blue 375.00
Pitcher, water, marigold 230.00
Spooner, blue................... 85.00
Spooner, claw feet, marigold...... 60.00
Table set, blue, 4 pcs. 350.00
Tumbler, blue................... 48.00
Tumbler, marigold ....35.00 to 45.00

Fentonia Water Set

Water set: pitcher & 6 tumblers;
  blue, 7 pcs. (ILLUS.) 750.00

FERN
Compote, marigold 110.00
Compote, 6" d., 5" h.,
  purple ....35.00 to 45.00
Dish, hat-shaped, red (Fenton) 375.00

FIELD FLOWER (Imperial)
Pitcher, water, amber 300.00
Pitcher, water, green 185.00
Pitcher, water, marigold 115.00
Pitcher, water, purple 400.00
Tumbler, green 55.00
Tumbler, marigold................ 32.50
Tumbler, purple 100.00

FIELD THISTLE (English)
Bowl, 10" d., marigold............ 50.00
Compote, marigold 195.00
Pitcher, water, marigold 250.00
Plate, 6" d., marigold............ 110.00
Plate, 9" d., marigold 450.00
Spooner, marigold............... 55.00
Tumbler, marigold............... 60.00
Vase, 7" h., marigold............. 45.00

FILE & FAN
Compote, blue opalescent......... 125.00
Compote, peach opalescent 130.00

FINECUT & ROSES (Northwood)
Candy dish, 3-footed, amber 55.00
Candy dish, 3-footed, green 55.00
Candy dish, 3-footed, ice blue 95.00
Candy dish, 3-footed, marigold 30.00
Candy dish, 3-footed,
  purple ....45.00 to 85.00
Candy dish, 3-footed, white 75.00

Rose bowl, aqua opalescent 700.00
Rose bowl, green 175.00
Rose bowl, ice blue . . . . 250.00 to 310.00
Rose bowl, marigold. 115.00
Rose bowl, purple. . . . . 65.00 to 100.00
Rose bowl, white. 250.00

FINE RIB (Northwood & Fenton)

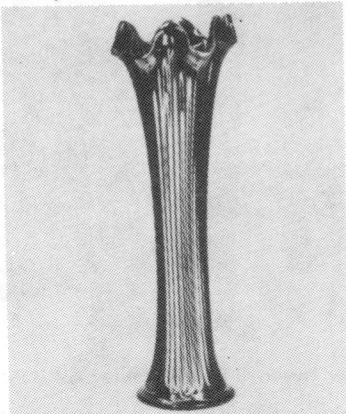

Fine Rib Vase

Vase, 6½" h., 5" d., squatty,
  marigold 32.00
Vase, 9" h., scalloped rim, blue 28.00
Vase, 9" h., fluted rim, ice green . . . 40.00
Vase, 9" h., 3½" d., marigold 20.00
Vase, 9" h., red (Fenton) 175.00
Vase, 10" h., amber (Fenton). 27.00
Vase, 10" h., red (Fenton) 235.00
Vase, 11" h., blue (ILLUS.) 40.00
Vase, 14" h., ice green 225.00
Vase, 15" h., blue. 50.00
Vase, 15" h., marigold. 22.00
Vase, 16" h., red, Fenton 350.00

FISHERMAN'S MUG

Fisherman's Mug

Marigold 225.00
Peach opalescent (ILLUS.). 1,085.00
Purple . . . . .80.00 to 125.00

FISHSCALE & BEADS
Bowl, 7" d., marigold 15.00

Bowl, 7" d., ribbon candy rim,
  purple 25.00
Plate, 7" d., marigold 35.00
Plate, 7" d., ruffled rim, peach
  opalescent. 100.00
Plate, 7" d., purple 300.00
Plate, 7" d., white 80.00
Plate, 8" d., clambroth 50.00

FLEUR DE LIS (Millersburg)

Fleur De Lis Bowl

Bowl, 10" d., green . . . . . . .165.00 to 225.00
Bowl, 10" d., marigold (ILLUS.) 165.00
Bowl, 10" d., purple . . . . . . .160.00 to 195.00

FLORAL & GRAPE (Dugan or Diamond Glass Co.)
Pitcher, water, blue 195.00
Pitcher, water, marigold 125.00
Pitcher, water, purple 150.00
Pitcher, water, white 275.00
Tumbler, blue. . . . . .25.00 to 35.00
Tumbler, marigold. 15.00
Tumbler, purple 32.50
Tumbler, white. 60.00
Water set: pitcher & 4 tumblers;
  purple, 5 pcs. 400.00
Water set: pitcher & 6 tumblers;
  marigold, 7 pcs. 245.00

FLORAL & WHEAT COMPOTE
Clambroth 35.00
Marigold 25.00
Peach opalescent. 70.00
White 70.00

FLOWERS & FRAMES
Bowl, 7" d., dome-footed, purple . . . 105.00
Bowl, 9" d., dome-footed, peach
  opalescent. 70.00
Bowl, 9" d., dome-footed, fluted,
  purple 75.00

FLUTE (Imperial)
Berry set: master bowl & 6 sauce
  dishes; purple, 7 pcs. 250.00

Bowl, 8" to 9" d., green 40.00
Breakfast set: individual size
  creamer & sugar bowl; purple,
   pr............................. 110.00
Creamer, clambroth 15.00
Creamer, marigold 29.00
Pitcher, water, clambroth 100.00
Pitcher, water, marigold 175.00
Pitcher, water, purple 325.00
Punch cup, green 12.50
Punch cup, marigold.............. 30.00
Punch cup, purple 28.00

Flute Punch Set

Punch set: bowl, base & 5 cups;
  purple, 7 pcs. (ILLUS.) 535.00
Salt dip, footed, individual size,
  marigold 40.00
Sauce dish, marigold 25.00
Sauce dish, purple 20.00
Sugar bowl, breakfast size, purple .. 70.00
Sugar bowl, cov., green 20.00
Table set: creamer, sugar bowl &
  toothpick holder; purple, 3 pcs.... 225.00
Toothpick holder, green 50.00
Toothpick holder, lavender 125.00
Toothpick holder, marigold 65.00
Toothpick holder, purple 75.00
Toothpick holder, vaseline 295.00
Tumbler, marigold................. 39.00
Tumbler, purple 90.00

FLUTE & CANE
Goblet, marigold.................. 85.00
Pitcher, milk, marigold 110.00
Pitcher, tankard, marigold 365.00

FOUR SEVENTY FOUR (Imperial)
Goblet, water, marigold 125.00
Pitcher, milk, green 180.00
Pitcher, milk, marigold 195.00
Pitcher, milk, purple.............. 200.00
Pitcher, water, green
  (ILLUS.) ....240.00 to 300.00
Pitcher, water, marigold ...125.00 to 190.00
Punch bowl & base, green, 2 pcs.... 390.00
Punch bowl & base, purple, 2 pcs. .. 900.00
Punch cup, green 25.00

Punch cup, marigold.............. 22.50
Punch cup, purple 45.00
Punch set: bowl, base & 4 cups;
  marigold, 6 pcs.................. 175.00
Punch set: bowl, base & 5 cups;
  green, 7 pcs. 350.00

Four Seventy Four Tumbler & Pitcher

Tumbler, green (ILLUS.) 75.00
Tumbler, marigold................. 25.00
Tumbler, purple 75.00
Vase, 16" h., green...............1,925.00

FROLICKING BEARS (U.S. Glass)

Frolicking Bears Pitcher

Pitcher, green (ILLUS.) ..3,000.00 to 6,000.00

FROSTED BLOCK
Bowl, scalloped & fluted,
  clambroth 26.50
Compote, clambroth 65.00
Creamer, clambroth 16.00
Plate, 7" sq., clambroth........... 18.00
Plate, 9" d., clambroth 25.00
Relish, marigold.................. 37.50
Rose bowl, clambroth............. 60.00

Rose bowl, marigold............. 25.00
Sugar bowl, clambroth............ 20.00

FRUIT SALAD
Punch bowl & base, purple, 2 pcs. . . 750.00
Punch cup, marigold.............. 15.00
Punch cup, peach opalescent 90.00

FRUITS & FLOWERS (Northwood)
Berry set: master bowl & 6 sauce
  dishes; purple, 7 pcs............ 230.00
Bon bon, stemmed, 2-handled, aqua
  opalescent..................... 400.00
Bon bon, stemmed, 2-handled,
  blue 110.00
Bon bon, stemmed, 2-handled,
  green 55.00
Bon bon, stemmed, 2-handled, ice
  blue 365.00
Bon bon, stemmed, 2-handled,
  marigold 40.00
Bon bon, stemmed, 2-handled,
  purple ....65.00 to 80.00
Bon bon, stemmed, 2-handled,
  white 375.00
Bowl, 7" d., purple 125.00
Bowl, 7" d., ruffled, ice green 300.00
Bowl, master berry, 10" d., ice
  green 750.00
Card tray, green 100.00
Plate, 7" d., blue................. 320.00
Plate, 7" d., green 130.00
Plate, 7" d., marigold 140.00
Plate, 7" d., purple 100.00
Plate, 7½" d., hand-grip, pastel
  marigold 185.00
Plate, 7½" d., hand-grip, purple.... 87.50
Sauce dish, purple ....28.00 to 35.00

GARDEN PATH

Garden Path Chop Plate

Bowl, 8" to 9" d., marigold......... 40.00
Bowl, 10" d., ruffled, marigold 75.00
Bowl, 10" d., ruffled, white 140.00
Plate, 7" d., peach opalescent 500.00

Plate, chop, 11" d., purple
  (ILLUS.) 1,775.00
Sauce dish, peach opalescent 115.00

GARLAND ROSE BOWL (Fenton)
Blue 75.00
Marigold 43.50

GAY NINETIES (Millersburg)
Pitcher, green...................5,550.00
Tumbler, purple 1,000.00

GOD & HOME

God & Home Tumbler & Pitcher

Pitcher, blue (ILLUS.).............1,200.00
Tumbler, blue (ILLUS.) 130.00

GODDESS OF HARVEST (Fenton)

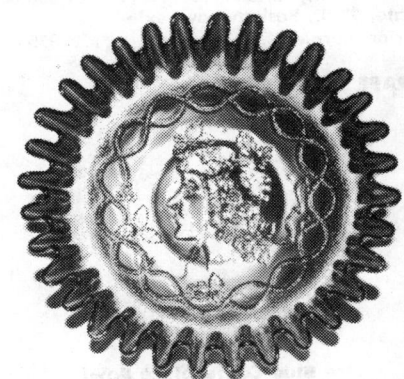

Goddess of Harvest Bowl

Bowl, marigold (ILLUS.)............3,500.00

GOLDEN HARVEST (U.S. Glass)
Decanter w/stopper, marigold...... 130.00
Decanter w/stopper,
  purple ....150.00 to 175.00
Wine, marigold 19.00
Wine, purple...................... 30.00
Wine set: decanter & 6 wines;
  purple, 7 pcs.................... 450.00

GOOD LUCK

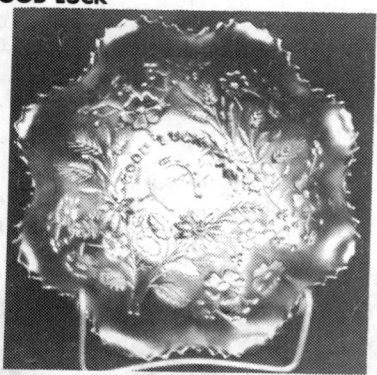

Good Luck Bowl

Bowl, 7" d., blue 210.00
Bowl, 7" d., ruffled, purple 128.00
Bowl, 8" to 9" d., fluted, aqua
  opalescent...................... 635.00
Bowl, 8" to 9" d., fluted, blue
  (ILLUS.).......................... 165.00
Bowl, 8" to 9" d., fluted, green 160.00
Bowl, 8" to 9" d., fluted, marigold .. 87.50
Bowl, 8" to 9" d., fluted, purple 150.00
Bowl, 8" to 9" d., fluted, teal blue
  (Northwood) 500.00
Bowl, 8" to 9" d., fluted, turquoise.. 225.00
Plate, 9" d., green ....400.00 to 475.00
Plate, 9" d., marigold 230.00
Plate, 9" d., purple.......180.00 to 260.00
Plate, 9" d., white 1,600.00
Plate, 9" d., Basketweave exte-
  rior, purple 375.00

GRAPE & CABLE

Ice Blue Centerpiece Bowl

Banana boat, blue ....220.00 to 265.00
Banana boat, green 225.00
Banana boat, ice blue 450.00
Banana boat, ice green 475.00
Banana boat, marigold 150.00
Banana boat, purple 165.00
Berry set: master bowl & 3 sauce
  dishes; green, 4 pcs. 200.00
Berry set: master bowl & 4 sauce
  dishes; purple, 5 pcs............. 130.00
Berry set: master bowl & 6 sauce
  dishes; green, 7 pcs. 210.00

Berry set: master bowl & 6 sauce
  dishes; purple, 7 pcs............. 250.00
Berry set: master bowl & 8 sauce
  dishes; purple, 9 pcs............. 400.00
Bon bon, 2-handled, blue 70.00
Bon bon, 2-handled, green 55.00
Bon bon, 2-handled, marigold 45.00
Bowl, 5" d., blue (Fenton).......... 25.00
Bowl, 5" d., marigold.............. 40.00
Bowl, 5" d., purple 32.50
Bowl, 6" d., red (Fenton).......... 425.00
Bowl, 7½" d., ball-footed, amber
  (Fenton) 100.00
Bowl, 7½" d., ball-footed, blue
  (Fenton) 30.00
Bowl, 7½" d., ball-footed, marigold
  (Fenton) 27.00
Bowl, 7½" d., ball-footed, purple
  (Fenton) 68.00
Bowl, 7½" d., ball-footed, vaseline
  (Fenton) 100.00
Bowl, 7½" d., ruffled, ice blue 500.00
Bowl, 7½" d., spatula-footed, green
  (Northwood) 45.00
Bowl, 7½" d., spatula-footed,
  marigold (Northwood) 28.00
Bowl, 7½" d., spatula-footed, purple
  (Northwood) 60.00
Bowl, 8" to 9" d., aqua opalescent
  (Northwood) 900.00
Bowl, 8" to 9" d., ball-footed,
  purple (Fenton) 55.00
Bowl, 8" to 9" d., ball-footed, red
  (Fenton) 1,200.00
Bowl, 8" to 9" d., spatula-footed,
  green (Northwood) 55.00
Bowl, 8" to 9" d., spatula-footed,
  marigold (Northwood) 65.00
Bowl, 8" to 9" d., spatula-footed,
  ruffled, purple
  (Northwood) ....50.00 to 65.00
Bowl, 8" to 9" d., stippled,
  ice blue 650.00
Bowl, berry or fruit, 9" d., green ... 67.50
Bowl, berry or fruit, 9" d., stippled,
  ice blue ....475.00 to 800.00
Bowl, berry or fruit, 9" d.,
  ice green...................... 650.00
Bowl, berry or fruit, 9" d.,
  marigold ....100.00 to 140.00
Bowl, berry or fruit, 9" d.,
  purple ....70.00 to 95.00
Bowl, orange, 10½" d., footed,
  Persian Medallion interior, blue
  (Fenton) 190.00
Bowl, orange, 10½" d., footed,
  Persian Medallion interior, green
  (Fenton) 235.00
Bowl, orange, 10½" d., footed,
  Persian Medallion interior,
  marigold (Fenton) 95.00
Bowl, orange, 10½" d., footed,
  Persian Medallion interior, purple
  (Fenton) 155.00

Bowl, orange, 10½" d., footed,
  ice blue 825.00
Bowl, orange, 10½" d., footed,
  marigold 120.00
Bowl, orange, 10½" d., footed,
  purple 225.00
Bowl, orange, 10½" d., footed,
  white 600.00
Bowl, 10½" d., ruffled, Basketweave exterior, green 110.00
Bowl, ice cream, 11" d., green 115.00
Bowl, ice cream, 11" d., marigold .. 90.00
Bowl, ice cream, 11" d., white 180.00
Breakfast set: individual size
  creamer & sugar bowl; green,
  pr. 135.00
Breakfast set: individual size
  creamer & sugar bowl; marigold,
  pr. 77.50
Breakfast set: individual size
  creamer & sugar bowl; purple,
  pr. 210.00
Butter dish, cov., green 162.50
Butter dish, cov., marigold 135.00
Butter dish, cov., purple 200.00
Candle lamp, green 585.00
Candle lamp, purple 385.00
Candle lamp shade, green 235.00
Candle lamp shade, marigold 210.00
Candle lamp shade, purple 235.00
Candlestick, green (single) ..80.00 to 110.00
Candlesticks, marigold, pr. 145.00
Candlesticks, purple, pr. 235.00
Centerpiece bowl, blue 350.00
Centerpiece bowl, green 285.00
Centerpiece bowl, ice blue
  (ILLUS.) 850.00
Centerpiece bowl, ice green 625.00
Centerpiece bowl,
  marigold ....175.00 to 225.00
Centerpiece bowl, purple 255.00
Centerpiece bowl, white 350.00
Cologne bottle w/stopper,
  marigold 145.00
Cologne bottle w/stopper, purple ... 250.00
Compote, cov., marigold, large 1,250.00
Compote, cov., purple, small 175.00
Compote, cov., purple,
  large ....350.00 to 475.00
Compote, open, green, large 400.00
Compote, open, purple, small 240.00
Compote, open, purple,
  large ....400.00 to 425.00
Cookie jar, cov., marigold 230.00
Cookie jar, cov., purple 275.00
Cookie jar, cov., white 525.00
Creamer, green 100.00
Creamer, purple 100.00
Creamer, individual size, green 60.00
Creamer, individual size, marigold .. 75.00
Creamer, individual size, purple 67.50
Cup & saucer, green 425.00
Cup & saucer, purple 220.00

Grape & Cable Cuspidor

Cuspidor, purple
  (ILLUS.) ....4,000.00 to 7,000.00
Decanter w/stopper, whiskey,
  marigold 650.00
Decanter w/stopper, whiskey,
  purple ....550.00 to 650.00
Dresser tray, green 160.00
Dresser tray, marigold 130.00
Dresser tray, purple ....175.00 to 230.00
Fernery, ice blue 1,200.00
Fernery, white 1,400.00
Hatpin holder, green ......150.00 to 200.00
Hatpin holder, marigold ...125.00 to 175.00
Hatpin holder, purple .....140.00 to 185.00
Hat shape, marigold 30.00
Hat shape, purple 50.00
Humidor, marigold 240.00
Humidor, purple 375.00
Ice cream dish, ice green 650.00
Ice cream set, purple, 7 pcs. 530.00
Nappy, single handle, green 60.00
Nappy, single handle, marigold 50.00
Perfume bottle w/stopper,
  marigold ....400.00 to 425.00
Perfume bottle w/stopper, purple .. 465.00
Pin tray, green.................... 180.00
Pin tray, marigold ....85.00 to 130.00
Pin tray, purple ....150.00 to 210.00
Pitcher, water, 8¼" h., green 225.00
Pitcher, water, 8¼" h., marigold ... 180.00
Pitcher, water, 8¼" h., purple 250.00
Pitcher, tankard, 9¾" h.,
  ice green 2,400.00
Pitcher, tankard, 9¾" h.,
  marigold 415.00
Pitcher, tankard, 9¾" h.,
  purple ....550.00 to 575.00
Plate, 5" to 6" d., purple (North-
  wood)........................... 130.00
Plate, 7½" d., turned-up hand grip,
  marigold 65.00
Plate, 7½" d., turned-up hand grip,
  purple 65.00
Plate, 8" d., footed, purple......... 85.00
Plate, 9" d., green 130.00
Plate, 9" d., spatula-footed, green .. 85.00
Plate, 9" d., spatula-footed,
  marigold 60.00

Plate, 9" d., purple.............. 85.00
Plate, 9" d., spatula-footed,
  purple 110.00
Plate, 9"d ., Basketweave exte-
  rior, green.............85.00 to 100.00
Plate, 9" d., Basketweave exte-
  rior, marigold.................. 80.00
Plate, 9" d., stippled, blue 340.00
Plate, 9" d., stippled, green........ 350.00
Plate, 9" d., stippled,
  ice blue......................1,700.00
Plate, 9" d., stippled, marigold 70.00
Plate, 9" d., stippled, purple 90.00
Plate, 9" d., stippled, teal
  blue..........................1,100.00
Powder jar, cov., green ...100.00 to 125.00
Powder jar, cov., marigold 62.50
Powder jar, cov., purple 110.00
Punch bowl & base, blue, 11" d.,
  2 pcs........................... 395.00
Punch bowl & base, marigold,
  11" d., 2 pcs................... 150.00
Punch bowl & base, purple, 11" d.,
  2 pcs........................... 400.00
Punch cup, aqua opalescent 260.00
Punch cup, stippled, blue 70.00
Punch cup, green 21.50
Punch cup, ice green 65.00
Punch cup, marigold............... 14.50
Punch cup, purple 20.00
Punch cup, white.................. 65.00
Punch set: 11" bowl, base & 6 cups;
  marigold, 8 pcs................. 360.00
Punch set: 11" bowl, base & 8 cups;
  marigold, 10 pcs................ 550.00
Punch set: 14" bowl, base & 6 cups;
  marigold, 8 pcs................. 665.00
Punch set: 14" bowl, base & 12 cups;
  purple, 14 pcs. 1,400.00
Punch set: 17" bowl, base & 8 cups;
  purple, 10 pcs. 1,550.00
Sauce dish, marigold 19.00
Sauce dish, purple 25.00
Sauce dish, white 350.00
Sherbet or individual ice cream dish,
  blue 25.00
Sherbet or individual ice cream dish,
  green 35.00
Sherbet or individual ice cream dish,
  ice green...................... 120.00
Sherbet or individual ice cream dish,
  marigold ....20.00 to 35.00
Sherbet or individual ice cream dish,
  purple 50.00
Spooner, green 110.00
Spooner, ice green 200.00
Spooner, marigold................. 60.00
Spooner, purple................... 95.00
Sugar bowl, cov., green 125.00
Sugar bowl, cov., marigold......... 75.00
Sugar bowl, cov., purple 120.00
Sugar bowl, individual size, green .. 85.00
Sugar bowl, individual size,
  marigold 60.00

Sugar bowl, individual size, purple.. 55.00
Sweetmeat jar, cov., marigold...... 750.00
Sweetmeat jar, cov., purple 215.00
Table set, purple, 4 pcs. ...400.00 to 600.00
Tumbler, green 35.00
Tumbler, marigold................. 24.00
Tumbler, purple............25.00 to 35.00
Tumbler, smoky 30.00
Tumbler, stippled, marigold 49.00
Tumbler, stippled, purple 75.00
Tumbler, tankard, blue 79.00
Tumbler, tankard, green 200.00
Tumbler, tankard, marigold 47.50
Tumbler, tankard, purple 55.00
Water set: pitcher & 6 tumblers;
  ice green, 7 pcs. 2,400.00
Water set: pitcher & 6 tumblers;
  marigold, 7 pcs. 320.00
Water set: pitcher & 6 tumblers;
  purple, 7 pcs................... 400.00
Water set: tankard pitcher & 6
  tumblers; purple, 7 pcs. 950.00
Whimsey teacup, purple 100.00
Whiskey set: whiskey decanter
  w/stopper & pr. shot glasses;
  marigold, 3 pcs................. 885.00
Whiskey shot glass, marigold 155.00
Whiskey shot glass,
  purple ....140.00 to 200.00
Wine, marigold 35.00

GRAPE & GOTHIC ARCHES (Northwood)

Grape & Gothic Arches Table Set

Berry set: master berry bowl & 6
  sauce dishes; marigold, 7 pcs..... 150.00
Butter dish, cov., green 250.00
Butter dish, cov., marigold 75.00
Creamer, blue 60.00
Pitcher, water, blue ......250.00 to 300.00
Pitcher, water, green 235.00
Pitcher, water, marigold 100.00
Sauce dish, green 28.00
Sauce dish, marigold 15.00
Spooner, blue..................... 60.00
Spooner, marigold................. 28.00
Sugar bowl, cov., blue............. 60.00
Sugar bowl, cov., green 67.50
Sugar bowl, cov., marigold......... 45.00
Table set, blue, 4 pcs.
  (ILLUS.)...................... 350.00
Table set, marigold,
  4 pcs..................175.00 to 195.00

Tumbler, blue	45.00
Tumbler, green	38.50
Tumbler, marigold	22.00
Water set: pitcher & 6 tumblers; blue, 7 pcs.	375.00

GRAPE & LATTICE

Tumbler, blue	38.00
Tumbler, marigold	22.00

GRAPE ARBOR (Northwood)

Bowl, 10" d., footed, marigold	75.00
Bowl, orange, footed, marigold	85.00
Bowl, orange, footed, purple	195.00
Hat shape, blue	100.00
Hat shape, ice green	375.00
Pitcher, water, ice blue	710.00
Pitcher, water, marigold	185.00 to 225.00
Pitcher, water, purple	500.00
Pitcher, water, white	550.00
Tumbler, blue	100.00
Tumbler, ice blue	120.00 to 150.00
Tumbler, marigold	35.00
Tumbler, purple	52.50
Tumbler, white	135.00
Water set: pitcher & 5 tumblers; purple, 6 pcs.	850.00
Water set: pitcher & 6 tumblers; ice green, 7 pcs.	8,500.00
Water set: pitcher & 6 tumblers; marigold, 7 pcs.	350.00

GRAPE DELIGHT

Grape Delight Rose Bowl

Nut bowl, 6-footed, blue	98.00
Nut bowl, 6-footed, marigold	75.00
Nut bowl, 6-footed, purple	72.50
Nut bowl, 6-footed, white	95.00 to 125.00
Rose bowl, 6-footed, blue	60.00
Rose bowl, 6-footed, marigold	50.00
Rose bowl, 6-footed, purple	50.00 to 70.00
Rose bowl, 6-footed, white (ILLUS.)	85.00 to 125.00

GRAPEVINE LATTICE

Bowl, 7" d., ruffled, marigold	28.00
Bowl, 7" d., ruffled, white	45.00
Hat shape, white	65.00
Pitcher, water, blue	225.00 to 400.00

Pitcher, water, marigold	160.00 to 230.00
Pitcher, water, white	850.00
Plate, 6" to 7" d., marigold	60.00
Plate, 6" to 7" d., peach opalescent	140.00
Plate, 6" to 7" d., purple	65.00
Plate, 6" to 7" d., white	75.00
Tumbler, marigold	37.50
Tumbler, purple	60.00

GREEK KEY (Northwood)

Greek Key Pitcher

Bowl, 8" to 9" d., fluted, green	58.00
Bowl, 8" to 9" d., ruffled, marigold	60.00
Bowl, 8" to 9" d., purple	65.00
Pitcher, water, marigold	700.00
Pitcher, water, purple (ILLUS.)	450.00
Plate, 9" d., marigold	275.00 to 300.00
Plate, 9" d., green	450.00
Tumbler, green	95.00
Tumbler, marigold	65.00 to 75.00
Tumbler, purple	85.00

HAMMERED BELL

Hammered Bell Shade

Chandelier shade, white (ILLUS.)	80.00

HARVEST FLOWER (Dugan or Diamond Glass)

Harvest Flower Tankard Pitcher

Pitcher, tankard, marigold
(ILLUS.) 1,600.00
Tumbler, marigold................. 100.00

HATTIE (Imperial)

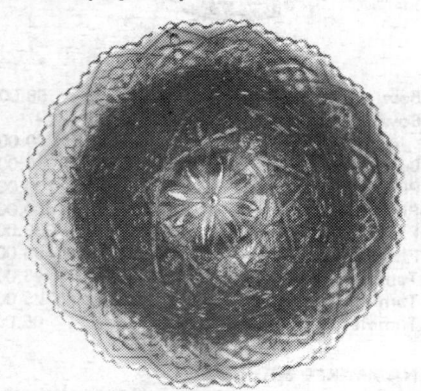

Hattie Bowl

Bowl, 8" to 9" d., marigold......... 40.00
Bowl, 8" to 9" d., purple........... 62.00
Bowl, 8" to 9" d., smoky (ILLUS.) ... 70.00
Plate, chop, 10½" d., amber.......1,000.00
Plate, chop, green................. 300.00
Plate, chop, marigold............. 200.00

HEADDRESS BOWL

Blue 55.00
Marigold 45.00

HEART & VINE (Fenton)

Bowl, 8" to 9" d., ribbon candy rim,
blue (ILLUS.) 50.00
Bowl, 8" to 9" d., green 65.00

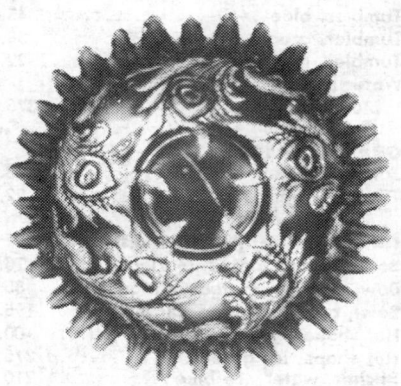

Heart & Vine Bowl

Bowl, 8" to 9" d., marigold......... 42.00
Bowl, 8" to 9" d., purple 50.00
Plate, 9" d., blue................. 230.00
Plate, 9" d., purple............... 130.00
Plate, 10" d., blue................ 150.00

HEARTS & FLOWERS (Northwood)

Hearts & Flowers Compote

Bowl, 8" to 9" d., ruffled, blue 475.00
Bowl, 8" to 9" d., ruffled, ice blue .. 270.00
Bowl, 8" to 9" d., ruffled,
ice green 350.00
Bowl, 8" to 9" d., ruffled,
marigold 43.50
Bowl, 8" to 9" d., ruffled, purple ... 85.00
Bowl, 8" to 9" d., ruffled, white 250.00
Compote, 6¾" h., aqua opalescent
(ILLUS.) 435.00
Compote, 6¾" h., blue 130.00
Compote, 6¾" h., green 550.00
Compote, 6¾" h., ice blue 162.50
Compote, 6¾" h., ice green........ 575.00
Compote, 6¾" h., marigold 62.50
Compote, 6¾" h., purple 175.00
Compote, 6¾" h., white 115.00
Plate, green 515.00
Plate, ice green 1,000.00
Plate, marigold 155.00
Plate, purple..................... 225.00

HEAVY GRAPE (Dugan or Diamond Glass - formerly Millersburg)

Bowl, master berry, 10" d., peach opalescent	550.00
Bowl, master berry, 10" d., purple	175.00

HEAVY GRAPE (Imperial)

Berry set: master bowl & 6 sauce dishes; marigold, 7 pcs.	110.00
Bowl, 5" d., clambroth	30.00
Bowl, 5" d., 2" h., marigold	20.00
Bowl, 5" d., 2" h., purple	32.50
Bowl, 7" d., fluted, green	30.00
Bowl, 7" d., purple	50.00
Bowl, 8" to 9" d., purple	28.00
Bowl, 10" d., marigold	65.00
Bowl, 10" d., purple	50.00
Fruit bowl & base, marigold, 2 pcs.	250.00
Nappy, handled, marigold	18.00
Plate, 7" to 8" d., blue	65.00
Plate, 7" to 8" d., green	47.50
Plate, 7" to 8" d., marigold	40.00
Plate, 7" to 8" d., purple	82.50
Plate, chop, 11" d., amber	200.00
Plate, chop, 11" d., green	100.00
Plate, chop, 11" d., marigold	148.00
Plate, chop, 11" d., purple	385.00

HEAVY IRIS - See IRIS, HEAVY

HOBNAIL (Millersburg)

Hobnail Butter Dish

Butter dish, cov., purple (ILLUS.)	550.00
Cuspidor, marigold	475.00
Cuspidor, purple	525.00 to 650.00
Pitcher, water, blue	1,050.00
Pitcher, water, marigold	1,550.00
Pitcher, water, purple	1,500.00
Rose bowl, marigold	250.00
Rose bowl, purple	270.00
Sugar bowl, cov., marigold	400.00
Tumbler, blue	1,000.00
Tumbler, marigold	750.00
Water set: pitcher & 1 tumbler; blue, 2 pcs.	2,350.00
Whimsey, jardiniere, purple	600.00

HOBSTAR (Imperial)

Hobstar Pickle Castor

Butter dish, cov., marigold	62.50
Compote, marigold	45.00
Cookie jar, cov., marigold	150.00
Creamer, marigold	42.50
Pickle castor, cov., marigold, complete w/silverplate frame (ILLUS.)	450.00
Spooner, marigold	35.00
Spooner, purple	85.00
Table set, marigold, 4 pcs.	110.00

HOBSTAR & FEATHER (Millersburg)

Hobstar & Feather Punch Set

Punch cup, green	28.50
Punch cup, marigold	20.00
Punch cup, purple	80.00
Punch set: bowl, base & 12 cups; marigold, 14 pcs. (ILLUS.)	1,525.00
Rose bowl, green, 7½" top d., 13" h.	2,000.00
Sauce dish, purple, 4" d.	190.00

HOBSTAR BAND

Celery vase, 2-handled, marigold	75.00
Pitcher, marigold	140.00
Tumbler, marigold	37.50

HOLLY, HOLLY BERRIES & CARNIVAL HOLLY

Bon bon, 2-handled, blue	65.00

Bon bon, 2-handled, green	50.00
Bon bon, 2-handled, purple	60.00
Bowl, 5" d., marigold	25.00
Bowl, 7" d., fluted, peach opalescent (Dugan)	50.00
Bowl, 7" d., purple	48.00
Bowl, 8" to 9" d., blue	55.00
Bowl, 8" to 9" d., green	70.00

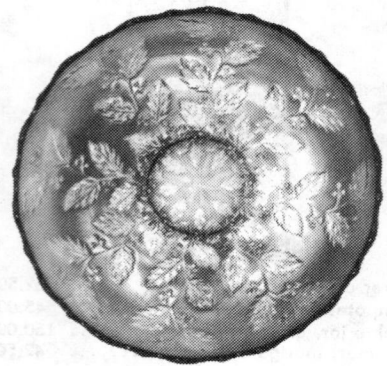

Holly Bowl

Bowl, 8" to 9" d., marigold (ILLUS.)	46.50
Bowl, 8" to 9" d., purple	52.50
Bowl, 8" to 9" d., red	635.00
Bowl, 8" to 9" d., vaseline	80.00
Bowl, 10" d., fluted, green	77.50
Bowl, 10" d., fluted, marigold	150.00
Bowl, 10" d., purple	75.00
Compote, small, blue	35.00
Compote, small, green	30.00
Compote, small, marigold	22.50
Compote, small, red	475.00
Compote, small, vaseline	48.00
Dish, hat-shaped, blue, 5¾"	30.00
Dish, hat-shaped, green, 5¾"	30.00
Dish, hat-shaped, marigold, 5¾" ...	22.00
Dish, hat-shaped, red, 5¾"	300.00
Dish, hat-shaped, red, 7"	240.00
Dish, hat-shaped, amber	92.00
Dish, hat-shaped, milk glass w/marigold overlay	60.00
Dish, hat-shaped, vaseline	25.00
Goblet, green	35.00
Goblet, marigold	17.00
Plate, 9" to 10" d., blue ...145.00 to	175.00
Plate, 9" to 10" d., green ....200.00 to	400.00
Plate, 9" to 10" d., marigold ....75.00 to	110.00
Plate, 9" to 10" d., purple	225.00
Plate, 9" to 10" d., white ...95.00 to	165.00
Sauceboat, handled, peach opalescent (Dugan)	80.00
Sauceboat, handled, purple	48.00
Vase, 6" h., pinched, peach opalescent	125.00

HOLLY STAR PANELED or HOLLY STAR (Northwood)

Bon bon, green	45.00
Bon bon, marigold	32.50

HOLLY WHIRL or HOLLY SPRIG (Millersburg, Fenton & Dugan)

Bowl, 7" d., marigold	55.00
Bowl, 7" d., ruffled, purple	40.00
Bowl, 7" d., vaseline	650.00
Bowl, 7½" w., tricornered, purple ..	45.00
Bowl, 8" to 9" d., ruffled, blue	45.00
Bowl, 8" to 9" d., green	55.00
Bowl, 8" to 9" d., marigold	35.00
Bowl, 8" to 9" d., purple	65.00
Card tray, 2-handled, green	57.50
Card tray, 2-handled, purple	85.00
Nappy, green	38.00
Nappy, marigold	60.00
Nappy, peach opalescent (Dugan) ..	48.00
Nappy, purple	55.00
Nappy, tricornered, green	80.00
Nappy, tricornered, purple	85.00
Nut dish, 2-handled, purple	62.50
Rose bowl, small, vaseline	400.00
Sauceboat, peach opalescent (Dugan)	55.00
Sauceboat, purple	33.00
Sauce dish, peach opalescent, 5½" d. (Dugan)	38.00
Sauce dish, purple, 5½" d	150.00

HOMESTEAD (Imperial)

Plate, amber ....625.00 to	700.00
Plate, blue	1,125.00
Plate, green	525.00
Plate, marigold	325.00
Plate, purple.....................	500.00
Plate, white	425.00

HONEYCOMB

Honeycomb Rose Bowl

Bon bon, marigold	30.00
Card tray, Beads & Flowers exterior, peach opalescent, 7"	65.00
Rose bowl, peach opalescent (ILLUS.)........................	225.00

HORSE HEADS or HORSE MEDALLION (Fenton)

Horse Heads Bowl

Bowl, 7" to 8" d., blue	130.00
Bowl, 7" to 8" d., green	140.00
Bowl, 7" to 8" d., marigold (ILLUS.)	70.00
Bowl, 7" to 8" d., purple	125.00
Bowl, jack-in-the-pulpit shaped, blue	120.00
Bowl, jack-in-the-pulpit shaped, marigold	100.00
Nut bowl, 3-footed, blue...130.00 to	175.00
Nut bowl, 3-footed, green	125.00
Nut bowl, 3-footed, marigold	82.50
Nut bowl, 3-footed, red	900.00
Nut bowl, 3-footed, vaseline	110.00
Plate, 7" to 8" d., blue	275.00
Plate, 7" to 8" d., marigold	140.00
Rose bowl, blue	200.00
Rose bowl, marigold	90.00

ILLINOIS SOLDIER'S & SAILOR'S PLATE
Blue	650.00
Marigold	550.00

ILLUSION
Bon bon, 2-handled, blue	55.00
Bon bon, 2-handled, marigold	45.00

IMPERIAL GRAPE (Imperial)

Imperial Grape Bowl

Berry set: master berry & 6 sauce dishes; marigold, 7 pcs.	210.00
Bowl, 7" d., 2½" h., green	30.00
Bowl, 7" d., 2½" h., marigold	27.50
Bowl, 7" d., 2½" h., ruffled, purple	35.00
Bowl, 8" to 9" d., aqua	50.00
Bowl, 8" to 9" d., green	45.00
Bowl, 8" to 9" d., marigold	22.50
Bowl, 8" to 9" d., purple	50.00
Bowl, 8" to 9" d., white	55.00
Bowl, 10" d., clambroth	40.00
Bowl, 10" d., marigold (ILLUS.)	32.50
Bowl, 10" d., purple	57.50
Compote, marigold	55.00
Cup & saucer, green	62.50
Cup & saucer, marigold	80.00
Decanter w/stopper, marigold	60.00
Decanter w/stopper, purple	120.00
Decanter w/stopper, smoky	100.00
Goblet, green	72.50
Goblet, marigold	32.50
Goblet, purple	55.00
Goblet, smoky	125.00
Pitcher, water, green	125.00
Pitcher, water, marigold	75.00
Pitcher, water, purple	200.00
Pitcher, water, smoky	300.00
Plate, 6" d., amber	160.00
Plate, 6" d., green	60.00
Plate, 6" d., marigold	35.00
Plate, 6" d., purple	70.00
Plate, 8" d., green	60.00
Plate, 9" d., ruffled, clambroth	35.00
Plate, 9" d., ruffled, green	130.00
Plate, 9" d., flat, marigold	115.00
Plate, 9" d., ruffled, marigold	37.50
Plate, 9" d., purple	310.00
Plate, 9" d., ruffled, white	45.00
Punch bowl, marigold	60.00
Punch bowl, purple	225.00
Punch bowl & base, marigold, 2 pcs.	250.00
Punch cup, green	25.00
Punch cup, marigold	10.00
Punch set: punch bowl, base & 5 cups; purple, 7 pcs.	450.00
Punch set: punch bowl, base & 6 cups; green, 8 pcs.	257.00
Punch set: punch bowl, base & 9 cups; marigold, 11 pcs.	245.00
Sauce dish, green	17.00
Sauce dish, ruffled, marigold	13.00
Sauce dish, smoky	32.50
Tumbler, green	27.50
Tumbler, marigold	18.00
Tumbler, purple	42.50
Water bottle, green	120.00
Water bottle, marigold	100.00
Water bottle, purple	130.00
Water set: pitcher & 6 tumblers; marigold, 7 pcs.	185.00 to 245.00
Water set: pitcher & 6 tumblers; purple, 7 pcs.	325.00

Wine, green ....25.00 to 35.00
Wine, marigold 20.00
Wine, purple...................... 30.00
Wine, smoky...................... 40.00
Wine set: decanter w/stopper & 6
  wines; green, 7 pcs............. 225.00
Wine set: decanter w/stopper & 6
  wines; marigold, 7 pcs.......... 240.00
Wine set: decanter w/stopper & 6
  wines; purple, 7 pcs. 270.00

INVERTED FEATHER (Cambridge)

Inverted Feather Cookie Jar

Compote, jelly, marigold.......... 55.00
Cookie jar, cov., green (ILLUS.)..... 200.00
Parfait, marigold 50.00
Pitcher, water, tankard, marigold ..4,000.00
Tumbler, green or marigold,
  each ....450.00 to 500.00

INVERTED STRAWBERRY (Cambridge)

Bowl, 7" d., green 49.00
Bowl, master berry, 10" d., purple .. 155.00
Candlestick, green (single) 125.00
Candlesticks, marigold, 7" h., pr. ... 380.00
Compote, open, 5" d., 6" h.,
  green 525.00
Compote, open, giant,
  marigold ....175.00 to 225.00
Compote, open, giant, purple 400.00
Creamer & sugar bowl, purple, pr... 325.00
Cuspidor, green.................. 600.00
Cuspidor, marigold ....425.00 to 500.00
Decanter, green, marked
  Near-Cut......................3,550.00
Pitcher, milk, purple 1,300.00
Pitcher, tankard, green...350.00 to 1,200.00
Pitcher, tankard, purple 800.00
Powder jar, cov., green............ 110.00
Sauce dish, marigold 28.50
Spooner, green 75.00
Sugar bowl, cov., green 100.00
Table set: creamer, sugar bowl &
  spooner; marigold, 3 pcs. 550.00
Tumbler, marigold................. 250.00
Tumbler, purple.................. 200.00

INVERTED THISTLE (Cambridge)

Compote, 8" h., ruffled, green 550.00
Pitcher, water, purple (ILLUS.) 2,000.00

Inverted Thistle Pitcher

Plate, chop, purple 1,750.00
Tumbler, purple.................. 310.00

IRIS

Compote, 6¾" d., blue 170.00
Compote, 6¾" d., green 65.00
Compote, 6¾" d., marigold 50.00
Compote, 6¾" d., purple 65.00
Goblet, buttermilk, green 80.00
Goblet, buttermilk, marigold 55.00
Goblet, buttermilk, marigold,
  souvenir....................... 69.00
Goblet, buttermilk, purple 55.00

IRIS, HEAVY (Dugan or Diamond Glass)

Pitcher, water, marigold 400.00
Pitcher, water, peach opalescent ... 900.00
Pitcher, water, white 1,000.00
Tumbler, marigold................. 52.50
Tumbler, purple.................. 58.00
Tumbler, white................... 175.00
Water set: pitcher & 4 tumblers;
  marigold, 5 pcs.................. 635.00
Water set: pitcher & 6 tumblers;
  purple, 7 pcs. 865.00

JARDINIERE (THE)

Marigold 325.00
Purple 600.00

JEWELED HEART (Dugan or Diamond Glass)

Bowl, master berry, 10½" d., fluted,
  peach opalescent............... 140.00
Dish, 2 turned-up sides, peach
  opalescent..................... 25.00
Pitcher, marigold.................. 650.00
Plate, 7" d., ruffled, peach
  opalescent..................... 38.00
Sauce dish, peach opalescent 22.50
Sauce dish, peach opalescent
  w/rayed interior 41.00
Sauce dish, purple 40.00
Tumbler, marigold................. 75.00

KITTENS (Fenton)

Bowl, cereal, blue	200.00
Bowl, cereal, marigold	100.00 to 140.00
Bowl, ruffled, marigold	120.00
Bowl, 4-sided, blue	240.00
Bowl, 4-sided, ruffled, marigold	70.00 to 110.00
Bowl, 4-sided, purple	175.00
Bowl, 6-sided, ruffled, marigold	100.00
Cup, marigold	145.00
Cup & saucer, marigold	175.00 to 250.00
Cuspidor, marigold	5,500.00
Dish, turned-up sides, marigold	105.00
Dish, turned-up sides, purple	175.00
Plate, 4½" d., marigold	90.00
Saucer, marigold	125.00
Spooner, blue	200.00
Spooner, marigold	175.00
Toothpick holder, blue	255.00
Toothpick holder, marigold	145.00
Vase, blue	210.00
Vase, marigold	125.00

LATTICE & GRAPE (Fenton)

Pitcher, water, blue	250.00
Pitcher, water, marigold	115.00
Pitcher, water, white	510.00
Tumbler, blue	40.00
Tumbler, marigold	20.00 to 30.00
Tumbler, white	85.00
Water set: pitcher & 2 tumblers; white, 3 pcs.	780.00
Water set: pitcher & 4 tumblers; marigold, 5 pcs.	225.00
Water set: tankard pitcher & 6 tumblers; blue, 7 pcs.	645.00

LATTICE & POINSETTIA (Northwood)

Bowl, cobalt blue	175.00
Bowl, ice blue	305.00
Bowl, marigold	95.00
Bowl, purple	145.00

LEAF & BEADS (Northwood)

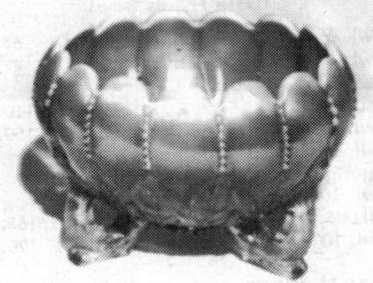

Leaf & Beads Rose Bowl

Nut bowl, handled, green	40.00
Nut bowl, handled, marigold	26.00
Nut bowl, handled, purple	40.00
Rose bowl, aqua	150.00

Rose bowl, aqua opalescent (ILLUS.)	230.00
Rose bowl, blue	95.00
Rose bowl, green	55.00 to 70.00
Rose bowl, ice blue opalescent	210.00
Rose bowl, ice green opalescent	1,600.00
Rose bowl, lavender	500.00
Rose bowl, marigold	52.50
Rose bowl, purple	70.00
Rose bowl, interior pattern, teal blue	1,000.00
Rose bowl, white	425.00

LEAF & FLOWERS or LEAF & LITTLE FLOWERS (Millersburg)

Compote, green, miniature	285.00
Compote, marigold, miniature	250.00
Compote, purple, miniature	250.00

LEAF CHAIN (Fenton)

Leaf Chain Bowl

Bowl, 6" d., marigold	30.00
Bowl, 7" d., aqua	120.00
Bowl, 7" d., blue	40.00
Bowl, 7" d., green	45.00
Bowl, 7" d., red	450.00
Bowl, 7" d., vaseline w/marigold overlay	60.00
Bowl, 7" d., white	55.00
Bowl, 8" to 9" d., aqua	120.00
Bowl, 8" to 9" d., blue (ILLUS.)	45.00
Bowl, 8" to 9" d., clambroth	45.00
Bowl, 8" to 9" d., green	40.00
Bowl, 8" to 9" d., light blue	80.00
Bowl, 8" to 9" d., marigold	35.00
Bowl, 8" to 9" d., white	85.00
Plate, 7" to 8" d., blue	80.00
Plate, 7" to 8" d., marigold	57.50
Plate, 9" d., green	85.00
Plate, 9" d., white	140.00

LEAF RAYS NAPPY

Marigold	17.50

Peach opalescent	40.00
Purple	22.50
White	45.00

LEAF TIERS

Berry set: 9" d. master bowl & 4 sauce dishes; marigold, 5 pcs.	75.00
Butter dish, cov., marigold	135.00
Pitcher, footed, marigold	295.00
Tumbler, marigold	65.00

LILY OF THE VALLEY (Fenton)

Lily of the Valley Pitcher

Pitcher, water, blue (ILLUS.)	3,900.00 to 4,500.00
Tumbler, blue	265.00
Tumbler, marigold	375.00

LINED LATTICE VASE

Purple	40.00
White, 10" h.	35.00

LION (Fenton)

Lion Bowl

Bowl, 5" d., marigold	150.00
Bowl, 7" d., blue (ILLUS.)	295.00
Bowl, 7" d., marigold	115.00
Plate, 7½" d., marigold	485.00

LITTLE BARREL PERFUME

Little Barrel Perfume

Green (ILLUS.)	80.00
Marigold	70.00
Smoky	85.00 to 120.00

LITTLE FISHES

Little Fishes Bowl

Bowl, 6" d., 3-footed, blue	65.00
Bowl, 6" d., 3-footed, marigold	47.50
Bowl, 6" d., 3-footed, purple	70.00 to 110.00
Bowl, 8" to 9" d., 3-footed, blue	150.00
Bowl, 8" to 9" d., 3-footed, marigold	120.00
Bowl, 10" d., 3-footed, blue (ILLUS.)	165.00
Bowl, 10" d., 3-footed, marigold	120.00

LITTLE FLOWERS

Berry set: master bowl & 3 sauce dishes; blue, 4 pcs.	75.00 to 100.00
Berry set: master bowl & 6 sauce dishes; green, 7 pcs.	270.00
Berry set: master bowl & 6 sauce dishes; marigold, 7 pcs.	195.00

Bowl, 5" d., blue 30.00
Bowl, 5" d., green 25.00
Bowl, 5" d., marigold . . . . 15.00 to 23.00
Bowl, 5" d., purple 30.00
Bowl, 8" to 9" d., blue 70.00
Bowl, 8" to 9" d., marigold 70.00
Bowl, 8" to 9" d., purple 75.00
Bowl, 10" d., purple 65.00
Bowl, 10" d., spatula-footed, red . . . 900.00
Nut bowl, blue 75.00
Nut bowl, marigold 65.00
Plate, 6" d., marigold 210.00

Little Flowers Chop Plate

Plate, chop, marigold
(ILLUS.) . . . . 350.00 to 600.00

LITTLE STARS BOWL (Millersburg)
Bowl, 7" d., green . . . . 90.00 to 140.00
Bowl, 7" d., fluted, marigold 70.00
Bowl, 7" d., purple 70.00
Bowl, 8" d., green 75.00
Bowl, 8" d., ruffled, marigold 95.00
Bowl, 8" d., ruffled,
purple . . . . 75.00 to 95.00

LOGANBERRY VASE (Imperial)
Amber 400.00
Green 195.00
Marigold 125.00
Purple 175.00

LONG THUMBPRINTS
Creamer & sugar bowl, marigold,
pr. 45.00
Vase, 7" h., green 32.00

LOTUS & GRAPE (Fenton)
Bon bon, 2-handled, blue 30.00
Bon bon, 2-handled, celeste blue . . . 185.00
Bon bon, 2-handled, marigold 32.50
Bon bon, 2-handled, purple 50.00
Bowl, 5" d., footed, blue 50.00
Bowl, 5" d., footed, marigold 35.00
Bowl, 5" d., footed, purple 57.00
Bowl, 8" to 9" d., blue 55.00
Bowl, 8" to 9" d., green 53.00

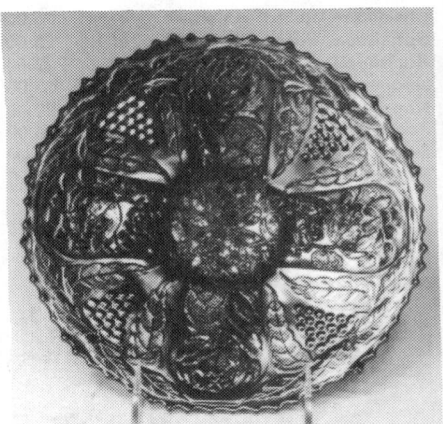

Lotus & Grape Plate

Plate, 9" d., blue (ILLUS.) 400.00
Plate, 9" d., green . . . . 475.00 to 625.00
Plate, 9" d., purple 360.00

LOUISA (Westmoreland)

Louisa Rose Bowl

Bowl, 8" to 9" d., 3-footed, peach
opalescent 415.00
Bowl, 8" to 9" d., 3-footed, teal
blue 40.00
Nut bowl, footed, blue 35.00
Nut bowl, footed, green 45.00
Nut bowl, footed, purple 52.50
Plate, 9½" d., footed, aqua 325.00
Plate, 9½" d., footed, teal blue 98.00
Rose bowl, footed, amber 60.00
Rose bowl, footed, green (ILLUS.) . . . 60.00
Rose bowl, footed, lavender 85.00
Rose bowl, footed, marigold 60.00
Rose bowl, footed, purple 57.50

LUSTRE FLUTE (Northwood)
Creamer & sugar bowl, green, pr. . . 50.00
Creamer & sugar bowl, marigold,
pr. 55.00

Hat shape, fluted, green, 5" d. 25.00
Hat shape, fluted, marigold, 5" d. . . 25.00
Hat shape, fluted, purple, 5" d. 32.50
Nappy, green 35.00
Nappy, marigold 20.00
Punch cup, green 16.00
Sugar bowl, green 20.00
Sugar bowl, marigold 15.00

LUSTRE ROSE (Imperial)

Lustre Rose Footed Bowl

Bowl, 8" to 9" d., 3-footed, amber . . 37.50
Bowl, 8" to 9" d., 3-footed, blue
  (ILLUS.) 65.00
Bowl, 8" to 9" d., 3-footed,
  clambroth 30.00
Bowl, 8" to 9" d., 3-footed, green . . . 40.00
Bowl, 8" to 9" d., 3-footed,
  marigold 40.00
Bowl, 8" to 9" d., 3-footed, purple . . 45.00
Bowl, 10½" d., 3-footed,
  marigold . . . . 40.00 to 50.00
Bowl, 10½" d., 3-footed, smoky 75.00
Bowl, 10½" d., 3-footed, white 130.00
Butter dish, cov., marigold 55.00
Creamer, marigold . . . . 30.00 to 40.00
Creamer, purple 75.00
Fernery, blue 65.00
Fernery, marigold 30.00
Fernery, purple 95.00
Fernery, smoky 70.00
Pitcher, water, clambroth 80.00
Pitcher, water, 8" h., marigold 52.50
Plate, 9" d., amber 85.00
Plate, 9" d., green 75.00
Plate, 9" d., marigold . . . . 45.00 to 60.00
Plate, 9" d., purple 95.00
Rose bowl, amber 85.00
Rose bowl, green 45.00
Spooner, green 40.00
Spooner, marigold 35.00
Spooner, purple 25.00
Sugar bowl, cov., marigold 45.00
Table set, marigold, 4 pcs. 160.00
Tumbler, green 30.00
Tumbler, marigold 17.50
Tumbler, purple 32.50
Water set: pitcher & 6 tumblers;
  marigold, 7 pcs. 150.00
Water set: pitcher & 6 tumblers;
  purple, 7 pcs. 595.00

MANY FRUITS (Dugan)

Punch bowl, 9¾" d., marigold 180.00
Punch bowl, 9¾" d., purple 245.00
Punch bowl & base, marigold,
  2 pcs. 270.00
Punch bowl & base, purple, 2 pcs. . . 400.00
Punch cup, blue 29.00
Punch cup, marigold 30.00
Punch cup, purple 22.50
Punch cup, white 65.00
Punch set: bowl, base & 5 cups;
  purple, 7 pcs. 525.00
Punch set: bowl, base & 6 cups;
  blue, 8 pcs. 500.00
Punch set: bowl, base & 6 cups;
  marigold, 8 pcs. 375.00
Punch set: bowl, base & 6 cups;
  white, 8 pcs. 1,600.00

MANY STARS (Millersburg)

Bowl, 8" to 9" d., green 300.00
Bowl, ice cream, 10" d., green 400.00
Bowl, ice cream, 10" d., marigold . . 395.00
Bowl, 10" d., purple 435.00

MAPLE LEAF (Dugan)

Maple Leaf Pitcher

Berry set: master berry bowl & 6
  small berry bowls; pedestaled,
  purple, 7 pcs. 225.00
Bowl, master berry or fruit,
  marigold 100.00
Bowl, ice cream, footed, large,
  purple 105.00
Butter dish, cov., purple 135.00
Creamer, marigold 45.00
Creamer, purple 60.00
Pitcher, water, purple (ILLUS.) 165.00
Spooner, marigold 50.00
Spooner, purple 65.00
Table set: cov. sugar bowl, creamer
  & spooner; purple, 3 pcs. 235.00
Table set, marigold, 4 pcs. 200.00
Tumbler, blue 50.00

Tumbler, marigold................ 25.00
Tumbler, purple 35.00
Water set: pitcher & 6 tumblers;
    marigold, 7 pcs................ 175.00
Water set: pitcher & 6 tumblers;
    purple, 7 pcs.................. 725.00

MARILYN (Millersburg)
Pitcher, water, green 675.00
Pitcher, water, marigold 300.00
Pitcher, water, purple 750.00
Tumbler, green 210.00
Tumbler, marigold................ 45.00
Tumbler, purple...........90.00 to 120.00
Water set: pitcher & 6 tumblers;
    purple, 7 pcs. 1,500.00

MARY ANN VASE (Dugan)
Marigold 65.00
Purple 105.00
Vaseline 350.00

MAYAN (Millersburg)
Bowl, 8" to 9" d., green 50.00
Bowl, 8" to 9" d., purple.......... 60.00

MEMPHIS (Northwood)

Memphis Punch Bowl

Punch bowl, 11½" d., marigold..... 62.50
Punch bowl & base, green, 2 pcs.... 175.00
Punch bowl & base, ice green,
    2 pcs. 2,950.00
Punch bowl & base, marigold,
    2 pcs. 180.00
Punch bowl & base, purple, 2 pcs.
    (ILLUS.)....................... 340.00
Punch bowl base, green 50.00
Punch bowl base, ice green 125.00
Punch bowl base, purple 32.50
Punch cup, green ....30.00 to 40.00
Punch cup, ice blue 60.00
Punch cup, ice green 60.00
Punch cup, marigold.............. 25.00
Punch cup, purple 25.00
Punch cup, white................. 60.00

Punch set: bowl, base & 4 cups; ice
    blue, 6 pcs. 2,000.00
Punch set: bowl, base & 5 cups;
    marigold, 7 pcs.................. 425.00
Punch set: bowl, base & 6 cups; pur-
    ple, 8 pcs.........495.00 to 525.00
Sauce dish, marigold 20.00

MIKADO (Fenton)
Compote, 10" d., blue .....250.00 to 300.00
Compote, 10" d., marigold 125.00
Compote, 10" d., purple 335.00

MILADY (Fenton)

Milady Pitcher & Tumbler

Pitcher, water, blue (ILLUS.)........ 650.00
Pitcher, water, marigold 475.00
Tumbler, blue (ILLUS.) 60.00
Tumbler, marigold ....60.00 to 85.00
Tumbler, purple................... 75.00
Water set: pitcher & 4 tumblers;
    blue, 5 pcs..................... 885.00

MILLERSBURG PIPE HUMIDOR
Green 3,375.00
Marigold 3,000.00

MIRRORED LOTUS
Bowl, 7" d., blue 65.00
Bowl, 7" d., ice green 250.00
Bowl, 7" d., marigold............. 55.00
Rose bowl, white................. 525.00

MITERED OVALS (Millersburg)
Vase, green......................1,700.00

MORNING GLORY (Millersburg)
Pitcher, tankard, green 9,000.00
Pitcher, tankard, purple
    (ILLUS.) ....6,350.00 to 7,500.00
Tumbler, green...................1,150.00

Morning Glory Tankard Pitcher

MULTI-FRUITS (Millersburg)
Pitcher, water, purple............7,100.00
Punch bowl & base, purple, 2 pcs. . . . 500.00
Punch cup, green 40.00

MULTI-FRUITS & FLOWERS (Millersburg)
Pitcher, water, green...5,250.00 to 7,500.00
Punch bowl & base, green,
  2 pcs. 1,000.00
Punch bowl & base, purple, 2 pcs. . . . 850.00
Punch cup, purple 35.00
Punch set: bowl, base & 6 cups;
  tulip-shaped, marigold, 8 pcs. ...1,200.00

NAUTILUS (Dugan)
Creamer, peach opal-
  escent ....180.00 to 250.00
Sugar bowl, peach opalescent 250.00
Sugar bowl, purple 165.00
Vase, peach opalescent............ 195.00

NESTING SWAN (Millersburg)
Bowl, 10" d., amber 225.00
Bowl, 10" d., green ....225.00 to 265.00
Bowl, 10" d., marigold.....165.00 to 210.00
Bowl, 10" d., purple ......200.00 to 285.00

NIPPON (Northwood)
Bowl, 8" to 9" d., 2¼" h., ice
  blue ....150.00 to 195.00
Bowl, 8" to 9" d., marigold........ 57.50
Bowl, 8" to 9" d., purple 52.50
Bowl, 8" to 9" d., fluted,
  white ....175.00 to 190.00
Plate, 9" d., marigold 195.00
Plate, 9" d., white 600.00

NU-ART
Plate, Chrysanthemum, amber...... 750.00
Plate, Chrysanthemum, green 350.00
Plate, Chrysanthemum,
  marigold ....550.00 to 650.00

Nu-Art Chrysanthemum Plate

Plate, Chrysanthemum, purple
  (ILLUS.)........................ 800.00
Plate, Chrysanthemum, white 695.00

OCTAGON (Imperial)

Octagon Decanter & Wine

Bowl, 10" sq., green.............. 49.00
Butter dish, cov., marigold 110.00
Compote, jelly, green 75.00
Compote, jelly, marigold........... 50.00
Creamer, marigold 30.00
Decanter w/stopper, marigold
  (ILLUS.)........................ 80.00
Goblet, water, marigold .....40.00 to 60.00
Pitcher, milk, marigold 95.00
Pitcher, water, 8" h., marigold 70.00
Pitcher, water, 8" h., purple 400.00
Pitcher, water, tankard, 9¾" h.,
  marigold 100.00
Pitcher, water, tankard, 9¾" h.,
  purple ....300.00 to 400.00
Sauce dish, marigold 17.00
Spooner, marigold................. 45.00
Sugar bowl, cov., marigold........ 50.00
Table set, marigold, 4 pcs. 225.00
Toothpick holder, marigold........ 170.00

Tumbler, green ....245.00 to 350.00
Tumbler, marigold................. 20.00
Tumbler, purple.................... 50.00
Vase, 8" h., marigold.............. 55.00
Water set: pitcher & 6 tumblers;
   marigold, 7 pcs. ....235.00 to 275.00
Wine, marigold (ILLUS.) 22.50
Wine, purple...................... 52.50
Wine set: decanter & 6 wines; mari-
   gold, 7 pcs. ....185.00 to 250.00

OHIO STAR (Millersburg)
Compote, jelly, marigold........... 400.00
Vase, marigold 300.00
Vase, purple...................... 375.00

OPEN ROSE (Imperial)
Berry set: master bowl & 6 sauce
   dishes; marigold, 7 pcs. 85.00
Bowl, 5" d., marigold............. 15.00
Bowl, 7" d., footed, green 40.00
Bowl, 7" d., footed, purple 40.00
Bowl, 8" to 9" d., amber 67.50
Bowl, 8" to 9" d., aqua 52.00
Bowl, 8" to 9" d., green 55.00
Bowl, 8" to 9" d., marigold........ 36.50
Bowl, 8" to 9" d., smoky........... 55.00
Bowl, 10" d., marigold............ 50.00
Bowl, 10" d., fluted, white 65.00
Plate, 9" d., amber............... 135.00
Plate, 9" d., green 75.00
Plate, 9" d., marigold 57.50
Plate, chop, purple............... 375.00
Rose bowl, amber................. 75.00
Spooner, marigold................ 29.00
Tumbler, marigold................ 20.00
Water set: pitcher & 6 tumblers;
   marigold, 7 pcs................. 200.00
Water set: pitcher & 6 tumblers;
   purple, 7 pcs................... 375.00

ORANGE TREE (Fenton)

Orange Tree Loving Cup

Bowl, 8" to 9" d., amber 60.00
Bowl, 8" to 9" d., blue............ 60.00
Bowl, 8" to 9" d., clambroth........ 45.00
Bowl, 8" to 9" d., green 70.00

Bowl, 8" to 9" d., marigold........ 30.00
Bowl, 8" to 9" d., purple 75.00
Bowl, 8" to 9" d., red............. 825.00
Bowl, 8" to 9" d., white.......... 98.00
Bowl, 10" d., 3-footed, blue 130.00
Bowl, 10" d., 3-footed, green 295.00
Bowl, 10" d., 3-footed,
   marigold ....70.00 to 80.00
Breakfast set: individual size
   creamer & cov. sugar bowl;
   blue, pr. ....90.00 to 100.00
Breakfast set: individual size
   creamer & cov. sugar bowl; mari-
   gold, pr. 70.00
Breakfast set: individual size
   creamer & cov. sugar bowl;
   purple, pr. 110.00
Breakfast set: individual size
   creamer & cov. sugar bowl; white,
   pr...... .... 125.00
Butter dish, cov., blue 225.00
Compote, 5" d., blue 65.00
Compote, 5" d., green 85.00
Compote, 5" d., marigold 25.00
Creamer, footed, blue 55.00
Creamer, footed, marigold 35.00
Creamer, footed, purple 55.00
Creamer, individual size, blue 52.50
Creamer, individual size, marigold .. 45.00
Creamer, individual size, purple 42.50
Creamer & cov. sugar bowl, footed,
   blue, pr. 140.00
Dish, ice cream, footed, blue....... 45.00
Dish, ice cream, footed, marigold... 20.00
Goblet, blue ....50.00 to 75.00
Goblet, green.................... 75.00
Goblet, marigold 25.00
Goblet, marigold, w/adver-
   tising ....50.00 to 75.00
Hatpin holder, blue............... 150.00
Hatpin holder, green 335.00
Hatpin holder, marigold 130.00
Hatpin holder, purple............. 165.00
Loving cup, blue 230.00
Loving cup, green 200.00
Loving cup, marigold
   (ILLUS.) ....125.00 to 160.00
Loving cup, purple 200.00
Loving cup, white 225.00
Mug, amber 125.00
Mug, aqua...................... 185.00
Mug, blue 38.00
Mug, green..................... 225.00
Mug, marigold 26.50
Mug, marigold w/blue
   base ....95.00 to 125.00
Mug, marigold w/green base 120.00
Mug, marigold w/vaseline
   base ....140.00 to 175.00
Mug, purple 110.00
Mug, red ....400.00 to 550.00
Mug, teal blue 175.00
Mug, vaseline................... 130.00
Pitcher, water, blue 325.00

Pitcher, water, marigold 275.00
Pitcher, water, white ..... 350.00 to 525.00
Plate, 9" d., flat, blue 180.00
Plate, 9" d., flat,
   clambroth .... 75.00 to 120.00
Plate, 9" d., flat, green 275.00
Plate, 9" d., flat, marigold 85.00
Plate, 9" d., flat, white 110.00
Powder jar, cov., blue 62.50
Powder jar, cov., green 195.00
Powder jar, cov., marigold ... 45.00 to 60.00
Powder jar, open, peach
   opalescent 195.00
Punch bowl & base, marigold,
   2 pcs. .... 110.00 to 135.00
Punch bowl & base, white, 2 pcs. 325.00
Punch cup, blue 20.00
Punch cup, marigold 10.00
Punch cup, purple 20.00
Punch cup, white 45.00
Punch set: bowl, base & 4 cups;
   white, 6 pcs. 525.00

Orange Tree Punch Set

Punch set: bowl, base & 6 cups;
   blue, 8 pcs. (ILLUS.) 400.00
Rose bowl, marigold 40.00
Rose bowl, red 575.00
Rose bowl, white 250.00
Sauce dish, footed, blue 25.00
Sauce dish, footed, marigold 15.00
Shaving mug, amber 125.00
Shaving mug, blue .... 40.00 to 60.00
Shaving mug, marigold 35.00
Shaving mug, purple 275.00
Shaving mug, red 550.00
Spooner, blue 75.00
Sugar bowl, blue 65.00
Sugar bowl, purple 52.50
Sugar bowl, white 75.00
Sugar bowl, open, breakfast size,
   marigold 25.00
Sugar bowl, open, breakfast size,
   white 50.00
Tumbler, blue 40.00
Tumbler, marigold 36.50
Tumbler, white .... 85.00 to 110.00
Wine, blue 45.00
Wine, green 175.00
Wine, marigold 30.00
Wine, purple 35.00

ORANGE TREE ORCHARD (Fenton)
Pitcher, blue 330.00
Pitcher, marigold 185.00
Pitcher, white 550.00
Tumbler, blue 45.00
Tumbler, marigold 40.00
Tumbler, white 165.00
Water set: pitcher & 3 tumblers;
   white, 4 pcs. 1,025.00

ORANGE TREE SCROLL
Pitcher, marigold 130.00
Pitcher, white 325.00
Tumbler, blue 110.00
Tumbler, marigold 50.00
Water set: pitcher & 6 tumblers;
   blue, 7 pcs. 900.00

ORIENTAL POPPY (Northwood)

Oriental Poppy Pitcher & Tumbler

Pitcher, water, green 750.00
Pitcher, water, marigold
   (ILLUS.) .... 275.00 to 400.00
Pitcher, water, white ..... 945.00 to 1,385.00
Tumbler, green 45.00
Tumbler, ice blue 175.00
Tumbler, ice green 200.00
Tumbler, marigold (ILLUS.) 35.00
Tumbler, purple 40.00
Tumbler, white 120.00
Water set: pitcher & 6 tumblers;
   purple, 7 pcs. .... 800.00 to 875.00

PALM BEACH (United States Glass Co.)
Butter dish, cov., white 210.00
Creamer, marigold 70.00
Creamer, white 80.00
Pitcher, water, marigold 437.50
Pitcher, water, white 725.00
Rose bowl, purple 125.00
Sauce dish, white 30.00
Spooner, marigold 85.00
Spooner, white 85.00
Tumbler, amber 80.00

Tumbler, marigold.................. 210.00
Tumbler, white.................... 155.00
Whimsey, banana boat, marigold,
   6" 90.00
Whimsey, banana boat, purple, 6" .. 115.00
Whimsey vase, white 250.00

PANSY (Imperial)

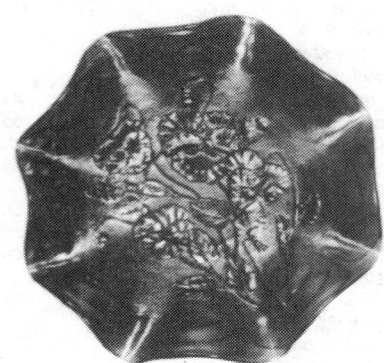

Pansy Bowl

Bowl, 8" to 9" d., amber 20.00
Bowl, 8" to 9" d., blue............. 35.00
Bowl, 8" to 9" d., green 45.00
Bowl, 8" to 9" d., marigold......... 30.00
Bowl, 9" d., fluted, purple (ILLUS.) .. 35.00
Creamer, marigold 22.50
Creamer, green 22.00
Creamer, purple 30.00
Creamer & sugar bowl, marigold,
   pr............................... 37.50
Dresser tray, marigold 33.00
Dresser tray, purple 65.00
Nappy, amber 38.00
Nappy, green 25.00
Nappy, lavender 25.00
Nappy, marigold 20.00
Pickle (or relish) dish, amber,
   9 x 6"........................... 60.00
Pickle (or relish) dish, blue,
   9 x 6"........................... 25.00
Pickle (or relish) dish, clambroth,
   9 x 6"........................... 20.00
Pickle (or relish) dish, green,
   9 x 6"........................... 27.50
Pickle (or relish) dish, marigold,
   9 x 6"........................... 20.00
Pickle (or relish) dish, purple,
   9 x 6"........................... 30.00
Pickle (or relish) dish, smoky,
   9 x 6"........................... 73.00
Sugar bowl, amber 35.00
Sugar bowl, marigold.............. 20.00
Sugar bowl, smoky 35.00

PANSY SPRAY

Bowl, 8" to 9" d., green 45.00
Bowl, 8" to 9" d., marigold......... 27.00

Bowl, 8" to 9" d., purple 45.00
Dresser tray, flat, oval, green 55.00
Dresser tray, flat, oval, marigold ... 45.00
Nappy, handled, green 18.00
Relish, marigold, 7½" 25.00

Pansy Spray Sugar Bowl

Sugar bowl, open, purple, 3½" h.
   (ILLUS.)......................... 50.00

PANTHER (Fenton)

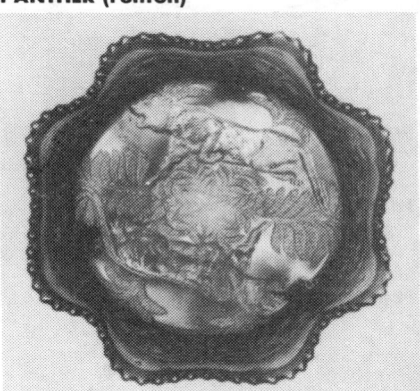

Panther Bowl

Berry set: master bowl & 6 sauce
   dishes; blue, 7 pcs.............. 700.00
Berry set: master bowl & 6 sauce
   dishes; marigold,
   7 pcs..................400.00 to 450.00
Bowl, 5" d., footed, aqua 250.00
Bowl, 5" d., footed, blue.......... 75.00
Bowl, 5" d., footed, marigold....... 36.50
Bowl, 5" d., footed, red........... 650.00
Bowl, 9" d., claw-footed, blue 265.00
Bowl, 9" d., claw-footed, marigold
   (ILLUS.)......................... 130.00
Bowl, 9" d., claw-footed, purple 150.00
Bowl, 9" d., claw-footed, white 625.00
Centerpiece bowl, blue 900.00

PEACH (Northwood)

Berry set: master bowl & 4 sauce
   dishes; white, 5 pcs. 325.00
Bowl, 9" d., white................ 145.00
Butter dish, cov., white 375.00
Sauce dish, white 50.00

Spooner, white.................... 98.00
Sugar bowl, cov., white ....90.00 to 125.00
Table set, white, 4 pcs............. 690.00
Tumbler, blue.................... 70.00
Tumbler, marigold 2,100.00
Tumbler, white................... 60.00

Peach Water Pitcher

Water set: pitcher & 5 tumblers;
  blue, 6 pcs. (ILLUS. of pitcher) ...1,250.00

PEACH & PEAR OVAL FRUIT BOWL
Marigold ....40.00 to 60.00
Purple 80.00

PEACOCK, FLUFFY (Fenton)

Fluffy Peacock Water Set

Pitcher, water, blue 650.00
Pitcher, water, green............. 585.00
Pitcher, water, marigold 325.00
Pitcher, water, purple 500.00
Tumbler, blue................... 65.00
Tumbler, green 55.00
Tumbler, marigold............... 45.00
Tumbler, purple................. 65.00
Water set: pitcher & 6 tumblers;
  purple, 7 pcs. (ILLUS.) 925.00

PEACOCK & DAHLIA (Fenton)
Bowl, 7" d., marigold........50.00 to 65.00

Bowl, 8" d., footed, green 49.00
Plate, 7½" d., marigold 175.00

PEACOCK & GRAPE (Fenton)
Bowl, 8" to 9" d., 3-footed, amber .. 160.00
Bowl, 8" to 9" d., 3-footed, blue 58.00
Bowl, 8" to 9" d., 3-footed, green... 55.00
Bowl, 8" to 9" d., 3-footed, ice
  green opalescent................ 595.00
Bowl, 8" to 9" d., 3-footed,
  lavender 125.00
Bowl, 8" to 9" d., 3-footed,
  marigold 42.50
Bowl, 8" to 9" d., 3-footed, purple .. 55.00
Bowl, 8" to 9" d., 3-footed,
  red ....550.00 to 675.00
Bowl, 8" to 9" d., 3-footed,
  vaseline 60.00
Bowl, 8" to 9" d., 3-footed, vaseline
  opalescent.................... 400.00
Bowl, 8" to 9" d., collared base,
  blue 55.00
Bowl, 8" to 9" d., collared base,
  peach opalescent............... 228.00
Bowl, 8" to 9" d., collared base,
  purple 50.00
Plate, 9" d., collared base, blue 400.00
Plate, 9" d., collared base,
  marigold 215.00
Plate, 9" d., 3-footed, green 110.00
Plate, 9" d., 3-footed, marigold..... 175.00
Plate, 9" d., 3-footed, purple 270.00

PEACOCK & URN
Berry set: master bowl & 4 sauce
  dishes; marigold, 5 pcs. 225.00
Berry set: master bowl & 6 sauce
  dishes; purple, 7 pcs.....650.00 to 675.00
Bowl, 7" d., ruffled, green
  (Millersburg)...........270.00 to 295.00
Bowl, 7" d., ruffled, marigold
  (Millersburg).................. 375.00
Bowl, 7" d., ruffled, purple
  (Millersburg)...........270.00 to 295.00
Bowl, 8" to 9" d., blue
  (Fenton)...............90.00 to 125.00
Bowl, 8" to 9" d., blue
  (Millersburg).................. 600.00
Bowl, 8" to 9" d., green (Fenton) ... 180.00
Bowl, 8" to 9" d., green
  (Millersburg)...........295.00 to 425.00
Bowl, 8" to 9" d., marigold
  (Fenton) 65.00
Bowl, 8" to 9" d., marigold
  (Millersburg).................. 140.00
Bowl, 8" to 9" d., purple
  (Fenton)...............110.00 to 135.00
Bowl, 8" to 9" d., purple
  (Millersburg).................. 210.00
Bowl, 8" to 9" d., white (Fenton) ... 150.00
Bowl, ice cream, 10" d., blue
  (Northwood) 300.00
Bowl, ice cream, 10" d., green
  (Northwood) 950.00

Bowl, ice cream, 10" d., ice blue
(Northwood) 585.00
Bowl, ice cream, 10" d., ice green
(Northwood) 800.00
Bowl, ice cream, 10" d., marigold
(Millersburg) 335.00
Bowl, ice cream, 10" d., marigold,
(Northwood) 150.00
Bowl, ice cream, 10" d., purple
(Northwood) 285.00
Bowl, ice cream, 10" d., white
(Northwood) ....320.00 to 365.00
Bowl, 10½" d., ruffled, blue
(Millersburg) 1,325.00
Bowl, 10½" d., ruffled, green 225.00
Bowl, 10½" d., ruffled, marigold ... 145.00
Bowl, 10½" d., ruffled,
purple ....150.00 to 225.00
Bowl, 10½" d., ruffled, vaseline
(Millersburg) 1,900.00
Compote, 5½" d., 5" h., aqua
(Fenton) 150.00
Compote, 5½" d., 5" h., blue
(Fenton) ....60.00 to 100.00
Compote, 5½" d., 5" h., marigold
(Fenton) 45.00
Compote, 5½" d., 5" h., purple
(Fenton) 55.00
Compote, 5½" d., 5" h., red
(Fenton) ....695.00 to 1,000.00
Compote, 5½" d., 5" h., vaseline
(Fenton) 160.00
Compote, 5½" d., 5" h., white
(Fenton) 300.00
Compote, blue (Millersburg Giant) .. 475.00
Compote, green (Millersburg
Giant) ....895.00 to 950.00
Compote, marigold (Millersburg
Giant)......................... 500.00
Compote, purple (Millersburg
Giant)......................... 845.00
Cuspidor, purple 4,168.00
Goblet, marigold (Fenton).......... 43.00
Ice cream dish, aqua opalescent,
small (Northwood) .....700.00 to 1,100.00
Ice cream dish, blue, small
(Northwood) 48.00
Ice cream dish, green, small 185.00
Ice cream dish, ice blue, small 135.00
Ice cream dish, marigold, small 40.00
Ice cream dish, purple, small....... 50.00
Ice cream dish, white, small 110.00
Ice cream set: large bowl & 4 small
dishes; ice blue, 5 pcs. 950.00
Ice cream set: large bowl & 4 small
dishes; marigold, 5 pcs. 375.00
Ice cream set: large bowl & 6 small
dishes; purple, 7 pcs. (Dugan) 650.00
Ice cream set: large bowl & 6 small
dishes; purple, 7 pcs.
(Northwood) ....500.00 to 645.00
Ice cream set: large bowl & 6 small
dishes; white, 7 pcs. 1,450.00
Plate, 6½" d., purple 235.00

Plate, 9" d., blue ....190.00 to 300.00
Plate, 9" d., marigold .....120.00 to 185.00
Plate, 9" d., purple............... 150.00
Plate, 9" d., white 250.00

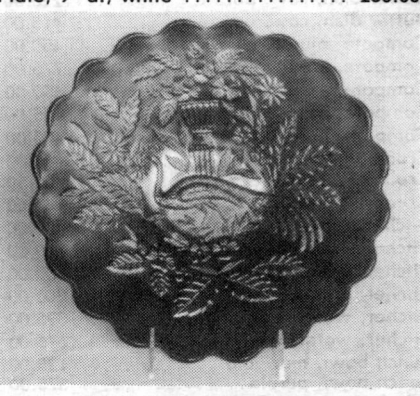

Peacock & Urn Chop Plate

Plate, chop, 11" d., marigold, North-
wood (ILLUS.) 350.00
Plate, chop, 11" d., purple
(Millersburg)............510.00 to 700.00
Plate, chop, 11" d., purple
(Northwood) 325.00
Sauce dish, blue (Millersburg) 130.00
Sauce dish, blue
(Northwood) ....60.00 to 95.00
Sauce dish, ice green, 6" d.
(Northwood) ....170.00 to 200.00
Sauce dish, marigold (Millersburg) .. 65.00
Sauce dish, marigold (Northwood) .. 40.00
Sauce dish, purple
(Millersburg)............150.00 to 195.00
Sauce dish, purple (Northwood) 72.50
Sauce dish, white (Northwood) 125.00

PEACOCK AT FOUNTAIN (Northwood)

Berry set: master bowl & 4 sauce
dishes; white, 5 pcs. 675.00
Berry set: master bowl & 5 sauce
dishes; marigold, 6 pcs. 185.00
Berry set: master bowl & 6 sauce
dishes; blue, 7 pcs............... 270.00
Berry set: master bowl & 6 sauce
dishes; marigold, 7 pcs. 175.00
Berry set: master bowl & 6 sauce
dishes; purple, 7 pcs.............. 215.00
Bowl, master berry, blue 125.00
Bowl, master berry, ice blue 500.00
Bowl, master berry,
marigold ....75.00 to 100.00
Bowl, master berry, purple......... 165.00
Bowl, orange, 3-footed, aqua
opalescent 2,000.00
Bowl, orange, 3-footed, blue 280.00
Bowl, orange, 3-footed, green 525.00
Bowl, orange, 3-footed, lavender ... 325.00
Bowl, orange, 3-footed,
marigold ....130.00 to 185.00

Bowl, orange, 3-footed,
  purple ....240.00 to 285.00
Butter dish, cov., marigold 135.00
Butter dish, cov., purple 225.00
Butter dish, cov., white 415.00
Compote, blue 450.00
Compote, ice blue ....700.00 to 775.00
Compote, ice green 650.00
Compote, marigold 425.00
Compote, purple ....350.00 to 425.00
Creamer, blue 105.00
Creamer, marigold 62.50
Creamer, purple 87.50
Pitcher, water, blue 400.00
Pitcher, water, green...1,500.00 to 1,750.00
Pitcher, water, ice blue 2,500.00
Pitcher, water, marigold...165.00 to 200.00
Pitcher, water, purple .....265.00 to 395.00
Pitcher, water, white 675.00
Punch bowl, marigold 125.00
Punch bowl, purple 375.00
Punch bowl & base, blue, 2 pcs. 365.00
Punch bowl & base, ice blue,
  2 pcs. 2,350.00
Punch bowl & base, marigold,
  2 pcs. 225.00
Punch bowl & base, purple,
  2 pcs..................480.00 to 500.00
Punch cup, blue................... 25.00
Punch cup, ice blue 75.00
Punch cup, marigold.............. 32.50

Peacock at Fountain Punch Cups

Punch cup, purple, each (ILLUS.) 30.00
Punch cup, white................. 55.00
Punch set: bowl, base & 4 cups; ice
  green, 6 pcs....................2,400.00
Punch set: bowl, base & 4 cups;
  purple, 6 pcs. 650.00
Punch set: bowl, base & 6 cups;
  marigold, 8 pcs................. 365.00
Sauce dish, blue 42.50
Sauce dish, marigold............. 16.00
Sauce dish, purple 45.00
Sauce dish, teal blue 110.00
Sauce dish, white 45.00
Spooner, blue.................... 125.00
Spooner, marigold................ 55.00
Spooner, purple.............75.00 to 95.00
Spooner, white.................. 100.00
Sugar bowl, cov., blue............ 125.00
Sugar bowl, cov., ice blue 220.00
Sugar bowl, cov., marigold...75.00 to 90.00
Sugar bowl, cov., purple 85.00
Table set, ice blue, 4 pcs........... 925.00

Table set, marigold, 4 pcs. 395.00
Table set, purple, 4 pcs. 550.00
Tumbler, blue.................... 42.50
Tumbler, green 450.00
Tumbler, ice blue 220.00
Tumbler, marigold................ 30.00
Tumbler, purple 38.00
Tumbler, white.................. 125.00
Water set: pitcher & 6 tumblers;
  blue, 7 pcs.................... 550.00
Water set: pitcher & 6 tumblers;
  marigold, 7 pcs................. 375.00
Water set: pitcher & 6 tumblers;
  purple, 7 pcs.................. 500.00

PEACOCKS ON FENCE (Northwood Peacocks)

Peacocks on Fence Plate

Bowl, 8" to 9" d., aqua opalescent .. 575.00
Bowl, 8" to 9" d., fluted, blue 325.00
Bowl, 8" to 9" d., fluted,
  green ....500.00 to 700.00
Bowl, 8" to 9" d., fluted, ice blue ... 375.00
Bowl, 8" to 9" d., fluted, ice
  green 375.00
Bowl, 8" to 9" d., fluted,
  marigold ....85.00 to 110.00
Bowl, 8" to 9" d., fluted,
  purple ....225.00 to 350.00
Bowl, 8" to 9" d., fluted,
  white ....275.00 to 350.00
Plate, 9" d., blue (ILLUS.) 365.00
Plate, 9" d., green 550.00
Plate, 9" d., ice blue 785.00
Plate, 9" d., ice green 300.00
Plate, 9" d., lavender............. 395.00
Plate, 9" d., marigold 200.00
Plate, 9" d., purple 375.00
Plate, 9" d., white ....225.00 to 295.00

PEACOCK STRUTTING (Westmoreland)

Breakfast set: individual size
  creamer & open sugar bowl;
  purple, pr....................... 65.00
Creamer, cov., individual size,
  purple 40.00

PEACOCK TAIL (Fenton)

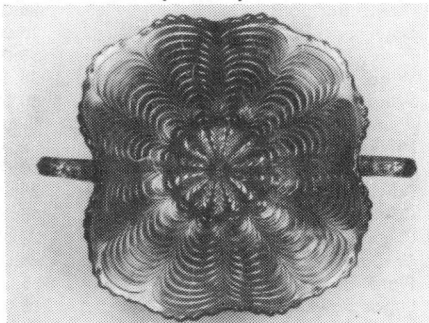

Peacock Tail Bon Bon

Bon bon, 2-handled, green	30.00
Bon bon, 2-handled, marigold (ILLUS.)	30.00
Bon bon, tricornered, green	35.00
Bon bon, tricornered, purple	40.00
Bowl, 5" d., ruffled, marigold	22.50
Bowl, 5" d., ruffled, purple	30.50
Bowl, 7" d., purple	22.50
Bowl, 7" d., red	385.00
Bowl, 9" d., blue	47.50
Bowl, 9" d., green	55.00
Bowl, 9" d., ribbon candy rim, purple	36.00
Bowl, 10½" d., marigold	47.00
Bowl, ice cream, red	600.00
Compote, 6" d., 5" h., green	38.00
Compote, 6" d., 5" h., marigold	40.00
Compote, 6" d., 5" h., purple	50.00
Plate, 6" d., marigold	28.00
Plate, 9" d., marigold	350.00
Sauce dish, green	35.00
Sauce dish, purple	28.00
Whimsey, hat-shaped, blue	26.50

PERFECTION (Millersburg)

Perfection Water Set

Pitcher, water, marigold	2,700.00
Pitcher, water, purple (ILLUS.)	2,000.00 to 3,000.00
Tumbler, green	500.00
Tumbler, purple (ILLUS.)	450.00

PERSIAN GARDEN (Dugan)

Berry set: 11" d. fruit bowl & 4 sauce dishes; peach opalescent, 5 pcs.	700.00
Berry set: master bowl & 6 sauce dishes; peach opalescent, 7 pcs.	400.00
Bowl, 5" d., white	52.50
Bowl, 9" d., ruffled, marigold	50.00
Bowl, ice cream, 11" d., peach opalescent	350.00
Bowl, ice cream, 11" d., purple	275.00
Bowl, ice cream, 11" d., white	200.00
Fruit bowl (no base), marigold, 11½" d.	70.00 to 85.00
Fruit bowl (no base), peach opalescent, 11½" d.	195.00
Fruit bowl (no base), purple, 11½" d.	135.00
Fruit bowl (no base), white, 11½" d.	275.00
Fruit bowl & base, peach opalescent, 2 pcs.	385.00
Fruit bowl & base, purple, 2 pcs.	300.00
Fruit bowl & base, white, 2 pcs.	240.00
Ice cream dish, white, small	55.00
Ice cream set: 11" d. master ice cream bowl & 4 small dishes; white, 5 pcs.	650.00
Plate, 6" to 7" d., blue	80.00
Plate, 6" to 7" d., marigold	52.50
Plate, 6" to 7" d., peach opalescent	180.00
Plate, 6" to 7" d., purple	175.00 to 200.00
Plate, 6" to 7" d., white	90.00
Plate, chop, 11" d., purple	1,400.00 to 2,000.00

PERSIAN MEDALLION (Fenton)

Persian Medallion Plates

Bon bon, 2-handled, amber	60.00
Bon bon, 2-handled, blue	40.00

Bon bon, 2-handled, green 60.00
Bon bon, 2-handled, marigold 25.00
Bon bon, 2-handled, purple 35.00
Bon bon, 2-handled, red 485.00
Bon bon, 2-handled, vaseline 60.00
Bowl, 5" d., green 36.00
Bowl, 5" d., marigold 45.00
Bowl, 5" d., purple 30.00
Bowl, 7" d., green 60.00
Bowl, 7" d., marigold 55.00
Bowl, 7" d., pie crust edge, purple.. 75.00
Bowl, 8" to 9" d., fluted,
    blue ....50.00 to 68.00
Bowl, 8" to 9" d., ribbon candy rim,
    blue 90.00
Bowl, 8" to 9" d., ribbon candy rim,
    green 60.00
Bowl, 8" to 9" d., marigold 45.00
Bowl, 8" to 9" d., ribbon candy rim,
    purple 65.00
Bowl, ice cream, 10½" d., purple ... 55.00
Bowl, 10½" d., fluted, blue 70.00
Compote, 6½" d., 6½" h., blue 60.00
Compote, 6½" d., 6½" h., green ... 45.00
Compote, 6½" d., 6½" h.,
    marigold 32.50
Compote, 6½" d., 6½" h.,
    purple ....85.00 to 125.00
Compote, 6½" d., 6½" h., white ... 400.00
Hair receiver, blue 105.00
Hair receiver, marigold 50.00
Plate, 6½" d., blue (ILLUS.
    left)......................50.00 to 85.00
Plate, 6½" d., green 115.00
Plate, 6½" d., marigold 40.00
Plate, 6½" d., purple 90.00
Plate, 6½" d., red slag 325.00
Plate, 6½" d., white 75.00
Plate, 9" d., blue................. 110.00
Plate, 9" d., marigold 125.00
Plate, 9" d., white 375.00
Plate, chop, 10½" d., blue (ILLUS.
    right) 300.00
Rose bowl, blue................... 65.00
Rose bowl, marigold.............. 45.00
Rose bowl, white.................. 115.00

PETAL & FAN (Dugan)
Berry set: master bowl & 6
    sauce dishes; peach opales-
    cent, 7 pcs...................... 250.00
Bowl, 5" d., peach opalescent 35.00
Bowl, 5" d., purple 30.00
Bowl, 11" d., peach opalescent 110.00
Bowl, 11" d., ruffled, purple........ 125.00
Plate, 6" d., ribbon candy edge,
    purple 105.00

PETER RABBIT (Fenton)
Bowl, 8" d., marigold............. 750.00
Plate, blue.......................2,000.00
Plate, green 3,000.00
Plate, marigold..................1,200.00

PILLOW & SUNBURST (Westmoreland)
Bowl, marigold................... 25.00
Bowl, purple 35.00
Plate, 8" d., aqua 38.00
Wine, marigold 25.00
Wine, purple.................... 50.00

PINEAPPLE
Bowl, 5" d., marigold............. 30.00
Bowl, 8" d., marigold............. 38.00
Compote, purple 45.00
Creamer, marigold, 4½" h. 28.00
Creamer, purple 38.00
Plate, 8" d., purple.............. 135.00
Sugar bowl, aqua 215.00

PINE CONE (Fenton)

Pine Cone Bowl

Bowl, 5" d., blue 35.00
Bowl, 5" d., marigold............. 25.00
Bowl, 5" d., purple 35.00
Bowl, 7" d., ruffled, blue 60.00
Bowl, 7" d., marigold 26.50
Bowl, 7" d., ruffled, purple
    (ILLUS.)....................... 40.00
Plate, 6½" d., blue........60.00 to 85.00
Plate, 6½" d., green ....90.00 to 125.00
Plate, 6½" d., marigold .....40.00 to 55.00
Plate, 6½" d., purple 125.00
Plate, 7½" d., blue ....140.00 to 185.00
Plate, 7½" d., marigold 75.00

PODS & POSIES or FOUR FLOWERS (Dugan)
Bowl, 6" d., peach opalescent 40.00
Bowl, 8" to 9" d., green 200.00
Bowl, 10" d., shallow, ruffled,
    lavender 225.00
Bowl, 10" d., peach opal-
    escent ....60.00 to 85.00
Bowl, 10" d., purple 145.00
Plate, 6" d., green 250.00
Plate, 6" d., peach opalescent 90.00

Plate, 6" d., purple 145.00
Plate, 9" d., green 525.00
Plate, 9" d., purple 400.00
Plate, chop, 11" d., peach
 opalescent.................... 450.00

Pods & Posies Plate

Plate, chop, 11" d., purple
 (ILLUS.) ....650.00 to 850.00

POINSETTIA (Imperial)
Pitcher, milk, amber............... 59.00
Pitcher, milk, green 250.00
Pitcher, milk, marigold 65.00
Pitcher, milk, smoky.............. 125.00

POINSETTIA & LATTICE
Bowl, 8" to 9" d., footed, stippled,
 marigold 130.00
Bowl, aqua opalescent 3,000.00
Bowl, ice blue 200.00
Bowl, marigold ....90.00 to 110.00
Bowl, purple.............200.00 to 225.00

PONY

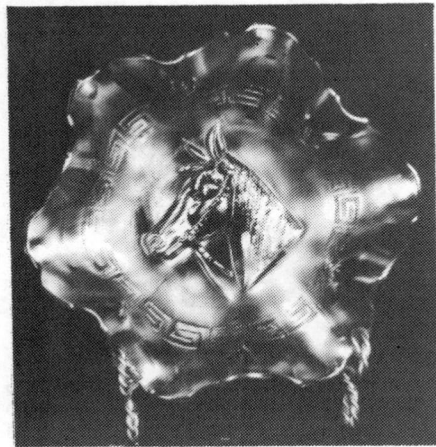

Pony Bowl

Bowl, 8" to 9" d., aqua 400.00
Bowl, 8" to 9" d., marigold......... 60.00
Bowl, 8" to 9" d., marigold w/aqua
 base 200.00
Bowl, 8" to 9" d., purple (ILLUS.) ... 130.00

POPPY (Millersburg)
Compote, green ....500.00 to 650.00
Compote, marigold 275.00
Compote, purple ....425.00 to 500.00

POPPY (Northwood)
Pickle dish, blue 75.00
Pickle dish, ice blue 150.00
Pickle dish, marigold 50.00
Pickle dish, white 225.00

POPPY SHOW (Northwood)

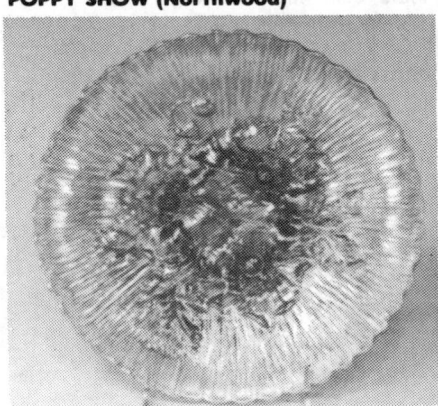

Poppy Show Plate

Bowl, 8" to 9" d., blue............. 300.00
Bowl, 8" to 9" d., clambroth........ 190.00
Bowl, 8" to 9" d., ice blue 400.00
Bowl, 8" to 9" d., ice green 600.00
Bowl, 8" to 9" d., marigold......... 160.00
Bowl, 8" to 9" d., purple 185.00
Bowl, 8" to 9" d., white............ 225.00
Plate, blue 445.00
Plate, green (ILLUS.) 1,200.00
Plate, ice blue 615.00
Plate, marigold 300.00
Plate, purple ....385.00 to 425.00
Plate, white ....325.00 to 475.00

POPPY SHOW VASE (Imperial)
Marigold ....285.00 to 350.00
Purple 950.00
Smoky ....275.00 to 550.00

PRIMROSE BOWL (Millersburg)
Green............................ 85.00
Marigold 75.00
Purple 85.00

PRINCESS LAMP
Purple, complete 1,000.00
Purple, base only 225.00

PRISMS

Compote, 7¼" d., 2½" h.,
  2-handled, marigold 50.00
Compote, 7¼" d., 2½" h.,
  2-handled, purple 55.00

QUESTION MARKS

Bon bon, footed, marigold, 6" d.,
  3¾" h. 32.50
Bon bon, footed, pastel marigold,
  6" d., 3¾" h. 35.00
Bon bon, footed, peach opalescent,
  6" d., 3¾" h. 65.00
Bon bon, footed, purple, 6" d.,
  3¾" h. 27.50
Bon bon, footed, white, 6" d.,
  3¾" h. 120.00
Plate, dome-footed, Georgia Peach
  exterior, purple 100.00

QUILL (Dugan or Diamond Glass Co.)

Quill Pitcher

Pitcher, water, purple (ILLUS.) 2,200.00
Tumbler, marigold................. 275.00
Tumbler, purple 400.00

RAINDROPS (Dugan)

Bowl, 9" d., dome-footed, peach
  opalescent..................... 60.00
Bowl, 9" d., dome-footed, purple ... 58.00

RAMBLER ROSE (Dugan)

Pitcher, water, marigold 135.00
Pitcher, water, purple 325.00
Tumbler, blue.................... 32.50
Tumbler, marigold................. 20.00
Tumbler, purple.................. 35.00
Water set: pitcher & 4 tumblers;
  blue, 5 pcs..................... 400.00
Water set: pitcher & 6 tumblers;
  marigold, 7 pcs. ....275.00 to 350.00

RANGER

Pitcher, milk, marigold 145.00
Sherbet, marigold 17.50
Whiskey shot glass, marigold 95.00

RASPBERRY (Northwood)

Pitcher, milk, green 195.00
Pitcher, milk, marigold 95.00
Pitcher, milk, purple 155.00
Pitcher, water, green 250.00
Pitcher, water, ice green 2,275.00
Pitcher, water, marigold 129.00
Pitcher, water, purple 225.00
Sauceboat, green 175.00
Sauceboat, purple 75.00
Tumbler, green 50.00
Tumbler, ice blue 245.00
Tumbler, ice green 1,000.00
Tumbler, marigold................. 32.50
Tumbler, purple.................. 37.50
Water set: pitcher & 6 tumblers;
  marigold, 7 pcs.................. 325.00
Water set: pitcher & 6 tumblers;
  purple, 7 pcs.................... 400.00

RAYS & RIBBONS (Millersburg)

Banana boat, green 850.00
Bowl, 8" to 9" d., green 57.50
Bowl, 8" to 9" d., purple 75.00
Bowl, 10" d., green 47.50
Bowl, 10" sq., green ......250.00 to 275.00
Bowl, 10" d., ice cream shape,
  turned-down rim, green 135.00
Bowl, 10" d., marigold............ 47.50
Bowl, 10" d., purple 65.00

RISING SUN

Pitcher, water, pedestal base,
  marigold 800.00
Tumbler, marigold................. 400.00
Water set: pitcher & 4 tumblers;
  marigold, 5 pcs. 2,950.00

ROBIN (Imperial)

Robin Mug

Mug, marigold (ILLUS.)............. 38.50
Pitcher, water, marigold 160.00
Tumbler, marigold................. 47.50
Water set: pitcher & 6 tumblers;
  marigold, 7 pcs. ....320.00 to 400.00

ROCOCO VASE
Bowl, 6" d., dome-footed, mari-
  gold ....18.00 to 25.00
Vase, clambroth 40.00
Vase, marigold 45.00
Vase, smoky.....................   62.50

ROSALIND (Millersburg)
Bowl, 10" d., ruffled,
  green ....125.00 to 150.00
Bowl, 10" d., marigold......75.00 to 100.00
Bowl, 10" d., purple 125.00
Compote, 6", small, ruffled, green .. 350.00
Compote, 6", small, ruffled,
  purple 485.00
Compote, 6" d., 9" h., tall, ruffled,
  purple 1,000.00
Plate, 9" d., green 575.00

ROSE COLUMNS VASE

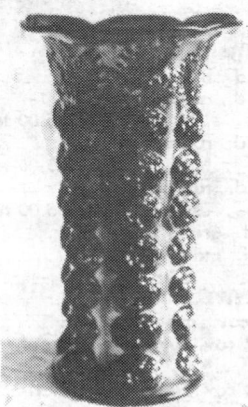

Rose Columns Vase

Amethyst 1,500.00
Amethyst, experimental, factory-
  painted roses decoration
  (ILLUS.) 3,250.00
Green............................. 925.00
Marigold..........................1,200.00

ROSE SHOW

Rose Show Variant Bowl

Bowl, 9" d., aqua opalescent 525.00
Bowl, 9" d., blue.........275.00 to 350.00
Bowl, 9" d., green 400.00
Bowl, 9" d., ice blue............ 300.00
Bowl, 9" d., ice green 500.00
Bowl, 9" d., ice green opalescent ... 700.00
Bowl, 9" d., marigold 110.00
Bowl, 9" d., purple 225.00
Bowl, 9" d., white............ 230.00
Plate, 9" d., blue............... 400.00
Plate, 9" d., green 600.00
Plate, 9" d., ice blue 1,000.00
Plate, 9" d., ice green 525.00
Plate, 9" d., marigold 255.00
Plate, 9" d., purple 400.00
Plate, 9" d., white 250.00

ROUND UP (Dugan)

Round Up Plate

Bowl, 9" d., low, fluted, blue.......   70.00
Bowl, 9" d., marigold.............   50.00
Bowl, 9" d., peach opalescent 325.00
Bowl, 9" d., purple 90.00
Bowl, 9" d., white 95.00
Plate, 9" d., blue (ILLUS.) 220.00
Plate, 9" d., ruffled, marigold 95.00
Plate, 9" d., flat, peach
  opalescent.................... 150.00
Plate, 9" d., ruffled, peach
  opalescent.................... 325.00
Plate, 9" d., purple 225.00
Plate, 9" d., white 225.00

RUSTIC VASE
Blue, 9" h.......................   40.00
Blue, 16" h......................   75.00
Blue, 19" h...................... 165.00
Blue, 21" h...................... 235.00
Blue, 23½" h..................... 270.00
Green, 11" h.....................   40.00
Green, 16" h.....................   70.00
Green, 18" h. (ILLUS.) 350.00
Marigold, 11" h. 30.00

Rustic Vase

Marigold, 16" h. 150.00
Marigold, 20" h. 175.00
Purple, 9" h. 40.00
Purple, 16" h. 100.00
White, 20" h. ....400.00 to 450.00

SAILBOAT (Fenton)
Bowl, 5" d., aqua 100.00
Bowl, 5" d., ruffled, blue 55.00
Bowl, 5" d., ruffled, green ...80.00 to 95.00
Bowl, 5" d., marigold 40.00
Bowl, 5" d., purple 70.00
Bowl, 5" d., ruffled, red 500.00
Compote, blue 100.00
Compote, marigold 45.00
Goblet, water, green 225.00
Goblet, water, marigold 185.00
Goblet, water, purple 350.00
Plate, 6" d., blue 350.00
Plate, 6" d., marigold 200.00
Wine, ice blue ....195.00 to 225.00
Wine, marigold 25.00
Wine, vaseline 125.00

SCALE BAND
Pitcher, marigold 85.00
Plate, 6" d., flat, marigold 22.00
Water set: pitcher & 6 tumblers;
    marigold, 7 pcs. 175.00

SCALES
Bowl, 7" d., marigold 22.50
Bowl, 7" d., peach
    opalescent ....40.00 to 55.00
Bowl, 7" w., tricornered, peach
    opalescent 125.00
Bowl, 7" d., purple 40.00
Bowl, 8" to 9" d., aqua opalescent .. 250.00
Bowl, 8" to 9" d., milk white
    w/marigold overlay 160.00
Bowl, 8" to 9" d., peach
    opalescent 85.00
Plate, 6½" d., marigold 40.00
Plate, 6½" d., purple ....25.00 to 40.00

SCOTCH THISTLE COMPOTE
Green 57.50
Purple 45.00

SCROLL EMBOSSED
Bowl, 8" to 9" d., green 45.00
Bowl, 8" to 9" d., marigold 35.00
Bowl, 8" to 9" d., purple 45.00
Bowl, 8" to 9" d., smoky 35.00
Compote, green 60.00
Compote, marigold 25.00
Compote, purple 110.00
Plate, 9" d., green ....55.00 to 75.00
Plate, 9" d., marigold 100.00
Plate, 9" d., purple 110.00
Sauce dish, purple, 5½" d. 11.50

SEACOAST PIN TRAY (Millersburg)
Green 325.00
Marigold 290.00
Purple 325.00

SEAWEED (Millersburg)
Bowl, 10" d., blue 900.00
Bowl, 10" d., ruffled,
    green ....175.00 to 200.00
Bowl, 10" d., ruffled, mari-
    gold ....225.00 to 275.00
Bowl, 10" d., ruffled,
    purple ....195.00 to 250.00
Plate, 9" d., green 550.00
Plate, 9" d., marigold 500.00

SHELL & JEWEL
Creamer, cov., green 28.00
Creamer & cov. sugar bowl, green,
    pr. 60.00
Creamer & cov. sugar bowl, mari-
    gold, pr. ....45.00 to 80.00
Sugar bowl, cov., green 28.00
Sugar bowl, cov., marigold 20.00

SHIP & STARS PLATE
Marigold 25.00

SINGING BIRDS (Northwood)
Berry set: master bowl & 6 sauce
    dishes; green, 7 pcs. 350.00
Bowl, master berry, purple 90.00
Butter dish, cov., green 285.00
Butter dish, cov., marigold 100.00
Butter dish, cov., purple 195.00
Creamer, marigold 50.00
Creamer, purple 77.50
Mug, aqua opalescent ....875.00 to 1,000.00
Mug, blue 75.00
Mug, green ....90.00 to 150.00
Mug, ice blue 775.00
Mug, lavender 125.00
Mug, marigold 45.00
Mug, stippled, marigold 130.00
Mug, purple (ILLUS. right) 65.00
Mug, purple, w/advertising, "Hotel
    Verdome" 130.00

Mug, white 600.00
Pitcher, green 275.00
Pitcher, marigold............... 220.00
Pitcher, purple 275.00
Sauce dish, green 35.00
Sauce dish, marigold 35.00
Sauce dish, purple 35.00
Spooner, marigold............... 50.00
Spooner, purple 85.00
Sugar bowl, cov., marigold........ 80.00
Table set: cov. sugar bowl, creamer
  & spooner; marigold, 3 pcs. 225.00
Table set: cov. butter dish, cov.
  sugar bowl, creamer & spooner;
  purple, 4 pcs. 900.00
Tumbler, green 42.50
Tumbler, marigold............... 26.50

Singing Birds Tumbler & Mug

Tumbler, purple (ILLUS. left)........ 50.00
Water set: pitcher & 6 tumblers;
  green, 7 pcs. 575.00
Water set: pitcher & 6 tumblers;
  marigold, 7 pcs................. 560.00
Water set: pitcher & 6 tumblers;
  purple, 7 pcs............650.00 to 700.00

SIX PETALS (Dugan)
Bowl, 7" w., tricornered, peach
  opalescent...................... 55.00
Bowl, 7" w., tricornered, purple 52.50
Bowl, 8" d., peach opalescent 75.00
Bowl, 8" d., purple 55.00
Bowl, 8" d., white................. 62.50

SKI STAR (Dugan)
Banana bowl, peach
  opalescent ....78.00 to 100.00
Basket, peach opalescent 395.00
Berry set: master bowl & 2 sauce
  dishes; peach opalescent, 3 pcs... 165.00
Bowl, 5" d., peach opalescent 35.00
Bowl, 5" d., fluted, peach
  opalescent...................... 65.00

Bowl, 5" d., ruffled, peach
  opalescent...................... 55.00
Bowl, 5" d., ruffled, purple...... 55.00
Bowl, 7" d., ruffled, purple......... 75.00
Bowl, 8" to 9" d., dome-footed,
  peach opalescent................ 85.00
Bowl, 8" to 9" d., dome-footed,
  purple 70.00
Bowl, 10" d., peach opalescent 110.00
Bowl, 11" d., peach opalescent 80.00
Bowl, tricornered, dome base,
  peach opalescent................ 85.00
Plate, 6" d., crimped rim, peach
  opalescent...................... 125.00
Plate, 8½" d., dome-footed,
  w/handgrip, peach
  opalescent ....125.00 to 160.00

SNOW FANCY
Creamer, marigold 40.00
Creamer & sugar bowl, marigold,
  pr............................. 75.00
Sugar bowl, marigold............. 37.50

SODA GOLD (Imperial)

Soda Gold Water Set

Console set: bowl & pr. candle-
  sticks; marigold, 3 pcs. 45.00
Cuspidor, marigold ....45.00 to 60.00
Pitcher, milk, marigold 195.00
Pitcher, water, marigold ...125.00 to 160.00
Pitcher, water, smoky 375.00
Tumbler, marigold ....25.00 to 40.00
Tumbler, smoky.............50.00 to 90.00
Water set: pitcher & 6 tumblers;
  marigold, 7 pcs. (ILLUS.) 275.00
Water set: pitcher & 6 tumblers;
  smoky, 7 pcs.................... 650.00

SOUTACHE (Dugan)
Bowl, 8" to 9" d., dome-footed,
  piecrust edge, peach opalescent .. 90.00
Plate, 9½" d., dome-footed, peach
  opalescent...................... 300.00

SPRINGTIME (Northwood)
Berry set: master bowl & 6 sauce
  dishes; green, 7 pcs. 280.00

Bowl, 5" d., green 45.00
Bowl, 5" d., marigold 25.00
Bowl, 5" d., purple 37.50
Bowl, master berry, green 150.00
Bowl, master berry, marigold 75.00
Butter dish, cov., green 400.00
Butter dish, cov., marigold 165.00
Butter dish, cov., purple 275.00
Creamer, marigold 85.00
Creamer, purple 110.00
Pitcher, green 495.00
Pitcher, marigold 425.00
Pitcher, purple............600.00 to 750.00
Spooner, green 150.00
Spooner, marigold................. 60.00
Spooner, purple 100.00
Sugar bowl, cov., purple 120.00
Table set, marigold, 4 pcs..500.00 to 535.00
Tumbler, green 135.00
Tumbler, marigold................. 55.00
Tumbler, purple................... 95.00
Water set: pitcher & 4 tumblers;
  green, 5 pcs....................1,100.00
Water set: pitcher & 4 tumblers;
  purple, 5 pcs................... 865.00

"S" REPEAT (Dugan)

Punch cup, purple 150.00
Punch set: bowl, base & 4 cups;
  purple, 6 pcs........1,200.00 to 1,500.00

STAG & HOLLY (Fenton)

Stag & Holly Bowl

Bowl, 7" d., spatula-footed,
  blue ....95.00 to 115.00
Bowl, 7" d., spatula-footed, green .. 125.00
Bowl, 7" d., spatula-footed,
  marigold 50.00
Bowl, 7" d., spatula-footed, red 1,050.00
Bowl, 8" to 9" d., spatula-footed,
  blue 115.00
Bowl, 8" to 9" d., spatula-footed,
  green 175.00
Bowl, 8" to 9" d., spatula-footed,
  marigold 65.00
Bowl, 8" to 9" d., spatula-footed,
  purple 85.00

Bowl, 10" to 11" d., 3-footed,
  amber 600.00
Bowl, 10" to 11" d., 3-footed, blue
  (ILLUS.)..................... 200.00
Bowl, 10" to 11" d., 3-footed,
  green 250.00
Bowl, 10" to 11" d., 3-footed,
  marigold 95.00
Bowl, 10" to 11" d., 3-footed,
  purple 195.00
Bowl, 10" to 11" d., 3-footed, red ... 850.00
Bowl, 10" to 11" d., 3-footed,
  vaseline 170.00
Plate, 9" d., marigold .....395.00 to 475.00
Plate, chop, 12" d., 3-footed,
  marigold 535.00
Rose bowl, blue, large............. 595.00
Rose bowl, marigold,
  large ....195.00 to 250.00

STAR & FILE (Imperial)

Bowl, 5" d., marigold.............. 25.00
Bowl, 7" d., marigold.............. 20.00
Bowl, 8" to 9" d., marigold......... 35.00
Card tray, 2 turned-up sides, mari-
  gold, 6¼" d.................... 22.50
Celery vase, 2-handled, marigold ... 27.50
Compote, jelly, clambroth.......... 50.00
Compote, jelly, marigold 55.00
Compote, large, marigold 35.00
Creamer, marigold 20.00
Creamer & sugar bowl, marigold,
  pr............................ 47.50
Pitcher, milk, smoky.............. 40.00
Pitcher, water, marigold 120.00
Plate, 6" d., marigold 45.00
Relish tray, 2-handled, marigold 45.00
Rose bowl, marigold.............. 52.50
Sugar bowl, marigold.............. 15.00
Tumbler, marigold................. 50.00
Water set: pitcher & 6 tumblers;
  marigold, 7 pcs................. 255.00
Wine, marigold 35.00
Wine decanter w/stopper,
  marigold 90.00
Wine set: decanter w/stopper & 6
  wines; marigold, 7 pcs. 285.00

STAR MEDALLION

Bowl, 5" sq., marigold 25.00
Bowl, 7" d., smoky 22.50
Bowl, 8" d., marigold 30.00
Bowl, 8" d., smoky 28.00
Chalice, clambroth 38.00
Goblet, marigold 35.00
Pitcher, milk, clambroth 35.00
Pitcher, milk, marigold 37.50
Pitcher, milk, smoky.............. 45.00
Plate, 9" to 10" d., clambroth 70.00
Plate, 9" to 10" d., marigold 35.00
Punch cup, marigold.............. 15.00
Rose bowl, marigold.............. 35.00
Sherbet, stemmed, marigold 25.00
Tumbler, marigold................. 30.00

Tumbler, tall, tankard form,
marigold 35.00

STAR OF DAVID (Imperial)

Star of David Bowl

Bowl, 8" to 9" d., collared base,
green (ILLUS.) 45.00
Bowl, 8" to 9" d., collared base,
marigold 45.00
Bowl, 8" to 9" d., collared base,
purple 62.50
Bowl, 9" d., flat, ruffled, purple 90.00

STAR OF DAVID & BOWS (Northwood)

Bowl, 7" d., dome-footed, green.... 70.00
Bowl, 7" d., dome-footed, purple ... 55.00
Bowl, 8" to 9" d., dome-footed,
fluted, purple 65.00

STIPPLED PETALS

Bowl, peach opalescent 55.00
Bowl, white...................... 60.00

STIPPLED RAYS

Stippled Rays Bowl

Berry set: master bowl & 4 sauce
dishes; green, 5 pcs. 150.00
Bon bon, 2-handled, green 40.00
Bon bon, 2-handled, ice green...... 80.00
Bon bon, 2-handled, marigold 40.00
Bon bon, 2-handled, purple 25.00

Bon bon, 2-handled, red 260.00
Bowl, 5" d., green 30.00
Bowl, 5" d., purple 37.50
Bowl, 5" d., red...........175.00 to 275.00
Bowl, 6" d., Amberina 100.00
Bowl, 7" d., blue 35.00
Bowl, 7" d., dome-footed, green.... 25.00
Bowl, 7" d., marigold 25.00
Bowl, 7" d., ruffled rim, red........ 350.00
Bowl, 8" to 9" d., amber 97.50
Bowl, 8" to 9" d., green 40.00
Bowl, 8" to 9" d., ribbon candy rim,
green 57.50
Bowl, 8" to 9" d., marigold 36.00
Bowl, 8" to 9" d., ribbon candy rim,
marigold 35.00
Bowl, 8" to 9" d., purple 47.50
Bowl, 8" to 9" d., ribbon candy rim,
purple 42.50
Bowl, 8" to 9" d., teal blue......... 20.00
Bowl, 10" d., green 55.00
Bowl, 10" d., ruffled, marigold 47.50
Bowl, 10" d., purple, Northwood
(ILLUS.)....................... 45.00
Bowl, 10" d., red slag (Fenton) 450.00
Bowl, 10" d., white.......275.00 to 300.00
Creamer & sugar bowl, marigold,
pr. 40.00
Plate, 6" to 7" d., blue 40.00
Plate, 6" to 7" d., marigold 20.00
Sugar bowl, open, blue 27.50
Sugar bowl, open, marigold 15.00
Sugar bowl, open, red
(Imperial) 320.00

STORK & RUSHES (Dugan or Diamond Glass Works)

Basket, handled, marigold 90.00
Bowl, master berry or fruit,
marigold 40.00
Butter dish, cov., marigold 125.00
Hat shape, marigold............... 25.00
Mug, aqua base w/marigold
overlay........................ 450.00
Mug, marigold 22.50
Mug, purple 85.00
Pitcher, water, blue 375.00
Pitcher, water, purple 365.00
Punch bowl & base, marigold,
2 pcs. 200.00
Punch cup, marigold............... 18.00
Punch cup, purple 18.50
Sauce dish, marigold 16.50
Sauce dish, purple 27.50
Spooner, marigold................ 60.00
Tumbler, blue.................... 30.00
Tumbler, marigold................ 22.50
Tumbler, marigold w/pale blue
base 125.00
Tumbler, purple 35.00
Water set: pitcher & 1 tumbler;
blue, 2 pcs. 500.00
Water set: pitcher & 6 tumblers;
marigold, 7 pcs.................. 400.00

STRAWBERRY (Fenton)

Bon bon, 2-handled, blue 40.00
Bon bon, 2-handled, green 42.50
Bon bon, 2-handled, ice green
   opalescent...................... 450.00
Bon bon, 2-handled, marigold 27.50
Bon bon, 2-handled, vaseline
   w/marigold iridescence 150.00

STRAWBERRY (Millersburg)

Bowl, 5" d., marigold.............. 20.00
Bowl, 5" d., purple 50.00
Bowl, 7" d., green 75.00
Bowl, 7" d., purple 105.00
Bowl, 8" to 9" d., purple 150.00
Bowl, 8" to 9" d., vaseline 450.00
Compote, amber 45.00
Compote, green................... 175.00
Compote, marigold 115.00
Compote, purple ....175.00 to 195.00
Compote, vaseline 640.00

STRAWBERRY & WILD STRAWBERRY (Northwood)

Northwood Strawberry Plate

Bowl, 5" d., fluted, blue 35.00
Bowl, 5" d., marigold.............. 27.50
Bowl, 5" d., fluted, purple 56.50
Bowl, 7" d., marigold.............. 48.50
Bowl, 7" d., purple 30.00
Bowl, 8" to 9" d., stippled, blue 90.00
Bowl, 8" to 9" d., stippled, ribbon
   candy rim, green 150.00
Bowl, 8" to 9" d., ruffled, Basket-
   weave exterior, green 85.00
Bowl, 8" to 9" d., marigold......... 37.50
Bowl, 8" to 9" d., purple 70.00
Bowl, 10" d., ice green 575.00
Bowl, 10" d., marigold 55.00
Bowl, 10" d., Basketweave exterior,
   marigold ....85.00 to 125.00
Bowl, 10" d., purple ....85.00 to 120.00
Bowl, 10" d., Basketweave exterior,
   purple 135.00
Plate, 6" to 7" d., w/handgrip,
   green 135.00

Plate, 6" to 7" d., w/handgrip,
   marigold 75.00
Plate, 6" to 7" d., w/handgrip,
   purple ....90.00 to 125.00
Plate, 9" d., green 100.00
Plate, 9" d., lavender............. 135.00
Plate, 9" d., marigold 80.00
Plate, 9" d., purple (ILLUS.) 120.00

STRAWBERRY SCROLL (Fenton)

Strawberry Scroll Pitcher

Pitcher, water, blue
   (ILLUS.) ....1,850.00 to 2,000.00
Pitcher, water, mari-
   gold ....1,000.00 to 1,500.00
Tumbler, blue..................... 200.00
Tumbler, marigold................. 135.00

STREAM OF HEARTS (Fenton)

Compote, marigold ....38.00 to 50.00

SUNFLOWER BOWL (Northwood)

Bowl, 8" d., footed, blue........... 250.00
Bowl, 8" d., footed, clambroth...... 75.00
Bowl, 8" d., footed, green 67.50
Bowl, 8" d., footed, marigold....... 45.00
Bowl, 8" d., footed, purple 50.00

SUNFLOWER PIN TRAY (Millersburg)

Clambroth........................ 195.00
Green............................ 240.00
Marigold 350.00
Purple 265.00

SWAN PASTEL NOVELTIES (Dugan)

Salt dip, blue 10.00
Salt dip, ice blue 30.00
Salt dip, ice green 35.00
Salt dip, marigold 72.00
Salt dip, peach opalescent 175.00
Salt dip, pink 32.50
Salt dip, purple 160.00
Salt dip, vaseline................. 55.00

SWIRL HOBNAIL (Millersburg)

Cuspidor, marigold 525.00

Swirl Hobnail Cuspidor

Cuspidor, purple (ILLUS.)...425.00 to 650.00
Rose bowl, marigold............... 300.00
Rose bowl, purple.........200.00 to 250.00
Vase, green 135.00
Vase, marigold ....220.00 to 250.00
Vase, purple ....200.00 to 235.00

SWIRL RIB

Pitcher, tankard, marigold 150.00
Tumbler, marigold ....20.00 to 25.00
Vase, 9½" h., peach opalescent 40.00
Vase, 10½" h., peach opalescent ... 37.00
Vase, 14½" h., peach opalescent ... 48.00
Vase, marigold 35.00

TEN MUMS (Fenton)

Ten Mums Pitcher

Bowl, 8" to 9" d., ribbon candy
　edge, blue...................... 80.00
Bowl, 8" to 9" d., ribbon candy
　edge, green 120.00
Bowl, 10" d., ruffled, blue 135.00
Bowl, 10" d., footed, green 80.00
Bowl, 10" d., footed, marigold...... 210.00
Bowl, 10" d., ribbon candy edge,
　purple ....80.00 to 110.00
Pitcher, water, marigold 375.00
Pitcher, water, white 1,200.00
Tumbler, blue..............65.00 to 95.00
Tumbler, marigold................. 45.00

Tumbler, white................... 210.00
Water set: pitcher & 5 tumblers;
　blue, 6 pcs. (ILLUS. of pitcher
　only) 2,900.00
Water set: pitcher & 6 tumblers;
　marigold, 7 pcs................. 850.00

TEXAS HAT

Marigold 25.00

THIN RIB VASE

7½" h., ice green (Northwood) 80.00
8" h., aqua 27.00
9" h., aqua opalescent............ 90.00
9" h., blue...................... 45.00
9½" h., aqua 30.00
11" h., aqua opalescent........... 110.00
12" h., white 110.00
13" h., ice blue 125.00

THISTLE

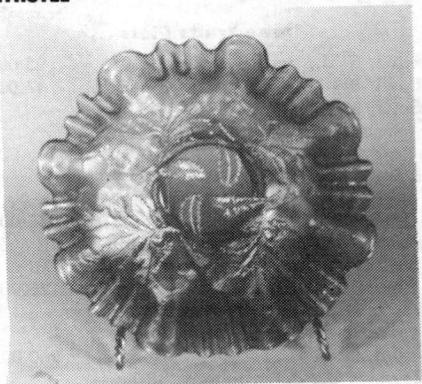

Thistle Bowl

Banana boat, blue................. 195.00
Banana boat, green 185.00
Banana boat, marigold ....100.00 to 150.00
Banana boat, purple ......165.00 to 200.00
Bowl, 8" to 9" d., ribbon candy
　edge, blue..................... 50.00
Bowl, 8" to 9" d., flared, green..... 45.00
Bowl, 8" to 9" d., ribbon candy
　edge, green 40.00
Bowl, 8" to 9" d., ribbon candy
　edge, marigold (ILLUS.) 40.00
Bowl, 8" to 9" d., ribbon candy
　edge, purple................... 42.50
Plate, 9" d., green.......800.00 to 1,000.00
Plate, 9" d., purple 1,250.00
Vase, 6" h., marigold............. 30.00

THISTLE & THORN (Sowerby's, England)

Bowl, 5" to 6" d., footed,
　marigold 35.00
Bowl, 9" d., footed, marigold....... 35.00
Creamer, marigold 32.00
Creamer & open sugar bowl, mari-
　gold, pr. 60.00

Plate, 3-footed, marigold 90.00
Sugar bowl, footed, marigold,
  5¼" h......................... 28.00

THREE FRUITS (Northwood)

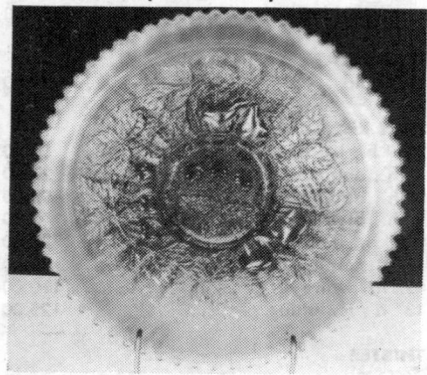

Three Fruits Plate

Bowl, 5" d., purple 25.00
Bowl, 8½" d., piecrust rim, purple .. 47.00
Bowl, 9" d., dome-footed, basketweave & grapevine exterior,
  green 115.00
Bowl, 9" d., dome-footed, basketweave & grapevine exterior, ice
  green 750.00
Bowl, 9" d., dome-footed, basketweave & grapevine exterior,
  marigold 75.00
Bowl, 9" d., dome-footed, basketweave & grapvine exterior,
  purple 200.00
Bowl, 9" d., dome-footed, basketweave & grapevine exterior,
  white 250.00
Bowl, 9" d., spatula-footed, aqua
  opalescent..................... 425.00
Bowl, 9" d., spatula-footed, blue ... 70.00
Bowl, 9" d., spatula-footed, ruffled,
  green 60.00
Bowl, 9" d., spatula-footed, ice
  green 385.00
Bowl, 9" d., spatula-footed,
  marigold 45.00
Bowl, 9" d., spatula-footed, pastel
  marigold ....40.00 to 60.00
Bowl, 9" d., spatula-footed, purple.. 70.00
Bowl, 9" d., spatula-footed, white .. 250.00
Bowl, 10" d., purple 73.00
Plate, 9" d., aqua opalescent
  (ILLUS.) 1,300.00
Plate, 9" d., blue................. 295.00
Plate, 9" d., green 175.00
Plate, 9" d., lavender............. 250.00
Plate, 9" d., marigold 125.00
Plate, 9" d., stippled, marigold 145.00
Plate, 9" d., purple............... 200.00
Plate, 9½" w., 12-sided, blue
  (Fenton)...................... 105.00

Plate, 9½" w., 12-sided, green
  (Fenton)................85.00 to 115.00
Plate, 9½" w., 12-sided, marigold
  (Fenton) 105.00
Plate, 9½" w., 12-sided, purple
  (Fenton) 145.00
Plate, teal blue 900.00

TIGER LILY (Imperial)

Pitcher, water, green 175.00
Pitcher, water, marigold ...100.00 to 125.00
Tumbler, aqua 210.00
Tumbler, blue.................... 87.50
Tumbler, green 35.00
Tumbler, marigold................ 25.00
Tumbler, purple 50.00
Water set: pitcher & 4 tumblers;
  marigold, 5 pcs................. 225.00

TORNADO VASE (Northwood)

Tornado Vase

Green............................ 160.00
Marigold 150.00
Purple (ILLUS.) 160.00

TOWN PUMP NOVELTY (Northwood)

Northwood Town Pump

Marigold ....1,000.00 to 1,300.00
Purple (ILLUS.) ....500.00 to 750.00

TREE TRUNK VASE (Northwood)

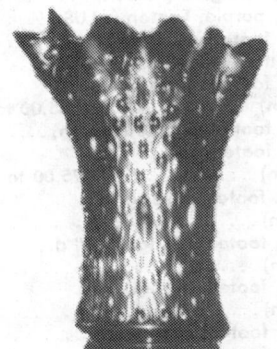

Northwood Tree Trunk Vase

7" h., ice green	130.00
8" h., green	35.00
9" h., aqua opalescent	275.00
9" h., green	60.00
10" h., aqua opalescent	300.00
10" h., ice blue	170.00
10" h., ice green	170.00
10" h., marigold	45.00
10" h., purple	35.00
10" h., teal blue	100.00
12" h., ice blue	175.00
12" h., 5" d., ice green	350.00
12" h., purple	35.00
13½" h., blue (ILLUS.)	85.00
15" h., purple, w/elephant foot	325.00 to 375.00
18" h., green	550.00
18" h., ice green	750.00
18" h., purple	350.00 to 385.00

TROUT & FLY (Millersburg)

Bowl, ice cream, green	320.00
Bowl, ice cream, lavender	950.00
Bowl, ice cream, marigold	250.00
Bowl, ice cream, purple	450.00
Bowl, ruffled, green	400.00
Bowl, ruffled, lavender	750.00
Bowl, ruffled, marigold	300.00
Bowl, ruffled, purple	400.00
Bowl, square, marigold	550.00
Bowl, square, purple	450.00

TWINS or HORSESHOE CURVE (Imperial)

Bowl, 6" d., green	16.00
Bowl, 6" d., marigold	17.50
Fruit bowl, marigold	50.00
Fruit bowl & base, marigold, 2 pcs.	100.00

TWO FLOWERS (Fenton)

Bon bon, stemmed, blue	85.00
Bowl, 7" to 8" d., footed, blue	55.00
Bowl, 7" to 8" d., footed, marigold	38.00
Bowl, 7" to 8" d., footed, red	1,050.00
Bowl, 10" d., footed, scalloped rim, blue	70.00
Bowl, 10" d., footed, scalloped rim, green	75.00

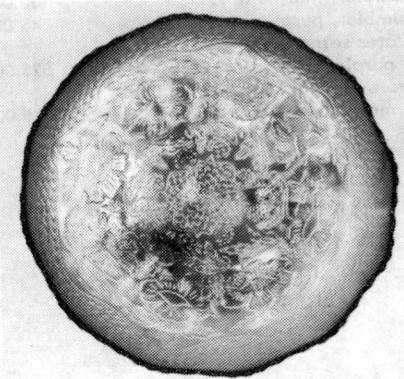

Two Flowers Bowl

Bowl, 10" d., footed, scalloped rim, marigold (ILLUS.)	50.00
Bowl, 10" d., footed, scalloped rim, purple	72.50
Bowl, 10" d., footed, vaseline	200.00
Bowl, 11½" d., footed, blue	125.00
Plate, 9" d., footed, marigold	340.00
Plate, chop, 13" d., 3-footed, marigold	475.00
Rose bowl, 3-footed, blue	110.00
Rose bowl, 3-footed, marigold	80.00
Rose bowl, 3-footed, purple	275.00

TWO FRUITS

Bon bon, divided, blue	85.00
Bon bon, divided, marigold	45.00

VENETIAN GIANT ROSE BOWL (Cambridge)

Venetian Giant Rose Bowl

Green (ILLUS.)	950.00

VICTORIAN
Bowl, 11" d., purple 250.00

VINEYARD
Pitcher, water, marigold 90.00
Tumbler, marigold. 30.00
Tumbler, purple 45.00
Water set: pitcher & 4 tumblers;
   purple, 5 pcs. . . . . 400.00 to 525.00
Water set: pitcher & 6 tumblers;
   marigold, 7 pcs. 175.00

VINTAGE

Vintage Epergne

Berry set: master bowl & 5 sauce
   dishes; green, 6 pcs. (Fenton) 110.00
Bon bon, 2-handled, blue (Fenton) . . 60.00
Bon bon, 2-handled, green
   (Fenton) 40.00
Bon bon, 2-handled, marigold
   (Fenton) 30.00
Bowl, 6" d., blue (Fenton) 35.00
Bowl, 6" d., marigold (Fenton) 16.00
Bowl, 6" d., purple (Fenton) 40.00
Bowl, 7" d., fluted, green (Fenton) . . 32.50
Bowl, 7" d., fluted, purple
   (Fenton) 30.00
Bowl, 7" d., purple (Millersburg) 60.00
Bowl, 8" to 9" d., footed, blue
   (Fenton) 50.00
Bowl, 8" to 9" d., green (Fenton) . . . 40.00
Bowl, 8" to 9" d., marigold
   (Fenton) . . . . 30.00 to 45.00
Bowl, 8" to 9" d., footed, purple
   (Fenton) 40.00
Bowl, 9" d., red (Fenton) 850.00
Bowl, 10" d., marigold, Hobnail ex-
   terior (Millersburg) 375.00
Bowl, ice cream, 10" d., red (Fen-
   ton) 600.00
Bowl, ice cream, 11" d., peach
   opalescent 650.00
Compote, 7" d., blue (Fenton) 45.00
Compote, 7" d., fluted, green
   (Fenton) 45.00
Compote, 7" d., marigold (Fenton) . . 40.00
Compote, 7" d., purple (Fenton) 45.00
Epergne, blue (Fenton) 110.00

Epergne, green (Fenton) 175.00
Epergne, marigold (Fenton) 80.00
Epergne, purple, Fenton (ILLUS.) 125.00
Fernery, footed, blue (Fenton) 46.50
Fernery, footed, green (Fenton) 50.00
Fernery, footed, marigold
   (Fenton) . . . . 35.00 to 50.00
Fernery, footed, purple (Fenton) 60.00
Fernery, footed, red
   (Fenton) . . . . 275.00 to 350.00
Nut dish, footed, blue, 6" d.
   (Fenton) 45.00
Nut dish, footed, marigold, 6" d.
   (Fenton) 50.00
Nut dish, footed, purple, 6" d.
   (Fenton) 60.00
Nut dish, footed, red 460.00
Nut dish, footed, white 95.00
Plate, 5" d., blue 65.00
Plate, 7" d., blue (Fenton) 75.00
Plate, 7" d., green (Fenton) 100.00
Plate, 7" d., marigold (Fenton) 75.00
Plate, 7" d., purple (Fenton) 110.00
Plate, 9" d., dome-footed,
   marigold 100.00
Powder jar, cov., marigold
   (Fenton) . . . . 40.00 to 55.00
Powder jar, cov., purple (Fenton) . . . 125.00
Sandwich tray, handled, marigold . . 28.00
Wine, marigold (Fenton) 18.00
Wine, purple (Fenton) 30.00

VINTAGE BAND
Mug, marigold 25.00
Tumbler, marigold. 500.00

WAFFLE BLOCK
Basket w/tall handle, clambroth,
   10" h. . . . . 40.00 to 65.00
Basket w/tall handle, marigold,
   10" h. 35.00
Creamer, clambroth 28.00
Cuspidor, clambroth 195.00
Pitcher, water, marigold 125.00
Punch bowl & base, clambroth 165.00
Punch cup, marigold 16.00
Punch set: bowl, base & 6 cups;
   marigold, 8 pcs. 125.00
Sugar bowl, clambroth 25.00
Sugar bowl, marigold. 30.00
Tumbler, marigold. 100.00

WATERLILY (Fenton)
Bon bon, marigold, 7½" d. 25.00
Bowl, 6" d., aqua 130.00
Bowl, 6" d., ruffled, aqua 85.00
Bowl, 6" d., blue 25.00
Bowl, 6" d., footed, marigold 15.00
Bowl, 6" d., vaseline w/marigold
   overlay . . . . 75.00 to 100.00
Bowl, 10" d., footed, marigold 40.00
Tumbler, marigold. 45.00

WATERLILY & CATTAILS

Waterlily & Cattails Pitcher

Banana boat, blue ....150.00 to 185.00
Banana boat, marigold 140.00
Bon bon, 2-handled, marigold,
   large.................... 60.00
Bowl, 5" d., marigold.............. 32.00
Dish, 3 turned up sides, marigold,
   6" d. 17.50
Pitcher, water, marigold (ILLUS.).... 575.00
Plate, 6" d., marigold 70.00
Sauce dish, marigold ....15.00 to 25.00
Toothpick holder, marigold...65.00 to 80.00
Tumbler, marigold................. 32.50
Whimsey, marigold 45.00

WHIRLING LEAVES BOWL (Millersburg)

Green, 9" d...................... 55.00
Marigold, 9" d. ....50.00 to 75.00
Purple, 9" d..................... 85.00
Green, 9½" w., tri-
   cornered ....90.00 to 150.00
Marigold, 9½" w., tri-
   cornered ....85.00 to 150.00
Purple, 9½" w., tricornered 175.00
Green, 10" d. 80.00
Marigold, 10" d. 65.00
Purple, 10" d...............75.00 to 90.00

WHITE OAK TUMBLERS

Tumbler, marigold................ 150.00

WIDE PANEL

Bowl, 12" d., marigold............. 45.00
Epergne, 4-lily, green .....425.00 to 700.00
Epergne, 4-lily, marigold.......... 525.00
Goblet, red..................... 100.00
Plate, chop, 14" d., marigold....... 60.00
Rose bowl, clambroth.............. 12.00
Salt dip, marigold 40.00
Vase, 13" h., ice blue 45.00

WILD ROSE

Bowl, 7" d., 3-footed, open heart
   rim, green (Northwood).......... 50.00

Bowl, 7" d., 3-footed, open heart
   rim, marigold (Northwood) 32.00
Bowl, 7" d., 3-footed, open heart
   rim, purple (Northwood) 45.00
Bowl, 8" to 9" d., marigold (Northwood)......................... 35.00
Lamp, 3 portrait medallions,
   w/original burner & etched chimney shade, green, small (Millersburg) 625.00
Lamp, w/original burner & etched
   chimney shade, purple (Millersburg) 500.00
Syrup pitcher, marigold 600.00

WILD STRAWBERRY (Northwood)

Bowl, 6" d., green 55.00
Bowl, 10" d., ice green............1,325.00
Bowl, 10" d., marigold............ 85.00
Bowl, 10" d., purple 125.00

WINDFLOWER

Bowl, 8" to 9" d., blue............. 45.00
Bowl, 8" to 9" d., ice green 275.00
Bowl, 8" to 9" d., marigold........ 25.00
Bowl, 8" to 9" d., purple 36.00
Plate, 9" d., blue..........75.00 to 90.00
Plate, 9" d., marigold 52.50
Sauceboat, marigold.............. 40.00

WINDMILL or WINDMILL MEDALLION (Imperial)

Windmill Bowl

Bowl, 7" d., green 45.00
Bowl, 7" d., marigold (ILLUS.) 37.50
Bowl, 7" d., purple 50.00
Bowl, 8" to 9" d., ruffled, purple ... 42.50
Bowl, 8" to 9" d., ruffled, vaseline .. 65.00
Bowl, 10" d., purple 75.00
Dresser tray, oval, marigold 40.00
Dresser tray, oval, purple 47.50
Pickle dish, green 22.50
Pickle dish, marigold 32.00
Pickle dish, purple 45.00
Pitcher, milk, marigold .....40.00 to 65.00

Pitcher, milk, purple............. 275.00
Pitcher, milk, smoky.............. 140.00
Pitcher, water, marigold........... 90.00
Plate, 8" d., marigold............. 20.00
Sauce dish, clambroth............. 30.00
Sauce dish, marigold.............. 15.00
Sauce dish, purple................ 23.50
Tumbler, green.................... 35.00
Tumbler, marigold................. 30.00
Tumbler, purple................... 100.00
Water set: pitcher & 1 tumbler;
    green, 2 pcs.................. 150.00
Water set: pitcher & 2 tumblers;
    purple, 3 pcs................1,200.00
Water set: pitcher & 6 tumblers;
    marigold, 7 pcs............... 225.00

WINE & ROSES

Wine & Roses Pattern

Pitcher, water, marigold
    (ILLUS.) ....285.00 to 425.00
Water set: pitcher & 6 tumblers;
    marigold, 7 pcs. ....325.00 to 435.00
Wine, blue 57.50
Wine, marigold (ILLUS.) 30.00
Wine set: decanter & 6 wines;
    marigold, 7 pcs. ....325.00 to 390.00

WISHBONE (Northwood)

Wishbone Plate

Bowl, 8" to 9" d., footed,
    blue ....75.00 to 85.00
Bowl, 8" to 9" d., footed, green 72.50
Bowl, 8" to 9" d., footed, ice
    green 875.00
Bowl, 8" to 9" d., footed, lavender.. 185.00
Bowl, 8" to 9" d., footed, lime
    green 80.00
Bowl, 8" to 9" d., footed, mari-
    gold 65.00
Bowl, 8" to 9" d., footed, purple.... 80.00
Bowl, 8" to 9" d., footed, white 425.00
Bowl, 10" d., footed, blue......... 650.00
Bowl, 10" d., piecrust rim, green ... 100.00
Bowl, 10" d., marigold......60.00 to 95.00
Bowl, 10" d., footed, ruffled,
    white 650.00
Epergne, green 180.00
Epergne, marigold................ 250.00
Epergne, purple.........325.00 to 450.00
Pitcher, water, purple............1,000.00
Plate, 8½" d., footed, marigold 225.00
Plate, 8½" d., footed, purple
    (ILLUS.)...................... 300.00
Plate, 8½" d., footed, tricornered,
    purple 375.00
Plate, chop, 11" d., mari-
    gold ....500.00 to 585.00
Tumbler, marigold................ 100.00
Tumbler, purple 180.00
Water set: pitcher & 4 tumblers;
    green, 5 pcs..................1,600.00
Water set: pitcher & 4 tumblers;
    purple, 5 pcs. 1,300.00

WISHBONE & SPADES
Banana bowl, ruffled, peach opales-
    cent, 10" l. 175.00
Bowl, 8" d., peach opales-
    cent ....60.00 to 75.00
Plate, 6½" d., peach opalescent 60.00
Plate, 6½" d., purple......125.00 to 140.00
Plate, chop, 11" d., purple 750.00
Plate set: 11" d. chop plate & six
    6½" d. plates; purple, 7 pcs...... 750.00
Sauce dish, peach opalescent 75.00

WREATH OF ROSES
Bon bon, 2-handled, blue, 8" d. 45.00
Bon bon, 2-handled, green, 8" d. ... 55.00
Bon bon, 2-handled, purple, 8" d.... 90.00
Compote, 6" d., blue............. 45.00
Compote, 6" d., fluted, green 40.00
Compote, 6" d., marigold 25.00
Compote, 6" d., fluted, purple...... 45.00
Punch bowl, Persian Medallion in-
    terior, blue 200.00
Punch bowl, Grape interior,
    purple 145.00
Punch bowl & base, Persian Medal-
    lion interior, marigold, 2 pcs. 200.00
Punch bowl & base, purple, 2 pcs. .. 255.00
Punch cup, Persian Medallion interi-
    or, amber 25.00

Punch cup, Persian Medallion interi-
  or, blue 35.00
Punch cup, Vintage interior, blue ... 20.00
Punch cup, green 25.00
Punch cup, Persian Medallion interi-
  or, green 30.00
Punch cup, Vintage interior,
  marigold 40.00
Punch cup, purple ....15.00 to 25.00
Punch set: bowl, base & 6 cups;
  green, 8 pcs. 360.00
Punch set: bowl, base & 6 cups;
  purple, 8 pcs. 375.00
Rose bowl, marigold.............. 35.00
Rose bowl, purple 50.00
Whimsey, tricornered, marigold 45.00

WREATHED CHERRY (Dugan)
Berry set: master bowl & 6
  sauce dishes; marigold,
  7 pcs. .... 210.00 to 250.00
Berry set: master bowl & 6 sauce
  dishes; white, 7 pcs. 395.00
Bowl, 8" d., 3-footed, marigold 35.00
Bowl, berry, 12 x 9" oval,
  marigold 78.00
Bowl, berry, 12 x 9" oval, peach
  opalescent...................... 275.00
Bowl, berry, 12 x 9" oval, purple ... 120.00
Bowl, berry, 12 x 9" oval, white 200.00
Butter dish, cov., purple 250.00
Creamer, marigold 45.00
Creamer, purple 65.00
Creamer, white.................. 80.00
Pitcher, water, purple 275.00
Pitcher, water, white w/red
  cherries 350.00
Sauce dish, oval, marigold 35.00
Sauce dish, oval, peach
  opalescent..................... 60.00
Sauce dish, oval, purple 45.00
Sauce dish, oval, white 47.50
Spooner, marigold................ 55.00
Spooner, purple 75.00
Spooner, white.................. 110.00
Tumbler, marigold................ 45.00
Tumbler, purple 72.50
Tumbler, white.................. 120.00

ZIG ZAG (Millersburg)
Bowl, 9½" d., marigold 125.00
Bowl, 9½" d., green 375.00
Bowl, 10" d., marigold 65.00
Bowl, 10" w., tricornered, piecrust
  rim, green...................... 215.00
Bowl, 10" w., tricornered,
  marigold 275.00
Bowl, 10" w., tricornered, purple ... 350.00
Pitcher, water, blue w/enameled
  decor 200.00
Pitcher, water, green 350.00
Pitcher, water, purple w/enameled
  decor 170.00

ZIPPERED HEART
Berry set: master bowl & 5 sauce
  dishes; purple, 6 pcs. 225.00
Rose bowl, green 450.00
Sauce dish, purple, 5" d. 25.00
Vase, 9" h., green 1,975.00

ZIPPERED LOOP LAMP (Imperial)

Zippered Loop Lamp

Lamp, hand, marigold, 4½" h. 650.00
Lamp, sewing, marigold, small 315.00
Lamp, sewing, blue, medium 250.00
Lamp, sewing, marigold, medium
  (ILLUS.)........................ 300.00
Lamp, sewing, smoky, medium 650.00
Lamp, sewing, marigold,
  large ....365.00 to 450.00

(End of Carnival Glass Section)

CHOCOLATE

Dolphin Covered Dish

*This glass is often called Caramel Slag. It
was made by the Indiana Tumbler and Goblet Company of Greentown, Ind., and other
glasshouses, beginning at the turn of this century. Various patterns were produced, highly popular among them being Cactus and
Leaf Bracket.*

Animal covered dish, Dolphin, saw-
tooth rim (ILLUS.) ......$325.00 to 475.00
Animal covered dish, Lamb 700.00
Banana bowl, Geneva patt. 250.00
Berry set: master bowl & 5 sauce
dishes; Cactus patt., 6 pcs........ 315.00
Bowl, 4½" d., Beaded Triangle
patt. 450.00
Bowl, 7" d., Cactus patt.,
Greentown 70.00
Bowl, 7" d., Chrysanthemum Leaf
patt. 350.00
Bowl, 8" d., Dewey patt.,
Greentown 180.00
Butter dish, cov., Geneva patt. 265.00
Butter dish, cov., Greentown Daisy
patt. 225.00
Butter dish, cov., Leaf Bracket patt.,
Greentown 145.00
Compote, jelly, Geneva patt........ 85.00
Compote, open, 6" d., Melrose
patt., scalloped rim 265.00
Compote, open, 9¼" d., Cactus
patt., Greentown............... 215.00
Cookie jar, cov., Cactus patt.,
Greentown 295.00
Creamer, child size, Austrian
patt. 325.00
Creamer, cov., Greentown Daisy
patt. 150.00
Creamer, Geneva patt. 195.00
Cruet w/original (broken) stopper,
Wild Rose with Bowknot patt. 255.00

Dresser Tray & Master Salt Dip

Dresser tray, Wild Rose with
Bowknot patt., Greentown,
10½ x 8" (ILLUS.) 310.00
Fern dish, Vintage patt., Fenton,
ca. 1910....................... 175.00
Frappe, Dewey patt. (no lid) 85.00
Frappe, Scalloped Flange patt.,
Greentown 50.00
Hatpin holder, Orange Tree patt.,
Fenton 225.00

Lemonade tumbler, Cactus patt.,
Greentown 70.00

Chocolate Glass Pitchers

Pitcher, water, File patt. (ILLUS.
center) 495.00
Pitcher, water, Racing Deer and
Doe patt....................... 200.00
Pitcher, water, Ruffled Eye patt.
(ILLUS. right).................. 495.00
Pitcher, water, Wild Rose with
Bowknot patt. (ILLUS. left) 495.00
Plate, 6¼" d., Serenade patt. 135.00
Plate, 8¼" d., Serenade patt. 165.00
Salt dip, master size, Honeycomb
patt. (ILLUS. w/dresser tray) 250.00
Salt shaker w/original top, Cactus
patt., Greentown (single) 65.00
Salt & pepper shakers w/original
top, Pleat Band patt., pr. 195.00
Sauce dish, Cattail & Waterlily patt.,
Fenton 85.00
Sauce dish, Chrysanthemum Leaf
patt., 4" d. 125.00
Sauce dish, Wild Rose with Bowknot
patt., Greentown................ 75.00
Spooner, Wild Rose with Bowknot
patt. 135.00
Sugar bowl, cov., Dewey patt....... 135.00
Table set: cov. butter dish, cov.
sugar bowl, creamer & spooner;
Dewey patt., Greentown, small
size, 4 pcs. 350.00
Tumbler, Fine Ribbed base 295.00
Tumbler, "Uneeda Milk Biscuit,"
Greentown, 5½" h. .....125.00 to 155.00

CHRYSANTHEMUM SPRIG, BLUE

*Some collectors of off-white to near yellow
Custard Glass have referred to this blue
opaque glass in the Chrysanthemum Sprig
pattern as "blue custard." This misnomer is
being replaced and this scarce glassware,
produced by the Northwood Glass Company
at the turn of the century, deserves a classifi-
cation of its own. Also see CUSTARD
GLASS.*

Berry set, master berry or fruit bowl
& 6 sauce dishes, 7 pcs........$1,400.00
Bowl, master berry or
fruit ....385.00 to 450.00

Blue Chrysanthemum Sprig Butter Dish

Butter dish, cov.
  (ILLUS.) ....350.00 to 1,000.00
Celery vase....................... 950.00
Compote, jelly ....300.00 to 500.00
Creamer ....285.00 to 375.00
Cruet w/original stopper........... 600.00
Pitcher, water ....675.00 to 800.00
Salt shaker w/original top (single) .. 185.00
Sauce dish ....150.00 to 200.00
Spooner.................275.00 to 325.00
Sugar bowl, cov.........375.00 to 425.00
Table set, cov. sugar bowl, creamer
  & spooner, 3 pcs................1,300.00
Table set, cov. butter dish, cov.
  sugar bowl, creamer & spooner,
  4 pcs. 1,795.00
Toothpick holder 325.00
Tumbler................155.00 to 195.00

CLUTHRA

Cluthra Vase

Cluthra glass is a cloudy-looking ware with bubbles and streaks or specks of color. Rather imitative of an earlier glass called Clutha and produced in Scotland. Cluthra was made in this country by Steuben Glass Works and

after 1924, by Vineland Glass Works. Some of the latter is marked Kimball. Also see STEUBEN.

Rose bowl, pink w/clear internal
  bubbles & white mottled streaks,
  applied clear rigaree portrusions
  at sides, 6" d., 6" h.............$135.00
Vase, 4" h., overall bubbles in shaded blue, orange & brown, signed
  Kimball 185.00
Vase, 6" h., gourd-shaped, mottled
  white 185.00
Vase, 7" h., bulbous base, mottled
  yellow, signed Kimball........... 225.00
Vase, 10" h., mottled blue
  w/streaked internal bubbles,
  signed Kimball 225.00
Vase, 10" h., 4¾" rim d., mottled
  white w/internal bubbles
  (ILLUS.)........................ 285.00

CORALENE

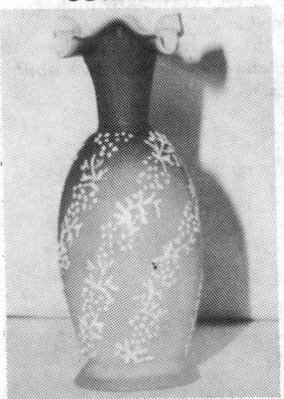

Coralene Vase

Coralene is a method of decorating glass, usually Satin glass, with the use of a beaded-type decoration customarily applied to the glass with the use of enamels, which were melted. Coralene decoration has been faked with the use of glue.

Console bowl, ruffled rim, yellow
  coralene seaweed on white exterior, blue lining, 9" d. $550.00
Vase, 3½" h., 3" d., yellow coralene wheat on shaded gold
  mother-of-pearl Diamond Quilted
  patt. satin, white lining 335.00
Vase, 5" h., yellow coralene sprigs
  on rose satin 500.00
Vase, 5 1/8" h., 4" d., yellow coralene stars at diamond intersections on shaded rose mother-of-
  pearl Diamond Quilted patt.
  satin 450.00

Vase, 5 3/8" h., 3 5/8" d., yellow coralene wheat on shaded yellow mother-of-pearl Snowflake patt. satin, white enameled dots at top edge, white lining 447.00

Vase, 5½" h., 2 5/8" d., yellow coralene stars on shaded rich pink mother-of-pearl Snowflake patt. satin, white enameled dots at top edge, white lining 437.00

Vase, 6¼" h., 3 1/8" d., coralene wheat on shaded rich golden yellow mother-of-pearl Snowflake patt. satin, white lining 462.00

Vase, 7¾" h., ruffled rim, diagonal rows of yellow coralene sprigs on shaded rose satin, white lining (ILLUS.) 475.00

Vase, 10" h., trumpet shape in brass base, green & blue coralene decor on pale to deep Peach Blow pink Diamond Quilted patt. satin 210.00

Vase, 11" h., blue, gold, green & white coralene florals, leaves & insects on Peach Blow pink satin 350.00

Water set: pitcher & 6 tumblers; coralene seaweed on pink satin, 7 pcs. 5,000.00

Creamer, pink band decor 110.00

Pickle castor, w/original silverplate footed frame & cover 295.00

Pickle castor, double, pink band decor, original silverplate frame marked "Racine S.P. Co. Triple Plate" 500.00

Pitcher, water, 8½" h., 7" d., pink band decor .... 185.00 to 295.00

Powder box, cov., pink band decor 145.00

Salt shaker w/original top, blue band decor, short (single) 60.00

Salt shaker w/original top, pink band decor, short (single) 50.00

Salt & pepper shakers w/original tops, pink band decor, tall, pr. ... 140.00

Spooner, pink band decor 142.50

Sugar bowl, cov., pink band decor .... 185.00 to 200.00

Syrup pitcher w/original top, pink band decor 225.00

Table set: cov. butter dish, cov. sugar bowl, creamer & spooner; pink band decor, 4 pcs...465.00 to 525.00

Tumbler, pink band decor 60.00

Water set: pitcher & 6 tumblers; pink band decor, 7 pcs. 550.00

COSMOS

Cosmos Butter Dish

A pattern of Cosmos flowers applied to milk-white glass gives this ware its name. The flowers are stained with various colors. Also see MINIATURE LAMPS under Lighting Devices.

Butter dish, cov., pink band decor (ILLUS.) ....$165.00 to 210.00

Cologne bottle w/original stopper, pink band decor 145.00

Condiment set, salt & pepper shakers & mustard on original glass stand 475.00

CRACKLE

Crackle Glass Pitcher

Sometimes called Iced Glass and also known by a trade name Craquelle, this type of ware has been made for centuries by submersing hot glass in cold water, reheating it and then blowing it to produce a crackled or frosted effect on the outside of the articles, or by other methods. The interior of the articles remains smooth. Also see SANDWICH GLASS.

Carafe, amber, h.p. floral decor, ground pontil $80.00

Pitcher, 5½" h., bulbous, cranberry
w/applied clear reeded handle ... 118.00

Pitcher, 7" h., bulbous, light blue
w/applied red-amber reeded handle (ILLUS.) 75.00

Pitcher, water, 7¾" h., 5¼" d., bulbous w/round mouth, cranberry
shaded to golden amber w/ap-
plied amber reeded handle 175.00

Pitcher, tankard, 10½" h., cranberry
w/applied clear reeded handle ... 195.00

Pitcher, water, Amberina (amber
shaded to fuchsia red) w/applied
amber reeded handle............ 300.00

Rose bowl, 8-crimp top, Rubina
Crystal (ruby shaded to clear),
4¼" d., 3 5/8" h. 88.00

Rose bowl, Rubina w/opaque white
crackle, 6" d. 50.00

Sweetmeat dish, melon-ribbed,
cranberry, in handled silverplate
holder, 7 7/8" d., 3¼" h. 88.00

Tumbler, Rubina Crystal 85.00

CRANBERRY

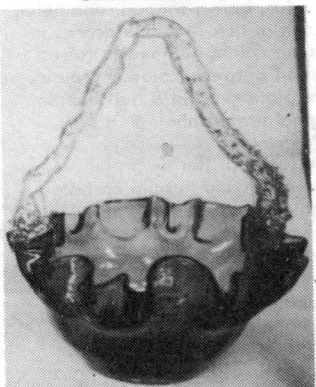

Cranberry Glass Basket

*Gold was added to glass batches to give
this glass its color on reheating. It has been
made by numerous glasshouses for years and
is currently being reproduced. Both blown
and molded articles were produced. A less expensive type of cranberry was made with the
substitution of copper for gold. Also see
BRIDE'S BASKETS, CRACKLE, CRUETS
and EPERGNES.*

Basket, ruffled rim, applied clear
thorn handle, 5½" d., 6½" h.
(ILLUS.).........................$125.00

Bowl, 6¼" d., 5¼" h., applied 3
clear reeded scroll feet & 6 applied clear berry prunts around
top edge, 3 clear shells on sides,
berry pontil.................... 255.00

Box w/hinged lid, ornate brass feet,
enameled white squares w/small
pink flowers within each on lid &
sides, 4" d., 4 3/8" h. 225.00

Butter dish, cov., applied clear shell
trim around center & thorny ball
finial, 6" d., 5¼" h. 125.00

Cologne bottle w/clear ball stopper,
enameled white, blue & yellow
florals w/green leaves outlined in
gold decor, 3 1/8" d., 7½" h. 195.00

Creamer & sugar bowl, applied
clear feet, gilt & enameled floral
decor, pr...................... 135.00

Cup & saucer, lacy gold leaves &
vines decor, applied clear handle
on cup 125.00

Decanter w/clear facet-cut stopper,
applied clear rope-twist handle,
undecorated, 9½" h. 125.00

Dresser set: pr. perfume bottles
w/clear ball stoppers, ring tree,
oval pin boat & 10½ x 7¾" oval
tray; gold palm trees, foliage &
scroll decor, 5 pcs. 275.00

Dresser tray, enameled blue & pink
florals & lacy gold foliage &
scrolls decor, 9½ x 6½" oblong .. 125.00

Finger bowl, Hobnail patt., polished
pontil 90.00

Finger bowl, paneled sides, square
top 98.00

Mug, applied clear handle,
enameled white florals w/blue
centers & bands of "sanded" gold
decor, 2½" d., 3½" h. 58.00

Mustard pot, in ornate silver holder
w/fleur-de-lis finial on lid........ 125.00

Perfume bottle w/original "bubble"
stopper, optic-ribbed panels,
5" h. 70.00

Pitcher, 4 3/8" h., 3" d., slightly bulbous w/round mouth, applied
vaseline handle, optic-ribbed
panels 75.00

Pitcher, 5 7/8" h., 3½" d., bulbous
w/square top, applied clear handle, Baby Inverted Thumbprint
patt.......................... 100.00

Pitcher, 6½" h., square mouth,
Reverse Swirl patt. 65.00

Pitcher, tankard, 8½" h., 4¼" d.,
applied clear reeded handle,
optic-ribbed panels 125.00

Rose bowl, 10-crimp top, enameled
white & pink florals, orange berries & green leaves decor,
4½" d., 4" h. 145.00

Salt dip, basket-shaped, ormolu
mounting & handle, 1¾" d.,
2¼" h. 68.00

Salt dip, applied vaseline ruffled
rim, silverplate holder & spoon,
2 5/8" d., 1 7/8" h., 3 pcs. 100.00

Salt dip, applied clear wishbone feet & shell trim around top, 2 7/8" d., 2¼" h. 55.00

Salt & pepper shakers, Optic Thumb-print patt. w/enameled daisies & leaves decor, in original ornate handled Wilcox silverplate holder w/tiny swan at each end 150.00

Salt & pepper shakers w/original tops, ring neck, Venetian Dia-mond patt., pr. 125.00

Sugar shaker w/pierced dome silver top, 10 panels, 5½" h. 60.00

Sugar shaker w/original top, ring neck, Venetian Diamond patt. 125.00

Syrup pitcher w/original pewter top, applied clear handle, Inverted Thumbprint patt. 135.00

Toddy cup, cover & "bubble" finial & saucer, applied clear handle, intaglio-cut florals & gold floral garlands decor 195.00

Tumbler, juice, overall ornate gold branches & leaves w/silver florals decor, 2¼" d., 4¼" h. 45.00

Tumble-up (water carafe w/tumbler top), Inverted Thumbprint patt. .... 100.00 to 130.00

Vase, 3¾" h., 4½" d., squat form, Hobnail patt. 79.00

Cranberry Vase

Vase, 6" h., applied ruffled rim, bul-bous body w/waisted neck & flar-ing rim, optic-ribbed panels, enameled decor (ILLUS.) 75.00

Vase, 6 5/8" h., 3 3/8" d., melon-ribbed, applied clear feet & clear ruffled leaves up from base 80.00

Vases, 6¾" h., 3¼" d., enameled small blue & white florals, gold heart designs w/white trim & white leaves decor, pr. 145.00

Vase, 9" h., 3 5/8" d., enameled white lily-of-the-valley decor, gold trim 85.00

Whiskey shot glass, barrel-shaped, bands of blue, blue & white florals & gold & white leaves decor, 2¼" d., 2¼" h. 55.00

Wine, clear stem, overall lacy gold decor, 5¼" h. 55.00

CROWN MILANO

Crown Milano Jam Pot

This glass, produced by Mt. Washington Glass Company late last century, is opal glass decorated by painting and enameling. It appears identical to a ware termed Albertine, also made by Mt. Washington.

Bowl, 5¼" sq., 1¼" h., turned-in sides, gold-encrusted florals cen-ter & at each corner, glossy finish $350.00

Cookie jar, barrel-shaped, enameled branch of oak leaves & acorns in autumn colors outlined in raised gold on Burmese-colored ground, silverplate rim, lid & bail handle, original paper label, 6" d., 9" h. 885.00

Cookie jar, h.p. florals & pink leaves outlined in gold on beige to gold ground, silverplate cover marked "M.W." 750.00

Cookie jar, h.p. florals & raised gold scrolls on white satin finish ground, silverplate rim, cover & bail handle, signed in lid 650.00

Decanter w/hollow stopper, enameled roses in full bloom on body, profuse gold scrolls on neck & stopper, glossy finish, 10" h. ... 735.00

Jam pot w/hinged lid, embossed foliate sprays & h.p. daisies on soft pink satin finish, signed "M.W." in lid (ILLUS.) 650.00

Mustard pot w/hinged lid, h.p. pas-tel roses & raised gold seaweed decor, signed "M.W." in lid, w/mustard spoon signed "Pair-point," 3¾" h. 450.00

Pickle castor, enameled pink & brown florals on shaded gold to yellow satin finish ground, origi-nal silverplate holder marked "Pairpoint" & original paper label on insert, 4½" d., 9" h. 795.00

Pitcher, squat form, applied "snail" handle, h.p. floral bouquets with-in diamond forms 985.00

Salt dip, 4-footed, melon-ribbed,
spray of pink & yellow pansies
w/gold highlights each side, pink-
washed collar................... 165.00
Sugar shaker w/original top, melon-
ribbed 350.00
Tray, rolled & serrated edges, h.p.
thistles & foliage outlined in raised
gold, glossy finish, signed, 9½ x
7"............................. 745.00
Tumbler, raised gold blossom swags
beneath ribbons & bows, glossy
finish 745.00
Urn w/crown-shaped lid, side handles, raised gold blossoms & foliage decor, signed, 16½" h......2,950.00
Vase, 4 5/8" h., scalloped gilt rim,
diamond-quilted body, h.p. pastel
& gilt floral decor, late 19th c..... 385.00
Vase, 9½" h., 5" w., triple gourd
form, brown, beige & gold acorns
& oak leaves decor & gold trim on
lustreless white ground, signed &
numbered 925.00
Vase, 12" h., stick-type w/bulbous
base & slender neck, orange
florals w/raised enamel dots on
shadow-scroll ground, unsigned .. 930.00
Vase, 14" h., 7" widest d., applied
"snail" handles, h.p. yellow, gold
& maroon spider mums w/blue &
lavender leaves outlined in purple
on Burmese-colored ground 985.00

CRUETS

Opalescent Hobnail Cruet

*We list here a random sampling of the
many cruets advertised for sale within the
past year. Also see CUSTARD, CUT,
OPALESCENT and PATTERN GLASS.*

Amber, blown, hourglass shape, applied amber handle, clear facet-
cut stopper, 5½" h. $45.00

Amber, blown, applied amber reeded & twisted handle, enameled
florals & leaves decor, original
amber ball-shaped stopper, 3" d.,
6¾" h. 110.00
Amber, blown, squared bulbous
shape w/four dimpled sides, applied sapphire blue handle & sapphire blue "bubble" stopper,
3 7/8" d., 8 1/8" h. 95.00
Amber, blown, applied electric blue
"spun rope" handle w/berry prunt
terminal, blue pedestal foot &
blue "bubble" stopper, 3 3/8" d.,
10¾" h. 95.00
Amber, pressed, Cathedral patt.,
original stopper ....65.00 to 80.00
Amber, pressed, Daisy & Button
with Crossbar patt., original
stopper 110.00
Amber, pressed Dice & Block patt.,
original stopper 65.00
Amethyst, pressed, Swag with
Brackets patt., original stopper ... 100.00
Amethyst to clear, pressed, Medallion Sprig patt., original stopper .. 165.00
Apple green, blown, enameled
white floral decor, applied green
handle, facet-cut stopper,
8" h. 60.00
Blue, pressed, Log & Star patt.,
original stopper, small size 85.00
Blue, pressed, Log & Star patt.,
original stopper, large size....... 65.00
Blue, pressed, Nestor patt., gold
trim, original clear stopper....... 95.00
Clear, pressed, Beaded Grape patt.,
original stopper 68.00
Cranberry, blown, flattened bulbous
shape, applied clear "spun rope"
handle, clear facet-cut stopper,
4 7/8" d., 9 5/8" h.............. 135.00
Cranberry, blown, Baby Inverted
Thumbprint patt., applied clear
handle, clear stopper 85.00
Cranberry opalescent, blown, Hob-
nail patt., applied clear handle,
original clear stopper, Hobbs,
Brockunier & Co. (ILLUS.) 210.00
Emerald green, pressed, Beaded
Grape patt., original stopper 95.00
Emerald green, pressed, Herring-
bone patt., original stopper 110.00
Emerald green, pressed, Shoshone
patt., original stopper 75.00
Emerald green, pressed, Sunbeam
patt., original stopper 135.00
Vaseline, blown, Inverted Thumb-
print patt., original stopper 78.00
Vaseline, pressed, Optic patt., origi-
nal stopper 105.00
White opalescent, pressed, Sunburst
on Shield patt., original stopper,
Northwood 450.00

CUP PLATES

"Bunker Hill" & "Victoria" Cup Plates

Produced in numerous patterns for almost 150 years, these little plates were designed to hold a cup while the tea or coffee was allowed to cool in a saucer. Cup plates were also made of ceramics. Where numbers are listed below, they refer to numbers assigned these plates in the book "American Glass Cup Plates," by Ruth Webb Lee and James H. Rose. A number of cup plates have been reproduced. Also see STAFFORDSHIRE CUP PLATES under Ceramics.

L & R No. 1, cobalt blue (tiny surface spall near rim) $70.00
L & R No. 22 . . . . 15.00 to 25.00
L & R No. 27 . . . . 27.00
L & R No. 29 . . . . 25.00
L & R No. 32 . . . . 27.00
L & R No. 37 . . . . 15.00 to 32.00
L & R No. 48 . . . . 39.50
L & R No. 53 . . . . 13.00
L & R No. 62-A 30.00
L & R No. 65 . . . . 30.00
L & R No. 69 (minor rim flakes) 75.00
L & R No. 78 . . . . 40.00
L & R No. 79 . . . . 13.00
L & R No. 109 . . . . 30.00
L & R No. 124-A 11.00
L & R No. 133 . . . . 55.00
L & R No. 150 . . . . 20.00
L & R No. 158 . . . . 165.00
L & R No. 158-A 35.00
L & R No. 169-A 25.00
L & R No. 164 . . . . 65.00
L & R No. 171, amethyst 575.00
L & R No. 171, clear 40.00
L & R No. 275, opalescent 85.00
L & R No. 292, opalescent 190.00
L & R No. 459-B, opalescent 30.00
L & R No. 465-J, opalescent opaque . . . . 100.00 to 160.00
L & R No. 465-L, opalescent 35.00
L & R No. 562-A 235.00
L & R No. 566 . . . . 30.00
L & R No. 575, Victoria (ILLUS. right) 40.00
L & R No. 586 . . . . 120.00
L & R No. 592 . . . . 210.00
L & R No. 594 . . . . 22.50
L & R No. 628, medium green 850.00

L & R No. 631 . . . . 30.00 to 50.00
L & R No. 636 . . . . 30.00
L & R No. 643-B, Bunker Hill (ILLUS. left) 35.00
L & R No. 662, deep clambroth opalescent 210.00
L & R No. 665-A 25.00
L & R No. 666 . . . . 25.00
L & R No. 670 . . . . 22.50
L & R No. 671 . . . . 115.00
L & R No. 676-B 25.00
L & R No. 677 . . . . 45.00
L & R No. 677-B 30.00
L & R No. 678 . . . . 130.00
L & R No. 681 . . . . 22.50

CUSTARD GLASS

This ware takes its name from its color and is a variant of milk-white glass. It was produced largely between 1890 and 1915 by the Northwood Glass Co., Heisey Glass Company, Fenton Art Glass Co., Jefferson Glass Co., and a few others. There are 21 major patterns and a number of minor ones. The prime patterns are considered Argonaut Shell, Chrysanthemum Sprig, Inverted Fan and Feather, Louis XV and Winged Scroll. Most custard glass patterns are enhanced with gold and some have additional enameled decoration or stained highlights. Unless otherwise noted, items in this listing are fully decorated.

ARGONAUT SHELL (Northwood)

Argonaut Shell Sugar Bowl & Creamer

Berry set, master bowl & 6 sauce dishes, 7 pcs. . . . . $500.00 to 580.00
Bowl, master berry or fruit, 10½" l., 5" h. . . . . 150.00 to 175.00
Butter dish, cov. 225.00
Compote, jelly, 5" d., 5" h. 115.00
Creamer (ILLUS. right) 120.00
Cruet w/original stopper 425.00
Pitcher, water . . . . 295.00 to 325.00
Salt & pepper shakers w/original tops, pr. 350.00
Sauce dish 65.00

Spooner....................75.00 to 110.00
Sugar bowl, cov. (ILLUS. left)....... 155.00
Table set, cov. butter dish, cov.
  sugar bowl, creamer & spooner,
  4 pcs.....................625.00 to 695.00
Toothpick holder 255.00
Tumbler ....55.00 to 80.00
Water set, pitcher & 6 tumblers,
  7 pcs. 800.00

BEADED CIRCLE (Northwood)

Beaded Circle Sugar Bowl & Creamer

Berry set, master berry bowl & 5
  sauce dishes, 6 pcs. 495.00
Bowl, master berry or fruit......... 225.00
Butter dish, cov. 235.00
Compote, jelly 350.00
Creamer (ILLUS. right) 170.00
Cruet w/original stopper.......... 650.00
Pitcher, water 460.00
Salt shaker w/original top
  (single)...................... 200.00
Salt & pepper shakers w/original
  tops, pr...................... 255.00
Sauce dish......................... 55.00
Spooner.....................80.00 to 95.00
Sugar bowl, cov. (ILLUS. left)....... 165.00
Tumbler 75.00
Water set, pitcher & 4 tumblers,
  5 pcs. 850.00

BEADED SWAG (A.H. Heisey)

Beaded Swag Sauce Dish

Goblet 52.50
Goblet, souvenir 80.00
Pickle dish (or tray) 250.00
Sauce dish, souvenir (ILLUS.) 35.00
Wine, w/advertising 75.00
Wine, souvenir.................... 65.00

CARNELIAN - See Everglades Pattern

CHERRY & SCALE or FENTONIA (Fenton)

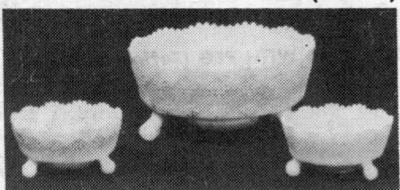

Cherry & Scale Berry Set

Berry set, master bowl & 4 sauce
  dishes, 5 pcs. (ILLUS. of part)..... 280.00
Butter dish, cov. 225.00
Creamer 110.00
Pitcher, water 325.00
Spooner 90.00
Sugar bowl, cov. 125.00
Tumbler 48.00
Water set, water pitcher & 6
  tumblers, 7 pcs.................. 600.00

CHRYSANTHEMUM SPRIG (Northwood)

Chrysanthemum Sprig Tumbler

Berry set, master bowl & 6 sauce
  dishes, 7 pcs. 500.00
Bowl, master berry or fruit,
  10½" oval 175.00
Butter dish, cov. ....195.00 to 250.00
Celery vase ....550.00 to 650.00
Compote, jelly 100.00
Compote, jelly (undecorated) 42.50
Condiment set, 4-footed tray, salt &
  pepper shakers w/original tops &
  toothpick holder, 4 pcs........... 945.00
Condiment tray 600.00
Creamer 95.00
Cruet w/original stopper........... 295.00
Pin tray 20.00
Pitcher, water 295.00
Salt & pepper shakers w/original
  tops, pr........................ 195.00
Sauce dish........................ 45.00
Spooner 98.00
Sugar bowl, cov. 225.00
Table set, 4 pcs. 700.00

Toothpick holder .... 225.00 to 295.00
Tumbler (ILLUS.)................... 55.00
Water set, pitcher & 6 tumblers,
   7 pcs. 700.00

DIAMOND WITH PEG (Jefferson)

Diamond with Peg Butter Dish

Berry set, master bowl & 6 sauce
   dishes, 7 pcs. 600.00
Bowl, master berry or fruit 225.00
Butter dish, cov. (ILLUS.) 200.00
Creamer 75.00
Creamer, souvenir 40.00
Mug, souvenir 45.00
Napkin ring, souvenir 160.00
Pitcher, tankard, 7½" h. 125.00
Pitcher, water, tankard 375.00
Punch cup 60.00
Salt & pepper shakers w/original
   tops, souvenir, pr. 95.00
Sauce dish...................... 35.00
Sauce dish, souvenir.............. 32.00
Spooner 95.00
Sugar bowl, cov. 165.00
Sugar bowl, cov., souvenir 105.00
Toothpick holder 80.00
Tumbler 40.00
Tumbler, souvenir 38.00
Vase, 6" h., souvenir 50.00
Water set, pitcher & 6 tumblers,
   7 pcs. 480.00
Whiskey shot glass,
   souvenir.................. 40.00 to 50.00
Wine 55.00
Wine, souvenir.................. 38.00

EVERGLADES or CARNELIAN (Northwood)

Berry set, master bowl & 6 sauce
   dishes, 7 pcs. 625.00
Bowl, master berry or fruit, footed
   compote....................... 195.00
Butter dish, cov. 370.00
Compote, jelly 350.00
Creamer 135.00
Cruet w/original stopper.......... 750.00
Pitcher, water (ILLUS.) 650.00
Salt shaker w/original top (single) .. 65.00
Salt & pepper shakers w/original
   tops, pr....................... 235.00

Everglades Water Pitcher

Sauce dish........................ 65.00
Spooner 120.00
Sugar bowl, cov. 150.00
Tumbler .... 80.00 to 95.00

FAN or NORTHWOOD FAN

Northwood Fan Pattern

Berry set, master bowl & 6 sauce
   dishes, 7 pcs. (ILLUS. of part)..... 450.00
Bowl, master berry or fruit........ 180.00
Butter dish, cov. 215.00
Creamer 100.00
Ice cream set, master bowl & 6
   individual ice cream dishes,
   7 pcs. 500.00
Pitcher, water .... 255.00 to 285.00
Sauce dish........................ 55.00
Spooner 60.00
Sugar bowl, cov. 95.00
Table set, cov. butter dish, cov.
   sugar bowl & spooner,
   3 pcs................... 350.00 to 450.00
Table set, 4 pcs. .... 550.00 to 700.00
Tumbler 60.00
Water set, pitcher & 6 tumblers,
   7 pcs.................. 650.00 to 700.00

FENTONIA - See Cherry & Scale Pattern

FLUTED SCROLLS

Bowl, master berry or fruit,
   footed .... 95.00 to 110.00
Creamer 50.00
Cruet w/original stopper.......... 185.00
Cruet w/replaced stopper 125.00
Pitcher, water, footed 250.00
Salt & pepper shakers w/original
   tops, pr....................... 95.00

Sauce dish	42.50
Sugar bowl, cov.	135.00
Spooner	50.00
Tumbler	37.50
Water set, pitcher & 6 tumblers, 7 pcs.	475.00

GENEVA (Northwood)

Geneva Salt Shaker

Banana boat, 4-footed, 11" oval	165.00
Berry set, oval master bowl & 6 sauce dishes, 7 pcs.	335.00
Bowl, master berry or fruit, 8½" oval, 4-footed	85.00 to 125.00
Bowl, master berry or fruit, 8½" d., 3-footed	90.00 to 155.00
Butter dish, cov.	110.00 to 155.00
Compote, jelly	92.50
Creamer	70.00
Cruet w/original stopper	290.00
Pitcher, water	200.00
Salt shaker w/original top (ILLUS.)	75.00
Sauce dish, oval	35.00
Sauce dish, round	42.00
Spooner	50.00
Sugar bowl, cov.	130.00
Syrup pitcher w/original top	250.00
Table set, 4 pcs.	395.00
Toothpick holder	135.00 to 175.00
Tumbler	47.50

GEORGIA GEM or LITTLE GEM (Tarentum)

Georgia Gem Tumbler

Berry set, master bowl & 6 sauce dishes, 7 pcs.	275.00
Bowl, master berry or fruit	95.00
Bowl, master berry or fruit (undecorated)	65.00
Butter dish, cov.	175.00 to 210.00
Celery vase	170.00
Creamer	35.00 to 55.00
Creamer & open sugar bowl, breakfast size, pr.	125.00
Cruet w/original stopper	250.00
Hair receiver, souvenir	55.00
Pitcher, water	310.00
Powder jar, cov.	45.00
Powder jar, cov., souvenir	47.50
Salt & pepper shakers w/original tops, pr.	80.00
Sauce dish	35.00
Spooner	55.00
Spooner, souvenir	60.00
Sugar bowl, cov.	80.00
Sugar bowl, open, breakfast size, souvenir	42.50
Table set, 4 pcs.	375.00
Toothpick holder	55.00
Toothpick holder, souvenir	40.00
Tumbler (ILLUS.)	48.00
Water set, pitcher & 4 tumblers, 5 pcs.	435.00

GRAPE & CABLE - See Northwood Grape Pattern

GRAPE & GOTHIC ARCHES (Northwood)

Grape & Gothic Arches Goblet

Berry set, master bowl & 6 sauce dishes, 7 pcs.	475.00
Bowl, master berry or fruit	175.00
Butter dish, cov.	200.00
Creamer	90.00
Goblet (ILLUS.)	50.00
Pitcher, water	285.00
Sauce dish	37.50

Spooner 85.00
Sugar bowl, cov. 110.00
Table set, 4 pcs. 375.00
Tumbler 55.00
Vase, 10" h. ("favor" vase made
    from goblet mold) 65.00
Water set, pitcher & 4 tumblers,
    5 pcs. 500.00

GRAPE & THUMBPRINT - See Northwood Grape Pattern

INTAGLIO (Northwood)

Intaglio Water Set

Berry set, 9" d. footed compote & 6
    sauce dishes, 7 pcs. 495.00
Bowl, fruit, 7½" d. footed
    compote 210.00
Bowl, fruit, 9" d. footed
    compote ....180.00 to 230.00
Butter dish, cov. 235.00
Compote, jelly ....85.00 to 125.00
Creamer ....115.00 to 145.00
Cruet w/original stopper ..300.00 to 365.00
Pitcher, water 325.00
Salt & pepper shakers w/original
    tops, pr......................... 195.00
Sauce dish.................50.00 to 75.00
Spooner..................75.00 to 110.00
Sugar bowl, cov. 150.00
Table set, 4 pcs. 575.00
Tumbler ....45.00 to 65.00
Water set, pitcher & 6 tumblers,
    7 pcs. (ILLUS.) ....500.00 to 800.00

INVERTED FAN & FEATHER (Northwood)

Berry set, master bowl & 6 sauce
    dishes, 7 pcs. 565.00
Bowl, master berry or fruit, 10" d.,
    5½" h., 4-footed 210.00
Butter dish, cov. (ILLUS.) 275.00
Compote, jelly 400.00
Creamer ....110.00 to 135.00
Cruet w/original stopper 630.00
Pitcher, water 475.00
Salt shaker w/original top (single) .. 175.00

Inverted Fan & Feather Butter Dish

Salt & pepper shakers w/original
    tops, pr......................... 400.00
Sauce dish....................... 45.00
Spooner..................95.00 to 135.00
Sugar bowl, cov. 180.00
Table set, 4 pcs. 800.00
Toothpick holder 435.00
Tumbler 75.00
Water set, pitcher & 6 tumblers,
    7 pcs. 750.00

IVORINA VERDE - See Winged Scroll Pattern

LITTLE GEM - See Georgia Gem Pattern

LOUIS XV (Northwood)

Louis XV Table Set

Berry set, master bowl & 6 sauce
    dishes, 7 pcs. 450.00
Bowl, berry or fruit,
    10 x 7¾" oval 135.00
Butter dish, cov. ....125.00 to 200.00
Creamer 80.00
Cruet w/original stopper........... 275.00
Pitcher, water ....150.00 to 210.00
Salt & pepper shakers w/original
    tops, pr......................... 140.00
Sauce dish, footed, 5" oval 40.00
Spooner 60.00
Sugar bowl, cov. ....75.00 to 130.00
Table set, 4 pcs. (ILLUS.)...425.00 to 475.00
Tumbler ....45.00 to 60.00
Water set, pitcher & 6 tumblers,
    7 pcs. 550.00

MAPLE LEAF (Northwood)
Banana bowl....................... 195.00
Berry set, master bowl & 6 sauce
    dishes, 7 pcs. 800.00

Bowl, master berry or fruit........ 380.00
Butter dish, cov. ....185.00 to 235.00

Maple Leaf Jelly Compote

Compote, jelly (ILLUS.)............. 400.00
Creamer ....60.00 to 85.00
Cruet w/original stopper 1,100.00
Pitcher, water 350.00
Salt & pepper shakers w/original
  tops, pr........................ 540.00
Sauce dish........................ 85.00
Spooner 75.00
Sugar bowl, cov. 185.00
Table set, 4 pcs. ....400.00 to 500.00
Toothpick holder ....495.00 to 650.00
Tumbler ....65.00 to 95.00
Water set, pitcher & 6 tumblers,
  7 pcs. 750.00

NORTHWOOD FAN - See Fan Pattern

**NORTHWOOD GRAPE, GRAPE & CABLE or
GRAPE & THUMBPRINT (Northwood)**

Northwood Grape Fernery

Banana boat 375.00
Bowl, 7½" d., ruffled rim ....40.00 to 70.00
Bowl, master berry or fruit, 11" d.,
  ruffled, footed 425.00
Butter dish, cov. 225.00
Cologne bottle w/original stopper .. 500.00
Cologne bottle (no stopper) 255.00
Cookie jar, cov., 2-handled 500.00
Creamer 100.00
Creamer, breakfast size 67.00
Creamer & open sugar bowl, break-
  fast size, pr..................... 135.00
Dresser tray ....195.00 to 275.00
Fernery, footed, 7½" d., 4½" h.
  (ILLUS.).......................... 150.00
Hatpin holder 450.00

Nappy, 2-handled 47.50
Pin dish 110.00
Pitcher, water 385.00
Plate, 7" d....................... 40.00
Plate, 8" w., 6-sided............. 70.00
Plate, 8" d....................... 55.00
Powder dish, cov. 215.00
Punch bowl & base, w/nutmeg
  stain, 2 pcs. 800.00
Punch cup 40.00
Sauce dish, flat 40.00
Sauce dish, footed 50.00
Spooner 95.00
Sugar bowl, cov. 125.00
Sugar bowl, open, breakfast
  size.....................65.00 to 80.00
Table set, cov. butter dish, cov.
  sugar bowl & creamer, 3 pcs. 475.00
Tumbler 70.00
Vase, 3½" h. 46.00
Water set, pitcher & 5 tumblers,
  6 pcs. 700.00

PRAYER RUG

Prayer Rug Nappy

Nappy, 2-handled, ruffled, 6" d.
  (ILLUS.)........................ 55.00
Plate, 7½" d. 12.50
Tumbler 80.00
Vase 50.00

PUNTY BAND (Heisey)

Punty Band Tumbler

Creamer, individual size, souvenir .. 45.00
Mug, souvenir 55.00
Salt & pepper shakers w/original
   tops, souvenir, pr. 80.00
Toothpick holder, souvenir 65.00
Tumbler, floral decor, souvenir
   (ILLUS.)........................ 46.50
Vase, 5½" h., souvenir 75.00
Wine, souvenir................... 50.00

RIBBED DRAPE (Jefferson)

Ribbed Drape Pattern

Butter dish, cov. 265.00
Compote, jelly 180.00
Creamer 110.00
Cruet w/original stopper.......... 325.00
Salt & pepper shakers w/original
   tops, pr. (ILLUS. left) 200.00
Sauce dish...................... 40.00
Spooner........................ 90.00
Sugar bowl, cov. (ILLUS. right)..... 145.00
Toothpick holder 95.00
Tumbler 75.00

RING BAND (Heisey)

Ring Band Pattern

Berry set, master bowl & 6 sauce
   dishes, 7 pcs.................... 365.00
Bowl, master berry or fruit........ 115.00
Butter dish, cov. 185.00
Celery vase...................... 300.00
Compote, jelly (ILLUS. left) 235.00
Condiment set, condiment tray, jelly
   compote, toothpick holder & salt
   & pepper shakers, 5 pcs......... 429.00

Condiment tray 140.00
Creamer 80.00
Creamer & sugar bowl, pr.......... 235.00
Cruet w/original stopper.......... 300.00
Mug, souvenir 45.00
Nappy (ILLUS. right) 40.00
Pitcher, water 230.00
Punch cup 60.00
Salt & pepper shakers w/original
   tops, souvenir, pr. 115.00
Spooner........................ 75.00
Sugar bowl, cov. 110.00
Syrup pitcher w/original
   top ....200.00 to 300.00
Table set, 4 pcs. 410.00
Toothpick holder, 2½" h. 110.00
Tumbler 55.00
Tumbler, souvenir 35.00
Water set, pitcher & 6 tumblers,
   7 pcs......................... 495.00

VICTORIA (Tarentum)

Victoria Celery Vase & Creamer

Berry set, master bowl & 5 sauce
   dishes, 6 pcs................... 575.00
Bowl, master berry or fruit........ 175.00
Butter dish, cov. 285.00
Celery vase (ILLUS. left) 300.00
Creamer (ILLUS. right) 85.00
Pitcher, water 350.00
Sauce dish...................... 55.00
Spooner........................ 85.00
Sugar bowl, cov. 165.00
Tumbler 60.00

WINGED SCROLL or IVORINA VERDE (Heisey)

Winged Scroll Hair Receiver

Berry set, master bowl & 6 sauce
   dishes, 7 pcs.   450.00
Bowl, fruit, 8½" d. 170.00
Butter dish, cov. 150.00
Cigar jar 165.00
Cigarette jar 120.00
Cologne bottle w/original stopper . .   245.00
Creamer 85.00
Cruet w/replaced stopper 175.00
Custard cup. 45.00
Dresser tray 150.00
Hair reciever (ILLUS.) 125.00
Nappy, folded side handle, 6" 58.00
Olive dish 45.00
Pitcher, water, 9" h., bulbous 245.00
Pitcher, water, tankard 225.00
Powder jar, cov. 80.00
Powder jar, cov., souvenir 55.00
Salt & pepper shakers w/original
   tops, pr. 175.00
Sauce dish, 4½" d. . . . . .28.00 to 40.00
Spooner . . . . .65.00 to 100.00
Sugar bowl, cov. 185.00
Syrup pitcher w/original top 295.00
Table set, 4 pcs. 580.00
Toothpick holder 100.00
Tray for smoke set 145.00
Tumbler 75.00
Vase, bud, 10" h. 95.00
Water set, tankard pitcher & 6
   tumblers, 7 pcs. 600.00

(End of Custard Glass Section)

CUT GLASS

*Cut glass most eagerly sought by collectors
is American glass produced during the so-
called "Brilliant Period" from 1880 to about
1915. Pieces listed below are by type of article in alphabetical order.*

BASKETS

Cross-cut vesicas of hobstars, hobnail & fan, scalloped & serrated
   rim, applied double-twisted han-
   dle, 8" d., overall 5" h. $425.00
Hawkes signed, "gravic" florals,
   buds & leaves, silverplate rim &
   bail handle, 6½" d., overall
   7" h. 275.00
Hobstars alternating w/pinwheel,
   base w/hobstar & fan, scalloped &
   serrated rim, applied double-
   twisted handle, 6 x 5¾",
   4½" h. 325.00
Hobstars, beading, strawberry dia-
   mond & fan, applied double-
   twisted handle, 11½" l., 6½" w.,
   overall 7" h. 750.00
Intaglio-cut roses (4) w/hobstar
   centers & buds, polished leaves,

band of Harvard patt. variant,
   star-cut base, notched rim, double
   row of bull's eye & almond cutting
   on handle, 10 1/8 x 5 7/8", over-
   all 14" h. 275.00
Irving Cut Glass Company's White
   Rose patt., satin-finish buds &
   roses w/hobstar centers &
   polished leaves, star-cut center,
   double egg & dart handle, 11 7/8
   x 6¾", overall 16¾" h. 450.00
Pinwheels (4), hobstars, beaded fan,
   strawberry diamond & other cutting, applied double-twisted han-
   dle, 6" d., overall 4½", pr. 375.00
Venetian patt. variant, applied
   double-twisted handle, 8" d.,
   6" h. 900.00

BOTTLES

Whiskey Jug

Barber, alternating panels of bull's
   eye & notched prism 110.00
Bitters, hobstar panels & vertical
   prism, hobstar base, hobstar on
   stopper, 7¾" h. 195.00
Whiskey, hobstars, diamond point,
   splits, etc., triple-notched strap
   handle, fluted neck, faceted ball
   stopper, 8½" h. (ILLUS.) 625.00
Worcestershire sauce, Brunswick
   patt., notched vertical flute
   w/band of hobstars around middle, hobstar base, flat stopper
   w/hobstar center, 7½" h. 300.00

BOWLS

Banana, Grecian patt. variant,
   11¼" l., 8" w. 400.00
Banana, hobstars, strawberry
   diamond & intaglio florals,
   scalloped & serrated rim,
   11½ x 7½ x 4½" 85.00

Banana, Harvard patt. w/hobstars
& strawberry diamond, 11½" l.,
8" w. ....200.00 to 325.00

Bishop's hat shape, swirling blaze
around radiant star center, daisies
& leaves, 2¼" w. undulating
brim, 9¾" d., 2¾" h............ 135.00

Eggnog, hobstars, cane, diamond &
fan, pedestal base w/teardrop in
stem & Florence hobstar on base,
11" d., overall 12" h., 2 pcs. 750.00

Fruit, Sinclaire signed, intaglio-cut
apples, pears & grapes, 14 x 8"
oblong 395.00

Orange, Cane patt. & other cutting,
fan-cut scalloped rim, large hobstar base, 9" d., 3½" h. 135.00

Orange, incurvate sides, large &
small hobstars, strawberry diamond, cane & stars, 24-point hobstar center, 9¾ x 6", 4¼" h...... 220.00

Blazed Star patt., 24-point hobstar
center surrounded by 4 cane rectangles, 8" d., 3¾" h. 195.00

Cluster of 24-point hobstars (7),
cane, strawberry diamond & fan,
9¼" d., 2¼" h. 175.00

Comet patt., 5 swirls w/three
16-point hobstars & strawberry
diamond bowties in each alternating w/swirls of cane, 20-point
hobstar center, 9" d., 4¼" h. 1,750.00

Egginton signed, hobstars (6)
between clear tusk-like cutting,
10" d. 1,000.00

Expanding Star patt., shallow,
8" d. 200.00

Florence patt., 10" d., 4½" h. 200.00

Harvard patt., serrated rim, 8" d.,
3¾" h.................195.00 to 250.00

Hawkes signed, "gravic" florals,
buds, foliage & ferns, scalloped
rim, 8" w., 3¾" h. 400.00

Hawkes' Venetian patt., 9¼" d.,
4" h........................... 425.00

Cut Glass Bowl

Hobstar, strawberry diamond & cane
elipses (4), separated by notched
prism & hobstars, scalloped & serrated rim, 9" d. (ILLUS.)......... 425.00

BOXES

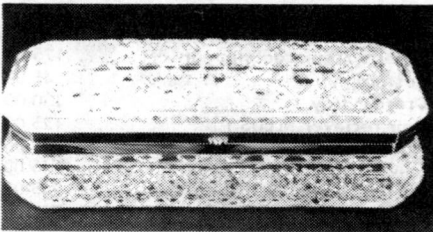

Cut Glass Glove Box

Dresser, cornflowers (3) & leaves on
hinged lid, ovals & splits on sides,
cornflower & leaves in base, silverplate fittings, 5¼" d.,
3½" h......................... 185.00

Dresser, strawberry diamond & fan
on hinged lid, ovals & split vesicas
on sides, 24-point rayed base, silverplate fittings, 5½" d.,
3¼" h......................... 275.00

Dresser, Libbey's Florence patt. on
hinged lid, panel-cut sides, sterling silver fittings, 6" d.......... 325.00

Dresser, Harvard patt. on hinged lid
& base, 7" d., 2¾" h........... 475.00

Glove, hobstars within square of
geometric cutting on hinged lid &
base, sterling silver fittings, 11" l.
(ILLUS.) 900.00

Glove, six-petal flowers & leaves on
lid & sides, star-cut base, silverplate fittings, 11 x 4¼", 3½" h. ... 650.00

Handkerchief, intaglio-cut florals on
hinged lid & sides, 7" sq. 325.00

Jewelry, Cane patt. w/strawberry
buttons & flowers w/hobnail
centers surrounded by foliage
hinged on lid, Cane patt. & fan
sides, 32-point rayed base, silverplate fittings, 10 x 6½", 4½" h. ... 700.00

Powder, flashed stars (4) separated
by fans on sides, star-cut base,
sterling silver lid w/embossed
scrolling & engraved florals &
foliage, 4" d., 3" h. 110.00

Powder, intaglio cut florals & sprays
of polished leaves on hinged lid &
base, silverplate fittings, 5¼" d.,
3" h. 135.00

Powder, Wild Rose patt., sterling
silver lid 150.00

BUTTER DISHES & TUBS

Covered dish, Harvard patt.
w/florals, dome lid & underplate........................... 310.00

Covered dish, hobstars alternating
w/panels of fan cutting, dome lid
& 6½" d. underplate 150.00
Covered dish, hobstars, cane & fan,
dome lid & 7½" d. underplate 265.00
Covered dish, hobstars, flashed fan,
cross-cut & strawberry diamond,
dome lid w/faceted knob & 8" d.
underplate 275.00
Covered dish, Libbey's Gloria patt.,
beading, hobstar & strawberry
diamond, dome lid & under-
plate 420.00
Covered dish, Russian patt., dome
lid & underplate 380.00
Tub, tab handles, flowers & foliage
w/hobnail & fan, scalloped rim,
6" d., 4½" h. 60.00
Tub, panels of engraved & cut sunflowers alternating w/panels of
button cutting 150.00

CANDLESTICKS & CANDLE HOLDERS

Candlesticks with Teardrops in Stems

Strawbery diamond & fan, 1½" h.,
pr. 80.00
Flute cutting in stem w/teardrop &
nozzle separated by facet-cut
knop, 6-sided base & top, 8" h.,
pr. (ILLUS.) 225.00
Green cut to clear, geometric motif,
8½" h., pr. 600.00
Intaglio-cut florals & foliage w/bull's
eyes, vertical flute & notch-cut
stem w/double teardrop, 64-point
rayed base, 3½" base d., 8¾" h.,
pr. 500.00
Star-cut base, tubular stem w/large
teardrop & rows of squared bull's
eyes, 9 7/8" h., pr. 275.00
Meriden's Pattern No. 126, hobstar
base, overall hobstar, strawberry
diamond & fan alternating w/ver-
tical row of cane, flute-cut bull's
eye above knobbed stem,
4" base d., 10" h., pr. 900.00

Hawkes signed, chain of bull's eye
on base & socket, intaglio florals
& flute on stem, 11¾" h., pr. 700.00
Libbey signed, rayed base, panel-cut
stem w/elongated teardrop above
faceted knob, 14" h., pr. 325.00

CARAFES

Straus' Drape Pattern

Clark signed, pinwheel & vesicas,
7½" h. 225.00
Egginton signed, Cambria patt.,
notched prism & step-cut neck,
6" d., 7½" h. 165.00
Harvard patt., horizontal step-cut
neck w/band of Harvard patt. at
rim, 24-point rayed base, 6" d.,
8" h. 275.00
Hawkes signed, Florence patt.,
6" d., 7½" h. 335.00
Hawkes' Venetian patt. 175.00
Hobstars, strawberry diamond &
fan, fluted, notched & ring-cut
neck, 24-point rayed base, 7" d.,
7" h. 200.00
Hobstars alternating w/cross-cut
diamond, fluted & notched neck,
16-point rayed base, 6" d.,
8¼" h. 135.00
Straus' Drape patt. (ILLUS.) 360.00

CELERY TRAYS & VASES

Tray, Chrysanthemum patt. variant,
large & small hobstars w/cane &
hobnail surrounding strawberry
diamond vesica, center radiants &
fan 115.00
Tray, Hawkes signed, Brilliant Period cutting, 11" l. ....130.00 to 165.00
Tray, Hoare signed, Harvard patt.
variant, 11¾" l. 135.00
Tray, large & small 16-point hobstars, cane, strawberry diamond &
stars, large 18-point hobstar
center, 11 5/8 x 4¾", 2 1/8" h. ... 110.00
Tray, two clusters of seven 8-point

hobstars w/hobnail, fan, flashed
fan & strawberry diamond, 11 5/8
x 5 5/8", 2" h. 85.00
Tray, Hunt signed, Royal patt.,
11 3/8 x 5½", 1 7/8" h. 195.00
Tray, intaglio-cut florals & leaves
center, hobstars, cane & fan at
ends, 13½ x 6½" 60.00
Tray, Libbey's Harvard patt., incurv-
ing sides, 11½ x 4" 125.00
Tray, Straus' Encore patt. 145.00
Vase, Dorflinger's St. Louis Diamond
patt., teardrop stem, 10¼" h. 285.00
Vase, large hobstars, fan &
V-shaped sections of cane &
hobnail, scalloped & ser-
rated rim, 24-point rayed
base, 4½" d., 6½" h. 285.00
Vase, Russian patt. w/hobstar button (Persian patt.), corset-shaped,
star-cut base, 4" d., 7¼" h. 295.00

CHAMPAGNES, CORDIALS & WINES
Champagne, Clark's Baker's Gothic
patt., hobstar base 175.00
Champagne, Hawkes signed, "gravic" berries, rayed base 25.00
Champagne, Libbey signed, Fern
patt., 4" h. 35.00
Champagne, Libbey's Harvard patt.,
knobbed stem w/elongated
teardrop 125.00
Champagne, Russian patt. variant
w/large clear horseshoe-shaped
device, lapidary-cut knob,
teardrop in stem, cut base,
2¼" top d., 7" h., set of 12 .....2,400.00
Cordial, Brunswick patt. variant,
hobstars & clear flutes w/horizon-
tal line cutting, notched stem,
3½" h. 55.00
Cordial, Hawkes' Louis XIV patt.,
set of 8 ....1,200.00
Cordial, hobstar, fan & crosshatching, 4" h. 65.00
Cordial, Russian patt. w/hobstar
button (Persian patt.), elongated
teardrop stem, 4" h. 85.00
Cordial, shooting star motif,
knobbed teardrop stem, 4" h.,
set of 8 .... 275.00
Cordial, Sinclaire signed, Flute
patt. 28.00
Cordial, Sinclaire signed, Greek Key
patt., starburst base, 3½" h.,
pr............................. 55.00
Cordial, strawberry diamond,
3¼" h. 27.50
Wine, green cut to clear, strawberry
diamond, flashed fan & star, clear
panel-cut & beaded stem & star-
cut foot, set of 10 ....1,100.00
Wine, Libbey signed, Brilliant Period
cutting, 8" h. 100.00

Wine, Libbey's Double Lozenge
patt., fan, hobstar & strawberry
diamond 55.00
Wine, Rhine-type, cranberry to
clear, block & fan cutting, rayed
base, 2 7/8" d., 7" h. 65.00
Wine, Rhine-type, green cut to
clear, Hawkes signed, Hobnail
patt., rayed base, 6½" h. 150.00
Wine, Russian patt., honeycomb
stem, rayed base, 4½" h. 115.00
Wine, Sinclaire signed, Flute
patt. 30.00

CHEESE DISHES

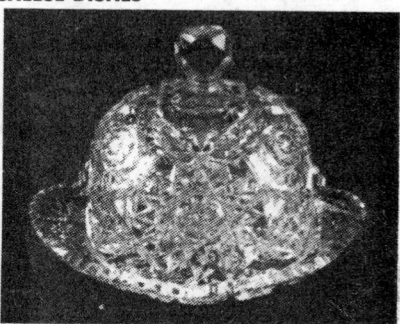

Brilliant Period Cheese Dish

Comet motif, pinwheel, hobstars &
zipper, 7" d. dome lid w/faceted
knob & 9" d. underplate w/scal-
loped & serrated rim 475.00
Elongated Harvard patt., dome lid &
underplate 400.00
Florence hobstar, hobstars, cane &
fan, 6" d. dome lid w/flute-cut
finial & 9" d. underplate w/scal-
loped & serrated rim 550.00
Hobstars, cane & strawberry diamond, 5 7/8" d. dome lid w/hob-
star knob & 8¾" d. underplate
w/hobstar center............... 475.00
Hobstars, strawberry diamond &
other cutting, dome lid w/faceted
knob & underplate w/scalloped &
serrated rim (ILLUS.)............ 385.00
Hobstars, strawberry diamond, clear
buttons & fan forming checkerboard motif, dome lid w/lapidary-
cut finial & 8" d. underplate
w/scalloped & serrated rim 425.00
Hobstars, strawberry diamond, star
& fan, 6¼" d., 5¾" h. dome lid
w/hobstar & strawberry diamond
finial & 8¾" d. underplate 425.00
Shield patt., three clusters each of
fans around strawberry diamond
hexagons centering a 12-point
hobstar w/shields of beading &
hobnail between, 6" d., 6" h.
dome lid & 8 7/8" d. underplate .. 400.00

Strawberry diamond lozenges, star
& other cutting, dome lid w/facet-
ed knob & 8½" d. underplate
w/serrated rim, overall 8" h...... 375.00

CLOCKS
Boudoir, Cane patt. & intaglio-cut
florals & leaves, sides w/step-
cutting, 3¾ x 3" base, 5½" h..... 235.00
Boudoir, Cane patt. w/strawberry
diamond buttons & nailhead,
4 x 3" base, 6" h............... 325.00
Boudoir, Harvard patt., w/straw-
berry diamond buttons & intaglio-
cut 8-petal flowers & leaves,
3 7/8 x 3 1/8" base, 5½" h....... 195.00
Boudoir, Harvard patt. & cosmos,
5½" h......................... 160.00
Boudoir, Harvard patt. overall, petticoat base, 4" d. base, 6½" h.... 375.00
Boudoir, cathedral-style, 8-point
hobstars, strawberry diamond,
prism, fan & star, 3½ x 2¼"
base, 5 1/8" h. 265.00
Mantel, Steeple case, Harvard patt.
& intaglio chrysanthemums,
9" h.......................... 850.00
Mantel, Harvard patt. around oblong
base, horizontal step cutting to
face, Harvard patt. over top, German movement, 9" w., 5" h. 450.00

COMPOTES

Compote with Harvard Pattern

Aberdeen patt. variant, clusters of
hobstars alternating w/hobstars &
strawberry diamond, base w/dou-
ble teardrop in stem, step-cutting
above band of strawberry diamond, hobstars, cane & fan,
32-point hobstar base, 8" d.,
10½" h., 2 pcs.................1,100.00
Clark signed, hobstars, fan, zipper &
star, scalloped rim, notched
panel- & step-cut stem

w/teardrop, star-cut foot, 6" d.,
8" h.......................... 165.00
Crosshatching & strawberry diamond
flaring to large pinwheels,
trumpet-shaped bowl, beaded
stem, pinwheel base, 8" d.,
9" h.......................... 210.00
Harvard patt. bowl, trumpet-shaped
stem w/step-cutting above hobstars & strawberry diamond,
7" d., 10¼" h. (ILLUS.).......... 485.00
Hawkes signed, "gravic" thistle,
stem w/faceted knob, scalloped
rim & foot, 6¾" d., 4¾" h. 450.00
Hawkes, starred rosettes & deep
prism cutting, cov., cut base 700.00
Hoare's Hindoo patt., 32-point hobstar base...................... 395.00
Hobstars, cane, strawberry diamond
& fan cutting on V-shaped bowl,
notched panel-cut stem, hobstar
base, 8 1/8" d., 9" h............. 275.00
Hobstars, hobnail & beading,
knobbed stem, fluted petticoat
base w/horizontal step-cutting,
scalloped & serrated rim & base,
8" d., 8½" h. 625.00
Hortensia patt. variant bowl & foot,
teardrop in stem, 8½" d.,
7 3/8" h. 375.00
Libbey, chain of hobstars w/alter-
nating strawberry diamond, serrated rim, 9" d., 8½" h. 460.00
Ribbon Star patt., large & small hobstars, cane, strawberry diamond &
star, notched panel-cut stem
w/teardrop, serrated hobstar
base, 5¾" d., 4¼" h. 175.00
Russian patt. & fan, scalloped & serrated rim, 6" d., 5½" h. 350.00
Sinclaire signed, Silver Threads
patt., hollow cone-shaped foot,
8" d., 8" h., pr. 850.00
Tuthill signed, Rosaceae patt., chain
of hobstars above satin finish engraved flowers, stem engraved
w/ferns on 6 flute-cut panels, foot
engraved w/flowers, 5¾" d.,
8 1/8" h. 375.00

CREAMERS & SUGAR BOWLS
Green cut to clear, cross-cut diamond & fan, 16-point rayed base,
creamer w/applied flute-cut handle, handleless sugar bowl, 3" &
2" h., pr. 615.00
Harvard patt., creamer w/flute- &
notch-cut lip, double-notched handles, scalloped rim, hobstar base,
2¾" & 3" h., pr. 375.00
Hobstars, tri-cornered, triple-
notched handles, scalloped rim,
pr............................ 425.00
Hunt signed, Royal patt., pr. 265.00

Libbey signed, Jewel patt., pr. 175.00
Libbey's Eulalia patt., ovoid, 3" d.,
  4½" h., pr. 375.00
Meriden Cut Glass Company's
  Beverly patt., double-notched handles, hobstar base, pr. 105.00
Plymouth patt. variant, flashed Florence stars & hobstars, flute-cut
  pedestal base, double-notched
  handles, scalloped & serrated rim,
  3½" h., pr. 500.00
Pyramidal star, hobstar, cane &
  beading, pedestal base, St. Louis
  Diamond handles, 5½" h., pr. 250.00
Tuthill signed, chain of hobstars &
  other cutting, pr. 275.00

CRUETS

Clark signed, hobstars, original
  stopper 125.00
Greek Key patt., original stopper ... 950.00
Hawkes signed, hobstars & other
  cutting w/strawberry leaves &
  intaglio-cut berries, notched neck,
  faceted stopper 125.00
Russian patt., original stopper 375.00
Tuthill's Poppy patt. 550.00

DECANTERS

Brilliant Period Cut Glass Decanters

Cordial, Harvard patt., bulbous,
  horizontal step-cutting at shoulder, 24-point rayed base,
  lapidary-cut ball stopper, 8" h.,
  pr. 700.00
Sherry, green cut to clear, Dorflinger's "Rock Crystal" Patt. No.
  7, sterling silver stopper marked
  "Gorham," 9½" h. ...1,500.00 to 1,750.00
Whiskey, vertical panels (2) of hobstars, fan & crosshatching separated by panels of pyramidal stars,
  matching stopper, 11¾" h. 425.00
Wine, Russian patt. w/starred buttons, applied handle, pedestal
  base 675.00

Bergen's Savoy patt., hobstar base,
  matching stopper............... 750.00
Cranberry cut to clear, pinwheels &
  other cutting.................... 165.00
Cross-cut diamond, strawberry diamond, star & fan, flute-cut shoulder & neck, star-cut base, faceted
  stopper, 17¼" h., 4¼" d. 135.00
Flute-cut body, slender neck, elongated handle, 32-point star-cut
  base, faceted stopper 125.00
Harvard patt. w/florals, bowling pin
  shape, 13½" h. 400.00
Hobstars, stars, strawberry diamond
  & fan, neck cut w/bull's eyes alternating w/vertical panels of
  notched prism, triple-notched handle, hobstar base, notched stopper w/teardrop, 17" h. 1,350.00
Intaglio-cut parrot tulips & leaves,
  bulbous, original stopper, 11½" h.
  (ILLUS. left); hobstars motif, original stopper, 12" h. (ILLUS. right),
  2 pcs. 385.00
Libbey's Wheat patt., matching stopper, 11" h. 225.00
Maple City Glass Company signed,
  Brilliant Period cutting 200.00
Pinwheels & flute, elongated St.
  Louis Diamond handle, faceted
  stopper, 13½" h. 400.00
Tuthill signed, Primrose patt., side
  handle, 12" h. 400.00

DISHES, MISCELLANEOUS

Cut Glass Relish

Bon bon, Meriden's No. 26 patt.,
  Florence hobstars & cane, flute-
  cut center stick handle w/faceted
  knob, scalloped & serrated rim,
  5¾" d. 225.00
Bon bon, Russian patt.............. 95.00
Candy, 2-handled, Expanding Star
  patt., 4-compartment, triple-
  notched handles, scalloped & serrated rim, 7" d. 300.00
Candy, 2-handled, hobstars, pinwheels & other cutting,
  4-compartment, 11¼" l. across
  handles 155.00
Fan-shaped, large 18-point hobstar

center, serrated rim, 6" l., 6" w.,
1 1/8" h. 65.00

Heart-shaped, sides w/pinwheels &
fan, base cut in 12-point stars,
strawberry diamond & fan, scalloped & serrated rim, 5½" w.,
4¾" l. 145.00

Heart-shaped, Florence hobstar &
cane, 9" w., 8" l. 175.00

Ice cream, pinwheels, fan & strawberry diamond w/pinwheel
center, 5" d., set of 6 . . . . 150.00

Libbey signed, Crossed Bars patt.,
8" d. 175.00

Meriden Cut Glass Company's
Beverly patt., Greek Key border,
daisy-type florals & foliage center,
double bull's eye cut center han-
dle, 10" d., 5½" h. 175.00

Oblong, Hawkes signed, Lexington
patt., 2-compartment, sterling silver "T" handle, 10½ x 5½" 75.00

Oblong, Ribbon Star patt.,
4-compartment, 12 x 8½" 425.00

Olive, comet each end w/engraved
flower petals between, cane
w/feathered fans, leaves & stems
center, 7½ x 3¾" 95.00

Oval, Russian patt., 10 x 7" 245.00

Relish, Harvard patt. sides, cornflowers & leaves center, applied
ring handles w/plain thumbrest,
8" l., 6" w. 155.00

Relish, hobstars & other cutting,
scalloped & serrated rim, 9½" l.,
5" w. (ILLUS.) 80.00

Relish, 2-handled, large & small
hobstars, flashed fan & hobnail,
4-compartment, double bull's eye
handles, 11¼" l. across handles,
2¾" h. 175.00

Sauce, Russian patt. w/starred button, 48-point rayed base, scal-
loped rim, 5¼" d., 1¼" h. 45.00

Shell-shaped, hobstars, beading, fan
& starred squares, 6" w.,
1½" h. 225.00

Square, Tuthill signed, Rosemere
patt., 6¾" sq., 1 3/8" h. 350.00

Venetian patt., 5 7/8" d., 1¼" h. 85.00

FERNERIES

Brilliant Period cutting, footed,
8" d. 165.00

Clark signed, thistles (unpolished
blazed fan) & leaves, 3 beaded &
panel-cut feet w/strawberry diamond bottoms, radiant star base,
8" widest d., 4" h. 135.00

Harvard patt. overall, footed,
large 135.00

Hobstars, 24-point rayed base,
footed, 7 x 4" 150.00

Hobstars & hobnail, hobstar

w/strawberry diamond points
base, 3-footed, 7¾" d., 4½" h. 275.00

Brilliant Period Fernery

Hobstars & fans, 3-footed, 8" d.
(ILLUS.) 145.00

Hobstars & other cutting, 3-footed,
8" w. 128.00

Tuthill signed, intaglio-cut primrose-
type flowers, buds & leaves between swirling motif of hobstars,
strawberry diamond & bowties,
3-footed, 7" d. w/incurving rim,
4" h. 395.00

GOBLETS

Hawkes signed, "gravic" Iris,
knobbed stem, engraved foot 45.00

Hawkes signed, Strawberry Dia-
mond & Fan patt., set of 12 . . . . . . 800.00

Hawkes' Louis XIV patt., set
of 8 . . . . .1,800.00

Hoare signed, Brilliant Period cutting, notched stem, rayed base . . . 80.00

Hobstars, cane & prism, teardrop
stem, star-cut base, 6½" h. 90.00

Libbey signed, Brilliant Period cutting, teardrop stem, set of 8 . . . . . 500.00

Russian patt., solid cranberry bowl,
clear stem, hobstar base 250.00

ICE BUCKETS & TUBS

Bucket, Cane patt. overall, serrated
rim, tab handles, 7" d. 295.00

Bucket, Harvard patt., w/matching
underplate 575.00

Bucket, clusters (4) of hobstars, fan,
strawberry diamond & beading,
ridged edge, 24-point hobstar
base, tab handles, 5" d.,
3 1/8" h. 110.00

Bucket, hobstars, flashed fan, strawberry diamond & other cutting,
large hobstar base, 6 7/8" d.,
5½" h. including 1 3/8" tab
handles 195.00

Bucket, hobstars & zipper, hobstar
bottom, triple-notched handles,
8½" w. across handles, 5" h. 275.00

Bucket, Libbey signed, double cross-
cut vesicas (4) filled w/hobstars,

hobnail & strawberry diamond, surrounded by star & feather flowers, notched fan & other cutting, star-cut base, 5 1/8" d., 4¾" h. 185.00

Bucket, Shield patt., 6" d., 4 5/8" h. including 1" tab handles 125.00

Tub, Clark signed, Prima Donna (Triple Square) patt., tab handles 850.00

Tub, Hoare signed, hobstars & prism flairs, ca. 1909 ....1,200.00

Tub, hobstars, stars & pinwheels, 5½" d., 5" h. including tab handles 200.00

Tub, hobstars, strawberry diamond & fan, single star cut tab handles, hobstar & beading on base, 4¾" d., 3" h., w/matching underplate 450.00

JARS & JARDINIERES

Harvard Pattern Tobacco Humidor

Chili sauce, Hawkes signed, Brilliant Period cutting, w/cover, ca. 1890 .... 125.00

Cookie, Dorflinger's Marlboro patt., hobstars, strawberry diamond & fan, star-cut base, matching cover, 6" d., 9" h. 675.00

Cookie, green cut to clear, pyramidal stars, fan & hobnail, hobstar base, sterling silver cover, 5¾" d., 7½" h. 850.00

Cookie, hobstars, cane, crosshatching & fan 1,400.00

Horseradish, 8-point hobstars (6) w/fans above & below, panel-cut neck, matching hollow stopper, 3½" d., 5¼" h. 110.00

Horseradish, Notched Panel patt., matching strawberry-shaped hollow stopper, 3" d., 5½" h. 50.00

Jardiniere, Sinclaire signed, Pattern No. 1023, flowers, fern leaves, hobstar & prism, 6½" d., 7½" h. 450.00

Marmalade, raspberries & foliage,

star-cut base, sterling silver domed cover w/spoon slot marked "Watson" 95.00

Mustard, large 8-point hobstars, beading & fan, star-cut base, cover w/lapidary-cut knob, star center & ridged edge, 2¾" d., 4" h. 45.00

Mustard, vertical notched prism, rayed base, cover w/faceted knob, w/matching underplate 130.00

Powder, bull's eye, button & fan, sterling silver cover w/Art Nouveau floral design, 4" h. 175.00

Powder, hobstars, cane & beading, hobstar base, sterling silver King's patt. cover 125.00

Powder, 3-footed, Russian patt. w/cross-hatched buttons, matching cover 250.00

Smelling salts, fan, star, strawberry diamond & block, star-cut bottom, hinged sterling silver lid w/applied beading marked "Mauser," w/interior glass stopper, 2 1/8" d., 3¼" h. 110.00

Smelling salts, 10-panel sides, star-cut base, hinged sterling silver "repousse" lid marked "LaPierre," w/interior glass stopper, 3½" h. 95.00

Tobacco, green cut to clear, hobstars & other Brilliant Period cutting, hobstar base, sterling silver cover, 6" d., 4" d. opening, 7" h. 975.00

Tobacco, Harvard patt., 5¼" w., 6¾" h. (ILLUS.) 725.00

Tobacco, 3 large & 3 small 16-point hobstars, strawberry diamond & fan, 16-point hobstar base, matching mushroom-shaped stopper, 4½" d., 7¼" h. 450.00

Tobacco, pinwheels, vertical notch-cut prism, fan & hobnail, 32-point rayed base, fitted lid w/pinwheel-cut knob, 6" d., 9" h. 575.00

KNIFE RESTS

Amber, faceted ball ends, large 75.00

Brilliant Period cutting, dumbbell shape, large 55.00

Faceted ball ends, notched panel bar 47.50

Flute-cut ball ends, notched panel bar, 3½" l. 30.00

Notched prism ball ends & bar, 5½" l. 50.00

Notched prism ball ends, panel-cut bar, 4" l. 30.00

LAMPS

Boudoir, mushroom-shaped shade, pinwheel, strawberry diamond &

fan cutting, fluted & notched
stem, scalloped & serrated rims,
7" d. shade, 13" h. 800.00
Boudoir, Gone-with-the-Wind-type,
Brilliant Period cutting, 14½" h. . . 275.00
Boudoir, mushroom-shaped shade,
Brilliant Period cutting, 16½" h. . . 345.00
Table, domed shade, florals, foliage
& trailing vines overall, 10" d.
shade, 18" h. 795.00
Table, Harvard patt., silver rim
w/prisms, 18" h. 1,100.00
Table, mushroom-shaped shade,
hobstars, cane & other cutting, St.
Louis Diamond stem, silverplate
ring w/notch-cut spear prisms,
18" h., pr. 5,000.00
Table, mushroom-shaped shade,
Hoare signed, hobstars, cane,
strawberry diamond & other cutting, matching baluster-shaped
stem & scalloped & serrated base
w/step-cut neck, silver rim
w/prisms, 12" d. shade, 21" h. 3,750.00

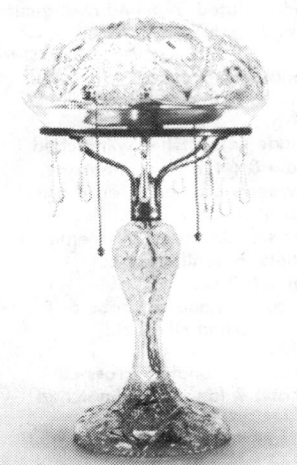

Cut Glass Table Lamp

Table, domed shade, hobstars &
single stars, silver rim w/teardrop
pendants (2 replaced), 2-light,
1890-1900, 21½" h. (ILLUS.) 2,970.00
Table, strawberry-shaped shade,
horizontal step-cutting at top,
florals, foliage & cane, scalloped
base, silver rim w/notch-cut spear
prisms, 10" d. shade, 7" d. base,
22" h. 900.00
Table, domed shade, Pairpoint
signed, Thistle & Butterfly patt.,
baluster-shaped stem, silver ring
w/prisms, 1910-15, 24" h. 3,200.00
Table, strawberry-shaped shade
w/flute & notch cutting, Harvard
patt., cane, florals, leaves & fern

in stem & scalloped base,
w/notch-cut spear prisms, 2-light,
12" d. shade, 7½" d. base,
25½" h. 2,200.00
Table, strawberry-shaped shade,
Meriden Cut Glass Co.'s Pattern
No. 136, flashed hobstar w/hob-
nail vesical, silver rim w/prisms
10" d. shade, 28" h. 2,650.00
Table, strawberry-shaped shade,
flute cut w/border of large
thumbprints, panels of cane, flowers & leaves in base, silver rim
w/prisms, 2-light, 12" d. shade,
9" d. base, 29" h. 1,900.00

MISCELLANEOUS

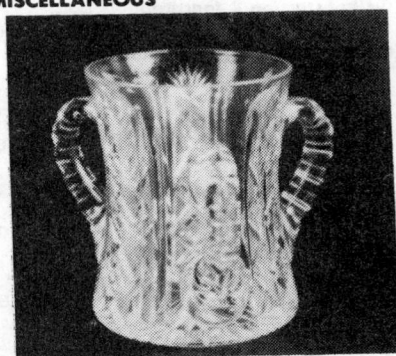

Cut Glass Loving Cup

Cake plate, Hawkes signed, Brilliant
Period cutting, center handle 95.00
Cake stand, overall tiny Harvard
patt., gallery rim, 9" oblong 360.00
Cake stand, Hoare's Saturn patt.,
blazed intaglio-cut poinsettia-type
flowers w/hobnail centers, foliage
& ferns, flute- & notch-cut stem,
scalloped rim, 10" d.,
6" h. . . . . .750.00 to 800.00
Cake stand, intaglio-cut & polished
florals & foliage, 16-point hobstar
base, 10¼" d., 3¼" h. 375.00
Canoe, Harvard patt., 6" l. 100.00
Canoe, Harvard patt. overall, fan
ends, 11 5/8 x 4¾", 3 1/8" h. 250.00
Canoe, Hoare signed, hobstars in
diamond field, 13" l. 185.00
Canoe, large hobstars (7), strawber-
ry diamond & stars, 11½ x 4½",
3 1/8" h. 250.00
Centerpiece bowl, Hawkes signed,
Brilliant Period cutting w/hobstars
at rim, 24-point hobstar base,
scalloped rim, 4" d. base flaring
to 9" d. top, 5" h. 395.00
Champagne cooler, hobstars in dia-
mond field & flashed fan, 6½" d.,
6" h. 250.00

Cheese & cracker server, cross-cut diamond cheese tray, underplate cut in chain of hobstars, cross-cut diamond & fan, large 16-point hobstar center, 9" d., 2 5/8" h. 95.00

Cheese & cracker server, chain of 8-point hobstars, strawberry diamond, cross-hatching & fans, large hobstar w/fans in base, 9¼" d., 2¾" h. 165.00

Coffee pot, cov., "Turkish Hookah" shape, single flower & leaves on either side, St. Louis Diamond spout, applied double-notched handle, scalloped foot cut w/hob-star & leaves, matching stopper w/hobstar top & teardrop, 7½" d., 16" h. 3,950.00

Cuspidor, corset-shaped, chain of hobstars w/strawberry diamond above & fans below, star-cut base, ridged top, 7¼" d., 3 1/8" h. 195.00

Cuspidor, Belmont patt. variant, crossed ellipticals, pinwheel & fan, rayed base, everted scal-loped rim 240.00

Cuspidor, lady's, hobstars, hobnail & strawberry diamond, wide sterling silver beaded rim 395.00

Epergne, Libbey signed, trumpet-shaped vase in bowl w/turned up almond-cut rim, blazed bull's eye, strawberry diamond & notched panel, star-cut base, 4 1/8" d., 5 7/8" h. 225.00

Finger bowl, Dorflinger's Picket Fence patt. 35.00

Finger bowl, Hawkes signed, Russian patt., 4½" d. 70.00

Finger bowl, Libbey signed, floral etching 85.00

Flask, lady's, irregular notched prisms, sterling silver "repousse" screw-on cap, 3" w., 5¾" h. 135.00

Flask, lay-down type, Russian patt., sterling silver screw-on cap, 11½" l. 285.00

Flask, large circle of beading w/hobstar, fan & crosshatching, sterling silver screw-on cap 155.00

Flower center, Hawkes signed, bull's eye, fan & hobstar, flaring scal-loped rim, large hobstar base, 7" d., 6" h. 350.00

Flower center, hobstars, strawberry diamond & fan step-cut neck, scal-loped rim, 8¼" d. 325.00

Flower center, Bergen's Glenwood patt., hobstars, strawberry dia-mond & other cutting, large hob-star base, 10" d., 5 5/8" h. 395.00

Flower center, hobstars, cane, strawberry diamond & beading,

fluted, notched & ring-cut neck, scalloped & serrated rim, 12" d., 9" h. 1,175.00

Hair receiver, hobstars, diamond & fan, sterling silver top, 4" d., 3¼" h. 85.00

Hair receiver, intaglio-cut flowers & trailing vines, band of thumbprints at base, star-cut bottom, sterling silver top w/engraved florals, 4" d. 110.00

Honey pot w/lid & underplate, verti-cal notched prism, rayed base, faceted ball finial, 3½" d. pot, 4½" d. plate, set 135.00

Humidor, bull's eye & zipper, hob-star bottom, 4½" d., 9½" h. 475.00

Humidor, Honeycomb patt., hobstar bottom, sterling silver cover 250.00

Ice cream set: 18 x 10" tray & twelve 7" d. dishes; Libbey's Wedgemere patt., 13 pcs. 6,000.00

Jug, Bergen's Glenwood patt., ap-plied strawberry diamond & fan handle, fluted, notched & ring-cut neck, 24-point rayed base, 7" h. ....750.00 to 825.00

Jug, hobstars, hobnail & cross-cut diamond, triple-notched handle, 7¾" h. 350.00

Lemonade set: pitcher w/notched handle & 6 tumblers; hobstars, strawberry diamond, fan & prism, 7 pcs. 500.00

Liqueur set: decanter & 6 stemmed cordials; overall cross-cut diamond, 7 pcs. 325.00

Loving cup, 3-handled, hobstar & prism, sterling silver rim, 4¾" h. 225.00

Loving cup, 3-handled, cross-cut diamond & fan, double-notched handles, 6" h. (ILLUS.) 220.00

Loving cup on standard, 3-handled, flashed hobstar w/strawberry dia-mond points, cane, fan & other cutting, triple-notched handles, 10" h. 800.00

Brilliant Period Mayonnaise Set

Mayonnaise bowl & underplate, dentil edge bowl w/chain of hobstars, hobnail radiants & 16-point hobstar base, matching underplate w/20-point hobstar, pr. (ILLUS.) .... 225.00 to 250.00

Mayonnaise bowl & underplate, 12-petal mitre-cut flowers & leaves alternating w/double column of Harvard patt. w/strawberry diamond buttons, 16-petal flower center, 5 1/8" d. bowl & 6 1/8" d. underplate, pr.................... 135.00

Mayonnaise bowl & underplate, Harvard patt., 6 x 4" oval bowl, 7½ x 5½" oval underplate, pr. 375.00

Mayonnaise bowl & underplate, hobstars, diamond & fan, pr. 165.00

Mayonnaise bowl w/pedestal base & underplate, Maple City Glass Co. signed, hobstars & other cutting, scalloped & serrated rims, pr. 290.00

Paperweight, model of a book, Russian patt., 3 7/8 x 2¼" 195.00

Perfume lamp, overall Brilliant Period cutting, candlestick base, clear glass chimney, 12½" h...... 395.00

Petit fours stand, hobstars alternating w/fields of cane & diamond, pedestal base w/hobstar bottom, 7½" d., 5" h. 250.00

Punch ladle, cross-cut diamond, fan & star handle w/large teardrop, silverplate stem & shell bowl signed "1880 Pairpoint Mfg. Co.," 14¼" l. 325.00

Punch ladle, 16-point hobstars (2), strawberry diamond & fan, notched panel-cut stem w/large teardrop, Pairpoint silverplate bowl, 17" l...................... 450.00

Punch ladle, stars, fan & beading, Stratford silverplate bowl 375.00

Punch ladle, 8-point hobstar, strawberry diamond & fan, notched flute-cut handle w/teardrop, silverplate bowl & stem, small...... 300.00

Salad bowl & underplate, miniature, hobstars & other Brilliant Period cutting, 2¾" d. bowl, 3¾" d. underplate, pr.................... 150.00

Salad serving set: sterling silver fork & spoon w/strawberry diamond & notched prism handles, marked Dorflinger, pr............ 325.00

Sauce boat, hobstars, step-cut lip, St. Louis Diamond handle, 7" l., 3¼" h. 100.00

Sauce bowl & underplate, Harvard patt., 5¾ x 3¾" oval bowl & 7 x 5" oval underplate, pr........ 275.00

Sherbets, Butterfly & Daisy patt., set of 6 .... 135.00

Sugar shaker, hobstars in diamond field w/fan, sterling silver lift-off cover, collar & top w/sifter regulator, 2" d., 5¼" h. 285.00

Sugar shaker, Brilliant Period cutting, ornate sterling silver top 145.00

Tantalus set, three 2½" d., 7¾" h. bottles, cross-cut blocks w/panel-cut necks, star-cut pedestal bases & star-cut stoppers w/teardrop, in cloverleaf-shaped metal holder w/Roman Key border & beaded loop handle, marked P.P. & S., overall 6¾" d., 8¾" h. 225.00

Tantalus set, three 9" h. Cane patt. bottles w/original stoppers in locking wood & metal frame, overall 13½ x 5", 11" h. 350.00

Whipped cream bowl, pedestal base, small hobstars, large blazed hobstars & vertical notched prisms, foot w/hobstars, scalloped & serrated rim, 6" d., 5¼" h. 650.00

Whipped cream bowl & underplate, Hawkes signed, bull's eye, cross & hobstar, pr...................... 375.00

Whiskey jug, hobstars overall, notched handle, pulled spout, rayed base, original stopper, 9" h. 395.00

Whiskey set: 6½" d., 5½" h. ship's decanter & six 2½" h. shot glasses; Hawkes' Brunswick patt., chain of hobstars, beading, flute & strawberry diamond, decanter w/St. Louis Diamond handle & mushroom-shaped stopper, 7 pcs. 900.00

NAPKIN RINGS

Brilliant Period cutting 90.00

Chain of hobstars ....45.00 to 60.00

Elongated 8-point hobstars (4) separated by crossed ellipticals w/star center, ridged edges, 2" d., 1¾" w. 55.00

Hawkes signed, Brilliant Period cutting 95.00

Huntley's Norway patt., hobstars & fan, 1 7/8" d., 1¾" w., set of 4 .. 195.00

Thistle patt., 2¼" d................. 45.00

NAPPIES

Chrysanthemum patt. variant, square, 2-handled 130.00

Dorflinger's Block Diamond patt., triangular, loop handle w/strawberry diamond thumbrest, 6½ x 5", 2" h...................... 125.00

Hawkes signed, "gravic" Iris, single handle, 6" d. 98.00

Hawkes signed, hobstars & engraved florals, single handle, 6" d. 50.00

Hoare's Quincy patt., 7" d. 250.00
Hobstars overall, loop handle 65.00
Hobstars, cane, cross-cut diamond &
  fan, 3-handled 135.00
Hobstars, fan & other cutting,
  2-handled 95.00
Hobstars & nailhead diamond, single
  handle, 6" d. 40.00
Hunt's Royal patt., unusual shape,
  interior handle 175.00
Libbey signed, 8-point hobstars (3),
  strawberry diamond & fan, 16-
  point hobstar base, single handle,
  5" d., 2 1/8" h. 55.00
Libbey signed, Brilliant Period cutting, 2-handled, 11" d. 165.00
Libbey signed, Sultana patt., heart-
  shaped 165.00
Star patt. 80.00

PERFUME & COLOGNE BOTTLES

Cologne, cross-cut diamond & fan,
  swirl-cut & fluted neck, 8-point
  star-cut base, original stopper,
  3" d., 6½" h. 95.00
Cologne, feathered stars, fan &
  other cutting, original stopper,
  2" d., 7" h. 45.00
Cologne, Harvard patt., original
  stopper, 7½" h. 85.00
Cologne, Hawkes signed, overall
  intaglio cutting, 14k gold
  stopper 495.00
Cologne, Hawkes' Russian & Pillar
  patt., original stopper, 6" h. 700.00
Cologne, hobstars & beading, faceted stopper, 6½" h. 50.00
Cologne, hobstars & fan, original
  stopper, 4½" d., 7½" h. 130.00
Cologne, hobstars, strawberry
  diamond & single stars, hobstar
  base, ball-shaped faceted stopper,
  5" h. 135.00
Cologne, bell-shaped, intaglio-cut
  florals & foliage, original stopper,
  7½" h. 135.00
Cologne, intaglio-cut floral panels
  alternating w/plain panels &
  columns of beading, rayed base,
  faceted stopper, 3 1/8" d.,
  7¾" h. 165.00
Perfume cross-cut diamond & single
  star, hinged sterling silver lid,
  2½" h. 75.00
Perfume, Dorflinger's No. 28 patt.,
  cross-cut diamond & strawberry
  diamond, bulbous, lapidary-cut
  stopper, 7½" h. 120.00
Perfume, Harvard patt., original
  matching stopper, 4½" h. 70.00
Perfumes, Tuthill signed, Wild Rose
  patt., Gorham sterling silver stopper w/engraved floral design,
  1910, 5" d., 4½" h., pr. 800.00

PITCHERS

"Gravic" Iris Water Pitcher

Champagne, notched prism, rayed
  base, notched handle, sterling silver rim w/"repousse" florals &
  scrolling, 10" h. 225.00
Champagne, 3 octagonal motifs,
  hobstar base, 3" w. Gorham
  sterling silver top 1,000.00
Cider, strawberry diamond panels
  topped w/small hobstars, chain of
  hobstars around base, step-cut
  handle w/bull's eyes, 5½" h. 220.00
Cider, cross-cut diamond & cane,
  honeycomb handle, 8" h. 169.00
Claret, jug-shaped, hobstars, beading, strawberry diamond & fan,
  hobstar base, St. Louis Diamond
  handle, scalloped & serrated rim,
  5" widest d., 12" h. 230.00
Cream, hobstars, stars & strawberry
  diamond, hobstar foot, applied
  double-notched handle, flute-cut
  lip, scalloped & serrated rim,
  4½" h. 95.00
Cream, hobstars, notched prism &
  cross-cut diamond, rayed base,
  applied notched handle, scalloped
  & serrated rim, 4¾" h. 125.00
Cream, strawberry diamond, fan &
  single stars, hobstar base, applied
  step-cut handle, flute- and notch-
  cut neck, scalloped rim,
  5¼" h. 170.00
Milk, bulbous, cross-cut diamond,
  strawberry diamond & fan, hobstar base, triple honeycomb handle, panel-cut, step-cut & ridged
  neck, 4" d., 5" h. 125.00
Milk, Hawkes signed, hobstars, hobnail, tiny Harvard patt. in diamond field & fan, rayed base,
  bull's eye handle, thumbprint
  under lip, serrated rim, 5½" d.,
  5" h. 325.00

Milk, Hawkes signed, Pinwheel
patt., bulbous, 6¾" h. 175.00
Tankard, hobstars, nailhead dia-
mond, fan, pinwheel & other cutting, star-cut base, thumbprint
handle, dentil rim, 9 7/8" h. 260.00
Tankard, large & small hobstars,
cane & strawbery diamond, 24-
point hobstar base, triple honeycomb handle, 6 1/8" d.,
10½" h. 295.00
Tankard, Harvard patt., ca. 1885,
12" h. 675.00
Tankard, Meriden Cut Glass Co.'s
Alhambra (Greek Key) patt., wide
sterling silver top, 12½" h. 2,000.00
Tankard, engraved & polished Vin-
tage patt., matching angular handle, ornate Gorham sterling silver
collar w/relief vintage motif,
5½" d., 16½" h. 1,500.00
Water, Hawkes' "gravic" Iris patt.,
8½" h. (ILLUS.) 300.00
Water, Hawkes' Grecian patt., vesi-
ca, fan & Russian patt., bulbous,
6" d., 8½" h. 1,200.00
Water, Libbey's Harvard patt., bul-
bous, applied Harvard patt.
handle, 8¾" h. 595.00
Water, Clark signed, Hobstar &
Diamond patt., double notched
handle, 9" h. 275.00
Water, notched prism, notched
double thumbprint handle, sterling silver top w/wide "repousse"
floral band, 10" h. 225.00
Water, Sunburst patt., 10" h. 350.00
Water, Pitkins & Brooks' Heart patt.,
pedestal base, 12" h. 1,500.00
Water, hobstars, beading & straw-
berry diamond, matching foot,
ornate sterling silver top,
12" h. 4,000.00
Water, Flashed Pinwheel patt.,
triple notched handle, 13" h. 450.00
Water, Harvard patt. variant overall,
pedestal base, 13½" h. 1,100.00
Water, large & small hobstars
w/bands of Harvard patt. at base
& top, 8" w. across handle,
15" h. 500.00

PLATES
6" d., Hawkes signed, Canterbury
patt. (Russian patt. w/starred
button) 250.00
6¾" d., crossed bars (3) of cane
w/twelve-point hobstar center &
hobstars, fan & flashed fan
between 65.00
7" d., blocks of strawberry diamond
& flat hobstars, fan border, scal-
loped & serrated rim 50.00

7" d., Hawkes signed, Gladys
patt. 195.00
7" d., hobstars, cross-cut diamond,
fan & other cutting, serrated
rim 125.00
7" d., Libbey signed, geometric
design of ovals & triangles of
cane, hobstars & strawberry
diamond 120.00
7" sq., Meriden's Patt. No. 227 F,
blocks of strawberry diamond &
flat hobstars, serrated rim 135.00
7" d., Tuthill signed, Brilliant Period
cutting 675.00
7¾" d., heart-shaped, hobstars &
fan 295.00
8½" d., Sinclaire's Adam patt. 675.00
9" d., Libbey's Atlantic patt. variant,
crossed bars of cross-cut diamond
within 6-point star, 6 hobstar
rosettes, scalloped & serrated
rim 200.00

Cut Glass Plate

10" d., cane border, intaglio-cut
flowers & polished leaves
(ILLUS.) 350.00
10" d., Hawkes signed, Kohinoor &
Hobstars (Lace) patt. 1,000.00
10" d., Libbey signed, wide border
of fine line cutting in a zigzag festoon design, large hobstar
center 295.00
10" d., Sinclaire's Assyrian
patt. 1,400.00
10¼" d., Hunt signed, chain of hob-
stars surrounding flowers &
leaves, large 32-point hobstar
center 225.00

PUNCH BOWLS
Dorflinger's Colonial patt., w/match-
ing base, 12" d., 9½" h., 2 pcs. . . 495.00
Empire Cut Glass Co., hobstars,
cane, notched prism & other cutting, scalloped & serrated rim,
matching flared base w/ringed
neck, 18" d., 2 pcs. 7,500.00

Expanding Harvard patt., scalloped
& serrated rim, 14" d., 15½" h. . .2,200.00
Harvard patt. panels alternating
w/hobstars & center radiants,
turned in rim, 12" d., 12" h. 800.00

Hoare Signed Punch Bowl

Hoare signed, chain of hobstars &
deep mitre cutting, scalloped &
serrated rim, matching flared
base, 10" d., 9¼" h., 2 pcs.
(ILLUS.). 950.00
Hobstars, cane & fan, scalloped &
serrated rim, matching flared
base, 18½" d., 12½" h., 2 pcs. . .1,200.00
Pinwheels & deep mitre cutting, serrated rim, matching base, 10" d.,
10" h., 2 pcs. 350.00
Red cut to clear, Hawkes' Brazilian
patt., matching base, 14" d.,
12½" h., 2 pcs. 1,900.00
Tuthill signed, Wild Rose patt.,
14" d., 13" h. 4,500.00

PUNCH CUPS
Bergen's Florida patt., prism & bull's
eye, 3" d., 2¼" h. 20.00
Brilliant Period cutting overall 20.00
Comet patt. 75.00
Diamond, fan & cane, set of 6 . . . . . . 180.00
Hawkes' Brunswick patt., pedestal
base 85.00
Hobstars, strawberry diamond &
fan, applied handle 20.00
Pineapple & Fan patt., 16-point star
base 13.00
Pitkin & Brooks' Prism patt. w/chain
of hobstars below rim 35.00
Straus' Corinthian patt. 24.00

ROSE BOWLS
Bergen's Cornucopia patt., 7½" d.,
4 5/8" h. 2,650.00
Diamond, fan & hobnail, 6½" d. 125.00
Egginton signed, Lotus patt.,
4-footed, flared rim 225.00

Hobstars & other cutting, 6" d. 125.00
Pinwheels, hobstars, strawberry dia-
mond & fan, 2¾" h. 80.00
Russian patt. w/strawberry diamond
button, 7½" d., 7" h. 150.00

SALT & PEPPER SHAKERS
Brilliant Period cutting, footed, ster-
ling silver top, pr. 60.00
Hawkes signed, Canterbury patt.
(Russian patt. w/starred button),
sterling silver top, pr. 150.00
Hobstars & other cutting, sterling
silver top, pr.   40.00
Step-cut & faceted, sterling silver
top, 2" h., pr.   16.00

SALT DIPS

Brilliant Period Salt Dips

Cross-cut diamond, star-cut base,
tab handles, ridged top, 3" d.,
2 1/8" h. 50.00
Crosshatching & fan, 1¾" d., each
(ILLUS.). 10.00
Harvard patt., canoe-shaped,
3½" l., ¾" h., set of 6 . . . . 150.00
Hobstars & vesicas of strawberry
diamond & fan, hobstar base,
scalloped & serrated rim, 3½" d.,
1¾" h. 125.00
Hobstars & other cutting, footed,
master size 75.00
Russian patt. w/starred button, leaf-
shaped, fluted & notched at one
end, 4¾" l., 2" w. 135.00
Strawberry diamond patt., pedestal
base, master size, 3" d., 3" h. 100.00

SPOONERS
Band of strawberry diamond hexa-
gons above large 6-petal flowers
& foliage, star-cut base, 3 3/8" d.,
4 5/8" h. 95.00
Brilliant Period cutting, corset-
shaped 125.00
Brilliant Period cutting, 2-handled. . . 150.00
Hobstars, fan & zipper, 4¼" h. 125.00
Hobstars separated by cane, straw-
berry diamond, crosshatching &
fan, 3½" d., 4½" h. 100.00
Hobstars & diamond, hobstar base . . 165.00
Hobstars, strawberry diamond &
notched prism 110.00

Spoonholder tray, hobstars, hobnail, strawberry diamond & star centering 18-point hobstar, 6¾" l., 4¾" w. (pinched in at middle), 1½" h. 85.00

SYRUP PITCHERS & JUGS

Brilliant Period cutting, star-cut base, silverplate lid & handle 65.00

Chain of hobstars & strawberry diamond w/fan, star-cut base, silverplate hinged lid w/shell finial & beaded handle & collar, 3¼" d., 4½" h. 150.00

Hawkes signed, Brilliant Period cutting 150.00

Notched prism, silverplate handle, collar & lid w/applied beading, 3" d., 4 1/8" h. 65.00

Strawberry diamond & fan, sterling silver lid 125.00

Vertical irregular band of notched prism, block & thumbprint around base, pear-shaped body, silverplate hinged lid, 3¾" h. 75.00

TOOTHPICK HOLDERS

Toothpick Holder with Paperweight Base

Brilliant Period cutting, pedestal base, 3¼" h. 75.00

Cross-cut diamond & fan, faceted paperweight base, scalloped rim, 2½" h. (ILLUS.) 40.00

Cross-cut diamond & fan, rayed pedestal base 95.00

Flashed hobstar 25.00

Harvard patt., rayed base, 2" h. 55.00

Hobstars, ovoid, pedestal base 65.00

TRAYS

Bread, 6 large 18-point hobstars, smaller hobstars, cane, strawberry diamond & beading, turned in sides, 11¾" l., 5½" w., 2¾" h. .. 325.00

Bread, 16-point hobstars, cross-cut strawberry diamond vesicas & fan, 12 x 5¼", 2 7/8" h. 175.00

Bread, Hawkes signed, "gravic" Strawberry, 12 x 8" 135.00

Cracker, large & small hobstars, cane, hobnail, strawberry diamond & fan, 11 1/8 x 4¼", 2 5/8" h. 175.00

Dresser, Russian patt. w/strawberry diamond buttons, 11 x 6¼" 260.00

Ice cream, overall hobstars, scalloped & serrated rim, 13½ x 8½" oval 185.00

Ice cream, Harvard patt. w/hobstars & single stars, 14 x 8" oblong 140.00

Ice cream, 24-point & 16-point hobstars w/fan & cross-cut vesicas of hobnail, strawberry diamond & star, 17 x 10 3/8", 2½" h. 550.00

Ice cream, Libbey signed, intaglio-cut strawberries & foliage, fields of tiny hobstars & triple mitre cane, 17½ x 10" shaped oval 850.00

Sandwich, Hallmark (United Jewelers, Inc.), butterflies, tulip blossoms & leaves, hobnail center, clear center handle w/divided curved top w/thumbprint cutting, scalloped half-moon cut rim, 9¾" d., 6½" h. 335.00

Cross-cut diamond & fan w/large 28-point hobstar center, 8 7/8" l., 5 5/8" w., 1 5/8" h. 135.00

Elongated Florence-type hobstars (6), cane, strawberry diamond, small hobstars, split zipper & fan, large 8-point Florence hobstar center, 13½" l., 9 5/8" w., 2 1/8" h. 350.00

Fry signed, "Nabisco," sides w/hobstars alternating w/strawberry diamond, 6-petal flower w/hobstar center & leaves in bottom, 8 3/8" l. including ¾" tab handles, 3¼" w., 1¾" h. 85.00

Fry Signed Tray

Fry signed, pinwheel, fan & other cutting, scalloped & serrated rim,

oak leaf shaped, 13 x 11", pr.
(ILLUS. of one) 1,000.00
Harvard patt. border, central hobstar, cut flowers w/polished
leaves & strawberry diamond vesicas, turned up rim w/rounded
ends, 13¼ x 8¼", 1¾" h. 175.00
Hawkes signed, swirl motif w/hob-
stars & star, serrated petal-form
rim, 12" d. 2,500.00
Hawkes' Grecian patt., clear vesicas, fan & Russian patt., irregular
scalloped & serrated rim,
12" d. 3,000.00
Hobstar rosettes, hobstars, cane,
fan & crossed vesicas of hobnail &
strawberry diamond, scalloped &
serrated rim, turned-in sides,
12 x 5"......................... 300.00
Hobstars, strawberry diamond &
beaded vesicas, 12¼" d 375.00
Hobstar, cane, strawberry diamond
& stars, step-cut tab handles,
13½ x 8½"..................... 450.00
Hobstars (4 large 32-point & 4 large
24-point), strawberry diamond,
pyramidal star, fan & beading,
24-point hobstar center, 14" d.,
2" h. 2,000.00
Lozenge-shaped central figures
w/cross-hatched background &
bull's eye in each, surrounded by
chain of hobstars, geometric outer
border, 13½" d. 750.00
Russian patt. w/starred button, serrated & scalloped rim, 8¼ x 7" ... 175.00
Sinclaire signed, Holly patt.,
15 x 11" 3,000.00

TUMBLERS

Shaped Tumblers

Iced tea, Clark's Triple Square patt.,
hobstar base.................... 75.00
Juice, Brilliant Period cutting, set
of 6 .... 150.00
Juice, Harvard patt. 25.00
Juice, Hawkes signed, Brilliant Period cutting, set of 12 .... 240.00
Juice, Hawkes' Louis XIV patt., set
of 6 .... 720.00
Juice, Hoare's Russian & Wheat
patt., rayed base, 3½" h........ 130.00

Juice, hobstars, clear & strawberry
diamond blocks & fan, 20-point
hobstar base, 3 3/8" h. 20.00
Juice, hobstars, strawberry diamond
& fan, star-cut base, 2 7/8" d.,
3¾" h. 30.00
Juice, hobstars, pinwheels, cane &
fan, rayed base, 3¾" h. 40.00
Juice, hobstars, prism & fan, each
(ILLUS. of three)............. 215.00
Juice, Russian patt., 4" h. 65.00
Water, Brilliant Period cutting 35.00
Water, cranberry cut to clear, Bril-
liant Period cutting 110.00
Water, Libbey signed, Brilliant
Period cutting................. 60.00
Water, Sinclaire's Queens patt. vari-
ant, bull's eye, hobstar & fan,
hobstar base, 3¾" h............ 155.00
Whiskey, rainbow cut to clear, Bril-
liant Period cutting 375.00

VASES

Brilliant Period Vase

Brilliant Period cutting, corset-
shaped, scalloped & serrated rim,
rayed base, 12" h. 185.00
Cane triangles (3) between cut flowers & leaves all above 3 large
hobnail vesicas between cut flowers & leaves, corset-shaped, star-
cut base, 5¾" d., 15¾" h. 225.00
Chain of hobstars, beading, fan &
strawberry diamond, scalloped &
serrated rim, 18" h. (ILLUS.) 2,090.00
Clark signed, hobstar, bull's eye &
diamond, pedestal base, hobstar
foot, 14" h.................... 375.00
Dorflinger's Kalana Poppy patt.,
12" h......................... 325.00
Egginton signed, Prism patt., cylindrical, chain of six 8-point hobstars w/strawberry diamond
centers above alternating columns

of ridging & splits, star-cut base,
2¼" d., 8" h. 95.00
Geometric cutting, chalice form,
teardrop in stem, faceted knob
above base, full scalloped hobstar
on foot, 12½" h. 375.00
Green cut to clear, Dorflinger's
Montrose patt., 3 columns of 6
bull's eyes w/beading & cane between, 16-point hobstar base,
5 1/8" d., 8 3/8" h. 875.00
Harvard patt., tulip-shaped,
lapidary-cut knob at base w/step-
cutting above, matching foot,
14" h. 450.00
Hawkes signed, Middlesex patt.,
large 8-point star w/clear button,
strawberry diamond & fan, 2-
handled, 10½" w. across handles,
6" h. 550.00
Hawkes signed, Queens patt., chain
of hobstars & bull's eye, trumpet-
shaped, 16" h. 1,250.00
Hawkes' "gravic" Tulip, sterling silver rim marked Jacobi & Jenkins,
10" h. 288.00
Hoare signed, Wheat patt., step-cut
neck, 5½" base d., 18½" h. 250.00
Hobstars overall, ovoid, 10½" h. .. 550.00
Hobstars & cane, flower form, pedestal base, notched stem w/tear-
drop, rayed base, 12" h. 250.00
Hobstars (16), strawbery diamond &
star, corset-shaped, large 24-point
hobstar base, 6" d., 17 7/8" h. 850.00
Libbey signed, hobstar, fan, strawberry diamond & zipper, rayed
base, 12" h. 325.00
Pitkin & Brooks signed, Oro patt.,
11" h. 450.00
Sinclaire signed, Pattern No. 1023,
florals, hobstars & prism, urn-
shaped, 8" h. 140.00
Sinclaire signed, Lily-of-the-Valley
patt., intaglio-cut blossoms & foliage, moon borders on foot & rim,
5" d., 13¼" h. 275.00
Sunburst motif, hobstars & step cutting, serrated rim, 20½" h. 475.00
Tuthill signed, Poppy patt. alternating w/geometric panels, trumpet-
shaped, 14" h. 995.00
Tuthill's Vintage patt., fluted
notched rim, footed, 9 7/8" widest
d., 6¼" h. 300.00
Zipper patt., attributed to Mt.
Washington, 1875-82, 10½" h. 600.00

WATER SETS

Pitcher & 2 tumblers, chain of hobstars, strawberry diamond & fan
w/splits & flutes below & engraved flowers & leaves above,
star-cut bottom, 9¼" h. corset-

shaped pitcher w/bull's eye handle & notched panel-cut spout,
3 pcs. 175.00
Pitcher & 4 tumblers, Hawkes
signed, Queens patt., 5 pcs. 1,150.00
Pitcher & 5 tumblers, Allen Cut
Glass Company's Lotus patt.,
9¼" h. tankard pitcher,
6 pcs. 400.00
Pitcher & 5 tumblers, hobstars,
feathered fan & crosshatching,
6 pcs. 550.00
Pitcher & 5 tumblers, Pinwheel &
Sheaf patt., 6 pcs. 290.00
Pitcher & six 3¾" h. tumblers, hobstars & crosshatching, 9" h. pitcher w/double bull's eye handle,
7 pcs. 250.00
Pitcher & 6 tumblers, Meriden Cut
Glass Company's Alhambra patt.,
7 pcs. 1,800.00

Cut Glass Water Set

Pitcher & 6 tumblers, pinwheel,
strawberry diamond & fan, 7 pcs.
(ILLUS.)........................ 375.00
Pitcher & 6 tumblers, Strauss' Drape
patt., 7 pcs. 600.00
Pitcher & 8 tumblers, pinwheel &
strawberry diamond, 9 pcs. 225.00
Pitcher & 9 tumblers, Libbey signed,
Comet patt. variant, 10 pcs. 275.00

(End of Cut Glass Section)

CUT VELVET

*Several glasshouses, including Mt.
Washington, produced this two-layered glass
with its velvety or acid finish and raised pattern. The inner casing is frequently white, and
the pattern was developed by blowing into
a mold.*

Bottle-vase, ribbed, rich blue, white
lining, 3¾" d., 8" h. $145.00
Bowl, ruffled rim, apricot 300.00
Creamer, bulbous w/round mouth,
applied opaque white handle, Diamond Quilted patt., heavenly
blue, white lining, 2¾" d.,
3¼" h. 195.00

Ewer, applied frosted handle, Diamond Quilted patt., deep blue,
white lining, 3½" d., 4¾" h. 140.00
Rose bowl, 6-crimp top, Diamond
Quilted patt., American Beauty
rose, white lining, 3 3/8" d.,
3½" h. . . . . .170.00 to 185.00
Rose bowl, 8-crimp top, Diamond
Quilted patt., deep rose, cream
lining, 3¾" d., 3¾" h. 195.00
Rose bowl, egg-shaped, 4-crimp top,
Diamond Quilted patt., heavenly
blue, white lining, 2 7/8" d.,
3 7/8" h. . . . . .148.00 to 165.00
Sugar shaker w/original top,
Diamond Quilted patt., blue,
6" h. 265.00
Vase, 4¼" h., pinched top, Diamond
Quilted patt., blue 185.00
Vase, 4¾" h., 5 5/8" d., Diamond
Quilted patt., tan, white
lining 175.00

Cut Velvet Stick Vase

Vase, 6" h., stick-type, Diamond
Quilted patt., amethyst on white
(ILLUS.) 210.00
Vase, 7" h., 3¼" d., ruffled top,
Diamond Quilted patt., heavenly
blue, white lining 135.00
Vase, 8" h., ribbed, blue, signed
Webb 225.00
Vase, 9½" h., ruffled rim, blue,
white lining. 175.00

CZECHOSLOVAKIAN

*At the close of World War I, Czechoslova-
kia was declared an independent republic and
immediately developed a large export indus-*
*try. Czechoslovakian glass factories produced
a wide variety of colored and hand-painted
glasswares from about 1918 until 1939, when
the country was occupied by Germany at the
outset of World War II. Between the wars,
fine quality blown glasswares were produced
along with a deluge of cheaper, vividly colored spatterwares for the American market.
Subsequent production was primarily limited to cut crystal or Bohemian-type etched
wares for the American market. Although it
was marked, much Czechoslovakian glass is
mistaken for the work of Tiffany, Loetz, or
other glass artisans it imitates. It is often
misrepresented and overpriced.*

Basket, cased, green & black,
signed, 6¾" w. $36.00
Bowl, 9" d., 5½" h., cased, orange
spatter interior, pink exterior 80.00
Cologne bottle w/original stopper,
green satin, 6" h. 45.00

Czechoslovakian Compote

Compote, cov., 6½" d., 10" h.,
enameled colorful florals on red
(ILLUS.) 85.00
Liqueur decanter, clear w/enameled
seaweed & fish decor 60.00
Liqueur set: 6-sided decanter & 6
angular liqueurs; transparent
w/engraved & ruby-flashed geo-
metric decor, ca. 1930, 7 pcs. 550.00
Perfume atomizer, cobalt blue
w/gold decor, complete w/bulb . . 40.00
Perfume bottle w/frosted floriform
stopper, amber w/etched design
on body, 5" h. 50.00
Perfume bottle w/brass lid & long
glass dauber, orange & black,
6" h. 45.00
Vase, 6¾" h., mottled green & red
over orange 30.00
Vase, 9½" h., bulbous bottom, scal-
loped top, bright yellow w/black
threading around mid-section 40.00
Vase, 10" h., red w/black handles . . 50.00
Vase, 13" h., green overlay w/silver
deposit birds decor 85.00

Wine decanter w/clear steeple-form
stopper & applied clear handle,
ruby cut to clear, signed,
17" h. 125.00

D'ARGENTAL

D'Argental Cameo Atomizer

Glass known by this name is so-called af-
ter its producer, who fashioned fine cameo
pieces in France late last century.

Cameo atomizer, carved dark brown
florals & leaves against shaded
rose to beige matte ground,
signed (ILLUS.) $375.00
Cameo bowl, 3" d., 2½" h., carved
scene w/lake, birch trees & 3 flying ducks against grey-green to
rust to translucent white satin
ground, signed 395.00
Cameo vase, 3½" h., 5" d., carved
brown flowers w/darker brown
leaves against yellow to white
frosted ground, signed 400.00
Cameo vase, 4" h., carved dark
brown florals against frosted
orange ground, signed 290.00
Cameo vase, 5" h., carved yellow,
orange & blue lighthouse scene
w/sea & rocky shore, signed 650.00
Cameo vase, 5 5/8" h., 3" d.,
carved purple scene w/gondola in
foreground & Venetian shoreline
background against translucent
white frosted ground, signed 675.00
Cameo vase, 8½" h., carved wine-
colored trumpet flowers against
yellow ground, fire-polished,
signed 650.00
Cameo vase, 9 5/8" h., 4 1/8" d.,
carved brown to rose-brown scene
w/trees, hills & lake against rich
frosted gold ground, signed 975.00
Cameo vase, 12" h., 3¾" w., carved

magenta iris leaves against gold
satin ground, signed 650.00
Cameo vase, 12 1/8" h., 4¾" d.,
carved shaded brown castle scene
w/trees against translucent frost-
ed gold ground, signed 898.00
Cameo vase, 13¾" h., baluster-
shaped, carved pink & green-
brown pendant flowering shrubs
against matte yellow ground,
signed 440.00

DAUM NANCY

Daum Nancy Bowl in Wrought Iron Frame

This fine glass, much of it cameo, was made
by Auguste and Antonin Daum, who found-
ed a factory in 1875 in Nancy, France. Most
of their cameo and enameled glass was made
from the final decade of last century.

Cameo bowl, 11 3/8" d., slightly
flaring base, rim cut in 4 shallow
flutes & carved w/aspen branches
& leaves at side & top border
against yellow shaded to green
& puce ground, late 19th c.,
signed $715.00
Cameo bowl-vase, carved purple to
white crows in flight against vivid
yellow ground, signed, 7½" d.,
4½" h. 1,150.00
Cameo bowl-vase, flaring cylinder,
carved lavender & brown berried
branches against mottled beige
ground w/yellow speckles, in
wrought iron stand, signed, over-
all 9½" h. (ILLUS.) 825.00
Cameo powder box, cov., carved &
enameled fleur-de-lis against
deep lavender ground, signed,
5" d., 3" h. 575.00

Cameo rose bowl, carved &
enameled barren forest scene
w/snow-laden trees & snow-
covered ground against mottled
gold to yellow satin finish ground,
signed, 4 7/8 x 5 5/8", 4¼" h. 995.00

Cameo salt dip, carved rust-red
florals & green leaves against yel-
low ground, signed 350.00

Cameo toothpick holder, barrel-
shaped, carved & enameled barren forest scene w/snow-laden
trees & snow-covered ground
against mottled frosted gold
ground, signed, 1 7/8" h. 375.00

Cameo toothpick holder, carved
rose Bleeding Hearts & green
leaves w/gold stems & trim
against frosted blue ground,
signed 275.00

Cameo tumbler, carved & enameled
autumn-colored Black-Eyed
Susans, signed, 4¾" h. 450.00

Cameo vase, 4 7/8" h., 2 1/8" sq.,
carved & enameled barren black
spring trees blowing in wind
amidst "pelting" rain against
frosted mottled pink shaded to
green ground, signed . . . . . , ... 995.00

Cameo vase, 5¾" h., baluster-
shaped, carved shamrock green
crocus blossoms & buds against a
shaded green to frosted "martele"
ground, ca. 1900, signed 1,045.00

Cameo vase, 6" h., carved brown
thistles against green ground,
signed 440.00

Cameo Vase with Jonquils

Cameo vase, 7" h., carved orange-
centered white jonquils w/mottled
green stems & leaves against
matte white ground shading to
deep purple at pedestal foot,
signed (ILLUS.) 1,210.00

Cameo vase, 11" h., pedestal foot,
carved snow white trees & leaves
w/touches of green in the leaves
& swans floating on water
against ice blue ground, signed . . 1,850.00

Cameo vase, 11" h., bulbous,
carved mountainous landscape
w/trees & water in shades of
maroon, red & mottled yellow,
signed 1,050.00

Cameo vase, 12 3/8" h., inverted
pyriform on circular foot, carved
lime green & pumpkin leafage,
poppy blossoms & buds against
grey mottled w/ochre, mustard &
lime green, ca. 1910, signed 990.00

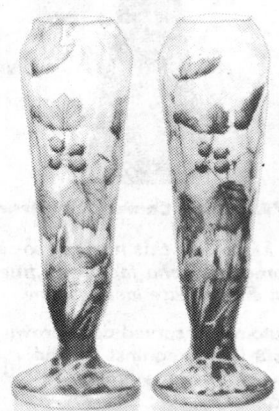

Daum Nancy Cameo Vases

Cameo vases, 15 1/8" h., carved &
enameled bushes & berries
against mottled amber-brown
ground, signed, pr. (ILLUS.) 3,600.00

Cameo vase, 16½" h., ovoid w/ir-
regular rim, mold-blown berry-
laden leafy branches against
ochre ground splashed w/red &
yellow, ca. 1910, signed 3,630.00

Cameo vase, 19½" h., bulging
spherical base w/slender cylindrical neck & circular foot, carved
dusty lavender iris blossoms, leafage, dragonfly, butterfly & bee
against shaded plum ground,
ca. 1900, signed 1,650.00

Compote, 9" h., wide mouth
w/pulled lip continuing to double
gourd form body, mottled rusty
orange shading to mottled blue
heightened w/pink, internally
decorated w/patches of bittersweet orange foil inclusions, deep
navy blue & pink domed foot, ca.
1930, signed 660.00

Rose bowl, mottled red & gold, ca.
1930, signed, 3" h. 165.00

DEPRESSION GLASS

The phrase "Depression Glass" is used by collectors to denote a specific kind of transparent glass produced primarily as tablewares, in crystal, amber, blue, green, pink, milky-white, etc., during the late 1920's and 1930's when this country was in the midst of a financial depression. Made to sell inexpensively, it was turned out by such producers as Jeannette, Hocking, Westmoreland, Indiana and other glass companies. We list all the major Depression Glass patterns.

ADAM (Process-etched)

Adam Salt & Pepper Shakers

Ash tray, clear, 4½" d.	$11.00
Ash tray, green, 4½" d.	15.00
Ash tray, pink, 4½" d.	19.00
Bowl, nappy, 4¾" sq., green	9.00
Bowl, nappy, 4¾" sq., pink	9.50
Bowl, nappy, 5¾" sq., green	20.00
Bowl, nappy, 5¾" sq., pink	19.00
Bowl, nappy, 7¾" sq., green or pink	14.00
Bowl, cov. vegetable, 9" sq., green	50.00
Bowl, cov. vegetable, 9" sq., pink	35.00
Bowl, 9" sq., green	25.00
Bowl, 9" sq., pink	16.00
Bowl, 10" oval vegetable, green	16.00
Bowl, 10" oval vegetable, pink	18.00
Butter dish, cov., green	220.00
Butter dish, cov., pink	69.00
Cake plate, green, 10" sq.	16.00
Cake plate, pink, 10" sq.	12.50
Candlesticks, green, 4" h., pr.	65.00
Candlesticks, pink, 4" h., pr.	53.00
Candy jar, cov., green	75.00
Candy jar, cov., pink	51.00
Coaster, clear	10.00
Coaster, green	11.00
Coaster, pink	15.00
Creamer, green	12.50

Creamer, pink	12.00
Creamer & cov. sugar bowl, green, pr.	41.00
Creamer & cov. sugar bowl, pink, pr.	34.00
Creamer & open sugar bowl, green, pr.	28.00
Creamer & open sugar bowl, pink, pr.	21.00
Cup & saucer, green	18.00
Cup & saucer, pink	19.50
Pitcher, 8" h., 32 oz., cone-shaped, clear	26.00
Pitcher, 8" h., 32 oz., cone-shaped, green	31.00
Pitcher, 8" h., 32 oz., cone-shaped, pink	24.00
Plate, sherbet, 6" sq., green	4.00
Plate, sherbet, 6" sq., pink	3.50
Plate, salad, 7¾" sq., green or pink	7.00
Plate, salad, round, pink	75.00
Plate, salad, round, yellow	120.00
Plate, dinner, 9" sq., green	13.00
Plate, dinner, 9" sq., pink	15.00
Plate, grill, 9" sq., green or pink	11.50
Platter, 12" l., green	13.00
Platter, 12" l., pink	11.00
Relish, 2-part, green, 8" oblong	11.00
Relish, 2-part, pink, 8" oblong	12.00
Salt & pepper shakers, footed, green, 4" h., pr.	72.50
Salt & pepper shakers, footed, pink, 4" h., pr. (ILLUS.)	41.00
Sherbet, green	21.00
Sherbet, pink	15.00
Sugar bowl, cov., green	31.00
Sugar bowl, cov., pink	24.00
Sugar bowl, open, green	11.00
Sugar bowl, open, pink	11.50
Tumbler, cone-shaped, green, 4½" h., 7 oz.	14.50
Tumbler, cone-shaped, pink, 4½" h., 7 oz.	16.00
Tumbler, cone-shaped, green, 5½" h., 9 oz.	24.00
Tumbler, cone-shaped, pink, 5½" h., 9 oz.	38.00
Vase, 7½" h., green	39.00
Vase, 7½" h., pink	179.00
Water set: pitcher & 4 tumblers; green, 5 pcs.	80.00

AMERICAN SWEETHEART (Process-etched)

Berry set: 9" bowl & 6 sauce dishes; Cremax, 7 pcs.	50.00
Bowl, berry, 3½" d., Cremax	65.00
Bowl, berry, 3½" d., pink	35.00
Bowl, cream soup, 4½" d., Monax	42.50
Bowl, cream soup, 4½" d., pink	27.00
Bowl, cereal, 6" d., Cremax	7.00
Bowl, cereal, 6" d., Monax	9.00
Bowl, cereal, 6" d., pink	8.50

Bowl, 9" d., Cremax	29.00
Bowl, 9" d., Monax	30.00
Bowl, 9" d., pink	17.00
Bowl, 10" oval vegetable, Monax	40.00
Bowl, 10" oval vegetable, pink	27.00
Bowl, soup w/flange rim, 10" d., Monax	34.00
Bowl, soup w/flange rim, 10" d., pink	25.00
Console bowl, Monax, 18" d.	295.00
Console bowl, ritz blue, 18" d.	802.00
Creamer, Monax	7.00
Creamer, pink	8.50
Creamer, ritz blue	90.00
Creamer & cov. sugar bowl, Monax, pr.	155.00
Creamer & open sugar bowl, Monax, pr.	12.00
Creamer & open sugar bowl, pink, pr.	15.00
Creamer & open sugar bowl, ritz blue, pr.	172.00
Creamer & open sugar bowl, ruby red, pr.	178.00
Cup & saucer, Monax	10.00
Cup & saucer, pink	12.00
Cup & saucer, ritz blue	121.00
Cup & saucer, ruby red	106.00
Lamp shade, Monax	342.50
Lamp shade & base, Monax	567.00
Lazy Susan, Monax, 15½" plate on metal stand	212.50
Pitcher, 7½" h., 60 oz., jug-type, pink	395.00
Pitcher, 8" h., 80 oz., pink	358.00
Plate, bread & butter, 6" d., Monax	3.50
Plate, bread & butter, 6" d., pink	2.50

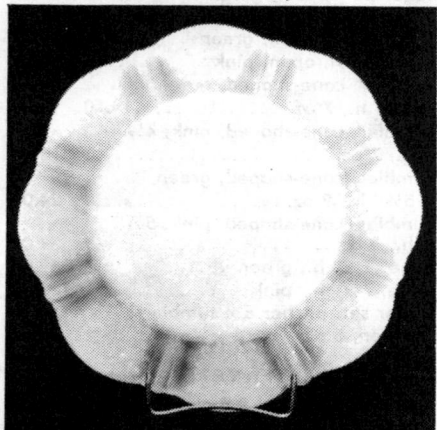

American Sweetheart Plate in Monax

Plate, salad, 8" d., Monax (ILLUS.)	5.75
Plate, salad, 8" d., pink	6.00
Plate, salad, 8" d., ritz blue	82.50
Plate, salad, 8" d., ruby red	62.00
Plate, luncheon, 9" d., Monax	7.00

Plate, luncheon, 9" d., pink	8.00
Plate, luncheon, 9" d., ritz blue	78.00
Plate, luncheon, 9" d., ruby red	58.00
Plate, dinner, 10" d., Monax	13.00
Plate, dinner, 10" d., pink	14.00
Plate, chop, 11" d., Monax	11.00
Plate, chop, 11" d., pink	10.00
Plate, salver, 12" d., Monax	11.00
Plate, salver, 12" d., pink	10.00
Plate, salver, 12" d., ritz blue	159.00
Plate, salver, 12" d., ruby red	155.00
Plate, 15" d., w/center handle, Monax	160.00
Plate, 15½" d., Monax	162.50
Plate, 15½" d., ruby red	252.00
Platter, 13" oval, Monax	34.00
Platter, 13" oval, pink or ritz blue	17.00
Platter, 13" oval, ruby red	90.00
Salt & pepper shakers, Monax, pr.	221.00
Salt & pepper shakers, pink, pr.	270.00
Sherbet, footed, Monax, 4" h.	13.00
Sherbet, footed, pink, 4" h.	10.50
Sherbet, low foot, Monax, 4¼" h.	13.00
Sherbet, low foot, pink, 4¼" h.	8.50
Sherbet, ice cream in metal holder, clear	3.00
Sherbet, ice cream in metal holder, Monax	6.00
Sherbet, ice cream in metal holder, pink	5.75
Sugar bowl, cov., Monax	165.00
Sugar bowl, open, Monax	6.00
Sugar bowl, open, pink	8.00
Sugar bowl, open, ruby red	64.00
Tid bit server, 2-tier, Monax	45.50
Tid bit server, 2-tier, pink	58.00
Tid bit server, 2-tier, ruby red	247.00
Tid bit server, 3-tier, Monax	55.00
Tid bit server, 3-tier, pink	85.00
Tid bit server, 3-tier, ruby red	545.00
Tumbler, pink, 3½" h., 5 oz.	34.00
Tumbler, pink, 4" h., 9 oz.	32.00
Tumbler, pink, 4½" h., 10 oz.	40.00

BLOCK or Block Optic (Press-mold)

Block Pattern Sherbet

Bowl, nappy, 4¼" d., green	4.50
Bowl, nappy, 5¼" d., green	7.00
Bowl, nappy, 5¼" d., pink	4.00

Bowl, nappy, 7" d., green or pink ..	11.00
Bowl, nappy, 8½" d., green	14.00
Butter dish, cov., oblong, green	30.00
Butter dish, cov., round, green	32.00
Candlesticks, green, pr.	45.00
Candlesticks, pink, pr.	31.50
Candlesticks, yellow, pr.	30.00
Candy jar, cov., green, 2¼" h.	29.50
Candy jar, cov., pink, 2¼" h.	29.00
Candy jar, cov., yellow, 2¼" h.	37.00
Candy jar, cov., clear, 6¼" h.	19.50
Candy jar, cov., green, 6¼" h.	28.00
Candy jar, cov., pink, 6¼" h.	36.50
Candy jar, cov., yellow, 6¼" h.	30.00
Compote, 4" d., cone-shaped, green	22.00
Compote, 4" d., cone-shaped, pink	17.00
Creamer, cone-shaped, green or pink	8.00
Creamer, cone-shaped, yellow	9.00
Creamer, round, footed, green	8.00
Creamer, round, footed, yellow	9.00
Creamer, straight sides, green	4.00
Creamer, straight sides, yellow.....	5.00
Creamer & open sugar bowl, green, pr.	15.50
Creamer & open sugar bowl, yellow, pr.	16.00
Creamer & open sugar bowl, cone-shaped, green, pr.	16.50
Creamer & open sugar bowl, cone-shaped, pink, pr.	17.00
Creamer & open sugar bowl, cone-shaped, yellow, pr.	19.50
Cup & saucer, clear	4.00
Cup & saucer, green or pink	8.00
Cup & saucer, yellow	7.00
Goblet, wine, clear, 4" h., 2 oz.	7.50
Goblet, wine, green, 4" h., 2 oz. ...	22.00
Goblet, wine, pink, 4" h., 2 oz.	12.00
Goblet, clear, 6" h.	7.50
Goblet, green, 6" h.	15.00
Goblet, pink, 6" h.	12.00
Goblet, yellow, 6" h.	11.00
Goblet, clear, 7¼" h.	7.50
Goblet, green, 7¼" h.	14.00
Goblet, pink, 7¼" h.	11.00
Goblet, yellow, 7¼" h.	17.00
Ice tub, clear	13.00
Ice tub, green	23.00
Ice tub, pink	40.00
Mug (or cup), green	25.00
Nite set: 3" tumbler bottle & 6" tumbler; green, set	45.00
Nite set bottle, green, 3"	11.00
Nite set bottle, pink, 3"	17.50
Pitcher, 7 5/8" h., 68 oz., green ...	28.50
Pitcher, 8" h., 80 oz., clear	13.00
Pitcher, 8" h., 80 oz., green	36.00
Pitcher, 8" h., 80 oz., pink	37.00
Pitcher, 8½" h., 54 oz., clear	18.00
Pitcher, 8½" h., 54 oz., green	30.00
Pitcher, 8½" h., 54 oz., pink	33.00

Plate, 6" d., clear	1.00
Plate, 6" d., green, pink or yellow..	2.00
Plate, luncheon, 8" d., green or pink	3.00
Plate, luncheon, 8" d., yellow	4.00
Plate, dinner, 9" d., clear	4.00
Plate, dinner, 9" d., green	11.00
Plate, dinner, 9" d., yellow	20.00
Plate, grill, 9" d., clear	4.00
Plate, grill, 9" d., green	10.00
Plate, sandwich, 10" d., clear	6.00
Plate, sandwich, 10" d., green	10.50
Plate, sandwich, 10" d., pink	13.00
Salt & pepper shakers, squat, green, pr.	34.00
Salt & pepper shakers, squat, pink, pr.	50.00
Salt & pepper shakers, squat, yellow, pr.	62.50
Salt & pepper shakers, footed, clear, pr.	25.00
Salt & pepper shakers, footed, green, pr.	21.00
Salt & pepper shakers, footed, pink, pr.	47.00
Salt & pepper shakers, footed, yellow, pr.	18.00
Sandwich server w/center handle, green	33.00
Sandwich server w/center handle, pink	31.00
Sherbet, round or V shaped, clear ..	2.50
Sherbet, round or V shaped, green (ILLUS.)	3.00
Sherbet, round or V shaped, pink ...	5.00
Sherbet, round or V shaped, yellow	6.50
Sherbet, stemmed, clear, 5" h.	5.00
Sherbet, stemmed, green, pink or yellow, 5" h.	9.00
Sugar bowl, cone-shaped, clear	4.00
Sugar bowl, cone-shaped, green or pink	7.00
Sugar bowl, cone-shaped, yellow ...	8.00
Sugar bowl, round, clear	3.00
Sugar bowl, round, green	7.00
Sugar bowl, round, pink	6.50
Sugar bowl, round, yellow	5.50
Sugar bowl, straight sides, green ...	7.50
Tumbler, whiskey, clear, 2½" h.	6.00
Tumbler, whiskey, green, 2½" h.	14.50
Tumbler, whiskey, pink, 2½" h.	9.50
Tumbler, juice, clear, 3" h., 5 oz.	3.75
Tumbler, juice, green, 3" h., 5 oz.	11.00
Tumbler, juice, pink, 3" h., 5 oz. ...	8.00
Tumbler, juice, footed, green, 3¼" h., 5 oz.	16.00
Tumbler, juice, footed, pink, 3¼" h., 5 oz.	8.00
Tumbler, clear, 9 oz.	3.50
Tumbler, green, 9 oz.	11.00
Tumbler, pink, 9 oz.	8.50
Tumbler, yellow, 9 oz.	8.00
Tumbler, footed, clear, 9 oz.	6.50

Tumbler, footed, green, 9 oz. 11.00
Tumbler, footed, pink, 9 oz. 9.50
Tumbler, footed, yellow, 9 oz. 12.00
Tumbler, iced tea, clear, 10 oz. 5.50
Tumbler, iced tea, green, 10 oz. 11.00
Tumbler, iced tea, pink, 10 oz. 8.00
Tumbler, iced tea, footed, green,
  6" h., 10 oz. 15.00
Tumbler, iced tea, footed, pink,
  6" h., 10 oz. 12.00
Tumbler, iced tea, footed, yellow,
  6" h., 10 oz. 12.50
Tumbler, green, 14 oz. 16.50
Tumbler, pink, 14 oz. 13.00

BUBBLE (Press-mold)

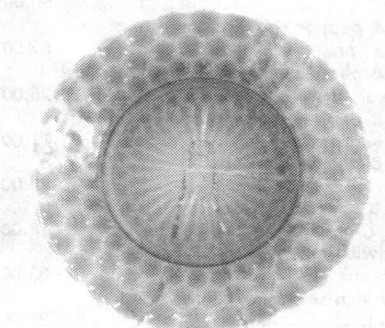

Bubble Dinner Plate

Berry set: master bowl & 6 sauce
  dishes; milk white, 7 pcs. 12.50
Berry set: master bowl & 8 sauce
  dishes; clear, 9 pcs. 17.50
Bowl, 4" d., blue 8.00
Bowl, 4" d., clear 2.00
Bowl, 4" d., pink 15.00
Bowl, 4" d., ruby red 4.50
Bowl, fruit, 4½" d., blue or green .. 5.00
Bowl, fruit, 4½" d., clear 3.00
Bowl, fruit, 4½" d., milk white 2.00
Bowl, fruit, 4½" d., ruby red 4.00
Bowl, cereal, 5¼" d., blue 6.00
Bowl, cereal, 5¼" d., clear 3.00
Bowl, cereal, 5¼" d., green 7.00
Bowl, soup, 7¾" d., blue 7.00
Bowl, soup, 7¾" d., clear 5.00
Bowl, soup, 7¾" d., green 15.00
Bowl, soup, 7¾" d., pink 4.75
Bowl, soup, 7¾" d., ruby red 5.75
Bowl, 8 3/8" d., blue or ruby red ... 8.00
Bowl, 8 3/8" d., clear 4.50
Bowl, 8 3/8" d., green 12.00
Bowl, 8 3/8" d., milk white 3.50
Bowl, 8 3/8" d., pink 4.75
Bowl, 9" d., flanged, milk white 30.00
Candlesticks, clear, pr. 11.00
Creamer, blue 18.00
Creamer, clear 5.00
Creamer, green 6.00

Creamer, milk white 2.00
Creamer, ruby red 3.00
Creamer & open sugar bowl, blue,
  pr. 30.00
Creamer & open sugar bowl, milk
  white, pr. 7.00
Cup & saucer, blue or pink 4.00
Cup & saucer, clear 3.00
Cup & saucer, green 6.50
Cup & saucer, ruby red 7.00
Dinner service for 6, w/serving
  pieces, blue, 56 pcs. 250.00
Pitcher w/ice lip, 64 oz., blue 35.00
Pitcher w/ice lip, 64 oz., clear...... 41.00
Pitcher w/ice lip, 64 oz., ruby red .. 32.00
Plate, bread & butter, 6¾" d.,
  blue 2.00
Plate, bread & butter, 6¾" d.,
  clear 1.50
Plate, bread & butter, 6¾" d.,
  green 3.00
Plate, dinner, 9¼" d., blue 4.00
Plate, dinner, 9¼" d., clear 3.00
Plate, dinner, 9¼" d., green 6.50
Plate, dinner, 9¼" d., ruby red
  (ILLUS.) 6.00
Plate, grill, 9¼" d., blue 8.00
Plate, grill, 9.¼" d., clear 4.00
Platter, 12" oval, blue or clear 7.00
Platter, 12" oval, green 10.00
Salt & pepper shakers, blue, small,
  pr. 10.00
Salt & pepper shakers, green, pr.... 45.00
Sugar bowl, open, blue 13.00
Sugar bowl, open, clear 4.00
Sugar bowl, open, green 5.00
Sugar bowl, open, milk white 2.00
Sugar bowl, open, ruby red 3.00
Tid bit server, blue 39.00
Tid bit server, ruby red 27.00
Tumbler, juice, clear, 6 oz. 5.50
Tumbler, juice, green, 6 oz. 17.50
Tumbler, juice, ruby red, 6 oz. 5.00
Tumbler, old fashioned, clear,
  9 oz. 6.00
Tumbler, old fashioned, green,
  9 oz. 4.00
Tumbler, old fashioned, ruby red,
  9 oz. 5.00
Tumbler, clear, 12 oz. 5.50
Tumbler, green, 12 oz. 6.00
Tumbler, ruby red, 12 oz. 6.50
Tumbler, iced tea, clear, 16 oz....... 10.50
Tumbler, iced tea, ruby red,
  16 oz. 8.50
Tumbler, footed, clear, 7" h. 8.00
Tumbler, footed, green, 7" h. 6.00
Water set: pitcher & 8 tumblers;
  ruby red, 9 pcs. 65.00

CAMEO (Process-etched)
Bowl, cream soup, 4¾" d., clear ... 3.00
Bowl, cream soup, 4¾" d., green... 49.00
Bowl, nappy, 5½" d., clear 5.00

Bowl, nappy, 5½" d., green	18.50
Bowl, nappy, 5½" d., yellow	19.00
Bowl, nappy, 7" d., green	28.50
Bowl, nappy, 8¼" d., green	21.50
Bowl, nappy, 8¼" d., yellow	21.00
Bowl, 9" oval vegetable, green	15.00
Bowl, 9" oval vegetable, pink	125.00
Bowl, 9" oval vegetable, yellow	33.00
Bowl, soup w/flange rim, 9" d., green	27.00
Butter dish, cov., green	137.00
Cake plate, footed, clear, 10" d.	12.00
Cake plate, footed, green, 10" d.	14.00
Cake plate, handled, green, 10½" d.	73.00
Candlesticks, green, 4" h., pr.	77.00
Candy dish, cov., low, green	36.50
Candy dish, cov., low, yellow	67.00
Candy jar, cov., green, 6½" h.	88.00
Compote, 4" h., cone-shaped, green	18.00
Console bowl, 3-footed, green, 11" d.	42.00
Console bowl, 3-footed, pink, 11" d.	19.50
Console bowl, 3-footed, yellow, 11" d.	50.00
Cookie jar, cov., green	35.00
Creamer, green, 3" h.	14.00
Creamer, yellow, 3" h.	12.50
Creamer, green, 4" h.	14.00
Creamer, pink, 4" h.	62.50
Creamer, yellow, 4" h.	16.00
Creamer & open sugar bowl, green, 3" h., pr.	25.00
Creamer & open sugar bowl, pink, 3" h., pr.	22.50
Creamer & open sugar bowl, yellow, 3" h., pr.	23.00
Creamer & open sugar bowl, green, 4" h., pr.	31.00
Cup & saucer, green	12.50
Cup & saucer, pink	7.75
Cup & saucer, yellow	8.00
Cup & saucer w/ring, green	95.00
Domino tray, green, 7" d.	95.00
Goblet, wine, green, 4" h.	44.00
Goblet, green, 6" h.	34.00
Ice bowl, green, 3½" h.	97.50
Juice set: pitcher & 6 tumblers; green, 7 pcs.	150.00
Mayonnaise bowl w/ladle, green, 2 pcs.	18.50
Mayonnaise bowl w/underplate, green, 2 pcs.	23.00
Mayonnaise set: bowl, underplate & ladle; green, 3 pcs.	35.00
Pitcher, syrup or milk, 5¾" h. 20 oz., green	134.00
Pitcher, juice, 6" h., 36 oz., green	44.00
Pitcher, 8½" h., 56 oz., jug-type, clear	15.00
Pitcher, 8½" h., 56 oz., jug-type, green	36.00

Plate, sherbet, 6" d., clear	2.00
Plate, sherbet, 6" d., green or yellow	2.50
Plate, 7" d., clear w/platinum rim	3.00
Plate, luncheon, 8" d., green	6.00
Plate, luncheon, 8" d., pink	20.00
Plate, luncheon, 8" d., yellow	5.00
Plate, salad, 8" sq., green	23.00
Plate, salad, 8" sq., yellow	7.00
Plate, dinner, 9½" d., clear or yellow	6.00
Plate, dinner, 9½" d., green	12.50
Plate, dinner, 9½" d., pink	31.00
Plate, sandwich, 10" d., green	10.00
Plate, sandwich, 10" d., pink	32.00
Plate, dinner, 10½" d., closed handles, green	9.00
Plate, dinner, 10½" d., closed handles, yellow	11.50
Plate, grill, 10½" d., closed handles, green	43.00
Plate, grill, 10½" d., closed handles, yellow	6.00
Plate, grill, 10½" d., green	6.50
Plate, grill, 10½" d., yellow	5.50
Platter, 10½" oval, green	12.50
Platter, 10½" oval, pink	5.00
Platter, 10½" oval, yellow	25.00
Platter, 12", closed handles, green	13.50
Platter, 12", closed handles, yellow	5.50
Relish, green, 7½"	15.50
Salt & pepper shakers, green, pr.	49.00
Sandwich server, green	10.50
Sherbet, green, 3"	10.00
Sherbet, pink, 3"	31.50
Sherbet, yellow, 3"	20.00
Sherbet, thin, high stem, green	22.00
Sherbet, thin, high stem, yellow	25.00
Sugar bowl, open, green, 3" h.	9.00
Sugar bowl, open, pink, 3" h.	65.00
Sugar bowl, open, yellow, 3" h.	10.00
Sugar bowl, open, green, 4" h.	15.00
Sugar bowl, open, yellow, 4" h.	12.00
Tumbler, juice, footed, green, 3 oz.	42.00
Tumbler, juice, green, 3" h., 5 oz.	18.50
Tumbler, juice, pink, 3" h., 5 oz.	61.00
Tumbler, juice, footed, green, 5 oz.	39.00
Tumbler, juice, footed, pink, 5 oz.	45.00
Tumbler, clear, 4" h., 9 oz.	5.00
Tumbler, green, 4" h., 9 oz.	19.00
Tumbler, pink, 4" h., 9 oz.	55.00
Tumbler, yellow, 4" h., 9 oz.	15.50
Tumbler, footed, green, 5" h., 9 oz.	20.00
Tumbler, footed, pink, 5" h., 9 oz.	45.00
Tumbler, footed, yellow, 5" h., 9 oz.	12.50
Tumbler, green, 4¾" h., 10 oz.	18.50
Tumbler, pink, 4¾" h., 10 oz.	60.00
Tumbler, yellow, 4¾" h., 10 oz.	25.50
Tumbler, green, 5" h., 11 oz.	21.00
Tumbler, yellow, 5" h., 11 oz.	45.50

Tumbler, footed, green, 6" h.,
  11 oz. 33.50
Tumbler, footed, yellow, 6" h.,
  11 oz. 12.00
Tumbler, green, 5¼" h., 14 oz. 34.00
Vase, 5¾" h., green 92.50

Cameo Vase

Vase, 8½" h., green (ILLUS.) 18.50
Water bottle, no stopper, green 25.00
Water bottle w/stopper, green 82.50
Water bottle, green frosted,
  8½" h. 29.00
Water bottle, dark green "White
  House Vinegar" base, 8½" h. 15.00
Water set: pitcher & 6 tumblers;
  green, 7 pcs. 200.00
Wine set: decanter & 5 wine
  goblets; green, 6 pcs. 275.00

CHERRY BLOSSOM (Process-etched)

Cherry Blossom Pitcher

Berry set: master bowl & 7 sauce
  dishes; green, 8 pcs. 75.00
Bowl, nappy, 4¾" d., Delfite 9.50
Bowl, nappy, 4¾" d., green 11.00
Bowl, nappy, 4¾" d., pink 8.00
Bowl, nappy, 5¾" d., Delfite 12.50
Bowl, nappy, 5¾" d., green 23.50

Bowl, nappy, 5¾" d., pink 20.00
Bowl, soup, 7¾" d., green 38.00
Bowl, soup, 7¾" d., pink 36.00
Bowl, nappy, 8½" d., Delfite 37.50
Bowl, nappy, 8½" d., green 19.50
Bowl, nappy, 8½" d., pink 15.50
Bowl, 9" d., handled, clear 15.50
Bowl, 9" d., handled, Delfite 13.00
Bowl, 9" d., handled, green 18.50
Bowl, 9" d., handled, pink 18.00
Bowl, 9" oval vegetable, green 26.00
Bowl, 9" oval vegetable, pink 20.00
Bowl, fruit, 10½" d., 3-footed,
  green 41.00
Bowl, fruit, 10½" d., 3-footed,
  pink 37.50
Butter dish, cov., green 71.00
Butter dish, cov., pink 62.00
Cake plate, green, 10¼" d. 17.00
Cake plate, pink, 10¼" d. 16.50
Coaster, green 9.00
Coaster, pink 11.00
Creamer, clear 9.50
Creamer, Delfite 14.00
Creamer, green 12.50
Creamer, pink 11.50
Creamer & cov. sugar bowl, green,
  pr. 28.50
Creamer & cov. sugar bowl, pink,
  pr. 29.00
Creamer & open sugar bowl, Del-
  fite, pr. 28.50
Creamer & open sugar bowl, green,
  pr. 19.00
Creamer & open sugar bowl, pink,
  pr. 20.00
Cup & saucer, Delfite 19.00
Cup & saucer, green 18.00
Cup & saucer, pink 15.00
Mug, green, 8 oz. 153.00
Mug, pink, 8 oz. 140.00
Pitcher, 6½" h., 36 oz., jug-type,
  overall patt., Delfite 84.00
Pitcher, 6½" h., 36 oz., jug-type,
  overall patt., green 38.00
Pitcher, 6½" h., 36 oz., jug-type,
  overall patt., pink 33.00
Pitcher, 8" h., 36 oz., cone-shaped,
  patt. top, Delfite 71.00
Pitcher, 8" h., 36 oz., cone-shaped,
  patt. top, green 34.50
Pitcher, 8" h., 36 oz., cone-shaped,
  patt. top, pink 34.00
Pitcher, 8" h., 42 oz., straight side,
  patt. top, Delfite (ILLUS.) 89.00
Pitcher, 8" h., 42 oz., straight side,
  patt. top, green 35.50
Pitcher, 8" h., 42 oz., straight side,
  patt. top, pink 31.50
Plate, sherbet, 6" d., Delfite 7.00
Plate, sherbet, 6" d., green 5.00
Plate, sherbet, 6" d., pink 4.50
Plate, salad, 7" d., clear 12.00
Plate, salad, 7" d., green 13.00

Plate, salad, 7" d., pink	12.50
Plate, dinner, 9" d., Delfite or pink	11.50
Plate, dinner, 9" d., green	14.00
Plate, grill, 9" d., green	15.50
Plate, grill, 9" d., pink	14.50
Platter, 11" oval, clear.............	12.00
Platter, 11" oval, Delfite	34.00
Platter, 11" oval, green	23.00
Platter, 11" oval, pink	21.50
Platter, 13" oval, Delfite or green ..	36.00
Platter, 13" oval, pink	35.50
Platter, 13" oval, divided, green	37.50
Platter, 13" oval, divided, pink	32.50
Salt & pepper shakers, green, pr....	995.00
Sandwich tray, handled, Delfite, 10½" d..........................	14.50
Sandwich tray, handled, green, 10½" d..........................	16.00
Sandwich tray, handled, pink, 10½" d..........................	13.00
Sherbet, Delfite	12.50
Sherbet, green....................	11.50
Sherbet, pink	10.00
Sugar bowl, cov., clear	17.00
Sugar bowl, cov., green	21.00
Sugar bowl, cov., pink	19.00
Sugar bowl, open, Delfite	15.00
Sugar bowl, open, green...........	9.00
Sugar bowl, open, pink	8.00
Tumbler, juice, footed, Delfite, 3½" h., 4 oz.	15.00
Tumbler, juice, footed, green, 3½" h., 4 oz.	15.50
Tumbler, juice, footed, pink, 3½" h., 4 oz.	11.50
Tumbler, patt. top, green, 3½" h., 5 oz............................	13.50
Tumbler, patt. top, pink, 3½" h., 5 oz............................	11.50
Tumbler, patt. top, clear, 4" h., 9 oz............................	7.00
Tumbler, patt. top, Delfite, 4" h., 9 oz............................	21.00
Tumbler, patt. top, green, 4" h., 9 oz............................	15.50
Tumbler, patt. top, pink, 4" h., 9 oz............................	12.50
Tumbler, footed, clear, 4½" h., 9 oz............................	10.00
Tumbler, footed, Delfite, 4½" h., 9 oz............................	14.00
Tumbler, footed, green, 4½" h., 9 oz............................	24.00
Tumbler, footed, pink, 4½" h., 9 oz............................	22.50
Tumbler, patt. top, Delfite, 5" h., 12 oz.	16.00
Tumbler, patt. top, green, 5" h., 12 oz............................	43.50
Tumbler, patt. top, pink, 5" h., 12 oz............................	34.50
Water set: pitcher & 6 tumblers; pink, 7 pcs....................	120.00

Water set: pitcher & 7 tumblers; green, 8 pcs.	120.00

JUNIOR SET:

Creamer, Delfite or pink	22.00
Creamer & sugar bowl, Delfite, pr................................	42.00
Creamer & sugar bowl, pink, pr. ...	47.50
Cup, Delfite	20.00
Cup, pink........................	28.00
Cup & saucer, Delfite or pink....	23.00
Cup, saucer & plate, pink, 3 pcs. ...	30.00
Plate, 6" d., Delfite	7.00
Plate, 6" d., pink	6.50
Saucer, Delfite	4.00
Saucer, pink	4.50
Sugar bowl, Delfite	20.00
Sugar bowl, pink	25.50
14 pc. set, Delfite	189.00
14 pc. set, pink	169.00

CLOVERLEAF (Process-etched)

Cloverleaf Sugar Bowl

Ash tray, black, 4" d..............	45.00
Ash tray, black, 5¾" d............	66.50
Bowl, dessert, 4" d., green or yellow	12.00
Bowl, dessert, 4" d., pink	9.00
Bowl, nappy, 5" d., green..........	16.00
Bowl, nappy, 5" d., yellow	22.00
Bowl, 7" d., green	29.00
Bowl, 7" d., yellow	35.50
Bowl, 8" d., green	38.00
Candy dish, cov., green...........	32.00
Candy dish, cov., yellow	88.00
Creamer, black	11.00
Creamer, green	7.00
Creamer, yellow	10.00
Creamer & open sugar bowl, black, pr................................	22.50
Creamer & open sugar bowl, green, pr................................	14.00
Creamer & open sugar bowl, yellow, pr................................	20.00
Cup & saucer, black	11.00
Cup & saucer, clear	5.50
Cup & saucer, green or pink	6.00
Cup & saucer, yellow	13.00
Plate, sherbet, 6" d., black........	24.00
Plate, sherbet, 6" d., green	4.00

Plate, sherbet, 6" d., yellow 4.50
Plate, salad, 8" d., black. 10.50
Plate, salad, 8" d., clear 2.75
Plate, salad, 8" d., green 4.00
Plate, salad, 8" d., pink 4.50
Plate, salad, 8" d., yellow 8.00
Plate, grill, 10" d., green 12.00
Plate, grill, 10" d., yellow. 12.50
Salt & pepper shakers, black, pr. 59.00
Salt & pepper shakers, green, pr.. . . .   25.50
Salt & pepper shakers, yellow, pr.. . .   78.00
Sherbet, black 13.00
Sherbet, clear. 4.00
Sherbet, green or pink 4.50
Sherbet, yellow 8.00
Sugar bowl, open, black or yellow . .   10.00
Sugar bowl, open, green (ILLUS.) . . .   7.50
Tumbler, green, 4" h., 9 oz.. . . . .   22.00
Tumbler, pink, 4" h., 9 oz. 14.50
Tumbler, green, 3¾" h., 10 oz.. . . . .   20.00
Tumbler, pink, 3¾" h., 10 oz. 21.00
Tumbler, footed, green, 5¾" h.,
   10 oz.. . . . .   15.50
Tumbler, footed, yellow, 5¾" h.,
   10 oz.. . . . .   19.50
Tumbler, footed, green, 6½" h.,
   13 oz.. . . . .   19.00
Tumbler, footed, yellow, 6½" h.,
   13 oz.. . . . .   21.00

COLONIAL or Knife & Fork (Press-mold)

Colonial Celery

Bowl, berry, 4" d., green 8.00
Bowl, berry, 4" d., pink. 19.50
Bowl, cream soup, 4½" d., green. . .   34.50
Bowl, cream soup, 4½" d., pink 28.00
Bowl, nappy, 4½" d., clear or
   pink 6.50
Bowl, nappy, 4½" d., green. 9.00
Bowl, nappy, 5½" d., green. 7.50
Bowl, nappy, 5½" d., pink 22.50
Bowl, soup, 7" d., clear. 13.50
Bowl, soup, 7" d., green 38.00
Bowl, soup, 7" d., pink 26.50
Bowl, 9" d., clear . . . . .7.00 to   9.50
Bowl, 9" d., green 17.00
Bowl, 9" d., pink 12.50
Bowl, 10" oval vegetable,
   clear. . . . . .9.50 to   14.00

Bowl, 10" oval vegetable, green or
   pink .15.00 to   22.00
Butter dish, cov., clear 26.50
Butter dish, cov., green. 44.00
Butter dish, cov., pink 250.00
Celery or spooner, clear 36.00
Celery or spooner, green (ILLUS.) . . .   97.00
Celery or spooner, pink. 95.00
Cheese dish, wooden base w/clear
   dome cover. 65.00
Creamer, clear. 7.50
Creamer, green 13.00
Creamer, pink . . . . .6.00 to   10.00
Cup & saucer, clear 6.50
Cup & saucer, green. 11.50
Cup & saucer, milk white 12.00
Cup & saucer, pink 8.50
Goblet, cordial, green, 3¾" h.,
   1 oz.. . . . .   25.00
Goblet, cordial, pink, 3¾" h.,
   1 oz.. . . . .   15.50
Goblet, wine, clear, 4½" h.,
   2½ oz.. . . . .   8.50
Goblet, wine, green, 4½" h.,
   2½ oz.. . . . .   18.00
Goblet, cocktail, clear, 4" h.,
   3 oz.. . . . .   7.00
Goblet, cocktail, green, 4" h.,
   3 oz.. . . . .   17.00
Goblet, cocktail, pink, 4" h.,
   3 oz.. . . . .   13.00
Goblet, claret, clear, 5" h., 4 oz. . . .   9.50
Goblet, claret, green, 5" h., 4 oz. . .   18.00
Goblet, clear, 5¾" h., 8½ oz.. . . . . .   10.50
Goblet, green, 5¾" h., 8½ oz. 22.50
Goblet, pink, 5¾" h., 8½ oz. 18.00
Pitcher, 7" h., 54 oz., clear. 20.00
Pitcher, 7" h., 54 oz., green 37.00
Pitcher, 7" h., 54 oz., pink 32.50
Pitcher, 7½" h., 67 oz., clear. 24.50

Colonial Pitcher

Pitcher, 7½" h., 67 oz., green
   (ILLUS.). 43.00
Pitcher, 7½" h., 67 oz., pink 40.00
Plate, sherbet, 6½" d., clear 2.50
Plate, sherbet, 6½" d., green 3.50
Plate, sherbet, 6½" d., pink 3.00
Plate, luncheon, 8½" d., clear 3.50

Plate, luncheon, 8½" d., green	6.00
Plate, luncheon, 8½" d., pink	5.50
Plate, dinner, 10" d., clear	14.00
Plate, dinner, 10" d., green	39.50
Plate, dinner, 10" d., milk white	11.00
Plate, dinner, 10" d., pink	26.00
Plate, grill, 10" d., clear	12.50
Plate, grill, 10" d., green	19.00
Plate, grill, 10" d., pink...........	15.50
Platter, 12" oval, clear.............	10.50
Platter, 12" oval, green	15.00
Platter, 12" oval, pink	17.00
Salt & pepper shakers, clear, pr.	45.00
Salt & pepper shakers, green, pr....	105.00
Salt & pepper shakers, pink, pr.	90.00
Sherbet, clear...................	4.50
Sherbet, green...................	9.50
Sherbet, pink	6.50
Sugar bowl, cov., clear	13.00
Sugar bowl, cov., green	24.50
Sugar bowl, cov., pink	25.00
Sugar bowl, open, clear	6.00
Sugar bowl, open, green	9.50
Sugar bowl, open, pink	5.00
Tumbler, whiskey, clear, 2½" h., 1½ oz.	4.00
Tumbler, whiskey, green, 2½" h., 1½ oz.	9.00
Tumbler, whiskey, pink, 2½" h., 1½ oz.	7.50
Tumbler, cordial, footed, clear, 3¼" h., 3 oz.	6.50
Tumbler, cordial, footed, green, 3¼" h., 3 oz.	14.00
Tumbler, cordial, footed, pink, 3¼" h., 3 oz.	10.00
Tumbler, juice, clear, 3" h., 5 oz.	4.00
Tumbler, juice, green, 3" h., 5 oz. ...	18.00
Tumbler, juice, pink, 3" h., 5 oz. ...	9.00
Tumbler, claret, footed, clear, 4" h., 5 oz.	8.00
Tumbler, claret, footed, green, 4" h., 5 oz.	16.00
Tumbler, claret, footed, pink, 4" h., 5 oz.	12.00
Tumbler, clear, 4" h., 9 oz.	5.00
Tumbler, green, 4" h., 9 oz........	20.00
Tumbler, pink, 4" h., 9 oz.	9.50
Tumbler, cordial, footed, clear, 5¼" h., 10 oz.	8.50
Tumbler, cordial, footed, green, 5¼" h., 10 oz.	32.50
Tumbler, cordial, footed, pink, 5¼" h., 10 oz.	16.50
Tumbler, clear, 10 oz.	12.00
Tumbler, green, 10 oz.	18.50
Tumbler, pink, 10 oz..............	13.50
Tumbler, iced tea, green, 12 oz.....	33.50
Tumbler, iced tea, pink, 12 oz.	21.00
Tumbler, lemonade, green, 15 oz. ..	70.00
Tumbler, lemonade, pink, 15 oz.....	30.00

COLUMBIA (Press-mold)

Bowl, cereal, 5" d., clear	9.00

Bowl, soup, 8" d., clear............	10.50
Bowl, salad, 8½" d., clear	11.50
Bowl, salad, 8½" d., pink..........	12.00
Bowl, 10½" d., ruffled rim, clear ...	12.00
Bowl, 10½" d., ruffled rim, pink....	12.50
Butter dish, cov., clear	14.00
Butter dish w/metal lid, clear	20.00
Cup & saucer, clear	5.00
Plate, bread & butter, 6" d., clear ..	1.50
Plate, luncheon, 9½" d., clear......	4.00
Plate, luncheon, 9½" d., pink	9.50
Plate, chop, 11¾" d., clear	6.50
Plate, chop, 11¾" d., pink	8.50

CUBE or Cubist (Press-mold)

Bowl, dessert, 4½" d., clear	1.00
Bowl, dessert, 4½" d., green.......	3.50
Bowl, dessert, 4½" d., pink	4.00
Bowl, 4½" d., deep, clear	3.50
Bowl, 4½" d., deep, green.........	4.50
Bowl, 4½" d., deep, pink	4.00
Bowl, salad, 6½" d., clear	4.00
Bowl, salad, 6½" d., green	9.00
Bowl, salad, 6½" d., pink..........	6.00
Bowl, 7 3/8" d., scalloped rim, clear	9.00
Bowl, 7 3/8" d., scalloped rim, green	12.00
Bowl, 7 3/8" d., scalloped rim, pink	8.50
Butter dish, cov., green	45.00
Butter dish, cov., pink	42.00
Candy jar, cov., green, 7½" h.	21.00
Candy jar, cov., pink, 7½" h.	18.50
Coaster, clear, 3¼" d.............	18.00
Coaster, green or pink, 3¼" d......	4.00
Creamer, clear, 2" h.	3.50
Creamer, green, 2" h.	5.50
Creamer, pink, 2" h.	2.50
Creamer, clear, 3" h.	2.00
Creamer, green, 3" h.	6.00
Creamer, pink, 3" h.	4.00
Cup & saucer, green.............	8.50
Cup & saucer, pink	6.00
Pitcher, 8¾" h., 45 oz., green or pink	137.50
Plate, sherbet, 6" d., clear	1.00
Plate, sherbet, 6" d., green	2.00
Plate, sherbet, 6" d., pink	1.50
Plate, luncheon, 8" d., green......	4.00
Plate, luncheon, 8" d., pink	3.50
Powder jar, cov., 3-footed, clear...	8.50
Powder jar, cov., 3-footed, green...	13.00
Powder jar, cov., 3-footed, pink	12.00
Salt & pepper shakers, clear, pr.	16.00
Salt & pepper shakers, green, pr....	24.00
Salt & pepper shakers, pink, pr.	22.00
Sherbet, clear...................	2.00
Sherbet, green...................	6.00
Sherbet, pink	4.50
Sugar bowl, cov., clear, 3" h.	3.00
Sugar bowl, cov., green, 3" h.......	12.50
Sugar bowl, cov., pink, 3" h.	9.50
Sugar bowl, open, clear or pink	2.00

Sugar bowl, open, green, 2" h. 6.50
Sugar bowl, open, green, 3" h. 5.50
Sugar bowl, open, pink, 3" h. 4.50
Tray for 3" h. creamer & sugar
 bowl, clear, 7½" 3.50
Tumbler, green, 4" h., 9 oz. 33.50
Tumbler, pink, 4" h., 9 oz. 31.00
Water set: pitcher & 4 tumblers;
 pink, 5 pcs. 200.00

DAISY or Number 620 (Press-mold)
Bowl, berry, 4½" d., amber 6.00
Bowl, berry, 4½" d., clear 3.50
Bowl, cream soup, 4½" d., amber . . 5.50
Bowl, cream soup, 4½" d., clear . . . 3.50
Bowl, cereal, 6" d., amber 18.00
Bowl, cereal, 6" d., clear . . . . .9.50 to 15.00
Bowl, berry, 7 3/8" d., amber 20.00
Bowl, berry, 9 3/8" d., amber 17.50
Bowl, berry, 9 3/8" d., clear 9.50
Bowl, 10" oval vegetable, amber . . . 12.00
Bowl, 10" oval vegetable, clear 5.00
Creamer, footed, amber 5.75
Creamer, footed, clear 3.00
Cup & saucer, amber or clear 5.00
Plate, sherbet, 6" d., amber or
 clear 1.50
Plate, salad, 7 3/8" d., amber 5.00
Plate, luncheon, 8 3/8" d., amber . . 4.50
Plate, luncheon, 8 3/8" d., clear 3.00
Plate, dinner, 9 3/8" d., amber 5.00
Plate, dinner, 9 3/8" d., clear 3.50
Plate, grill, 10 3/8" d., amber 9.00
Plate, grill, 10 3/8" d., clear 3.50
Plate, 11½" d., amber 8.00
Plate, 11½" d., clear 4.50
Platter, 10¾", amber 9.50
Platter, 10¾", clear 6.50
Relish, 3-part, amber, 8 3/8" 14.00
Relish, 3-part, clear, 8 3/8" 7.50
Sherbet, amber 5.50
Sherbet, clear 4.00
Sugar bowl, open, footed, amber . . . 5.00
Sugar bowl, open, footed, clear 3.50
Tumbler, footed, amber, 9 oz. 13.50
Tumbler, footed, clear, 9 oz. 7.00
Tumbler, footed, amber, 12 oz. 29.00
Tumbler, footed, clear, 12 oz. 13.50

DIAMOND QUILTED or Flat Diamond (Press-mold)
Bowl, cream soup, 4¾" d., blue 12.50
Bowl, cream soup, 4¾" d., green . . . 8.00
Bowl, cream soup, 4¾" d., pink 7.50
Bowl, cereal, 5" d., pink 5.00
Bowl, 5½" d., single handle,
 black 12.00
Bowl, 5½" d., single handle, blue . . 11.00
Bowl, 5½" d., single handle,
 green 7.00
Bowl, 5½" d., single handle, pink . . 6.00
Bowl, 7" d., black 16.50
Bowl, 7" d., blue 14.00
Bowl, 7" d., green or pink 8.00

Candlesticks, black or blue, pr. 20.00
Candlesticks, green or pink, pr. 12.50
Candy jar, cov., footed, pink 70.00
Coaster, pink, 3" d. 4.00
Console bowl, rolled edge, pink 28.00
Creamer, black 12.50
Creamer, blue or pink 8.00
Creamer, green 9.00
Creamer, red 35.00
Cup & saucer, black 11.50
Cup & saucer, green 3.00
Cup & saucer, pink 8.00
Goblet, champagne, pink, 6" h.,
 9 oz. 8.50
Ice bucket, blue . . . . .25.00 to 32.00
Mayonnaise set: 3-footed dish, plate
 & ladle; pink, 3 pcs. 45.00
Plate, sherbet, 6" d., black 5.00
Plate, sherbet, 6" d., blue 3.50
Plate, sherbet, 6" d., green or
 pink 2.50
Plate, salad, 7" d., black or green . . 5.00
Plate, salad, 7" d., blue 5.50
Plate, salad, 7" d., pink 2.50
Plate, luncheon, 8" d., black or
 blue 9.50
Plate, luncheon, 8" d., green 3.50
Plate, luncheon, 8" d., pink 4.00
Plate, 14" d., green 30.00
Punch bowl w/stand, green,
 2 pcs. 275.00
Sherbet, black 8.00
Sherbet, blue 9.00
Sherbet, green 5.00
Sherbet, pink 4.50
Sugar bowl, open, black 10.00
Sugar bowl, open, blue 8.00
Sugar bowl, open, green 7.00
Sugar bowl, open, pink 5.50
Tumbler, whiskey, green, 1½ oz. 6.50
Tumbler, footed, pink, 6 oz. 6.00

DIANA (Press-mold)

Diana Demitasse Cup & Saucer

Bowl, cereal, 5" d., amber or pink . . 3.50
Bowl, cereal, 5" d., clear 3.00
Bowl, cream soup, 5½" d., amber . . 6.50
Bowl, cream soup, 5½" d., clear . . . 4.50

Bowl, cream soup, 5½" d., pink	....	3.00
Bowl, salad, 9" d., amber	....	7.50
Bowl, salad, 9" h., clear	....	5.50
Bowl, salad, 9" h., pink	....	8.50
Bowl, 12" d., scalloped rim, amber	....	8.50
Bowl, 12" d., scalloped rim, clear	...	6.00
Bowl, 12" d., scalloped rim, pink	...	9.50
Candy jar, cov., round, amber	......	26.00
Candy jar, cov., round, clear	....	10.50
Candy jar, cov., round, pink	....	21.00
Coaster-ash tray, amber, 3½" d.	....	6.50
Coaster-ash tray, clear, 3½" d.	......	5.50
Coaster-ash tray, pink, 3½" d.	.....	4.50
Console bowl, amber, 11" d.	....	9.00
Console bowl, clear, 11" d.	....	4.50
Console bowl, pink, 11" d.	....	7.00
Creamer, oval, amber	....	6.50
Creamer, oval, clear	....	3.50
Creamer, oval, pink	....	5.50
Cup & saucer, demitasse, amber	....	7.50
Cup & saucer, demitasse, clear (ILLUS.)	....	5.00
Cup & saucer, demitasse, pink	.....	15.00
Cup & saucer, amber	....	8.00
Cup & saucer, clear	....	5.50
Cup & saucer, pink	....	7.00
Plate, bread & butter, 6" d., amber	.	2.50
Plate, bread & butter, 6" d., clear or pink	....	1.50
Plate, dinner, 9½" d., amber	....	6.50
Plate, dinner, 9½" d., clear	....	4.00
Plate, dinner, 9½" d., pink	....	6.00
Plate, 11¾" d., amber or pink	.....	6.00
Plate, 11¾" d., clear	....	5.00
Platter, 12" oval, amber	....	9.00
Platter, 12" oval, clear	....	7.50
Platter, 12" oval, pink	....	5.50
Salt & pepper shakers, amber, pr.	..	68.00
Salt & pepper shakers, clear, pr.	...	23.50
Salt & pepper shakers, pink, pr.	....	32.50
Sherbet, amber	....	7.00
Sherbet, pink	....	9.50
Sugar bowl, open, oval, amber	.....	4.00
Sugar bowl, open, oval, clear	......	3.50
Sugar bowl, open, oval, pink	....	4.50
Tumbler, amber or pink, 4 1/8" h., 9 oz.	....	22.00
Tumbler, clear, 4 1/8" h., 9 oz.	.....	14.00
Water set: pitcher & 6 tumblers; green, 7 pcs.	....	125.00

DOGWOOD or Apple Blossom or Wild Rose (Process-etched)

Bowl, cereal or dessert, 5½" d., clear	....	6.00
Bowl, cereal or dessert, 5½" d., Cremax	....	7.50
Bowl, cereal or dessert, 5½" d., green	....	15.00
Bowl, cereal or dessert, 5½" d., pink	....	14.50
Bowl, nappy, 8½" d., Cremax	......	27.50

Bowl, nappy, 8½" d., green	....	56.00
Bowl, nappy, 8½" d., pink	....	32.00
Bowl, fruit, 10¼" d., Cremax	.....	60.00
Bowl, fruit, 10¼" d., green	....	100.00
Bowl, fruit, 10¼" d., pink	....	197.50
Cake plate, green, 13" d.	....	65.00
Cake plate, pink, 13" d.	....	63.00
Creamer, thin, green, 2¾" h.	......	36.00
Creamer, thin, pink, 2¾" h.	......	10.00
Creamer, thick, pink, 3¼" h.	......	12.00
Cup & saucer, Cremax	....	32.00

Dogwood Cup & Saucer

Cup & saucer, green (ILLUS.)	....	16.50
Cup & saucer, pink	....	11.00
Dinner service for 6, pink, 46 pcs.	..	450.00
Pitcher, 8" h., jug-type, green	......	39.50
Pitcher, 8" h., jug-type, pink	.......30.00 to	45.00
Pitcher, 8" h., jug-type, hand-decorated, clear	....	170.00
Pitcher, 8" h., jug-type, hand-decorated, green	....	430.00
Pitcher, 8" h., jug-type, hand-decorated, pink	....	115.00
Plate, bread & butter, 6" d., green	..	3.50
Plate, bread & butter, 6" d., pink	...	4.50
Plate, luncheon, 8" d., clear	....	3.00
Plate, luncheon, 8" d., green	......	4.50
Plate, luncheon, 8" d., pink	....	4.00
Plate, dinner, 9¼" d., pink	....	16.50
Plate, grill, 10½" d., overall patt., green	....	18.00
Plate, grill, 10½" d., overall patt., pink	....	12.50
Plate, grill, 10½" d., border patt., green	....	10.00
Plate, grill, 10½" d., border patt., pink	....	11.50
Plate, salver, 12" d., Monax or pink	....	19.00
Platter, 12" oval, pink	....	290.00
Sherbet, low foot, pink	....	16.00
Sugar bowl, open, thin, green, 2½" h.	....	27.00
Sugar bowl, open, thin, pink, 2½" h.	....	9.50
Sugar bowl, open, thick, green, 3¼" h.	....	30.00
Sugar bowl, open, thick, pink, 3¼" h.	....	9.50

Tid bit server, 2-tier, pink	45.00	Candy dish, 3-section, green, 6"	6.50
Tumbler, plain, pink, 3½" h., 5 oz.	3.50	Candy jar, cov., green or pink, 8" h.	27.00
Tumbler, decorated, green, 4" h., 10 oz.	60.00	Coaster, green, 3" d.	16.00
Tumbler, decorated, pink, 4" h., 10 oz.	22.00	Coaster, pink, 3" d.	9.00
Tumbler, plain, green, 4" h., 10 oz.	4.00	Creamer, green	10.00
Tumbler, plain, pink, 4" h., 10 oz.	5.00	Creamer, pink	8.00
Tumbler, decorated, green, 4¾" h., 11 oz.	59.50	Creamer & open sugar bowl, green, pr.	14.00
Tumbler, decorated, pink, 4¾" h., 11 oz.	30.00	Creamer & open sugar bowl, pink, pr.	18.00
Tumbler, plain, green, 4¾" h., 11 oz.	10.00	Cup & saucer, green	9.50
Tumbler, plain, pink, 4¾" h., 11 oz.	5.00	Cup & saucer, pink	8.00
Tumbler, decorated, pink, 5" h., 12 oz.	31.00	Pitcher, 5" or 6" h., 36 oz., jug-type, green	29.00
Tumbler, plain, pink, 5" h., 12 oz.	8.50	Pitcher, 5" or 6" h., 36 oz., jug-type, pink	28.00
Water set: 80 oz. pitcher & 4 tumblers; pink, 5 pcs.	275.00	Pitcher, 7" h., 47 oz., pink	200.00
Water set: decorated pitcher & 6 decorated tumblers; pink, 7 pcs.	275.00	Plate, sherbet, 6" d., green	3.50
Water set: plain pitcher & 6 plain tumblers; green, 7 pcs.	80.00	Plate, sherbet, 6" d., pink	2.50
		Plate, salad, 7" d., green	11.50
		Plate, salad, 7" d., pink 9.50 to	12.00
		Plate, dinner, 9" d., green	10.00
		Plate, dinner, 9" d., pink	7.50
		Plate, grill, 9" d., green	10.00
		Plate, grill, 9" d., pink	8.50
		Platter, 12" oval, green or pink	13.50
		Relish, clear or green, 4 x 4"	7.00
		Relish, pink, 4 x 4"	6.00
		Relish, green, 4 x 8"	10.50
		Relish, pink, 4 x 8"	7.50

DORIC (Press-mold)

Doric Butter Dish

Doric Relish

Bowl, nappy, 4½" d., Delfite	6.00
Bowl, nappy, 4½" d., green or pink	5.00
Bowl, cereal, 5½" d., green	24.50
Bowl, cereal, 5½" d., pink	22.00
Bowl, nappy, 8¼" d., clear or pink	10.00
Bowl, nappy, 8¼" d., green	12.50
Bowl, 9" d., handled, green or pink	11.00
Bowl, 9" oval vegetable, green or pink	12.00
Butter dish, cov., green	72.00
Butter dish, cov., pink (ILLUS.)	65.00
Cake plate, green or pink, 10" d.	12.50
Candy dish, 3-section, Delfite or pink, 6"	4.50

Relish, green or pink, 8 x 8" (ILLUS.)	13.00
Relish, square inserts in metal holder, green	37.00
Relish, square inserts in metal holder, pink	45.00
Relish, 4-part, handled, green	36.00
Relish, 4-part, handled, pink 35.00 to	40.00
Salt & pepper shakers, clear, pr.	22.00
Salt & pepper shakers, green, pr.	29.50
Salt & pepper shakers, pink, pr.	26.00
Sandwich tray, handled, green, 10" d.	11.50

Sandwich tray, handled, pink,
  10" d. 10.50
Sherbet, Delfite 5.00
Sherbet, green 9.00
Sherbet, pink 7.50
Sugar bowl, cov, green or pink 26.50
Tumbler, green, 4½" h., 9 oz. 51.00
Tumbler, pink, 4½" h., 9 oz. 28.50
Tumbler, footed, green, 4" h.,
  10 oz. 49.00
Tumbler, footed, pink, 4" h.,
  10 oz. 25.00
Tumbler, footed, green, 5" h.,
  13 oz. 51.50
Tumbler, footed, pink, 5" h.,
  13 oz. 35.50

DORIC & PANSY (Press-mold)

Doric & Pansy Cup & Saucer

Bowl, 4½" d., clear, green or
  pink 6.50
Bowl, 4½" d., ultramarine 10.00
Bowl, 8" d., clear 16.00
Bowl, 8" d., pink 17.50
Bowl, 8" d., ultramarine 60.00
Bowl, 9" d., handled, clear 16.50
Bowl, 9" d., handled, ultramarine . . . 21.00
Butter dish, cov., ultramarine 565.00
Creamer, ultramarine 177.50
Cup & saucer, clear 9.50
Cup & saucer, ultramarine (ILLUS.) . . 17.50
Plate, sherbet, 6" d., green or
  ultramarine 8.00
Plate, sherbet, 6" d., pink 6.00
Plate, salad, 7" d., ultramarine 27.50
Plate, dinner, 9" d., green or
  ultramarine 19.00
Salt & pepper shakers, ultramarine,
  pr. 340.00
Sugar bowl, open, pink 50.00
Sugar bowl, open, ultramarine 150.00
Tray, handled, clear, 10" 16.00
Tray, handled, green, 10" 9.00
Tray, handled, ultramarine, 10" 21.00
Tumbler, ultramarine, 4½" h.,
  9 oz. 34.00

PRETTY POLLY PARTY DISHES

Creamer, pink 25.50
Creamer, ultramarine 30.00
Creamer & sugar bowl, pink, pr. . . . 40.00

Creamer & sugar bowl, ultramarine,
  pr. . . . . 55.00 to 70.00
Cup, pink 20.50
Cup, ultramarine 29.00
Cup & saucer, pink 21.50
Cup & saucer, ultramarine 33.00
Plate, pink 5.00
Plate, ultramarine 7.00
Saucer, pink or ultramarine 5.00
Sugar bowl, pink 22.00
Sugar bowl, ultramarine 28.50
14 piece set, pink 167.50
14 piece set, ultramarine 210.00

ENGLISH HOBNAIL (Handmade - not true Depression)

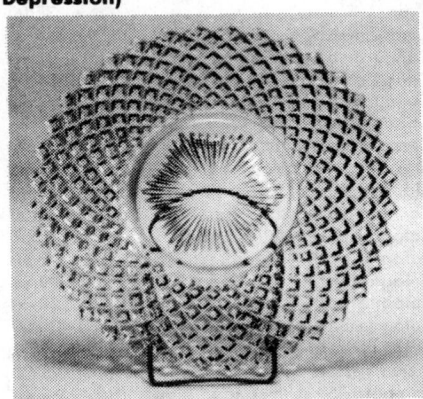

English Hobnail Luncheon Plate

Ash tray, clear, 4½" d. 20.00
Ash tray, pink, 4½" d. 26.00
Bowl, nappy, 4½" d., amber 7.75
Bowl, nappy, 4½" d., clear 4.50
Bowl, nappy, 4½" d., green 7.00
Bowl, nappy, 4½" d., pink 11.50
Bowl, nappy, 4½" sq., pink 14.00
Bowl, cream soup, 4¾" d., clear . . . 6.00
Bowl, cream soup, 4¾" d., pink 11.00
Bowl, mayonnaise, 6" d., clear 6.50
Bowl, mayonnaise, 6" d., green 9.50
Bowl, nappy, 6½" d., clear 6.50
Bowl, nappy, 6½" d., green 9.00
Bowl, nappy, 6½" d., pink 8.00
Bowl, 6¾" d., turquoise 22.50
Bowl, fruit, 8" d., 2-handled, footed,
  amber 35.00
Bowl, fruit, 8" d., 2-handled, footed,
  clear 17.50
Bowl, fruit, 8" d., 2-handled, footed,
  green 25.50
Bowl, fruit, 8" d., 2-handled, footed,
  pink 28.00
Bowl, fruit, 8" d., 2-handled, footed,
  turquoise 34.00
Bowl, nappy, 8" d., green 26.00
Bowl, 12" d., canted (bell) sides,
  clear 35.00

Bowl, 12" d., canted (bell) sides, turquoise	77.00
Bowl, 12" d., flared, blue	50.00
Bowl, 12" d., flared, clear	14.50
Bowl, 12" d., flared, green	23.00
Bowl, 12" d., flared, turquoise	30.00
Candlesticks, amber, 3½" h., pr.	19.00
Candlesticks, clear, 3½" h., pr.	22.50
Candlesticks, green, 3½" h., pr.	28.00
Candlesticks, turquoise, 3½" h., pr.	67.50
Candlesticks, amber or green, 8½" h., pr.	75.00
Candlesticks, clear, 8½" h., pr.	30.00
Candlesticks, pink, 8½" h., pr.	40.00
Candlesticks, turquoise, 8½" h., pr.	38.00
Candy dish, cov., amber	35.00
Candy dish, cov., clear	27.50
Candy dish, cov., cobalt blue	275.00
Candy dish, cov., green or pink	45.00
Celery tray, clear, 12" l.	7.50
Celery tray, clear, 12" l.	7.50
Cigarette jar, cov., clear	13.50
Cigarette jar, cov., pink	22.00
Coaster, clear, 5½" d.	4.00
Cologne bottle, blue	30.00
Cologne bottle, clear	22.50
Cologne bottle, green	29.50
Cologne bottle, pink	27.00
Cologne bottle, turquoise	31.00
Cologne bottles w/stoppers, turquoise, pr.	125.00
Compote, 5" d., rounded sides, clear	12.00
Creamer, clear	7.00
Creamer, pink	17.00
Creamer, turquoise	33.75
Creamer & open sugar bowl, amber, pr.	20.00
Cruet, oil, clear, 2 oz.	45.00
Cruet, oil, clear, 6 oz.	21.00
Cruet, oil, pink, 6 oz.	25.00
Cup & saucer, clear	8.50
Cup & saucer, green	35.00
Cup & saucer, pink	40.00
Dish, cov., 3-footed, blue	14.00
Dish, cov., 3-footed, clear	35.00
Dish, cov., 3-footed, green	43.00
Dish, cov., 3-footed, pink	47.50
Egg cup, clear	15.00
Finger bowl, clear, 4½" d.	4.50
Finger bowl, pink, 4½" d.	9.00
Flip jar, cov., amber	225.00
Goblet, cordial, clear, 1 oz.	7.50
Goblet, wine, clear, 2 oz.	8.50
Goblet, cocktail, clear, 3 oz.	6.50
Goblet, claret, clear, 5 oz.	6.50
Goblet, claret, green, 5 oz.	20.00
Goblet, claret, pink, 5 oz.	12.50
Goblet, clear, 6¼" h., 8 oz.	7.50
Goblet, green, 6¼" h., 8 oz.	22.50
Goblet, pink, 6¼" h., 8 oz.	19.50
Goblet, topaz, 6¼" h., 8 oz.	12.00
Goblet, turquoise, 6¼" h., 8 oz.	44.00
Ivy ball, clear	10.00
Lamp, clear, 6¼" h.	35.00
Lamp, green, 6¼" h.	70.00
Lamp, pink, 6¼" h.	58.00
Lamp, amber, 9¼" h.	105.00
Lamp, clear, 9¼" h.	24.50
Lamp, green, 9¼" h.	74.00
Lamp, pink, 9¼" h.	103.00
Lamp, turquoise, 9¼" h.	120.00
Marmalade jar, cov., clear	15.00
Marmalade jar, cov., pink	21.00
Nut cup, individual size, footed, amber	4.00
Nut cup, individual size, footed, blue	11.50
Nut cup, individual size, footed, clear	6.50
Nut cup, individual size, footed, green	9.50
Nut cup, individual size, footed, pink	12.00
Nut cup, individual size, footed, turquoise	25.00
Pitcher, 38 oz., clear	38.00
Pitcher, 38 oz., pink	250.00
Pitcher, ½ gal., straight sides, amber	125.00
Plate, sherbet, 6" d., clear or pink	3.00
Plate, sherbet, 6" d., green	4.00
Plate, luncheon, 8" d., clear (ILLUS.)	4.50
Plate, luncheon, 8" d., green or pink	7.00
Plate, luncheon, 8" d., turquoise	15.00
Plate, luncheon, 8" sq., clear	5.00
Plate, luncheon, 8" sq., green	8.00
Plate, luncheon, 8" sq., turquoise	16.00
Plate, dinner, 10" d., clear	7.50
Plate, dinner, 10" d., green	16.50
Plate, dinner, 10" d., pink	18.50
Plate, 10" d., clear	17.50
Puff box, cov., blue	38.00
Puff box, cov., clear	35.00
Puff box, cov., green	27.50
Puff box, cov., pink	28.00
Puff box, cov., turquoise	44.50
Relish, 3-part, clear, 8" d.	18.00
Relish, 5-part, clear, 10" d.	29.50
Rose bowl, clear, 4"	15.00
Salt & pepper shakers, amber, green or pink, pr.	55.00
Salt & pepper shakers, clear, pr.	21.00
Salt & pepper shakers, turquoise, pr.	116.00
Sherbet, low foot, clear	5.00
Sherbet, high foot, clear	6.00
Sugar bowl, open, clear	5.00
Sugar bowl, open, footed, clear	7.00
Sugar bowl, open, footed, pink	12.50
Sugar bowl, open, footed, turquoise	25.00
Tid bit server, 2-tier, clear	18.50
Tumbler, whiskey, clear, 3 oz.	5.50

Tumbler, clear, 3¾" h., 5 oz. 5.50
Tumbler, footed, clear, 7 oz. 6.00
Tumbler, amber, 3¾" h., 8 oz. 6.00
Tumbler, clear, green or pink,
  3¾" h., 8 oz. 8.00
Tumbler, footed, clear, 9 oz. 7.50
Tumbler, footed, green, 9 oz. 15.00
Tumbler, clear, 4" h., 10 oz. 6.00
Tumbler, clear, 5" h., 12 oz. 8.00
Tumbler, pink, 5" h., 12 oz. 12.00
Tumbler, footed, clear, 12½ oz. 9.00
Vase, 5¾" h., clear 20.00
Vase, 7¼" h., green 29.50

FLORAL or Poinsettia (Process-etched)

Floral Pitcher & Tumblers

Bowl, berry, 4" d., green 11.00
Bowl, berry, 4" d., pink............ 9.50
Bowl, nappy, 7½" d., green........ 12.50
Bowl, nappy, 7½" d., pink......... 13.00
Bowl, cov. vegetable, 8" d., green .. 28.50
Bowl, cov. vegetable, 8" d., pink ... 22.50
Bowl, 9" oval vegetable, green 13.00
Bowl, 9" oval vegetable, pink 10.50
Butter dish, cov., green............ 69.00
Butter dish, cov., pink 61.00
Candlesticks, green, pr............. 58.00
Candlesticks, pink, pr............. 49.00
Candy jar, cov., green 27.00
Candy jar, cov., pink 24.50
Coaster, green, 3¼" d. 6.75
Coaster, pink, 3¼" d. 6.00
Creamer, green 9.50
Creamer, pink 8.50
Cup & saucer, green 13.50
Cup & saucer, pink 12.00
Ice tub, oval, pink, 3½" h. 500.00
Pitcher, 5½" h., 24 oz., green 375.00
Pitcher, 8" h., 32 oz., cone-shaped,
  green (ILLUS.).................. 23.50
Pitcher, 8" h., 32 oz., cone-shaped,
  pink 21.00
Pitcher, lemonade, 10¼" h., 48 oz.,
  jug-type, green 212.00
Pitcher, lemonade, 10¼" h., 48 oz.,
  jug-type, pink................. 171.00
Plate, sherbet, 6" d., green 3.50

Plate, sherbet, 6" d., pink 3.00
Plate, salad, 8" d., green 7.00
Plate, salad, 8" d., pink 6.50
Plate, dinner, 9" d., green 12.75
Plate, dinner, 9" d., pink 10.50
Platter, 10¾" oval, green 11.00
Platter, 10¾" oval, pink 9.50
Powder jar, cov., green........... 210.00
Refrigerator dish, cov., green 42.00
Refrigerator dish, cov., Jadite 19.00
Refrigerator dish, cov., pink........ 8.50
Relish, 2-part, green............... 11.00
Relish, 2-part, pink 9.00
Salt & pepper shakers, footed,
  green, 4" h., pr. 32.50
Salt & pepper shakers, footed, pink,
  4" h., pr....................... 29.50
Salt & pepper shakers, green, 6" h.,
  pr............................. 32.00
Salt & pepper shakers, pink, 6" h.,
  pr............................. 29.00
Sherbet, green.................... 10.00
Sherbet, pink 9.00
Sugar bowl, cov., green 20.00
Sugar bowl, cov., pink............ 16.00
Sugar bowl, open, green.......... 8.00
Sugar bowl, open, pink 6.75
Tray, handled, green, 6" sq. 13.00
Tray, handled, pink, 6" sq......... 16.00
Tumbler, footed, green, 4" h.,
  5 oz........................... 13.50
Tumbler, footed, pink, 4" h., 5 oz. ... 12.00
Tumbler, green, 4½" h., 9 oz....... 157.50
Tumbler, footed, green, 4¾" h.,
  7 oz. (ILLUS.) 12.50
Tumbler, footed, pink, 4¾" h.,
  7 oz.......................... 10.00
Tumbler, footed, green, 5¼" h.,
  9 oz.......................... 28.50
Tumbler, footed, pink, 5¼" h.,
  9 oz.......................... 25.00
Vase, 6 7/8" h., octagonal, green .. 425.00
Water set: cone-shaped pitcher & 6
  footed tumblers; pink, 7 pcs...... 80.00

(OLD) FLORENTINE or Poppy No. 1 (Process-etched)

Florentine Butter Dish

Bowl, berry, 5" d., clear 5.25
Bowl, berry, 5" d., cobalt blue 16.50
Bowl, berry, 5" d., green 9.00

Bowl, berry, 5" d., pink 10.00
Bowl, berry, 5" d., yellow 9.50
Bowl, nappy, 6" d., green 29.00
Bowl, nappy, 6" d., pink 14.00
Bowl, 8½" d., green 24.00
Bowl, 8½" d., pink 26.00
Bowl, 8½" d., yellow 21.50
Bowl, cov. vegetable, 9½" oval,
    green 33.50
Bowl, cov. vegetable, 9½" oval,
    pink 44.50
Bowl, 9½" oval vegetable, green . . . 16.50
Bowl, 9½" oval vegetable, pink 18.00
Bowl, 9½" oval vegetable, yellow . . 19.00
Butter dish, cov., clear 115.00
Butter dish, cov., green (ILLUS.) 110.00
Butter dish, cov., pink 135.00
Butter dish, cov., yellow 107.00
Candy dish, cov., clear 75.00
Coaster-ash tray, green 20.00
Coaster-ash tray, pink 31.50
Coaster-ash tray, yellow 34.50
Creamer, plain rim, clear 6.50
Creamer, plain rim, green 8.00
Creamer, ruffled rim, clear 13.75
Creamer, ruffled rim, cobalt blue . . . 44.00
Creamer & cov. sugar bowl, pink,
    pr. 37.00
Creamer & cov. sugar bowl, yellow,
    pr. 25.50
Cup & saucer, clear 6.00
Cup & saucer, green or yellow 8.50
Cup & saucer, pink 9.00
Pitcher, 6½" h., 36 oz., jug-type,
    clear or green 30.00
Pitcher, 6½" h., 36 oz., jug-type,
    pink 38.00
Pitcher, 6½" h., 36 oz., jug-type,
    yellow 40.00
Pitcher, 7½" h., 54 oz., clear 41.00
Pitcher, 7½" h., 54 oz., green 68.00
Pitcher, 7½" h., 54 oz., pink 98.00
Pitcher, 7½" h., 54 oz., yellow 125.00
Plate, sherbet, 6" d., clear 2.50
Plate, sherbet, 6" d., green 4.50
Plate, sherbet, 6" d., pink 3.75
Plate, sherbet, 6" d., yellow 3.00
Plate, luncheon, 8" d., clear 4.00
Plate, luncheon, 8" d., green 5.50
Plate, luncheon, 8" d., pink 7.50
Plate, luncheon, 8" d., yellow 6.50
Plate, dinner, 9¾" d., clear 6.00
Plate, dinner, 9¾" d., green 10.50
Plate, dinner, 9¾" d., pink 12.50
Plate, dinner, 9¾" d., yellow 11.00
Plate, grill, 9¾" d., clear 6.50
Plate, grill, 9¾" d., green 7.50
Plate, grill, 9¾" d., pink 10.00
Plate, grill, 9¾" d., yellow 9.50
Platter, 11½" oval, clear 9.00
Platter, 11½" oval, green 12.50
Platter, 11½" oval, pink or yellow . . 12.00
Salt & pepper shakers, clear, pr. 25.00
Salt & pepper shakers, green, pr. . . . 28.00

Salt & pepper shakers, pink, pr. 45.00
Salt & pepper shakers, yellow, pr. . . 41.50
Sherbet, clear 4.50
Sherbet, green or yellow 7.50
Sherbet, pink 7.00
Sugar bowl, cov., clear 18.00
Sugar bowl, cov., green 25.00
Sugar bowl, open, clear 6.00
Sugar bowl, open, cobalt blue 35.50
Sugar bowl, open, green 6.50
Sugar bowl, open, pink 9.50
Sugar bowl, open, yellow 8.00
Tumbler, juice, footed, clear,
    3¼" h., 5 oz. 7.00
Tumbler, juice, footed, green,
    3¼" h., 5 oz. 14.50
Tumbler, juice, footed, pink,
    3¼" h., 5 oz. 10.50
Tumbler, juice, footed, yellow,
    3¼" h., 5 oz. 14.00
Tumbler, water, footed, clear, 4" h.,
    9 oz. 6.75
Tumbler, water, footed, green,
    4" h., 9 oz. 8.00
Tumbler, water, footed, pink, 4" h.,
    9 oz. 18.00
Tumbler, water, footed, yellow,
    4" h., 9 oz. 12.50
Tumbler, iced tea, footed, clear,
    5" h., 12 oz. 8.50
Tumbler, iced tea, footed, green,
    5" h., 12 oz. 13.50
Tumbler, iced tea, footed, pink,
    5" h., 12 oz. 20.50
Tumbler, iced tea, footed, yellow,
    5" h., 12 oz. 17.00

FLORENTINE or Poppy No. 2 (Process-etched)

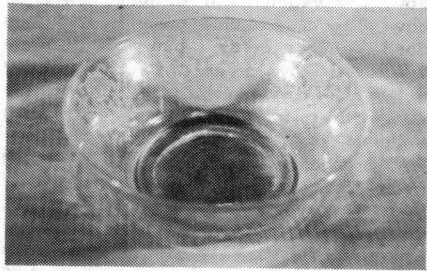

Florentine Cereal Bowl

Ash tray, clear, 2½" d. 8.00
Ash tray, green, 2½" d. 13.50
Ash tray, yellow, 2½" d. 22.50
Bowl, berry, 4½" d., clear or
    green 8.50
Bowl, berry, 4½" d., pink 6.00
Bowl, berry, 4½" d., yellow 12.50
Bowl, cream soup w/plain rim,
    4¾" d., clear 6.00
Bowl, cream soup w/plain rim,
    4¾" d., green 8.50

Bowl, cream soup w/plain rim,
   4¾" d., pink.................. 8.00
Bowl, cream soup w/plain rim,
   4¾" d., yellow.............. 13.00
Bowl, 5½" d., yellow 31.00
Bowl, cereal, 6" d., clear or pink ... 10.00
Bowl, cereal, 6" d., green.......... 15.50
Bowl, cereal, 6" d., yellow
   (ILLUS.)...................... 27.00
Bowl, nappy, 8" d., green.......... 15.50
Bowl, nappy, 8" d., pink 16.50
Bowl, nappy, 8" d., yellow 21.00
Bowl, cov. vegetable, 9" oval,
   clear...................... 29.00
Bowl, cov. vegetable, 9" oval,
   green 33.00
Bowl, cov. vegetable, 9" oval,
   yellow 43.00
Bowl, 9" oval vegetable, clear...... 16.00
Bowl, 9" oval vegetable, green or
   yellow 21.00
Butter dish, cov., green........... 95.00
Butter dish, cov., pink 45.00
Butter dish, cov., yellow 110.00
Candlesticks, green, 3" h., pr....... 51.50
Candlesticks, yellow, 3" h., pr...... 47.50
Candy dish, cov., clear 61.00
Candy dish, cov., green........... 91.00
Candy dish, cov., pink 87.50
Candy dish, cov., yellow 124.00
Celery, oval, clear 22.00
Coaster, green, 3¼" d............. 10.00
Coaster, yellow, 3¼" d. 14.00
Coaster-ash tray, clear, 3¾" d..... 11.00
Coaster-ash tray, green, 3¾" d. 14.00
Coaster-ash tray, yellow, 3¾" d. ... 18.50
Coaster-ash tray, green, 5½" d. 18.50
Coaster-ash tray, yellow, 5½" d. ... 23.00
Compote, 3½" d., blue 45.00
Compote, 3½" d., clear........... 9.00
Compote, 3½" d., green 22.50
Compote, 3½" d., pink 10.00
Condiment set: creamer, sugar
   bowl, salt & pepper shakers &
   8½" d. tray; yellow, 5 pcs........ 115.00
Creamer, clear.................. 5.00
Creamer, green................. 6.75
Creamer, pink.................. 3.00
Creamer, yellow 8.50
Cup & saucer, clear............. 6.50
Cup & saucer, green or pink 9.00
Cup & saucer, yellow 9.50
Custard cup, clear.............. 30.50
Custard cup, green 75.00
Custard cup, yellow 59.00
Gravy boat, yellow 36.50
Gravy boat w/platter, pink,
   11½" oval 75.00
Gravy boat w/platter, yellow,
   11½" oval 67.00
Nut dish, handled, ruffled rim,
   blue 32.50
Nut dish, handled, ruffled rim,
   clear...................... 16.50

Nut dish, handled, ruffled rim,
   green 49.50
Nut dish, handled, ruffled rim,
   pink 8.00
Nut dish, handled, ruffled rim,
   yellow 19.00
Pitcher, 6" h., 24 oz., cone-shaped,
   yellow 97.50
Pitcher, 7¼" h., 30 oz., cone-
   shaped, clear 17.00
Pitcher, 7¼" h., 30 oz., cone-
   shaped, green 24.00
Pitcher, 7¼" h., 30 oz., cone-
   shaped, yellow............. 18.50
Pitcher, 7½" h., 36 oz., footed,
   cone-shaped, clear 17.50
Pitcher, 7½" h., 36 oz., footed,
   cone-shaped, green 29.00
Pitcher, 7½" h., 36 oz., footed,
   cone-shaped, yellow......... 21.00
Pitcher, 7½" h., 54 oz., straight
   sides, clear 41.00
Pitcher, 7½" h., 54 oz., straight
   sides, green 55.00
Pitcher, 7½" h., 54 oz., straight
   sides, pink 96.00
Pitcher, 7½" h., 54 oz., straight
   sides, yellow 120.00
Pitcher, 8" h., 76 oz., jug-type,
   clear...................... 50.00
Pitcher, 8" h., 76 oz., jug-type,
   green 63.00
Pitcher, 8" h., 76 oz., jug-type,
   pink 225.00
Pitcher, 80 oz., bulbous, pink...... 185.00
Plate, sherbet, 6" d., clear 2.00
Plate, sherbet, 6" d., green 2.50
Plate, sherbet, 6" d., pink 4.00
Plate, sherbet, 6" d., yellow 3.00
Plate, 6¼" d., w/indentation,
   clear...................... 7.00
Plate, 6¼" d., w/indentation,
   green 3.00
Plate, 6¼" d., w/indentation,
   pink 4.00
Plate, 6¼" d., w/indentation,
   yellow 20.50
Plate, luncheon, 8½" d., clear...... 4.25
Plate, luncheon, 8½" d., green or
   yellow 5.50
Plate, dinner, 10" d., clear 6.50
Plate, dinner, 10" d., green 9.00
Plate, dinner, 10" d., yellow 10.00
Plate, grill, 10½" d., clear 6.25
Plate, grill, 10½" d., green 8.50
Plate, grill, 10½" d., yellow........ 9.00
Platter, 11" oval, clear............ 8.00
Platter, 11" oval, green or yellow... 12.00
Relish, clear, 10"................ 10.00
Relish, green, 10" 16.50
Relish, yellow, 10" 18.00
Relish, 3-part, clear 12.00
Relish, 3-part, green 14.00
Relish, 3-part, pink 15.50

Relish, 3-part, yellow 18.00
Salt & pepper shakers, clear, pr. . . . 24.00
Salt & pepper shakers, green, pr. . . . 32.00
Salt & pepper shakers, yellow, pr. . . 36.50
Sherbet, clear. 5.00
Sherbet, green or pink 5.75
Sherbet, yellow 8.00
Sugar bowl, cov., green 18.00
Sugar bowl, cov., yellow 22.00
Sugar bowl, open, clear 5.25
Sugar bowl, open, green 5.50
Sugar bowl, open, yellow 6.75
Tray, yellow, 8½" d. 65.50
Tumbler, clear, 3½" h., 5 oz. 5.50
Tumbler, green, 3½" h., 5 oz. 9.50
Tumbler, pink, 3½" h., 5 oz. 8.00
Tumbler, yellow, 3½" h., 5 oz. 14.00
Tumbler, footed, clear, 3½" h.,
 5 oz. 6.00
Tumbler, footed, green or pink,
 3½" h., 5 oz. 8.75
Tumbler, footed, yellow, 3½" h.,
 5 oz. 9.50
Tumbler, blue, 4" h., 9 oz. 52.00
Tumbler, clear, 4" h., 9 oz. 7.50
Tumbler, green, 4" h., 9 oz. 9.00
Tumbler, pink, 4" h., 9 oz. 9.50
Tumbler, yellow, 4" h., 9 oz. 13.00
Tumbler, footed, clear, 4½" h.,
 9 oz. 8.00
Tumbler, footed, green, 4½" h.,
 9 oz. 14.50
Tumbler, footed, pink, 4½" h.,
 9 oz. 9.25
Tumbler, footed, yellow, 4½" h.,
 9 oz. 15.00
Tumbler, iced tea, clear, 5" h.,
 12 oz. 16.50
Tumbler, iced tea, green, 5" h.,
 12 oz. 28.50
Tumbler, iced tea, pink, 5" h.,
 12 oz. 24.50
Tumbler, iced tea, yellow, 5" h.,
 12 oz. 33.00
Tumbler, footed, clear, 5" h.,
 12 oz. 13.50
Tumbler, footed, green, 5" h.,
 12 oz. 16.50
Tumbler, footed, yellow, 5" h.,
 12 oz. 22.00
Vase (or parfait), 6" h., clear 16.50
Vase (or parfait), 6" h., green 42.00
Vase (or parfait), 6" h., yellow 49.00

GEORGIAN or Lovebirds (Process-etched)

(All items in green only.)

Bowl, berry, 4½" d. 5.00
Bowl, cereal, 5¾" d. 13.00
Bowl, 6½" d. 42.50
Bowl, berry, 7½" d. 40.00
Bowl, 9" oval vegetable 43.50
Butter dish, cov. 62.50

Creamer & cov. sugar bowl, 3" h.,
 pr. 35.00
Creamer & cov. sugar bowl, 4" h.,
 pr. 23.50
Creamer & open sugar bowl, 3" h.,
 pr. 14.00
Creamer & open sugar bowl, 4" h.,
 pr. 15.50
Cup & saucer 9.50
Hot plate, center design, 5" d. 34.50
Plate, sherbet, 6" d. 2.75
Plate, luncheon, 8" d. 5.75
Plate, dinner, 9¼" d. 16.00
Plate, 9¼" d., center design only . . . 15.00
Platter, 11" oval 44.50
Sherbet 8.25
Tumbler, 4" h., 9 oz. 36.50
Tumbler, iced tea, 5¼" h., 12 oz. . . . 65.00

HOBNAIL (Press-mold)

Bowl, nappy, 5½" d., clear 4.75
Creamer & sugar bowl, clear, pr. . . . 5.00
Cup & saucer, clear 3.75
Cup & saucer, pink 5.00
Decanter w/stopper, clear, 32 oz. . . 13.00
Goblet, clear, 10 oz. 5.00
Pitcher, milk, 18 oz., clear 12.00
Pitcher, 8" h., 55 oz., clear 16.00
Pitcher, 67 oz., jug-type, clear 16.00
Plate, sherbet, 6" d., clear 1.00
Plate, sherbet, 6" d., pink 1.75
Plate, luncheon, 8½" d., clear 2.50
Plate, luncheon, 8½" d., pink 3.50
Sherbet, clear 2.50
Sherbet, pink 3.50
Tumbler, whiskey, clear, 1½ oz. 3.50
Tumbler, wine, footed, clear,
 3 oz. 4.50
Tumbler, clear, 5 oz. 3.50
Tumbler, footed, clear, 5 oz. 4.00
Tumbler, clear, 9 oz. 4.00
Tumbler, pink, 9 oz. 5.00
Tumbler, clear, 10 oz. 5.50
Tumbler, clear, 15 oz. 5.50

HOLIDAY (Press-mold)

Holiday Berry Bowl

(All items in pink only. Later iridescent pieces not included.)

Bowl, berry, 5 1/8" d. (ILLUS.) 6.50
Bowl, cereal or flat soup, 7¾" d. . . . 27.50
Bowl, fruit, 8½" d. 13.50
Bowl, 9½" oval vegetable 11.00
Butter dish, cov. 33.50
Cake plate, footed, 10½" d. 57.00
Candlesticks, 3" h., pr. 53.00
Console bowl, 10" d. 58.00
Creamer 5.50
Cup & saucer, plain base 7.00
Cup & saucer, rayed base 7.50
Pitcher, milk, 4½" h., 16 oz. 43.00
Pitcher, 6¾" h., 52 oz. 26.00
Plate, sherbet, 6" d. 2.75
Plate, dinner, 9" d. 9.00
Plate, chop, 13 5/8" d. 60.00
Platter, 11 3/8 x 8" 10.50
Sandwich tray, 10½" d. 9.00
Saucer, plain or rayed base 3.00
Sherbet 5.00
Sugar bowl, cov. 15.00
Sugar bowl, open 6.50
Tumbler, footed, 4" h., 5 oz. 26.50
Tumbler, 4" h., 10 oz. 14.00
Tumbler, footed, 6" h., 9 oz. 65.00
Water set, pitcher & 6 tumblers,
   7 pcs. 125.00

HOMESPUN or Fine Rib (Press-mold)

Bowl, 4½" d., closed handles,
   pink 4.00
Bowl, cereal, 5" d., clear 5.00
Bowl, cereal, 5" d., pink 7.50
Bowl, berry, 8¼" d., pink 8.50
Butter dish, cov., clear 27.00
Butter dish, cov., pink 39.00
Coaster-ash tray, pink 4.50
Creamer, footed, clear 7.00
Creamer & sugar bowl, footed, pink,
   pr. 13.50
Cup & saucer, pink 6.00
Pitcher, 96 oz., ball tilt-type, pink . . 61.00
Plate sherbet, 6" d., pink 2.25
Plate, dinner, 9¼" d., pink 9.00
Platter, 13", closed handles, pink . . . 10.00
Sherbet, clear. 4.00
Sherbet, pink 6.50
Tumbler, juice, footed, clear, 4" h.,
   5 oz. 4.00
Tumbler, juice, footed, pink, 4" h.,
   5 oz. 5.50
Tumbler, water, pink, 4" h.,
   9 oz. 7.50
Tumbler, footed, pink, 6¼" h.,
   9 oz. 9.00
Tumbler, iced tea, clear, 5¼" h.,
   13 oz. 7.00
Tumbler, iced tea, pink, 5¼" h.,
   13 oz. 17.00
Tumbler, footed, pink, 6½" h.,
   15 oz. 14.00

CHILD'S TEA SET

Cup & saucer, clear 20.00

Plate, clear 4.50
Plate, pink 5.00
Saucer, clear or pink 5.00
Teapot, pink 67.50
14 piece set, pink 175.00

IRIS or Iris & Herringbone (Press-mold)

Iris Tumbler

Berry set: 11" d. flared fruit bowl &
   6 sauce dishes; clear, 7 pcs. 25.00
Bowl, fruit, 4½" d., amber
   iridescent 6.00
Bowl, fruit, 4½" d., clear 28.50
Bowl, nappy, 5" d., amber
   iridescent 6.00
Bowl, nappy, 5" d., clear 4.75
Bowl, nappy, 6" d., amber
   iridescent 10.00
Bowl, nappy, 6" d., clear 35.50
Bowl, soup, 7½" d., amber
   iridescent 22.50
Bowl, soup, 7½" d., clear 66.00
Bowl, fruit, 8" d., beaded rim,
   amber iridescent 12.50
Bowl, fruit, 8" d., beaded rim,
   clear 52.00
Bowl, fruit, 8" d., ruffled rim, amber
   iridescent or clear 7.75
Bowl, nappy, 9½" d., amber irides-
   cent or clear 8.00
Bowl, 11" d., amber iridescent 7.50
Bowl, 11" d., clear 29.50
Bowl, fruit, 11" d., flared, amber
   iridescent or clear 7.50
Butter dish, cov., amber iridescent . . 29.00
Butter dish, cov., clear 27.00
Candlesticks, 2-branch, amber
   iridescent, pr. 21.50
Candlesticks, 2-branch, clear, pr. . . . 16.00
Candy jar, cov., clear 65.00
Coaster, clear 30.50
Creamer & cov. sugar bowl, amber
   iridescent, pr. 17.00
Creamer & cov. sugar bowl, clear,
   pr. 17.50
Creamer & open sugar bowl, amber
   iridescent, pr. 15.00

Creamer & open sugar bowl, clear,
pr. 11.50
Cup & saucer, demitasse, amber
iridescent 125.00
Cup & saucer, demitasse, clear 69.50
Cup & saucer, amber iridescent. 11.00
Cup & saucer, clear 12.50
Goblet, wine, amber iridescent,
4" h., 3 oz. 13.00
Goblet, wine, clear, 4" h., 3 oz. 11.50
Goblet, wine, amber iridescent,
4½" h., 3 oz. 12.50
Goblet, wine, clear, 4½" h., 3 oz. . . 12.00
Goblet, amber iridescent, 5¾" h.,
4 oz. 14.50
Goblet, clear, 5¾" h., 4 oz. 13.00
Goblet, clear, 5¾" h., 8 oz. 14.00
Goblet, amber iridescent, 7" h. 22.50
Goblet, clear, 7" h. 11.50
Lamp shade, clear, 11½" 22.50
Nut bowl w/metal insert, frosted
w/pink roses, 11½" 24.00
Nut set: bowl w/metal holder,
cracker & picks; clear, set 43.00
Pitcher, 9½" h., jug-type, amber
iridescent 21.50
Pitcher, 9½" h., jug-type, clear 18.00
Plate, sherbet, 5½" d., amber
iridescent 4.25
Plate, sherbet, 5½" d., clear 7.50
Plate, luncheon, 8" d., clear. 32.00
Plate, dinner, 9" d., amber
iridescent 18.50
Plate, dinner, 9" d., clear 29.50
Plate, sandwich, 11¾" d., amber
iridescent 10.50
Plate, sandwich, 11¾" d., clear 9.50
Sherbet, amber iridescent, 2½" h. . . . 7.50
Sherbet, clear, 2½" h. 11.00
Sherbet, amber iridescent, 4" h. 8.00
Sherbet, clear, 4" h. 10.00
Tumbler, clear, 4" h. 46.00
Tumbler, footed, amber iridescent
or clear, 6" h. 10.00
Tumbler, footed, clear, 7" h.
(ILLUS.). 13.50
Vase, 9" h., amber iridescent 12.00
Vase, 9" h., clear 12.50
Vase, 9" h., pink 48.50
Water set: pitcher & 6 tumblers;
amber iridescent, 7 pcs. 82.50
Water set: pitcher & 6 tumblers;
clear, 7 pcs. 123.00

LACE EDGE or Open Lace (Press-mold)

Bowl, cereal, 6½" d., clear 7.25
Bowl, cereal, 6½" d., pink 11.00
Bowl, nappy, 7¾" d., plain or
ribbed, pink 22.00
Bowl, 9½" d., plain or ribbed, clear
or pink. 11.50
Butter dish (bon bon or preserve),
cov., pink (ILLUS.) 43.00

Lace Edge Butter Dish

Candlesticks, pink, pr. 134.00
Candlesticks, pink frosted, pr. 39.50
Candy jar, cov., ribbed, clear,
4" h. 32.50
Candy jar, cov., ribbed, pink,
4" h. 29.00
Compote, cov., 7" d., pink 28.50
Compote, open, 7" d., pink 14.00
Console bowl, 3-footed, pink,
10½" d. 115.00
Cookie jar, cov., pink, 5" h. 42.50
Creamer, pink 13.50
Cup & saucer, clear 17.50
Cup & saucer, pink 23.00
Fish bowl, clear, ½ gal. 14.00
Flower bowl w/crystal block, pink . . 18.00
Flower bowl w-o/crystal block,
pink 15.00
Plate, bread & butter, 7¼" d.,
pink 11.50
Plate, salad, 8½" d., clear 3.75
Plate, salad, 8½" d., pink 11.50
Plate, dinner, 10½" d., clear or
pink 16.00
Plate, grill, 10½" d., pink 11.00
Platter, 12¾" oval, clear. 10.00
Platter, 12¾" oval, pink 18.50
Platter, 12¾" oval, 5-part, clear 17.50
Platter, 12¾" oval, 5-part, pink 16.00
Relish, pink, 7½" d. 49.50
Relish, 3-part, clear, 10½" d. 12.00
Relish, 3-part, pink, 10½" d. 13.00
Relish, 4-part, pink, 13" d. 28.50
Sherbet, pink 51.00
Sugar bowl, open, pink 13.00
Tumbler, pink, 4½" h., 9 oz. 8.50
Tumbler, footed, pink, 5" h.,
10½ oz. 41.00
Vase, 7" h., pink. 225.00
Vase, 7" h., pink frosted 74.50

LORAIN or Basket or Number 615 (Process-etched)

Bowl, cereal, 6" d., green. 28.50
Bowl, cereal, 6" d., yellow 37.50
Bowl, salad, 7¼" d., green 26.00
Bowl, salad, 7¼" d., yellow 40.50
Bowl, berry, 8" d., green 65.00
Bowl, berry, 8" d., yellow. 140.00
Bowl, 9¾" oval vegetable, green . . . 28.00
Bowl, 9¾" oval vegetable, yellow . . 42.50

Cake plate, yellow, 11½" d. 30.00
Creamer, footed, clear 11.00
Creamer, footed, green 10.50

Lorain Creamer & Sugar Bowl

Creamer & open sugar bowl, footed,
   yellow, pr. (ILLUS.) 36.50
Cup & saucer, clear 9.00
Cup & saucer, green 12.50
Cup & saucer, yellow 15.00
Plate, sherbet, 5½" d., clear 4.00
Plate, sherbet, 5½" d., green 3.00
Plate, sherbet, 5½" d., yellow 5.00
Plate, salad, 7¾" d., clear 6.00
Plate, salad, 7¾" d., green 6.50
Plate, salad, 7¾" d., yellow 9.50
Plate, luncheon, 8 3/8" d., green ... 10.50
Plate, luncheon, 8 3/8" d., yellow .. 19.00
Plate, dinner, 9 3/8" d., yellow 40.50
Plate, dinner, 10¼" d., green 29.50
Plate, dinner, 10¼" d., yellow 43.00
Platter, 11½", green 20.50
Platter, 11½", yellow 29.00
Relish, 4-part, clear, 8" 8.00
Relish, 4-part, green, 8" 14.00
Relish, 4-part, yellow, 8" 23.50
Sherbet, green 14.50
Sherbet, yellow 25.50
Sugar bowl, open, footed, clear 9.50
Sugar bowl, open, footed, green ... 11.00
Tumbler, footed, clear, 4¾" h.,
   9 oz. 14.50
Tumbler, footed, green, 4¾" h.,
   9 oz. 14.00
Tumbler, footed, yellow, 4¾" h.,
   9 oz. 18.50
Tumbler, footed, green, 5 1/8" h.,
   12 oz. 18.50
Tumbler, footed, yellow, 5 1/8" h.,
   12 oz. 22.00

MADRID (Process-etched)

Madrid Cream Soup Bowls

Ash tray, green, 6" sq. 72.50
Bowl, cream soup, 4¾" d., amber,
   each (ILLUS.) 9.50

Bowl, cream soup, 4¾" d., clear ... 7.00
Bowl, cream soup, 4¾" d., green... 11.00
Bowl, nappy, 5" d., amber 4.50
Bowl, nappy, 5" d., clear 3.00
Bowl, nappy, 5" d., green or pink .. 5.50
Bowl, soup, 7" d., amber 8.00
Bowl, soup, 7" d., clear or green ... 7.50
Bowl, 8" d., amber 11.00
Bowl, 8" d., blue 65.00
Bowl, 8" d., clear 9.25
Bowl, 8" d., green 16.50
Bowl, fruit, 9 3/8" d., amber 15.00
Bowl, fruit, 9 3/8" d., green 19.00
Bowl, fruit, 9 3/8" d., pink 10.00
Bowl, salad, 9½" d., amber or
   green 20.00
Bowl, salad, 9½" d., blue 67.00
Bowl, 10" oval vegetable, amber ... 11.50
Bowl, 10" oval vegetable, blue 28.00
Bowl, 10" oval vegetable, clear..... 7.75
Bowl, 10" oval vegetable, green ... 14.50
Bowl, 11¾" d., blue 40.00
Bowl, 11¾" d., green 13.00
Bowl, 11¾" d., pink 20.00
Butter dish, cov., amber 58.50
Butter dish, cov., clear 135.00
Butter dish, cov., green 66.00
Cake plate, amber or pink,
   11½" d. 11.00
Cake plate, clear, 11½" d. 14.50
Candlesticks, amber, carnival or
   pink, 2" h., pr. 14.50
Candlesticks, clear, 2" h., pr. 12.00
Console bowl, flared, amber,
   11" d. 10.50
Console bowl, flared, carnival or
   pink, 11" d. 9.50
Console bowl, flared, clear, 11" d... 15.00
Console set: bowl & pr. candle-
   sticks; carnival, 3 pcs. 23.00
Cookie jar, cov., amber 32.00
Cookie jar, cov., clear or pink 25.00
Creamer, amber 5.50
Creamer, blue 12.50
Creamer, clear................... 4.75
Creamer, green 8.50
Cup & saucer, amber or clear 6.50
Cup & saucer, blue 21.50
Cup & saucer, green............. 10.00
Cup & saucer, pink 7.25
Gravy boat & platter,
   amber .... 895.00 to 1,000.00
Hot dish coaster, amber, 5" d. 21.50
Hot dish coaster, clear, 5" d. 23.50
Hot dish coaster, green, 5" d. 30.00
Hot dish coaster w/ring, amber 31.50
Hot dish coaster w/ring, clear..... 21.00
Hot dish coaster w/ring, green 30.00
Jam dish, amber, 7" d. 14.00
Jam dish, blue, 7" d. 27.00
Jam dish, clear, 7" d............. 9.00
Jello mold, amber, 2" h. 7.25
Pitcher, juice, 5" h., 36 oz.,
   amber 29.00

Pitcher, juice, 5" h., 36 oz.,
  pink 31.00
Pitcher, 8" h., 60 oz., square,
  amber 33.00
Pitcher, 8" h., 60 oz., square, blue .. 130.00
Pitcher, 8" h., 60 oz., square,
  green 115.00
Pitcher, 8" h., 60 oz., square, pink .. 31.00
Pitcher, 8½" h., 80 oz., jug-type,
  amber 45.00
Pitcher w/ice lip, 8½" h., 80 oz.,
  amber 52.50
Plate, bread & butter, 6" d., amber
  or clear 2.50
Plate, bread & butter, 6" d., blue ... 7.50
Plate, bread & butter, 6" d., green .. 3.00
Plate, salad, 7½" d., amber or
  green 7.50
Plate, salad, 7½" d., blue 16.00
Plate, salad, 7½" d., clear 5.50
Plate, luncheon, 9" d., amber 5.00
Plate, luncheon, 9" d., blue 16.00
Plate, luncheon, 9" d., clear 4.00
Plate, luncheon, 9" d., green 7.50
Plate, dinner, 10½" d., amber 23.00
Plate, dinner, 10½" d., blue 48.50
Plate, dinner, 10½" d., clear 25.00
Plate, dinner, 10½" d., green 28.00
Plate, grill, 10½" d., amber or
  pink 8.00
Plate, grill, 10½" d., clear 6.75
Plate, grill, 10½" d., green 12.00
Platter, 11½" oval, amber or pink .. 10.00
Platter, 11½" oval, blue 26.50
Platter, 11½" oval, clear 8.75
Platter, 11½" oval, green 13.00
Relish, amber or pink, 10½" d. 9.00
Salt & pepper shakers, amber,
  3½" h., pr. 34.50
Salt & pepper shakers, blue,
  3½" h., pr. 120.00
Salt & pepper shakers, clear,
  3½" h., pr. 46.00
Salt & pepper shakers, green,
  3½" h., pr. 49.50
Salt & pepper shakers, pink,
  3½" h., pr. 40.00
Salt & pepper shakers, footed,
  amber, 3½" h., pr. 56.00
Salt & pepper shakers, footed,
  blue, 3½" h., pr. 115.00
Salt & pepper shakers, footed,
  clear, 3½" h., pr. 46.00
Salt & pepper shakers, footed,
  green, 3½" h., pr. 66.00
Sherbet, amber 5.25
Sherbet, blue 10.00
Sherbet, clear 4.25
Sherbet, green or pink 6.50
Sugar bowl, cov., amber 32.00
Sugar bowl, cov., blue 125.00
Sugar bowl, cov., clear 30.00
Sugar bowl, cov., green 50.00
Sugar bowl, open, amber 5.00

Sugar bowl, open, blue 13.50
Sugar bowl, open, clear 4.00
Sugar bowl, open, green or pink ... 6.50
Tumbler, juice, amber, 3 7/8" h.,
  5 oz. 11.25
Tumbler, juice, blue, 3 7/8" h.,
  5 oz. 18.00
Tumbler, juice, green, 3 7/8" h.,
  5 oz. 47.50
Tumbler, footed, amber, 4" h.,
  5 oz. 14.50
Tumbler, footed, green, 4" h.,
  5 oz. 37.50
Tumbler, amber, 4½" h., 9 oz. 11.00
Tumbler, blue, 4½" h., 9 oz. 21.00
Tumbler, clear or pink, 4½" h.,
  9 oz. 10.50
Tumbler, green, 4½" h., 9 oz. 19.00
Tumbler, footed, amber, 5¼" h.,
  10 oz. 17.00
Tumbler, footed, blue, 5¼" h.,
  10 oz. 21.00
Tumbler, footed, green, 5¼" h.,
  10 oz. 27.00
Tumbler, amber, 5½" h., 12 oz. 14.00
Tumbler, blue, 5½" h., 12 oz. 32.00
Tumbler, green, 5½" h., 12 oz. 29.00

MANHATTAN or Ribbed Horizontal (Press-mold)

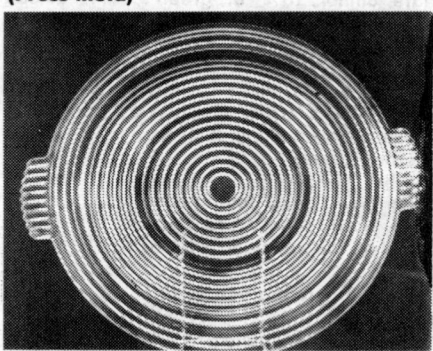

Manhattan Plate

Ash tray, clear 6.00
Bowl, dessert, 4½" d., clear 4.00
Bowl, fruit, 5 3/8" d., handled, clear
  or pink 8.00
Bowl, 7½" d., clear 8.50
Bowl, 8" d., 2-handled, clear 10.00
Bowl, 9" d., clear or pink 12.00
Bowl, fruit, 9½" d., clear 15.00
Bowl, fruit, 9½" d., pink 17.50
Candlesticks, double, square, clear,
  4¼" h., pr. 7.00
Candy dish, cov., clear 17.50
Candy dish, cov., pink 5.50
Candy dish, open, 3-legged, clear .. 19.00
Candy dish, open, 3-legged, pink ... 5.00
Coaster, clear, 3½" d. 4.25
Compote, 5¾" h., clear 11.00

Compote, 5¾" h., pink	14.50
Cookie jar, cov., clear	31.00
Creamer, clear	4.25
Creamer, pink	5.75
Creamer & open sugar bowl, clear, pr.	10.00
Creamer & open sugar bowl, pink, pr.	11.50
Cup & saucer, clear	10.50
Pitcher, juice, 42 oz., clear	15.00
Pitcher w/ice lip, 80 oz., ball tilt type, clear	19.50
Pitcher w/ice lip, 80 oz., ball tilt type, pink	34.00
Plate, sherbet, 6" d., clear	2.50
Plate, sherbet, 6" d., pink	7.50
Plate, salad, 8½" d., clear	6.25
Plate, dinner, 10½" d., clear	8.25
Plate, 14" d., clear (ILLUS.)	12.50
Relish, 4-part, clear, 14"	11.50
Relish, 4-part, pink, 14"	37.50
Relish, 5-part, clear, 14"	24.50
Relish, 5-part, clear w/ruby inserts or pink, 14"	32.50
Relish tray insert, clear	3.00
Relish tray insert, pink or ruby	4.00
Salt & pepper shakers, round or square, clear, 2" h., pr.	13.00
Salt & pepper shakers, round or square, pink, 2" h., pr.	30.00
Sherbet, clear or pink	5.00
Sugar bowl, open, clear	4.25
Sugar bowl, open, pink	5.75
Tumbler, footed, clear, 10 oz.	7.00
Tumbler, footed, green, 10 oz.	10.50
Tumbler, footed, pink, 10 oz.	9.00
Vase, 8" h., clear	8.00
Vase, 8" h., pink	15.00
Water bottle, cov., clear	19.50

MAYFAIR or Open Rose (Process-etched)

Mayfair Vegetable Bowl

Bowl, cream soup, 5" d., blue	43.00
Bowl, cream soup, 5" d., pink	27.00
Bowl, fruit, 5½" d., blue	28.50
Bowl, fruit, 5½" d., pink	13.50
Bowl, nappy, 7" d., blue	36.50
Bowl, nappy, 7" d., pink	17.00
Bowl, 9½" oval vegetable, blue	40.00
Bowl, 9½" oval vegetable, green (ILLUS.)	75.00
Bowl, 9½" oval vegetable, pink	17.00

Bowl, cov. vegetable, 10" d., blue	80.00
Bowl, cov. vegetable, 10" d., pink	68.00
Bowl, 10" d., blue	37.00
Bowl, 10" d., pink	15.00
Bowl, 10" d., handled, blue	35.50
Bowl, 10" d., handled, pink or pink frosted	13.50
Bowl, 11¾" d., blue	44.50
Bowl, 11¾" d., green	22.50
Bowl, 11¾" d., pink	36.50
Bowl, fruit, 12" d., flared, blue	50.00
Bowl, fruit, 12" d., flared, green	23.50
Bowl, fruit, 12" d., flared, pink	34.50
Butter dish, cov., blue	230.00
Butter dish, cov., pink	43.50
Cake plate, footed, blue, 10" d.	45.00
Cake plate, footed, green or pink, 10" d.	18.00
Cake plate, handled, blue, 12" d.	42.50
Cake plate, handled, green, 12" d.	40.00
Cake plate, handled, pink or pink frosted, 12" d.	25.00
Candy jar, cov., blue	160.00
Candy jar, cov., pink	32.00
Candy jar, cov., pink frosted	30.00
Celery dish, blue, 10" d.	25.00
Celery dish, pink, 10" d.	20.00
Celery dish, 2-part, blue, 10" d.	30.00
Celery dish, 2-part, pink, 10" d.	95.00
Cookie jar, cov., blue	145.00
Cookie jar, cov., green	625.00
Cookie jar, cov., pink	30.00
Cookie jar, cov., pink frosted	32.50
Creamer, blue	46.00
Creamer, green	135.00
Creamer, pink	14.00
Cup, blue	29.00
Cup, pink	10.50
Cup & saucer, blue	43.00
Cup & saucer, pink	18.50
Decanter w/stopper, pink, 10" h.	98.00
Goblet, pink, 4" h., 2½ oz.	75.00
Goblet, wine, pink, 4½" h., 3 oz.	58.00
Goblet, cocktail, pink, 4" h., 3½ oz.	63.00
Goblet, champagne, blue, 5¼" h., 4½ oz.	65.00
Goblet, champagne, pink, 5¼" h., 4½ oz.	75.00
Goblet, water, pink, 5¾" h., 9 oz.	41.00
Goblet, water, thin, blue, 7¼" h., 9 oz.	105.00
Goblet, water, thin, pink, 7¼" h., 9 oz.	115.00
Juice set: pitcher & 6 tumblers; pink, 7 pcs.	200.00
Pitcher, juice, 6" h., 37 oz., blue	85.00
Pitcher, juice, 6" h., 37 oz., clear	9.50
Pitcher, juice, 6" h., 37 oz., pink	29.00
Pitcher, 8" h., 60 oz., jug-type, blue	98.00
Pitcher, 8" h., 60 oz., jug-type, pink	33.50

Pitcher, 8½" h., 80 oz., jug-type,
  blue 120.00
Pitcher, 8½" h., 80 oz., jug-type,
  pink 55.00
Plate, bread & butter, 6" w., blue .. 12.00
Plate, bread & butter, 6" w., pink .. 7.50
Plate, sherbet, 6½" d., blue 8.50
Plate, sherbet, 6½" d., green 45.00
Plate, sherbet, 6½" d., pink 7.00
Plate, sherbet, 6½" d., off-center
  indentation, blue or pink 17.50
Plate, luncheon, 8½" d., blue 26.50
Plate, luncheon, 8½" d., pink 14.00
Plate, luncheon, 8½" d., yellow 85.00
Plate, dinner, 9½" d., blue 38.00
Plate, dinner, 9½" d., pink 36.50
Plate, dinner, 9½" d., yellow 6.75
Plate, grill, 9½" d., blue 25.00
Plate, grill, 9½" d., pink 22.00
Plate, grill, 11½" d., yellow 87.50
Plate, 12" d., 2-handled, blue 42.00
Plate, 12" d., 2-handled, pink or
  pink frosted 20.00
Platter, 12" oval, pierced handles,
  blue 36.50
Platter, 12" oval, pierced handles,
  clear 13.00
Platter, 12" oval, pierced handles,
  pink 16.50
Relish, 2-part, blue 41.00
Relish, 2-part, clear 12.00
Relish, 4-part, blue 31.50
Relish, 4-part, pink 20.50
Relish, 4-part, pink frosted 13.50
Salt & pepper shakers, blue, pr. 190.00
Salt & pepper shakers, pink, pr. 41.50
Salt & pepper shakers, pink frosted,
  pr. 34.00
Salt & pepper shakers, footed, blue,
  pr. 155.00
Sandwich server w/center handle,
  blue, 12" 45.00
Sandwich server w/center handle,
  green, 12" 18.00
Sandwich server w/center handle,
  pink or pink frosted, 12" 23.50
Sherbet, blue, 2¼" h. 54.00
Sherbet, pink, 2¼" h. 115.00
Sherbet, pink, 3¼" h. 11.00
Sherbet, footed, blue, 4¾" h. 55.00
Sherbet, footed, pink, 4¾" h. 56.50
Sherbet w/underplate, blue, 2¼" h.
  sherbet 72.50
Sugar bowl, cov., blue 1,250.00
Sugar bowl, open, blue 45.50
Sugar bowl, open, green.......... 98.00
Sugar bowl, open, pink 13.50
Sugar bowl, open, pink frosted 9.00
Tumbler, whiskey, green, 2¼" h.,
  1½ oz. 40.00
Tumbler, whiskey, pink, 2¼" h.,
  1½ oz. 47.00
Tumbler, juice, footed, pink,
  3¼" h., 3 oz. 50.00

Tumbler, juice, blue, 3½" h.,
  5 oz. 72.00
Tumbler, juice, pink, 3½" h.,
  5 oz. 30.00
Tumbler, water, blue, 4¼" h.,
  9 oz. 75.00
Tumbler, water, pink, 4¼" h.,
  9 oz. 22.50
Tumbler, footed, blue, 5¼" h.,
  10 oz. 95.00
Tumbler, footed, pink, 5¼" h.,
  10 oz. 23.50
Tumbler, blue, 4¾" h., 11 oz. 95.00
Tumbler, water, footed, pink,
  4¾" h., 11 oz. 78.50
Tumbler, iced tea, blue, 5¼" h.,
  13½ oz. 110.00
Tumbler, iced tea, pink, 5¼" h.,
  13½ oz. 27.00
Tumbler, iced tea, footed, blue,
  6½" h., 15 oz. 105.00
Tumbler, iced tea, footed, pink,
  6½" h., 15 oz. 24.50
Vase, 5½ x 8½", sweetpea, hat-
  shaped, blue................... 67.50
Vase, 5½ x 8½", sweetpea, hat-
  shaped, pink................... 100.00
Water set: pitcher & 6 tumblers;
  blue, 7 pcs. 695.00
Water set: pitcher & 6 tumblers;
  pink, 7 pcs.................... 150.00

MISS AMERICA (Press-mold)

Miss America Water Pitcher

Bowl, nappy, 4½" d., clear 5.00
Bowl, nappy, 4½" d., green........ 7.25
Bowl, nappy, 4½" d., pink 12.50
Bowl, cereal, 6¼" d., clear 5.50
Bowl, cereal, 6¼" d., green........ 7.50
Bowl, cereal, 6¼" d., pink 11.50
Bowl, fruit, 8" d., curved top,
  clear 27.50
Bowl, fruit, 8" d., curved top, pink.. 41.50
Bowl, fruit, 8" d., curved top, ruby.. 125.00
Bowl, fruit, 8¾" d., deep, clear 22.00
Bowl, fruit, 8¾" d., deep, pink 40.00
Bowl, 10" oval vegetable, clear..... 10.50
Bowl, 10" oval vegetable, pink 14.50

Butter dish, cov., clear	165.00
Butter dish, cov., pink	350.00
Cake plate, footed, clear, 12" d.....	15.00
Cake plate, footed, pink, 12" d.	27.00
Candy dish w/metal lid, clear, 6¼" d.	20.00
Candy jar, cov., clear.............	45.00
Candy jar, cov., pink	88.50
Celery tray, clear, 10½" oblong	7.50
Celery tray, pink, 10½" oblong	13.00
Coaster, clear, 5¾" d..............	10.00
Coaster, green, 5¾" d.	6.00
Coaster, pink, 5¾" d.	16.50
Compote, 5" d., clear.............	10.00
Compote, 5" d., pink	12.50
Creamer, clear....................	6.25
Creamer, pink	11.50
Creamer & open sugar bowl, clear, pr.............................	12.00
Creamer & open sugar bowl, pink, pr.............................	22.50
Cup & saucer, clear	9.00
Goblet, wine, clear, 3¾" h., 3 oz...........................	15.00
Goblet, wine, pink, 3¾" h., 3 oz...........................	45.00
Goblet, wine, ruby, 3¾" h., 3 oz...........................	175.00
Goblet, juice, clear, 4¾" h., 5 oz...........................	15.00
Goblet, juice, pink, 4¾" h., 5 oz...........................	47.50
Goblet, water, clear, 5½" h., 10 oz..........................	15.00
Goblet, water, pink, 5½" h., 10 oz..........................	32.50
Goblet, water, ruby, 5½" h., 10 oz..........................	150.00
Pitcher, 8½" h., 65 oz., clear......	52.00
Pitcher, 8½" h., 65 oz., pink	78.00
Pitcher w/ice lip, 8½" h., 65 oz., clear...........................	50.00
Pitcher w/ice lip, 8½" h., 65 oz., pink (ILLUS.)	90.00
Plate, sherbet, 5¾" d., clear	2.75
Plate, sherbet, 5¾" d., pink	4.25
Plate, bread & butter, 6¾" d., clear...........................	2.50
Plate, bread & butter, 6¾" d., green	7.00
Plate, bread & butter, 6¾" d., pink	8.00
Plate, salad, 8½" d., clear	4.75
Plate, salad, 8½" d., pink	12.00
Plate, dinner, 10¼" d., clear	9.50
Plate, dinner, 10¼" d., pink	17.00
Plate, grill, 10¼" d., clear	6.50
Plate, grill, 10¼" d., pink..........	11.50
Platter, 12" oval, clear............	11.00
Platter, 12" oval, pink	13.50
Relish, 4-part, clear, 8½" d.........	7.00
Relish, 4-part, pink, 8½" d.	11.50
Relish, divided, clear or pink, 12" d.........................	13.50

Salt & pepper shakers, clear, pr.	19.50
Salt & pepper shakers, green, pr....	200.00
Salt & pepper shakers, pink, pr.....	37.50
Sherbet, clear.....................	6.00
Sherbet, pink	11.00
Sugar bowl, open, clear	5.50
Sugar bowl, open, green	6.00
Sugar bowl, open, pink	11.50
Tid bit server, 2-tier, clear	13.00
Tumbler, clear, 4" h., 5 oz.	11.00
Tumbler, pink, 4" h., 5 oz.	32.50
Tumbler, clear, 4½" h., 10 oz.	14.00
Tumbler, green, 4½" h., 10 oz.	12.00
Tumbler, pink, 4½" h., 10 oz.	25.00
Tumbler, clear, 6¾" h., 14 oz.	18.00
Tumbler, green, 6¾" h., 14 oz.	19.00
Tumbler, pink, 6¾" h., 14 oz.	42.50
Tumbler, ruby, 6¾" h., 14 oz.	41.00

MODERNTONE (Press-mold)

Moderntone Pattern

Ash tray, blue, 5½" d.	12.50
Ash tray w/match holder, blue, 7¾" d........................	140.00
Bowl, cream soup, 4¾" d., amethyst	8.00
Bowl, cream soup, 4¾" d., blue	11.00
Bowl, nappy, 6½" d., blue	27.50
Bowl, soup, 7½" d., blue	75.00
Bowl, nappy, 8¾" d., amethyst.....	15.00
Bowl, nappy, 8¾" d., blue	25.00
Butter dish w/metal lid, blue	60.00
Creamer, amethyst	5.50
Creamer, blue (ILLUS. right)	7.50
Creamer & sugar bowl w/metal lid, blue, pr.	32.50
Cup, amethyst	6.25
Cup, blue........................	6.75
Cup & saucer, amethyst...........	7.25
Cup & saucer, blue	8.50
Custard or jello cup, amethyst......	8.25
Custard or jello cup, blue	10.00
Nut bowl, handled, ruffled rim, amethyst, 5" d.	9.00
Nut bowl, handled, ruffled rim, blue, 5" d.......................	15.00
Plate, sherbet, 5¾" d., amethyst ...	2.50
Plate, sherbet, 5¾" d., blue	3.00
Plate, salad, 6¾" d., amethyst	4.25
Plate, salad, 6¾" d., blue	5.50
Plate, luncheon, 7¾" d., amethyst or blue.......................	5.00
Plate, dinner, 8 7/8" d., amethyst or blue	8.00

Plate, 10½" d., amethyst	14.00
Plate, 10½" d., blue	20.50
Platter, 11" oval, amethyst	18.75
Platter, 11" oval, blue	21.50
Platter, 12" oval, amethyst	20.00
Platter, 12" oval, blue	29.00
Punch bowl w/metal holder, blue	35.00
Punch set: punch bowl in metal holder, 8 cups & ladle w/blue knob; blue, 11 pcs.	130.00
Salt & pepper shakers, amethyst, pr.	31.50
Salt & pepper shakers, blue, pr. (ILLUS.)	22.50
Sherbet, amethyst	6.25
Sherbet, blue	7.25
Sugar bowl, open, amethyst	5.50
Sugar bowl, open, blue (ILLUS. left)	6.50
Sugar bowl w/metal lid, blue	37.50
Teapot, cov., "Little Hostess," amethyst	32.50
Tea set, "Little Hostess," 16 pcs.	50.00 to 60.00
Tumbler, whiskey, blue, 1½ oz.	14.00
Tumbler, amethyst, 5 oz.	28.00
Tumbler, blue, 5 oz.	21.50
Tumbler, amethyst, 4" h., 9 oz.	16.50
Tumbler, blue, 4" h., 9 oz.	14.50
Tumbler, amethyst, 12 oz.	45.00

MOONSTONE (Press-mold)

Moonstone Vase

(All items clear to opalescent only.)

Bon bon, heart-shaped, 6½" w.	7.50
Bowl, dessert, 5½" d., crimped	5.50
Bowl, 5½" d., straight	7.50
Bowl, 6½" d., handled, crimped	5.50
Bowl, 7¾" d.	7.50
Bowl, 9½" d., crimped	12.50
Candle holders, 4¼" h., pr.	13.00
Candy jar, cov.	20.00
Cigarette box, cov.	13.50
Creamer	5.00
Creamer & sugar bowl, pr.	11.50

Cruet w/stopper	16.25
Cup & saucer	8.00
Dish, cloverleaf-shaped, 6" w.	7.25
Goblet, 10 oz.	12.50
Perfume bottle w/stopper, 5¼" h.	11.50
Plate, sherbet, 6¼" d.	2.50
Plate, luncheon, 8" d.	7.50
Plate, 10" d., crimped	15.00
Plate, 11" d.	14.00
Puff box, cov.	14.00
Relish, divided	7.50
Salt & pepper shakers, pr.	32.50
Sherbet	5.00
Sugar bowl	4.50
Tumbler, 3½" h., 4 oz.	6.50
Tumbler, footed, 5½" h.	14.00
Vase, 3½" h. (ILLUS.)	10.00
Vase, 5" h.	8.25

MOROCCAN AMETHYST (Early 1960's - not true Depression)

Moroccan Amethyst Cup & Saucer

Basket	28.00
Bowl, fruit, 4¾" d.	3.75
Bowl, cereal, 5¾" d.	5.00
Candy jar, cov.	19.00
Cocktail shaker w/chrome lid	18.50
Creamer	8.00
Cup & saucer (ILLUS.)	4.50
Plate, 6" w.	3.75
Plate, salad, 7¼" w.	3.50
Plate, dinner, 9 3/8" w.	5.25
Punch cup	4.00
Relish	7.25
Tid bit server, 2-tier	17.00
Tid bit server, 3-tier	14.50
Tumbler, juice, 2½" h., 4 oz.	3.75
Tumbler, old fashioned, 3¼" h., 8 oz.	3.50
Tumbler, water, 4½" h., 11 oz.	4.00

NORMANDIE (Process-etched)

Bowl, nappy, 5" d., amber	3.75
Bowl, nappy, 5" d., carnival	4.00
Bowl, nappy, 5" d., pink	5.00
Bowl, 6½" d., amber	8.00

Bowl, 6½" d., carnival 5.75
Bowl, 6½" d., pink 16.50
Bowl, nappy, 8½" d., amber 11.00
Bowl, nappy, 8½" d., carnival 9.50
Bowl, nappy, 8½" d., pink 13.50
Bowl, 9½" oval vegetable, amber or
　carnival 12.00
Creamer, amber or carnival 5.50
Creamer, pink 8.00
Cup & saucer, amber or pink 7.00

Normandie Cup & Saucer

Cup & saucer, carnival (ILLUS.) 6.00
Pitcher, 8" h., 80 oz., amber 45.00
Pitcher, 8" h., 80 oz., clear 50.00
Pitcher, 8" h., 80 oz., pink 75.00
Plate, bread & butter, 6" d., amber,
　carnival or pink 2.25
Plate, salad, 8" d., amber 7.00
Plate, salad, 8" d., pink 8.00
Plate, luncheon, 9¼" d., amber 6.50
Plate, luncheon, 9¼" d., carnival or
　pink 7.00
Plate, dinner, 10½" d., amber 20.00
Plate, dinner, 10½" d., carnival 12.50
Plate, dinner, 10½" d., pink 31.50
Plate, grill, 10½" d., amber 9.00
Plate, grill, 10½" d., carnival 6.50
Plate, grill, 10½" d., pink 22.00
Platter, 12" oval, amber 11.00
Platter, 12" oval, carnival 9.50
Platter, 12" oval, pink 13.00
Salt & pepper shakers, amber, pr. . . . 32.50
Salt & pepper shakers, pink, pr. 51.50
Sherbet, amber or pink 5.50
Sherbet, carnival 4.50
Sherbet, clear 2.25
Sugar bowl, cov., amber 69.00
Sugar bowl, open, amber 4.50
Sugar bowl, open, carnival 5.50
Tumbler, amber, 4" h., 5 oz. 9.50
Tumbler, pink, 4" h., 5 oz. 27.00
Tumbler, amber, 4½" h., 9 oz. 9.00
Tumbler, pink, 4½" h., 9 oz. 24.50
Tumbler, amber, 5" h., 12 oz. 13.00

NUMBER 612 or Horseshoe (Acid-etched)

Bowl, berry, 4½" d., green 19.00
Bowl, berry, 4½" d., yellow 16.00
Bowl, cereal, 6½" d., green 20.00
Bowl, cereal, 6½" d., yellow 18.00
Bowl, salad, 7½" d., green 16.50
Bowl, salad, 7½" d., yellow 17.50

Bowl, berry, 9" d., green 23.50
Bowl, berry, 9" d., yellow 27.50
Bowl, 10½" oval vegetable, green . . 13.50
Bowl, 10½" oval vegetable,
　yellow 22.50
Butter dish, cov., green 650.00
Candy dish in metal holder, motif on
　lid, pink 97.50
Creamer, footed, green 11.00
Creamer, footed, yellow 13.00
Cup & saucer, green 8.50
Cup & saucer, yellow 10.50
Pitcher, 8½" h., 64 oz., green 190.00
Pitcher, 8½" h., 64 oz., yellow 245.00
Plate, sherbet, 6" d., green 2.75
Plate, sherbet, 6" d., yellow 3.75
Plate, salad, 8 3/8" d., green 6.00
Plate, salad, 8 3/8" d., yellow 6.50
Plate, luncheon, 9 3/8" d., green . . . 8.00
Plate, dinner, 10 3/8" d., green 14.00
Plate, dinner, 10 3/8" d., yellow 10.00
Plate, grill, 10 3/8" d., green 20.50
Plate, 11¼" d., green or yellow 11.50
Platter, 10¾" oval, green 12.00
Platter, 10¾" oval, yellow 15.00
Relish, 3-part, footed, green 18.00
Relish, 3-part, footed, yellow 22.50
Sherbet, green 9.50
Sherbet, yellow 11.00
Sugar bowl, open, footed, green . . . 8.50
Sugar bowl, open, footed, yellow . . . 9.50
Tumbler, footed, green, 9 oz. 14.00
Tumbler, footed, yellow, 9 oz. 15.00
Tumbler, footed, green, 12 oz. 75.00
Tumbler, footed, yellow, 12 oz. 100.00

OLD CAFE (Press-mold)

Old Cafe Mint Trays

Ash tray, ruby 4.00
Bowl, nappy, 3¾" d., clear or
　pink 3.00
Bowl, nappy, 3¾" d., ruby 2.00
Bowl, nappy, 5" d., handled, clear
　or pink 4.00
Bowl, nappy, 5½" d., clear w/ruby
　cover 9.50
Bowl, nappy, 5½" d., pink 11.00
Bowl, 9" d., handled, clear 6.50
Bowl, 9" d., handled, pink 6.00
Bowl, 9" d., handled, ruby 8.00
Candy dish, cov., clear 3.00

Candy dish, cov., pink	4.50
Candy dish, cov., ruby	8.00
Cookie jar, cov., pink	40.00
Cup & saucer, pink	8.00
Cup & saucer, ruby cup, clear saucer	6.75
Lamp, pink	12.00
Mint tray, low, flared, clear, 8"	3.50
Mint tray, low, flared, pink, 8" (ILLUS. right)	5.00
Mint tray, low, flared, ruby, 8" (ILLUS. left)	9.00
Olive dish, clear, 6" oblong	5.00
Olive dish, pink, 6" oblong	4.00
Pitcher, 8" h., 80 oz., pink	65.00
Plate, sherbet, 6" d., clear	3.00
Plate, sherbet, 6" d., pink	5.50
Plate, dinner, 10" d., pink	13.00
Sherbet, clear	3.00
Sherbet, pink	6.00
Tumbler, juice, clear, 3" h.	4.00
Tumbler, juice, pink, 3" h.	5.00
Tumbler, clear, 4" h.	4.00
Tumbler, pink, 4" h.	6.50
Vase, 7¼" h., clear	4.50

OYSTER & PEARL (Press-mold)

Bowl, 5¼" heart shape, clear	4.00
Bowl, 5¼" heart shape, pink	6.00
Bowl, 5¼" heart shape, red	12.50
Bowl, 5¼" heart shape, white w/green	8.50
Bowl, 5¼" heart shape, white w/pink	6.50
Bowl, 5¼" d., handled, clear	4.00
Bowl, 5¼" d., handled, pink	4.50
Bowl, 5¼" d., handled, red	7.50
Bowl, 5¼" d., handled, white	3.50
Bowl, 6½" d., handled, clear	4.00
Bowl, 6½" d., handled, pink	8.00
Bowl, 6½" d., handled, red	12.00
Candlesticks, clear or white w/pink, pr.	15.00
Candlesticks, green, pr.	8.00
Candlesticks, pink, pr.	14.50
Candlesticks, red, pr.	27.00
Candlesticks, white, pr.	10.00
Candlesticks, white w/green, pr.	13.00
Console bowl, clear or pink, 10½" d.	15.50
Console bowl, red, 10½" d.	25.50
Console bowl, white, 10½" d.	10.00
Console bowl, white w/green or w/pink, 10½" d.	15.00
Console set: bowl & 2 candlesticks; red, 3 pcs.	32.00
Console set: bowl & 2 candlesticks; white w/green or w/pink, 3 pcs.	19.00
Plate, 13½" d., clear	10.50
Plate, 13½" d., pink	12.50
Plate, 13½" d., red	19.50
Relish, divided, clear, 10¼" oval	4.50
Relish, divided, pink, 10¼" oval	6.00

Vase, jadite	8.50
Vase, white	14.50
Vase, white w/pink	13.00

PARROT or Sylvan (Process-etched)

Parrot Sherbet

Bowl, berry, 5" d., amber	13.00
Bowl, berry, 5" d., green	15.00
Bowl, soup, 7" d., amber	24.50
Bowl, soup, 7" d., green	26.50
Bowl, berry, 8" d., green	45.00
Bowl, 8¼" sq., green	68.00
Bowl, 10" oval vegetable, amber	37.50
Bowl, 10" oval vegetable, green	35.00
Butter dish, cov., green	230.00
Creamer & cov. sugar bowl, green, pr.	102.00
Creamer & open sugar bowl, amber, pr.	46.00
Creamer & open sugar bowl, green, pr.	35.50
Cup & saucer, amber	30.50
Cup & saucer, green	32.50
Jam dish, amber	24.00
Plate, sherbet, 5¾" d., amber	9.00
Plate, sherbet, 5¾" d., green	14.50
Plate, salad, 7½" d., green	16.50
Plate, dinner, 9" d., amber	24.00
Plate, dinner, 9" d., green	26.00
Plate, grill, 10½" d., amber	15.50
Plate, grill, 10½" d., green	20.50
Platter, 11¼" oblong, amber	31.00
Platter, 11¼" oblong, green	23.50
Salt & pepper shakers, green, pr.	185.00
Sherbet, cone-shaped, amber	13.00
Sherbet, cone-shaped, green	14.00
Sherbet, amber, 4¼" h. (ILLUS.)	11.50
Sherbet, green, 4¼" h.	14.00
Tumbler, green, 4¼" h., 10 oz.	92.00
Tumbler, green, 5½" h., 12 oz.	100.00
Tumbler, footed, cone-shaped, amber, 5¾" h.	110.00
Tumbler, footed, cone-shaped, green, 5¾" h.	115.00

PATRICIAN or Spoke (Process-etched)

Bowl, cream soup, 4¾" d., amber	9.50

Bowl, cream soup, 4¾" d., clear ... 6.00
Bowl, cream soup, 4¾" d., green... 12.00
Bowl, cream soup, 4¾" d., pink 14.50
Bowl, nappy, 5" d., amber 7.00
Bowl, nappy, 5" d., clear or green .. 6.50
Bowl, nappy, 5" d., pink 8.50
Bowl, cereal, 6" d., amber 13.00
Bowl, cereal, 6" d., clear 11.50
Bowl, cereal, 6" d., green.......... 15.00
Bowl, cereal, 6" d., pink 14.50
Bowl, nappy, 8½" d., amber 25.00
Bowl, nappy, 8½" d., clear 13.00
Bowl, nappy, 8½" d., green........ 19.50

Patrician Bowl

Bowl, nappy, 8½" d., pink (ILLUS.).. 15.50
Bowl, 10" oval vegetable, amber or
    pink 17.50
Bowl, 10" oval vegetable, clear..... 12.50
Bowl, 10" oval vegetable, green 15.50
Butter dish, cov., amber 62.50
Butter dish, cov., clear 57.00
Butter dish, cov., green........... 82.50
Butter dish, cov., pink 160.00
Cookie jar, cov., amber........... 57.00
Cookie jar, cov., clear 65.00
Cookie jar, cov., green 195.00
Creamer & cov. sugar bowl, amber,
    pr............................. 40.00
Creamer & cov. sugar bowl, green,
    pr............................. 57.50
Creamer & cov. sugar bowl, pink,
    pr............................. 61.00
Creamer & open sugar bowl, amber,
    pr............................. 11.00
Creamer & open sugar bowl, clear,
    pr............................. 8.50
Creamer & open sugar bowl, green
    or pink, pr.................... 15.00
Cup & saucer, amber, green or
    pink 12.00
Cup & saucer, clear 8.00
Jam dish, amber, 6"............... 18.50
Jam dish, green, 6" 22.00
Jam dish, pink, 6"................ 12.00

Pitcher, 8" h., 60 oz., amber 67.00
Pitcher, 8" h., 60 oz., clear........ 46.00
Pitcher, 8" h., 60 oz., green 69.00
Pitcher, 8" h., 60 oz., pink 135.00
Pitcher, 8½" h., 68 oz., clear...... 55.00
Pitcher, 8½" h., 68 oz., pink 95.00
Pitcher, 8½" h., 80 oz., jug-type,
    amber 78.00
Pitcher, 8½" h., 80 oz., jug-type,
    clear 71.50
Pitcher, 8½" h., 80 oz., jug-type,
    green 82.00
Plate, bread & butter, 6" d.,
    amber 6.00
Plate, bread & butter, 6" d., clear,
    green or pink 3.50
Plate, salad, 7½" d., amber, green
    or pink........................ 8.50
Plate, salad, 7½" d., clear 6.50
Plate, luncheon, 9" d., amber, green
    or pink........................ 6.00
Plate, luncheon, 9" d., clear....... 5.00
Plate, dinner, 10½" d., amber or
    clear.......................... 5.00
Plate, dinner, 10½" d., green 25.50
Plate, dinner, 10½" d., pink 19.00
Plate, grill, 10½" d., amber 6.50
Plate, grill, 10½" d., clear 4.50
Plate, grill, 10½" d., green 9.50
Plate, grill, 10½" d., pink.......... 10.00
Platter, 11½" oval, amber 16.00
Platter, 11½" oval, clear........... 10.00
Platter, 11½" oval, green 11.50
Platter, 11½" oval, pink 15.00
Salt & pepper shakers, amber, pr. .. 36.50
Salt & pepper shakers, clear, pr. ... 32.50
Salt & pepper shakers, green, pr.... 39.00
Salt & pepper shakers, pink, pr. 70.00
Sherbet, amber 6.50
Sherbet, clear.................... 5.50
Sherbet, green 8.00
Sherbet, pink 7.50
Tumbler, amber or clear, 4" h.,
    5 oz........................... 20.00
Tumbler, green or pink, 4" h.,
    5 oz........................... 22.00
Tumbler, amber or green, 4½" h.,
    9 oz........................... 18.00
Tumbler, clear or pink, 4½" h.,
    9 oz........................... 19.00
Tumbler, footed, amber, 5" h.,
    10 oz.......................... 30.50
Tumbler, footed, clear, 5" h.,
    10 oz.......................... 32.50
Tumbler, footed, green, 5" h.,
    10 oz.......................... 35.00
Tumbler, iced tea, amber, 5" h.,
    12 oz.......................... 25.50
Tumbler, iced tea, green, 5" h.,
    12 oz.......................... 26.50
Tumbler, iced tea, pink, 5" h.,
    12 oz.......................... 28.50
Tumbler, iced tea, amber, 5 3/8" h.,
    14 oz.......................... 26.00

Tumbler, iced tea, clear, 5 3/8" h.,
14 oz. 20.00
Tumbler, iced tea, green, 5 3/8" h.,
14 oz. 28.00
Tumbler, iced tea, pink, 5 3/8" h.,
14 oz. 46.00
Water set: pitcher & five 4½" h.
tumblers; amber, 6 pcs. 145.00

PETALWARE (Press-mold)
Bowl, cream soup, 4½" d., clear,
Monax or pink 5.50
Bowl, cream soup, 4½" d.,
Cremax 6.50
Bowl, cereal, 5¾" d., clear 3.50
Bowl, cereal, 5¾" d., Cremax or
pink 4.50
Bowl, cereal, 5¾" d., Monax 5.00
Bowl, 8¾" d., clear 12.00
Bowl, 8¾" d., Cremax 14.50
Bowl, 8¾" d., Monax or pink 12.50
Bowl, 9¼" oval vegetable,
Cremax 9.00
Bowl, 9¼" oval vegetable, Monax .. 16.50
Bowl, 9¼" oval vegetable, pink 12.50
Creamer, Cremax or Monax 4.50
Creamer, pink 2.50
Cup & saucer, clear 3.00
Cup & saucer, Cremax 5.50
Cup & saucer, Monax or pink 5.00
Lamp, clear 90.00
Lamp shade, Monax, 6" h. 7.00
Lamp shade, pink, 10" h. 8.00
Mustard jar w/metal cover, blue ... 10.50
Plate, bread & butter, 6" d., clear .. 1.00
Plate, bread & butter, 6" d.,
Cremax, Monax or pink 2.00
Plate, salad, 8" d., clear 1.75
Plate, salad, 8" d., Cremax 3.50
Plate, salad, 8" d., Monax or pink .. 3.00
Plate, dinner, 9" d., clear 3.50
Plate, dinner, 9" d., Cremax or
Monax 4.50
Plate, dinner, 9" d., pink 5.50
Plate, salver, 11" d., clear 3.00
Plate, salver, 11" d., Cremax 6.50
Plate, salver, 11" d., Monax 5.50
Plate, salver, 11" d., pink 11.00
Plate, salver, 12" d., clear 4.00
Platter, 13" oval, clear 7.50
Platter, 13" oval, Cremax 9.00
Platter, 13" oval, Monax or pink 10.50
Sherbet, Cremax 5.00
Sherbet, Monax 7.50
Sherbet, pink 6.00
Sugar bowl, open, footed, Cremax .. 5.00
Sugar bowl, open, footed, Monax
or pink 4.50
Tid bit server, clear 12.00
Tid bit server, Monax 21.50

PINEAPPLE & FLORAL or Number 618 or Wildflower (Press-mold)
Ash tray, clear, 4½" 11.50

Bowl, berry, 4½" d., amber 19.50
Bowl, berry, 4½" d., clear 31.50
Bowl, cream soup, 4 5/8" d.,
amber 13.50
Bowl, cream soup, 4 5/8" d., clear .. 16.00
Bowl, cereal, 6" d., clear 17.00
Bowl, salad, 7" d., clear 3.75
Bowl, 10" oval vegetable, amber ... 13.00
Bowl, 10" oval vegetable, clear 16.50
Compote, diamond-shaped, amber .. 7.50
Compote, diamond-shaped, clear ... 2.00
Creamer & open sugar bowl,
diamond-shaped, amber or clear,
pr. 12.00
Cup & saucer, amber or clear 8.50
Plate, sherbet, 6" d., amber 4.00
Plate, sherbet, 6" d., clear 2.75
Plate, salad, 8 3/8" d., amber 6.00
Plate, salad, 8 3/8" d., clear 5.00
Plate, dinner, 9 3/8" d., amber 10.00
Plate, dinner, 9 3/8" d., clear 8.50
Plate, grill, 10½" d., clear 12.50
Plate, 11½" d., amber 12.00
Plate, 11½" d., clear 10.50
Platter, 11", closed handles,
amber 12.00
Platter, 11", closed handles, clear .. 9.00
Relish, divided, clear, 11½" 10.00
Sherbet, amber 9.50
Sherbet, clear 13.00
Tumbler, clear, 4" h., 9 oz. 22.00
Tumbler, iced tea, clear, 4½" h.,
12 oz. 38.00

PRINCESS (Process-etched)

Princess Cookie Jar

Ash tray, green, 4" 55.00
Bowl, nappy, 4½" d., green 16.50
Bowl, nappy, 4½" d., pink 12.00
Bowl, 5½" d., amber or green 17.50
Bowl, 5½" d., pink 13.00
Bowl, 5½" d., pink frosted 6.50
Bowl, 5½" d., yellow 20.00
Bowl, salad, 9" octagon, green 22.00
Bowl, salad, 9" octagon, pink 25.50
Bowl, salad, 9" octagon, yellow 88.00
Bowl, 9½" hat shape, green 22.00
Bowl, 9½" hat shape, pink 30.00

Bowl, 10" oval vegetable, green	15.00
Bowl, 10" oval vegetable, pink	14.00
Bowl, 10" oval vegetable, yellow ...	41.00
Butter dish, cov., green	62.00
Butter dish, cov., pink	60.00
Cake stand, footed, green, 10" d. ..	13.50
Cake stand, footed, pink, 10" d.	12.50
Candy jar, cov., green	32.50
Candy jar, cov., pink	38.50
Coaster, green, 4"	19.00
Coaster, yellow, 4"	6.00
Cookie jar, cov., green (ILLUS.)	32.00
Cookie jar, cov., green frosted	28.00
Cookie jar, cov., pink	36.00
Creamer, amber	6.00
Creamer & cov. sugar bowl, green, pr.	27.00
Creamer & cov. sugar bowl, pink or yellow, pr.	29.50
Creamer & open sugar bowl, green, pr.	16.00
Creamer & open sugar bowl, pink, pr.	12.00
Creamer & open sugar bowl, yellow, pr.	14.00
Cup & saucer, amber, pink or yellow	8.00
Cup & saucer, green	11.00
Pitcher, 6" h., 37 oz., jug-type, green	31.00
Pitcher, 6" h., 37 oz., jug-type, pink	25.00
Pitcher, 8" h., 60 oz., jug-type, amber	49.00
Pitcher, 8" h., 60 oz., jug-type, green	33.00
Pitcher, 8" h., 60 oz., jug-type, pink	29.00
Pitcher, 8" h., 60 oz., jug-type, yellow	55.50
Plate, sherbet, 6" d., amber or green	4.00
Plate, sherbet, 6" d., pink or yellow	3.00
Plate, salad, 8" d., amber..........	5.50
Plate, salad, 8" d., green	7.00
Plate, salad, 8" d., pink or yellow	6.00
Plate, dinner, 9½" d., amber.......	8.00
Plate, dinner, 9½" d., green	16.00
Plate, dinner, 9½" d., pink	10.50
Plate, dinner, 9½" d., yellow	9.00
Plate, grill, 9½" d., amber	4.50
Plate, grill, 9½" d., green	9.00
Plate, grill, 9½" d., pink..........	7.00
Plate, grill, 9½" d., yellow	5.50
Plate, grill, 11½" d., handled, amber or yellow	6.00
Plate, grill, 11½" d., handled, green	9.00
Plate, grill, 11½" d., handled, pink	6.50
Plate, 11½" d., handled, green.....	15.00
Plate, 11½" d., handled, pink	10.00

Platter, 12" oval, green or pink.....	13.50
Platter, 12" oval, yellow	28.00
Relish, divided, green	16.50
Relish, divided, pink..............	10.50
Relish, divided, yellow	12.00
Salt & pepper shakers, green, 4½" h., pr....................	37.00
Salt & pepper shakers, pink, 4½" h., pr....................	35.00
Salt & pepper shakers, yellow, 4½" h., pr....................	67.00
Salt & pepper (or spice) shakers, green, 5½" h., pr.	27.50
Salt & pepper (or spice) shakers, yellow, 5½" h., pr.	54.00
Sherbet, green	12.00
Sherbet, pink	10.00
Sherbet, yellow	23.00
Sugar bowl, cov., amber	18.00
Sugar bowl, open, amber	7.00
Sugar bowl, open, pink frosted	2.75
Tumbler, green or yellow, 3½" h., 5 oz........................	19.00
Tumbler, pink, 3½" h., 5 oz.	13.00
Tumbler, green or yellow, 4" h., 9 oz........................	16.50
Tumbler, pink, 4" h., 9 oz.	12.00
Tumbler, footed, green, 5¼" h., 10 oz.......................	20.50
Tumbler, footed, pink or yellow, 5¼" h., 10 oz.	15.00
Tumbler, footed, green, 6½" h., 12 oz.......................	52.00
Tumbler, footed, pink, 6½" h., 12 oz.......................	28.50
Tumbler, footed, yellow, 6½" h., 12 oz.......................	19.00
Tumbler, green, 5" h., 12½ oz......	24.00
Tumbler, pink, 5" h., 12½ oz.	15.00
Tumbler, yellow, 5" h., 12½ oz.	18.50
Vase, 8" h., green or pink	20.00
Vase, 8" h., pink frosted	12.00
Water set: pitcher & 4 tumblers; green, 5 pcs.	110.00

QUEEN MARY or Ribbed Vertical (Press-mold)

Queen Mary Cup & Saucer

Ash tray, oval, clear	2.50
Ash tray, square, clear	4.00
Bowl, nappy, 4" d., clear or pink ...	2.50
Bowl, nappy, 4" d., handled, clear ..	2.50

Bowl, nappy, 4" d., handled, pink ..	3.00
Bowl, dessert, 4½" d., clear	1.50
Bowl, dessert, 4½" d., pink	2.50
Bowl, 5½" d., 2-handled, clear	2.25
Bowl, 5½" d., 2-handled, pink.....	4.00
Bowl, 6" d., clear or pink	4.50
Bowl, nappy, 7" d., clear	4.50
Bowl, nappy, 7" d., pink	6.00
Bowl, 8¾" d., clear	7.50
Bowl, 8¾" d., pink	10.00
Butter (or jam) dish, cov., clear	18.00
Butter (or jam) dish, cov., pink ...	76.00
Candlesticks, clear, 4½" h., pr.	10.50
Candy jar, cov., clear	13.50
Candy jar, cov., pink	21.00
Celery dish, oval, clear	5.50
Celery dish, oval, pink	16.50
Cigarette jar, clear, 2 x 3" oval.....	8.50
Coaster, clear or pink, 3½" d.	2.00
Coaster-ash tray, clear, 4¼" d.....	2.25
Coaster-ash tray, pink, 4¼" d.	9.00
Coaster-ash tray, ruby, 4¼" d.	4.00
Compote, 5¾" d., clear	7.00
Creamer, clear or pink	4.00
Cup & saucer, clear	4.50
Cup & saucer, pink (ILLUS.).........	7.00
Pickle dish, clear.................	5.00
Plate, sherbet, 6" d., clear or pink..	2.00
Plate, 6¾" d., clear	2.25
Plate, 6¾" d., pink...............	5.50
Plate, salad, 8½" d., clear	3.50
Plate, salad, 8½" d., pink	6.00
Plate, dinner, 10" d., clear	11.50
Plate, dinner, 10" d., pink	20.00
Plate, 12" d., clear	7.00
Plate, 12" d., pink...............	15.00
Plate, 14" d., clear	5.50
Punch cup, pink..................	4.00
Punch set: punch bowl & 10 cups; pink, 11 pcs......................	65.00
Relish, 3-part, clear, 12" d.........	6.00
Relish, 4-part, clear, 14" d.........	8.00
Salt & pepper shakers, clear, pr. ...	16.00
Salt & pepper shakers, clear w/red tops, pr.......................	20.00
Salt & pepper shakers, pink, pr.	12.00
Sherbet, clear...................	3.00
Sherbet, pink	4.50
Sugar bowl, open, clear or pink	4.50
Tumbler, juice, clear, 3½" h., 5 oz............................	2.50
Tumbler, juice, pink, 3½" h., 5 oz............................	5.00
Tumbler, water, clear, 4" h., 9 oz. ..	4.00
Tumbler, water, pink, 4" h., 9 oz. ..	6.00
Tumbler, footed, clear, 5" h., 10 oz............................	11.00
Tumbler, footed, pink, 5" h., 10 oz............................	20.00
Vase, ruffled rim, clear	6.50

RAINDROPS or Optic Design (Press-mold)

(All items listed are green.)

Bowl, berry, 4½" d.	4.00
Bowl, cereal, 6" d.	5.75
Creamer	6.00
Cup & saucer	5.50
Plate, sherbet, 6" d.	2.00
Plate, luncheon, 8" d.	4.50
Sherbet	4.00
Tumbler, whiskey, 1 7/8" h........	4.00
Tumbler, 3" h., 4 oz.	4.00
Tumbler, 11 oz.	7.50

RIBBON (Press-mold)

(While pattern was also made in black, all items listed are green.)

Bowl, 4" d.	12.00
Bowl, 8" d.	12.50
Candy dish, cov.	24.50
Creamer & open sugar bowl, footed, pr..............................	9.00
Cup & saucer	6.00
Plate, sherbet, 6¼" d.	1.75
Plate, luncheon, 8" d.	3.50
Salt & pepper shakers, pr.	13.50
Sherbet	3.50
Tumbler, 5½" h., 10 oz.	13.00
Tumbler, 6½" h., 13 oz.	14.00

RING or Banded Rings (Press-mold)

Bowl, 5" d., clear	3.50
Bowl, 8" d., green	7.00
Butter tub or ice bucket, clear......	8.00
Butter tub or ice bucket, green	17.00
Cocktail shaker, clear	10.50
Cocktail shaker, green............	12.00
Creamer & open sugar bowl, footed, clear, pr......................	8.75
Creamer & open sugar bowl, footed, green, pr......................	11.00
Cup & saucer, clear	4.50
Cup & saucer, green	3.75
Decanter w/stopper, clear	10.50
Decanter w/stopper, green	18.50
Goblet, clear, 7" h. 9 oz.	5.00
Goblet, green, 7" h., 9 oz.	7.50
Pitcher, 8" h., 60 oz., clear.........	9.50
Pitcher, 8" h., 60 oz., green	10.00
Pitcher, 8½" h., 80 oz., clear	11.50
Pitcher, 8½" h., 80 oz., green	15.00
Plate, sherbet, 6¼" d., clear	1.50
Plate, sherbet, 6¼" d., green	2.25
Plate, 6½" d., off-center ring, clear.........................	1.50
Plate, 6½" d., off-center ring, green.........................	2.50
Plate, luncheon, 8" d., clear........	5.50
Plate, luncheon, 8" d., green	3.00
Salt & pepper shakers, clear, 3" h., pr..............................	18.50
Sandwich server w/center handle, clear	9.50
Sandwich server w/center handle, green	13.00
Sherbet, low, clear	3.25

Sherbet, low, green	4.50
Sherbet, footed, clear, 4¾"	3.50
Tumbler, whiskey, clear, 2" h., 1½ oz.	3.50
Tumbler, clear, 3½" h., 5 oz.	2.50
Tumbler, green, 3½" h., 5 oz.	4.00
Tumbler, clear, 4¼" h., 9 oz.	2.50
Tumbler, green, 4¼" h., 9 oz.	4.25
Tumbler, clear, 5 1/8" h., 12 oz.	3.50
Tumbler, green, 5 1/8" h., 12 oz.	5.00
Tumbler, cocktail, footed, clear, 3½" h.	3.25
Tumbler, cocktail, footed, green, 3½" h.	4.00
Tumbler, water, footed, clear, 5½" h.	3.75
Tumbler, iced tea, footed, clear or green, 6½" h.	4.00

ROULETTE or Many Windows (Press-mold)

Bowl, fruit, 9" d., green	9.00
Cup & saucer, green	5.50
Pitcher, 8" h., 64 oz., green	35.50
Pitcher, 8" h., 64 oz., pink	20.50
Plate, sherbet, 6" d., green	1.50
Plate, luncheon, 8½" d., clear	3.00
Plate, luncheon, 8½" d., green	3.50
Plate, 12" d., green	8.00
Sherbet, green	3.75
Tumbler, whiskey, green, 2½" h., 1½ oz.	7.00
Tumbler, whiskey, pink, 2½" h., 1½ oz.	6.00
Tumbler, juice, pink, 3¼" h., 5 oz.	3.50
Tumbler, water, green, 4 1/8" h., 9 oz.	10.50
Tumbler, water, pink, 4 1/8" h., 9 oz.	9.00
Tumbler, footed, green, 5½" h., 10 oz.	14.50
Tumbler, iced tea, green or pink, 5 1/8" h., 12 oz.	8.50

ROYAL LACE (Process-etched)

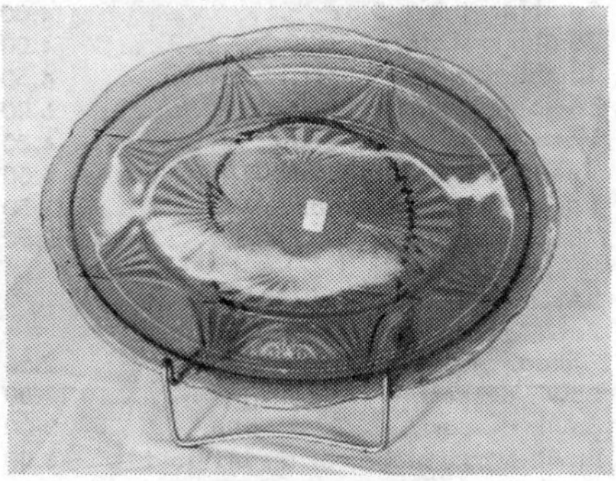

Royal Lace Platter

Bowl, cream soup, 5" d., blue	21.50
Bowl, cream soup, 5" d., clear	8.00
Bowl, cream soup, 5" d., green	19.00
Bowl, cream soup, 5" d., pink	11.00
Bowl, nappy, 5" d., blue	23.00
Bowl, nappy, 5" d., clear	11.50
Bowl, nappy, 5" d., green	18.50
Bowl, nappy, 5" d., pink	15.50
Bowl, nappy, 10" d., blue	35.00
Bowl, nappy, 10" d., green	19.50
Bowl, nappy, 10" d., pink	15.50
Bowl, 10" d., 3-footed, rolled edge, blue	42.00
Bowl, 10" d., 3-footed, rolled edge, pink	34.00
Bowl, 10" d., 3-footed, ruffled edge, blue	260.00
Bowl, 10" d., 3-footed, ruffled edge, clear	17.50
Bowl, 10" d., 3-footed, ruffled edge, pink	20.50
Bowl, 10" d., 3-footed, straight edge, blue	46.00
Bowl, 10" d., 3-footed, straight edge, clear	15.50
Bowl, 10" d., 3-footed, straight edge, pink	20.00
Bowl, 11" oval vegetable, blue	40.00
Bowl, 11" oval vegetable, clear	13.50
Bowl, 11" oval vegetable, green	19.50
Bowl, 11" oval vegetable, pink	16.00
Butter dish, cov., blue	275.00
Butter dish, cov., clear	50.00
Butter dish, cov., green	210.00
Butter dish, cov., pink	115.00
Candlesticks, rolled edge, blue, pr.	95.00
Candlesticks, rolled edge, clear, pr.	30.00
Candlesticks, rolled edge, green, pr.	56.50
Candlesticks, rolled edge, pink, pr.	38.50
Candlesticks, ruffled edge, blue, pr.	94.00
Candlesticks, ruffled edge, clear or green, pr.	35.00
Candlesticks, ruffled edge, pink, pr.	32.50
Candlesticks, straight edge, blue, pr.	80.00
Candlesticks, straight edge, clear, pr.	22.50
Candlesticks, straight edge, green, pr.	57.50
Candlesticks, straight edge, pink, pr.	36.50
Cookie jar, cov., blue	205.00
Cookie jar, cov., clear	30.00
Cookie jar, cov., green	55.50
Cookie jar, cov., pink	34.00
Creamer, clear	7.00
Creamer & cov. sugar bowl, blue, pr.	120.00
Creamer & cov. sugar bowl, green, pr.	52.00

Creamer & cov. sugar bowl, pink,
pr. 42.00
Creamer & open sugar bowl, blue,
pr. 43.50
Creamer & open sugar bowl, green,
pr. 27.50
Cup & saucer, blue 27.00
Cup & saucer, clear 8.50
Cup & saucer, green 17.00
Cup & saucer, pink 13.00
Nut dish, pink, 5" d. 105.00
Pitcher, 54 oz., straight sides,
blue 83.50
Pitcher, 54 oz., straight sides,
green 70.00
Pitcher, 54 oz., straight sides,
pink 56.00
Pitcher, 8" h., 68 oz., blue 108.00
Pitcher, 8" h., 68 oz., clear 37.00
Pitcher, 8" h., 68 oz., pink 46.00
Pitcher, 8" h., 80 oz., blue 120.00
Pitcher, 8" h., 80 oz., green 76.00
Pitcher, 8" h., 80 oz., pink 52.50
Pitcher, 8½" h., 96 oz., blue 145.00
Pitcher, 8½" h., 96 oz., clear 43.00
Pitcher, 8½" h., 96 oz., green 97.50
Pitcher, 8½" h., 96 oz., pink 68.00
Plate, sherbet, 6" d., blue 7.50
Plate, sherbet, 6" d., clear or pink .. 3.50
Plate, sherbet, 6" d., green 5.50
Plate, luncheon, 8½" d., blue 25.00
Plate, luncheon, 8½" d., clear 5.00
Plate, luncheon, 8½" d., green or
pink 12.00
Plate, dinner, 10" d., blue 27.50
Plate, dinner, 10" d., clear 8.00
Plate, dinner, 10" d., green 14.50
Plate, dinner, 10" d., pink 13.50
Plate, grill, 10" d., blue 20.50
Plate, grill, 10" d., green 12.50
Plate, grill, 10" d., pink 11.50
Platter, 13" oval, blue (ILLUS.) 37.00
Platter, 13" oval, clear 13.50
Platter, 13" oval, green 25.00
Platter, 13" oval, pink 15.00
Salt & pepper shakers, blue, pr. 195.00
Salt & pepper shakers, clear, pr. ... 35.50
Salt & pepper shakers, green, pr. ... 95.00
Salt & pepper shakers, pink, pr. 41.50
Sherbet, blue 22.50
Sherbet, clear 7.00
Sherbet, green 16.50
Sherbet, pink 9.50
Sherbet in metal holder, blue 18.50
Sherbet in metal holder, clear 7.00
Sugar bowl, cov., clear 27.50
Sugar bowl, open, clear 7.00
Toddy set: cov. cookie jar, 8
tumblers, metal tray & ladle;
blue, 11 pcs. 180.00
Tumbler, blue, 3" h., 5 oz. 25.00
Tumbler, clear, 3" h., 5 oz. 8.00
Tumbler, green, 3" h., 5 oz. 18.00
Tumbler, pink, 3" h., 5 oz. 14.00

Tumbler, blue, 4" h., 9 oz. 22.00
Tumbler, clear, 4" h., 9 oz. 8.00
Tumbler, green, 4" h., 9 oz. 18.00
Tumbler, pink, 4" h., 9 oz. 11.00
Tumbler, blue or green, 4¾" h.,
12 oz. 40.00
Tumbler, pink, 4¾" h., 12 oz. 15.00
Tumbler, blue, 5 3/8" h., 13 oz. 44.00
Tumbler, clear, 5 3/8" h., 13 oz. 30.00
Tumbler, green, 5 3/8" h., 13 oz. ... 50.00
Tumbler, pink, 5 3/8" h., 13 oz. 34.00

ROYAL RUBY (Press-mold)

(All items in ruby red.)

Ash tray, 4½" sq. 3.50
Bowl, berry, 4¼" d. 3.50
Bowl, 5¼" d. 6.00
Bowl, soup, 7½" d. 8.00
Bowl, 8" oval vegetable 14.50
Bowl, berry, 8½" d. 10.00
Console bowl, 11½" d. 18.00
Creamer, flat 5.00
Creamer, footed 4.50
Creamer & sugar bowl, flat, pr. 9.00
Creamer & sugar bowl, footed, pr. .. 12.00
Cup & saucer 4.50
Goblet, ball stem 6.50
Pitcher, 22 oz., tilted or upright 17.00
Pitcher, 42 oz., tilted or upright 18.50
Pitcher, 3-qt., tilted or upright 25.00
Plate, sherbet, 6½" d. 3.00
Plate, salad, 7" d. 3.50
Plate, luncheon, 7¾" d. 4.00
Plate, dinner, 9" d. 6.50
Punch bowl 24.50
Punch bowl & base 45.00
Punch cup 2.00
Punch set, punch bowl, base & 12
cups, 14 pcs. 80.00
Salt & pepper shakers, pr. 62.50
Sherbet 5.50
Sugar bowl, flat 4.50
Sugar bowl, footed 7.50
Tumbler, cocktail, 3½ oz. 4.50
Tumbler, juice, 5 oz. 4.00
Tumbler, water, 9 oz. 4.00
Tumbler, water, 10 oz. 4.50
Tumbler, iced tea, 13 oz. 6.00
Vase, 4" h., ball-shaped 4.00
Vase, bud, 5½" h., ruffled top 5.50
Vase, 6½" h., bulbous 7.50
Wine, 2½ oz. 6.50

SANDWICH (Press-mold)

Bowl, dessert, 4 7/8" d., amber,
clear or desert gold 2.50
Bowl, dessert, 4 7/8" d., green 2.00
Bowl, dessert, 4 7/8" d., pink 3.00
Bowl, 6" d., amber or desert gold .. 6.00
Bowl, 6" d., clear 8.50
Bowl, 6" d., pink 7.00
Bowl, salad, 6½" d., amber or
desert gold 6.00

Bowl, salad, 6½" d., clear	4.50
Bowl, salad, 6½" d., green	21.50
Bowl, nappy, 7" d., clear	6.00
Bowl, nappy, 7" d., green	28.00
Bowl, 8" d., clear	6.00
Bowl, 8" d., desert gold	5.00
Bowl, 8" d., green	36.00
Bowl, 8" d., pink	10.50
Bowl, 8½" d., red	23.00
Bowl, 8½" oval vegetable, amber	6.00
Bowl, 8½" oval vegetable, clear	4.00
Bowl, 8½" oval vegetable, green	40.00
Bowl, 8½" oval vegetable, pink	17.00
Bowl, 9" d., amber	10.00
Bowl, 9" d., clear	11.50
Butter dish, cov., amber	37.50
Butter dish, cov., clear	22.00
Cookie jar, cov., amber	26.00
Cookie jar, cov., clear or desert gold	24.00
Cookie jar, cov., green	14.00
Creamer, green	13.00
Creamer & cov. sugar bowl, clear, pr.	14.50
Creamer & open sugar bowl, clear, pr.	5.50
Cup & saucer, amber	4.50
Cup & saucer, clear	3.00
Cup & saucer, desert gold	4.00
Cup & saucer, green	19.00
Custard cup, clear	3.00
Custard cup, green	2.00
Pitcher, juice, 6" h., 36 oz., clear	43.00
Pitcher, juice, 6" h., 36 oz., green	82.00
Pitcher w/ice lip, 2-qt., clear	40.00
Pitcher w/ice lip, 2-qt., green	160.00
Plate, 4½" d., amber	1.50
Plate, 4½" d., green	1.75
Plate, dessert, 7" d., amber	3.00
Plate, dessert, 7" d., clear	5.00
Plate, dessert, 7" d., desert gold	2.25
Plate, 8" d., clear	2.75
Plate, dinner, 9" d., amber or desert gold	4.50
Plate, dinner, 9" d., clear	8.50
Plate, dinner, 9" d., green	40.00
Plate, snack, 9" d., clear	3.75
Plate, serving, 12" d., amber	8.00
Plate, serving, 12" d., clear	14.00

Sandwich Punch Bowl and Base

Punch bowl & base, clear (ILLUS.)	25.00
Punch cup, clear	1.75
Punch set: punch bowl & 7 cups; clear, 8 pcs.	40.00
Punch set: punch bowl, base, 10 cups & ladle; white, 13 pcs.	20.00
Punch set: punch bowl & 13 cups; white, 14 pcs.	30.00
Sherbet, clear	4.00
Sugar bowl, cov., green	16.50
Sugar bowl, open, green	12.50
Tumbler, clear, 5 oz.	4.00
Tumbler, green, 5 oz.	2.50
Tumbler, water, clear, 9 oz.	5.00
Tumbler, water, green, 9 oz.	3.00
Tumbler, footed, clear, 9½ oz.	13.00
Vase, green	14.00
Water set: ice lip pitcher & 6 tumblers; green, 7 pcs.	125.00

SHARON or Cabbage Rose (Chip-mold)

Bowl, cream soup, 5" d., amber	15.50
Bowl, cream soup, 5" d., green	27.00
Bowl, cream soup, 5" d., pink	24.00
Bowl, nappy, 5" d., amber	4.50
Bowl, nappy, 5" d., green	7.00
Bowl, nappy, 5" d., pink	6.00
Bowl, cereal, 6" d., amber	10.50
Bowl, cereal, 6" d., green or pink	13.00
Bowl, soup, 7½" d., amber or pink	23.50
Bowl, nappy, 8½" d., amber	4.00
Bowl, nappy, 8½" d., green	18.00
Bowl, nappy, 8½" d., pink	15.00
Bowl, 9½" oval vegetable, amber	9.00
Bowl, 9½" oval vegetable, green	15.00
Bowl, 9½" oval vegetable, pink	12.00
Bowl, fruit, 10½" d., amber	13.50
Bowl, fruit, 10½" d., green or pink	20.00
Butter dish, cov., amber	37.50
Butter dish, cov., green	65.00
Butter dish, cov., pink	33.00
Cake plate, footed, amber, 11½" d.	14.50
Cake plate, footed, clear, 11½" d.	9.00
Cake plate, footed, green, 11½" d.	49.00
Cake plate, footed, pink, 11½" d.	21.00
Candy jar, cov., amber	30.00
Candy jar, cov., green	135.00
Candy jar, cov., pink	32.00
Cheese dish, cov., amber	150.00
Cheese dish, cov., pink	580.00
Creamer, amber	7.00
Creamer, green	12.00
Creamer, pink	9.00
Cup & saucer, amber	9.00
Cup & saucer, green	13.50
Cup & saucer, pink	11.50
Jam dish, amber, 7½"	20.00
Jam dish, green, 7½"	29.50
Jam dish, pink, 7½"	83.00

Pitcher, 9" h., 80 oz., amber 87.00
Pitcher, 9" h., 80 oz., pink 95.00
Pitcher w/ice lip, 9" h., 80 oz.,
    amber 87.50
Pitcher w/ice lip, 9" h., 80 oz.,
    clear 45.00
Pitcher w/ice lip, 9" h., 80 oz.,
    green 325.00
Pitcher w/ice lip, 9" h., 80 oz.,
    pink 92.00
Plate, bread & butter, 6" d.,
    amber 2.50
Plate, bread & butter, 6" d., green.. 3.75
Plate, bread & butter, 6" d., pink ... 3.00
Plate, salad, 7½" d., amber 9.50
Plate, salad, 7½" d., green 12.00
Plate, salad, 7½" d., pink 16.00
Plate, dinner, 9¼" d., amber 8.00
Plate, dinner, 9¼" d., green 11.50
Plate, dinner, 9¼" d., pink 10.00
Platter, 12¼" oval, amber 10.00
Platter, 12¼" oval, green 14.00
Platter, 12¼" oval, pink 12.00
Salt & pepper shakers, amber or
    pink, pr. 31.00
Salt & pepper shakers, green, pr.... 49.00
Sherbet, amber 7.50
Sherbet, green 20.00
Sherbet, pink 8.50
Sugar bowl, cov., amber 18.00
Sugar bowl, cov., green 32.00
Sugar bowl, cov., pink 26.00
Sugar bowl, open, amber 6.00
Sugar bowl, open, green 8.50
Sugar bowl, open, pink 7.50
Tumbler, amber or pink, 4" h.,
    9 oz. 18.50
Tumbler, green, 4" h., 9 oz. 58.00
Tumbler, amber, 5¼" h., 12 oz. 26.50
Tumbler, green, 5¼" h., 12 oz. 51.00
Tumbler, pink, 5¼" h., 12 oz. 30.00
Tumbler, footed, amber, 6½" h.,
    15 oz. 60.00
Tumbler, footed, clear, 6½" h.,
    15 oz. 17.00
Tumbler, footed, pink, 6½" h.,
    15 oz. 32.00

SIERRA or Pinwheel (Press-mold)
Bowl, berry, 4" d., green or pink ... 6.00
Bowl, cereal, 5½" d., green or
    pink 6.50
Bowl, berry, 8½" d., green 15.50
Bowl, berry, 8½" d., pink 11.50
Bowl, 9½" oval vegetable, green ... 33.00
Bowl, 9½" oval vegetable, pink 23.00
Butter dish, cov., green or pink 45.00
Creamer, green 10.00
Creamer, pink 8.50
Cup & saucer, green or pink 10.50
Pitcher, 6½" h., 32 oz., green 61.00
Pitcher, 6½" h., 32 oz., pink 40.00
Plate, dinner, 9" d., green 12.00
Plate, dinner, 9" d., pink 9.00

Platter, 11" oval, green 24.00
Platter, 11" oval, pink 15.50
Salt & pepper shakers, green, pr.... 30.00
Salt & pepper shakers, pink, pr. 26.00
Serving tray, 2-handled, pink 8.50
Sugar bowl, cov., green or pink 21.00
Tumbler, footed, green, 4½" h.,
    9 oz. 43.00
Tumbler, footed, pink, 4½" h.,
    9 oz. 23.00

SPIRAL (Press-mold)

(All items in green only.)

Bowl, berry, 4¾" d. 3.50
Bowl, mixing, 7" d. 16.50
Candlesticks, low, pr. 14.50
Candy dish, cov. 17.00
Creamer, footed 7.75
Ice or butter tub 15.00
Mug 35.00
Pitcher, 7 5/8" h., 58 oz. 26.50
Plate, sherbet, 6" d. 1.50
Plate, luncheon, 8" d. 3.25
Preserve, cov. 14.50
Salt & pepper shakers, pr. 21.50
Sandwich server w/center handle... 19.00
Sherbet 3.50
Sugar bowl, flat 5.50
Sugar bowl, footed 10.00
Tumbler, water, 5" h., 9 oz. 6.00
Tumbler, iced tea, 5¼" h., 12 oz.... 10.00

SWIRL (Press-mold)

Swirl Double Candlesticks

Bowl, nappy, 5¼" d., Delfite or
    ultramarine 6.50
Bowl, nappy, 5¼" d., pink 5.00
Bowl, nappy, 9" d., Delfite 12.00
Bowl, nappy, 9" d., pink 9.00
Bowl, nappy, 9" d., ultramarine 13.50
Bowl, fruit, 10" d., handled, footed,
    ultramarine 22.00
Butter dish, cov., pink 115.00
Butter dish, cov., ultramarine 170.00
Candlesticks, double, ultramarine,
    pr. (ILLUS.) 28.50
Candy dish, cov., pink 58.00
Candy dish, cov., ultramarine 70.00

Candy dish, open, 3-footed, pink, 5½" d. 6.50
Candy dish, open, 3-footed, ultramarine, 5½" d. 7.50
Coaster, pink, 1 x 3¼" 6.50
Coaster, ultramarine, 1 x 3¼" 8.50
Coaster, pink (Goodyear Tire) 15.00
Console bowl, footed, ultramarine, 10½" d. 18.00
Creamer & open sugar bowl, Delfite, pr. 13.00
Creamer & open sugar bowl, pink, pr. 11.00
Creamer & open sugar bowl, ultramarine, pr. 15.50
Cup & saucer, pink 6.50
Cup & saucer, ultramarine 8.50
Plate, sherbet, 6½" d., Delfite or ultramarine 3.00
Plate, sherbet, 6½" d., pink 1.75
Plate, salad, 7¼" d., ultramarine 8.00
Plate, 8" d., ultramarine 8.50
Plate, dinner, 9½" d., Delfite 8.00
Plate, dinner, 9½" d., pink 5.00
Plate, dinner, 9½" d., ultramarine 9.50
Plate, 12½" d., pink 8.00
Plate, 12½" d., ultramarine 13.00
Platter, 12" oval, Delfite 17.00
Salt & pepper shakers, ultramarine, pr. 26.50
Sherbet, pink 5.00
Sherbet, ultramarine 9.50
Soup bowl w/lug handles, ultramarine 15.50
Tumbler, pink, 4" h., 9 oz. 8.50
Tumbler, ultramarine, 4" h., 9 oz. 14.00
Tumbler, footed, pink, 9 oz. 7.00
Tumbler, footed, ultramarine, 9 oz. 20.00
Tumbler, pink, 4¾" h., 12 oz. 15.00
Tumbler, ultramarine, 4¾" h., 12 oz. 29.00
Vase, 6½" h., pink 9.00
Vase, 8½" h., ultramarine 13.50
Water set: pitcher & 6 tumblers; pink, 7 pcs. 67.50

TEA ROOM (Press-mold)

Banana split dish, clear, 7½" 47.50
Banana split dish, green, 7½" 56.00
Banana split dish, pink, 7½" 79.00
Bowl, salad, 8¾" d., green 72.50
Bowl, salad, 8¾" d., pink 46.00
Bowl, 9½" oval vegetable, green 49.00
Bowl, 9½" oval vegetable, pink 38.00
Candlesticks, green, pr. 47.50
Candlesticks, pink, pr. 37.00
Celery or pickle dish, green, 8½" .. 17.50
Creamer & cov. sugar bowl, clear or pink, pr. 24.00
Creamer & cov. sugar bowl, green, pr. 27.50
Creamer & open sugar bowl on tray, pink 54.00
Cup & saucer, green 34.50
Cup & saucer, pink 42.00
Goblet, clear, 9 oz. 40.00
Goblet, green or pink, 9 oz. 63.00
Ice bucket, green 64.00
Ice bucket, pink 51.00
Lamp, electric, green, 9" 42.00
Lamp, electric, pink, 9" 61.00
Mustard, cov., clear 43.00
Parfait, green 76.00
Parfait, pink 35.00
Pitcher, 64 oz., green 105.00
Pitcher, 64 oz., pink 87.50
Plate, sherbet, 6½" d., pink 20.00
Plate, luncheon, 8¼" d., green or pink 31.00
Relish, divided, clear 14.00
Relish, divided, green or pink 15.00
Salt & pepper shakers, clear, pr. 43.50
Salt & pepper shakers, green or pink, pr. 41.00
Sandwich server w/center handle, green or pink 110.00
Sherbet, footed, ice cream, green .. 25.00
Sherbet, footed, ice cream, pink 22.00
Sherbet, low-footed sundae, clear .. 22.00
Sherbet, low-footed sundae, green 18.00
Sherbet, low-footed sundae, pink 16.50
Sherbet, tall-footed sundae, clear 21.50
Sherbet, tall-footed sundae, green .. 32.00
Sherbet, tall-footed sundae, pink 26.00
Sugar bowl, cov., footed, amber, 4½" h. 47.50
Tumbler, footed, green, 6 oz. 19.00
Tumbler, green or pink, 8½ oz. 17.50
Tumbler, footed, clear, 9 oz. 17.50
Tumbler, footed, green, 9 oz. 21.00
Tumbler, footed, pink, 9 oz. 14.00
Tumbler, green, 12 oz. 40.00
Tumbler, pink, 12 oz. 35.00
Vase, 6" h., ruffled rim, green 74.00
Vase, 6" h., ruffled rim, pink 48.50
Vase, 9" h., ruffled rim, clear 18.50
Vase, 9" h., ruffled rim, green 51.00
Vase, 11" h., ruffled rim, green 95.00

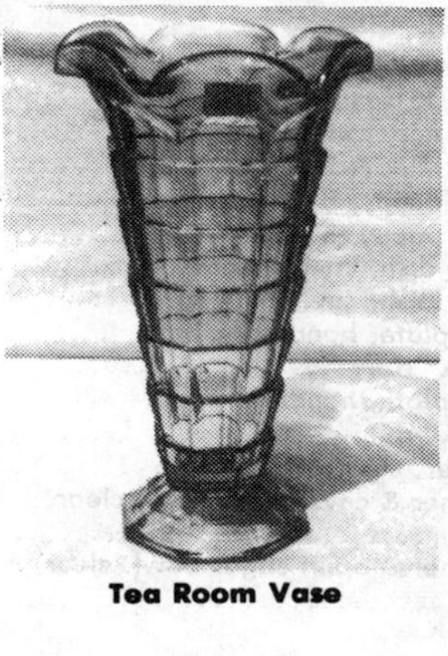

Tea Room Vase

TWISTED OPTIC (Press-mold)

Vase, 11" h., ruffled rim, pink (ILLUS.)	105.00
Water set: pitcher & 6 tumblers; pink, 7 pcs.	180.00

TWISTED OPTIC (Press-mold)

Bowl, cereal, 5" d., pink	7.00
Candlesticks, amber, green or pink, 3", pr.	12.00
Candy jar, cov., green	15.00
Coaster, pink	2.75
Console bowl, rolled edge, pink, 12" d.	12.00
Creamer, green	6.00
Creamer, pink	4.75
Cup & saucer, amber	5.00
Plate, sherbet, 6" d., green	1.50
Plate, luncheon, 8" d., amber or green	3.00
Plate, luncheon, 8" d., pink	2.50
Plate, luncheon, 8" d., yellow	4.75
Preserve jar w/slot in lid, green	15.00
Sandwich server w/center handle, amber	14.00
Sherbet, green	4.50
Sherbet, pink	4.00
Sugar bowl, open, green	4.50

WATERFORD or Waffle (Press-mold)

Waterford Pattern

Ash tray, clear, 4"	3.00
Bowl, dessert, 4¾" d., clear	3.50
Bowl, dessert, 4¾" d., pink	5.50
Bowl, nappy, 5¼" d., clear	8.00
Bowl, nappy, 5¼" d., pink	14.00
Bowl, nappy, 8¼" d., clear	6.00
Bowl, nappy, 8¼" d., pink	11.00
Butter dish, cov., clear	17.50
Butter dish, cov., pink	150.00
Cake plate, handled, clear, 10¼" d.	4.50
Cake plate, handled, pink, 10¼" d.	8.00
Coaster, clear, 4"	1.50
Creamer & cov. sugar bowl, clear, pr.	7.50
Creamer & open sugar bowl, clear, pr.	4.50

Cup & saucer, clear (ILLUS.)	5.50
Goblet, clear, 5¼" h.	10.50
Goblet, clear, 6" h.	8.50
Lamp, clear, 4" h.	24.00
Pitcher, 42 oz., jug-type, clear	14.50
Pitcher w/ice lip, 80 oz., clear	20.00
Pitcher w/ice lip, 80 oz., pink	100.00
Plate, sherbet, 6" d., clear	1.25
Plate, sherbet, 6" d., pink	3.75
Plate, salad, 7½" d., clear	2.50
Plate, salad, 7½" d., pink	6.75
Plate, dinner, 9 5/8" d., clear	4.50
Plate, dinner, 9 5/8" d., pink	10.00
Plate, 10¼" d., handled, pink	8.00
Plate, 13¾" d., clear	7.50
Plate, 13¾" d., pink	13.50
Relish, 5-section, clear w/ruby inserts, 13¾" d.	16.00
Salt & pepper shakers, clear, short, pr.	5.00
Salt & pepper shakers, clear, tall, pr.	5.00
Sherbet, clear	2.50
Sherbet, pink	6.50
Sugar bowl, open, pink	6.00
Tumbler, footed, clear, 3½" h., 5 oz.	5.50
Tumbler, footed, clear, 5" h., 10 oz. (ILLUS.)	7.00
Tumbler, footed, pink, 5" h., 10 oz.	8.00

WINDSOR DIAMOND or Windsor (Press-mold)

Windsor Diamond Butter Dish

Ash tray, Delfite, 5¾" d.	37.00
Ash tray, pink, 5¾" d.	27.50
Bowl, nappy, 4¾" d., clear	2.75
Bowl, nappy, 4¾" d., green	5.50
Bowl, nappy, 4¾" d., pink	4.50
Bowl, cream soup, 5" d., green	13.50
Bowl, cream soup, 5" d., pink	16.00
Bowl, cereal, 5 1/8" d., green	15.00
Bowl, cereal, 5 1/8" d., pink	12.00
Bowl, 5 3/8" d., pink	11.00
Bowl, 7" d., footed, pink	19.00
Bowl, 8" d., 2-handled, pink	9.00
Bowl, nappy, 8½" d., pink	8.50
Bowl, 9½" d., handled, green	14.00
Bowl, 9½" d., handled, pink	9.00
Bowl, 9½" oval vegetable, clear or pink	8.50

Bowl, 9½" oval vegetable, green ... 14.50
Bowl, fruit, 10½" d., clear 11.00
Bowl, fruit, 10½" d., pink, sharp
points 125.00
Bowl, 11¾ x 7" boat shape, clear .. 11.50
Bowl, 11¾ x 7" boat shape, green
or pink 19.00
Bowl, 12½" d., pink 70.00
Butter dish, cov., clear 18.50
Butter dish, cov., green 65.00
Butter dish, cov., pink (ILLUS.) 34.00
Cake plate, footed, clear, 10¾" d... 3.50
Cake plate, footed, green,
10¾" d. 13.00
Cake plate, footed, pink, 10¾" d. .. 10.50
Cake plate, green, 13½" d. 16.00
Candlesticks, clear, 3" h., pr. 10.00
Candlesticks, pink, 3" h., pr. 70.00
Candy jar, cov., clear 10.00
Coaster, green, 3" d. 10.00
Coaster, pink, 3" d. 6.00
Creamer, flat, clear 3.50
Creamer, flat, green 6.50
Creamer, flat, pink 5.50
Creamer, footed, clear 2.50
Creamer, footed, green 9.50
Creamer, footed, pink 7.50
Cup & saucer, clear 4.00
Cup & saucer, green or pink 8.50
Pitcher, milk, 4½" h., 16½ oz.,
clear 13.00
Pitcher, milk, 4½" h., 16½ oz.,
pink 105.00
Pitcher, juice, 5" h., 20 oz., clear ... 9.00
Pitcher, juice, 5" h., 20 oz., pink... 16.00
Pitcher, 6¾" h., 52 oz., clear...... 11.00
Pitcher, 6¾" h., 52 oz., green 38.00
Pitcher, 6¾" h., 52 oz., pink 17.00
Plate, sherbet, 6" d., green 3.50
Plate, sherbet, 6" d., pink 3.00
Plate, salad, 7" d., green 10.00
Plate, salad, 7" d., pink 12.00
Plate, dinner, 9" d., clear 3.50
Plate, dinner, 9" d., green or pink .. 9.00
Plate, chop, 13 5/8" d., clear....... 6.50
Plate, chop, 13 5/8" d., green 14.50
Plate, chop, 13 5/8" d., pink 13.50
Platter, 11½" oval, clear........... 3.75
Platter, 11½" oval, green or pink ... 10.00
Relish, divided, clear, 11½" 5.00
Salt & pepper shakers, clear, pr. ... 11.50
Salt & pepper shakers, green, pr.... 35.00
Salt & pepper shakers, pink, pr. 24.50
Sandwich tray, handled, clear,
10¼" d. 6.00
Sandwich tray, handled, green or
pink, 10¼" d.................. 9.50
Sherbet, green 9.00
Sherbet, pink 6.50
Sugar bowl, cov., flat, pink 13.00
Sugar bowl, cov., footed, clear 4.50
Sugar bowl, cov., footed, green 19.00
Sugar bowl, cov., footed, pink...... 15.50
Sugar bowl, open, clear 3.50

Sugar bowl, open, green 6.50
Sugar bowl, open, pink 5.50
Tray, pink, 4" sq. 22.00
Tray, pink, 8" sq. 63.00
Tray, green, 9 x 4 1/8" 15.50
Tray, pink, 9¾ x 8½" 27.50
Tray, handled, green or pink, 9¾ x
8½" 32.00
Tray, green, 13½" 14.50
Tray, pink, 13½" 11.00
Tumbler, clear, 3¼" h., 5 oz. 3.50
Tumbler, green, 3¼" h., 5 oz....... 25.00
Tumbler, pink, 3¼" h., 5 oz. 8.50
Tumbler, clear, 4" h., 9 oz. 3.50
Tumbler, green, 4" h., 9 oz. 18.00
Tumbler, pink, 4" h., 9 oz. 8.00
Tumbler, footed, clear, 4" h.,
9 oz.......................... 3.75
Tumbler, green, 5" h., 12 oz........ 24.00
Tumbler, pink, 5" h., 12 oz. 13.00

(End of Depression Glass Section)

DE VEZ & DEGUE

Pieces signed "Degue"

Cameo glass with the name De Vez was made in Pantin, France, by Saint-Hilaire, Touvier De Varreaux and Company. Some pieces made by this firm were signed "Degue," after one of the firm's glassmakers. The official company name was "Cristallerie de Pantin."

Cameo atomizer, carved mountains,
lake, cottage & boat, signed
DeVez, 8" h. $425.00
Cameo bowl, 4" w., 3½" h.,
diamond-shaped, carved green to
rose lake scene w/mountainous
background, large tree in foreground, birds & small islands
against frosted gold translucent
ground, signed DeVez 650.00
Cameo bowl, 12" d., 6½" h., vasi-
form w/tapering base, carved
tomato red to aqua blue Indian

paintbrush blossoms & leafage against mottled mint green ground, ca. 1925, signed Degue .. 715.00

Cameo bowl-vase, carved navy blue to rose scene w/man in boat fishing, house on shore & tree branches framing scene against frosted gold ground, signed DeVez, 3 7/8" d., 4¼" h. 675.00

Cameo chalice, carved sapphire blue Art Deco circle-in-square designs against acid-etched emerald green ground shading to sapphire blue spreading foot, ca. 1925, signed Degue (ILLUS. left) 1,320.00

Cameo vase, 4½" h., squat form w/narrow neck, carved frosted dragonfly against clear to shaded vibrant red ground, signed Pantin.......................... 550.00

Cameo vase, 5½" h., carved brown scene w/three elk, water, trees & house against mottled orange ground w/lattice design at top, signed 990.00

Cameo vase, 5¾" h., 3 7/8" d., carved deep green to pink scene w/trees in foreground, water & mountainous background w/village & trees against soft translucent frosted blue ground, signed DeVez 707.00

Cameo vase, 6½" h., baluster-shaped, carved cherry red blossoming poppies against pale yellow ground w/internal iridescence, ca. 1910, signed DeVez 385.00

Cameo vase, 7½" h., carved soft green & tan stylized long-necked birds against yellow ground, signed 675.00

Cameo vase, 8" h., 3 3/8" d., carved deep green to rose Roman temple in cove w/trees, water & hills & branches framing top of scene against frosted gold ground, signed DeVez 695.00

Cameo vase, 8" h., 3½" d., carved green to peach sailboat scene against frosted pearly translucent ground, signed DeVez 995.00

Cameo vase, 8¾" h., 3 3/8" d., carved navy blue to soft yellow island scene w/water, mountainous background & trees against frosted shell pink translucent ground, signed DeVez 650.00

Cameo vase, 9¼" h., 2 3/8" d., carved sailboat scene w/boats in harbor, village shoreline & moonlit sky against purple shaded to soft aqua to translucent white satin ground, signed DeVez 695.00

Cameo vase, 10½" h., carved deep rose-red poppies & 3 butterflies against frosted iridescent ground w/rose & gilt highlights, signed Pantin.......................... 575.00

Cameo vase, 12" h., 4¼" d., carved navy blue to rose sailboat scene against frosted gold ground, signed DeVez 807.00

Cameo vase, 12 3/8" h., swelling ovoid, carved salmon & green scene w/village nestled in a mountain cove & sailboats & trees in foreground against pale blue ground, ca. 1900, signed DeVez .. 605.00

Cameo vase, 13 5/8" h., 4¾" d., carved navy blue to creamy yellow mountain scene framed by leafy pine trees w/pine cones against pale pink frosted ground, signed DeVez 1,250.00

Cameo vase, 14¼" h., teardrop-shaped w/flaring flattened rim, carved lime green & chocolate brown intersecting triangles against pale peach ground, signed Degue (ILLUS. right) 990.00

Degue Cameo Vase

Cameo vase, 15" h., ovoid w/short flaring neck, carved mottled rose abstract triangles & horizontal banding against acid-etched grey ground, ca. 1925, signed Degue (ILLUS.)........................ 990.00

DUNCAN & MILLER

Duncan & Miller Glass Company, a successor firm to George A. Duncan & Sons Company, was operated by George A. Duncan & Edwin C. Miller in Washington, Pa., from the late 19th century and produced many types of pressed wares and novelty pieces, many of which are now eagerly sought by collectors.

George A. Duncan was a pioneer glass manufacturer, associated earlier with several firms. Also see ANIMALS under Glass.

Teardrop Pattern Dish

Ash tray, model of a duck, ruby,
7" $95.00
Bowl, 9" d., ruffled rim, Canterbury
patt., pink opalescent 35.00
Bowl, 10" d., Sanibel patt., vaseline
opalescent 50.00
Butter dish, cov., Teardrop patt.,
clear, ¼ lb. 20.00
Champagne, Mardi Gras patt.,
clear 26.00
Compote, First Love patt.,
clear 65.00
Condiment set: 2 cruets w/stoppers,
salt & pepper shakers & tray;
Teardrop patt., clear, 5 pcs. 40.00
Console set: bowl & pr. candle
holders; Teardrop patt., clear,
3 pcs. 47.50
Dish, heart-shaped, divided, Tear-
drop patt., clear (ILLUS.) 14.00
Goblet, Lily of the Valley patt.,
clear 30.00
Mint dish, Sanibel patt., cranberry
pink 25.00
Nappy, Sanibel patt., blue, 7" 40.00
Pitcher, tankard, Mardi Gras patt.,
clear 99.00
Pitcher, water, Teardrop patt.,
clear 72.50
Plate, 13" d., American Way patt.,
ruby 55.00
Platter, Hobnail patt., cranberry 35.00
Punch set: bowl, 12 cups, ladle &
tray; Caribbean patt., clear
w/ruby handles, 15 pcs. 250.00
Spooner, Mardi Gras patt.,
clear 45.00
Swan, clear, 3½" l. 17.00
Swan, chartreuse w/clear neck,
7" l. 28.00
Swan, milk white w/cobalt blue
neck, 7½" l. 300.00
Swan, emerald green w/clear neck,
10½" l. 40.00
Swan, ruby w/clear neck, 12" l. 60.00
Syrup pitcher w/original top, Mardi
Gras patt., clear 89.00

Torte plate, Teardrop patt., clear,
18" d. 32.00
Tray, Sanibel patt., blue opalescent,
13" 30.00
Tumbler, iced tea, footed, Teardrop
patt., clear, 5¼" h. 10.00
Wine, Hobnail patt., clear 10.00
Wine, Teardrop patt., clear 14.00

DURAND

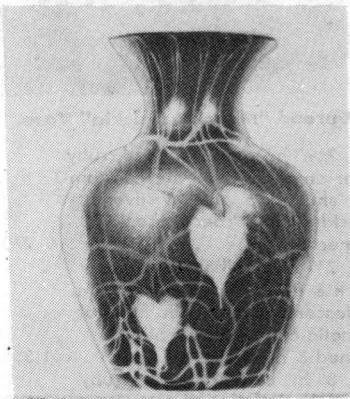

Durand Vase

Fine decorative glass similar to that made by Tiffany and other outstanding glasshouses of its day was made by the Vineland Flint Glass Works Co. in Vineland, N.J., first headed by Victor Durand, Sr., and subsequently by his son Victor Durand, Jr., in the 1920's.

Bowl-vase, iridescent peacock blue,
signed, 7½" d. $695.00
Goblet, gold ruby w/pulled peacock
feathering, 6 5/8" h. 275.00
Perfume bottle, iridescent orange
lustre, signed, 6½" h. 195.00
Vase, 4½" h., flared ruffled ring,
King Tut patt. w/gold scrolling
swirls on soft green, gold lining,
signed 675.00
Vase, 5" h., bulbous, iridescent
gold, signed 185.00
Vase, 6 3/8" h., cased green over
opal w/opal heart & clinging vine
decor (ILLUS.) 500.00
Vase, 6½" h., bulbous w/narrow
neck & flaring rim, iridescent
orange lustre, signed 300.00
Vase, 6½" h., classical shape, gold
lustre w/opal heart & clinging
vine decor 485.00
Vase, 7" h., bulbous, iridescent
gold 400.00
Vase, 7¼" h., deep iridescent blue
w/silver-blue highlights, signed .. 425.00

Durand "Moorish Crackle" Vase

Vase, 7½" h., melon-shaped, ruby
over ambergris w/iridescent amber shaded to violet & silver
crackled "lava" decor, ca. 1928,
signed (ILLUS.) 770.00

Vase, 7¾" h., bulbous w/narrow
neck & flaring turned-down rim,
iridescent gold w/wide band of
intaglio-cut florals on body,
signed & numbered 1,350.00

Vase, 8" h., beaker-shaped, ruby
w/white pulled feathering 540.00

Vase, 8" h., triple-cased iridescent
butterscotch 275.00

Vase, 8 1/16" h., King Tut patt.
w/iridescent gold scrolling trails
on green, orange rim, signed 462.00

Vase, 8¼" h., King Tut patt., green
w/iridescent platinum swirls,
white lining, signed 975.00

Vase, 8½" h., oval form, iridescent
gold w/pulled white & blue
feathering & overlaid w/gold
threading, signed 750.00

Vase, 9" h., King Tut patt., white
w/iridescent gold swirling
scrolls......................... 450.00

Vase, 12" h., ribbed bulbous bottle
shape, blue w/lavender & gold
highlights 750.00

Wine, ruby w/pulled peacock
feathering, 5½" h. 250.00

FENTON

*Fenton Art Glass Company began produc-
ing glass at Williamstown, West Virginia, in
January 1907. Organized by Frank L. and
John W. Fenton, the company began operations in a newly built glass factory with an
experienced master glass craftsman, Jacob
Rosenthal, as their factory manager. Fenton*

*has produced a wide variety of collectible
glassware through the years, including Carnival (which see). Still in production today,
their current productions may be found at
finer gift shops across the country.*

Fenton Art Glass Vase

Basket, Coin Dot patt., blue, 5" $35.00
Basket, Hobnail patt., cranberry
opalescent, 10½" 100.00
Bowl, 10½" d., double crimped rim,
Diamond Optic patt., mulberry ... 65.00
Bowl, 11½" oval, swan handles,
black 100.00
Candlesticks, Hobnail patt., blue
opalescent, pr................... 25.00
Candy jar, cov., Jade green,
9½" h.......................... 33.00
Console set: bowl w/cupped rim &
pr. 8" h. candlesticks; Mandarin
red (opaque), 3 pcs. 125.00
Console set: ruffled bowl & pr. can-
dle holders; Hobnail patt., vase-
line opalescent, 3 pcs. 85.00
Creamer & sugar bowl, Hobnail
patt., green opalescent, pr. 75.00
Cruet w/original stopper, Coin Dot
patt., cranberry, 6¾" h. 55.00
Flower frog, "September Morn
Nymph," opaque black w/Jade
green base 165.00
Pitcher, 4½" h., Hobnail patt., blue
opalescent...................... 23.00
Pitcher, water, Hobnail patt., cran-
berry opalescent 165.00
Pitcher, water, Swirl patt., cranberry
opalescent, applied clear reeded
handle, fluted top 85.00
Rose bowl, Hobnail patt., topaz
opalescent, 4" 35.00
Sugar shaker w/original top, Coin
Dot patt., cranberry 45.00
Tumble-up (water carafe w/tumbler
lid), blue opalescent............ 70.00

Vase, 7" h., Fern patt., blue
  satin 65.00
Vase, 8" h., Dot Optic patt.,
  cranberry 85.00
Vase, 8½" h., "Mosaic Inlaid" art
  glass, mottled red, orange & yellow on cobalt blue w/threading,
  original label (ILLUS.) 200.00
Water set: "cannonball" pitcher & 6
  tumblers; Drapery patt., ruby
  w/enameled decor & gold trim,
  7 pcs. 345.00
Water set: pitcher & 6 tumblers;
  Hobnail patt., blue opalescent,
  7 pcs. 225.00
Whimsey, top hat, Coin Dot patt.,
  lime opalescent 85.00

FINDLAY ONYX

Findlay Onyx Bowl

This ware was produced by Dalzell, Gill-more & Leighton Co., of Findlay, O., about 1889. Some pieces are layered glass and others homogeneous with a molded raised pattern. It was produced in several colors with lustred patterns contrasting with the body color.

Bowl, 8" d., master berry or fruit,
  creamy ivory w/silver (ILLUS.) $600.00
Butter dish, cov., creamy ivory
  w/silver (or platinum), 6" d.,
  4½" h. 1,235.00
Celery vase, creamy ivory w/silver,
  6½" h. .... 350.00 to 500.00
Creamer, raspberry red w/white
  opalescent pattern 850.00
Marmalade jar, cov., raspberry red
  w/white opalescent pattern,
  3 7/8" h. 785.00
Pitcher, water, creamy ivory
  w/silver 600.00
Salt shaker w/original top, creamy
  ivory w/silver (single) 195.00
Spooner, raspberry red w/white
  opalescent pattern ...... 425.00 to 550.00
Sugar bowl, cov., creamy ivory
  w/silver, 4½" d., 6" h. 485.00
Sugar bowl, raspberry red w/white
  opalescent (no lid) 570.00

Sugar shaker w/original top, creamy
  ivory w/silver 365.00
Syrup pitcher w/original top, creamy
  ivory w/silver 575.00
Toothpick holder, creamy ivory
  w/platinum 385.00
Tumbler, barrel-shaped, cased
  orange-amber w/opalescent lining
  & pattern, 3 5/8" h. 800.00

FIREGLOW

Fireglow Vases

Somewhat resembling English Bristol glass, Fireglow usually transmits a reddish-brown color when held to light. Pieces have been attributed to Boston & Sandwich Glass Co. and other glasshouses.

Dish, cov., enameled bird & floral
  decor, 6¼" $50.00
Rose petal jar, cov., enameled
  plums & pears, green & gold
  leaves decor, 4" d., 6½" h. 195.00
Vase, 4" h., cylindrical, enameled
  roses & leaves decor 75.00
Vases, 8" h., enameled red & white
  florals on blue-grey ground, pr.
  (ILLUS.) 175.00
Vase, 11" h., 4½" d., enameled
  birds, flowers & ornate lacy
  brown top border, satin finish 195.00
Vases, 13½" h., pedestal base, gold
  portrait decor, pr. 245.00

FOSTORIA

Fostoria Glass Company, founded in 1887, is still in operation today in Moundsville, West Va. It has produced numerous types of fine wares through the years, many of which are now being collected. Also see ANIMALS under Glass.

Bowl, 9" oval, Versailles patt.,
blue $40.00
Bowl, cream soup, footed, 2-handled, Versailles patt., blue 24.00
Cake plate, 2-handled, Trojan patt., topaz, 10" d. 25.00
Candlesticks, Baroque patt., topaz, 4" h., pr. 30.00
Candlesticks, Kashmir patt., topaz, 5½" h., pr. 30.00
Candy dish, cov., 3-part, Baroque patt., topaz 65.00

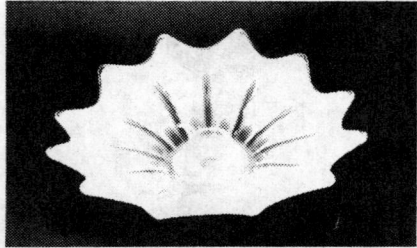

Fostoria Centerpiece Candleholder

Centerpiece candleholder, Heirloom patt., pink opalescent, 9" d. (ILLUS.) 18.00
Champagne, June patt., blue or yellow, each 32.00
Cocktail, Versailles patt., blue or topaz, each 26.50
Console set: console bowl & pr. candlesticks; Versailles patt., pink, 3 pcs. 70.00
Creamer & sugar bowl, June patt., topaz, pr. 46.00
Creamer & sugar bowl on tray, Colony patt., clear, 3 pcs. 23.00
Cruet w/original stopper, Versailles patt., pink 350.00
Cup & saucer, demitasse, June patt., topaz 42.50
Cup & saucer, Versailles patt., pink 22.50
Decanter w/original stopper, Hermitage patt., topaz 95.00
Goblet, June patt., topaz 32.00
Goblet, Trojan patt., topaz 20.00
Goblet, Versailles patt., pink....... 25.00
Ice bucket, Baroque patt., topaz 65.00
Plate, 8¾" d., Versailles patt., topaz 8.00
Platter, 12" oval, Versailles patt., blue 45.00
Sherbet, Versailles patt., pink 20.00
Tumbler, footed, Buttercup patt., clear, 12 oz. 20.00
Tumbler, footed, June patt., pink, 9 oz. 25.00

FRANCES WARE

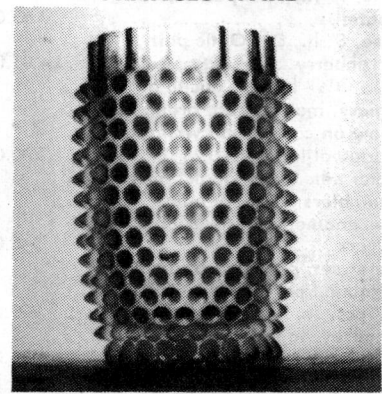

Frances Ware Celery Vase

This was made by Hobbs, Brockunier & Co., Wheeling, West Va., in the 1880's. It is frosted or clear glass with stained amber tops or rims and was both mold-blown and pressed. It usually has a pattern of hobnails or swirled ribs.

Berry set: 9" oval bowl & 12 sauce dishes; frosted swirl w/amber rim, 13 pcs. $375.00
Bowl, berry, 7½" sq., frosted hobnail w/amber rim ....60.00 to 80.00
Bowl, berry, 9 x 7" oval, clear hobnail w/amber rim 65.00
Butter dish, cov., frosted hobnail w/amber rim 95.00
Celery tray, frosted hobnail w/amber rim, 12 x 7" 85.00
Celery vase, frosted hobnail w/amber rim (ILLUS.) 110.00
Creamer, clear hobnail w/amber rim 70.00
Creamer, frosted hobnail w/amber rim 85.00
Finger bowl, frosted swirl w/amber rim 25.00
Ice cream tray, frosted hobnail w/amber rim, 14 x 9½" 225.00
Lemonade set: cloverleaf-shaped tray, pitcher, waste bowl & 2 tumblers; frosted hobnail w/amber rim, 5 pcs. 425.00
Pitcher, milk, 5" h., clear hobnail w/amber rim 165.00
Pitcher, milk, 5½" h., frosted hobnail w/amber rim 185.00
Pitcher, water, frosted hobnail w/amber rim ....150.00 to 185.00
Sauce dish, clear hobnail w/amber rim, 4" sq. 28.00
Sauce dish, frosted hobnail w/amber rim, 4" sq. ....25.00 to 32.00
Spooner, clear hobnail w/amber rim 50.00

Spooner, frosted hobnail w/amber
rim 42.50
Sugar bowl, cov., frosted hobnail
w/amber rim 75.00
Sugar bowl, cov., frosted swirl
w/amber rim ....85.00 to 110.00
Sugar bowl, open, frosted hobnail
w/amber rim 55.00
Syrup pitcher w/original lid, frosted
hobnail w/amber rim 150.00
Toothpick holder, frosted hobnail
w/amber rim 55.00
Toothpick holder, frosted swirl
w/amber rim 90.00
Tumbler, clear hobnail w/amber
rim 35.00
Tumbler, frosted hobnail w/amber
rim 45.00
Water set: pitcher & 4 tumblers;
clear hobnail w/amber rim,
5 pcs. 295.00

FRY

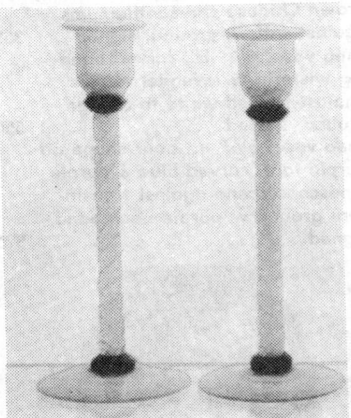

Pearl Art Glass Candlesticks

*Numerous types of glass were made by the
H.C. Fry Company, Rochester, Pa. One type
of its art line was called Foval (and also Pearl
Art Glass) and was blown in the mid-1920's.
Cheaper was its silky-opalescent ovenware
made for utilitarian purposes but also now being collected. The company also made fine cut
glass.*

Basket, Foval, opaline w/applied
Jade green rim & handle,
7½" h. $87.00
Cake pan, ovenware, 8" sq. 12.00
Candlesticks, Foval, twisted stems,
opaline w/Jade green trim,
10" h., pr. (ILLUS.) 450.00
Casserole dish, cov., ovenware,
opalescent, 8" oval 28.00

Compote, 6" d., 7" h., Foval, opaline w/Jade green stem 69.50
Cup & saucer, Foval, opaline
w/Delft blue handle 46.00
Cup & saucer, Foval, opaline
w/Jade green handle 38.00
Custard cup, ovenware,
opalescent..................... 4.00
Juice reamer, ovenware,
opalescent..................... 33.00
Loaf pan, ovenware, 9 x 5"
oblong 12.00
Mugs, Foval, opaline w/vertical
opalescent blue stripes & applied
Delft blue handles, pr........... 100.00
Pie plate, ovenware, opalescent,
w/patent dates ....12.00 to 25.00
Pitcher, water, Foval, opaline
w/vertical blue opalescent stripes
& applied Delft blue handle 100.00
Pitcher, water, clear "crackle," applied Jade green handle, polished
pontil 110.00
Teapot, cov., Foval, opaline w/ap-
plied Delft blue knob finial, handle & spout ....200.00 to 225.00
Tea set: cov. teapot & 3 c/s; Foval,
opaline w/Delft blue trim,
7 pcs. 375.00
Vase, 5" h., Foval, opaline w/Delft
blue foot, rolled rim embellished
w/three silver deposit designs ... 250.00
Vase, 8" h., Foval, opaline w/Jade
green ball connector in stemmed
base 115.00
Vase, 10" h., 6½" flaring rim d.,
Foval, opaline w/three applied
aqua leaves decor ....95.00 to 135.00
Vase, 10" h., cone-shaped, Foval,
opaline w/Jade green base 175.00
Vase, 10¾" h., 5" base d., narrow
neck, Foval, opaline w/applied
Jade green trim................ 125.00
Wine, Foval, opaline w/applied
Delft blue stem 65.00

GALLE'

*Galle' glass was made in Nancy, France, by
Emile Galle', a founder of the Nancy School
and a leader in the Art Nouveau movement
in France. Much of his glass, both enameled
and cameo, is decorated with naturalistic motifs. The finest pieces were made in the last
two decades of the 19th century and the opening years of the present one. Pieces marked
with a star preceding the name were made between Galle's death in 1904 and 1914. Also
see GALLE' POTTERY and FURNITURE
for Art Nouveau style Tables designed by
Galle'.*

Galle' Cameo Bowl-Vase

Cameo bowl, 8½" d., low trefoil form, short circular foot, carved orange & Chinese red wildflowers & leafage against lemon yellow shading to Chinese red ground, ca. 1900, signed $1,100.00

Cameo bowl-vase, carved mauve florals against pink ground, signed, 4½" d., 4¾" h. (ILLUS.) . . 775.00

Cameo box, cov., carved cherry red leafy, berried branches against frosted clear & orange ground, signed w/star, 1904-14, 6" d. 725.00

Cameo decanter w/matching hollow stopper, oviform, ribbed transparent yellow foot, carved red branch of pendant cherry blossoms & cherry clusters against translucent ground, signed, 9¼" h. 770.00

Cameo liqueur, carved dusty rose nasturtium blossoms & leafage against clear ground on bowl, pale avocado short cylindrical standard & circular foot, fire-polished, ca. 1900, signed, 3" h. . . . 770.00

Cameo powder box, cov., carved green leaves against lemon ground, signed & w/original paper label, 7" d., 2¾" h. 850.00

Cameo vase, 3" h., oval, carved & enameled cream, azure, rust, pink, green & brown blossoms & leafage w/gilt details against pale green ground, ca. 1900, signed . . . 880.00

Cameo vase, 3½" h., footed pear shape, carved dark amethyst florals & leaves against frosted ground, signed 450.00

Cameo vase, 3¾" h., bell-shaped, carved purple vine against lemon yellow ground, signed 200.00

Cameo vase, 4¾" h., bulbous, carved pale blue & magenta pond scene against matte white ground shading to orange at the top & bottom, signed 528.00

Cameo vase, 5" h., 3½ x 3", carved rust florals against lemon yellow ground, signed 450.00

Cameo vase, 5" h., baluster-shaped, internally decorated w/emerald & turquoise green, rust & gilt foil streaks, wheel-carved butterflies (3) in flight against transparent lemon yellow hammered ground, ca. 1895, signed 1,980.00

Cameo vase, 5" h., bulbous bottom, carved dark red vine against burnt orange ground, signed 350.00

Cameo vase, 5" h., cylindrical, carved mauve florals against cream ground, fire-polished, signed w/star, 1904-14 . . . . 330.00

Cameo vase, 5¾" h., 3½" d., carved brown to green scene w/waterlily buds & pods in foreground & leafy green trees on background shore against frosted shell pink ground, signed 595.00

Cameo vase, 6½" h., 3 1/8" d., banjo form, carved deep brown to green ferns against frosted ground, signed w/star 350.00

Cameo vase, 6½" h., baluster-shaped, carved deep yellow & brown Chinese chrysanthemums against saffron ground, signed . . . 352.00

Cameo vase, 6½" h., carved hanging wisteria w/lavender leaves against frosted white to orange ground, signed 550.00

Cameo vase, 6½" h., pear shape on purple foot, carved blue & purple landscape scene against translucent ground w/purple neck band, signed 825.00

Mold-Blown Cameo Vase

Cameo vase, 9 3/8" h., mold-blown & cameo-carved orange & orange-brown flowering clematis sprays against frosted white & canary yellow ground, signed (ILLUS.) . . . 2,860.00

Cameo vase, 10¼" h., shouldered cylinder, carved purple sprays of hydrangea blossoms & leafage against grey & purple ground, signed w/star, 1904-14 . . . . 770.00

Mold-Blown Cameo Vase

Cameo vase, 11¾" h., mold-blown
& cameo-carved lavender & deep
violet pendant branches of cherry
clusters against grey to yellow
ground, ca. 1925, signed
(ILLUS.) 5,720.00

Cameo Polar Bear Vase

Cameo vase, 14" h., ovoid, carved
opaque & creamy white Arctic
scene w/three polar bears & icebergs against translucent sapphire
blue ground, signed 20,900.00
Cameo vase, 15 5/8" h., baluster-
shaped, mold-blown & cameo-
carved deep violet & smoky blue
plum-laden branches against frosted yellow ground, ca. 1900,
signed 3,575.00
Cameo vase, 16¼" h., lozenge-
shaped, flaring rim, carved dark
green aquatic scene of slender
arrowheads & marsh grass above
numerous lily pads against streaked blue & green ground, signed . .9,900.00

Cameo vase, 17" h., baluster-shaped,
carved pink & burgundy magnolia
sprays against yellow-tinted matte
white ground, signed 2,750.00
Cameo vase, 17½" h., slender cylindrical neck, flattened circular foot,
carved lime green undulating ferns
& grasses against pale grey streaked w/lemon yellow ground, 1904-10,
signed w/star 1,650.00
Cameo vase, 19 5/8" h., baluster-
shaped, carved violet & green blossoming leafy stalks against grey
shading to cornflower blue ground,
1904-14, signed w/star 1,870.00
Cameo vase, 20" h., teardrop form
w/trefoil rim, carved pale & dark
pink flowering columbines & leaves
w/opal iridescence against beige
ground, signed 4,620.00
Cameo vase, 23¼" h., stick-type,
carved deep cherry red berry-laden
boughs against yellow to frosted
ground, signed w/star 1,850.00
Cameo vase, 23½" h., bulbous w/tall
cylindrical neck, carved brown floral sprays against matte white &
saffron ground, signed 1,320.00
Compote, 7¼" d., enameled forget-
me-nots on clear ground, in gilt
metal base 750.00
Decanter set: whiskey decanter & 6
shot glasses; enameled florals on
dark tan ground, each shot glass
w/different toast in French,
signed, 7 pcs. 1,750.00
Vase, 8" h., stick-type, twisted &
fluted base, enameled thistle &
cross of Lorraine, signed 600.00
Vase, 10½" h., 3 pinched-in sides,
enameled gold, blue, green & yellow florals, leaves & intricate
designs on rust-brown & tan moss
agate ground, signed 1,800.00

GOOFUS

*This is a name collectors have given a
pressed glass whose colors were sprayed on
and then fired. Most pieces have intaglio or
convex designs and were produced by the
Northwood Glass Co.*

Bowl, 9" d., relief-molded dogwood
blossoms, red & gold $20.00
Bowl, 9" d., relief-molded red floral
plumes on gold 16.00
Bowl, 9" d., relief-molded peaches &
pears, red & gold 35.00
Bowl, 9½" d., relief-molded straw-
berries, red & gold 25.00

Bowl, 10" d., fluted rim, relief-molded cherries, red & gold 26.00

Bowl, fruit, Three Fruits patt., red & gold w/opalescent rim 25.00

Dresser tray, relief-molded red roses on gold, 11" l. 36.00

Jar, relief-molded Statue of Liberty, 12" h. 125.00

Plate, 5" d., relief-molded thistles & foliage, red & gold 15.00

Plate, 10½" d., relief-molded red floral star on gold 18.00

Plate, 10½" d., relief-molded red grapes on gold.................. 18.00

Goofus Plate with Roses

Plate, 10½" d., relief-molded red roses on gold (ILLUS.) 22.00

Plate, 11" d., relief-molded cherries, red & gold 15.00

Powder box, cov., cabbage rose, white 35.00

Syrup pitcher w/original top, relief-molded red grapes on gold 35.00

Vase, 6" h., relief-molded cabbage roses, white 24.00

Vase, 7" h., relief-molded red poppies on gold 15.00

Vase, 10½" h., relief-molded peacock on gold 80.00

Vase, 13" h., 8" d., relief-molded long-stemmed red roses on gold.. 65.00

GREENTOWN

Greentown glass was made in Greentown, Ind., by the Indiana Tumbler & Goblet Co. from 1894 until 1903. In addition to its famed Chocolate and Holly Amber glass, which see, it produced other types of clear and colored glass. Miscellaneous pieces are listed here. Also see CHOCOLATE, HOLLY AMBER and PATTERN GLASS.

Animal covered dish, Dolphin, cobalt blue $395.00

Bowl, 6¼" d., Herringbone Buttress patt., amber 100.00

Bowl, 6¼" d., Pattern No. 11, blue w/gold 125.00

Bowl, 7½" d., Cord Drapery patt., clear 35.00

Bowl, 10 x 4" oblong, Holly patt., clear 125.00

Butter dish, cov., Dewey patt., amber 60.00

Butter dish, cov., Dewey patt., canary yellow.................... 95.00

Butter dish, cov., Teardrop & Tassel patt., clear 50.00

Butter dish, cov., Teardrop & Tassel patt., cobalt blue 135.00

Butter dish, cov., Teardrop & Tassel patt., white opaque 100.00

Cake plate, Cord Drapery patt., clear, 9¾" d. 32.50

Compote, open, 5¼" d., Cactus patt., clear 200.00

Compote, open, 7 5/8" d., high stand, Austrian patt., clear 65.00

Compote, jelly, Austrian patt., canary yellow.................... 110.00

Condiment tray, serpentine, Dewey patt., canary yellow, large 55.00

Cordial, Austrian patt., clear, 3" h. ....38.00 to 50.00

Cordial, Overall Lattice patt., clear........................... 35.00

Cordial, Shuttle patt., clear 35.00

Nile Green Indian Head Creamer

Creamer, Indian Head, Nile green (ILLUS.)........................ 475.00

Creamer, Dewey patt., canary yellow, 5" h. 65.00

Creamer, Early Diamond patt., clear........................... 23.00

Creamer, Teardrop & Tassel patt., green 80.00

Dewey Pattern Cruet

Cruet w/original stopper, Dewey
  patt., amber (ILLUS.) 110.00
Cruet w/original stopper, Dewey
  patt., clear 95.00
Goblet, Austrian patt., clear 42.00
Goblet, Beehive patt., clear 57.50
Goblet, Brazen Shield patt.,
  clear 30.00
Goblet, Diamond Prisms patt.,
  clear 65.00
Goblet, Herringbone Buttress patt.,
  clear 125.00
Goblet, Overall Lattice patt.,
  clear 30.00
Goblet, Shuttle patt., clear 45.00

Clear Holly Pattern Mug

Mug, Holly patt., clear, 4½" h.
  (ILLUS.) 55.00
Mug, Indoor Drinking Scene, Nile
  green, 5¾" h. 90.00
Mug, Serenade patt., blue, 5" h. . . . 75.00
Nappy, cov., Austrian patt., clear . . . 55.00
Pitcher, tankard, Pattern No. 11,
  clear w/amber stain 145.00

Pitcher, water, Cord Drapery patt.,
  green 225.00
Pitcher, water, Racing Deer patt.,
  clear . . . . 100.00 to 145.00
Pitcher, water, Squirrel patt.,
  clear 100.00
Pitcher, water, Teardrop & Tassel
  patt., blue 250.00
Plate, 6¼" d., Serenade patt., milk
  white 35.00
Plate, footed, Dewey patt., amber . . 40.00
Punch cup, Austrian patt., clear
  w/gold 16.50
Punch cup & saucer, Shuttle patt.,
  clear 42.00
Relish, Holly patt., clear 45.00
Salt & pepper shakers w/original
  tops, Cord Drapery patt., clear,
  pr. 90.00
Salt & pepper shakers w/original
  tops, Shuttle patt., clear, pr. 40.00
Sauce dish, Austrian patt., clear 10.00
Sugar bowl, cov., Teardrop & Tassel
  patt., blue 135.00
Sugar bowl, cov., Teardrop & Tassel
  patt., clear 45.00
Syrup pitcher w/original top, Wild
  Rose with Bowknot patt., frosted
  clear, decorated 125.00
Toothpick holder, Holly patt.,
  clear 85.00
Toothpick holder, Pattern No. 11,
  clear w/gold 35.00
Toothpick holder, dog's head, frost-
  ed clear 90.00

Nile Green Dog's Head Toothpick

Toothpick holder, dog's head, Nile
  green (ILLUS.) 155.00
Tumbler, Austrian patt., canary
  yellow 85.00
Tumbler, Austrian patt., green 125.00
Tumbler, Brazen Shield patt., blue . . 45.00
Wine, Austrian patt., canary
  yellow 100.00
Wine, Austrian patt., emerald
  green 75.00
Wine, Beehive patt., clear 45.00
Wine, Cord Drapery patt.,
  clear 75.00
Wine, Overall Lattice patt., clear . . . 15.00
Wine, Shuttle patt., clear 12.00

GUTTATE

Guttate is a mold-blown glassware made by the Consolidated Lamp & Glass Company at Fostoria, Ohio, during the late 1890's. A beautifully designed pattern, it was made primarily in opaque pastel colors, sometimes cased in clear to form a glossy finish and sometimes in a satin finish with a white lining. It is also found in transparent cranberry. Because of its appealing design, it is popular and somewhat scarce. Cased cranberry items available today are new pieces currently being reproduced along with a variety of tumblers. Collectors should exercise caution.

Butter dish, cov., white w/gold trim	$50.00 to 75.00
Creamer, pink satin	55.00
Cruet w/original stopper, pink satin	265.00
Cruet w/original stopper, white	155.00
Pitcher, water, pink cased in clear or pink satin, each	145.00
Pitcher, water, white w/gold trim ..	85.00
Salt shaker w/original top, squatty, pink cased in clear (single).......	65.00
Salt & pepper shakers w/original tops, pink satin, pr.	90.00
Salt & pepper shakers w/original tops, white, pr.	50.00
Sugar bowl, cov., cranberry	125.00
Sugar shaker w/original top, pink cased in clear	150.00
Syrup pitcher w/original top, cranberry......................	250.00
Syrup pitcher w/original top, pink cased in clear	165.00
Tumbler, pink cased in clear	50.00
Tumbler, pink satin...............	40.00
Tumbler, white glossy ....27.50 to 38.00	
Water set: pitcher & 4 tumblers; white w/gold, 5 pcs.	235.00

HEISEY

Numerous types of fine glass were made by the A. H. Heisey Glass Co., Newark, O., from 1895. The company's trademark — an H enclosed within a diamond — has become known to most glass collectors. The company's name and molds were acquired by Imperial Glass Co., Bellaire, O., in 1958, and some pieces have been reissued. The glass listed below consists of miscellaneous pieces and types. Also see ANIMALS under Glass and PATTERN GLASS.

Beer mug, elephant handle, clear, signed, 4½" h....................	$175.00
Beer mug, Old Sandwich patt., Sahara (yellow), 12 oz.	150.00

Berry set: 8" d. master bowl & four 4" sauce dishes; Colonial patt., clear, 5 pcs.	50.00
Berry set: master bowl & 5 sauce dishes; Greek Key patt., clear, 6 pcs.	150.00
Bowl, 4½" d., Empress patt., Sahara	9.50
Bowl, 10" d., Empress patt., Alexandrite (orchid)	750.00
Bowl, 11" d., dolphin-footed, Empress patt., Moongleam (green) ..	110.00
Bowl, 11" d., flared, Lariat patt., clear	25.00
Bowl, 12½" d., Rib & Panel patt., Moongleam	55.00
Breakfast set: individual creamer & sugar bowl on oval tray; Crystolite patt., clear, 3 pcs.	40.00
Butter pat, Fandango patt., clear	25.00
Butter pat, Old Sandwich patt., clear	15.00
Candelabra, 2-light, Trident patt., clear, orchid-etched, pr.	85.00
Candlesticks, Waverly patt., clear, 4½" h., pr.	35.00
Candlesticks, Plantation patt., clear, 5" h., pr.	55.00
Champagne, Greek Key patt., clear	35.00
Champagne, Tyrolean patt., clear, 6 oz.	28.50
Cigarette jar, footed, Crystolite patt., clear	20.00
Cocktail, Bantam Rooster stem, clear	300.00
Compote, 9" d., 6" h., Puritan patt., clear	30.00
Compote, cov., 8" h., Pleat & Panel patt., Flamingo (pink) w/silver overlay........................	125.00

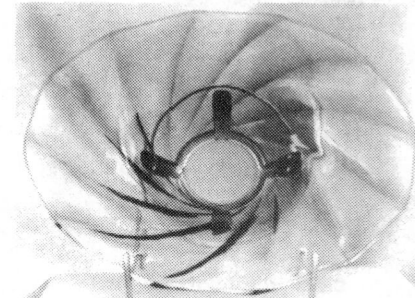

Heisey Twist Pattern Bowl

Console bowl, Twist patt., Moongleam, 12" l. (ILLUS.)	40.00
Creamer & sugar bowl, Old Sandwich patt., Sahara (yellow), pr....	66.00
Cruet w/original stopper, Greek Key patt., clear, 4 oz.	90.00

Dresser set: powder box, 2 cologne
   bottles & tray; Crystolite patt.,
   clear, 4 pcs. 235.00
Egg cup, Prince of Wales - Plumes
   patt., clear 85.00
Garniture set: pr. dolphin footed
   vases & 11" d. centerpiece bowl;
   Alexandrite (orchid), 3 pcs. 1,500.00
Goblet, Creole patt., Sahara 49.00
Goblet, Spanish patt., cobalt blue .. 73.00
Marmalade jar & underplate,
   Ridgeleigh patt., clear 75.00
Mayonnaise bowl, footed, Waverly
   patt., clear, orchid-etched 34.00
Mugs, Tally Ho patt., clear, 4¾" h.,
   pr. 300.00
Mustard jar w/underplate & spoon,
   Twist patt., Moongleam (green) .. 115.00
Pitcher, tankard, Beaded Swag
   patt., ruby-stained 95.00
Pitcher, Empress patt., Flamingo
   (pink) 100.00
Plate, 8" sq., Empress patt., Tanger-
   ine (orange) 85.00
Plate, 14" d., Waverly patt., clear,
   orchid-etched 40.00
Platter, 15" oval, Lariat patt.,
   clear 37.00
Punch set: bowl, base & 8 cups;
   Sunburst & Panel patt., clear,
   10 pcs. 300.00
Punch set: bowl, base & 12 cups;
   Prince of Wales - Plumes patt.,
   clear, 14 pcs. 435.00
Relish, 4-section, Plantation patt.,
   clear, 8" d. 55.00
Rose bowl, Fancy Loop patt., clear,
   4" 65.00
Salt & pepper shakers w/original
   tops, Empress patt., clear, pr. 69.00

Colonial Pattern Salt Dip

Salt dip, Colonial patt., clear, 2" h.
   (ILLUS.) 5.00
Sandwich tray w/center handle,
   Empress patt., Sahara, 12" d. 48.00
Sherbet, Charter Oak patt.,
   Flamingo 15.00
Sherbet, Duquesne patt., Tangerine,
   5 oz. 145.00
Spooner, Prince of Wales - Plumes
   patt., clear 95.00
Syrup pitcher w/original top,
   Crystolite patt., clear 58.00

Table set: cov. butter dish, cov.
   sugar bowl, creamer & spooner;
   Pineapple & Fan patt., clear,
   4 pcs. 150.00
Toothpick holder, Fancy Loop patt.,
   clear 65.00
Toothpick holder, Fandango patt.,
   clear 95.00
Toothpick holder, Greek Key patt.,
   clear 200.00
Toothpick holder, Prison Stripe patt.,
   clear 95.00
Torte plate, Waverly patt., clear,
   orchid-etched, 14" d. 45.00
Tumbler, Tally Ho patt., clear,
   12 oz., 5" h. 25.00
Tumbler, iced tea, Tyrolean patt.,
   clear, 12 oz. 35.00
Vase, 7" h., crimped top, Lariat
   patt., clear w/ruby staining 90.00
Vase, 9" h., footed, Empress patt.,
   Sahara 98.00
Vase, 10" h., Pineapple & Fan patt.,
   clear 32.00
Water bottle, Prince of Wales -
   Plumes patt., clear 140.00
Whiskey shot glass, Steeple Chase
   patt., clear 28.00

HISTORICAL & COMMEMORATIVE

Columbus Plate

*Reference numbers are to Bessie M. Lind-
sey's book, "American Historical Glass."
Also see BREAD PLATES & TRAYS,
MILK WHITE and PATTERN GLASS.*

Admiral Dewey plate, bust portrait
   of Dewey & stars transfer center,
   openwork club border, milk
   white, 7" d., No. 393 .... $30.00
"America" tumbler, clear, etched
   w/hymn title & first stanza,
   3¾" h., No. 458 .... 30.00

Bathtub dish, milk white, No. 166... 22.50

Bible match holder, clear, No. 199 .. 45.00

Bunker Hill cup plate, "Bunker Hill
Battle fought June 17, 1775 - Cor-
nerstone laid by Lafayette, June
17, 1825 - Finished by the Ladies,
1841 - From the Fair to the
Brave," clear, 3¾" d., No. 45 .... 26.00

Carpenter's Hall (Washington Centennial patt.) bread platter, clear,
No. 28 .... 82.50

Civil War tumbler, cannon, cannon-
balls & trench mortar, reverse
w/American eagle, shield, 34-star
flag & sword, clear, 4¾" h.,
No. 148 ....90.00 to 125.00

Columbus plate, bust portrait of
Columbus center, openwork club
border, milk white, 9½" d., No. 7
(ILLUS.)......................... 42.50

Covered Wagon covered dish, clear,
6" l., 3" w., 5" h., No. 128 ...... 170.00

Emblem lamp, applied handle, 2
shields around bowl, inscribed on
metal collar "Pat'd Apr. 19, 1875,
M'ch 21, 1876," clear, 4" d.,
3½" h., No. 63 .... 115.00

Garfield Memorial mug, handled,
embossed bust of Garfield, date
of birth & death, clear, 2 5/8" h.,
No. 294 .... 48.50

Gladstone mug, "For the Millions,"
clear, 2½" h., No. 441 .... 85.00

Grand Army of the Republic goblet,
insignia one side, inscribed "21
Encampment September 27, 28, St.
Louis, Mo." reverse, 6¾" h.,
No. 506 .... 42.50

Grand Army of the Republic platter,
insignia medal "Grand Army of
the Republic Veteran - 1861-66"
center, decorative border w/fur-
ther inscriptions, clear, 11 1/8 x
7 5/8", No. 505 .... 100.00

Grant Peace plate, bust portrait of
Grant center, maple leaf border,
apple green, 10½" d., No. 289 ... 60.00

Grant Peace plate, bust portrait of
Grant center, maple leaf border,
blue, 10½" d., No. 289 ....45.00 to 55.00

Henry Clay cup plate, profile portrait of Clay center w/name framing portrait, clear, 3½" d.,
No. 264 .... 26.00

Industry bowl, log cabin & cider barrel center, border w/man plow-
ing, sailing ship & factory against
stippled ground, clear, 6¼" d.,
No. 267 ....160.00 to 190.00

Jacob's Coat bowl, clear, 9¼" d.,
3 1/8" h., No. 212 .... 22.50

Jenny Lind match safe, "Pat'd. June
13, 1876," frosted, pierced to
hang, 4½" l., No. 426 .... 55.00

John Hancock platter, shell handles,
milk white, small, No. 40
variant 295.00

John Paul Jones flask, amber,
No. 48 .... 25.00

Kaiser Wilhelm I plate, bust portrait
of Kaiser center, laurel & oak leaf
border, clear, 9¾" sq., No. 445 .. 68.00

Knights of Labor mug, clear, 6" h.,
No. 513 .... 35.00

Knights of Labor Platter

Knights of Labor platter, clear,
11¾" l, No. 512 (ILLUS.) 75.00

Knights of Labor platter, vaseline,
11¾" l., No. 512 .... 150.00

Liberty Bell goblet, "Declaration of
Independence" & "1776-1876" one
side, "100 Years Ago" reverse,
6¼" h., No. 35 ....48.00 to 70.00

Liberty Bell patt. plate, closed handles, scalloped rim w/thirteen
original states & "100 Years Ago,"
clear, 10¼" d., No. 37 .....80.00 to 95.00

Lincoln statuette, frosted, 6" h.,
No. 277 .... 275.00

Log Cabin bank, milk white,
3 x 3½ x 4", No. 190 .... 65.00

Log Cabin patt. creamer, clear,
4¼" h., No. 183 ....125.00 to 195.00

Log Cabin patt. spoonholder, clear,
4¼" h., No. 184 .... 90.00

Log Cabin patt. water pitcher, clear,
8" h., No. 186 .... 290.00

Louisiana Purchase tumbler, 4 features of St. Louis Exposition in
relief, clear, 5" h., No. 107 ...... 14.00

Masonic loving cup, "Syria - Pittsburgh, Pa." & "St. Paul, Minnesota, 1908," clear w/silvered scimi-
tar blades w/gold hilts, grain &
star inscription, white crescent,
black rope edge at base, ruby-
stained rim, 2¾" d., 5¼" h.,
No. 510 .... 65.00

McKinley (William B.) covered cup,
bust portrait opposite handle,
"Protection & Prosperity," clear,
overall 5" h., No. 335 . . . .   55.00

McKinley plate, bust portrait of
McKinley framed by Gothic pat-
tern border, black amethyst, 9" d.
No. 341 . . . .   69.00

McKinley plate, bust portrait of
McKinley center, openwork Gothic
patt. border, milk white, 9" d.,
No. 341 . . . .   75.00

McKinley Memorial platter, "It's
God's Way" etc., clear, 10½ x 8",
No. 356 . . . .   40.00

McKinley-Roosevelt tumbler, etched
oval portrait medallions of candi-
dates, clear, 3¾" h., No. 353 . . . .   60.00

McKinley statuette, frosted, 5½" h.,
No. 354 . . . . .90.00 to 145.00

Mephistopheles water pitcher, clear,
No. 206 variant 95.00

Old Abe (eagle) covered compote,
clear, No. 478 . . . .   180.00

Old Statehouse Philadelphia tray,
clear, round, No. 32 . . . . . . .65.00 to 75.00

Old Statehouse Philadelphia tray,
electric blue, round, No. 32 . . . . . .   100.00

Palm Leaf Fan dish, 3-footed, stippled floral sprays & Dewdrop patt.
border, clear, 6" d., No. 174 . . . . .   25.00

Pershing paperweight, bust portrait
center, inscribed "General John J.
Pershing, 1917," amethyst flat
disc, 4" d., No. 404 . . . .   30.00

Pershing paperweight, bust portrait
center, inscribed "General John J.
Pershing, 1917," clear flat disc,
4" d., No. 404 . . . .   37.00

Pope Leo covered dish, milk white,
5" d., 5½" h., No. 241 . . . .   125.00

Prospect Point plate, milk white,
7" d., No. 491 . . . .   30.00

Railroad Train Platter

Railroad train platter, Union Pacific
Engine No. 350, clear, 12 x 9",
No. 134 (ILLUS.) 80.00

Rock of Ages bread tray, clear,
No. 236 . . . .   55.00

Rock of Ages bread tray, clear
w/opaque white inlaid center,
No. 236 . . . .   150.00

Roosevelt (Theodore) platter,
portrait center, teddy bears,
etc. border, clear, 10¼ x 7¾",
No. 357 . . . . .50.00 to 90.00

Ruth statuette, frosted, marked "Gillinder & Sons Centennial Exposi-
tion" on base, 4½" h., No. 216 . . .   135.00

Sothern (Edward Hugh) match safe,
hanging-type, bust portrait of the
American actor, Sothern, in full
relief, frosted, 4½" h., No. 432 . . .   55.00

Statue of Liberty toothpick holder,
hand holding torch, amber,
4¼" h., No. 529 . . . .   75.00

Statue of Liberty toothpick holder,
hand holding torch, blue, 4¼" h.,
No. 529 . . . .   100.00

Symbolical platter, Plymouth Rock
"1620," sinking "1776" ship & sun
rising above water & full-rigged
"1876" ship, clear, No. 20 . . . .   110.00

Taft (William H.) campaign plate of
1908, milk white, 7½" d.,
No. 358 . . . .   75.00

Taft-Sherman hat, opaque white
w/painted red & blue decor,
3 5/8" widest d., No. 363 . . . .   72.50

Tennessee mug, Cherokee rose &
clematis blossoms within shield
one side & American 16-star flag
reverse, camphor, 3½" h.,
No. 102 . . . .   45.00

Three Presidents platter, bust portraits of Garfield, Washington &
Lincoln, inscribed "In Rembrance,"
clear, 12½ x 10", No. 249 . .60.00 to 75.00

Three Presidents platter, bust portraits of Garfield, Washington &
Lincoln, inscribed "In Rembrance,"
clear w/frosted center, 12½ x
10", No. 249 . . . .   95.00

Three Shields covered dish, shield-
shaped, clear, 8½" l., 5½" w.,
No. 60 . . . .   90.00

Washington Bi-Centennial Bottle

Washington Bi-Centennial bottle,
oval portrait medallion of
Washington front & American eagle w/olive branches & thunderbolts in oval medallion reverse,
"1732-1932," clear, qt., No. 262
(ILLUS.) 20.00
Washington Centennial patt. platter
w/bear paw handles, frosted center, "First in War," etc., 12 x 8½",
No. 27 ....90.00 to 110.00
Whisk-broom dish, Daisy & Button
patt. below handle, amber, 5" w.,
7½" l., No. 175 .... 40.00
Whittier's Birthplace tumbler, clear
shaded to amber w/enameled
scene of Whittier's home, 5" h.,
No. 407 .... 20.00

Hobb's Block patt., amber &
frosted 90.00
Bowl, 9" d., vaseline overlay w/ap-
plied cranberry edging at ruffled
rim, ca. 1885 (ILLUS.) 200.00
Bowl, 9½" l., ruffled & folded rim,
Rubina Crystal (ruby to clear) 95.00
Lemonade set: pitcher, 2 tumblers,
waste bowl & tray; Hobb's Hobnail
patt., frosted & amber, 5 pcs. 425.00
Sauce dish, Hobb's Hobnail patt.,
frosted Rubina Crystal (ruby to
clear), square.................... 50.00
Syrup pitcher w/original top, rubina
(ruby to clear) opalescent 225.00
Tumbler, Hobb's Block patt., frosted
& amber rim.................... 38.00
Tumbler, Hobb's Hobnail patt.,
Rubina Verde (ruby shaded
to green) 85.00

HOBBS, BROCKUNIER & CO.

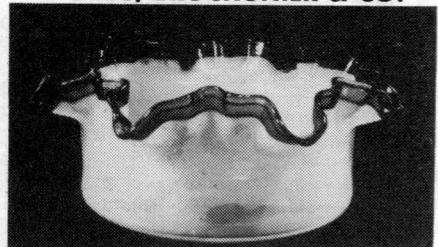

Hobbs, Brockunier & Co. Bowl

About 1845, the Wheeling, West Virginia
glasshouse of Hobbs, Barnes & Co. was
founded by two former employees of the New
England Glass Company, John L. Hobbs and
James B. Barnes. They were soon joined by
their sons, John H. Hobbs and James F.
Barnes. The firm became Hobbs, Brockunier
& Co. in 1863 as John L. and John H. Hobbs
and Charles Brockunier took charge of the
company and hired, in that same year, the
former superintendent of the New England
Glass Company, William Leighton, Sr., to
take charge of production. Leighton revolutionized the glass industry the following year,
1864, when he devised a formula for soda lime
glass. In the 1880's, the firm produced Victorian art glass lines including Amberina,
Frances Ware, Peach Blow, Rubina Crystal,
Rubina Verde and Tortoise Shell, which see.
Also see OPALESCENT GLASS for blown
patterns such as Christmas Snowflake, Coin
Spot, Hobnail and others.

Berry set: square master bowl & 5
sauce dishes; Hobb's Hobnail
patt., frosted Rubina Crystal (ruby
to clear), 6 pcs. $235.00
Bowl, cov., 6 x 5" oval, 4½" h.,

HOLLY AMBER

Holly Amber Toothpick Holder

Holly Amber was produced by the Indiana
Tumbler and Goblet Co. A molded glass, it
is characterized by a glossy finish, shadings
that range from opalescent to brownish amber, and holly leaf patterns. It is also called
Golden Agate. It is scarce and therefore expensive. Collectors are alerted to the fact that
the St. Clair Glass Company has reproduced
some Holly Amber pieces.

Bowl, 7½ x 4½" oval, 2" h........$358.00
Bowl, 8½" d. 675.00
Butter dish, cov...................1,125.00
Compote, jelly, cov., 4½" d. 975.00
Compote, cov., 6½" d 1,100.00
Cruet w/original stopper 1,400.00
Mug, handled, 4" h. 395.00
Parfait, 6" h. 425.00
Pickle tray, 2-handled, 6½ x 4" 350.00
Sauce dish ....225.00 to 250.00
Syrup jug w/original tin lid........ 750.00
Toothpick holder (ILLUS.).......... 475.00
Tray, water, 9¼" d.......600.00 to 975.00
Tumbler, 4" h. ....325.00 to 350.00

IMPERIAL

Imperial Free Hand Ware Vase

Imperial Glass Company, Bellaire, Ohio, was organized in 1901 and was in continuous production, except for very brief periods, until its closing in June, 1984. It had been a major producer of Carnival Glass (which see) earlier in this century and also produced other types of glass, including an Art Glass line called "Free Hand Ware" during the 1920's and its "Jewels" about 1916. The company acquired a number of molds of other earlier factories, including the Cambridge and A. H. Heisey companies, and had reissued numerous items through the years.

Free Hand Ware vase, 4½" h.,
5½" d., cobalt blue w/imbedded
iridescent white vines & leaves . . . $150.00
Free Hand Ware vase, 6¼" h.,
cobalt blue w/white opal lining . . .   95.00
Free Hand Ware vase, 6¾" h.,
3½" d., deep blue w/imbedded
opal hearts & vines, orange lustre
lining . . . . 185.00 to 255.00
Free Hand Ware vase, 5 7/8" h.,
white satin finish w/imbedded
blue-green seaweed fronds &
trailing threads, orange lustre
lining at neck, w/partial label on
base (ILLUS.) 330.00
Free Hand Ware vase, 7" h., cobalt
blue w/iridescent marigold lining
at throat 90.00
Free Hand Ware vase, 7¾" h., lus-
tred blackish brown w/imbedded
gold lustre leaves & tendrils,
w/part original label 275.00
Free Hand Ware vase, 8" h.,
6¼" d., iridescent red ruffled
trumpet-shaped top w/iridescent
brown stretched throat & "verre
de soie" foot 225.00
Free Hand Ware vase, 8½" h.,
3" d., mirrored iridescent blue
w/opal mosaic 175.00

Free Hand Ware vase, 8¾" h., yellow w/white iridescent drag
loops, iridescent orange lustre
lining 110.00
Free Hand Ware vase, 9" h.,
3½" d., dark blue w/stretched
brown iridescence at wide flaring
neck 125.00
Free Hand Ware vase, 9" h., deep
iridescent blue w/white drag
loops 300.00
Free Hand Ware Vase, 10" h., emer-
ald green w/imbedded opal
hearts & vines, orange lustre
throat interior 150.00
Free Hand Ware vase, 10" h.,
trumpet-shaped, green to purple
mirror finish 300.00
Free Hand Ware vase, 11" h., irides-
cent emerald green w/imbedded
white hearts & vines, orange
lustre throat interior,
w/label . . . . 285.00 to 300.00
Free Hand Ware vase, 11" h., irides-
cent bronze 110.00
Free Hand Ware vase, 11½" h.,
golden bronze exterior, blue
interior 95.00
Free Hand Ware vase, 11½" h., red-
dish gold lustre w/white drag
loops, original label 225.00
Jewels bowl, 9" d., 4" h., iridescent
amber 75.00
Jewels creamer, amethyst w/pearl
green lustre 65.00
Jewels vase, 8" h., flared rim,
silver iridescence over
mulberry . . . . 85.00 to 125.00

IOWA CITY GLASS

This ware, made by the Iowa City Glass Manufacturing Co., Iowa City, Iowa, from 1880 to about 1883, was produced in many shapes and patterns.

Bread plate, "Elaine," frosted cen-
ter, 1-0-1 border $90.00
Goblet, Deer & Doe patt., clear 95.00
Mug, child's, Lamb patt. w/two
standing lambs, 2" h. 125.00
Platter, "Be Industrious," beehive
frosted center, 1-0-1 border 75.00
Mustard jar, cov., Running Elk patt.
w/Owl finial on lid 125.00
Plate, 5½" d., "Be Playful," kitten
center, stippled bird handles 95.00
Plate, 7¾" d., "Be Affectionate,"
cow & calf center, frosted bird
handles 95.00
Wine, Geometric Block patt. 65.00

JACK-IN-PULPIT VASES

Jack-in-Pulpit Vase

Glass vases in varying sizes and resembling in appearance the flower of this name have been popular with collectors since the 19th century. They were produced in various solid colors and in shaded wares.

Blue opaque shaded to maroon at
  hobnail effect edge w/crimped
  rim (ILLUS.) $85.00
Cased, white exterior, blue spangled interior w/silver mica flecks,
  clear binding at ruffled edge,
  5 5/8" h. 95.00
Cased, white exterior, green interi-
  or, applied clear feet, 5" widest
  d., 7" h. 88.00
Cased, white exterior, shaded green
  hobnail effect interior, 7¼" h..... 100.00
Cased, white exterior, shaded purple interior, 6¼" widest d.,
  7 3/8" h. 95.00
Cased, yellow opaque exterior, rose
  interior, 4½" widest d., 9" h. 95.00
Cased, heavenly blue exterior,
  white interior, applied clear scallop shell trim around edge of
  foot, 15¾" h. 195.00
Green opalescent stripe, applied
  green leaf & pink floral, 9" h. 125.00
Pink & yellow opalescent stripe, bulbous bottom, 3¼" widest d.,
  5 3/8" h. 85.00
Pink, yellow & blue opalescent
  stripes in clear, 4¼" widest d.,
  8¼" h. 100.00
Spangled, purple, green & white
  spatter w/silver mica flecks,
  6½" h. 65.00
Spatter, green & white, Diamond
  Quilted patt. on base, 9 3/8" h. ... 88.00
Spatter, white & peach spatter on
  green, Venetian Diamond patt. on
  base, 5½" widest d., 9 3/8" h. 95.00
Vaseline opalescent, 6" h. 58.00
Vaseline opalescent, Swirl patt.,
  applied pink spiral rigaree trim,
  7¾" h. 95.00

KELVA

Kelva Box

Kelva was made early in this century by the C.F. Monroe Co., Meriden, Conn., and was a type of decorated opal glass very like the same company's Wave Crest and Nakara wares. This type of glass was produced until about the time of the first World War. Also see NAKARA and WAVE CREST.

Box w/hinged lid, mottled dark
  green w/h.p. pink florals &
  enameled beading decor, signed,
  3" d. $335.00
Box w/hinged lid, 6-sided, blown-
  mold rose in full relief on lid,
  mottled green ground, chased silverplate fittings, signed, 3¾" w.,
  3" h. (ILLUS.) 600.00
Box w/hinged lid, moss green
  w/deep rose, white, yellow &
  blue floral decor, signed, 6" w.,
  3½" h. 450.00
Box w/hinged lid, blown-mold rose
  in full relief on lid, mottled green
  w/h.p. florals & scrolls on sides,
  8" d. 850.00
Cigar jar, cov., mottled apple green
  w/h.p. pink wild roses & "Cigars"
  lettered in gold, signed 450.00
Dresser box w/mirror in hinged lid,
  mottled green, 4½" d., 2½" h. 270.00
Jewelry box w/hinged lid, mottled
  green w/pink floral decor on lid,
  original lining in lid only, signed,
  5" d. 350.00
Jewelry box w/hinged lid, 6-sided,
  blown-mold maple leaf in relief
  on lid, mottled green, original
  lining, signed 5" w. 400.00
Vase, 13" h., hexagonal, marbled
  robin's egg blue w/h.p. full-blown
  pink roses decor & white
  enameled dotted rim, signed 495.00
Vase, 17½" h., ormolu rim band
  w/applied ornate ormolu handles,
  footed ormolu base, mottled
  green w/overall h.p. full-blown
  roses decor, signed 1,800.00

KEW BLAS

Kew Blas Vase

Glass of this name was made by the Union Glass Works, Somerville, Mass. These iridescent wares were similar to those produced by other art glass firms during the same period in the 1890's.

Bowl, 8½" d., ruffled edge, blue
    interior, dark green exterior,
    signed $800.00
Plate, 6" d., iridescent gold,
    signed 195.00
Vase, 3½" h., rose bowl shape,
    green & gold hooked design on
    butterscotch ground, gold lining,
    signed 525.00
Vase, 3¾" h., wide base tapering to
    a flared out ruffled top, iridescent
    amber fishscale design, signed ... 375.00
Vase, bud, 4¾" h., baluster-shaped,
    iridescent peach w/darker
    feathering 385.00
Vase, 5" h., 6" d., squat cylinder
    w/wide crimped rim, green swirl
    on white, iridescent gold lining ... 350.00
Vase, 5½" h., 2¾" d., green & gold
    pulled design, gold interior 750.00
Vase, 6" h., iridescent apricot
    w/gold pulled feathering, tooled
    prunts at throat (ILLUS.) 825.00
Vase, 8½" h., 5½" w., double
    gourd shape, iridescent gold,
    unsigned 250.00

LALIQUE

Fine glass, including numerous extraordinary molded articles, has been made by the glass house established by Rene' Lalique early in this century in France. The firm was car- ried on by his son, Marc, until his death in 1977 and is now headed by Marc's daughter, Marie-Claude. All Lalique glass is marked, usually on, or near the bottom with either an engraved or molded signature. Unless otherwise noted we list only those pieces marked "R. Lalique" produced before the death of Rene' Lalique in 1945. Also see COMMEMORATIVE PLATES.

Ash tray, "Tobago," molded band of
    scarabs, frosted amber, 5½" d. . . .$528.00
Ash tray, "Zephyrs," molded w/two
    children's faces blowing currents
    of air, frosted yellow, 3 1/8" d. ... 330.00
Bottle w/stopper, "Meplat Sirenes,"
    flattened ovoid, molded in medi-
    um relief w/outer border of nude
    figure on a floral ground, stopper
    molded in full relief as a kneeling
    nude w/blossoms in her hair,
    frosted, ca. 1925, 14" h.........2,310.00
Bowl, 5" d., "Coquilles," molded
    clam shell, blue-tinted opales-
    cence, early 1930's 95.00

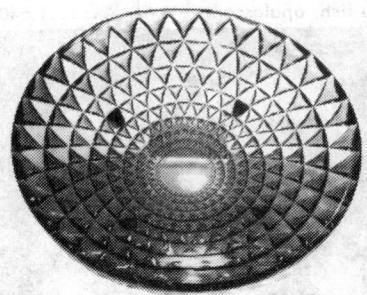

"Rosale" Bowl by Rene' Lalique

Bowl, 12½" d., "Rosale," 4 triangu-
    lar feet, molded graduated
    pyramid bands, blue (ILLUS.).....2,420.00
Bowl, 15½" widest d., "Flora Bella,"
    flattened rim, molded on ex-
    terior in medium relief w/gradu-
    ated bands of overlapping
    leafage, sapphire blue,
    ca. 1932 ....2,200.00
Box, cov., "Amours," cover molded
    w/cherubs, grey-stained frosted,
    3¼" oval 385.00
Box, cov., "Paon," molded peacock
    amongst leafy branches, blue-
    stained, 4¾" d. 770.00
Box, cov., "Sirenes," cover molded
    w/two water nymphs w/long hair
    amidst bubbles, opalescent,
    w/blue silk-covered body,
    10" d. 1,760.00
Carafe, "Masque," spherical w/con-
    cave sides, molded shallow relief
    Bacchus masks washed in brown,

original silver stopper cast
w/grapes & leafage, ca. 1932,
12½" h. 1,980.00

Cologne bottle w/stopper, "Dans la
Nuit," stars molded in relief,
cobalt blue, signed "Worth,"
5½" h. 145.00

Cologne bottle w/double doves
stopper, "L'Air du Temps," opalescent, 32 oz. 45.00

Figure of "Suzanne," nude but for
drapery descending from her outstretched arms, amber, ca. 1932,
9½" h. 4,620.00

Hood ornament, "Chevaux," model
of 5 parallel prancing horses,
amethyst-tinged, 6" l. 3,520.00

Hood ornament, "Faucon," model of
a falcon (hawk), clear, chrome-
metal mount w/green filter,
8" h. 1,210.00

Hood ornament, "La Vitesse," figure
of a nude symbolizing speed,
frosted, ca. 1925, 7½" h. 3,080.00

Hood ornament, "Perche," model of
a fish, opalescent, 6½" l. 1,540.00

"Masque de Femme" Luminaire

Luminaire, "Masque de Femme,"
frosted female mask supported
on chrome base, 12" sq.
(ILLUS.) 3,300.00

Luminaire, "Yeso," semi-circular
panel w/intaglio-molded goldfish,
frosted, w/electrified base,
20½" l. 5,500.00

Perfume atomizer, relief nudes
w/garlands of flowers, brass fittings, 3" h. ....240.00 to 275.00

Perfume bottle w/stopper, "Epines,"
molded thorny branches, brown-
washed, 3¾" h. 295.00

Perfume bottle, flattened spherical
form, molded w/five bands of triangles, amber-stained, "Worth,"
6¼" h. 550.00

Plate, 10½" d., "Coquilles," molded
shells (4), soft blue 210.00

Powder box, "Emiliane," molded
florals, light brown stain, 4" d. ... 185.00

Vase, 5" h., "Chamois," oviform,
molded stylized antelopes,
frosted 352.00

Vase, 6" h., "Esterel," ovoid, molded leafy branches, frosted
amber 1,210.00

Vase, 6¾" h., "Gui," mistletoe berries & leafage molded in low
relief, cased deep emerald green,
ca. 1932 .... 935.00

Vase, 7" h., "Formose," spherical,
footed, molded pattern of swimming fish in medium relief, blue-
stained opalescent 440.00

Vase, 7¾" h., "Courges," spherical,
molded gourds, frosted blue 3,520.00

"Bali" Vase

Vase, 8" h., "Bali," serrated
cylinder, molded w/flying birds in
low relief, frosted & brown
stained (ILLUS.) 3,740.00

Vase, 8¼" h., "Plumes," oviform,
molded frosted feathers outlined
in green stain................... 990.00

"Antinea" Vase

Vase, 8½" h., "Antinea," opalescent green figures supporting
clear vase (ILLUS.) 1,100.00
Vase, 9¼" h., "Monnaie Du Pape,"
cylindrical, molded "paper money"
leaves & branches, brown-stained
& frosted 770.00
Vase, 9¼" h., "Monnaie Du Pape,"
ovoid, molded "paper money"
leaves & branches, olive green,
ca. 1930 .... 2,200.00
Vase, 10" h., "Aigrettes," ovoid,
upper section molded in low relief
w/exotic birds in flight against
undulating grasses, frosted,
ca. 1932 .... 770.00
Vase, 10" h., "Perruches," ovoid,
molded in low relief w/pairs of
lovebirds perched on prunus
branches, reddish amber,
ca. 1932 .... 3,300.00
Vase, 10½" h., "Archers," ovoid,
molded nude archers & eagles,
cased & frosted yellow 3,520.00
Vase, 11½" h., "Salomonides,"
ovoid, molded fish, frosted 1,430.00

LEAF MOLD

*Though the maker of this attractive glass
pattern remains elusive, the Leaf Mold pattern becomes more popular with collectors
each year. Thought to have been made in the
1890's, there are several colors and color com-
binations available and it was made in both
satin and shiny finish as well as in a cased
version.*

Bowl, master berry, cranberry spatter, satin finish .... $65.00 to 75.00
Cologne bottle w/original stopper,
vaseline w/cranberry spatter,
satin finish .... 125.00 to 150.00
Creamer, pink, satin finish 90.00
Salt & pepper shakers w/original
tops, cased cranberry w/mica
flecks, pr. .... 125.00 to 145.00
Sauce dish, vaseline w/cranberry &
white spatter 30.00
Sugar shaker w/original top, blue,
satin finish 125.00
Sugar shaker w/original top,
vaseline w/cranberry
spatter .... 160.00 to 170.00
Syrup jug w/original top, vaseline
w/cranberry spatter 245.00
Toothpick holder, cranberry, satin
finish 85.00
Tumbler, vaseline w/cranberry &
white spatter 90.00

LEAF UMBRELLA

*This attractive pattern is attributed to the
Northwood Company and dates from 1889. A
complete table service was made in cranberry glass and cased-glass in shades of blue,
pink and yellow. Some cased cranberry and
white spatter glass is also found and sometimes the wares were given a satin finish. A
somewhat brittle glassware that readily
flakes, items offered for sale have sometimes
had the rims polished or smoothed.*

Berry set: master bowl & 4 sauce
dishes; cranberry, 5 pcs. $265.00
Bowl, master berry, cased cranberry
& white spatter 95.00
Butter dish, cov., cased cranberry &
white spatter 225.00
Creamer, applied clear handle,
cranberry 100.00
Creamer, cased blue, 4" h. 68.00
Pitcher, water, cased blue, satin
finish 375.00
Pitcher, water, cased cranberry &
white spatter 295.00
Pitcher, water, cased pink-mauve ... 360.00
Pitcher, water, cased yellow 340.00
Pitcher, water, cranberry .. 225.00 to 285.00
Salt shaker w/original top, cased
blue 60.00
Salt shaker w/original top, cased
yellow 50.00
Salt shaker w/original top,
cranberry..................... 45.00
Sauce dish, cranberry .... 25.00 to 40.00
Sugar shaker w/original top, cased
blue 165.00
Sugar shaker w/original top,
cranberry..................... 230.00
Sugar shaker w/original top, cased
cranberry & white spatter 275.00
Syrup pitcher w/original top,
cranberry..................... 325.00
Toothpick holder, cased blue 120.00
Toothpick holder, cased cranberry
spatter 115.00
Toothpick holder, cranberry 85.00
Tumbler, cranberry 45.00
Tumbler, cased pink-mauve 100.00
Water set: pitcher & 6 tumblers;
cranberry, 7 pcs. 675.00

LE GRAS

*Cameo and enameled glass somewhat simi-
lar to that made by Galle', Daum Nancy and
other factories of the period was made at the
Le Gras works in Saint Denis, France, late
last century and until the outbreak of World
War I.*

Le Gras Cameo Vase

Cameo bowl, 4¼" oval, carved
   scene w/eleven ships, mountains
   & water against pink to orange
   ground, signed................$295.00
Cameo bowl-vase, flattened oval
   shape, carved & enameled village
   on hill, lake & mountains in background & trees in foreground,
   signed, 5¼ x 3¼", 4½" h....... 295.00
Cameo bowl-vase, boat-shaped,
   carved & enameled scene w/lake,
   boats & trees, signed, 12 x 5",
   6¼" h......................... 600.00
Cameo bride's basket, carved burgundy maple leaves against camphor ground, silverplate frame
   w/vines & leaves, hinged handle,
   signed, 8" d.................. 385.00
Cameo vase, 4¼" h., carved tan &
   brown leaves against cream
   ground, signed (ILLUS.).......... 550.00
Cameo vase, 7½" h., carved &
   enameled peach, beige & brown
   boat scene w/two fishermen in
   the largest boat, signed......... 450.00
Cameo vase, 10¾" h., carved &
   enameled red berries & leaves
   decor against frosted ground..... 750.00
Cameo vases, 13½" h., carved &
   enameled boat on lake scene
   w/trees & mountains against chartreuse & orange ground, pr. 1,200.00
Cameo vases, 13¾" h., carved lake
   & forest scene in shades of green,
   brown & orange, signed, pr. 950.00
Cameo vase, 16" h., carved russet
   grapevine against peach ground,
   signed 500.00
Cameo vase, 17½" h., tapered
   ovoid w/waisted foot, carved ray
   & sunburst motifs in varying
   shades of deep to light green,
   ca. 1925, signed............. 522.50
Cameo vase, 21" h., cylindrical,
   topaz, carved elongated drapery
   swags, signed 1,210.00

Cameo vase, 23" h., carved maroon,
   green & shaded brown cockle
   shells, seaweed & kelp against
   cream ground, signed 1,450.00

LE VERRE FRANCAISE

Cameo Vase

*This glass was made in France by Charles
Schneider and fairly large quantities of the
cameo ware were exported to the United
States in the early part of this century. Much
of it was sold by Ovingtons, New York City.
See SCHNEIDER for further details on this
company.*

Cameo vase, 6 5/8" h., elongated
   teardrop on short circular foot,
   carved chocolate brown stylized
   bellflowers & leafage against mottled lemon yellow to tango red
   ground, ca. 1925, signed........$385.00
Cameo vase, 7¼" h., sloping body,
   straight neck, applied mottled
   deep amethyst scrolling handles,
   carved amethyst band of cats at
   various lazy pursuits above brickwork against mottled tango red
   shading to lemon yellow acid finish ground, mottled deep amethyst circular foot, ca. 1925,
   signed 935.00
Cameo vase, 8" h., baluster-shaped,
   carved blue to orange stylized
   florals against acid-etched yellow
   ground, signed.................. 275.00
Cameo vase, 8¾" h., cylindrical
   w/short rolled foot, carved sapphire blue panels of pendant stylized blossoms against clear
   mottled w/pale blue shading to
   sapphire blue ground, ca. 1920,
   signed 467.00
Cameo vase, 9½" h., ovoid on short
   circular foot, carved tango red to
   deep mottled purple stylized

mushrooms & grasses against
acid-etched pale lemon yellow
splashed w/turquoise, ca. 1925,
signed 522.00
Cameo vase, 11½" h., shouldered
ovoid, carved sapphire blue stylized exotic blossoms against mottled grey streaked w/dusty rose &
grey-blue acid finish ground,
w/cut brickwork at neck & foot,
ca. 1925, signed (ILLUS.) 660.00
Cameo vase, 12¼" h., 8½" d., tulip-
shaped w/wide mouth & tapering
towards raised foot, carved rows
(2) of orange-petaled florals &
slender stems against mottled
orange ground, purple base,
signed 522.50
Cameo vase, 13½" h., inverted pyriform, carved tango red shading to
mottled amethyst carnations, leafage & grasses against acid-etched
clear ground enclosing lemon yellow & sky blue mottling, ca. 1925,
signed 935.00
Candlesticks, domed circular base,
baluster stem striped w/pale lemon yellow & amethyst, mottled
chocolate brown to pumpkin out-
wardly flaring candle cup, ca.
1920, 11 1/8" h., pr............. 770.00

LIBBEY

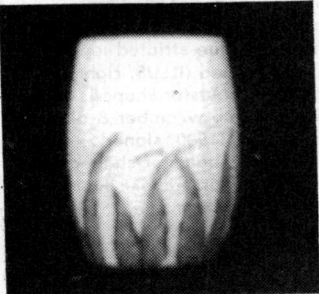

Maize Tumbler

In 1878, William L. Libbey obtained a lease
on the New England Glass Company of Cambridge, Mass., changing the name to the New
England Glass Works, W.L. Libbey and Son,
Proprietors. After his death in 1883, his son,
Edward D. Libbey, continued to operate the
company in Cambridge until 1888 when the
factory was closed. Edward Libbey moved to
Toledo, Ohio, and set up the company subsequently known as Libbey Glass Co. During
the 1880's, the firm's master technician,
Joseph Locke, developed the now much
desired colored art glass lines of Agata,

Amberina, Peach Blow and Pomona. Renowned for its Cut Glass of the Brilliant
Period, the company continues in operation
today as Libbey Glassware, a division of
Owens-Illinois, Inc.

Champagne, clear bowl w/green
threading, clear twisted stem,
signed, 6½" h..................$125.00
Cocktail, clear bowl, black silhouette of kangaroo in stem 145.00
Cocktail, clear bowl, opalescent silhouette of giraffe in stem,
signed 145.00
Cocktail, clear bowl, opalescent silhouette of squirrel in stem 90.00
Compote, 7" h., twisted stem,
Expanded Zipper patt., turquoise, signed 275.00
Finger bowl, clear w/etched florals,
signed 85.00
Goblet, clear bowl, opalescent silhouette of monkey in stem...... 95.00
Maize salt shaker w/original brass
top, creamy white w/gold-edged
green husks, 4½" h. 185.00
Maize sugar shaker, custard color
w/gold-edged green husks,
5½" h........................ 265.00
Maize sugar shaker, creamy white
w/gold-edged blue husks 195.00
Maize tumbler, creamy white
w/gold-edged yellow husks
(ILLUS.)....................... 285.00
Milk jug, applied strap handle, clear
w/blue Nailsea-type loopings,
signed 275.00
Punch cup, Morovingian patt. w/red
pull-ups, signed 110.00
Salt shaker w/original top, egg-
shaped, opaque white satin, lettered "Columbian 1893 Souvenir"
in gold script, 2¾" l. 150.00
Vase, 8" h., clear w/black silhouette of rabbit in stem 395.00
Wine, clear bowl, opalescent silhouette of kangaroo in stem 135.00

LOETZ

Iridescent glass, some of it somewhat
resembling that of Tiffany and other contemporary glasshouses, was produced by the Bohemian firm of J. Loetz Witwe of Klostermule
and is referred to as Loetz. Some cameo pieces
were also made. Not all pieces are marked.

Bowl, 9½" d., amethyst & turquoise
w/iridescent oil splotches $250.00
Bowl, 10" d., 2-handled squat form,
iridescent peacock blue w/green
highlights, signed 500.00

Compote, pale green to deep purple
bowl w/ruffled edges in metal
dolphin base, signed 275.00
Inkwell w/brass hinged lid & trim,
iridescent purple, blue & gold,
unsigned 195.00
Inkwell, iridescent cranberry,
w/hinged brass lid & brass lily
pad base, signed 295.00
Rose bowl, flared top, iridescent
green, unsigned, 5" d. 130.00
Vase, 4¼" h., ruffled rim, iridescent
green, signed 220.00

Loetz Vases

Vases, 4 7/8" h., baluster-shaped,
yellow-green w/silvery-blue wave
designs & oil splotches, ca. 1900,
unsigned, pr. (ILLUS. of one
left) 660.00
Vase, 5½" h., 2¾" d., cylindrical
w/flaring rim, footed, iridescent
green w/blue highlights,
unsigned 185.00
Vase, 5½" h., deep iridescent am-
ber overlaid w/continuous bands
of iridescent blue & green wave
designs, ca. 1900, unsigned
(ILLUS. center) 495.00
Vase, 6½" h., square pyramid form,
ultra-iridescent blue, green &
lavender, signed 130.00
Vase, 6 5/8" h., tapered, pale yel-
low w/medial band of apple
green dripping into deep salmon
pink & iridescent silvery blue continuing to form zipper patterns,
neck w/silvery blue lappets,
ca. 1900, signed 4,675.00
Vase, 6¾" h., gourd form, 3 applied
handles at waist, yellow-green
w/blue, olive green & violet
splotches dripping from top &
light silvery blue splotches at the
base & waist, ca. 1900,
unsigned 2,090.00

Vase, 7" h., baluster-shaped, green
shaded to purple w/iridescent
waves splashed w/silver-blue oil
splotches, signed 550.00
Vase, 7" h., free form, iridescent
blue & purple, unsigned 150.00
Vase, 8" h., peach w/iridescent
pulled feathering, signed 275.00
Vase, 8" h., ovoid w/flat shoulder &
waisted neck, deep red w/silvery
blue iridescent concentric waves,
ca. 1900, unsigned 715.00
Vase, 8¼" h., floriform w/crimped
lip, striated green, amber, blue &
gold iridescence, ca. 1900,
unsigned 440.00
Vase, 8¼" h., tulip top, twisted
body, flared base, Amberina
w/iridescent oil splotches & applied w/iridescent gold snake,
unsigned 270.00
Vase, 9" h., 4 pinched-in sides, blue
w/overall iridescent purple &
green snakeskin design,
unsigned 450.00
Vase, 9" h., ovoid w/slender neck,
deep amber tinged w/silvery blue
iridescent concentric waves,
ca. 1900, signed 550.00
Vase, 9½" h., irregular baluster form
w/pinched & squared sides, pale
yellow w/silvery blue hearts &
vertical trailings, ca. 1900,
signed 1,100.00
Vase, 11 7/8" h., bulbous base,
cylindrical body, shaded from
azure to pale sky blue w/irides-
cent silvery-blue striated lappets,
ca. 1900, signed (ILLUS. right) 1,100.00
Vase, 12" h., baluster-shaped, deep
iridescent blue w/amber & blue
chevrons, ca. 1900, signed 1,100.00
Vase, 13¼" h., baluster-shaped,
lime green w/irregular silvery
blue whiplash patt., ca. 1900,
unsigned 715.00

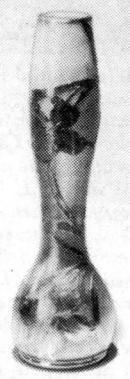

Vase with Silver Overlay

Vase, 13¾" h., iridescent gold,
w/sterling silver floral & sinuous
leaf overlay marked "Alvin Corp."
(ILLUS.) 1,045.00
Vase, 14" h., dimpled sides, fluted
top, green w/lavender swirls,
unsigned 190.00
Vase, 18½" h., green w/iridescent
blue oil splotches, unsigned 750.00

MARBLE

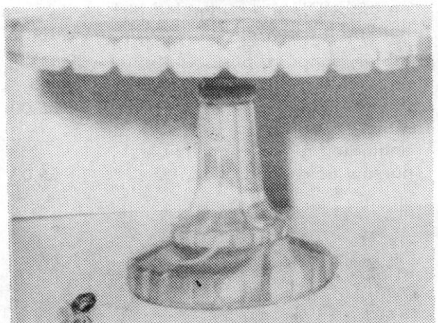

Marble Glass Cake Stand

*Slag and Agate glass are other names ap-
plied to this variegated glass ware made from
the middle until the close of the last century
and now being reproduced. It is characterized
by variegated streaks of color. Pink slag was
made only in the Inverted Fan & Feather Pattern and is rare.*

Animal covered dish, squirrel on
acorn, blue $145.00
Bowl, 5 1/8 x 3 7/8", 4¼" h., hel-
met shape on pedestal foot,
purple 55.00
Butter dish, cov., paneled, Block &
Star patt., purple 60.00
Butter dish, cov., overall diamonds
& shields, purple, 7 1/8" d.,
5" h. 85.00
Cake stand, plain, purple, 9" d.
(ILLUS.) . . . . .130.00 to 150.00
Compote, jelly, Scroll with Acanthus
patt., purple 45.00
Compote, jelly, Shell patt., purple . . 75.00
Compote, jelly, Spool patt., purple . . 45.00
Compote, jelly, threaded, purple . . . 55.00
Creamer, Flower & Panel patt.,
purple 85.00
Cruet w/original stopper, Inverted
Fan & Feather patt., pink 950.00
Goblet, purple 38.00
Match holder, ball-footed, stippled
body, fluted collar, purple, 3" h.
(ILLUS.). 40.00

Marble Glass Match Holder

Plate, 10¼" d., lattice edge,
purple 90.00
Punch cup, Inverted Fan & Feather
patt., pink, 2½" h. 235.00
Sauce dish, Inverted Fan & Feather
patt., pink, 5" d. 235.00
Spooner, Swan patt., butterscotch
(brown) 55.00
Spooner, Scroll with Acanthus patt.,
purple 55.00
Table set: cov. butter dish, cov.
sugar bowl, creamer & spooner;
Flower & Panel patt., purple,
4 pcs. . . . . .400.00 to 500.00
Toothpick holder, Inverted Fan &
Feather patt., pink 625.00
Toothpick holder, Scroll with Acan-
thus patt., purple 87.00
Vase, 4½" h., footed, parrots decor,
purple 75.00
Vase, Maple Leaf Chalice patt.,
purple 35.00

MARY GREGORY

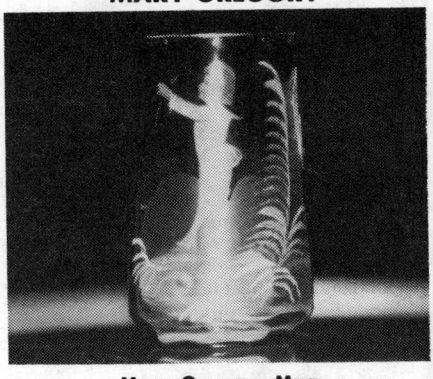

Mary Gregory Mug

*Glass enameled in white with silhouette-
type figures, primarily children, is now
termed Mary Gregory. Glass of this kind was*

decorated at the Boston & Sandwich Glass Works, reportedly by a decorator named Mary Gregory, but also was made in numerous other factories in this country and abroad. Bohemian pieces are said to have tinted faces. This type is now being widely reproduced. Also see BARBER BOTTLES.

Box w/hinged lid, cobalt blue, white
enameled boy, white dot trim
around sides, 3½" d., 2½" h. $155.00
Box w/hinged lid, ormolu feet,
cobalt blue, white enameled girl
holding bird on lid, white sprays
around sides, 5 3/8" d., 3" h. 395.00
Box w/hinged lid, footed, sapphire
blue, white enameled boy holding
sailboat on lid & sprays around
sides, 3½" d., 4" h. 245.00
Box w/hinged lid, sapphire blue,
white enameled boy w/hat feeding 2 small ducks on pond,
5 3/8" d., 4 5/8" h. 525.00
Compote, 6¼" d., 4¼" h., cobalt
blue, white enameled girl w/but-
terfly net, in footed ormolu frame
w/rings on sides 145.00
Cordial set: decanter w/original
clear "bubble" stopper & applied
handle, 8 mugs & 12¾ x 9½"
tray; sapphire blue, white
enameled girl w/hat holding a
flower, 10 pcs. 495.00
Creamer, applied clear handle, sapphire blue, white enameled girl
w/basket, 4¼" h. 120.00
Dresser tray, cobalt blue, white
enameled boy pushing another
boy in cart, 9¾ x 6¾" 225.00
Dresser tray, cranberry, white
enameled boy sitting on stump
fishing & girl sitting in rowboat,
10 3/8 x 7¾" 275.00
Jewelry box w/hinged lid, ormolu
feet & rim, sapphire blue, white
enameled girl feeding bird on lid
& floral garlands on sides, 6" d.,
5 5/8" h. 495.00
Mug, barrel-shaped, golden amber
w/applied amber handle, white
enameled boy, 2¾" d., 4" h. 75.00
Mug, emerald green w/applied
green handle, white enameled
figure & ferns, 1880's (ILLUS.) 45.00
Perfume bottle w/original bubble
stopper, sapphire blue, white
enameled boy w/tinted features &
2 birds, 2¾" d., 5½" h. 145.00
Perfume bottle w/original stopper,
clear, white enameled girl beneath tree & w/ferns on ground .. 165.00
Pin dish, sapphire blue, white
enameled boy, w/brass mounts,
3¾" d., 1 3/8" h. 98.00

Pitcher, 6½" h., emerald green,
white enameled boy w/flowers ... 165.00
Pitcher, water, 8¾" h., 5½" d.,
squared bulbous shape w/round
mouth, amber w/applied sapphire
blue handle, white enameled
girl 295.00
Rose bowl, cranberry, white
enameled girl, gold trim,
2½" h. 135.00
Tumbler, juice, cranberry, white
enameled boy, 2 1/8" d., 4" h. ... 55.00
Tumbler, flattened oval shape, gold-
en amber, white enameled girl
holding basket, 4" h. 115.00
Tumbler, sapphire blue, white
enameled girl carrying basket of
flowers, 2½" d., 5" h. 85.00
Tumbler, cobalt blue, white
enameled girl picking flower,
narrow gold band at top 95.00

Mary Gregory Vase

Vase, 2½" h., cobalt blue, white
enameled girl (ILLUS.) 85.00
Vases, 3" h., 1¾" d., cranberry,
white enameled boy on one & girl
on other, each w/birds in flight &
typical fernery, facing pr. 165.00
Vase, 4¾" h., 1¾" d., clear
pedestal foot, cranberry, white
enameled girl 110.00
Vase, bud, 6¼" h., 2¼" d., cranberry, white enameled girl 85.00
Vase, 7 1/8" h., 3½" d., scalloped
top, sapphire blue, white
enameled boy 130.00
Vase, 7¾" h., 3½" d., cranberry,
white enameled boy w/hat 130.00
Vase, 10" h., cylindrical, lime green,
white enameled boy, ormolu
stand & collar 225.00
Vase, 13¾" h., 6¼" d., medium
green opaque, white enameled
girl w/pitcher at pump & young
man w/hat standing nearby 272.00

MC KEE

McKee Range Set

The McKee name has been associated with glass production since 1834, first producing window glass and later bottles. In the 1850's a new factory was established in Pittsburgh, Pa., for production of flint and pressed glass. The plant was relocated at Jeannette, Pa. in 1888, and operated there as an independent company, almost continuously until 1951 when it sold out to Thatcher Glass Manufacturing Company. Many types of collectible glass were produced by McKee through the years including Depression, Pattern, Milk White and a variety of utility kitchen wares.

Bird house, "Wren's Honeymoon Hut," green	$60.00
Bowl, 4¾" d., footed, Art Deco style, black amethyst	15.00
Bowl, 5" d., Rock Crystal, ruby-flashed	22.00
Bowl, 8½" d., Jade green opaque	6.00
Champagne, Rock Crystal, clear	8.00
Console set: 12½" footed bowl & pr. 2-light candlesticks; Rock Crystal, clear, 3 pcs.	45.00
Cordial, Rock Crystal, clear	15.00 to 22.00
Goblet, Rock Crystal, clear	10.00 to 13.50
Goblet, Rock Crystal, pink	17.50
Juice reamer, Chalaine blue opaque	235.00
Range set, milk white shakers w/original tops, 4 pcs. (ILLUS.)	25.00
Refrigerator dish, cov., Jade green opaque, 8½ x 4"	15.00
Relish, Rock Crystal, clear, oval	10.00
Salt & pepper shakers w/original tops, black amethyst, pr.	30.00
Sherbet, Rock Crystal, clear	8.00
Strawholder jar, cov., clear	75.00
Sundae glasses, low footed, Rock Crystal, ruby-flashed, set of 5	150.00
Tom & Jerry set: bowl & 12 cups; milk white w/red lettering, 13 pcs.	38.00 to 45.00
Tumbler, Flower Band patt., green, 3½" h.	12.00
Whiskey tumbler w/coaster base, "Bottoms Up," custard color	55.00
Whiskey tumbler w/coaster base, "Bottoms Up," Jade green opaque	65.00 to 100.00
Wine, Rock Crystal, clear	16.00

MERCURY

Mercury Cup & Saucer

This glass has a silvery appearance due to a coating of silver nitrate in double-walled objects. A gold effect was obtained by placing the silver nitrate in amber glass. The hole through which the solution was injected was subsequently sealed. It was made in this country and England from the middle of the 19th century.

Candelabra, 2-light, pr.	$150.00
Candle holder, pedestal base, amber interior for gold-washed effect	35.00
Candlesticks, low, pr.	35.00
Cup, demitasse, applied clear handle	22.00
Cup & saucer, etched scrolling foliage (ILLUS.)	135.00
Curtain tiebacks w/original pewter shanks, etched grape design, pr.	45.00
Darner, mushroom-shaped, blue cast w/enameled floral decor, brass trim, large	55.00
Doorknobs, brass trim & connecting rods, 2½" d., 2 pr.	10.00
Egg cup	12.00
Goblet, etched vintage design, amber interior for gold-washed effect, 6 7/8" h.	25.00
Pitcher, 10" h., applied clear handle, bulbous base w/etched florals & leaves, clear top	290.00
Vase, 7" d., ball-shaped, blue cast	25.00
Vase, bud, 9½" h.	15.00

MILK WHITE

This is opaque white glass that resembles the color of and was used as a substitute for white porcelain. Opacity was obtained by adding oxide of tin to a batch of clear glass. It has been made in numerous forms and shapes *in this country and abroad from about the first quarter of last century. It is still being produced, and there are many reproductions of earlier pieces. Also see ABC PLATES, COSMOS, HISTORICAL and PATTERN GLASS.*

Three Owls Plate

Animal covered dish, "American Hen," w/eggs inscribed "Porto Rico," "Cuba," & "Philippines," 6" l., 4" h. $55.00

Animal covered dish, Blue Head Hen on lacy base, amber glass eyes, Atterbury 155.00

Animal covered dish, "The British Lion" on base, 6¼" l. 95.00

Animal covered dish, Deer on "fallen tree" base, Flaccus, 6¾" l. 195.00

Animal covered dish, Dove on split-ribbed base, McKee 100.00

Animal covered dish, Flat-Earred Rabbit on split-ribbed base, McKee, 5½" l. 150.00

Animal covered dish, Fox on ribbed top & ribbed base, Atterbury 125.00

Animal covered dish, Jack Rabbit w/laid-back ears on ribbed base, Flaccus 125.00

Animal covered dish, Lamb on "Bo Peep" base, 6" l. base, 4¼" h. 172.50

Animal covered dish, Lamb on ribbed base, McKee, 5½" l. 185.00

Animal covered dish, Lion on ribbed cover & lacy-edge base, Atterbury ....90.00 to 125.00

Animal covered dish, Mule-Earred Rabbit on octagonal picket base, McKee, 5½" l. 65.00

Animal covered dish, Open Neck Swan on split-ribbed base, McKee, 5½" l. 275.00

Animal covered dish, Robin on Nest, 6¼" d..................100.00 to 150.00

Bowl, 9" d., open lattice edge 35.00

Bowl, 9¼ x 8¾" sq., open edge border 38.00

Covered dish, Cruiser ship, 6" l. 45.00

Covered dish, Fish on Skiff base, 7½" l. 42.50

Covered dish, Robed Santa Claus on Sleigh, 5½" l. 90.00

Easter egg, embossed & gilt cross & h.p. floral decor, 6" l. 22.00

Plate, 7" d., Niagara Falls 28.00

Plate, 7" d., Three Bears, w/traces of original brown, green & gilt ... 32.50

Plate, 7" d., Three Owls (ILLUS.).... 30.00

Plate, 7¼" d., Dart patt. openwork border 14.00

Plate, 7¼" d., "Easter," rabbits & eggs, scroll border 40.00

Plate, 7¼" d., "Easter Greetings," Easter rabbit & egg, lacy open-work border 62.50

Plate, 7¼" d., Gothic patt. open-work border 7.50

Plate, 7¼" d., Little Red Hen patt., openwork lacy border 35.00

Plate, 7¼" d., "No Easter Without Us," rooster & hens 35.00

Plate, 7¼" d., Shell & Club border 12.00

Plate, 7¼" d., Spring Meets Winter patt., openwork border 50.00

Plate, 7¼" d., Sunken Rabbit patt. 35.00

Plate, 7½" d., "Easter" ducks, scroll border 35.00

Plate, 7½" d., "Easter Opening," 2 chicks emerging from eggs & lily-of-the-valley 52.50

Plate, 7½" d., "Easter Sermon," preacher practicing sermon be-neath tree as rabbits listen 65.00

Plate, 7½" d., h.p. floral border on fishnet-weave ground........... 30.00

Plate, 7½" d., Hare & Cloverleaf center, scalloped & beaded border 38.00

Plate, 7½" d., Indian Head center, Beaded Loop border 40.00

Rabbit & Horseshoe Plate

Plate, 7½" d., Rabbit & Horseshoe
(ILLUS.).......................... 32.50
Plate, 7½" d., Wicket patt. open-
work border 14.00
Plate, 8" d., Angel & Harp patt.,
openwork single forget-me-not
border 25.00
Plate, 8" d., Arch patt. border...... 12.00
Plate, 8¼" d., Three Puppies patt.,
open leaf border 80.00
Plate, 9" d., Acanthus Leaf
patt. 38.00
Plate, 10" d., Scroll & Eye openwork
border 15.00

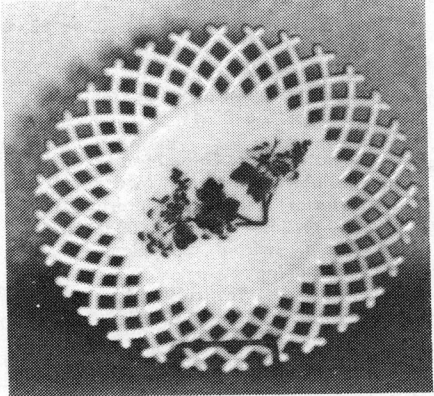

Lattice Edge Plate

Plate, 10½" d., Trumpet Vine patt.
enameled center, Lattice Edge
border (ILLUS.).............45.00 to 55.00
Platter, 13¼ x 9¾", Retriever patt.,
lily pad border...........75.00 to 105.00
Platter, 13¾ x 10½", flattened fish
form w/scale details ......55.00 to 85.00
Salt & pepper shakers w/original
tops, Creased Bale patt., pr. 25.00

Creased Neck Salt & Pepper Shakers

Salt & pepper shakers w/original
tops, Creased Neck patt., h.p.
trumpet vine florals, 4" h., pr.
(ILLUS.)......................... 50.00

Salt dip, master size, footed, Blackberry patt....................... 15.50
Salt dip, master size, model of an
open sleigh, 4" l. 48.50
Smoke bell (for hanging kerosene
parlor lamp), fluted edge, flint,
large........................... 85.00
Spooner, Acanthus Leaf patt., base
marked "Pat'd Apr. 23, '78,"
4 5/8" h. 55.00
Spooner, Blackberry patt. 52.50
Sugar bowl, cov., Blackberry
patt. 48.00
Syrup pitcher w/original hinged lid,
Alba patt., enameled floral
decor 45.00
Syrup pitcher w/original hinged lid,
Apple Blossom patt. 125.00
Syrup pitcher w/original hinged lid,
Torquay patt., h.p. yellow
stripe 85.00
Syrup pitcher w/original hinged lid,
Tree of Life patt. 75.00
Tray, Lady & Fan patt., 7 x 5¼" 35.00
Tray, Child & Shell patt.,
8¾ x 6¼" 90.00
Vase, 5" h., Poppy patt., poppies in
high relief, early 20th c. 25.00

MILLEFIORI

Millefiori Scent Bottle

*Millefiori glass is decorated or patterned,
with tiny slices of thin multicolored glass
canes and is familiar in paperweights, often
filled with closely packed canes. These flower pattern canes have also been used in the
production of other objects for many years
and the technique is ancient. This type of
glass is still being made in Murano, Italy, and
elsewhere. Also see PAPERWEIGHTS.*

Fruit knives, each handle w/assort-
ed millefiori canes & gold threads,
2 dated "1847" on a single cane &
several canes signed "F.C.," now
mounted w/silverplate blades &
sterling silver ferrules at the junc-
ture, 8¼" l., set of 6 (restorations) $715.00
Pitcher w/hinged silverplate lid,
5" h., multicolored canes 150.00

Punch cup, applied opaque blue
handle, multicolored canes
throughout, ca. 1910 . . . . 150.00
Rose bowl, crimped rim, multi-
colored canes 225.00
Scent bottle, multicolored canes set
in pattern at right angles to each
other, attributed to St. Louis or
Baccarat, 2½" h. (ILLUS.) 210.00
Vase, 4½" h., applied double ribbon
handles 75.00

MONART

*This glass was produced by John Mon-
crieff, Ltd., in Perth, Scotland, between 1924
and 1957. Much of it was signed on a paper
label.*

Bowl, 9½" d., white "crackle"
w/eight petal chocolate design on
orange rim $105.00
Candle holder, 2-tone green w/gold
mica flecks, original label
(single) 60.00
Candle holders, mottled blue shaded
to lavender, 3" h., pr. 75.00
Vase, 7" h., urn-shaped, clear
w/vivid yellow lacy inclusions &
bubbles 85.00
Vase, 7¼" h., green w/silvery
beige spatter swirls 95.00
Vase, 14½" h., blue w/iridescent
treebark designs 145.00
Vase, 16" h., orange w/green mica
flecks at neck & gold Cluthra-type
bubbles in body (now drilled as
lamp base) 450.00

MONOT & STUMPF

*A glassworks was established by E.S.
Monot at La Villette, near Paris, in 1850. This
operation was moved to Pantin in 1858 and
became Monot & Stumpf as Mr. F. Stumpf
joined the firm in 1868. Monot's son also en-
tered the firm and, in 1873, it became Monot,
Pere et Fils, et Stumpf. According to an article by Albert Christian Revi, recognized
authority on glasswares and paperweights,
their iridescent wares were called "Chine
Metallique," a patented process they used beginning in 1878. The firm continued business
in Pantin into the early 1890's but by the beginning of the 20th century the company had
become Cristallerie de Pantin and was operated by Saint-Hilaire, Touvier, de Varreux &
Company.*

Rose bowl, 4-crimp top, "Chine
Metallique," soft opalescent pink-
striped effect exterior, lustred
gold interior, 4" d., 3 1/8" h. $110.00
Salt dip, 4-crimp top, "Chine Metallique," caramel opalescent exteri-
or, lustred gold interior, 1 7/8" d.,
1½" h. 65.00
Salt dip, fluted square top, "Chine
Metallique," opalescent pink-
striped effect exterior, lustred
gold interior, 2" d., 1½" h. 65.00
Salt dip, "Chine Metallique," soft
opalescent pink-striped effect exterior, lustred gold interior, 2¼ x
1¾" oval, 1¼" h. . . . . 65.00 to 85.00
Salt dip, fluted top, "Chine Metal-
lique," soft opalescent pink-
striped effect exterior w/lustred
gold interior, 2 3/8" d.,
1 1/8" h. 70.00
Salt dip, fluted top, "Chine Metal-
lique," opalescent pink-striped effect exterior, lustred gold interior,
2½" d., 1¼" h. . . . . 50.00 to 65.00
Vase, 4½" h., swirled, cranberry,
iridescent lining 195.00
Vase, 7¾" h., 7¾" d., ruffled fan-
shaped top, "Chine Metallique,"
soft opalescent pink-striped
effect 250.00

MONT JOYE

Mont Joye Bowl

*Cameo and enameled glass bearing this
mark was made in Pantin, France, by the
same works that produced pieces signed De
Vez.*

Bowl, 7 x 4" oblong, 2" h., enameled violets decor, gold trim,
signed $225.00
Bowl, 10" l., translucent green
w/enameled bluebirds & berry-
laden branches decor (ILLUS.) 280.00
Cameo rose bowl, carved &
enameled violets against frosted
clear ground, 4" d., 4½" h. 400.00
Cameo vase, 8½" h., carved &
enameled leaves & deep red pop-

pies against frosted clear "icy"
ground 430.00
Cameo vase, 10" h., carved thistle
highlighted in gold against clear
to opalescent green ground 250.00
Cameo vase, 12" h., carved &
enameled gold florals & green
leaves against frosted rose
ground, unsigned 325.00
Cameo vase, carved & enameled silver & gold oak leaves & textured
green acorns, signed 345.00
Vase, 5½" h., deep green w/raised
enameling, signed.............. 145.00
Vase, Rubina Crystal w/enameled
floral decor, signed 225.00

MOSER

Moser Cameo Vase with Elephants

*High-quality Art Nouveau glass was
produced from around the turn of the century by Moser, Ludwig & Sohne in Carlsbad
and Mierhofen. Much of the base glass was
amethyst in color, but this expert craftsman
turned out various types of glass, some with
exquisite enameling.*

Bowl, 7¼" d., 5 5/8" h., shaded
pink opalescent w/enameled
multicolored oak leaves & foliage, applied lustred acorns,
signed $1,100.00
Box w/hinged lid, amethyst w/ap-
plied amber salamander feet &
applied gold-trimmed salamander
on lid, enameled pink florals &
green foliage decor, 4½" d.,
4 3/8" h. 575.00
Box w/hinged lid, cranberry
w/enameled white figure of
woman carrying cornucopia &

grapes w/gold vines & berries,
signed, 6" d., 3¾" h........... 650.00
Cameo vase, 7¼" h., flaring sides,
carved sienna branches of pendant pods against translucent
amber shading to brown at foot,
signed 330.00
Cameo vase, 8" h., carved &
enameled maroon medial African
landscape band w/family of
elephants, grassy plains & palm
trees against transparent lime
green ground, ring-turned base,
heightened w/gilding overall
(ILLUS.) 1,100.00
Cologne bottle w/original stopper,
cranberry w/encrusted gold
leaves decor outlined in white
enamel & w/blue & white enamel
dotted blossoms, 10¾" h........ 395.00
Cup & saucer, cobalt blue or
emerald green w/overall gold-
encrusted decor, signed, each 150.00
Finger bowl, triangular, Amberina
w/enameled multicolored oak
leaves & applied acorns (6), gold
trim, signed, 4½" w., 2¾" h. 495.00
Goblet, cranberry w/overall enameled foliage, dragonfly & lady-
bug decor, 4" h. 255.00
Goblet, green cut to clear, signed .. 95.00
Jewel casket w/hinged lid, sapphire
blue, applied ormolu feet, rim &
side handles, enameled multicolored oak leaves decor & applied lustred acorns & fly, unsigned, 4¼ x 3¼" oblong,
4½" h. 795.00
Liqueur, cranberry w/applied clear
pedestal foot, enameled multicolored oak leaves & applied single lustred acorn, signed,
1¼" d., 2½" h. 195.00
Liqueurs, cobalt blue bowl intaglio-
cut to clear, clear ornately cut
stem & base, signed, 5¼" h., set
of 12 .... 500.00
Marmalade jar, cov., Rubina Crystal,
decorated, signed 375.00
Mug, medium green w/applied
green handle & enameled multicolored oak leaves & bee, applied lustred acorns, unsigned,
2 5/8" d., 3¼" h. 295.00
Mug, medium green w/applied
green handle & enameled multicolored oak leaves & applied
lustred acorns 295.00
Perfume bottle w/matching ball-
shaped stopper, green w/enam-
eled multicolored leaves w/pink &
white berries, gold trim, unsigned, 2¾" d., 5¼" h. 165.00

Moser Perfume Bottle

Perfume bottle w/metal screw-on
stopper & metal footed frame,
cased pink opalescent w/enam-
eled white florals, yellow scrolls &
small round bull's eyes cut light
brown to clear, signed, 5¼" h.
(ILLUS.) 135.00
Perfume bottle w/brass stopper &
collar, cranberry cut to clear,
signed, 9½" h. 235.00
Pitcher, 5¼" h., quatrefoil rim,
cranberry w/applied amber reeded handle & enameled berries &
leaves decor 495.00
Pitcher, 8¼" h., bulbous, cranberry
w/overall enameled butterflies,
florals, dragonflies & gold
webbing 395.00
Pitcher, 9" h., Inverted Thumbprint
patt., sapphire blue w/encrusted
gold decor, signed 395.00
Tumbler, juice, melon-ribbed, shaded blue w/band of enameled
white florals, yellow scrolls & red
& green jeweling, signed, 2¼" d.,
3½" h. 200.00

MT. WASHINGTON

*A wide diversity of glass was made by the
Mt. Washington Glass Company, of New
Bedford, Mass., between 1869 and 1900. It
was succeeded in 1900 by the Pairpoint Cor-
poration. Miscellaneous types are listed be-
low, but also see AMBERINA, BURMESE,
CROWN MILANO, CUT, CUT VELVET,
PEACH BLOW, ROYAL FLEMISH and
SMITH BROTHERS.*

Candlesticks, soft peach shaded to
lustreless white ribbed columns

w/h.p. peach pink florals, in ornate silverplate base signed "Pairpoint" & dated Aug. 22, 1893,
12½" h., w/removable bobeches,
pr. $395.00
Compote, 10" d., 14" h., "Napoli,"
interior-painted orange blossoms,
oranges & leaves on clear cranberry outlined in gold on exterior,
in Art Nouveau silverplate
base 1,150.00

Mt. Washington Cookie Jar

Cookie jar, lustreless white w/h.p.
florals & leaves outlined in raised
gold & w/textured leaf-outlined
base, silverplate rim, cover & bail
handle (ILLUS.) 595.00
Cookie jar, melon-ribbed, dusty pink
w/h.p. blackberries & blossoms
decor, silverplate rim, cover &
bail handle 275.00
Flower frog, mushroom-shaped,
beige satin finish w/h.p. green,
brown & gold autumn leaves
decor, 5" d., 2¾" h. 175.00
Lamp, kerosene-type, "Lava," glossy
black w/profuse inclusions of
pink, blue, green, white & mauve-
colored chips, w/burner 1,500.00
Mustard jar, narrow-ribbed, lustreless white w/h.p. lavender, blue
& green floral decor, silverplate
lid 65.00
Mustard jar w/hinged pagoda-
shaped silverplate lid, fig mold
variant, pink shaded to white
w/h.p. leaves decor, lid signed
Pairpoint 235.00
Pitcher, 5½" h., cranberry "overshot" w/h.p. white lily decor 265.00
Pitcher, 6½" h., bulbous, "Verona,"
clear w/h.p. goldfish & multicolored seaplants & leaves &
gold trim exterior 900.00

Pitcher, tankard, "Verona," clear
w/h.p. realistic apple blossoms &
green leaves outlined in gold on
exterior 675.00

Plate, 10" d., lustreless white
w/h.p. holly & birds decor 85.00

Potpourri (rose petal) jar, shaded
light to deep peach pink w/h.p.
rose hips & shaded green leaves,
engraved silverplate pierced cover
w/turn-knob finial to twist & re-
lease aroma, 5" h. 230.00

Salt shaker, model of a chick w/sil-
verplate head, glossy textured
white w/h.p. rose sprays decor... 335.00

Salt shaker w/original top, cockle
shell shape, pink
(single) ....195.00 to 245.00

Salt shaker w/original top, egg-
shaped, shaded cream to pale
blue satin finish w/h.p. shasta
daisies decor (single) ......50.00 to 65.00

Salt shaker w/original top, melon-
ribbed, blue satin finish w/h.p.
pink, blue & brown floral decor
(single)........................ 62.50

Salt & pepper shakers w/original
tops, cockle shell shape, pr. 600.00

Sugar shaker w/original top, egg-
shaped, lustreless white w/h.p.
large clusters of blue forget-me-
nots & jeweling ....195.00 to 225.00

Sugar shaker w/original top, egg-
shaped, yellow shaded to burnt
orange w/h.p. yellow daisies
decor 215.00

Sugar shaker w/original top, melon-
ribbed, pale blue shaded to cream
w/h.p. pink & white floral decor.. 230.00

Sugar shaker w/original top, melon-
ribbed, white satin finish w/h.p.
autumn leaves decor 325.00

Sweetmeat jar, "Verona," clear
w/h.p. white & blue florals &
stained blue vertical ribs exterior,
original silverplate rim & cover
signed "M.W.," 6" h. 225.00

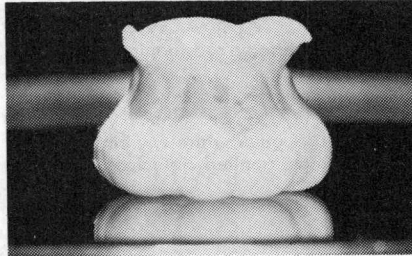

Mt. Washington Toothpick Holder

Toothpick holder, melon-ribbed,
shaped rim, lustreless white, h.p.
floral decor (ILLUS.) 400.00

Toothpick holder, hat-shaped, lustreless white w/h.p. autumn
leaves decor 234.00

Vase, 4½" h., 5" widest d., globular, applied handles at sides,
"Lava," glossy black w/profuse inclusions of pink, blue, green &
mauve-colored chips 1,500.00

Vase, 8" h., 4" top d., waisted cylinder w/pulled ears at rim, clear
w/h.p. Easter lilies, buds &
leaves outlined in gold on
exterior 375.00

Vase, 9¼" h., applied handles,
"Lava," glossy black w/profuse inclusions of soft pink, blue, green,
grey, blue-grey, light green,
white & mauve,......1,000.00 to 2,000.00

Vase, 10" h., "Verona," clear w/h.p.
grasshoppers, wheat sheaves &
stems on exterior 750.00

Vase, 10½" h., lustreless white
shaded to soft yellow w/h.p.
roses, leaves, branches, butterfly
& bee decor 450.00

Vase, bud, 13½" h., ruby "overshot," in bronzed metal holder
w/crane & dragonfly, ca. 1870.... 385.00

Vase, "Napoli," clear w/interior-
painted frog, reeds & rushes outlined in gold on exterior 785.00

MULLER FRERES

Muller Freres Cameo Vase

*The Muller Brothers made acid-etched cam-
eo and other fine glass at Luneville, France,
starting in 1910 and until the outbreak of
World War II in Europe. Also see SHADES
under Glass.*

Cameo vase, 5 7/8" h., 4½" d.,
carved rose orchid-like florals &
leaves against green frosted to
mottled ground, signed $1,100.00

Cameo vase, 6 5/8" h., 3¾" d.,
carved deep maroon to rose
scene of shepherd w/staff & hat
tending flock of sheep against
mottled gold translucent satin
ground, tree branches frame top
of scene, signed 1,112.00

Cameo vase, 7¾" h., 4¼" d., carved
scene w/stork by water in foreground & black to blue to gold
hills at front & house on reverse,
against translucent frosted gold
ground, signed 1,395.00

Cameo vase, 8 5/8" h., 4 5/8" d.,
carved dark marooon to rose river
landscape w/trees against mottled white frosted ground,
signed 650.00

Cameo vase, 9 1/8" h., cylindrical
w/waisted neck, carved deep
blue-grey & deep raspberry red
magnolia blossoms & leaves
against frosted citron yellow
ground, ca. 1910, signed
(ILLUS.) 2,860.00

Cameo vase, 11½" h., carved
burnt orange, gold & brown
chrysanthemums against white
ground, signed 2,800.00

Cameo vase, 11¾" h., stick-type
w/long narrow neck, carved dark
blue forest scene w/girl resting
before tree against lemon yellow
ground, signed 800.00

Cameo vase, 14" h., carved black
forest & deer scene against red
ground, signed 1,250.00

Etched Glass Luminiere

Luminiere, oblong clear panel
deeply etched w/scene of 4 polar
bears prowling on icebergs in
Arctic landscape, fitted into
stepped chrome metal base, ca.
1930, signed, overall 33½" l.
(ILLUS.) 4,950.00

NAILSEA

*Glass was made at Nailsea, near Bristol,
England, from 1788 to 1873. Although the
bulk of the products were similar to Bristol*

*wares, collectors today visualize Nailsea
primarily as a glass characterized by swirls
and loopings, usually white, on a colored
ground. Much glass attributed to Nailsea was
made in glasshouses elsewhere. Also see
KITCHENWARES.*

Cologne bottle w/original tall stopper, opaque white w/blue loop-
ings, 6½" h. $125.00

Flask, clear w/red, white & blue
loopings, 6¼" l. 110.00

Flask, clear w/pink & white loop-
ings, 8" l. 120.00

Flask, blue w/white loopings,
9" l. 125.00

Fluid lamp w/original double wick
burner, clear font w/white loopings, w/matching shade & ruffled
base w/applied cranberry thread-
ing, 13" h. 995.00

Nailsea Pitcher

Pitcher, 7½" h., applied handle,
clear w/pink & white swirled
loopings, ground pontil, 19th c.
(ILLUS.) 247.00

Powder flask, clear w/amethyst
loopings & opaque white chalky
lining, applied clear foot, neck
ring & lip, 11½" h. 300.00

Rolling pin, clear w/red loopings,
12" l. 110.00

Rolling pin, white w/red loopings,
14½" l. 118.00

Rolling pin, clear w/red & white
loopings, 17" l. 125.00

Sugar bowl, opqaue white w/pink &
red loopings, applied clear foot. . . 200.00

NAKARA

*Like Kelva (which see), Nakara ware was
made early in this century by C.F. Monroe
Company. For details see WAVE CREST.*

Nakara Box

Box w/hinged lid, bishop's hat
  mold, h.p. florals & white
  enameled dots on mauve shaded
  to tan ground, signed, 3¾" d.....$340.00
Box w/hinged lid, reserve scene of
  cupids on lid on glossy red shaded
  to tan ground, signed, 3¾" d.,
  2½" h........................ 365.00
Box w/hinged lid, octagonal mold,
  reserve scene on lid of Kate
  Greenaway figures at tea on
  shaded blue to beige ground
  w/white enameled beading &
  florettes, 4½" d. (ILLUS.) 900.00
Jewelry box w/hinged lid, reserve
  portrait of Queen Louise, original
  lining, 8" d.....................1,000.00
Jewelry box w/hinged lid & inside
  mirror, crown mold, roses decor
  on moss green, original lining,
  signed, 8½" d. ....675.00 to 750.00
Pin dish, hexagonal, ormolu rim &
  handles, enameled panels (4) of
  florals on pink 195.00
Ring box w/hinged lid, octagonal
  mold, enameled white dotted
  swags & florals w/lavender
  centers on soft green, signed,
  2½" d...................... 395.00
Trinket box, open, swirl mold, soft
  pink clover on robin's egg shaded
  to blue ground, signed 185.00
Vase, 14" h., footed, pink roses outlined in white enameled dots on
  shaded pink to blue ground,
  signed ....525.00 to 575.00
Vase, 15¾" h., 6" d., h.p. florals on
  shaded green to pale beige
  ground, signed.................. 675.00
Watch box w/hinged lid, apple blossoms spray on shaded lavender to
  olive green ground, original
  lining, 3½" d. 325.00
Whisk broom holder, ormolu trim,
  pink floral decor on soft blue
  ground, signed.................. 850.00

NASH

Nash Chintz Pattern Vases

*This glass was made by A. Douglas Nash
Corp., which purchased the Corona Works
from L.C. Tiffany in December, 1928. Nash,
who formerly worked for Tiffany, produced
outstanding glass for a brief period of time
since the manufacture ceased prior to March
of 1931, when A. Douglas Nash became associated with Libbey Glass in Toledo, Ohio.
This fine quality ware is scarce.*

Bowl, 4¾ x 3½" oval, 2½" h., footed, shaded green to clear,
  signed $100.00
Bowl, 8 3/8" d., Chintz patt., rose
  petal pink w/lavender stripes 120.00
Bowl, 13" d., footed, twisted green
  & lavender stripes, mirror lustre
  finish, signed 250.00
Candlesticks, ball stem, Chintz patt.,
  blood red w/grey, 4" h., pr. 450.00
Cordial, Alexandrite (shaded yellowish to rose blue), signed,
  5 7/8" h. 200.00
Goblet, ball stem, Chintz patt.,
  bright green & blue, signed,
  6¼" h. 110.00
Parfait, peach pastel stain, signed,
  6½" h. 125.00
Plate, 10¾" d., Chintz patt., chartreuse stripes 80.00
Plate, 11¼" d., Chintz patt., iridescent gold & blue striping 90.00
Tumbler, Alexandrite (shaded yellowish to rose to blue), signed,
  5½" h. 90.00
Vase, 4¾" h., 5" d., globular,
  Chintz patt., opalescent, yellow &
  brown stripes, signed............ 200.00
Vase, 6" h., circular foot, textured
  stem, flaring rim, iridescent gold,
  signed 165.00
Vase, 6¾" h., irregular ribbing,
  blue, signed 525.00

Vase, 8" h., Chintz patt., green &
   brown, signed 400.00
Vase, 9" h., ball stem, Chintz patt.,
   blood red & grey, signed........ 475.00
Vase, 9¼" h., Chintz patt., orange,
   unsigned (ILLUS. right) 175.00
Vase, 10" h., Chintz patt., black &
   orange, signed (ILLUS. left) 350.00
Vase, 12" h., trumpet form, Chintz
   patt., blue, green & clear........ 450.00
Wine, clear w/blue band around
   top, signed, 7 5/8" h............ 110.00

OPALESCENT

*Presently, this is one of the most popular
areas of glass collecting. The opalescent effect was attained by adding bone ash chemi-
cals to areas of an item while still hot and
refiring this object at tremendous heat. Both
pressed and mold-blown patterns are available to collectors and we distinguish the types
in our listing below.* Opalescent Glass From
A to Z *by William Heacock, is the definitive
reference book for collectors. Also see* ART
GLASS BASKETS, EPERGNES *and* PAT-
TERN GLASS.

MOLD-BLOWN OPALESCENT PATTERNS

BUTTONS & BRAIDS
Pitcher, water, blue $135.00
Pitcher, water, cranberry 235.00
Pitcher, water, green 115.00
Water set: pitcher & 5 tumblers;
   blue, 6 pcs..................... 275.00

CHRISTMAS SNOWFLAKE
Lamp, cranberry 380.00
Pitcher, water, rope handle,
   cranberry...................... 365.00
Tumbler, cranberry 90.00

CHRYSANTHEMUM BASE SWIRL

Chrysanthemum Base Swirl Pattern

Creamer, blue 125.00
Spooner, blue ....75.00 to 100.00
Syrup pitcher w/original top, blue,
   satin finish 175.00

Toothpick holder, cranberry
   (ILLUS.)....................... 90.00

COINSPOT

Coinspot Tumbler

Barber bottle w/original stopper,
   cranberry..................... 95.00
Pitcher, water, blue 100.00
Pitcher, water, green 80.00
Pitcher, water, white 78.00
Sugar shaker w/original top, blue .. 85.00
Sugar shaker w/original top,
   cranberry..................... 125.00
Tumbler, cranberry (ILLUS.) 60.00
Vase, 7" h., white................ 38.00
Water set: pitcher & 6 tumblers;
   pitcher w/round ruffled rim, cran-
   berry, 7 pcs.................... 265.00
Water set: pitcher & 6 tumblers;
   white, 7 pcs................... 230.00

DAISY & FERN

Daisy & Fern Water Set

Barber bottle w/original stopper,
   cranberry..................... 85.00
Cruet w/original stopper, blue 65.00
Cruet w/original stopper, white 45.00
Pitcher, water, bulbous, cranberry .. 215.00
Pitcher, water, square ruffled neck,
   cranberry..................... 160.00

Pitcher, water, white 125.00
Sauce dish, blue . . . .'. 30.00
Syrup pitcher w/original top, blue . . 120.00
Syrup pitcher w/original top,
   white 79.00
Tumbler, cranberry 45.00
Tumbler, white 30.00
Water set: pitcher & 6 tumblers;
   cranberry, 7 pcs. (ILLUS. of part) . . 485.00

HOBNAIL, HOBBS

Hobnail Pitcher

Berry set: master bowl & 6 sauce
   dishes; square, vaseline, 7 pcs. 200.00
Bowl, 12" d., ruffled rim,
   cranberry 75.00
Celery vase, vaseline 95.00
Cruet w/original stopper, blue 210.00
Cruet w/original stopper,
   cranberry 325.00
Cruet w/original stopper, vaseline . . 225.00
Cruet w/original stopper, white 95.00
Finger bowl, cranberry 48.00
Pitcher, 5½" h., 5½" w., applied
   clear handle, cranberry (ILLUS.) . . 225.00
Pitcher, 9½" h., quatrefoil rim,
   cranberry . . . . 200.00 to 285.00
Pitcher, water, square mouth, ap-
   plied handle, vaseline 170.00
Pitcher, water, bulbous, square top,
   white 165.00
Sauce dish, vaseline 40.00
Water set: pitcher & 6 tumblers;
   cranberry, 7 pcs. 175.00

NINE-PANEL COINSPOT

Sugar shaker w/original top, blue . . 85.00
Sugar shaker w/original top,
   green 120.00
Syrup pitcher w/original top,
   blue 90.00
Syrup pitcher w/original top,
   green . . . . 85.00 to 140.00
Syrup pitcher w/original top,
   white 47.50

POINSETTIA

Pitcher, water, tankard, 13" h.,
   blue . . . . 165.00 to 225.00
Pitcher, water, tankard, 13" h.,
   green 125.00
Tumbler, blue 43.00
Tumbler, green 33.00
Water set: bulbous pitcher
   w/crimped rim & 7 tumblers;
   blue, 8 pcs. 425.00

POLKA DOT

Barber bottle, blue 125.00
Barber bottle, cranberry 125.00
Cruet w/original stopper, cran-
   berry 120.00
Pitcher, water, cranberry 185.00
Pitcher, water, white 110.00
Syrup pitcher w/original top, blue . . 175.00
Syrup pitcher w/original top,
   cranberry 220.00
Syrup pitcher w/original top,
   white 60.00
Toothpick holder, cranberry 75.00
Tumbler, cranberry 48.00

REVERSE SWIRL

Reverse Swirl Syrup Pitcher

Bowl, berry, 9" d., white 45.00
Carafe, blue 35.00
Celery vase, blue 68.00
Cruet w/original stopper, cran-
   berry 235.00
Mustard jar, canary yellow 34.50
Pitcher, water, canary yellow 145.00
Pitcher, water, tankard, cranberry . . 295.00
Pitcher, water, tankard, white 102.00
Salt shaker w/original top, blue or
   canary yellow 25.00
Sauce dish, blue 20.00
Spooner, blue 55.00
Sugar bowl, cov., blue 115.00
Sugar shaker w/original top, blue . . 120.00
Sugar shaker w/original top, canary
   yellow 85.00

Sugar shaker w/original top,
cranberry 125.00
Syrup pitcher w/original top, blue .. 125.00
Syrup pitcher w/original top, cran-
berry (ILLUS.) 220.00
Toothpick holder, blue 85.00
Toothpick holder, white 40.00
Tumbler, juice, white 25.00
Tumbler, canary yellow 38.00
Tumbler, cranberry 45.00
Tumbler, white.................... 65.00
Vase, 5" h., cranberry 60.00
Vase, 6¼" h., 2-handled, cran-
berry 48.00
Vase, 8" h., cranberry 48.00
Water set: pitcher & 4 tumblers;
white, 5 pcs. 165.00
Whiskey shot glass, white 22.00

RIBBED LATTICE

Ribbed Lattice Creamer

Celery vase, cranberry 87.00
Creamer, blue (ILLUS.) 95.00
Cruet w/original stopper, blue 150.00
Cruet w/original stopper, cran-
berry 165.00
Cruet w/original stopper, white 55.00
Pitcher, water, white 130.00
Pitcher, water, tankard, cranberry .. 275.00
Salt shaker w/original top,
cranberry 45.00
Sugar shaker w/original top, blue .. 90.00
Sugar shaker w/original top,
cranberry 110.00
Sugar shaker w/original top,
white ....50.00 to 75.00
Syrup pitcher w/original top, blue .. 160.00
Syrup pitcher w/original top,
cranberry 265.00
Syrup pitcher w/original top,
white 95.00
Toothpick holder, blue 65.00
Toothpick holder, cranberry 72.50
Toothpick holder, white............ 30.00
Tumbler, cranberry 65.00
Tumbler, white.................... 50.00

SEAWEED

Barber bottle, blue 130.00
Barber bottle, cranberry ...120.00 to 135.00

Barber bottle, white 85.00
Butter dish, cov., blue 200.00
Celery vase, blue 85.00
Cruet w/original stopper, blue 135.00
Cruet w/original stopper, white 85.00
Finger bowl, blue 45.00
Pitcher, water, blue, satin finish 255.00
Pitcher, water, cranberry 275.00
Pitcher, water, white 125.00
Salt shaker w/original top,
cranberry 42.50
Spooner, cranberry, satin finish 90.00
Sugar bowl, cov., cranberry, satin
finish 110.00
Sugar shaker w/original top, blue .. 95.00
Syrup pitcher w/original top, blue .. 235.00
Tumbler, blue.................... 55.00

SPANISH LACE

Spanish Lace Bowl

Bowl, 7" d., ruffled rim, blue
(ILLUS.)........................ 80.00
Pitcher, 5½" h., blue 60.00
Pitcher, water, 9" h., canary
yellow 145.00
Pitcher, water, tankard, 11½" h.,
cranberry 385.00
Pitcher, water, fluted rim, blue 265.00
Pitcher, water, white 110.00
Pitcher, water, tankard, green 450.00
Rose bowl, blue.................. 65.00
Rose bowl, canary yellow 50.00
Rose bowl, white, 4½" 55.00
Spooner, blue..............60.00 to 75.00
Spooner, cranberry 75.00
Sugar shaker w/original top, blue .. 130.00
Sugar shaker w/original top, canary
yellow ....85.00 to 110.00
Sugar shaker w/original top,
cranberry 145.00
Sugar shaker w/original top,
white 50.00
Syrup pitcher w/original top, blue .. 115.00
Syrup pitcher w/original top,
cranberry 165.00
Tumbler, blue ....35.00 to 45.00
Vases, 6" h., 4" w., ruffled top,
blue, pr. 135.00
Water set: pitcher & 4 tumblers;
cranberry, 5 pcs. 375.00

STARS & STRIPES
Barber bottle w/original stopper,
   blue 180.00
Barber bottle w/original stopper,
   cranberry 210.00
Barber bottle, white 155.00
Finger bowl, white 15.00
Tumbler, blue..................... 60.00
Tumbler, cranberry 45.00
Tumbler, white................... 45.00

STRIPE
Barber bottle, cranberry 95.00
Cruet w/original stopper, cran-
   berry 125.00
Cruet w/original stopper, white 145.00
Syrup pitcher w/original top, blue .. 185.00
Syrup pitcher w/original top, canary
   yellow 125.00

SWIRL
Barber bottle w/original stopper,
   blue 110.00
Barber bottle, cranberry, 10¼" h. .. 65.00
Bowl, master berry, white 50.00
Cruet w/original stopper, cran-
   berry 160.00
Lamp shade, white, 7½" h. 37.50
Pitcher, 4¼" h., bulbous, applied
   blue handle, blue 48.00
Pitcher, 6¼" h., bulbous, applied
   blue handle, blue 75.00
Pitcher, water, 9¼" h., square ruf-
   fled top, applied clear handle,
   cranberry .... 165.00 to 210.00
Pitcher, water, blue 155.00
Pitcher, water, white .... 95.00 to 110.00
Rose bowl, canary yellow 45.00
Rose bowl, white.................. 37.50
Straw holder w/original lid,
   cranberry 325.00
Sugar shaker w/original top, blue .. 84.00
Syrup pitcher w/original top, blue .. 105.00
Syrup pitcher w/tin top, canary
   yellow 125.00
Toothpick holder, blue 42.50
Tumbler, cranberry 35.50
Tumbler, white................... 29.00
Vase, 7" h., 10" d., scalloped rim
   w/ruffled edge, green 39.50
Water set: pitcher & 4 tumblers;
   blue, 5 pcs. 195.00
Water set: pitcher & 5 tumblers;
   green, 6 pcs. 235.00
Whimsey, hat, white 70.00
Whimsey, pipe, blue, 18" l. 110.00

WINDOWS, PLAIN
Pitcher, water, blue 125.00
Pitcher, water, cranberry 245.00
Pitcher, water, applied clear handle,
   white 150.00
Salt shaker w/original top,
   cranberry..................... 40.00

Syrup pitcher w/original top, blue .. 135.00
Toothpick holder, white 40.00
Tumbler, blue..................... 37.50
Vase, 9" h., ruffled top, blue 60.00
Water set: pitcher w/straight top &
   2 tumblers; cranberry, 3 pcs. 300.00

WINDOWS, SWIRLED
Finger bowl, blue, 4½" d. 35.00
Pitcher, water, white 135.00
Salt shaker w/original top,
   cranberry..................... 32.00
Salt & pepper shakers w/original
   tops, blue, pr. 85.00
Sugar shaker w/original top, cran-
   berry ....175.00 to 195.00
Syrup pitcher w/original top, blue,
   tall 210.00
Syrup pitcher w/original top, cran-
   berry, tall 250.00
Syrup pitcher w/original top, white,
   tall 75.00
Toothpick holder, cranberry 85.00
Tumbler, blue..................... 85.00
Tumbler, cranberry 57.50
Tumbler, white................... 28.00

Pressed Opalescent Patterns

ALASKA - See Pattern Glass

ARGONAUT SHELL
Berry set: master bowl & 4 sauce
   dishes; white, 5 pcs. 190.00
Berry set: master bowl & 6 sauce
   dishes; blue, 7 pcs............... 300.00
Bowl, 7" d., dome footed, ruffled,
   blue 70.00
Compote, jelly, blue 67.00
Compote, jelly, white............. 45.00
Creamer, blue 110.00
Cruet w/original stopper, blue 270.00
Cruet w/original stopper, white 110.00
Spooner, blue..................... 35.00
Sugar bowl, cov., blue 175.00
Table set: cov. butter dish, cov.
   sugar bowl, creamer & spooner;
   blue, 4 pcs. 895.00
Table set, white, 4 pcs. 490.00
Tumbler, white................... 30.00
Water set: pitcher & 5 tumblers;
   white, 6 pcs.................... 315.00

ASTRO
Bowl, 8½" d., blue 30.00
Bowl, 8½" d., footed, white........ 20.00
Bowl, 9" d., footed, green 38.00
Bride's bowl, ruffled, blue 45.00

AURORA BOREALIS
Vase, blue....................... 34.00
Vase, green 25.00
Vase, white 12.00

BEATTY RIB

Beatty Rib Bowl

Berry set: master bowl & 7 sauce
  dishes; white, 8 pcs. 95.00
Bowl, 8" d., white (ILLUS.) 45.00
Celery vase, blue 42.00
Celery vase, white 45.00
Creamer, blue 26.00
Creamer, individual size, white 40.00
Finger bowl, blue 30.00
Mug, blue 38.00
Pitcher, water, blue 205.00
Salt dip, white 22.00
Sauce dish, blue 7.50
Sugar shaker w/original top, blue . . 90.00
Table set, blue, 4 pcs. 285.00
Toothpick holder, blue 29.00
Toothpick holder, white 24.00
Tumbler, blue 45.00

BEATTY SWIRL

Beatty Swirl Pitcher

Bowl, master berry, white 40.00
Butter dish, cov., blue 135.00
Pitcher, water, blue (ILLUS.) 160.00
Spooner, white 35.00
Tumbler, blue 45.00
Water tray, canary yellow 85.00

CIRCLED SCROLL

Bowl, 8½" d., white 55.00

Creamer, blue 62.50
Creamer, green 62.50
Creamer, white 36.00
Cruet w/original stopper, green 245.00
Sauce dish, footed, blue, 4¼" d. . . . 31.00
Spooner, blue 65.00
Sugar bowl, cov., blue 130.00
Tumbler, green 55.00

DIAMOND SPEARHEAD

Diamond Spearhead Butter Dish

Butter dish, cov., vaseline (ILLUS.) . . 175.00
Celery vase, vaseline 80.00
Creamer, vaseline, 2¾" h. 55.00
Goblet, blue 76.00
Sauce dish, vaseline 12.00
Spooner, green 75.00
Spooner, vaseline 59.00
Sugar bowl, cov., green 135.00
Sugar bowl, cov., vaseline 95.00
Toothpick holder, green 50.00
Toothpick holder, vaseline 60.00

DRAPERY

Creamer, blue 35.00
Creamer, white 35.00
Pitcher, water, blue 145.00
Sauce dish, blue 27.00
Sauce dish, white 15.00
Spooner, white 30.00
Sugar bowl, cov., white 55.00
Table set, blue, 4 pcs. 265.00
Tumbler, blue 35.00
Water set: pitcher & 4 tumblers;
  blue, 5 pcs. 280.00
Water set: pitcher & 6 tumblers;
  blue, 7 pcs. 385.00
Water set: pitcher & 6 tumblers;
  white, 7 pcs. 190.00

EVERGLADES

Butter dish, cov., blue w/gold
  trim 175.00
Butter dish, cov., canary yellow 275.00
Compote, jelly, blue w/gold trim . . . 160.00
Compote, jelly, white 47.50
Creamer, canary yellow 75.00
Cruet w/original stopper, canary
  yellow w/gold trim 325.00

Sauce dish, blue w/gold trim	25.00
Sauce dish, canary yellow	35.00
Sauce dish, white	15.00
Spooner, canary yellow	75.00
Sugar bowl, cov., blue w/gold trim	110.00
Sugar bowl, cov., canary yellow	145.00

Everglades Pattern

Table set, blue w/gold trim, 4 pcs. (ILLUS. of part)	495.00
Tumbler, blue w/gold trim	75.00

FANCY FANTAILS
Rose bowl, 4-legged, white w/cranberry edge	52.50

FLORA
Berry set: master bowl & 6 sauce dishes; canary yellow, 7 pcs.	295.00
Bowl, master berry, blue	75.00
Butter dish, cov., canary yellow	195.00 to 245.00
Butter dish, cov., white	95.00
Candy dish, tri-cornered, white, 7" w.	25.00
Celery vase, blue	95.00 to 125.00
Compote, jelly, blue	125.00
Creamer, blue	65.00
Sauce dish, blue	35.00
Spooner, blue	75.00
Spooner, white	45.00
Sugar bowl, cov., blue	95.00
Sugar bowl, cov., canary yellow	125.00

FLUTED BARS & BEADS

Fluted Bars & Beads Vase

Rose bowl, green w/cranberry rim	38.00
Vase, blue (ILLUS.)	35.00
Vase, green	32.00
Vase, vaseline w/cranberry rim	37.50

FLUTED SCROLLS

Fluted Scrolls Pattern

Berry set: master bowl & 6 sauce dishes; vaseline, 7 pcs.	200.00 to 230.00
Bowl, 7½" d., turned-down side, blue	45.00
Bowl, master berry, blue	60.00
Bowl, master berry, vaseline	85.00
Butter dish, cov., blue	155.00 to 200.00
Butter dish, cov., vaseline	150.00 to 200.00
Butter dish, cov., white	125.00
Card tray, vaseline, 7" w.	60.00
Card tray, white, 7" w.	35.00
Creamer, blue	50.00
Creamer, vaseline w/enameled florals	75.00
Creamer, white	33.50
Cruet w/replaced stopper, blue	125.00
Cruet w/original stopper, vaseline (ILLUS.)	150.00
Epergne, blue	120.00
Pitcher, water, blue	195.00 to 250.00
Pitcher, water, vaseline	200.00
Pitcher, water, white	87.50
Puff jar, cov., blue	50.00
Puff jar, cov., vaseline	50.00
Puff jar, cov., white	30.00
Rose bowl, blue	55.00
Rose bowl, white	45.00
Salt & pepper shakers w/original tops, blue, pr.	75.00
Sauce dish, blue w/enameled florals	32.50
Sauce dish, vaseline	25.00
Sauce dish, white w/enameled florals	27.00
Spooner, blue	55.00
Spooner, vaseline w/enameled florals	95.00
Spooner, white	42.50
Sugar bowl, cov., blue	80.00
Sugar bowl, cov., vaseline	80.00
Sugar bowl, cov., vaseline w/enameled florals	135.00

Table set, blue, 4 pcs. 485.00
Table set, vaseline, 4 pcs.
(ILLUS.). 400.00
Tumbler, blue w/enameled florals . . 65.00
Tumbler, vaseline w/enameled
florals. 65.00
Water set: pitcher & 4 tumblers;
vaseline, 5 pcs. 445.00

GONTERMAN SWIRL

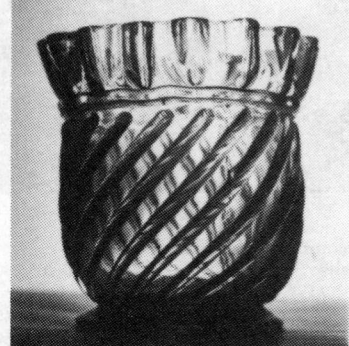

Gonterman Swirl Spooner

Bowl, master berry, 10" d.,
blue top. 135.00
Celery vase, amber top 80.00
Celery vase, blue top. 85.00
Compote, jelly, amber top 110.00
Creamer, applied amber handle,
amber top 95.00
Pitcher, water, amber
top . . . . .150.00 to 250.00
Spooner, amber top (ILLUS.) 85.00
Spooner, blue top 95.00
Sugar bowl, cov., amber
top . . . . .85.00 to 120.00
Sugar bowl, cov., blue top 160.00
Syrup pitcher w/original lid, amber
top 250.00
Toothpick holder, amber top 120.00
Toothpick holder, blue top . .85.00 to 115.00
Water set: pitcher & 5 tumblers;
amber top, 6 pcs. 575.00

HILLTOP VINES
Candy dish, green. 32.50

HOBNAIL, NORTHWOOD
Creamer, white 35.00
Creamer & sugar bowl, white, pr. . . 55.00
Nappy, ruffled, blue. 12.00
Pitcher, water, 8" h., 7" d., bulbous,
square mouth, applied clear han-
dle, white 125.00
Powder jar, cov., white 15.00
Salt & pepper shakers w/original
tops, blue, pr. 15.00
Spooner, white. 25.00
Tumbler, blue. 10.00

Vase, 5½" h., fluted rim, canary
yellow 25.00

HOBNAIL & PANELED THUMBPRINT

Hobnail & Paneled Thumbprint Table Set

Butter dish, cov., blue 145.00
Creamer, blue 45.00
Pitcher, water, blue 145.00
Sauce dish, blue 30.00
Spooner, blue. 60.00
Spooner, canary yellow 55.00
Sugar bowl, cov., canary yellow 90.00
Table set, blue, 4 pcs. 425.00
Table set, canary yellow, 4 pcs.
(ILLUS.). 345.00
Tumbler, blue. 25.00

HOBNAIL-IN-SQUARE
Bowl, master berry, 10" d.,
white 85.00
Pickle castor, white insert in silver-
plate holder w/apples decor 125.00
Tumbler, white. 25.00

HONEYCOMB & CLOVER
Bowl, master berry, blue 32.50
Bowl, master berry, green 35.00
Bowl, master berry, white 30.00
Pitcher, water, blue 265.00
Pitcher, water, white 175.00
Tumbler, green 55.00

IDYL
Berry set: master bowl & 6 sauce
dishes; green, 7 pcs. 50.00
Creamer, blue 45.00
Creamer, green 50.00
Creamer, white 25.00
Pitcher, water, green 245.00
Spooner, blue 80.00
Spooner, green 75.00
Sugar bowl, open, green. 40.00
Toothpick holder, green 110.00

INTAGLIO
Berry set: master bowl & 6 sauce
dishes; blue, 7 pcs. 400.00
Bowl, master berry, pedestal base,
blue 75.00
Compote, jelly, blue 30.00
Compote, jelly, canary yellow 40.00
Compote, jelly, white. 30.00

Creamer, blue 45.00
Creamer, white 22.50
Creamer & sugar bowl, blue, pr. ... 110.00
Creamer & sugar bowl, white, pr. .. 65.00
Cruet w/original stopper, blue 110.00
Cruet w/original stopper, white 85.00
Pitcher, water, blue 185.00
Pitcher, water, white 85.00
Sauce dish, blue 17.50
Sauce dish, white 15.00
Spooner, blue.................... 60.00
Spooner, white................... 35.00
Table set, blue, 4 pcs. 850.00
Tumbler, white................... 30.00
Water set: pitcher & 6 tumblers;
   blue, 7 pcs..................... 525.00

INVERTED FAN & FEATHER
Bowl, 7" d., footed, canary
   yellow 125.00
Creamer, blue 65.00
Rose bowl, blue.................. 32.00
Sauce dish, blue 30.00
Tumbler, blue.................... 47.50
Vase, canary yellow 65.00

IRIS WITH MEANDER
Bowl, master berry, blue 90.00
Butter dish, cov., blue 100.00
Compote, jelly, blue.............. 30.00
Compote, jelly, canary yellow 60.00
Creamer, blue 100.00
Salt & pepper shakers w/original
   tops, canary yellow, pr. 145.00
Sauce dish, blue 18.00
Sauce dish, canary yellow......... 20.00
Spooner, blue.................... 75.00
Toothpick holder, blue.......50.00 to 85.00
Toothpick holder, canary yellow 75.00
Toothpick holder, green 42.50
Toothpick holder, white........... 35.00
Tumbler, green 25.00
Water set: pitcher & 6 tumblers;
   blue, 7 pcs..................... 350.00

JACKSON
Bon bon, blue, 8" w. 20.00
Butter dish, cov., canary yellow 110.00
Creamer, blue 35.00
Creamer, canary yellow 50.00
Cruet w/original stopper, canary
   yellow 135.00
Pitcher, water, blue 195.00
Salt shaker w/original top, blue
   (single)........................ 35.00
Salt & pepper shakers w/original
   tops, canary yellow, pr. 60.00
Sugar bowl, cov., blue............ 92.50
Table set, blue, 4 pcs. 285.00

JEFFERSON WHEEL
Bowl, 9" d., footed, ruffled rim,
   blue 25.00
Bowl, 9" d., ruffled rim, green 45.00

JEWEL & FAN
Bowl, 7" d., fluted rim, green 20.00
Dish, blue, 7" oval 28.50
Dish, blue, 8½" oval 32.50
Dish, green, 8½" oval 27.50
Rose bowl, blue.................. 60.00
Sauce dish, green, oval 32.50

JEWEL & FLOWER

Jewel & Flower Pattern

Berry set: master bowl & 6 sauce
   dishes; blue w/gold trim, 7 pcs. ... 250.00
Bowl, master berry, canary yellow .. 55.00
Butter dish, cov., canary yellow 175.00
Butter dish, cov., white 95.00
Creamer ....45.00 to 60.00
Creamer, canary yellow 100.00
Sauce dish, canary yellow......... 35.00
Sauce dish, white 25.00
Pitcher, water, canary yellow 400.00
Spooner, blue 75.00
Spooner, canary yellow 90.00
Spooner, white................... 35.00
Sugar bowl, cov., canary yellow 175.00
Table set, blue w/gold, 4 pcs....... 475.00
Water set: pitcher & 5 tumblers;
   canary yellow, 6 pcs.
   (ILLUS.) ....800.00 to 900.00

JEWELED HEART
Berry set: master bowl & 5 sauce
   dishes; green, 6 pcs. 200.00
Bowl, 10" d., blue 35.00
Pitcher, water, green 250.00
Pitcher, water, white 125.00
Sauce dish, blue, 5½" d.......... 28.00
Sauce dish, white, 5½" d. 11.00
Tumbler, blue.................... 40.00
Water set: pitcher & 6 tumblers;
   blue, 7 pcs...................... 850.00

MANY LOOPS
Bowl, 8" d., blue 40.00
Bowl, 8" d., green.........30.00 to 35.00
Bowl, 8" d., white................ 27.50

MAPLE LEAF
Compote, jelly, blue.............. 40.00
Compote, jelly, green 37.50

NETTED ROSES

Bowl, 8½" d., ruffled, blue 30.00
Bowl, 8½" d., ruffled, white 55.00

NORTHWOOD'S BLOCK

Bowl, footed, turned-up sides,
   blue 37.50
Celery vase, blue 45.00

OPAL OPEN

Compote, blue 28.50
Cuspidor, blue 28.50
Rose bowl, pedestal base, blue..... 40.00

OPEN O'S

Compote, jelly, white............. 26.00
Vase, green 26.00

PALM BEACH

Berry set: master bowl & 6 sauce
   dishes; canary yellow, 7 pcs. 295.00
Bowl, master berry, blue 70.00
Creamer, blue 95.00
Finger bowl, blue 115.00
Nappy, blue 65.00
Pitcher, water, canary yellow 350.00
Spooner, blue.................... 47.00
Tumbler, canary yellow 85.00

PANELED HOLLY

Paneled Holly Spooner

Spooner, blue (ILLUS.) 50.00
Table set, white w/red & green
   decor, 4 pcs..................... 325.00

PEARLS & SCALES

Compote, blue 35.00
Compote, green.................. 27.50

PIASA BIRD

Cuspidor, lady's, white 32.50
Rose bowl, blue.................. 50.00
Vase, 12" h., blue................ 55.00
Vase, 12" h., white.........55.00 to 65.00

PUMP & TROUGH

Novelty vase, blue 90.00
Novelty vase, white 80.00

Northwood's Trough

Trough, blue (ILLUS.) 35.00

REFLECTING DIAMONDS

Bowl, 9" d., ruffled edge, blue 40.00
Bowl, 9" d., ruffled edge, green 35.00

REGAL

Berry set: master bowl & 4 sauce
   dishes; green, 5 pcs. 110.00
Bowl, master berry, blue 85.00
Butter dish, cov., blue 195.00
Butter dish, cov., green........... 165.00
Celery vase, blue ....85.00 to 95.00
Compote, jelly, blue 75.00
Creamer, blue 60.00
Sauce dish, blue 29.00
Spooner, blue.............50.00 to 60.00
Sugar bowl, cov., green 110.00
Tumbler, blue...........55.00 to 65.00
Tumbler, green 42.50

RIBBED SPIRAL

Bowl, 8¼" d., blue............... 36.50
Bowl, 9" d., canary yellow 37.50
Compote, jelly, blue.............. 47.00
Creamer, blue 52.50
Pitcher, water, blue 195.00
Plate, canary yellow............. 23.00
Sauce dish, blue 25.00
Spooner, blue................... 55.00
Toothpick holder, blue............ 75.00
Toothpick holder, canary yellow 65.00
Toothpick holder, white........... 55.00

RUFFLES & RINGS

Bowl, 8" to 9½" d., 3-footed,
   blue ....35.00 to 58.00
Bowl, 8" to 9½" d., 3-footed,
   green ....25.00 to 48.00
Bowl, 8" to 9½" d., 3-footed,
   white ....20.00 to 40.00

SCROLL WITH ACANTHUS

Bowl, master berry, 9½" d., blue... 65.00
Bowl, master berry, 9½" d., white.. 45.00
Compote, jelly, blue.............. 30.00
Compote, jelly, green 35.00
Creamer, canary yellow 52.50
Cruet w/original stopper, blue 135.00
Spooner, canary yellow 45.00
Tumbler, blue................... 55.00

SHELL

Berry set: master bowl & 6 sauce
dishes; blue, 7 pcs.............. 395.00
Compote, jelly, blue 175.00
Creamer & sugar bowl, green, pr. .. 110.00
Sauce dish, blue 25.00

SPOOL

Compote, jelly, blue 26.00
Compote, jelly, green 25.00

SWAG WITH BRACKETS

Berry set: master bowl & 5 sauce
dishes; blue, 6 pcs............... 165.00
Butter dish, cov., blue 165.00
Butter dish, cov., green....155.00 to 180.00
Compote, jelly, canary yellow 75.00
Compote, jelly, green 30.00
Creamer, blue or green, each 45.00
Cruet w/original stopper, canary
yellow 245.00
Pitcher, water, canary yellow 220.00
Salt shaker w/original top, blue
(single)........................ 75.00
Spooner, canary yellow or green,
each 45.00
Sugar bowl, cov., blue 75.00
Sugar bowl, cov., green .....65.00 to 75.00
Sugar bowl, cov., white 50.00
Toothpick holder, blue 150.00
Tumbler, blue..................... 55.00
Tumbler, canary yellow 45.00
Tumbler, green 55.00
Water set: pitcher & 6 tumblers;
canary yellow, 7 pcs. 489.00

TOKYO

Bowl, master berry, blue or green,
each .... 50.00 to 65.00
Butter dish, cov., green........... 125.00
Butter dish, cov., white 135.00
Compote, jelly, blue 45.00
Compote, jelly, green ....25.00 to 37.00
Creamer, blue 35.00
Creamer, green ....40.00 to 55.00
Creamer, white 37.50
Cruet w/original stopper, blue 150.00
Dish, ruffled rim, green, 7½" d..... 20.00
Dish, footed, white, 8" d. 30.00
Dish, footed, blue, 8¾" d. 37.50
Pitcher, water, green 115.00
Pitcher, water, white 65.00
Spooner, green 40.00
Spooner, white.................... 47.50
Sugar bowl, cov., white......50.00 to 75.00
Table set: cov. butter dish, cov. sug-
ar bowl & creamer; blue, 3 pcs. .. 375.00

VINTAGE

Bowl, 8" d., up-turned rim, white ... 35.00
Bowl, 8¼" d., green 28.00
Compote, blue 38.00
Plate, blue 25.00

WATERLILY WITH CATTAILS

Waterlily with Cattails Tumbler

Bowl, 8" d., white................. 20.00
Bowl, master berry, blue 60.00
Butter dish, cov., blue 185.00
Creamer, blue 40.00
Creamer, green 35.00
Spooner, blue..................... 40.00
Sugar bowl, cov., blue 125.00
Tumbler, blue..................... 35.00
Tumbler, white (ILLUS.) 22.50

WILD BOUQUET

Wild Bouquet Jelly Compote & Tumbler

Berry set: master bowl & 5 sauce
dishes; white, 6 pcs. 145.00
Bowl, master berry, blue 95.00
Compote, jelly, blue (ILLUS. left).... 80.00
Creamer, green 60.00
Cruet w/original stopper, blue 295.00
Cruet w/original stopper, white ... 135.00
Pitcher, water, blue ....175.00 to 235.00
Spooner, blue.............65.00 to 85.00
Spooner, green ....60.00 to 70.00
Sugar bowl, cov., canary yellow 135.00
Toothpick holder, blue 225.00
Tumbler, blue (ILLUS. right) 75.00
Tumbler, green 70.00

WREATH & SHELL

Berry set: master bowl & 6 sauce
dishes; blue or vaseline, 7 pcs.,
each set...................... 250.00

Butter dish, cov., blue . . . . . 165.00 to 185.00
Cookie jar, cov., blue 325.00

Wreath & Shell Creamer & Sugar Bowl

Creamer, blue (ILLUS. left) 70.00
Cuspidor, lady's, vaseline 45.00
Pitcher, water, vaseline. 385.00
Rose bowl, footed, blue 65.00
Rose bowl, footed, white 30.00
Sauce dish, vaseline 22.00
Spooner, vaseline . . . . 50.00 to 75.00
Sugar bowl, cov., blue (ILLUS.
  right) 160.00
Table set, vaseline, 4 pcs. 400.00
Toothpick holder, white 85.00
Tumbler, blue. 55.00
Tumbler, blue, enameled decor 60.00
Tumbler, vaseline . . . . 45.00 to 55.00

ORREFORS

Engraved Orrefors Glass

This Swedish glasshouse, founded in 1898 for production of tablewares, has made decorative wares as well since 1915. By 1925, Orrefors had achieved an international reputation for its Graal glass, an engraved art glass developed by master glass blower Knut Bergqvist and artist-designers Simon Gate and Edward Hald. Ariel glass, recognized by a design of controlled air traps, and the heavy Ravenna glass, usually tinted, were both de-

veloped in the 1930's. While All Orrefors glass is collectible, pieces signed by early designers and artists are now bringing high prices. Also see COMMEMORATIVE PLATES.

Bowl, 5" w., 2½" h., Graal, blue on
  clear, rosy pink bottom, artist-
  signed $225.00
Bowl, 7" w., Ravenna, deep trans-
  parent blue inlaid w/clear & tint-
  ed red circles, ca. 1950 . . . . 550.00
Bowl, 9½" d., Ariel, applied clear
  foot, internal decoration of red &
  clear banded scrolls, designed by
  Ingeborg Lundin, ca. 1968 . . . . 385.00
Centerpiece bowl, Ravenna, deep
  blue enclosing concentric rows of
  pale yellow lappets touched
  w/oxblood, mid-20th c., 13" d. . . . 1,760.00
Decanter w/stopper, engraved
  w/seated man holding a cocktail
  glass one side & w/three crowns
  & "V Anno 1930" reverse,
  designed by Edward Hald, ca.
  1930, 8" h. (ILLUS. left) 528.00
Decanter w/blue stopper, clear
  paneled sides engraved w/Nep-
  tune holding up tiny sea mermaid,
  designed by Simon Gate, engraved by Karl Rossler, ca. 1934,
  8¼" h. 715.00
Vase, 5¾" h., Graal, bulbous, clear
  w/internally decorated deep
  green swimming fish & underwater plants, designed by Edward
  Hald, ca. 1950 . . . . 467.00
Vase, 6" h., Ariel, cylindrical, inter-
  nally decorated w/powder &
  medium blue striations and wave
  motifs "slashed" w/colorless
  glass, ca. 1950 . . . . 770.00
Vase, 6¾" h., Ariel, cylindrical
  w/squared sides, air-trapped
  designs of abstracted profiles
  in violet & cornflower blue,
  designed by Ingeborg Lundin,
  ca. 1950 . . . . 3,575.00
Vase, 8¼" h., clear w/black foot,
  transparent ribbed body engraved
  w/mermaid, designed by Simon
  Gate (ILLUS.) 528.00

PAIRPOINT

Originally organized in New Bedford, Massachusetts, in 1880, as the Pairpoint Manufacturing Company, on land adjacent to the famed Mount Washington Glass Works, this company first manufactured silver and plated wares. In 1894, the two famous factories merged as the Pairpoint Corporation and enjoyed renowned success for more than forty years. The company was sold in 1939, to a group of local businessmen and eventually bought out by one of the group who turned the management over to Robert M. Gunderson. Subsequently, it operated as the Gunderson Glass Works until 1952 when, after Gunderson's death, the name was changed to Gunderson-Pairpoint. This factory closed in 1956. Subsequently, Robert Bryden took charge of this glass works, at first producing glass for Pairpoint abroad and eventually, in 1970, began glass production in Sagamore, Massachusetts. Bryden's Pairpoint company continues in operation today manufacturing fine quality blown and pressed glass. Also see BURMESE, CUT and PEACH BLOW.

Early Pairpoint Cookie Jars

Bowl, 12" d., 4½" h., ruby w/clear "controlled bubble" ball connector in stem, Gunderson-Pairpoint, 1950's $68.00

Candlesticks, flattened rim on urn-shaped sockets, baluster stem, amber w/clear "controlled bubble" ball connector to base, Gunderson-Pairpoint, 12" h., pr......................85.00 to 110.00

Candlesticks, Auroria (reddish amber), engraved Hampton patt.,1950's, 12" h., pr. 425.00

Centerpiece bowl, clear w/green "controlled bubble" paperweight base, 10" d. 125.00

Centerpiece bowl, pedestal base, amber w/engraved Vintage (grape clusters & vine) patt., 12" d., 7" h. ....145.00 to 185.00

Compote, 7½" d., ruby w/clear "controlled bubble" ball connector in stem, 1950's 62.50

Compote, 12" w., 6½" h., amber w/clear "controlled bubble" ball connector in stem, 1950's 115.00

Compote, Diamond Quilted patt., Rosaria (cranberry) w/clear "con-

trolled bubble" ball in stem, large 125.00

Cookie jar, orange-washed opaline w/enameled floral decor, silver-plate rim, cover & bail handle, Pairpoint Corporation, late 19th c., overall 9½" h. 325.00

Cookie jar, lustreless white 4-lobe body w/h.p. rose garlands & ribbons above shaped stripe border, silverplate pierced rim, cover & shaped finial, late 19th c. (ILLUS. right) 600.00

Cookie jar, melon-ribbed, lustreless white w/enameled florals & scroll decor, silverplate "repousse" rim, cover & twisted wire bail handle, late 19th c. (ILLUS. left) 550.00

Cookie jar, shaded pink to yellow w/h.p. florals & leaves decor, fitted silverplate base & silverplate cover signed w/"P" in diamond trademark 275.00

Cup plate, "The Study Gallery," canary yellow, Bryden-Pairpoint, 1981 .... 8.50

Goblet, green w/clear "controlled bubble" ball in stem, 1950's, 11½" h....................... 85.00

Grape juice (or punch) bowl, deep bowl w/flaring rim, pedestal base, Auroria (amber), engraved Vintage (grape clusters & vine) patt., early 20th c. 99.00

Ice bucket, clear w/engraved Polar Bear, nickel silver rim, bail handle & drainer 110.00

Perfume bottle w/original stopper, clear twisted bottle & twisted stopper w/cranberry trim, 6½" h. 170.00

Perfume bottle, ruby w/white enameled floral decor & clear long steeple stopper, 7" h....... 65.00

Perfume bottle w/tall stopper, clear paperweight base threaded w/red & white ribbon 150.00

Pitcher, 3" h., amethyst, enameled decor, Bryden-Pairpoint, 1970's ... 35.00

Plates, salad, 8" d., clear w/engraved Vintage patt. on wide border, 1950's, set of 6 .... 75.00

Salt shaker w/original top, inverted pear shape, "Pairpoint Delft" w/typical Delft blue decor on white opaline, 1890-1920 (single)......................... 145.00

Vase, 7½" h., jack-in-pulpit type, Peach Blow color, Bryden-Pairpoint, 1970's 85.00

Vase, 10½" h., bulbous w/slender neck, white opaque w/h.p. floral decor, Pairpoint Corporation, ca. 1900 .... 120.00

Vase, 12" h., amethyst, engraved
Vintage patt., Pairpoint Corpora-
tion, early 20th c. 145.00
Vase, 12" h., cranberry w/clear
"controlled bubble" ball connec-
tor, 1950's . . . . .135.00 to 175.00
Vase, 12" h., 8" top d., expanding
cylinder, light amber, engraved
Vintage patt., Pairpoint Corpora-
tion, early 20th c. 195.00

PATE DE VERRE

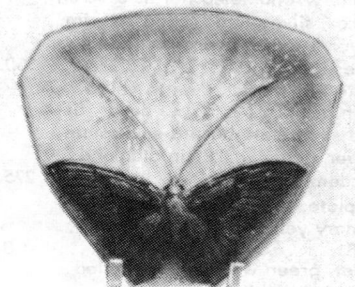

Pate de Verre Dish

*Pate de Verre, or "paste of glass," was
molded by very few glass artisans. In the pate
de verre technique, powdered glass is mixed
with a liquid to make a paste which is then
placed in a mold and baked at a high temper-
ature. These articles have a finely-pitted or
matte finish and are easily distinguished from
blown glass. Duplicate pieces are possible
with this technique.*

Ash tray, oval, central medallion of
bust of a classical maiden in yellow & brown on clear shading to
blue & purple at molded rim,
signed Gabriel Argy-Rousseau,
6 5/16" l. $352.00
Bowl, 3½" d., deep olive green,
molded at lip w/band of low relief oak leafage in shades of
dusty rose & grey, ca. 1925,
signed G. Argy-Rousseau 550.00
Bowl, 5¼" h., expanding circle on
ringed foot, ochre streaked w/vio-
let, molded in medium relief on
exterior w/carnival masks & fans,
ca. 1925, signed G. Argy-
Rousseau 1,760.00
Dish, shaded mustard yellow, mot-
tled emerald & blue green
chameleon in full relief at one
side, signed A. Walter, Nancy &
Berge, Sc., 4¾" d. 2,090.00
Dish, triangular, mottled turquoise
blue splashed w/lemon yellow &

molded w/high relief moth in
in deep amber, turquoise, forest
green & dark brown on one side,
ca. 1925, signed A. Walter,
Nancy & Sc. Berge, 6¼" w.
(ILLUS.) 1,870.00
Inkwell, cov., lime green sides
streaked w/sapphire blue & cinna-
mon molded in low relief w/olive
green & deep amber maple
leaves, pine boughs & florettes,
circular cover cast w/snail, ca.
1925, signed A. Walter, Nancy &
Berge Sc., 3½" h. 1,155.00
Paperweight, modeled as a curious
frog seated before a pond on
base cast w/leafage & a snail,
shades of deep emerald green &
mustard yellow, ca. 1920, signed
Daum Nancy, 4½" d. 660.00
Tray, molded as a yellow sunflower
w/deep purple center & turned-up
petals, signed G. Argy-Rousseau,
3½" w. 600.00
Vase, 4" h., ovoid, grey streaked
w/purple & green, molded in
medium relief w/white berries &
ochre & green leaves, ca. 1925,
signed G. Argy-Rousseau 1,017.00
Vase, 6¼" h., flared, tiered & rib-
bed cylinder, transparent body
streaked w/purple & aquamarine,
signed Decorchemont 1,210.00

Pate de Verre Vases

Vase, 7½" h., shoulders w/broad
band of rust-red florals within
black borders & 3 yellow florette
medallions on matte yellow
ground, signed Gabriel Argy-
Rousseau (ILLUS. left) 1,100.00
Vase, 9½" h., molded w/two bands
of lotus blossoms in burgundy on
a streaked purple & burgundy
clear ground, signed Gabriel
Argy-Rousseau (ILLUS. right) 1,320.00

PATTERN GLASS

Though it has never been ascertained whether glass was first pressed in the United States or abroad, the development of the glass pressing machine revolutionized the glass industry in the United States and this country receives the credit for improving the method to make this process feasible. The first wares pressed were probably small flat plates of the type now referred to as "lacy" Sandwich, the intricacy of the design concealing flaws.

In 1827, both the New England Glass Co., Cambridge, Massachusetts and Bakewell & Co., Pittsburgh, took out patents for pressing glass furniture knobs and soon other pieces followed. This early pressed glass contained red lead which made it clear and resonant when tapped (flint). Made primarily in clear, it is rarer in blue, amethyst, olive green and yellow.

By the 1840's, early simple patterns such as Ashburton, Argus and Excelsior appeared. Ribbed Bellflower seems to have been one of the earliest patterns to have had complete sets. By the 1860's, a wide range of patterns were available.

In 1864, William Leighton of Hobbs, Brockunier & Co., Wheeling, West Virginia, developed a formula for "soda lime" glass which did not require the expensive red lead for clarity. Although "soda lime" glass did not have the brilliance of the earlier flint glass, the formula came into widespread use because glass could be produced cheaply.

By 1900, patterns had become ornate in imitation of the expensive brilliant cut glass.

ACTRESS

Actress Sugar Bowl & Creamer

Bowl, 6" d., footed	$25.00 to 50.00
Bowl, 8" d., Adelaide Neilson	85.00
Bread tray, Miss Neilson, 12½" l.	80.00 to 100.00
Butter dish, cov., Fanny Davenport & Miss Neilson	85.00

Cake stand, Maud Granger & Annie Pixley, 10" d., 7" h.	155.00
Celery vase, Pinafore scene	155.00
Cheese dish, cov., "Lone Fisherman" on cover, "The Two Dromios" on underplate	200.00 to 245.00
Cologne bottle w/original stopper, 11" h.	48.50
Compote, cov., 6" d., 10" h.	120.00
Compote, cov., 8" d., 12" h.	140.00 to 235.00
Compote, cov., 10" d., 14½" h., Fanny Davenport & Maggie Mitchell	150.00
Compote, open, 6" d., 11" h.	145.00
Compote, open, 7" d., 7" h., Miss Neilson	145.00
Creamer, Miss Neilson & Fanny Davenport (ILLUS. right)	50.00 to 75.00
Goblet, Lotta Crabtree & Kate Claxton	90.00
Marmalade jar, cov., Maud Granger & Annie Pixley	70.00 to 85.00
Mug, Pinafore scene	47.50
Pickle dish, Kate Claxton, "Love's Request is Pickles," 9¼ x 5¼"	52.50
Pitcher, water, 9" h., Miss Neilson & Maggie Mitchell	250.00
Platter, 11½ x 7", Pinafore scene	110.00
Relish, Maud Granger, 9 x 5"	65.00
Salt dip, master size	68.00
Salt shaker w/original pewter top (single)	45.00
Sauce dish, Maggie Mitchell & Fanny Davenport, 4½" d., 2½" h.	22.50
Spooner, Mary Anderson & Maud Granger	78.00
Sugar bowl, cov., Lotta Crabtree & Kate Claxton (ILLUS. left)	90.00

ADONIS (Pleat & Tuck or Washboard)

Bowl, berry, canary yellow, small	12.00
Creamer, green	15.00

ALABAMA (Beaded Bull's Eye with Drape)

Butter dish, cov., w/silver rim	57.50
Celery tray	25.00
Compote, cov., 5" d.	62.50
Creamer	35.00
Creamer, individual size	13.00
Cruet w/original stopper	55.00
Honey dish, cov.	47.50
Pitcher, water	95.00
Relish, 8 1/8 x 5"	18.00 to 22.00
Spooner	35.00
Sugar bowl, cov.	42.50
Syrup pitcher w/original top	100.00
Toothpick holder	55.00
Tray, water, 10½"	42.50
Tumbler	22.00

ALASKA (Lion's Leg)

Banana boat, blue opalescent	255.00
Banana boat, emerald green	72.50

Banana boat, vaseline opalescent... 225.00

Berry set: master bowl & 6 sauce
dishes; blue or vaseline opalescent, 7 pcs.............325.00 to 375.00

Bowl, master berry, blue
opalescent ....90.00 to 125.00

Bowl, master berry, green
w/enameled florals 130.00

Bowl, master berry, vaseline
opalescent...,................... 92.00

Butter dish, cov., blue opalescent... 225.00

Butter dish, cov., green w/enameled
florals........................... 165.00

Butter dish, cov., vaseline opalescent 250.00

Card tray, blue opalescent 28.50

Card tray, vaseline opalescent 30.00

Celery tray, blue opalescent
w/enameled florals 232.00

Celery tray, vaseline opalescent 75.00

Compote, open, 7½" d., 3¼" h.,
ruffled rim, blue opalescent 65.00

Creamer, blue opalescent 75.00

Creamer, clear to opalescent....... 32.00

Creamer, green 32.50

Creamer, vaseline opalescent 78.00

Cruet w/original stopper, blue
opalescent w/enameled florals ... 250.00

Cruet w/original stopper, green
w/enameled florals 175.00

Cruet w/original stopper, vaseline
opalescent...................... 250.00

Pitcher, water, blue opalescent 300.00

Pitcher, water, clear w/enameled
florals & gold trim.............. 110.00

Pitcher, water, vaseline opalescent 450.00

Salt shaker w/original top, blue
opalescent (single) 55.00

Salt shaker w/original top, clear to
opalescent (single) 25.00

Salt shaker w/original top, green
(single)........................ 29.00

Salt shaker w/original top, vaseline
opalescent (single) 55.00

Sauce dish, blue opalescent 35.00

Sauce dish, clear to opalescent 22.50

Sauce dish, green w/enameled
florals & leaves 45.00

Sauce dish, vaseline opalescent 32.50

Alaska Spooner

Spooner, blue opalescent (ILLUS.) ... 52.50

Spooner, clear to opalescent 30.00

Spooner, green 42.50

Spooner, green w/enameled
florals......................... 65.00

Spooner, vaseline opalescent....... 60.00

Spooner, vaseline opalescent
w/enameled florals 95.00

Sugar bowl, cov., blue
opalescent ....125.00 to 145.00

Sugar bowl, cov., vaseline
opalescent...................... 150.00

Sugar bowl, open, clear to
opalescent...................... 40.00

Sugar bowl, open, vaseline
opalescent...................... 85.00

Table set: creamer, open sugar
bowl, spooner & cov. butter dish;
blue opalescent, 4 pcs. 750.00

Table set: creamer, open sugar
bowl, spooner & cov. butter dish;
vaseline opalescent, 4 pcs........ 615.00

Tumbler, blue opalescent 73.00

Tumbler, green 40.00

Tumbler, vaseline opalescent....... 65.00

Wine, blue opalescent 90.00

ALEXIS - See Priscilla Pattern

**ALMOND THUMBPRINT (Pointed Thumb-
print)**

Bowl, 4½" d., 4 7/8" h., footed,
non-flint....................... 20.00

Butter dish, cov., ruby-stained, non-
flint........................... 102.00

Champagne, non-flint.............. 25.00

Salt dip, master size, flint.......... 12.00

Spooner, fluted, non-flint 20.00

Wine, flint....................... 30.00

AMAZON (Sawtooth Band)

Child's Sugar Bowl & Creamer

(Items may be plain or with etched designs)

Banana stand 50.00

Bowl, 9" d. 22.00

Butter dish, cov. 50.00

Cake stand, 8" d. 36.00

Cake stand, 9¼" d. 40.00

Celery vase....................... 35.00

Champagne........................ 28.50

Compote, cov., 7" d., 11½" h....... 62.50

Compote, open, jelly 24.00
Compote, open, 6" d., high stand ... 20.00
Compote, open, 8¾" d., 7¼" h. 42.00
Cordial 35.00
Creamer .... 26.00 to 35.00
Creamer, chlid's miniature (ILLUS.
    right) 27.50
Creamer & cov. sugar bowl,
    pr. .... 35.00 to 45.00
Cruet w/bar in hand stopper,
    amethyst 250.00
Cruet w/bar in hand stopper,
    clear 33.50
Dish, cov., oval w/lion's head han-
    dles & knob 75.00
Egg cup 14.00
Goblet 30.00
Nappy 25.00
Pitcher, water 60.00
Salt dip, master size .... 12.50 to 18.00
Sauce dish, flat or footed ..... 4.50 to 11.50
Spooner .... 25.00 to 30.00
Sugar bowl, cov. 37.50
Sugar bowl, child's miniature (ILLUS.
    left) 30.00
Syrup pitcher w/original top 42.50
Table set: cov. butter dish, creamer,
    cov. sugar bowl & spooner; child's
    miniature, 4 pcs. 150.00
Tumbler .... 15.00 to 25.00
Wine .... 25.00 to 30.00

AMBERETTE (English Hobnail Cross or Klondike)

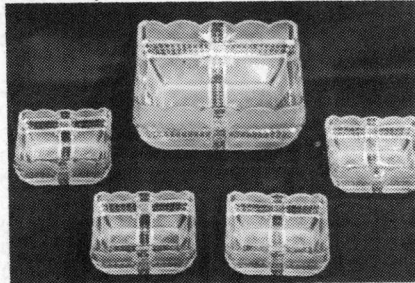

Amberette Berry Set

Berry set: master bowl & 4 sauce
    dishes; frosted w/amber cross,
    5 pcs. (ILLUS.) 385.00
Berry set: 8" sq. master bowl & 6
    sauce dishes; clear w/amber
    cross, 7 pcs. 175.00
Bowl, fruit, 8½" sq., frosted
    w/amber cross 250.00
Bowl, 11" sq., flared, clear w/amber
    cross 150.00
Bread plate, clear w/amber cross,
    11 x 8½" oval 135.00
Butter dish, cov., clear w/amber
    cross 115.00
Butter dish, cov., frosted w/amber
    cross .... 270.00 to 350.00

Celery tray, frosted w/amber cross,
    10 7/8 x 4½", 2 7/8" h. 185.00
Celery vase, clear w/amber cross .. 135.00
Celery vase, frosted w/amber
    cross 195.00
Creamer, frosted w/amber cross ... 210.00
Cruet w/original amber stopper,
    frosted w/amber cross 550.00
Goblet, clear w/amber cross 125.00
Pitcher, water, clear w/amber
    cross 285.00
Pitcher, water, frosted w/amber
    cross 545.00
Punch cup, clear w/amber cross 60.00
Punch cup, frosted w/amber cross .. 110.00
Relish, clear w/amber cross, boat-
    shaped, 9 x 4" 118.00
Relish, frosted w/amber cross,
    9 x 4" w/silverplate holder,
    overall 6" h. 145.00
Salt shaker w/original top, clear
    w/amber cross (single) 69.00
Salt & pepper shakers w/original
    tops, frosted w/amber cross,
    pr. 250.00
Sauce dish, flat or footed, frosted
    w/amber cross .... 78.50 to 85.00
Spooner, clear w/amber cross 50.00
Spooner, frosted w/amber cross 165.00
Sugar bowl, cov., clear w/amber
    cross, 6¾" h. 185.00
Sugar bowl, cov., frosted w/amber
    cross, 4" d., 6¾" h. 240.00
Syrup pitcher w/original top, frosted
    w/amber cross 525.00
Table set, frosted w/amber cross,
    4 pcs. 1,100.00
Toothpick holder, clear w/amber
    cross 145.00
Toothpick holder, frosted w/amber
    cross 350.00
Tumbler, clear w/amber cross 135.00
Tumbler, frosted w/amber cross 145.00
Vase, 8" h., trumpet-shaped, clear
    w/amber cross 85.00
Vase, 10" h., trumpet-shaped, frost-
    ed w/amber cross 300.00
Wine, frosted w/amber cross 495.00

APOLLO

(Items may be plain or with etched designs)

Bowl, 8" d. 20.00
Butter dish, cov. 50.00
Celery tray 22.50
Celery vase 45.00
Compote, open, 7" d., low stand ... 25.00
Compote, open, 8" d., 8" h. 37.00
Creamer .... 30.00 to 40.00
Goblet .... 27.50 to 40.00
Lamp, kerosene-type, amber,
    9" h. 190.00
Lamp, kerosene-type, blue, 9" h. ... 190.00

Lamp, kerosene-type, canary yel-
low, 9" h. 165.00
Pitcher, water, bulbous 65.00
Plate, 9½" sq. 26.50
Salt dip, master size.............. 25.00
Sauce dish, flat or footed .....6.00 to 10.50
Spooner ....30.00 to 35.00
Sugar bowl, cov. 45.00
Sugar bowl, open 35.00
Sugar shaker w/original top 45.00
Syrup pitcher w/original top 42.50
Tray, water...................... 45.00
Tumbler 21.50

ARGUS (Thumprint by Bakewell, Pears & Co.)

Argus Spillholder

Ale glass, footed, flint, 5½" h. 70.00
Butter dish, footed, flint, 8" d. 85.00
Celery vase, flint 50.00
Champagne, flint.................. 50.00
Champagne (Hotel Argus), non-
flint............................ 18.50
Compote, cov., 12" d., high stand,
flint............................ 125.00
Creamer w/applied handle, flint.... 70.00
Egg cup, flint 25.00
Goblet, flint ....35.00 to 45.00
Goblet (Barrel Argus), flint......... 40.00
Goblet, Five-Row................. 55.00
Goblet (Hotel Argus), non-flint 25.00
Goblet, master size, flint 45.00
Mug, applied handle, flint 60.00
Pitcher, water, 8¼" h., applied han-
dle, flint........................ 200.00
Punch bowl, pedestal base, scal-
loped rim, 11½" d., 9½" h. 160.00
Salt dip, master size, flint.......... 27.50
Spillholder, flint (ILLUS.) 45.00
Spooner, flint 48.50
Sugar bowl, cov., flint 65.00
Sugar bowl, open, flint ......35.00 to 40.00
Tumbler (Barrel Argus), flint 30.00
Tumbler, bar-type, flint 48.00
Tumbler, footed, flint, 4" h. 40.00
Tumbler, footed, flint, 5" h. 60.00
Tumbler, whiskey, handled......... 57.50

Wine, flint, 4" h. 45.00
Wine (Barrel Argus) 35.00
Wine (Hotel Argus), non-
flint....................15.00 to 22.00

ART (Job's Tears)

Art Compote

Banana stand 125.00
Basket, fruit 165.00
Bowl, 7" d., flared rim, footed 27.00
Bowl, 8½" d. 40.00
Butter dish, cov. 50.00
Butter dish, cov., ruby-stained...... 65.00
Cake stand, 9" d. 52.50
Cake stand, 10¼" d. 55.00
Celery vase 30.00
Compote, cov., 7" d. 70.00
Compote, open, 8" d., high stand... 35.00
Compote, open, 9" d., 7¼" h....... 45.00
Compote, open, 10" d., 9" h.
(ILLUS.)................55.00 to 68.00
Creamer ....40.00 to 50.00
Cruet w/original stopper 65.00
Goblet 27.50
Pitcher, milk 140.00
Pitcher, milk, ruby-stained 125.00
Pitcher, water, bulbous 85.00
Plate, 10" d. 55.00
Relish, 7¾ x 4¼" 22.00
Relish, ruby-stained 65.00
Sauce dish, flat or footed ....14.00 to 20.00
Spooner 28.50
Sugar bowl, cov. ....35.00 to 45.00
Tumbler 20.00

ASHBURTON

Ale glass, flint, 5" h. 87.50
Ale glass, flint, 6½" h. 65.00
Bitters bottle w/original pewter
lid 55.00
Bowl, 6½" d., low, footed, flint 72.50
Carafe, flint 175.00
Celery vase, scalloped rim, canary
yellow, flint 400.00
Celery vase, plain rim, clear, flint .. 60.00
Celery vase, scalloped rim, clear,
flint............................ 120.00

Champagne, flint................... 45.00
Champagne, creased ovals, flint 60.00
Champagne, cut ovals, flint 75.00
Champagne, double knob stem,
  flint.............................. 68.00
Claret, flint, 5¼" h. 55.00
Compote, open, 7½" d., low
  stand 65.00
Cordial, flint, 4¼" h. 70.00
Cordial, non-flint 38.00
Cordial, vaseline, flint 140.00
Creamer, applied handle, flint...... 165.00
Cup plate, 3" d. 20.00
Decanter w/original stopper, flint,
  qt................................. 75.00
Decanters w/original stoppers,
  canary yellow, flint, pr.......... 700.00
Decanter, bar lip & facet-cut neck,
  qt................................. 62.50
Decanter, bar lip & facet-cut neck,
  canary yellow, qt................. 600.00
Egg cup, clambroth, flint 125.00
Egg cup, flint ....24.00 to 35.00
Egg cup, non-flint 16.50
Egg cup, double, flint.............. 95.00
Flip glass, handled, flint 185.00
Goblet, flint, barrel-shaped 55.00
Goblet, flint, flared 56.50
Goblet, non-flint ....18.00 to 30.00
Goblet, disconnected ovals......... 26.50
Goblet, "giant," straight stem,
  flint.............................. 55.00
Honey dish, 3½" d. 9.50
Mug, applied handle, 3" h.......... 67.50
Pitcher, water, applied hollow
  handle, flint 450.00
Plate, 6 5/8" d., flint 60.00
Sauce dish, flint................... 10.00
Spooner, flint 115.00

Ashburton Sugar Bowl

Sugar bowl, cov., flint (ILLUS.)...... 140.00
Sugar bowl, open, non-flint 35.00
Toddy jar, cov..................... 110.00
Tumbler, bar, flint................. 60.00

Tumbler, water, flint 55.00
Tumbler, water, footed 67.50
Tumbler, whiskey, applied handle,
  flint............................ 150.00
Wine, barrel-shaped, flint 41.50
Wine, flint.................30.00 to 40.00
Wine, cut ovals 65.00
Wine, non-flint................... 22.50
Wine, emerald green, flint 425.00
Wine, peacock green, flint 525.00

ATLANTA - See Lion Pattern

ATLAS (Crystal Ball or Cannon Ball)

Atlas Tankard Pitcher

Bowl, cov., large, flat, clear....... 35.00
Bowl, open, 9" d., clear 20.00
Butter dish, cov, clear 45.00
Cake stand, clear, 8" d. 22.50
Cake stand, clear, 9" d. 45.00
Cake stand, ruby-stained, 10" d..... 95.00
Celery vase, clear 25.00
Champagne, clear, 5½" h. 25.00
Compote, cov., 8" d., 8" h., clear ... 55.00
Cordial, clear 32.50
Creamer, flat or pedestal base,
  clear 22.50
Creamer & open sugar bowl, clear,
  pr............................... 50.00
Goblet, clear 25.00
Pitcher, milk, tankard, applied
  handle, clear 42.50
Pitcher, water, tankard, applied
  handle, clear (ILLUS.) 55.00
Salt dip, individual size, clear 7.50
Salt dip, master size, clear 20.00
Salt & pepper shakers w/original
  tops, clear, pr.................. 20.00
Sauce dish, flat or footed,
  clear.......................7.50 to 12.50
Sauce dish, flat or footed, ruby-
  stained 20.00
Spooner, clear 26.00
Spooner, ruby-stained, w/gold
  trim 35.00

Sugar bowl, cov., clear 38.00
Sugar bowl, open, clear 20.00
Toothpick holder, clear 20.00
Tumbler, clear 30.00
Wine, clear 25.00

AURORA (Diamond Horseshoe)

(Items may be plain or with etched designs)

Celery vase...................... 32.50
Creamer, applied handle.......... 38.00
Decanter w/stopper, ruby-stained .. 140.00
Goblet 30.00
Pitcher, water, tankard, 9½" h. 40.00
Pitcher, water, tankard, 12" h. 45.00
Salt & pepper shakers w/original
   tops, pr........................ 30.00
Tray, wine, 10" d...........20.00 to 30.00
Tray, wine, ruby-stained,
   10" d...................40.00 to 55.00
Wine............................ 18.00
Wine, ruby-stained 35.00
Wine set: decanter w/original ruby
   stopper, 6 wines & tray; ruby-
   stained, 8 pcs. 350.00

AZTEC

Aztec Creamer

Bon bon, footed, 7" d., 4½" h. 13.50
Butter dish, cov. 40.00
Carafe, water.................... 37.50
Champagne....................... 15.00
Cordial 17.00
Creamer (ILLUS.) 26.50
Creamer, individual size 16.00
Cruet w/original stopper........... 35.00
Goblet 28.00
Punch cup 5.00
Punch set, 13" d. bowl w/base & 12
   cups, 14 pcs.................... 110.00
Relish 15.00
Salt & pepper shakers w/original
   tops, pr........................ 35.00
Sugar bowl, cov. 25.00
Toothpick holder 18.50
Tumbler 20.00
Tumbler, whiskey 12.00
Wine............................ 18.50

BABY FACE

Butter dish, cov., 5¼" d............ 150.00

Compote, cov., 5¼" d.,
   6½" h. ....125.00 to 140.00
Compote, cov., 8" d., 13" h., scalloped rim....................... 250.00
Compote, open, 8" d., 4¾" h. 85.00

Baby Face Compote

Compote, open, 8" d., 8" h.
   (ILLUS.)....................... 95.00
Creamer 110.00
Goblet ....85.00 to 150.00
Pitcher, water 175.00
Spooner 95.00

BABY THUMBPRINT - See Dakota Pattern

BALDER (Kamoni or Pennsylvania - Late)

Balder Creamer & Sugar Bowl

Bowl, berry or fruit, 8½" d., clear
   w/gold trim ....20.00 to 24.50
Bowl, 9" d., 2½" h., clear 29.50
Butter dish, cov., clear 35.00
Carafe, clear 36.00
Celery tray, clear, 11 x 4½" 24.50
Cheese dish, cov., clear 62.50
Creamer, clear w/gold trim, small,
   3" h. 18.00
Creamer, green w/gold trim, small,
   3" h. 65.00
Creamer, clear, large, 4" h......... 28.00
Creamer & open sugar bowl, indi-
   vidual size, clear w/gold trim,
   pr. (ILLUS.) 38.00
Cruet w/original stopper, clear 49.00
Decanter w/original stopper, clear,
   10¾" h. 75.00
Goblet, clear 23.00

Mustard jar w/pewter lid, clear 40.00
Pitcher, water, clear.............. 45.00
Plate, 8" d., clear 29.50
Punch cup, clear 10.00
Relish, clear 11.50
Salt & pepper shakers w/original
   tops, clear, pr.................. 22.00
Sauce dish, boat-shaped, clear 22.00
Sauce dish, round or square,
   clear.....................8.50 to 15.00
Spooner, clear 20.00
Sugar bowl, cov., clear 40.00
Sugar bowl, open, clear 25.00
Sugar bowl, open, breakfast size,
   clear 10.00
Syrup pitcher w/original top, clear.. 37.50
Table set, clear, 4 pcs. 140.00
Toothpick holder, clear 26.50
Toothpick holder, green 50.00
Tumbler, juice, clear 8.50
Tumbler, juice, green............. 21.00
Tumbler, water, blue, souvenir 42.00
Tumbler, water, clear w/gold trim .. 24.50
Tumbler, water, ruby-stained 50.00
Tumbler, whiskey, clear 13.50
Tumbler, whiskey, green w/gold
   trim............................ 26.00
Whiskey shot glass, clear 61.50
Wine, clear 16.50
Wine, green w/gold trim 42.50

BALTIMORE PEAR

Baltimore Pear Creamer

Bowl, 6" d. 29.00
Bowl, berry or fruit, 9" d. 40.00
Bread plate, 12½" l. 60.00
Butter dish, cov. 62.50
Cake plate, side handles, 10"
   octagon 31.50
Celery vase...................... 40.00
Compote, cov., 7" d., high stand ... 75.00
Compote, cov., 8½" d., low stand .. 45.00
Compote, open, jelly 28.50
Creamer (ILLUS.) 25.00
Creamer & open sugar bowl, pr..... 50.00

Goblet 26.00
Pitcher, milk..................... 60.00
Pitcher, water ....75.00 to 90.00
Plate, 9" d....................... 28.00
Relish, 8¼" l.................... 15.00
Sauce dish, flat or footed ....10.00 to 15.00
Spooner......................... 28.00
Sugar bowl, cov. 42.50
Sugar bowl, open 25.00

BAMBOO - See Broken Column Pattern

BANDED BEADED GRAPE MEDALLION
Creamer 50.00
Goblet 35.00
Spooner 28.50

BANDED BUCKLE
Spooner 26.50
Tumbler, bar..................... 55.00

BANDED PORTLAND (Portland w/Diamond Point Band)

Banded Portland Dresser Jar

Bowl, berry, 9" d. 32.00
Butter dish, cov. 50.00
Butter pat 18.00
Candlesticks, pr. 80.00
Carafe, water.................... 82.50
Celery tray, gold-stained, 12 x 5"... 22.50
Cologne bottle w/original stopper .. 48.00
Compote, cov., jelly 35.00
Compote, open, 8¼" d., 8" h., scal-
   loped rim...................... 40.00
Compote, open, 10" d., high stand.. 50.00
Creamer 35.00
Creamer, individual size 13.50
Creamer & sugar bowl, individual
   size, yellow-stained, pr. 90.00
Dresser jar, cov., 3½" d. (ILLUS.) ... 35.00
Dresser set: large tray, pin tray, pr.
   cov. pomade jars, pr. cologne bot-
   tles w/original stoppers & ring
   tree; clear w/gold, 7 pcs. 195.00
Goblet 35.00
Pickle dish, 6 x 4"................ 15.00
Pin dish, cov., 2¼" 25.00

Pin tray, souvenir	15.00
Pitcher, water	50.00
Pitcher, child's	33.50
Punch cup, gold rim	17.00
Relish, 8½ x 4" oval	10.00
Ring tree, gold-stained	40.00
Salt & pepper shakers w/original tops, pr.	45.00
Sauce dish	11.50
Spooner	35.00
Sugar bowl, cov., gold-stained	36.00
Sugar bowl, individual size	20.00
Sugar bowl, individual size, green-stained	25.00
Sugar shaker w/original top	40.00
Syrup jug w/original top	50.00
Toothpick holder	20.00
Tumbler	28.00
Vase, 6" h., flared	16.50
Vase, 9" h.	20.00
Wine	30.00
Wine, gold-stained	35.00
Wine set, tray & 6 wines, 7 pcs.	145.00

BANDED PORTLAND W/COLOR - See Portland Maiden Blush Pattern

BAR & DIAMOND - See Kokomo Pattern

BARBERRY

Barberry Compote

Bowl, 6" oval	20.00
Bowl, 8" oval	22.50
Bread plate	23.00
Butter dish, cov., shell finial	45.00
Cake stand, 9½" d.	35.00
Celery vase	32.50
Compote, cov., 6" d., high stand, shell finial	45.00
Compote, cov., 8" d., low stand, shell finial	48.50
Compote, open, 8½" d., 7" h. (ILLUS.)	25.00
Creamer	32.50
Cup plate	35.00
Egg cup	22.50

Goblet	26.00
Goblet, buttermilk	18.50
Pitcher, water, 9½" h., applied handle	75.00 to 110.00
Plate, 6" d., amber	38.00
Plate, 6" d., clear	16.50
Salt dip, master size	20.00
Sauce dish, flat or footed	6.50 to 15.00
Spooner, footed	25.00
Sugar bowl, cov., shell finial	45.00
Sugar bowl, open	27.50
Syrup jug w/original top	85.00 to 110.00
Tumbler, footed	22.50
Wine	25.00

BARLEY

Barley Compote

Bowl, 10" oval	20.00
Bread platter, plain rim, 11½ x 9½"	28.00
Bread platter, scalloped rim, 11½ x 9½"	35.00
Butter dish, cov.	32.50
Cake stand, 8" d.	25.00
Cake stand, 9" d.	25.00
Celery vase	22.50
Compote, cov., 7" d., high stand	60.00
Compote, open, 6" d., high stand	30.00
Compote, open, 8½" d., 6¼" h. (ILLUS.)	30.00
Compote, open, 8½" d., 8" h.	35.00
Compote, open, 8¾" d., 6½" h., scalloped rim	35.00
Creamer	25.00
Goblet	22.50 to 30.00
Pickle castor w/frame & tongs	82.50
Pitcher, milk	30.00
Pitcher, water	50.00
Plate, 6" d.	35.00
Platter, 13 x 8"	25.00
Relish, 8 x 6"	15.00 to 20.00
Sauce dish, flat or footed	9.00 to 12.00
Spooner	21.50
Sugar bowl, cov.	27.00
Table set, creamer, open sugar bowl & cov. butter dish, 3 pcs.	110.00
Wheelbarrow sugar cube dish w/metal wheels	65.00 to 75.00
Wine, 3¾" h.	30.00

BARRED HOBSTAR - See Checkerboard Pattern

BARRED STAR - See Spartan Pattern

BASKETWEAVE
Cup & saucer, amber	32.00
Goblet, amber	24.50
Goblet, clear	17.00
Goblet, vaseline	30.00
Mug, clear, 3" h.	12.00
Pitcher, water, vaseline	60.00
Plate, 8¾" d., handled, clear	11.00
Tray, water, scenic center, vaseline, 12"	50.00

BEADED BAND
Creamer	18.00
Goblet	28.00
Sugar bowl, cov.	40.00

BEADED BULL'S EYE WITH DRAPE - See Alabama Pattern

BEADED DEWDROP - See Wisconsin Pattern

BEADED GRAPE (California)

Beaded Grape Toothpick Holder

Bowl, 5½" sq., green	16.50
Bowl, 7½" sq., clear	20.00
Bowl, 7½" sq., green	28.00
Bowl, 8" sq., clear	25.00
Bowl, 8" sq., green	38.00
Bowl, 8½ x 6¼" rectangle, green	30.00
Bread tray, clear, 10 x 7"	25.00
Butter dish, cov., sq., clear	65.00
Butter dish, cov., sq., green	96.50
Cake stand, clear, 9" sq.	67.50
Cake stand, green, 9" sq., 6" h.	85.00
Celery tray, clear	30.00
Celery tray, green	45.00
Compote, open, 8½" sq., high stand, clear	75.00
Creamer, clear	25.00
Creamer, green	55.00
Cruet w/original stopper, clear	68.00
Cruet w/original stopper, green	95.00 to 125.00

Dish, clear, 8¼" sq.	30.00
Dish, green, 5½" sq.	20.00
Egg cup, clear	16.00
Goblet, clear	35.00
Goblet, green	42.50
Pitcher, water, round, green	66.50
Pitcher, water, square, green	95.00 to 120.00
Plate, 8" sq., clear	26.00
Plate, 8" sq., green	40.00
Relish, clear, 7 x 4"	20.00
Salt & pepper shakers w/original tops, clear, pr.	28.00
Salt & pepper shakers w/original tops, green, pr.	85.00
Sauce dish, clear	10.50
Sauce dish, green	13.50
Spooner, clear	30.00
Spooner, green	35.00 to 45.00
Sugar bowl, cov., clear	46.50
Sugar bowl, cov., green	60.00
Toothpick holder, clear (ILLUS.)	27.50
Toothpick holder, green	48.50
Tumbler, clear	25.00
Tumbler, green	40.00
Vase, 7" h., green	47.50
Wine, clear	35.00
Wine, green	65.00

BEADED GRAPE MEDALLION
Bowl, oval	24.50
Butter dish, cov.	42.50
Celery vase	55.00
Compote, cov., 8¼" d., low stand	75.00
Creamer, applied handle	40.00
Egg cup	23.50
Goblet	27.50
Goblet, buttermilk	35.00
Goblet, lady's	27.50
Pitcher, water, applied handle	80.00
Salt dip, flat	15.00
Sauce dish	8.00
Spooner	26.50
Sugar bowl, cov.	46.50
Sugar bowl, open	30.00
Vegetable dish, cov., footed, dated 1869	75.00
Wine	50.00

BEADED LOOP (Oregon)
Berry set, master bowl & 5 sauce dishes, 6 pcs.	50.00
Bowl, 9¼ x 6¾" oval	22.00
Bread platter	25.00
Butter dish, cov.	50.00
Cake stand, 9" d.	28.00
Cake stand, 10½" d.	45.00
Celery vase, 7" h.	29.00
Compote, open, jelly	45.00
Compote, open, 7½" d.	20.00
Creamer, clear	21.50
Creamer, ruby-stained	48.00
Cruet w/faceted stopper	67.50
Goblet	32.50

Honey dish	8.00
Pickle dish, boat-shaped, 9" l.	15.00
Pitcher, milk, 8½" h.	40.00
Pitcher, water, tankard	47.50
Relish	12.00
Salt shaker w/original top (single)	20.00
Sauce dish, flat or footed .....6.50 to	13.00
Spooner, clear	28.00
Spooner, ruby-stained	40.00
Sugar bowl, cov., clear	30.00
Sugar bowl, cov., ruby-stained	47.50
Syrup pitcher w/original top	65.00
Toothpick holder	32.50
Tumbler	42.50
Wine	32.50

BEADED MEDALLION - See Beaded Mirror Pattern

BEADED MIRROR (Beaded Medallion)

Butter dish, cov.	40.00
Castor bottle, mustard	13.50
Castor bottle w/original stopper, oil	25.00
Celery vase	36.50
Egg cup	18.50
Goblet	20.00
Goblet, buttermilk	22.00
Salt dip	18.00
Sauce dish, flat	6.00
Spooner	22.50
Sugar bowl, cov.	45.00
Sugar bowl, open	20.00

BEADED TULIP

Goblet	38.00
Pitcher, water	60.00
Wine	28.00

BEARDED HEAD - See Viking Pattern

BEARDED MAN (Old Man of the Woods or Neptune)

Bearded Man Compote

Butter dish, cov.	52.50
Celery vase	35.00

Compote, cov., 9" h. (ILLUS.)	60.00
Creamer	40.00
Pitcher, water, 2-qt.	58.00
Spooner	40.00
Sugar bowl, open	50.00

BELLFLOWER

Bellflower Goblets

Bowl, 6" d., 1¾" h., single vine	75.00
Bowl, 8" d., 4½" h., scalloped rim .....63.50 to	75.00
Bowl, 9 x 6" oval, rayed base	115.00
Butter dish, cov.	80.00
Castor bottle w/original stopper	28.00
Celery vase, fine rib, single vine	115.00
Celery vase, w/cut bellflowers	160.00
Champagne, barrel-shaped, fine rib, knob stem, plain base	100.00
Champagne, straight sides, plain stem, rayed base ....70.00 to	90.00
Cologne bottle w/stopper, clambroth	160.00
Compote, open, 4¾" d., low stand, scalloped rim	88.00
Compote, open, 7" d., 5" h., fine rib, double vine	125.00
Compote, open, 8" d., 5" h., scalloped rim, single vine .....50.00 to	80.00
Compote, open, 9½" d., 8½" h., scalloped rim, single vine ....100.00 to	125.00
Creamer, fine rib, double vine, applied handle...........80.00 to	135.00
Decanter w/bar lip, fine rib, single vine, pt.	185.00
Decanter w/bar lip, single vine, qt.	140.00
Decanter w/original stopper, cut shoulder, qt.	160.00
Egg cup, coarse rib	22.50
Egg cup, fine rib, single vine ....30.00 to	37.50
Goblet, barrel-shaped, fine rib, single vine, knob stem	45.00
Goblet, barrel-shaped, fine rib, single vine, plain stem (ILLUS. left)	30.00
Goblet, coarse rib	30.00
Goblet, double vine ....45.00 to	55.00

Goblet, fine rib, sun-colored
amethyst 75.00
Goblet, single vine, rayed base
(ILLUS. right).................. 40.00
Goblet, buttermilk 55.00
Honey dish, single vine 115.00
Lamp, kerosene-type, clear font,
milk glass base, flint, 9½" h. 165.00
Lamp, whale oil, brass stem, marble
base ....95.00 to 125.00
Pitcher, milk, double vine 350.00
Pitcher, water, 8¾" h., coarse rib,
double vine.................... 325.00
Pitcher, water, single vine 250.00
Plate, 6" d., fine rib, single vine.... 55.00
Salt dip, cov., master size, footed,
beaded rim, fine rib, single vine.. 75.00
Salt dip, open, master size, footed,
scalloped rim, single vine 38.00
Sauce dish, double vine........... 20.00
Sauce dish, single vine 25.00
Spillholder....................... 30.00
Spooner, low foot, double vine 55.00
Spooner, scalloped rim, single
vine 45.00
Sugar bowl, cov., single vine 95.00
Sugar bowl, open, coarse rib,
double vine.................... 68.00
Sugar bowl, open, single vine 48.00
Syrup pitcher w/original top, ap-
plied handle, fine rib, single
vine 410.00
Tumbler, bar ....50.00 to 70.00
Tumbler, coarse rib, double vine ... 77.50
Tumbler, fine rib, single vine...... 82.50
Tumbler, whiskey 135.00
Wine, barrel-shaped, knob stem,
fine rib, single vine, rayed base .. 82.50
Wine, straight sides, plain stem,
rayed base 60.00

BIGLER

Bigler Goblet

Bowl, 10" d. 75.00
Celery vase ....75.00 to 100.00
Champagne...................... 95.00

Cordial 60.00
Decanter w/bar lip, pt. 55.00
Goblet, 6" h. (ILLUS.) 38.50
Lamp, whale oil, 10" h........... 155.00
Plate, 4" d...................... 11.00
Salt dip, master size............. 20.00
Tumbler ....50.00 to 60.00
Whiskey, handled 100.00
Wine........................... 45.00

BIRD & FERN - See Hummingbird Pattern

BIRD & STRAWBERRY (Bluebird)

Bird & Strawberry Sauce Dish

Berry set: master bowl & 6 sauce
dishes; footed, clear, 7 pcs....... 125.00
Bowl, 5½" d., w/color............ 35.00
Bowl, 7½" d., footed, clear 60.00
Bowl, 7½" d., footed, w/color..... 82.50
Bowl, 9½ x 6" oval, footed, clear... 52.50
Bowl, 10" d., flat, clear 42.50
Bowl, 10" d., flat, w/color & gold
trim ....95.00 to 110.00
Butter dish, cov., clear .....85.00 to 110.00
Butter dish, cov., w/color 255.00
Cake stand, clear, 9" to 9½" d. 50.00
Celery tray, clear, 10" l. 35.00
Celery vase, pedestal base, clear,
7½" h......................... 65.00
Compote, cov., 6" d., low stand,
clear 50.00
Compote, cov., 6½" d., 9½" h.,
clear 85.00
Compote, cov., 7" d., high stand,
clear 110.00
Compote, open, 4½" d., 5" h.,
clear 70.00
Compote, open, 8" d., 6" h., scal-
loped & ruffled rim, w/color 110.00
Creamer, clear................... 50.00
Creamer, w/color................ 135.00
Dish, heart-shaped, clear ....35.00 to 42.00
Goblet, clear 40.00
Pitcher, water, clear.............. 185.00
Pitcher, water, w/color 275.00
Plate, 12" d., clear 70.00
Punch cup, clear 17.50
Relish, clear, 8¼" oval 22.00
Sauce dish, flat or footed, clear
(ILLUS.)..................20.00 to 25.00

Spooner, clear 45.00
Spooner, w/color.................. 125.00
Sugar bowl, cov., clear 55.00
Sugar bowl, open, clear 30.00
Table set: creamer, cov. butter dish
    & spooner; clear, 3 pcs........... 350.00
Table set, w/color, 4 pcs......... 450.00
Tumbler, clear 45.00
Tumbler, w/color................. 55.00
Water set: pitcher & 6 tumblers;
    w/color, 7 pcs.................. 900.00
Wine, clear ....40.00 to 55.00

BIRD IN RING (Butterfly & Fan)
Bread tray 39.00
Spooner 25.50

BLEEDING HEART

Bleeding Heart Cake Stand

Bowl, cov., 9½" d. 55.00
Bowl, 7¼" oval 27.50
Boel, 9¼" oval................... 30.00
Brandy snifter.................... 45.00
Butter dish, cov. 46.50
Cake stand, 9½" d. (ILLUS.) 58.50
Cake stand, 10" d. 80.00
Compote, cov., 7" d., w/Bleeding
    Heart finial 65.00
Compote, cov., 9" d., 12" h.
    w/Bleeding Heart finial 110.00
Compote, open, 8½" d., low
    stand 25.00
Compote, open, 8½" d., high
    stand 30.00
Creamer 47.50
Egg cup 40.00
Goblet, buttermilk 25.00
Goblet, knob stem 32.50
Honey dish ....12.50 to 17.00
Mug, 3" h........................ 38.50
Pitcher, water 100.00
Relish, 5 1/8 x 3 5/8" oval 30.00
Salt dip, master size, footed 42.50
Sauce dish, flat 12.50
Spooner.......................... 32.50
Sugar bowl, cov. 52.50
Sugar bowl, open 20.00

Tumbler, flat..................... 75.00
Tumbler, footed 25.00
Wine, plain stem 42.50
Wine, knob stem 155.00

BLOCK

(Also see Red Block)

Carafe, clear 25.00
Celery, clear..................... 15.00
Creamer, large, clear............. 8.00
Cruet w/original stopper, clear 20.00
Pitcher, water, clear.............. 65.00
Punch cup, applied handle, clear ... 8.00
Sauce dish, flat, clear 5.00
Tumbler, clear 40.00
Water set: pitcher & 6 tumblers;
    clear w/gold, 7 pcs. 110.00
Wine, clear 14.50

BLOCK & FAN

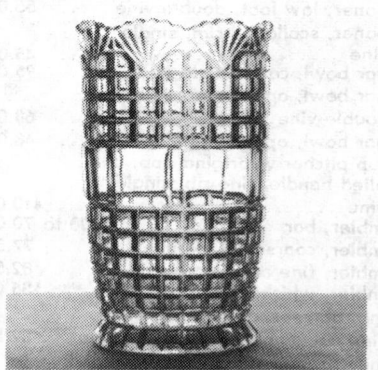

Block & Fan Celery Vase

Bowl, berry, 8" d., footed 22.50
Bowl, 9¾" d. 32.50
Bowl, 10 x 6" rectangle 50.00
Butter dish, cov. 45.00
Cake stand, 10" d. 35.00
Carafe, water.................... 50.00
Celery tray 30.00
Celery vase (ILLUS.) 27.50
Compote, open, 8" d., high stand ... 37.50
Cookie jar, cov. 65.00
Creamer 22.50
Cruet w/original stopper, small,
    6" h.......................... 24.00
Cruet w/original stopper, medium .. 35.00
Cruet w/original stopper, large..... 29.50
Finger bowl...................... 29.50
Goblet 57.50
Ice bucket 42.50
Pitcher, milk 35.00
Pitcher, water 45.00
Plate, 6" d. 21.50
Plate, 10" d. 19.50
Relish, 9¾ x 6" oval............... 25.00

Rose bowl 25.00
Salt & pepper shakers w/original
  tops, pr. 40.00
Sauce dish, flat or footed . . . . .8.00 to 12.50
Sauce dish, footed, ruby-stained 25.00
Spooner 25.00
Sugar bowl, cov. 40.00
Sugar bowl, open 18.00
Sugar shaker w/original top 35.00
Syrup pitcher w/original top, 7" h. . .   55.00
Tumbler 30.00
Wine 45.00

BLOCK & STAR - See Valencia Waffle Pattern

BLUEBIRD - See Bird & Strawberry Pattern

BOW TIE
Bowl, berry, 8" d. 27.50
Bowl, 10" d., 5" h. 75.00
Butter dish, cov. . . . . .55.00 to 65.00
Butter pat 25.00
Cake stand, 9" d. 55.00
Compote, open, 5½" d., 10½" h. . . .   60.00
Compote, open, 8" d., low stand 47.50
Compote, open, 9¼" d., high
  stand 55.00
Compote, open, 10½" d., 10¼" h. . .   70.00
Creamer 45.00
Goblet 42.50
Marmalade jar w/cover 45.00
Marmalade jar (no cover) 30.00
Pitcher, milk 65.00
Pitcher, water 70.00
Punch bowl, 1-pc. 100.00
Relish, rectangular 20.00
Salt dip, master size 35.00
Sauce dish, flat 18.00
Spooner 35.00
Sugar bowl, cov. 55.00
Sugar bowl, open 35.00
Tumbler 45.00

BROKEN COLUMN (Irish Column, Notched Rib or Bamboo)
Banana stand, clear 100.00
Basket, applied handle, clear, 15" l.,
  12" h. 150.00
Bowl, 7¼" d., clear 45.00
Bowl, 9" d., clear . . . . .35.00 to 40.00
Butter dish, cov., clear 60.00
Cake stand, clear, 9" d. 58.00
Cake stand, clear, 10" d. 80.00
Carafe, water, clear 72.50
Celery vase, clear 42.50
Celery vase, clear w/red notches . . .   135.00
Champagne, clear 65.00
Claret, clear 45.00
Compote, cov., 4¾" d., clear. 56.00
Compote, cov., 5¼" d., 10½" h.,
  clear. 57.50
Compote, cov., 5¼" d., 10½" h.,
  clear w/red notches 225.00

Compote, cov., 7" d., 12" h.,
  clear . . . . .100.00 to 120.00
Compote, cov., 8" d., high stand,
  clear 150.00
Compote, open, jelly, clear w/red
  notches 110.00
Compote, open, 5" d., 6" h., clear . .   35.00
Compote, open, 6" d., flared rim,
  clear 50.00
Compote, open, 6" d., clear w/red
  notches 135.00
Compote, open, 7" d., clear 36.00
Cookie jar, cov., clear 70.00
Creamer, clear.   37.50
Creamer, clear w/red notches 110.00
Cruet w/original stopper, clear 57.50
Decanter w/original stopper, clear,
  10½" h. 85.00

Broken Column Goblet

Goblet, clear (ILLUS.) 37.50
Marmalade jar w/original cover,
  clear 62.50
Pickle castor, clear, w/frame &
  tongs 95.00
Pickle castor, clear w/red notches,
  w/frame & tongs 425.00
Pitcher, water, clear. 90.00
Pitcher, water, clear w/red
  notches 210.00
Plate, 5" d., clear 32.50
Plate, 7" d., clear 32.50
Plate, 8" d., clear 35.00
Powder jar, cov., clear 25.00
Punch cup, blue 55.00
Punch cup, clear 15.00
Relish, clear, 5 x 3¾" 15.00
Relish, clear, 6½" l. 20.00
Relish, clear, 8 x 5" 30.00
Salt shaker w/original top, clear
  (single) 30.00
Sauce dish, clear 15.00
Sauce dish, clear w/red notches 37.50
Spooner, clear 25.00
Spooner, clear w/red notches 110.00
Sugar bowl, cov., clear 55.00
Syrup pitcher w/metal top, clear . . .   125.00

Syrup pitcher w/metal top, clear
  w/red notches .... 380.00 to 425.00
Tumbler, clear 38.50

BRYCE - See Ribbon Candy Pattern

BUCKLE

Buckle Goblet

Butter dish, cov.	68.00
Cake stand, 9¾" d., 5¼" h.	30.00
Champagne, flint................	60.00
Compote, cov., 6" d., 8½" h........	80.00
Creamer, applied handle, flint.....	110.00
Creamer, small size, non-flint	25.00
Egg cup, flint	30.00
Egg cup, non-flint	25.00
Goblet, flint	30.00
Goblet, non-flint (ILLUS.)	22.50
Goblet, buttermilk, non-flint	24.00
Lamp, kerosene-type, w/clambroth base	125.00
Pitcher, water, bulbous, applied handle, flint	525.00
Pitcher, water, bulbous, applied handle, non-flint	85.00
Salt dip, master size, footed, flint ..	30.00
Sauce dish, flint...................	10.00
Sauce dish, non-flint..............	7.00
Spooner, flint	40.00
Spooner, non-flint	26.00
Sugar bowl, cov., w/acorn finial, flint........................	65.00
Sugar bowl, open, flint	45.00
Sugar bowl, open, non-flint	19.00
Tumbler, bar, flint................	55.00
Tumbler, non-flint	30.00
Wine, non-flint..................	27.50

BUCKLE WITH STAR

Bowl, 8" oval	15.00
Butter dish, cov.	35.00
Cake stand, 9" d.	25.00
Celery vase.....................	24.50
Compote, cov., 7" d.	60.00

Compote, open, 7" d., 5½" h.	19.50
Creamer	24.00
Goblet	25.00
Pitcher, water, applied handle	80.00
Relish, 7¼ x 5 1/8" oval	10.00
Salt dip	25.00
Sauce dish, flat or footed .... 5.00 to 12.00	
Spillholder......................	60.00
Spooner	20.00
Sugar bowl, cov.	35.00

Buckle with Star Open Sugar

Sugar bowl, open (ILLUS.)	22.00
Tumbler, bar.....................	55.00
Wine............................	36.00

BULL'S EYE

Celery vase, flint..................	72.50
Cordial, flint	45.00
Creamer, applied handle, flint......	110.00
Decanter w/bar lip, flint, qt.	120.00
Egg cup, flint	45.00
Goblet, flint .... 50.00 to 60.00	
Goblet, giant bull's eye, flint	65.00
Lamp, kerosene-type, marble base, brass stem, 9" h.	110.00
Salt dip, master size, footed, flint ..	32.50
Spillholder......................	40.00
Spooner, flint	35.00
Spooner, non-flint	18.00
Sugar bowl, cov., flint	135.00
Tumbler, bar, flint...............	85.00
Tumbler, flat, flint...............	75.00
Wine, knob stem, flint	42.00

BULL'S EYE VARIANT - See Texas Bull's Eye Pattern

BULL'S EYE WITH DIAMOND POINT

Celery vase......................	140.00
Cologne bottle	85.00
Creamer, applied handle..........	175.00
Goblet (ILLUS.)	95.00
Honey dish	23.00
Lamp, kerosene-type, applied handle	150.00

Bull's Eye with Diamond Point Goblet

Salt dip, master size	29.00
Salt dip, basket-shaped	85.00
Sauce dish	15.00
Spillholder	75.00
Spooner	80.00
Tumbler, bar	110.00
Tumbler, water	150.00
Tumbler, whiskey	125.00
Wine	120.00

BULL'S EYE WITH FLEUR DE LIS

Bull's Eye with Fleur De Lis Goblet

Celery vase, 11" h.	85.00
Creamer	65.00
Goblet (ILLUS.)	70.00
Lamp, kerosene-type, pear-shaped font w/brass standard on marble base	175.00
Pitcher, water	485.00
Salt dip, master size	52.50
Sugar bowl, open	55.00

BUTTERFLY & FAN - See Bird in Ring Pattern

BUTTON ARCHES

Button Arches Bowl

Basket w/ruby-stained handle	25.00
Berry set: 8" d. master bowl & 6 sauce dishes; ruby-stained, 7 pcs.	135.00
Bowl, 8" d. ruby-stained, souvenir (ILLUS.)	45.00
Butter dish, cov., clear	48.00
Butter dish, cov., ruby-stained	95.00
Butter dish, cov., ruby-stained, souvenir	65.00
Compote, open, jelly, 4½" h., ruby-stained	45.00
Creamer, clear	20.00
Creamer, ruby-stained	40.00
Creamer, individual size, ruby-stained	18.50
Goblet, clambroth	22.00
Goblet, clear	20.00
Goblet, ruby-stained	37.50
Goblet, ruby-stained, souvenir	28.50
Mug, child's, ruby-stained, souvenir	25.00
Mug, clear, souvenir	22.50
Mug, ruby-stained, souvenir, 3½" h.	30.00
Pitcher, 7" h., ruby-stained, souvenir	60.00
Pitcher, tankard, 8¾" h., clear	100.00
Pitcher, water, tankard, 12" h., clear	85.00
Pitcher, water, tankard, 12" h., ruby-stained	125.00
Plate, 7" d., clear	7.00
Punch cup, clear	9.00
Punch cup, ruby-stained	17.50
Salt shaker w/original top, clear (single)	7.50
Salt shaker w/original top, ruby-stained (single)	22.50
Sauce dish, green	9.00
Sauce dish, ruby-stained	22.00
Spooner, clear	27.50
Spooner, ruby-stained	32.50
Sugar bowl, cov., clear	30.00
Sugar bowl, cov., ruby-stained, etched	65.00 to 80.00
Syrup pitcher w/original top, ruby-stained	125.00
Table set, ruby-stained, 4 pcs.	235.00
Toothpick holder, clambroth, souvenir	30.00

Toothpick holder, clear	14.50
Toothpick holder, ruby-stained	35.00
Toothpick holder, ruby-stained, souvenir........................	30.00
Tumbler, clear	22.50
Tumbler, ruby-stained	22.50
Tumbler, ruby-stained, souvenir	27.50
Water set: pitcher & 5 tumblers; clear w/frosted band & gold, 6 pcs............................	225.00
Water set: tankard pitcher & 5 tumblers; ruby-stained, souvenir, 6 pcs.	245.00
Whiskey shot glass, ruby-stained ...	14.50
Wine, clambroth	25.00
Wine, clear	15.00
Wine, ruby-stained	25.00
Wine, ruby-stained, souvenir	35.00

CABBAGE LEAF

Butter dish, cov., frosted...........	500.00
Celery vase, clear & frosted........	65.00
Custard cup, frosted, marked Libbey Glass Co., "Columbian Expo" on base	80.00
Pitcher, water, frosted.............	135.00
Rose bowl, amber	175.00
Sauce dish, frosted, w/rabbit center........................	35.00

CABBAGE ROSE

Cabbage Rose Pickle

Bitters bottle, 6½" h...............	85.00
Bowl, berry, 8½" oval	26.00
Butter dish, cov.	42.50
Cake stand, 11" d.	45.00
Cake stand, 12½" d.	69.00
Celery vase....................	50.00
Champagne.....................	50.00
Compote, cov., 7" d.	75.00
Compote, cov., 8" d., high stand ...	110.00
Compote, cov., 8½" d., 7" h........	95.00
Compote, open, 8½" d., high stand	36.50
Compote, open, 9¼" d., 7½" h.....	34.00
Cordial	55.00
Creamer, applied handle...........	55.00
Egg cup	30.00
Goblet........................	42.50
Goblet, buttermilk	40.00
Pickle or relish, 8½" l. (ILLUS.)	35.00
Pitcher, water	100.00

Salt dip, master size...............	20.00
Sauce dish........................	10.00
Spooner	28.00
Sugar bowl, cov.	55.00
Tumbler	40.00
Wine.........................	32.50

CABLE

Cable Egg Cup

Bowl, 9" d.	70.00
Butter dish, cov.	100.00
Celery vase......................	65.00
Champagne......................	275.00
Compote, open, 5¼" d., high stand	62.50
Compote, open, 7" d., 5" h........	40.00
Compote, open, 8" d., 4¾" h.......	50.00
Compote, open, 9" d., 4½" h.......	55.00
Creamer	495.00
Decanter w/bar lip, qt. .....95.00 to	125.00
Decanter w/stopper, qt.	195.00
Egg cup (ILLUS.)	50.00
Egg cup, clambroth, flint	550.00
Goblet	65.00
Honey dish, 3½" d., 1" h...........	15.00
Lamp, whale oil, 8¾" h............	135.00
Pitcher, water, 9½" h., applied handle ....350.00 to	500.00
Plate, 6" d.	65.00
Salt dip, individual size	20.00
Salt dip, master size	45.00
Sauce dish......................	28.00
Spooner	37.50
Sugar bowl, cov.	95.00
Wine.........................	77.50

CABLE WITH RING

Lamp, kerosene hand-type w/ring handle	175.00
Sugar bowl, cov., flint	78.00

CALIFORNIA - See Beaded Grape Pattern

CAMEO - See Classic Medallion Pattern

CANADIAN

Bowl, berry, 7" d., 4½" h., footed ..	75.00

Bread plate, handled, 10" d. 35.00
Butter dish, cov. 85.00
Cake stand, 9¾" d., 5" h. 35.00
Celery vase.   55.00
Compote, cov., 7" d., 11" h.. . . . . . .   92.50
Compote, cov., 8" d., low stand 76.50
Compote, open, 7" d., 6" h. 35.00
Compote, open, 8" d., 5" h. 45.00
Cordial. 36.50
Creamer 42.50
Goblet 50.00
Pitcher, milk, 8" h. 75.00
Pitcher, water 95.00
Plate, 6" d., handled 25.00
Plate, 8" d., handled 35.00
Sauce dish, flat or
  footed . . . . 16.00 to 30.00
Spooner 45.00
Sugar bowl, cov. 70.00

Canadian Wine

Wine (ILLUS.) 37.50

CANE
Bowl, 9½" oval, amber 15.00
Bread platter, amber 25.00
Candlestick, clear (single) 15.00
Celery vase, clear 32.50
Compote, open, 5¼", amber 27.50
Creamer, amber 30.00
Creamer, blue 35.00
Creamer, clear. . . . . 18.00 to 25.00
Goblet, amber 30.00
Goblet, apple green 45.00
Goblet, blue 35.00
Goblet, clear 18.00
Goblet, vaseline 40.00
Match holder, model of a cauldron,
  amber 18.00
Match holder, model of a cauldron,
  blue 16.00
Mustard jar, cov., amber 37.00

Pitcher, water, amber 57.50
Pitcher, water, apple green 47.00
Pitcher, water, blue 65.00

Cane Water Pitcher

Pitcher, water, clear (ILLUS.) 40.00
Relish, amber, 7½ x 3½" 22.50
Relish, clear, 8 x 5¼" oval 12.50
Sauce dish, flat, apple green 9.50
Sauce dish, footed, clear 15.00
Spooner, amber 42.00
Spooner, apple green 35.00
Sugar bowl, cov., amber 55.00
Sugar bowl, cov., clear 40.00
Toddy plate, amber, 4½" d. 14.00
Toddy plate, apple green, 4½" d. . . .   14.00
Toddy plate, blue, 4½" d. 17.50
Toddy plate, clear, 4½" d. 14.00
Tumbler, apple green 28.50
Tumbler, blue. 25.00
Tumbler, clear 16.50
Waste bowl, amber 32.50
Waste bowl, apple green 30.00
Whimsey, slipper, amber 30.00

CANNON BALL - See Atlas Pattern

CAPE COD

Cape Cod Spooner

Bowl, 6" d., handled 20.00
Bread platter 45.00
Compote, cov., 8" d., 12" h........ 115.00
Compote, open, 8" d., 5½" h....... 36.00
Decanter w/original stopper 160.00
Goblet 35.00
Pitcher, water 65.00
Plate, 8"d ., open handles 55.00
Sauce dish, flat or
    footed ....14.00 to 18.50
Spooner (ILLUS.).................. 35.00

CARDINAL BIRD

Cardinal Bird Sauce Dish

Butter dish, cov. 65.00
Butter dish, cov., 3 identified
    birds.......................... 110.00
Creamer 33.50
Goblet 35.00
Honey dish, cov., 3½" h. 35.00
Honey dish, open 18.50
Sauce dish, flat or footed (ILLUS. of
    footed sauce).............14.00 to 21.00
Spooner.......................... 32.50
Sugar bowl, cov. 60.00
Sugar bowl, open 30.00

CATHEDRAL

Cathedral Compote

Bowl, 6" d., crimped rim, vaseline .. 35.00
Bowl, 8" d., amber 48.00
Bowl, 8" d., blue 40.00
Bowl, 8" d., vaseline 32.50
Butter dish, cov., clear 50.00

Cake stand, blue, 10" d., 4½" h. ... 52.50
Cake stand, vaseline 68.00
Compote, cov., 7¼" d., 10½" h.,
    clear 75.00
Compote, open, 7" d., high stand,
    fluted rim, amethyst............ 145.00
Compote, open, 7½" d., fluted rim,
    amber 40.00
Compote, open, 9" d., 5½" h.,
    amber 50.00
Compote, open, 9" d., 7" h.,
    amethyst 75.00
Compote, open, 9" d., 5½" h.,
    blue 65.00
Compote, open, 9" d., 7" h., clear .. 48.00
Compote, open, 10" d., 6" h.,
    amethyst 80.00
Compote, open, 10½" d., 8" h.,
    shaped rim, clear (ILLUS.) 55.00
Creamer, clear 24.00
Creamer, ruby-stained 50.00
Cruet w/original stopper, amber ... 70.00
Dish, ruffled rim, ruby-stained,
    5" d., 2" h. 24.00
Goblet, amber 40.00
Goblet, amethyst................. 70.00
Goblet, clear 27.50
Goblet, vaseline 52.50
Pitcher, water, clear.............. 125.00
Pitcher, water, ruby-stained 145.00
Relish, fish-shaped, amber 35.00
Relish, fish-shaped, blue 35.00
Relish, fish-shaped, ruby-stained.... 55.00
Relish, fish-shaped, vaseline 35.00
Salt dip, canoe-shaped, vaseline 17.50
Sauce dish, flat or footed,
    amethyst 35.00
Sauce dish, flat or footed, blue 22.00
Sauce dish, flat or footed, clear 12.50
Sauce dish, flat or footed, ruby-
    stained...................15.00 to 22.00
Sauce dish, flat or footed,
    vaseline..................17.00 to 24.00
Spooner, amber.................. 40.00
Spooner, clear................... 32.50
Sugar bowl, cov., clear 55.00
Sugar bowl, cov., ruby-stained 65.00
Tumbler, amber.................. 31.00
Tumbler, blue.................... 40.00
Tumbler, clear................... 22.50
Tumbler, ruby-stained 35.00
Wine, amber..................... 37.50
Wine, blue 55.00
Wine, clear 25.00
Wine, vaseline................... 40.00

CERES (Goddess of Liberty)

Compote, open, 6" d., low stand,
    clear.......................... 25.00
Creamer, clear................... 22.50
Mug, amber 25.00
Mug, blue 22.50
Mug, clear....................... 17.50
Sugar bowl, cov., clear 45.00

CHAIN

Chain Sauce Dish

Bread plate	27.00
Butter dish, cov.	35.00
Compote, cov., 7½" d., 8" h.	36.00
Compote, cov., 7½" d., 12" h.	45.00
Creamer	18.50
Goblet	20.00
Plate, 7" d.	14.50
Relish, 8" oval	11.00
Sauce dish, flat or footed (ILLUS. of footed sauce)	8.50
Spooner	25.00
Sugar bowl, cov.	30.00
Sugar bowl, open	20.00
Wine	20.00

CHAIN & SHIELD

Creamer	30.00
Goblet	35.00
Pitcher, water	50.00
Platter, oval	25.00

CHAIN WITH STAR

Chain with Star Plate

Bread plate, handled	27.50
Butter dish, cov.	32.50
Cake stand, 8¾" d., 4¾" h.	27.00
Cake stand, 10" d.	32.50
Compote, open, 8" d., 6½" h.	22.50
Compote, open, 9½" d.	29.00
Creamer	20.00
Goblet	22.50
Pitcher, water	55.00
Plate, 7" d. (ILLUS.)	16.00

Relish	14.00
Sauce dish	11.50
Spooner	18.00
Sugar bowl, cov.	37.50
Sugar bowl, open	27.00
Syrup pitcher (no lid)	45.00
Wine	27.50

CHANDELIER (Crown Jewel)

Chandelier Celery Vase

Bowl, 8" d., 3¼" h.	25.00
Butter dish, cov.	60.00
Cake stand, 10" d.	70.00
Celery vase (ILLUS.)	35.00
Compote, open, 6½" d.	38.00
Compote, open, 8" d., high stand, etched	95.00
Compote, open, 9¼" d., 7¾" h.	68.00
Creamer	32.50
Finger bowl	16.00
Goblet	50.00
Inkwell	60.00 to 85.00
Pitcher, water	68.00
Salt dip, footed	30.00
Sauce dish, flat	16.50
Spooner	27.50
Sugar bowl, cov.	40.00
Sugar shaker w/original top	60.00
Tumbler	40.00
Wine	32.00

CHECKERBOARD (Barred Hobstar)

Bowl, 9" d., flat	20.00
Butter dish, cov.	42.50
Celery tray	30.00
Compote, jelly	25.00
Creamer	12.00 to 20.00
Goblet	20.00
Honey dish, cov., 5" w.	45.00
Pitcher, milk	35.00
Pitcher, water	30.00
Plate, 7" d.	21.50
Punch cup	5.00
Sauce dish, flat	10.00
Sauce dish, flat, ruby-stained, gilt trim, 4½" d.	14.50

Spooner 22.50
Sugar bowl, cov. 25.00
Tumbler 17.00
Water set: pitcher & 4 tumblers;
   ruby-stained, 5 pcs. 210.00
Wine 14.00

CHERRY THUMBPRINT - See Paneled Cherry with Thumbprints Pattern

CLASSIC

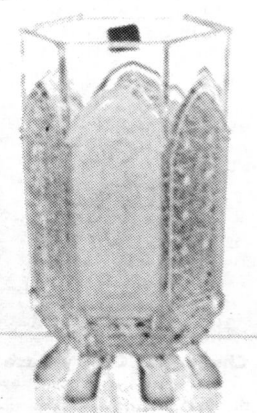

Classic Celery Vase

Berry set, master bowl & 4 sauce
   dishes, 5 pcs. 275.00
Bowl, cov., 7" hexagon, open log
   feet 110.00
Butter dish, cov., collared base 125.00
Butter dish, cov., open log feet 175.00
Celery vase, collared base . . 90.00 to 150.00
Celery vase, open log feet
   (ILLUS.) . . . . 180.00 to 225.00
Compote, cov., 6½" d., collared
   base 150.00
Compote, cov., 6½" d., open log
   feet 240.00
Compote, cov., 7½" d., 8" h., open
   log feet 250.00
Compote, cov., 10" d., open log
   feet 295.00
Compote, cov., 12½" d., collared
   base 325.00
Compote, open, 7¾" d., open log
   feet 175.00
Creamer, collared base 95.00
Creamer, open log feet 150.00
Goblet 200.00
Pitcher, milk, 8½" h., open log
   feet . . . . 375.00 to 550.00
Pitcher, water, collared base 250.00
Pitcher, water, 9½" h., open log
   feet 295.00
Plate, 10" d., "Blaine," signed
   Jacobus 185.00
Plate, 10" d., "Cleveland" 185.00
Plate, 10" d., "Logan" . . . . . 165.00 to 225.00

Plate, 10" d., "Warrior" . . . . . 95.00 to 125.00
Plate, 10" d., "Warrior," signed
   Jacobus 160.00
Sauce dish, collared base 30.00
Sauce dish, open log feet 38.00
Spooner, collared base 80.00
Spooner, open log feet . . . . . 90.00 to 150.00
Sugar bowl, cov., collared base 150.00
Sugar bowl, cov., open log feet 175.00
Sugar bowl, open, log feet 150.00

CLASSIC MEDALLION (Cameo)

Classic Medallion Spooner

Bowl, 6¾" d., 3½" h., footed 38.00
Celery vase 30.00
Compote, open, 7" d., 3¾" h. 22.50
Creamer 25.00
Pitcher, water 52.50
Sauce dish, footed 13.00
Spooner (ILLUS.) 26.50
Sugar bowl, open 20.00

COLLINS - See Crystal Wedding Pattern

COLONIAL (Empire Colonial)

Colonial Claret

Celery vase, flint	75.00
Champagne, flint	55.00
Claret, 5½" h. (ILLUS.)	50.00
Creamer, applied handle, flint	120.00
Goblet, flint	55.00
Salt dip, master size	17.50
Spillholder	40.00
Spooner	40.00
Sugar bowl, cov.	95.00
Tumbler, footed, clear, flint ..25.00 to	45.00
Wine, flint	75.00

COLORADO

Colorado Bowl

Berry set: master bowl & 6 sauce dishes; green w/gold, 7 pcs.	165.00
Bowl, 6" d., clear	20.00
Bowl, 7" d., flat, green	23.00
Bowl, 7" d., footed, scalloped rim, blue	25.00
Bowl, 7½" d., footed, turned-up sides, blue w/gold	55.00
Bowl, 7½" d., footed, turned-up sides, green	30.00
Bowl, 8½" d., footed, crimped edge, green	35.00
Bowl, 9" d., footed, 3-turned up sides, clear (ILLUS.)	29.00
Bowl, 9" d., green w/gold	42.00
Bowl, 10" d., footed, fluted, green	39.00
Butter dish, cov., blue w/gold	200.00
Butter dish, cov., clear	52.50
Butter dish, cov., green ....100.00 to	125.00
Candy dish, clear	9.50
Candy dish, green, souvenir	20.00
Card tray, clear	25.00
Card tray, green w/gold	32.50
Celery vase, clear	35.00
Celery vase, green w/gold	48.00
Compote, open, 6" d., 4" h., crimped rim, clear	20.00
Compote, open, 8" d., 7" h., beaded rim, green	77.50
Compote, open, 9½" d., blue	95.00
Compote, open, 10½" d., 7" h., green w/gold	135.00
Creamer, blue w/gold	95.00
Creamer, clear w/ruby-staining, individual size	40.00
Creamer, green w/gold, small	32.50
Creamer, green w/gold, large	60.00

Cup, clear	11.00
Cup, green	30.00
Cup, green, souvenir	30.00
Cup & saucer, green, souvenir	40.00
Custard cup, green, large	28.00
Dish, clear, 6" sq.	15.00
Match holder, green	35.00
Mug, clear, souvenir	18.50
Mug, green	25.00
Nappy, tricornered, blue w/gold	32.50
Nappy, tricornered, clear	17.50
Nappy, tricornered, green w/gold	32.50
Pitcher, 6" h., blue w/gold	115.00
Pitcher, 6" h., green w/gold	42.00
Pitcher, water, blue w/gold	400.00
Pitcher, water, green w/gold	190.00 to 225.00
Plate, 7" d., footed, clear	17.50
Plate, 8" d., blue	60.00
Punch cup, clear	13.50
Punch cup, green w/gold, souvenir	28.00
Salt & pepper shakers w/original tops, green, pr.	95.00
Sauce dish, clear	14.00
Sauce dish, green w/gold	32.50
Spooner, clear	25.00
Spooner, green w/gold	55.00
Sugar bowl, cov., large, clear	32.00
Sugar bowl, cov., large, green	80.00
Sugar bowl, open, large, green	25.00
Sugar bowl, open, individual size, blue	26.50
Sugar bowl, open, individual size, green	27.50
Table set, green w/gold, 4 pcs.	350.00
Toothpick holder, blue w/gold	46.50
Toothpick holder, clear w/gold	27.50
Toothpick holder, green w/gold	35.00
Tumbler, green w/gold	24.00
Vase, 12" h., blue w/gold ..95.00 to	145.00
Vase, 12" h., trumpet-shaped, green	65.00
Violet vase, blue	35.00
Wine, clear	20.00
Wine, green w/gold	37.50

COLUMBIAN COIN

Berry set: master bowl & 6 sauce dishes; gilded coins, 7 pcs.	295.00
Butter dish, cov., gilded coins	165.00
Celery vase, frosted coins	85.00
Celery vase, gilded coins	80.00
Champagne, frosted coins	65.00
Champagne, gilded coins	85.00
Claret, clear coins	90.00
Claret, frosted coins	140.00
Claret, gilded coins	75.00
Compote, open, 8" d., clear coins	80.00
Creamer, frosted coins	235.00
Creamer, gilded coins	150.00
Epergne	775.00
Goblet, frosted coins	80.00
Goblet, gilded coins	75.00

Lamp, kerosene-type, milk white,
   10" h. 450.00

Columbian Coin Lamp

Lamp, kerosene-type, frosted coins,
   12" h. (ILLUS.) 160.00
Mug, beer, handled, gilded coins ... 75.00
Pickle dish........................ 90.00
Pitcher, milk, frosted coins 75.00
Pitcher, milk, gilded coins 155.00
Pitcher, water, 10" h., frosted
   coins........................... 185.00
Pitcher, water, 10" h., gilded
   coins.................. 125.00 to 145.00
Salt & pepper shakers w/original
   tops, frosted coins, pr. 100.00
Sauce dish, flat or footed, gilded
   coins........................... 32.50
Spooner, frosted coins 42.50
Spooner, gilded coins 55.00
Sugar bowl, cov., frosted coins 135.00
Syrup pitcher w/original top, frosted
   coins........................... 135.00
Table set, gilded coins, 4 pcs. 350.00
Toothpick holder, gilded coins 72.50
Tumbler, gilded coins.............. 55.00
Wine, frosted coins.......... 55.00 to 80.00

COMET (Early)

Goblet 75.00
Pitcher, water, tankard 400.00
Spooner 85.00
Tumbler, bar...................... 95.00
Tumbler, bar, canary yellow 750.00
Tumbler, water 110.00
Tumbler, whiskey, handled......... 110.00

COMPACT - See Snail Pattern

CORD & TASSEL

Bowl, oval 20.00
Butter dish, cov. 48.00
Cake stand, 9½" d. 45.00
Castor bottle..................... 32.00
Compote, cov., 8" d. 50.00
Compote, open, 8" d., low stand ... 26.50
Creamer (ILLUS.) 29.00

Cord & Tassel Creamer

Goblet 28.00
Mug 25.00
Pitcher, water 95.00
Salt & pepper shakers w/original
   tops, pr. 55.00
Sauce dish, flat 10.00
Spooner 32.50
Sugar bowl, open 28.00
Wine............................. 31.50

CORD DRAPERY

Cord Drapery Compote

Bowl, cov., clear 165.00
Bowl, 7½" d., 2¾" h., clear 35.00
Bowl, 8½" oval, clear 27.50
Bowl, 10" d., 3½" h., clear 45.00
Butter dish, cov., clear 55.00
Butter dish, cov., green........... 150.00
Cake plate, clear, 10" d........... 42.50
Celery vase, clear 20.00
Compote, cov., jelly, blue 55.00
Compote, cov., jelly, clear 45.00
Compote, cov., 6½" d., clear...... 65.00
Compote, open, jelly, clear
   (ILLUS.)........................ 18.00
Compote, open, 7½" d., 5½" h.,
   clear 40.00
Compote, open, 8½" d., 6¼" h.,
   clear 48.00

Creamer, clear....................	31.50
Cruet w/original stopper, amber ...	265.00
Cruet w/original stopper, clear	90.00
Goblet, clear	55.00
Mug, clear........................	27.00
Pickle, amber, 9¼ x 5¼" oval	37.00
Pickle, clear, 9¼ x 5¼" oval	22.50
Pitcher, water, amber	165.00
Pitcher, water, clear...............	57.50
Punch cup, clear	16.00
Relish, clear, 7 x 4"	21.50
Relish, clear, 9¼ x 5¾"	22.50
Salt & pepper shakers w/original tops, clear, pr...................	92.50
Sauce dish, flat or footed, clear...................8.50 to	11.50
Spooner, clear	35.00
Sugar bowl, cov., clear	38.50
Syrup pitcher w/original top, amber	265.00
Toothpick holder, clear	75.00
Tumbler, clear	45.00
Wine, clear......................	75.00

CORDOVA

Butter dish, cov.	50.00
Celery vase.......................	45.00
Cologne bottle, 5" h.	20.00
Compote, open, 8" d.............	35.00
Compote, open, 10" d., high stand..	42.50
Creamer	17.50
Creamer, individual size	35.00
Creamer & cov. sugar bowl, pr.	65.00
Inkwell...........................	75.00
Mug	14.00
Pitcher, milk......................	30.00
Pitcher, water	45.00
Punch cup	6.50
Salt shaker w/original top (single) ..	15.00
Spooner	30.00
Sugar bowl, cov. ....35.00 to	40.00
Sugar bowl, cov., individual size....	40.00
Syrup pitcher w/pewter top ....85.00 to	125.00
Toothpick holder	21.50
Tumbler	15.00
Vase, bud	15.00

COTTAGE (Dinner Bell or Finecut Band)

Bowl, berry, 7" d., green	16.00
Bowl, berry, 9¼ x 6½" oval, clear..	15.00
Butter dish, cov., clear	45.00
Cake stand, amber	65.00
Cake stand, blue	55.00
Cake stand, clear	31.00
Celery vase, clear.................	27.50
Champagne, clear.................	37.00
Compote, cov., 7" d., high stand, clear	30.00
Compote, open, jelly, 4½" d., 4" h., blue	28.50
Compote, open, jelly, 4½" d., 4" h., clear	19.00

Compote, open, jelly, 4½" d., 4" h., green	32.50
Creamer, amber	37.50
Creamer, clear...................	22.50
Cruet w/original stopper, clear	37.00
Cup & saucer, clear	35.00
Goblet, amber	47.50
Goblet, clear	25.00
Pitcher, milk, clear	35.00
Pitcher, water, clear, 2-qt.	40.00
Plate, 5" d., clear	11.50
Plate, 6" d., clear	15.00
Plate, 7" d., clear	18.00
Plate, 8" d., clear	22.00
Plate, 9" d., clear	32.50
Salt shaker w/original top, clear (single).........................	25.00
Sauce dish, clear.................	8.00
Saucer, clear, 6" d...............	8.00
Saucer, green, 6" d...............	20.00
Spooner, clear	20.00
Sugar bowl, cov., clear	47.00
Sugar bowl, open, clear	16.00
Syrup pitcher w/original top, clear..	65.00
Tray, water, clear	25.00

Cottage Tumbler

Tumbler, clear (ILLUS.).............	18.50
Waste bowl, clear	38.00
Wine, clear......................	18.00

CROESUS

Berry set: master bowl & 6 sauce dishes; green, 7 pcs.	300.00
Berry set: master bowl & 6 sauce dishes; purple, 7 pcs.............	435.00
Bowl, 6¾" d., 4" h., footed, green	95.00
Bowl, 6¾" d., 4" h., footed, purple	185.00
Bowl, 8" d., green	100.00
Bowl, 8" d., purple	175.00
Butter dish, cov., clear	75.00
Butter dish, cov., green.....95.00 to	150.00
Butter dish, cov., purple	170.00
Celery vase, green w/gold	135.00
Compote, open, jelly, purple	225.00
Condiment tray, clear	18.00
Condiment tray, green.............	35.00

Creamer, green 85.00
Creamer, purple 150.00
Creamer, individual size, purple,
   3" h............................. 100.00
Creamer & cov. sugar bowl, green,
   pr............................... 225.00
Cruet w/original stopper, clear 75.00
Cruet w/original stopper, green 175.00
Cruet w/original stopper, purple ... 350.00
Cruet w/original stopper, miniature,
   green, 4" h. 140.00
Pitcher, water, green......200.00 to 250.00
Pitcher, water, purple 550.00
Plate, 8" d., scalloped rim, green
   w/gold 110.00
Salt & pepper shakers w/replaced
   tops, green, pr. 140.00
Sauce dish, clear 13.50
Sauce dish, green w/gold 32.50
Sauce dish, purple w/gold 48.50
Spooner, green 67.50
Spooner, purple 90.00
Sugar bowl, cov., clear 75.00
Sugar bowl, cov., green ...115.00 to 130.00
Sugar bowl, cov., purple...160.00 to 200.00
Table set, green, 4 pcs.......... 425.00
Table set, purple, 4 pcs. 550.00
Toothpick holder, green 82.50

Croesus Toothpick Holder

Toothpick holder, purple (ILLUS.) ... 95.00
Tumbler, green 45.00
Tumbler, purple 70.00
Water set: pitcher & 5 tumblers;
   green, 6 pcs. 425.00
Water set: pitcher & 6 tumblers;
   purple, 7 pcs. 850.00

CROWN JEWEL - See Chandelier Pattern

CRYSTAL BALL - See Atlas Pattern

CRYSTAL WEDDING (Collins)

(Items may be plain or with etched designs)

Banana stand, 10" h. 100.00
Berry set, 8" sq. bowl & 6 sauce
   dishes, 7 pcs. 125.00
Bowl, cov., 7" sq. 75.00

Butter dish, cov. 52.50
Butter dish, cov., amber-stained 100.00
Butter dish, cov., ruby-stained 75.00
Cake stand, 9" sq., 8" h............ 50.00
Cake stand, 10" sq. ....65.00 to 85.00

Crystal Wedding Celery Vase

Celery vase (ILLUS.) 45.00
Compote, cov., 5" sq. 52.50
Compote, cov., 6" sq.,
   9½" h....................45.00 to 65.00
Compote, cov., 7" sq. 85.00
Compote, open, 4" sq., 6" h....... 22.50
Compote, open, 7" sq., 8¾" h. 75.00
Compote, open, 8" sq., low stand .. 36.00
Creamer ....30.00 to 42.50
Creamer, ruby-stained 62.50
Creamer & cov. sugar bowl, pr. 75.00
Creamer & cov. sugar bowl, amber-
   stained, pr..............180.00 to 195.00
Cruet w/original stopper, amber-
   stained....................... 175.00
Goblet 45.00
Lamp base, kerosene-type, square
   font, 10" h. 375.00
Pitcher, milk 125.00
Pitcher, water 155.00
Salt dip 35.00
Sauce dish........................ 12.00
Spooner 25.00
Spooner, ruby-stained 55.00
Sugar bowl, cov., ... 50.00
Sugar bowl, cov., amber-stained.... 65.00
Sugar bowl, cov., ruby-stained 85.00
Sugar bowl, open, scalloped rim 30.00
Syrup pitcher w/original top, ruby-
   stained....................... 210.00
Tumbler 32.50
Wine............................. 68.00

CUPID & VENUS (Guardian Angel)

Bowl, 6½" d. 20.00
Bowl, 9" d., scalloped rim, footed .. 35.00
Bread plate, amber, 10½" d........ 115.00
Bread plate, clear, 10½" d. 30.00

Butter dish, cov. . . . . .55.00 to 65.00
Cake plate 40.00
Celery vase 38.50
Champagne 85.00
Compote, cov., 7" d., low stand 55.00
Compote, cov., 9½" d., low stand . . 95.00
Compote, cov., 10" d., high stand . . 97.50
Compote, open, 6" d., low stand . . . 30.00
Compote, open, 8½" d., low stand,
    scalloped rim 35.00
Creamer 32.50
Goblet 57.50
Honey dish, 3½" d. 7.50
Marmalade jar, cov. 38.50
Mug, 2½" h. 22.50
Mug, 3½" h. 26.50
Pickle castor w/resilvered frame,
    cover & tongs 80.00
Pitcher, milk, amber 190.00
Pitcher, milk, clear 55.00
Pitcher, water, ...65.00 to 75.00

Cupid & Venus Footed Sauce Dish

Sauce dish, footed, 3½" to 4½" d.
    (ILLUS.) 10.00
Spooner 36.50
Sugar bowl, cov. 65.00
Sugar bowl, open 27.50
Wine 70.00

CURRANT
Cake stand, 11" d. 60.00
Celery vase 42.50
Creamer 32.50
Egg cup . . . . .20.00 to 25.00
Goblet 22.50
Goblet, buttermilk 40.00
Honey dish, 3½" d. 16.00
Pitcher, water 70.00
Spooner 22.50
Wine 16.50

CURRIER & IVES
Bitters bottle, clear 38.00
Bowl, master berry or fruit,
    10" oval, flat w/collared base,
    clear 40.00
Bread plate, Balky Mule on Railroad
    Tracks, blue 85.00

Bread plate, Balky Mule on Railroad
    Tracks, clear 55.00
Bread plate, children sawing felled
    log, frosted center 75.00
Compote, cov., 7½" d., high stand
    clear 95.00
Compote, open, 7½" d., 9" h.,
    scalloped rim, clear 45.00
Cordial, clear, 3¼" h. 25.00
Creamer, clear 30.00
Cup, clear 10.00
Cup, vaseline 35.00
Cup & saucer, clear 35.00
Decanter w/original stopper, clear . . 55.00
Goblet, clear 25.00
Lamp, kerosene-type, clear,
    9½" h. 70.00

Currier & Ives Kerosene Lamp

Lamp, kerosene-type, clear, 11" h.
    (ILLUS.) 75.00
Pitcher, milk, clear 57.50
Pitcher, water, amber 120.00
Pitcher, water, clear 48.50
Relish, clear, 10" oval . . . . . . .16.00 to 20.00
Salt shaker w/original top, amber
    (single) 45.00
Salt shaker w/original top, clear
    (single) 19.00
Salt shaker w/original top, vaseline
    (single) 52.50
Salt & pepper shakers w/original
    tops, blue, pr. 90.00
Sauce dish, flat or footed, amber . . . 20.00
Sauce dish, flat or footed, blue 28.50
Sauce dish, flat or footed,
    clear .7.00 to 12.50
Spooner, clear 30.00
Sugar bowl, cov., clear 35.00
Syrup jug w/original top, clear 55.00
Tray, wine, clear, 9½" d. . . . .40.00 to 48.00
Tray, water, Balky Mule on Railroad
    Tracks, blue, 12" d. 110.00
Tray, water, Balky Mule on Railroad
    Tracks, clear, 12" d. . . . . . . .45.00 to 58.00

Tray, water, Balky Mule on Railroad
   Tracks, vaseline, 12" d...100.00 to 125.00
Waste bowl, clear 42.00
Wine, clear ....15.00 to 18.00
Wine set: decanter w/original stop-
   per & 6 wines; clear, 7 pcs. 180.00

CURTAIN

Curtain Pattern Salt Shaker

Bowl, cov., 8" d. 60.00
Butter dish, cov. 50.00
Cake stand, 9½" d. 36.50
Celery boat 48.50
Celery vase 36.50
Compote, open, 10" d., 8" h........ 42.50
Condiment set, pr. salt & pepper
   shakers & mustard jar, 3 pcs. 65.00
Creamer 35.00
Goblet 35.00
Salt shaker w/original top (ILLUS.) .. 15.00
Sauce dish, flat or footed, 4¾" d. .. 8.00
Spooner 25.00
Sugar bowl, cov. 32.00
Tumbler 20.00

CURTAIN TIE BACK

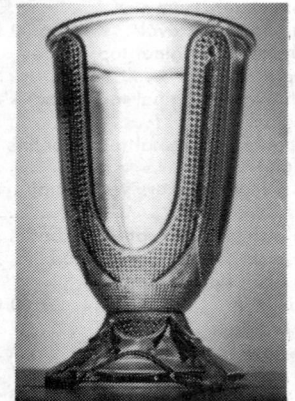

Curtain Tie Back Celery Vase

Bowl, 7½" sq., flat 18.00
Bread tray 35.00

Butter dish, cov. 38.00
Cake stand, 9" d., 6½" h. 25.00
Celery vase (ILLUS.) 30.00
Creamer 25.00
Goblet 17.00
Pitcher, water 55.00
Relish 10.00
Sauce dish, flat or footed, 3¾" d. .. 10.00
Spooner 28.00
Sugar bowl, cov. 30.00
Sugar bowl, open 15.00

CUT LOG

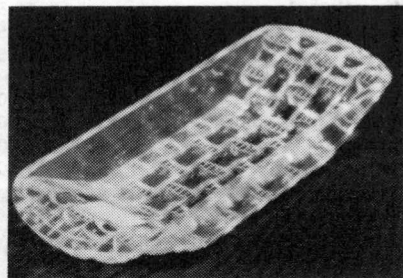

Cut Log Relish

Bowl, 8½" d., scalloped rim 27.50
Bowl, master berry or fruit,
   10½" d., footed 40.00
Butter dish, cov. ....65.00 to 70.00
Cake stand, 9" d., 6" h. 57.50
Cake stand, 10" d. 60.00
Celery tray 15.00
Celery vase 35.00
Compote, cov., 5½" d., 7½" h. 55.00
Compote, cov., 7" d., 8½" h........ 60.00
Compote, cov., 7" d., 10" h........ 75.00
Compote, cov., 8" d., 12½" h....... 95.00
Compote, open, 5" d. 32.50
Compote, open, 6" d., 4¾" h. 37.50
Compote, open, 8" d., 5" h. 40.00
Compote, open, 10" d., 8½" h.,
   scalloped rim ....75.00 to 85.00
Creamer 40.00
Creamer, individual size 15.00
Cruet w/original stopper, small 37.50
Cruet w/original stopper, large..... 45.00
Goblet 40.00
Mug 18.00
Nappy, handled, 5" d. 20.00
Olive dish ....15.00 to 22.50
Pitcher, water, tankard 75.00
Relish, boat-shaped, 9¼" l.
   (ILLUS.) 30.00
Salt shaker w/original tin top
   (single) 45.00
Sauce dish, flat or footed ....25.00 to 30.00
Spooner 30.00
Sugar bowl, cov. 60.00
Sugar bowl, cov., individual size.... 35.00
Sugar bowl, open 20.00
Tumbler 45.00

Tumbler, juice 25.00
Wine........................... 25.00

DAHLIA

Dahlia Water Pitcher

Bowl, 9 x 6" oval, clear............ 16.50
Bread platter, clear, 12 x 8"........ 32.50
Butter dish, cov., clear 40.00
Cake stand, amber, 9" d........... 65.00
Cake stand, clear, 9" d........... 22.50
Cake stand, amber, 10½" d. 75.00
Champagne, clear................ 55.00
Creamer, clear.................. 18.00
Creamer, green 30.00
Egg cup, double, clear 55.00
Goblet, clear................... 40.00
Goblet, vaseline 65.00
Mug, amber 40.00
Mug, clear..................... 27.50
Mug, child's, blue 40.00
Pitcher, milk, applied handle,
   clear 37.00
Pitcher, water, blue (ILLUS.)........ 100.00
Pitcher, water, clear.............. 48.00
Pitcher, water, vaseline .....75.00 to 95.00
Plate, 7" d., amber................ 42.50
Plate, 7" d., blue................. 36.00
Plate, 7" d., clear 20.00
Plate, 9" d., w/handles, blue....... 50.00
Plate, 9" d., w/handles, clear 20.00
Plate, 9" d., w/handles, vaseline ... 38.50
Relish, clear, 9½ x 5".............. 13.00
Sauce dish, flat, amber 9.00
Sauce dish, flat, blue 12.00
Sauce dish, flat, clear 10.00
Spooner, amber.................. 45.00
Spooner, blue................... 50.00
Spooner, clear 22.50
Sugar bowl, open, clear 20.00
Wine, clear..................... 36.00

DAISY & BUTTON
Bowl, 8" sq., amber 50.00

Bowl, 8" w., tricornered, vaseline .. 50.00
Bowl, berry or fruit, 8½" d., clear .. 42.50
Bowl, 10 x 7" rectangle, 2¼" h.,
   vaseline 45.00
Bread tray, amber ....22.00 to 35.00
Bread tray, clear 20.00
Bread tray, vaseline 25.00
Butter chip, fan-shaped, clear 9.50
Butter chip, round, amber.......... 9.00
Butter chip, round, clear 5.00
Butter chip, square, amber........ 22.00
Butter dish, cov., scalloped base,
   blue 60.00
Butter dish, cov., square, clear 40.00
Butter dish, cov., square, vaseline .. 80.00
Butter dish, cov., model of Victorian
   stove, blue 52.50
Butter tub, cov., 2-handled,
   vaseline...................... 55.00
Canoe, amber, 8" l. 40.00
Canoe, Amberina, 8" l. 495.00
Canoe, apple green, 8" l. 35.00
Canoe, clear, 8" l. 25.00
Canoe, vaseline, 8" l. 90.00
Canoe, canary yellow, 12" l. 50.00
Canoe, clear w/ruby-stained but-
   tons, 12" l. 55.00
Canoe, amber, 13" l. 60.00
Castor set, 3-bottle, clear, in glass
   frame w/toothpick holder at top.. 50.00
Castor shaker bottle w/original top,
   amber 18.00
Celery vase, triangular, green...... 35.00
Cheese dish, cov., clear 52.00
Cologne bottle w/original stopper,
   clear 22.50
Compote, open, 8½" d., 7¾" h.,
   canary yellow................. 75.00
Compote, open, 8½" d., scalloped
   rim, clear 40.00
Compote, open, 9" d., scalloped
   rim, petticoat base, clear 65.00
Creamer, amber 25.50
Creamer, clear................... 20.00
Goblet, amber 30.00
Goblet, blue.................... 32.50
Goblet, clear 19.00
Hat shape, amber, 2½" h. 30.00
Hat shape, apple green, 2½" h. 35.00
Hat shape, blue, 2½" h. 28.00
Hat shape, clear, 2½" h. 20.00
Hat shape, vaseline, 2½" h. 35.00
Hat shape, blue, from tumbler mold,
   4¾" widest d. 40.00
Hat shape, canary yellow, from
   tumbler mold, 5" widest d.,
   3¾" h. 48.00
Humidor, cov., amber 185.00
Match holder, cauldron w/original
   bail handle, amber 29.50
Match holder, wall-hanging scuff,
   amber, 4½" l. 30.00
Match holder, wall-hanging scuff,
   clear......................... 18.00

Pickle castor, sapphire blue insert,
w/silverplate frame & tongs...... 250.00
Pitcher, water, bulbous, applied
handle, clear 55.00
Plate, 7" sq., amber.........14.50 to 22.50
Plate, 7" sq., clear 13.50
Plate, 10" d., scalloped rim,
amber 28.00
Plate, 10" d., blue.............. 35.00
Platter, 13 x 9" oval, open handles,
amber 37.50
Platter, 13 x 9" oval, open handles,
blue 39.50
Relish, "Sitz bathtub," amber 140.00
Relish, "Sitz bathtub," clear 65.00
Salt dip, master size, blue, 3½" d... 12.50
Salt dip, master size, vaseline,
3½" d........................ 23.00
Salt & pepper shakers w/original
tops, clear, pr................ 20.00
Sauce dish, amber, 4" to
5" sq.....................12.50 to 30.00
Sauce dish, blue, 4" to
5" sq.....................13.50 to 32.00
Sauce dish, clear, 4" to
5" sq......................9.00 to 12.00
Sauce dish, cloverleaf-shaped,
amber 14.50
Sauce dish, octagonal, vaseline..... 38.00
Sauce dish, tricornered, clear 16.00
Slipper, "1886 patent," clear 45.00
Smoke bell, amber 65.00
Spooner, amber.............30.00 to 40.00
Spooner, blue.................... 40.00
Spooner, clear.................. 30.00
Spooner, hat-shaped, amber 32.00
Sugar bowl, cov., amber 40.00
Sugar bowl, cov., barrel-shaped,
blue 45.00
Sugar bowl, open, purple 55.00
Toothpick holder (or salt dip),
"Bandmaster's cap," blue 35.00

Bandmaster's Hat Toothpick

Toothpick holder (or salt dip),
"Bandmaster's cap," vaseline
(ILLUS.)....................... 45.00
Toothpick holder, 3-footed, amber
or electric blue 35.00
Toothpick holder, 3-footed,
Amberina 175.00

Toothpick holder, 3-footed,
vaseline 39.50
Toothpick holder, urn-shaped,
clear 28.00
Toothpick holder, amber, w/brass
rim & base 20.00
Toothpick holder, blue, w/brass rim
& base 20.00
Tumbler, water, blue 28.00
Tumbler, water, clear 17.00
Tumbler, water, clear w/ruby-
stained buttons 35.00
Tumbler, water, vaseline 22.50
Vase, 6" h., hand holding cornu-
copia, blue 50.00
Vase, 6" h., hand holding cornu-
copia, clear w/ruby-stained
buttons...................... 58.50
Waste bowl, clear 30.00
Water set: bulbous pitcher & 2
tumblers; clear, 3 pcs............ 185.00
Whimsey, sleigh, amber,
7¾ x 4½"..................... 115.00
Whimsey, "whisk broom" dish,
amber 37.50
Whimsey, "whisk broom" dish,
vaseline 32.50
Wine, vaseline 45.00

DAISY & BUTTON WITH CROSSBARS (Mikado)

Daisy & Button with Crossbars Tray

Berry set: master bowl & 4 sauce
dishes; blue, 5 pcs.............. 85.00
Bread tray, blue, 12 x 9" (ILLUS.) ... 42.00
Bread tray, clear 25.00
Butter dish, cov., clear 45.00
Cake stand, blue 85.00
Cake stand, clear 55.00
Celery vase, amber 39.00
Celery vase, blue 40.00
Celery vase, clear 27.00
Celery vase, vaseline 50.00
Compote, open, 7" d., 4" h.,
amber 26.50
Compote, open, 8½" d., 7½" h.,
amber 45.00
Compote, open, 8½" d., 7½" h.,
blue 45.00

Compote, open, 8½" d., 7½" h., clear	32.50
Compote, open, 9½" d., clear	35.00
Compote, open, 10" d., amber	60.00
Creamer, amber	37.00 to 45.00
Creamer, blue	45.00
Creamer, clear	25.00 to 35.00
Creamer, individual size, amber	23.50
Creamer, individual size, blue	30.00
Creamer, individual size, clear	15.00
Creamer & open sugar bowl, amber, pr.	70.00
Cruet w/original stopper, amber	110.00 to 125.00
Cruet w/original stopper, clear	35.00
Cruet w/original stopper, vaseline	125.00
Finger bowl, blue	25.00
Goblet, amber	35.00
Goblet, blue	38.00
Goblet, clear	25.00
Goblet, vaseline	45.00
Mug, amber, 3" h.	18.00
Mug, canary yellow, 3" h.	22.50
Mug, clear, 3" h.	12.50
Pitcher, milk, amber	48.00
Pitcher, milk, clear	50.00
Pitcher, water, amber	82.50
Pitcher, water, blue	90.00
Pitcher, water, clear	65.00
Relish, blue, 8 x 4½"	20.00
Sauce dish, flat or footed, amber	12.00 to 15.00
Sauce dish, flat or footed, canary yellow	14.50
Sauce dish, flat or footed, vaseline	22.00
Spooner, amber	50.00
Spooner, blue	55.00
Spooner, clear	23.50
Sugar bowl, cov., blue	55.00
Sugar bowl, cov., clear	25.00
Toothpick holder, clear	28.00
Tumbler, amber	22.00
Tumbler, blue	30.00
Tumbler, clear	17.50
Tumbler, vaseline	25.00
Vase, vaseline	45.00
Waste bowl, canary yellow	22.50
Water set: pitcher & 8 tumblers; amber, 9 pcs.	185.00
Wine, clear	30.00

DAISY & BUTTON WITH NARCISSUS

Bowl, 9½ x 6" oval, footed	38.00 to 45.00
Butter dish, cov.	50.00
Creamer	45.00
Decanter, no stopper	65.00
Goblet	18.00 to 22.50
Nappy, leaf-shaped	65.00
Pitcher, water (ILLUS.)	70.00
Sauce dish, flat or 3-footed	8.00 to 15.00
Spooner	30.00
Sugar bowl, cov.	42.00
Tray, 10½" d.	25.00 to 35.00

Daisy & Button with Narcissus Pitcher

Tumbler	18.00
Wine	20.00

DAISY & BUTTON WITH THUMBPRINT PANELS

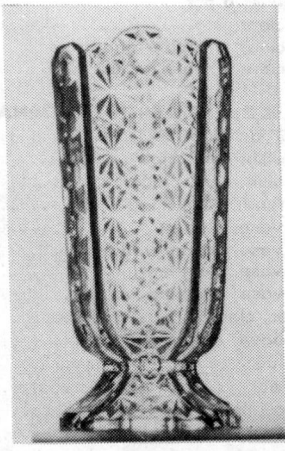

Daisy & Button with Thumbprint Panels

Bowl, 8" sq., clear	25.00
Bowl, 11" d., collared base, clear w/amber panels	51.50
Butter dish, cov., clear	78.00
Cake basket, clear w/amber panels, 11 x 7", 5½" h.	125.00 to 165.00
Cake stand, clear, 9½" d.	48.00
Celery vase, clear	30.00
Celery vase, clear w/amber panels (ILLUS.)	78.00
Champagne, clear w/amber panels	25.00
Compote, cov., 6¾" d., 10½" h., clear	62.50
Creamer, footed, clear	20.00
Cruet w/original stopper, clear	28.00
Dish, triangular, clear, 5" w., 2" h.	10.00

Finger bowl, clear 22.50
Goblet, clear 27.50
Goblet, clear w/amber panels 65.00
Goblet, clear w/blue panels 45.00
Pitcher, water, applied handle, clear
    w/amber panels 160.00
Pitcher, water, applied handle, clear
    w/blue panels 65.00
Sauce dish, flat or footed, clear,
    5" sq. . . . . .5.00 to 12.50
Sauce dish, flat or footed, clear
    w/amber panels, 5" sq. . . . .15.00 to 30.00
Salt shaker w/original top, clear
    w/amber panels (single) 85.00
Spooner, clear w/amber panels 55.00
Spooner, vaseline 48.00
Sugar bowl, open, clear w/amber
    panels 36.00
Syrup jug w/original top, clear
    w/amber panels 125.00
Tumbler, amber 22.50
Tumbler, blue 25.00
Tumbler, clear 20.00
Water set: pitcher & 5 tumblers;
    vaseline, 6 pcs. 295.00
Wine, clear 18.50
Wine, clear w/amber panels 33.50
Wine, clear w/blue panels 40.00

DAISY & BUTTON WITH "V" ORNAMENT

Bowl, 9" d., clear 45.00
Butter dish, cov., blue 80.00
Butter dish, cov., clear 45.00
Cake stand, blue, 9" d. 75.00
Celery vase, amber 45.00
Celery vase, canary yellow 65.00
Celery vase, clear 26.50
Celery vase, vaseline 60.00
Creamer, clear 30.00
Finger bowl, blue 45.00
Mug, blue 22.50
Mug, clear 15.00
Mug, vaseline 25.00
Mug, miniature, vaseline 26.00
Pitcher, water, amber 90.00
Pitcher, water, blue 90.00
Pitcher, water, clear 48.00
Sauce dish, amber 17.50
Sauce dish, blue 15.00
Sauce dish, clear 10.00
Spooner, clear 20.00
Sugar bowl, cov., blue 49.00
Sugar bowl, open, vaseline 30.00
Toothpick holder, amber 25.00
Toothpick holder, blue 28.00
Toothpick holder, clear 25.00
Toothpick holder, vaseline 35.00
Tumbler, amber 25.00
Tumbler, clear 15.00
Waste bowl, amber 28.50
Waste bowl, clear 22.50
Waste bowl, vaseline 28.00

DAISY IN PANEL - See Two Panel Pattern

DAKOTA (Baby Thumbprint)

Dakota Creamer

(Items may be plain or with etched designs)

Basket, 10" l., 2" h. 165.00
Butter dish, cov. 55.00
Cake stand, 8" d. . . . . .30.00 to 55.00
Cake stand, 9¼" d. 48.00
Cake stand, 10¼" d. . . . . .45.00 to 55.00
Celery vase, flat base 37.50
Celery vase, pedestal base 45.00
Compote, cov., jelly, 5" d., 5" h. . . . 55.00
Compote, cov., 6" d., high stand . . . 65.00
Compote, cov., 7" d., 11" h. 55.00
Compote, cov., 8" d., 12" h. 72.50
Compote, open, jelly, 5" d., 5" h. . . . 35.00
Compote, open, 6" d. . . . . .30.00 to 40.00
Compote, open, 7" d. 42.50
Compote, open, 8" d., low
    stand .32.50 to 38.00
Compote, open, 8" d., 9" h. . .55.00 to 70.00
Compote, open, 10" d. 75.00
Creamer (ILLUS.) . . . . .37.00 to 55.00
Cruet w/original stopper . . . . .50.00 to 75.00
Finger bowl 45.00
Goblet .25.00 to 30.00
Goblet, ruby-stained 47.50
Lamp, kerosene-type 140.00
Mug, ruby-stained, 3½" h. 35.00
Pitcher, water 75.00
Pitcher, water, ruby-
    stained . . . . .125.00 to 190.00
Plate, 10" d. 85.00
Salt & pepper shakers w/original
    tops, pr. 90.00
Sauce dish, flat or footed . . . .12.00 to 24.00
Sauce dish, flat or footed, ruby-
    stained 22.50
Shaker bottle w/original top,
    5" h. 35.00
Shaker bottle w/original top, hotel
    size, 6½" h. 65.00
Spooner 33.50
Sugar bowl, cov. 55.00
Sugar bowl, open 25.00
Tray, water, piecrust rim, 13" d. 75.00

Tumbler 40.00
Tumbler, ruby-stained 45.00
Waste bowl 50.00
Wine 25.00
Wine, ruby-stained ....35.00 to 45.00

DARBY - See Pleat & Panel Pattern

DART

Dart Creamer

Compote, cov., 8½" d., high
  stand 35.00
Compote, open, jelly 17.00
Creamer (ILLUS.) 27.50
Goblet 24.00
Sauce dish, footed 8.50
Spooner 20.00
Sugar bowl, cov. 32.50

DEER & DOG

Deer & Dog Water Pitcher

(Each piece etched w/scene of deer, dog & hunter)

Butter dish, cov., pedestal base &
  frosted dog finial 130.00

Celery vase, scalloped rim, signed
  "Gillinder" 95.00
Compote, cov., 8" oval, 8¾" h.,
  frosted dog finial 135.00
Compote, open, 8" d. 90.00
Cordial 95.00
Creamer 75.00
Goblet, straight sides 57.50
Goblet, U-shaped 80.00
Marmalade jar, cov. 65.00
Pitcher, milk, 9" h. 165.00
Pitcher, water, applied reeded
  handle (ILLUS.) 195.00
Sauce dish, footed 20.00
Spoooner 52.50
Sugar bowl, cov., frosted dog
  finial 110.00
Wine ....60.00 to 85.00

DEER & PINE TREE

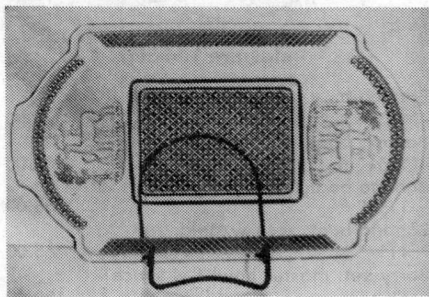

Deer & Pine Tree Bread Tray

Bread tray, amber, 13 x 8" 80.00
Bread tray, apple green, 13 x 8" 78.00
Bread tray, blue, 13 x 8" .....58.00 to 75.00
Bread tray, clear, 13 x 8" (ILLUS.) ... 42.50
Bread tray, vaseline, 13 x 8" 80.00
Butter dish, cov., clear 65.00
Cake stand, clear 77.50
Celery vase, clear 52.50
Compote, cov., 8" sq., 6" h., clear .. 68.00
Compote, cov., 8" sq., 12" h.,
  clear 80.00
Compote, open, 8" sq., high stand,
  clear 48.00
Creamer, clear 65.00
Finger bowl, clear 55.00
Goblet, clear 40.00
Mug, child's, amber 45.00
Mug, child's, vaseline 55.00
Mug, large, apple green 65.00
Mug, large, clear 40.00
Pitcher, milk, clear 70.00
Pitcher, water, clear ....85.00 to 95.00
Sauce dish, flat or footed,
  clear ....15.00 to 25.00
Spooner, clear 35.00
Sugar bowl, cov., clear 50.00
Tray, water, handled, amber,
  15 x 9" 68.00

Tray, water, handled, apple green,
15 x 9" 68.00
Tray, water, handled, clear,
15 x 9" 55.00

DELAWARE (Four Petal Flower)

Delaware Tumbler

Banana boat, amethyst w/gold,
11¾" l. 125.00
Banana boat, clear w/gold,
11¾" l. 50.00
Banana boat, green w/gold,
11¾" l. 55.00
Banana boat, rose w/gold,
11¾" l. 65.00
Berry set: master bowl & 4 sauce
dishes; green w/gold, 5 pcs. 120.00
Berry set: master bowl & 4 sauce
dishes; rose w/gold, 5 pcs. 175.00
Bowl, 8" d., green w/gold 32.50
Bowl, 8" d., rose w/gold 46.50
Bowl, 9" d., green w/gold 52.50
Bowl, 9" d., rose w/gold 75.00
Bowl, 10" octagon, green w/gold ... 57.50
Bride's basket, boat-shaped open
bowl, rose w/gold, w/silverplate
frame, 11½" oval 135.00
Bride's basket, boat-shaped open
bowl, green w/gold, miniature ... 175.00
Butter dish, cov., clear 60.00
Butter dish, cov., green w/gold..... 105.00
Butter dish, cov., rose w/gold 140.00
Celery vase, clear w/gold.......... 37.00
Celery vase, green w/gold 65.00
Celery vase, rose w/gold 72.50
Claret jug, green w/gold 175.00
Creamer, clear w/gold 37.50
Creamer, green w/gold 52.50
Creamer, rose w/gold 65.00
Creamer, individual size, clear
w/gold 25.00
Creamer & open sugar bowl, rose
w/gold, pr....................... 95.00
Creamer & sugar bowl, breakfast
size, rose w/gold, pr. 125.00
Cruet w/original stopper, clear 87.50
Dresser tray, clear 30.00

Dresser tray, rose w/gold 65.00
Marmalade dish w/silverplate
holder, green w/gold 38.50
Marmalade dish w/silverplate
holder, rose w/gold 95.00
Pin tray, clear, 7 x 3½" 15.00
Pin tray, green w/gold 55.00
Pin tray, rose w/gold 65.00
Pitcher, milk, green w/gold ..60.00 to 85.00
Pitcher, tankard, clear w/cranberry
& green florals & gold trim 125.00
Pitcher, tankard, green w/gold 85.00
Pitcher, tankard, rose w/gold 150.00
Pitcher, water, bulbous, rose
w/gold 125.00
Pomade jar w/jeweled cover, rose
w/gold 215.00
Punch cup, clear 15.00
Punch cup, green w/gold 25.00
Punch cup, rose w/gold........... 28.50
Salt shaker w/original top, rose
w/gold (single) 45.00
Sauce dish, boat-shaped, green
w/gold 25.00
Sauce dish, boat-shaped, rose
w/gold 38.50
Sauce dish, round, green w/gold ... 24.00
Sauce dish, round, rose w/gold..... 25.00
Spooner, clear w/gold 35.00
Spooner, green w/gold 40.00
Spooner, rose w/gold 57.50
Sugar bowl, cov., clear 65.00
Sugar bowl, cov., green w/gold 130.00
Sugar bowl, cov., rose w/gold...... 100.00
Sugar bowl, individual size, green .. 55.00
Table set: cov. butter dish, cov.
sugar bowl & spooner; rose
w/gold, 3 pcs. 365.00
Table set, green w/gold,
4 pcs. 395.00
Table set, rose w/gold, 4 pcs. 500.00
Toothpich holder, clear 30.00
Toothpick holder, clear w/rose-
stained florals & gold 65.00
Toothpick holder, green w/gold 77.50
Toothpick holder, rose w/gold...... 95.00
Tumbler, clear w/rose-stained
florals 32.50
Tumbler, custard w/stained florals
(ILLUS.)........................ 45.00
Tumbler, green w/gold 45.00
Tumbler, rose w/gold 40.00
Vase, 6" h., green w/gold 39.50
Vase, 6" h., rose w/gold........... 70.00
Vase, 8" h., green w/gold 115.00
Vase, 9½" h., rose w/gold......... 125.00
Water set: pitcher & 6 tumblers;
green w/gold, 7 pcs. 260.00
Water set: pitcher & 6 tumblers;
rose w/gold, 7 pcs. .....295.00 to 310.00

DEW & RAINDROP
Berry set, master bowl & 6 sauce
dishes, 7 pcs. 80.00

Bowl, 6½" d.	28.00
Bowl, berry, 8" d.	38.00
Butter dish, cov.	50.00
Compote, open, jelly	35.00
Cordial	14.50
Creamer	32.50
Goblet	30.00
Pitcher, water	40.00 to 55.00

Dew & Raindrop Punch Cup

Punch cup (ILLUS.)	9.00
Salt & pepper shakers w/original tops, pr.	40.00
Sauce dish, flat or footed	10.00 to 12.00
Spooner	35.00
Sugar bowl, cov.	50.00
Tumbler	15.00 to 22.00
Vase, bud, 6" h.	20.00
Wine	19.00

DEWDROP

Butter dish, cov., clear	30.00
Cake stand, clear, 8½" d.	20.00
Cordial, clear	40.00
Creamer, clear	25.00
Egg cup, double, clear	20.00
Goblet, clear	20.00
Mug, applied handle, clear	27.50
Relish, clear	15.00
Sauce dish, clear	7.00
Spooner, clear	25.00
Sugar bowl, open, clear	50.00
Tumbler, blue	27.50
Tumbler, clear	14.50
Wine, clear	25.00

DEWDROP WITH STAR

Bowl, 7" d.	14.00
Bowl, 9" d., footed	15.00
Butter dish, cov.	45.00
Cake stand, 9" d.	45.00
Celery vase	40.00
Cheese dish, cov.	95.00
Compote, cov., 5" d.	60.00
Compote, open,, 9" d., 9" h.	45.00
Creamer, applied handle	25.00
Pitcher, water, 8" h.	95.00
Plate, 5" d.	12.00
Plate, 7" to 8" d.	12.50
Relish, 9" l.	15.00
Sauce dish, flat (ILLUS.)	10.00

Dewdrop with Star Sauce Dish

Sugar bowl, cov.	50.00

DEWEY (Flower Flange)

(Also see Chocolate Glass)

Bowl, 8" d., amber	30.00
Bowl, 8" d., green	45.00
Bowl, 8" d., yellow	45.00
Butter dish, cov., amber	65.00
Butter dish, cov., clear	55.00
Butter dish, cov., green	75.00
Butter dish, cov., yellow	95.00
Butter dish, cov., amber, miniature	60.00 to 75.00
Creamer, amber	35.00
Creamer, clear	30.00
Creamer, green	45.00
Creamer, yellow	55.00
Cruet w/original stopper, amber	120.00
Cruet w/original stopper, clear	95.00
Cruet w/original stopper, green	185.00
Cruet w/original stopper, Nile green	750.00

Dewey Cruet

Cruet w/original stopper, yellow
(ILLUS.)......................... 125.00
Mug, amber 65.00
Mug, clear....................... 25.00
Mug, green 42.50
Mug, yellow 55.00
Parfait, green................... 33.50
Parfait, yellow 50.00
Pitcher, water, amber............ 95.00
Pitcher, water, clear............. 67.50
Plate, footed, amber 42.00
Plate, footed, clear............. 15.00
Plate, footed, green 45.00
Plate, footed, yellow 55.00
Relish, serpentine shape, amber,
small 30.00
Relish, serpentine shape, clear,
small 20.00
Relish, serpentine shape, green,
small 33.50
Relish, serpentine shape, yellow,
small 45.00
Relish, serpentine shape, amber,
large......................... 56.00
Relish, serpentine shape, yellow,
large......................... 55.00
Salt shaker w/original top, green
(single)...................... 55.00
Sauce dish, amber 20.00
Sauce dish, green 25.00
Sauce dish, yellow 25.00
Spooner, amber.................. 60.00
Spooner, green 35.00
Sugar bowl, cov., clear 25.00
Sugar bowl, cov., green 45.00
Sugar bowl, cov., yellow.......... 80.00
Sugar bowl, cov., individual size,
amber 45.00
Sugar bowl, cov., individual size,
clear......................... 32.50
Sugar bowl, cov., individual size,
green 45.00
Sugar bowl, cov., individual size,
yellow 65.00
Tumbler, clear 50.00
Tumbler, green 45.00
Tumbler, yellow................. 55.00
Water set: pitcher & 6 tumblers;
clear, 7 pcs. 250.00

DIAGONAL BAND

Berry set, master bowl & 5 sauce
dishes, 6 pcs. 48.00
Bread plate, "Eureka," clear,
13 x 7½"..................... 40.00
Butter dish, cov. 35.00
Cake stand 30.00
Celery vase..................... 22.50
Compote, cov., 7½" d., 9¼" h...... 45.00
Compote, open, 7½" d., high
stand 16.50
Creamer 22.50
Goblet (ILLUS.)................. 18.00
Pitcher, milk 32.00

Diagonal Band Goblet

Pitcher, water 37.50
Plate, 8" d....................... 10.50
Relish, 6 7/8" oval 7.50
Salt dip, footed 25.00
Salt & pepper shakers w/original
tops, pr....................... 30.00
Sauce dish, flat or footed .....5.50 to 9.00
Spooner........................ 22.50
Sugar bowl, open 15.00
Wine........................... 22.50

DIAGONAL BAND & FAN

Diagonal Band & Fan Relish

Butter dish, cov. 40.00
Goblet 20.00
Plate, 6" d....................... 6.00
Plate, 8" d....................... 13.50
Relish, 8" oval (ILLUS.)............ 15.00
Sauce dish, footed 13.50
Spooner........................ 22.50
Wine........................... 17.50

**DIAMOND & BULL'S EYE BAND - See
Reverse Torpedo Pattern**

DIAMOND & SUNBURST

Celery vase...................... 35.00
Compote, cov., 7" d., high
stand 45.00
Compote, open, jelly 15.00
Goblet (ILLUS.).................. 22.00
Salt dip, master size 20.00
Spooner........................ 21.50
Sugar bowl, open 25.00

Diamond & Sunburst Goblet

Sugar shaker	22.00
Syrup jug w/original top, applied handle	45.00
Tumbler	25.00
Wine.............................	20.00

DIAMOND BAR - See Lattice Pattern

DIAMOND HORSESHOE - See Aurora Pattern

DIAMOND MEDALLION (Finecut & Diamond or Grand)

Diamond Medallion Creamer

Bread plate, 10" d.	21.50
Butter dish, cov.	35.00
Cake stand, 9" d.	28.00
Cake stand, 10" d.	30.00
Celery vase.......................	27.50
Compote, cov., 7" d., high stand	36.00
Compote, open, 6" d., 6" h.	19.50
Compote, open, 7" d., high stand	22.50

Creamer, footed (ILLUS.)	22.50
Goblet	22.50
Pitcher, water	45.00
Relish, 7½" oval	12.00
Salt & pepper shakers w/original tops, pr.....................	35.00
Sauce dish, flat or footed .....6.00 to	9.00
Spooner	22.50
Sugar bowl, cov.	35.00
Sugar bowl, open	15.00
Wine...........................	28.00

DIAMOND POINT

Diamond Point Creamer

Bar bottle, flint	55.00
Bowl, 6" d. ....20.00 to	25.00
Butter dish, cov., flint	95.00
Castor set, 6-bottle, w/silverplate frame	165.00
Celery vase, pedestal base w/knob stem, flint	70.00
Champagne, flint..................	92.50
Claret, flint	130.00
Compote, open, 7" d., 7" h., non-flint	37.50
Compote, open, 7½" d., low stand, non-flint......................	25.00
Creamer, applied handle, flint (ILLUS.)......................	130.00
Creamer & cov. sugar bowl w/applied handle, flint, pr.	180.00
Decanter w/original stopper, qt.....	87.50
Egg cup, canary yellow, flint	210.00
Egg cup, clambroth, flint	115.00
Egg cup, clear, flint	40.00
Goblet, flint	55.00
Goblet, non-flint	20.00
Honey dish, flint	16.50
Pitcher, tankard, applied handle, flint, qt.	180.00
Plate, 6" d., non-flint	13.50
Salt dip, cov., master size.........	27.50
Sauce dish, 3½" to 5½" d.....6.00 to	12.50
Spillholder, flint.................	47.50
Spooner, flint............40.00 to	55.00
Spooner, non-flint	22.50

Sugar bowl, cov., flint 90.00
Tumbler, flint 47.50
Tumbler, bar, flint 65.00
Tumbler, whiskey, handled, flint,
   3" h. 65.00
Wine, flint 52.50
Wine, non-flint 13.50

DIAMOND POINT WITH PANELS - See Hinoto Pattern

DIAMOND QUILTED

Diamond Quilted Champagne

Bowl, 6" d., amber 10.00
Bowl, 6" d., footed, amethyst 20 00
Bowl, 7" d., amber 19.00
Bowl, 9" d., amber 50.00
Butter dish, cov., amber . . . . . 42.00 to 50.00
Butter dish, cov., vaseline 85.00
Celery vase, amber 40.00
Champagne, clear 21.50
Champagne, turquoise blue
   (ILLUS.) 30.00
Compote, cov., 8" d., 13" h.,
   amber 115.00
Compote, cov., 8" d., 13" h.,
   clear 75.00
Compote, open, 6" d., 6" h.,
   amber 35.00
Compote, open, 8" d., low stand,
   vaseline 52.00
Creamer, amethyst 40.00
Goblet, amber 26.50
Goblet, amethyst 35.00
Goblet, blue 35.00
Goblet, turquoise blue 40.00
Goblet, vaseline 40.00
Mug, amethyst 30.00
Pitcher, water, blue 80.00
Salt shaker w/original top, blue
   (single) 35.00
Sauce dish, flat or footed, amber . . . 10.00
Sauce dish, flat or footed,
   amethyst . . . . 11.00 to 20.00

Sauce dish, flat or footed, turquoise
   blue . . . . 9.50 to 15.00
Sauce dish, flat or footed,
   vaseline . . . . 11.00 to 20.00
Spooner, amber 30.00
Spooner, turquoise blue 40.00
Spooner, vaseline 30.00
Sugar bowl, cov., amber 45.00
Sugar bowl, cov., blue 47.50
Sugar bowl, cov., vaseline 45.00
Sugar bowl, open, turquoise blue . . . 30.00
Tumbler, juice, amber 20.00
Tumbler, amber 45.00
Tumbler, vaseline . . . . 25.00 to 35.00
Wine, amber 22.50
Wine, amethyst 48.00
Wine, blue 38.00
Wine, clear 15.00
Wine, vaseline 25.00

DIAMOND THUMBPRINT

Diamond Thumbprint Compote

Butter dish, cov. . . . . 140.00 to 200.00
Cake stand, 12" d. 195.00
Celery vase 168.00
Champagne 350.00
Compote, open, 7" d., 4½" h.,
   extended scalloped rim 65.00
Compote, open, 8" d., 6" h. 75.00
Compote, open, 9" d., low stand . . . 90.00
Compote, open, 10½" d., 7½" h.
   (ILLUS.) 285.00
Creamer, applied handle 215.00
Cup plate 50.00
Goblet 325.00
Lamp, whale oil, original burner,
   brass stem, marble base 265.00
Pitcher, water 425.00
Punch bowl, scalloped rim, pedestal
   base, 11½" d., 9 1/8" h. 425.00
Spillholder, clear 40.00
Spillholder, vaseline 875.00
Spooner 85.00
Sugar bowl, cov. 125.00
Tumbler 95.00
Tumbler, bar, 3¾" h. 75.00
Tumbler, whiskey, handled 300.00
Wine 245.00

DINNER BELL - See Cottage Pattern

DORIC - See Indiana Pattern

DOUBLE LEAF & DART - See Leaf & Dart Pattern

DOUBLE LOOP - See Ribbon Candy Pattern

DOUBLE WEDDING RING

Double Wedding Ring Footed Tumbler

Champagne	52.50
Goblet	32.50
Lamp, kerosene, hand-type w/flat base, applied handle	80.00
Tumbler, bar	90.00
Tumbler, footed (ILLUS.)	80.00

DRAPERY

Drapery Spooner

Butter dish, cov.	40.00
Cake plate, sq., footed	40.00 to 45.00
Creamer, applied handle	32.50
Egg cup	19.50
Goblet	26.50
Goblet, buttermilk	20.00
Pitcher, water, applied handle	75.00
Plate, 6" d.	19.00
Sauce dish, flat	10.00
Spooner (ILLUS.)	28.50
Sugar bowl, cov.	40.00

Sugar bowl, open	25.00
Tumbler	27.00

EGG IN SAND

Egg in Sand Goblet

Bread tray, handled, clear	32.50
Butter dish, cov., clear	48.00
Creamer, clear	25.00
Goblet, amber	45.00
Goblet, blue	40.00
Goblet, clear (ILLUS.)	28.00
Pitcher, milk, clear	45.00
Pitcher, water, amber	70.00
Pitcher, water, clear	50.00
Relish, clear, 9 x 5½"	17.00
Sauce dish, clear	12.00
Spooner, amber	47.50
Spooner, clear	22.50
Sugar bowl, cov., clear	37.50
Tray, water, clear, 12½" oblong	38.50
Tumbler, clear	36.00

EGYPTIAN

Egyptian Pickle Dish

Berry set, master bowl & 5 sauce dishes, 6 pcs.	150.00
Bowl, 8½" d.	48.00
Bread platter, Cleopatra center, 12 x 9"	50.00
Bread platter, Salt Lake Temple center	295.00
Butter dish, cov.	67.50
Celery vase	62.50
Compote, cov., 6" d., 6" h., sphinx base	135.00

Compote, cov., 7" d., 12" h., sphinx
  base 180.00
Compote, cov., 8" d., high stand,
  sphinx base 210.00
Compote, open, 6" d., low stand ...   50.00
Compote, open, 7½" d., sphinx
  base 62.50
Creamer 40.00
Goblet ....40.00 to 50.00
Pickle dish (ILLUS.) 20.00
Pitcher, water ....135.00 to 180.00
Plate, 10" d. 46.50
Plate, 12" d. 75.00
Relish, 8½ x 5½" 22.50
Sauce dish, flat or
  footed ....9.00 to 16.50
Spooner 38.50
Sugar bowl, cov. 67.50
Sugar bowl, open 25.00
Table set, 4 pcs. 225.00

**EMERALD GREEN HERRINGBONE - See
Paneled Herringbone Pattern**

EMPIRE COLONIAL - See Colonial Pattern

**ENGLISH HOBNAIL CROSS - See Amberette
Pattern**

ESTHER

Esther Sauce Dish

(Items may be plain or with etched designs)

Berry set: master bowl & 8 sauce
  dishes; green, 9 pcs. 245.00
Butter dish, cov., clear 70.00
Butter dish, cov., clear w/amber
  stain 110.00
Butter dish, cov., green 135.00
Celery vase, clear 70.00
Celery vase, green 135.00
Compote, cov., high stand, clear ... 80.00
Compote, open, 5" d., 6½" h.,
  clear 65.00
Compote, open, 5" d., 6½" h.,
  green 62.50
Cookie jar, cov., clear w/amber
  stain 225.00
Creamer, clear.................... 70.00
Creamer, green 135.00
Cruet w/ball-shaped stopper,
  green 190.00

Cruet w/original stopper, clear,
  miniature...................... 28.00
Cruet w/original stopper, green,
  miniature...................... 95.00
Goblet, clear 50.00
Goblet, green.................... 90.00
Pitcher, water, clear w/amber
  stain 250.00
Pitcher, water, green 140.00
Plate, 12" d., footed, scalloped rim,
  clear 65.00
Salt & pepper shakers w/original
  tops, green, pr. 98.00
Sauce dish, clear (ILLUS.) 18.50
Spooner, clear 45.00
Spooner, green 55.00
Sugar bowl, cov., clear 40.00
Sugar bowl, cov., clear w/amber
  stain & etching 80.00
Sugar bowl, cov., green 60.00
Sugar bowl, open, clear 20.00
Syrup jug w/original spring lid,
  clear w/amber stain & etching ... 360.00
Table set, green, 4 pcs............ 325.00
Toothpick holder, clear 40.00
Toothpick holder, clear w/amber
  stain & etching 72.50
Toothpick holder, green 82.50
Tray, ice cream, green 150.00
Tumbler, clear 32.50
Tumbler, green 50.00
Wine, clear 28.50

EUREKA
Bowl, 9½" d. 30.00
Bread tray....................... 32.50
Compote, open, jelly 55.00
Compote, open, jelly, ruby-stained.. 75.00
Creamer 45.00
Creamer, ruby-stained 65.00
Egg cup 15.00
Goblet 25.00
Salt dip, master size............. 24.50
Spooner 40.00
Sugar bowl, cov. 55.00
Sugar bowl, open 25.00
Toothpick holder 35.00
Tumbler, footed 25.00
Wine............................. 25.00

EXCELSIOR
Bar bottle, pt. ....35.00 to 50.00
Butter dish, cov. 100.00
Cake stand, flint, 9¼" h. 175.00
Candlestick, flint (single).......... 96.00
Celery vase...................... 80.00
Cordial 35.00
Creamer 55.00
Egg cup 22.50
Egg cup, double.................. 45.00
Egg cup, double, opalescent, flint... 225.00
Flip glass, 8" h. (ILLUS.)......... 200.00
Goblet, "Barrel".................. 42.50
Goblet, flint 50.00

Excelsior Flip

Lamp, kerosene, hand-type, applied
   finger loop handle 95.00
Pitcher, water, flint 325.00
Salt dip, master size.............. 18.50
Spillholder, flint 75.00
Sugar bowl, cov. 75.00
Syrup pitcher, applied handle 110.00
Syrup pitcher w/original top,
   green 750.00
Tumbler, bar, flint, 3½" h.......... 52.50
Tumbler, footed, flint 47.50
Wine, flint 40.00

EYEWINKER

Eyewinker Salt Shaker

Banana boat, flat, 8½" l. 85.00
Butter dish, cov. 70.00
Cake stand, 8½" to
   9½" d...................50.00 to 75.00
Celery vase, 6½" h................ 65.00
Compote, cov., 6½" d., 11" h...... 52.50
Compote, open, 4" d., 5" h........ 31.50
Compote, open, 6½" sq., 8½" h..... 70.00
Compote, open, 7½" d., 4½" h..... 40.00
Compote, open, 9½" d., 6½" h..... 90.00
Creamer 42.50
Creamer, miniature 50.00
Lamp, kerosene-type, 8" h. (no
   burner) ....95.00 to 125.00

Pitcher, milk..................... 85.00
Plate, 7" d., 1½" h., turned-up
   sides......................... 27.50
Plate, 9" sq., 2" h., turned-up
   sides......................... 37.50
Salt shaker w/original top (ILLUS.) .. 22.50
Sauce dish, square 13.50
Spooner 35.00
Sugar bowl, cov. 60.00

FEATHER (Indiana Swirl or Finecut & Feather)

Feather Bowl

Banana boat, footed, clear 75.00
Bowl, 7" oval, clear ....15.00 to 25.00
Bowl, 7½" d., clear (ILLUS.) 22.00
Bowl, 8" d., clear 25.00
Bowl, 9¼" oval, flat, clear 17.50
Butter dish, cov., clear 52.50
Butter dish, cov., green............ 125.00
Cake stand, clear, 8" d. 33.50
Cake stand, clear, 9½" d. 40.00
Cake stand, clear, 11" d. 60.00
Celery vase, clear 35.00
Compote, cov., 7" d., 10½" h.,
   clear 85.00
Compote, cov., 8½" d., 12" h.,
   clear 125.00
Compote, open, jelly, 5" d.,
   clear ....18.00 to 23.50
Compote, open, 8" d., clear 40.00
Cordial, clear, 3" h. 70.00
Creamer, clear.................... 27.50
Creamer, green 65.00
Cruet w/original stopper, green 185.00
Cruet w/replaced stopper, clear 30.00
Goblet, clear 47.50
Goblet, clear w/amber staining 150.00
Honey dish, clear, 3½" d........... 15.00
Pitcher, milk, clear 46.50
Pitcher, water, clear ....45.00 to 58.00
Pitcher, water, green 190.00
Plate, 9¼" d., clear 30.00
Plate, 10" d., clear 32.50
Relish, clear, 8¼" oval 18.00

Salt shaker w/replaced top, green
(single)........................ 65.00
Salt & pepper shakers w/original
tops, clear, pr................... 37.50
Sauce dish, flat or footed,
clear ....10.00 to 15.00
Spooner, clear 25.00
Spooner, green 60.00
Sugar bowl, cov., clear 37.50
Sugar bowl, cov., green 80.00
Syrup pitcher w/original top, clear.. 100.00
Toothpick holder, clear 60.00
Toothpick holder, green 185.00
Tumbler, clear 40.00
Tumbler, green 75.00
Wine, clear 32.50

FESTOON

Festoon Cake Stand

Berry set, 9½" d. master bowl & 6
sauce dishes, 7 pcs. 70.00
Bowl, berry, 8" rectangle 25.00
Bowl, berry, 9 x 5½" rectangle 30.00
Butter dish, cov. 55.00
Cake stand, high pedestal, 9" d..... 32.50
Cake stand, high pedestal, 10" d.
(ILLUS.)......................... 45.00
Creamer 27.50
Finger bowl, 4½" d., 2" h. 30.00
Marmalade jar, cov. 28.00
Pickle castor, silverplate frame &
cover w/bird finial 85.00
Pitcher, water 75.00
Plate, 7½" d. 27.50
Plate, 9¼" d. 25.00
Relish, 7 x 4" 15.00
Sauce dish........................ 6.50
Spooner 32.50
Sugar bowl, cov. 45.00
Sugar bowl, open 15.00
Table set, 4 pcs. 185.00
Tray, water, 10" d. 32.50
Tumbler ....22.50 to 30.00
Water set, pitcher, tray & 4
tumblers, 6 pcs.................. 195.00
Water set, pitcher, tray & 5
tumblers, 7 pcs.................. 210.00

Water set, pitcher, tray & 6
tumblers, 8 pcs.................. 225.00

FINECUT

Finecut Salt & Pepper Shakers

Bowl, 8¼ x 5 1/8", flat, clear 12.00
Bread tray, amber................. 40.00
Butter dish, cov., clear 45.00
Cake stand, clear 30.00
Celery vase, footed, 2-handled,
clear 25.00
Celery vase, vaseline, ornate square
base silverplate holder 115.00
Compote, cov., 9¼" d., 7" h.,
amber 135.00
Creamer, blue 37.50
Creamer, clear 16.00
Cruet w/matching stopper, amber .. 165.00
Goblet, amber 45.00
Goblet, blue 55.00
Goblet, clear 20.00
Goblet, vaseline 42.00
Pickle dish, clear, 9 x 6" 12.00
Pitcher, water, amber 95.00
Pitcher, water, clear.............. 40.00
Plate, 6" d., blue................. 20.00
Plate, 6" d., clear................. 8.00
Plate, 7" d., amber............... 15.00
Plate, 7" d., clear 20.00
Plate, 7" d., vaseline 20.00
Plate, 10" d., blue................ 46.00
Relish, boat-shaped, amber 35.00
Salt & pepper shakers w/original
tops, clear, pr. (ILLUS.) 25.00
Sauce dish, clear w/vaseline base .. 7.00
Spooner, amber................... 35.00
Spooner, clear 17.00
Spooner, vaseline 38.00
Sugar bowl, cov., clear 35.00
Toothpick holder, hat shape on
plate, clear 26.00
Toothpick holder, hat shape on
plate, vaseline 30.00
Tray, ice cream, lion's head han-
dles, amber 40.00
Tray, water, clear 45.00
Tumbler, clear 13.50
Tumbler, vaseline 28.00

Waste bowl, vaseline	32.50
Whimsey, shoe on skate, amber	30.00
Whimsey, slipper, amber, 4" l.	30.00
Whimsey, slipper, blue, 4" l.	30.00
Whimsey, slipper, blue, 6" l.	30.00
Wine, clear	13.00

FINECUT & BLOCK

Finecut & Block Pitcher

Bowl, fruit, 9" d., collared base, clear	35.00
Butter dish, cov., 2-handled, clear ..	75.00
Cake stand, clear	35.00
Celery tray, clear, 11" l.	27.50
Celery tray, clear w/blue blocks, 11" l.	60.00
Celery tray, clear w/pink blocks, 11" l.	60.00
Compote, cov., low stand, clear	35.00
Compote, open, jelly, all blue	50.00
Compote, open, jelly, clear	18.00
Compote, open, jelly, clear w/amber blocks.................	75.00
Compote, open, jelly, clear w/blue blocks........................	50.00
Compote, open, 7¾" d., clear w/blue blocks	65.00
Compote, open, 8½" d., 6½" h., clear	32.50
Cordial, clear	85.00
Creamer, clear....................	32.00
Creamer, clear w/amber blocks	67.00
Creamer, clear w/blue blocks....................48.00 to 65.00	
Creamer, clear w/pink blocks	65.00
Creamer, clear w/yellow blocks	76.50
Egg cup, single, clear..............	30.00
Goblet, clear	37.50
Goblet, clear w/amber blocks	53.50
Goblet, clear w/blue blocks	65.00
Goblet, clear w/pink blocks	50.00
Goblet, buttermilk, clear ....25.00 to 35.00	
Goblet, buttermilk, clear w/blue blocks.........................	52.00

Goblet, buttermilk, clear w/pink blocks.........................	85.00
Goblet, buttermilk, clear w/yellow blocks.........................	60.00
Ice cream tray, clear w/amber blocks.........................	85.00
Ice cream tray, clear w/yellow blocks.........................	75.00
Pitcher, water, all amber (ILLUS.) ...	85.00
Pitcher, water, clear...............	42.50
Pitcher, water, clear w/amber blocks.........................	85.00
Pitcher, water, clear w/blue blocks.........................	90.00
Pitcher, water, clear w/pink blocks.........................	125.00
Pitcher, water, clear w/yellow blocks.........................	85.00
Plate, 5¾" d., clear	23.50
Punch cup, clear	12.00
Relish, handled, all blue, 7½"	27.50
Relish, handled, clear w/blue blocks, 7½"	50.00
Salt dip, clear w/blue blocks	20.00
Salt dip, clear w/pink blocks	20.00
Sauce dish, all amber	18.50
Sauce dish, clear	8.50
Sauce dish, clear w/amber blocks ..	20.00
Sauce dish, clear w/yellow blocks ..	17.50
Spooner, clear	30.00
Spooner, clear w/amber blocks.....	45.00
Spooner, clear w/blue blocks	55.00
Sugar bowl, cov., clear w/yellow blocks.........................	125.00
Tumbler, all blue.................	30.00
Tumbler, clear	17.50
Tumbler, clear w/blue blocks	42.00
Tumbler, clear w/yellow blocks	50.00
Waste bowl, all amber	45.00
Wine, clear	30.00
Wine, clear w/blue blocks	55.00

FINECUT & DIAMOND - See Diamond Medallion Pattern

FINECUT & FEATHER - See Feather Pattern

FINECUT & PANEL (Paneled Finecut)

Bowl, 8" oval, clear	18.00
Bread tray, amber, 13 x 9"........	50.00
Bread tray, blue, 13 x 9"..........	45.00
Bread tray, clear, 13 x 9"	30.00
Butter dish, cov., amber	65.00
Compote, open, high stand, amber	47.50
Compote, open, high stand, clear...	32.00
Creamer, amber	35.00
Goblet, amber	40.00
Goblet, clear	20.00
Goblet, clear w/amber bars..35.00 to 50.00	
Pitcher, milk, vaseline	50.00
Pitcher, water, amber	85.00
Plate, 6" d., amber...............	25.00
Plate, 6" d., blue.................	30.00

Finecut & Panel Plate

Plate, 6" d., vaseline (ILLUS.)	25.00
Plate, 7" d., clear	12.00
Relish, clear, 7 x 3½"	22.50
Salt shaker w/original top, clear (single)	10.00
Sauce dish, amber	11.00
Sauce dish, clear	8.00
Sauce dish, vaseline	12.50
Spooner, vaseline	30.00
Tray, water, blue	55.00
Tumbler, clear	18.00
Tumbler, vaseline	38.00
Wine, amber	32.50
Wine, blue	35.00
Wine, clear	17.50
Wine, vaseline	32.50
Wine set: decanter & 4 wines; vaseline, 5 pcs.	185.00

FINECUT BAND - See Cottage Pattern

FINE RIB

Butter dish, cov.	75.00
Castor set, complete w/frame	190.00
Celery vase, flint	42.00
Champagne, flint	62.50
Champagne, cut ovals, flint	85.00
Compote, open, 7¾" d., 7" h., flint	50.00
Compote, open, 10¼" d., 8¼" h., scalloped foot, flint	185.00
Cordial, flint	40.00
Creamer, flint, 6" h.	325.00
Decanter w/bar lip, qt.	95.00
Egg cup, flint	42.00
Egg cup, double, flint	35.00
Goblet, flint	75.00
Goblet, non-flint	35.00
Honey dish, flint, 3½" d.	14.00
Pitcher, water, bulbous, applied handle, flint	425.00
Salt dip, individual size, flint	13.50
Salt dip, master size, footed, scalloped rim, flint	38.00
Spoonholder, flint	52.50
Sugar bowl, cov., flint	95.00
Sugar bowl, open, non-flint	29.00

Tumbler, flint	65.00
Tumbler, whiskey, non-flint	38.00
Wine, flint	45.00
Wine, cut ovals, flint	98.00

FISHSCALE

Fishscale Plate

Berry set, master bowl & 5 flat sauce dishes, 6 pcs.	48.50
Bowl, cov., 8½" d.	35.00
Bowl, cov., 9½" d.	42.50
Bowl, 7½" d.	16.00
Bowl, 8" d.	18.00
Bowl, 8½" d.	20.00
Bread platter	26.00
Butter dish, cov.	47.50
Cake stand, 8" d.	36.00
Cake stand, 9" d.	28.00
Celery vase	30.00
Compote, cov., 7½" d.	45.00
Compote, open, jelly	14.50 to 20.00
Compote, open, 8" d., high stand	24.50
Condiment tray, rectangular	35.00
Creamer	27.50
Goblet	28.50
Lamp, kerosene-type w/finger grip	65.00
Lamp base, kerosene-type, pedestal base, original burner	81.00
Pitcher, milk	32.50
Pitcher, water	40.00
Plate, 7" d.	18.00
Plate, 8" d.	22.00
Plate, 9" sq. (ILLUS.)	28.50
Relish, 8½ x 5"	20.00
Salt shaker w/original top (single)	27.50
Sauce dish, flat or footed	5.50 to 12.00
Spooner	22.50
Sugar bowl, cov.	43.50
Tray, water, round	35.00
Tumbler	45.00

FLORIDA - See Paneled Herringbone Pattern

FLORIDA PALM

Florida Palm Goblet

Cake stand, 9½" d.	25.00
Celery vase	18.00
Compote, cov., 7" d., high stand	50.00
Compote, open, 9" d.	30.00
Creamer	20.00
Goblet (ILLUS.)	25.00
Plate, 9" d.	15.00
Relish	12.00
Spooner	20.00
Sugar bowl, cov.	35.00
Tumbler, footed	28.00
Wine	23.50

FLOWER FLANGE - See Dewey Pattern

FLOWER POT (Potted Plant)

Flower Pot Creamer

Bread tray	55.00
Butter dish, cov.	40.00
Cake stand, 10½" d.	45.00
Compote, open, 7¼" h.	18.00
Creamer (ILLUS.)	27.50
Creamer, vaseline	45.00
Goblet	40.00
Pitcher, milk	40.00

Pitcher, water	58.00
Salt shaker w/original top (single)	20.00
Sauce dish	8.50
Sugar bowl, cov.	37.50
Spooner	22.00
Spooner, vaseline	45.00

FLUTE

Flute Claret

Ale glass	50.00
Bar bottle, qt.	70.00
Bar bottle, blue, flint, qt.	250.00
Bar bottle, applied ring below rim, canary yellow, 11¼" h.	310.00
Celery vase	80.00
Champagne	21.50
Claret (ILLUS.)	20.00
Compote, open, 8¼" d., 3" h.	27.00
Compote, open, 9½" d., 3½" h.	35.00
Compote, open, 10" d.	75.00
Cordial	30.00
Decanter w/bar lip & original pewter-rimmed glass stopper, amethyst, flint	600.00
Egg cup	20.00
Egg cup, double	24.00
Egg cup, handled	65.00
Goblet, Bessimer	20.00
Goblet, Brooklyn	35.00
Goblet, Connecticut or New England	17.50
Goblet	29.00
Sugar bowl, open	35.00
Tumbler, amethyst, 10 panels	100.00
Tumbler, 3½" h.	16.00
Tumbler, whiskey, handled	27.50
Whiskey shot glass, footed	25.00
Wine, New England	20.00
Wine, Pittsburgh, flint	45.00

FLYING ROBIN - See Hummingbird Pattern

FOUR PETAL

Creamer & cov. sugar bowl, pr.	135.00

Four Petal Sugar Bowl

Sugar bowl, cov. (ILLUS.) 70.00
Sugar bowl, open 35.00

FOUR PETAL FLOWER - See Delaware Pattern

FROSTED CIRCLE

Frosted Circle Sauce Dish

Bowl, 6" d. 28.00
Bowl, 8" d., 3¼" h. 25.00
Butter dish, cov. 45.00
Cake stand, 9½" d. 40.00
Celery tray 20.00
Compote, cov., 5" d., 9" h. 43.50
Compote, open, 7" d., 6" h. 23.00
Compote, open, 9" d., 8½" h. 50.00
Compote, open, 10" d., high stand,
   scalloped rim 55.00
Creamer 35.00
Goblet 35.00
Pitcher, water, tankard 65.00
Plate, 9" d. 22.00
Punch cup 15.00
Relish, 8 x 4½" 20.00
Salt shaker w/original top (single) . .   35.00
Salt & pepper shakers w/original
   tops, pr. 47.50
Sauce dish (ILLUS.) 10.00
Spooner . . . . .25.00 to   35.00
Sugar bowl, cov. 45.00

Sugar shaker w/original top 37.50
Syrup pitcher w/original top 110.00
Tumbler 35.00
Wine 35.00

FROSTED LEAF

Celery vase 150.00
Creamer 395.00
Egg cup 90.00
Goblet 82.50
Salt dip 50.00
Sauce dish 22.50

FROSTED LION (Rampant Lion)

Frosted Lion Butter Dish

(Items may be plain or with etched designs)

Bowl, cov., 6 7/8 x 3 7/8" oblong,
   collared base 110.00
Bowl, cov., 7 7/16 x 4 5/8" oblong,
   collared base 110.00
Bowl, cov., 8 7/8 x 5½" oblong, col-
   lared base 125.00
Bowl, open, oval 73.00
Bread plate, rope edge, closed han-
   dles, 10½" d. 72.50
Butter dish, cov., rampant lion finial
   (ILLUS.) . . . . .85.00 to 100.00
Celery vase 87.50
Compote, cov., 6¾" oval, 7" h., col-
   lared base, rampant lion finial . . . 130.00
Compote, cov., 7" d., 11" h., lion
   head finial 165.00
Compote, cov., 7¾" oval, low col-
   lared base, rampant lion finial . . . 125.00
Compote, cov., 8" d., 13" h., ram-
   pant lion finial . . . . .145.00 to 195.00
Compote, cov., 8½ x 7¾" oval, low
   collared base, rampant lion
   finial 72.50
Compote, open, 7¾" d., high
   stand 65.00
Compote, open, 8" oblong, low
   stand 96.50
Creamer 70.00

Egg cup 57.50
Goblet .55.00 to 70.00
Marmalade jar, cov., rampant lion
 finial. . . . . .85.00 to 110.00
Paperweight, embossed "Gillinder &
 Sons, Centennial" 110.00
Pickle dish 60.00
Pitcher, water 350.00
Platter, 10½ x 9" oval, lion
 handles 80.00
Relish 35.00
Salt dip, cov., master size, collared
 base, rectangular 250.00
Sauce dish, 4" to 5" d. . . . . . . .15.00 to 35.00
Spooner 57.50
Sugar bowl, cov., rampant lion
 finial 75.00
Syrup pitcher w/original top 300.00
Wine, 4 1/8" h. . . . . .125.00 to 150.00

FROSTED RIBBON
Bowl, low 22.00
Bread platter 35.00
Butter dish, cov. 45.00
Celery vase. 45.00
Cologne bottle w/stopper 45.00
Compote, cov., 6½" d. 61.50
Compote, open, 10" d., 9½" h. 40.00
Creamer 37.50
Creamer & cov. sugar bowl, pr. 95.00
Goblet 22.50
Pitcher, water 55.00
Salt dip, master size, double 10.00
Sauce dish. 9.50
Spooner 29.50
Sugar bowl, cov. 45.00

FROSTED ROMAN KEY (With Flutes or Ribs)

Frosted Roman Key Pattern

Bowl, 9¾" d., 3½" h. 42.50
Butter dish, cov. 55.00
Celery vase. 67.50
Champagne. 55.00
Compote, cov., 7" d. 75.00
Compote, open, 7¾" d. 95.00
Compote, open, 9" d., 8" h. 60.00
Cordial 45.00
Creamer, applied handle (ILLUS.
 left). 56.00

Egg cup 30.00
Goblet (ILLUS. right) 40.00
Goblet, buttermilk 42.50
Plate, 6½" d., dated Aug. 27,
 1864 . . . . 75.00
Salt dip, master size. 32.00
Sauce dish. 14.00
Spooner 25.00
Sugar bowl, cov. 90.00
Sugar bowl, open 26.00
Tumbler, bar. 85.00
Tumbler, footed 75.00
Wine 67.50

FROSTED STORK
Bowl, 9" oval, 101 border 50.00
Bread plate, round 55.00
Butter dish, cov. 70.00
Creamer 62.50
Finger bowl. 90.00
Goblet . . . . .55.00 to 60.00
Pickle castor w/original frame 245.00
Platter, 12 x 8" oval 48.00
Platter, deer & doe border 75.00
Relish, 101 border 58.00
Sauce dish. 32.00
Spooner 45.00
Sugar bowl, cov., stork finial 95.00
Tray, water, 15½ x 11" 125.00
Waste bowl. 40.00

FROSTED WAFFLE - See Hidalgo Pattern

GALLOWAY (Virginia)
Bowl, 6½" d. . . . . .18.00 to 22.50
Bowl, 9¾" d., flat 35.00
Bowl, ice cream, 11" d., 3½" h. 45.00
Butter dish, cov. 50.00
Butter dish, cov., ruby-stained 110.00
Cake stand, 9¼" d., 6" h. 65.00
Carafe 55.00
Celery vase. 30.00
Celery vase, ruby-stained 75.00
Compote, open, 4¼" d., 6" h. 25.00
Compote, open, 10" d., 8" h., scal-
 loped rim. 55.00
Creamer 25.00
Creamer, individual size 15.00
Cruet w/stopper 35.00
Goblet 70.00
Mug, 4½" d.. . . . . 36.00
Nappy, handled, gold rim, 5" d. 16.00
Olive dish, 6 x 4" . . . . .16.50 to 25.00
Pitcher, milk 40.00
Pitcher, lemonade, applied handle . . 70.00
Pitcher, water, 9"h. . . . . .50.00 to 75.00
Pitcher, water, ruby-stained 125.00
Pitcher, child's 25.00
Pitcher, child's, ruby-stained 85.00
Plate, 6½" d. 20.00
Plate, 8" d. 20.00
Punch bowl, 14" d. 145.00
Punch cup 10.00
Relish, 8¼" l. 15.00

Relish, ruby-stained 29.50
Salt dip, master size, scalloped rim,
  2" d. 24.00
Salt & pepper shakers w/original
  tops, gold rim, 3" h., pr. 35.00
Sauce dish, flat or footed . . . . . 9.00 to 15.00
Spooner 24.50
Spooner, amber-stained 35.00
Sugar bowl, cov. 42.50
Sugar shaker w/original top 37.50
Syrup pitcher w/metal spring top . . . 57.50
Syrup pitcher w/metal spring top,
  ruby-stained 135.00
Toothpick holder 24.50
Tumbler 18.50
Vase, 9½" h. 15.00
Vase, 12" h. 22.50
Waste bowl 25.00
Water set, pitcher & 6 tumblers,
  7 pcs. 230.00
Water set, child's, pitcher & 4
  tumblers, 5 pcs. 50.00
Wine 35.00

GARFIELD DRAPE

Garfield Drape Bread Plate

Bread plate, "We Mourn Our
  Nation's Loss," 11½" d. (ILLUS.) . . 55.00
Butter dish, cov. 59.00
Cake stand, 9½" d. 47.50
Celery vase, pedestal base 47.50
Compote, cov., 6" d., low stand 50.00
Compote, cov., 8" d., 12½" h. 125.00
Creamer 32.50
Creamer & open sugar bowl, pr. . . . 65.00
Goblet . . . . 28.00 to 40.00
Pitcher, milk 55.00
Pitcher, water 68.50
Plate, 10" d. 60.00
Sauce dish, flat or footed . . . . . 8.50 to 10.00
Spooner 28.00
Sugar bowl, cov. 60.00
Tumbler 30.00

GEORGIA - See Peacock Feather Pattern

GOBLETS WITH BIRDS & ANIMALS

Bear climber, etched 65.00
Deer & Doe w/lily-of-the-valley,
  pressed . . . . 95.00 to 110.00
Dog w/rabbit in mouth, etched 65.00
Ostrich Looking at Moon, pressed . . 79.00
Owl-Possum, pressed 95.00
Pigs in Corn, pressed 350.00
Squirrel, pressed 300.00
Stork & flowers, etched 50.00

GODDESS OF LIBERTY - See Ceres Pattern

GOOD LUCK - See Horseshoe Pattern

GOOSEBERRY

Gooseberry Compote

Butter dish, cov. 50.00
Compote, cov., 6" d. 35.00
Compote, cov., 7" d. (ILLUS.) 65.00
Creamer 30.00
Creamer & open sugar bowl, pr. 80.00
Goblet 22.50
Mug 26.00
Mug, child's, blue opaque 25.50
Sauce dish 8.00
Spooner 18.00
Tumbler, bar 30.00
Tumbler, water . . . . 25.00 to 30.00

GOTHIC

Bowl, master berry or fruit, flat 69.00
Celery vase 95.00
Champagne 125.00
Compote, open, 8" d., 4" h. 65.00
Creamer, applied handle 90.00
Egg cup (ILLUS.) 42.50
Goblet 60.00
Honey dish 22.50
Sauce dish 14.00
Spooner 45.00
Sugar bowl, cov. 80.00
Tumbler 95.00
Wine, 3¾" h. 96.50

Gothic Egg Cup

GRAND - See Diamond Medallion Pattern

GRAPE & FESTOON

Grape & Festoon Spooner

Butter dish, cov., stippled leaf	50.00
Celery vase, stippled leaf	45.00
Compote, cov., 8" d., high stand, acorn finial, stippled leaf	115.00
Compote, open, 8" d., low stand	75.00
Creamer, stippled leaf	40.00
Egg cup, stippled leaf	18.00
Goblet, stippled leaf	27.50
Goblet, buttermilk, stippled leaf	33.00
Goblet, veined leaf	22.50
Pitcher, milk, 7" h., stippled leaf	65.00
Pitcher, water, stippled leaf	85.00
Plate, 6" d., stippled leaf	20.00
Relish, stippled leaf	7.50
Salt dip, footed, stippled leaf	23.50
Sauce dish, flat, stippled leaf, 4" d.	8.00
Sauce dish, flat, veined leaf	12.50
Spooner, stippled leaf (ILLUS.)	24.00
Spooner, veined leaf	22.50
Sugar bowl, cov., stippled leaf	50.00
Sugar bowl, open, stippled leaf	25.00

GRAPE & FESTOON WITH SHIELD

Compote, cov., 8" d., low stand	39.50
Creamer, applied handle	35.00
Goblet, w/shield & grapes	25.00
Goblet, w/American shield	50.00
Mug, 1 7/8" h.	16.50
Mug, cobalt blue, 1 7/8" h.	26.00
Mug, 3¼" h.	18.50
Sauce dish, flat or footed	6.00 to 12.00
Spooner	26.50

GRASSHOPPER (Locust)

(Items may be plain or with etched designs)

Bowl, cov., 8" d., footed	27.50
Bowl, open, 7" d., footed	21.00
Bowl, open, 8" d.	20.00
Bowl, open, 11" d., shallow	15.00
Butter dish, cov.	50.00
Celery vase, w/insect	38.00
Compote, cov., 8¼" d.	52.50
Creamer	30.00 to 38.00
Goblet, w/insect, amber	85.00
Goblet, w/insect	32.50
Marmalade jar, cov., w/insect	115.00
Pitcher, water	75.00
Plate, 8½" d., footed	25.00
Salt dip	20.00
Sauce dish, footed	8.00
Spooner	45.00
Spooner, w/insect	50.00
Sugar bowl, cov., w/insect	55.00
Sugar bowl, open, w/insect	42.00
Table set, creamer without insect & spooner & cov. sugar bowl w/insect, 3 pcs.	125.00

GREEK KEY (Heisey's Greek Key)

Butter dish, cov.	125.00
Celery tray	48.00
Creamer & open sugar bowl, pr.	55.00
Goblet	45.00
Humidor, cov.	285.00
Ice tub, small	95.00
Ice tub, hotel size	135.00
Pitcher, tankard, 1½ qt.	95.00 to 110.00
Punch bowl & pedestal base, 2 pcs.	250.00
Punch cup	20.00
Salt dip, master size	20.00
Sauce dish	20.00
Soda fountain (straw-holder) jar	128.00
Tumbler	85.00

GUARDIAN ANGEL - See Cupid & Venus Pattern

HALEY'S COMET

Celery	35.00
Goblet	32.50
Pitcher, water	80.00
Tumbler	26.00

Haley's Comet Wine

Wine (ILLUS.) ....18.00 to 25.00

HAMILTON
Bar bottle, qt. 135.00
Butter dish, cov. 80.00
Cake stand 175.00
Compote, open, 7" d.............. 46.00
Compote, open, 8" d., 5½" h....... 65.00
Compote, open, 8" d., 8" h., scal-
   loped rim...................... 70.00
Creamer 75.00
Egg cup 40.00
Goblet ....40.00 to 52.50
Pitcher, water ....255.00 to 335.00

Hamilton Sauce Dish

Sauce dish (ILLUS.) 15.00
Spooner......................... 35.00
Sugar bowl, cov. 125.00
Tumbler, bar...................... 65.00
Tumbler, water 80.00
Tumbler, whiskey, applied handle .. 90.00
Wine............................. 90.00

HAMILTON WITH LEAF
Butter dish, cov., frosted leaf 80.00
Compote, open, 6" d., 4½" h....... 78.00
Compote, open, high stand, large .. 85.00
Creamer, frosted leaf............. 55.00
Egg cup, clear leaf 55.00
Goblet, clear leaf 45.00
Goblet, frosted leaf 55.00
Lamp base, kerosene-type, scal-
   loped foot, clear leaf 80.00
Spooner, clear leaf 30.00
Sugar bowl, cov., clear leaf 75.00
Sweetmeat dish, cov., clear leaf.... 75.00
Tumbler, clear leaf 55.00
Tumbler, frosted leaf 125.00
Tumbler, bar, clear leaf 70.00
Tumbler, bar, frosted leaf.......... 125.00

HAND (Pennsylvania, Early)
Bowl, 9" d. 36.50
Bread plate, 10½ x 8" oval 20.00
Butter dish, cov. 75.00
Cake stand 55.00
Celery vase...................... 40.00
Compote, cov., 8" d., high stand ... 95.00
Compote, open, 7¾" d., 6¾" h..... 42.50
Compote, oen, 9" d., low stand 28.00
Cordial 75.00
Creamer 37.50
Creamer, child's.................. 45.00
Goblet 40.00
Marmalade jar, cov................ 40.00
Mug 45.00
Pitcher, water 75.00
Sauce dish, 4½" d. 12.00
Spooner......................... 25.00
Sugar bowl, cov. 67.50
Wine............................ 35.00

HARP

Harp Spillholder

Goblet, flared sides 650.00
Goblet, straight sides............. 250.00
Spillholder (ILLUS.) 85.00

HEART WITH THUMBPRINT
Banana boat, clear, 7½ x 6½" 85.00
Banana boat, clear, 11 x 6½" 75.00

Barber bottle w/original pewter stopper, clear	125.00
Berry set: master bowl & 6 sauce dishes; clear, 7 pcs.	130.00
Bowl, 7" sq., 3½" h., clear	37.50
Bowl, 9" d., clear	25.00
Bowl, 10" d., scalloped rim, clear	30.00
Bread plate, clear, 11¾" d.	45.00
Butter dish, cov., clear	75.00
Cake stand, clear, 9" d., 5" h.	125.00
Carafe, clear	55.00
Card tray, folded edge, clear, 6" w.	24.50
Card tray, clear, 8 x 4¼"	27.50
Card tray, green	35.00
Celery vase, clear	49.00
Compote, open, 8½" d., high stand, clear	85.00
Cordial, clear, 3" h.	55.00
Creamer, clear	26.50
Creamer, individual size, clear	20.00
Creamer, individual size, green w/gold	36.50
Creamer & open sugar bowl, individual size, green w/gold, pr.	80.00
Creamer, sugar bowl & tray, individual size, clear, 3 pcs.	57.50
Cruet w/original stopper, clear	65.00
Goblet, clear	45.00
Goblet, green w/gold	90.00
Ice bucket, clear	57.50
Lamp, kerosene-type, clear, 8" h.	137.00
Mustard jar w/silverplate cover, clear	95.00
Nappy, heart-shaped, clear	33.50
Olive dish, handled, green	42.50
Pitcher, water, clear	50.00
Plate, 6" d., clear	20.00
Plate, 12" d., clear	45.00
Powder jar w/silverplate cover, clear	65.00

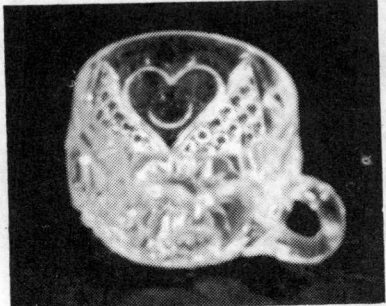

Heart with Thumbprint Punch Cup

Punch cup, clear (ILLUS.)	13.50
Relish, clear w/gold	17.50
Rose bowl, clear, 3¾" d.	25.00
Rose bowl, clear, 5" d.	32.50
Salt shaker w/original top, clear (single)	50.00

Sauce dish, clear	10.00 to 22.50
Sauce dish, green	32.00
Spooner, clear	39.50
Sugar bowl, cov., clear, large	45.00
Sugar bowl, open, clear	24.50
Sugar bowl, open, individual size, clear w/pewter rim	16.50
Sugar bowl, open, individual size, green w/gold	30.00
Syrup jug w/pewter top, clear	68.50
Tray, clear, 8 1/8 x 4 1/8"	30.00
Tumbler, water, clear	35.00
Tumbler, water, ruby-stained	115.00
Vase, 6" h., trumpet-shaped, clear	35.00
Vase, 6" h., green	36.00
Vase, 7" h., green	65.00
Vase, 8" h., clear	45.00
Vase, 10" h., trumpet-shaped, clear	47.50
Wine, clear	45.00

HEARTS OF LOCH LAVEN - See Shuttle Pattern

HEAVY PANELED FINECUT (Paneled Diamond Cross)

Cake stand, 9" d.	18.00
Spooner	45.00

HERCULES PILLAR (Pillar Variant)

Hercules Pillar Cordial

Ale glass, clear	30.00
Butter dish, cov., clear	32.00
Celery vase, clear	47.00
Champagne, clear	35.00
Cordial, clear, 3¾" h. (ILLUS.)	38.00
Syrup jug w/pewter top, amber, 8" h.	115.00
Syrup jug w/original top, blue	130.00
Toothpick holder, amber	100.00
Tumbler, clear	45.00
Whiskey taster, clear	13.50
Wine, clear	35.00

HERRINGBONE (Herringbone with Star & Shield Motif)

Celery vase	30.00
Creamer	27.00
Goblet	22.00
Goblet, buttermilk	23.00
Salt dip, master size	14.00
Sauce dish	10.50
Spooner	20.00
Sugar bowl, cov.	24.00
Wine	15.00

HERRINGBONE BAND

Egg cup	18.50
Goblet	13.50
Sauce dish, 4" sq.	9.50
Spooner, pedestal base, scalloped rim	21.00
Sugar bowl, open	15.00
Wine	20.00

HICKMAN (Le Clede)

Hickman Creamer

Banana stand, clear	65.00
Bowl, 5" d., green w/gold	8.00
Bowl, 7" sq., clear	15.00
Bowl, 7 x 6", green w/gold	25.00
Butter dish, cov., clear	35.00
Cake stand, clear, 9¼" d.	35.00
Celery dish, boat-shaped, green	28.00
Champagne, clear	21.50
Compote, cov., 5" d., clear	36.00
Compote, cov., 7" d., high stand, clear	53.00
Compote, open, jelly, green	16.00
Compote, open, 7½" d., 5½" h., clear	20.00
Compote, open, 8" d., 6½" h., clear	31.50
Cookie jar, cov., clear	45.00
Creamer, clear w/gold	24.50
Creamer, green (ILLUS.)	26.50
Creamer & open sugar bowl, individual size, oval, green, pr.	38.00
Cruet w/ball-shaped stopper, clear	42.50
Dish, pulled-out corners, clear, 6½" sq.	11.00
Doughnut stand, scalloped rim, clear, 8" d.	45.00

Goblet, clear	30.00
Goblet, green w/gold	35.00
Ice tub, clear	57.50
Mustard jar w/cover & underplate, clear, 2 pcs.	45.00
Pickle dish, clear, 8 x 4"	14.50
Pitcher, clear w/gold	55.00
Plate, 8½ x 7½", diamond-shaped, flat, clear	13.00
Plate, 9¼" d., clear	12.50
Punch cup, clear	7.50
Punch cup, green	12.50
Punch set: punch bowl & 13 cups; clear, 14 pcs.	125.00
Relish, clear, 5½" l.	15.00
Rose bowl, clear	30.00
Salt dip, clear	10.00
Salt shaker w/original top, clear (single)	9.50
Salt shaker w/original top, green (single)	18.00
Sauce dish, clear	8.00
Spooner, clear	22.50
Sugar bowl, cov., clear	38.00
Sugar bowl, cov., green	45.00
Sugar shaker w/original top, clear	40.00
Table set, clear w/gold, 4 pcs.	175.00
Toothpick holder, clear	55.00
Tumbler, clear	27.50
Vase, 10" h., clear	38.50
Wine, clear	25.00
Wine, green	30.00

HIDALGO (Frosted Waffle)

Hidalgo Compote

(Items may be plain or with etched designs)

Bowl, 10" sq.	22.00
Butter dish, cov.	45.00
Celery dish, boat-shaped, 13" l.	46.00
Celery vase	25.00 to 40.00
Celery vase, clear w/amber staining	32.50
Compote, open, 7" d. (ILLUS.)	20.00

Creamer ....22.50 to	40.00
Cruet w/original stopper...........	60.00
Egg cup	30.00
Goblet ....15.00 to	20.00
Pitcher, milk....................	39.50
Pitcher, water	55.00
Relish, shell-shaped	15.00
Sauce dish, handled	12.00
Spooner	33.50
Sugar bowl, cov.	30.00
Sugar shaker w/original top	45.00
Syrup pitcher w/original top	70.00
Tumbler	15.00

HINOTO (Diamond Point with Panels)

Hinoto Creamer

Butter dish, cov.	90.00
Celery vase....................	42.50
Champagne.....................	75.00
Compote, open, 7½" d., 2½" h.	27.50
Creamer (ILLUS.)	75.00
Dresser set, 6 pcs.	95.00
Egg cup, handled................	23.00
Goblet	45.00
Pitcher, tankard, 9" h., applied handle	110.00
Spooner	32.50
Sugar bowl, cov.	45.00
Tumbler, footed.................	40.00
Tumbler, whiskey, handled, footed	45.00
Wine...........................	57.50

HOBNAIL

(Also see Hobnail under OPALESCENT GLASS.)

Bowl, 4¾" d., 3" h., amber	8.00
Bowl, 7½" d., ruffled rim, blue	35.00
Butter dish, cov., amber	35.00
Cake stand, pedestal base, square, clear	85.00
Celery vase, footed, vaseline.......	95.00
Cologne bottle, clear, 6½" h.	22.00
Creamer, fluted top, applied handle, amber, 3 x 2"...................	17.50

Creamer, scalloped & ornamented top, clear, 6" h.	45.00
Cruet w/original stopper, clear, 4½" h.	22.50
Dish in silverplate holder, vaseline	95.00
Finger bowl, ruffled rim, clear......	10.00
Goblet, clear	15.00
Lamp, kerosene-type w/finger grip, clear.........................	48.00
Lamp, kerosene-type w/finger grip, opaque white w/amber foot & handle, 4¼" d., 6" h............	110.00

Hobnail Mug

Mug, amber (ILLUS.)	22.50
Pitcher, 7½" h., amber	45.00
Pitcher, 8" h., square top, clear	60.00
Pitcher, water, Rubina	125.00
Punch cup, clear	20.00
Salt shaker w/original top, clear (single).....................	5.00
Sauce dish, square, ruby-stained ...	45.00
Spooner, ruffled rim, amber........	32.00
Spooner, clear	26.50
Toothpick holder, amber	20.00
Toothpick holder, blue	24.50
Toothpick holder, vaseline	35.00
Tumbler, 10-row, blue	31.00
Tumbler, 10-row, clear...........	25.00
Tumbler, 10-row, Rubina Frosted ...	95.00
Tumbler, ruby-stained	45.00
Tumbler, vaseline	46.50
Wine, amber....................	20.00
Wine, blue	25.00

HOBNAIL WITH FAN

Hobnail with Fan Bowl

Bowl, 6" d., clear 20.00
Bowl, 7" d., blue (ILLUS.) 55.00
Celery vase, clear 38.00
Creamer, blue 20.00
Goblet, clear 30.00
Sauce dish, clear 8.00
Spooner, blue..................... 45.00

HOBNAIL WITH THUMBPRINT BASE

Hobnail with Thumbprint Base

Butter dish, cov., clear 55.00
Butter dish, cov., child's, amber 95.00
Creamer, amber (ILLUS.) 37.50
Creamer, blue 45.00
Creamer, child's, amber 15.00
Creamer, child's, blue 23.00
Pitcher, 7" h., clear w/ruby-stained
    rim 45.00
Pitcher, 8" h., amber 90.00
Pitcher, 8" h., blue 72.50
Spooner, blue.................... 45.00
Sugar bowl, cov., clear 35.00
Waste bowl, amber 40.00

HONEYCOMB

Honeycomb Vase

Ale glass 42.00
Barber bottle w/pewter top 45.00
Butter dish & cover w/knob finial,
    flint........................... 60.00
Butter dish, cov., non-flint 45.00
Cake stand, 10½" d. 35.00
Celery vase, flint 25.00
Celery vase, Laredo, flint 35.00
Celery vase, New York, non-flint ... 18.00
Celery vase, Vernon, flint, 9" h. 65.00
Champagne, flint.................. 50.00
Compote, cov., 9¼" d., 11½" h.,
    flint........................... 90.00
Compote, 7" d., 5" h., flint......... 35.00
Compote, open, 7" d., 7" h., flint ... 55.00
Compote, open, 8" d., 6¼" h.,
    flint........................... 55.00
Compote, open, 8¾" d., 7" h. 45.00
Compote, open, 11" d., 8" h., flint .. 135.00
Cordial, flint, 3¼" h. 25.00
Creamer, applied handle, flint...... 30.00
Decanter w/bar lip, flint, 10½" h. ... 75.00
Decanter w/original stopper, flint,
    13" h. 150.00
Egg cup 20.00
Finger bowl, flint................. 45.00
Goblet, flint 17.50
Goblet, non-flint 12.00
Goblet, Banded Vernon 22.00
Goblet, Barrel w/knob stem 18.00
Goblet, buttermilk 24.00
Goblet, Laredo................... 25.50
Goblet, New York 20.00
Mug 30.00
Pitcher, water, 8½" h., molded han-
    dle, polished pontil, flint......... 100.00
Pitcher, water, 9" h., applied han-
    dle, flint...................... 90.00
Pomade jar, cov., flint 48.00
Relish 30.00
Salt dip, pedestal base, flint 35.00
Sauce dish, flint.................. 11.00
Spillholder, flint 22.00
Spooner, flint.................... 33.50
Spooner, non-flint 18.00
Sugar bowl, cov., flint 75.00
Sugar bowl, open, scalloped rim.... 35.00
Syrup pitcher w/pewter top 126.50
Toothpick holder 24.00
Tumbler, bar..................... 25.00
Tumbler, Vernon, flint 55.00
Tumbler, whiskey, Vernon 125.00
Vase, 7½" h., 4" d., Vernon,
    flint........................... 45.00
Vases, 10¼" h., Vernon, flint, pr.
    (ILLUS. of one) 150.00
Wine, flint....................... 24.00
Wine, non-flint................... 15.00

HORN OF PLENTY
Bar bottle w/original stopper, qt..... 130.00
Bar bottle w/pewter pour spout,
    8" 135.00
Bowl, 9 x 6¼" oval............... 145.00

Butter dish, cov. 145.00
Butter dish & cover w/Washington's
   head finial 1,100.00
Celery vase....................... 100.00
Champagne........................ 160.00
Compote, cov., 8¼" oval, 5¾" h.... 350.00
Compote, open, 7" d., 3" h. 110.00

Horn of Plenty Compote

Compote, open, 8" d., 8" h.
   (ILLUS.)......................... 125.00
Compote, open, 9" d., 8½" h. 200.00
Creamer, applied handle, 5½" h. 235.00
Creamer, applied handle, 7" h. 155.00
Decanter w/original stopper, pt..... 180.00
Dish, low foot, 7¼" d.............. 85.00
Dish, low foot, 8" d............... 95.00
Egg cup, 3¾" h. 42.50
Goblet 70.00
Honey dish, cov. 17.50
Honey dish, open 10.50
Lamp, w/whale oil burner, 11" h.... 175.00
Peppersauce bottle w/stopper 142.50
Pitcher, water 575.00
Plate, 6" d. 65.00
Relish, 7 x 5" oval................ 30.00
Salt dip, master size, oval ..95.00 to 150.00
Sauce dish...............16.00 to 25.00
Spillholder....................... 48.50
Spooner 45.00
Sugar bowl, cov. 90.00
Tumbler, bar..................... 70.00
Tumbler, water, 3 5/8" h. 95.00
Tumbler, whiskey, 3" h. 85.00
Tumbler, whiskey, handled........ 235.00
Wine............................ 135.00

HORSESHOE (Good Luck or Prayer Rug)

Bowl, cov., 8 x 5" oval, flat, triple
   horseshoe finial 195.00
Bowl, open, 8 x 5" oval, footed..... 37.50
Bread tray, single horseshoe
   handles 35.50
Bread tray, double horseshoe
   handles 60.00
Butter dish, cov. 50.00
Cake stand, 8" d., 6½" h. 45.00
Cake stand, 9" d. 52.50
Cake stand, 10" d. 65.00
Celery vase................37.00 to 45.00

Cheese dish, cov., w/woman churn-
   ing butter in base 235.00
Compote, cov., 6" d., 10½" h....... 135.00
Compote, cov., 8" d., 11" h......... 80.00
Compote, cov., 12" d. 95.00
Compote, open, 8" d., 7¾" h. 35.00
Creamer, hotel-type, 6½" h. 95.00
Creamer, regular.................. 32.50
Creamer, individual size 38.50
Doughnut stand 57.50
Goblet, knob stem 35.00
Goblet, plain stem 30.00
Marmalade jar, cov................ 97.50
Marmalade jar, open 29.50
Pitcher, water 75.00
Plate, 7" d. 30.00
Plate, 8" d. 41.50
Plate, 10" d. 42.50
Relish, 8 x 5" 12.00
Relish, 9 x 5½" 19.50
Salt dip, individual size 19.00
Salt dip, master size, horseshoe
   shape 90.00
Sauce dish, flat or footed .....8.00 to 18.00

Horseshoe Spooner

Spooner (ILLUS.)................. 27.50
Sugar bowl, cov. 50.00
Waste bowl, 4" d., 2½" h. 55.00
Wine....................145.00 to 180.00

HUBER

Huber Compote

(Items may be plain or with etched designs)

Celery vase	38.50
Champagne, straight sides	40.00
Compote, open, 7" d.	55.00
Compote, open, 8" d. (ILLUS.)	75.00
Cordial	27.50
Creamer	80.00
Egg cup	14.00
Egg cup, double	30.00
Goblet	21.50
Goblet, barrel	13.50
Goblet, buttermilk	16.50
Salt dip, master size	17.50
Sugar bowl, cov.	57.50
Tumbler, bar	22.50
Vase	18.50
Wine	15.00

HUMMINGBIRD (Flying Robin or Bird & Fern)

Butter dish, cov., clear	50.00
Celery vase, amber	55.00
Celery vase, clear	35.00
Compote, open, 7" d., clear	48.00
Creamer, amber	52.50
Creamer, blue	50.00
Creamer, clear	28.50
Goblet, amber	57.50
Goblet, blue	60.00
Goblet, clear	30.00
Pitcher, milk, blue	120.00
Pitcher, milk, clear	47.50
Pitcher, water, amber	127.50
Pitcher, water, blue	100.00
Pitcher, water, clear	85.00
Sauce dish, clear	12.00
Sugar bowl, cov., clear	55.00
Sugar bowl, open, clear	20.00
Spooner, blue	50.00
Spooner, clear	30.00
Tray, water, amber	170.00
Tumbler, amber	50.00
Tumbler, clear	32.50
Waste bowl, clear	35.00
Water set: pitcher & 6 tumblers; amber, 7 pcs.	350.00

HUNDRED EYE

Creamer, clear	18.50
Goblet, clear	15.50
Mug, blue	25.00
Wine, clear	9.00

ILLINOIS

Basket, applied reeded handle, 11½ x 7"	100.00
Bowl, 5¼" sq.	12.00
Bowl, 8" sq.	35.00
Butter dish, cov., 7" sq. (ILLUS.)	60.00
Candlestick (single)	70.00
Celery tray	40.00
Compote, open	145.00
Creamer, small	18.50

Illinois Butter Dish

Creamer, large	35.00
Cruet w/original stopper	40.00
Marmalade jar in silverplate frame w/spoon, 3 pcs.	135.00
Pitcher, water, tankard	50.00 to 65.00
Pitcher, water, silverplate rim, green	72.50
Plate, 7" sq.	20.00
Relish, 8½ x 3"	13.50
Salt dip, individual size	12.50
Sauce dish	15.00
Soda fountain (straw-holder) jar, cov., 12½" h.	180.00
Soda fountain (straw-holder) jar, cov., green, 12½" h.	300.00
Spooner	27.50
Sugar bowl, cov.	50.00
Sugar bowl, open	35.00
Sugar bowl, cov., individual size	30.00
Syrup pitcher w/original pewter top	95.00
Table set, cov. butter dish, open sugar bowl, creamer & spooner, 4 pcs.	197.50
Toothpick holder	27.50
Vase, 5¾" h.	26.00

INDIANA (Doric)

Butter dish, cov.	75.00
Creamer	23.00
Sugar bowl, open	23.00

INDIANA SWIRL - See Feather Pattern

INVERTED FERN

Butter dish, cov.	57.50
Champagne	115.00
Compote, open, 8" d.	55.00
Creamer, applied handle	122.00
Egg cup	22.50
Goblet (ILLUS.)	30.00 to 40.00
Honey dish, 4" d.	12.50
Salt dip, master size, footed	35.00
Sauce dish, 4" d.	7.50
Spooner	36.00
Sugar bowl, cov.	75.00
Tumbler	95.00
Wine	57.50

Inverted Fern Goblet

INVERTED LOOPS & FANS - See Maryland Pattern

IOWA (Paneled Zipper & Zippered Block)

Bowl, 9" d., 5½" h., ruby-stained	135.00
Carafe, water	35.00
Lamp, kerosene-type	95.00 to 125.00
Nappy, handled	10.00
Olive dish	18.00
Punch cup	12.00
Salt & pepper shakers w/original tops, pr.	35.00
Sauce dish, flat	8.50
Spooner	16.50
Sugar bowl, cov., small	20.00
Table set, ruby-stained, 4 pcs.	235.00
Toothpick holder	22.50
Toothpick holder, ruby-stained	75.00
Tumbler	22.50
Tumbler, ruby-stained	35.00
Vases, gold trim, pr.	18.00
Wine	24.50

IRISH COLUMN - See Broken Column Pattern

IVY IN THE SNOW

Bowl, 8 x 5½", flat	9.00
Butter dish, cov.	50.00
Cake stand, 8" d.	37.50
Cake stand, amber-stained ivy sprigs, 10" sq.	125.00
Celery vase, 8" h.	27.50
Compote, cov., 8" d., 13" h. (ILLUS.)	60.00
Compote, open, jelly	20.00
Creamer	17.50
Egg cup	28.00
Goblet	25.00
Pitcher, 5½" h., ruby-stained ivy sprigs, souvenir	65.00
Pitcher, water	47.50
Plate, 6" d.	10.00
Plate, 10" d.	19.00

Ivy in the Snow Compote

Relish	20.00
Sauce dish, flat or footed	7.00 to 10.00
Spooner	30.00
Sugar bowl, open	15.00
Syrup jug w/original top	62.50
Tumbler	25.00
Wine	35.00

JACOB'S LADDER (Maltese)

Jacob's Ladder Creamer

Bowl, 6¾" d., 4¾" h., footed	25.00
Bowl, 7¼" d., footed	30.00
Bowl, 7¾" oval, flat	15.00
Butter dish, cov., Maltese Cross finial	60.00
Cake stand, 10½" d.	50.00
Candlesticks, pr.	38.00
Castor set: cruet w/original Maltese Cross stopper, salt & pepper shakers & mustard jar w/original tops; pewter frame, 5 pcs.	200.00

Celery vase........................ 35.00
Cologne bottle w/original Maltese
   Cross stopper, footed........... 125.00
Compote, cov., 7¼" d. 58.50
Compote, cov., 9½" d., high
   stand 175.00
Compote, open, 7" d., low stand ... 28.00
Compote, open, 7½" d., 7½" h..... 35.00
Compote, open, 8½" d., scalloped
   rim 27.50
Compote, open, 9" d.,
   7" h....................25.00 to 40.00
Compote, open, 9½" d., 9¼" h..... 45.00
Compote, open, 10" d., 5" h....... 35.00
Creamer (ILLUS.) 35.00
Cruet w/original stopper, footed ... 80.00
Egg cup 15.00
Goblet 55.00
Pickle dish, Maltese Cross handle,
   blue 65.00
Pickle dish, Maltese Cross handle,
   clear 13.00
Pitcher, milk, 7" h. 40.00
Pitcher, water, applied handle 150.00
Plate, 6" d. 22.50
Relish, Maltese Cross handles,
   10 x 5½"...................... 16.50
Salt dip, master size, footed 24.00
Sauce dish, flat or footed .....7.00 to 8.50
Spooner.......................... 38.50
Sugar bowl, cov. 43.50
Sugar bowl, open 28.00
Syrup jug w/pewter top 75.00
Wine............................. 32.50

JEWEL & DEWDROP (Kansas)

Jewel & Dewdrop Compote

Berry set, master bowl & 6 sauce
   dishes, 7 pcs.................... 75.00
Bowl, 8½" d...................... 40.00
Bread tray, "Our Daily Bread,"
   10½" oval 48.00
Butter dish, cov. 55.00
Cake stand, 8" d. 65.00
Cake stand, 9" d. 55.00
Cake stand, 10" d. 68.00
Celery vase....................... 38.00
Compote, cov., 9½" d. 55.00
Compote, open, jelly 23.50

Compote, open, 7½" d., 5" h.
   (ILLUS.)....................... 40.00
Compote, open, 9½" d............. 75.00
Creamer 38.00
Dish, cov., 4½" d. 45.00
Goblet 40.00
Mug 18.50
Pitcher, milk 50.00
Pitcher, water 50.00
Plate, 7" sq. 15.00
Relish, 8½" oval 20.00
Sauce dish, 4" d. 15.00
Syrup jug w/original top 125.00
Toothpick holder 42.50
Tumbler, water, footed 37.50
Whiskey taster, 2-handled 40.00
Wine............................. 48.00
Wine, ruby-stained, w/gilt trim 70.00

JEWEL & FESTOON (Loop & Jewel)

Jewel & Festoon Small Open Sugar Bowl

Butter dish, cov. 35.00
Champagne........................ 42.00
Creamer 22.00
Creamer, individual size 32.00
Dish, 5½" sq. 7.50
Dresser bottle w/matching stopper,
   7½" h......................... 50.00
Goblet 16.50
Pickle dish........................ 17.50
Punch cup 18.00
Sauce dish........................ 12.00
Spooner 29.00
Sugar bowl, cov. 29.00
Sugar bowl, open, individual size
   (ILLUS.)....................... 25.00
Toothpick holder 30.00
Vase, 8¾" h. 40.00
Wine............................. 30.00

JEWEL BAND (Scalloped Tape)

Bowl, cov., 8" rectangle (ILLUS.) 35.00
Bread platter 25.00
Cake stand, 9½" d. 35.00
Celery vase, 8" h. 22.50
Compote, cov., 8¼" d., 12" h....... 45.00
Creamer 27.50
Goblet 18.50
Pitcher, water, 9¼" h.............. 39.00

Jewel Band Covered Bowl

Relish, 7" l.	9.50
Sauce dish, flat or footed . . . . . 8.00 to	10.00
Sugar bowl, cov.	30.00
Wine	20.00

JEWELED MOON & STAR (Moon & Star with Waffle)

Bowl, 6¾" d., flat	13.50
Cake stand, 8½" d.	29.50
Cake stand, w/amber & blue staining, 8½" d.	125.00
Carafe	45.00
Celery	37.50
Creamer, w/amber & blue staining	50.00
Cruet	19.50
Goblet, gilt trim	45.00
Pitcher, water, bulbous, applied handle	140.00
Salt shaker w/original top (single)	25.00
Sauce dish	3.50
Spooner, w/amber & blue staining	60.00
Sugar bowl, cov.	120.00
Tumbler, gilt trim	24.50

JOB'S TEARS - See Art Pattern

JUMBO and JUMBO & BARNUM

Jumbo Spoon Rack

Butter dish & cover w/frosted elephant finial, oblong	550.00
Butter dish & cover w/frosted elephant finial, round	450.00
Castor holder (no bottles)	100.00
Compote, cov., 12" h., frosted elephant finial . . . . 325.00 to	475.00
Compote, open, 12" h.	250.00
Creamer . . . . 95.00 to	125.00
Creamer, w/Barnum head at handle	250.00
Goblet	400.00
Marmalade jar w/Barnum head handles & cover w/frosted elephant finial	237.50
Pitcher, water, w/elephant in base	695.00
Spooner	95.00
Spoon rack (ILLUS.)	975.00
Sugar bowl w/Barnum head handles & cover w/frosted elephant finial	425.00
Toothpick holder, "Baby Mine"	70.00

KAMONI - See Balder Pattern

KANSAS - See Jewel & Dewdrop Pattern

KENTUCKY

Cake stand, clear, 9½" d.	37.50
Cruet w/original stopper, clear	36.50
Pitcher, water, clear	55.00
Punch cup, green . . . . 12.00 to	18.00
Salt & pepper shakers w/original tops, clear, pr.	20.00
Sauce dish, footed, blue w/gold	16.00
Sauce dish, footed, clear	6.50
Sauce dish, footed, green	12.50
Sugar bowl, cov., clear	30.00
Toothpick holder, clear	26.50
Toothpick holder, green	110.00
Tumbler, green	21.50
Wine, clear	24.00
Wine, green	45.00

KING'S CROWN (Also see Ruby Thumbprint)

King's Crown Punch Cup

Banana stand, clear	50.00
Bowl, 9¼" oval, scalloped rim, round base, clear	50.00
Butter dish, cov., clear	37.50

Celery vase, clear	40.00
Compote, cov., 6" d., 6" h., clear	85.00
Compote, open, jelly, clear	35.00
Compote, open, 8½" d., high stand, clear	67.50
Compote, open, 9" d., low stand, clear	37.50
Cordial, clear	48.00
Creamer, clear	45.00 to 60.00
Creamer, individual size, clear	18.50
Cup & saucer, clear	45.00
Goblet, clear	27.50
Goblet, clear w/amethyst thumbprints	22.00
Goblet, clear w/green thumbprints	23.00
Lamp, kerosene-type, stem base, clear	85.00
Mustard jar, cov., clear	38.00
Pitcher, tankard, 13" h., clear	95.00
Pitcher, bulbous, clear	115.00
Plate, 7" d., clear	20.00
Punch cup, clear (ILLUS.)	18.00
Salt dip, individual size, clear	10.00
Salt dip, master size, footed, clear	22.50
Sauce dish, clear, 4" d.	7.50
Sauce dish, boat-shaped, clear	22.50
Spooner, clear	40.00 to 50.00
Toothpick holder, clear	25.00
Tumbler, blue	75.00
Tumbler, clear	25.00
Wine, clear	22.50

KLONDIKE - See Amberette Pattern

KOKOMO (Bar & Diamond)

Bowl, 8½" d., footed	22.50
Butter dish, cov., pedestal base	30.00
Cake stand	40.00
Compote, cov., 7½" d., low stand	28.00
Compote, cov., 7½" d., high stand	45.00
Compote, open, 7½" d., low stand	20.00
Creamer, applied handle	25.00
Cruet w/stopper	22.50
Decanter	65.00
Goblet	25.00 to 35.00
Pitcher, water, tankard	40.00
Salt & pepper shakers w/original tops, pr.	24.00
Sauce dish, footed	7.50
Spooner	22.50
Sugar bowl, cov.	45.00
Tray, water	27.50
Wine	24.00

LATTICE (Diamond Bar)

Bowl, 8" oval	18.00
Bread plate, "Waste Not - Want Not," 10" d.	40.00
Cake stand, 8¼" d., 5" h.	36.00
Cake stand, 12½" d.	48.00

Compote, cov., 7½" d., high stand	50.00
Creamer	35.00
Goblet	22.50
Pitcher, water	40.00

Lattice Plate

Plate, 7" d. (ILLUS.)	15.00
Spooner	25.00
Sugar bowl, cov.	29.00
Syrup pitcher w/original tin top	70.00
Wine	20.00

LEAF & DART (Double Leaf & Dart)

Leaf & Dart Tumbler

Bowl, 8¼" d., low foot	25.00
Butter dish, cov., pedestal base	85.00
Celery vase, pedestal base	35.00
Compote, open, jelly	35.00
Creamer, applied handle	35.00
Cruet w/original stopper	110.00
Egg cup	18.00
Goblet	28.50
Honey dish, 3½" d.	5.00
Pitcher, milk	120.00
Pitcher, water, applied handle	95.00

Salt dip, cov., master size......... 68.00
Salt dip, open, master size........ 24.50
Sauce dish...................... 8.50
Spooner........................ 22.50
Sugar bowl, cov. 42.50
Sugar bowl, open 20.00
Tumbler, footed (ILLUS.) 25.00
Water set, pitcher & 5 footed
   tumblers, 6 pcs................. 290.00
Wine......................30.00 to 38.00

LE CLEDE - See Hickman Pattern

LIBERTY BELL

"Signer's" Platter

Berry set, flat master bowl & 6 flat
   sauce dishes, 7 pcs. 195.00
Bread platter, "John Hancock,"
   shell handles, clear,
   11½ x 7 1/8"...........85.00 to 120.00
Bread platter, shell handles, without
   John Hancock signature, clear,
   11½ x 7 1/8" 170.00
Bread platter, "John Hancock,"
   shell handles, milk white,
   11½ x 7 1/8" 295.00
Bread platter, "John Hancock,"
   twig handles, milk white,
   13½ x 9½" 250.00
Bread platter, "Signer's," twig
   handles (ILLUS.)..........95.00 to 135.00
Butter dish, cov..........110.00 to 140.00
Butter dish, cov., miniature 160.00
Creamer, applied handle ...95.00 to 110.00
Goblet ....48.00 to 70.00
Mug, snake handle 375.00
Pickle dish, closed handles, 1776-
   1876, w/thirteen original states,
   9¼ x 5½" oval 50.00
Pitcher, water 650.00
Plate, 6" d., closed handles, scal-
   loped rim, w/thirteen original
   states 80.00
Plate, 6" d., no states,
   dated 57.50
Plate, 8" d., closed handles, scal-
   loped rim, w/thirteen original
   states 45.00
Plate, 10" d., closed handles, scal-

loped rim, w/thirteen original
   states 95.00
Platter, 13 x 8¼", twig handles,
   w/thirteen original
   states ....55.00 to 75.00
Table set, 4 pcs. 495.00

LILY-OF-THE-VALLEY

Lily-of-the-Valley Sauce Dish

Butter dish, cov. 75.00
Celery vase..................... 55.00
Champagne..................... 48.00
Compote, cov., 8½" d., high
   stand 85.00
Creamer, 3-footed, molded handle .. 80.00
Creamer, plain base, applied
   handle 65.00
Cruet w/original stopper 80.00
Egg cup 35.00
Goblet 37.50
Honey dish 12.00
Pitcher, milk, applied handle 85.00
Pitcher, water, bulbous, applied
   handle 110.00
Relish, 8 x 5½" 18.00
Salt dip, cov., master size,
   3-footed 125.00
Salt dip, open, master size,
   3-footed 27.50
Sauce dish (ILLUS.) 10.00
Spooner 38.00
Sugar bowl, cov., 3-footed 75.00
Tumbler, flat.................... 9.50
Wine......................... 130.00

LINCOLN DRAPE & LINCOLN DRAPE WITH TASSEL

Celery vase.................... 90.00
Compote, cov., 6" d., high
   stand 275.00
Compote, open, 7½" d., 3½" h..... 52.00
Compote, open, 8" d., medium
   stand ....60.00 to 77.00
Goblet 52.50
Goblet w/tassel................. 120.00
Lamp, kerosene-type, miniature 125.00
Salt dip, master size.............. 35.00
Salt dip, master size, w/tassel 125.00

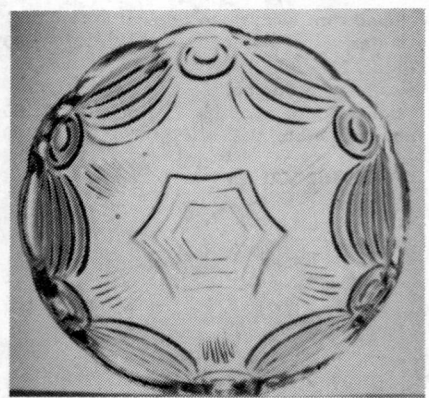

Lincoln Drape Sauce Dish

Sauce dish, 4" d. (ILLUS.)	20.00
Spillholder.......................	52.50
Spooner	52.50
Sugar bowl, cov.	85.00
Syrup pitcher w/original pewter top	125.00
Syrup pitcher w/original top, opaque white	650.00
Wine.............................	55.00

LION (Square Lion's Head or Atlanta)

Bowl, 8 x 5" oblong, flat	55.00
Bread plate, "Give Us...," 12" sq. ....46.00 to	75.00
Butter dish, cov.	65.00
Cake stand, large	82.50
Celery vase.................60.00 to	80.00
Compote, cov., 5" sq., 6" h........	85.00
Compote, cov., 7" sq., low stand ...	95.00
Compote, cov., 7" sq., high stand...	100.00
Compote, open, 6" sq., 7½" h....................27.50 to	40.00
Compote, open, 8" sq., high stand	75.00
Creamer	40.00
Cup & saucer, miniature	47.50
Dish, cov., oblong................	85.00
Egg cup	50.00
Goblet	65.00
Lamp, kerosene-type	175.00
Pitcher, water	110.00
Platter, handled..................	80.00
Relish, boat-shaped	35.00
Salt dip, master size.............	40.00
Sauce dish.......................	23.00
Spooner	50.00
Sugar bowl, cov.	95.00
Syrup pitcher w/original top	240.00
Toothpick holder	38.50
Tumbler	45.00

LION, FROSTED - See Frosted Lion Pattern

LION'S LEG - See Alaska Pattern

LOCUST - See Grasshopper Pattern

LOG CABIN

Log Cabin Sugar Bowl

Butter dish, cov.	250.00
Compote, open, 6 x 4", high stand	350.00
Creamer, 4¼" h. ....90.00 to	150.00
Pitcher, water	325.00
Sauce dish, flat oblong	85.00
Spooner ....85.00 to	110.00
Sugar bowl, cov., 8" h. (ILLUS.)	250.00
Sugar bowl, cov., vaseline	675.00

LOOP (Seneca Loop)

Loop Goblet

Bowl, 9" d., flint	80.00
Butter dish, cov., flint	150.00
Celery vase, flint.................	60.00
Celery vase, non-flint.............	20.00
Champagne, non-flint.............	15.00

Compote, cov., 9½" h., flint 70.00
Compote, open, 5¾" d., flint....... 45.00
Compote, open, 8" d., 6" h., non-
flint........................... 30.00
Compote, open, 9" d., 7" h.,
flint.......................... 125.00
Cordial, non-flint, 2¾" h. 18.50
Creamer, flint.................... 50.00
Decanter, non-flint 35.00
Egg cup, flint 26.00
Egg cup, non-flint 12.00
Goblet, flint (ILLUS.) 30.00
Goblet, non-flint 16.50
Lamp, kerosene-type, applied
handle 49.00
Pitcher, water, applied handle,
flint....................145.00 to 170.00
Pitcher, water, non-flint 60.00
Salt dip, individual size, flint 18.00
Salt dip, master size, flint.......... 25.00
Sauce dish, non-flint.............. 6.50
Spooner, flint 25.00
Spooner, non-flint 17.50
Sugar bowl, cov., flint 125.00
Sugar bowl, cov., non-flint 29.50
Syrup jug w/original pewter top,
applied handle, flint 95.00
Tumbler, flint 18.00
Tumbler, bar, non-flint............ 14.00
Wine, flint 25.00
Wine, non-flint................... 16.00

LOOP & DART

Loop & Dart Compote

Bowl, 8 x 5" oval, round
ornaments 15.00
Bowl, 9 x 6" oval, round
ornaments 19.50
Butter dish, cov., diamond
ornaments..............35.00 to 45.00
Butter dish, cov., round ornaments,
flint........................... 80.00
Celery vase, round ornaments 27.00

Champagne, diamond ornaments ... 35.00
Champagne, round ornaments 78.00
Compote, cov., 8" d., 10" h., round
ornaments (ILLUS.) 85.00
Compote, cov., 8" d., low stand,
round ornaments 65.00
Compote, open, 8" d., 4½" h.,
round ornaments 42.50
Cordial, 3¾" h. 22.00
Creamer, applied handle, diamond
ornaments 28.00
Creamer, applied handle, round
ornaments 38.00
Egg cup, diamond ornaments 18.00
Egg cup, round ornaments 22.50
Goblet, diamond ornaments 18.50
Goblet, round ornaments 25.00
Goblet, buttermilk, diamond
ornaments 20.00
Goblet, buttermilk, round
ornaments 35.00
Lamp, kerosene-type, round orna-
ments on font, milk white glass
base 85.00
Pitcher, water, round
ornaments.............85.00 to 90.00
Plate, 6" d., round ornaments 35.00
Relish, diamond ornaments 15.00
Relish, round ornaments 25.00
Salt dip, master size, diamond
ornaments 15.00
Salt dip, master size, round
ornaments 28.50
Sauce dish, diamond ornaments 5.00
Sauce dish, round ornaments....... 7.00
Spooner, diamond ornaments 18.50
Spooner, round ornaments 26.50
Sugar bowl, cov., diamond
ornaments 36.50
Sugar bowl, cov., round
ornaments 57.50
Tumbler, flat or footed, diamond
ornaments...............30.00 to 35.00
Tumbler, flat or footed, round
ornaments...............25.00 to 30.00
Wine, diamond ornaments 35.00
Wine, round ornaments 25.00

**LOOP & JEWEL - See Jewel & Festoon
Pattern**

LOOP & PILLAR - See Michigan Pattern

LOOP WITH DEWDROPS
Butter dish, cov. 27.50
Creamer 22.50
Goblet 25.00
Pitcher, water 65.00
Sugar bowl, cov. 25.00
Tumbler 17.00
Wine............................ 25.00

**LOOP WITH STIPPLED PANELS - See Texas
Pattern**

LOOPS & DROPS - See New Jersey Pattern

LOOPS & FANS - See Maryland Pattern

MAGNET & GRAPE

Butter dish, cov., frosted leaf, flint	185.00
Celery vase, frosted leaf, flint	175.00
Champagne, frosted leaf, flint	125.00
Compote, open, 7½" d., high stand, stippled leaf, non-flint	68.00
Creamer, frosted leaf, flint	160.00
Egg cup, clear leaf, non-flint	18.00
Egg cup, frosted leaf, flint	85.00
Goblet, clear leaf, non-flint	22.50
Goblet, frosted leaf, flint	75.00
Goblet, frosted leaf & American Shield, flint	300.00
Goblet, stippled leaf, non-flint	27.50
Salt dip, frosted leaf, flint	50.00
Sauce dish, frosted leaf, flint	18.00
Sauce dish, stippled leaf, non-flint	4.50
Spooner, frosted leaf, flint	77.50
Spooner, stippled leaf, non-flint	25.00
Sugar bowl, cov., frosted leaf, flint	95.00
Sugar bowl, cov., stippled leaf, non-flint	60.00
Tumbler, frosted leaf, flint	85.00
Wine, stippled leaf, non-flint	40.00

MAINE (Stippled Flower Panels)

Maine Jelly Compote

Bowl, master berry, 8½" d., clear	40.00
Bowl, master berry, 8½" d., green	35.00
Butter dish, cov., clear	42.50
Cake stand, green, 8½" d.	42.50
Compote, cov., small, green	65.00
Compote, open, jelly, green (ILLUS.)	25.00
Compote, open, 7" d., clear	35.00
Compote, open, 8" d., green	58.00
Creamer, clear	28.50
Pitcher, milk, green	85.00
Pitcher, water, clear	50.00
Pitcher, water, clear w/red & green stain	125.00

Platter, oval, clear	38.00
Relish, clear, 7¼" l.	15.00
Sauce dish, clear	12.50
Spooner, clear	30.00
Sugar bowl, cov., green	60.00
Syrup pitcher w/original top, clear	55.00
Tumbler, clear w/red & green stain	45.00
Wine, clear	32.50

MALTESE - See Jacob's Ladder Pattern

MANHATTAN

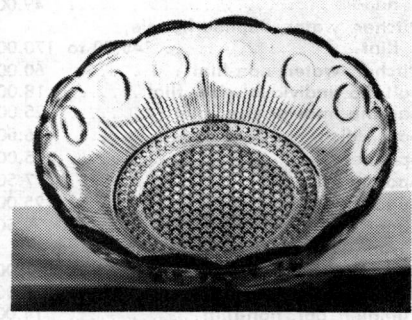

Manhattan Bowl

Berry set, master bowl & 3 flat sauce dishes, 4 pcs.	35.00
Bowl, 6" d.	27.00
Bowl, 9" d. (ILLUS.)	20.00
Butter dish, cov.	55.00
Butter dish, cov., clear w/pink stain	85.00
Cake stand, 10" d.	30.00
Carafe, water	40.00
Cookie jar, cov.	60.00
Cookie jar, cov., clear w/pink stain	85.00
Creamer	12.50
Creamer, individual size	20.00
Creamer & open sugar bowl, pr.	35.00
Creamer & open sugar bowl, individual size, pr.	32.50
Cruet w/original stopper	30.00
Goblet	20.00
Pickle dish w/advertising, 8 x 6" oval	25.00
Plate, 4½" d., w/handle	8.00
Plate, 5" d., clear w/pink stain	27.50
Plate, 10¾" d.	18.50
Punch bowl, 14" d., 8" h.	110.00
Punch cup	8.50
Relish, 6" l.	10.00
Sauce dish, flat	8.00
Sauce dish, flat, clear w/pink stain	12.00
Sugar bowl, cov., clear w/pink stain	45.00
Toothpick holder	27.50
Vase, 7" h.	15.00

Violet bowl	22.50
Wine	30.00

MAPLE LEAF (Leaf)
Berry set: oval master bowl, oval tray & 6 leaf-shaped sauce dishes; amber, 8 pcs.	95.00
Bowl, 9" oval, footed, clear	26.00
Bowl, 10 x 6" oval, footed, amber	40.00
Bowl, 10 x 6" oval, footed, clear	36.00
Bowl, 10 x 6" oval, footed, green	55.00
Bowl, 10 x 6" oval, footed, vaseline	65.00
Bowl, 10" square, crimped rim, blue	85.00
Bowl, 12 x 7½" oval, amber	70.00
Bread plate, Grant, "Let Us Have Peace," amber, 9½" d.	65.00
Bread plate, Grant, "Let Us Have Peace," blue, 9½" d.	75.00
Bread plate, Grant, "Let Us Have Peace," clear, 9½" d.	40.00
Bread plate, Grant, "Let Us Have Peace," vaseline, 9½" d.	60.00
Bread tray, vaseline w/frosted maple leaves, 13¼ x 9¼"	60.00
Butter dish, cov., clear	80.00
Celery vase, frosted stem, scalloped rim, clear	38.00
Compote, open, jelly, green	45.00
Creamer, blue	65.00
Creamer, clear	37.50
Creamer, vaseline	50.00
Goblet, amber	85.00 to 110.00
Goblet, frosted tree trunk stem, clear	150.00
Goblet, vaseline	90.00 to 110.00
Pitcher, water, clear	67.50
Platter, 10½" oval, blue	45.00
Platter, 10½" oval, clear	40.00
Platter, 10½" oval, vaseline	45.00
Sauce dish, leaf-shaped, clear, 5½" l.	16.00
Spooner, blue	55.00
Spooner, clear	40.00
Spooner, green	45.00
Spooner, vaseline	65.00
Sugar bowl, cov., blue	95.00
Sugar bowl, open, clear	40.00

MARYLAND (Inverted Loops & Fans or Loops & Fans)
Banana bowl, flat, 11¼ x 5"	25.00
Bread platter	25.00
Butter dish, cov.	65.00
Cake stand, 8" d.	37.00
Celery vase	25.00
Compote, cov., 7" d., high stand	48.00
Compote, open, jelly	14.50
Compote, open, medium	32.50
Creamer	16.00
Goblet	25.00 to 35.00
Pickle dish	16.50

Pitcher, milk	39.00
Pitcher, water	60.00
Plate, 7" d.	10.00
Relish	13.50
Salt & pepper shakers w/original tops, pr.	65.00
Sauce dish	8.50
Spooner	30.00

Maryland Tumbler

Tumbler (ILLUS.)	26.00
Wine	40.00

MASCOTTE

Mascotte Footed Sauce Dish

Bowl, 9" d., 2¾" h.	35.00
Butter dish, cov.	45.00
Butter dish, cov., horseshoe-shaped, "Maude S."	100.00
Butter pat	10.00
Cake basket w/handle	55.00 to 70.00
Cake stand	35.00
Celery vase	35.00
Cheese dish, cov.	65.00
Compote, cov., 9" d., high stand	175.00
Compote, open, jelly	25.00
Creamer	30.00 to 38.00
Creamer & cov. sugar bowl, pr.	75.00
Goblet	22.50 to 35.00
Pitcher, water	70.00
Salt shaker w/original top (single)	9.00
Sauce dish, flat	8.50 to 12.00
Sauce dish, footed (ILLUS.)	14.00 to 20.00
Spooner	25.00
Sugar bowl, cov.	35.00 to 45.00
Sugar bowl, open	25.00
Tumbler	15.00
Wine	25.00

MASSACHUSETTS

Massachusetts Butter Dish

Banana boat, 8½ x 6½"	55.00
Bar bottle, 11" h.	62.50
Bowl, 6" sq.	16.00
Butter dish, cov. (ILLUS.)	52.50
Carafe	36.00
Cologne bottle w/stopper	37.50
Cordial	52.50
Creamer	22.50
Creamer, breakfast size	15.00
Cruet w/original stopper	40.00
Cruet w/original stopper, miniature	55.00
Decanter w/stopper	9.00
Goblet	45.00
Ice cream tray, 8"	16.50
Mug, 3½" h.	27.50
Olive dish, 5 x 3½"	8.50
Pitcher, water	75.00
Plate, 5" sq., serrated rim	19.00
Plate, 6" sq., w/advertising	16.50
Plate, 8" sq.	20.00 to 30.00
Punch bowl, pedestal base, small size	95.00
Punch cup	12.00
Relish, 8½" l.	12.50
Rum jug, 5" h.	75.00
Spooner	20.00
Sugar bowl, open, 2-handled	17.50
Toothpick holder	45.00
Tumbler, juice	20.00
Tumbler, water	30.00
Vase, 6½" h., trumpet-shaped	13.00
Vase, 6½" h., trumpet-shaped, cobalt blue w/gold	40.00 to 60.00
Vase, 9" h., trumpet-shaped, green	33.00
Vase, 10" h., trumpet-shaped, green	38.00
Whiskey shot glass	15.00
Whiskey set, bar bottle & 6 shot glasses, 7 pcs.	125.00
Wine	42.50

MELROSE

Butter dish, cov.	45.00
Cake stand, 8" d.	27.50
Celery vase	20.00

Compote, open, jelly, 5½" d.	15.00
Compote, open, 7" d., 7" h.	25.00
Creamer	30.00
Goblet	15.00
Pitcher, water	35.00
Plate, 8" d.	9.00
Spooner	30.00
Sugar bowl, cov.	38.00
Tray, water, 11½" d.	38.00
Wine	15.00 to 25.00

MICHIGAN (Paneled Jewel or Loop & Pillar)

Michigan Goblet

Bowl, cov., master berry or fruit, clear	75.00
Bowl, 7½ x 5¼" oval, clear	12.50
Bowl, 9" d., clear	25.00
Bowl, 9" d., clear w/pink stain	55.00
Bowl, 10" d., clear	35.00
Butter dish, cov., clear	45.00
Butter dish, cov., clear w/pink stain	200.00
Butter dish, cov., clear w/yellow stain & enameled florals	190.00
Carafe, water, clear	150.00
Carafe, water, clear w/pink stain	150.00
Celery vase, clear	30.00 to 35.00
Celery vase, clear w/pink stain & gold	75.00
Champagne, clear w/blue stain	50.00
Champagne, clear w/yellow stain	50.00
Compote, open, jelly, 4½" d., clear	23.00
Compote, open, 10" d., clear	45.00
Creamer, clear, 4" h.	30.00
Creamer, clear w/pink stain, 4" h.	65.00
Creamer, individual size, clear	15.00
Creamer, individual size, clear w/yellow stain & enameled florals	24.00
Creamer & open sugar bowl, individual size, clear, pr.	45.00

Finger bowl, clear	14.50
Goblet, clear (ILLUS.)	36.50
Goblet, clear w/pink stain & gold	38.00
Honey dish, clear, 3½" d.	8.00
Mug, clear	15.00
Mug, clear w/pink stain & gold	35.00
Olive dish, clear w/pink stain	32.50
Parfait, clear	30.00
Pickle dish, clear	12.00
Pitcher, water, 8" h., clear	47.50
Pitcher, water, 12" h., clear	60.00
Pitcher, water, 12" h., clear w/pink stain	135.00
Punch cup, clear w/enameled decor	9.00
Relish, clear	20.00
Salt & pepper shakers w/original tops, clear, pr.	38.00
Sauce dish, clear	10.00
Sauce dish, clear w/pink stain	20.00
Sauce dish, clear w/yellow stain & enameled florals	21.00
Spooner, clear	25.00
Spooner, clear w/pink stain	50.00
Spooner, clear w/yellow stain & enameled florals	45.00
Sugar bowl, cov., clear	50.00
Sugar bowl, individual size, clear	26.00
Syrup jug w/pewter top, clear	100.00
Table set, clear w/pink stain, 4 pcs.	400.00
Toothpick holder, clear	25.00
Toothpick holder, clear w/enameled florals	45.00
Toothpick holder, clear w/yellow stain	50.00
Toothpick holder, clear w/yellow stain & enameled florals	68.00
Tumbler, clear	25.00
Tumbler, clear w/pink stain & gold	50.00
Vase, 6" h., clear	10.00
Vase, 6" h., clear w/pink stain & gold	17.50
Vase, 8" h., clear	18.00
Vase, 8" h., clear w/green stain & white enameled dots	35.00
Water set: pitcher & 6 tumblers; clear, 7 pcs.	150.00
Water set: pitcher & 6 tumblers; clear w/pink stain, 7 pcs.	325.00
Wine, amber	32.50
Wine, clear	27.50
Wine, clear w/yellow stain	35.00

MIKADO - See Daisy & Button with Cross-bars Pattern

MINERVA

Bread tray, 13" l.	69.00
Butter dish, cov.	75.00
Cake stand, 9" d.	68.00
Cake stand, 10½" d.	95.00

Compote, cov., 8" d., low stand	80.00
Compote, cov., 8" d., high stand	135.00
Compote, open, 10" d., 9" h.	55.00
Creamer	42.50
Creamer & open sugar bowl, pr.	75.00
Goblet	80.00
Marmalade jar, cov.	150.00
Pickle dish, "Love's Request is Pickles," oval	25.00
Pitcher, milk, 7½" h.	72.50
Pitcher, water	150.00
Plate, 8" d., J.C. Bates portrait center, scalloped rim	50.00
Plate, 9" d., handled	57.00
Plate, 10" d., Mars center	50.00

Minerva Relish

Relish, 8 x 5" oblong (ILLUS.)	27.50
Sauce dish, flat or footed	14.00 to 20.00
Spooner	36.50
Sugar bowl, cov.	60.00
Sugar bowl, open	30.00

MINNESOTA

Banana bowl, flat	50.00
Basket w/applied reeded handle	65.00
Berry set, 10" d. master bowl & 5 sauce dishes, 6 pcs.	55.00
Bowl, 8½" d.	30.00
Butter dish, cov.	45.00
Carafe	35.00
Celery tray, 13" l.	25.00
Compote, open, 9" sq.	47.50
Creamer, 3½" h.	23.50
Creamer, individual size	16.50
Cruet w/original stopper	32.50
Cup, large	17.00
Flower frog, green, 2 pcs.	45.00
Goblet	25.00
Mug	19.00
Olive dish, oval	12.50
Pickle dish	10.00
Pitcher, water, tankard	85.00
Plate, 7 3/8" d., turned-up rim	12.50

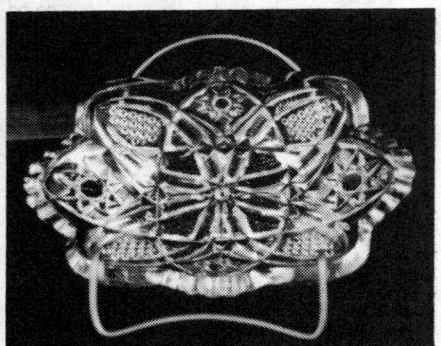

Minnesota Relish

Relish, 5 x 3" (ILLUS.)	9.00
Relish, 8¾ x 6½" oblong	13.00
Sauce dish	15.00
Spooner	17.00
Sugar bowl, cov.	29.50
Syrup pitcher w/original top	55.00
Toothpick holder, 3-handled	22.50
Tumbler	18.00
Wine	26.00

MIRROR

Mirror Pomade Jar

Bar bottle	40.00
Celery vase	75.00
Champagne	31.00
Compote, open, 7" d., 7" h.	85.00
Compote, open, 10" d., 7½" h.	120.00
Goblet, bulb stem	65.00
Pomade jar w/ground stopper, 3½" h. (ILLUS.)	35.00
Salt dip, cov., master size	95.00
Spillholder	40.00
Spooner	22.00
Sugar bowl, cov.	60.00
Tumbler, bar	30.00
Tumbler, footed	45.00
Wine	25.00 to 37.50

MISSOURI (Palm & Scroll)

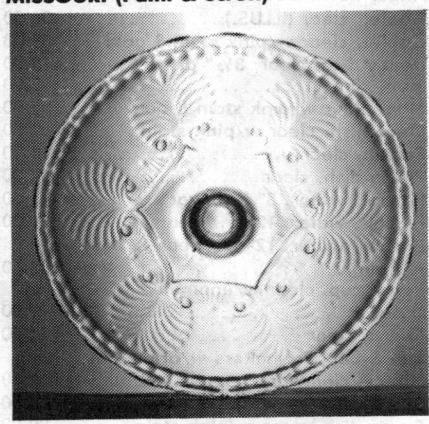

Missouri Doughnut Stand

Bowl, 8¾" d., green	30.00
Butter dish, cov., clear	50.00
Butter dish, cov., green	65.00
Cake stand, clear, 9" d., 4¾" h.	38.00
Calery vase, clear	30.00
Compote, jelly, clear	22.50
Creamer, clear	25.00
Creamer, green	40.00
Cruet w/original stopper, clear	45.00
Crueet w/original stopper, green	160.00
Doughnut stand, clear, 6" d. (ILLUS.)	35.00
Goblet, clear	47.50
Mug, green	40.00
Pitcher, milk, clear	45.00
Pitcher, water, clear	65.00
Pitcher, water, tankard, green	80.00
Relish, clear	10.00
Sauce dish, clear	10.50
Sauce dish, green	14.00
Spooner, clear	25.00
Spooner, green	40.00
Sugar bowl, cov, clear	50.00
Sugar bowl, cov., green	55.00
Table set, clear, 4 pcs.	197.00
Wine, clear	40.00
Wine, green	40.00

MOON & STARS

Moon & Stars Pattern

Berry set, master bowl & 6 sauce
   dishes, 7 pcs. 95.00
Bowl, cov., 7" d. 30.00
Bowl, 8" d. 28.00
Bowl, fruit, 9" d., footed 30.00
Bowl, 10 x 7", teardrop-shaped 42.00
Bread tray, scalloped rim,
   10¾ x 6½" 24.50
Butter dish, cov. (ILLUS. left) 57.50
Cake stand, 9" d. 35.00
Cake stand, 10" d. 48.00
Cake stand, 11½" d. 70.00
Carafe, water 40.00
Celery vase 42.50
Champagne 32.00
Compote, cov., 6" d., 10" h. 45.00
Compote, cov., 6" d., low stand 50.00
Compote, cov., 8" d., 12" h. 52.50
Compote, open, 7" d., 7½" h. 32.50
Compote, open, 8" d.,
   8" h. 33.50 to 47.50
Compote, open, 9" d., 6½" h. 40.00
Compote, open, 10" d., high stand . . 125.00
Creamer (ILLUS. right) 45.00
Goblet 35.00
Lamp, kerosene-type, table model,
   amber 190.00
Lamp, kerosene-type, table model,
   blue 190.00
Lamp, kerosene-type, table model,
   clear font, milk white base,
   15" h. 145.00
Pickle dish, 8" l. . . . . 15.00 to 20.00
Relish, oblong 20.00
Salt dip, individual size, footed 12.00
Salt & pepper shakers w/original
   tops, pr. 50.00
Sauce dish, flat or
   footed . . . . 7.50 to 15.00
Spillholder 37.50
Spooner 45.00
Sugar bowl, cov. (ILLUS. center) 65.00
Syrup pitcher w/original top 75.00
Tumbler, flat 45.00
Tumbler, footed, flint 67.50
Wine 35.00

**MOON & STARS WITH WAFFLE - See
Jeweled Moon & Star Pattern**

MORNING GLORY
Compote, 9" d., 8" h. 165.00
Egg cup 325.00
Syrup pitcher w/original pewter top,
   opaque white 85.00

NAIL
Cake stand, clear 50.00
Celery vase, clear w/ruby
   staining 55.00
Cordial, clear 45.00
Decanter, clear 40.00
Pitcher, water, clear 65.00

Sauce dish, flat or footed,
   clear . . . . 7.50 to 11.00
Wine, clear, etched 68.00

NAILHEAD

Nailhead Goblet

Bowl, 6" d. 16.00
Butter dish, cov. . . . . 30.00 to 46.50
Cake stand, 10½" d. 30.00
Celery vase 50.00
Compote, cov., 6¼" d., 6¼" h. 40.00
Compote, cov., 6¼" d., 9½" h. 45.00
Compote, open, 6½" d., 6¾" h. 25.00
Compote, open, 9" d., 6½" h. 35.00
Compote, open, 10" d.,
   7" h. 45.00 to 50.00
Creamer & open sugar bowl, pr. 30.00
Goblet (ILLUS.) 22.50
Pitcher, water 47.50
Plate, 7" sq. 16.50
Plate, 9" sq. 18.50
Sauce dish, 4" 8.00
Spooner 22.50
Sugar bowl, cov. 25.00
Tumbler 36.50
Wine . . . . 15.00 to 22.50

NEPTUNE - See Bearded Man Pattern

NESTOR

Nestor Butter Dish

Butter dish, cov., blue, gold trim
(ILLUS.)........................ 65.00
Cruet w/original stopper, blue, gold
trim............................ 100.00
Cruet w/stopper, green............ 70.00
Sauce dish, purple, gold trim....... 25.00
Tumbler, blue, gold trim.......... 75.00
Tumbler, purple, gold trim......... 28.00

NEW ENGLAND PINEAPPLE

New England Pineapple Egg Cup

Bowl, 8" d., footed, scalloped rim .. 80.00
Cake stand....................... 115.00
Castor bottle..................... 35.00
Champagne....................... 175.00
Compote, cov., 5" d., 8½" h........ 150.00
Compote, open, 7" d., 4" h......... 65.00
Compote, open, 8" d., 5" h......... 75.00
Creamer, applied handle........... 165.00
Decanter w/bar lip, qt. 120.00
Decanter w/original stopper 225.00
Egg cup (ILLUS.).................. 32.50
Goblet........................... 50.00
Goblet, lady's.................... 70.00
Honey dish....................... 20.00
Plate, 6" d....................... 85.00
Salt dip, individual size 25.00
Salt dip, master size.............. 36.00
Sauce dish....................... 12.00
Spooner.......................... 40.00
Sugar bowl, cov. 95.00
Tumbler, bar..................... 95.00
Tumbler, water................... 85.00
Tumbler, whiskey, applied handle .. 145.00
Wine............................ 135.00

NEW JERSEY (Loops & Drops)

Compote, open, jelly ....20.00 to 30.00
Compote, open, 7" d., 3½" h....... 12.50
Creamer 35.00
Cruet w/original stopper........... 45.00
Goblet 35.00
Olive dish 18.00
Plate, 8" d. 12.00
Plate, 11" d. 18.50
Relish 15.00

Sauce dish, flat 11.50
Sugar bowl, cov. 40.00
Toothpick holder 40.00
Tumbler 22.00
Water set, pitcher & 6 tumblers,
7 pcs. 165.00
Wine............................ 30.00

NORTHWOOD DRAPERY - See Opalescent Glass

NOTCHED RIB - See Broken Column Pattern

OAKEN BUCKET (Wooden Pail)

Oaken Bucket Pitcher

Butter dish, cov., blue 100.00
Butter dish, cov., clear 45.00
Creamer, amber 40.00
Creamer, amethyst 85.00
Creamer, blue 75.00
Creamer, clear 35.00
Creamer, vaseline 40.00
Match holder w/original wire
handle, amber, 2 5/8" d.,
2 5/8" h. 19.50
Pitcher, water, amber 82.50
Pitcher, water, amethyst (ILLUS.) ... 137.50
Pitcher, water, blue ....75.00 to 110.00
Pitcher, water, clear.............. 57.50
Salt dip, clear................... 12.00
Spooner, amber 40.00
Spooner, blue 47.50
Spooner, vaseline 55.00
Sugar bowl, cov., blue 45.00
Sugar bowl, cov., clear 35.00
Sugar bowl, cov., vaseline 55.00
Sugar bowl, open, amber 20.00
Sugar bowl, open, blue 20.00
Sugar bowl, open, miniature,
amethyst 22.50
Toothpick holder, blue 22.50
Toothpick holder, clear 27.50
Toothpick holder, vaseline 27.50
Tumbler, clear 15.00

OAK LEAF BAND

Oak Leaf Band Goblet

Bowl, 8 x 5½" oval	9.50
Butter dish, cov.	45.00
Goblet (ILLUS.)	32.50
Mug, applied handle, 3½" h.	37.50
Pitcher, 6" h.	36.00
Relish	10.00
Sauce dish, 5" d.	16.00

OLD MAN OF THE MOUNTAIN - See Viking Pattern

OLD MAN OF THE WOODS - See Bearded Man Pattern

ONE HUNDRED ONE

One Hundred One Creamer

Creamer, 4¾" h. (ILLUS.)	24.50
Goblet	30.00
Sugar bowl, cov.	45.00

OPEN ROSE

Compote, open, 7½" d.	32.50
Creamer	40.00
Egg cup	21.50
Goblet	19.50
Goblet, buttermilk	22.00
Goblet, lady's	28.00
Relish, 8 x 5½"	12.50
Sauce dish	10.00
Spooner (ILLUS.)	27.50

Open Rose Spooner

Sugar bowl, cov.	50.00
Sugar bowl, open	25.00
Tumbler	28.00
Tumbler, applied handle	65.00
Water set, pitcher & 6 goblets, 7 pcs.	325.00

OREGON NO. 1 - See Beaded Loop Pattern

OREGON NO. 2 (Skilton)

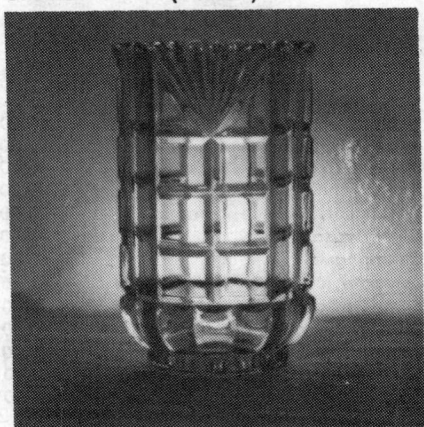

Skilton Celery Vase

Bowl, 7¾" d., 2½" h., clear	12.50
Butter dish, cov., clear	40.00
Cake stand, clear, 9" d.	35.00
Celery vase, clear (ILLUS.)	27.50
Compote, open, 5½" d., 4½" h., clear	22.50
Compote, open, 8½" d., low stand, clear	35.00

Compote, open, 8½" d., low stand,
  ruby-stained 55.00
Decanter, whiskey, clear........... 29.00
Pitcher, milk, clear 25.00
Pitcher, water, tankard, clear 40.00
Pitcher, water, tankard, ruby-
  stained........................ 125.00
Relish, clear 15.00
Sauce dish, clear 10.00
Spooner, ruby-stained 40.00
Syrup pitcher w/original top, clear .. 45.00
Tumbler, ruby-stained 35.00
Wine, clear 32.50

OWL IN FAN - See Parrot Pattern

PALM & SCROLL - See Missouri Pattern

PALMETTE

Palmette Goblet

Bowl, 8" d., flat.................. 25.00
Butter dish, cov. 52.50
Butter pat 45.00
Cake stand 45.00
Castor set, 5-bottle, complete 125.00
Celery vase 31.50
Champagne........................ 68.00
Compote, cov., 8" d., high stand ... 67.50
Compote, open, 8" d., low stand ... 30.00
Creamer, applied handle........... 60.00
Cup plate 45.00
Egg cup 22.00
Goblet (ILLUS.)................... 32.50
Lamp, kerosene-type, table model
  w/stem 72.50
Lamp, kerosene-type, table model
  w/stem, milk white 85.00
Pitcher, water, applied handle 95.00
Relish 17.50
Salt dip, master size, footed 20.00
Salt & pepper shakers w/original
  tops, 5½" h., pr................. 55.00
Sauce dish................. 6.50 to 10.00
Spooner 32.50

Sugar bowl, cov. 40.00
Sugar bowl, open 20.00
Syrup pitcher w/original top,
  applied handle 110.00
Tumbler, bar...................... 58.00
Tumbler, water, footed 55.00

PANELED CANE
Creamer & cov. sugar bowl, clear,
  pr.............................. 32.00
Goblet, amber 25.00
Goblet, clear 22.00

**PANELED CHERRY WITH THUMBPRINTS
(Cherry Thumbprints)**

Paneled Cherry Sugar Bowl & Creamer

(All pieces in clear glass w/red-stained cherries & gilt cable trim)

Berry set, master bowl & 6 sauce
  dishes, 7 pcs. 135.00
Butter dish, cov. .... 85.00 to 110.00
Celery dish 45.00
Creamer (ILLUS.) 45.00
Pitcher, water .... 110.00 to 125.00
Punch cup, footed 26.00
Sauce dish................. 12.00 to 15.00
Spooner 45.00
Sugar bowl, cov. (ILLUS.)........... 45.00
Tumbler 25.00
Water set, pitcher & 6 tumblers;
  7 pcs. 225.00

PANELED DAISY

Paneled Daisy Pickle Dish

Bowl, 7 x 5" oval................. 10.00
Bowl, berry, 8¼ x 5¾" oval 25.00
Butter dish, cov. 45.00
Cake stand, tall pedestal, 8" d...... 30.00
Cake stand, 11½" d. 45.00
Celery vase 32.50
Compote, cov., 5" d., high stand ... 40.00

Creamer	35.00
Goblet	25.00
Mug	30.00
Pickle dish, handled (ILLUS.)	15.00
Pitcher, water	45.00
Plate, 7½" sq.	16.00
Plate, 9" sq.	24.00
Relish, 7 x 5" oval	12.50
Sauce dish, flat or footed	6.00 to 12.00
Spooner	25.00

PANELED DEWDROP

Bowl, 8½" oval	24.00
Bread platter, 12½ x 9½"	60.00
Butter dish, cov.	65.00
Celery vase	35.00
Compote, open	35.00
Cordial, 3¼" h.	30.00
Creamer	25.00
Creamer, individual size	20.00
Goblet	28.00
Marmalade jar, cov.	42.50
Mug, applied handle	35.00
Pitcher, milk	42.50
Plate, 7" d.	15.00
Plate, 9" d.	30.00
Sauce dish, flat or footed	6.00 to 10.00
Spooner	35.00
Sugar bowl, cov.	38.00
Wine	21.50

PANELED DIAMOND CROSS - See Heavy Paneled Finecut Pattern

PANELED FINECUT - See Finecut & Panel Pattern

PANELED FORGET-ME-NOT

Paneled Forget-Me-Not Cake Stand

Bread platter, 11 x 7" oval	30.00
Butter dish, cov.	35.00
Cake stand, 10" d. (ILLUS.)	32.50
Celery vase	35.00
Compote, cov., 6" d., 9½" h.	45.00
Compote, cov., 7" d., 10" h.	65.00
Compote, cov., 8" d., high stand	50.00 to 75.00

Compote, open, 8½" d., 12" h., scalloped rim	45.00
Compote, open, 10" d., 7½" h.	38.00
Creamer	27.50
Goblet	32.50
Marmalade jar, cov.	36.00
Pitcher, milk	47.50
Pitcher, water	60.00
Relish, handled, 7¾ x 4½"	15.00
Relish, handled, 9 x 5"	20.00
Salt & pepper shakers w/original tops, pr.	65.00
Sauce dish, flat or footed	15.00
Spooner	22.00
Sugar bowl, cov.	40.00
Sugar bowl, open	18.00
Water set, pitcher & 6 tumblers, 7 pcs.	265.00
Wine	38.50

PANELED GRAPE

Butter dish, cov.	68.00
Compote, open, 6½" h.	65.00
Creamer	25.00
Goblet	25.00
Sauce dish	10.00
Sugar bowl, cov., small	25.00
Sugar bowl, open	25.00
Tumbler	18.00

PANELED HEATHER

Paneled Heather Jelly Compote

Bowl, 8¼" d., 3¾" h.	24.00
Butter dish, cov., ruby-stained	40.00
Cake plate, 9½" d., 4" h.	32.00
Compote, cov.	40.00
Compote, open, jelly (ILLUS.)	20.00
Compote, open, 8" d.	27.50
Creamer	22.50
Goblet	24.00
Pitcher, water	38.00
Plate, 12" d.	15.00
Sauce dish, flat or footed	7.00 to 10.00
Spooner	18.00
Sugar bowl, open	18.00
Table set, h.p. florals, gilt trim, 4 pcs.	175.00
Tumbler	30.00
Wine	18.50

PANELED HERRINGBONE (Emerald Green Herringbone or Florida)

Paneled Herringbone Water Pitcher

Berry set: 9" d. master bowl & 6 sauce dishes; green, 7 pcs.	95.00
Bowl, 7½" d., green	35.00
Bowl, oval vegetable, green, large	45.00
Butter dish, cov., green	45.00
Cake stand, green, 9½" d.	42.00
Cake stand, clear, 10½" d.	25.00
Celery vase, green	55.00
Compote, open, jelly, 5½" sq., green	25.00
Creamer, clear	20.00
Creamer, green	30.00
Cruet w/original stopper, green	100.00
Goblet, clear	14.50
Goblet, green	32.50
Mustard pot, cov., clear	22.50
Nappy, green	19.00
Pitcher, water, clear	35.00
Pitcher, water, green (ILLUS.)	65.00
Plate, 7" sq., green	17.00
Plate, 9" sq., clear	15.00
Relish, green, 6" sq.	15.00
Relish, green, 8½" sq.	18.00
Salt shaker w/original top, green (single)	20.00
Sauce dish, green	11.50
Sugar bowl, open, green	28.00
Syrup pitcher w/original top, green	225.00
Tumbler, green	23.50
Water set: pitcher & 4 tumblers; green, 5 pcs.	120.00
Water set: pitcher & 6 goblets; green, 7 pcs.	215.00
Wine, clear	26.00
Wine, green	55.00

PANELED JEWEL - See Michigan Pattern

PANELED STAR & BUTTON - See Sedan Pattern

PANELED THISTLE

Basket w/applied handle, 7 x 4¾", 2½" h.	35.00
Bowl, cov., 5½" d., 4" h., w/bee	48.00
Bowl, 5½" d., 2½" h., footed	15.00
Bowl, 7" oval, 1¾" h.	20.00
Bowl, 9" d., deep, w/bee	34.50
Butter dish, cov., w/bee	40.00 to 55.00
Cake stand, 9½" d., 5" h.	32.50
Celery vase	30.00
Champagne, flared, w/bee	37.00
Compote, open, 5" d., low stand	18.50
Compote, open, 5" d., high stand	23.50
Compote, open, 7½" d., 7" h.	35.00
Compote, open, 9" d., 6½" h.	35.00

Paneled Thistle Creamer

Creamer (ILLUS.)	30.00
Cruet w/stopper	40.00
Goblet	26.50
Honey dish, cov., square	50.00
Honey dish, open	10.00
Pitcher, milk	32.50
Pitcher, water, w/bee	68.00
Plate, 7" sq.	16.00
Plate, 7" sq., w/bee	20.00
Plate, 9½" d.	36.00
Punch cup	16.00
Relish, 8½ x 4"	12.50
Rose bowl, 5" d., 2¾" h.	21.50
Rose bowl, extra large	50.00
Salt dip, master size	9.00
Salt dip, master size, w/bee	15.00
Salt & pepper shakers w/original tops, pr.	42.50
Sauce dish, flat or footed	10.00 to 20.00
Spooner, handled	18.50
Sugar bowl, cov.	30.00
Sugar bowl, open	16.50
Toothpick holder	29.00
Vase, 8" h., trumpet-shaped	35.00
Wine	20.00

PANELED ZIPPER - See Iowa Pattern

PARROT (Owl in Fan)

Goblet	32.50

Pitcher, water 75.00
Spooner 25.00
Wine.............................. 50.00

PAVONIA (Pineapple Stem)

Pavonia Tumbler

(Items may be plain or with etched designs)

Butter dish, cov. 60.00
Butter dish, cov., ruby-stained 110.00
Cake stand, 10" d. 47.50
Celery vase....................... 37.50
Compote, open, jelly 38.00
Creamer 45.00
Creamer, ruby-stained 65.00
Cup plate......................... 28.00
Finger bowl, 7" d................. 36.00
Goblet 30.00
Mug, applied handle 15.00
Pitcher, water, tall tankard 70.00
Pitcher, water, tall tankard, ruby-
   stained......................... 95.00
Salt dip, master size.............. 18.50
Sauce dish, flat or
   footed ....7.00 to 12.00
Spooner ....35.00 to 45.00
Sugar bowl, cov. 55.00
Sugar bowl, cov., ruby-stained 75.00
Table set, 4 pcs. 265.00
Table set, ruby-stained & etched,
   4 pcs. 325.00
Tray, water 60.00
Tumbler (ILLUS.).................. 25.00
Tumbler, ruby-stained ....30.00 to 40.00
Waste bowl....................... 45.00
Waste bowl, ruby-stained 110.00
Wine.....................25.00 to 32.50

PEACOCK FEATHER (Georgia)

Berry set, master bowl & 6 sauce
   dishes, 7 pcs. 75.00
Bon bon dish, footed 25.00
Butter dish, cov. 42.50

Cake stand, 8½" d., 5" h. 35.00
Cake stand, 10" d. 50.00
Celery tray, 11¾" l. 35.00
Compote, open, jelly 28.00
Compote, open, 6½" d., high
   stand 25.00

Peacock Feather Compote

Compote, open, 7½" d. (ILLUS.) 30.00
Compote, open, 8" d., high
   stand 42.00
Creamer 22.00
Cruet w/original stopper 50.00
Cup plate......................... 25.00
Decanter, no stopper 30.00
Lamp, kerosene-type, low hand-type
   w/handle, blue, 5¼" h. 135.00
Lamp, kerosene-type, table model
   w/handle, blue, 9" h. ...225.00 to 255.00
Lamp, kerosene-type, table model
   w/handle, 9" h...........40.00 to 65.00
Lamp, kerosene-type, table model,
   blue, 12" h...................... 235.00
Mug.............................. 19.00
Pitcher, water 52.50
Salt & pepper shakers w/original
   tops, pr........................ 50.00
Sauce dish........................ 9.00
Spooner 36.00
Sugar bowl, cov. 45.00

PENNSYLVANIA, EARLY - See Hand Pattern

PENNSYLVANIA, LATE - See Balder Pattern

PICKET

Picket Sauce Dish

Bread tray, 13 x 8"................ 67.50
Butter dish, cov. ....45.00 to 55.00
Celery 55.00
Compote, open, 7" sq., 7" h. 35.00
Creamer 42.50
Goblet 35.00

Lamp, kerosene-type, clear
  w/amber stain 195.00
Pitcher, water 85.00
Salt dip, master size............. 32.50
Sauce dish (ILLUS.) 8.00
Spooner 30.00
Sugar bowl, cov. 40.00
Toothpick holder 30.00
Wine 50.00

PILLAR
Ale glass, 6½" h. 42.50
Claret 55.00
Compote, open, 8" d............... 55.00
Creamer 70.00
Decanter w/bar lip, pt. 52.50
Goblet ....40.00 to 50.00
Saucer, footed, 8" d. 95.00
Wine 45.00

PILLAR & BULL'S EYE

Pillar & Bull's Eye Decanter

Decanter w/bar lip, 10" h. (ILLUS.).. 80.00
Goblet ....45.00 to 70.00
Pitcher, water, applied handle 325.00
Tumbler 65.00
Wine ....50.00 to 65.00

PILLAR VARIANT - See Hercules Pillar Pattern

PILLOW & SUNBURST
Creamer 20.00
Creamer & sugar bowl, pr........... 32.50
Plate, 10¼" d. 30.00
Spooner 30.00

PILLOW ENCIRCLED

(Called Ruby Rosette when ruby-stained.)

Bowl, 8" d., clear 28.00
Bowl, 8" d., Ruby Rosette 52.50
Butter dish, cov., clear 65.00
Butter dish, cov., Ruby Rosette 75.00

Celery vase, clear 25.00
Celery vase, Ruby Rosette 50.00
Compote, clear 40.00
Creamer, clear..................... 30.00
Creamer, Ruby Rosette 37.50
Creamer & cov. sugar bowl, clear,
  pr........................... 75.00
Cruet w/original stopper, Ruby
  Rosette...................... 135.00
Lamp, kerosene, w/stem, clear,
  10¼" h. 36.50
Pitcher, milk, Ruby Rosette 85.00
Pitcher, water, tankard, clear 36.00
Pitcher, water, tankard, Ruby
  Rosette ....95.00 to 105.00
Sauce dish, footed, clear.......... 16.00
Sauce dish, footed, Ruby Rosette ... 20.00
Spooner, clear ....25.00 to 30.00
Spooner, Ruby Rosette ......45.00 to 55.00
Sugar bowl, cov., clear 32.50
Sugar bowl, cov., Ruby Rosette 37.50
Sugar shaker, clear (no top)........ 18.00
Table set: cov. butter dish, sugar
  bowl & spooner; Ruby Rosette,
  3 pcs. 285.00
Tumbler, clear 15.00
Tumbler, Ruby Rosette 30.00
Water set: tankard pitcher & 6 tum-
  blers; Ruby Rosette w/etching,
  7 pcs. 240.00

PINEAPPLE & FAN
Celery tray 25.00
Creamer 30.00
Sugar shaker 27.50

PINEAPPLE STEM - See Pavonia Pattern

PLEAT & PANEL (Darby)

Pleat & Panel Goblet

Bowl, cov., 8 x 5" 42.50
Bowl, 7" d., 4½" h., footed 22.50
Bread tray, closed handles,
  13 x 8½"..................... 36.00
Butter dish, cov., footed 55.00
Cake stand, 9" to 10" sq. ....40.00 to 45.00
Celery vase, footed 35.00

Compote, cov., 7" sq.,
10½" h. ....45.00 to 65.00
Creamer 26.00
Goblet (ILLUS.)................... 25.00
Lamp, kerosene, stem 85.00
Pickle dish...................... 20.00
Pitcher, water ....45.00 to 55.00
Plate, 5" sq. 20.00
Plate, 6" sq..................... 17.50
Plate, 7" sq., amber 32.50
Plate, 7" sq., amethyst 95.00
Plate, 7" sq., clear 20.00
Plate, 8" sq., clear 25.00
Platter w/open handles ......30.00 to 50.00
Relish, 7 x 4½" 12.50
Relish, 9½" l.................... 25.00
Salt dip, master size............. 18.00
Salt shaker w/original top (single) .. 25.00
Sauce dish, flat, handled........... 10.50
Sauce dish, footed ....12.00 to 20.00
Spooner 25.00
Sugar bowl, cov................. 45.00
Sugar bowl, open 12.50
Waste bowl...................... 25.00

PLEAT & TUCK - See Adonis Pattern

PLUME

Plume Compote

Berry set: 8½" sq. master bowl &
five 4½" sq. sauce dishes; clear,
6 pcs. 80.00
Bowl, 6" d., clear 22.50
Bowl, 8" d., shallow, clear 28.00
Bowl, 8½" sq., master berry,
clear ....25.00 to 35.00
Butter dish, cov., clear 48.00
Cake stand, clear, 9" d.,
5¾" h....................45.00 to 50.00
Celery vase, clear 25.00
Compote, cov., 6½" d., 12" h.,
clear 95.00
Compote, open, 7" d., 6¾" h.,
clear 35.00
Compote, open, 8" d., 8" h., clear .. 45.00
Compote, open, 9" d., 6½" h., clear
(ILLUS.)........................ 48.00
Creamer, applied handle, clear 30.00
Creamer, ruby-stained 55.00
Creamer & cov. sugar bowl, clear,
pr.............................. 65.00
Goblet, clear 30.00

Goblet, ruby-stained & etched 55.00
Pitcher, water, clear.............. 70.00
Pitcher, water, ruby-stained 140.00
Relish, clear 25.00
Sauce dish, flat or footed,
clear....................8.50 to 12.50
Sauce dish, ruby-stained 20.00
Spooner, clear 26.50
Spooner, ruby-stained 55.00
Sugar bowl, cov., clear 30.00
Sugar bowl, cov., ruby-stained 90.00
Sugar bowl, open, clear 20.00
Sugar bowl, open, ruby-stained..... 37.50
Tumbler, clear 35.00
Waste bowl, clear 45.00
Water set: pitcher & 6 tumblers;
clear, 7 pcs. 165.00

POINTED THUMBPRINT - See Almond Thumbprint Pattern

POLAR BEAR

Polar Bear Waste Bowl

Bread tray, frosted 175.00
Claret 120.00
Goblet, clear 125.00
Goblet, clear & frosted 110.00
Pitcher, water, frosted ....250.00 to 350.00
Tray, water, clear, 16" l.......... 95.00
Tray, water, frosted,
16" l. ....195.00 to 250.00
Waste bowl, clear 87.50
Waste bowl, frosted (ILLUS.) 110.00

POPCORN

Popcorn Cake Stand

Butter dish, cov.	52.50
Cake stand, 11" d. (ILLUS.)	66.50
Celery vase, 6½" h.	40.00
Cheese dish, cov., 11 x 8"	185.00
Creamer w/raised ears	47.50
Creamer & cov. sugar bowl, pr.	110.00
Goblet w/raised ears	42.50
Goblet	30.00
Pickle dish, oval	12.50
Pitcher, water	80.00
Spooner w/raised ears	40.00
Spooner	35.00
Sugar bowl, cov.	40.00
Wine w/raised ears	58.00
Wine	35.00

PORTLAND

Portland Creamer

Basket w/high handle	125.00
Bowl, 9" d.	25.00
Butter dish, cov.	50.00
Cake stand, 10½"	45.00
Carafe	30.00
Celery tray	21.50
Celery vase	35.00
Compote, cov., 6½" d., high stand	115.00
Compote, open, 7½" d., 5½" h.	48.00
Cordial	30.00
Creamer (ILLUS.)	20.00
Creamer & open sugar bowl, oval, pr.	28.00
Cruet w/original stopper	25.00
Dresser jar, cov., 5" d.	22.50
Goblet	22.50
Lamp, kerosene, 9" h.	65.00
Pitcher, water	75.00
Pitcher, water, miniature	20.00
Punch cup	12.00
Relish, boat-shaped, 9" l.	12.50
Relish, boat-shaped, 12" l.	18.50
Salt & pepper shakers w/original tops, pr.	30.00
Sauce dish, 4½" d.	7.50
Spooner	27.50
Sugar bowl, cov.	36.50
Sugar bowl, open	17.50
Syrup pitcher w/original top	125.00
Toothpick holder	25.00
Tumbler	18.50

Vase, 6" h., scalloped rim	14.00
Vase, 9" h.	30.00
Wine	20.00

PORTLAND MAIDEN BLUSH (Banded Portland with Color)

Portland Maiden Blush Sauce

Bowl, 9" d.	26.50
Butter dish, cov.	165.00
Celery tray, 10" oval	65.00
Celery vase	67.50
Creamer	75.00
Creamer, breakfast size	30.00
Goblet	50.00
Marmalade jar w/silverplate cover, frame & spoon, 3 pcs.	95.00
Perfume bottle w/original stopper	85.00
Pin tray, souvenir	12.50
Pitcher, tankard, 11" h.	150.00
Pitcher, water, child's	35.00
Powder jar, cov.	85.00
Punch cup	18.00 to 25.00
Relish, 6½ x 4"	25.00
Relish, boat-shaped, 8¾ x 4¼"	32.50
Salt & pepper shakers w/original tops, pr.	125.00
Sauce dish, 4½" d. (ILLUS.)	30.00
Sugar bowl, cov., large	115.00
Sugar shaker w/original top	120.00
Table set, 4 pcs.	285.00
Toothpick holder	42.50
Tumbler	27.00
Vase, 4" h.	25.00
Vase, 6" h.	27.50
Wine	55.00

PORTLAND WITH DIAMOND POINT BAND - See Banded Portland Pattern

POST (Square Panes)

Bowl, cov., 6¾" d., footed	45.00
Bowl, 8" sq.	25.00
Butter dish, cov.	42.50
Cake stand, 9½" d.	60.00
Celery vase	42.50
Compote, cov., 7½" d., high stand	70.00
Creamer	40.00
Goblet	42.50
Lamp, kerosene, 8½" h.	65.00
Pitcher, water	75.00
Spooner	28.00
Sugar bowl, cov.	47.50

POTTED PLANT - See Flower Pot Pattern

POWDER & SHOT

Butter dish, cov.	65.00
Creamer, applied handle, flint	95.00
Egg cup, flint	45.00
Goblet, flint	60.00
Goblet, buttermilk	37.50
Sauce dish	20.00
Spooner	42.50
Sugar bowl, cov.	90.00
Sugar bowl, open	35.00

PRAYER RUG - See Horseshoe Pattern

PRESSED LEAF

Pressed Leaf Spooner

Bowl, 7" oval	40.00
Butter dish, cov.	50.00
Champagne	21.50
Compote, cov., acorn finial, low stand	37.50
Creamer, applied handle	35.00
Egg cup	25.00
Goblet	22.50
Goblet, buttermilk, non-flint	25.00
Pitcher, water, applied handle	78.50
Relish, 7 x 5"	12.50
Salt dip, master size	15.00
Sauce dish	9.00
Spooner (ILLUS.)	20.00
Sugar bowl, cov.	40.00
Sugar bowl, open	19.00
Wine	32.50

PRIMROSE

Butter dish, cov., clear	40.00
Cake plate, 2-handled, clear, 9" d.	18.00
Cake stand, blue, 10" d.	47.00
Card tray, amber w/wire frame, 4½" d.	32.00
Compote, cov., 5" d., milk white	28.00
Creamer, clear	30.00
Goblet, clear	40.00

Pickle dish, clear	14.50
Pitcher, milk, amber	65.00
Pitcher, milk, clear	27.50
Pitcher, water, clear	37.50
Plate, 4½" d., amber or blue	12.00
Plate, 4½" d., clear	10.00
Plate, 6" d., clear	13.50
Plate, 7" d., amber	16.00
Platter, 12 x 8", amber	22.50
Relish, amber, 9¼ x 5"	18.00
Relish, clear	15.00
Sauce dish, flat, blue	10.00

Primrose Sauce Dish

Sauce dish, flat or footed, clear (ILLUS.)	8.00 to 12.00
Spooner, clear	25.00
Sugar bowl, cov., clear	42.50
Tray, water, clear, 11" d.	27.50
Wine, amber	37.50
Wine, clear	17.50 to 25.00
Wine, opaque turquoise	60.00

PRINCESS FEATHER (Rochelle)

Princess Feather Goblet

Bowl, cov., 7½" d.	35.00
Butter dish, cov.	51.50
Celery vase	35.00 to 42.50
Compote, open, 8" d., low stand	32.50
Creamer	52.50
Egg cup	32.50
Goblet (ILLUS.)	26.50
Goblet, buttermilk	25.00

Honey dish 12.50
Lamp, kerosene, clear, 12" h. 50.00
Lamp, kerosene, cobalt blue,
  12" h. 200.00
Pitcher, water, bulbous, applied
  handle, flint 85.00
Plate, 6" d. 35.00
Plate, 9" d. 27.50
Relish, 7 x 5" oval 17.50
Sauce dish 10.00
Sauce dish, blue, flint 145.00
Spooner 27.50
Sugar bowl, cov. ....45.00 to 55.00
Sugar bowl, open 29.50

PRISCILLA (Alexis)

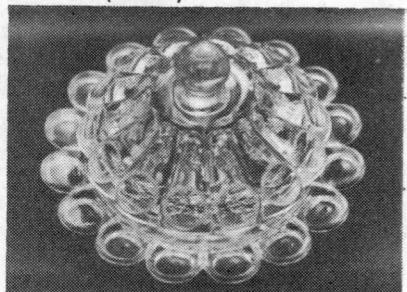

Priscilla Butter Dish

Banana stand 75.00
Bowl, 8" d., 3½" h., straight sides,
  flat 45.00
Bowl, 8" d., 3½" h., w/pattern on
  base 75.00
Bowl, 8¾" d., 3 3/8" h., flared
  sides 55.00
Bowl, 9" d., shallow 45.00
Bowl, 9 7/8" d., 2" h. 35.00
Bowl, 10¾" d., shallow 35.00
Butter dish, cov. (ILLUS.) 145.00
Cake stand, 9" to 10" d., high
  stand................... 60.00 to 90.00
Compote, cov., jelly 50.00
Compote, cov., 6" d., 10" h...55.00 to 65.00
Compote, open, 4¾" d., 4 7/8" h.,
  flared sides...................... 35.00
Compote, open, 6 7/8" d., 7" h. 45.00
Compote, open, 8" d., 8" h. 58.00
Compote, open, 8½" d., 8¾" h. 53.00
Compote, open, 8¾" d., 9¾" h.,
  flared rim 55.00
Compote, open, 10" d., 5¼" h.,
  scalloped rim 32.00
Cookie jar, cov. 175.00
Creamer 42.50
Creamer, individual size 32.50
Cruet w/original stopper 55.00
Doughnut stand, 5¾ x 4¼" 47.50
Goblet 52.50
Nappy, handled 28.00
Pitcher, water ....85.00 to 115.00
Punch cup 15.00

Relish ....20.00 to 28.00
Rose bowl, 3¾" h. 30.00
Sauce dish, flat, 4½" to
  5" d..................8.00 to 12.00
Spooner 31.50
Sugar bowl, cov. 40.00
Sugar bowl, cov., individual size.... 32.50
Sugar bowl, open 17.50
Syrup pitcher w/original pewter
  top 135.00
Table set, 4 pcs. 235.00
Toothpick holder 37.50
Tumbler 28.00
Wine............................. 25.00

PRISM

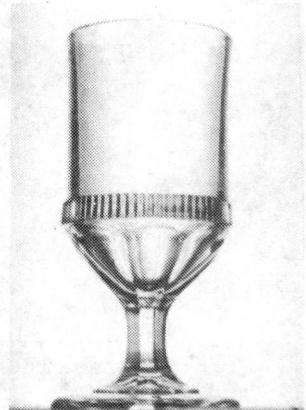

Prism Claret

Bowl, 7" d., flat................. 8.00
Celery vase...................... 30.00
Champagne....................... 45.00
Claret, 6" h. (ILLUS.)............ 22.00
Compote, open, 7" d., 5" h. 65.00
Compote, 7½" triangle, 4½" h. 45.00
Creamer 55.00
Egg cup 25.00
Egg cup, double.................. 26.50
Goblet 35.00
Pitcher, water 100.00
Plate, 7½" d. 25.00
Sauce dish....................... 16.00
Spooner 36.50
Sugar bowl, open 18.00
Tumbler, buttermilk 35.00
Wine............................. 38.00

PRISM WITH DIAMOND POINT
Goblet 25.00
Salt dip, master size.............. 17.50
Tumbler, bar..................... 65.00

PSYCHE & CUPID
Bread tray 40.00
Butter dish, cov. 65.00
Celery vase....................... 38.00

Compote, open, 5" d., 6¾" h.	45.00
Creamer	42.50
Goblet	36.50
Pitcher, water	65.00 to 75.00
Plate, 7" d., milk white	20.00
Relish, 9½ x 6½"	32.50
Sauce dish, footed	11.50
Spooner	38.00
Sugar bowl, cov.	42.50
Sugar bowl, open, footed, 6½" h.	32.50

PYGMY - See Torpedo Pattern

RED BLOCK

Red Block Spooner

Bowl, berry or fruit, 8" d.	65.00
Butter dish, cov.	70.00
Creamer, large	57.50
Decanter, whiskey, w/original stopper, 12" h.	175.00
Goblet	30.00
Mug	22.50
Pitcher, 8" h., bulbous	95.00
Pitcher, tankard, 9 5/8" h.	125.00
Rose bowl	55.00
Salt dip, individual size, 2-handled	48.00
Salt & pepper shakers w/original tops, pr.	90.00
Spooner (ILLUS.)	50.00
Sugar bowl, cov.	60.00
Sugar bowl, open	35.00
Table set, 4 pcs.	225.00
Tumbler	25.00
Tumbler, amber blocks	35.00
Water set, pitcher & 6 tumblers, 7 pcs.	225.00
Wine	30.00

REVERSE TORPEDO (Diamond & Bull's Eye Band)

Banana stand	115.00
Bowl, cov., 9" d. (ILLUS.)	75.00
Bowl, 5¾" d., piecrust rim	35.00
Bowl, 7½" d., piecrust rim	70.00
Bowl, 9" d., piecrust rim	65.00
Bowl, 10¼" d., piecrust rim	72.50

Reverse Torpedo Covered Bowl

Bowl, 11¼" d., 7" h., footed	85.00
Butter dish, cov.	80.00
Cake stand	62.50 to 85.00
Celery vase	70.00
Compote, cov., jelly	37.50
Compote, cov., 6" d., high stand	95.00
Compote, cov., 7" h., low stand	85.00
Compote, open, 5" d., flared rim	45.00
Compote, open, 9" d., 7" h., turned-over piecrust rim	80.00
Compote, open, 10" d., 6½" h.	70.00
Creamer	62.50
Goblet	85.00
Salt & pepper shakers w/original tops, pr.	55.00
Sauce dish	20.00
Spooner	55.00
Sugar bowl, cov.	70.00
Tumbler	85.00

RIBBED GRAPE

Ribbed Grape Plate

Compote, open, 8" d., 5" h.	90.00
Creamer, applied handle	130.00
Goblet	37.50
Plate, 6" d. (ILLUS.)	25.00
Sauce dish, 4" d.	15.00

Spooner 38.50
Sugar bowl, cov. 95.00

RIBBED IVY
Bitters bottle w/original tulip-
   shaped stopper 175.00
Bowl, 8" d., 2" h. 67.50
Butter dish, cov. 95.00
Celery 225.00
Champagne........................ 140.00
Compote, cov., 6" d., high stand ... 130.00
Compote, open, 7" d., low stand .. 55.00
Compote, open, 7½" d., high stand,
   rope edge rim 92.50
Creamer, applied handle........... 110.00
Egg cup 30.00
Goblet 50.00
Salt dip, cov., master size........ 115.00
Salt dip, open, master size, beaded
   rim 40.00
Sauce dish........................ 13.50
Spooner 40.00
Sugar bowl, cov. 87.50
Sweetmeat, cov. 325.00
Tumbler, bar ....105.00 to 125.00
Tumbler, water 80.00
Tumbler, whiskey ....68.00 to 95.00
Tumbler, whiskey, handled.......... 150.00
Wine.....................95.00 to 110.00

RIBBED PALM

Ribbed Palm Goblet

Bowl, 8" d., footed 40.00
Butter dish, cov. 90.00
Celery vase....................... 65.00
Champagne........................ 95.00
Creamer ....145.00 to 160.00
Egg cup ....25.00 to 35.00
Goblet (ILLUS.).................... 40.00
Goblet, buttermilk 35.00
Honey dish 12.50
Pitcher, water, 9" h., applied
   handle 250.00

Plate, 6" d. 60.00
Salt dip, footed, individual size 20.00
Salt dip, master size.............. 27.50
Sauce dish....................... 10.00
Spillholder....................... 45.00
Spooner 42.50
Sugar bowl, cov. 75.00
Sugar bowl, open 27.50
Tumbler 110.00
Wine............................. 47.50

RIBBON (Early Ribbon)

Ribbon Spooner

Bread tray 28.00
Butter dish, cov. ....62.50 to 75.00
Cake stand, 8½" to 10" d. ....36.00 to 60.00
Celery vase....................... 47.50
Cheese dish, cov. 145.00
Compote, cov., 8" d. 70.00
Compote, open, 7" d., low stand ... 32.50
Compote, open, 8 x 5¼" rectangu-
   lar bowl, 7" h., frosted dolphin
   stem on dome base 225.00
Compote, open, 10½" d., 11" h.,
   w/original silverplate frame of
   dolphins 165.00
Creamer 32.00
Creamer & cov. sugar bowl, pr. 110.00
Goblet 35.00
Pitcher, water 70.00
Plate, 7" d. 35.00
Platter, 13 x 9" 60.00
Pomade jar, cov., squat 28.00
Sauce dish, flat or footed .....8.00 to 18.00
Spooner (ILLUS.)................. 32.50
Sugar bowl, cov., 4¼" d., 7¾" h. .. 62.50
Tray, water, 15" 115.00
Wine............................. 110.00

RIBBON CANDY (Bryce or Double Loop)
Bowl, cov., 6¼" d., footed 35.00
Bowl, 8" d., flat................... 20.00
Butter dish, cov. 45.00

Cake stand, 8" to 10½" d. . . .27.00 to 40.00
Celery vase.......................... 28.00
Compote, cov., 5" d., 8½" h........ 47.50
Compote, open, jelly 25.00
Creamer 20.00
Creamer & open sugar bowl, pr..... 38.00
Doughnut stand 35.00
Goblet 30.00
Pitcher, milk..................... 55.00
Pitcher, water 70.00
Plate, 8½" d. 14.00
Plate, 9½" d. 17.00
Plate, 10½" d..................... 32.00

Ribbon Candy Plate

Plate, 12" d. (ILLUS.) 45.00
Relish, 8½" l...................... 11.00
Salt & pepper shakers w/original
    tops, pr....................... 55.00
Spooner 22.50
Sugar bowl, cov. 35.00
Syrup pitcher w/original top 95.00
Wine.............................. 27.50

RISING SUN

Rising Sun Toothpick Holder

Berry set: master bowl & 4 sauce
    dishes; green suns, 5 pcs......... 75.00
Bowl, master berry, pink suns 30.00
Celery vase, gold suns............. 18.00
Celery vase, pink suns............. 32.50
Compote, open, jelly, purple suns .. 22.00
Compote, open, 7" d., 6" h., clear .. 18.50

Creamer, clear.................... 22.00
Cruet w/stopper, clear 28.00
Goblet, clear 27.50
Goblet, gold suns 20.00
Goblet, green suns 25.00
Goblet, pink suns 26.00
Goblet, purple suns 25.00
Pitcher, water, clear............. 75.00
Pitcher, water, gold suns 35.00
Punch cup, green suns............. 20.00
Spooner, gold suns 18.00
Sugar bowl, open, scalloped rim,
    green suns 22.00
Toothpick holder, 3-handled, clear .. 18.00
Toothpick holder, 3-handled, gold
    suns (ILLUS.)................. 25.00
Toothpick holder, 3-handled, green
    suns 30.00
Toothpick holder, 3-handled, purple
    suns 25.00
Tumbler, clear 15.00
Tumbler, gold suns 13.50
Tumbler, green suns............... 25.00
Tumbler, pink suns 22.00
Tumbler, whiskey, clear 8.50
Water set: pitcher & 4 tumblers;
    green suns, 5 pcs. ......140.00 to 195.00
Water set: pitcher & 6 tumblers;
    gold suns, 7 pcs. 95.00
Wine, clear 16.00
Wine, green suns 30.00
Wine, pink suns................... 30.00
Wine, purple suns 30.00

ROCHELLE - See Princess Feather Pattern

ROMAN KEY - See Frosted Roman Key Pattern

ROMAN ROSETTE

Roman Rosette Creamer

Bowl, 7" d. 22.50
Bowl, 8" d. 25.00
Bread platter, 11 x 9" 29.50
Butter dish, cov. 47.00

Butter dish, cov., ruby-stained 105.00
Cake stand, 9" to 10" d. .....45.00 to 55.00
Castor set, salt & pepper shakers &
   cov. condiment jar, set 36.50
Celery vase 20.00
Compote, cov., 5" d. 47.50
Compote, cov., 6" d., 10" h......... 62.50
Compote, open, 5" d., jelly 25.00
Compote, open, 7" d., 8" h......... 23.50
Cordial 32.50
Creamer (ILLUS.) 27.00
Creamer & open sugar bowl, pr..... 35.00
Goblet 42.50
Honey dish, cov. ....42.50 to 60.00
Marmalade dish, footed 38.00
Marmalade dish, footed, ruby-
   stained 45.00
Mug, 3" h.......................... 15.00
Pitcher, milk 40.00
Pitcher, water 70.00
Plate, 6" d., fiery opalescent, flint .. 140.00
Plate, 7" d.......................... 18.00
Plate, 8" d., flint 45.00
Relish, 9 x 6" 20.00
Salt & pepper shakers w/original
   tops, pr....................... 32.00
Sauce dish.......................... 10.00
Spooner 23.00
Sugar bowl, cov. 32.50
Toddy plate, 5½" d................. 35.00
Toddy plate, purple, flint, 5½" d.... 325.00
Wine................................ 45.00

ROSE IN SNOW

Rose in Snow Spooner

Berry set: 8¼" sq. footed bowl & 4
   footed sauce dishes; clear,
   5 pcs........................... 75.00
Bowl, 7" d., footed, clear 22.50
Butter dish, cov., round, clear 40.00
Butter dish, cov., square, clear 47.50
Cake plate, handled, clear, 10" d. .. 35.00
Cake stand, clear, 9" d. 77.50
Cologne bottle w/original stopper,
   clear 90.00

Compote, cov., 6" d., 8" h., clear ... 70.00
Compote, cov., 7" d., 8" h., clear ... 85.00
Compote, cov., 8" d., 10" h., clear .. 80.00
Compote, open, 5" d., 5½" h.,
   clear 55.00
Compote, open, 5¾" d., vaseline ... 55.00
Compote, open, 6" d., low stand,
   clear 20.00
Compote, open, 7" d., low stand,
   clear 24.00
Creamer, round, blue.............. 55.00
Creamer, round, clear 36.00
Creamer, square, clear 37.50
Creamer, square, vaseline 60.00
Creamer & open sugar bowl, round,
   clear, pr....................... 90.00
Creamer & open sugar bowl,
   square, clear, pr. 95.00
Goblet, amber 40.00
Goblet, clear 32.50
Mug, clear, 3½" h................. 35.00
Mug, applied handle, "In Fond
   Remembrance," clear 40.00
Pitcher, water, applied handle,
   amber 110.00
Pitcher, water, applied handle,
   clear 80.00
Pitcher, water, vaseline........... 165.00
Plate, 5" d., clear 30.00
Plate, 6" d., clear 22.50
Plate, 7" d., clear ....19.50 to 25.00
Powder jar, cov., clear 21.00
Relish, clear, 8 x 5½" oval 16.50
Relish, clear, 9¼ x 6¼" 18.50
Relish, double, clear.............. 75.00
Sauce dish, flat or footed,
   clear....................10.00 to 17.50
Spooner, round, clear (ILLUS.) 28.50
Spooner, square, clear............ 35.00
Sugar bowl, cov., round, clear...... 40.00
Sugar bowl, cov., square, clear..... 45.00
Sugar bowl, open, square, clear 20.00
Table set, square, clear, 4 pcs. 170.00
Tumbler, clear 38.00
Wine, clear 20.00

ROSE SPRIG

Bowl, 9" d., footed, clear 25.00
Bowl, 9 x 8¼" oval, footed, clear... 35.00
Bread tray, 2-handled, blue 35.00
Bread tray, 2-handled, yellow 40.00
Cake stand, amber, 9" octagon,
   6½" h........................ 60.00
Cake stand, blue, 9" octagon,
   6½" h........................ 65.00
Cake stand, clear, 9" octagon,
   6½" h........................ 58.00
Cake stand, yellow, 9" octagon,
   6½" h........................ 85.00
Celery vase, amber 45.00
Celery vase, clear................ 35.00
Compote, cov., high stand, clear,
   large.......................... 75.00
Compote, open, 7" oval, amber 36.00

Compote, open, 7" d., 5" h.,
  yellow 35.00
Compote, open, 9" d., high stand,
  amber 37.50
Creamer, yellow 40.00
Goblet, amber 32.50
Goblet, blue 48.00
Goblet, clear 24.50
Pitcher, milk, amber.............. 55.00
Pitcher, water, clear............. 42.50
Plate, 6" sq., handled, amber 26.50
Plate, 6" sq., handled, blue 30.00
Plate, 6" sq., handled, clear........ 20.00
Relish, boat-shaped, amber,
  8" l. ....25.00 to 32.00
Relish, boat-shaped, blue, 8" l. 37.50
Relish, boat-shaped, clear, 8" l. 22.00
Relish, boat-shaped, yellow, 8" l.... 32.50
Sauce dish, flat, amber 15.00
Sauce dish, flat, clear 12.50
Sauce dish, footed, clear.......... 8.00

Rose Sprig Handled Tumbler

Tumbler, applied handle, clear
  (ILLUS.)........................ 45.00
Wine, blue 50.00
Whimsey, sleigh (salt dip), amber,
  4 x 6 x 4" 45.00

ROSETTE

Rosette Jelly Compote

Bowl, 7½" d. 20.00
Bread plate, handled, 11" d. 25.00
Butter dish, cov. 40.00
Cake stand, 8½" to 11" d. ...20.00 to 35.00
Celery vase...................... 25.00
Compote, cov., 6" d., 9" h......... 70.00
Compote, open, jelly, 4½" d., 5" h.
  (ILLUS.)........................ 22.00
Creamer 28.50
Pitcher, milk 40.00
Pitcher, water, tankard 55.00
Plate, 7" d...................... 22.50
Plate, 9" d., 2-handled........... 20.00
Relish, fish-shaped 15.00
Salt shaker w/replaced top
  (single)........................ 23.00
Sauce dish...................... 8.00
Spooner 32.50
Sugar bowl, cov. 37.50
Wine........................... 25.00

ROYAL IVY
Berry set: master berry bowl & 4
  sauce dishes; frosted rubina
  crystal, 5 pcs................... 175.00
Bowl, 8" d., rubina crystal 95.00
Bowl, 8" d., frosted rubina crystal .. 120.00
Bowl, fruit, 9" d., craquelle (cran-
  berry & vaseline spatter)......... 125.00
Bowl, fruit, 9" d., frosted rubina
  crystal 100.00
Butter dish, cov., clear & frosted ... 175.00
Butter dish, cov., frosted craquelle.. 137.50
Butter dish, cov., rubina crystal..... 175.00
Butter dish, cov., frosted rubina
  crystal 215.00
Creamer, clear & frosted.......... 50.00
Creamer, rubina crystal........... 100.00
Cruet w/original stopper, rubina
  crystal 275.00
Cruet w/original stopper, frosted
  rubina crystal 325.00
Cruet, no stopper, clear & frosted .. 95.00
Pickle castor, clear & frosted insert,
  complete w/frame 140.00
Pickle castor, cased spatter (cran-
  berry & vaseline) insert, complete
  w/silverplate frame & tongs...... 350.00
Pitcher, water, cased spatter 225.00
Pitcher, water, clear & frosted...... 125.00
Pitcher, water, craquelle 450.00
Pitcher, water, frosted craquelle.... 400.00
Pitcher, water, rubina
  crystal ....165.00 to 225.00
Pitcher, water, frosted rubina
  crystal ....250.00 to 285.00
Rose bowl, cased spatter 295.00
Rose bowl, rubina crystal 60.00
Rose bowl, frosted rubina crystal ... 85.00
Rose bowl, craquelle 110.00
Salt shaker w/original top, rubina
  crystal (single) 36.50
Salt shaker w/original top, frosted
  rubina crystal (single) 45.00

Sauce dish, rubina crystal 30.00
Sauce dish, frosted rubina
  crystal . . . . .35.00 to 40.00
Spooner, clear & frosted 45.00
Spooner, frosted rubina crystal 75.00
Sugar bowl, cov., rubina crystal 130.00
Sugar bowl, cov., frosted rubina
  crystal 135.00
Sugar shaker w/original top, cased
  spatter 175.00
Sugar shaker w/original top, clear
  & frosted . . . . .58.00 to 75.00
Sugar shaker w/original top, rubina
  crystal 110.00
Sugar shaker w/original top, frosted
  rubina crystal 135.00
Syrup pitcher w/original top, cased
  spatter 500.00
Syrup pitcher w/original top, clear &
  frosted 155.00
Syrup pitcher w/original top, rubina
  crystal 250.00
Syrup pitcher w/original top, frosted
  rubina crystal 450.00
Table set, cased spatter, 4 pcs. 875.00
Table set, craquelle, 4 pcs. 850.00
Table set, clear & frosted, 4 pcs. . . . 335.00
Table set, frosted rubina crystal,
  4 pcs. 495.00
Toothpick holder, craquelle 125.00
Toothpick holder, rubina crystal 85.00
Toothpick holder, frosted rubina
  crystal 125.00
Tumbler, clear & frosted 25.00
Tumbler, craquelle 80.00
Tumbler, frosted rubina crystal 65.00
Water set: pitcher & 5 tumblers;
  cased spatter, 6 pcs. 850.00
Water set: pitcher & 6 tumblers;
  rubina crystal, 7 pcs. . . . .400.00 to 500.00
Water set: pitcher & 6 tumblers;
  frosted rubina crystal,
  7 pcs. . . . . .500.00 to 600.00

ROYAL OAK

Royal Oak Dresser Jar

Butter dish, cov., frosted crystal 65.00
Butter dish, cov., rubina crystal 135.00

Butter dish, cov., frosted rubina
  crystal . . . . .165.00 to 195.00
Creamer, frosted crystal 95.00
Creamer, rubina crystal 85.00
Dresser jar, cov., frosted crystal,
  5" w., 5½" h. (ILLUS.) 150.00
Dresser jar w/original silverplate
  cover, frosted rubina crystal, pon-
  til, 4½" d., 5¼" h. 85.00
Pickle castor, frosted rubina crystal
  insert, w/silverplate frame &
  cover 245.00
Pitcher, 8½" h., frosted crystal 100.00
Pitcher, water, rubina crystal 250.00
Pitcher, water, frosted rubina
  crystal 300.00
Salt shaker w/original top, rubina
  crystal (single) 50.00
Salt & pepper shakers w/original
  tops, frosted rubina crystal, pr. 150.00
Sauce dish, frosted crystal 12.50
Sauce dish, rubina crystal 35.00
Spooner, frosted crystal 65.00
Spooner, rubina crystal 60.00
Spooner, frosted rubina crystal 100.00
Sugar bowl, cov., frosted crystal 55.00
Sugar bowl, cov., rubina crystal 140.00
Sugar bowl, cov., frosted rubina
  crystal 130.00
Sugar shaker w/original top, rubina
  crystal 125.00
Sugar shaker w/original top, frosted
  rubina crystal 165.00
Syrup pitcher w/original (repaired)
  top, rubina crystal 275.00
Table set, frosted rubina crystal,
  4 pcs. 600.00
Toothpick holder, frosted crystal 47.50
Toothpick holder, rubina crystal 82.50
Toothpick holder, frosted rubina
  crystal 125.00
Tumbler, frosted crystal 75.00
Tumbler, frosted rubina crystal 80.00
Water set: pitcher & 5 tumblers;
  frosted crystal, 6 pcs. 425.00

RUBY ROSETTE - See Pillow Encircled Pattern

RUBY THUMBPRINT

(Items may be plain or with etched designs)

Berry set, master bowl & 4 sauce
  dishes, 5 pcs. 135.00
Berry set, boat-shaped master bowl
  & 6 boat-shaped sauce dishes,
  7 pcs. 235.00
Bowl, 8½" d. 45.00
Bowl, master berry or fruit, 10" l.,
  boat-shaped 125.00
Butter dish, cov. 125.00
Cake stand, 10" d. 125.00
Castor bottle 25.00

Castor set, 5-bottle,
w/frame .... 325.00 to 425.00
Celery vase 55.00
Champagne 35.00
Cheese dish, cov., 7" d. 55.00
Claret 46.50
Compote, open, jelly, 5¼" h. 42.50
Compote, open, 7" d. 95.00
Cordial 28.00
Creamer 52.50
Creamer, individual size 26.00
Cup & saucer 58.00
Dish, cov., 8" d., 7" h. 68.00
Goblet 38.00
Match holder 20.00
Mustard jar, cov. 58.00
Mustard jar, cov., etched "World's
Fair, 1893" 127.50
Olive dish 125.00
Pitcher, milk, 7½" h., bulbous 120.00
Pitcher, milk, tankard, 8 3/8" h. 85.00
Pitcher, water, tankard, 11" h. 175.00
Plate, 7½" d. 22.00
Punch cup 20.00
Salt dip, individual size 145.00
Salt shaker w/original top (single) .. 28.00
Salt & pepper shakers w/original
tops, pr. 70.00
Sauce dish, boat-shaped 26.50
Sauce dish, round 20.00
Spooner 60.00
Sugar bowl, cov. 77.50
Sugar bowl, open 32.50
Table set, 4 pcs. .... 250.00 to 350.00
Toothpick holder 25.00
Toothpick holder, etched "World's
Fair Chicago 1893" 30.00
Water set, tankard pitcher & 6
tumblers, 7 pcs. 385.00
Wine 26.50

SANDWICH STAR

Sandwich Star Spillholder

Butter dish, cov. 195.00

Compote, open, 8½" d., low
stand 60.00
Compote, open, 12" d., 9½" h. 265.00
Decanter w/bar lip, pt. 70.00
Decanter w/bar lip, qt. 85.00
Lamp, whale oil, 6-sided font,
10½" h. 125.00
Spillholder (ILLUS.) 65.00
Spillholder, clambroth 450.00
Spillholder, electric blue ... 565.00 to 750.00
Spooner, clear 95.00

SAWTOOTH

Sawtooth Celery Vases

Butter dish, cov., flint 80.00
Butter dish, cov., non-flint 35.00
Cake stand, non-flint, 9½" d.,
4½" h. 52.50
Celery vases, knob stem, flint, pr.
(ILLUS.) 140.00
Celery vase, knob stem, non-flint ... 23.50
Champagne, knob stem, flint 55.00
Champagne, non-flint 32.00
Compote, cov., 8" d., low stand,
flint 125.00
Compote, cov., 9¼" d., 4" h., non-
flint 48.00
Compote, cov., 9½" d., 14" h.,
flint 200.00
Compote, cov., 9½" d., 14" h., non-
flint 62.50
Compote, open, 8" d., 6" h., non-
flint 36.00
Compote, open, 8¼" d., 8¼" h.,
flint 37.50
Compote, open, 9" d., flint 45.00
Cordial, non-flint 20.00
Creamer, applied handle, flint 80.00
Creamer, applied handle, opaque
white, flint, 5¼" h. ..... 160.00 to 300.00
Creamer, applied handle, non-flint .. 30.00
Decanter w/acorn stopper, flint,
½ pt. 85.00

Egg cup, flint 42.50
Goblet, knob stem, flint 40.00
Goblet, knob stem, non-flint 20.00
Pitcher, water, applied handle,
    flint 140.00
Pitcher, water, applied handle,
    opaque white, flint 345.00
Salt dip, cov., individual size,
    footed, flint 35.00
Salt dip, individual size, footed,
    flint 18.00
Salt dip, cov., master size, footed,
    flint 80.00
Salt dip, cov., master size, footed,
    milk white, flint 65.00
Salt dip, master size, flint 30.00
Salt dip, master size, non-flint 15.00
Salt dip, master size, milk white,
    non-flint 19.50
Salt shaker w/original top, milk
    white, non-flint (single) 19.50
Spillholder, flint 85.00
Spooner, flint 45.00
Spooner, non-flint 25.00
Sugar bowl, cov., flint 75.00
Tumbler, bar, flint, 4½" h. 50.00
Tumbler, bar, non-flint 35.00
Vase, 9 7/8" h. 25.00
Wine, flint 35.00
Wine, non-flint 27.50

SAWTOOTH BAND - See Amazon Pattern

SCALLOPED TAPE - See Jewel Band Pattern

SEDAN (Paneled Star & Button)

Sedan Sauce Dish

Butter dish, cov. 38.00
Compote, open, high stand 20.00
Creamer 20.00
Goblet 22.00
Mug, miniature 12.50
Pitcher, water 45.00
Salt dip, master size 12.50
Sauce dish, flat, 4½" d.
    (ILLUS.) 8.00
Spooner 25.00

Sugar bowl, cov. 45.00
Wine 15.00

SENECA LOOP - See Loop Pattern

SHELL & JEWEL (Victor)

Shell & Jewel Pitcher

Bowl, 8" d., clear 20.00
Bowl, 10" d., clear 25.00
Butter dish, cov., clear 60.00
Cake stand, clear, 10" d., 5" h. 45.00
Compote, cov., 8½" d., high stand,
    clear 75.00
Compote, open, 7" d., 7½" h.,
    clear 40.00
Creamer, clear 40.00
Pitcher, milk, blue 75.00
Pitcher, water, blue or green 99.00
Pitcher, water, clear (ILLUS.) 55.00
Relish, oblong, clear 18.00
Sauce dish, amber 15.00
Sauce dish, clear ....7.00 to 10.00
Spooner, clear 26.50
Sugar bowl, cov., clear 42.50
Tumbler, amber 35.00
Tumbler, blue 40.00
Tumbler, clear 18.00
Tumbler, green 36.00
Water set: pitcher & 6 tumblers;
    amber, 7 pcs. 260.00
Water set: pitcher & 6 tumblers;
    blue, 7 pcs. 245.00
Water set: pitcher & 6 tumblers;
    clear, 7 pcs. 150.00

SHELL & TASSEL

Berry set: 10" oval master berry
    bowl & 6 square footed sauce
    dishes; clear, 7 pcs. 190.00
Bowl, 11½ x 6½" oval, amber 90.00
Bowl, 11½ x 6½" oval, clear 45.00
Bread tray, clear, 13 x 9" 50.00
Bride's basket, 8" oval clear bowl in
    silverplate frame 125.00
Butter dish, cov., round, dog finial,
    clear 110.00
Cake stand, shell corners, clear,
    8" sq. 45.00

Cake stand, shell corners, clear,
9" sq. 50.00
Cake stand, shell corners, clear,
10" sq. 65.00
Cake stand, shell corners, clear,
12" sq. 80.00
Celery vase, round, handled, clear . . 47.50
Celery vase, square, clear 48.00
Compote, open, jelly, clear 50.00
Compote, open, 6½" sq., 6½" h.,
clear 32.50
Compote, open, 7½" sq., 9" h.,
clear 45.00

Shell & Tassel Compote

Compote, open, 8½" sq., 8" h.,
clear (ILLUS.) 72.50
Compote, open, 10" sq., 8" h.,
clear . . . . 60.00 to 75.00
Creamer, round, clear 30.00
Creamer, square, clear 40.00
Creamer & sugar bowl, square,
clear, pr. 120.00
Goblet, round, knob stem, clear 35.00
Oyster plate, clear, 9½" d. 210.00
Pitcher, water, round, clear 60.00
Pitcher, water, square, clear 68.00
Plate, shell-shaped w/three shell-
shaped feet, clear, large 67.50
Platter, 11 x 8" oblong, clear 62.50
Relish, clear, 8 x 5" 40.00
Salt dip, shell-shaped, clear 20.00
Sauce dish, flat or footed, clear,
4" to 5" d. . . . . 8.50 to 12.50
Spooner, round, clear 37.00
Spooner, square, clear 32.50
Sugar bowl, cov., round, dog finial,
clear 85.00
Sugar bowl, cov., square, shell
finial, clear 75.00
Table set, clear, 4 pcs. 295.00
Tray, ice cream, clear 55.00

SHERATON
Bowl, 6 5/8 x 4 7/8", amber 23.00
Bowl, 10 x 8", 8-sided, clear 18.50
Bread platter, amber, 10 x 8" 42.50

Bread platter, blue, 10 x 8" 32.50
Bread platter, clear, 10 x 8" 25.00
Butter dish, cov., blue 50.00
Butter dish, cov., clear 35.00
Cake stand, clear, 10½" d. 32.00
Celery vase, clear 20.00
Compote, open, 7" d., 5" h.,
amber 28.00
Compote, open, 7" d., 5" h., clear . . 25.00

Sheraton Compote

Compote, open, 8" d., 7¾" h.,
clear (ILLUS.) 28.00
Compote, open, 10" d., clear 45.00
Creamer, blue 37.00
Creamer, clear 30.00
Goblet, blue 42.50
Goblet, clear 25.00
Pitcher, milk, clear 25.00
Pitcher, water, amber 55.00
Pitcher, water, clear 45.00
Plate, 7" sq., amber 20.00
Relish, handled, amber 16.50
Relish, handled, clear 14.50
Sauce dish, blue, 4" d. 12.00
Sauce dish, clear, 4" d. 9.00
Spooner, amber 30.00
Spooner, blue 35.00
Spooner, clear 22.00
Sugar bowl, cov., clear 25.00
Tumbler, clear 22.00
Wine, clear 22.50

SHOSHONE
Cake stand, green 55.00
Creamer, amber-stained 48.00
Plate, 11½" d., reticulated rim, milk
white 35.00
Relish, 7½" l. 12.00

SHOVEL
Compote, open, jelly 18.00
Goblet (ILLUS.) 20.00
Tumbler 16.00
Wine 18.00

SHRINE
Bowl, 8¼" d. 31.50
Butter dish, cov. 45.00

Champagne	58.50
Compote, open, jelly	22.50
Creamer	32.50
Goblet	37.50
Lamp, kerosene, w/finger grip, pedestal base, 10" h.	145.00
Mug	38.50
Pickle dish	16.50
Pitcher, cider, ½ gal.	110.00 to 135.00
Pitcher, water	50.00
Plate, 6" d., scalloped rim	46.00
Salt shaker w/original top (single)	28.50
Sauce dish	13.00
Spooner	26.50
Sugar bowl, cov.	47.50
Tumbler, 4" h.	37.50

SHUTTLE (Hearts of Loch Laven)

Shuttle Mug

Bowl, berry, large	30.00
Butter dish, cov.	50.00
Celery vase	36.00
Champagne	35.00
Cordial, small	20.00
Creamer, tall tankard	35.00
Goblet	40.00
Mug, amber	50.00
Mug (ILLUS.)	28.00
Punch cup	10.00 to 14.00
Salt shaker w/original top (single)	42.50
Wine	12.50

SKILTON - See Oregon Pattern

SMOCKING

Smocking Creamer & Sugar Bowl

Butter dish, cov.	90.00
Champagne, knob stem	85.00
Creamer, applied handle	105.00
Creamer w/applied handle & cov. sugar bowl, pr. (ILLUS.)	275.00
Goblet	50.00
Spillholder	39.50
Spooner	37.50

SNAIL (Compact)

Snail Goblet

Banana stand, 10" d., 7" h.	165.00
Bowl, 7" d., low	30.00
Bowl, berry, 8" d., 4" h.	32.50
Bowl, 9" d., 2" h.	25.00
Butter dish, cov.	95.00
Cake stand, 10" d.	87.50
Celery vase	60.00
Compote, cov., 7" d., 11½" h.	130.00
Creamer	55.00
Cruet w/original stopper	100.00
Cruet w/original stopper, ruby-stained	225.00
Goblet (ILLUS.)	65.00
Honey dish, cov.	95.00
Pickle dish, 8 x 5½"	28.00
Pitcher, water, tankard	95.00
Plate, 7" d.	27.50
Punch cup	30.00
Relish, 7" oval	25.00
Rose bowl, large	50.00
Salt dip, individual size	20.00
Salt dip, master size, 3" d.	50.00
Salt & pepper shakers w/original tops, pr.	55.00
Salt & pepper shakers w/original tops, ruby-stained, pr.	95.00
Sauce dish	9.00 to 15.00
Spooner	30.00
Spooner, ruby-stained	85.00
Sugar bowl, cov.	60.00
Sugar bowl, open	20.00
Sugar shaker w/original top, ruby-stained	160.00

Syrup jug w/original brass top 80.00
Syrup jug (no top) 65.00
Tumbler ....40.00 to 47.50

SNAKESKIN & DOT
Celery vase, clear 35.00
Compote, cov., clear 60.00
Creamer, clear 35.00
Goblet, clear 30.00
Plate, 4½" d., amber 9.00
Plate, 7" d., milk white 15.00
Plate, 9" d., clear 25.00
Sugar bowl, cov., clear 45.00

SPARTAN (Barred Star)
Cordial 15.00
Goblet 25.00
Sauce dish, flat 10.00
Sugar bowl, cov. 60.00
Tumbler 17.50

SPIREA BAND
Bowl, 8" oval, flat, blue 32.50
Butter dish, cov., amber 50.00
Butter dish, cov., blue 57.50
Butter dish, cov., clear 40.00
Cake stand, amber, 8½" d. 45.00
Cake stand, blue, 10½" d. 56.00
Compote, cov., 7" d., high stand,
   blue 65.00
Compote, cov., 7" d., high stand,
   clear 40.00
Compote, open, 7" d., low stand,
   amber 26.00
Creamer, amber 36.50
Creamer, blue 32.50
Creamer, clear 20.00
Goblet, amber 30.00
Goblet, blue 37.50
Goblet, clear 24.00
Pitcher, water, amber 42.50
Pitcher, water, blue 90.00
Pitcher, water, clear 45.00
Platter, 10½ x 8½", amber 25.00
Platter, 10½ x 8½", clear 20.00
Relish, amber, 7 x 4½" 10.00
Relish, amber, 9 x 5½" 18.50
Salt shaker w/original top, blue
   (single)........................ 37.50
Salt & pepper shakers w/original
   tops, amber, pr. 30.00
Sauce dish, flat or footed,
   amber ....6.00 to 12.00
Sauce dish, flat or footed,
   blue ....11.00 to 14.00
Spooner, amber 26.50
Spooner, blue 33.00
Spooner, clear 18.00
Spooner, vaseline 26.00
Sugar bowl, cov., blue 55.00
Sugar bowl, cov., clear 32.50
Sugar bowl, open, amber 22.00
Tumbler, blue 35.00
Wine, amber 25.00

Wine, blue 35.00
Wine, clear 18.50

SPRIG

Sprig Relish

Berry set, 8½" d. master bowl & 6
   sauce dishes, 7 pcs. 80.00
Bowl, 9" oval 35.00
Bread platter, 11" oval 32.00
Butter dish, cov. 47.50
Cake stand 42.50
Celery vase 36.50
Compote, cov., 6" d., high stand ... 50.00
Compote, cov., 8" d., low stand ... 45.00
Compote, open, 6¾" d., 5½" h. 17.50
Compote, open, 7" d., low stand ... 28.50
Compote, open, 8" d., high stand ... 25.00
Compote, open, 10" d., high stand .. 42.50
Creamer 25.00
Goblet ....27.50 to 40.00
Pickle castor, clear insert, resilvered
   frame & tongs 85.00
Pitcher, water 50.00
Relish, 8¾" oval (ILLUS.) 22.00
Salt dip, master size 45.00
Sauce dish, flat or footed .....7.50 to 11.00
Spooner 23.50
Sugar bowl, cov. 48.00
Sugar bowl, open 20.00
Wine 32.50

SQUARE LION'S HEAD - See Lion Pattern

SQUARE PANES - See Post Pattern

STAR ROSETTED

Star Rosetted Goblet

Bowl, 7¼ x 5" oval................ 6.50
Butter dish, cov. 40.00
Cake (or bread) plate, "A Good
  Mother Makes A Happy Home"... 55.00
Creamer 30.00
Goblet (ILLUS.)................... 28.00
Relish, 3-handled, 9¾ x 5"........ 6.50
Sauce dish, flat or footed 4.50
Spooner......................... 25.00
Sugar bowl, cov. 40.00

STATES (THE)
Bowl, 7" d., 3-handled 55.00
Bowl, 9" d. 60.00
Butter dish, cov. 55.00
Card tray, 7 3/8 x 5" 15.00
Celery 30.00
Cocktail, flared 24.00
Compote, open, 9¼" d., 9" h...... 80.00
Creamer 25.00
Creamer, individual size 29.00
Creamer & sugar bowl, individual
  size, pr....................... 42.50
Goblet, clear 35.00
Nappy, 2-handled 22.50
Olive dish 17.50
Pitcher, water 60.00
Punch cup 12.50
Relish, cov., w/silver holder & ladle,
  4" d. 125.00
Salt & pepper shakers w/original
  tops, pr....................... 40.00
Sauce dish...................... 12.00
Spooner 28.00
Sugar bowl, cov. 40.00
Sugar bowl, open, individual size ... 17.50
Toothpick holder 37.50
Tumbler 18.50
Water set, pitcher & 6 tumblers,
  7 pcs......................... 125.00
Wine........................... 27.50

STEDMAN
Champagne...................... 35.00
Creamer 40.00
Egg cup 20.00
Goblet 30.00
Sauce dish, flat 14.00
Spooner 40.00
Syrup pitcher, applied handle,
  4¼" d., 8¼" h................ 100.00
Wine........................... 45.00

STIPPLED CHAIN
Creamer 30.00
Goblet 22.50
Relish, 8¼ x 6 1/8"............. 7.50
Salt dip, master size............. 19.50
Sauce dish...................... 4.50
Spooner 22.50
Tumbler 20.00

STIPPLED CHERRY
Bowl, master berry, 8" d. 28.00

Bread platter 26.00
Butter dish, cov. 42.00
Creamer 22.50
Pitcher, water 55.00
Plate, 6" d. 20.00
Sauce dish, flat 6.50
Spooner 25.00
Tumbler 22.00

STIPPLED DOUBLE LOOP
Butter dish, cov. 40.00
Goblet 28.00
Spooner 22.00
Sugar bowl, cov. 35.00
Tumbler 15.00

STIPPLED FLOWER PANELS - See Maine Pattern

STIPPLED FORGET-ME-NOT

Stippled Forget-Me-Not Compote

Butter dish, cov. 48.00
Cake stand, 8" to 9" d. 42.50
Celery vase..................... 40.00
Compote, cov., 8" d., high stand ... 55.00
Compote, open, 6" d., 6½" h.
  (ILLUS.)...................... 32.50
Compote, open, 8" d............. 45.00
Goblet 32.50
Mug 20.00
Pitcher, milk.................... 36.00
Pitcher, water 55.00
Plate, 7" d., w/baby in tub reaching
  for ball on floor center 55.00
Plate, 7" d., w/kitten center 45.00
Plate, 9" d., closed handles 36.00
Salt dip, master size, oval 35.00
Salt shaker w/original top (single) .. 25.00
Sauce dish...................... 17.00
Syrup pitcher w/original top 80.00
Tray, water..................... 75.00
Tumbler 30.00
Wine........................... 45.00

STIPPLED GRAPE & FESTOON
Celery vase..................... 27.50
Compote, 8" d., low stand 38.50
Creamer, w/clear leaf 38.50

Goblet 25.00
Pitcher, water 98.00
Spooner, w/clear leaf 28.50
Sugar bowl, open 25.00

STIPPLED IVY
Butter dish, cov. 45.00
Compote, open, jelly, flint 35.00
Creamer, applied handle.......... 35.00
Egg cup 28.00
Goblet 27.50
Salt dip, master size.............. 30.00
Sauce dish, flat 8.00
Spooner 27.50
Sugar bowl, cov. 35.00
Tumbler, water 30.00

STIPPLED ROMAN KEY
Goblet 36.50
Tumbler 18.00

SUNK HONEYCOMB
Creamer, ruby-stained, 4½" h. 25.00
Cruet w/original stopper, ruby-
　　stained, enameled floral decor ... 135.00
Mug, ruby-stained, 3" h. 12.50
Pitcher, 6½" h., ruby-stained,
　　souvenir 20.00
Punch cup, clear 6.50
Salt shaker w/original top, clear
　　(single)...................... 6.50
Salt shaker w/original top, ruby-
　　stained (single) 19.50
Syrup pitcher w/original top, ruby-
　　stained...................... 65.00
Toothpick holder, ruby-stained,
　　souvenir 40.00
Wine, clear, etched 15.00
Wine, ruby-stained 32.50
Wine, ruby-stained, etched........ 40.00

SWAN

Swan Spooner

Butter dish, cov., swan finial,
　　clear 90.00

Celery vase, clear 60.00
Compote, cov., 8" d., 12" h., clear .. 120.00
Compote, open, 8½" h., clear 45.00
Creamer, clear.................. 55.00
Dish, cov., clear 55.00
Goblet, canary yellow 70.00
Goblet, clear 50.00
Marmalade jar, cov., clear 57.50
Mug, footed, clear 27.50
Mug, footed, ring handle, opaque
　　blue 68.00
Mug, footed, ring handle, opaque
　　purple 68.00
Mustard jar, cov., amber 75.00
Pitcher, water, clear............. 220.00
Sauce dish, flat or footed,
　　clear.....................9.00 to 15.00
Spooner, clear (ILLUS.)........... 55.00
Sugar bowl, cov., clear 195.00
Sugar bowl, open, clear 40.00

TEARDROP & TASSEL

Teardrop & Tassel Tumbler

Berry set: master bowl & 5 sauce
　　dishes; cobalt blue, 6 pcs. 145.00
Bowl, 7½" d., clear 40.00
Bowl, 7½" d., teal blue........... 60.00
Bowl, master berry or fruit, cobalt
　　blue 45.00
Butter dish, cov., clear 55.00
Butter dish, cov., cobalt blue 135.00
Butter dish, cov., emerald green.... 130.00
Butter dish, cov., teal blue 160.00
Compote, cov., 9½" d., clear...... 75.00
Compote, open, 5" d., clear 28.00
Compote, open, Nile green
　　opaque...................... 250.00
Creamer, clear.................. 26.50
Creamer, Nile green opaque 80.00
Creamer, teal blue 100.00
Goblet, clear 95.00
Pitcher, water, clear............. 67.50
Pitcher, water, emerald green...... 195.00
Pitcher, water, teal blue 250.00
Relish, clear 25.00
Relish, emerald green 45.00
Relish, Nile green opaque 55.00
Salt shaker w/original top, clear
　　(single)...................... 65.00
Sauce dish, clear 12.00

Sauce dish, cobalt blue 20.00
Spooner, clear 30.00
Sugar bowl, cov., clear 45.00
Sugar bowl, cov., cobalt blue...... 135.00
Tumbler, clear (ILLUS.)........... 25.00
Tumbler, cobalt blue 45.00
Tumbler, teal blue 50.00
Water set: pitcher & 6 tumblers;
   cobalt blue, 7 pcs. 550.00

TEASEL
Celery 20.00
Goblet 25.00
Plate, 7" to 9" d.............12.00 to 20.00
Sauce dish...................... 5.50
Sugar bowl, open 30.00
Tumbler 10.00
Wine........................... 12.00

TEXAS (Loop with Stippled Panels)

Texas Toothpick Holder

Bowl, 8" oval ....25.00 to 32.00
Butter dish, cov., ruby-stained...... 165.00
Cake stand, 9½" to 10¾" d. 75.00
Compote, cov., 6" d., 11" h........ 90.00
Creamer 18.00
Creamer, individual size 15.00
Creamer & sugar bowl, individual
   size, pr. 37.50
Cruet w/original stopper........... 70.00
Cruet w/original stopper, ruby-
   stained...................... 165.00
Goblet 45.00
Goblet, ruby-stained.............. 95.00
Pitcher, water, 8½" h............. 120.00
Plate, 8¾" d. 62.50
Relish, handled, 8½" l. 22.50
Salt dip, master size, footed, 3" d.,
   2¾" h. 22.50
Sauce dish, flat or footed ....12.00 to 28.00
Spooner 50.00
Sugar bowl, cov. 60.00
Sugar bowl, open, individual size ... 15.00
Toothpick holder (ILLUS.)........... 32.50
Vase, bud, 8" h. 20.00
Vase, 9" h. 37.50
Vase, 10" h. 27.50
Wine........................... 55.00
Wine, ruby-stained 95.00

TEXAS BULL'S EYE (Bull's Eye Variant)
Celery vase..................... 32.00
Egg cup 15.00
Goblet 25.00
Lamp, kerosene-type, footed, hand-
   type w/finger grip 37.50
Sugar bowl, open 30.00
Tumbler 22.50
Wine.......................... 15.00

THOUSAND EYE

Thousand Eye Celery Vases

Bowl, 8" d., 4½" h., footed, blue
   opaque....................... 55.00
Bowl, 11½" sq., 1¾" h., folded
   corners, clear 45.00
Bread tray, blue 37.50
Bread tray, clear 28.00
Butter dish, cov., apple green 85.00
Butter dish, cov., blue 82.50
Butter dish, cov., clear 37.50
Butter dish, cov., vaseline 70.00
Cake stand, amber, 8½" to
   10" d. ....47.50 to 60.00
Cake stand, apple green, 8½" to
   10" d. 67.50
Cake stand, blue, 8½" to 10" d. 86.00
Cake stand, clear, 8½" to 10" d. ... 27.50
Celery vase, 3-knob stem, apple
   green 57.50
Celery vase, 3-knob stem, clear 45.00
Celery vase, 3-knob stem, clear to
   opalescent w/purple tint 50.00
Celery vase, plain stem, amber..... 50.00
Celery vase, plain stem, clear, each
   (ILLUS. of pair) 35.00
Cologne bottle w/matching stopper,
   clear 26.00
Compote, cov., 12" h., clear........ 115.00
Compote, cov., 3-knob stem, apple
   green, large 120.00
Compote, open, 6" d., low stand,
   amber 18.00
Compote, open, 6" d., low stand,
   apple green 30.00
Compote, open, 6" d., low stand,
   blue 37.50
Compote, open, 7½" d., 3-knob
   stem, amber.................. 47.50

Compote, open, 7½" d., 3-knob
  stem, blue...................... 55.00
Compote, open, 7½" d., 5" h.,
  blue 48.00
Compote, open, 7½" d., 5" h.,
  clear 25.00
Compote, open, 8" d., 3¾" h.,
  apple green 37.50
Compote, open, 8" d., 6" h., 3-knob
  stem, amber 35.00
Compote, open, 8" d., 6" h., 3-knob
  stem, apple green 45.00
Compote, open, 8" d., 6" h., 3-knob
  stem, blue.................... 65.00
Compote, open, 8" d., 6" h., 3-knob
  stem, clear 40.00
Compote, open, 10" d., 6½" h.,
  apple green 45.00
Creamer, amber 38.00
Creamer, clear.................. 25.00
Creamer, vaseline 47.50
Cruet w/original 3-knob stopper,
  amber 60.00
Cruet w/original 3-knob stopper,
  apple green 110.00
Cruet w/original 3-knob stopper,
  clear.......................... 45.00
Cruet w/original 3-knob stopper,
  vaseline 125.00
Dish, apple green, 7 x 5" 25.00
Egg cup, blue 75.00
Egg cup, clear 25.00
Egg cup, vaseline 65.00
Goblet, amber 35.00
Goblet, apple green 33.50
Goblet, blue 42.50
Goblet, clear 28.00
Hat shape, clear, small 12.00
Hat shape, vaseline, small 24.00
Inkwell, cov., amber 85.00
Inkwell, cov., clear, 2" sq. 30.00
Lamp, kerosene-type, pedestal
  base, amber, 14" h. to collar, (22"
  to chimney top) 165.00
Lamp, kerosene-type, pedestal
  base, blue, 12" h. 165.00
Lamp, kerosene-type, flat base, ring
  handle, clear ....105.00 to 120.00
Mug, amber, 3½" h. 22.50
Mug, clear, 3½" h................ 12.50
Mug, vaseline, 3½" h........25.00 to 35.00
Pitcher, milk, 3-knob stem, clear ... 35.00
Pitcher, water, 3-knob stem,
  amber 210.00
Pitcher, water, 3-knob stem, apple
  green 85.00
Pitcher, water, clear.............. 57.50
Plate, 6" d., apple green........... 22.50
Plate, 6" d., clear 12.00
Plate, 8" d., amber............... 25.00
Plate, 8" d., apple green.......... 25.00
Plate, 8" d., clear 20.00
Plate, 10" sq., w/folded corners,
  clear.......................... 26.50

Platter, 11 x 8", blue 42.50
Platter, 11 x 8", clear............. 28.00
Salt shaker w/original top, apple
  green (single)................... 30.00
Salt shaker w/original top, clear
  (single)........................ 20.00
Salt shaker w/original top, vaseline
  (single)........................ 30.00
Salt & pepper shakers w/brass tops,
  blue, pr. 80.00
Sauce dish, flat or footed,
  amber ....9.00 to 12.00
Sauce dish, flat or footed, apple
  green ....10.00 to 14.00
Sauce dish, flat or footed,
  blue ....12.00 to 25.00
Sauce dish, flat or footed,
  clear.....................7.00 to 9.50
Sauce dish, flat or footed,
  vaseline ....15.00 to 27.00
Spooner, 3-knob stem, amber 32.50
Spooner, 3-knob stem, apple
  green 35.00
Spooner, 3-knob stem, blue 35.00
Spooner, 3-knob stem, clear 18.00
Sugar bowl, cov., 3-knob stem,
  blue 55.00
Sugar bowl, cov., clear 40.00
Sugar bowl, open, 3-knob stem,
  clear.......................... 42.50
Syrup pitcher w/original pewter top,
  footed, apple green 85.00
Toothpick holder, amber 32.50
Toothpick holder, clear 22.50
Toothpick holder, vaseline 35.00
Tray, water, amber, 12½" d........ 90.00
Tray, water, apple green, 12½" d... 80.00
Tray, amber, 14" oval 60.00
Tray, apple green, 14" oval 85.00
Tumbler, amber.................. 22.50
Tumbler, blue.................... 35.00
Tumbler, clear 18.50
Water set: oval tray, pitcher & 5
  tumblers; apple green, 7 pcs. 240.00
Whimsey, model of a 4-wheeled
  cart......................... 115.00
Wine, amber..................... 25.00
Wine, clear...................... 22.50

THREE FACE
Bread plate 78.00
Butter dish, cov. 105.00
Cake stand, 8" to
  10½" d.................125.00 to 170.00
Celery vase...................... 97.50
Champagne...................... 127.50
Claret........................... 135.00
Compote, cov., 4½" d., 6½" h...... 75.00
Compote, cov., 6" d. 125.00
Compote, cov., 8" d., 13" h........ 160.00
Compote, cov., 10" d. 145.00
Compote, open, 6" d., 7½" h........ 70.00
Compote, open, 8½" d., 8½" h. 95.00
Compote, open, 9½" d., 9½" h. 165.00

Creamer 85.00
Creamer w/mask spout 125.00
Creamer w/mask spout & cov. sugar
  bowl, pr. 265.00
Goblet 82.50

Three Face Lamp

Lamp, kerosene-type, pedestal
  base, 8" h. (ILLUS.) 145.00
Pitcher, water 295.00
Salt dip 50.00
Salt & pepper shakers w/original
  tops, pr........................ 85.00
Sauce dish...................... 18.50
Spooner 65.00
Sugar bowl, cov. 115.00
Sugar bowl, open 75.00
Table set, creamer, cov. sugar bowl
  & spooner, 3 pcs. 285.00
Toothpick holder 45.00
Wine........................... 98.00

THREE PANEL

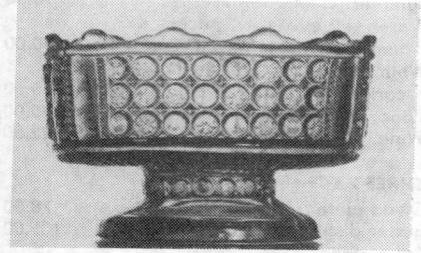

Three Panel Sauce Dish

Berry set: 9" d. master bowl & 6
  footed sauce dishes; clear,
  7 pcs. 95.00
Berry set: master bowl & 8 sauce
  dishes; amber, 9 pcs. 150.00
Bowl, 7" d., footed, amber 25.00
Bowl, 7" d., footed, blue.......... 35.00
Bowl, 7" d., footed, clear 20.00
Bowl, 9" d., footed, amber 30.00
Bowl, 9" d., footed, clear 20.00

Bowl, 9" d., footed, vaseline 45.00
Bowl, 10" d., amber 47.50
Bowl, 10" d., blue 50.00
Bowl, 10" d., vaseline 46.00
Butter dish, cov., amber 65.00
Butter dish, cov., blue 60.00
Butter dish, cov., clear 40.00
Celery vase, amber 40.00
Celery vase, blue 37.50
Celery vase, clear 35.00
Compote, open, 7" d., low stand,
  amber 25.00
Compote, open, 7" d., low stand,
  blue 32.50
Compote, open, 7" d., low stand,
  clear 20.00
Compote, open, 8½" d., low stand,
  blue 37.00
Compote, open, 8½" d., low stand,
  vaseline 32.50
Creamer, amber 32.50
Creamer, blue 47.50
Creamer, clear................. 22.00
Creamer, vaseline.............. 35.00
Goblet, amber 30.00
Goblet, blue 37.50
Goblet, clear 32.50
Goblet, vaseline 40.00
Lamp, kerosene-type, amber 135.00
Mug, amber 27.50
Mug, blue 37.50
Mug, clear.................... 22.00
Mug, vaseline................. 35.00
Pitcher, water, amber 85.00
Pitcher, water, blue 100.00
Sauce dish, footed, amber
  (ILLUS.)...................... 17.50
Sauce dish, footed, blue 15.00
Sauce dish, footed, vaseline........ 15.00
Spooner, amber................. 40.00
Spooner, clear 22.50
Spooner, vaseline 27.50
Sugar bowl, cov., amber 55.00
Sugar bowl, cov., blue.......... 65.00
Sugar bowl, cov., clear 28.00
Sugar bowl, cov., vaseline 65.00
Table set, amber, 4 pcs. 195.00
Tumbler, amber................. 35.00

THUMBPRINT - See Argus Pattern

THUMBPRINT, EARLY

Bitters bottle..................... 135.00
Bowl, 8" d., flat................. 85.00
Butter dish, cov................. 135.00
Celery vase, plain base 90.00
Compote, cov., 6" d., 7½" h........ 225.00
Compote, open, 5" d., 5½" h., scal-
  loped rim..................... 75.00
Compote, open, 7½" d., 7¼" h.,
  scalloped rim 90.00
Compote, open, 8½" d., high stand,
  scalloped rim 175.00
Compote, open, 12½" d., 11¼" h... 400.00

Creamer 85.00
Decanter, 11" h. 100.00
Egg cup 40.00
Goblet, baluster stem ......50.00 to 75.00
Honey dish 16.00
Pitcher, water, 8¼" h............. 275.00
Salt dip, master size, footed 27.50
Sauce dish...................... 9.00
Spillholder..................... 45.00
Spooner 48.50
Tumbler, bar.................... 30.00

Early Thumbprint Footed Tumbler

Tumbler, footed (ILLUS.) 48.50
Tumbler, whiskey, handled,
  footed 150.00
Wine, baluster stem 50.00

TONG

Tong Celery Vase

Celery vase (ILLUS.) 40.00
Spillholder..................... 30.00
Sugar bowl, cov. 50.00

TORPEDO (Pygmy)

Banana stand, clear 55.00
Bowl, cov., master berry, clear 85.00
Bowl, 7" d., flat, clear 17.50
Bowl, 7" d., flat, ruby-stained 37.50

Bowl, 8" d., clear 18.50
Bowl, 8" d., ruby-stained 35.00
Bowl, 9" d., clear 32.50
Bowl, 9½" d., clear 45.00
Butter dish, cov., clear 75.00
Cake stand, clear, 9" to
  11" d. ....55.00 to 82.50
Celery vase, clear................ 40.00
Compote, cov., jelly, clear 42.50
Compote, cov., 8" d., 14" h., clear .. 125.00
Compote, open, jelly, 5" d., 5" h.,
  clear ....35.00 to 45.00
Compote, open, 8" d., high stand,
  flared rim, clear 55.00
Compote, open, 9" d., low stand,
  clear 55.00
Creamer, clear.................. 30.00
Cruet w/original faceted stopper,
  clear 52.50
Cup & saucer, clear 60.00
Decanter w/original stopper, clear.. 110.00

Torpedo Goblet

Goblet, clear (ILLUS.) 50.00
Honey dish, cov., clear 20.00
Lamp, kerosene, hand-type w/finger
  grip, clear, w/burner & chimney .. 67.50
Lamp, kerosene-type, pedestal
  base, clear, 8½" h. 75.00
Marmalade jar, cov., clear 55.00
Pitcher, milk, 7" h., clear 50.00
Pitcher, milk, 8½" h., clear 72.50
Pitcher, milk, 8½" h., ruby-
  stained 90.00
Pitcher, water, 10" h., clear 75.00
Pitcher, water, 10" h., ruby-
  stained 90.00
Pitcher, water, tankard, 12" h.,
  clear 80.00
Salt dip, individual size, clear,
  1½" d. 32.50
Salt dip, master size, clear 40.00
Sauce dish, clear................ 15.00
Spooner, clear 38.50
Sugar bowl, cov., clear 75.00
Sugar bowl, open, clear 25.00
Syrup jug w/original top, clear 75.00

Syrup jug w/original top, ruby-
stained 160.00
Tray, clear, 9¾" d. 75.00
Tumbler, ruby-stained 45.00
Waste bowl, clear 45.00
Wine, clear 70.00

TREE OF LIFE - PITTSBURGH (Tree of Life with Hand)

Pittsburgh Tree of Life Creamer

Butter dish, cov. 55.00
Cake stand, 8¾" d. . . . . .70.00 to 95.00
Compote, cov., 6" d., 8" h., frosted
hand & ball stem 65.00
Compote, open, 5½" d., 5½" h.,
clear hand & ball stem 39.00
Compote, open, 5½" d., 5½" h.,
frosted hand & ball stem 47.50
Compote, open, 8" d., 8½" h.,
frosted hand & ball stem 57.50
Compote, open, 9" d., frosted hand
& ball stem 75.00
Compote, open, 10" d., 10" h.,
frosted hand & ball stem 95.00
Creamer, w/hand & ball handle
(ILLUS.) 45.00
Creamer & sugar bowl, pr. 95.00
Pitcher, water, 9" h. 60.00
Relish, oval 29.00
Sauce dish, flat or
footed . . . . .12.00 to 20.00
Spooner 45.00
Sugar bowl, cov. 52.50
Tumbler 23.00
Wine. 28.00

TREE OF LIFE - PORTLAND

Berry set: master bowl & 4 sauce
dishes; blue, 5 pcs. 325.00
Bowl, 5½" d., flat, clear 12.00
Bowl, signed "Davis," green, in sil-

verplate holder marked "Meriden
Britannia Co.". 235.00
Bread tray, clear 40.00
Butter dish, cov., clear 55.00
Butter pat, blue 25.00
Butter pat, clear 13.00
Butter pat, vaseline 25.00
Cake stand, signed "Davis," clear,
9" to 11½" d. . . . . .45.00 to 60.00
Celery vase, clear, in metal
holder 75.00
Champagne, clear 60.00
Compote, open, 6" d., 6" h., clear . . 35.00
Compote, open, 7¾" d., signed
"P.G. Co.," clear 85.00
Compote, open, 7¾" d., 11" h.,
Infant Samuel stand, signed
"Davis," clear 175.00
Compote, open, 8½" d., 6½" h.,
signed "Davis," clear 120.00
Compote, open, 9½" d., Infant
Samuel stand, clear 200.00
Creamer, signed "Davis," clear 65.00
Creamer, cranberry, in silverplate
holder 85.00
Creamer & sugar bowl w/silverplate
cover, clear, in silverplate holder,
pr. 110.00
Dish, leaf-shaped, clear, 6¾ x 5" . . . 13.50
Epergne, Infant Samuel stand,
signed "Davis," clear, 2 pcs. 125.00
Goblet, clear . . . . .32.50 to 42.00
Goblet, signed "Davis,"
clear . . . . .50.00 to 65.00
Mug, applied handle, clear,
3½" h. 25.00
Pitcher, water, applied handle,
clear 100.00
Pitcher, water, applied handle,
signed "Davis," amber . . .225.00 to 250.00
Plate, 6½" d., clear 18.00
Plate, 12" l., 3-footed, shell-shaped,
clear 85.00
Salt dip, flat, clear, 3" d. 10.00
Salt dip, footed, opaque green 95.00
Sauce dish, melon-ribbed, clear,
4½" to 5½" d. 18.00
Sauce dish, leaf-shaped, amber 11.50
Sauce dish, leaf-shaped, clear 15.00
Spooner, clear, in handled silver-
plate holder w/two Griffin
heads 57.50
Sugar bowl, cov., clear 55.00
Sugar bowl, clear, in silverplate
holder 70.00
Toothpick holder, vaseline 55.00
Tray, ice cream, clear, 14"
rectangle 42.50
Tray, ice cream, vaseline, 14"
rectangle 85.00
Tumbler, clear, 4½" h. 22.50
Tumbler, footed, clear, 6" h. 40.00
Waste bowl, clear 15.00

Portland Tree of Life Waste Bowl

Waste bowl, cranberry, flint
(ILLUS.) 145.00
Wine, clear 45.00

TULIP WITH SAWTOOTH

Tulip with Sawtooth Celery Vases

Butter dish, cov., non-flint 80.00
Celery vase, flint 70.00
Celery vase, non-flint, each (ILLUS.
of pair) 30.00
Champagne, non-flint 40.00
Compote, cov., 6" d., high stand,
flint 120.00
Compote, open, 7" d., low stand,
non-flint 75.00
Compote, open, 9¾" d., 4½" h.,
non-flint 70.00
Creamer, applied handle, flint 85.00
Decanter w/tulip-form stopper, flint,
12" h., pt. . . . . 120.00 to 180.00
Decanter w/bar lip, flint, pt. 68.00
Goblet, flint 50.00
Goblet, non-flint 27.50
Marmalade jar, cov., non-flint 30.00
Pitcher, water, flint 175.00
Salt dip, master size, scalloped rim,
flint 25.00
Sauce dish, flat, non-flint,
3 7/8" d. 8.00
Spooner, flint 35.00

Spooner, non-flint 28.00
Sugar bowl, open, non-flint 32.50
Tumbler, bar, flint 85.00
Tumbler, bar, non-flint 27.50
Tumbler, footed, flint 55.00
Wine, flint 60.00
Wine, non-flint 22.50

TWO PANEL (Daisy in Panel)

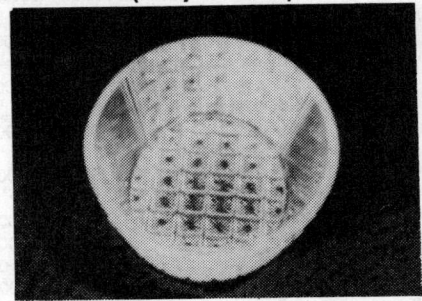

Two Panel Sauce Dish

Bowl, cov., 7" oval, vaseline 55.00
Bowl, 7 x 5½" oval, amber 25.00
Bowl, 10 x 8" oval, blue 65.00
Bowl, 10 x 8" oval, vaseline 50.00
Bread tray, apple green 35.00
Bread tray, blue 45.00
Bread tray, clear 27.00
Butter dish, cov., blue 90.00
Butter dish, cov., vaseline 55.00
Celery vase, amber 30.00
Celery vase, blue 50.00
Compote, cov., 8 x 6½", 11" h.,
vaseline 85.00
Compote, open, 9" oval, amber 37.00
Compote, open, 9" oval, blue 40.00
Compote, open, 9" oval, 4" h.,
vaseline 45.00
Creamer, amber 38.00
Creamer, apple green 40.00
Creamer, blue 35.00
Creamer, clear 22.50
Creamer, vaseline 35.00
Goblet, amber 32.50
Goblet, apple green 35.00
Goblet, blue 37.50
Goblet, clear 28.00
Goblet, vaseline 35.00
Lamp, kerosene-type, pedestal
base, amber 80.00
Lamp, kerosene-type, pedestal
base, blue 125.00
Lamp, kerosene-type, pedestal
base, vaseline 130.00
Marmalade jar, cov., clear 36.50
Marmalade jar, cov., vaseline 65.00
Pitcher, water, amber 50.00
Pitcher, water, apple green 55.00
Pitcher, water, blue 95.00
Pitcher, water, clear 35.00
Pitcher, water, vaseline 75.00

Relish, amber 16.00
Relish, blue 22.50
Relish, vaseline 22.50
Salt dip, master size, amber 20.00
Salt dip, master size, apple
  green 18.50
Salt dip, master size, vaseline 22.00
Salt dip, individual size, apple
  green 15.00
Sauce dish, flat or footed,
  amber 12.00
Sauce dish, flat or footed, apple
  green ....13.50 to 22.00
Sauce dish, flat or footed,
  blue ....14.00 to 18.00
Sauce dish, flat or footed,
  clear ....7.50 to 15.00
Sauce dish, flat or footed,
  vaseline (ILLUS.) ....15.00 to 19.00
Spooner, amber 35.00
Spooner, blue 37.50
Spooner, clear 25.00
Spooner, vaseline 32.50
Sugar bowl, cov., amber 50.00
Sugar bowl, open, vaseline 35.00
Tray, water, cloverleaf shape, vase-
  line, 10½ x 8¾" oval 55.00
Tray, water, amber, 15 x 10" oval .. 47.50
Tumbler, amber 25.00
Tumbler, blue or vaseline 32.50
Waste bowl, amber 30.00
Water set: pitcher & 6 tumblers;
  blue, 7 pcs. 300.00
Wine, amber 35.00
Wine, apple green 35.00
Wine, blue 35.00
Wine, clear 17.50
Wine, vaseline 35.00

Butter dish, dollars & half dollars ... 500.00
Cake stand, clear dollars, 10" d 265.00
Cake stand, frosted dollars, 10" d... 475.00
Candy dish, cov., 6" d. 275.00
Celery vase, frosted quarters 350.00
Champagne, frosted dimes 325.00
Compote, cov., 6 7/8" d., high
  stand, frosted coins 475.00
Compote, cov., 8" d., 11½" h.,
  frosted coins (ILLUS.) 525.00
Compote, cov., 9" d., frosted
  coins 650.00
Compote, open, 7" d., 5¾" h., frost-
  ed dimes & quarters 400.00
Compote, open, 8" d., 6½" h.,
  frosted coins 450.00
Compote, open, 9¼" d., 7" h., frost-
  ed half dollars on bowl, quarters
  on stem 375.00
Epergne, frosted dollars 1,200.00
Goblet, frosted dimes 395.00
Lamp, kerosene-type, round font,
  frosted dollars in base 850.00
Lamp, kerosene-type, round font,
  pedestal base, frosted quarters... 485.00
Mug, frosted coins 345.00
Pickle dish, clear coins, 7½ x 3¾".. 220.00
Pitcher, water, frosted dollars 485.00
Relish, frosted coins 185.00
Sauce dish, frosted quarters,
  4" d..................125.00 to 175.00
Spooner, clear quarters 225.00
Spooner, frosted quarters 375.00
Sugar bowl, cov., frosted coins 450.00
Toothpick holder, frosted coins 190.00
Tumbler, frosted dollar in base 175.00
Wine, frosted half dimes 450.00

U.S. COIN

U.S. Coin Compote

Bowl, 8" oval, frosted coins 315.00
Bread tray, dollars & half
  dollars ....345.00 to 425.00

VALENCIA WAFFLE (Block & Star)

Valencia Waffle Pattern

Bread platter, clear 27.00
Butter dish, cov., amber 70.00
Butter dish, cov., apple green 60.00
Butter dish, cov., clear 42.50
Butter dish, cov., ruby-stained...... 110.00
Cake stand, amber 70.00
Cake stand, clear, 10" d. 70.00

Celery vase, blue	42.50
Celery vase, clear	37.50
Celery vase, yellow	35.00
Compote, cov., 6" d., 10" h., clear	75.00
Compote, cov., 7" sq., low stand, amber	62.50
Compote, cov., 7" sq., low stand, apple green	75.00
Compote, cov., 7" sq., low stand, blue	77.50
Compote, cov., 7" sq., low stand, clear	55.00
Compote, cov., 8" sq., 9" h., amber	90.00
Creamer, clear	38.00
Creamer, vaseline	32.50
Goblet, amber	35.00
Goblet, clear	24.00
Pitcher, water, 7½" h., amber	65.00
Pitcher, water, apple green	95.00
Pitcher, water, blue	70.00
Pitcher, water, clear	40.00
Relish, amber, 10¾ x 7½"	30.00
Relish, clear, 10¾ x 7½"	10.00
Salt dip, master size, amber	22.50
Salt dip, master size, blue	25.00
Salt dip, master size, clear	12.00
Salt dip, master size, yellow	26.00
Salt & pepper shakers w/original tops, apple green, pr.	50.00
Sauce dish, footed, amber	13.50
Sauce dish, footed, blue	12.00
Sauce dish, footed, clear	12.50
Spooner, amber	40.00
Spooner, blue	37.50
Spooner, clear	18.00
Syrup jug w/original top, amber	100.00
Syrup jug w/original top, blue	90.00
Tray, water, amber, 13¼ x 9½", amber	37.50 to 45.00

VICTOR - See Shell & Jewel Pattern

VICTORIA

Victoria Compote

Compote, cov., 8" d., low foot (ILLUS.)	150.00
Compote, cov., 8" d., high stand	200.00
Compote, cov., 10½" d., 15¼" h.	215.00

VIKING (Bearded Head or Old Man of the Mountain)

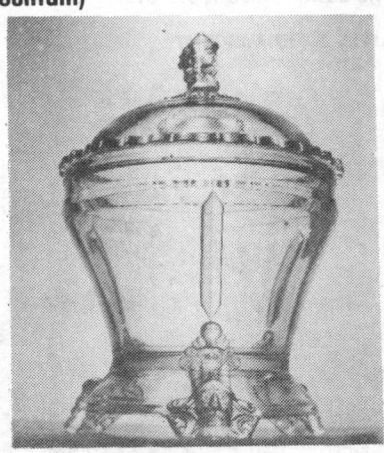

Viking Sugar Bowl

Apothecary jar w/original stopper	95.00
Bowl, cov., 8" oval	45.00
Bowl, cov., 9" oval	55.00
Bowl, 7" d., 4" h.	25.00
Bread tray, cupid hunt scene center	50.00
Butter dish, cov.	55.00
Cake stand, 10" d.	67.50
Celery vase	38.50
Compote, cov., 7" d., low stand	45.00
Compote, cov., 8" d., low stand	70.00
Compote, cov., 9" d., low stand	75.00
Compote, cov., 12" h.	150.00
Compote, open, 8" d., high stand	62.50
Creamer	48.00
Dish, cov., 8" oval	85.00
Egg cup	35.00
Marmalade jar, footed, etched (no cover)	27.50
Mug, applied handle	65.00
Pickle dish, 7" l.	45.00
Pitcher, water, 8¾" h.	85.00
Salt dip, master size	47.50
Sauce dish, footed	12.00
Shaving mug, milk white	45.00
Spooner	30.00
Sugar bowl, cov. (ILLUS.)	57.50

VIRGINIA - See Galloway Pattern

WAFFLE

Celery vase, flint	42.50
Compote, open, 7" d., 5¼" h.	32.50
Compote, open, 9½" d., 8" h.	75.00
Creamer, applied handle	135.00
Cruet	27.50

Egg cup 40.00
Goblet 75.00
Salt dip, master size............... 27.50
Sugar bowl, cov. 60.00
Syrup pitcher, applied handle 85.00
Tumbler, bar..................... 75.00
Waste bowl, ruffled top........... 75.00

WAFFLE & THUMBPRINT

Waffle & Thumbprint Spillholder

Bowl, 7¼" d., flint 30.00
Celery vase, flint ....85.00 to 100.00
Compote, open, 6" d., 6" h., flint ... 85.00
Cordial, flint 85.00
Creamer, applied handle, flint...... 250.00
Decanter, no stopper, flint, pt. 70.00
Decanter w/original matching stop-
  per, canary yellow, qt. 275.00
Egg cup, flint 32.50
Goblet, flint 57.50
Lamp, w/original 2-tube burner,
  hand-type w/applied handle, flint,
  3" h............................ 135.00
Lamp, w/original whale oil burner,
  flint, 11" h.............135.00 to 170.00
Pitcher, water, flint 300.00
Spillholder, flint (ILLUS.) 115.00
Sugar bowl, cov., flint 175.00
Tumbler, bar, flint................ 62.50
Tumbler, footed, flint 125.00
Tumbler, whiskey, flint 92.00
Wine, flint....................... 50.00

WASHBOARD - See Adonis Pattern

WASHINGTON (Early)

Claret, flint..................... 135.00
Decanter w/original stopper, qt..... 225.00
Egg cup, flint 65.00
Goblet, flint ....60.00 to 80.00
Lamp, kerosene-type, cast iron
  base 125.00
Pitcher, water, flint 225.00
Salt dip, individual size 12.50
Salt dip, master size, flat, round.... 27.50

WASHINGTON CENTENNIAL

"Carpenter's Hall" Platter

Bowl, 8½" oval 22.50
Bread platter, Carpenter's Hall,
  clear (ILLUS.) 100.00
Bread platter, Carpenter's Hall,
  frosted 125.00
Bread platter, George Washington
  center, clear............85.00 to 100.00
Bread platter, George Washington
  center, frosted..........95.00 to 110.00
Bread platter, Independence Hall
  center, clear................... 85.00
Butter dish, cov., footed 87.50
Cake stand, 8½" to 11½" d. 45.00
Celery vase..................... 40.00
Champagne...................... 42.50
Compote, cov., 8½" d., 12" h....... 105.00
Compote, open, 7½" d., 8" h....... 42.00
Compote, open, 8" d., 6½" h....... 37.50
Creamer, applied handle........... 80.00
Egg cup 42.50
Goblet 42.50
Honey dish 12.00
Lamp, kerosene-type, brass stem &
  marble base 90.00
Pickle dish..................... 25.00
Pitcher, milk 80.00
Pitcher, water 90.00
Relish, bear paw handles, dated
  1876 .... 42.50
Salt dip, master size.............. 25.00
Sauce dish, flat or footed 9.00
Spooner 35.00
Sugar bowl, cov. 75.00
Sugar bowl, open 20.00
Toothpick holder 60.00
Tumbler, bar................... 65.00
Tumbler 72.50
Wine.......................... 40.00

WEDDING BELLS

Bowl, 8" d., flat, ruby-stained 32.50

Bowl, master berry, clear, w/gold
trim.......................... 28.00
Butter dish, cov., clear 30.00
Celery tray, pink-stained.......... 27.50
Celery vase, clear................. 27.50
Creamer, 4-footed, clear........... 48.00
Goblet, clear..................... 50.00
Pitcher, water, clear.............. 60.00
Pitcher, water, alternate ruby-
stained panels 85.00
Punch cup, clear 15.00
Salt shaker w/original top, clear
(single)........................ 20.00
Spooner, clear 40.00
Sugar bowl, cov., clear 55.00
Toothpick holder, clear, gold trim... 55.00
Toothpick holder, pink-stained...... 80.00
Tumbler, clear 18.00
Water set: pitcher & 4 tumblers;
clear, 5 pcs. 135.00
Wine, clear 17.50
Wine, pink-stained 40.00

WEDDING RING
Decanter w/stopper, qt. 55.00
Goblet 47.50
Sauce dish, 4" d. 8.50
Tumbler 45.00
Wine............................. 37.50

WESTWARD HO

Westward Ho Butter Dish

Bread platter ....92.50 to 110.00
Butter dish, cov. (ILLUS.) 175.00
Celery vase....................... 125.00
Compote, cov., 5" d., 9" h......... 98.00
Compote, cov., 6" d., 12" h........ 145.00
Compote, cov., 6¾ x 4½" oval 150.00
Compote, cov., 7¾ x 5" oval,
10" h. 160.00
Compote, cov., 8" d., low stand 275.00
Compote, cov., 8" d., 11½" h....... 250.00
Compote, cov., 8 x 5½" oval,
12" h.......................... 290.00

Compote, cov., 8" d., 14" h........ 290.00
Compote, cov., 10 x 6½" oval, low
stand 235.00
Compote, open, 6" d., high stand ... 130.00
Compote, open, 8 1/16" d., 8" h. ... 65.00
Creamer 110.00
Creamer & cov. sugar bowl, pr. 275.00
Creamer & open sugar bowl, pr.... 175.00
Goblet ....55.00 to 95.00
Marmalade jar, cov............... 150.00
Pickle dish, oval 55.00
Pitcher, milk, 8" h. 250.00
Pitcher, water 250.00
Relish, deer handles.............. 115.00
Sauce dish, footed 27.50
Spooner 85.00
Sugar bowl, cov...........150.00 to 165.00
Sugar bowl, open 35.00
Water set, pitcher & 6 goblets,
7 pcs.......................... 595.00

WHEAT & BARLEY

Wheat & Barley Plate

Bowl, cov., 8" d., flat, clear 40.00
Bread plate, amber................ 25.00
Butter dish, cov., blue 75.00
Butter dish, cov., clear 35.00
Cake stand, amber, 8" to 10" d. 35.00
Cake stand, clear, 8" to
10" d....................36.50 to 45.00
Compote, cov., 8½" h., high stand,
clear 55.00
Compote, open, jelly, blue 28.00
Compote, open, jelly, clear 18.50
Compote, open, jelly, vaseline 35.00
Compote, open, 8¾" d., 6¾" h.,
clear 35.00
Creamer, blue 45.00
Creamer, clear 22.50
Goblet, amber 37.50
Goblet, blue 40.00
Goblet, clear 25.00
Mug, amber 32.50
Mug, blue 40.00
Mug, clear....................... 20.00
Pitcher, milk, blue 65.00
Pitcher, milk, clear 35.00
Pitcher, water, amber 85.00
Pitcher, water, blue 72.50

Pitcher, water, clear	40.00
Pitcher, water, vaseline	98.00
Plate, 7" d., amber	28.00
Plate, 7" d., blue	30.00
Plate, 7" d., clear	18.00
Plate, 9" d., closed handles, amber (ILLUS.)	35.00
Plate, 9" d., closed handles, blue	27.50
Plate, 9" d., closed handles, clear	22.50
Salt shaker w/original top, blue (single)	37.50
Salt & pepper shakers w/original tops, clear, pr.	30.00
Sauce dish, flat, handled, amber	12.00
Sauce dish, flat, handled, clear	10.00
Sauce dish, footed, amber	14.50
Sauce dish, footed, clear	15.00
Spooner, amber	32.50
Spooner, blue	30.00
Spooner, clear	18.00
Sugar bowl, cov., amber	45.00
Sugar bowl, cov., clear	32.00
Tumbler, amber	32.50
Tumbler, blue	30.00
Tumbler, clear	22.50

WILDFLOWER

Wildflower Sauce Dish

Bowl, 5¾" sq., clear	10.00
Bowl, 6½" sq., blue	22.50
Bowl, 7" sq., footed, amber	29.00
Bowl, 7" sq., clear	14.50
Bowl, 8" sq., 5" h., footed, apple green	22.50
Bowl, 8" sq., 5" h., footed, blue	50.00
Butter dish, cov., amber	75.00
Butter dish, cov., flat, clear	35.00
Butter dish, cov., collared base, vaseline	60.00
Cake stand, amber, 9½" to 11"	48.50 to 65.00
Cake stand, apple green, 9½" to 11"	60.00 to 95.00
Cake stand, blue, 9½" to 11"	50.00 to 85.00
Cake stand, clear, 9½" to 11"	30.00 to 45.00
Cake stand, vaseline, 9½" to 11"	60.00 to 95.00
Celery vase, amber	57.50
Celery vase, blue	62.50
Celery vase, clear	28.00
Champagne, amber	57.50
Compote, cov., 6" d., blue	70.00
Compote, cov., 6" d., clear	35.00
Compote, cov., 7" d., amber	50.00
Compote, cov., 8" d., amber	85.00
Compote, open, 7" d., low stand, apple green	23.50
Compote, open, 7" d., low stand, blue	38.00
Compote, open, 9½" d., amber	45.00
Compote, open, 10½" d., 7½" h., blue	105.00
Compote, open, 10½" d., 8¼" h., amber	75.00
Creamer, amber	27.50
Creamer, apple green	40.00
Creamer, blue	35.00
Creamer, clear	22.50
Creamer, vaseline	40.00
Goblet, amber	32.50
Goblet, apple green	35.00
Goblet, blue	25.00
Goblet, clear	20.00
Goblet, vaseline	40.00
Pitcher, water, amber	52.50
Pitcher, water, apple green	75.00
Pitcher, water, blue	75.00
Pitcher, water, clear	40.00 to 55.00
Pitcher, water, vaseline	58.00
Plate, 7" sq., apple green	24.50
Plate, 10" sq., amber	35.00
Plate, 10" sq., apple green	32.50
Plate, 10" sq., blue	35.00
Plate, 10" sq., clear	28.00
Platter, 11 x 8", apple green	45.00 to 69.00
Platter, 11 x 8", clear	35.00
Relish, amber	17.50
Relish, apple green	19.50
Relish, clear	22.50
Salt shaker w/original top, vaseline (single)	45.00
Salt & pepper shakers w/original tops, amber, pr.	50.00
Salt & pepper shakers w/original tops, blue, pr.	70.00
Salt & pepper shakers w/original tops, clear, pr.	45.00
Sauce dish, flat or footed, amber	9.00 to 12.00
Sauce dish, flat or footed, apple green	13.50
Sauce dish, flat or footed, blue	10.00 to 30.00
Sauce dish, footed, clear (ILLUS.)	10.00
Sauce dish, flat or footed, vaseline	15.00
Spooner, amber	30.00
Spooner, apple green	35.00
Spooner, clear	27.50
Spooner, vaseline	35.00
Sugar bowl, cov., amber	45.00
Sugar bowl, cov., blue	48.00
Sugar bowl, cov., clear	35.00

Sugar bowl, open, amber	19.00
Sugar bowl, open, apple green	35.00
Sugar bowl, open, clear	20.00
Syrup pitcher w/original top, amber	175.00
Syrup pitcher w/original top, apple green	185.00
Syrup pitcher w/original top, blue	165.00
Syrup pitcher w/original top, vaseline	130.00
Tray, dresser, amber, 9 x 4"	30.00
Tray, water, amber, 13 x 11"	47.50
Tray, water, apple green, 13 x 11"	55.00
Tray, water, clear, 13 x 11"	35.00
Tray, water, vaseline, 13 x 11"	45.00
Tumbler, amber	30.00
Tumbler, apple green	28.00
Tumbler, blue	27.50
Tumbler, clear	24.00
Tumbler, vaseline	30.00
Tumbler, yellow	27.50
Water set: pitcher, tray & 6 tumblers; apple green, 8 pcs.	325.00

WILLOW OAK

Willow Oak Water Pitcher

Bowl, cov., 7" d., flat, clear	32.50
Bowl, 7" d., amber	20.00
Bowl, 7" d., blue	30.00
Bowl, 7" d., clear	14.50
Bowl, 8" d., 2½" h., clear	19.50
Bread plate, amber, 11" d.	25.00
Bread plate, clear, 11" d.	19.00
Butter dish, cov., amber	65.00
Butter dish,, cov., blue	65.00
Butter dish, cov., clear	40.00
Cake stand, amber, 8" to 10" d.	40.00 to 60.00
Cake stand, blue, 8" to 10" d.	42.00 to 85.00
Cake stand, clear, 8" to 10" d.	32.50
Celery vase, amber	47.00
Celery vase, clear	35.00
Compote, cov., 6½" d., 9" h., clear	47.50

Compote, open, 6" d., scalloped top, clear	35.00
Compote, open, 7" d., high stand, blue	60.00
Compote, open, 7" d., high stand, clear	25.00
Creamer, amber	37.50
Creamer, blue	42.50
Creamer, clear	22.50
Goblet, amber	37.50
Goblet, blue	45.00
Goblet, clear	35.00
Mug, amber	35.00
Mug, blue	42.50
Mug, clear	34.00
Pitcher, milk, amber	65.00
Pitcher, milk, clear	40.00
Pitcher, water, amber (ILLUS.)	85.00
Pitcher, water, blue	65.00
Pitcher, water, clear	50.00
Plate, 7" d., amber	35.00
Plate, 9" d., handled, amber	30.00
Plate, 9" d., handled, blue	45.00
Plate, 9" d., handled, clear	20.00
Salt shaker w/original top, blue (single)	85.00
Salt shaker w/original top, clear (single)	25.00
Sauce dish, flat or footed, clear	10.00 to 18.00
Spooner, amber	40.00
Spooner, blue	38.00
Spooner, clear	25.00
Sugar bowl, cov., amber	62.50
Sugar bowl, cov., clear	35.00
Sugar bowl, open, clear	20.00
Tray, water, clear, 10½" d.	27.50
Tumbler, amber	35.00
Tumbler, blue	37.50
Tumbler, clear	32.50

WINDFLOWER

Bowl, 7 x 5" oval	27.50
Butter dish, cov.	55.00
Celery vase	40.00
Compote, cov., 8½" d., low stand	60.00
Creamer	27.50
Egg cup	20.00
Goblet	47.50
Pitcher, water	65.00
Sauce dish	10.00
Spooner	30.00
Sugar bowl, cov.	29.00
Sugar bowl, open	18.00
Tumbler, bar	35.00
Tumbler, water	40.00
Wine	35.00

WISCONSIN (Beaded Dewdrop)

Bowl, 6½" d.	37.00
Bowl, 8" d.	25.00
Bowl, 8½" oblong	35.00
Bread tray	45.00
Butter dish, cov.	80.00

Cake stand, 9¾" d.	47.50
Celery tray, flat, 10 x 5"	40.00
Celery vase	40.00
Compote, cov., 10½" d.	65.00
Compote, open, 6½" d., 6½" h.	22.50
Compote, open, 7½" d., 5½" h.	37.50
Creamer, individual size	49.00
Cup & saucer	45.00
Dish, cov., oval	29.00
Goblet	42.50
Mug, 3½" h.	35.00
Nappy, handled, 4" d.	22.00
Olive dish, 2-handled	35.00
Pickle dish	18.50
Pitcher, milk	48.00

Wisconsin Pitcher

Pitcher, water, 8" h. (ILLUS.)	65.00
Plate, 5" sq.	15.00
Plate, 6½" sq.	27.50
Punch cup	15.00
Relish, 8½ x 4"	22.50
Salt & pepper shakers w/original tops, pr.	45.00
Sauce dish	10.00
Spooner	30.00
Sugar bowl, cov., 5" h.	37.50
Sugar shaker w/original top	65.00
Syrup pitcher w/original top, 6½" h.	56.00
Toothpick holder	35.00
Tumbler	38.00
Wine	52.50

WOODEN PAIL - See Oaken Bucket Pattern

ZIPPER

Bowl, 8" oval	18.00
Bowl, 10" d.	17.50
Butter dish, cov.	40.00
Celery vase	18.00
Cheese dish, cov.	55.00
Compote, cov., low stand	40.00
Creamer	20.00
Cruet w/original stopper	38.00

Cruet w/original stopper, ruby-stained	145.00
Goblet	20.00
Humidor, cov.	45.00
Marmalade jar, cov.	35.00
Pitcher, water	35.00
Punch cup	7.00
Relish	15.00
Sauce dish, flat or footed	6.00 to 8.00
Spooner	20.00
Sugar bowl, cov.	25.00
Sugar bowl, open	15.00
Sugar shaker w/silverplate top	28.00
Toothpick holder	15.00
Toothpick holder, ruby-stained	25.00
Wine	16.00

ZIPPERED BLOCK - See Iowa Pattern

(End of Pattern Glass Section)

PEACH BLOW

Several types of glass lumped together by collectors as Peach Blow were produced by half a dozen glass houses. Hobbs, Brockunier & Co., Wheeling, West Va., made Peach Blow as a plated ware that shaded from red at the top to yellow at the bottom and is referred to as Wheeling Peach Blow. Mt. Washington Glass Works produced an homogeneous Peach Blow shading from a rose color at the top to pale blue in the lower portion. The New England Glass Works' Peach Blow, called Wild Rose, shaded from rose at the top to white. Gunderson—Pairpoint Co. also reproduced some of the Mt. Washington Peach Blow in the early 1950's, and some glass of a somewhat similar type was made by Steuben Glass Works, the Boston & Sandwich Factory and by Thomas Webb & Sons and Stevens & Williams of England. Sandwich Peach Blow is a one-layered glass and the English is two-layered. A relative newcomer to the fold is called New Martinsville "Peach Blow." It is a single-layered glass.

GUNDERSON - PAIRPOINT

Cup & saucer, applied reeded handle	$175.00 to 250.00
Ewer, 6" h.	135.00
Toothpick holder, fluted rim	125.00 to 145.00
Vase, 9¼" h., trefoil rim	275.00

MOUNT WASHINGTON

Pitcher, 7½" h., 8½" widest d., applied handle, acid finish	1,050.00
Toothpick holder, cylindrical w/squared rim, enameled daisies	

& leaves decor, gold stripe on
rim............................2,750.00
Vase, 8" h., stick-type 2,000.00

NEW ENGLAND

New England Peach Blow Tumbler

Celery vase, cylindrical w/squared
  top, scalloped rim, acid finish,
  4¾" h........................... 450.00
Cruet w/original stopper, glossy fin-
  ish, 5½" h...................... 575.00
Darner, glossy finish ......150.00 to 185.00
Finger bowl, glossy finish, 4½" d.,
  2¾" h........................... 435.00
Finger bowl, 10 folded-in pleats at
  rim, 5½" d., 2½" h.............. 265.00
Pear, glossy finish, w/stem intact... 200.00
Punch cup, applied reeded handle,
  acid finish, 2½" h. ......175.00 to 275.00
Rose bowl, crimped rim, lettered
  "World's Fair 1893" in gold 395.00
Spooner, 4¾" h................... 495.00
Sugar bowl, lettered "World's Fair
  1893" in gold 450.00
Toothpick holder, folded-in tricor-
  nered top, acid finish, 2¼" h. 485.00
Tumbler, acid finish, 3¾" h.
  (ILLUS.)........................ 365.00
Vase, 7" h., dimpled sides, acid
  finish 425.00

WEBB

Creamer, applied clear handle, bulbous w/round mouth, glossy,
  creamy white lining, 2½" d.,
  3½" h........................... 225.00
Dish, shell-shaped w/ruffled rim,
  glossy, dull gold floral decor,
  creamy white lining, 9½ x 6¾",
  2½" h........................... 302.00
Jar, cov., acid finish, gold
  prunus branches & pine needles
  decor, creamy white lining,
  4½" h.................595.00 to 650.00
Scent bottle w/hallmarked silver
  screw-on cap, acid finish, gold

prunus blossoms & butterfly decor, 3 5/8" d., 4¾" h. 495.00
Sweetmeat jar, acid finish, gold
  encrusted prunus decor, creamy
  white lining, silverplate rim,
  cover & bail handle, 3¾" d.,
  4½" h..................395.00 to 475.00
Vase, 3¼" h., acid finish, gold blossoms & leaves one side, dragonfly
  reverse, creamy white lining 255.00
Vase, 4¼" h., 4¼" d., glossy, gold
  & silver leaves & butterfly in flight
  decor, enameled blue trim,
  creamy white lining 295.00
Vase, 5¾" h., 4¼" d., glossy, applied clear loop feet & clear
  rigaree, branches & berries on
  body, creamy white lining 495.00
Vase, 6 7/8" h., 5 3/8" d., acid finish, gold encrusted daisies &
  leaves & large dragonfly, creamy
  white lining..................... 650.00
Vase, 7" h., 3 3/8" d., stick-type,
  glossy, gold branches, florals &
  small butterfly decor, creamy
  white lining..................... 235.00

Webb Peach Blow Vase

Vase, 7 5/8" h., acid finish, gold encrusted florals, leaves & small
  butterfly decor, creamy white lining (ILLUS.) 850.00
Vase, 8¼" h., bottle-shaped, acid
  finish, creamy white lining 260.00
Vases, 10¼" h., acid finish, gold
  & silver branches & paired birds
  decor, creamy whtie lining,
  pr. 1,000.00

WHEELING
Condiment set: ball-shaped salt &
  pepper shakers & open sugar

bowl; in original silverplate holder marked Hartford Silver Plate
Co.,set 1,250.00

Wheeling Peach Blow Creamer

Creamer, white lining (ILLUS.) 385.00
Cruet w/original facet-cut amber
stopper, applied reeded amber
handle, glossy, oyster white lining, 6¾" h. .... 850.00 to 1,250.00
Cruet w/original facet-cut amber
stopper, applied reeded amber
handle, acid finish,
7" h. .... 1,050.00 to 1,395.00
Morgan vase replica, glossy,
7¾" h. 945.00
Pitcher, 4 5/8" h., square top, applied amber handle, glossy, oyster
white lining 500.00
Pitcher, 5" h., Drape patt., oyster
white lining 850.00
Pitcher, water, 7" h., square top,
applied amber handle, oyster
white lining 825.00
Pitcher, water, 8" h., Hobnail patt.,
oyster white lining 1,695.00
Pitcher, water, 10" h., square top,
applied amber handle, glossy,
oyster white lining 1,250.00
Sugar bowl, glossy, oyster white lining, 3½" h. 725.00
Sugar shaker w/original silverplate
pull-off top, glossy,
5" h. .... 425.00 to 550.00
Tumbler, glossy finish, oyster white
lining, 3 7/8" h. .... 275.00 to 395.00
Vase, 4½" h., glossy, oyster white
lining 325.00
Vase, 7½" h., ruffled rim w/applied
amber, rigaree, Drape patt.,
glossy, white lining 395.00
Vase, 8¼" h., stick-type w/bulbous
base & long narrow neck, acid finish, oyster white lining 950.00
Vase, 9" h., double gourd form
w/stick-type neck, glossy finish,
oyster white lining 600.00

Vase, 10½" h., stick-type w/bulbous
base & long narrow neck, glossy,
oyster white lining 1,025.00
Water set: pitcher & 6 tumblers;
glossy, oyster white lining,
7 pcs. 2,500.00

PEKING

Peking Cameo Glass Vase

*This is Chinese glass, some of it cameo-
carved, that has attracted collector interest.*

Goblet, amethyst $69.00
Teacup, amethyst 39.00
Vase, 4½" h., cameo-carved deep
blue bird in a tree one side &
mountain scene reverse against
white ground 225.00
Vase, 4¾" h., cameo-carved cobalt
blue to white intricate design
w/green & yellow birds, foliage
& mountains 375.00
Vases, 6" h., 4½" w., cameo-carved
magenta florals & birds against
white ground, pr. 1,400.00
Vase, 8" h., cameo-carved green
honeycomb against white
ground 170.00
Vases, 8½" h., ovoid, cameo-carved
quatrefoil panels of birds & florals
reserved on an incised trellis
ground between pendant leaves
& petals, yellow, pr. 1,650.00
Vase, 9" h., cameo-carved yellow-
orange bird on branch against
white ground, late 19th c.
(ILLUS.) 600.00
Vases, 9" h., cameo-carved turquoise honeycomb against white
ground, pr. 500.00
Vases, 12" h., cameo-carved red foo
lions, florals & carp on white
ground, pr. 475.00

PELOTON

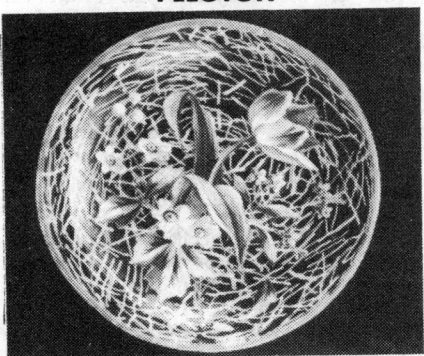

Peloton Plate with Enameled Florals

Made in Bohemia, Germany and England in the late 19th century, this glassware is characterized by threads or filaments of glass rolled into the glass body of the object in random patterns. Some of these wares were decorated.

Barber bottle, clear w/cranberry "coconut" threading (no stopper)....................... $82.00
Cookie jar, ribbed body, clear w/yellow, blue & red "coconut" threading, satin finish, silverplate rim, cover & bail handle......... 750.00
Pitcher, 5¼" h., applied clear handle, clear w/pink, blue & yellow "coconut" threading............ 485.00
Pitcher, water, 12" h., 5" d., applied clear handle, amber w/multi-colored "coconut" threading...... 550.00
Plate, 5½" d., clear w/"coconut" threading & enameled colorful floral decor, ca. 1880 (ILLUS.)..... 88.00
Rose bowl, 4 pulled-up points at rim, clear shell feet, opaque white w/pink, blue, yellow & white "coconut" threading....... 295.00
Vase, 3¼" h., bulbous w/flared & crimped rim, lavender-grey w/pink, blue & yellow "coconut" threading...................... 210.00
Vase, 3 7/8" h., 4¾" d., squat bulbous form w/folded-over tricornered top, opaque white w/pink, blue, yellow & white "coconut" threading, cased in clear........ 295.00
Vase, 4½" h., 2½ x 5", fan-shaped on clear pedestal base w/embossed patterning, lavender-pink w/white, pink, blue & yellow "coconut" threading........... 225.00
Vase, 7" h., 5¾" d., folded-over tricornered top, embossed ribbing, clear to opalescent w/pink, blue, white & yellow "coconut" threading..................... 333.00

PHOENIX

This ware was made by the Phoenix Glass Co. of Beaver County, Pa., which produced various types of glass from the 1880's. One special type that attracts collectors now is a molded ware with a vague resemblance to cameo in its "sculptured" decoration.

Vase, 7" h., sculptured white bell-flowers on aqua blue ground..... $70.00
Vase, 7" h., sculptured white starflowers on rose-pink ground, original paper label............. 85.00
Vase, 7½" h., sculptured white cosmos & vertical stripes on blue ground........................... 85.00
Vase, 7½" h., sculptured yellow ferns & green leaves on white ground, original label........... 65.00
Vase, 8¼" h., sculptured white Praying Mantis & leaves on pale green ground................... 120.00
Vase, 9¼" h., pillow-shaped, sculptured white flying geese on cocoa brown ground..........160.00 to 225.00
Vase, 9¼" h., sculptured yellow wild rose (dogwood) blossoms & green leaves on white ground..................95.00 to 140.00
Vase, 9½" h., pillow-shaped, sculptured flying geese, frosted & pearly white...........150.00 to 165.00
Vase, 9½" h., pillow-shaped, sculptured pearly white flying geese on red ground, original sticker...... 195.00
Vase, 9½" h., pillow-shaped, sculptured white flying geese on blue ground................185.00 to 235.00

Phoenix Vase with Dancing Nudes

Vase, 11" h., sculptured white dancing nudes on blue ground (ILLUS.)........................ 298.00
Vase, 12" h., sculptured white philodendron leaves on light blue ground...................60.00 to 95.00
Vase, 18" h., sculptured white thistles on blue ground............. 250.00

PIGEON BLOOD

Synora Lace Pattern

This name refers to the color of the glass, which was blood-red, and many wares have been lumped into this category.

Bowl, Torquay patt., silverplate rim,
 large ....$85.00 to 135.00
Celery vase, pedestal base......... 40.00
Creamer, Torquay patt., silverplate
 rim & handle 75.00
Pitcher, water, bulbous, ruffled rim,
 applied clear ribbed handle,
 w/gold aventurine flecks 195.00
Pitcher, water, applied clear ribbed
 handle, pulled white feathering .. 200.00
Plates, 6" w. hexagon, set of 6..... 100.00
Plate, 7½" d. 20.00
Salt & pepper shakers w/original
 tops, Bulging Loops patt.,
 pr...................... 95.00 to 120.00
Salt & pepper shakers w/original
 tops, Synora Lace patt., pr.
 (ILLUS.)....................... 95.00
Vase, 8½" h. 85.00

POMONA

Pomona Punch Cup

First produced by the New England Glass Works in the 1880's, Pomona has a frosted ground on clear glass decorated with mineral stains, most frequently amber-yellow, sometimes pale blue. It may be recognized by its background of finely-etched lines crossing one another. Some pieces bore floral decorations. Two types were made. One called "first

grind" was etched by acid that cut into the numerous etched lines made with a needle on glass that had been given an acid resistant coating. A cheaper method, "second grind," consisted of rolling the glass article in particles of acid-resisting material which were picked up by it. The glass was then etched by acid which attacked areas not protected by the resistant particles. A favorite design on Pomona was the cornflower.

Bowl, 5" w., 2½" h., scalloped top,
 blue cornflower decor, 1st grind ..$195.00
Bowl, 5½" d., ruffled rim, cornflower decor, 2nd grind............. 105.00
Bowl, 8" d., amber-stained crimped
 rim, cornflower decor, 2nd
 grind......................... 255.00
Bowl, 8" d., amber-stained ruffled
 rim, Inverted Thumbprint patt.,
 2nd grind...................... 145.00
Creamer, all clear, 1st grind....... 155.00
Creamer, amber stain, 2nd grind ... 95.00
Cruet w/clear ball-type stopper, applied clear handle, blueberries &
 gold leaves decor, 2nd grind,
 5½" h. 485.00
Cruet w/original ball stopper, toed
 base, Inverted Thumbprint patt.,
 2nd grind...................... 250.00
Finger bowl & underplate, 2nd
 grind.......................... 155.00
Lemonade pitcher, blue cornflower
 decor, 1st grind, 12" h. 885.00
Lemonade set: 9¼" h. tankard
 pitcher & 6 tall mugs w/applied
 handles; amber stain, 1st grind,
 7 pcs. 1,100.00
Pickle castor, cornflower decor, 1st
 grind, complete w/silverplate
 frame, cover & tongs 300.00
Pitcher, 6¼" h., square top, cornflower decor, 1st grind 350.00
Pitcher, tankard, 7" h., Expanded
 Diamond patt., amber stain, front
 w/amber-stained pansy & blue-
 stained stem & leaf decor, reverse
 w/amber & blue-stained butterfly,
 2nd grind...................... 365.00
Pitcher, 8½" h., Expanded Diamond
 patt., 2nd grind 125.00
Pitcher, tankard, 9" h., fluted upper
 portion, cornflower decor, 1st
 grind.......................... 182.50
Pitcher, tankard, 9½" h., amber
 stain, blue & amber-stained butterflies hovering over wheat
 stalks decor, 2nd grind 545.00
Pitcher, tankard, 11¾" h., 4" d.,
 amber-stained top, blue-stained
 cornflowers decor, 2nd grind 810.00
Punch cup, amber-stained rim, blue
 cornflower decor, 1st grind,
 2 5/8" d., 2¾" h. (ILLUS.) 100.00

Punch cup, amber-stained rim, cornflower decor, 2nd grind 80.00
Toothpick holder, scalloped amber-
stained rim pulled in by applied
clear rigaree at collar, 1st grind . . 265.00
Toothpick holder, tricornered,
amber-stained rim, 1st grind 135.00
Tumbler, amber-stained top, blue-
stained cornflower decor, 1st
grind, 3¾" h. . . . . 125.00 to 155.00
Tumbler, blue cornflower decor, 2nd
grind 75.00
Tumbler, juice, amber-stained rim,
acanthus leaf decor 115.00

1st Grind Pomona Vase

Vase, 5¼" h., crimped amber-
stained rim, Inverted Thumbprint
body, blue-stained cornflower
decor, 1st grind (ILLUS.) 350.00
Water set: pitcher & 6 tumblers; 1st
grind, 7 pcs. 750.00

QUEZAL

Quezal Agate Glass Vase

*These wares resembled those of Tiffany and
other lustred "Art" glass houses of the late*
19th and early 20th centuries and were made
by the Quezal Art Glass and Decorating Co.
of Brooklyn, N.Y., early in the century and
until its closing in the mid-20's. Also see
SHADES under Glass.

Compote, 5" h., iridescent gold,
signed $275.00
Nut dish, iridescent gold, signed &
numbered, 3" d. 175.00
Punch cup, scroll handle, iridescent
gold, signed 225.00
Salt dip, ribbed, iridescent gold,
signed, 2¾" d., 1" h. 150.00
Vase, 3½" h., 6" d., iridescent blue,
ground pontil, signed 425.00
Vase, 4¼" h., bulbous w/everted
lip, marbleized carmel, brown,
yellow-green & green w/beige
striations, 1905-25, signed
(ILLUS.) 550.00
Vase, 5" h., short flaring neck,
iridescent amber w/petal terminals above opal body w/two
bands of iridescent amber striated
feathering, iridescent forest green
zigzags at shoulder, 1901-25,
signed 660.00
Vase, 5½" h., opal w/pulled green
lustre threads edged in gold,
iridescent gold interior 750.00
Vase, 6½" h., iridescent gold
w/blue highlights 600.00
Vase, 7" h., iridescent lavender-
green, signed 850.00
Vase, 7¼" h., iridescent gold, silver
top rim & silver overlay Art
Nouveau florals 385.00
Vase, 8¾" h., stretched & ruffled
top, iridescent green w/pulled
gold feathering, signed &
numbered 975.00
Vase, 10" h., trumpet-shaped,
iridescent gold w/pink highlights,
signed 460.00

Quezal Vase

Vase, 12" h., floriform, iridescent
gold lustre w/pulled feathering
(ILLUS.)......................... 990.00
Vase, 12½" h., 5" widest d., iridescent blue w/purple & silver
highlights & imbedded white
hearts & trailing vines, signed ...2,100.00
Whimsey, model of a pipe,
12" l..........................1,300.00

w/mountains & fir trees in distance against pale tangerine
shaded to grey ground, ca. 1920,
signed 495.00
Cameo wine, clear knobbed stem &
foot, carved rose landscape
w/trees & tower along river
against frosted ground on bowl,
signed, 7¾" h.................. 450.00

RICHARD

Richard Cameo Vase

This is cameo glass made in France.

Cameo jar & cover w/finial, cylindrical, carved orange scene of castle
reflected in mountain lake
w/trees & distant peaks surrounded by clouds against white
ground, signed, 4" d., 6" h. $595.00
Cameo vase, 4" h., carved deep
blue floral spray against citron
shaded to deep blue at foot,
signed (ILLUS.) 300.00
Cameo vase, 8" h., bulbous, carved
navy blue scene of castle, bridge,
mountains, trees & water against
citron ground, signed 450.00
Cameo vase, 9" h., stick-type w/bul-
bous base, carved fuchsia florals
against blue ground, signed 395.00
Cameo vase, 9 7/8" h., 2 5/8" d.,
carved green to pink figure of
lady in headdress dancing
w/hands in air & w/scarves &
florals around her against soft
frosted blue translucent ground,
signed 1,000.00
Cameo vase, 10¼" h., 6½" d.,
carved scene of mountains, trees
& water against golden orange
ground shading to deep blue at
foot, signed 785.00
Cameo vase, 16" h., baluster-
shaped, carved plum scene of
arched toll bridge across river

ROYAL FLEMISH

Royal Flemish Cookie Jar

*This ware, made by Mt. Washington Glass
Co., is characterized by very heavy enameled
gold lines dividing the surface into separate
areas or sections. The body, with a matte finish, is variously decorated.*

Bottle-vase w/domed cover, onion
form body w/elongated neck &
upright handles, raised gold
mythological beasts, cupid, scrollwork & gold line segments over
puce & green panels, late 19th c.,
original paper label, 13½" h. ...$2,970.00
Cookie jar, gold line segments
separating vari-colored panels &
gold Roman coin medallions
decor, silverplate rim, cover &
bail handle (ILLUS.)............. 990.00
Vase, 5¾" h., squat bulbous body &
bulbous collar enameled w/gold
pansies, body painted w/colorful
pansies outlined in gold & w/gold
maidenhair fern tracery 1,450.00
Vase, 8" h., 6¾" widest d., bulbous
w/collared neck, large raised gold
fierce mythological winged gar-
goyle w/long scaly tail front &
small fish-like creature reverse,
gold line segments separating tan
& brown panels 2,450.00
Vase, 13½" h., slightly expanding

cylinder w/raised gold band at collared neck, raised gold scaly dragon front & large gold beastly fish reverse 3,500.00

Sugar shaker w/original top 79.00
Vases, 9½" h., 3¾" d., gold-trimmed 6-crimp rim, h.p. yellow, white & lavender mums & gold foliage decor, pr. 275.00

RUBINA CRYSTAL

Rubina Crystal Bowl

This glass, sometimes spelled "Rubena," is a flashed ware, shading from ruby to clear. Some pieces are decorated, others are plain. Also see EPERGNES.

Bowl, 5" d., ruffled rim, ca. 1885 (ILLUS.) $65.00
Claret jug w/embossed metal footed base, handle & hinged lid, acid-etched & cut florals & bowknot, 4½" d., 12¾" h. 145.00
Cologne bottle w/clear facet-cut stopper, blown Optic Panels patt., 2½" d., 6" h. 65.00
Cruet w/original stopper, bulbous, Inverted Thumbprint patt. 85.00
Cruet w/original stopper, Medallion Sprig patt. 250.00
Jar w/hinged lid, intaglio-cut body w/overall applied threading, foot-ed brass base & brass collar w/side handles, 4 1/8" d., 7¾" h. 225.00
Mustard pot, square, silverplate hinged lid & silverplate spoon, 1 3/8" sq., 3¼" h., 2 pcs. 45.00
Pitcher, 7½" h., "overshot" 125.00
Pitcher, water, 9" h., applied clear handle, blown Optic Panels patt., polished pontil 125.00
Pitcher, applied reeded shell han-dle, enameled daisies, bluebells, leaves & asters decor, attributed to Mt. Washington 375.00
Pitcher, water, Paneled Sprig patt. . . . 175.00
Rose bowl, 6-crimp top, applied wafer foot, enameled white lace decor, 4" d., 5¾" h. 140.00
Salt shaker w/original top, threaded 85.00
Sauce dish, square, Hobnail patt., Hobbs, Brockunier & Co. 50.00

RUBINA VERDE

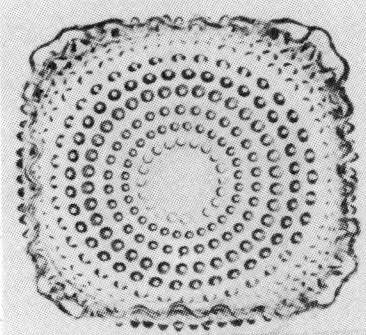

Rubina Verde Hobnail Pattern Bowl

This glass shades from ruby or deep cran-berry to green. Also see BRIDE'S BASKETS.

Basket, ruffled rim $225.00
Bowl, master berry, 8" sq., Hobnail patt. (ILLUS.) 125.00
Cruet w/original facet-cut stopper & tri-pour spout, Inverted Thumb-print patt., 6¾" h. . . . . . . 325.00 to 450.00
Pitcher, 7" h., applied green handle, enameled apple blossoms, branches, leaves & butterfly decor 325.00
Pitcher, 8" h., Optic Panels patt. . . . 295.00

Rubina Verde Complete Punch Set

Punch set: cov. punch bowl, 10 cups & 17" d. tray; paneled bodies & crimped rim on punch bowl, 12 pcs. (ILLUS.) 800.00
Tumbler, Hobb's Hobnail patt. 75.00
Tumbler, enameled decor 85.00
Vase, 6½" h., 4½" widest d., bul-

bous, Reverse Rubina Verde,
enameled blue, green, yellow &
purple floral decor 155.00
Vase, 12 1/8" h., 5¼" d., cylindrical
w/ruffled rim, enameled multicolored florals, green leaves,
lacy gold sprigs & blue ribbon
bow 165.00

RUBY

Lacy Medallion Pattern Mug

*This name derives from the color of the
glass — a deep red. Much ruby glass was
flashed or stained and was produced as souvenir items late last century and in the
present one. Most items listed below are
flashed glass. Also see PATTERN GLASS.*

Berry set: master bowl & 6 sauce
dishes; Carnation patt., gold trim,
souvenir, 7 pcs. $165.00
Berry set: master bowl & 6 sauce
dishes; Leaf & Star patt., 7 pcs.... 195.00
Berry set: master bowl & 6 sauce
dishes; New Jersey patt., 7 pcs. .. 175.00
Berry set: master bowl & 6 sauce
dishes; Pioneer's Victoria patt.,
7 pcs. 165.00
Berry set: master bowl & 6 sauce
dishes; Spearpoint Band patt.,
7 pcs. 100.00
Bowl, master berry, 8" d., Pillow
Encircled patt. 50.00
Bowl, master berry, 10½ x 7½"
oval, New Jersey patt. 115.00
Butter dish, cov., Beaded Swag
patt. ....95.00 to 110.00
Butter dish, cov., Pavonia patt.
w/leaf & berry etching 110.00
Butter dish, cov., Pioneer's Victoria
patt. 95.00
Butter dish, cov., Red Block
patt. ....65.00 to 75.00
Celery vase, Box in Box patt. 75.00
Celery vase, Nail patt.............. 55.00
Cordial, Button Arches patt.,
souvenir...................... 25.00

Cordial, Diamond Peg patt.,
souvenir...................... 25.00
Creamer, individual size, Button
Arches patt. 18.00
Creamer, individual size, Sunk
Honeycomb patt. 29.00
Creamer, individual size, Truncated
Cube patt. 32.50
Creamer, Button Arches patt.,
souvenir, 4" h. 32.00
Creamer, Buttressed Sunburst
patt. 47.00
Creamer, Heart Band patt.,
souvenir...................... 25.00
Creamer, Nail patt. 45.00
Creamer, Pavonia patt. w/leaf &
berry etching 65.00
Creamer, Red Block patt. 55.00
Creamer, Triple Triangle patt. 35.00
Cruet w/original stopper, Beaded
Swirl with Lens patt. 110.00
Cruet w/original stopper, Sunk
Honeycomb patt. 95.00
Goblet, Pioneer's Victoria patt.,
etched 45.00
Goblet, Red Block patt. ......28.00 to 36.00
Mug, Button Arches patt.,
souvenir.................25.00 to 30.00
Mug, Lacy Medallion patt., souvenir
(ILLUS.)......................... 25.00
Napkin ring, Diamond Peg patt.,
souvenir...................... 85.00
Pitcher, water, tankard, Block &
Lattice patt. 150.00
Pitcher, water, tankard, Majestic
patt. 115.00
Spooner, Buttressed Sunburst patt... 42.00
Spooner, Champion patt............. 30.00
Spooner, Nail patt. 75.00
Sugar bowl, cov., Buttressed Sun-
burst patt...................... 55.00
Sugar bowl, cov., Loop & Block
patt. 55.00
Sugar bowl, cov., Riverside's Victo-
ria patt., 5" d., 6½" h. ...85.00 to 100.00
Table set: cov. butter dish, cov.
sugar bowl, creamer & spooner;
Royal Crystal patt., 4 pcs......... 245.00
Toothpick holder, Harvard patt.,
souvenir...................... 30.00

Heart Band Toothpick Holder

Toothpick holder, Heart Band patt.,
  souvenir (ILLUS.) 30.00
Toothpick holder, cuspidor-shaped,
  Jersey Swirl patt. 30.00
Toothpick holder, Ladder with Dia-
  mond patt. 90.00
Toothpick holder, Majestic patt. 75.00
Toothpick holder, Rib & Bead patt. . .   35.00
Toothpick holder, Scroll with Cane
  Band patt. 50.00
Tray, Barred Ovals patt.,
  10¾ x 4¾" 55.00
Tumbler, Block & Lattice patt. 25.00
Tumbler, Diamond with Peg patt.,
  souvenir. 32.50
Tumbler, Heart Band patt. 20.00
Tumbler, Late Block patt. 25.00
Tumbler, Late Fleur-de-Lis patt.,
  gold trim 36.50
Tumbler, Loop & Block patt. 30.00
Tumbler, Millard patt., etched 35.00
Tumbler, O'Hara Diamond patt.
  w/fern & berry etching 30.00
Tumbler, Pineapple & Fan patt.,
  souvenir. 35.00
Tumbler, Roanoke patt. 30.00
Tumbler, Royal Crystal patt. 26.50
Tumbler, Sunburst patt. 10.00
Tumbler, Teardrop & Thumbprint
  patt. 22.00
Tumbler, Thumbprint patt. 37.00
Tumbler, Zipper Slash patt. 30.00
Water set: pitcher & 5 tumblers;
  Leaf & Star patt., 6 pcs. 275.00
Wine, Arched Ovals patt. 25.00
Wine, Aurora patt. 32.00
Wine, Bull's Eye Band patt.,
  souvenir. 17.00
Wine, Campanula patt., souvenir . . .   30.00
Wine, Pioneer's Victoria patt. 32.00
Wine, Scalloped Swirl patt.,
  etched 42.00
Wine, Sunk Honeycomb patt. 35.00
Wine, Thumbprint patt., etched 45.00
Wine, Triple Triangle patt. . . .25.00 to   35.00
Wine, Truncated Cube patt. 25.00

SAINT LOUIS

*The Saint Louis glass factory in France has
been producing fine glass since the late 18th
century. It is now known as the Compagnie
des Verrieres et Crystalleries de Saint-Louis
with showrooms in Paris.*

Cameo vase, 10" h., carved brown
  to ivory florals, leaves & butter-
  flies decor $1,275.00
Cologne bottle w/ornate facet-cut
  gold-trimmed stopper, cranberry
  shaded to clear w/overall ice-

stippled effect & gold bands
  decor, 2½" d., 6" h. 85.00
Vases, 4¾" h., baluster-shaped,
  spiraling design of cobalt blue
  ribbons alternating w/twisted
  white latticinio threading in
  clear, exterior w/horizontal
  ribbed design 1,430.00
Vase, 6" h., paperweight-type,
  base composed of concentric
  millefiori weight in shades of
  green, salmon pink, blue & white
  on an upset muslin ground,
  below a clear facet-paneled
  vase w/etched border of fruiting vines & applied rim w/deep
  salmon pink twisted ribbon
  entwined w/white latticinio 1,540.00

SANDWICH

Acanthus Pattern Candlesticks

*Numerous types of glass were produced at
the Boston & Sandwich Glass Works, Cape
Cod, Mass., from 1826 to 1888. Those listed
here represent a sampling. Also see PAT-
TERN GLASS.*

Bowl, 6¼" d., lacy, log cabin &
  cider barrel center, "Industries" . .$245.00
Candlesticks, Acanthus patt., hex-
  agonal clambroth stepped base &
  baluster stem, hexagonal starch-
  blue candle socket, 1840-50,
  9½" h., pr. (ILLUS.) 715.00
Cologne bottle w/stopper, Star &
  Punty patt., canary yellow 275.00
Compote, 8½" d., low stand, Fine
  Rib patt., clear, flint 45.00
Curtain tiebacks w/original pewter
  shanks, amber flower forms, pr. . .   42.00
Curtain tiebacks w/original pewter
  shanks, green flower forms, pr. . .   65.00
Drawer pulls, clear flower forms,
  flint, set of 4 . . . .   85.00

Egg cup, Ashburton patt., clambroth, flint..................... 165.00

Sandwich Fishbowl

Fishbowl, clear bowl etched w/fish
& aquatic plants, set on swirled
knop & acid finish dolphin stem,
clear molded round base w/scal-
loped edge, ca. 1870, 16½" h.
(ILLUS.)...................... 550.00

Goblets, Ripple patt., clear,
pr............................. 50.00

Honey dish, lacy, Roman Rosette
patt., clear 67.50

Plate, 6" d.., lacy, Roman Rosette
patt., fiery opalescent 160.00

Plate, 9½" octagon, Thistle & Beehive patt., clear................ 125.00

Salt dip, "Lafayette Boat," medium
blue 850.00

Salt dip, "Lafayette Boat," sapphire
blue opaque 800.00

Salt shaker, "Christmas" salt w/agi-
tator & dated top, canary yellow
or electric blue, each 110.00

Salt shaker, "Christmas" salt w/agi-
tator & dated top, sapphire blue .. 60.00

Salt shaker, "Christmas" salt w/agi-
tator & dated top, vaseline....... 100.00

Sauce dish, lacy, Crossed Swords
patt., red-amber 275.00

Sauce dish, lacy, Plume & Diamond
patt., light blue, 5" d. 295.00

Sauce dish, lacy, Princess Feather
patt., opalescent, 4¼" d. 168.00

Smelling salts bottle, Sunburst patt.,
emerald green 250.00

Spillholder, lacy, clear, flint 225.00

String holder, clear w/frosted florals
& applied cobalt blue roping on
rim, disc on top w/hole to pull
string 295.00

Water set: gooseneck pitcher w/ice
bladder & 4 footed tumblers; cranberry "overshot," 5 pcs. 1,100.00

SATIN

*Satin and Mother-of-Pearl wares were made
by numerous glasshouses over a large part
of the world. They continue in production today. Also see ART GLASS BASKETS and
BRIDE'S BASKETS.*

Basket, applied frosted thorn handle, rose shaded to pink mother-
of-pearl Herringbone patt.,
7½" h.........................$315.00

Bowl-vase, ruffled rim, shaded
heavenly blue mother-of-pearl
Diamond Quilted patt. w/enam-
eled bluebird & floral decor,
white lining, ormolu foot, 6¼" d.,
9 1/8" h. 895.00

Cologne bottle w/frosted stopper,
cylindrical w/flared & crimped collar, pink mother-of-pearl Diamond
Quilted patt. w/enameled white
butterfly hovering among blossoms decor, gold highlights,
3¾" h. 385.00

Cookie jar, pink mother-of-pearl
Herringbone patt. w/enameled
yellow & gold ferns & flowers decor, silverplate rim, cover & bail
handle, 9½" h. 600.00

Creamer, applied frosted handle &
wafer foot, crimped top, blue
mother-of-pearl Ribbon patt.,
white lining, 3 1/8" d., 2¾" h. ... 250.00

Ewer, applied thorn handle, rose
shaded to white mother-of-pearl
Diamond Quilted patt., 14" h. 450.00

Finger bowl & underplate, Amberina mother-of-pearl Diamond
Quilted patt., cream lining, pr. ... 900.00

Pitcher, milk, 7" h., 5½" d., bulbous
w/oval top, applied frosted handle, aqua w/enameled pink & yellow florals & green foliage, gold
tracery 225.00

Satin Glass Pitcher

Pitcher, water, quatrefoil top, applied amber reeded handle, shaded blue (ILLUS.) 225.00

Rose bowl, tricornered top, frosted wafer foot, brown mother-of-pearl Ribbon patt., white lining, 2 5/8" d., 2¾" h. 305.00

Rose bowl, 8-crimp top, American Beauty Rose mother-of-pearl Ribbon patt., white lining, 3¾" d., 2¾" h. 240.00

Rose bowl, 10-crimp top, frosted wafer foot, blue mother-of-pearl Flower & Acorn patt., white lining, 3 5/8" d., 3 1/8" h. 265.00

Sugar shaker w/silverplate top, bridal white mother-of-pearl Raindrop patt., Webb, 3½" h. 465.00

Sweetmeat jar, melon ribbed, soft blue mother-of-pearl Raindrop patt., silverplate rim, cover & bail handle, 5½" h. 435.00

Tumbler, shaded deep pink mother-of-pearl Diamond Quilted patt. w/enameled blue daisies & yellow & green leaves decor, white lining, 2 7/8" d., 3 7/8" h. 195.00

Tumbler, pink shaded to white mother-of-pearl Diamond Quilted patt. 75.00

Tumbler, rubina (shaded red to white) mother-of-pearl Herringbone patt., white lining 110.00

Vase, 4 7/8" h., 5½" d., tricornered top, dimpled sides, American Beauty Rose mother-of-pearl Ribbon patt., white lining 507.00

Vase, 6" h., 4" d., brown mother-of-pearl "Federzeichung" patt., white lining 1,650.00

Satin Glass Vase

Vase, 7" h., blue mother-of-pearl Diamond Quilted patt., attributed to Webb (ILLUS.) 150.00

Vase, 7" h., shaded red to white w/enameled gold florals, foliage,

Satin Vase with Gold Enamel

vines & dragonflies decor, white lining (ILLUS.) 325.00

Vase, 8 1/8" h., 5" d., applied frosted handles, ruffled top, shaded peach mother-of-pearl Herringbone patt., white lining 225.00

Vase, 11¾" h., 5¾" d., shaded green mother-of-pearl Coin Spot patt. w/enameled pink & white florals, green & tan leaves & gold branches decor, white lining, Webb 995.00

Water set: pitcher & 4 tumblers; butterscotch mother-of-pearl Herringbone patt., Webb, 5 pcs 400.00

SCHNEIDER

Ewer & Vase by Schneider

This ware is made in France at Cristallerie Schneider, established in 1913 near Paris by Ernest and Charles Schneider. Some pieces of cameo were marked "Le Verre Francais" and others were signed "Charder." Also see LE VERRE FRANCAIS.

Bowl, 4 3/8" d., 2½" h., mottled
brown shaded to yellow,
signed $118.00
Candlestick, swirled amethyst stem
& base, green Cintra candle cup,
signed & w/Ovington label,
11½" h. (single) 225.00
Compote, 12½" d., 3" h., shaded
orange to yellow bowl, purple-
striped stem & base, signed 350.00
Ewer, lobed neck & pulled spout,
clear mottled w/white, mustard
yellow & dusty rose, applied angled purple handle & body w/ap-
plied purple petals at sides &
leafage at base, 1922-24,
13 3/8" h. (ILLUS. left) 825.00
Vase, 8 3/8" h., translucent char-
treuse spherical body raised on
grey-striped mottled amethyst
stem & circular domed base, ca.
1920, signed 605.00
Vase, 11 3/8" h., chalice form, clear
w/mottled tango red shaded to
form maroon clouds at upper
edge above lemon yellow stylized
floral clusters & splashes of emerald green, deep mottled amethyst
spreading circular foot, ca. 1930,
signed 715.00
Vase, 13½" h., ribbed globular
body w/long expanding ovoid
neck, brilliant tango red w/ap-
plied mottled amethyst scalloped
base at clear circular foot
streaked w/mottled lemon yellow,
ca. 1925, signed 3,850.00
Vase, 16" h., angular baluster form
on compressed circular foot, grey
rim & neck w/mottled peach &
yellow continuing to waves of Chinese red streaked through pumpkin orange & grey body, ca. 1920,
signed (ILLUS. right) 770.00

Schneider Chalice Form Vases

Vases, 16¼" h., tango red body
mottled w/deep purple, knopped
amber stem, slightly domed mottled purple, lavender & white-
striped foot, ca. 1920, signed, pr.
(ILLUS.) 1,870.00
Vase, 16½" h., tapering cylinder
w/scalloped rim, mottled lime
green w/vertical stripes of mottled blue, applied band of tangerine waves at base continuing to
deep plum foot, ca. 1920,
signed 2,850.00

SHADES

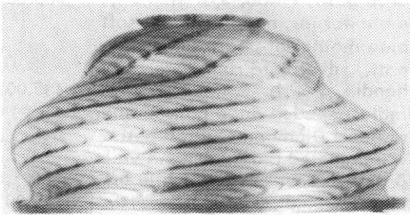

Quezal Shade

*The popularity of collecting fine early Art
Glass gas and electric shades has recently
soared and values have escalated accordingly. Listed below, by manufacturer or type of
glass, is a random sampling of shades offered
for sale within the past six months.*

Fostoria, opal w/gold pulled design,
gold lining, set of 5 . . . .$600.00
Lustre Art, iridescent gold w/pulled
opal feathering & overall gold
threading, pr. 225.00
Lustre Art, iridescent gold w/gold
zipper over opal pulled design,
ruffled rim, set of 4 . . . . 600.00
Lustre Art, opal w/gold banding,
gold lining, bell-shaped, 5" h., set
of 4 . . . . 375.00
Muller Freres, molded stylized pea-
cocks & florals, 6" d. 145.00
Nuart, iridescent marigold Carnival
glass, set of 7 . . . . 245.00
Quezal, damascened in iridescent
green & blue, 14" d. (ILLUS.) 462.00
Quezal, iridescent gold w/green
snakeskin 100.00
Quezal, iridescent gold w/opal
snakeskin at top & iridescent
green w/gold pulled design, rose
highlights 135.00
Quezal, iridescent green w/border
of golden ivy leaves & white
flowerheads, baluster-shaped,
11½" h. 352.00

Quezal, iridescent pea green
w/orange drape outlined in dark
green, gold lining 300.00
Quezal, opal w/gold lining, ribbed
trumpet form, 5½" h. 175.00
Quezal, opal w/gold fishnet design,
gold lining..................... 295.00
Quezal, opal w/gold zipper, corset-
shaped, 4" h. 130.00
Quezal, opal w/pulled gold feathering outlined in green, dimpled ... 160.00
Quezal, opal w/green foliate vines
& overall gold threading, gold
lining 165.00
Quezal, opal w/yellow drape out-
lined in green, gold lining 165.00
Steuben, Calcite, gold lining, set
of 4 .... 395.00
Steuben, Calcite w/blue feathering,
rose gold lining 300.00
Steuben, Calcite w/green feathering
outlined in gold, gold lining, scalloped rim...................... 170.00
Steuben, iridescent gold Aurene,
Calcite lining, trumpet-shaped 75.00
Steuben, iridescent gold Aurene
w/green drape................. 145.00
Steuben, iridescent green Aurene on
Calcite w/platinum applied border, melon ribbed, 10" 2,250.00
Steuben, iridescent green Aurene
w/pulled gold looping, ruffled
rim, 5" d. 350.00
Steuben, opal w/lime green drape
outlined in gold, gold
lining 165.00
Tiffany, iridescent gold, lily form,
4½" h., pr. 1,100.00
Tiffany, iridescent gold, tulip-
shaped, ribbed................. 350.00
Tiffany, opal w/overall green
damascene swirl 575.00
Tiffany, translucent yellow w/wide
gold rim, ovoid, ribbed 352.00

Basket, red opaque w/heavy sterling silver overlay designs, 4" d.,
6" h. $650.00
Candle holders, black amethyst
w/silver deposit, 2½" h., pr...... 18.00
Console bowl, footed, clear w/silver
deposit morning glories decor 65.00
Decanter, handled, vaseline
w/heavy sterling silver overlay
florals........................ 375.00
Loving cup, 3-handled, cranberry
w/sterling silver overlay decor ... 495.00
Perfume bottle w/sterling silver top,
green cylinder w/sterling silver
Art Nouveau style overlay,
2¼" h. 160.00
Perfume bottle w/original stopper,
cranberry w/sterling silver overlay decor, 3½" h. 235.00
Perfume bottles w/original stoppers,
clear w/sterling silver Art Nouveau overlay of scrolling florals &
vines, 4" & 6" h., pr. 330.00
Pitcher, 2½" h., cranberry w/ster-
ling silver overlay decor 150.00
Pitcher, 10¾" h., 5" d., applied
green handle w/silver overlay,
green opaline body w/sterling silver overlay florals, leaves &
scrolling branches decor 350.00
Plate 8 1/8" d., clear w/wide silver
deposit border & intaglio-cut butterfly hovering over carnation
blossom, buds & foliage center,
marked "Silver Deposit D157" 110.00
Rum jug w/side spout, silver stopper & silver-covered handle,
green w/sterling silver overlay of
bulldog........................ 295.00
Sherbet & underplate, clear w/silver
deposit, pr..................... 35.00
Vase, 10" h., elongated cylinder,
emerald green w/silver overlay
undulating tulips & leaves within
panels 550.00

SILVER OVERLAY & SILVER DEPOSIT

*Silver Deposit and Silver Overlay have
been made commercially since the last quarter of the 19th century. Silver is deposited on
the glass by various means, the most widely
adopted utilizing an electric current. The
glass was very popular during the first three
decades of this century, and some pieces are
still being produced. During the late 1970's,
silver commanded exceptionally high prices
and this was reflected in a surge of interest
in silver overlay glass, especially in pieces
marked "sterling" or "925" on the heavy silver overlay.*

Emerald Green Vases with Silver Overlay

Vases, 10" & 12" h., emerald green
w/sterling silver overlay Art Nouveau scrolling tendrils & vines,
each w/engraved monogram, pr.
(ILLUS. of one right) 660.00
Vase, 14" h., emerald green w/ster-
ling silver overlay sinuous iris
blossoms & leaves, heart-form
reserve w/engraved inscription
(ILLUS. left) 440.00
Vase, 14" h., frosted clear w/ster-
ling silver overlay florals &
leaves, polished pontil 450.00
Water set: pitcher & 6 tumblers;
blue w/silver deposit, 7 pcs. 155.00
Whiskey bottle, deep amber w/ster-
ling silver overlay designs & label,
12½" h. 250.00

SMITH BROTHERS

Smith Brothers Powder Jar

*This company first operated as a decorat-
ing department of the Mt. Washington Glass
Works in the 1870's and later on as an independent business in New Bedford, Mass.
The firm was noted for its outstanding
decorating work on glass and also carried on
a glass cutting trade.*

Bowl, 4" d., 2½" h., melon-ribbed,
enameled light blue scrollwork &
orange florals on white satin finish, signed $295.00
Bowl, 4½" d., 2½" h., melon-
ribbed, beaded rim, w/raised gold
florals on creamy white satin
finish 225.00
Bowl, 8" d., pansies outlined in gold
on white ground, signed 175.00
Creamer & cov. sugar bowl, gold
blossoms w/raised gold edges on
cream ground, w/silverplate
mounts & signed "S.B." in lid of
sugar bowl, pr. 585.00
Creamer & cov. sugar bowl, melon-
ribbed, gold apple blossoms &

leaves & enameled jeweling on
cream ground, w/silverplate
mounts & lid, signed, pr. 585.00
Fernery, melon-ribbed, violets &
leaves decor on glossy white,
original metal insert, signed,
10" l. 675.00
Mustard pot w/original hinged silverplate lid & handle, narrow-
ribbed body, floral decor on
white 110.00
Perfume bottle w/silverplate floral-
embossed hinged lid, swirled
body, floral decor on shaded
ground, 5" h. 420.00
Plate, 6½" d., h.p. "Santa Maria"
ship............................ 345.00
Powder jar, cov., melon-ribbed,
sprays of foliage on white ground,
signed (ILLUS.) 285.00
Rose bowl, melon-ribbed, orange
daisies & blue scrollwork decor on
white, signed, 4½" d. 245.00
Sweetmeat jar, melon-ribbed, 5
sprays of tiny daisies on creamy
white ground, silverplate melon-
ribbed lid w/embossed collar &
bail handle, signed, 5½" d.,
5" h. 635.00
Toothpick holder, narrow-ribbed,
pastel florals on lustreless white,
blue enameled dots around rim,
2¼" h. 135.00

Smith Brothers Vases

Vases, 8" h., cylindrical, colorful
heron & rushes on creamy ivory
ground, signed, in original silverplate footed holders, pr.
(ILLUS.)........................ 400.00
Vase, 8 1/8" h., 3" d., cylindrical,
black & white heron & green foliage on soft blue ground,
unsigned 95.00
Vase, 8¾" h., pillow-shaped, leafy
stem w/full-blown rose & blue ribbon streamers on front, smaller
rose & single streamer reverse,
signed 385.00

SPANGLED

Spangled Glass Rose Bowl

Spangled glass incorporated particles of mica or metallic flakes and variegated colored glass particles imbedded in the transparent glass. Usually made of two layers, it might have either an opaque or transparent casing. The Vasa Murrhina Glass Company of Sandwich, Mass., first patented the process for producing Spangled glass in 1884 and this factory is known to have produced great quantities of this ware. It was, however, also produced by numerous other American and English glasshouses. This type, along with Spatter, which see below, is often erroneously called "End of Day." Also see ART GLASS BASKETS and JACK-IN-PULPIT VASES.

Basket, ruffled rim, applied clear
  thorn handle, butterscotch w/mica
  flecks, 5½" sq. $175.00
Basket, applied amber twisted handle & edge, ribbed body, pink
  w/silver mica flecks, cased,
  4¼" d., 7" h. 125.00
Basket, applied clear handle &
  edge, deep rose shading to white
  w/silver mica flecks, 7½" d.,
  8¾" h. 235.00
Basket, applied clear handle, pink,
  green & white spatter w/mica
  flecks, cased, 11½" h. 165.00
Box, cov., amber w/splotches of
  dark amber & brown & copper
  mica flecks 425.00
Cruet w/clear faceted stopper, pale
  blue to clear w/white spatter &
  silver mica flecks, Hobbs, Brockunier & Co. 435.00
Pitcher, water, 8½" h., 7" widest d.,
  melon-ribbed, applied clear handle, peach blow pink cased in
  clear w/mica flecks, white lining,
  attributed to Mt. Washington 425.00
Rose bowl, 8-crimp top, deep rose
  w/silver mica flecks in coral-like
  pattern, white lining (ILLUS.) 120.00
Tumbler, yellow & white spatter
  w/gold mica flecks, 4" h. 40.00

Vase, 5¼" h., green, white & blue
  spatter w/green aventurine mica
  flecks 65.00
Vase, 5½" h., 3½" w., applied clear
  ruffled edge, pink, yellow & blue
  spatter w/silver mica flecks,
  white lining, attributed to Mt.
  Washington 425.00
Vase, 7" h., 4" d., applied clear
  thorn handles, rose w/mica
  flecks, white lining 115.00
Vase, 7 7/8" h., 4 5/8" d., jack-in-
  pulpit type, green w/oxblood &
  white spatter & mica flecks 88.00
Vase, 8¼" h., 5 1/8" d., applied
  clear thorn handles, square top,
  deep rose w/silver mica flecks in
  coral-like pattern, white lining ... 130.00
Vase, 9½" h., bulbous base, slender
  neck w/applied clear fluted edge,
  cranberry w/gold mica flecks 150.00
Vase, 11½" h., ruffled top, brown,
  orange & tan spatter w/silver
  mica flecks, white lining 150.00
Vase, 12½" h., 6" widest d., applied
  clear edge, blue, pink & yellow
  stripes w/silver mica flecks, white
  lining, attributed to Mt.
  Washington 650.00

SPATTER

Spatter Glass Basket

This variegated-color ware is similar to Spangled glass but does not contain metallic flakes. The various colors are applied on an opaque white or colored body. Much of it was made in Europe and England. It is sometimes called "End of Day." Also see ART GLASS BASKETS and JACK-IN-PULPIT VASES.

Basket, applied clear handle, blue
  w/multicolored swirled spatter,
  4" d., 5" h. (ILLUS.) $90.00
Basket, applied sapphire blue thorn

handle, Swirl patt., blue w/pale
blue spatter, 4½" d., 8" h. 175.00
Basket, fan-shaped, applied clear
handle, soft blue w/brown, white,
pink & yellow spatter, white lin-
ing, 5 x 3", 4 5/8" h. 88.00
Bowl, pinched rim w/applied clear
edging, red & yellow spatter in
white opaque cased in clear,
ground pontil, large 235.00
Box w/hinged lid, footed, pink, blue
& yellow spatter in white, white
lining, 6" d., 5½" h. 275.00
Creamer & sugar bowl, applied
clear petal feet & applied clear
handle on creamer, maroon, blue,
white, green & cream spatter,
small, pr. 88.00
Pitcher, 1 7/8" h., 1 3/8" d., bulbous
w/round mouth, applied clear
handle, yellow & white spatter
w/enameled yellow scrolls, gold
band & gold trim 70.00
Pitcher, 6½" h., 6" d., bulbous
w/round mouth, applied clear
reeded handle, embossed swirls,
dark red spatter in yellow, yellow
lining 195.00
Pitcher, water, 7½" h., applied
clear reeded handle, embossed
swirls, rainbow spatter in clear,
white lining. 150.00
Pitcher, tankard, 9" h., orchid & yel-
low spatter cased in clear. 110.00
Pitcher, water, applied clear ribbed
handle, ruffled rim, brown &
white spatter in clear, polished
pontil 150.00
Tumbler, blue & white spatter in
clear, 2¾" d., 3¾" h. 35.00
Tumbler, Swirl patt., white w/pink,
orange & yellow spatter,
3¾" h. 55.00
Tumbler, Baby Thumbprint patt.,
cranberry & white spatter 60.00

Spatter Glass Vase

Vase, 5" h., 4 applied clear petal
feet, bulbous w/ring below
straight cylindrical neck, multicolored spatter, white lining
(ILLUS.). 65.00
Vases, 7½" h., jack-in-the-pulpit
type, blue & brown spatter in
clear, pr. 100.00
Vase, 7¾" h., Ribbed Swirl patt.
w/ruffled rim & applied clear
edging, pink, yellow & orange
spatter cased in clear 80.00
Vase, 8½" h., ruffled, amethyst
w/cranberry & white spatter 75.00
Water set: pitcher & 5 tumblers;
Venetian Diamond patt., pink &
white spatter in clear,
6 pcs. 135.00
Water set: 7½" h. pitcher w/tricor-
nered spout & applied clear handle & 6 tumblers; red & opaque
white spatter in clear, 7 pcs. 215.00

STEUBEN

*The Steuben glass listed below was made
at the Steuben Glass Works, now a division
of Corning Glass, between 1903, when the factory was organized by T.G. Hawkes, Sr., the
late Frederick Carder, and others, until about
1933. Mr. Carder devised many types of glass
and revived many old techniques. Also see
SHADES under Glass.*

ACID CUT BACK

Unsigned Acid Cut Back Vase

Bowl, 6" d., incurved lip, plum Jade
cut w/four classical male profile
medallions & urns $440.00
Bowl, 8" d., incurved lip, plum Jade
cut w/floral medallions alternat-

ing w/roundels on diapered
design, signed 1,650.00
Plate, Rosaline cut to Alabaster
roses (9) 135.00
Rose bowl, Rosaline cut to Alabaster
Fircone patt., catalogued
No. 6078 .... 895.00
Vase, 6" h., black Jade cut to
Alabaster Pussy Willows,
signed 1,500.00
Vase, 6½" h., rose bowl shape,
Rosaline cut to Alabaster Marlene
patt., signed 875.00
Vase, 10" h., green Jade cut to
Alabaster w/birds, branches &
flowers, signed 700.00
Vase, 14½" h., baluster-shaped,
black cut to light blue dragon &
designs w/stylized leafage at
neck, ca. 1920, unsigned, some
chips (ILLUS.) 1,430.00

ANIMALS

Bear seated on haunches on oblong
block, signed F. Carder, 1920's,
8¼" l., 5¾" h. 522.50
Bird, w/wings outspread & perched
on ball, signed, 11½" w. wingspan, 5½" h. 275.00
Duck, stylized vertical version,
signed, 8½" h. 275.00
Elephant standing on ball, signed,
4½" h. 295.00
Koala Bear, in fitted red leather
case, 5¾" h. 750.00
Pigeons, cut feathers on wings &
tails, signed, 6½" h., pr. 950.00

AURENE

Gold Aurene Bowl-Vase

Ash tray w/pedestal cup center,
gold Aurene, Carder line drawing,
No. 2106, signed 185.00
Basket, rosette buttons on handle,
blue Aurene w/deep purple highlights, signed & numbered,
3 3/8 x 2½", 3½" h. 1,650.00

Bowl, 10" d., 3-footed, incurved-lip,
blue Aurene, Carder shape
No. 2586 .... 450.00
Bowl-vase, footed, 3-handled, gold
Aurene, signed, 6½" h. (ILLUS.) .. 425.00
Candlesticks, twisted stem, gold
Aurene, signed, 8" h., pr. 650.00
Candlesticks, twisted stem, blue
Aurene, signed & numbered,
10" h., pr. 900.00
Cologne bottle, blue Aurene w/blue
Jade & black 5-petal flower stop-
per, 6¾" h. 750.00
Cologne bottle w/teardrop form
stopper, blue Aurene 350.00
Cordial, twisted stem, gold Aurene,
3¾" h. .... 165.00 to 185.00
Creamer & sugar bowl, applied
ribbed handle, Diamond Quilted
patt., gold Aurene w/blue &
lavender highlights, signed, pr.... 600.00
Goblet, twisted stem, gold Aurene
w/blue highlights, signed 300.00
Perfume atomizer, melon-ribbed,
gold Aurene, 5" h. 250.00
Punch cup, footed, gold Aurene,
signed 240.00
Rose bowl, ribbed body, scalloped
turned-in rim, gold Aurene,
signed, 3" h. 275.00
Salt dip, footed, gold Aurene,
signed & numbered .....185.00 to 200.00
Sherbet & underplate, gold Aurene,
signed, pr. ....195.00 to 295.00
Toothpick holder, pinched form,
blue Aurene, signed 355.50
Vase, 6" h., globular w/waisted
neck, blue Aurene w/band of
applied abstract white threading
below shoulder, signed 1,900.00
Vase, 6" h., jack-in-pulpit type, gold
Aurene, signed 695.00
Vase, bud, 6" h., trumpet-shaped,
blue Aurene w/purple highlights,
signed .... 395.00 to 425.00
Vase, 6" h., single prong tree trunk,
blue Aurene, signed 350.00
Vase, 6¼" h., 3-prong tree stump,
gold Aurene, signed 450.00
Vase, 6¼" h., 3-prong tree trunk,
blue Aurene, signed 850.00
Vase, 7½" h., gold Aurene w/iri-
descent amber striated peacock
feathering devices w/pale green
"eyes," iridescent amber interior
lip, 1905-20, signed 1,980.00
Vase, bud, 8" h., blue Aurene,
signed 325.00
Vase, 8" h., 3" w., stick-type, gold
Aurene w/pink & blue highlights,
signed 225.00
Vase, 9" h., fan-shaped, blue
Aurene, signed 1,300.00

Aurene Vase

Vase, 9" h., gold Aurene
(ILLUS.). 800.00
Vase, 10" h., trumpet-shaped, blue
Aurene, signed & w/paper label . . 850.00

CLUTHRA

Cluthra Vase

Bowl, 3¼" d., lavender w/random
trapped air bubbles 125.00
Vase, 6¾" h., shaded white to
green, w/random trapped air bub-
bles, signed 275.00
Vase, 8½" h., amethyst w/random
trapped air bubbles 625.00
Vase, 10" h., 9½" widest d., white
w/random trapped air bubbles . . . 550.00
Vase, 10" h., flattened oval form,
shaded white to raspberry w/ran-
dom trapped air bubbles 725.00
Vase, 10¼" h., deep amethyst
w/random trapped bubbles
(ILLUS.). 700.00

IVRENE

Ivrene Vase

Compote, 7" d., pearly iridescence,
black base, signed 310.00
Vase, 4½" h., fluted & flaring top,
donut in base, pearly iridescence,
signed 175.00
Vase, 5¼" h., ribbed body, flaring
rim, signed 125.00
Vase, 6" h., ribbed oval body w/ruf-
fled rim on wafer stem & pedestal
foot, signed 225.00
Vase, 6½" h., jack-in-pulpit type,
signed 425.00
Vase, 8" h., 10" d., signed 275.00
Vase, 8½" h., fan-shaped, black
base 375.00
Vase, 10¼" h., experimental shape,
pedestal foot, unsigned (ILLUS.) . . 550.00
Vase, 10¼" h., ribbed body, evert-
ed lip, signed 185.00

JADE

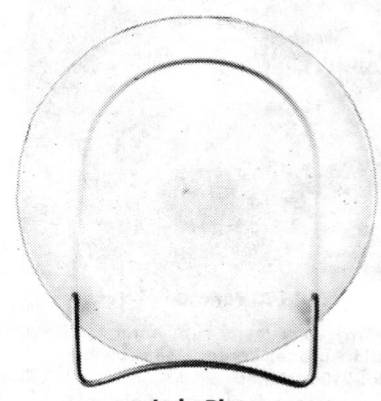

Jade Plate

Bowl, 13" d., green Jade on
Alabaster base. 155.00

Centerpiece bowl, green Jade,
etched York patt.,
9½" d. . . . . .175.00 to 195.00
Compote, cov., 10" d., 10" h., green
Jade & Alabaster 325.00
Parfait, yellow Jade w/Alabaster
pedestal 40.00
Plate, 8" d., green Jade (ILLUS.) 145.00
Sherbet & underplate, green Jade,
pr. 150.00
Vase, 5½" h., 3-prong tree stump,
green Jade, signed . . . . . .225.00 to 295.00
Vase, 6" h., swirled square, green
Jade, signed 165.00
Vase, 11½" h., 3-sided cone shape,
green Jade w/Alabaster foot,
signed 275.00
Wine, green Jade w/twisted Alabas-
ter stem, signed, 7¼" h. 95.00

POMONA GREEN

Pomona Green Fruit Bowl

Centerpiece flower bowl, puffy base
w/four hollow columns supporting
wide shallow top, signed,
10½" d., 5½" h. 125.00
Bowl, fruit, 10" d., 6" h., applied
Bristol Yellow domed base & loop
handles, signed (ILLUS.) 160.00
Cologne bottle w/self-threaded
stopper, ribbed, signed, 5½" h. . . 125.00
Goblet, signed, 6" h. 30.00
Jar w/domed self-threaded stopper,
diagonally ribbed body, pedestal
foot, signed, 7" h. 150.00
Lemonade tumbler, applied Topaz
wafer foot, 5" h. 20.00
Vase, 5¾" h., brandy snifter shape,
diagonally ribbed top, applied To-
paz foot, signed 90.00
Vase, 6½" h., 3-prong thorny tree
stump, signed 185.00
Vase, 8½" h., ribbed fan shape
w/ball stem, signed 120.00
Vase, 10" h., diagonally ribbed,
signed 115.00
Wine, green top & foot, clear stem,
signed, 4½" h. 35.00

ROSALINE

Bowl, 6" d., 6" h., ball-footed,
signed Carder 325.00
Bowl, 14" d., flanged rim 155.00

Candlestick, Rosaline cup, Alabaster
foot, short, signed (single) 110.00
Candlestick, twisted stem, 8¼" h.
(single) 250.00
Charger, wheel-etched florals sepa-
rated by striated panels, early
20th c., signed Carder, 13¾" d. . . 192.50

Rosaline & Alabaster Compote

Compote, 6½" d., 4" h., Rosaline
w/Alabaster foot (ILLUS.) 175.00
Compote, 8" d., Rosaline w/Alabas-
ter foot . . . . .175.00 to 225.00
Compote, 10" d., low stand, Rosa-
line w/Alabaster foot 475.00
Cup & saucer, Rosaline w/Alabaster
handle 130.00
Ewer, Rosaline w/Alabaster handle,
8" h. 135.00
Ewer, Rosaline w/Albaster base &
twisted Alabaster handle, 13" h. . . 295.00
Finger bowl, Swirl patt. 110.00
Perfume bottle, Rosaline w/Alabas-
ter stopper & foot, 8" h. 185.00
Pitcher, 7¾" h., applied Alabaster
handle 400.00
Plate, 8¼" d., signed 75.00
Puff box & cover w/Alabaster knob,
5" w., 5½" h. 400.00
Sherbet & underplate, sherbet
w/Alabaster stem & foot, pr. 185.00
Shrimp bowl, Rosaline w/Alabaster
foot 235.00
Vase, 6" h., trumpet-shaped, Rosa-
line w/Alabaster pedestal base,
signed 165.00
Vase, 7 5/8" h., 8 3/8" w., fan-
shaped, Rosaline w/Alabaster
foot 200.00
Vase, 9¼" h., 7½" d., Rosaline
w/engraved florals & Alabaster
foot 675.00
Wine, Rosaline w/twisted Alabaster
stem 245.00

TOPAZ

Bowl, 9½" d., swirl design,
signed 75.00
Candlestick, w/navy blue banding at
rims, 5" h., single (ILLUS.) 45.00

Topaz Candlestick

Candlesticks, hollow Topaz ribbed
stem w/double balls, Marina Blue
ribbed top & bottom, signed,
10" h., pr. 325.00
Candy dish & cover w/knob finial,
Topaz body & cover, twisted blue
stem, signed, 6" h. 125.00
Centerpiece bowl, signed. 365.00
Salt dip, pedestal base 85.00
Tumblers, Flemish blue rim, signed,
5" h., set of 4. . . . . 175.00
Vase, 8" h., ribbed body, roll-over
rim, signed 95.00
Wine. 85.00

STEVENS & WILLIAMS

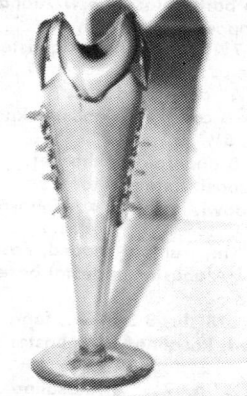

Stevens & Williams Vase

*This long-established English glass house
has turned out scores of types of glass
through the years. The following represents
a cross-section of its wares. Also see AP-
LIQUED GLASS.*

Basket, applied amber feet & handle, cream opaque exterior w/ap-
plied green & amber ruffled
leaves, pink interior w/amber
edging, 5" d., 9" h. $365.00
Bowl, 7¾" d., 5½" h., footed, blue
translucent Diamond Quilted patt.
w/applied clear scalloped shell
top 185.00
Vase, 3¾" h., 5" d., off white shad-
ing to deep rose at fluted rim, applied blue branch & leaves & rose
florette. 140.00
Vase, 4¼" h., 4½" d., fluted rim,
cased, cream w/heavenly blue lining, applied clear stem & leaf on
body 130.00
Vase, 4½" h., melon-ribbed, cran-
berry w/five applied clear feet . . . 105.00
Vase, 6 1/8" h., 4½" d., box-
pleated top, embossed basketweave patt., pink satin w/cream
lining 425.00
Vase, 6¾" h., 3 7/8" d., 8-crimp
rim, cased, cream w/pink lining,
applied cranberry stem & ruffled
green & amber leaves 150.00
Vase, 6¾" h., 3½" d., cased, off
white w/rose lining & amber edging at top, applied amber branch
w/green & amber leaves & pink &
white florettes 140.00
Vases, 7¼" h., 4¼" d., cased,
cream opaque w/deep rose lining,
applied amber scalloped edge & 3
rose, amber & green leaves on
body, pr. 350.00
Vases, 8" h., 4-sided folded petal
rim, shaded pink to clear w/ap-
plied green rigaree on sides, pr.
(ILLUS. of one) 165.00
Vase, 10" h., urn-shaped, cased,
creamy opaque w/pink lining &
applied amber scalloped edge at
ruffled rim, body w/applied rose-
streaked amber oak leaves &
amber acorn. 200.00

STIEGEL & STIEGEL-TYPE

*This glass was made at the American Flint
Glass Works of "Baron" Henry W. Stiegel
at Manheim, Pennsylvania, from 1765 until
the 1770's. It is difficult to attribute pieces
positively to Stiegel.*

Bottle, case-type, blown half-post
method, enameled polychrome
floral decor, pewter top (w/cap
missing), 5½" h. $225.00
Bottle, blown half-post method, rec-
tangular, rounded sloping collar,
clear w/engraved tulips, leaves &

tendrils, pontil, 4½ x 3",
9 3/8" h. 60.00
Flip glass, enameled polychrome
florals, 3 7/8" h. 310.00
Flip glass, clear w/engraved mums
& hollyhocks, pontil, 6 7/8" d.,
8¾" h. 90.00
Mug, applied strap handle, copper
wheel engraved flower, clear,
4 5/8" h 155.00

Stiegel-Type Mug

Mug, applied handle, copper wheel
engraved medallion of paired
birds, clear, 5½" h. (ILLUS.) 225.00
Mug, applied foot & handle, copper
wheel engraved tulip, clear,
5½" h. 125.00
Mug, applied handle, spreading
foot, enameled florals & bird,
18th c., 7" h. 785.00
Tumbler, enameled yellow, red,
white, green & blue leaves &
florals & a white crowing pea-
cock, 3 1/8" d., 3¾" h. 275.00

TIFFANY

Tiffany Flower Bowl & Frog

*This glassware, covering a wide diversity
of types, was produced in glasshouses operated by Louis Comfort Tiffany, America's
outstanding glass designer of the Art Nouveau period, from the last quarter of the 19th
century until the early 1930's. Tiffany revived
early techniques and devised many new ones.
Also see SHADES under Glass.*

Bon bon dish, pastel lavender,
signed, 8" d., 1½" h. $385.00
Bowl, 3¼" h., sloping sides & wide
mouth, paperweight-type, clear
w/imbedded white narcissus blossoms w/yellow & red millefiori
centers & mottled wintergreen
vines & leafage, ca. 1925, signed
L.C.T. Favrile. 3,300.00
Bowl, 6" d., scalloped rim, irides-
cent gold, signed. 375.00
Bowl, 6½" h., inverted teardrop
form, paperweight-type, clear
w/imbedded milky white snow-
drop blossoms & undulating lime
green leafage & trailings, ca.
1903, signed L.C.T. 4,400.00
Bowl, 6½" d., swirl-ribbed, deep
iridescent purple, signed 325.00
Champagne, transparent amber
w/mirror-like phantom lustre,
signed 110.00
Compote, 6¾" d., sea foam green
"rice grain" center shaded to
iridescent white stretched edge,
clear stem & base, signed 525.00
Cordials, iridescent gold, signed
L.C.T., pr. 295.00
Creamer, iridescent pastel green
shaded to opalescent, signed 385.00
Finger bowl & underplate,
paperweight-type, clear w/imbed-
ded dusty rose, amber & green
stylized lotus blossoms & leafage,
1892-1928, signed L.C.T. Favrile,
7¼" d. underplate, 2 pcs. 880.00
Flower bowl & 2-tier flower frog,
iridescent gold w/phantom lustre
spider web design, each piece
signed & numbered, 3¼" h. frog
& 10" d. bowl, pr. (ILLUS.) 1,100.00
Nut dish, iridescent pastel blue interior, opalescent exterior,
signed 225.00
Nut set: master bowl & 6 individual
nut cups w/ruffled rims; iridescent
gold, signed & numbered,
7 pcs. 1,200.00
Perfume bottle w/original stopper,
iridescent gold w/blue highlights,
signed L.C. Tiffany Favrile,
4¼" h. 450.00
Pitcher, 3" h., applied foot & han-
dle, pastel pink to opalescent,
signed & numbered 425.00

Pitcher, 3" h., deep iridescent blue,
signed 475.00

Plate, 8½" d., pastel pink or pastel
lavender w/opalescent rays from
center, signed, each 275.00

Plate, 11" d., scalloped rim, pastel
turquoise w/opalescent rays from
center, signed .... 225.00 to 245.00

Punch cup, raised & twisted pulled
prunts, iridescent gold w/fiery
mirror finish, signed 200.00

Salt dip, iridescent gold w/pale blue
highlights, signed L.C.T.
Favrile .... 145.00 to 195.00

Salt dip, ruffled edge, iridescent
gold interior, shiny opalescent exterior, signed 185.00

Salt dip, paperweight-type, iridescent gold w/twisted & pulled
prunts, signed 185.00

Tiffany Toothpick Holder

Toothpick holder, dimpled sides,
iridescent gold, signed L.C.T.,
2" h. (ILLUS.) 225.00

Toothpick holder, light green to
iridescent blue w/red stripe,
signed L.C.T., 2½" 200.00

Tray, upright scalloped edge, iridescent blue, signed, 7¼" d. 285.00

Tumbler, iridescent gold lustre,
signed 400.00

Vase, 1 7/8" h., gourd form w/bulg-
ing neck, tomato red exterior,
iridescent yellow interior, unsigned, 1892-1928 .... 1,540.00

Vase, 2" h., compressed ovoid, 2
rows of raised dots, emerald
green w/silvery amber iridescent
spotting against sapphire blue
ground, ca. 1915, signed L.C.T.
Tiffany-Favrile 1,870.00

Vase, 7" h., "Cypriote," bottle-
shaped w/flaring lip, iridescent
pale amber w/overall deep amber,
blue, green & ochre irregular
iridescent pitted effect, 1892-1928,
signed L.C.T. 3,025.00

Vase, 7" h., "lava," freeform pear

shape, lower half w/twelve horizontal iridescent gold bands intercepted by random oval protrusions,
upper half w/brilliant gold & rainbow iridescence beneath irregular
circular rim, signed L.C. Tiffany
Favrile 18,700.00

Tiffany Vases

Vase, 7 1/8" h., "Tel el Armana," 3
applied C-scroll handles, iridescent peacock blue w/gold collar &
overlapping green & blue herringbone bands, signed L.C. Tiffany,
Favrile (ILLUS. right) 2,860.00

Vase, 7¼" h., expanding cylinder,
paperweight-type, clear w/medium
lemon yellow nasturtium blossoms
& lime green trailing vines & leafage, interior w/deep amber-pink
iridescence, ca. 1906, signed
L.C.T. 2,750.00

Vase, 8¼" h., baluster-shaped,
paperweight-type, clear w/burnt
orange nasturtium blossoms w/mille-
fiori centers & deep avocado green
leafage & trailings reserved on a
blue-grey ground, iridescent amber
interior, ca. 1916, signed L.C.
Tiffany Favrile 9,350.00

Vase, 8¼" h., "Cypriote," pyriform,
deep amber w/overall amber &
brown iridescent cypriote pitting,
further decorated w/deep iridescent amber-pink leafage & vines,
ca. 1895, signed L.C.T. & w/rem-
nants of original paper label 4,675.00

Vase, 9" h., "Tel El Amarna," avocado green body decorated at
shoulder w/iridescent amber-blue
heart form leafage & spidery tendrils & at iridescent amber neck
& rolled lip w/opalescent & forest
green zigzag motifs, ca. 1925,
signed L.C. Tiffany Favrile &
w/original paper label 2,750.00

Vase, 11" h., "millefiori," double
gourd form, millefiori-centered

iridescent gold flower amidst dark
green leaves & trailing stems on
iridescent orange-gold ground,
signed L.C. Tiffany, Favrile &
numbered & w/original paper
label (ILLUS. left) 1,760.00
Vase, 11¾" h., floriform, opales-
cent shading to amber-orange at
spherical foot w/upright undulating
emerald green leafage, iridescent
amber interior, ca. 1900, signed
L.C.T. 1,980.00
Vase, 13¼" h., jack-in-pulpit-type,
deep iridescent blue, signed L.C.
Tiffany Favrile 4,180.00
Vase, 16 3/8" h., jack-in-pulpit-type,
iridescent gold, signed L.C.T. &
w/paper label 2,420.00

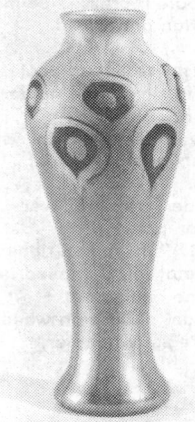

Tiffany Vase with Peacock Feathering

Vase, 20" h., green pulled peacock
feathering, signed & numbered
(ILLUS.) 4,125.00
Whiskey shot glass, iridescent gold,
signed L.C.T. 185.00

TIFFIN "BLACK SATIN"

*Among the wares made by the Tiffin Glass
Co., Tiffin, O., was a type collectors call
"black satin." This is the type of ware listed
below. Similar glass was made by the
United States Glass Company's plant in
Pittsburgh, Pa.*

Basket, 8" h. $35.00
Bowl, cov., 7½" d. 50.00
Bowl, 11" d. 40.00
Compote, 10", red poppies decor . . . 65.00
Console bowl, rolled rim, 12" d.,
4" h. .35.00 to 45.00
Pin tray, molded stag trampling a
wolf, 6 x 5" oval 30.00

Rose bowl, relief-molded poppies . . . 40.00
Vase, 5" h., bulbous, poppies
decor 30.00
Vase, 9" h., 8" widest d., red cora-
lene poppies decor 95.00
Vases, 10" h., relief-molded poppies
decor, applied brass collars &
footrims, pr. 80.00

TORTOISE SHELL

Tortoise Shell Glass Ice Bucket

*Tortoise Shell glass is primarily amber with
splotches of darker amber or brown and
resembles the actual tortoise shell, hence the
name. Some of this ware is attributed to
Sandwich, but it was also made in numerous
European glasshouses. Readily identified by
its peculiar coloring, it is admired by many
collectors.*

Bowl, 7¾" d., 3½" h. $85.00
Card holder, pedestal base, 3" w.,
2¾" h. 58.00
Ice bucket, expanding cylinder
w/tab handles (ILLUS.) 90.00
Pitcher, 8½" h., applied amber
handle 125.00
Pitcher, 10 1/8" h., applied handle . . 135.00
Plate, 11¼" d. 110.00
Potpourri (rose petal) jar, cov., am-
ber, brown & cream splotches,
clear lining 195.00
Toothpick holder, bulging base, at-
tributed to Hobbs, Brockunier &
Co. 95.00
Vase, 8" h., paneled, ca. 1910 . . . . . . 50.00
Vase, 12" h., bottle-shaped,
unmarked 75.00

VAL ST. LAMBERT

*This Belgian glass works was founded in
1790. Items listed here represent a sampling
of its numerous types of production.*

Bowl, 8" d., clear w/engraved floral
swags, signed $55.00
Cameo toothpick holder, carved
cranberry to frosted clear design
w/inscription "Janvier 4 - 1873-
1898," gold trim, signed 265.00
Coasters, clear w/engraved fruit in
base, signed, set of 4 .... 37.50
Decanter w/stopper, square, clear
w/cut cross-hatched design 85.00
Dresser set: pr. dresser boxes, hair
receiver, pr. cologne bottles
w/stoppers & tray; lemon yellow
& crystal, signed, 6 pcs. 350.00
Figure of Madonna, clear,
10" h. 75.00
Jar & cover w/facet-cut knob, cranberry cut to clear narrow panels
on body & star-cut base, 3½" d.,
5½" h. 70.00
Paperweight, iceberg form, clear,
signed, 4¼" l. 30.00
Vase, 8½" h., footed, Art Deco
style, amber 95.00
Wine, cranberry overlay on clear ... 49.00

leaves on body, 4¾" d.,
8¼" h. 135.00
Finger bowl, blown, paneled
body 40.00
Goblet, pressed Basketweave
patt. 30.00
Goblet, pressed Inverted Thumbprint
with Stars patt. 35.00
Lemonade pitcher, applied reeded
handle, narrow neck w/ruffled &
scalloped rim, Inverted Thumb-
print patt., 10½" h. 85.00
Marmalade jar w/silverplate frame,
cover & spoon, 5½" d., 6" h. 95.00
Salt shaker w/original top, pressed
Riverside's Ranson patt. (single) .. 30.00
Salt shaker w/original top, pressed
Wildflower patt. (single) 45.00
Sauce dish, footed, pressed Belmont
Daisy & Button patt., 4" d.
(ILLUS.)....................... 37.50
Sweetmeat dish, scalloped opalescent edge, in silverplate holder,
6½" d., 6" h. 95.00
Table set: cov. butter dish, cov. sug-
ar bowl & spooner; Petticoat
patt., 3 pcs. 195.00
Toothpick holder, pressed River-
side's Ranson patt. 55.00
Vase, 4" h., 3¼" d., melon-ribbed
w/flower petal top & applied leaf
feet, vaseline opalescent 55.00
Whimsey, model of boat on wheels,
w/English Registry number,
9½" l., 2¼" h.................. 135.00

VASELINE

Belmont Daisy & Button Pattern

*This glass takes its name from its color,
which is akin to that of petroleum jelly used
for medicinal purposes. Pieces below are miscellaneous. Also see JACK-IN-PULPIT
VASES, OPALESCENT and PATTERN
GLASS.*

Candlestick, 4¼" d., 7" h. (single) .. $65.00
Celery vase, pedestal foot, raised
ribs, vaseline opalescent 110.00
Cruet w/original stopper, Optic
patt., gold trim 110.00
Dish, canoe-shaped, War of Roses
patt., vaseline opalescent,
w/English Registry number,
9½" l. 95.00
Ewer, flattened bulbous shape,
vaseline opalescent w/applied
amber handle & applied amber

VENETIAN & VENETIAN-TYPE

*Venetian glass has been made for six cen-
turies on the island of Murano, where it continues to be produced today. The skilled glass
artisans developed numerous techniques, subsequently imitated elsewhere.*

Bowl, blue & white opaque swirled
stripes, small $95.00
Goblet, pale translucent green
w/applied blue rigaree at baluster
stem, 7" h. 20.00
Model of a swan, clear w/gold mica
flecks, 12" l. 35.00
Tumblers, clear w/enameled Etruscan warriors decor, 2¼" h., pr. .. 110.00
Vase, 7" h., model of red winged
dolphin rising up to form jack-in-
pulpit top, clear leaf base........ 40.00
Vase, 10" h., 6" d., swirled body,
translucent green, signed 110.00
Vases, 11" h., pale blue w/applied
amber feet & amber salamanders
on body & rigaree at rim, pr...... 170.00

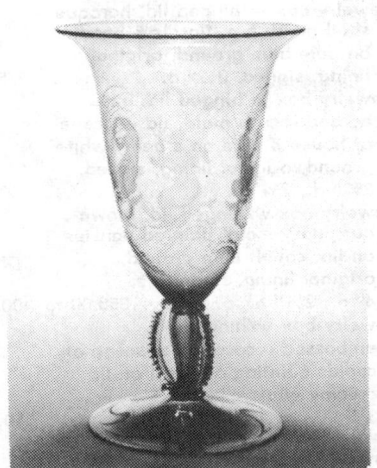

Engraved Venetian Glass Vase

Vase, 14 5/8" h., pale translucent
blue engraved w/three mermaids
above ground cut w/sea sprays,
waves & stars, baluster stem enclosed by 3 rigaree bands to engraved circular foot, designed by
Guido Balsamo Stella for Salir,
ca. 1930 (ILLUS.) 1,430.00
Water set: pitcher & 8 footed tumblers; amber w/overall silver
deposit scene of gondolas &
figures, 9 pcs. 185.00

VERLYS

Verlys Bowl

*This glass is a relative newcomer for col-
lectors and is not old enough to be antique,
having been made for less than half a century in France and the United States, but fine
pieces are collected. Blown and molded pieces
have been produced.*

Ash tray, sculptured lovebirds,
clear, signed, 4½ x 3½" $50.00
Bowl, 5½" d., sculptured roses,
amber (ILLUS.) 60.00
Bowl, 6" d., Pinecone patt., clear ... 55.00

Bowl, 13½" d., sculptured flying
seagulls & fish amidst swirling
waves, frosted amber & amber,
signed 175.00
Bowl, 13½" d., sculptured flying
seagulls & fish amidst swirling
waves, frosted & clear, signed ... 150.00
Bowl, 13¾" d., shallow, sculptured
waterlilies & leaves, frosted &
clear, signed.................... 140.00
Bowl, 14½ x 11¾" oval, 1 7/8" h.,
clear w/etched leaves, signed 75.00
Bowl, Tassels patt., Directoire
blue 175.00
Candlestick, Waterlily patt., Directoire blue (single) 25.00
Candy box, cov., sculptured florals,
smoky, 7" d..................... 185.00
Charger, sculptured birds & bees,
frosted & clear, 11½" d. 70.00
Dish, 3-footed, Pinecone patt., clear,
6" d. 40.00
Vase, 8" h., square, frosted & clear
design, signed 75.00
Vase, 9" h., bulbous, sculptured
sunflowers, frosted & clear,
signed 150.00
Vase, Alpine Thistle patt., dusty
rose, signed 275.00

WAVE CREST

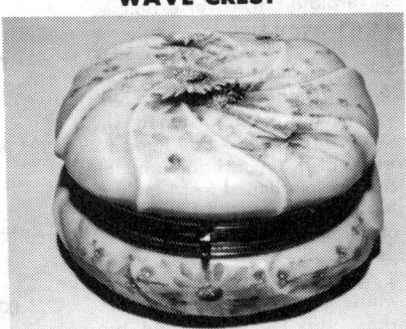

Helmschmied Swirl Box

*Now much sought after, Wave Crest was
produced by the C.F. Monroe Co., Meriden,
Conn., in the late 19th and early 20th centuries from opaque white glass blown into
molds. It was then hand-decorated in enamels
and metal trims were often added. Boudoir
accessories such as jewel boxes, hair
receivers, etc., were predominant. Also see
KELVA and NAKARA.*

Box w/hinged lid, Helmschmied
Swirl (or Erie Twist) mold, blue
florals & white beading on pale
yellow ground, unsigned,
3¼" d. $225.00

Box w/hinged lid, Baroque Shell mold, h.p. pink florals on blue shading to white ground, signed, 4" d., 3" h. 325.00

Box w/hinged lid, blown-out zinnia mold, painted zinnia lid, glossy blue ground, signed, 5" d. 375.00

Box w/hinged lid, Helmschmied Swirl mold, enameled florals on pale pink shading to pale blue ground, unsigned, 5¼" d., 3" h. ... 295.00

Box w/hinged lid, Helmschmied Swirl mold, h.p. florals w/raised enamel centers on creamy white, unsigned, 7½" d. (ILLUS.) 350.00

Card holder, ormolu rim, embossed rococo mold, h.p. florals on soft blue ground, signed, 4½" w. 265.00

Collars & cuffs box w/hinged lid, puffy Egg Crate mold, lid w/h.p. robin on creamy white, ormolu rims & lion mask feet, 6½" w., 6¾" h. 1,550.00

Comb & brush holder w/trinket tray, pink florals on yellow ground, 8¾ x 4½", 4½" h. 810.00

Cookie jar, plain mold, floral decor on creamy white, silverplate rim, cover & bail handle, marked "C.F.M." in lid, 8" h. 295.00

Cookie jar, puffy egg crate mold, blue delphiniums w/enameled centers on creamy white ground, silverplate rim, cover & bail handle, unsigned, 5½" sq., 9½" h. ....250.00 to 265.00

Cookie jar, plain mold, pink florals & faint cupid transfer on robin's egg blue ground, unsigned, silverplate rim, cover & bail handle 325.00

Dresser dish, open, ormolu handles & rim, Helschmied Swirl mold, h.p. orange & white florals on creamy white, 4½" d. 85.00

Dresser dish, open, ormolu handles & rim, pansies decor on creamy white, signed, 9½" d., 2½" h. ... 225.00

Ferner, puffy Egg Crate mold, h.p. violets & gold trim on white ground, 7" sq. 315.00

Ferner, Embossed Rococo mold, blue florals on creamy white ground, original liner, 9 x 5" 260.00

Glove box w/hinged lid, Embossed Rococo mold, pink & white roses & green leaves on creamy yellow ground, ormolu rims & feet, signed, 9½ x 6", 5" h. 950.00

Hair receiver w/silverplate cover, florals on creamy white, 4¼" d. ... 225.00

Humidor w/hinged lid, Embossed Rococo mold, "Cigars" & h.p. florals on pale blue ground, signed 350.00

Jewelry box w/hinged lid, baroque shell mold, h.p. florals & beading on pale blue ground, original lining, signed, 3½" d. 275.00

Jewelry box w/hinged lid, embossed rococo mold, lid w/scene of house & lake on creamy white ground, original lining, signed, 3¾" d., 2¾" h. 350.00

Jewelry box w/hinged lid, blown-out pansy mold, painted pansies on lid, cobalt blue ground, original lining, signed, 4" d., 2½" h. ....350.00 to 400.00

Jewelry box w/hinged lid, embossed rococo mold, scene of cupids painting at easel on lid, creamy white ground, 5½" w., 3" h. 550.00

Jewelry box w/hinged lid, ormolu rim & feet, puffy egg crate mold, h.p. florals on creamy white w/mauve borders, original lining, signed, 6½" w., 6½" h. 775.00

Jewelry box w/hinged lid, ormolu rim & feet, Helmschmied Swirl mold, h.p. florals on creamy white, original lining, 7" d. 595.00

Jewelry box w/hinged lid, embossed rococo mold, floral decor on pale blue ground, red satin lining, signed, 7" oblong 675.00

Jewelry box w/hinged lid, ormolu rim & feet, Helmschmied Swirl mold, dark yellow roses on shaded blue ground, original lining, 7½" d., 6" h. 575.00

Photo receiver, puffy Egg Crate mold, enameled pink florals on creamy white ground, ormolu rim & footed base, 6 x 4½" 350.00

Pin tray, ormolu handles, Helmschmied Swirl mold, florals on white ground, unsigned 100.00

Ring box w/hinged lid, h.p. cupid on lid, 2½" d. 295.00

Salt & pepper shakers w/original tops, Helmschmied Swirl mold, florals on deep pink ground, pr. ... 160.00

Smoker's set, cigar jar flanked by match holders on footed ormolu frame, h.p. florals on creamy white 525.00

Spooner, Helmschmied Swirl mold, apple blossoms on pink shaded to white ground, ormolu collar & handles ....165.00 to 195.00

Sugar bowl w/silverplate rim, handles & cover, pink & blue florals on creamy white, unsigned 210.00

Sugar shaker w/original silverplate top, Helmschmied Swirl mold, panels of florals & blue shadow scrolls on creamy white......... 350.00

Syrup pitcher w/original silverplate
top, Helmschmied Swirl mold,
enameled spray of pink wild roses
on pale blue, unsigned 435.00
Toothpick holder, ormolu base,
enameled florals on creamy
white, 2 3/8" h................. 285.00

Wave Crest Toothpick Holder

Toothpick holder, ormolu base, h.p.
pale blue florals w/pale green
stems on creamy white, signed,
2½" h. (ILLUS.) 195.00
Vase, 6" h., 2-handled ormolu rim,
h.p. reserve cartouche w/florals
each side, ormolu footed base ... 250.00

WEBB

Webb Vase & Sugar Shaker

*This glass is made by Thomas Webb &
Sons, of Stourbridge, one of England's most
prolific glasshouses. Numerous types of glass,
including cameo, have been produced by this
firm through the years. The company also devised various types of novelty and "art" glass
during the late Victorian period. Also see
PEACH BLOW and SATIN.*

Bowl, 7" d., 5" h., pearlized w/ap-
plied green threading $90.00
Bowl, 10" d., scalloped rim, blue exterior w/raised enamel decor,
white lining, signed 145.00
Cameo bowl, 3½ x 2", carved white
plums, foliage & vines & geometric collar against red satin
ground 425.00
Cameo cookie jar, carved opaque
white florals, branches & leaves
against red satin ground, silverplate rim, cover & bail handle,
5¾" h., 5½" h. 2,010.00
Cameo inkwell, flaring rounded
base, 3 carved white medallions
centered amidst flowering
branches against ivory ground,
hallmarked silver domed lid &
original glass insert, signed,
3½" h. 1,250.00
Cameo scent bottle w/hallmarked
silver hinged lid, lay-down type,
carved opaque white leaves
against heavenly blue frosted
ground, 3¾" l................. 595.00
Cameo scene bottle w/hallmarked
silver hinged cap & inside glass
stopper, lay-down type, carved
white flower front & butterfly
reverse against olive green
ground 625.00
Cameo scent bottle w/hallmarked
silver cap, carved white florals
against pale blue ground,
2¾" h. 550.00
Centerpiece bowl, flattened oval,
enameled green & tan leaves, yellow florals & green foliage on
heavenly blue shaded to tan w/in-
side top also in shaded blue, 12½
x 5 7/8" oval, 7" h. 350.00
Rose bowl, turned-in & crimped rim,
rose-pink w/twenty-four evenly
spaced vertical air traps rising
from base like silk ribbons of lustrous rose-red, enameled gold
prunus blossoms decor, 4½" d.,
2¾" h......................... 585.00
Sugar shaker, pale apricot mother-
of-pearl Herringbone patt.,
pierced silver slip-on cover (ILLUS.
right) 375.00
Toothpick holder, enameled floral
spray on yellow satin ground,
white lining, in silverplate
pedestal frame................. 395.00
Tumbler, raised white enameled
decor on yellow ground, signed,
4" h.......................... 30.00
Vase, 5" h., 3½" d., pleated top,
gold prunus blossoms & gold
branches decor, shaded brown
satin ground, cream lining 505.00

Vase, 6" h., cased, deep red
w/enameled heavy gold & silver-
gilt monkey, butterfly & floral
decor 295.00
Vase, 9½" h., ruffled & crimped
rim, blue, gold & white coralene
florals & green foliage on dark to
light gold satin stripe ground
(ILLUS. left) 625.00

(End of Glass Section)

GRANITEWARE

Cruller Pan with Liner

This is a name given to metal (customarily iron) kitchenwares covered with an enamel
coating. Featured at the 1876 Philadelphia
Centennial Exposition, it became quite popular for it was lightweight, attractive, and easy
to clean. Although it was made in huge quantities and is still produced, it has caught the
attention of a younger generation of collectors and prices have steadily risen over the
past five years. There continues to be a con-
sistent demand for the wide variety of these
utilitarian articles turned out earlier in this
century and rare forms now command high
prices. Also see CHILDREN'S DISHES &
MUGS, SALESMAN'S SAMPLES, SIGNS
& SIGNBOARDS and WORLD FAIR COL-
LECTIBLES.

Baking pan, oblong, brown & white
swirls $45.00
Baking pan, oblong, cobalt blue &
white swirls .... 30.00 to 38.00
Baking pan, oblong, grey mottled,
signed "Granite Iron Ware" &
dated July 3, 1877 .... 38.00
Basin, emerald green & white
swirls 40.00
Basin, white interior, blue exterior,
10" d. 22.00

Basting spoon, cream & garnet
red 10.00
Batter jug w/tin lid & bail handle,
straight spout w/tin cap, grey
mottled .... 40.00 to 50.00
Bottle warmer, grey speckled,
w/cord & socket plug 45.00
Cake pan, aqua & white marbleized,
9" d. 20.00
Cake pan, iris blue marbleized 48.00
Cake pan, tube-type, grey mottled .. 16.00
Camping (or picnic) set: large pot &
metal-clamp-on lid w/four 8" d.
plates, four 5" d. dishes, 4 cups &
serving bowl; green, 14 pcs. 110.00
Candleholder, chamberstick-type
w/saucer base & ring handle, red
& black speckled 45.00
Candleholder, chamberstick-type
w/saucer base & ring handle, sky
blue 35.00
Candleholder, chamberstick-type
w/large beehive-ridged chamberstick base & ring handle, grey
mottled, 7½" d. 95.00
Canning kettle w/bail handle,
chocolate brown & white mottled
splotches, marked "Majestic" 50.00
Cruller (deep fat) frying pan w/in-
side pan, grey mottled, 2-pc.
(ILLUS.)....................... 80.00
Dipper, blue & white mottled 22.50
Dipper, grey mottled .... 12.00 to 20.00
Dipper, sky blue & white swirls
w/black handle 15.00
Dipper, turquoise & white swirls 38.00
Dish pan, blue & white swirls 25.00
Dish pan, 2-handled, dark green &
white marbleized veins, 19" d.
(minor wear at base) 60.00
Double boiler w/lid, cobalt blue
w/white speckles .... 25.00 to 38.00
Double boiler w/lid, emerald green
& white marbleized veins 78.00
Double boiler w/lid, turquoise &
white mottled.................. 62.00

Fruit Bowl

Fruit bowl, reticulated sides, crysto-
lite, dark green w/white veins,
white lining (ILLUS.) 45.00
Funnel, apple green & white mar-
bleized, large 35.00
Funnel, canning-type, lavender &
white speckled, large 32.00
Grater, cast iron, white, marked
"Helvetia" 40.00
Gravy boat, blue & white mottled .. 200.00
Ladle, turquoise blue & white
marbleized 22.50
Liquid measure, grey mottled,
1-cup 30.00
Liquid measure, grey mottled,
1-gal. 40.00
Lunch bucket, miner's type, grey
mottled 55.00
Milk can, blue & white speckled,
14" h. 85.00
Milk can, child's, grey
mottled 25.00
Milk cooling basin, turquoise blue &
white marbleized 35.00
Milk pail, brown & white
marbleized 70.00
Milk pail, cobalt blue & white
marbleized 110.00

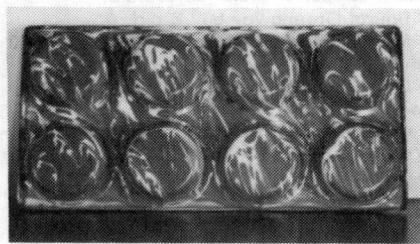

Graniteware Muffin Pan

Muffin pan, 8-cup, blue & white
marbleized (ILLUS.) 60.00
Muffin pan, 12-cup, grey
mottled ....18.00 to 25.00
Mug, turquoise blue & white
marbleized, large 38.00
Pie pan, cobalt blue & white
marbleized 15.00
Pie pan, grey mottled 8.50
Pie pan, shamrock green & white
marbleized 30.00
Pitcher, milk, convex, grey
mottled 75.00
Pitcher, water, blue & white
mottled 62.00
Plate, child's, Dutch boy w/white
geese decor on blue, 7" d. 35.00
Pudding pan, blue & white mar-
bleized, 7 x 2" 32.00
Roaster, brown & white
marbleized 38.00
Salt box, hanging-type, grey
mottled 55.00

Sauce pan, child's, grey
mottled 15.00
Skimmer, apple green & white
marbleized 38.00
Soap dish w/drain insert, blue &
white marbleized 50.00
Soap dish w/drain insert, green &
white marbleized 70.00
Soap dish w/drain insert, grey
mottled 28.00
Sugar bowl, cov., grey mottled
w/pewter trim 190.00
Sugar shaker, white & blue
speckled 75.00
Syrup pitcher, turquoise blue &
white marbleized 75.00
Tea kettle, cobalt blue & white
marbleized 145.00
Teapot, cov., bulbous, blue mottled
w/pewter trim, marked "Manning-
Bowman" 175.00
Teapot, cov., grey mottled, 1-cup ... 75.00

Graniteware Tea Steeper

Tea steeper w/tin lid, grey mottled
(ILLUS.) 45.00
Tumbler, blue & white marbleized .. 75.00
Wash board, wooden frame w/co-
balt blue corrugated scrubbing
surface & soap-saver top, "Por-
celain Enamel Washboard, Nat'l.
Washboard Co." 72.00
Wash boiler, blue & white swirls,
31" l. (no lid) 127.50

GREENAWAY (Kate) ITEMS

Numerous objects in pottery, porcelain, glass and other materials were made in or with the likenesses of the appealing children created by the famous 19th century English artist, Kate Greenaway. These are now eagerly sought along with the original Greenaway books.

Almanack for 1886, published by
George Routledge & Sons $65.00

Almanack for 1924

Almanack for 1924 (ILLUS.) 50.00
Almanack for 1925 . . . .   45.00
Almanack for 1926 . . . .   35.00
Book, "A Day in a Child's Life,"
  music by Myles B. Foster, illus-
  trated by Greenaway, published
  by George Routledge & Sons,
  1881 . . . .   85.00
Book, "Kate Greenaway's Birthday
  Book for Children," verses by Mrs.
  Sale Barker, illustrated by
  Greenaway, 1880 . . . . 35.00 to 50.00
Book, "Little Ann and Other
  Poems," by Jane and Ann Taylor,
  illustrated by Greenaway, ca.
  1883 . . . .   75.00
Butter pat, decal of Greenaway chil-
  dren playing 35.00
Creamer, child's, decal of Greena-
  way children 25.00
Feeding set, child's: cup, saucer &
  6" d. plate; china, Greenaway
  children decor, 3 pcs. 90.00
Greeting card, "Happy New Year,"
  14 Greenaway children 35.00
Match holder w/striker, china,
  figural Greenaway girl helping
  her little sister over a log beside
  container 85.00
Mug, silverplate, low relief Greena-
  way children around sides, engraved w/name & "1882" 60.00
Mush set: pitcher, bowl & 7" d.
  plate; china, Greenaway children
  decor, Germany, 3 pcs. 80.00
Plate, decal of children playing
  w/kite, Doulton & Royal Doulton . .   75.00
Prints, Greenaway children &
  verses, in oblong frame w/double
  oval openings . . . . .100.00 to 125.00
Reward of Merit cards, set of 4
  (ILLUS. of one) . . . . .20.00 to 35.00

Reward of Merit Card

Salt & pepper shakers, china, figural
  Greenaway boy & girl, 4" h.,
  pr. 135.00
Salt & pepper shakers, silverplate,
  figural Greenaway boy & girl,
  Meriden Silverplate Co., pr. 49.00
Serving plate, glass, frosted center,
  Greenaway children decor 95.00
Toothpick holder, silverplate,
  Greenaway girl holding large
  acorn-shaped urn, Tufts 125.00

HAIRWORK PICTURES & WREATHS

Hair Wreath

This sentimental Victorian pastime enabled ladies to preserve strands of human hair, especially that of a relative or close friend, in the form of a floral wreath or bouquet. Intricate braids, twisted and crocheted locks and curlicue arrangements, sometimes worked in shades ranging from ash blonde to deep brunette for contrast, were set in deep shadowbox frames, often on a white slipper satin background, and proudly displayed. Today these curiosities are finding favor with some collectors of Victoriana.

Bouquet of flowers, original walnut
deep shadowbox frame, 12 x 9" .. $85.00
Bouquet of flowers w/beaded
centers, black shadowbox frame,
17½ x 13½" 55.00
Bouquet of flowers, walnut shadowbox frame, 23 x 22½" ....85.00 to 100.00
Floral spray w/leaves, walnut
shadowbox frame, 12 x 10" 95.00
Florals & leaves applied to round
leather circle, 16" d. 150.00
Flowers, each labeled "Mother,"
"Father," or "Mary," etc., walnut
deep shadowbox frame,
15 x 13" 50.00
Wreath of flowers & leaves, various
colors of braided & crocheted hair
wired into wreath, round giltwood
shadowbox frame, 17" d., 3¼"
deep 85.00
Wreath of flowers, horseshoe-
shaped wreath, walnut deep
shadowbox frame w/gilt liner,
22½ x 19" 75.00
Wreath of flowers w/butterfly,
leaves, etc., original deep
shadowbox frame, 24½ x 20½" .. 195.00
Wreath of flowers, various colors of
braided & twisted hair, shadowbox frame, 24¾ x 20¾" (ILLUS.).. 105.00
Wreath of flowers, various colors
braided hair, on beige silk background, walnut shadowbox frame,
ca. 1850, 26 x 16" 250.00
Wreath of flowers, stems & birds,
on shirred pink silk background,
shadowbox frame, 26 x 24" 155.00

HATPIN HOLDERS

Bavarian china, boys eating fruit
decor, gold trim................ $47.50
German china, 2-handled, green,
pink & yellow roses w/green
leaves on white ground, 3½" d.,
5" h............................ 40.00
German china, lavender & white
florals w/green leaves on salmon
pink shaded to white ground 38.00
Limoges china, white w/ornate gold
trim........................... 55.00
Nippon china, relief-molded coiling
serpent on mottled pastel ground,
5" h........................... 40.00
Nippon china, h.p. violets & green

foliage decor, gold beading &
trim, w/attached pin tray 60.00
Nippon china, h.p. sailing ships
decor 85.00
R.S. Germany china, hexagonal,
molded feet, pink & green floral
decor on white ground, 4½" h.... 55.00
R.S. Germany china, bulbous, white
roses decor.................... 45.00
R.S. Germany china, pink & white
roses on shaded green ground ... 48.00
R.S. Prussia china, h.p. floral decor,
w/attached covered pin box 300.00
R.S. Prussia china, h.p. bluebirds
decor 450.00
R.S. Prussia china, 3-footed, h.p.
floral decor................... 165.00
Royal Bayreuth china, figural
owl 350.00
Royal Bayreuth china, Fox Hunt
scene 250.00
Royal Bayreuth china, Rose Tapestry
w/three-color roses 140.00
Schafer & Vater jasper ware, white
relief Art Nouveau lady's head
front & reverse on lavender
ground, gold beading & trim 130.00
Sterling silver, Art Nouveau style
floral top 38.00
Torquay pottery, "Motto Ware," blue
& green decor 65.00

HATPINS

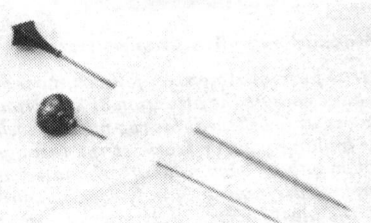

Brass & Gold-Finish Metal Hatpins

Advertising "Economy Stove-Range,"
gilt head w/logo, 10" l.......... $18.00
Bakelite, black, 2 opposing arrows
studded w/rhinestones, 2½ x 1½"
top 12.00
Brass, 6" l. (ILLUS. top) 12.00
Brass, oval filigree top in the form
of a horseshoe & bit, rhinestone-
studded, 9" l.................. 20.00
Brass, reticulated edge w/pink &
blue glass insets, relief beetle
center, 1¾" d., 12" l............ 35.00
Carnival glass, flying bat,
purple 30.00

Carnival glass, Phoenix Bird........ 32.00
Carnival glass, rooster, purple 28.00
Gold, 14k, w/faceted amber glass
   inset, 9" l...................... 32.00
Gold, 14k, w/faceted lavender glass
   insets, 8½" l.................... 25.00
Gold-finish metal, flower form,
   4½" l. (ILLUS. bottom) 10.00
Rhinestone-studded, 1¼" sq. top,
   10" l. 25.00
Rhinestones surrounding faceted
   sapphire blue inset.............. 20.00
Silverplate, embossed rim w/faceted
   deep blue glass inset, 1 5/8" d.,
   12" l. 28.00
Sterling silver set w/abalone
   shell 12.00
Sterling silver, bird on spring "nodding" device 68.00

HOOKED RUGS

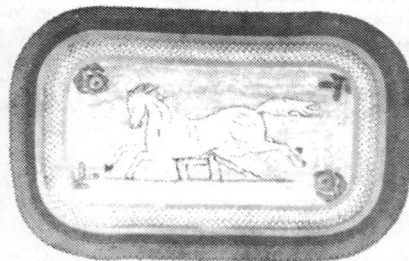

Hooked Rug with Leaping Horse

A true form of American folk art, hooked rugs have caught the attention of numerous collectors. It is believed this rug-making technique (pulling yarn or fabric strips through a woven fabric background) originated in America. Jute burlap (gunny-sacking) provides the ideal background material and after this fabric was brought out around the 1850's, rug hooking became quite a vogue. It provided the opportunity to thriftily use up leftover burlap sacks and the remnants of discarded clothing to produce attractive floor coverings. Geometric and floral design rugs are the most common while animals, houses, figures, landscapes and ships are scarcer. Bold colorful, original designs are most appealing to collectors, but those hooked on stamped burlap patterns even during the 20th century, are also avidly sought.

Blossoms & buds within diamond-
   shaped reserve, corners
   w/elaborate scrolling, red, pink,
   grey, beige & brown, 19th c.,
   60 x 52"....................... $660.00

Calico cat in shades of orange &
   black seated on salmon pink &
   green ottoman on grey-beige
   ground, borders & foliate scrolls
   in black, maroon, olive green &
   salmon pink, 45 x 28½" (some
   wear & old repairs) 220.00
Dog reclining, orange, brown &
   white animal on shaded red rug,
   colorful florals on olive ground on
   short side borders, 39 x 19"
   (rebacked)..................... 160.00
Eagle w/spread wings, rabbits (3)
   running & "Blackhawk," multicolored, (new) black backing
   extends beyond hooked area,
   40 x 25"....................... 945.00
Floral design in beige, blue & pink
   on black ground, 31 x 18"........ 125.00
Frigate, colorful 4-masted vessel
   sailing on sea blue water under a
   brilliant blue sky 600.00
Geometric design in shades of blue,
   lavender, green, orange & maroon, dark border, 46 x 28½" 165.00
Horse leaping a fence, white animal
   on olive green ground w/flowers
   & foliage in corners, wide braided
   border in shades of brown, olive
   green & red, some wear & fading,
   48 x 31" (ILLUS.) 310.00

Kittens Rug

Kittens (2) flanking ball of thread
   within shaped reserve, brown,
   beige, slate blue, grey &
   magenta, 19th c., 49½ x 29½"
   (ILLUS.) 1,430.00

Hooked Rug with Reclining Lion

Lion reclining within an oval rope-
   twist surround, foliate corners,
   black, brown, beige, green & dark

blue, pattern by Ebenezer Ross,
19th c., 60 x 32" (ILLUS.) 715.00
Mermaids (2) w/starfish & shells on
blue-green ground, central inscription "Over the bounding
wave what could be more delightful to the eyes of a lonely sailor
man altho their snares are spite-
ful," 1920-30, 54 x 36". 1,760.00
Pot of red & yellow tulips within
shaped reserve, shaded green
ground against green & black diagonal stripes within black bor-
ders, 37 x 25" 95.00
Roosters (2) in dark colors on grey &
purple ground within multicolored
striped border, 39 x 26" 425.00
Scottie dogs, black animals on shad-
ed light grey ground within multicolored striped borders, 1930's,
32 x 20" 425.00
Shore birds standing on grey &
brown striped sandy ground highlighted w/a blue wave design,
31 x 23½" 350.00
Stag in landscape w/tree stump &
squirrel, rich shades of brown,
green & blue, oval foliate border
in red & black, backed in bars of
colored fabric, red end fringe,
53 x 28" 175.00
Three-masted ship on choppy blue
sea w/castle & 2 ships in background, black border w/nautical
design in faded yellow, blue &
brown, 36 x 28" 160.00

HORN

*The hard keratinous substance that forms
the horns and hoofs of animals can be worked
to produce a wide range of items, both
utilitarian and decorative. Powder horns are
probably the most readily recognized items
available, but spoons, tumblers, jewelry and
haircombs also abound. The ugly horn furniture, popular in this country during the
1880's, incorporates whole animal horns of the
Texas Longhorn and other steers to form the
framework. Excluding furniture, most horn
items, even those with scratch-carved decoration, are moderately priced. Also see
STOOLS under Furniture.*

Chalice, on turned walnut pedestal
base, 12" h. $25.00
Magnifying glass, w/sterling silver
handle 95.00
Shoe horn, carved bird head handle
w/inlaid eyes, polished 39.00

Snuff box w/hinged lid, silverplate
fittings forming thistle design on
lid, 3¾" l. 30.00
Spoon, Revolutionary War period . . . 25.00
Thimble holder 22.00

HORSE & BUGGY COLLECTIBLES

Buggy Wrench

Bridle, leather head harness
w/beaded throat latch & lead
rosette trim $125.00
Bridle bit, black steel, engraved &
silver-mounted, marked "Crockett-
Kelly" 175.00
Bridle bit, blue & silver aluminum,
engraved & silver-mounted,
marked "Crockett-Kelly" 90.00
Bridle bit, nickel-plated w/sterling
silver "concho," marked
"Crockett" 250.00
Bridle rosettes, horse's head under
convex glass, brass back,
pr. . . . . .25.00 to 40.00
Bridle rosettes, lead-backed shield
shape, pr. 10.00
Buggy, wooden 1-seat model,
wooden hubs w/offset wooden
spokes, manufactured by "Excelsior Carriage Co., Watertown,
New York," ca. 1860 . . . . .1,050.00
Buggy, wooden, "Studebaker," 1854
model 1,200.00
Buggy seat, child-size, wooden,
w/hand-colored stenciling on
sides & back, 36" w. 70.00
Buggy steps, cast iron, 8" l.,
pr. . . . . .15.00 to 25.00
Buggy wrench, cast iron, ca. 1885,
6½" l. (ILLUS.) 20.00
Carriage lap robe, bearskin w/inset
glass eyes 45.00
Carriage lap robe, woven
mohair 95.00
Carriage lap robe, woven wool,
horse heads (2) superimposed on
race track scene 45.00
Chaps, fringed leather, pr. 375.00
Chaps, white wool, "Hamley Saddle
Co.," 1918, pr. 550.00
Conestoga wagon grease bucket . . . 85.00
Conestoga wagon jack, wood &
tooled wrought iron, w/date
"1797" in iron, 24" h. 125.00

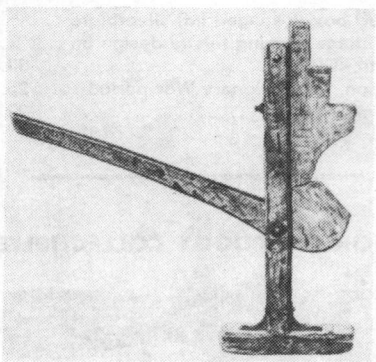

Wagon Jack

Conestoga wagon jack, wood &
  wrought iron, dated 1865
  (ILLUS.)........................ 185.00
Curry comb 5.00

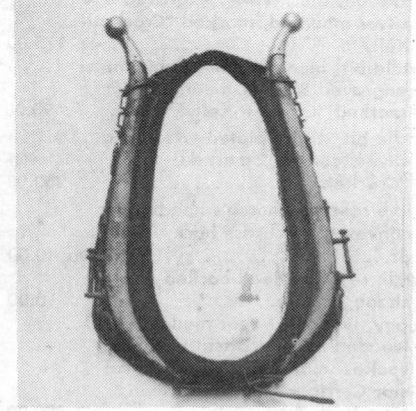

Horse Collar

Horse collar, leather-covered wood
  w/wooden hames & brass end
  knobs (ILLUS.) ....30.00 to 55.00
Horse hames, steel w/brass knobs,
  pr............................. 7.00
Horse hitching posts, cast iron,
  model of lion's head w/ring in
  mouth, square standard w/split
  end designed to be fitted on
  wooden post, 17" h., pr......... 230.00
Horse hitching post, cast iron, figure
  of black stable boy, retouched
  original paint, 38" h. ....500.00 to 750.00
Horse hitching post, cast iron, figure
  of jockey standing, by J.L. Mott,
  ca. 1890, 49" h. 2,200.00
Horse hitching post, cast iron, figure
  of a jockey standing & holding out
  ring, wearing cap, short buttoned
  jacket, jodpurs & high leather
  boots, very old polychrome
  repaint, 50½" h........750.00 to 1,200.00

Horse hitching post, cast iron,
  model of a horse's head on post,
  simple details in mane & head,
  53" h...................330.00 to 385.00
Horse hitching post, cast iron, well-
  detailed model of horse's head
  w/ring in mouth on post, traces of
  old paint, 53" h. ....450.00 to 495.00
Horse hitching post, cast iron,
  model of stylized tree trunk
  w/sawed-off branches, worn
  black paint, overall 67½" h.
  (some rust) 245.00
Horse hitching post, cast iron,
  clenched fist top on post 125.00
Horse hitching weight, cast iron 17.50
Lariat, woven rawhide, 35" l....... 125.00
Lariat, woven rawhide, 54" l....... 140.00
Pony trap, wooden 2-wheeled cart,
  w/original coach lamps, Ballina-
  more, Ireland, 19th c...........1,400.00
Quirt (riding whip), braided
  multicolored horsehair,
  30" l. ....150.00 to 250.00
Spurs, wrought iron w/leather
  straps, pr..................... 45.00
Spurs, steel w/sterling silver inlay,
  pr............................. 100.00
Stirrup, wooden, each ....8.00 to 12.00
Surrey, wooden, 2-seat model,
  red "tufted" upholstery, fringed
  leather top....................2,000.00
Sweat scraper, hand-carved hickory,
  double-ended handle, 19th c...... 55.00
Wagon wheels, wooden, w/wooden
  hubs & spokes & iron rim banding,
  according to size.........25.00 to 150.00

HUMPHREY (MAUD) ARTWORK

*Maud Humphrey was an accomplished art-
ist whose illustrations appeared in more than
twenty children's books and numerous wom-
en's magazines during the 1890's and in the
early years of the 20th century. Although
many of her illustrations are unsigned, most
of her book illustrations carry at least her initials if not the full signature. The mother of
actor Humphrey Bogart, she died in Hollywood, in 1940, at the age of 72.*

Book, "Baby's Record," 1898 ....$150.00
Calendar, 1904, advertising, "Equita-
  ble Life Society," little girls, 6
  color-illustrated pages 285.00
Calendar sheet, 1899, May-June,
  beautiful children 32.50
Christmas card for subscription to
  "Youth's Companion" 20.00
Poster, advertising, "Fairy Soap,"

entitled "Kitty's Bath," 2 pretty little girls about to bathe a white angora cat, copyright Fairbanks Co., Chicago, dated 1899, 23½ x 13½" 225.00
Print, entitled "Baby & Rose Petals" 75.00
Print, entitled "Birthday Party," original frame 195.00
Print, entitled "Flirtation," Stokes Co., No. 892 .... 125.00
Print, entitled "Miss Muffet's Christmas Party," dated 1894, framed, 14½ x 10¼" 135.00
Print, entitled "Mistress Mary," dated 1891 .... 45.00
Print, untitled, pretty little girl & toddler sweeping, 10 x 8" 22.50

ICART PRINTS

Don Juan

The works of Louis Icart, the successful French artist whose working years spanned the Art Nouveau and Art Deco movements, first became popular in the United States shortly after World War I. His limited edition etchings were much in vogue during those years that the fashion trends were established in Paris. These prints were later relegated to closet shelves and basements but they have now re-entered the art market and are avidly sought by collectors. Listed by their American titles, those appearing below have been sold within the past eighteen months.

Attic Room, 1940, 16½ x 14" $660.00
Baby Doll, 1924, 17½ x 13" oval 330.00
Carmen, 1927, 13½ x 20" 330.00

Casanova, 1928, 14 x 21" 495.00
Don Juan, 1928, 14 x 21" (ILLUS.) ... 660.00

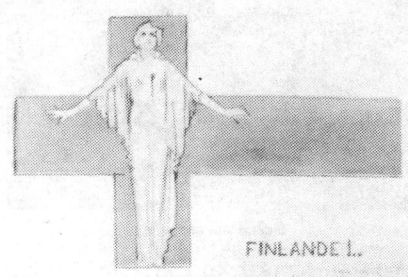

Finlande

Finlande, 1940, 21 x 14" (ILLUS.)......................... 605.00
Fountain (The), 1937, 8 x 20" 1,850.00
Gay Senorita, 1939, 21½ x 18¼" ... 525.00
Golden Veil, 1930, 20 x 15".............1,100.00 to 1,700.00
Guardians, 1936, 15" d............. 770.00
Hydrangeas, Lilacs, 1929, 21 x 17" oval 605.00
Lady of the Camelias, 1927, 21 x 17" oval ....462.00 to 600.00
Lilies, 1934, 19½ x 28" 935.00
Love's Blossom, 1937, 25 x 17"..............1,320.00 to 1,980.00
Love Seat (The) - The Sofa, 1937, 25 x 17" 3,080.00
Madame Bovary, 1929, 20 x 16" oval ....495.00 to 750.00
Masked, 1933, 8½ x 13" 605.00

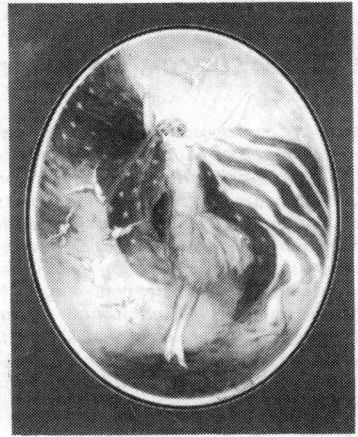

Miss America

Miss America, 1927, 13 x 20" oval (ILLUS.) 1,430.00
Miss California, 1927, 13 x 20" oval 1,750.00
Nurse, 1917, 15½ x 19½"......... 440.00
Pink Alcove, Pink Divan, 1929, 13 x 10½" oval 440.00

Scheherazade

Scheherazade, 1927, 20 × 13"
(ILLUS.)......................... 660.00
Seville, 1928, 13 × 20" 550.00
Silk Robe (The), The Silk Dress,
1926, 18½ × 15"................1,800.00
Sleeping Beauty, 1929, 19½ × 15½"
oval ....880.00 to 995.00
Spanish Dancer, 1929, 13 × 20½" ... 600.00
Speed, 1933, 25 × 15½" 1,980.00
Thais, 1927, 20 × 16"
oval ....1,540.00 to 2,420.00
Tosca, 1928, 13 × 21" cathedral 495.00
Unmasked, 1933, 8½ × 13"......... 880.00
Venus, 1928, 19½ × 14" oval 715.00
Venus in the Waves, 1931,
16 × 19"........................ 550.00
Waterfall, 1936, 8 × 20" 1,850.00
White Underwear, 1925, 19 × 15" ... 880.00
Wisteria, 1940, 21 × 17½".......... 990.00
Youth, 1930, 15½ × 24" 1,540.00

ICE CREAM SCOOPS & SERVERS

During the past decade, the ice cream scoop and ice cream server have become very popular with a growing number of collectors and prices have soared. While the nickel-plated brass scoop with a lever-operated blade that eases the ball-shaped scoop of ice cream from the server seems to be the most popular, there is also interest in the earlier cone-shaped tin scoops and in pewter or aluminum servers. Collectors can select a scoop that served up a small penny-size ice cream cone, a larger nickel-size cone, or a square slice for an ice cream sandwich.

"Arnold No. 50".................... $18.00
"Dover No. 20," old-style w/two-
way action to level off scoop,
nickel-plated brass w/wooden
handle, 10½" l.........100.00 to 170.00
"Eire Specialty," cone-shaped,
nickel-plated brass, size 6 .... 52.50
"Gem, Troy, New York," nickel-
plated brass 35.00

"Gilchrist No. 30," nickel-plated
brass, w/unusual squeeze han-
dle,, ca. 1930, 10½" l.....30.00 to 45.00
"Gilchrist No. 31," aluminum
w/wooden handle,
8½" l. ....25.00 to 38.00
"Gilchrist No. 33," cone-shaped,
nickel-plated brass w/wooden
handle ....50.00 to 85.00
"Hamilton Beach," chrome w/long
Bakelite handle ....20.00 to 32.00
"Hamilton Beach," chrome
w/wooden handle 40.00
"ICI PI" (Icy Pie) ice cream slice for
ice cream sandwiches, nickel-
plated brass w/wooden
handle ....95.00 to 175.00
"Indestructo No. 4," w/1928
patent ....20.00 to 35.00
"Kingery," cone-shaped,
1895-1908 ....135.00 to 225.00
"Medco," nickel-plated brass,
wooden handle, 2½" d. ball-
shaped scoop 35.00
"Mosteller," cone-shaped, nickel-
plated brass ....48.00 to 55.00
"Trojan No. 16," nickel-plated brass
w/wooden handle.............. 50.00
Nickel-plated brass w/squeeze-type
handle & gear, "Made in
Germany" 32.00
Tin, cone-shaped, bent wire
handle ....15.00 to 25.00
Tin, cone-shaped w/inside blade to
ease ice cream from
scoop ....20.00 to 35.00

INDIAN RELICS

Navajo Blanket

Arrowheads, black, framed, set of
250 ....$350.00

Blanket, Navajo, woven in Bayeta
yarn in shades of red, green, natural white, indigo blue & grey,
46 x 30½" (ILLUS.) 2,900.00
Blanket, Navajo, woven in German-
town wool, 2-tone & checkered ser-
rations w/pr. lozenges & arrows
either side in white, yellow, pale
pink, deep red, green & purple
w/maroon detailing on red ground,
w/multicolored yarn fringe,
76 x 46½" 2,530.00
Ceremonial necklace, Zuni, single
strand, dark brown pen shell &
turquoise heshe interspersed
w/foxes, bears & birds carved
from serpentine, coral, jet, abalone shell & mother-of-pearl 180.00
Cradleboard, Sioux, beaded hide,
stitched around the sides in yellow,
bright blue, light green & translucent red against white beaded
ground w/pattern of concentric
lozenges, terraced diamonds enclosing crosses & concentric right
triangles, bar & rectangle pattern
on the crest beaded in similar
colors, 25¼" l. 1,210.00
Headdress, Hopi, cloth, painted
w/black & white striped pattern, 2
tall cones projecting from the top
& bound at points w/dried corn-
husks, panel of black horsehair
attached to interior, 13½" h.
(used by the Koshare or Hano
Clown) 1,100.00
Magazines, Harper's Weekly, 1877,
"The Surrender of Chief Joseph,"
illustrated, set of 4 .... 60.00
Moccasins, Plains, quilled hide,
divided on front into rectangular
quadrants of yellow & shades of
deep purple quillwork enclosing
crosses in alternating colors, a
narrow strip of pale green quillwork around the fronts, 9½" l.,
pr. 1,320.00
Peace medal, bronze, obverse
w/bust of John Tyler & inscription
"John Tyler, President of the
United Sates, 1841," reverse
w/clasped hands, crossed peace
pipe, tomahawk & inscription
"Peace and Friendship," 3" d. 440.00
Peace medal, "Benjamin Harrison -
President U.S.A., 1889" obverse,
"Peace," Indian & settler reverse,
3 x 2¼" oval 750.00
Pipe, Plains, black stone bowl
carved in the form of a buffalo,
cylindrical wooden stem decorated w/brass tacks, 28½" l...... 475.00
"Possible" bag, Plains, beaded &
quilled hide, front decorated

w/linear quillwork design consisting of 3 red bands containing purple & yellow rectangles, sides &
top flap w/opaque & translucent
beading, w/fringe of tin cone
dangles & red horsehair tails,
19" l. 880.00
Rug, Navajo, Ganado area, woven
red, grey, black, orange & white
serrated & vertically stacked triangle designs, 56 x 33" 200.00
Saddle bags, double, Sioux, beaded
& fringed hide, w/slit across center
bordered by multicolored beaded
panels & triangles, side panels
each stitched w/stylized butterflies
flanked by terraced triangles in
yellow, dark blue, translucent
green & pink on a powder blue
beaded ground, 65½" l.........2,090.00
Spoon, Plains, carved horn w/details
filled in w/resin, handle wrapped
w/fine braided quill in orange,
purple & yellow, 11½" l......... 155.00

Northern Plains Beaded Vest

Vest, man's, Northern Plains, beaded cloth, decorated w/cobalt blue,
sky blue, red, green & faceted
brass beading, 1900-25, 21" l.
(ILLUS.)...................... 400.00

INVALID FEEDERS

Staffordshire Invalid Feeder

The invalid feeder is a descendent of the 18th and 19th century English silver pap boat, a low boat-shaped vessel that narrowed to a pouring lip at one end and was used to feed semi-liquid food (pap) to infants. The virtually spill-proof invalid feeder was conceived by enclosing the spout and adding a handle to the opposite end and was utilized in feeding both infants and invalids. Made in a variety of materials, including glass, Staffordshire earthenware pottery, and ironstone china, the invalid feeder is an unusual and popular collectible today.

Amethyst glass, blown, w/applied
   clear filler hole & handle, 8¼" l.
   (interior residue) $150.00
Bone china, overall floral decor, gilt
   trim, English, 5¾" l. 20.00
China, cobalt blue & red floral
   decor, gilt trim, 3 3/8" l.,
   2½" h. 40.00
China, white florals outlined in gold
   on pink lustre ground, 6 3/8 x 3",
   2¼" h. 35.00
China, blue floral decor. 25.00
China, pink & gold floral decor 45.00
Davenport china, Muleteer patt.,
   blue 195.00
Haviland china, white, ca. 1880,
   6½" l. 45.00
Haviland china, white w/embossed
   floral decor 20.00
Ironstone china, light blue transfer
   decor, 5½" l. 40.00
Ironstone, all white . . . . 5.00 to 20.00
Meissen porcelain, Blue Onion patt.,
   gilt trim, 5¾" l. . . . . 35.00 to 45.00
Pewter, bird-shaped, 5" l. 65.00
Royal Copenhagen porcelain, blue &
   white, 7¼ x 2¾", 2½" h. 45.00
Staffordshire pottery, floral decor,
   medium blue transfer, 7" l.
   (ILLUS.) 60.00

IVORY

Also see FANS, SEWING ADJUNCTS and STANHOPES.

Centerpiece, carved in high relief
   depicting a basket of flowering
   prunus & peony, twig handle attached to a loose ring chain suspended from a stand carved as a
   writhing dragon, 14" h. $660.00
Figure of a scholar, seated w/hand
   resting on raised knee, Chinese,
   Ming Dynasty, 3 7/8" h.
   (ILLUS.) 4,070.00

Carved Ivory Figure of a Scholar

Figure of a cavalier, wearing loose
   trousers & plumed hat & playing a
   trumpet, on ivory socle, Continental, probably Dieppe, late 19th c.,
   7¼" h. 550.00
Figure group, Kuan Yin seated &
   holding a small child on her lap,
   dressed in long cowled robes
   w/etched floral borders & holding
   a prayer bead in one hand,
   Chinese, 19th c., 7 1/8" h. 770.00

Carved Ivory Figure Group

Figure group, The Three Graces,
   after Antonio Canova, raised on
   molded ivory socle, enclosed
   w/glass dome on a wooden base,
   cracks to ivory & glass dome, late
   19th c., 9¼" h. (ILLUS.) 2,200.00
Jar, cov., ovoid, carved in high
   relief w/battle scenes below
   waisted neck carved w/figures at
   leisure separated by monster
   mask loose ring handles, high

cover carved w/finial depicting a warrior beside a prancing horse, 19th c., 18" h. 1,100.00

Models of Buddhistic lions, each seated on its haunches, one w/paw on a cub, other w/paw on a ball, each on high, waisted rectangular plinths, 12" h., pr. 1,100.00

Table screen, carved in relief one side w/monk & attendant standing in the courtyard of a pavilion awaiting the arrival of a deity riding on a white crane, reverse w/flowering plum tree, bamboo blossoms & ornate butterflies, stand w/four cabriole legs joined by a foliate scroll below a pierced frieze, Chinese, 18th c., 10 5/8" h.....................1,320.00

Table screen, carved w/scene of a gentleman beside his horse blowing his horn in the woods, castle in the distance, within scrolled & mask-carved border, raised on turned standard ending in scrolled feet headed by animal masks, Continental, late 19th-early 20th c., 17" h.............1,100.00

Tankard, sides carved w/amoretti playing war, 2 riding goats, mounted in silver, lid marked by Heinrich Georg Kock & engraved w/armorial device, German, 18th c., 9¾" h. 2,860.00

Tusk, curved body carved & undercut w/figures of dignitaries & warriors traveling along a mountain path, 19th c., 22½" l. 990.00

JEWELRY (Victorian)

Gold Bangle Bracelet

Bar pin, 18k gold, enameled "en grisaille" w/cupid center, 2" l. ...$275.00

Bar pin, jet w/seed pearl floral sprays 195.00

Bracelet, bangle-type, gold, bright-cut engraving & initials (ILLUS.) ... 200.00

Bracelet, bangle-type, sterling silver oval tubular style, engraved, ca. 1900 .... 75.00

Bracelet, sterling silver, styled in the Eastern taste, Shiebler Silver Co., 1890-1900 .... 60.00

Brooch, carnelian cameo in 18k gold mount, 1¾" l. 245.00

Cameo Brooch

Brooch, cameo, carved shell, 14k gold frame, now fitted w/swivel to wear as pendant, 2" oval (ILLUS.)......................... 275.00

Brooch, ivory, carved in the form of a hand w/lacy cuff, 2" 65.00

Cuff links, gold, oval convex panels connected by an oblong link, engraved w/italic script monogram within bright-cut border, late 18th c., pr. 715.00

Earrings, sardonyx cameo in textured 2-tone gold mount, 1¼" l. drop, pr. 225.00

Hair comb, coin silver, Spanish type w/engraved convex top, marked Pure Silver Coin, 4¾ x 2" 95.00

Locket, 14k gold set w/four diamonds, ca. 1865................. 175.00

Mourning bracelet, braided human hair w/gold-filled fittings, locket-type inset w/hinged top opening to reveal lock of hair 45.00

Mourning locket, jet w/cluster of embossed roses & "In Memory," picture of young boy & lock of braided hair interior............. 250.00

Mourning pin, spray of jet forget-me-nots & leaves, pink gold stems, 1 5/8" 28.00

Mourning pin, yellow gold w/lock of blonde hair under beveled glass, black enamel border, intricate filigree frame, 1¼ x 1" 65.00

Necklace, amber (cherry red) graduated facet-cut beads, 23" l. 160.00

Necklace, pink angel skin coral beads w/carved floral drop, 16" l. 65.00

Necklace, 14k gold, rope chain,
24" l. 390.00
Necklace, creamy white cultured
pearls, 14k green gold clasp
w/cultured pearl surrounded by 5
prong-set sapphires 310.00
Necklace, green Peking glass beads,
20" l. 45.00
Necklace, rose quartz beads alternating w/small 14k gold beads ... 110.00
Necklace, sterling silver set w/lapis
lazuli 350.00
Pendant, 10k gold, Tiffany-type
prong-set miner-cut diamond
w/pearl drop, 1 7/8" l. 142.00
Pin, gold, owl w/diamond eyes sitting on branch, 1 3/8" l. 750.00
Pin, 14k gold, set w/cabochon
amethyst 135.00
Pin, 22k gold, central pearl surrounded by 4 garnets 175.00
Ring, friendship-type, 9k gold, narrow tapered band w/two clasped
hands 33.00
Ring, girl's, 9k gold, prong-set oval
amethyst, carved scrolls at
sides 58.00
Ring, lady's, 9k gold, emerald center surrounded by 8 prong-set
garnets, carved sides 299.00
Ring, lady's, 9k gold, crescent shape
set w/garnets 60.00
Ring, lady's, 9k gold, ruby center
w/sapphire either side, carved
double hearts at sides 127.00
Ring, lady's, 9k gold, prong-set sapphire in deeply carved floral
center 292.00
Ring, lady's, 9k gold, coiled snake
w/ruby eyes & sapphire in
head 195.00
Ring, lady's, 9k gold, bezel-set garnet, love knot sides 85.00
Ring, lady's, 9k rose gold, 3 prong-
set seed pearls w/sapphire either
side, wide scroll-carved band 170.00
Ring, lady's, 10k gold, band set
w/marquise-cut green
tourmaline 39.00
Ring, lady's, 14k gold, bezel-set
cameo-carved coral within ivy leaf
border 240.00
Ring, lady's, 14k gold, double coiled
snake w/ruby eyes 110.00

Man's Gold Ring

Ring, man's, 14k gold, 8-prong set
sapphire, ca. 1890
(ILLUS.) .... 150.00 to 200.00
Watch chain, lady's, gold-filled, slide
w/opal one side & pearl reverse,
50" l. 135.00
Watch chain, lady's, gold-filled,
w/four hand-set opals on slide ... 85.00
Watch chain, lady's, gold-filled, ruby
w/opal either side & surrounded
by circle of 10 seed pearls on
slide 70.00
Watch chain, lady's, braided human
hair, slide set w/garnet & seed
pearls 75.00
Watch chain, man's, 14k gold,
ornate links, 18" l. ...... 180.00 to 215.00
Watch chain, man's, 18k gold, rope
chain, 32" l. 475.00
Watch chain, man's, braided human
hair w/gold-filled
fittings .... 30.00 to 45.00
Watch chain slide, 14k gold, shield-
shaped, engraved, 7/16" 73.00
Watch chain slide, 14k gold, shield-
shaped, turquoise in carved starburst center, ½" 111.00

KEWPIE COLLECTIBLES

Bisque Kewpie "Thinker"

*Rose O'Neill's Kewpies were so popular in
their heyday that numerous objects depicting them were produced and are now collectible. The following represents a sampling.*

Booklet, "Jell-O & the Kewpies,"
1915 .... $25.00
Bottle, clear glass, figural Kewpie,
2½" h. 20.00
Bowl, china, 7 action Kewpies,
signed Rose O'Neill, Royal Rudolstadt, Prussia, 8" d. 150.00
Cake decoration, celluloid, Kewpie

bride & groom, signed Rose O'Neill, pr. 50.00

Clock, jasper ware case, dome-top, white relief action Kewpies on green, signed Rose O'Neill 550.00

Creamer, jasper ware, 7 white relief action Kewpies on blue, signed ... 165.00

Door knocker, brass, figural Kewpie, 3" h. 110.00

Figures, Kewpie bride & groom, celluloid, signed O'Neill, 3¾" h., pr. 70.00

Figures, Kewpie boy & girl in graduation attire, celluloid, 4" h., pr. .. 100.00

Figure, Kewpie Indian, bisque, 4½" h. 385.00

Figure, Kewpie "Thinker," bisque, 5½" h. (ILLUS.) 325.00

Figure, Kewpie bride in original dress, composition, paper labels, 9" h. 135.00

Flannel square, "Kick Frog," pink background, signed & dated 1914, 5 x 7" 17.00

Handkerchief, white silk w/pink satin border, transfer of Kewpie bride & groom standing beside car, Kewpie soldier & Kewpie farmer, ca. 1910 .... 35.00

Mug, china, 2 action Kewpies on green lustre ground, signed Rose O'Neill Wilson, Kewpie, Germany, 2½" h. 65.00

Perfume bottle, porcelain, figural Kewpie, Germany 38.00

Plate, 3 action Kewpies on green lustre ground, signed Rose O'Neill, Kewpie, Germany, 5½" d. 65.00

Postcard, "Tis Xmas, Dear" 32.00

Postcard, Santa Claus & 14 Kewpies, signed Rose O'Neill 35.00

Soap, figural Kewpie, original box 145.00

Teapot, cov., china, action Kewpies on pink lustre ground 180.00

Teaspoon, sterling silver, Kewpie handle 85.00

Tea towel, linen, stamped for embroidery, 3 action Kewpies on border & "He Loves Me, Kewpie" 50.00

Toothpick holder, pewter, Kewpie beside basket holder 59.00

Tray, cloverleaf form, jasper ware, pink relief action Kewpies on green, signed Rose O'Neill, Royal Rudolstadt, 7" .... 275.00 to 335.00

Vase, 6½" h., jasper ware, white relief action Kewpies on green, signed Rose O'Neill 550.00

KITCHENWARES

Stove-Top Toaster

Also see ADVERTISING ITEMS, BASKETS, BOTTLE OPENERS, BOTTLES & FLASKS, BUTTER MOLDS & STAMPS, CANS & CONTAINERS, CASTORS & CASTOR SETS, CERAMICS, CHARACTER COLLECTIBLES, CLOCKS, COFFEE GRINDERS, COOKBOOKS, COOKIE CUTTERS, CORKSCREWS, FIREPLACE & HEARTH ACCESSORIES, FOOD, CANDY & MISC. MOLDS, FRUIT JARS, FURNITURE (cabinets & ice boxes), GLASS, GRANITEWARE, ICE CREAM SCOOPS, METALS, MOTHER-OF-PEARL HANDLED FLATWARE, NUTCRACKERS, ROYCROFT ITEMS, SCALES, SHAKER COLLECTIBLES, STRING HOLDERS, TRAYS, WOODENWARES and WORLD FAIR COLLECTIBLES.

Apple corer, tin, tubular T-shaped handle $13.00

Apple parer, cast iron, "Bonanza, Goodell Co., Antrim, New Hampshire," 16" l. 80.00

Apple parer, cast iron, 4-gear, "Reading Hardware Co., Reading, Pennsylvania," 1878 first patent date 50.00

Apple parer, cast iron, 7-gear, "Sinclair Scott Co.," 1868 patent 60.00

Bean slicer, cast iron, marked "Germany" 24.00

Bowl, utilitarian crockery, Apricot patt., yellow & green, 5½" d. 40.00

Bowl, utilitarian crockery, Wedding Ring patt., blue & white, 5½" d... 55.00

Bowl, utilitarian crockery, Flying Bird patt., blue & white, 8" d. 70.00

Bread box, tin, original blue paint, 19½ x 13½" 90.00

Bread (dough) mixer, "Universal No. 4, Landers, Frary & Clark, New Britain, Connecticut," tin bucket shape w/crank handle in lid, 1910-20 .... 25.00 to 30.00

Bread toaster, stove-top model, tin, pyramid style, 6" sq. base, 5" h. (ILLUS.) 15.00

Cylinder Churn

Butter churn, cylinder crank-type, wooden staves w/iron hoop bandings, late 19th c., 25" h. (ILLUS.) .. 195.00

Butter churn, pine floor model, U-shaped tub w/tin liner & lift-up lid, sides w/cut-out feet, cast iron crank w/wooden handle grip & wooden paddle blades, worn blue paint, 13 x 13", 31½" h. 190.00

Butter churn, cylinder floor model, wooden stave construction, tin lid, iron crank, original cream-colored paint w/stenciled label "The Blanchard Churn, Patented June 4, 1878, Concord, N.H.," 19 x 15¾", 32½" h. 180.00

Butter churn, wooden floor model w/dasher, stave construction, 19th c., 35" h. ....165.00 to 250.00

Butter crock w/lid & bail handle, utilitarian crockery, Basketweave & Daisy patt., blue & white 115.00

Butter crock w/lid & bail handle, utilitarian crockery, Block patt., blue & white................... 145.00

Butter crock w/lid, utilitarian crockery, Scroll patt., blue & white 92.50

Butter crock w/lid, utilitarian crockery, Waffle patt., blue & white ... 160.00

Butter crock w/lid, utilitarian crockery, Wildflower patt., blue & white 145.00

Cabbage (or slaw) cutting board, applied edge molding & chip-carved designs at bottom edge & crest, worn old red paint, 6¾" w., 18¼" l. 75.00

Cabbage (or slaw) cutting board, pine, 1-blade, cut-out heart design in crest & chip-carved decor, worn old red paint, early 19th c., 7" w., 21½" l. 350.00

Cabbage cutting board, walnut, applied molding at edge, rounded crest for hanging, 7" w., 21" l. ....25.00 to 40.00

Cabbage (or kraut) stomper, wooden w/some burl, whittled handle, 36" l. 35.00

Candy thermometer, "Moeller Instrument Co.," in copper case 65.00

Canister, cov., china, barrel-shaped, "Oatmeal," Blue Onion patt., marked "Germany," 6½" h. 55.00

Canister, cov., yellowware, "Beans" 85.00

Canister, emerald green transparent glass, embossed "Sugar," metal screw-on lid, 1930's, 7¼" h. 20.00

Can opener, cast iron ram's head end, wooden handle............ 28.00

Carpet beater, bent iron wire loop w/heart shapes center, wooden handle 29.00

Cauldron, cast iron, 3-legged, iron wire bail handle, 5" d., 4" h. 65.00

Charcoal iron, cast iron, w/woman's head finial & cast w/ornate scrollwork & designs of wolf & children, probably Scandinavian origins 75.00

Cherry pitter, cast iron, "Enterprise No. 1," 12" h.................... 25.00

Cherry pitter, cast iron, "Enterprise No. 16" 22.50

Cherry pitter, cast iron, double action, "Home Cherry Stoner," pat'd 1917, table clamp-on model 27.50

Chopping bowl, hand-hewn wooden oblong w/shaped handles at rim, painted dark green exterior, 24" l. 165.00

Coffee pot, cov., tin, straight spout, off-center handle, 11½" h. 55.00

Early Tin Colander

Colander, tin, footed, strap handles at sides, 13½" d. (ILLUS.) 22.50

Cornstick pan, cast iron, "Krusty Korn Kobs, Jr., Wagner Ware, Sidney, Ohio, Pat'd, July 6, 1920," 8½ x 4¼"..................... 30.00

Cornstick pan, cast iron, 7-ear, "Griswold Crispy Cornsticks, No. 273" 25.00

Cornstick pan, cast iron, "Griswold No. 262," miniature 60.00

Cream top spoon, tin, ca.
1925 ....8.00 to 15.00
Cream whip, cov., tin, cast iron &
wood, "Fries," ca. 1890, 6" l.,
4½" w., 8" h.............48.00 to 65.00
Croquette mold (cone-shaped mold
used for shaping chicken or ham),
tin, ca. 1880 .... 18.00

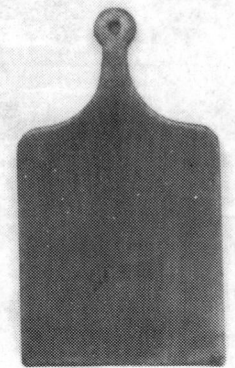

Cutting Board

Cutting board, lollipop handle, early
19th c., 10" w., overall 18½" l.
(ILLUS.)......................... 85.00
Deep fry "bird's nest" basket, tinned
wire nested baskets, 4" d. outer
basket, ca. 1935 .... 20.00
Dipper, brass bowl w/wrought iron
handle & simple hanging hook,
17" to 20" l., each........55.00 to 90.00
Dish cover (fly cover), domed wire
screen, 9½" to 10½" d.,
each ....30.00 to 40.00
Dough box on stand, pine, oblong
1-board top w/breadboard ends,
dough trough w/square corner
posts mortised & pinned through
sides continuing to form legs,
traces of old worn blue paint,
37 x 22½", 27¾" h. 500.00
Dough box on stand, pine, lift-off
lid, canted & dovetailed dough
trough on stand w/turned splayed
poplar legs, 38½ x 21" box on
stand 350.00
Dough box on stand, walnut,
1-board lid w/breadboard ends,
dovetailed canted dough trough
on ring- and baluster-turned legs,
36 x 16" box, overall 31" h. 295.00
Dough scraper, steel blade w/short
hollow copper handle, 18th c. 95.00
Dough scraper, wrought iron, 19th
c., 3" w., 3¾" l. 23.00
Dough scraper, wrought iron
w/turned wood handle & brass
ferrule, 18th c.................. 40.00
Doughnut cutter, tin 6.50

Doughnut cutter, tin, rolling-type ... 27.50
Doughnut cutter, wooden w/elon-
gated knob handle 85.00
Doughnut & pastry cutter, handled,
tin & wire, ca. 1890, 3" d.,
6½" l. 15.00
Drying rack, wooden, "The Easy
Clothestree," 3-tier w/folding
arms on tripod base, worn origi-
nal white paint w/partial decal,
67¾" h........................ 65.00
Dust pan, tin, hand-seamed 20.00
Egg basket, wire, tulip-shaped 28.00
Egg boiling rack, wire, 6 revolving
compartments, early 1900's 20.00
Egg poacher, 3-egg, cast iron & tin,
"S. & Co., N.Y., Nov. 2, 1885" 30.00
Egg poacher, 6-egg, tin & wire,
"Kreamer Mfg. Co.,"
1880's ....25.00 to 45.00
Egg scale, red-painted sheet metal,
"Jiffy Way," ca. 1940 .... 14.00
Eggbeater, iron & wire, "A & J" (Ed-
ward Katzinger Company), 1923
patent ....7.00 to 10.00
Eggbeater, cast iron & tin, "Dover,"
1880's to early 1900's,
12½" l. ....15.00 to 25.00
Eggbeater, cast iron & tin, "Holt's,"
ca. 1900 ....15.00 to 25.00
Eggbeater, chromed steel w/green
wooden handle, "Ladd Ball Bearing," 1920's 7.50

Taplin Eggbeater

Eggbeater, "Taplin Light Running,"
ca. 1908 (ILLUS.) 12.00
Flatware: 6 knives & 6 forks; steel
w/pewter-inlaid ebony handles,
marked "J. Russell & Co.,"
12 pcs. 80.00
Fluting iron, cast iron, "Crown"..... 35.00
Fluting iron, cast iron, "Eclipse -
American Machine Co., Philadel-
phia, Pat'd 1875 & 1880," table
clamp-on model w/slugs 85.00
Fluting iron, cast iron, "Geneva
Hand Fluter," dated 1866 or 1871,
2 pcs....................60.00 to 75.00
Fluting iron, cast iron, "Magic" 65.00
Fluting iron, cast iron, "Mrs. Knox's
Fluting Machine, w/gilt stenciling,
"Every Lady Should Have One,"
1866 .... 145.00

Fluting iron, cast iron, "Shepherd
Hardware," 1880's patent 100.00
Food chopper, wrought steel continuous U-shaped blade fitted
w/wooden handle, 4¾" w. 75.00
Food chopper, crescent-shaped steel
blade marked "B. Denton, Patent,
Auburn, N.Y.," wooden handle,
6 3/8" w......................... 25.00
Food chopper, crescent-shaped steel
blade, wooden handle, 8" l....... 15.00
Food chopper, crescent-shaped steel
blade, turned wooden handle,
10¾" l. 22.50
Food grinder, cast iron, "Enterprise," 1888 ....15.00 to 25.00
Food grinder, "Griswold No. 1110".. 35.00
Food grinder, "Keen Kutter," 1906 .. 20.00
Fruit (or berry) crushing press, cast
iron, "Enterprise Mfg. Co.," crank
handle & auger-type worm
through cone, 1880's............ 50.00
Fruit jar holder, wire 7.00

Blue Onion Pattern Funnel

Funnel, china, Blue Onion patt.,
4" h. (ILLUS.) 29.00
Funnel, copper.................... 24.00
Funnel, copper, w/mechanical
strainer 42.50
Funnel for fruit jar, tin, 1897 .... 12.00
Garlic press, hand-carved cherry-
wood, 2 hinged sections 75.00
Gas iron, blue graniteware,
"Coleman"...................... 38.50
Gas iron, "Diamond Kero" 48.00
Gas iron, "The Monitor" 22.00
Gas iron, "Strause Gas Iron Co.,
Philadelphia" 45.00
Goffering iron, brass barrel rests on
S-shaped wrought iron stand (no
rod)........................... 125.00
Grater, hand-punched tin on hand-
hewn wooden frame, 8½" to
10½" l., each............45.00 to 65.00
Grater, table clamp-on model, tin &
iron, "Lorraine," green 16.00

Ice cream maker, child's, "Peerless
Iceland Freezer Co.," ca. 1900,
5" d., 6¼" h. 125.00
Juice reamer, clear glass, ribbed ... 5.00
Juice reamer, green opalescent
glass, "Sunkist" 100.00

"Sunkist" Juice Reamer

Juice reamer, milk white glass,
"Sunkist" (ILLUS.)............... 20.00
Kettle pourer, tin, pat'd. May 12,
1898, 10" w., 16" l.............. 29.00
Knife scouring box, wooden,
19th c. 75.00
Ladle, hammered brass bowl
w/wrought iron handle, 15" to
18" l., each ....75.00 to 95.00
Lady finger pan, 6-compartment,
sheet tin, 19th c., 9½ x 4½" 35.00
Lady finger pan, 6-compartment, tin,
"Kreamer," early 20th c. 20.00
Lady finger pan, 12-compartment,
tin, 9¼" sq. 20.00
Lefse roller (corrugated wooden roll-
ing pin) ....25.00 to 45.00
Lemon squeezer, cast iron, "Arcade
No. 2" 38.00
Lemon squeezer, cast iron, hinged,
"Landers, Frary & Clark," 2-part .. 18.00
Lemon squeezer, cast iron,
"Townsend" 29.00
Lemon squeezer, cast iron,
"Universal".................... 10.00
Lemon squeezer, cast iron w/iron-
stone insert, "The Arcade" 26.00
Lemon squeezer, cast iron
w/wooden insert, "Pearl,"
8" l. 20.00
Lemon squeezer, maple, hinged,
2-part, 1870-80, 10¾" l.....35.00 to 45.00
Liquid measure, tin, 1-qt. 12.00
Liquid measure, copper, flaring
sides, hay stack form, block-
braced handle, 2-qt. 85.00
Mangling board, horse handle
w/remnants of black paint &
carved initials "AMRED," "AO" &
date "1801," trapezoidal board
w/floral urn, fan & chip carving,
Scandinavian, early 19th c.,
22" l. 412.50
Measuring cup, green "Jadite"
glass, pressed sunflower in bottom, "Jeanette," 2-cup.......... 15.00
Meat cleaver, "Keen Kutter" 30.00

Meat fork, wrought iron, 2-tine,
shaped handle, 16¼" l........... 12.50

Meat juice press, cast iron, "Columbia," late 19th c. 35.00

Meat tenderizer, cast iron, 7½" l. ... 13.00

Meat tenderizer, cast iron head
dated "Oct. 1892," wooden handle, 10" l. 20.00

Meat tenderizer, stoneware head,
wooden handle, w/patent date of
Dec. 25, 1877 .... 65.00

Meat tenderizer, yellowware head,
oak handle, dated Dec. 1877 ..... 45.00

Muffin pan, cast iron, scroll handles,
8-compartment, 4 fruit (pear & apple) & 4 vegetable (beet & squash)
molds, 13 x 8" 195.00

Muffin pan, cast iron, 6-cup,
"Griswold" 25.00

Muffin pan, cast iron, 11 oval cups.. 19.00

Muffin pan, cast iron, 12-cup, handled, "Griswold" ....30.00 to 40.00

Muffin Tin

Muffin pan, tin, 6-cup (ILLUS.) 10.00

Muffin pan, tin, 24-cup, "Lockwood,"
17 x 11½" 12.00

Noodle cutter, table clamp-on
model, cast iron, marked
"Germany" 85.00

Nutmeg grater, cast iron round disc
w/hinged cover & black wooden
handle center 65.00

Nutmeg grater, punched tin w/slid-
ing wooden barrel 130.00

Nutmeg grater w/hinged lid,
punched tin, cylindrical pocket-
style w/fold-out side, 3" h....... 120.00

Nutmeg grater, punched tin, pocket-
style, japanned finish........... 95.00

Nutmeg grater, punched tin,
w/crank & spring plunger, "Pat
Sep 4, 1877," 4½" h. 130.00

Nutmeg grater, tin, wire & wood,
"Edgar, pat'd Aug. 18, 1891,"
5¼" w., 5 7/8" l. 85.00

Oven peel, wrought iron, heart-
shaped blade, handle w/ram's
head curls, 18th c., 33" l. 125.00

Pan, copper, hand-hammered, brass
ring handle, 11" d., 1½" h.
(ILLUS.)........................ 95.00

Copper Pan

Pastry (or bread) board, tin, w/slot
for wooden rolling pin, 22 x 22"
board, 2 pcs. 155.00

Pastry stamp, cast iron, basket of
flowers, ½" thick, 5" l. 65.00

Pastry stamp, cast iron, cornucopia
of fruit, ½" thick, 5" l. 65.00

Pastry wheel, brass wheel & handle,
4 3/8" l...................... 10.00

Pastry wheel, brass, wheel at each
end, 4½" l..................... 20.00

Pastry wheel, blue & white porcelain wheel, turned wood handle, 6¾" l. 125.00

Peach peeler, cast iron, 3-gear,
heart design, "Sinclair Scott Co.,
Baltimore"................45.00 to 65.00

Pickle scoop, glass w/wooden
handle 24.00

Pitcher, utilitarian crockery, Apricot
patt., blue & white 125.00

Pitcher, utilitarian crockery, Banded
Scroll patt., blue & white 115.00

Pitcher, utilitarian crockery, Basketweave patt., blue & white 165.00

Pitcher, utilitarian crockery, Cherry
Band patt., blue & white,
8½" h......................... 135.00

Pitcher, utilitarian crockery, Daisy
patt., blue & white 245.00

Pitcher, utilitarian crockery, Deer
with Fawn patt., blue & white,
8¼" h. 145.00

Pitcher, utilitarian crockery, Grape
patt., blue & white 110.00

Pitcher, utilitarian crockery, Indian
Head patt., blue & white........ 190.00

Pitcher, utilitarian crockery, Wildflower patt., blue & white........ 125.00

Pitcher, utilitarian crockery, Windmill & Bush patt., blue & white ... 130.00

Poppyseed grinder, spun brass,
turquoise-painted cast iron &
wood, ca. 1890, 9¼" l. 35.00

Potato baking rack, tin, ca. 1900,
 2 1/8" w., 15¼" l. 25.00
Potato masher, cast iron 17.00
Raisin seeder, cast iron, "Enter-
 prise," 1890's 30.00
Raisin seeder, cast iron, "The Gem,"
 table model, 1895 .... 33.50
Rice ball, wire mesh, hinged,
 5½" d. 19.00
Roaster, cov., utilitarian crockery,
 Flying Bird patt., blue & white 160.00
Rolling pin, blown glass, amber,
 14" l. ....95.00 to 140.00
Rolling pin, blown glass, amethyst .. 95.00
Rolling pin, blown glass, Camphor
 large 60.00
Rolling pin, blown Nailsea-type
 glass, blue loops on white,
 14" l. 118.00
Rolling pin, china, Blue Onion patt.
 transfer, wooden handles 145.00
Rolling pin, pressed glass, clear,
 w/metal screw-on end cap 11.00
Rolling pin, pressed glass, clear
 w/maple handles, Cambridge
 Glass Co., dated 1921 .... 45.00
Rolling pin, pressed glass, milk
 white w/wooden handles, Imperial Mfg. Co. ....40.00 to 65.00
Rolling pin, cherrywood, 1-piece
 w/elongated knob handles,
 18½" l. 20.00

Curly Maple Rolling Pin

Rolling pin, curly maple, painted
 wooden handles (ILLUS.) 55.00
Rolling pin, curly maple, 1-piece
 w/bulbous-turned handles,
 17¼" l. 95.00
Rolling pin, maple, mule-earred
 handles 32.00
Rolling pin, walnut, wooden peg
 handles, 21" l. 85.00
Sad iron, cast iron, primitive,
 5½" l. 17.50
Sad iron, cast iron, removable
 wooden handle, 6½" l. .....15.00 to 25.00
Sad iron, cast iron, "Sensible
 No. 1" 24.00
Salt box, wooden 85.00
Salt crock, wall-type, utilitarian
 crockery, Apple Blossom patt.,
 blue & white................... 135.00
Salt crock, wall-type, utilitarian
 crockery, Blackberry patt., blue &
 white 120.00
Salt crock, wall-type, utilitarian

crockery, Butterfly patt., blue &
 white 130.00
Salt crock, wall-type, utilitarian
 crockery, Grape patt., blue &
 white 65.00
Salt crock, wall-type, utilitarian
 crockery, Peacock patt., blue &
 white 200.00
Sauce pan, copper w/hand-forged
 iron handle, dovetailed, 2-qt. 130.00
Sauce pan w/handle, cast iron,
 "Griswold" 16.00
Sausage grinder, cast iron, dated
 March, 1859 .... 55.00
Sausage stuffer, pewter, w/wooden
 plunger 25.00

Tin Skimmer & Scoop

Scoop, tin, tubular handle (ILLUS.
 right) 12.00
Scrub board, wooden frame w/glass
 corrugated insert, "Good
 Housekeeper" 22.00
Scrub board, wooden frame w/mot-
 tled blue graniteware corrugated
 insert 32.00
Scrub board, wooden frame w/tin
 corrugated insert, "Scanti Handi,"
 small 6.00
Skimmer, pierced brass bowl & well-
 shaped wrought iron handle
 w/hook end ....65.00 to 145.00
Skimmer, tin, 10½" l. (ILLUS. left) .. 15.00
Skimmer, wooden, primitive pierced
 bowl, naturally crooked handle
 w/hanging ring, 31" l. 80.00
Sleeve iron, detachable handle,
 1890's 30.00

Soap Saver

Soap saver, "Androck" (ILLUS.) 10.00
Spoon, carved cherrywood, round
  bowl, shaped handle, 18th c...... 85.00
Springerle roller, carved wood,
  pinned in wooden yoke, daisy
  design, mid-19th c. 150.00
Strawberry huller, tin, ca. 1900 ..... 8.00
Sugar nippers (or cutter), cast iron,
  ca. 1830 .... 40.00
Sugar nippers, hand-wrought steel,
  polished, good form, 7¾" l....... 70.00

Tailor's Iron

Tailor's iron, twisted handle, 12-lb.
  (ILLUS.)....................... 38.00
Tallow skimmer, cast iron.......... 24.00
"Taster" spoon, brass bowl & well-
  shaped wrought iron handle,
  5 7/8" l....................... 285.00
"Taster" spoon, wrought iron,
  shaped bowl & tooled handle,
  dated "1835".................... 550.00
Tea steeper, cov., tin............. 25.00
Vinegar barrel pump, wooden...... 35.00
Wash boiler, copper, w/tin lid &
  wooden handles ....75.00 to 95.00
Wash boiler, tin w/copper bottom,
  tin lid & wooden handles 30.00

KNIVES

Advertising Pocket Knife

*Also see ADVERTISING ITEMS, ART
NOUVEAU, BOY SCOUT ITEMS and
STANHOPES.*

Advertising, "Franklin Fire Ins. Co.,"
  1-blade pocket knife, silverplate .. $77.00
Advertising, "Frisco Lines," Remington pocket knife 60.00
Advertising, "The Travelers Insurance Co.," full-length passenger
  train reverse, nickel silver
  (ILLUS.)....................... 75.00
Case XX U.S.A. 1-blade "Sod

Buster" pocket knife, black com-
  position handle, 1967-70,
  No. 2138, 5 5/8" l. closed 25.00
Case Tested XX 1-blade pocket
  knife, stag handle, pre-1940,
  No. 5165, 5½" l. closed.......... 125.00
Case XX U.S.A. 2-blade pocket
  knife, bone handle, 1965-70,
  No. 6249, 3 15/16" l. closed 50.00
Case XX 3-blade pocket knife, stag
  handle, 1950-65, No. 5383, 3½" l.
  closed........................ 60.00
Case XX 3-blade pocket knife, bone
  handle, 1960-65, No. 6344, 3¼" l.
  closed........................ 32.00
Case Tested XX 3-blade pocket
  knife, pearl handle, stainless steel
  blades, pre-1950, No. 83088SS,
  3 1/8" l. closed 125.00
Coin silver 1-blade pocket knife,
  fruit-filled cornucopia in high
  relief on handle, 3¼" l.
  closed........................ 55.00
Fleam (lancet) knife, 2-blade, in
  leather case 48.00
Fleam (lancet) knife, 3-blade, in
  brass case 45.00
Ka-Bar 3-blade pocket knife, bone
  handle, w/dog's head emblem ... 400.00
Keen Kutter pocket knife,
  No. K209 .... 40.00
Kutmaster, Girl Scout knife 9.00
Remington 1-blade "Barlow" pocket
  knife, buffalo horn handle,
  No. R1240, 5" l. closed.......... 150.00
Remington pocket knife, pyremite
  handle, No. R2295 .... 50.00
Remington 3-blade "Stockman"
  pocket knife, pyremite handle,
  No. 3565, 4" l. closed........... 97.50
Remington 2-blade pocket knife,
  bone handle, bullet shield,
  No. R4353, 4¼" l. closed........ 850.00
Remington pocket knife, bone han-
  dle, No. 6673 .... 85.00
Remington 2-blade pocket knife
  w/bail, pearl handle, No. 6904,
  2½" l. closed 23.00
Silver 1-blade pocket knife, cornucopia, scrolling leaves in relief on
  handle, Albert Coles, English hallmark, 5 7/8" l. closed 38.00
Sterling silver 2-blade pocket knife,
  Gorham Silver Co. 85.00
Valley Forge Cut. Co. 2-blade
  pocket knife, nickel silver
  handle 250.00
Wadsworth pocket knife, mother-of-
  pearl handle 10.00
Winchester 2-blade pocket knife,
  stag handle, No. 2980, 3 5/8" l. .. 80.00

LIGHTING DEVICES

Also see CANDLESTICKS & CANDLE HOLDERS, FAIRY LAMPS, CARNIVAL & PATTERN GLASS.

CHANDELIERS

18th Century Candle Chandelier

Candle chandelier, brass, 6-light, baluster-turned shaft set w/six scrolling candle arms w/dished drip pans & slender baluster-form nozzles, early 18th c., 19" h. (ILLUS.) $2,475.00

Candle chandelier, brass, 3-light, ring-turned shaft set w/three scrolling candle arms w/molded drip pans above ball & teardrop pendant, 20th c., 22½" h. 1,100.00

Candle chandelier, brass, 3-tier, 24-light, graduated ball & sphere-turned shaft set w/three tiers of 8 scrolling candle arms each, 19th c., 47" d., 51½" h. 5,500.00

Craftsman Chandelier by Stickley

Chandelier, copper & glass, hammered copper frame & domed top set w/sixteen amber glass square panels extending down sides, suspended on heavy chain, stamped "The Craftsman Workshop, Gustav Stickley," 20¼" d., 20¼" h. without chain (ILLUS.) ...6,875.00

Chandelier shade, Galle' signed cameo glass, carved sapphire blue & purple pendant plum branches against yellow ground, original rods & ceiling cap, 15 5/8" d. 2,860.00

Chandelier shade, Galle' signed cameo glass, carved sapphire blue & purple daisies against bright yellow ground, original black-painted metal mount & ceiling cap, 21 3/8" d. 7,150.00

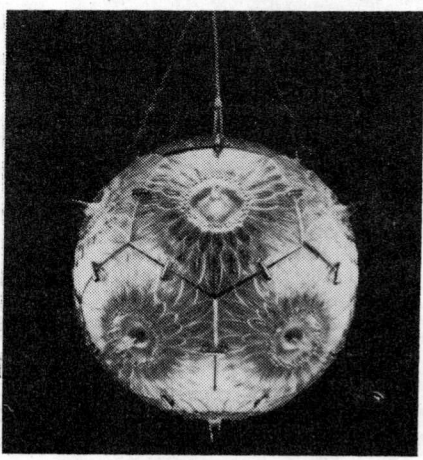

Lalique "Sunflower" Chandelier

Chandelier shade, Lalique signed, brown-stained frosted glass in Sunflower patt., pentagonal sections molded w/large sunflower in each, 19½" d. (ILLUS.) 5,500.00

Chandelier shade, Tiffany signed leaded glass "Nasturtium" patt. octagonal shade, profusion of deeply mottled yellow, orange & burgundy trellised blossoms & green leaves on streaked turquoise blue & sky green ground, 25" d. (no chains) 7,700.00

Chandelier shade, Tiffany signed leaded glass "Trumpet Creeper" patt. conical shade, brightly mottled orange flower clusters pendant from brown branches amidst green leaves on textured pale blue ground, original sockets, rod & chains, 29" d............18,700.00

Chandelier shade, Tiffany signed

leaded glass "Black-Eyed Susan"
patt. conical shade, overall Black-
Eye Susan's amidst green leaves
on sage green shaded to opaque
white ground, 29" d. (replaced
sockets & chains) 12,100.00

LAMPS, MISCELLANEOUS

Argand Lamps

Argand lamps, single, black finish
metal fluid chamber on base
w/lateral arm supporting burner &
frosted & cut glass pyriform
shade, w/clear prisms, labeled
"Messenger & Sons, London & Birmingham, Manufactured for
Jones, Lows & Ball, Boston," 1839,
12½" h., pr. (now electrified) 715.00
Argand lamps, single, gilt-metal
urn-shaped fluid chamber
w/Greek Key decor on base
w/lateral arm supporting burner
& pyriform acid-etched clear
glass shade, w/prisms, ca. 1830,
17" h., pr. 3,850.00
Argand lamps, double, bronze, urn-
shaped fluid chamber on base
w/lateral arm supporting burners
& acid-etched frosted glass
pyriform shades, w/prisms, pr.
(ILLUS.) 2,250.00
Argand lamps, gilt-metal urn-
shaped fluid chamber w/brass
acorn finial on shaped base
w/lateral arm supporting burners
& engraved frosted glass pyriform shades, original glass
prisms, signed "J. & I. Cox,"
New York, ca. 1830, double lamp
& pr. single lamps, 3 pcs. 1,870.00
Astral lamp, 3-footed bronze base &
fluted stem, original font, acid-
etched New England Glass Co.
shade, 24½" h. 695.00
Astral lamp, bronze square base
w/disc feet, acanthus leaf &
fluted stem, original engraved
frosted glass shade, 1815-20
(ILLUS.) 2,100.00

Astral Lamp

Art Deco lamp, chrome base
w/figural nude lady each side of
frosted cobalt blue shade raised
on 3 circular tiers 145.00

Art Nouveau Reverse-Painted Lamp

Art Nouveau table lamp, reverse-
painted scenic shade, patinated
metal base, 23" h. (ILLUS.) 285.00
Banquet lamp, marble base, brass
columnar stem w/gilding & Corinthian capital, Argand-type burner
& font, cut & frosted glass shade,
w/double row of prisms, signed
"Cornelius & Co., Philad., Patent
April 1st, 1843," overall 26½" h.
(now electrified) 550.00
Banquet lamp, brass base, stem &
fittings, deep red overlay glass
font cut to clear design of floral
panels & circles, frosted cut to
clear glass shade, 26¾" h........ 300.00
Betty lamp, double, cast & wrought
iron, European 70.00

Bigelow & Kenard signed table
lamp, leaded glass shade w/red &
green florals, Grueby Pottery
signed base, 18" h. 5,000.00

Boudoir lamps, "Aladdin" signed,
pressed Alacite glass Plume patt.
base, original flared silk-covered
shades, pr. 45.00

Bouillotte Lamp

Bouillotte lamp, 3-light, brass &
toleware, circular brass base
fitted w/three candle arms & tole
shade adjustable on rod standard
w/loop finial, signed "Baker
Arnold & Co., Philadelphia" on
base, ca. 1810, 26¼" h.
(ILLUS.) 3,300.00

Bouillotte lamp, 3-light, Louis XVI,
silverplate, dished circular base
w/beaded edge, fluted central
column supporting 3 scrolling
"hunting horn" form candle arms
& w/painted tole shade adjustable on rod standard, France,
late 18th c., 26½" h. 1,650.00

Bradley & Hubbard signed organ
(or piano) lamp, kerosene-type,
brass & onyx base, raspberry
satin glass ball-shaped 11" h.
shade, overall 50" h. 1,075.00

Bradley & Hubbard signed table
lamp, kerosene-type, embossed
brass cylindrical base, coral pink
& white striped cased satin glass
upturned shade w/crimped edge,
clear glass chimney, 18" h. 325.00

Bradley & Hubbard signed table
lamp, electric, caramel slag glass
panels in domical shade, patinated metal base, ca. 1915,
22½" h. . . . . .300.00 to 550.00

Desk lamp, "Emeralite," brass base
& adjustable stem, single knuckle,
cased green over white glass
shade . . . . .295.00 to 325.00

Duffner & Kimberly signed table
lamp, leaded green glass domical

shade, bronze base & standard
cast w/acanthus leaves, 20" h. 2,250.00

Gone-with-the-Wind Lamp

Gone-with-the-Wind lamp, red satin
glass ball-shaped shade & brass-
footed matching base w/h.p. floral decor, brass slip-in font, original Nangatuck burner (ILLUS.) 715.00

Gone-with-the-Wind lamp, beige-
pink glass ball-shaped shade &
brass-footed glass base w/em-
bossed scrolls & reserve panels of
h.p. colorful florals, original slip-
in font, burner & clear glass chimney, 10½" d., 21½" h. (now elec-
trified) 575.00

Gone-with-the-Wind lamp, opaline
glass ball-shaped shade & base
w/decal scene of cottage, mill &
swans on green-washed ground,
24" h. (now electrified but with oil
font not drilled) 350.00

Gone-with-the-Wind lamp, red satin
glass Beaded Drape patt. ball-
shaped shade & base, original
slip-in brass font & burner 695.00

Lacemaker's lamp, blown clear
glass, domed base w/applied rim,
hollow baluster stem w/applied
handle, spherical font w/drip pan
& tin drop-in burner, 10½" h. 525.00

Lacemaker's lamp, blown cranberry
"overshot" glass shade, handled
brass base, 10½" d., 16" h. 390.00

Lacemaker's lamp, blown cranberry
glass Inverted Thumbprint patt.
shade w/ruffled top, handled
brass base, 8½" d., 17½" h. 487.00

Lacemaker's lamp, cased shaded
rose glass shade embossed
w/leaves, scrolls & overlapping
petals, white lining, handled brass
base, 10" d., 18" h. 510.00

Mechanical lamp, "Moderator" model, ornate brass cylindrical base, original narrow-ribbed milk white glass ball-shaped shade, ca. 1850, 19" h. 795.00

Mechanical lamp, Wanzer "side-winder" 30-hour model, brass base, original burner, dated 1886 (no shade) 395.00

Moe Bridges signed table lamp, 15" d. reverse-painted shade w/autumn sunset scene, patinated metal base, 22" h. 525.00

Moe Bridges signed table lamp, 18" d. reverse-painted shade w/exotic birds amidst lush tropical vegetation, patinated metal 2-handled urn-form base molded w/polychromed stylized florettes, early 20th c., 23½" h. 1,760.00

Pairpoint signed boudoir lamp, 5" d. "puffy" glass Butterfly & Daisy Balmoral patt. shade w/reverse-painted purple, lilac & yellow butterflies & florals, silver finish metal base 1,650.00

Pairpoint "Puffy" Boudoir Lamp

Pairpoint signed boudoir lamp, 8" d. "puffy" frosted glass Apple Blossom patt. lamp reverse-painted at lower border in shades of pink, blue, green, yellow & w/black edge, baluster-shaped silver finish metal base molded w/stylized leaves, 14½" h. (ILLUS.) 1,100.00

Pairpoint signed table lamp, 16" d. reverse-painted flaring glass shade w/Italianate landscape, Sans Souci scene on acid-etched ground, patinated metal base w/fluted details, ca. 1910, 22" h. (ILLUS.) 1,210.00

Pairpoint Reverse-Painted Lamp

Pairpoint signed table lamp, 16" d. 8-panel caramel slag glass domical shade, patinated metal base, 24" h. 850.00

Peg lamp, tin petticoat-type w/acorn-shaped font & original whale oil burner, original brown japanned finish, 4¼" h. 95.00

Peg lamps, shaded lemon yellow overlay satin finish font & mushroom shade w/ruffled top edge & white lining, original brass candlestick holder base, 6" d., overall 17" h., pr. 1,118.00

Rush light holder, wrought iron shaft w/candle socket as counter balance set in wooden block base, 18th c., 10½" h. 385.00

Spout lamp, single spout, pewter, 10¾" h. (minor dents) 65.00

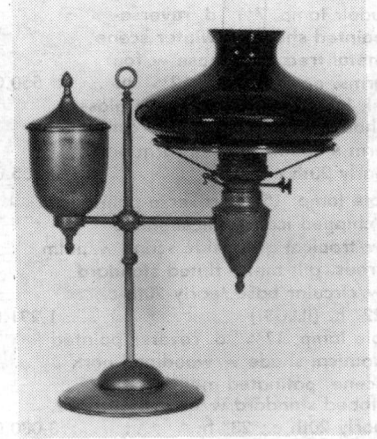

Student Lamp

Student lamp, single, brass reservoir & lamp adjustable on rod standard & domed base, signed Bradley & Hubbard, original green & white overlay glass shade, clear glass chimney (ILLUS.) 495.00

Student lamp, single, nickel-plated brass reservoir & lamp adjustable on rod standard & domed base, signed "German Student Co.," 10" d. blue-violet opaline glass shade & clear glass chimney, dated 1870 . . . . 795.00

Student lamp, double, brass reservoir & lamp adjustable on rod standard & domed base, (replaced) pale blue opaline glass shades & clear glass chimneys 900.00

HANDEL LAMPS (All Signed)

Handel Lamp with Reverse-Painted Shade

Boudoir lamp, 7½" d. reverse-painted shade w/winter scene, metal tree trunk base w/four arms, early 20th c., 12½" h. 550.00

Desk lamp, cylindrical green glass shade, bronze adjustable curved arm standard w/leaf-form base, early 20th c., 14" h. 465.00

Table lamp, 15" d. reverse-painted "chipped ice" domical shade w/tropical oceanside scene w/palm trees, gilt metal fluted standard w/circular base, early 20th c., 22" h. (ILLUS.) 1,291.00

Table lamp, 17¾" d. reverse-painted domical shade w/woodland park scene, patinated metal lightly ribbed standard w/quatrefoil base, early 20th c., 23" h. 3,080.00

Table lamp, 3-light, 18" d. reverse-

painted scenic shade, patinated metal standard & base, early 20th c. 925.00

Table lamp, 20" d. mottled green & yellow leaded glass shade, patinated metal base, early 20th c., 24" h. 975.00

Handel Leaded Glass Lamp

Table lamp, leaded glass domical shade w/striated amber, honey & white rectangular tiles (some w/damage) & diagonally inset border, bronze cylindrical standard & spreading circular base, early 20th c., 25½" h. (ILLUS.) 825.00

SANDWICH WHALE OIL LAMPS

Blue Punty patt. font, acid finish, brass stem, marble base, pr. 1,200.00

Blue Star & Punty patt. font, cross spiral brass stem, marble base, 9¾" h. 385.00

Clear Tulip patt. font, clambroth base, pr. 600.00

Overlay cranberry cut to white & clear font, brass stem, marble base 300.00

Overlay opaque white cut to clear punties on ball-shaped font, crossed spiral brass stem, marble base, 8¾" h. 365.00

TIFFANY LAMPS (All Signed)

Bridge lamp, counter-balance type, domical cased deep blue shade w/concentric bands of silver-blue iridescence above continuous silver-blue coiling band, on double S-scroll support terminating in counter-balance orb, bronze cylindrical standard terminating in 5

splayed legs & spade feet, 1899-
1920, 54¾" h. 4,400.00
Candlestick lamp, iridescent gold
glass ruffled umbrella-type shade
& swirl-ribbed base, early 20th c.,
17" h. . . . . .995.00 to 1,200.00

Tiffany Desk Lamp

Desk lamp, 7½" d. green & gold
Favrile glass Wave pattern shade,
patinated bronze base, early 20th
c., 13" h. (ILLUS.) 1,045.00
Desk lamp, counter-balance type,
7" d. hemispherical Damascene
glass shade w/iridescent silver-
blue swirls on emerald green
ground enchanced w/gold highlights, bronze base, early 20th c.,
14½" h. . . . . .2,420.00 to 4,180.00
Desk lamp, "turtleback," swivel
shade set w/two iridescent green
Favrile glass turtleback tiles within
a beaded rope-twist mount, bronze
base w/band of matching green
glass cabochons, early 20th c.,
14½" h. . . . . .2,420.00 to 3,300.00
Floor lamp, "Clematis," 19" d. leaded
glass conical shade w/green-centered
white dogwood sprays amidst green
leaves against blue-grey mottled
sky ground, bronze base, early
20th c., 64¼" h. (replaced
sockets) 16,500.00
Floor lamp, "Daffodil," 19" d. leaded
glass domical shade w/mottled
lemon & pale yellow & pumpkin
daffodil blossoms w/emerald &
wintergreen leafage reserved
against striated medium, deep &
grey-blue ground, bronze cylindrical standard w/applied stringing
& leaf-molded circular base, petal
form feet, early 20th c., 63" h. . . .18,150.00
Floor lamp, "Peony Border," 24" d.
leaded glass domical shade w/lower

band of yellow-centered vivid pink,
red, magenta & white blossoms
w/mottled green leaves against
deeply mottled blue-green ground,
ribbed standard w/green-brown
patina, w/pigtail finial, early
20th c., 76½" h. . . .38,500.00 to 44,000.00
Lily lamp, 7-light, iridescent amber
lily-form shades, bronze stems &
circular lily pad base, early 20th c.,
21" h. . . . . .4,400.00 to 9,350.00

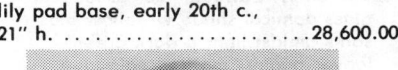

Tiffany Lily Lamp

Lily lamp, 10-light, iridescent amber
lily-form shades, bronze stems &
lily pad base, early 20th c.,
21" h. . . . . .7,150.00 to 9,900.00
Lily lamp, 12-light, iridescent gold
lily-form shades, bronze base,
early 20th c.,
20" h. . . . . .8,800.00 to 13,200.00
Lily lamp, 18-light, iridescent gold
lily-form shades, bronze stems &
lily pad base, early 20th c.,
21" h. 28,600.00

Tiffany "Nautilus" Lamp

Nautilus lamp, original nautilus seashell shade fitted w/leaded trim,
patinated bronze ribbed base
(ILLUS.) 1,750.00
Table lamp, "Apple Blossom," 16" d.
leaded glass hemispherical shade
w/yellow-centered pink & white
apple blossom sprays amidst
streaked emerald green leaves on
bright mottled green ground,
bronze ribbed base w/greenish
patina, early 20th c., 23" h. 15,400.00
Table lamp, "Apple Blossom," 25" d.
leaded glass domical shade w/yel-
low-centered red, pink & white
apple blossoms amidst bright emerald green leaves & brown branches
against "fractured" pale blue sky
ground, bronze tree form base
w/greenish brown patina, early
20th c., 30" h..................28,600.00
Table lamp, "Begonia," 13" d.
leaded glass domical shade w/ir-
regular rim w/profusion of yellow-
centered dark pink & crimson blossoms amidst pale green leaves
pendant from openwork branches
on pale blue "fractured" glass
ground, bronze elongated tree
form base w/greenish brown patina,
early 20th c., 21½" h..........57,200.00
Table lamp, "Black Eyed Susan,"
16" d. leaded glass shade w/black-
centered yellow flowerheads, light
& dark green stems against green
& white mottled ground, bronze
3-light base w/ribbed standard &
ball feet, early 20th c., 22" h. ...7,150.00
Table lamp, "Colonial," 16" d. leaded
glass conical shade w/radiating
bands of rounded oblong yellow-
ochre striated tiles, bronze urn-
form standard & dished square
foot, 1899-1928, 23" h. 4,675.00
Table lamp, "Daffodil," 20" d. leaded
glass domical shade w/yellow blossoms amidst light & dark green
leaves against mottled pale blue
shading to green-blue ground,
bronze standard cast w/twisting
vines issuing from flat circular
base, early 20th c., 27¼" h. 20,900.00
Table lamp, "Geometric," 16" d.
leaded glass domical shade w/radi-
ating bands of mottled mint green &
medial band of mottled lemon yellow
ivy leaves, bronze 3-arm support
above waisted ribbed standard
w/domed circular base on 5 ball
feet, early 20th c.,
23" h...............2,860.00 to 3,740.00
Table lamp, "Greek Border," 20" d.
leaded glass conical shade w/low-
er band of green & yellow Greek

Key motifs on mottled green
ground, bronze standard & base,
early 20th c., 25½" h...........9,900.00
Table lamp, "Lotus," 26" d. leaded
glass conical flaring ribbed shade
w/bands of geometric striated green
panels, bronze cylindrical waisted
standard w/flaring circular base
on 5 ball feet, early 20th c.,
27½" h........12,100.00 to 13,200.00
Table lamp, "Nasturtium," 20" d.
leaded glass shallow domical
shade w/mottled orange, red &
burgundy blossoms amidst streaked & mottled green leaves against
textured orange-yellow & green
ground, bronze base, early 20th c.,
25¼" h..........14,300.00 to 17,600.00

Tiffany "Poppy" Lamp

Table lamp, "Poppy," 16" d. leaded
glass conical shade w/streaked
orange & yellow blossoms amidst
green leaves against mottled yellow ground, bronze ribbed standard, circular base, early 20th c.,
22" h. (ILLUS.) 17,600.00
Table lamp, "Zodiac," 22" d. leaded
glass domical shade w/rectangular
panels of mottled blue within
green surrounds reserved against
mottled amber ground set w/cir-
cular medallions pierced w/Zodiac
signs & centering a medial belt
set w/dark blue turtleback bosses,
bronze urn-form standard & circular base w/beaded border, early
20th c., 30" h. .....16,500.00 to 18,700.00

MINIATURE LAMPS

*Numbers following our listing of lamps are
those assigned to the various miniature
lamps pictured in Frank R. & Ruth E. Smith's
book, "Miniature Lamps," now often referred
to as Smith's Book I.*

Miniature Lamps

Amberina glass paneled base &
   globe-chimney shade, Hornet
   burner, 8¼" h., No. 439 . . . . 715.00
Blue mother-of-pearl Satin glass
   Raindrop patt., ball-shaped base
   w/applied frosted feet & upturned
   fluted shade, Nutmeg burner,
   clear glass chimney,
   8½" h., No. 601 . . . . 900.00
Blue opaque glass ball-shaped base
   w/embossed designs, known as
   "Katy Did" at turn-of-the-century,
   Nutmeg burner & nickel-plated
   reflector, clear glass chimney,
   3" h., No. 56 . . . .   85.00
Blue opaque glass pedestal base,
   pressed clear glass font, Olmsted
   burner, milk white glass chimney-
   shade, No. 11 . . . . 275.00 to 400.00
Brass "Beauty Night Lamp," em-
   bossed wall lamp, w/filling spout
   on wall reservoir & lion's mouth
   supporting tube to burner, green
   glass beehive chimney-shade,
   No. 77 . . . .   65.00
Clear glass Bull's Eye patt. stem
   lamp, Acorn burner, clear glass
   chimney, 5¾" h., No. 110 . . . .   35.00
Clear glass "Little Harry's Night
   Lamp" embossed on ball-shaped
   base, Olmsted burner, white opaline glass chimney-shade, 6" h.,
   No. 15 . . . .   95.00
Clear glass Greek Key patt. stem
   lamp & globe-chimney shade,
   Acorn burner, 8½" h.,
   No. 166 . . . . .75.00 to 100.00
Cobalt blue glass base w/medial
   metal banding joined to metal
   hanger & reflector w/mirror, foreign burner, clear glass chimney,
   2¼" h., No. 58 . . . .   75.00
Cranberry glass pedestal base &
   globe-chimney shade w/ruffled &
   crimped rim, enameled white berries & leaves decor, foreign burn-
   er, 9¾" h., No. 460 . . . . 425.00
Custard glass Leon's Ribbed patt.
   base & globe-chimney shade,

Acorn burner, 6" h.,
   No. 177 . . . . .285.00 to 320.00
Milk white glass font embossed
   "Nutmeg" w/narrow brass band
   forming removable handle, Nutmeg burner, clear glass chimney,
   2¾" h. base, No. 29 . . . .   55.00
Milk white glass base w/applied
   handle & enameled red berries &
   green leaves & blue bands, Nutmeg burner, clear glass chimney,
   3" h., No. 39 . . . .   70.00
Milk white glass "Shag" or "Christ-
   mas Tree" patt. w/gold ribs on
   base & shade, Acorn burner,
   6¾" h., No. 125 . . . . 165.00
Milk white glass Cosmos patt. base
   & umbrella shade w/pink-stained
   band & colored florals, Nutmeg
   burner, 7½" h., No. 286 (ILLUS.
   right) . . . . .250.00 to 375.00
Milk white glass Plume patt. base &
   umbrella shade w/gilt highlights,
   Nutmeg burner, clear glass chim-
   ney, 7½" h., No. 203 . . . . 195.00
Milk white glass "Swan" lamp, swan-
   molded base & umbrella-type shade
   w/embossed swan on lake scene,
   Nutmeg burner, clear glass chim-
   ney, 7½" h., No. 499 . . . . .1,300.00
Milk white glass base & shade
   w/embossed Beaded Swirl & seg-
   mented rib design, called Brady's
   Night Lamp, Nutmeg burner,
   made by Consolidated Lamp &
   Glass Co., Pittsburgh, 7¾" h.,
   No. 217 . . . . 425.00
Milk white glass Drape patt. square
   base & globe shade w/shaded
   pink wash, original burner, clear
   glass chimney, 8½" h., No. 231 . . 225.00
Milk white glass base & globe-
   chimney w/embossed & melon-
   ribbed panels painted w/alternat-
   ing colors, sometimes called "Centennial Lamp," Hornet burner,
   8½" h., No. 202 . . . . 285.00
Milk white glass base w/embossed
   lion's heads in gilt & globe-
   chimney shade w/h.p. florals,
   Nutmeg burner, clear glass chim-
   ney, 8½" h., No. 268 . . . . 395.00
Milk white glass 8-sided base & ball
   shade w/embossed scrolls &
   florals highlighted w/pink, blue,
   yellow & green enameling, sometimes called "Paneled Cosmos,"
   Nutmeg burner, 8½" h.,
   No. 241 . . . . .295.00 to 375.00
Milk white glass footed base
   w/painted blue & white florals &
   frosted glass globe-chimney
   w/conforming decor, Hornet burner, often called "Nellie Bly" by

collectors, 9" h., No. 219 (ILLUS. center) 250.00

Milk white glass 3-tier banquet lamp on brass pedestal base w/h.p. floral decor, P. & A. Victor burner, clear glass chimney, 17" h., No. 306 . . . . 495.00

Pink cased glass base & globe-chimney w/embossed scroll designs, Hornet burner, 8¾" h., No. 374 . . . . 650.00

Pink Satin glass squared base & puffy-molded Artichoke variant shade, Nutmeg burner, by Consolidated Lamp & Glass Co., Pittsburgh, 7" h., No. 380 (ILLUS. left) . . . . 400.00 to 550.00

Red Satin glass "Artichoke" lamp w/melon-ribbed base & artichoke-molded ball-shaped shade, Nutmeg burner, clear glass chimney, 8" h., Color Plate III 550.00

Spatter glass (green & brown mottled) Beaded Rib patt. base & globe-chimney shade, Hornet burner, 8 3/8" h., No. 368 . . . . 650.00

Yellow & brown porcelain figure of man beside barrel base, English burner, clear glass chimney, 3½" h. base, No. 487 . . . . 450.00

LANTERNS

Early Tin Candle Lantern

Barn lantern, kerosene-type, "Dietz Crystal," soldered tin, red globe, 6½" h. 95.00

Barn lantern, kerosene-type, "Dietz No. 2 Blizzard," tin w/copper base, clear globe 35.00

Barn lantern, kerosene-type,

"Ham's," tin w/brass bottom, 15" h. 75.00

Bicycle lantern, brass w/red & green glass panels, "Badger Brass Co., Kenosha, Wis.," 1899 patent 65.00

Bicycle lantern, carbide-type, "Majestic," 1899 & 1900 patent dates . . . . 50.00 to 75.00

Candle lantern, folding-type, tin w/original mica sides, original brown japanned finish & gold stenciling, marked "Minors Pat. Jan. 24, 1865," w/compartment for candle & matches, 5" h. 85.00

Candle lantern, tin, square w/glass sides, pyramidal punchwork decorated top & crimped-edge circle below strap handle, painted green & red, 19th c., 7¾" h. (ILLUS.) 385.00

Candle lantern, tin, square w/glass sides, pyramidal punchwork top & strap handle, marked "F. Parkers Patents of 1859 & 1855, Boston, Mass.," old black paint, 12" h. plus handle 105.00

Candle lantern, pierced tin cylinder w/conical top & ring handle (so-called Paul Revere lantern), old black repaint, 12¾" h. . . 150.00 to 225.00

Miner's lantern, tin, teakettle-type . . 25.00

Miner's lantern, brass, carbide-type, "Justrite," cap-type 40.00

Ship's lantern, brass, w/glass chimney, hand-polished, 6" d., 14" h. 195.00

Ship's Lanterns

Ship's lanterns, brass & copper, quarter-round chamber enclosing clear glass globe, one w/brass plaque inscribed "Port," Scotland, 22 1/8" h., pr. (ILLUS.) 165.00

Skater's lantern, brass, w/clear glass pear-shaped globe & wire bail handle, overall 11½" h. . . . . 60.00 to 75.00

Skater's lantern, tin, w/clear glass pear-shaped globe & wire bail

handle, "Dietz," w/patent dates
from 1904 through 1914 . . . .　50.00
Skater's lantern, tin, w/blue glass
pear-shaped globe & wire bail
handle, marked "Jewel," 6¾" h.
plus handle (some rust) . . . .　165.00
Skater's lantern, tin, w/clear glass
pear-shaped globe & wire bail
handle, marked "Jewel," 6¾" h.
plus handle . . . . .42.50 to 50.00
Torchlight parade lantern, brass font
& burner on turned wood handle,
overall 28" l. . . . .　65.00

TINDER BOXES & PISTOLS

Brass tinder box, Queen Anne style,
pierced porringer-type handle
w/heart design, dovetailed base &
cover w/candle socket, 1730-50,
4¾" d., 2¾" l. handle . . . .　475.00
Sheet iron tinder box w/tin damper,
hand-forged iron striker & flint,
4¾ x 3", 1¾" h. . . . .　275.00
Tinned sheet iron tinder box, w/iron
striker, flint & damper, oblong
box w/clasp closure & carrying
ring, 4½ x 3", 1½" h. . . . .　265.00
Tin tinder box, cylindrical w/wire
loop handle at side & candle
holder on lid, w/iron striker, flint
& interior cover for same,
4¼" h. . . . .　200.00
Tinder lighter pistol, flintlock,
wrought iron w/hinged compartment in the side & candle socket
attached, simple carving on wood-
en pistol grip, 11¼" l. . . . .　380.00
Tinder lighter pistol, flintlock, brass
& steel mechanism w/walnut pistol grip, marked "I. Davidson" on
right side, England, 18th c.,
6" l. . . . .　687.50

(End of Lighting Devices Section)

LITHOPHANES

Lithophanes are pictorial panes of porcelain cast in molds, the layer of clay varying in thickness so that when light is transmitted through the panels, the picture is seen in highlights and shadows. Said to have been invented in France in the 1830's they were also made elsewhere. The panes are utilized in lamps, steins and also as scenic plaques.

Lamp shade, 5 panels w/scenes of
children at various pursuits, ornately embossed brass frame-

work, marked P.P.M., 10" w. at
base, 5¼" h. $550.00
Night lamp (or tea warmer), 4 sce-
nic panels, all white, w/original
base & burner, 5¼" sq., 7½" h. . . .　500.00
Night lamp (or tea warmer), 4
panels w/scenes of children . . . . . .　395.00
Panel, scene of 2 women in a door-
way w/dog & pigeons in yard,
marked P.R. w/sickle & num-
bered, framed, 5 1/8 x 4¼" . . . . . .　110.00
Panel, scene of hunter & maiden
w/flock of geese, 5 1/8 x
4 3/8" . . . .　65.00
Panel, village scene w/figures,
church & houses, marked C. 108,
5½ x 4" . . . .　82.00

Lithophane Panel

Panel, classical figures & a sibyl attempting to entrap cupids,
marked K.P.M., 6 x 4¾"
(ILLUS.) . . . .　209.00
Panel, "Blessed Virgin Mary," 6" w.,
7½" h. . . . .　195.00
Panel, "Sacred Heart of Jesus,"
6" w., 7½" h. . . . .　195.00
Panels, one depicting a man & lady
running, the other w/scene of a
lady holding a crying cupid, each
4¾ x 4", together in lighted
wooden frame . . . .　240.00

LOCKS & KEYS

Door lock, brass, lock incorporating
single revolving dead bolt & sliding
night lock, engraved case w/cypher
of Duke of Leeds & motto "Honi

16th Century Brass Door Lock

Soit Qui Mal Y Pense," w/ovoid
engraved knobs, George II,
1720-30 (ILLUS.) $4,675.00
Door lock, brass, rectangular case
w/dead bolt, night lock & molded
loop pull, Georgian, 18th c. 825.00
Key, folding-type, brass & steel,
"M.W. & Co." . . . . .12.00 to 18.00
Key, skeleton-type, "Keen Kutter"
(E.C. Simmons) 10.00
Padlock, brass, "Captain Broadfoot
R.E.," circular, ca. 1854, w/key . . . 225.00
Padlock, brass, "Cottrill," ca. 1884,
5" 180.00
Padlock, brass, "E.C. Simmons -
Keen Kutter," emblem-shaped,
w/key . . . . .75.00 to 85.00
Padlock, brass, "Giant," Smith &
Egge Mfg. Co., dated 1877, w/two
keys 50.00
Padlock, brass, "I.H.C.," 6-lever 185.00
Padlock, brass, "Mars," Corbin 17.50
Padlock, brass, "Ne Plus Ultra,"
Fraim Slaymaker 12.00
Padlock, brass, "No-Key," 8 push-
button type, American Keyless
Lock Co. 32.50
Padlock, brass, "Texaco," w/em-
bossed star 20.00
Padlock, brass, "U.S.N." . . . .8.00 to 15.00
Padlock, brass, "Victorian Chubb,"
ca. 1880, w/key, 4" 130.00
Padlock, brass, "Winchester" 150.00
Padlock, brass, "Yale & Towne" 9.00
Padlock, railroad, brass, "Monon,"
heart-shaped 75.00

LORGNETTES, OPERA GLASSES
& SPECTACLES

Lorgnette, gilt silver, reticulated,
marked "Barr Bros." $125.00
Lorgnette, 14k gold, Art Nouveau
style (ILLUS.) 625.00

Gold Art Nouveau Lorgnette

Lorgnette, 14k gold, ornate 245.00
Lorgnette, 14k gold, long handle . . . 100.00
Lorgnette, gold-filled, folding-type
w/push button & handle,
ca. 1920 . . . . .50.00 to 70.00
Lorgnette, ivory 50.00
Lorgnette, sterling silver, w/chain &
case .85.00 to 95.00
Lorgnette, sterling silver inlaid
w/mother-of-pearl, 8" l. 75.00
Lorgnette, tortoise shell 65.00
Opera glasses, mother-of-pearl &
brass, marked "France" . . . .45.00 to 65.00
Opera glasses, mother-of-pearl &
gold-plated brass, detachable
handle, marked "Henrichen &
Greenberg, Portland" 85.00
Opera glasses, mother-of-pearl &
gold-plated brass, engraved
"Amy, 1904" & marked "L'Ing &
Godghaux, 156 Rue de Rivoli,
Paris," folding handle, w/plush
bag 60.00
Opera glasses, mother-of-pearl &
gold-plated brass, marked
"LeMaire Paris" . . . . .40.00 to 60.00
Pince nez, 14k gold & tortoise shell
frame 25.00
Pince nez, 14k gold-filled, w/chain &
clip 15.00
Spectacles, coin silver frames,
marked "Hyde," ca. 1830 . . . . 125.00
Spectacles, coin silver frames, ca.
1840, w/tin case 52.00
Spectacles, coin silver frames
w/sliding side pieces, granny-
type 45.00
Spectacles, 10k gold frames w/slid-
ing side pieces, granny-type 90.00
Spectacles, 14k gold, Ben Franklin
style 35.00

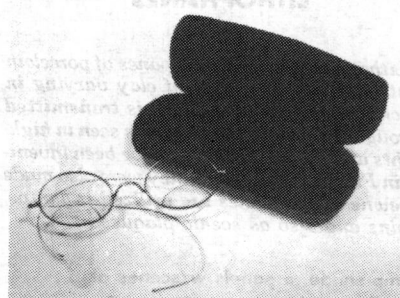

Granny-type Bifocal Spectacles

Spectacles, gold wire frames,
granny-type, bifocal lenses,
w/leather-covered tin case
(ILLUS.) 30.00
Spectacles, gold-plated, Ben Franklin style, bifocal lenses .....7.00 to 15.00
Spectacles, lady's, 14k white gold
w/engraving, folding-type........ 85.00

MAGAZINES

July 1925 Modern Priscilla

Cosmopolitan, 1900, July, Paris Ex-
position featured $12.00
Delineator, 1904, November 35.00
Demorest, 1867, full year bound 65.00
Golf Illustrated, 1934, September ... 10.00
Good Housekeeping, 1918, April,
Kewpies & April Fools 12.00
Harper's Weekly, 1862, 16 Winslow
Homer engravings, full year
bound 700.00
Hearst's International, 1922, Febru-
ary, Alphonse Mucha cover 60.00
Hollywood, 1938, December, Shirley
Temple cover.................... 45.00
Hygeia, 1927-49, 23 buckram-bound
volumes 325.00
Judge, 1906, McKinley political car-
toon cover..................... 27.00
McCall's, 1941, August 4.00
McClure's, 1897, June, "Langley on
the Flying Machine," photographs
& article....................... 15.00
Modern Priscilla, 1925, July
(ILLUS.)....................... 6.50
Motion Picture, 1943, September 10.00
Motor World, 1916, December 6 .... 7.00
Movieland Pin-ups, 1955, Vol. 1,
No. 1 .... 25.00

Movie Mirror, 1933, April, Katherine
Hepburn cover 8.00
National Geographic, 1926, full
year 25.00
New Detective, 1947, January,
Vol. 1, No. 1 .... 25.00
New England Fireside, 1888, May,
needlework, fashion prints & lawn
tennis article 32.00
Photoplay, 1929, August, Greta Gar-
bo cover 10.00
Pictorial Review, 1919, January, cov-
er & double page illustration of
children by Charles Twelvetrees,
Dolly Dingle & fashion plates 40.00
Playboy, 1965, February, Beatles
interview 20.00
Playgirl, 1973, June, Vol. 1,
No. 1 ....15.00 to 20.00
Popular Science, 1928, January,
Zeppelin article 9.50
Radio Age, 1925, July 5.00
Saturday Evening Post, 1900, March
3 through June 30, Harrison Fisher
& J.C. Leyendecker covers,
Maxfield Parrish Colgate ad, 18
issues bound................... 65.00
Saturday Evening Post, 1929, March
9, Norman Rockwell cover "Doctor
& Doll" 250.00
Scientific American, 1886, January
through June, 6 months bound ... 125.00
TV Forecast, 1950, August 12, Gene
Autry cover & article 17.50
TV Guide, Lucy's baby, Vol. 1,
No. 1 .... 95.00
TV Guide, 1951, February 10, Bert
Parks cover, Capt. Video Super
Weapons article 50.00
Vogue, 1938, January, article on
Steichen w/photographs, & Erte'
fashions 15.00

August 1963 Woman's Day

Woman's Day, 1963, August, w/"Dictionary of Sandwich Glass"
(ILLUS.)....................... 12.00

Woman's Day, 1965, July, antique
paperweights article............ 9.00
Woman's Home Companion, 1910,
October, Dolly Dingle &
Kewpies...................... 18.50
Woman's Home Companion, 1915,
December, full page Jessie Wilcox
Smith illustration of children at
Christmas 13.00
Woman's Home Companion, 1921,
April, Peter Piper color ad by
Parrish, Djer Kiss & color
fashions...................... 50.00
Youth's Companion, 1894, October
25, premium issue............. 15.00

Magic lantern slides, Civil War, set
of 26......................... 115.00
Magic lantern slides, World War I,
set of 29 .... 75.00
Magic lantern slides, assorted set of
31 .... 45.00
Magic lantern slides, "Italy," American Museum of Natural History,
colored, 4 x 3", set of 47 .... 75.00
Magic lantern slides, modes of
transportation, set of 49 .... 185.00
Magic lantern slides, children's
story, "Little Black Sambo," complete set, in original box........ 125.00

MAGIC LANTERNS

Tin Magic Lantern

*These devices were used to project slide pic-
tures on a screen and were popular from the
late 19th to the early 20th century. Prices
range from $60.00 to $250.00, or more.*

Magic lantern, "E.P. Germany," tin,
kerosene-type, w/eight glass
slides $125.00
Magic lantern, "Magica Lanternica,"
folding-type box, w/paper label .. 100.00
Magic lantern, red enameled tin,
kerosene-type, w/six slides, in
original box, Germany (ILLUS.) ... 195.00
Magic lantern, tin, kerosene-type
w/original burner & numerous
assorted slides, in original
dovetailed wooden box 140.00
Magic lantern slide, "Temperance
Union" 3.00
Magic lantern slides, "Metropolitan
Life Insurance Company," 1896,
for Beseler Lantern, set of 17 .... 125.00
Magic lantern slides, American
Indian life, set of 25 .... 85.00

MARBLES

Assorted Swirl Marbles

China, hand-painted, German,
½" d., 125 in original box $75.00
China, unglazed, ¾" d. 10.00
Glass, Akro Agate, 36 marbles &
pouch in original metal box
w/Akro Agate trademark,
1930's 67.00
Glass, cat's eye, 1" d., set of 12 .... 14.00
Glass, comic strip type, "Betty
Boop," "Bimbo" & "Koko,"
set of 3 .... 165.00
Glass, "onionskin," dark green &
white swirls, 1¼" d. 75.00
Glass, "onionskin," overall swirled
blue & white, 4 lobes, clear cen-
ter, 2 3/16" d. 275.00
Glass, sulphide, w/chipmunk eating
carrot, 2½" d. 500.00
Glass, sulphide, w/dog,
1 7/8" d. ....75.00 to 100.00
Glass, sulphide, w/donkey, 2" d. ... 155.00
Glass, sulphide, w/duck on water,
large......................... 350.00
Glass, sulphide, w/eagle, 1½" d.... 140.00
Glass, sulphide, w/frog, 1½" d. 125.00
Glass, sulphide, w/guinea hen,
1¼" d. 125.00
Glass, sulphide, w/white, blue,
green & black hen, 1½" d. (small
chips) 710.00
Glass, sulphide, w/horse,
1 7/8" d. 130.00
Glass, sulphide, w/lamb 100.00

Glass, sulphide, w/lion standing,
  greenish glass, 1½" d. 90.00
Glass, sulphide, w/numeral "5,"
  2¼" d. .... 45.00'
Glass, sulphide, w/owl standing 85.00
Glass, sulphide, w/parrot 150.00
Glass, sulphide, w/rooster 75.00
Glass, sulphide, w/sheep, 2" d. 75.00
Glass, sulphide, w/Spitz dog,
  large........................... 85.00
Glass, sulphide, w/tiger,
  2 3/16" d. 125.00
Glass, sulphide, w/young boy,
  large........................... 270.00
Glass, swirl, w/red, white & blue
  ribbon core center & yellow outer
  swirls, 1¼" d. 32.50
Glass, swirl, w/divided core,
  orange, white & blue, 1¼" d. 30.00
Glass, swirl, w/dark yellow latticino
  core & green, black, white & red
  outer swirls, 1½" d. 27.50
Glass, swirl, w/latticino core, red,
  white & blue, 1 5/8" d. 40.00
Glass, swirl, w/yellow, sage green,
  red & white core w/four swirled
  groups of 3 threads each radiating
  from the pontils, 1 7/8" d. 130.00
Glass, swirl, w/white latticino core
  w/eight swirled ribbons of yellow,
  red & brown radiating from the
  pontils, 1 15/16" d............... 130.00
Glass, swirl, w/yellow latticino center & blue & white outer swirls,
  2¼" d. 45.00

MATCH SAFES & CONTAINERS

Advertising Wall Match Holder

*Also see ADVERTISING ITEMS and
BISQUE.*

Advertising container, wall-type,
  chalkware, "Admiration Cigars,"
  man in the moon............... $75.00

Advertising container, wall-type, tin,
  "Juicy Fruit," Wm. Wrigley, Jr.
  pictured, 3½ x 1¼", 5" h.
  (ILLUS.)....................... 75.00
Advertising safe, pocket-type, brass,
  "James Wilde Fashionable Clothi-
  ers, Chicago" 48.00
Advertising safe, pocket-type, gutta
  percha, "Arm & Hammer Baking
  Soda" 85.00
Bisque container, table model, model of a skull on a book 35.00
Brass container, table model, model
  of an owl w/glass eyes, 2¾" h. ... 55.00
Brass safe, pocket-type, model of a
  pig 110.00
Bronze container, table model,
  figural sailor w/dolphin at his feet
  & covered sea chest on his back
  standing beside barrel-shaped
  container, 7½" h. 165.00
Cast iron container, table model,
  model of an egg on slender stem
  w/bird's foot, 5¼" h............. 105.00
Cast iron container, wall-type, father & children resting at wayside
  in relief, ca. 1890 .... 75.00
Cast iron container, wall-type, double pocket, foliate openwork
  backplate cast w/fluted urns,
  w/striker at base, 1867 patent
  date, 7 x 5" 55.00
German silver safe, pocket-type,
  bust of an Art Nouveau lady
  w/flowing hair & flowers 35.00

Glass Match Container

Glass container, table model, model
  of a bucket w/original wire bail
  handle, amber (ILLUS.).......... 25.00
Glass container, table model, model
  of a boot, brown, satin finish,
  3" h. 45.00
Glass container, table model, model
  of an open valise w/straps, milk
  white, 3¼ x 2¾" 45.00

Porcelain container, table model, figural child, w/striker 45.00

Pot metal container, table model, black man playing banjo & wearing jockey cap w/smoke coming from cigar, white w/gilt trim, 7" h. 250.00

Pot metal safe, pocket-type, "Skating, Smoking, Teddy Bear," 1910. . 49.00

Silver safe, pocket-type, English hallmarks, ca. 1907, 1½" d. 70.00

Silverplate container w/brass insert, table model, figural devil's head, 3" h. 35.00

Sterling silver safe, pocket-type, applied gold octopus on chased ocean waves in relief, marked "Gorham" 125.00

Sterling silver safe, pocket-type, Indian head in relief 90.00

Sterling silver safe, pocket-type, engraved "Liberty 1904," enamel trim 285.00

Stoneware container, table model, model of a beehive 75.00

Tin container, table model, model of a top hat w/hinged lid, worn original green paint w/black band, 2 3/8" h. 50.00

Tin container, wall-type, backplate w/scalloped crest, double pocket, w/striker at base 15.00

Wooden container, wall-type, barrel-shaped pocket, backplate w/heart-shaped crest carved w/cross-hatched hearts, pipe, jackknife & monogram, chip-carved & cross-hatched borders, 5½" h. 130.00

MEDICAL QUACKERY ITEMS

Numerous devices and contrivances offered last century and early in the present one as "cures" or palliatives for a host of ailments and subsequently found to be worthless, dangerous or at least unequal to their claims are now sought by some collectors. The following represents a sampling of items being collected.

Davis & Kidder's Magneto Electric machine, shock treatment device, w/original brass-bound mahogany box & instructions, ca. 1860 . . . . . $135.00

Detroit Medical, battery-operated shock treatment device, w/wood-lined tin case 950.00

Dr. Spalding's electric belt, w/original box, 1895 . . . . 20.00

Fisher Type "FO" machine, mahogany cabinet w/porcelain front & beveled glass lift top, w/attachments & instructions, 51" h. . . . . 850.00 to 1,000.00

Shock Treatment Device

Magneto-electric machine, pocket size, consisting of magnet, coil & geared wheels w/exterior rose-wood crank, adjustment knob at one end & pr. brass holding rods w/wires, in mahogany case w/brass key plate, interior of lid w/directions below engravings of machine in use, English, mid-19th c., 5 1/8" l. (ILLUS.) 440.00

Master Violet Ray Kit, No. 11, w/original box & instructions, 1924 . . . . 23.00

Mills Electric Treatment, coin-operated counter model, battery-operated shock treatment device, ornate case & dial, ca. 1900 . . . . . 3,450.00

Potter's Faradic Cure, w/original box & instruction book 40.00

Renulife violet ray generator, w/original box 40.00

Renulife violet ray & ozone shock treatment machine 67.50

Violetta medical raygun 20.00

METALS

Also see ABC PLATES, ADVERTISING ITEMS, ART DECO, ART NOUVEAU, AUTOMOBILE ACCESSORIES, AVIATION COLLECTIBLES, BABY MEMENTOES, BASEBALL MEMORABILIA, BELLS,

*BOOKENDS, BOOKMARKS, BOOT-
JACKS, BOTTLE OPENERS, BREWERI-
ANA, BRONZES, BROWNIES, BUCKLES,
BUSTER BROWN COLLECTIBLES, BUT-
TON HOOKS, BUTTONS, CANDLE-
STICKS & CANDLE HOLDERS, CANS &
CONTAINERS, CARD CASES, CASH
REGISTERS, CAT COLLECTIBLES,
CHARACTER COLLECTIBLES, CIGAR &
CIGARETTE CASES & HOLDERS,
CIGAR & TOBACCO CUTTERS, COCA-
COLA ITEMS, COFFEE GRINDERS,
CORKSCREWS, COUNTRY STORE COL-
LECTIBLES, COW CREAMERS, DISNEY
COLLECTIBLES, DOLL FURNITURE,
DOOR KNOCKERS, DOOR STOPS,
EPERGNES, FABERGE, FARM COL-
LECTIBLES, FIREPLACE & HEARTH
ITEMS, FLUE COVERS, FOOD, CANDY
& MISCELLANEOUS MOLDS, FOOT
SCRAPERS, FRAMES, FURNITURE,
GREENAWAY ITEMS, HATPINS,
HORSE & BUGGY COLLECTIBLES, ICE
CREAM SCOOPS, JEWELRY, KEWPIE
ITEMS, KITCHENWARES, KNIVES,
LIGHTING DEVICES, LOCKS & KEYS,
LORGNETTES, MATCH SAFES, NUT-
CRACKERS, POWDER HORNS &
FLASKS, ROYCROFT ITEMS, SALE-
MAN'S SAMPLES, SCALES, SEWING
ADJUNCTS, SIGNS & SIGNBOARDS,
SOUVENIR SPOONS, SPELTER WARES,
STRING HOLDERS, SUNDIALS, TOYS,
TRAYS, WORLD FAIR COLLECTIBLES,
WRITING ACCESSORIES and ZEPPE-
LIN COLLECTIBLES.*

BRASS

Calipers, figural lady's legs w/gar-
ters & shoes, 5" l. $95.00
Candle holder, chamberstick-type
w/saucer base & sea serpent handle, Bradley & Hubbard, ca. 1910,
6" d., 4" h. 75.00
Candle sconce, elaborate octagonal
backplate chased w/floral & geometric designs, cast single candle
arm & nozzle, Continental,
18th c., 21" h. 495.00
Candlewick trimmer & snuffer,
scissors-type, circular base
w/knopped stem, ring handle,
19th c., overall 7½" h. 225.00
Candlewick trimmer & snuffer,
scissors-type on tray, engraved
details, early 20th c., 9 5/8" l.
tray 75.00
Chestnut roaster, square pan
w/pierced lid, well-shaped brass
handle w/ring end, 21" l. 205.00
Cup, figural rabbit handle, cast
w/grapes & leaves in relief
around sides & w/rabbits at top
border, 4¾" d., 4½" h. 100.00

Cuspidor, 8½" d., 2 pcs. 45.00
Cuspidor, lion head handles, 12" d.,
10" h. 120.00
Cyclist's cup, folding-type, nickel-
plated, embossed tandem
bicycle 30.00
Dish cross, burnished, 13 x 13" 55.00
Flag pole finial, figural American
eagle, 5½" wing spread 35.00
Kettle, spun brass w/iron bail han-
dle, 12" d., 8½" h. 65.00
Kettle, spun brass w/iron bail han-
dle, stamped "Hiram W. Hayden,
Waterbury, Conn., Pat. Dec. 16,
1851," 15" d. 135.00
Letter rack, cast w/cherubs &
florals, Bradley & Hubbard,
large 75.00
Letter rack, cast w/stag, hunting
dogs & fence, Bradley &
Hubbard 65.00

Brass Pail

Pail, spun brass w/iron bail handle,
stamped "The Ansonia Brass Co.,
Hayden's Patent," 13½" d.,
15½" h. (ILLUS.) 95.00
Pail, spun brass w/iron bail handle
fastened w/copper rivets,
stamped "Moore & Company,
American Brass Kettle, Hamilton,
Ontario," 18" d., 30" h. 88.00
Pipe tamper, model of a hand hold-
ing an Irish clay pipe, 2 1/8" h. . . 155.00
Pipe tamper, figural Dickens'
character, "The Artful Dodger,"
2 1/8" h. 55.00
Pipe tamper, model of a horse's
head, detailed mane, 2 3/8" h. . . . 145.00
Pipe tamper, flattened bust of
George Washington, 2½" h. 135.00
Sauce pan, pouring lip, hollow iron
handle, 18th c. small 85.00
Spoon mold for pewter spoons,
ca. 1740 . . . . 180.00

Stencil for barrel, "Apple Brandy,"
16" d. 125.00
Stencil for shipping crate, "Daisy
Brand, Mild Cure, Ottumwa,
U.S.A.," 18 x 14" 225.00

18th Century English Brass Tankard

Tankard, baluster-shaped w/hinged
dome lid & scrolled handle, circular base, w/initials "JAL" on underside, England, 18th c., 8" h.
(ILLUS.) 6,050.00
"Taster" spoon, signed "J. Schmidt"
& dated "1842" 400.00
Tea kettle, cov., oval, bulbous body
w/button feet, gooseneck spout,
shaped swing handle, 5¼" h. plus
handle 70.00
Tea kettle, cov., globular, goose-
neck spout, shaped swing handle,
10" h. 165.00

Queen Anne Style Tea Urn

Tea urn, Queen Anne style, pear-
shaped body on scrolling legs
w/paw feet, domed lid w/urn finial, C-scroll handle, cast spigot
w/dolphin turn, tin lining, prob-
ably England, 13" h. (ILLUS.) 385.00

Telescope, 5-draw, 2" d., 36" l. 225.00
Tobacco box, oblong w/stepped
base on bracket feet & stepped
8-sided top w/turned finial, over-
all 6" h. 175.00
Umbrella (or cane) holder, em-
bossed interior scenes w/figures
& dog on sides & 3 copper bands
at high collar, 14" d., 29" h. 350.00

BRONZE

Desk Set by Tiffany Studios

Ash tray - matchbox combination,
Zodiac patt., signed Tiffany
Studios 135.00
Blotter, rocker-type, Abalone patt.,
signed Tiffany Studios 110.00
Blotter ends, Chinese patt., signed
Tiffany Studios, 19" l., pr. 165.00
Blotter ends, Grapevine patt.,
signed Tiffany Studios, pr. 125.00
Blotter ends, Zodiac patt., dark
patina, signed Tiffany Studios,
pr. 185.00
Book rack, expandable-type, Pine
Needle patt., signed Tiffany
Studios 435.00
Box w/hinged lid, Pine Needle
patt., green glass liner, ball-
footed, dark patina, signed Tif-
fany Studios, 5½" l. 250.00
Calendar frame, easel-type, Vene-
tian patt., "dore" finish, signed
Tiffany Studios & numbered,
6½ x 6" 225.00
Card tray, w/inlaid sterling silver
Art Deco design 40.00
Desk set: letter rack, inkwell &
rocker-blotter; Abalone patt.,
signed Tiffany Studios & num-
bered, 3 pcs. 675.00
Desk set: letter rack, inkwell, rock-
er blotter, stamp box, perpetual
calendar, pr. blotter ends & pen
tray; American Indian patt.,
"dore" finish, 8 pcs. 2,565.00
Desk set: letter rack, double ink-
well, pr. blotter ends, pen tray,
note pad holder, match box & letter opener; Venetian patt., signed
Tiffany Studios, 8 pcs. (ILLUS.) . . . 1,600.00

Frame, Venetian patt., signed Tiffany Studios, 9" w., 12" h. 650.00
Humidor, cov., square form, cast w/Indian's facial masks, w/different expression on each, on all sides & lid 795.00
Letter rack, Bookmark patt., "dore" finish, signed Tiffany Studios 275.00
Letter rack, 2-tier, Grapevine patt., green-brown patina, green glass insets, signed Tiffany Studios 375.00
Magnifying glass, Zodiac patt., signed Tiffany Studios & numbered 95.00
Note pad holder, Grapevine patt., green patina, signed Tiffany Studios 295.00
Paperweight, model of a dog's head, impressed "Shando," signed Tiffany Studios, 2¼" h. 242.00
Paperweight, model of a hippotamus, signed Tiffany Studios 225.00
Pen tray, Abalone patt., signed Tiffany Studios 110.00
Pen tray, Grapevine patt., signed Tiffany Studios 155.00
Pen tray, Spider Webb patt., w/butterscotch glass insets, signed Tiffany Studios 80.00
Stamp box w/hinged lid, Grapevine patt., signed Tiffany Studios 165.00
Stamp box w/hinged lid, Pine Needle patt., green glass insets, 3-compartment, signed Tiffany Studios, 4 x 2¼" 175.00

"Peacock" Table Mirror

Table mirror, oval beveled mirror plate within framework set w/band of iridescent peacock blue "eyes," w/peacock plumage cast in low relief on back, swiveling on base cast w/matching plumage & set w/six leaded glass peacock "eyes," signed Tiffany Studios, ca. 1906, 18¼" h. (ILLUS.) 9,350.00

Tray, Flower & Wave patt. w/abalone shell discs in relief at border, "dore" finish, signed Tiffany Studios, 13½" d. 175.00
Urns, cov., cast in high relief at frieze w/dead game, leaves & dogs chasing wounded stag, each base w/entwining foliage, birds & lizards & w/heron finial on one & falcon finial on other, dark brown patina, signed P.J. Mene, second half 19th c., 15¼" h., pr. 1,430.00

Neoclassical Bronze Urn

Urns, cast w/foliate wreath at rim, figures at various pursuits around body, base cast w/acanthus leaves & flowerheads & handles cast as female figures, berry & foliate socle & molded plinth base, 19th c., 31½" h. (ILLUS. of one) 3,575.00
Vase, cast w/birds & animals in relief, Japan, 19th c., 9" h., pr. 180.00
Vase, sterling silver inlaid cat-o'-nine tails decor, signed Heinz Art Metal, 1915-22, 10" h. 100.00

COPPER

Cheese maker's vat, rounded bottom, collared neck & rim, solid dovetail construction, 54" d., 30" h. 350.00
Chocolate pot, cov., straight spout at side, wooden handle, 9" h. 35.00
Coal scuttle, helmet-shaped, domed circular foot, w/brass bail handle & applied ring-turned brass handle at rear, 19th c., 19" h. 285.00
Desk set: cov. inkwell, pen tray, letter knife, oblong blotter holder, rocker blotter, cov. stamp box, double letter rack & ash tray; hand-hammered, some pieces signed Gustav Stickley, 8 pcs. 350.00
Funnel, 5½" oval, 4" h. 35.00

Measure, haystack-type, dovetail
construction, stamped "Imperial
2," 8¼" h. 125.00
Pail, dovetail construction, 10" h. 85.00

Heavy Copper Pan

Pan, heavy, dovetail construction,
applied handle at side, 9¾" d.,
3¾" h. (ILLUS.) 135.00
Pan, large oval w/cast iron handles
at each end, tin lining 170.00
Pen tray, hand-hammered, signed
Hubbard 25.00
Saucepan, dovetail construction,
shaped copper handle, 6¼" d.,
3¼" h. 125.00
Saucepan, dovetail construction,
small 75.00
Sheet pan, hand-seamed, 20 x 12".. 55.00
Skillet, loop handle, 3" d.
miniature...................... 26.00
Spatula, pierced oval blade,
w/hanging ring on handle,
10½" l. 95.00
Stamp box, cov., hand-hammered,
signed Gustav Stickley 210.00
Tea kettle, cov., dovetail construction, globular body, gooseneck
spout, fixed handle
w/maker's mark "G.T. Rissler,"
6¾" h. plus handle............. 245.00
Tea kettle, cov., dovetail construction, slightly swollen sides, gooseneck spout, fixed overhead
handle, 11½" h. 180.00

Copper Tea Kettle

Tea kettle, cov., cylindrical, gooseneck spout, stepped lid w/acorn
finial, tubular handle, first half
19th c., 13" h. (ILLUS.) 220.00
Tea kettle, cov., dovetail construction, globular, gooseneck spout,
lid w/turned finial, bail handle
w/heart-shaped terminals, late
18th-early 19th c., 11" d.,
13½" h. 275.00
Tea kettle, on brass stand w/alcohol
burner, 8" d. kettle, overall
12¾" h. 165.00
Tray, hand-hammered, 14" l. 45.00

Whiskey Still

Whiskey still, small (ILLUS.) 150.00
Whiskey strainer, strap handle, long
spout, 1-qt. 70.00

IRON

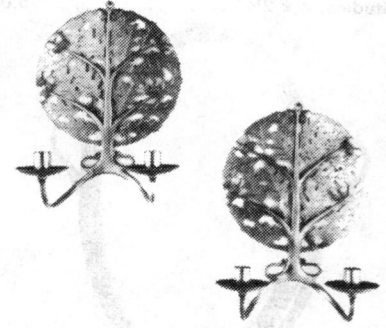

Iron Candle Sconces

Ash tray, cast, figural pr. open
cupped hands, old gilt paint,
w/green leaves & grapes at wrist,
ca. 1860, 7½" l.................. 95.00
Book press, cast, worn red & black
paint, 12½ x 9½" bed, overall
18½ x 12" (some rust) 100.00
Book rack, expandable-type, cast,
Indian decor each end, opening to
22½" 37.50
Candle sconces, cast & wrought,
2-light, circular backplate pierced
w/veined oak leaves & applied

w/realistic acorns on branching
tree trunk, outward scrolling arms
w/candle cups & drip pans (now
drilled for electricity), designed by
Ernest Gimson, ca. 1905, 14¼" h.,
pr. (ILLUS.) 770.00
Candlewick trimmer & snuffer,
hand-wrought, scisscors-type,
18th c. 60.00
Dipper, cast bowl, hand-wrought
well-shaped handle, 15" l. 45.00
Ember tongs, hand-wrought, accordion scissors-type, 21" l. 65.00
Fork, 2-tine, hand-wrought, shaped
handle, dated 1835 .... 77.00
Fork, 3-tine, hand-wrought, shaped
handle, 16¼" l. 40.00
Fork, 3-tine, hand-wrought, well-
shaped handle, 24½" l. 75.00
Fork, 3-tine, hand-wrought, decorative cut-out in center tine, straight
handle w/ring end, 31¾" l. 160.00

19th Century Fountain

Fountain, cast, figural putti riding dolphin supporting spray
nozzle on fluted pedestal cast
w/acanthus leaves & florals,
stamped "Robert Wood & Co.
Makers, Phila.," painted green,
late 19th c., 25½" d., 40" h.
(ILLUS.) 2,530.00
Masonry tie-rod end, cast, star
form 22.50
Model of a frog, cast, outstretched
back leg, worn green & gold
paint, 7" l. 50.00
Model of dog, cast, seated well-
proportioned animal w/good
details & perky ears, inset
glass eyes, old worn white
paint, 23" h. 4,500.00

Model of Lion

Model of lion, cast, standing on oblong base, England, early 19th c.,
46" l. (ILLUS.) 4,730.00
Oven peel, hand-wrought, ram's
horn handle ends, 32¾" l. 60.00
Oxen shoe, hand-wrought 4.50
Panel from rendering kettle, cast,
embossed pair of steer's heads &
grain, 25 x 13½" 175.00
Paperweight, cast, model of cash
register 25.00
Paperweight, cast, model of frog, "I
Croak for the Jackson Wagon,"
traces of old green repaint,
4¾" l. 175.00
Porringer, cast, lacy tab handle,
marked "Kenrick," 4½" d. 85.00
Pot, cast, 3-footed, bail handle, im-
pressed "No. 2 - 3 Qts., Savery &
Co., Philadelphia," 7¼" h. 135.00
Pot lifter, hand-wrought, 19th c. 18.00
Shooting gallery target, cast, model
of a song bird, worn paint,
3¾" h. .... 40.00 to 50.00
Shooting gallery target, cast, model
of rooster, worn orange paint,
5" h. 85.00
Shooting gallery target, cast, model
of a duck, 5¾" h. (pitted) 45.00
Shooting gallery target, cast, model
of a squirrel, 6" h. .... 60.00 to 85.00
Shooting gallery target, cast, figure
of a soldier w/gun, 8" h. 85.00
Shooting gallery target, cast, model
of a gorilla, 14" h. 152.00
Shooting gallery target, cast, model
of an eagle, worn red, white &
blue repaint, 15" h. 155.00
Shooting gallery target, cast, model
of a greyhound racing, molded in
the half-round w/flat back &
pierced w/target hole in center of
body, red paint over original polychrome, early 20th c., 27" l. 1,320.00
Skewer holder, hand-wrought, twisted stem, 15½" l. 55.00
Spatula, hand-wrought, flat blade,
detailed handle .... 50.00 to 95.00

Stove foot, cast, grotesque winged
  mask form, 8½" h. (single) 20.00
Stove plate, cast, scene from "Elijah
  & the Ravens" & dated 1760, attributed to the Shearwell Furnace,
  Bucks County, Pennsylvania 1,155.00
Tea kettle, cov., cast, globular,
  gooseneck spout, swivel lid, bail
  handle, 19th c. ....75.00 to 100.00
Theatre curtain weights, cast, replicas of tassels, 10½" h., pr. 195.00
Utensil rack, hand-wrought, flat bar
  w/hanging hooks enhanced
  w/simple scrollwork details,
  17" w. 175.00
Wall brackets, cast, pierced scroll,
  palmette & foliate motifs supporting round plant dish, painted
  white, ca. 1890, 21½" d., 32" h.,
  pr............................. 100.00
Yard or garden ornament, model of
  a rabbit, cast, early white repaint,
  11½" h. 150.00

PEWTER

Pewter Charger by Nathaniel Austin

Basin, Richard Austin, Boston, ca.
  1800, 8" d. 550.00
Basin, Thomas Danforth III, Connec-
  ticut & Philadelphia, ca. 1800,
  8" d. 275.00
Basin, Townsend & Compton, Lon-
  don, 18th c., 13" d. 302.00
Beaker, Boardman & Hart, New
  York, ca. 1830, 3" h. 220.00
Beaker, Timothy Boardman & Co.,
  New York, ca. 1825, 5¼" h....... 880.00
Candle holder, chamberstick-type,
  saucer base w/ring handle,
  Roswell Gleason, Dorchester,
  Massachusetts, ca. 1835, 3" h..... 495.00
Charger, "lovebird" mark, Philadel-
  phia, late 18th c., 13" d. 935.00
Charger, Blakslee Barnes, Philadel-
  phia, ca. 1815, 13½" d. 715.00
Charger, German "angel & stag"
  touchmark, 13" d. 135.00

Charger, Nathaniel Austin,
  Charlestown, Massachusetts, late
  18th c., 15" d. (ILLUS.) 605.00
Charger, Thomas Badger, Boston,
  ca. 1800, 15" d. 825.00
Charger, William Billings, Provi-
  dence, Rhode Island, ca. 1800,
  15" d. 715.00
Charger, Henry Will, New York, late
  18th c., 15" d. 1,430.00
Charger, "crowned rose" touchmark
  & "London," 16 3/8" d........... 200.00
Coffee pot, cov., pear-shaped body,
  pedestal base, wooden C-scroll
  handle & turned finial on lid, Dix-
  on & Son, England, 11½" h. 175.00
Coffee pot, cov., Freeman Porter,
  Westbrook, Maine, 1835-60....... 295.00
Coffee pot, cov., ebony handle &
  finial, Reed & Barton, 1840 & on .. 225.00
Coffee pot, cov., tapering cylinder,
  gooseneck spout, domed lid, H.
  Yale, Wallingford, Connecticut,
  1822-31 .... 375.00
Dish, deep, George Lightner, Balti-
  more, Maryland, ca. 1810,
  11¼" d. 220.00
Dish, William Billings, Providence,
  Rhode Island, ca. 1800, 11½" d. .. 770.00
Dish, deep, Thomas Danforth II,
  Middletown, Connecticut, ca.
  1770, 13¼" d. 467.00
Dish, deep, Thomas Danforth III,
  Philadelphia, ca. 1800, 13¼" d.... 357.00
Dish, deep, Edwin Danforth, Mid-
  dletown & Hartford, Connecticut,
  ca. 1790, 13½" d. 467.00
Flagon, Boardman & Co., New
  York, New York, ca. 1825,
  11" h. 1,430.00
Flagon, Thomas D. & Sherman
  Boardman, Hartford, Connecticut,
  ca. 1820, 13½" h. 1,870.00
Measure, tankard, brass rim, W.R.
  Loftus, London, qt., 6" h. 140.00

Mug by Nathaniel Austin

Mug, Nathanial Austin, Charlestown, Massachusetts, late 18th c.,
  6" h. (ILLUS.) 1,320.00

Mug, Joseph Danforth, Middletown,
Connecticut, ca. 1785, 6" h. 880.00
Mug, Samuel Hamlin, Providence,
Rhode Island, late 18th-early
19th c., 6" h. 2,200.00
Pitcher & cover w/acorn finial, pear-
shaped body, low foot, S-scroll
handle, Homan & Co., Cincinnati,
Ohio, 1847-90, 11½" h. 150.00
Pitcher, water, Rufus Dunham,
Westbrook, Maine, 1837-60 ...... 225.00
Plate, Ashbil Griswold, Meriden,
Connecticut, 1807-35, 7¾" d. 165.00
Plate, Blakslee Barnes, Philadelphia,
ca. 1810, 8" d. 110.00
Plate, Ashbil Griswold, Meriden,
Connecticut, ca. 1810, 8" d. 220.00
Plate, George Lightner, Baltimore,
Maryland, ca. 1810, 8" d. 247.00
Plate, Jacob Whitmore, Middletown,
Connecticut, 3rd quarter 18th c.,
8" d. 220.00
Plate, Frederick Bassett, New York,
ca. 1825, 9¼" d. .... 385.00 to 412.00
Plate, Boardman & Co., New York
City, ca. 1825, 9¼" d. 275.00
Plate, John Danforth, Norwich, Con-
necticut, ca. 1780, 9½" d. 385.00
Porringer, Richard Lee Sr. or Jr.,
Springfield, Vermont, ca. 1800,
4" l. 275.00
Porringer, William Calder, Provi-
dence, Rhode Island, ca. 1820,
6" l. 605.00
Porringer, William Billings, Provi-
dence, Rhode Island, ca. 1800,
7¼" l. 880.00
Porringer, Thomas & Sherman
Boardman, Hartford, Connecticut,
ca. 1820, 7½" l. 440.00

American Pewter Porringers

Porringer, William Calder, Providence, Rhode Island, ca. 1830,
7½" l. (ILLUS. left) 385.00
Porringer, Samuel Hamlin, Providence, Rhode Island, late 18th c.,
8" l. (ILLUS. right) 825.00
Saucer, Thomas Danforth III,
Philadelphia or Connecticut, late
18th c., 6" d. 357.00

Drum-Form Teapot

Teapot, cov., drum form, unmarked
American, possibly New York,
6½" h. (ILLUS.) 3,630.00
Teapot, cov., bulbous body, footed,
gooseneck spout, wooden C-scroll
handle, hinged domed lid, Sellew
& Co., Cincinnati, Ohio, 1832-60,
7¼" h. 325.00
Teapot, cov., William Calder, Providence, Rhode Island, ca. 1830,
8" h. 357.00

PLATED SILVER (Hollowware)

Silverplate Butter Dish

Bowl, canoe-shaped, "repousse"
leafy vines on sides & large Kate
Greenaway-type boy seated on
rim, vaseline glass insert, Wilcox
Silver Plate Co., Meriden,
Connecticut 350.00
Bread tray, chased vintage decor,
Homan Silver Plate Company, Cin-
cinnati, Ohio. 48.00
Butter dish w/roll-top cover, classi-
cal decor, Simpson, Hall, Miller &
Co., Wallingford, Connecticut
(ILLUS.). 200.00
Cake basket, cherubs decor, Victori-
an, Derby Silver Co., Derby,
Connecticut 185.00
Coffee urn, "repousse" florals & foli-
age decor, Simpson, Hall, Miller &
Co. 375.00
Condensed milk can holder, ornate

"repousse" decor, original glass
liner 90.00
Crumb knife, Assyrian patt. 25.00
Cup & saucer, engraved & bright-cut
butterflies & floral decor, James
W. Tufts, Boston, Massachusetts .. 40.00
Embroidery scissors, figural Salem
Witch, "Salem, 1692," Germany .. 68.00
Flask w/screw-on cap, canteen-
shaped w/puffy fluted sides, engraved w/golfer wearing knickers, holding golf sticks on
shoulder & drinking from flask,
4¾ x 4½" 160.00
Humidor, cov., chased w/mythologi-
cal figure holding reins of large
horse, Meriden Brittania
Company 355.00
Letter rack, desk-type, 4 paw feet,
tall center divider, reticulated
sides, Tiffany & Co., New York,
5" w., 2¾" h.................... 110.00
Mustard pot, reticulated sides, cobalt blue glass liner, E.G. Webster
& Son, Brooklyn, New York 70.00
Nut bowl, leaf-shaped w/little cabbage feet, figural squirrel seated
at one end, Pairpoint Mfg. Co.,
New Bedford, Massachusetts,
1890's 125.00
Pitcher, chased floral band, Wilcox
Silver Plate Co., 7" h. 35.00
Plateau mirror, beveled mirror plate
within framework applied w/cos-
mos blossoms, footed, 12" d...... 110.00
Plateau mirror, cut floral & foliage
decor on beveled mirror plate
within chased scrolls & strawberries framework w/ornate feet,
14" d. 165.00
Punch set: 14½" d., 11" h. bowl
w/pedestal base, 19" l. tray, ladle
w/double spout bowl & twisted
handle & 12 cups; engraved & applied w/shells, berries, florals &
foliage, F. B. Rogers Silver Co.,
Taunton, Massachusetts, 15 pcs. .. 475.00
Syrup pitcher & cover w/lady's head
finial, Simpson, Hall, Milller &
Co., 1865, 8¼" h. 58.00
Teapot, cov., serpent spout, chased
floral band, Pairpoint 250.00
Wine coolers, Victorian, 2-handled
campana shape, openwork grapevine body, shellwork base, w/lin-
er & detachable rim, late 19th c.,
10¾" h., pr. 1,430.00

PLATED SILVER (Flatware)
ADAM (W.D. Smith Silver Co.)
Butter serving knife 3.50
Dinner fork 4.50
Gravy ladle....................... 10.00
Iced tea spoon 5.00

Meat fork 10.00
Salad fork 4.50
Salad serving spoon 12.00
Sugar spoon 3.50

BERKSHIRE (1847 Rogers Bros.)
Berry forks, set of 6 .... 150.00
Butter spreaders, set of 6 .... 48.00
Dinner knife 22.50
Gravy ladle...................... 23.50
Seafood fork 8.00
Soup ladle, 13¼" l. 55.00

CHARTER OAK (1847 Rogers Bros.)

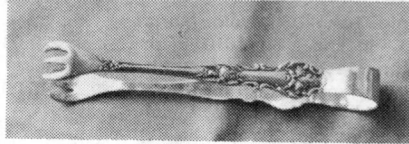

Charter Oak Pattern Sugar Tongs

Butter serving knife 16.00
Butter spreaders, set of 6 .... 58.00
Cold meat fork.................... 22.00
Cream ladle 20.00
Dinner fork 11.00
Dinner knife, hollow handle 22.00
Grapefruit spoon 15.00
Oyster forks, set of 6 .... 75.00
Salad serving fork & spoon 140.00
Seafood fork..................... 17.50
Sugar shell 14.00
Sugar tongs, 4½" l. (ILLUS.) 20.00
Teaspoon........................ 9.00

MOSELLE (American Silver Co.)
Butter serving knife 28.00
Cold meat fork.................... 75.00
Meat fork 40.00
Sugar shell 30.00
Teaspoon........................ 10.00

VINTAGE (1847 Rogers Bros.)

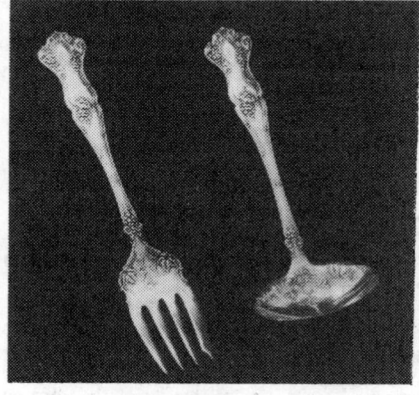

Vintage Pattern

Baby spoon, curved handle 22.50
Berry serving spoon . . . . .28.00 to 40.00
Bouillon spoon 12.00
Butter spreader 13.00
Carving set, 3 pcs. 60.00
Cheese scoop, hollow handle 40.00
Chocolate muddler 65.00
Dinner fork 10.00
Dinner knife, hollow handle 12.00
Food pusher 40.00
Fruit knife, hollow handle 30.00
Grapefruit spoon 18.00
Gravy ladle (ILLUS.) 32.00
Marmalade spoon 25.00
Meat fork (ILLUS.) 25.00
Oyster forks, set of 6 . . . .   80.00
Oyster ladle 100.00
Salad serving fork & spoon 75.00
Tablespoon 15.00
Teaspoon 11.00

SILVER - COIN

Coin Silver Mug

Beaker, cylindrical w/flaring molded
  rim & molded base, engraved
  name, N. Harding & Co., Boston,
  ca. 1830, 3¼" h. 137.50
Berry spoon, shell-shaped bowl,
  engraved name & dated "1871,"
  8" l. 42.00
Butter knife, master size, Albert
  Coles, New York, ca. 1860 . . . .   65.00
Butter knife, master size, Fiddle
  Thread patt., R. & W. Wilson,
  Philadelphia, ca. 1840 . . . .   55.00
Creamer & cov. sugar bowl, pear-
  shaped w/banded decor, Ball,
  Tompkins & Black, New York City,
  1839-51, pr. 750.00
Cup, tapered, reeded banding, P.L.
  Krider, Philadelphia, 1850-60,
  3½" h. 225.00
Cup, Albert Coles, New York City,
  1844-76 . . . . 175.00
Dessert spoon, Butler & McCarthy,
  Philadelphia, ca. 1850 . . . .   25.00
Dessert spoon, Gale, Wood &
  Hughes, New York City,
  ca. 1835 . . . .   25.00
Dinner fork, French Thread patt.,

Ball, Black & Co., New York City,
  1851, 7¾" l. 31.50
Dinner knives, Jones, Ball & Poor,
  Boston, 1846, 11½" l., set of 12 . . 750.00
Egg spoons, French Thread patt.,
  Wm. Gale & Son, New York City,
  set of 4 . . . .   95.00
Fish slice, relief scrolls on handle,
  pierced & bright-cut figural fish
  blade, S.T. Crosby, Boston,
  ca. 1850, 11½" l. 225.00
Fish slice, Olive patt., pierced fish
  form blade, Jones, Ball & Co.,
  Boston, ca. 1850, 12" l. 300.00
Fruit knife w/folding blade, florals,
  beading & monogram on blade,
  unmarked 22.00
Gravy boat, Greek Key border, Wm.
  Gale, New York City, 1799-1867 . . 395.00
Gravy ladle, Gelston, Ladd & Co.,
  New York City, 1839-44,
  7 7/8" l. 95.00
Ice cream set: ice cream slice & 12
  ice cream spoons; Church &
  Rogers, Hartford, Connecticut,
  ca. 1860, 13 pcs. 475.00
Meat fork, overall etching, Newell
  Harding & Co., Boston, ca. 1840 . . 150.00
Mug, scroll handle, Newel Harding
  & Co., Boston, ca. 1840 (ILLUS.) . . . 135.00
Mustard ladle, J. Blackman & Co.,
  Bridgeport, Connecticut, 1808-72 . .   32.00
Mustard ladle, Palmer & Batchelder,
  Boston, 1854-60 . . . .   29.00
Nut pick, Olive patt., Bailey & Co.,
  Philadelphia, ca. 1850 . . . .   25.00
Pastry server, bright-cut blade,
  Bigelow Bros. & Kennard, Boston,
  ca. 1840, 11" l. 195.00
Plate, Eoff & Shepard, New York
  City, ca. 1850, 8" d. 525.00
Porridge spoon, mid-rib front, T.
  Coverly, Boston & Newport, Rhode
  Island, ca. 1760 . . . . 395.00
Salt shovel, master size, Norton &
  Seymour, Syracuse, New York,
  ca. 1850 . . . .   21.00
Salt spoon, master size, ornately en-
  graved handle, gold-washed bowl,
  Albert Coles, New York City 24.00
Salt spoon, master size, Jones, Low
  & Ball, Boston, 1839 . . . .   38.00
Salt spoon, master size, Olmstead,
  Farmington, Connecticut,
  ca. 1810 . . . .   35.00
Sardine fork, Strawberry patt.,
  Palmer & Batchelder, Boston,
  ca. 1860 . . . . 125.00
Sauce ladle, Jedediah Baldwin,
  Massachusetts, Connecticut, New
  Hampshire & New York,
  ca. 1810 . . . .   50.00
Sauce ladle, Goodwin & Dodd, Hart-
  ford, Connecticut, ca. 1812 . . . .   36.00

Serving fork, 5-tine, Newell Harding
& Co., Boston, 1796-1852, 9" l..... 140.00

Serving spoon, Olive patt., scalloped
bowl, Mulford & Wendell, Albany,
New York, ca. 1850, 8 5/8" l. 75.00

Serving spoon, shell-ribbed & scalloped bowl, full figure knight's
head at handle tip, Ball, Black &
Co., New York City, ca. 1850,
11" l. 400.00

Soup ladle, Emperor patt. w/mono-
gram, hand-chased, gold-washed
bowl w/bright-cut work, Knowles
& Ladd 425.00

Sugar shell, shell-ribbed bowl,
Farrington & Hunnewell, Boston,
ca. 1840 .... 38.00

Sugar shell, shell-ribbed bowl,
Butler & McCarthy, Philadelphia,
ca. 1845 .... 38.00

Sugar shovel, Gorham & Thurber,
Providence, Rhode Island,
ca. 1850 .... 35.00

Sugar sifter, twist in mid-handle,
bust medallion end, scalloped &
pierced gold-washed bowl, Albert
Coles, New York City 85.00

Sugar sifter, Fiddle patt., Bailey &
Kitchen, Philadelphia, ca. 1840 ... 115.00

Sugar tongs w/spoon ends, B.C.
Frobisher, Boston, 6 1/8" l. 55.00

Sugar tongs, J.C. Farr, Philadelphia,
ca. 1824 .... 65.00

Sugar tongs, Fiddle Shell patt., A.
Jacobs, Philadelphia, ca. 1816 .... 95.00

Tablespoon, Chedell, Auburn, New
York, ca. 1827 .... 55.00

Coin Silver Tablespoon

Tablespoon, engraved initials on
handles, S. & E. Roberts, ca. 1830,
8 5/8" l. (ILLUS.) 40.00

Tablespoon, bright-cut engraving, R.
Wilson, New York City, ca. 1800 .. 125.00

Teaspoon, Appleton Co., ca. 1840... 12.00

Teaspoon, Bailey & Parker, Owen,
Vermont, ca. 1845 .... 25.00

Teaspoon, J. Black, Philadelphia,
ca. 1820 .... 18.00

Teaspoon, T. Bradbury & Sons,
Newburyport, Massachusetts,
ca. 1815 .... 24.00

Teaspoon, J. David, Jr., Philadelphia, ca. 1790 .... 85.00

Teaspoon, S. Drowne, Portsmouth,
New Hampshire, ca. 1790 .... 75.00

SILVER, AMERICAN, ENGLISH & OTHERS (Hollowware)

Russian Silver Cake Basket

Beaker, George III, tapered sides,
engraved w/monogram, Peter &
Ann Bateman, London, 1798,
3½" h......................... 352.00

Bowl, flared sides, molded spreading foot, base engraved w/con-
temporary monogram, Samuel
Casey, South Kingston, Rhode
Island, ca. 1760, 5¾" rim d. 15,400.00

Bowl, George III, vase-shaped circular bowl raised from domed pedestal base, 2 circled reeded
upright handles terminating
w/paterae, engraved w/applied
coat of arms, Wm. Burwash &
Richard Sibley, London, 1808,
11" d. 2,860.00

Box, cov., George III, cylindrical,
engraved w/armorials on lid &
front, gilt interior, John Holloway,
London, 1790, 3 3/8" d. 880.00

Cake basket, George IV, lobed &
fluted sides w/shell & foliate rim
& swing handle, shaped pedestal
foot, John Angell, London, 1826,
12" d. 825.00

Cake basket, chased to simulate
basketweave w/an overlaid napkin, cable handles, 4 wirework
feet, basketweave gilded, Khleb-
nikov, Moscow, 1878, 14¾" l.
(ILLUS.) 3,960.00

Caudle cup, cov., James II, vase
form on molded foot, domed
cover w/acorn finial, scroll handles, Robert Cooper, London,
1686, 7" h....................2,090.00

Cheese scoop, George III, Bacchanalian patt., shaped handle
decorated on the front w/bac-
chanal figures & a lion surrounded
by grapevine, reverse w/a trophy
of crossed thyrsi, amphora, tambourine & basket of flowers,
engraved w/crest & motto, Paul
Storr, London, 1816, 9" l........1,210.00

Cigarette cup, cylinder supported by
4 laurel wreaths & mounted on a

circular base raised on 4 bun feet, etched w/naked infants playing in a forest, Faberge, Moscow, ca. 1900, 4 1/8" h. 2,420.00

Coffee pot & cover w/bell finial, George II, plain tapering cylinder, engraved w/armorials in a baroque cartouche, faceted swan's neck spout, Edward Vincent, London, 1731, 8¾" h. 1,870.00

Creamer, pyriform w/scalloped rim & curved spout, 3 stepped pad scroll feet w/shell knees, acanthus-capped scroll handle, Thomas Arnold, Newport, Rhode Island, 1760-75, 4 1/8" h. 4,180.00

Creamer & cov. 2-handled sugar bowl, George IV, melon form, scroll handles mounted on applied foliate cartouches rising from shells, William Elliott, London, 1824, pr. 467.00

Dish cross, George III, swiveling arms & sliding double-scroll supports chased w/leaves & w/large shell terminals, w/crested lamp, William Grundy, London, ca. 1760, 12" l. 990.00

Entree dish & domed cover w/mounted knight finial, George IV, rectangular w/serpentine sides, angles w/shells & leaves, William Elliott, London, 1826, 12½" l. 2,750.00

American Silver Marrow Spoon

Marrow spoon, double-ended, tapered flat handle, Clark & Company, Augusta, Georgia, 1830-42, 7 1/8" l. (ILLUS.) 770.00

Marrow spoon, John Cullen, Dublin, Ireland, 1769. . . . . 350.00

Mug, George III, baluster form w/molded rim & domed stepped base, leaf-capped double-scroll handle, front engraved w/inscription, maker's mark W.C., London, 1780, 5 1/8" h. 440.00

Nutmeg grater, flattened cylindrical case, hinged front & cover open to removable grater, Hester Bateman, London, ca. 1790, 2¾" h. 312.50

Pitcher, vase-shaped body w/flaring

cylindrical neck, scroll handle w/mask thumbpiece, beaded borders, engraved w/stylized foliage & scrolls, Bigelow Bros. & Kennard, Boston, Massachusetts, ca. 1845, 9¾" h. 1,100.00

Platter, shaped oblong form, ribbon-tied reeded rims w/scrolling acanthus, border engraved w/contemporary armorials, Mortimer & Hunt, London, 1842, 16" l. 1,210.00

Platter, George III, shaped oval w/gadroon rim, border engraved w/armorials, Sebastian & James Crespell, London, 1766, 21" l. 2,200.00

Platter, well-and-tree, William IV, shaped oval form w/gadroon rim interrupted by shells & leaves at intervals, 4 paw feet headed by acanthus, border engraved twice w/armorials, Charles Marsh, Dublin, Ireland, 1833, 22½" l. 2,420.00

Porringer, circular w/everted rim & pierced keyhole handle, engraved w/monogram, Thomas Knox Emery, Boston, Massachusetts, 1802-13, 6¾" d. 770.00

Salt dips, George II, deeply fluted shell form raised on 3 shell feet, applied w/rococo cartouches, Edward Wood, London, 1740, 3 5/8" l., pr. 467.00

Salver, George III, beaded rim, border of conjoining circles, center engraved w/crest within rayed oval cartouche, on 3 panel supports, Peter & Ann Bateman, London, 1796, 11 7/8" d. 1,760.00

Salver, rim cast, pierced & chased w/grapevine enclosing lions, urns, cornucopiae & bacchanal masks, center engraved w/monogram surrounded by scrolling foliage linking spread eagles, raised on 3 paw feet headed by roses & acanthus, Hamilton, Crichton & Co., Edinburgh, Scotland, 1875, 18¼" d. 2,970.00

Sauce tureens, cov., George III, plain boat shape w/reeded rim & loop handle, reeded & foliate ring finial, John Scofield, London, 1790, 9 5/8" l. across handles, pr. 1,320.00

Soup ladle, George III, Fiddle patt., engraved w/crest, Dublin, Ireland, 1808 . . . . 286.00

Soup plates, George III, shaped circular form, gadroon rim w/alternating acanthus leaves & beads, border engraved w/armorials, Paul Storr, London, 1811-14, 10 3/8" d., set of 12 . . .15,400.00

Soup tureen, cov., oval, molded

foot & rim, pendant ring handles
applied w/grape clusters, domed
cover applied w/grape cluster
& beaded foliage over embossed
& chased foliage, hammered surface, Georg Jensen, Copenhagen,
Denmark, ca. 1925, 13 7/8" l. 4,510.00
Stuffing spoon, Shell patt., Edinburgh, Scotland, ca. 1860 .... 225.00
Sugar box, rectangular w/incurved
hinged cover engraved w/crest,
front engraved w/date "1791,"
fitted w/lock, Continental (probably Polish), ca. 1791, 6¼" l. 825.00
Sugar shaker, ornate pierced domed
top, Samuel Wood, London,
1761 .... 550.00
Tablespoon, handle w/bright-cut
wrigglework borders, & monogram in oval cartouche above
flowerhead & pendant husks, long
molded drop on reverse of egg-
shaped bowl, Paul Revere, Jr.,
Boston, Massachusetts, ca. 1785,
8¼" l. 4,950.00
Tea & coffee set: cov. coffee pot,
cov. teapot, cov. sugar bowl,
creamer, waste bowl, kettle on
stand & tray; bombe form chased
& applied w/vignettes of putti
playing & rococo decor, leaf-
capped scroll handles & hinged
domed covers w/flower spray
finials, raised on 4 slender leaf-
decorated scroll supports headed
by winged putto masks, tray
w/conforming border & cut-out
handles, center monogram, Shreve
& Co., San Francisco, California,
ca. 1911, 7 pcs. 4,950.00

18th Century Silver Teapot

Teapot, pear-shaped w/fluted
faceted body & partly octagonal
spout, octagonal handle sockets,
domed cover similarly decorated
& w/baluster wood finial,
Johann Christoffer Buschman,

Bremen, Germany, ca. 1740,
6½" h. (ILLUS.) 7,700.00
Tray, Martele', shaped oval w/cut-
out handles, undulating rim embossed & chased w/two scantily
draped maidens & a continuous
vine of roses, Gorham Co.,
Providence, Rhode Island, 1907,
15¼" l. 2,640.00
Vases, Martele', flaring cylinder
w/scalloped & lobed brim above
swelled cylindrical stem, over a
domed base on a scalloped &
lobed foot, entire surface
hammer-faceted, w/"repousse"
& chased daisies, leaves & stylized stems, Gorham Co., Providence, Rhode Island, 1900-04,
14½" h., pr. 5,280.00
Wine taster, Louis XV, thread rim,
side engraved "Ctne. Fombert,"
mushroom-shaped thumbpiece
engraved w/cupid holding arrow
below the words "Il seitindra
jamais," w/ring handle, Mathieu
Lamoureaux, Rouen, France, 1770,
3 1/8" d. 2,420.00

SILVER, AMERICAN FLATWARE PATTERNS
AMERICAN BEAUTY (George W. Shiebler)
Bon bon spoon, pierced bowl 35.00
Butter pick 35.00
Claret ladle 195.00
Horseradish spoon 50.00
Salad fork 45.00
Soup spoon 26.00

CANTERBURY (Towle Mfg. Co.)
Berry serving spoon, gold-washed
bowl 95.00
Cold meat fork 75.00
Cream ladle 35.00
Lemon fork 18.00
Sardine fork 30.00
Strawberry fork 25.00

CHRYSANTHEMUM (Tiffany & Co.)
Asparagus tongs, individual size 265.00
Crumb knife 495.00
Dinner knife 60.00
Fruit knife 55.00
Sandwich tongs 550.00
Sugar sifter 245.00
Teaspoon 38.00
Tomato server 485.00

ETON (R. Wallace & Sons)
Butter serving knife 45.00
Citrus spoon 20.00
Dinner fork 28.00
Salad fork 50.00
Soup spoon, oval 45.00
Sugar tongs 26.00

IMPERIAL QUEEN (Whiting Mfg. Co.)
Berry serving spoon 75.00
Cracker scoop 295.00
Dinner fork 37.00
Ice cream slice 175.00
Punch ladle 350.00
Stuffing spoon 325.00

KINGS (Dominick & Haff)
Butter spreader 20.00
Cream soup spoon 38.00
Dinner fork 45.00
Dinner knife 40.00
Luncheon fork 29.00
Luncheon knife 32.00

LILY OF THE VALLEY (Gorham Mfg. Co.)

Lily of the Valley Pattern

Crumb knife, gold-washed blade . . . 175.00
Ice cream spoons, set of 6 . . . . 175.00
Sauce ladle (ILLUS.) 45.00
Sugar shell (ILLUS.) 35.00

VERSAILLES (Gorham Mfg. Co.)
Asparagus server, footed 550.00
Cheese knife 95.00
Dinner fork 50.00
Fish slice 225.00
Gravy ladle 115.00
Jelly server 65.00
Luncheon fork 32.00
Mustard ladle 75.00
Salad serving spoon & fork 325.00
Sugar tongs 45.00
Waffle server 235.00

WAVE EDGE (Tiffany & Co.)
Cheese scoop 175.00
Cream ladle 165.00
Ice cream server, hatchet-shaped . . . 475.00
Salad fork 65.00
Sherbet spoon 50.00
Sugar shell 48.00
Tablespoon 50.00

TIN & TOLE

Toleware Basket

Basket, tole, oval w/notched rim &
  attached handles at sides, stenciled grapes & leaves overall on
  red ground, France, 19th c., 12" l.
  (ILLUS.) 770.00
Beeswax mold, tin, tapering square,
  3" h. 65.00
Bonnet box, cov., tin, original
  mustard yellow paint 90.00
Bread tray, tole, free-hand yellow,
  white & blue foliage on vivid red
  ground, 12¾ x 8" 1,375.00
Butter churn, dasher-type, tin, flared
  top, original mustard yellow
  paint, 23" h. 260.00
Cake box, cov., original gold-
  stenciled "Cake" on brown
  japanned finish 25.00
Candle box, wall-type, cylindrical
  w/hinged lid & original hanging
  tabs 225.00
Candle mold, tin, single "cathedral"
  size, braced base, 18" h. 295.00
Candle mold, tin, 2-tube, oblong
  tray top w/ring handles,
  11½" l. 55.00
Candle mold, tin, 3-tube, crimped
  top 175.00
Candle mold, tin, 4-tube, 8½" h. . . . 50.00
Candle mold, tin, 6-tube, tray top
  w/handles at sides,
  11" h. . . . . 60.00 to 75.00
Candle mold, tin, 12-tube, 2 rows of
  6, w/strap handles each side,
  11" h. . . . . 80.00 to 100.00
Candle mold, tin, 18-tube, 2 rows
  of 9 in wooden frame,
  10½" h. . . . . 100.00 to 155.00
Candle sconce, tin, crimped circular
  top above plain backplate w/in-
  vected circles at top & half-round
  candle shelf below, 14" h. 150.00
Candle snuffer & tray, tin, cone-
  shaped snuffer, green-painted
  tray, 2 pcs. 85.00
Christmas tree candle holders, tin,
  clip-on type, marked "Germany,"
  set of 12 . . . . 28.00

Pennsylvania Punched Tin Coffee Pots

Coffee pot w/conical lid & braced strap handle, tin, punched wriggleswork design of large stylized American eagle & American flag on standard one side & w/meandering stylized tulips & florals reverse, w/wriggleswork maker's signature on handle, Pennsylvania, early 19th c., 10¾" h. (ILLUS. left) 2,640.00

Coffee pot w/domed lid & braced strap handle, tin, punched design of large stylized tulip flanked by crowned peacocks perched on scrolling leafage & w/peacocks flanking a tulip tree below, inscribed w/name "Mary Shade - March th 18 AD 1848" on base & signed "W. Shade" on handle, dated 1848, 11¼" h. (ILLUS. right).......................2,420.00

Coffee pot, cov., tin, attached metal plaque "The Continental - 1858" .. 165.00

Pennsylvania Tole Coffee Pot

Coffee pot w/domed lid & braced strap handle, tole, tapering cylinder, gooseneck spout, freehand large red fruit specimens w/yellow leafage on black ground, Pennsylvania, 19th c., 11" h. (ILLUS.) 935.00

Comb box, wall-type, tin, early 20th c. ....12.00 to 20.00

Cottage cheese sieve, tin, heart-shaped, punched dot & dash design, 3 conical feet, 6" w., 5" h. ... 275.00

Cracker cutter & pricker combination, tin, scalloped rim, arched handle, rolled edge, round 85.00

Cup, tole, straight sides, strap handle, stenciled "A Gift" on red-orange ground, 2 1/8" h. 45.00

Document box w/flat lid, tole, white band w/free-hand red & blue florals & yellow striping on dark brown japanned ground, miniature size, 4¼" l. 200.00

Document box w/domed lid, tole, free-hand red & white swags on original dark brown japanned ground, original bail handle, 8 5/8" l........................ 90.00

Egg shipping box, cov., tin, double-decker, w/packing instructions, ca. 1940, 13 x 9 x 9" 20.00

Flask, tole, gilt-stenciled & brush stroke decor of Indian "pow-wow," early 19th c., 4½" l. 135.00

Hand warmer, tin 45.00

Kitchenette (so-called tin kitchen), tole, "Perfect Pantry" stenciled on lower front drawers, compartmented bins for flour, sugar, etc., gilt-stenciled decor & labels plus original clock, Perfect Pantry Co., St. Louis, 1904 patent, large size ....800.00 to 1,200.00

Knitting needle case, tole, free-hand yellow & red decor on dark brown japanned ground, 9" l. (some wear) 100.00

Lunch bucket, tin, oblong, w/interior tray, cup & vessel for liquids 20.00

Milk (or cream) can, cov., tin, wire bail handle, 5½" d., 10" h. 20.00

Oil lamp filler can, tin, cylinder w/conical top & chained cap, narrow spout, high loop handle w/tipping handle below, 5" d., 9" h. 72.00

Pencil box w/sliding lid, tin, "Columbia for a Good Scholar," w/slate pencil 20.00

Plate, tin, attributed to the Shakers, 11" d........................... 55.00

Rolling pin, tin, pull-out wooden handles to reveal tin flour scoop & cookie cutter inside 55.00

Sugar shaker, tin, strap handle, 3¾" h........................... 17.50

Teapot, cov., tin, blocked oval w/pewter handle & finial, 5" h. ... 65.00

Tea tray, tole, free-hand colorful bucolic landscape w/manor house, shepherds, etc., England, 19th c., 27½" oval (now on bamboo-turned stand, 19" h.) 3,300.00

Plate Warming Stand

Warming stand for plates, tole,
  slightly domed top above case
  w/door opening to shelves, sides
  w/brass carrying handles, on
  cabriole legs, penny feet, gilt-
  stenciled decor on black ground,
  19th c., 15" w., 28½" h.
  (ILLUS.) 1,210.00

(End of Metals Section)

MINIATURES (Paintings)

Miniature Portrait of a Gentleman

Bust portrait of gentleman on copper, wearing royal blue coat
  w/gold braid, ornate white wig,
  gilt brass locket frame, France,
  18th c., 1¾" oval $192.50
Bust portrait of gentleman in pale
  brown jacket w/white cravat &
  waistcoat on ivory, in gold-
  rimmed pendant frame w/plaited
  human hair & enamel reverse,
  signed & dated James Peale, ca.
  1805, 2 5/8" oval (ILLUS.) 990.00
Bust portrait of gentleman on ivory,

wearing blue jacket & yellow
  waistcoat & w/curly light brown
  hair, in the manner of Karl von
  Saar, in gilt-metal frame, ca.
  1820, 3¾" oval 660.00
Bust portrait of Dutch gentleman in
  dark frock coat on ivory, Dutch
  dealer's label reverse, early
  1800's, 2½" oval within black
  recessed frame w/gilt trim, overall 6" square.................... 125.00
Bust portrait of lady on ivory, inlaid
  ivory & tortoise shell frame, 3½ x
  4" oval 185.00
Bust portrait of young man w/wavy
  brown hair on ivory, brass & black
  velvet-edged frame w/wooden
  back, 2 5/8 x 3" oval 175.00
Bust portrait of young woman on
  ivory, wearing white dress & gold
  chain necklace, signed "P. Strad-
  ley," in original cardboard &
  (worn) red velvet frame w/gilt-
  brass liner, 5 3/8 x 6" 275.00
Child w/blonde hair on porcelain,
  framed, 2½ x 2" 180.00
Full-length figure of woman wearing
  plum-colored gown w/ornate lace
  trim on ivory, signed "Striber," inlaid ivory frame................. 265.00
Madonna w/flowing hair on porcelain, ca. 1780, 3 3/8" oval...... 486.00
Three-quarter figure of young lady
  w/burgundy dress w/lace collar,
  French School, artist-signed &
  dated 1830, original brass
  frame, 4" square 450.00

MINIATURES (Replicas)

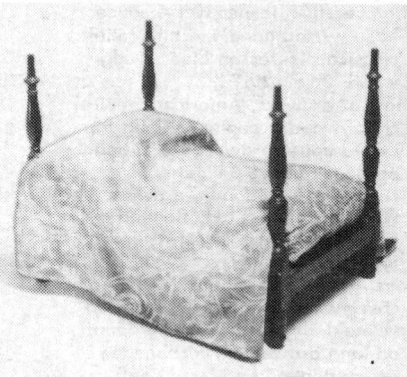

Miniature Federal Tall Poster Bed

Also see SALESMAN'S SAMPLES.

Basket, buttocks-type, 6-rib construction, woven splint, 2 3/8" l...$105.00

Bed, Federal tall poster, mahogany,
baluster- and ring-turned head &
footposts, tapering feet, early
19th c., 10" w., 14" l., 12" h.
(ILLUS.)...................... 495.00

Bench, painted & decorated, 2-
chairback style w/shaped & scalloped roll-over crestrail above
medial stayrail & 3 uprights,
downswept arms, plank seat,
turned legs w/stretchers, free-
hand acorns & red tulips crestrail
decor on black ground highlighted
w/gold striping, Pennsylvania....2,550.00

Blanket chest, painted pine, hinged
lid w/molded edge lifting to well
w/till, bracket feet, rosmaaling
on white ground, painted interior,
19½" l. 225.00

Blanket chest, painted pine, oblong
top lifting to deep well, painted
ochre w/dark brown sponge-
daubing worked in a continuous
diagonal line stripe design overall, black painted sheet metal
lock, New England, ca. 1830,
24 x 12", 9¼" h. 880.00

Bowl, cut glass, 2-handled, hobstars
& fan, 11½" w. across handles 110.00

Bowl, redware, clear glaze
w/brown-sponged design, 3¼" d.,
1½" h. 165.00

Bride's basket, ruffled cranberry
glass bowl, silverplate frame
marked "Reliance Quadruplate
Silver," 5¾" w., 5½" h. 195.00

Chair, Windsor "fan-back" armchair,
shaped crestrail w/scrolling ears
above 7-spindle back, shaped
seat, baluster-turned splayed
legs, branded "Wallace Nutting".. 990.00

Chamberstick, jasper ware, saucer
base w/ring handle, white relief
classical figures on blue, Wedgwood, 3" d., 2½" h. 70.00

Chest of drawers, American Empire,
cherrywood & poplar, oblong top
above upper drawer w/cockbead-
ed edges above 3 slightly
recessed & graduated drawers
w/conforming details flanked by
reeded columns, baluster-turned
legs, ball feet, Kentucky 2,600.00

Chest of drawers, Sheraton-style,
cherrywood & poplar, oblong top
w/molded edge above 4 graduated long drawers w/cockbeaded
edges flanked by applied half-
round ring-turned columns continuing to ring-turned feet,
24¼" w., 23" h. (replaced brass
rosette handles)................. 775.00

Condiment set: triangular tray
w/raised sides, cov. mustard pot
w/spoon slot, cruet w/faceted
stopper & shaker bottle w/glass
screw-on top; cut glass, pinwheel
& vertical notch cutting 3½ x 3"
tray, 4 pcs. 150.00

Document box w/domed lid, tole,
free-hand red, white, yellow &
green floral & fruit decor
w/sprouting tendrils & dark green
heart-shaped foliage on black
ground, Maine, early 19th c.,
6¼" l., 4½" h.................. 605.00

Fainting couch, Victorian, Eastlake
substyle, ebony finish w/gilding,
worn original tufted upholstery
w/built-in bolster, 24" l. 425.00

Parlor set: settee & 2 arm chairs;
sterling silver, French rococo style
w/embossed cupids on seats,
1¾" h., 3 pcs. 180.00

Pitcher, tankard, cut glass, bull's
eye, cross-cut diamond & fan, applied notched handle, 16-point
rayed base, 2" d., 2½" h......... 70.00

Pitcher, redware, clear glaze,
2¾" h......................... 65.00

Pitcher, ruby glass w/applied handle, bulbous w/round mouth,
enameled gold florals & trim,
1 3/8" d., 1 7/8" h.............. 65.00

Shaving stand, wooden, rectangular
mirror plate tilting on scrolled
supports above rectangular base
w/single drawer, original black
paint w/gold trim, 9¼" h. 210.00

Skillet, graniteware, blue mottled .. 65.00

Tea & coffee service: cov. teapot,
cov. coffee pot, creamer, sugar
bowl, hot water kettle on warming stand & tray; sterling silver
w/turquoise finials, marked
Heochen D.F. 925, 7 pcs.......... 350.00

Tea kettle, graniteware, mottled
blue 75.00

Miniature Dome-Top Trunk

Trunk, dome-top, wooden, top
painted w/large basket of red &

white flowers flanked by red &
white birds on green leafage,
front painted w/red & white flowers & bow-knotted swags & red &
white bird w/a flower in its beak,
sides w/flowerheads, all on black
ground, probably Continental,
early 19th c., 17¾ x 12", 10¾" h.
(ILLUS.) 935.00
Utensil set: dipper, 2-tined fork &
spatula; wrought iron, well-
shaped handles, each 4 7/8" l.,
3 pcs. 415.00
Window seat, American Empire, ma-
hogany, scrolled acanthus-carved
roll-over arm supports, upholstered seat, carved winged hairy
paw feet, ca. 1840, 20" l. 935.00

MOTHER-OF-PEARL FLATWARE

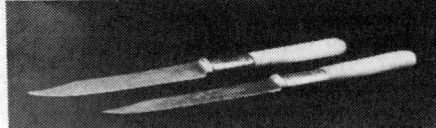

Fruit Knives

*Mother-of-pearl refers to the lustrous pearly
internal layer of certain mollusk shells. It was
applied as a decoration to papier mache objects, fans, card cases and a variety of items
or made into buttons and jewelry. Considered
exceptionally fashionable throughout the
19th century, it was also used to form the handles of table silverware. While a variety of
flatware pieces are available, fruit knives appear to be the most common form. Sometimes
the ferrules, or metal rings used for securing
the joint, are of sterling quality.*

Berry spoon $45.00
Bread knife, silver ferrule, serrated
blade, 12½" l. . . . . .12.00 to 18.00
Butter serving knife 20.00
Butter spreaders, sterling silver fer-
rules, set of 6 . . . . .65.00 to 75.00
Butter spreaders, sterling silver fer-
rules, sabre blades, set of 6 . . . . . 40.00
Carving set: 2-tined fork & slicing
knife; sterling silver ferrules,
original case, pr. 90.00
Cheese server, sterling silver
ferrule 20.00
Cold meat fork . . . . .18.00 to 25.00
Cream ladle, 6" l. 11.50
Dessert forks, set of 6 . . . . 92.00
Dinner forks, embossed sterling fer-
rules, A. Stowell, Boston, Massachusetts, set of 12 in original
flannel wrapper 245.00

Dinner knifes, marked J. Russell &
Co., 1834, No. 12, set of 6 . . . . 90.00
Dinner knives, silver ferrules &
flame-shaped tips, Landers, Frary
& Clark, set of 8 . . . . 160.00
Dinner knives, embossed sterling
silver ferrules, A. Stowell, Boston,
Massachusetts, set of 12 in origi-
nal flannel wrapper 245.00
Fish server & fork, sterling silver
ferrules, ornate engraved scroll-
work, pr. 55.00
Fish set: 12 knives & 12 forks; en-
graved fish swimming through
seaweed, 24 pcs. 250.00
Flatware service for six, 6 each
luncheon knives & forks, 12 pcs.
in original box 195.00
Fruit knives, sterling silver ferrules,
"World Brand," set of 4 . . . . 25.00
Fruit knives, floral "repousse" ster-
ling silver ferrules, engraved
blades, 6" l., set of 6 (ILLUS. of
part) 85.00
Fruit ladle, 9" l. 15.00
Gravy ladle 35.00
Luncheon knives, silver blades,
Meriden Cutlery Co., set of 6 . . . . . 75.00
Mustard spoon 15.00
Nut picks, wide elaborate sterling
silver ferrules, set of 6 . . . .40.00 to 60.00
Olive fork 8.00
Petit four server, 5¾" l. 6.00
Pickle fork . . . . .12.00 to 18.00
Pie server, ornate sterling silver
ferrule 18.00
Preserve spoon 8.00
Serving spoon, sterling silver fer-
rule, round bowl 15.00
Steak knives, Gorham Mfg. Com-
pany, ca. 1865, set of 12 . . . . 360.00
Sugar shell, sterling silver ferrule,
silverplate bowl, pat. Sept. 8-14 . . 22.00
Tomato server, pierced blade,
8" l. 19.00

MUCHA (Alphonse) ARTWORK

*A leader in the Art Nouveau movement,
Alphonse Maria Mucha was born in Moravia
(now part of Czechoslovakia) in 1860. Display-
ing considerable artistic talent as a child, he
began formal studies locally, later continuing
his work in Munich and then Paris, where it
became necessary for him to undertake commercial artwork. In 1894, the renowned actress Sarah Bernhardt commissioned Mucha
to create a poster for her play "Gismonda"
and this opportunity proved to be the turn-*

ing point in his career. While continuing his association with Bernhardt, he began creating numerous advertising posters, packaging designs, book and magazine illustrations and "panneaux decoratifs" (decorative pictures). Commissioned assignments and a lecture series in the United States followed. Mucha died in his native Czechoslovakia in 1939.

Alphonse Mucha Advertising Poster

Poster, "Aurora," 1899, printed
  by F. Champenois, Paris,
  18¼ x 34½" $1,320.00
Poster, "Autome," 1896,
  39¼ x 20" .1,200.00
Poster, "Bernhardt - American Tour,
  Direction of Abbey, Schoeffel &
  Grau," 1896, framed, 78 x 29"
  (slight creasing at middle) 4,620.00
Poster, "Bieres de la Meuse,"
  ca. 1897, 55 x 36¼" 3,300.00
Poster, "Carnation," 1897, framed,
  40 3/8 x 16½" 2,300.00
Poster, "Crepuscule," 1899, printed
  by F. Champenois, Paris,
  18 1/8 x 34 5/8" 1,320.00
Poster, "Gismonda, Bernhardt,
  American Tour," 1895, framed,
  29½ x 77½" 4,180.00
Poster, "Job," cigarette paper
  advertisement, 1898, printed by
  F. Champenois, Paris, 60¼ x
  40 1/8" (ILLUS.) 4,675.00
Poster, "La Dame aux Camelias,
  Sarah Bernhardt," 1896, printed by
  F. Champenois, Paris,
  80 x 28¾" 850.00
Poster, "La Danse," 22¼ x 13¾". . .2,200.00
Poster, "La Musique," 1898,
  23½ x 15" .2,090.00
Poster, "La Plume Magazine," 1899,
  21 1/8 x 9 3/8" 1,485.00
Poster, "La Poesie," 22 3/8 x 14". . .2,860.00

"Leslie Carter" by Mucha

Poster, "Leslie Carter," 1908,
  82½ x 30¾" (ILLUS.) 4,400.00
Poster, "Lily," 1897, framed,
  40¼ x 16 3/8" 1,600.00
Poster, "Monaco-Monte Carlo," 1897,
  printed by F. Champenois, Paris,
  framed, 23 x 43¼" 3,300.00
Poster, "Night's Repose,"
  1899, framed,
  40½ x 14 5/8" . . . . . . .1,650.00 to 1,870.00
Poster, "Reverie," 1896, printed by
  F. Champenois, Paris, framed,
  25 1/8 x 18¾" . . . . . . .3,850.00 to 4,400.00
Poster, "Societe Populaires des
  Beauxarts," 1897, 23 5/8 x
  17 1/8" 1,650.00
Print, covers (front & back) of the
  architectural journal "L'Habitation
  Pratique," 1903, framed, 14 x
  11½" 275.00
Print, design for Lefevre-Utile "Bis-
  cuits Champagne" container, 1897,
  framed 850.00
Prints, designs for 3 Lefevre-Utile
  biscuit containers, 1897, in single
  frame, largest 3 5/8 x 7¾" 275.00
Print, reclining woman & bear,
  printed in colors, from Documents
  Decoratifs, published by Librairie
  Centrale des Beaux Arts, Paris,
  1902, framed, 14 5/8 x 9¼" 770.00
Prints, "Reverie du Soir" & "Repos
  de la Nuit," framed, 18 x 8",
  pr. 1,200.00
Print, "Salome," 1897, 16 x 12½" . . . 605.00
Prints, "Tete Byzantine-Brunette"
  & "Tete Byzantine-Blonde," framed,
  11 x 13½", pr. 4,400.00

MUSIC BOXES

Gem Roller Organ

Bremond (Swiss) cylinder music
  box, 6-tune, inlaid rosewood case,
  11" l. cylinder $2,500.00
Bremond (Swiss) "interchangeable"
  cylinder music box, on matching
  table w/twelve 6-tune cylinders
  & original tune sheet listing all
  72 melodies in lid 8,000.00
Criterion (F. Otto & Sons) disc
  music box, double comb, oak
  table model case w/cabinet base,
  w/twenty 15½" discs 3,100.00
Gem Roller Organ, w/five cobs
  (ILLUS.) 500.00
Jacot (Swiss) Music Box Co. cylin-
  der music box, 10-tune, grain-
  painted case w/pseudo inlay,
  ca. 1886, 7½" l. cylinder, 19" l.
  box, 7" h. 1,200.00
Komet (Weissbach & Co., Leipzig,
  Germany) disc music box, ornate
  walnut case, 21½" disc 3,750.00
Mermod Freres (Swiss) cylinder
  music box, 8-tune, oak case,
  26" l. 1,800.00
Mermod Freres (Swiss) cylinder
  music box, 12-tune, oak case,
  original tune card, ca. 1895 . . . . . .2,200.00
Mira (Mermod Freres) disc music
  box, single comb, mahogany case,
  w/twenty 12" discs 1,600.00
New Century (Mermod Freres)
  "shifting disc" (2 tunes per disc
  in 2 revolutions) music box,
  cherrywood finish mahogany case,
  18½" disc (restored) 6,500.00
Nicolas Freres (Swiss) cylinder
  music box, 6-tune, mahogany
  case, 11" cylinder . . . .1,450.00 to 2,900.00
Olympia (F.G. Otto & Sons, Jersey
  City, New Jersey) disc music box
  No. 4, 76-note, carved mahogany
  case w/original finish, w/three
  15¾" discs (restored) 2,350.00
Paillard (Swiss) cylinder music box,
  8-tune, double spring, 18"
  cylinder 3,750.00

Polyphon (Polyphon Musikwerke,
  Leipzig, Germany) disc music box,
  walnut case, w/seventeen 11"
  discs 1,350.00
Polyphon disc music box, inlaid
  walnut case, w/fifty-five 16"
  discs 9,000.00
Polyphon upright disc music box,
  ornate walnut case, 24½" disc,
  58" h. (restored) 19,700.00
Regina (American subsidiary of Poly-
  phon Musikwerke, Rahway, New
  Jersey) disc music box, single
  comb, tempo control lever, crank-
  wound at center, mahogany case,
  ca. 1900, 8" disc 750.00
Regina disc music box, table
  model, oak case, w/ten 15½"
  discs 3,200.00

Regina Corona Upright Music Box

Regina Corona upright disc music
  box w/automatic changer,
  Style 35, case w/leaded art
  glass front, 15½" disc
  (ILLUS.) . . . . .8,500.00 to 14,000.00
Regina Orchestral disc music box,
  No. 6 parlor model, oak case,
  27" disc, 34 x 20" case,
  12½" h. 5,495.00
Regina library table model music
  box, Style 62, duplex combs, desk-
  style case w/four drawers for disc
  storage concealed behind cabinet
  doors, painted scenes on lid of
  case & carved lion masks at cor-
  ners, 20½" disc, 1904-06 . . . . .9,500.00
Reginaphone (Regina) disc music
  box, Style 150 w/nickel-plated
  outside "morning glory" horn,
  serpentine oak case, w/twenty
  15½" discs . . . . .3,800.00 to 4,700.00
Stella (Mermod Freres) disc music
  box, single comb, mahogany case

Stella Disc Music Box

w/leaf-carved panel over single
drawer, w/seventy-two 17¼" discs,
some teeth missing from comb,
28 x 21" case, 13" h. (ILLUS.) 1,980.00
Symphonion (Leipzig, Germany) disc
music box, Style 120, single comb,
mahogany case w/carved mold-
ing, ca. 1905, 13½" disc 770.00
Symphonion "Eroica" triple-disc music
box, Style 38 (Three-Disc Sym-
ponion), walnut case...........8,000.00

MUSICAL INSTRUMENTS

Tenor Banjo

Banjo (tenor), "Bacon Silver
Bell" $1,250.00
Banjo, "S.S. Stewardt," 5-string,
ca. 1885 .... 325.00
Banjo, "Waverly," 4-string, 11" d.
drum head, 18½" l. handle 145.00
Banjo (tenor), "Weymann"
(ILLUS.) 1,210.00
Banjo, 4-string, bird's eye maple.... 75.00
Banjo, rosewood w/solid mother-of-
pearl neck & nickel-plated trim ... 195.00
Banjo-mandolin, 8 ivory keys, bird's
eye maple w/inlaid mother-of-
pearl star, 10¼" drum head,
15" l. handle.................... 115.00

Bugle, brass, World War I vintage .. 25.00
Clavier, piano keyboard, ca. 1915... 195.00
Concertina, "Bardonian," wooden,
made in Leipsig, Germany,
ca. 1905 .... 325.00
Concertina, hexagonal rosewood
ends, 10 bone buttons one end, 11
on other, original wallpaper lined
case w/lock & key 125.00
Flute, boxwood, 4-key, ivory mounts
& silver keys w/pewter plugs, by
Johann Christian Blume, London,
late 18th-early 19th c., 20¾" 440.00
Flute, wood & metal, original
wooden case w/worn leather
covering, 26" l. 60.00
Harmonica, "Hohner - Little Lady" .. 20.00
Harmonica, "Hohner - Marine Band
No. 1896," original box & instruc-
tion book...................... 45.00
Harmonica, "Hohner - Melodica".... 22.50
Harmonica, "Masterphone".......... 60.00
Harmonica, "Strauss Loutone No.
500," original illustrated box 70.00
Harp, "Lyon & Healy - Salzedo
Model," curly maple body & neck,
47 strings, 7 pedals, ca. 1930,
72½" h. 6,600.00
Harp, neoclassical-style, giltwood,
19th c..........................1,650.00
Harpsichord, "Flemish," cherrywood
case, turned legs, w/bench 895.00
Mandolin, child's, alternating mahogany & maple ribs, inlaid tortoise shell guard plate, mahogany
neck & ebonized fingerboard,
original finish, ca. 1875, 13" l..... 150.00
Mandolin, "C.F. Martin," rosewood
w/engraved German silver fittings, w/case 325.00
Melodeon, "Jewett & Goodman,"
rosewood case w/octagonal legs
(restored) 650.00
Melodeon, "Mason & Hamlin," rosewood case, ca. 1850 (restored &
refinished)..................... 775.00
Melodeon, "George A. Prince &
Co.," rosewood case w/detach-
able legs & pedals for transport-
ing, 30" w............750.00 to 1,200.00
Oboe, "Cabart Paris," wooden
(needs new pads) 400.00
Organ, "Kimbal," oak, ornate
w/beveled mirror in superstructure.......................1,200.00
Piano, baby grand, "Bosendorfer,"
ebony, 1870-90 (restored).......10,000.00
Piano, baby grand, "Steinway & Co.,"
No. 200316," ebonized wood,
ca. 1920, w/bench, 66" w........4,675.00
Piano, square grand, "Chickering,"
rosewood, 1865-70 (restored &
refinished) 18,000.00
Piano, square grand, "Emerson,"

rosewood, carved legs, 82" l.,
41" deep 2,000.00
Piano, square grand, "Kimball," walnut, 1892, w/stool 5,000.00
Piano, square grand, "Steinway,"
rosewood, 1870's .....5,000.00 to 8,500.00
Piano, upright, "Fischer," mahogany, ca. 1915 ....5,250.00
Piano, upright, "Steinway," burl
walnut, 1893, 56" h.
(restored) ....2,200.00 to 5,600.00
Pitch pipe, "Congdon's," Germany,
dated 1890 .... 7.50
Snare drum, w/label of maker
"John F. Stratton," New York,
ca. 1875 .... 71.50
Tambourine, brass rim & jingling
discs, w/oil painting of cat on
stretched surface, 8" d. 65.00
Violin, "Hopf," w/case 125.00
Violin, "Mathias Hornsteiner,"
1872 .... 250.00
Violin, by "Angelo Serafino," copy
of Joseph Guarnerius Fecit
Cremono Anno 1716 model, made
in Germany 1,500.00
Violin, "Stainer," w/bow & case 750.00
Zither, "Nebel," w/case 50.00
Zither, inlaid ebony, Germany,
ca. 1880 .... 150.00

China, lettered, "To A Friend" in
gold (cup only) 25.00
China, Limoges, h.p. floral decor,
large (cup only) 32.50
China, Limoges, rococo-molded, h.p.
pastel florals & gold scrollwork ... 43.00
China, Nippon, h.p. delicate pink
roses & green leaves borders
w/geometric design between,
gold trim, Rising Sun mark (cup
only) 58.00
China, Nippon, h.p. scenic decor ... 75.00
China, pink lustre ground w/band of
florals 45.00
China, R.S. Prussia, green, pink &
white florals, gold trim 85.00
China, R.S. Prussia, self-footed rococo mold, colorful roses on shaded
violet ground, gold trim
(ILLUS.) 185.00
Majolica, Bird & Fan patt. 135.00
Silverplate, engraved florals,
Meriden Silverplate Co.
(cup only) 77.50
Silverplate, bright-cut designs, Vic-
tor Silver Co. (cup only) 65.00

MUSTACHE CUPS & SAUCERS

R.S. Prussia Mustache Cup

China, Blue Onion patt., 19th c. $85.00
China, Capo di Monte, left-handed,
nude children & garlands decor ... 165.00
China, Dresden, colorful floral
decal 37.00
China, Haviland & Co., factory-
decorated gold tracery & lip &
saucer edge 110.00
China, lettered "Fireman" & w/decal
scene (cup only) 100.00
China, lettered "Think of Me," pink
lustre trim, Germany 35.00

NUTCRACKERS

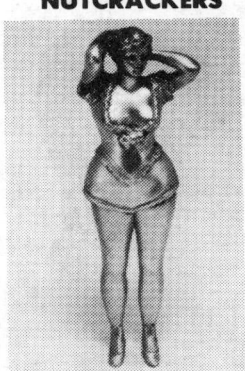

"Naughty Nellie" Nutcracker

Brass, figural Punch & Judy $45.00
Brass, model of an eagle's head 30.00
Bronze, model of dog on base,
marked "L.A. Althoff &
Co." ....85.00 to 125.00
Cast iron, "Little Giant," 1890's 15.00
Cast iron, model of an alligator,
green paint finish, 10" l. 25.00
Cast iron, model of bulldog, original
paint.......................... 65.00
Cast iron, model of a dog w/long
tail, overall 12" l. 52.50
Cast iron, model of a squirrel, old
black paint, 4¾" h. 80.00

Cast iron, model of a squirrel,
marked "Tyler, Texas & Chicago,"
1913 patent 39.00
Nickel-plated cast iron, model of
wolf's head, June 1920 patent, on
wooden base 75.00
Nickel-plated cast iron, vice-type,
"Perfection," ca. 1915 .....12.00 to 15.00
Silverplate, figural "Naughty Nellie,"
8½" l., pr. (ILLUS. of one) 357.00
Sterling silver, LaMarquise patt.,
Tiffany & Co., New York 95.00
Sterling silver, Shell & Thread patt.,
Tiffany & Co., New York 195.00
Wooden, carved model of friar's
head, large..................... 45.00
Wooden, carved model of a seated
squirrel 160.00
Wooden, carved well-detailed bust
of Indian chief w/feathered head-
dress, 8" l. 75.00
Wooden, cup-shaped w/turn-screw,
chip-carved, overall 8" l......... 25.00

OCCUPIED JAPAN

Occupied Japan Figurine

*American troops occupied the country of
Japan from September 2, 1945 until April 28,
1952, following World War II. All wares made
for export during this period were required
to be marked "Made in Occupied Japan."
Now these items, mostly small ceramic and
metal trifles of varying quality, are sought
out by a growing number of collectors.*

Bank, china, model of an elephant,
5 x 3½".......................... $10.00
Cigarette lighter, table model,
metal, replica of a baseball,
5" h. 25.00

Cup & saucer, demitasse, dragons in
relief on red ground 20.00
Cup & saucer, footed cup, light blue
& yellow leaf stem decor, gold
outlining 35.00
Dinner service for 8, w/serving
pieces, Naomi patt., Noritake,
63 pcs. 585.00
Figure of a Colonial man, china,
w/mandolin, multicolored garments, 5" h. (ILLUS.)............. 17.00
Figure of a Colonial lady, bisque,
pastel coloring, 10½" h. 40.00
Figures of a Samurai warrior & a
Geisha girl, bisque, 10½" h.,
pr............................ 48.00
Figure group, bisque, lovers about
to kiss, pastel garments,
5½" h. 22.00
Lamps, boudoir, china, figural
Colonial lady & gentleman, pastel
coloring, pr. 80.00
Match holder, wall-type, china, boy
& girl leaning from window &
holding baskets 40.00
Mug, china, rabbit handle, tavern
scenes decor................... 20.00

Occupied Japan Needle Book

Needle book, "Lady Prim," w/three
packages of needles & threader,
multicolor cover, 4½ x 4¾"
(ILLUS.)........................ 10.00
Parasol, paper, multicolored, 30" d.,
21" l. 50.00
Planter, china, figure of Hummel-
type boy playing violin beside
container 12.00
Plaques, wall-type, bisque, Colonial
lady & gentleman, 6¼ x 5½",
pr............................. 65.00
Salt & pepper shakers, china, figural
Dutch boy & girl, pr............. 10.00
Tape measure, celluloid, model of a
cat........................... 24.00
Tea set: cov. teapot, creamer & cov.
sugar bowl; windmill decor,
3 pcs. 40.00

Tea set, child's, floral decor on tan
lustre ground, original box,
11 pcs. 100.00
Toby mug, china, full-figure seated
man w/book 20.00
Toy, windup celluloid soldier 60.00
Toy, windup boy on scooter 35.00
Toy, windup tin donkey, cloth
covered, ears & tail move, origi-
nal paper label 35.00
Toy, windup tin "Hobo Clown
Skating" 150.00
Toy, windup tin Teddy Bear, original
box 85.00
Wall pockets, circular w/lacy edges,
flamingos, water lilies & lily pad
decor, pr. 58.00
Whimsey, china, lady's slipper,
floral decor, 2¾" l. 10.00

PAISLEY SHAWLS

Paisley Shawl

*This term "Paisley" shawl is a generic one
that encompasses not only the shawls woven
in Paisley, Scotland, but also shawls made in
India, other areas of Scotland, and elsewhere
on the European continent. However, all
these shawls, in various shapes, sizes and
styles, have a common ancestry in the shawls
exported to England from Kashmiri, India
during the 1770's. The Kashmir shawls, made
of fine colorfully-dyed Kashmir (cashmere)
wool yarns immediately became a popular
fashion and the European weaving centers began copying the style by the late 1770's. In
1800, Paisley joined in this production and
within twenty years was producing such a
sizeable number of shawls the Paisley name
came to be identified with the shawls and,
likewise, the pattern most closely associated*

*with the Paisley shawl, the Kashmiri "pine"
motif, became the Paisley pattern. Queen Victoria revived interest in wearing the Paisley
shawl during the 1840's to help stimulate the
depressed weaving industry and the fashion
peaked by 1865 before the bustle arrived on
the scene making the long shawl obsolete
within a few years.*

Black center w/name embroidered
in white, colorful border composed of rainbow-colored blocks,
w/1" fringe, 68" sq. $395.00
Black medallion center, red & purple
border, 72" sq. 70.00
Black center, colorful border,
78 x 76" 185.00
Black center, colorful border,
124 x 64" 175.00
Black center, colorful border, 1863
French label, 130 x 60" 75.00
Black center, soft muted colors at
borders, 132 x 61" 110.00
Black center, colorful paisley motif
borders, 140 x 62" 120.00
Ivory center & ground, colorful
14" w. border & 6" l. fringe,
72 x 70" 50.00
Ivory center & ground, red & blue
Paisley-type border, 72 x 70" 75.00
Red center set w/turquoise medal-
lion, colorful Paisley-type border,
72" sq. 130.00
Red & gold paisley overall design,
130 x 64" 198.00
Red, blue, green & purple paisley
design on orange ground 250.00
Red cruciform center w/central
medallions, colorful border, pr. . . . 300.00
White center, blue w/red, green &
yellow Paisley patt. border, 64"
sq. w/fringe (ILLUS.) 400.00

PAPER COLLECTIBLES

*Also see ADVERTISING ITEMS,
ALMANACS, AVIATION COLLECTI-
BLES, BASEBALL MEMORABILIA, BIG
LITTLE BOOKS, BOY SCOUT ITEMS,
BREWERIANA, BROWNIE, BUSTER
BROWN, CAMPBELL KID, CAT &
CHARACTER COLLECTIBLES, CHRIST-
MAS TREE ORNAMENTS, COCA-COLA
ITEMS, COMIC BOOKS, DISNEY COL-
LECTIBLES, FANS, FISHER GIRLS,
FRACTURS, GREENAWAY ITEMS,
HUMPHREY ARTWORK, MAGAZINES,
MUCHA ARTWORK, PAPER DOLLS,
PARRISH ARTWORK, POSTCARDS,*

POSTERS, SCRAPBOOKS & ALBUMS, SHAKER ITEMS, SIGNS & SIGN-BOARDS, SUNBONNET BABY COLLECTIBLES, TOYS, TWELVETREES ILLUSTRATIONS, WORLD FAIR COLLECTIBLES, YARD LONG PICTURES and ZEPPELIN COLLECTIBLES.

Admission ticket, "Notre Dame vs. Navy" football game, 1948, Baltimore Stadium, colorful football players in action $12.00
Book, "The Wedding Book," color illustrations by Frances Brundage . . 35.00
Booklet, souvenir, "Tournament of Roses Parade," 1939, Shirley Temple as Grand Marshall, w/mailing envelope 20.00
Brochure, "Lake Michigan Auto Ferry," 1937, illustrated 6.00
Business directory & almanac, "Cincinnati, Ohio," 1858, pocket-size . . 45.00

Pocket Calendars

Calendar for 1901, pocket-type, 3 x 2", each (ILLUS.) 2.00
Calendar for 1913, printed in Germany, embossed floral border & large bell opening up to beautiful little girls holding streamers 50.00

"The King of the Forest"

Calligraphic specimen, pen & ink drawing of lion on blue-tinted paper, inscribed "Penmanship: The King of the Forest, Executed by William Elliot Brown, Sept. 20, 1860, Manchester," 21¼ x 16½", framed (ILLUS.) 3,190.00
Calligraphic specimen, pen & ink drawing of allegorical figure riding reindeer & holding banner inscribed "Pen Work of F.M. Doyle" above 2 decorative banners inscribed "Learn to Write," 19th c., framed, 29½ x 23½" 550.00
Circus program, "Barnes Bros. Circus," 1946, 40 pp. 10.00
Circus program, "Ringling Bros., Barnum & Bailey," Dorothy Herbert cover, 1934 . . . . 20.00
Circus program, "Ringling Bros., Barnum & Bailey," chariot race cover, 1935 . . . . 15.00
City Directory, "Denison, Texas," 1887 . . . . 125.00
City Directory, "Portland, Maine," 1929, 1,396 pp. 12.00
Doll house, "The Dolls Playhouse," by Clara Williams, published by Stokes Co., 1915, cardboard foldout house w/pages of cut-out furniture & dolls, set 125.00
Easter card, folding-type w/tissue paper honeycomb, bunny in basket 12.00
Hidden name card 3.00
Land grant, Iowa tract, signed by President James Buchanan, dated 1859 . . . . 65.00
Movie program, "Ben Hur," 1925 . . . . 28.00
Movie program, "Fantasia," 1940 . . . 40.00
Movie program, "Gone with the Wind," illustrated, 20 pp., 9 x 12" 40.00
Newspapers, assorted pre-Civil War issues, 1821-1860, each 2.00
Newspapers, assorted Civil War issues, each 3.00
Newspaper, rag sheet type, "New Hampshire & Vermont Journal," 1798 . . . . 28.00
Newspaper, "Chicago Sun," 1945, w/headline "Hitler Suicide" 7.00
Newspaper, "Chicago Sunday Herald," 1917, May 20, James Montgomery Flagg illustration, "I Want You," 16½ x 24" 75.00
Newspaper, "Chicago Tribune," 1945, August 13, w/headline "President Dies" 5.00
Newspaper, "Los Angeles Herald Examiner," 1963, November 22, w/headline "Kennedy Assassinated" 10.00
Newspaper, "Los Angeles Herald

Examiner," 1963, November 26,
w/headline "Texas Charges
Ruby" 10.00
Newspaper, "New York Herald Trib-
une," 1932, May, w/headline
"Amelia Earhart Lands in
London" 22.50
Print, "The Bloody Massacre Per-
petrated in King Street, Boston on
March 5th, 1770," hand-colored
engraving, published by Paul Re-
vere, Boston, 1770, on 18th c. laid
paper, 10½ x 9 3/8" 25,300.00
Program, "Army-Navy Football
Game," 1936, Howard Chandler
Christy cover, 100 pp. 30.00
Program, "Buffalo Bill Wild West
Show," 1895, 65 pp. 45.00
Program, "Follies Bergere," 1930 ... 30.00
Program, heavyweight boxing cham-
pionship, "Joe Louis vs. Harry
Thomas," 1938, April 1, Chicago .. 30.00
Program, "Ice Follies," 1943,
32 pp. ....6.50 to 10.00
Program, "Indianapolis 500 Auto
Race," 1946, w/scorecard 25.00
Ration book, World War II ....2.00 to 5.00
Revenue bond, "New York City,"
1858 .... 15.00
Stock certificate, "First National
Bank of Chicago," 1863, 8 x 10" .. 40.00
Stock certificates, "Marconi Wire-
less," 1913, set of 4 .... 35.00

PAPER DOLLS

Roy Rogers & Dale Evans Paper Dolls

"Abraham Lincoln, His Boyhood
Home," uncut sheets w/log cabin
& figures, ca. 1923 .... $18.00
Advertising, "Canadian Spool Cotton," Wedding series, set of 7, in
original envelope 60.00
Advertising, "Clark's O.N.T.," Dolls
of All Nations series - Italian Girl
or Turkish Girl, each 5.00

Advertising, "Electric Lustre Starch,"
Red Riding Hood, mechanical 13.00
Advertising, "Enameline Stove Pol-
ish," College series, set of 7 ..... 60.00
Advertising, "Enterprise Coffee Co.,"
Little Bo Peep................... 20.00
Advertising, "Kiss-Me-Gum," In Fan-
cy Dress or Off to Town, uncut,
each 30.00
Advertising, "Lion Coffee," assorted
set of 30 dolls w/costumes 100.00
"Annette In Hawaii," uncut book,
Whitman No. 1961, 1961 .... 27.00
Arlene Dahl, uncut book, Saalfield
No. 1587, 1953 .... 25.00
Baby Sparkle Plenty, uncut book,
Saalfield, 1948 .... 32.00
Barbie, uncut book, Whitman,
1962 .... 20.00
Big Valentine Book, uncut book,
Saalfield, 1946 .... 15.00
Blondie, uncut book, Whitman
No. 993, 1945 .... 75.00
Claire McCardell, 2 dolls & designer
wardrobe, uncut book, Whitman,
1956 .... 30.00
Debbie Reynolds, uncut book, Whit-
man No. 1955, 1955 .... 45.00
Dionne Quintuplets, uncut books,
Whitman No. 1055, 1936, set
of 5............................. 165.00
Dolly Dingle, uncut magazine sheet,
various 1923 issues, each sheet... 10.00
Doris Day, uncut book, Whitman
No.1977, 1957.................. 48.00
Eva St. Claire & Topsey, McLoughlin
Bros., ca. 1863 .... 150.00
Fanny Davenport, jointed, 1880's ... 75.00
Gene Autry, uncut book, Whitman,
1951 .... 40.00
George Montgomery & Dinah Shore,
uncut book, Whitman No. 1970,
1959 .... 35.00
"Happiest Millionaire," uncut book,
Saalfield No. 4487, 1967 .... 9.50
"Household Servants," uncut 'Ladies'
Home Journal" magazine sheet,
1918 .... 10.00
Indians, uncut book, Whitman
No. 1504, 1938................. 22.00
"In Old New York," uncut book,
Saalfield No. 4411, 1957 .... 18.00
Jetsons, uncut book, 1965......... 11.50
The Kelly Sisters, uncut book, Saal-
field No. 2466, 1944 .... 12.00
"Laugh In Party," uncut book, Saal-
field No. 1325, 1969 .... 14.00
Lil Abner, Saalfield No. 1549 .... 25.00
"Little Women," uncut book, Saal-
field No. 1377................... 10.00
Marlo Thomas, uncut book, Saalfield
No. 1379 .... 10.00
Martha Washington, uncut book,
w/brief history of the Washing-

tons, 2 dolls & 10 dresses, ca.
1945 .... 325.00

"Mouseketeer" Linda, uncut book,
Whitman No. 1957, 1958 .... 30.00

"Our Gang," uncut "Ladies' Home
Companion" magazine sheet,
1925 .... 25.00

Partridge Family, uncut book, Whitman No. 5137, 1971 .... 10.00

Pigtails, 6 dolls, uncut book, Merrill
No. 3444-10, 1949 .... 25.00

Punch & Judy, uncut book, 1911 .... 35.00

Roy Rogers & Dale Evans, uncut
book, Whitman No. 1950, 1956
(ILLUS.)........................ 12.50

Shirley Temple Standing Dolls, uncut
book, Saalfield No. 1715, 1935.... 100.00

Susie's Pets, Series No. 3, McLoughlin Bros........................ 150.00

Tina & Tony, uncut book, Samuel
Lowe No. 131 .... 15.00

Tuck (Raphael), Fairy Tale Series of
Dressing Dolls, 1893 .... 65.00

Twiggy, uncut book, Whitman
No. 2809, 1962 .... 25.00

"Umbrella Girls," uncut book, Merrill No. 2562 .... 17.00

PAPERWEIGHTS

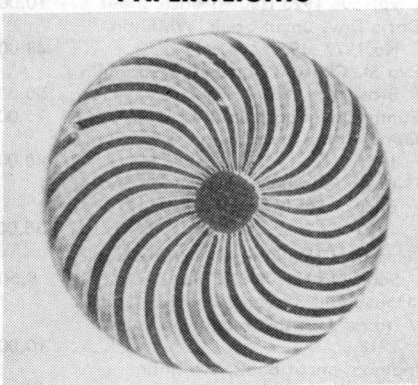

Clichy Swirl Paperweight

*Also see ADVERTISING ITEMS and
WORLD FAIR COLLECTIBLES.*

Baccarat, "Gentian" weight, clear
w/three deep salmon pink ribbed
flowers lined in opaque white
growing from green stalks w/two
long leaves at the base & numerous leaves about the flowers,
star-cut base, 2 7/8" d.........$8,800.00

Baccarat, faceted sulphide weight,
clear w/head of young Queen
Victoria looking to sinister, in-

scribed "Victoria I Reine de la
Grande Bretagne," translucent red
ground, sides cut w/diamond-
shaped facets, 3¼" d. 880.00

Baccarat, sulphide of Andrew Jackson, green ground, 1971 .... 145.00

Banford (Bob), "Pansy" weight, clear
w/three-dimensional blossom
amidst green foliage, star-cut
base, 2½" d. 500.00

Clichy, swirl weight, alternating
opaque white & lilac threads radiating from a central turquoise
blue, pink, blue & white setup,
3" d. (ILLUS.) 660.00

Kaziun (Charles), miniature "Rose"
weight on pedestal base, clear
w/gold foil bee resting on pink
rose centered by 3 petals & 3 blue
& white caned rosettes, set on a
cobalt blue ground, 2 1/8" h...... 302.50

Millville, "Ship" weight on pedestal
base, clear w/flat motif of finely
ground opaque white glass depicting a clipper ship w/dark pink flag
sailing on a bluish-grey sea, cut
w/three large circular printies on
the curve, on circular glass base,
4" h. 1,320.00

Mount Washington, magnum "Rose"
weight, clear w/large shaded pink
& yellow rose in full bloom growing from a straight green stalk
w/two large pink buds either side
w/four serrated leaves & 4 larger
leaves about the flower,
4 1/8" d......................22,000.00

Whittmore (Francis), "Rose" weight
on pedestal base, angled pink &
white petals w/four green leaves,
20th c., 3" h. 275.00

Ysart (Paul), clear w/solitary shaded
brown fish swimming over multicolored ground................. 385.00

PAPIER MACHE

*Various objects including decorative ad-
juncts were made of papier mache, which is
a substance made of pulped paper mixed with
glue and other materials or layers of paper
glued and pressed and then molded. Also see
DISNEY COLLECTIBLES, DOLLS and
TOYS.*

Box w/hinged cover, scene of 4
ladies near house & bamboo trees
reserved on lid, gilt trim,
11 x 7".........................$175.00

Candy container, model of a chick

dressed as English bobby (policeman), 4" h. 50.00

Candy container, figure of Father Christmas, marked "Germany," 4½" h. 95.00

Candy container, model of a duck standing, covered in yellow flannel & w/blue apron, glass eyes, 4½" h. 85.00

Candy container, model of a chick standing, covered w/fluffy feathers, glass eyes, metal feet, Germany, 5½" h. 210.00

Candy container, figure of Father Christmas in long white coat, Germany, 7" h. 165.00

Candy container, model of a stork w/wire feet, Germany, 7" h. 75.00

Candy container, model of a bunny emerging from egg, marked "Germany," 7 3/8" h. 85.00

Candy container, model of a rabbit w/glass eyes, dressed in painted clown suit, lift-off head, 8" h. 42.50

Candy container, figure of Father Christmas, well-painted face & white-painted coat w/mica glitter trim & red hood, holding small feather tree, 11" h. 425.00

Candy container, model of a chick fully dressed in formal attire & top hat, ca. 1910 .... 35.00

Figure of Father Christmas in long red coat & blue pants, Germany, 7" h. 135.00

Figure of Santa Claus, original red flannel clothing, early 1900's, 27" h. 200.00

Jack-o-lantern, original paper lining, 8½" d., 7½" h. ....15.00 to 20.00

Papier Mache Milliner's Model

Milliner's hat stand, h.p. features & hair, together w/Shaker bonnet, 2 pcs. (ILLUS.).................. 425.00

Model of a rabbit w/glass eyes, wearing jacket & patched pants, marked "Germany," 6½" h. 65.00

Model of a dog in reclining position w/swivel head held erect, glass eyes & curly fur-like covering, France, late 19th c., 18" l. 285.00

Model of a Dachshund dog, realistically painted in shaded brown tones, 20th c., 27" l. 135.00

Pail w/wire bail handle, Jack & Jill decor on blue, small 20.00

Pen box, chinoiserie decor on black lacquer finish ground, 8" l........ 9.00

Tray, serpentine outline, gilt chinoiserie scene w/pagodas, birds, butterflies & flowering peonies on black ground, Victorian, 19th c., 25 x 20" (on bamboo-turned stand of later date) 1,320.00

Tray, serpentine outline, gilt scrolling foliage, bellflowers & fruit clusters on black ground, Victorian, 19th c., 32½ x 24½" (on gilt bamboo-turned stand of later date)......................... 990.00

PARRISH (Maxfield) ARTWORK

Illustration by Maxfield Parrish

*During the 1920's and 1930's, Maxfield Parrish (1870-1966) was considered the most popular artist-illustrator in the United States. His illustrations graced the covers of the most noted magazines of the day–*Scribner's, Century, Life, Harper's, Ladies' Home Journal *and others. High quality art prints, copies of his original paintings usually in a range of sizes, graced the walls of homes and* *offices across the country. Today all Maxfield Parrish artwork, including magazine covers, advertisements and calendar art, is considered collectible but it is the fine art prints that command the most attention.*

Book, "A Golden Treasury of Songs
  & Lyrics," illustrated by Maxfield
  Parrish, 1911, 1st edition . . $75.00 to 90.00
Book, "Bolanyo," by Opie Reed,
  illustrated by Maxfield Parrish,
  1902 . . . . 85.00
Book, "King Albert's Book," illustrat-
  ed by Maxfield Parrish, 1914 . . . . . 45.00
Book, "Knave of Hearts," by Louise
  Sanders, illustrated by Maxfield
  Parrish, 1925, hard bound 575.00
Book, "The Lure of the Garden," by
  Hildegard Hawthorne, illustrated
  by Maxfield Parrish, 1911 . . . . 35.00
Calendar, 1926, for Edison-Mazda,
  entitled "Enchantment" . . . 90.00 to 110.00
Calendar, 1939, for Brown & Bigelow
  Publishing Co., entitled "Early
  Autumn" 150.00
Calendar, 1943, for Brown & Bigelow
  Publishing Co., entitled "A Perfect
  Day," overall 22 x 16" 195.00
Calendar, 1947, for Brown & Bigelow
  Publishing Co., entitled "Evening,"
  overall 22 x 16" 195.00
Greeting cards, for Brown & Bigelow
  Publishing Co., 6 different
  scenes 30.00
Jigsaw puzzle, "The Prince," in
  original box 140.00
Magazine cover, "Collier's," April
  17, 1909 . . . . 20.00
Magazine cover, "Ladies' Home
  Journal," January, 1896 . . . . 32.50
Magazine cover, "Scribner's," April,
  1899 . . . . 40.00
Playing cards, for Edison-Mazda, en-
  titled "Ecstasy," w/original box . . . 115.00

Print, "Canyons," original frame,
  12 x 15" 110.00
Print, "Cleopatra," medium 450.00
Print, "Contentment," large 375.00
Print, "Dawn," framed, 10 x 12" 150.00
Print, "Daybreak," 6 x 10" 45.00
Print, "Dreaming," original frame,
  18 x 30" 320.00
Print, "Dream Light," small 95.00
Print, "Enchantment," small 135.00
Print, "Fly Away Horse," 7 x 9" 30.00
Print, "Garden of Allah,"
  15 x 30" . . . . 150.00 to 215.00
Print, "Golden Hours," framed,
  16 x 24" . . . . 250.00 to 335.00
Print, "Hilltop," large 325.00
Print, "Lampseller of Bagdad,"
  9½ x 19" 55.00
Print, "The Land of Make Believe,"
  original frame, 8½ x 11" 65.00

Print, "Morning," large 125.00
Print, "Old King Cole," framed,
  small 65.00
Print, "Pandora's Box," 1908,
  Collier's Publishing Co.,
  11½ x 15" 40.00
Print, "Path to Home," 10 x 9" 45.00
Print, "Perfect Day," framed,
  12 x 14" 75.00
Print, "The Prince," original frame,
  large 525.00
Print, "Venetian Lamplighter,"
  small 85.00
Print, "Waterfall," 1930, framed,
  21½ x 16" 225.00
Sign, outdoor-type, metal,
  for Edison-Mazda, "Conver-
  sation Figures," lighted
  hood . . . . 1,250.00 to 2,000.00

PHONOGRAPHS

Columbia Disc Phonograph

Berliner Trade-Mark Gramo-
  phone $1,550.00
Columbia Type A Graphophone 275.00
Columbia Type AG, 5" l. cylinder . . . 925.00
Columbia Type AZ Graphophone . . . 365.00
Columbia Type BD Disc Grapho-
  phone, morning glory horn
  (ILLUS.) 1,200.00
Columbia Type BJ, nickel-plated
  horn 550.00
Columbia Type BNWM Grapho-
  phone, mahogany horn 900.00
Columbia Type BX Graphophone 290.00
Columbia Type Q Graphophone,
  1903 . . . . 250.00
Edison Amberola Model 1 . . . . 1,900.00
Edison Amberola Model 3, oak cabi-
  net, Opera Model mechanisms . . . 1,200.00

Edison Amberola 30 .... 225.00
Edison Amberola 75, oak case 450.00
Edison Concert Model console 1,600.00
Edison Fireside Model, w/wooden
  cygnet horn.................... 950.00
Edison Fireside Model A, K
  reproducer ....350.00 to 450.00
Edison Gem Model A,
  w/horn ....300.00 to 400.00
Edison Home Model A, oak suitcase
  model w/"Edison Home Phonograph" in decal banner, 1898,
  w/brass & black horn ...500.00 to 725.00
Edison Standard Model A, oak case
  w/decals & brass bell
  horn ....300.00 to 425.00
Edison Triumph Model, oak, 2 & 4
  minute play, w/cygnet
  horn..................950.00 to 1,600.00
Edison Triumph Model, oak case, 2
  minute play, (repainted) cygnet
  horn 750.00
Harmony Talking Machine.......... 475.00
Harvard Talking Machine, w/long
  tone arm 650.00
Kalamazoo Duplex................1,350.00
Kameraphone (phonograph in cam-
  era case), complete............1,425.00
Monarch Junior Gramophone....... 465.00
Perfektone, in wicker cabinet by
  Haywood-Wakefield .....500.00 to 875.00
Victor Model I, w/outside
  horn ....550.00 to 675.00
Victor Model II, "humpback,"
  w/wooden horn 1,200.00
Victor Model II, brass horn 550.00
Victor Model III, 22" l. black
  horn 600.00
Victor Model IV, mahogany case &
  matching mahogany horn........1,800.00
Victor Model V, brass bell horn 390.00
Victor Model V, oak case & match-
  ing horn, refinished............1,800.00
Victor Model V, oak case & large
  black metal horn.....1,000.00 to 1,200.00
Victor Model D, nickel-plated brass
  horn 950.00
Victor Model M, brass bell horn &
  ridged tone arm 1,275.00
Victor Model 0, w/amber morning
  glory horn..............650.00 to 850.00
Victor Schoolhouse Model, oak
  case, wooden horn, w/"Siam
  Sue" jointed wooden figure that
  dances while machine is
  playing 2,000.00
Victor Victrola No. 2, oak table-top
  model, doors open for speaker,
  dated 1904, 14½ x 13" base,
  7" h........................... 200.00
Zonophone, glass sides 1,700.00

PHOTOGRAPHIC ITEMS

Eastman Kodak No. 6 Camera

Albumen print, Civil War soldiers &
  chaplain, wearing Masonic
  aprons, 3¼ x 4¼" $60.00
Ambrotype, ninth plate (2 x 2½"),
  violin player, w/case 145.00
Ambrotype, sixth plate (2¾ x 3¼"),
  Civil War Confederate officer
  wearing loose fitting frock coat &
  kepi 200.00
Ambrotype, sixth plate, post-
  mortem baby 50.00
Ambrotype, quarter plate (3¼ x
  4¼"), man & dog, thermoplastic
  frame........................ 70.00
Ambrotype, half plate (4¼ x 5½"),
  gentleman, thermoplastic frame .. 30.00
Ambrotype, whole plate (6½ x
  8½"), Niagara Falls scene 345.00
Book, "Photography-Principles &
  Practice," by Noblette, 1930 ...... 12.00
Cabinet photograph, Deadwood,
  South Dakota blacksmith shop interior w/men & horses, 8 x 10"... 35.00
Cabinet photograph, fireman holding trumpet, 1880 .... 38.00
Camera, E. & H. T. Anthony & Co.,
  carte de visite 4-tube multilens ..1,200.00
Camera, Argus Model A, Art Deco
  design, 1936-41, w/original leather case & instruction booklet 20.00
Camera, Eastman Kodak No. 0,
  folding-type, blue bellows,
  1902-06....................... 45.00
Camera, Eastman Kodak No. 6 Improved, folding model, Universal
  lens in B & L iris diaphragm shut-
  ter, 48 exposures, roll film or
  8½ x 6½" plates, 1893-95
  (ILLUS.)...................... 990.00
Camera, Eastman Kodak Girl Scout
  model, w/case & instruction book,
  1929-34....................... 110.00
Camera, Expo Pocket Watch,
  1904 ....125.00 to 150.00
Carte de visite, Abraham Lincoln, by
  E. & H.T. Anthony, 1865.......... 495.00
Carte de visite, Mrs. Mary Lincoln,

by Spirit Photographer Mumler,
1865 . . . .   65.00
Daguerreotype, ninth plate, image
of man playing accordion 75.00
Daguerreotype, sixth plate, image
of Civil War soldier w/trumpet, in
thermoplastic case 45.00
Daguerreotype, sixth plate, image
of post-mortem infant 125.00
Daguerreotype, half plate, image of
sea captain, in ogee frame 100.00

Daguerreotype Case

Daguerreotype case, thermoplastic,
Bowl of Fruit patt. (ILLUS.) 77.00
Daguerreotype case, thermoplastic,
fortune teller design 87.00
Daguerreotype case, thermoplastic,
soldier's farewell design, 4 x 5" . .   125.00
Glass negatives, village street scene
& drugstore interior, 1905, 5 x 7",
each 20.00
Photograph, Civil War, Meade's
Headquarters at Gettysburg, 1863,
by Gardner & O'Sullivan 300.00
Photograph, Civil War, Military Telegraph Construction Corps, men
stringing telegraph wire 195.00
Photograph, girl on wicker settee
w/beautiful dressed doll & Teddy
Bear, 1900's 37.00
Photograph, Teddy Roosevelt in
Spanish-American War uniform,
4½ x 6½" 10.00
Tintype, ninth plate, Civil War offi-
cer wearing slouch hat w/Infantry
insignia & holding sword,
w/case 35.00
Tintype, sixth plate, child holding
baby, thermoplastic case 25.00
Tintype, quarter plate, Civil War soldier, battlefield background 45.00
Tintype, whole plate, man in buggy
drawn by white horse 60.00
Tintype, Annie Oakley 250.00
Tintype, gentleman in boxing
stance, w/case 85.00

PIN CUSHION DOLLS

German Pin Cushion Dolls

*These china half figures were never intend-
ed to use as dolls, but rather to serve as ornamental tops to their functional pin cushion
bases which were discreetly covered with silk
and lace skirts. They were produced in a wide
variety of forms and quality, all of which are
now deemed collectible, and were especially
popular during the first quarter of this
century.*

Bisque half figure of a "flapper"
w/one arm extended, wearing a
yellow bodice & gold ribbin in her
hair, 7¼" h. $35.00
Bisque half figure of a lady w/arms
extended away from body, ornate
hairstyle, red eye liner, 3½" d.,
5¼" h. 170.00
Bisque half figure of a nude lady
w/hands away from body, deeply
waved black hair w/chignon in
back, Goebel Crown mark,
3" h. 125.00
China half figure of Carmen, yellow
bodice, lustre shawl & hat, Ger-
man, 4" h. 50.00
China half figure of Jenny Lind,
arms extended from body, Goebel
Crown mark, 5¾" h. 500.00
China half figure of "La Belle
Chocolatiere" (The Chocolate
Lady), 4¾" h. 1,300.00
China half figure of a lady w/short
bouffant hairstyle, painted camisole top, impressed "Germany,
3553," 3½" h. (ILLUS. left) 50.00
China half figure of a lady
w/Colonial hairstyle, painted
camisole top, impressed "Germany, 6087," 3½" h. (ILLUS.
right) 55.00
China half figure of a lady w/flow-
ers in her long blonde hair, hands
away from body, 2" d., 3½" h. 110.00
China half figure of a lady holding
pink rose w/applied petals in outstretched hand, grey hair applied

w/wreath of pink roses, marked
"Dressel & Kister," 3 7/8" h. 195.00
China half figure of a lady w/up-
swept hair & arms extended away
from body, impressed "14753,"
2½" d., 5" h. 125.00
China half figure of Marie Antoinette, wearing deep blue bodice w/gold trim, one hand raised
to her bosom, 4¾" h. 375.00
China half figure of a nude "flapper" wearing a tight-fitting cloche
over her dark hair, holding a compact in one hand & powder puff in
the other, 5¼" h. 255.00
China half figure of a nude lady
w/blue feather in her grey hair,
4½" h. 165.00
China half figure of a nude lady
w/arms away from body, upswept
blonde hair w/long curls at each
side, 6" h. 170.00
China half figure of a Spanish
Senorita, large black satin cushion
w/flounces of black lace, 7" w.,
9½" h. 55.00
China half figure of a young black
woman, black wig, movable arms
on elastic cord, 5" h. 400.00
Whisk broom doll, china half figure
of Carmen, green dress & orange
shawl w/yellow fringe & hat &
green satin sash & blue flower,
marked "Made in Germany,"
3½" h. 95.00

POSTCARDS

Advertising Postcard

Advertising, "Black & White Scotch
Whiskey," polo players, Raphael
Tuck $35.00

Advertising, "Cherry Smash" 100.00
Advertising, "Cracker Jack," bears .. 35.00
Advertising, "Doe-Wah-Jack
(Dowagiac, Michigan) Round Oak
Stoves," Tribal Responsibility se-
ries, "Doe-Wah-Jack Watching the
Invader" (ILLUS.) 40.00
Advertising, "Paragan Amusement
Park," roller coaster, rides & band
stand, set of 40 .... 75.00
Advertising, "Sleepy Eye - The
Meritorious Flour," Indian scout
gazing at sunset rays 42.00
Birthday Greetings, young girl
w/large hat, 1900 .... 10.00
Birthday Greetings, assorted set
of 48 .... 186.00
Children, Ellen H. Clapsaddle, as-
sorted set of 7 .... 28.00
Christmas Greetings, Frances Brund-
age, Santa Claus carrying bag
filled w/toys, Series No. 208 ..... 20.00
College series, F. Earl Christy,
No. 7 .... 6.50
Colonial Heroes, American Historical
Art Co., Lange & Schwalback,
No. 9 .... 10.00
Commemorative, Hudson-Fulton
Celebration, Hudson & ship Half
Moon, postmarked 1909 ....4.00 to 6.00
Disaster, passenger train car being
pulled from river, "early morning
train from here to Pittsburg,"
postmarked New Castle, Pa.,
1919 ....8.00 to 10.00
Easter Greetings, children's faces in
lilies 8.00
Foreign country, Cuba, set
of 30 .... 25.00
Fourth of July, Ellen H.
Clapsaddle ....5.00 to 8.00

Kathryn Elliott Halloween Postcard

Halloween Greetings, signed
Kathryn Elliott (ILLUS.) 6.00

Hold-to-light, Natural Bridge, St.
  Louis, Missouri 12.00
Human hair-type, beautiful
  woman 25.00
Indians, "John Smith - Age 130,"
  real photograph, early 1900's 10.00
Irish Peat Moss, "Irish Life," scenes
  of Irish people at work & play, set
  of 12, in original wrapper 250.00
Memorial Day, Raphael Tuck,
  Confederate series, unused,
  set of 12 .... 110.00
Mining towns & mines, assorted set
  of 18 .... 43.00
Movie star, Bette Davis or Loretta
  Young, each 5.00
Movie star, Rudolph Valentino
  astride horse 10.00
Nazi, Hitler at the 1936 Berlin Auto
  Show .... 15.00 to 20.00
New Year Greetings, Raphael Tuck,
  little girl w/snowball 4.00
Puzzle, White House & Teddy
  Roosevelt, turn card to change
  scene 30.00
Railroad depots, set of 15 .... 90.00
Real photo, child w/teddy bear in
  wicker chair .... 6.00 to 8.00
St. Patrick's Day, Kilkenny castle,
  harp & staff 5.00

Embroidered Postcard

World War I, Medical Corps, American flags w/caduceus center, embroidered (ILLUS.) 8.00
World War I, "The Star Spangled
  Banner," embroidered 12.50

POSTERS

Also see MUCHA ARTWORK.

Ammunition, "Winchester Repeating
  Arms Co.," scene of black men (2)
  & dog frightened by skunk beside
  hollow log on which their shotgun
  rests, 1908 copyright, original
  frame, 28 x 20" $195.00

Cigarettes, "Chesterfields," cardboard, Rita Hayworth in scene
  from movie "Down to Earth,"
  w/large pack of cigarettes at
  side, 1940's, 20½ x 20½" 90.00
Circus, "Great Victorian Troupe
  Sword Swallowers," group performing, 40 x 28" 235.00
Circus, "Ringling Bros. - The Four
  McCrees," troupe performing,
  28 x 18" 75.00

"Medinger Cycles"

Cycles, "Medinger," chromolithograph
  of 1890's cyclists, by George Bottini,
  printed by Bataille, Paris, 1897,
  49 7/8 x 34¾" (ILLUS.) 2,200.00

1937 Paris International Exposition

Exposition, "1937 Paris Arts et Techniques Exposition Internationale,"
  lithograph on paper, artwork by
  Leonette Capiello, minor creases,
  48½ x 42½" (ILLUS.) 385.00
Farm equipment, "John Deere,"
  company emblem, pictures various corn shellers, team of horses,

barn, silo & men working, 1929,
37 x 25".......................... 225.00
Gin, "Gordon's," Humphrey Bogart
in scene from the movie, "The
African Queen," w/case of Gordon's Gin, 22 x 16"............. 30.00

"Harper's Magazine"

Magazine, "Harper's Magazine," by
Fred Hyland, promoting DuMauri-
er's serial "The Martian," chromolithograph on paper, 1896,
center crease, 29½ x 19½"
(ILLUS.)........................ 275.00
Patent medicine, "Indian Root Pills,"
1920's, 21 x 14"................ 135.00
Tobacco, "Bull Durham Smoking
Tobacco," scene of 2 black hunt-
ers w/bull in background, heavy
cardboard, unframed,
29½ x 21"...................... 495.00
Tobacco, "Mail Pouch," railroad en-
gineer on train, "For a Steady
Nerve," 1907, 22 x 16"........ 125.00
World War I, "Fight or Buy Bonds,"
Howard Chandler Christy, 1917,
40 x 30" (edge tears)........... 100.00
World War I, "Fourth Liberty Loan,"
scene of Hun dragging girl, by E.
Young, "Remember Belgium,"
30 x 20"....................... 45.00
World War I, "Motor Corps of
America," women drivers,
40 x 20"....................... 95.00
World War I, "Navy Gee! I Wish I
Were a Man," Howard Chandler
Christy, 1918 (tiny tear & few
water spots)................... 300.00
World War I, General Pershing in
France w/Uncle Sam & their ar-
mies, by E. C. Renesch, Chicago,
1917, 20 x 16"................. 50.00

POWDER HORNS & FLASKS

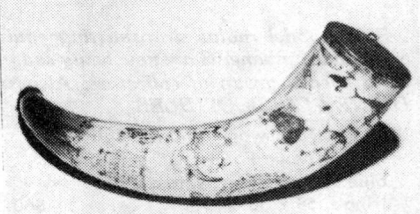

Early 19th Century Powder Horn

Brass flask, embossed shell design,
7" l............................. $62.50
Brass flask, embossed scene of
hunter & dog under tree, 9½" l.
(minor dents & some soldered
repair at seams)............... 55.00
Brass flask, embossed hanging
game.......................... 75.00
Copper flask, embossed crossed
flags & arm aiming gun, marked
"Massachusetts Arms Co.,
Chicopee Falls," 4¼" l.......... 95.00
Copper flask w/copper fittings,
plain, 4¾" l.................... 45.00
Copper flask w/brass fittings, embossed rococo shell design, 9" l... 55.00
Horn, engraved spread-winged
American eagle & shield, fully-
rigged sailing ship, interlacing
hearts, figure of mermaid inscribed "Naptun," a soldier riding
a seahorse, compasses, a horse
tied at stake & a large fort-like
building w/mounted guns, faceted
spout w/raised ring & wooden
base w/iron cleat, probably Pennsylvania, early 19th c., 13" l.
(ILLUS.).......................1,540.00
Horn, engraved landscape w/house,
deer & tiger one side & sailing
ship, double-coiled snake & 2
ladies reverse, scalloped design
at edge, brass ferrule, probably
American, 13¾" l.............. 247.50
Horn, engraved spread-winged
American eagle above monogram,
3 chip-carved rings at faceted
neck, brass plate at base, 19th c.,
18" l.......................... 357.50
Horn, molded into 8-sided container,
original wooden plug stopper,
8½" l.......................... 55.00
Horn, plain, wooden end & carved
wooden tip, 12½" l............. 55.00
Horn, plain, turned wooden end
w/brass studs, 13" l............ 50.00
Leather & brass flask, ca. 1860..... 54.00

RADIOS & ACCESSORIES

Early model radios, transmitting equipment and components are now being sought by a special group of collectors. Also see DISNEY COLLECTIBLES

Banner, "Farnsworth Phonograph-
Radio Known For Tone," gold on
blue satin banner w/tassels &
fringe, 58 x 38½" $60.00
Book, "Experimental Radio," by
Ramsey, 1929, Bloomington 10.00
Book, "How To Make A Neutrodyne
Receiver," soft cover, 1924,
63 pp. 9.00
Book, "Radio Amateur's Handbook,"
parts & drawings, soft cover,
560 pp. 18.00
Book, "Rider's Radio Service Manual," Vols. 1 through 22 .... 220.00
Catalogue, "Allied Radio," 1934 .... 6.00
Catalogue, "Beckley Ralston," radio,
battery & accessories, early
1920's, 65 pp. 75.00
Radio, Air King Products Model 824,
table model, wooden cabinet
(refinished), standard & short
wave bands, magic eye tuning,
1930's 150.00
Radio, Airline Model AC 62-425,
1930's 35.00
Radio, Atwater Kent Model 12, 1923,
breadboard case 450.00
Radio, Atwater Kent Model 20 "Big
Box," ca. 1925 .... 75.00 to 95.00
Radio, Atwater Kent Model 37, 1927,
w/tubes 125.00
Radio, Crosley Model 51,
1924 .... 85.00 to 95.00
Radio, Crosley "Cathedral"
Model 158 .... 95.00
Radio, Crosley "Pup," 1925 .... 315.00
Radio, Crosley Model YF, 1922 ...... 150.00
Radio, Detrola Model 568-1, w/short
wave band, metal cabinet 25.00
Radio, Echophone "Cathedral"
Model 225.00
Radio, FADA Model 652, yellow
bakelite case w/red trim 450.00
Radio, Federal crystal set 250.00
Radio, Freed-Eiseman Model 50,
1926, w/tubes, battery-operated .. 85.00
Radio, Garod "RAF" 140.00
Radio, General Electric Model H-77
console, AM & 2 short wave
bands, push-button controls,
1930's, wooden cabinet 350.00
Radio, General Electric Model K63,
1933 .... 180.00
Radio, Grunow Model 500,
w/chrome grille 90.00
Radio, Hallicrafters World Wide
portable model, A.C./D.C. 75.00

Radio, Howe crystal set 200.00
Radio, Kennedy (Colin B.) Model XV,
1925 .... 245.00
Radio, Majestic console model, Art
Deco style w/built-in bookshelves,
late 1920's 300.00
Radio, Metro "Super 7" Model,
1925 .... 200.00
Radio, Philco "Cathedral" Model 20,
1930 .... 180.00 to 250.00
Radio, Philco Model 510, 1928 ...... 390.00
Radio, Philmore crystal set, green
w/glass dome over crystal, origi-
nal box 150.00
Radio, RCA "Radiola 18," 1927,
w/Grebe "Cathedral" speaker 375.00
Radio, RCA "Radiola 60" cabinet
model, 1928, 8-tube, 10 x
10 x 29" .... 325.00 to 375.00
Radio, RCA Model 128, 1934,
3-band 200.00
Radio, Silver-Marshall "Cathedral"
Model 275.00
Radio, Stromberg Carlson Model
635, w/matching Temple 15
speaker 150.00
Radio, Westinghouse "Grandfather
Clock" Model WR-8-R, 1929 .... 325.00
Radio, Zenith Model 6-B-129, 1936,
battery-operated, 22" h. 115.00
Radio, Zenith Model 5S338, table
model 135.00
Radio horn speaker, "Dictograph" .. 120.00
Radio speaker, Operadio, 1925 ..... 60.00

REVERSE PAINTINGS ON GLASS

Reverse Painting of Puritan Lady

Also see SIGNS & SIGNBOARDS.

Children (2) gathering eggs in hen
house, entitled "Marz," original
frame, 12 x 9½" $275.00

Cock fight scenes entitled "Beginning to Death," 4 panels, overall 19 x 13" 195.00

Flamenco dancers, Art Deco style figures rendered in wrinkled tinsel & outlined in black, heightened w/magenta, gold & blue paint, ca. 1920, 12 x 16" 55.00

Floral arrangement of spring flowers in soft shades of pink & yellow w/green foliage, oval frame 85.00

Frankfurt, Germany, river scene w/boats, bridges, tree-lined banks & city buildings, mother-of-pearl insets, convex glass, 7¼ x 15" 275.00

Lady wearing colorful gown & large hat, entitled "Die Kirliamche," original frame, 10 7/8 x 8" (minor flaking) 225.00

"Nikolaus, Kaizer Aller Russina," three-quarter length portrait of gentleman wearing green uniform w/blue sash & gold detail against brown ground, original frame, 12 x 9½" (background flaking) ... 200.00

Puritan lady w/prayerbook, easel-type frame, 1900 copyright, Ullman Mfg. Co., New York, 9½" w. (ILLUS.) 75.00

"Whampoa Anchorage," town of Whampoa & the famed Nine-stage Pagoda on center island, Chinese, 19th c., framed, 17¾ x 14¼" 302.00

Woman w/flowers in her hair, entitled "Mailanderin," framed, 11½ x 9½" 135.00

Young woman w/ornately coiffed dark hair, wearing red gown & posed against blue ground, entitled "Silvia," original frame, 10¼ x 7¾" (minor flakes) 100.00

ROYCROFT ITEMS

Elbert Hubbard, eccentric entrepreneur of the late 19th century, founded Roycroft Shops and established a craft community in East Aurora, New York in 1895. Individuals were trained in the trades of bookbinding, leather tooling and printing. Craft-style furniture in the manner of Gustav Stickley and known as "Aurora Colonial" furniture was produced. A copper workshop, begun in 1908, turned out numerous items. All of these, along with the Buffalo Pottery china which was produced exclusively for use at the Roycroft Inn and carries the Roycroft symbol, constitute a special category associated with the Arts and Crafts movement. Also see FURNITURE.

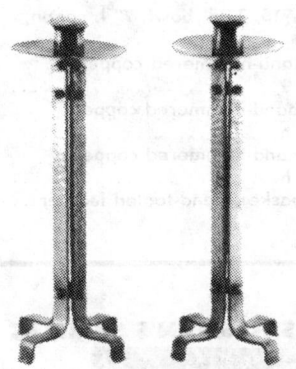

Roycroft Copper Candlesticks

Ash trays, hand-hammered copper, in base w/match holder, set of 4 .... $55.00

Bean pot, cov., brown glazed pottery, 4½" ....20.00 to 30.00

Book, "The Notebook of Elbert Hubbard," by Elbert Hubbard II, 1926 .... 45.00

Bookends, hand-hammered copper, owls in relief, pr. 95.00

Bookends, hand-hammered copper, slanted sides, strap & loop in relief, 4" w., 5" h., pr. 80.00

Bowl, hand-hammered copper, 9" d. 70.00

Box, hand-hammered copper, 5 x 3½" 70.00

Candlesticks, hand-hammered copper, wide bobeche on 4 vertical strips forming standard & feet, early 20th c., 12" h., pr. (ILLUS.) 715.00

Desk lamp, hand-hammered copper, deep domical shade, cylindrical standard w/flaring base, early 20th c., 13" h. 467.50

Desk set: cov. inkwell w/glass insert, letter holder & pr. blotter ends; hand-hammered copper, 4 pcs. ....95.00 to 125.00

Humidor & cover, hand-hammered copper w/green enameled abstract geometric design & ropework front, Roycroft logo reverse, 6" h. 175.00

Inkwell, cov., hand-hammered brass 75.00

Letter opener, hand-hammered brass & copper 35.00

Magazine, "The Roycrofter," 1927, November 5.50

Nut bowl & spoon, hand-hammered copper, wide mouth on squat form w/three hammered out feet, flattened spoon w/arched handle,

ca. 1915, 7" d. bowl, 7" l. spoon,
2 pcs. 275.00
Tray, hand-hammered copper,
14 x 9" 65.00
Vase, hand-hammered copper,
4¾" h. 40.00
Vase, hand-hammered copper,
9½" h. 95.00
Wastebasket, hand-tooled leather .. 175.00

SALESMAN'S SAMPLES

"Favorite" Cooking Range

The traveling salesman or "drummer" has all but disappeared from the American scene. In the latter part of the 19th century and up to the late 1930's they traveled the country making calls on potential customers, carrying with them small replicas of their products. Today these smaller versions of kitchenwares, farm equipment, and even bath tubs, are of interest to collectors and are available in a wide price range.

Basin, graniteware, turquoise &
white marbleized. $32.00
Bath tub, steel tub w/ornate feet,
embossed "Booths Pat., Steel Clad
Bath, Detroit, Michigan," 5½" l. ... 72.00
Bookcase, oak, 2-stack, lift-up glass
front, "Globe Wernicke, Cincinnati," 17" w., 4¾" deep, 19½" h. 165.00
Boot w/heel, rubber, embossed
elephant on one side, "Woonsocket Rubber Co." on other side,
2½" h. 15.00
Bowl, graniteware, grey mottled,
"Royal Granite," 5" d. 50.00
Burial vault, aluminum, "Clark" 37.50
Butcher knives, 24 knives & Catalog
No. 28 dated 1940 in original suitcase, "Foster Bros.," manufactured by John Chatillon & Sons,
26 pcs. 225.00

Button hooks, sterling silver handles, 12 in mahogany display
case, 13 pcs. 250.00
Canoe, fishing, aluminum, 42 x
13½" 75.00
Cedar chest, cedarwood, "Lane,"
9 x 4½ x 3½" 25.00
Cooking range, cast iron, "Favorite,"
6-hole top, water reservoir, 18 x
10", 23" h. (ILLUS.) 700.00
Cooking range, cast iron, "Bucks
No. 2 Junior," 18 x 12", 24" h.
(42 lbs.) 750.00
Cooking range, cast iron, "Charter
Oak No. 580" (no reservoir
cover) 1,100.00
Cooking range, blue enamel,
"Karr" 3,300.00
Crock, "Western Stoneware Co.,"
blue & white.................... 200.00
Cuspidor, graniteware, grey
w/white interior, weighted bottom, 3¼" top d., 2½" h. 95.00
Fabric swatch book, "ABC Percale,
Arthur Beir & Co., N.Y.," 1932 .... 38.00
Fluting iron, "Geneva Fluter Iron,
Pat. 1866," 3¾ x 2" 85.00
Food grinder, cast iron, "Rollman
No. 61," 1915, 6" 27.50
Hat, felt, "Stetson," original box 11.00
Ice box, wooden, double doors
w/pressed design, brass fittings,
zinc liner & drain, 10 x 7½",
18" h. 210.00
Meat grinder, 5½" 45.00
Moccasins, Indian-type, "Brown Shoe
Co., St. Louis, Missouri" 70.00
Organ stool, oak, refinished,
13" h. 110.00
Plate, graniteware, blue shaded,
stamped "Bluebelle Ware" 30.00
Plate, graniteware, cobalt blue &
white marbleized, stamped "Blue
Diamond Ware" 45.00
Rubbers, "Boston Rubber Shoe Co.,"
black & red, pr. 18.00
Scythe w/grain cradle, 4 curved
wooden tines & handle w/iron
blade, 8 x 4", 10" h. 150.00
Tea kettle, cast iron, swivel top
w/porcelain knob, wire bail handle, "Wagner Ware," 4" h. 52.50
Waffle iron, cast iron, "Wagner, Sidney, Ohio, pat. 1910," 4 3/8" d. .. 125.00
Wash boiler, hand soldered tin,
4 x 3" 26.00
Wash tub, galvanized metal, "U. S.
Steel," 4" d. 40.00
Washing machine, barrel-type, "The
Queen Washing Machine, J. H.
Knoll, Reading, Pa." 265.00

SCALES

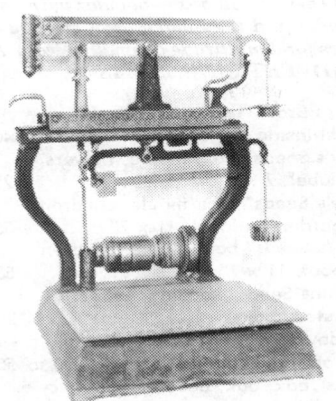

Countertop Computing Scale

Advertising scale, "Wrigley's Spearmint Pepsin Gum," w/shaped brass scoop, 4-lb. $225.00

Apothecary scale, walnut w/marble platform, brass pans, "Henry Troemner, Philad.," 18 x 8½", 7" h. 175.00

Apothecary scale, balance-type, brass pans, marble top, 6 x 19 x 5 3/8" 110.00

Baby weighing scale, brass & iron, w/basket, 24-lb. 40.00

Butcher's steelyard scale, "French Meats," 36" l. 135.00

Butter scale, wooden, turned post supporting balancing arm w/suspended wooden trays, 18" l. beam 85.00

Candy scale, cast iron & brass w/tin scoop, "Fairbanks," 45.00

Candy scale, lollypop-type w/indicating chart in glass-faced housing, "Toledo Model 8300T" 575.00

Chemical scale, balance-type, fully enclosed in wooden case, ca. 1900 . . . . 175.00

Coin-operated sidewalk scale, "Mills' Beam," 1-cent play 900.00

Coin-operated sidewalk scale, "Weight Teller, Caille," w/original instructions & key, 1-cent play . . .2,450.00

Countertop scale, computing-type, cast iron & brass, "Burrow, Stewart & Milne Co., Hamilton, Ont." on brass bar, w/brass pan & 2 weights, 14" l. 65.00

Countertop scale, computing-type, "The Computing Scale Co., Dayton, Ohio" (ILLUS.) 150.00

Countertop scale, oak w/marble platform, brass pans 100.00

Egg grading scale, "Mascot" 25.00

Farrier's scale, wrought iron & brass, "C. Hurtz," 12" l. 30.00

Fur trader's hide scale, brass, "Boker" 35.00

Fur trader's hide scale, wrought iron w/brass weight inserts 75.00

Gold scale, marble base, glass case w/cherrywood trim, "Chainomatic Gold Scale, Christian Becker" . . . . . . 165.00 to 275.00

Grain scale, brass, "Winchester," w/two buckets 300.00

Kitchen scale, "Turnbull's Family Scale" 65.00

Photographer's scale, w/five weights, "Eastman Kodak" 45.00

Physician's scale, cast iron base w/wheels, mahogany post w/brass rod for height measurement, brass mechanism, "Fairbanks," 1895 patent 1,000.00

Postage scale, hand-held, brass, "J. Cooke & Son" 95.00

Postage scale, platform-type, "Liberty, Triner Scale Co., Chicago," 4-lb. 40.00

Spring scale, hanging-type, iron w/polished brass face plate, "Chatillon's Improved Circular Spring Balance," 60-lb., 4½" w., 11" h. 65.00

Spring scale, hanging-type, 2-sided glass-covered face w/chrome frame, enamel pan, "Detector" . . . . .125.00 to 150.00

Spring scale, cast iron w/brass face, "Pelouze Mfg. Co.," 17" 25.00

Steelyard scale, wrought iron, 15" l. 55.00

SCRAPBOOKS & ALBUMS

Album, musical-type, velvet cover w/ornate brass Victorian-style clasp $110.00

Album, musical-type (plays "After the Ball" & "Oh Promise Me"), celluloid cover picturing steamship . . 200.00

Album, photograph, celluloid cover, colorful portrait of lady decor, ca. 1900, 13 x 9" . . . . .35.00 to 48.00

Album, photograph, green plush w/heart-shaped mirror insert & gilt brass trim front, on gilt metal stand w/drawer . . . . .80.00 to 95.00

Album, ice-skating enthusiast, over 30 photos of famous skaters, other newspaper clippings & single (dated 1929) postcard w/"Sonja Henie" signature 75.00

Victorian Album

Album, hardbound cloth cover
w/embossed lilies & centered
w/portrait of child, w/over 100
trade cards, McLoughlin's coffee
advertising paper dolls, diecuts &
scraps of florals, animals, etc.,
dated 1887 on back of album
(ILLUS.) 140.00
Album, w/over 100 trade cards in-
cluding blacks, children w/dolls &
metamorphic types 52.50
Album, w/150 postcards, assorted
Shrine, Knights Templar, Denver,
Colorado & Peoria, Illinois scenes
of parades, bands, etc. 75.00
Album, w/200 postcards, including
Brundage, Clapsaddle, Santa
Claus, Thanksgiving, Easter & Hal-
loween greetings. 180.00
Album, w/600 assorted trade cards,
ca. 1880 (some loose pages) 190.00
Scrapbook, w/275 advertising, die-
cut, greeting & calling cards,
some w/early comic characters &
blacks, 1865-1890. . . . . 95.00
Scrapbook, w/over 400 trade cards,
including "Waldorf Astoria" cards,
cigarette cards w/military scenes,
etc., late 1930's 600.00
Scrapbook, brown cloth cover em-
bossed w/cockatoos, w/58 pages
of die-cut flowers, children & miscellaneous items, dated 1883 . . . . . 85.00

SEED BOXES

These early factory-made wooden boxes once were used to display or to store garden and flower seeds. The sturdy construction
and colorful labels (often still intact), have
made these small boxes popular with collectors who find they make ideal storage containers for a multitude of small objects. Also
see ADVERTISING ITEMS.

"Brigg's Bros." box, oak, colorful
label inside lid, 10½ x 7" $40.00
"Ferry's Seeds" box, maple, flowers
on label, 7 x 5" 25.00
"Ferry's Seeds" box, maple, children
in garden on label, 11 x 7". 55.00
"Ferry's Seeds" box, maple, children
in boat, 11 x 7" 55.00
"Hawkins Seeds, Reading, Vt." fold-
ing store box 125.00
"Mandeville & King" box, oak, flow-
ers on label . . . . .35.00 to 55.00
"Pages" box, oak, dovetail construc-
tion, label w/lady in colonial
dress & flowers inside lid . .45.00 to 65.00
"Philips (J.M.) Sons, Mercersburg,
Pa." box, maple, original colorful
paper label w/fruit, vegetables in
lid & divided interior w/unused
seed packets & pictures of flowers
& vegetables (some edge wear),
28½ x 12". 205.00
"Rice's Popular Flower Seed" box,
oak, girl w/flowers on label,
6 x 5½" 37.50
"Rice's Flower Seed" box, oak, par-
quet top, 10½ x 6". . . . . . . .35.00 to 55.00
"Shaker's Garden Seeds, Mt. Leba-
non, New York" box, poplar &
pine w/original leather hinges &
worn red paint, 23¼" l 510.00
"Sibley (Hiram) Seed Company" box,
w/scene of factory on label inside
lid 65.00

SEWING ADJUNCTS

Beaded Pin Cushion

Also see ADVERTISING ITEMS, PIN CUSHION DOLLS, SALESMAN'S SAMPLES, SHAKER COLLECTIBLES and WORLD FAIR COLLECTIBLES.

Darner, turned wood, egg shape w/handle, early 20th c., 6" l.	$5.00 to 10.00
Embroidery scissors, stork handles, woven sweetgrass holder, Germany	22.50
Needle case, silver, France, early 19th c.	55.00
Pin cushion, beaded cloth, star-shaped, dove of peace, American flags & date "1919" worked in multicolored beading, 9" w. (ILLUS.)	65.00
Pin cushion, brass, model of a pig	85.00
Pin cushion, metal, model of a jockey's cap	30.00
Sewing bird, nickel-plated brass, single cushion, 5" h.	115.00
Sewing bird, wrought iron, single cushion, w/heart-shaped thumb-screw, 6" h.	125.00

Figural Sewing Caddy

Sewing caddy, turned wood, figural woman, hat holds thimble, thread & needles inside skirt, red & black (ILLUS.)	22.00
Tape measure, brass & silverplate, model of a fish	47.00
Tape measure, celluloid, figural black mammy w/ladybug pull	48.00
Tape measure, celluloid, model of a rooster	35.00
Thimble, 14k gold, chased house scene in band	105.00
Thimble, sterling silver, chased lily-of-the-valley band	70.00
Thread caddy, cast iron, 12-spool, rotating-type, w/pin cushion top	50.00

SHAKER COLLECTIBLES

Shaker Carrier

The Shakers, a religious sect founded by Ann Lee, first settled in this country at Watervliet, N.Y., near Albany, in 1774 and by 1880 there were nine settlements in America. Workmanship in Shaker crafts is an extension of their religious beliefs and features plain and simple designs reflecting a chaste elegance that is now much in demand though relatively few early items are available. Also see BASKETS and FURNITURE.

Advertisement, printed, "Shaker Hair Restorer, D. C. Brainard, Mount Lebanon, N.Y.," matted & framed, 12¾ x 9 3/8"	$65.00
Apple butter scoop, carved walnut, 1-piece, 2½" deep, 11¾" l.	285.00
Bean sorter, wooden, w/adjustable slats, 10 x 18½"	135.00
Berry basket, wooden, round bent-wood top & base rims, slat sides, 6½" d., 3¼" h.	110.00
Blueberry box, wooden, Sabbathday Lake Community, 8½ x 5½"	65.00
Bonnet, black (faded to brown) silk w/embroidered floral designs, blue polished linen lining (worn)	55.00
Bonnet, woven dark brown palm & straw, black ribbon & black silk trim, 9" l. flounce, South Union, Kentucky	185.00 to 300.00
Bottle, clear glass w/salmon label printed "Lime Water, Prepared at Shaker Village, Mer. Co. N.H." in black, 8" h. (minor sickness)	80.00
Bucket, cov., wooden stave construction (never had a finish), lid w/worn black & white printed label "Shaker Apple Sauce, Enfield, N.H.," wire bail handle & wooden grip, 6¾" h.	250.00
Carpet beater	55.00
Carrier, bentwood oval w/fixed handle, 2-finger lappet construction	

w/copper tacks, old varnish fin-
ish, 13¼ x 9¾", 2 5/8" h.
(ILLUS.) 325.00
Cheese drainer, tin, pierced round
holes in sides & bottom, 18" d.,
6" h. 220.00
Clothes hanger, wooden, South
Union, Kentucky, 20¾" w. 50.00
Coffee pot, cov., tapering cylinder,
handle at right angle to spout,
Sabbathday Lake, Maine, 11" h. . . 240.00
Darner, wooden, mushroom shape,
handle threads into socket,
4¾" l. 45.00
Flour scoop, wooden, w/pierce-
carved handle . . . . .85.00 to 135.00
Food cover, wood & wire, 17"
across. 45.00
Herb drying rack, 3-bar, mortise &
tenon construction, carved shoe
feet, grey paint, 34" w.,
48" h. . . . . .400.00 to 440.00
Knife tray, 2-section, tiger stripe
maple (handle reglued) 140.00
Pantry box, cov., bentwood oval, 3-
finger lappet construction w/sin-
gle finger in lid & 2 lappets in
base, copper tacks, worn light
blue paint over white, Canterbury,
New Hampshire, 6 3/8 x 4¼" 255.00
Pantry box, cov., bentwood oval, 2-
finger lappet construction, copper
tacks, old worn green paint, 8 x
5¼". 400.00
Pin cushion, turned wooden base,
worn blue plush top, original yellow varnish, Sabbathday Lake,
Maine, 2 7/8" h. 65.00
Sap bucket, wooden, stave construc-
tion w/iron bands & hanger, worn
old yellow paint, bottom impressed "N.E. Shakers, Enfield,
Conn.," 11¼" h. 145.00
Sieve, bentwood round sides, woven
horsehair strainer, old worn natural finish, attributed to Sabbathday Lake, Maine, 14¼" d. 200.00
Step-stool, painted hardwood,
2-tier 595.00
Tape loom, table model for weaving
binding for bonnets, Alfred,
Maine. 375.00

SIGNS & SIGNBOARDS

Also see BREWERIANA and POSTERS.

Apothecary, cast zinc, model of a
mortar & pestle, 24" d. $550.00

Butcher Shop Sign

Butcher shop, "Hodson Superior
Pork Butcher," carved & gilded
pine, enormous hog carved in the
half-round & hollowed, obverse
gessoed, gilded & painted, suspended from wrought iron
hangers, 19th c., 55" l., 37" h.
(ILLUS.) .4,675.00
Candy, "Sparrow Candy," self-
framed tin, Queen seated at table
w/box of chocolates, garden
scene background 1,200.00
Cigarettes, "Hassan," cardboard
under glass, original frame,
29 x 23". 185.00
Clothing, "Munsingwear,"
lithographed canvas, twin girls
modeling underwear for grandmother, 1914, original frame,
36 x 28". . . . . .350.00 to 425.00
Clothing, "Rex Collars," reverse
painting on glass, well-dressed
man w/opera glasses & various
types of collars, "2 for 25¢" 265.00
Dye, "Diamond Dye," self-framed
tin, w/Bessie Pease Gutman illustration entitled "A Busy Day in
Dollville" 450.00

"Century Fence" Sign

Fencing, "Century Fence, St. Paul,
Minnesota," graniteware, white
lettering on blue, 12 x 4"
(ILLUS.). 15.00
Flour, "Washburn Flour Mills, Min-
neapolis, Minn.," lithographed
paper, flour mill w/railroad cars,
show wagons & carriages, Minneapolis in background, original
ornate frame, 46 x 38" 950.00
Fur trading, "The Alaska Fur Co.,"

carved wood, model of a seal
atop shaped plank, gold lettering,
suspended from ornate wrought
iron hanger, 1890's, 55 x 54" 3,500.00
Gum, "California Fruit Chewing
Gum," paper under glass, young
boy in sailor suit w/toy sailboat,
framed 150.00
Insurance, "Atlas Assurance Co.,"
graniteware, Atlas holding the
world, multicolored, 15 x 8" 175.00

"Providence-Washington Insurance Co."

Insurance, "Providence-Washington
Insurance Company of Providence,
R.I.," self-framed tin, colorful
portrait of George Washington
(ILLUS.) 425.00

"Yale Locks" Wooden Sign

Locksmith, "Yale Locks," carved &
painted wood, key cut from single
plank, gilded ground, wrought
iron banding, late 19th-early
20th c., 41½" l. (ILLUS.) 1,760.00
Motorcycle, "Indian," tin,
36 x 11½" 200.00
Optometrist, "Eyes Examined -
Glasses Fitted," reverse painting
on glass, wire rim glasses pic-
tured, 1890-1915 . . . . 185.00 to 265.00
Paint, "Murphy Da-cote Enamel,"
self-framed tin, patio scene above
early auto & 10 color samples,
lithograph by H.D. Beach Co.,
Coshocton, Ohio, ca. 1925,
27 x 19" (ILLUS.) 715.00

"Murphy Da-cote Enamel"

Patent medicine, "Dr. Jayne's Expectorant," chromolithographed paper, stern image of Thomas
Jefferson adds credence to claims
for product, Knapp Co. Litho-
graphers, New York, 1893 copy-
right 330.00
Railroad, "Southern Railways," self-
framed tin, scene of high bridge
over Kentucky River 725.00
Railroad, "Union Pacific," cardboard,
scene of Zion National Park,
framed 125.00
Razors, "Twenty Grand Razor
Blades," die-cut tin, old style
razor shape 120.00
Seamstress, "Dressmaking & Altera-
tions," reverse painting on glass,
double-sided, orange, black &
white, wooden frame & original
wire hanging bracket 235.00
Seeds, "Mandeville & King Superior
Flower Seeds," paperboard, beautiful girl looking through colorful
flowers 325.00
Shipping lines, "Cunard Line," self-
framed tin, ship "Caronia" w/deck
plan & saloon rates, 1912,
37 x 28" 300.00
Shoe polish, "Bixby's Shoe Polish,"
die-cut tin frog in tuxedo, top hat
& spats holding can of Bixby's
Shoe Polish, 1880's, 24" h. 650.00
Shoes, "Hamilton Brown Shoe Co.,"
lithographed tin, 3 factory scenes,
ca. 1900, 44 x 31" 450.00
Soap, "Jap Rose Soap," cardboard,
Oriental children bathing doll,
framed, 28 x 36" 275.00
Soap, "Pear's," paperboard under
glass, comical baby in tub,
framed, 23 x 18" 125.00
Soap, "20 Mule Team Borax," self-

framed tin, 20-mule team pulling
wagons loaded w/Borax, by
Bachrach & Cordes, San Francisco,
California, 1896 copyright,
33 x 23" 750.00
Soft drink, "Cherry Smash," graniteware, flange-type, 18" d. 250.00
Soft drink, "Golden Sarsaparilla
10c," celluloid over tin, picturing
bottle & early glass, ca.
1910 .... 90.00 to 175.00

"Hires in Bottles"

Soft drink, "Hire's," self-framed tin,
flapper girl dressed in red on yellow ground (ILLUS.) 550.00
Soft drink, "Howell's Root Beer,"
self-framed tin, elf w/bottle, 6
colors, 1930's 160.00
Soft drink, "Pepsi Cola," tin, 6-pack
of bottles w/paper labels 245.00
Soft drink, "Whistle," paperboard,
scene of 3 elfin men in tub filled
w/bottles of Whistle, 1940's,
30 x 21" 30.00
Stoves, "Herald Ranges," tin,
detailed cook stove, ca. 1890 ..... 885.00
Textiles, "Southern Roller Mills,"
lithographed tin, scene of warehouse, wagon yard, horse-drawn
street car & children chasing
dogs, ca. 1885 .... 345.00
Thread, "Clark's O.N.T.," cardboard,
woman in Matador costume,
21 x 14½" 225.00
Thread, "Clark's O.N.T. Spool Cotton," self-framed tin, 2 small girls
w/spool of cotton, 1888 .... 900.00
Thread, "J & P Coats Best 6-Cord
Spool Cotton," paperboard, lovely
lady pictured 450.00
Thread, "Williamantic," paperboard,
woman in red, shawl over head,
15½ x 12" 65.00
Tires, "Goodrich Silvertowns,"
graniteware, double-sided, multicolored, 18 x 17" 65.00
Tobacco, "Cherry Smoking Tobacco,"
chromolithographed paper, pretty
girl 500.00

"Honest Scrap Chewing Tobacco"

Tobacco, "Honest Scrap Chewing
Tobacco," self-framed cardboard,
scene of dog & black cat about to
"scrap" (ILLUS.) 750.00
Tobacco, "Honeymoon," embossed
tin, man & woman sitting in
moon, ca. 1910, oak frame 375.00
Tobacco, "Tiger Tobacco," paperboard, tiger peering through
glass, original frame 800.00
Tobacco, "U.S. Marine Cut Plug,"
paper under glass, sailor in port-
hole, 34 x 24" 675.00
Toys, "Wood Bildo Toy Blocks," self-
framed tin, small boy & girl playing w/blocks, 19th c. 650.00
Veterinary medicine, "Campbell's
Horse Foot Remedies," paper,
"Axtell" (World Champion race
horse) & black stable boy,
26 x 19" 155.00
Whiskey, "Belle of Anderson Sour
Mash," reverse painting on glass,
nudes at public bath, framed,
41 x 32" 1,450.00
Whiskey, "Empire Whiskey," reverse
painting on glass, image of Abraham Lincoln at top 375.00
Whiskey, "Green River Whiskey,"
chromolithographed paper, black
man inviting us to enjoy whiskey
his mule carries, both were bred
in Old Kentucky, lithographed by
Chas. W. Shonk, Chicago, 1st
quarter 20th c., 20" d. 550.00
Whiskey, "Old Jed Clayton," chromolithographed paper, black man
pouring whiskey for hunters 400.00
Whiskey, "Overholt Rye," canvas,
fisherman pouring drink, wooden
frame, 1913, 38 x 27" 295.00
Whiskey, "Yellowstone Whiskey,"
self-framed tin, "Three Pleasures
of Life" 750.00
Yeast, "Fleishmann," paper under
glass, boy & girl under tree,
19½ x 13½" 100.00

Hawaiian
SOUVENIR SPOONS

by Dorothy T. Rainwater

The earliest proven date on an Hawaiian souvenir spoon is December 25, 1891. This 14 carat gold spoon is marked H. F. Wichman of Honolulu. There is a single palm tree and five fern fronds engraved on the handle. "Muriel" is engraved below the crown of the tree, with Honolulu and the date on the reverse.

The Wichman company, still outstanding jewelers of Hawaii, were early promoters of souvenir spoons. Their first advertisement of Hawaiian souvenir spoons appeared in *Paradise of the Pacific* in January 1893 when they offered "The Celebrated Hawaiian Spoons."

Conversations with old-time Honolulu jewelers revealed that many souvenir spoons were made in Honolulu. Dies were cut by mainland manufacturers and the spoons stamped from these dies in Hawaii. When no dies were used but the spoons were individually crafted, coin spoons epecially, were often made there by Chinese artists and craftsmen whose names, unfortunately, have been lost to history.

Other Honolulu jewelers who made souvenir spoons, or had spoons made especially for them were H. Gustave Biart, M. R. Counter, Harry Culman, Dawkins-Benny, W. H. Foster, Grossman-Moody, Thomas Lindsay, Henry W. Rietow, August and Joseph Vierra, Wall & Daugherty and the Westlin Company.

The names of many well-known mainland silver and jewelry companies such as Gorham, J. T. Inman, Daniel Low, Joseph Mayer, Paye & Baker, Charles M. Robbins, Shepard Manufacturing Company, Shreve & Bros., Sterling Silver Manufacturing Company, R. Wallace & Sons, Watrous Mfg. Co., Watson-Newell Company and E. J. Towle are found on Hawaiian spoons.

Many spoons bear no mark at all. Some of these were made in Honolulu. The makers were identified by old-time residents, especially by the late Chris Benny, a jeweler who could look at an Hawaiian coat of arms and tell who had made it.

The story of Hawaii, its tropical flowers, trees and fruits, the gracious Hawaiian people, their colorful customs and the proud saga of Hawaiian royalty have been told through spoons.

Around 500-600 A. D. a group of Polynesian people arrived in the Hawaiian Islands from the Marquesas and Tahiti bringing with them their families, possessions, plants and animals and their skills. For more than a thousand years the Hawaiians lived a Stone Age life. Their clothing was tapa cloth, made from the inner bark of various plants; their houses were thatched with grass; their most important crop was taro, from which poi, their staple food, is made. Poi was supplemented by foods from the other plants they brought with them, some kinds of seaweed, fish, shellfish and turtles.

In 1778 Captain James Cook was the first to make the islands known to the rest of the world. A few years after Cook's discovery, Kamehameha I brought the islands under one rule. He is commemorated by a bronze statue in Honolulu which shows him wearing his feather cloak.

The arrival of outsiders brought many changes. *Kahilis* (feather standards) gave way to flags as symbols of royalty, feather cloaks to uniforms and royal orders and seals were introduced. Hawaii's coat of arms was based on a design suggested by the College of Heralds in London in 1850. It too, has undergone changes. Unchanged is the motto which was uttered by Kamehameha III in 1843, *Ua mau ke ea o ka aina i ka pono* (The life of the land is perpetuated in righteousness).

In 1883, the Hawaiian government minted its own coins. Following annexation, an Act of Congress provided for the redemption of Hawaiian coins in United States' coins at par value and recoinage of the redeemed coins into United States' silver coins. After January 1, 1904 King Kalakaua's coins were no longer legal tender. Only a small portion showed up for redemption. Hundreds, perhaps thousands, were made into souvenirs.

When Hawaii became the 50th State on August 21, 1959, with very little change, the seal of the Territory of Hawaii became the seal of the State of Hawaii.

(Editor's Note: *Dorothy T. Rainwater is considered one of the foremost experts on souvenir spoons. Together with Donna H. Felger, she has authored two books on the subject,* American Spoons - Souvenir and Historical *and* A Collector's Guide to Spoons Around the World, *both considered essential references for the serious souvenir spoon collector. In addition, Mrs. Rainwater has also written the* Encyclopedia of American Silver Manufacturers *and, together with her husband, Ivan,* American Silverplate, *both excellent references for collectors.)*

* * * * *

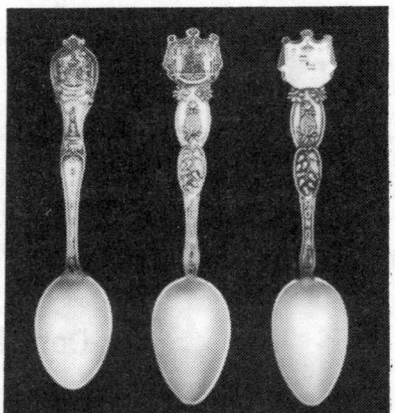

Hawaiian Coat of Arms

bowl, Joseph Mayer & Bros.
(ILLUS. right). 38.00

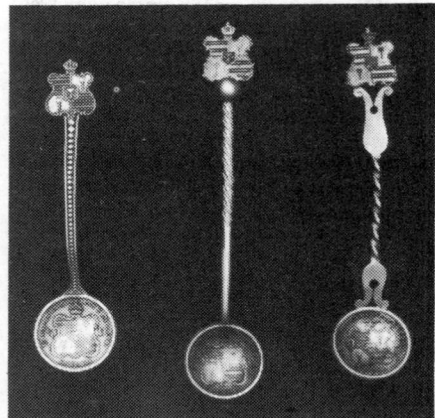

Spoons with 1883 Hawaiian Coins

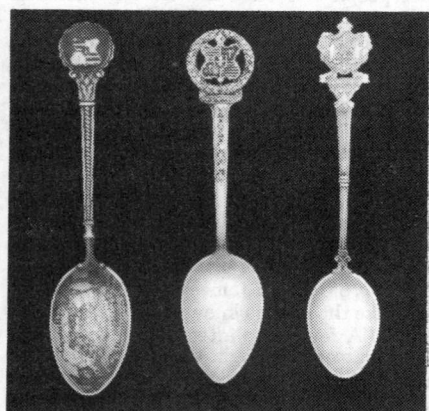

Spoons with Hawaiian Coat of Arms

Hawaiian coat of arms on handle
    terminal, "Grass Hut" &
    "Honolulu" in bowl, Watson-
    Newell Co. (ILLUS. left) $40.00
Hawaiian coat of arms on handle
    terminal, plain bowl, Robbins Co.,
    each (ILLUS. center & right) 30.00
Hawaiian coat of arms on handle
    terminal, plain bowl, J.T. Inman
    Co. & Joseph Mayer & Bros.,
    each (ILLUS. left & center respec-
    tively). 30.00
Hawaiian coat of arms w/enameled
    decor on handle terminal, plain

Hawaiian coat of arms on handle,
    terminal, *hapaha* coin (1883
    Hawaiian quarter) bowl; Paye
    & Baker Mfg. Co. left; H.F. Wich
    man center; unmarked but at-
    tributed to Wichman right; each
    (ILLUS.). 60.00
Hawaiin coat of arms on handle ter-
    minal, "Honolulu" on handle
    shank, *opihi* shell bowl, Wich-
    man (ILLUS. left) 40.00
Hawaiian coat of arms on handle
    terminal, stem shank, leaf bowl
    engraved "Honolulu," Wichman
    (ILLUS. center) 40.00
Hawaiian coat of arms on handle
    terminal, "Honolulu" on handle
    shank, engraved name in bowl,
    Wichman (ILLUS. right). 35.00

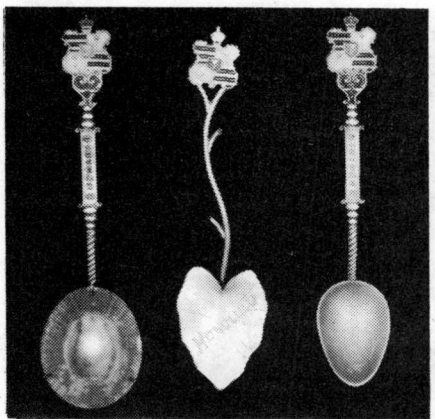

"Honolulu" Spoons

Statue of King Kamehameha I figural handle, applied split *hapaha* (1883 Hawaiian quarter) in bowl (ILLUS. left below) 55.00

Spoons with Enameled Bowls

Cal." (Schaezlein & Burridge, San Francisco, California); each (ILLUS.) ....95.00 to 125.00

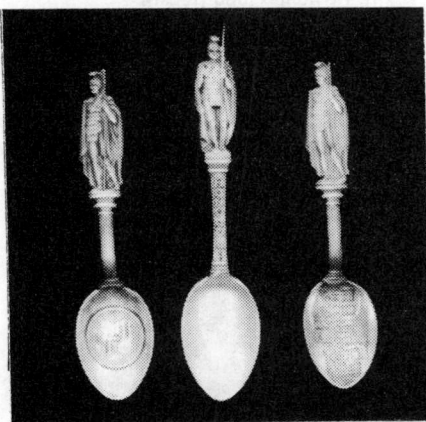

King Kamehameha I Figural Handles

Statue of King Kamehameha I figural handle, "Honolulu" on pedestal shank, plain bowl, marked *winged* "R" for Robbins Co. (ILLUS. center) 50.00

Statue of King Kamehameha I figural handle, Aliiolani Hale (Government office building in Honolulu as it appeared in 1893) in bowl, identified by the late Chris Benny as Wichman (ILLUS. right) 55.00

Statue of King Kamehameha I on pedestal figural handle, enameled Hawaiian coat of arms in round bowl, marked variously (1) Sterling and "CMR" in a diamond (Robbins Co.); (2) Sterling/H.F. Wichman; (3) Sterling "S. & B.S.F.

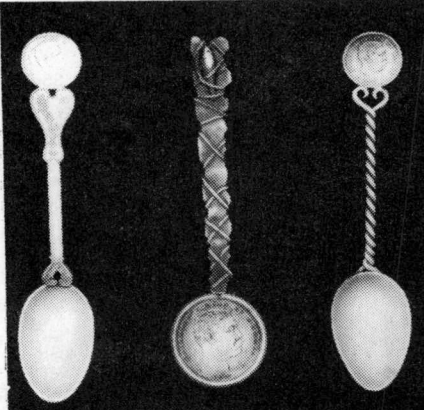

Spoons with Hawaiian Coins

Hapalua (1883 Hawaiian half dollar) bowl, rope-entwined handle w/applied fish, unmarked (ILLUS. center) 75.00

Umi kaneta (1883 Hawaiian dime) on handle terminal, plain bowl, unmarked, each (ILLUS. at sides) 45.00

Poi bowl on sugar cane handle, taro leaf bowl, Wichman 35.00

Net fisherman figural handle, beach scene w/fisherman in bowl, Watson-Newell for Wichman 50.00

Pineapple on handle, scene of "Surfing" off Diamond Head in bowl, Watson-Newell (ILLUS. left) 35.00

Banana stalk on handle, scene of "Waikiki Beach, Honolulu" in

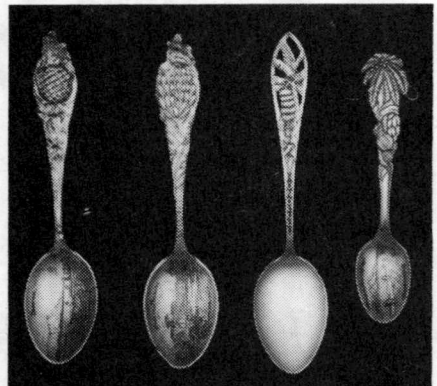

Symbolic of the Tropical Fruits

bowl, Watson-Newell (ILLUS.
center left) 35.00
Banana tree cut-out handle,
"Honolulu" on shank, plain bowl
(ILLUS. center right) 35.00
Coconut tree, bananas & pineapple
handle, "Diamond Head" beach
scene & "Honolulu" in bowl
(ILLUS. right).................... 35.00

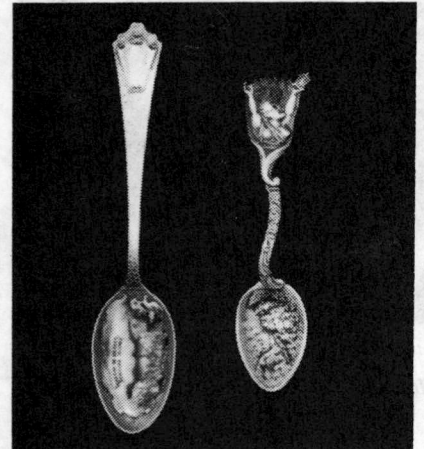

Volcano Spoons

Scroll medallion applied to hammered effect handle, scene of
"Kilauea" crater (traditional
home of Pele the Goddess of
Volcanoes) in bowl, Sterling Silver
Mfg. Co. (ILLUS. left) 30.00
Pele, Goddess of Volcanoes figural
handle, "Hawaii" on curved
shank, scene of erupting volcano
in bowl, Gorham Co. for H.F.
Wichman (ILLUS. right)........... 55.00
Honolulu harbor, old view with sailing ships on shaped handle, plain

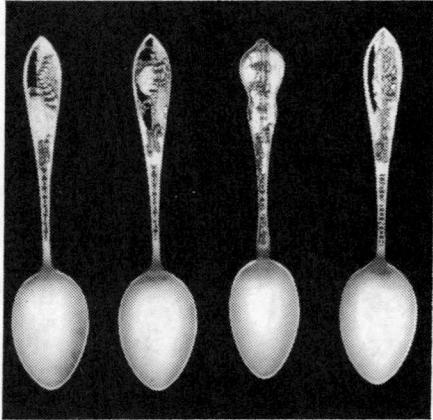

Souvenir Spoons by Robbins Company

bowl, Robbins Co. (ILLUS. center
right) 25.00
Cut-out handles depicting (left to
right): Hawaiian luau (feast);
primitive Hawaiian "grass hut"
home; Honolulu harbor with
modern (1915) view; plain
bowls, all by Robbins Co., each
(ILLUS.)........................ 30.00

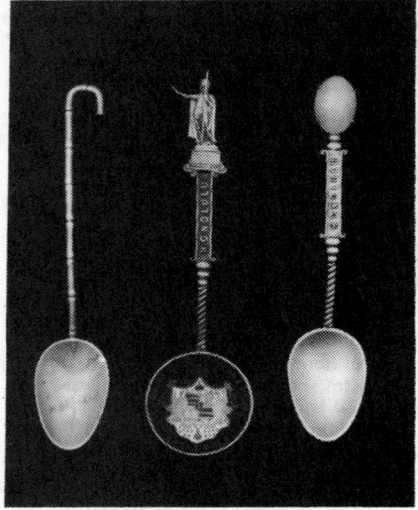

Spoons by Wichman

Sugar cane handle (ILLUS. left) 25.00
Statue of King Kamehameha I han-
dle terminal, "Honolulu" on
shank, enameled bowl w/Hawai-
ian coat of arms & motto (ILLUS.
center) 55.00
Jade oval on handle terminal,
"Honolulu" above twisted shank,
plain bowl (ILLUS. right) 40.00

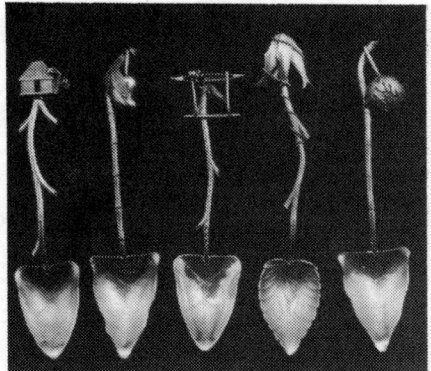

Spoons marked "Wichman Co."

Typical Hawaiian symbols on handle
terminals, left to right: grass hut,
mango, outrigger canoe, fishes
and breadfruit; stalk or sugar
cane shanks, taro leaf bowl,
except No. 4, all marked
Wichman Co., each
(ILLUS.) . . . . 35.00 to 45.00

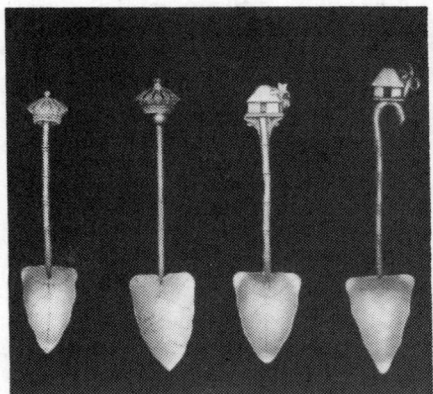

Crown & Grass Hut Spoons

bowl, Wichman Co. (ILLUS. center
left) 35.00
Grass hut, sugar cane shank, taro
leaf bowl, Gorham Co. (ILLUS.
center right) 32.50
Grass hut modeled in the full round,
sugar cane shank, taro leaf bowl,
Wichman Co. (ILLUS. right) 37.50

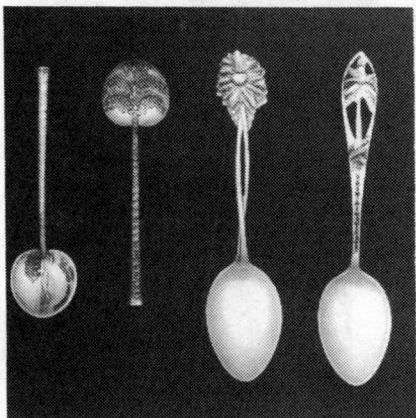

Hawaiian Palm Tree Spoons

Hawaiian palm tree w/scene in
bowl, controlled by H.C. Culman
(ILLUS. of front & reverse at
left) 35.00
Hawaiian palm tree w/entwined cut-
out shank, plain bowl, Robbins
Co. (ILLUS. center right) 35.00
Hawaiian palm tree cut-out handle,
"Honolulu" on shank, plain bowl,
Robbins Co. (ILLUS. right) 35.00
Kalakaua (Ruler of Hawaii 1874-91)
crown, sugar cane shank, taro
leaf bowl, Gorham Co. (ILLUS.
left) 30.00
Kalakaua crown modeled in the full
round, straight shank, taro leaf

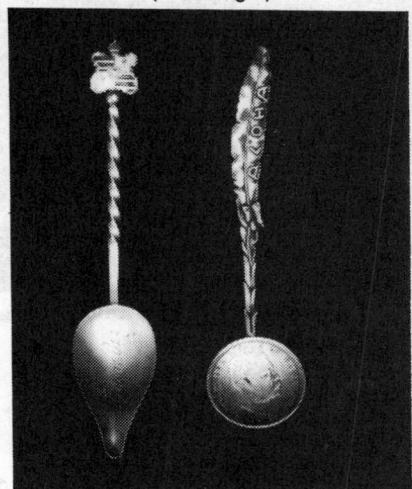

Unusual Spoons

Hawaiian coat of arms handle terminal, twisted shank, unusual bowl
engraved "Honolulu," probably
made in Hawaii (ILLUS. left) 40.00
Ti-leaf handle w/"Aloha," *hapaha*
(1883 Hawaiian quarter) bowl,
marked "Sterling/Shreve & Co."
(ILLUS. right) 80.00
"State of Hawaii" w/coat of arms,
motto, King Kamehameha I statue
& "1959" on handle terminal,
"State 50" & "Hawaii" on shank,
plain bowl, die cut by Hans Rei-

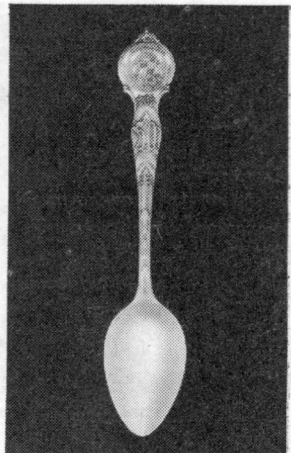

Hawaiian Statehood Spoon

chel from design suggested by the
author, E.J. Towle Company of
Seattle (ILLUS.)................. 35.00

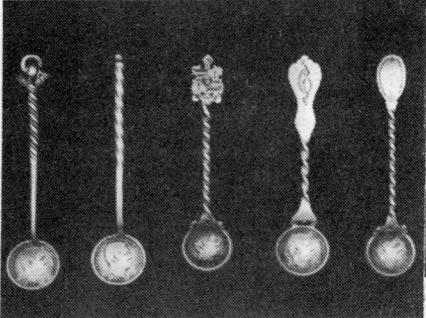

Salt Spoons with 1883 Hawaiian Dimes

Salt spoons w/*Um kaneta* (1883
Hawaiian dime w/portrait of the
ruler David Kalakaua) as bowl,
twisted handles in various forms,
center spoon marked "H.C." for
Harry Culman & others unmarked,
each (ILLUS.).............30.00 to 35.00

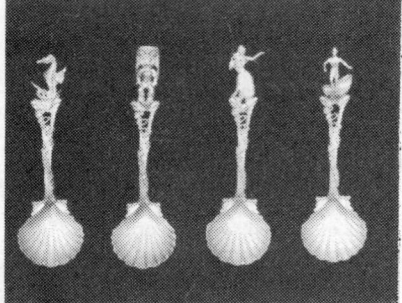

Salt Spoons with Shell Form Bowls

Salt spoons w/shell-shaped bowls &
figural handle terminals depicting
(left to right): sea horse, Hawaiian temple image (carved wood
original in Bishop Museum,
Honolulu), hula dancer & surf
rider; all controlled by Dawkins-
Benny & sometimes found mounted w/pinback clasps, each
(ILLUS.)....................20.00 to 30.00

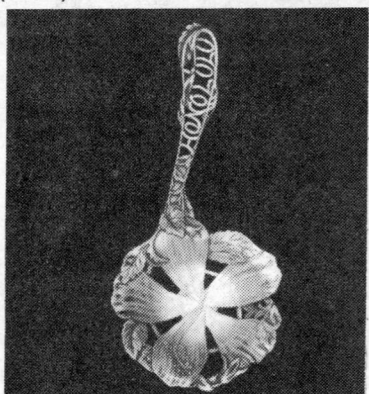

Bon Bon Spoon

Bon bon spoon, ornate cut-out
"Honolulu" handle, hibiscus (state
flower) cut-out bowl, made by
Watson Co. for Wall & Daugherty
of Honolulu (ILLUS.) 60.00

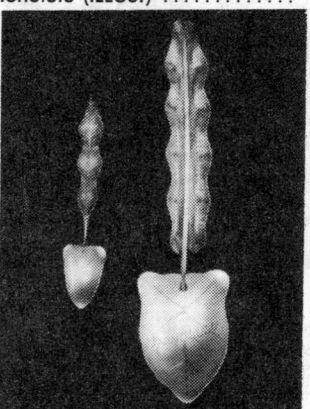

Spoons with Banana Leaf Handles

Banana leaf handles, taro leaf
bowls, unmarked but identified by
the late Chris Benny as Hawaiian-
made: 5" teaspoon size, $40; 8¾"
serving spoon size (ILLUS.
of pr.)........................ 85.00

(End of Special Focus)

SPELTER WARES

"Spelter" is a synonym for zinc and collectible spelter wares are simply cast zinc pieces cheaply produced during the 19th century in imitation of the more costly bronze figures and other decorations in vogue during that period.

Bookends, German Shepherd dog reclining on weighted base, 4 x 2½ x 5", pr. $40.00

Bookends, figure of Indian w/bow kneeling on rockwork base w/teepee and shrubbery at backplate, 7½" w., 8" h., pr. 195.00

Bust of a young lady, head tilted to side, upswept wispy curling hairstyle w/ornate comb, low neckline w/large rose pinned at shoulder by puffy sleeves, pedestal on marble base, 11" h. 125.00

Figure of a dancer, bare-breasted female in short tunic holding a gilt hoop, after a model by Fayral, on black marble base, 18" h. 605.00

Figure of a classical maiden holding a wine ewer in her arm, wine press at her side, black wooden plinth, unmarked, 21" h. 140.00

Inkwell, model of an elephant w/hinged back 75.00

Model of a stag, 3½" h., 6" l. 35.00

Model of a lion, signed "Coinchon," 8¾" l. 125.00

Model of a Russian Wolfhound dog, 13½" l. 195.00

SPINNING WHEELS

Flax Wheel

Flax wheel, maple, wheel w/turned spokes, base w/ring- and

baluster-turned splayed legs (ILLUS.) $260.00

Flax wheel, oak & maple, wheel w/elaborately turned spokes & clamps, on splayed turned legs, English or American, late 18th or early 19th c., overall 43" h. 198.00

Flax wheel, original blue paint, New York state origins 495.00

Flax wheel, walnut, wheel w/sausage-turned spokes, base w/sausage-turned legs joined by flattened stretchers w/initials & dated 1791 . . . . 412.50

Flax wheel, yellow-washed hardwood, wheel w/twelve spokes, base w/turned legs, complete 400.00

Spinning jenny, 2 wheels within framework of turned spindles 425.00

Wool wheel, hickory & ash, chipcarved details on block, pine bobbin box, 30¾" wheel, overall 42" h. 185.00

Wool wheel, walnut, wheel w/ten spokes on turned upright, 3-legged platform base, Pennsylvania, ca. 1840 . . . . 325.00

Wool wheel, wheel w/ten spokes on ring- and baluster-turned upright, base w/splayed legs, 44½" d. wheel, overall 59" h. 225.00

SPOOL, DYE & ALLIED CABINETS

"Dr. Lesure's Famous Remedies"

Creamery supplies, "DeLaval," wooden case w/lithographed tin front depicting cream separator & "Agency for DeLaval Cream Separators" & opening to drawers & shelves . . . . $430.00 to 500.00

Dye, "Diamond," oak case
w/lithographed tin front w/scene
of fairies 725.00
Dye, "Diamond," oak case
w/lithographed tin front w/scene
of woman dyeing clothing........ 950.00
Dye, "Dy-O-La," wooden case
w/lithographed tin front door &
back, 17 x 12½" 235.00
Dye, "Perfection," oak case w/em-
bossed tin front.........390.00 to 450.00
Dye, "Turkish," maple case
w/lithograhed paper insert front,
large .... 600.00 to 750.00
Needles, "Watson's," ash, 1-drawer,
w/original pulls & gold lettering,
15½ x 11 3/8", 2¾" h. 45.00
Sewing notions, "Daggett's Roll
Braid," walnut, 2-drawer, w/sten-
ciling, 24 x 8½ x 17" 220.00
Spool, "Beldings Silk," oak,
3-drawer 175.00
Spool, "Clark's O.N.T. Spool Cotton," oak, 2-drawer, original
brass pulls..................... 225.00
Spool, "Clark's," walnut, 6-drawer,
w/ruby glass drawer fronts 650.00
Spool, "J & P Coats," cherrywood,
6-drawer 650.00
Veterinary medicines, "Dr. Lesure's
Famous Remedies," wooden,
lithographed tin front panel
w/horse portrait (ILLUS.) 775.00
Veterinary medicines, "Humphrey's
Veterinary Specifics," tin,
w/lithographed scene of horses,
cows, sheep & other animals
above list of treatable
complaints 2,800.00

STANHOPES

Advertising Knife with Stanhope Lens

*Stanhopes are optical novelties, sometimes
referred to as "peephole" viewers, that take
their name from the English scientist, Lord
Charles Stanhope, who developed the tiny
(under 1/8" d.) round lens with two convex
faces enclosed in a metal tube to enlarge im-
ages concealed in bone, ivory or celluloid*

*jewelry and miniatures. Most were designed
as souvenir items of various locations such
as Niagara Falls, but some held religious im-
ages or risque views.*

Binoculars (miniature), mother-of-
pearl, w/view of Abraham Lincoln
& Lord's Prayer $40.00
Binoculars (miniature), w/view of
nude women................... 60.00
Binoculars (miniature), w/views of
the Graf Zeppelin in France & the
Empire State Building 110.00
Binoculars (miniature), ivory,
w/double panoramic view of
Gibralter 60.00
Cross, bone, w/portrait of a Russian
Orthodox church dignitary 70.00
Cross, sterling silver w/rhinestone
sets & chain, w/Lord's Prayer 25.00
Cross, wooden, religious scene of
the apparition at Knock Chapel,
Ireland 10.00
Hatpin, metal, w/six views of
Niagara Falls in head........... 45.00
Knife, pocket-type, mother-of-pearl
handle inlaid w/silver shield cen-
tered w/risque scene of girl
smoking cigarette in viewer, early
1900's, 3" l.................... 125.00
Knife, pocket-type w/corkscrew, ad-
vertising "Anheuser-Busch" beer,
w/portrait of Adolphus Busch in
viewer (ILLUS.) 135.00
Letter opener, celluloid, creamy
ivory, w/view of Blarney Castle
(Ireland) in handle 30.00
Letter opener, celluloid, w/view of
Niagara Falls in handle 30.00
Mechanical pencil, green metal,
w/German scene............... 12.75
Needle case, bone, ornately carved,
w/view of Niagara Falls, 5½" l. ... 75.00
Telescope (miniature), bone, w/view
of the Corn Palace, Sioux City,
Iowa 25.00
Telescope (miniature), bone, cam-
paign item, w/portrait of General
U.S. Grant, ¾" l. 45.00
Telescope (miniature), ivory, cam-
paign item, w/view of President
Garfield & family, ¾" l. 65.00

STEINS

Character, "Fat Man," pottery, full
figure standing & holding tools,
brown, yellow & grey garments,
by Steinzeugwerke, marked
"1566," early 20th c............$475.00

Von Maltke & Mephisto

Character, "Mephisto," porcelain, red, black, tan & brown garments, marked "Musterschutz" (copyright protection) on base, ca. 1900, hat feather repaired & chips on rim, ½ liter (ILLUS. right) 1,275.00

Character, "Monkey," seated position w/hangover expression on face & tail forming handle, brown animal wearing black top hat & holding pale blue scroll w/German proverb, by Steinzeugwerke, impressed "Germany" & "1261," early 20th c. 285.00

Character, "Munich Child," pottery, figure of child standing & holding stein & hops, tan & black garments, pewter-rimmed bust-form lid, marked "Joseph M. Mayer - Munchen," ca. 1900 . . . . 450.00

Postman & Sea Captain Character Steins

Character, "Postman," porcelain, ½ liter (ILLUS. left) 1,750.00

Character, "Sea Captain," stoneware, blue salt glaze, marked "LB. & C," ½ liter (ILLUS. right) 750.00

Character, "Soccer Ball," pottery, ball-shaped w/pewter-rimmed lid, tan & grey glaze, marked "Rochlitz Sporthaus," ca. 1900, ½ liter 325.00

Character, "Von Moltke," porcelain,

tan & brown, marked "Musterschutz," ca. 1900, small repaired chip, ½ liter (ILLUS. left col. 1) . .1,025.00

Glass, amber, enameled figure of lovely lady & man on front, applied amber handle, pewter lid & thumblift, dated 1898 on lid, 4" d., 7½" h. 272.00

Glass, amber, encased in openwork pewter, pewter lid, thumblift & handle, 2¾" d., 8½" h. 272.50

Glass, cranberry, encased in openwork pewter w/small ornate bust portrait medallions of lady, ornate pewter lid, thumblift & handle, 6¼" d., 17½" h. 695.00

Glass, cranberry, threaded, applied cranberry handle, pewter lid, thumblift & base, ½ liter 290.00

Glass, green, enameled multicolored shield, armor & crown & overall florals, applied green handle, pewter lid & thumblift, 5½" d., 14½" h. 562.00

Glass, milk white, enameled floral decor, applied milk white handle, pewter lid, thumblift & base, ca. 1800, ¼ liter 350.00

Majolica, tree trunk body, pewter lid & thumblift, 1 liter 160.00

Munich Stein

Mettlach, No. 2002, Munich stein, etched Munich maid & rooftop scene, inlaid pewter lid, ½ liter (ILLUS.). 450.00

Mettlach, No. 2049, etched chessboard & pieces, inlaid pewter lid, ½ liter 2,550.00

Mettlach, No. 2097, etched music scale, notes & lyrics, inlaid pewter lid, ½ liter 325.00

Mettlach, No. 2101, etched scene of man carrying stein & boar's head

on tray, inlaid rooftop on pewter
lid, ½ liter 450.00
Mettlach, No. 2247, relief-molded &
etched scene of peasants dancing,
inlaid pewter lid, 3/10 liter 275.00
Mettlach, No. 2277, etched scene of
Nurnberg, inlaid pewter lid,
½ liter 350.00
Mettlach, No. 2324, etched scene of
early football game, inlaid pewter
lid w/football finial, ½ liter 1,800.00
Mettlach, No. 2382, Thirsty Knight,
etched knight drinking in cellar
one side & riding off into night reverse, inlaid pewter lid, ½ liter .. 700.00
Mettlach, No. 2691, etched scene of
man w/guitar in wine cellar, inlaid pewter lid, master size,
2¾ liter 1,225.00

Mettlach Stein

Mettlach, No. 2807, etched tavern
scene, inlaid pewter lid, ½ liter
(ILLUS.)....................... 550.00
Mettlach, No. 2931, relief-molded
scene of man & woman w/verse,
inlaid pewter lid, ½ liter 385.00
Mettlach, No. 2959, etched scene of
boy bowling, inlaid pewter lid,
½ liter 750.00
Mettlach, No. 3089, "Diogenes,"
etched scene of Diogenes sitting
in barrel, signed Schlitt, inlaid
pewter lid, ½ liter 925.00
Mettlach, No. 3089, "Troll," etched
w/troll on barrel holding bottle,
signed Schlitt, inlaid pewter lid,
½ liter 1,950.00
Regimental, porcelain, "Ulan - 20th
Regiment - 1905-1908," 13" h.,
½ liter 625.00
Regimental, porcelain, "Hussar -
14th Regiment - 1908-1911,"
14" h., ½ liter 975.00

Regimental, porcelain, "Kurrisair -
4th Regiment, 1909-1912," 14" h.,
½ liter 1,075.00

Salt-Glazed Stein

Salt-glazed stoneware, 3 panels of
relief-molded figures, inlaid pewter lid, 4" d., 5" h. (ILLUS.) 175.00
Salt-glazed stoneware, cobalt blue
on grey w/incised scene of
roosters facing one another, pewter lid w/crest on thumblift,
½ liter 65.00

STRING HOLDERS

Cast Iron String Holder

*Before the widespread use of paper bags,
grocers and merchants wrapped their goods
in paper, securing it with string, and a string
holder, usually of cast iron, was a necessity
in the store. Homemakers also found many
uses for string and the ceramic or chalkware
wall-type holder became a common kitchen
feature. Also see ADVERTISING ITEMS.*

Advertising, "Jaxon Soap," cast
iron, model of a cauldron $65.00
Advertising, "S.S.S. for the Blood,"
cast iron, model of a cauldron 115.00
Cast iron, bell-shaped, hanging-
type 30.00

Cast iron, dome-shaped w/open-
work ovals, wire bail closure, old
black repaint, 4¾" h. 25.00

Cast iron, dome-shaped w/intersect-
ing arches, 5" h. (ILLUS. left) 35.00

Cast iron, dome-shaped w/vertical
slots, designed for tall cone of
string, 8½" h. (ILLUS. right) 30.00

Cast iron, model of a beehive
(ILLUS. center) 55.00

Cast iron, reticulated ball shape on
triangular base, old black repaint,
overall 6½" h. 25.00

Ceramic, head of an Art Deco
lady 45.00

Ceramic, head of a black bellhop ... 75.00

Ceramic, head of a black mammy .. 25.00

Ceramic, head of a cat w/red bow
tie 26.00

Chalkware, head of a black woman
wearing turban 45.00

Chalkware, head of chef .....14.00 to 20.00

Chalkware, head of Dutch
girl ....12.00 to 18.00

Chalkware, model of an apple,
pear, or a strawberry, each 18.00

Graniteware, ball-shaped,
w/advertising 12.00

Sewer tile pottery, modeled as a
grotesque face, 5¼" h. (chips) ... 250.00

Tin, canister form, hole in top
w/brass bars & cutter blade 130.00

SUNBONNET BABY COLLECTIBLES

Sunbonnet Babies Postcard

*Bertha L. Corbett, creator of these faceless
children, proved a figure did not need a face
to express character. Her pastel drawings appeared in "Sunbonnet Primer" by Eulalie Osgood Grover, published in 1900. Later Miss
Corbett did a series showing the babies at
work, one for each day of the week, and they
became so popular advertisers began using
them. Numerous objects including cards and
prints with illustrations of, or in the shape
of the Sunbonnet Babies are now being collected. Also see ROYAL BAYREUTH
CHINA.*

Bedspread, summer weight cotton,
Sunbonnet Babies in pastel
shades, lavender grid & border,
1930's $65.00

Book, "Sunbonnet Babies ABC
Book," by Eulalie Osgood Grover,
illustrated by Bertha Corbett, published by Rand McNally, 1934..... 42.00

Book, "Sunbonnet Babies Book," by
Eulalie Osgood Grover, illustrated
by Bertha Corbett, 1902....60.00 to 85.00

Book, "Sunbonnet Babies in Mother
Goose Land," by Eulalie Osgood
Grover, color illustrations by
Bertha Corbett, 1927, 7 x 5¾".... 45.00

Feeding dish, china, "Wash Day" ... 70.00

Pillow cover, appliqued Sunbonnet
Baby one side, Overall Boy
reverse, 1920's, 19" sq. 25.00

Plate, china, Sunbonnet Babies
decor, 9" d. 75.00

Postcard, "Going to Church" 9.00

Postcard, "Wash Day" 8.00

Postcard, "Motto" series w/singing
Sunbonnet Babies & "Should auld
acquaintance be forgot?,"
Bernhardt Wall, framed (ILLUS.) .. 16.00

Postcards, "Days of the Week" series, 1906 copyright by the Ullman
Mfg. Co., set of 7 .... 75.00

Postcards, assorted set of 18 .... 225.00

Print, "Cleaning Day," by B. L.
Corbett, framed 20.00

Print, "Fishing," by B. L. Corbett,
original frame 32.00

Print, "Wash Day," by B. L. Corbett,
bird's eye maple frame, 1904,
17 x 14"...................... 62.00

Quilt, 20 diamond-shaped blocks
appliqued w/Sunbonnet Babies
alternating w/solid color blocks,
dated 1932, 90 x 76"............ 350.00

SUNDIALS

Brass Sundial & Compass

Brass, Butterfield-type w/recessed
compass & folding bird gnomon,
base w/list of towns & their lati-
tudes, N. Bion, Paris, early 18th
c., 3" l. dial, in original fitted fish-
skin case (ILLUS.) $632.00

Brass, inscribed "Count None But
the Sunny Hours," 1920's 85.00

Brass, octagonal dial w/engraved
numerals surrounding sunface,
sickle & hourglass, border inscribed "As time & houres paffeth
awaye so douth the life of man
decaye," 8" w. (w/later engraving) 55.00

Brass, square dial w/engraved
numerals & folding gnomon, central recessed compass, mounted
on wooden base, 2½" sq......... 95.00

Lead, square plate w/incised clock
face, marked "Jas. Cutler, Salem,
1779," 19th c., 9¼" sq. 95.00

Pocket-type w/compass, in turned
wooden case, 2¼" d............ 30.00

TEXTILES

BATTENBURG LACE

Bedspread & pillow sham, Battenburg lace on net, pastel blue lining, 106 x 94" spread & 75 x 36"
sham, pr....................... $325.00

Collar, child's 7.50
Collar, lady's, circular, 8" w. 19.00
Doilies, 9" sq., pr. 15.00
Doily, 5" linen center, overall
11½" sq. 30.00
Doily, 14" d. 30.00
Dresser scarf, 46 x 16" 75.00
Dresser scarf, 52 x 18" 85.00
Piano scarf 95.00
Pillow sham, 80 x 27" 85.00
Table centerpiece, linen center,
wide Battenburg lace border,
26" sq. 85.00
Tablecloth, linen center, 11" w. Bat-
tenburg lace border, 35" d. 50.00
Tablecloth, linen center, 41" d. 95.00
Tablecloth, linen center, 12" w. Bat-
tenburg lace heart design border,
48" d.......................... 175.00
Tablecloth, coarse Irish linen center,
Battenburg lace heart & vintage
border, 52" d. 150.00
Tablecloth, linen center, Batteburg
lace vintage border, 62" d....... 140.00
Tablecloth, linen center, 68" d. 175.00
Tablecloth, linen center w/Batten-
burg lace butterfly border & Cluny
lace edging, 74 x 52" 155.00

Table runner, linen center, wide
Battenburg lace border,
46 x 16"...................... 85.00

BEDSPREADS

Crib-size, pink pongee on white silk
backing, French knot embroidery,
scalloped edges w/fold-down top
& delicate corners 45.00

Crib size, white marseilles cotton
fabric w/trapunto work 95.00

Candlewick embroidery on linen
w/overall pattern of small motifs
including birds, florals, stars &
castles, central reserve signed in
the weaving "Soy D. Josef Her-
nandez Moreno, Ano De 1790" ... 187.00

Hand-crocheted white cotton, filet
design of cherubs, 78 x 72" w/8"
flounce....................... 90.00

Hand-crocheted white cotton filet,
medallions & other designs, scalloped edge, 78" sq. 57.00

Hand-crocheted white cotton Popcorn in Diamond patt., 84" w. 155.00

Hand-crocheted ivory cotton filet,
block design, 90 x 80" 95.00

Hand-crocheted ecru cotton Popcorn
patt., w/fringe on 2 sides, 98 x
86" 225.00

Hand-crocheted white cotton filet,
scalloped edges, 104 x 92" 125.00

Hand-crocheted white cotton Popcorn & Star patt., scalloped edges,
deep fringe, large.............. 195.00

Linen cut-work & embroidery, ecru
net insets & embroidered silk
thread multicolored florals,
102 x 84"..................... 60.00

Linen cut-work & embroidery,
creamy ivory, lace medallion
center, extra large size 225.00

CHILDREN'S HANDKERCHIEFS

Acanthus leaf border, entitled "Les-
sons No. 6" w/seven poems,
printed in black on white cotton,
by the Boston Chemical Printing
Co., early 19th c. 185.00

Alphonse & Gaston cartoon characters, scene printed on cotton 35.00

Fireman, satin-stitched on cotton,
early 20th c. 4.00

Red Riding Hood & Wolf, scene
printed on cotton, 12" sq. 25.00

Regular Fellows, stamped on cotton,
1930's 15.00

Skippy, stamped on cotton, 1930's .. 22.50

Teddy Bear, embroidered on white
cotton........................ 10.00

Handkerchief book, "Hanker Ven-
tures," 6 cotton handkerchiefs
w/Disney characters & verses,
1939 .... 75.00

Comfortable, Colorful, Collectible
JACQUARD COVERLETS

Special Focus!

by John W. Heisey

Are you looking for something to collect---something colorful, limited in quantity yet almost individual in design---something somewhat unique? If you answer yes, let me suggest Jacquard coverlets.

Coverlets---those woven bed coverings---have been around for hundreds of years. But Jacquard coverlets are something new. They appeared in this country in the late 1820's and few were produced after the Centennial of 1876. In the years in between, they were quite the rage. Now they are antiques.

Quite frequently coverlets are thought of as quilts, but they aren't. There's a great difference. Quilts are usually made of two layers of thin cloth with a filling of batting or stuffing between, all sewn together with either plain or fancy stitches.

Coverlets are woven on a loom in either one thickness or two. If of only one layer or thickness, it is known as *single woven*. If two layers are used, it is *double woven*. The advantage of a double woven coverlet comes from its construction. The two layers are woven simultaneously, threads crossing back and forth from one layer to the other. This ties the fabric together and makes small air pockets which give added warmth without too much extra weight. Such heavier coverlets were usually made in states where English and Scots weavers worked---usually New York, Indiana, Illinois and Michigan. Dutch weavers in New Jersey likewise made double woven coverlets.

Single woven coverlets were generally the work of German and native-born American weavers and were usually made in Pennsylvania, Maryland, Ohio and a few in Illinois and Indiana, to name the main states.

Before Jacquard coverlets were made in America, housewives and professional weavers turned out single and double woven coverlets. However, the looms used for such cloth were simpler and cheaper. Due to their construction, threads strung on the loom (the

warp) could only be manipulated in groups. The *weft* or filling threads passed across the warp threads and made up the design as they skipped or "shot over" the warp threads. This was called an *overshot* coverlet and could be either a single or a double woven one. Since all threads were lifted only in groups, any design was geometric, being composed of squares or oblongs of colored threads.

Another type of coverlet made in America, usually in Pennsylvania, was called *summer and winter*. Although the weft threads skipped across the warp threads, they crossed over smaller numbers of such threads and the result was a more densely woven cloth. Like all coverlets, the colors were reversed on each side, but the designs were slightly different from the usual overshot ones.

With the introduction of the Jacquard mechanism, all this changed. Individual warp threads could now be lifted by small cords passing up to needles pressing against a piece of cardboard. Holes punched in this card controlled the lifting of warp threads, thus giving greater range and intricacy to the designs. At last the weaver could "draw" flowers, animals, birds, people, buildings, writing---anything seemed possible.

Inscriptions became practical and desired. Now the weaver could date and sign his work, weave in the client's name and note the location. The client could choose a prepared design, or the weaver could design a special one. The variety of border and interior patterns and designs, plus a large range of colors (natural dyes before the Civil War) resulted in almost one-of-a-kind coverlet masterpieces.

The Jacquard mechanism was costly and so were the cards. A weaver who bought such specialized equipment could not weave just when the spirit moved him. He had to weave almost full time to pay for his equipment. Housewives seldom were able to buy such an apparatus and could seldom work with it full time. Besides, women did not have the stamina or strength to use such equipment. As a result, men were the Jacquard coverlet weavers. The only woman known to have been a professional Jacquard coverlet weaver was Sarah Latourette (1822-1914) who worked in Fountain County, Indiana.

Early looms were narrow and coverlets were generally made in two strips sewn down the middle. Later looms were full size, so seamless coverlets could be made. The standard size of any coverlet, overshot or Jacquard, was for a double bed (almost 6 feet wide and at least that long or longer).

The first Jacquard coverlets featured a repetitive interior pattern, often of a quartet of flowers inside a wreath, or stars, or other repeated designs. The border designs were often of flowers, birds and rose trees or grapevines.

After the Civil War the emphasis changed. Large central medallions became popular. These were often surrounded by floral wreaths or with basketwork-like "filler" designs inside interior borders. The outer borders were usually geometric, floral, or of rope or Greek Key designs. Names, dates, weavers' names, plus the location of the weaver, were commonly placed in a block in each bottom corner, or along the bottom edge. Coverlets were made with fringes or without fringes woven in, or with a strip of woven fringed applied later.

The earliest dyes were natural (red from cochineal or madder and blue from indigo). Wool for the filling or weft was usually dyed, while the cotton warp was left natural or bleached white. When chemical dyes became available just before the Civil War, a whole new range of colors and hues became possible. Basic colors were supplemented by almost pastel hues of all shades.

Homespun and home-dyed yarn was used in the earlier coverlets. This yarn was often heavy and unevenly spun. Dyes didn't color it evenly at times either. Later coverlets used factory spun yarn which was thinner and more evenly spun. As a result, coverlets became lighter in weight and not as durable.

Starting and adding to a coverlet collection can be easy or difficult, depending on the goals of the collector. While overshot coverlets are fairly low-priced and readily available, it is difficult to date them. Jacquard coverlets, on the other hand, are usually signed and dated, and are higher priced as a result.

If the collector wishes to specialize in collecting Jacquard coverlets, there is almost unlimited choice. One can collect coverlets from only one area, county or state. The work of an individual weaver may make up a single collection. Patriotic, Masonic, floral, animal or other special designs may suggest a collecting goal. It's up to the collector to choose.

A collection may start with imperfect examples (coverlets with holes, stains or tears) which are usually cheaper to buy. Later, these less desirable pieces can be replaced by more perfect examples.

Surprisingly, many coverlet collectors are men, and they usually specialize in Jacquards. This may be because men were the weavers, or because of the intricacy of the equipment used in weaving.

Collectors can learn much about their collections by talking with antique dealers, other collectors, or weavers. They can join coverlet collectors' groups, such as the newly-formed Society of American Coverlet Collectors, and they can read and buy books about coverlets and coverlet weavers.

A collector might wish to begin a collection with a representative grouping of different types of coverlets. This would consist of at least one example of a single woven overshot, double woven overshot, single woven Jacquard, double woven Jacquard, summer and winter, and a Centennial coverlet. From this general beginning, he can branch out.

In collecting, know how much you can afford to spend on each type of coverlet. Remember that while they are antique, they may not appreciate in value as much as you hope. Get them for collecting's sake, not just for an investment. Set your top price and stick with it. This way you can keep your collecting urges under control. Your collection won't own you.

Properly caring for coverlets should be high on a collector's priority list. Since most coverlets can't be displayed all the time, they are usually packed away. However, every coverlet should be aired and/or displayed at least twice a year. When refolding them, try not to refold along the same folds as before. This can help prevent permanent creases and excessive wear of the fabric.

Don't wash coverlets unless absolutely necessary. Modern detergents may harm the fabric or cause colors to run or fade. If the cloth must be cleaned, it should be done by hand. Use a mild soap and squeeze—*don't wring*—the water out. Then spread flat in shade and turn frequently while drying naturally. Don't dryclean!

Storing coverlets in chests or drawers is suitable, but don't wrap them in plastic. Use plain tissue paper rather than newsprint when wrapping them, and keep them dry. Moth crystals or flakes can be used with safety. Think twice about having a coverlet repaired. While a good repair person can match up colors perfectly now, remember that yarns will fade, and the repair will show later. This can decrease the value of the coverlet.

Enjoy your collection and share it with others. Put it on display at various times and places. Go to see other coverlets on exhibit or display. Talk coverlets with other collectors, antique dealers and museum curators.

Visit museums that have coverlet displays and/or collections. For instance, you can see, examine and learn from the collection at Shelburne Museum, Shelburne, Vermont. An old Jacquard loom in working condition and a collection of more than 60 Jacquard coverlets from a number of weavers who worked in various states are displayed. The museum is open all year round.

Learn what you can about the coverlets in your own collection and about those you would like to obtain. You'll have more pleasure in collecting and you'll appreciate coverlets more. Remember, coverlets are a form of American folk art and a part of a vanishing breed. Do your best to preserve them for future generations.

(Editor's Note: A Checklist of American Coverlet Weavers, *published by the Colonial Williamsburg Foundation, Williamsburg, Virginia, was compiled by our author, John W. Heisey. This well-researched book about the early weavers in this country provides an excellent reference for the serious coverlet collector.*)

*   *   *   *   *

(Included in our illustrations are a number of coverlets on display at various museums. Since these museum-quality coverlets are not for sale, no values have been assigned. These illustrations have been included to give our readers a broad view of the various styles of Jacquard weave coverlets available.)

Coverlet by Robert Alexander

Single weave, 1-piece, blue wool, natural cotton, lacy-type floral medallions center, border w/peacocks on 2 sides & horse & rider w/dogs on other, corners w/house & signed "Robert Alexander, Canfield, Ohio," on display at Abby Aldrich Rockefeller Folk Art Center, Williamsburg, Virginia (ILLUS.)

Single weave, 1-piece, blue, red, olive green & gold wool, natural linen, lacy-type floral medallions center, border of peacocks on 2 sides & rider w/dogs other, corners w/house & signed "Robert Alexander, Canfield, Ohio," 80 x 70" $550.00

Coverlet with Eagles in Corners

Single weave, 1-piece, red, blue & lavender wool, white cotton, central medallion w/eagles in spandrels, vintage border, unidentified weaver, minor stains, 86 x 82" (ILLUS.) 350.00

Coverlet by Simon Riegel

Single weave, 1-piece, red & blue wool, white cotton, Pennsylvania Dutch sunburst medallions alternating w/floral medallions, paired birds & rose tree border, corners signed "Made by S. Riegel, German Township for Barbara Heck 1867," 92½ x 78", photograph courtesy of Abby Aldrich Rockefeller Folk Art Center, Williamsburg, Virginia (ILLUS.)

Coverlet dated 1856

Single weave, 1-piece, blue & red wool, white cotton, bold floral designs in squares center, floral border, corners signed "L.W. 1856," 96 x 80" (ILLUS.) 400.00

Coverlet by John Klinhinz

Single weave, 2-piece, blue wool, white cotton, scalloped circles alternating w/leafy spandrels cen-

ter, vases of flowers 2 sides & paired birds & rose tree borders, corners signed "John Klinhinz, Ohio, 1852," 81½ x 73", photograph courtesy of Abby Aldrich Rockefeller Folk Art Center, Williamsburg, Virginia (ILLUS.)

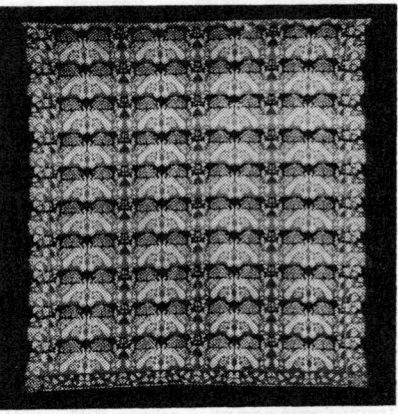

Paired Peacocks Coverlet by Pearson

Single weave, 2-piece, dark & light blue & red wool, white cotton, paired peacocks center (usually used on borders), floral vine border, corners signed "James Pearson, Medina County, Ohio, 1835," 82 x 78", photograph courtesy of Abby Aldrich Rockefeller Folk Art Center, Williamsburg, Virginia (ILLUS.)

Single weave, 2-piece, blue wool, white cotton, stylized floral medallions center, vintage border, unidentified weaver, 84 x 76" 325.00

Single weave, 2-piece, red & blue wool, natural linen, floral medallions center, lion & bird border, corners w/tree & "Zoar," 84 x 78" (minor wear & 3" section of fringe w/damage) 2,450.00

Single weave, 2-piece, compass star medallions center, bird border, corners signed "Coverlet, Wm. H. Van Gordon, Weaver, Covington, Miami Co., Ohio, 1851," 86 x 64" 850.00

Single weave, 2-piece, blue & red wool, white cotton, starflowers center, birds border, unidentified weaver, 86 x 76" 300.00

Single weave, 2-piece, red & blue wool, white cotton, unusual alternating block design center, houses & rose trees in 2 borders & paired birds & rose tree in third, corners signed "John Royer,

Coverlet by John Royer, Pennsylvania

New Holland, 1837," 87 5/8 x
84½", photograph courtesy of
Shelburne Museum, Shelburne,
Vermont (ILLUS.)

Sidewheeler Ships in Border

Single weave, 2-piece, blue wool,
white cotton, paired birds alternating w/pots of roses & grape
clusters center, stylized florals in
2 borders & sidewheeler ships
above signature "B. Lichty, Bristol,
Wayne County, Ohio, 1845" in
third, 88 x 74" (ILLUS.) 1,550.00
Single weave, 2-piece, rust-red
wool, white cotton, birds feeding
young in nest center, roses border, unidentified weaver,
88 x 76" 325.00

Single weave, 2-piece, blue wool,
white cotton, geometric medallions center, vintage & rose border, corners signed "Lima, Ohio"
(John Meily, 1842-50), 90 x 74" ... 325.00

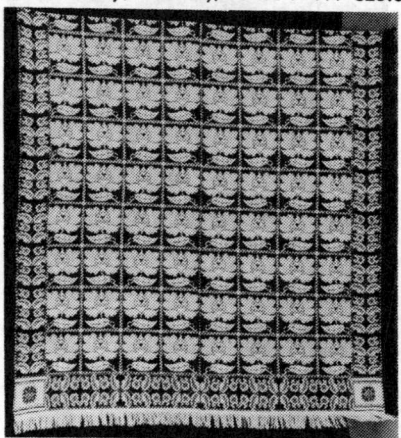

Bud & Leaf Pattern Coverlet

Single weave, 2-piece, blue wool,
white cotton, flower bud & leaf
design center, fern & floral border, corners w/sixteen-point compass rose trademark (often found
in a single location in south central Pennsylvania), ca. 1850, possibly Pennsylvania, 91½ x 85½",
photograph courtesy of Abby Aldrich Rockefeller Folk Art Center,
Williamsburg, Virginia (ILLUS.)
Single weave, 2-piece, blue, red &
green wool, white cotton, geometric medallion motifs center,
house border, corners signed
"Sidney, Shelby County, Ohio," attributed to Henry Enders, 93 x 72"
(minor wear & fading) 775.00
Single weave, 2-piece, red, blue &
olive green wool, natural cotton,
tile pattern & sunbursts center,
tree border, signed "David Brown,
C. Smellser 1844" in borders,
96 x 76" 400.00
Single weave, 2-piece, red, blue &
green wool, white cotton, snowflake medallions center, paired
birds & tree border, corners
signed "Made by John S. Goodman, Black Creek, Luzern Co. for
Hiram Keen, Penn.," 96 x 86" 400.00
Single weave, 2-piece, red & blue
wool, white cotton, compass flower & 4-rose cluster medallions
center, eagle & fruit tree inner
border, corners signed "Wove by
J.S. for L. Frank, 1840" (possibly

1840 Coverlet

Jacob Shalk), outer border of
stars, photograph courtesy of
Abby Aldrich Rockefeller Folk Art
Center, Williamsburg, Virginia
(ILLUS.)

Lion Trademark of Harry Tyler in Corners

Double woven, 1-piece, blue wool,
white cotton, compass & starflowers & flower medallions center,
picket fence & fruit tree border,
w/"Jefferson Co., N.Y.," corners
signed w/lion trademark of "Harry Tyler, 1840," 83 x 74", photograph courtesy of Shelburne
Museum, Shelburne, Vermont
(ILLUS.)
Double woven, 1-piece, blue & red
wool, white cotton, "Silver Dollar"
eagles center, double heart, floral
& leaf border, unidentified weav-

"Silver Dollar" Coverlet

er, ca. 1850, 91 x 77", photograph
courtesy of Shelburne Museum,
Shelburne, Vermont (ILLUS.)
Double woven, 1-piece, blue & red
wool, white cotton, "Silver Dollar"
eagles center, double heart, floral
& leaf border, unidentified weav-
er, 1837-1845, 92 x 77" 2,750.00

Patriotic Coverlet

Double woven, 1-piece, blue wool,
white cotton, patriotic motif
w/four "Liberty" heads in central
medallion & American eagle
w/shield & olive branch below "E
Pluribus Unum" banner in corners
w/"1863" & signed "Woven at Pal-
myra, N.Y. by Ira Hadsell" on 1
border edge, photograph courtesy
of Shelburne Museum, Shelburne,
Vermont (ILLUS.)
Double woven, 1-piece, red & gold-

enrod yellow wool, white cotton,
floral motif blocks center, house &
bird in tree border, corners
signed "Sold by S. Kuter and
Manufactured for---1839," 93 x 73"
(minor stains)................... 525.00

Double woven, 1-piece, blue wool,
white cotton, floral medallions
center, floral borders on 3 sides,
corners signed "Kuder & Hall, Le-
high County, Pennsylvania, 1861,"
96 x 74"...................... 385.00

"Foundation of Independence" Coverlet

Double woven, 1-piece, blue wool,
white cotton, large floral medallions center, Masonic emblems,
eagle & Independence Hall border, corners signed "Agriculture
and Manufacturers are the Foundation of our Independence, July
4, 1830" and w/name "Sarah
Holister" in outer borders, some
moth holes & stains, 98 x 76"
(ILLUS.)........................ 550.00

Double woven, 1-piece, blue wool,
white (darkened to light tan) cotton, floral rosette medallions center, Masonic emblems, eagles,
stars & Independence Hall border,
corners w/quote of General
LaFayette & w/name "A. Culver,"
101 x 84" 1,400.00

Double woven, 1-piece, blue wool,
white cotton, floral medallions
center, Masonic emblems, eagles &
Independence Hall border, corners
signed "Agriculture and Manufacturers are the Foundation of our
Independence, July 4, 1826, Genl.
Lafayette" & w/name of "M.

Brown" on border edge, 104 x 76"
(wear & ragged edges) 500.00

Leopard & Monkey Border Coverlet

Double woven, 2-piece, blue wool,
white cotton, tulip-stars & floral
designs center, leopard & monkey
border, unidentified weaver, 81 x
77¼", photograph courtesy of
Abby Aldrich Rockefeller Folk Art
Center, Williamsburg, Virginia
(ILLUS.)

Coverlet by Unidentified Weaver

Double woven, 2-piece, blue & red
wool, white cotton, floral block
design center, paired birds &
trees border, corners w/floral
rosettes, unidentified weaver,
82 x 74" (ILLUS.) 495.00

Double woven, 2-piece, blue & red

wool, white cotton, floral medallions center, bird & pine tree
border, corners dated 1840 &
w/owner's name, unidentified
weaver, 82 x 75" (minor wear) ... 510.00

Double woven, 2-piece, brick red &
blue wool, natural linen, floral
medallions alternating w/geomet-
ric motifs center, floral border,
corners signed "J. Klein, Hamilton
Co. Indiana, 1855," 83 x 76"...... 450.00

Double woven, 2-piece, blue & red
wool, white cotton, geometric design center, pine tree border,
unidentified weaver, 86 x 72" 450.00

Birds Feeding Young in Nest

Double weave, 2-piece, blue wool,
white cotton, birds feeding young
in nest & bowl of flowers center,
"Christian & Heathen" border,
w/"Piqua 1851" in outer edge,
unidentified weaver, 88 x 74"
(ILLUS.)........................ 875.00

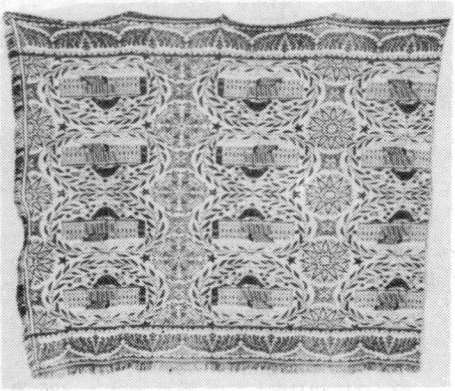

"Capitol in Washington" Coverlet

Double woven, 2-piece, red & blue
wool, natural linen, "Capitol in
Washington 1846" & buildings center, olive branch border, unidentified weaver, minor damage,
along top edge, 90 x 76"
(ILLUS.)........................ 650.00

Coverlet by Archibald Davidson

Double woven, 2-piece, blue wool,
white cotton, floral medallions
center, running stag & tree borders 2 sides & American eagles &
Capitol Building third, corners
signed "Ithaca Carpet Factory by
Archibald Davidson, 1838," 90½ x
80", photograph courtesy of Shelburne Museum, Shelburn, Vermont (ILLUS.)

Coverlet by James Alexander

Double woven, 2-piece, blue wool,
white cotton, floral medallions

center, patriotic borders w/Masonic emblems, eagles & monkeys on 2 sides & Independence Hall, eagles & monkeys on third, corners signed "American and Independence Declared July 4, 1776, Wove in 1840," by James Alexander, Orange County, New York, photograph courtesy of Shelburne Museum, Shelburne, Vermont (ILLUS.)

Double woven, 2-piece, blue wool, white cotton, birds feeding young in nest & bowls of flowers center, "Christian & Heathen" border, 94 x 80" (minor stains, wear & some moth damage)............ 425.00

Patriotic Emblems in Borders

Double woven, 2-piece, blue wool, white cotton, floral medallions center, patriotic emblems border, corners w/owner's name & "1822," attributed to James Alexander, Orange County, New York, 95 x 76½", photograph courtesy of Abby Aldrich Rockefeller Folk Art Center, Williamsburg, Virginia (ILLUS.)

Double woven, 2-piece, blue wool, white cotton, floral medallions center, American eagles border w/"Under This We Prosper" at edges of 2, corners w/"1846" above General Washington astride horse & "United We Stand - Divided We Fall" above "Washington, J. Cunningham, Weaver, N. Hartford, Oneida Co., N.York," photograph courtesy of Abby Aldrich Rockefeller Folk Art Center, Williamsburg, Virginia (ILLUS.)

Washington in Corners

Double woven, 2-piece, blue wool, white cotton, floral medallions center, American eagle border, corners w/"1840" above General Washington astride horse & "United We Stand - Divided We Fall" above "Washington, J. Cunningham, Weaver, N. Hartford, Oneida Co., N.York"............2,400.00

Owner's Name in Border

Double woven, 2-piece, blue wool, white cotton, American eagles & floral blocks center, animals, bird in tree, roosters & churches in borders w/owner's name, "Ann P. Cole, 1832," corners w/floral block, by David D. Haring, Bergen County, New Jersey, 96 x 72", photograph courtesy of Shelburne Museum, Shelburne, Vermont (ILLUS.)

Coverlet with Giraffes in Border

Double woven, 2-piece, blue wool, white cotton, florals center, roses & other flowers in 2 borders & giraffes, house & bird in tree in third, corners signed "1849 F. Hesse," photograph courtesy of Abby Aldrich Rockefeller Folk Art Center, Williamsburg, Virginia (ILLUS.)

Coverlet with Lions Border

Double woven, 2-piece, blue wool, white cotton, floral medallions & diamonds center, lions border, corners signed "B. French, Weaver, Waterville, 1835" & owner's name, photograph courtesy of Abby Aldrich Rockefeller Folk Art Center, Williamsburg, Virginia (ILLUS.)

(End of Special Focus)

PENNY RUGS

Table runner, round dark wool "pennies" embroidered w/yellow & shrimp pink sunburst centers & w/buttonhole-stitched yellow edges mounted on red felt center & applied w/border of wool tweed "tongues" w/bias edges, 28 x 15½" center, overall 38 x 23¼" 58.00

Table runner, red, mustard yellow & black wool rounds w/some black & white wool tweed, mounted on natural heavy homespun fabric, 39½ x 18½" 90.00

Table runner, multicolored wool felt "Liberty Bells" within red latticework on black ground, applied scalloped pink border, mounted on linen, 42 x 18" 115.00

Floor runner, brown & dark teal blue wool felt fishscale patt. w/embroidered center panel, mounted on burlap backing, 41 x 26½" 55.00

Floor runner, folk art type, conjoined wool felt circles, early 20th c., 60 x 26" 100.00

Floor runner, wool felt hexagonal medallions, faded dark colors, 125 x 28" 260.00

QUILTS

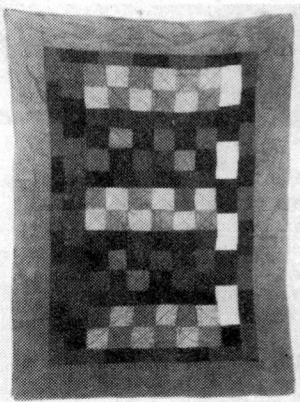

Amish Crib Quilt

Quilt, crib-size, pieced Block patt., blue, purple, black & grey square cotton patches in random pattern w/criss-cross quilting center & grapevine quilting at borders, Amish, ca. 1930, 46 x 34" (ILLUS.) 275.00

Quilt, crib-size, pieced Lightning Bolt Bars patt., red & green calico, 47 x 38" 275.00

Quilt, crib-size, pieced Nine Patch

patt. in several shades of blue, wide black cotton sateen border, Amish, 38½ x 35" 225.00

Quilt, crib-size, pieced Star of the East patt., lavender, pink, grey & beige cotton patches w/cable & flowerhead quilting, Amish, 20th c., 50 x 40" 770.00

Applique Quilt

Quilt, appliqued floral swag design, red, pink & green on white home-spun, some stains, 89 x 89" (ILLUS.) 550.00

Quilt, appliqued American Eagle center, bold vining floral border, solid red, yellow & teal blue cali-co on white field, 92 x 82" (minor stains) 600.00

Quilt, appliqued English Poppy patt., red & green on white, ca. 1900 . . . 350.00

Quilt, appliqued Princess Feather patt., slate blue & red on white field, tulip & vine border, ca. 1900 . . . . 650.00

Quilt, appliqued & pieced Rose Wreath patt., red & green on white field, red binding, ca. 1850 . . . . 325.00

Quilt, "linsey-woolsey," navy blue field worked w/wreaths, floral vine, blossoms & diagonal line quilting, reverses to beige, New England, ca. 1796, 100 x 96" 5,225.00

Quilt, pieced Cathedral Window patt., multicolored on unbleached cotton, 93 x 76" 550.00

Quilt, pieced Cherry Basket patt., multicolored prints w/goldenrod handles on white, 81 x 73" 265.00

Quilt, pieced & embroidered Crazy Quilt patt., multicolored velvet & satin, w/two centrally placed chicks in 3-dimensional clipped yarn, 64 x 54" 850.00

Joseph's Coat Pattern Quilt

Quilt, pieced Joseph's Coat patt., green, purple, blue, brown, red, orange & yellow cotton patches w/criss-cross, cable, diamond & Greek Key quilting, Mennonite, Lancaster County, Pennsylvania, ca. 1900, 81 x 81" (ILLUS.) 1,210.00

Quilt, pieced Postage Stamp patt., 1" square pastel cotton patches, 1930-40, 76 x 76" 335.00

Quilt, pieced Robbing Peter to Pay Paul patt., red cotton print on white, 86 x 76" 175.00

Quilt, pieced Snowball patt., blue circular cotton patches against grey, black & colorful diamond patt. ground within green inner & blue outer borders, w/decorative stitching in white thread, Amish, early 20th c., 72 x 57½" 385.00

Sunshine & Shadow Pattern Quilt

Quilt, pieced Sunshine & Shadow patt., purple, blue, grey, green, rose & pink wool & cotton patches, field w/criss-cross & borders w/flower basket quilting, Amish, Lancaster County, Pennsylvania, ca. 1890, 72 x 72" (ILLUS.) 1,100.00

Quilt, pieced Turkey Tracks patt., red, green & chartreuse tiny calico prints on white, quadruple border, queen size 310.00

SAMPLERS

American Sampler

Alphabets on homespun, signed "Joanna Prescott, Age 8, 1804," framed, 7 x 7" 295.00

Alphabets, Arabic numbers & cross-stitched design, signed "Florence Murphy, St. Roses Convent, May 1883," 11 x 8", framed........... 300.00

Alphabets above florals in shades of green, blue, gold & white on homespun fabric, signed & dated 1842, 18¼ x 10½", framed....... 300.00

Alphabets & large manor house flanked by stylized trees within meandering vine, signed & dated 1835, framed (ILLUS.) 330.00

Brick house flanked by willow trees w/verse above within meandering strawberry vine border, colorful silk stitches on linen, signed "Eliza Smith's Work, Sep. 18, 1821" (Carlisle, Pennsylvania), framed 1,045.00

Garden scene w/house & various decorative motifs within meandering strawberry vine border on canvas, signed & dated 1812, framed, 19¾ x 17¾" 2,200.00

TOYS

Also see ADVERTISING ITEMS, AVIATION COLLECTIBLES, BABY MEMENTOES, BANKS, BASEBALL MEMORABILIA, BROWNIE, BUSTER BROWN & CAMPBELL KID COLLECTIBLES, CANDY CONTAINERS, CARPET BALLS, CAT & CHARACTER COLLECTIBLES, CHILDREN'S DISHES, COCA-COLA COLLECTIBLES, DISNEY COLLECTIBLES, DOLL FURNITURE & ACCESSORIES, DOLLS, GAMES, KEWPIE ITEMS, MAGIC LANTERNS, MARBLES, OCCUPIED JAPAN ITEMS, PAPER DOLLS, PAPIER MACHE, SUNBONNET BABY ITEMS, WORLD FAIR & ZEPPELIN COLLECTIBLES and the "Special Focus" on TRAMP ART.

Airplane, pressed steel, single engine model "NX107," Boycraft, 1950's, 18" wingspan $75.00

Alphabet board (or wheel), tin & wood, letters & numbers on track, Foxy Toys, 1917 .... 32.50

Automobile, Ford Model A Coupe, cast iron w/nickel-plated wheels, Arcade (Freeport, Illinois, 1888-1946), 5" l................. 165.00

Automobile, 1938 Pontiac, cast iron, Arcade, 6" l.................... 300.00

Battery-operated, "Big Top Champ Circus Clown"................... 75.00

Battery-operated, "Bongo Monkey" 125.00

Battery-operated, "Bubble Blowing Bunny" 50.00

Battery-operated, "Bubble Blowing Popeye," Linemar, 11½" h. 300.00

Bell ringer toy, "Hello-Hello," telephone chimes, cast iron 1,750.00

Bell ringer toy, "The Landing of Columbus," cast iron, gilt finish .. 350.00

Bell ringer toy, "Uncle Sam & John Bull," cast iron, 1890's 650.00

Wooden Blocks

Blocks, alphabet-type, wooden, embossed & printed alphabet, num-

bers & scenes, 2" sq. cubes, set of
12 (ILLUS. of part) 25.00
Blocks, nesting-type, paper-covered
scenes of children, animals, Bible
& nursery rhyme characters, alphabet & numbers, Chaffee & Sel-
chow Publishers, New York,
1920's, set of 9 ....90.00 to 115.00
Blocks, puzzle-type, paper-covered
wood, animal pictures, McLough-
lin Bros. (1850-1920), set of 8 ..... 175.00
"Britains" (soldiers), British Motorcy-
clist Dispatch Riders, Set No. 200,
khaki uniforms, 4 pcs. 242.00
"Britians" (soldiers), Zulu War
scene, set of 50 .... 300.00
Bus, "Greyhound," die-cast metal,
Tootsietoy (Dowst, Chicago, Illinois, 1922-61), 6" l. 45.00
Bus, pressed steel, Buddy "L,"
1930's 450.00
Cannon on pr. 6-spoke wheels, cast
iron, unmarked, 9" l. 68.00
Cap bomb, "Admiral Dewey," cast
iron, 1898 .... 95.00
Cap pistol, "Bigger Bang," cast
iron 45.00
Cap pistol, "Eagle," cast iron,
1891 .... 55.00
Cash register, tin, "Little Folks,"
Humpty Dumpty pictured 55.00
Cement mixer, cast iron, painted
green, rubber tires, rear axle
controls the movement, Kenton
(Kenton, Ohio), ca. 1930, 9" l. ...1,320.00
Cement mixer, pressed steel,
Buddy "L," 1930's 325.00

Schoenhut Circus Buffaloes

Circus animal, Buffalo, wooden
(missing cloth mane), glass eyes,
Schoenhut, regular size (ILLUS.
right) 300.00
Circus animal, Buffalo, wooden,
carved mane, painted eyes,
Schoenhut, regular size (ILLUS.
left)........................... 250.00
Circus animal, Lion, wooden w/cloth
mane, glass eyes, Schoenhut,
regular size 425.00
Circus animal, Rabbit, wooden,
painted eyes, Schoenhut, regular
size 375.00
Circus performer, Clown, wooden,
Schoenhut, regular size 85.00

Circus performer, Crackerjack
Clown, wooden, Schoenhut, 8" ... 80.00
Circus performer, "Negro Dude,"
wooden, Schoenhut,
8¾" h..................150.00 to 250.00

Rare Hubley Circus Wagon

Circus wagon w/two-horse team,
driver & revolving monkey cage,
cast iron, original paint, Hubley
(Lancaster, Pennsylvania),
1919-26, 16" l. (ILLUS.) 19,800.00

Clockwork Bears

Clockwork mechanism bear, black
furry animal w/glass eyes, turns
head & opens mouth while hitting
a drum & cymbal, Ives, 14" h.
(ILLUS. left) 550.00
Clockwork mechanism bear, brown
furry animal w/muzzled open
mouth, turns head while walking,
Ives, 9½" l. (ILLUS. right) 412.00

"Dreadnaught" Coaster Wagon

Coaster wagon, wooden, w/iron-
rimmed wooden spoke wheels,
original finish & stenciling
"Dreadnaught Ball Bearing
Coaster," late 19th c.
(ILLUS.).......................... 700.00

Drum, color-printed tin sides, World
War I era military scenes, 8" d.,
8" h............................. 37.50

Dump truck, cast iron, red cab, blue
dumpster, white (crackled) rubber
tires on wheels, stamped "Champion" & "Geneva," ca. 1930,
7¾" l. 82.50

Fire "aerial" truck, pressed steel,
Buddy "L" 495.00

Fire hook & ladder truck w/bells &
headlights, pressed steel, white
side wall tires, original paint,
Structo, 18" l................... 175.00

Friction-type toy, "Jupiter Rocket -
JP7A," automatic upright landing,
Masuya Toy, Japan, 1960's,
9½" l. 95.00

Horse-drawn pony cart w/female
driver, cast iron, black w/yellow
wheels, ca. 1890, 10" l........... 330.00

Hotel set, "Pretty Village," chromolithographed heavy paperboard, 8 buildings, uncut figures,
McLoughlin Brothers (New York),
ca. 1897, set 175.00

Ice truck, Buddy "L" (Moline Pressed
Steel Company, East Moline, Illinois), pressed steel, 1930's...... 95.00

Ironing board, "Little Bo Peep,"
wooden 12.50

Jack-in-the-box, composition head
clown w/top hat, 1930's 215.00

Jazz dancers, "Jolly Jigger," Dutch
boy & girl, activated by depress-
ing their platform, Schoenhut
(Philadelphia, Pennsylvania),
patented 1910.................. 750.00

Jumping rope w/wooden soldier-
form handles, Germany.......... 12.00

Jumping Jack, lithographed paper
on wood, Harlequin boy, ca. 1885,
15" h. 95.00

Kitten, stuffed printed cloth, Arnold
Printworks, 1890's.........50.00 to 90.00

Log truck, cast iron, Hubley (Lancaster, Pennsylvania), 1940's 125.00

Motorcycle w/policeman driver,
"Champion," cast iron, blue paint,
white rubber tires, Champion
(Geneva, Ohio), ca. 1930,
7¼" l. 140.00

Noah's ark, painted wood ark
w/removable top & hinged door
on wheels & 31 composition
figures & animals, 29" l. ark, set
(ILLUS.)....................... 475.00

Noah's Ark

Pull toy, roosters (3) on platform
w/wheels, papier mache roosters
on spring legs, wooden base
w/iron wheels, worn original
paint, 8" h. 225.00

Lamb Pull Toy

Pull toy, lamb on wheels, wooly
leather lamb w/glass eyes (&
weight to activate bobbing action)
on cast iron wheels, Germany,
1890's (ILLUS.)................. 285.00

Tin Railway Station

Railway station, tin, "American
Flyer," green roof, red bricks,
grey base, 1940's, 5½ x 9½ x5½"
(ILLUS.)....................... 35.00

Record player, "Bing Pigmyphone,"
elves & Negro minstrels on sides,
w/six records.................. 225.00

Tramp Art

by Connie Morningstar

With more time than money, more patience than talent, they practiced a craft form since ignominiously dubbed Tramp Art. Few were tramps in the literal sense; most were whittlers more than artists. Believed to have originated in Germany or Scandinavia, the form appeared in America about 1870 and was practiced mostly in the eastern states until about 1930.

Tramp Art can be identified principally by its V-shaped, U-shaped, notched, or chip-carved wood. The usual tool was a pocket knife; the usual wood, the mahogany or cedar from old cigar boxes. Sometimes fruit crate pine was used instead. The box itself often formed the body to which flat, notched-edge strips were gradated shingle-style and glued or nailed together to create designs with a three-dimensional effect. This chip-carving and layering are unique to the craft and set Tramp Art apart from other forms of Folk Art.

Applied and inlaid decorations are other common features of the style. Geometric patterns dominate, but hearts and flowers, stars, bird and animal motifs were used also. Patriotic designs appear occasionally; religious symbols, infrequently. Vivid, garish colors dominate the few items that were painted. Additional decoration might include upholstery tacks, brass or porcelain knobs, beads, colored stones, or stained glass. As with all things, the decoration of such pieces followed the trend of the times--those of the Victorian era evidencing a "more is better" philosophy while pieces created in the 1920's were toned down considerably.

Full-sized furniture items with Tramp Art decoration are rare but include desks, bureaus, bedsteads, lounges, cupboards, and sideboards. Tall case clocks with Seth Thomas works are known. But by far, the most common items are small boxes and picture frames. Miniatures and doll furniture seem to lend themselves well to Tramp Art manipulation. Pin cushions, match holders, and wall pockets are common. Other items include plant stands, ferneries, small tables, lamp bases, banks, doll houses, and bird-

cages. Among the most unusual is a model of the Brooklyn Bridge. An intricately carved, mirrored-front wardrobe made in 1925 by Robert Meredith Jones of Granville, N.Y., carries his complete genealogy inscribed in Welsh inside the cabinet.

The Jones piece with its unmistakable identity is indeed a rarity. Very few pieces were signed, giving rise, no doubt, to their being attributed to anonymous craftsmen on the move. The term "Tramp Art" came into use during the 1940's--many years after the craft's popularity had waned. While it is quite likely that some practitioners were itinerant handymen, it is more logical to assume that Tramp Art was the work of anyone with time on his hands, a knife in his pocket, and an available source of scrap wood. Given the tempo of the times, it also seems reasonable that the craft persisted into the Depression years of the early 1930's.

Wood carving was an honored craft in northern Europe during the early part of the 19th century. Helaine Fendelman, the leading authority on Tramp Art, believes the form was introduced here by young German immigrants who were accustomed to travelling about in the old country, bartering their wood-carving skills for room and board. Once in America, they tended to follow the same pattern and, naturally, felt more comfortable in German-speaking communities of the East. While Tramp Art is found all over America, most of it seems to come from Pennsylvania and New York. That region remains the best hunting ground for the collector.

Little notice was taken of Tramp Art before Ms. Fendelman began her research in the early 1970's. Then suddenly pieces that had been relegated to the attic or junk pile became sought after objects and prices escalated accordingly. Shortly after her book came out in 1975, a full-sized Tramp Art decorated desk, when it could be found, would sell for $3500. An exhibit at the Museum of American Folk Art in New York in October of that year sparked interest further.

Unfortunately, no major auctions of Tramp Art have tested the market recently and prices vary widely, often within the same area. Rare, large, whimsical, or signed pieces can be expected to command the highest prices. A full-sized, tall case clock, for example, might bring $1500 or so; a plant stand such as the one shown on the cover, perhaps $1000. A Tramp Art drop-front, pedestal desk of Michigan provenance carried a price tag of $4750 at a Syracuse, New York, show last January. On the other hand, some of the more plentiful small boxes can be had for under $20.

Look for Tramp Art at garage sales, flea markets, and in small shops. It is seldom advertised. Specialty doll shops will be most likely to have miniature furniture and houses.

Tramp Art pieces need tender care. Their many-faceted surfaces collect dust readily so one might be tempted to use the vacuum. Experts advise against it, suggesting instead that nothing more powerful than a feather duster be used. Water should be avoided also because it might dissolve the glue.

The definitive work on the subject is Helaine W. Fendelman's *Tramp Art, An Itinerant's Folk Art* published by E. P. Dutton & Co., Inc., New York City, in 1975. Paperback copies are available now for $6.95 plus $1 postage from the author, 1248 Post Road, Scarsdale, NY 10583.

Museums with collections of Tramp Art include the Pennsylvania Dutch Folk Culture Society, Inc., Lenhartsville, PA; Abby Aldrich Rockefeller Folk Art Collection, Williamsburg, VA; The United States Tobacco Museum, Greenwich, CT; and the Museum of American Folk Art, New York City.

(Editor's Note: *Connie Morningstar, author of several books on furniture, including* Early Utah Furniture, *has also written numerous articles for various periodicals and is a regular columnist for* THE ANTIQUE TRADER WEEKLY *newspaper. Delving into the records of early cabinet makers, furniture shops and factories, she has become respected for her thorough research which enables her to write with accuracy, clarity and authority about American furniture styles and trends.*)

* * * * *

Tramp Art Box

Box, cov., 8 chip-carved layers on lid w/squared finial, 5 chip-carved layers on sides, varnish finish, 7" sq., 5½" h. (ILLUS.) $45.00

Tramp Art Box with Gold Paint

Box, cov., divided interior, 7 chip-carved graduated layers on lid w/applied pierced handle & 7 layers on sides, made from "King Edward" cigar box, painted gold, 8½ x 5", 5½" h. (ILLUS.) 15.00
Box, cov., diamond-shaped, chip-carved graduated layers on lid & sides, 9 x 7" 65.00
Box, cov., applied chip-carved triangular layers of wood on lid & sides, old dark finish, 11" l., 7½" h. 40.00
Box w/hinged lid, applied graduated chip-carved layers forming pyramid shape on lid & sides, red-orange stain, 8 x 5½", 5½" to top of layered lid 65.00
Box w/hinged lid, applied chip-carved diamond-shaped layers on lid & sides, w/mirror inside, 8 x 7" 35.00
Box w/hinged lid, color-printed paper scene within chip-carved framework on lid 40.00
Box w/three lift-top compartments above 2 short drawers w/white porcelain knobs, chip-carved pyramidal layers on top & chip-carved layered drawers 125.00

Unusual Tramp Art Chest

Chest w/hinged lid, oblong top lifting to stained pine interior, top & sides w/applied elaborate chip-carved layers of circles, stars, reel devices, etc., on turned bun feet, ca. 1930, 18" w., 15½" h. (ILLUS.) 990.00

Chest of drawers, child's playtime item, superstructure w/arch-top mirror in jig-sawed framework above oblong top over case w/three drawers, applied chip-carved layers on drawers, stiles & bracket feet, early 20th c., 9" w., 16" h. (some edge pieces missing) 77.00

Child's Chest of Drawers

Chest of drawers w/mirror, child size, superstructure w/double-arched cresting centered w/chip-carved layered roundels above shelf on curving supports over mirror; lower section w/oblong top above 2 short drawers w/applied layered roundels & pr. cupboard doors w/layered triangular sections forming panels, ca. 1930, 16" w., 11" deep, 33½" h. (ILLUS.) 1,430.00

Clock shelf w/drawer below, applied layers of chip-carving to supports & drawer front 37.50

Comb case, wall-type, plain crest above open box w/chip-carved layers on box 55.00

Comb case, wall-type, mirrored back, chip-carved layers on open box 135.00

Cross, w/Stanhope viewer center, applied circle & scroll cut-outs, dated "Aug. 21, 1879," 1¼" l. 65.00

Crucifix, cross w/four chip-carved layers applied w/metal figure of

Religious Tramp Art

Christ & heart form below, on square pedestal w/chip-carved edges & applied heart & roundel layers, 3-tier notched base, overall 20" h. (ILLUS.) 45.00

Doll cradle, jig-sawed edges & chip-carved layers on sides, 15" l. 35.00

Tramp Art Doll House

Doll house, 4-room, made from "California Prune" crate, roof w/empty thread spool as chimney, chip-carved trim on rooms & outside edges, applied chip-carved trim at glass windows, cream paint w/dark green notched trim, 14" w., 6½" deep, 16" h. (ILLUS.) 125.00

Doll house dresser, superstructure w/mirror, chip-carved layers forming framework & chip-carved layers on drawer fronts, 8" h. 40.00

Fraternal order (I.O.O.F.) blackball
ballot box, chip-carved layers &
Odd Fellows insignia 30.00
Jewelry box w/hinged lid opening
to tray in case w/drawer below,
applied pyramid-shaped chip-
carved layers, natural w/green
trim, 11 x 8½", 5½" h. 85.00
Magazine rack, wall-type, latticework design w/white porcelain
buttons & brass studs at
intersections 50.00
Match holder, wall-type, chip-carved
layers, overall 7¼" h. 40.00
Match holder, wall-type, w/hinged
lid, ornate backplate, chip-carved
layers highlighted w/colorful
paint 75.00

Bridge Model

Model of a bridge, possibly replica
of Brooklyn Bridge, 24" l., photograph courtesy of Barton Fendelman (ILLUS.)
Picture frame, 7 chip-carved layers,
original paint in medium to light
grey, 10 x 8", 2" deep 47.00
Picture frame, chip-carved layers,
varnish finish, 10½ x 8" 50.00
Picture frame, cross-bar style, chip-
carved layers, 11¼ x 10" 30.00
Picture frame, cross-bar style, fish-
shaped cut-outs at corners, gold
paint, 14 x 12" 15.00

Tramp Art Frame

Picture frame, chip-carved layers,
painted white, 14" sq. (ILLUS.) 55.00
Picture frame, chip-carved layers
w/star centered in crest & extended corners, natural finish,
15 x 12" 55.00

Frame with Velvet Insets

Picture frame, 8 panels, red velvet-
padded squares at corners & velvet oblongs enhanced by dia-
mond-and-scallop-carved sections,
15 x 12" (ILLUS.) 22.00

Frame with Eagle Crest

Picture frame, chip-carved layered
American eagle crest on cross-bar
style frame w/eaglets in upper
corners, 15½" w., 20½" h.,
photograph courtesy of Helaine
Fendelman (ILLUS.)

Picture frame, cross-bar type, chip-
carved layers, old brown, green &
rose paint w/gilt corner blocks,
22½ x 17½" (w/old chromolitho-
graph print of young boy) 175.00

Picture frame, chip-carved layers,
colorful paint, 20 x 16" 140.00

Picture frame, intricately chip-
carved layers w/scrolling crest
above compass star roundel &
tulip corners, applied stars,
diamonds & roundels overall,
highlighted w/inset red velvet
panels, 34" sq., photograph

Picture Frame with Tulip Corners

courtesy of Helaine Fendelman
(ILLUS.)

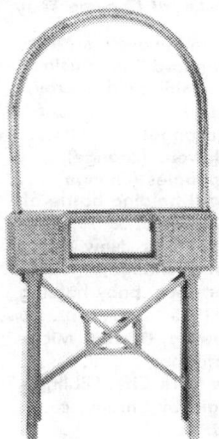

Tramp Art Imitative of Wicker

Plant stand, chip-carved layers forming pseudo wicker effect, 30" w.,
10" deep, overall 66" h., photograph courtesy of Helaine Fendelman (ILLUS.)
Secretary-bookcase, wooden w/chip-
carved details, 3-part construction:
upper part w/shaped cresting
centering bust portrait of maker
w/inscription "Made by C.E. Little-
field, 1896," above pr. glazed
cupboard doors opening to fitted
compartment; middle section w/pr.
glazed sliding doors; lower section
w/two pr. cupboard doors, each
centered w/chromolithographed
print of whimsical scene, signed
& dated 1896, 55½" w., 85" h.
(ILLUS.) 3,850.00
Sewing box w/inset 1½ x 1" velvet
pin cushion on top, chip-carved

Tramp Art Secretary Bookcase

layers on hinged lid opening to
well above conforming case
w/single drawer, painted black &
silver, 10 x 8", 8" h. 45.00
Shelf, wall-type, double picture
frame back, ornate, 24" w. 90.00
Wall box, hanging-type, applied
chip-carved heart & roundels,
sawtooth edges & inverted "V"
hanger, 8" w., 15" h. 85.00
Wall mirror, chip-carved layers
w/graduated stepped pyramid
form corners, 9½ x 7½" (contemporary mirror plate) 110.00
Wall mirror, outside sawtooth edge,
applied chip-carved diamond form
layers, 12¾" w., 10" h. 70.00

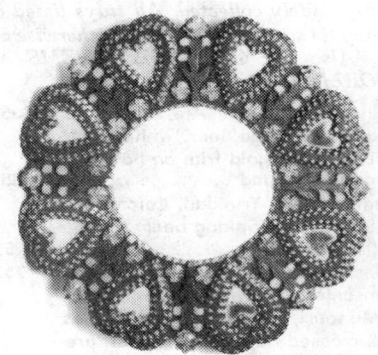

Mirror with Heart Details

Wall mirror, applied cut-out tree silhouettes & button details alternating w/chip-carved heart forms,
highlighted w/red & gilt paint &

w/original cigar box labels peeking out from beneath, 16½" d., photograph courtesy of Helaine Fendelman (ILLUS.)

Wall mirror, chip-carved layers w/applied layered star form top, 34 x 28" oval 50.00

Wall plaque w/mirror, comb & match box compartments, canted upper corners, applied cut-out silhouettes of fish, deer, squirrels, other animals & medallions above comb case & 1½" sq. match holder, double-layered chip-carved front, natural patina, 14" w., 24" h................... 145.00

(End of Special Focus)

TRAYS, SERVING & CHANGE

Tray with Steamship

Both serving & change trays once used in taverns, cafes and the like and usually bearing advertising for a beverage maker are now being widely collected. All trays listed are heavy tin serving trays, unless otherwise noted. Also see COCA-COLA ITEMS and WORLD FAIR COLLECTIBLES.

Billy Baxter Ginger Ale, bird $35.00
Blatz Milwaukee Beer, white lettering logo & gold trim on navy blue ground, round 35.00
Century Beer, Trinidad, Colorado, old couple drinking beer (change) 125.00
Chesterfield Cigarettes (change) 75.00
Consumer's Brewing Co., St. Louis, Missouri, Admiral Dewey, eagles & crossed flags border, oval, pre-prohibition 775.00
Crescent Brewing, Nampa, Idaho, factory scene w/rail cars & loading dock center, white lettering on reddish ground border 450.00
Cunard Steamers - "Carmania-Caronia," steamship center, light

overall wear, 38¾ x 28"
(ILLUS.)........................ 110.00
Dawson's Ale & Lager, lady & gentleman dining 125.00

DeLaval Change Tray

DeLaval Cream Separators, "The World's Standard," lady using separator, small child nearby, change (ILLUS.) ....50.00 to 65.00
Dick's Beer (change)............... 120.00
Dr. Pepper, kittens (change) 150.00
Dr. Pepper, puppies (change) 160.00
Dr. Pepper, girl holding bottle of soft drink...................... 135.00
Doelger (Peter) Beer, New York, factory scene (change).....75.00 to 90.00
Duesseldorfer Beer, baby holding bottle, ca. 1915 .... 350.00
East Side Brewing, Detroit, Michigan, Oriental boy 60.00
Ebling's, New York City, "Ebling's Extra," w/girl by Christy, ca. 1935, 13" d. 70.00
Edelweiss Beer, lovely girl, pre-prohibition ....125.00 to 175.00
Fehr's "Ambrosia" Beer, Greek mythological setting, "Nectar of the Gods," 1917................. 275.00
Garland Stoves & Ranges, G. Koehring & Bros. Hardware & Kitchen Furnishings, 878-82 Virginia Ave. (change) 40.00
Globe-Wernicke Sectional Bookcases, man, woman & bookcase (change) 40.00
Golden State Beer (Milwaukee Brewery of), San Francisco, chrysanthemum girl, pre-prohibition 225.00
Golden State Beer, San Francisco, 3 businessmen seated around table & drinking, pre-prohibition, 12" d.......................... 395.00
Gretz Beer, Philadelphia, man on highwheeler bike, post-prohibition 45.00

Hanley's "Peerless Ale," Providence, Rhode Island, "The Connoisseur," gentleman closely examining clear glass beer schooner, 1930's, 12" d. . . . . .75.00 to 115.00

Heptol Splits, cowboy on bucking bronco after C.M. Russell, 1904 (change) 225.00

Hire's Root Beer, soda jerk behind counter & slogan "Things is Getting Higher" 375.00

Hoefler Ice Cream, woman eating ice cream, oval 200.00

Home (F.P.) Lighting, woman beside stove (change) 45.00

Hommel's Champagne, 2 bottles of champagne, gold, pink & green, Shonk, Sandusky, Ohio, ca. 1905, 4" d. (change) 45.00

Hornell Brewing Co., Hornell, New York, "Hornell Lager Beer & Crystal Ale" 55.00

Hyroler Whiskey, man in top hat (change) 37.50

Indianapolis Brewing Co., elderly gentleman near fireplace drinking, pre-prohibition 95.00

Jacob Rupert Beer & Ale, 2 hands holding up beer mugs, 1930's, oval 50.00

Kenny (C.D.) Coffee, "America's Pride," flag raising at Valley Forge (change) 65.00

Lion Beer, Buffalo, New York, lion rolling barrel of beer 325.00

Lucky Lager Brewing Co., San Francisco, western Hemisphere (change) 25.00

Change Tray

Rockford High-Grade Watches, lady center, "For Sale by Engels & Drissen, Green Bay, Wis.," 5 x 3½", change (ILLUS.) 55.00

TWELVETREES (Charles) ARTWORK

Postcard collectors are familiar with the work of this artist and the comical children he portrayed. Charles Twelvetrees' illustrations also appeared in early 20th century advertisements, on magazine covers, calendar tops and frameable prints. While most postcards, many of them suitable for framing, can be found for under $10, his collectible prints are steadily rising in value.

Blotter, kids on front, 1932 . . . . $7.50

Bridge score pad, illustrated cover . . 4.00

Calendar, 1916, postcard size, Twelvetrees' child, signed 27.50

Calendar top, little girl 6.50

Fan, advertising, "666" salve, cardboard, quartette of children 6.00

Magazine cover, "Pictorial Review," 1925 . . . . 6.00

Print, advertising, "The 666 Clinic," little tots doctoring their dog w/salve, framed, 11½ x 9½" 12.00

Print, entitled "Let's Quit Fighting & All Be Friends," 10 children wearing hats of 10 countries fighting with one another, original frame, 21 x 9" 75.00

Print, entitled "The Doctor," framed 15.00

Print, entitled "I Am Some Bear," nude baby wearing bearskin hat & muff, dated 1914, framed 25.00

Print, entitled "Mother Ain't No Suffragette," framed 35.00

Print, untitled, scene w/little boy, original frame, 12½ x 9½" 18.00

Print, untitled, scene of child riding pig, blue background, matted & framed, 24 x 17" 60.00

Print, untitled, babies & pup blown into sky by March wind, framed . . 20.00

Prints: baby; baby w/bottle; baby & pet piggy; each framed, set of 3 . . . . 85.00

WOODENWARES

Maple Bowl

The patina and mellow coloring, along with the lightness and smoothness that come only with age and wear, attract collectors to old woodenwares. The earliest forms were the simplest and the shapes of items whittled out in the late 19th century varied little in form from those turned out in the American colonies two centuries earlier. Burl is a growth, or wart, on some trees in which the grain of the wood is twisted and turned in a manner which strengthens the fibers and causes a beautiful pattern to be formed. Treenware is simply a term for utilitarian items made from "treen," another word for wood. While maple was the primary wood used for these items, they are also abundant in pine, ash, oak, walnut, and other woods. "Lignum Vitae" is a West Indies species of wood that can always be identified by the contrasting colors of the dark heartwood and light sapwood and by its heavy weight, which causes it to sink in water. Also see ADVERTISING ITEMS, BOOTJACKS, CANES, CHARACTER COLLECTIBLES, COFFEE GRINDERS, COUNTRY STORE COLLECTIBLES, DECOYS, DOLL FURNITURE, FARM COLLECTIBLES, FRAMES, HORSE & BUGGY ITEMS, MATCH SAFES & CONTAINERS, NUTCRACKERS, SEWING ADJUNCTS, SHAKER COLLECTIBLES, SIGNS & SIGNBOARDS, TOYS, WRITING ACCESSORIES and YARN WINDERS as well as the "Special Focus" segments on TRAMP ART and WOOD SCULPTURE.

Apple butter scoop, hand-hewn from single block of wood $130.00
Ballot box, cherrywood, w/turned maple handle 50.00
Bowl, burl, 13" d., 3½" h. 475.00
Bowl, turned maple, old red-painted exterior, 14 x 13" warped d., 3½" h. 100.00
Bowl, curly maple, factory-turned, 15" d. 85.00
Bowl, maple, factory-made, 19" d. (ILLUS.) 65.00
Bowl, almond-shaped, hand-hewn from single block of wood, worn scrubbed finish, 24 x 15" 105.00
Box w/sliding lid, walnut, dovetail construction, applied molding at base, 9½ x 5", 5" h. 125.00
Bread (or pastry) board, round w/protruding handle, 1-board, 19" d., 3¾" l. handle 85.00
Breadboard, curly maple, 23¾ x 17" (minor split) 215.00
Breadboard, poplar, 1-board construction w/tombstone top drilled for hanging, 33½ x 16¾" 77.50
Bread cutting board, round, carved "Our Daily Bread" at border . . . . 60.00 to 70.00

Bucket, stave construction w/wire bandings, wire bail handle w/wooden grip, worn original yellow paint, 8" d., 6¼" h. 70.00
Butter carrier, cov., bentwood round, original green paint, wire bail handle w/wooden grip 140.00
Butter churn, dasher-type, stave construction w/bentwood arrow point locked lap bandings, original lid & dasher, old red-painted finish, 21" h. 600.00
Butter paddle, factory-made 15.00
Butter paddle, maple, hand-hewn rounded bowl & wide handle w/hook, 8¾" l 45.00
Butter paddles, factory-made, corrugated "Scotch Hands," 20th c., pr. . . . . 15.00 to 20.00
Butter worker, tiger stripe maple, hand-hewn w/bowl at right angle to handle, 10" l . . . . 85.00 to 125.00

Cake Board

Cake board, walnut or mahogany, carved w/figure of horseman astride steed within elaborately carved surround, signed "Watkins, New York," early 19th c., 11 x 11¼" sq. (ILLUS.) 825.00
Candle box w/sliding beveled edge lid, poplar, original red paint, 19th c., 14 x 8¾", 5¾" h. 145.00
Candle drying ladder, mortised & pinned construction, grid w/three rods, 18th c. 350.00
Canteen, stave construction, footed, w/wire bail handle, painted red, ca. 1810, 9" d. 175.00
Cheese curd breaker, wooden hopper w/wooden crank & roller w/wooden teeth, old red-washed stain 130.00
Cheese curd breaker knife, hand-carved sword shape, 25" l 75.00
Cheese drainer, pine, square canted

sides & bottom pierced w/round holes, 23 x 21", 8½" h. 250.00

Cheese drainer, Windsor-style, canted spindle sides & spindle bottom 495.00

Cheese ladder, mortised & pinned, 18th c., 26 x 10" 95.00

Cheese press, w/pulleys & wooden-toothed gear, painted red, 12" deep, 19" w., 46" h. 375.00

Cigar mold, 10-cigar, pine, 18 x 7", 2-piece . . . . .25.00 to 40.00

Cigar mold, 20-cigar, marked "Miller-Peters Mfg." & dated 1897, 2-piece 55.00

Clothes line frame (winder), hand-hewn hickory, mortised rod construction, 18th c. 57.00

Cookie roller, chip-carved pinned wooden yoke, hand-carved floral & leaf design roller, early 19th c. 155.00

Cuspidor, burl maple, hand-hewn round 350.00

Cutlery Tray

Cutlery tray, birch, nailed construction, canted sides, center divider pierced w/hand grip (ILLUS.). 40.00

Cutlery tray w/lid flaps, cherry-wood, dovetail construction, 2-compartment w/center divider handle pierced w/hand grip, 13 3/8 x 12½" (minor damage to one corner) 295.00

Dish drying rack, pine, mortised & pinned construction, 36 x 29" 450.00

Dough Bowl

Dough bowl, maple, 20 x 11" (ILLUS.). 140.00

Dough knife, pistol grip handle, 25" l. 75.00

Dough trough, cov, pine, canted sides & arched ends, old worn blue paint w/varnished finish, 32½ x 17½" 205.00

Dough trough on stand, cov., poplar, dovetail construction: trough w/canted sides & bread-board lid; stand w/scalloped apron & turned splayed legs; 42¼ x 23" 505.00

Drying rack, folding floor model, 3-section, mortised construction, each section 42" w., 57" h. 135.00

Grain measure, bentwood w/cast iron handles, old worn red paint, 14" d., 7½" h. (some edge wear & crack in bottom) 45.00

Grain measure, bentwood oak round, top band applied w/rose-head nails, fine patina, 15¾" d., 5¼" h. 125.00

Grain palette, hand-hewn w/two holes for thumb & finger, 6 x 17" 75.00

Grain shovel, hand-hewn from single block of wood, 34" l. 155.00

Jar, cov., turned treenware, low foot, old worn yellow varnish, attributed to Pease of Ohio, 6½" h. (1" age crack in lid) 110.00

Jar, cov., turned treenware, bulbous sides, collared base, domed lid w/well-shaped finial, brass wire bail handle, lightly speckled finish, attributed to Pease of Ohio, 8½" h. 425.00

Lemon squeezer, maple, factory-made w/two hinged section, ca. 1880 . . . . .45.00 to 60.00

Mallet, burl octagonal head, hickory handle, 8" l. 45.00

Muddler or toddy stick, birch, 1-piece 15.00

Noggin (pitcher hewn from single block of wood), maple, angled sides, 19th c., 4½" h. 175.00

Oven peel, pine, lollipop shape, 24½" l. 60.00

Oven peel, pine, hand-hewn from single block of wood, 18th c., 53" l. 220.00

Pail, cov., stave construction w/brass bandings & wire bail handle w/wooden grip, lid w/knop, natural finish, 5" d., 4½" h. 57.00

Pail, stave construction w/wire bandings & wire bail handle w/wooden grip, 14" d., 7" h. 20.00

Pantry box, cov., bentwood oval, single finger-lapped seam, original natural finish, 4" oval 80.00

Pantry box, cov., bentwood oval, 2 finger-lapped seam, original red-brown paint, 6" oval 145.00

Pantry box, cov., bentwood oval,
single finger-lapped seam, original natural finish, 7½" oval 140.00
Pantry box, cov., bentwood round,
straight-lapped seam w/copper
tacks, original green finish,
9½" d. 135.00

Pantry Boxes

Pantry boxes, cov., bentwood round
& oval forms, finger-lapped
seams, 4 round & 4 oval boxes
ranging from 5" to 13" d., set of 8
(ILLUS. of part) 770.00
Pencil box w/hinged lid, oak 18.00
Pie peel, short handle, beveled
edges, 1-piece 85.00
Piggin (stave-constructed bucket
w/single stave extending beyond
rim for form handle at side), bentwood bandings, natural finish,
10" h. plus handle 90.00
Porringer, cherrywood, hand-carved,
2-handled, carved rope-chain
around body & hex sign on base,
dated "May 14, 1846," 5" d. 140.00
Quilting frame, trestle base w/shoe
feet, natural finish 45.00
Rolling pin, tiger stripe maple, well-
shaped knob handles, 1-piece,
16¾" l. 70.00
Rundlet (or rum keg), oak, 4
wrought iron bands, green paint
over original red stain, 1770-1810,
6¼" d. 95.00
Salt box, hanging-type, pine, slant-
top lift lid & curving tab crest
pierced to hang, 11½" w.,
7" deep, 16¼" h. (old brown paint
removed & loose hinge) 65.00
Salt dip, burl, pedestal base,
19th c. 250.00
Sap bucket, original red
paint .... 20.00 to 35.00
Sap funnel, maple, turned,
1-piece 95.00
Scoop w/handle, hand-hewn dough
trough form bowl, 9¾ x 25" 125.00
Scrubbing stick, tiger stripe maple,
corrugated scrubbing board
w/arched handle carved from single block of wood, 18th c.,
37" l. 295.00
Shoulder yoke, hand-carved, old
blue paint 45.00
Soft soap dish, hand-hewn oblong,
18th c. 85.00

Soft soap scoop, hand-hewn from
single block of wood, long handle, 39" l. 250.00

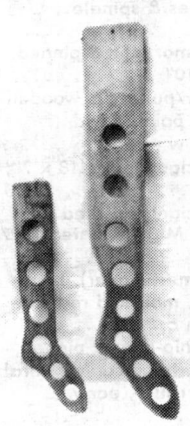

Stocking Stretchers

Stocking stretchers, child's or lady's,
maple, each (ILLUS.) 30.00
Stocking stretcher, man's, maple,
"size 11" .... 20.00 to 30.00
Sugar firkin (bucket of stave construction) w/lid, bentwood bandings & swing handle, natural
finish, 6½" d., 7" h. 72.00
Sugar firkin w/lid, bentwood bandings secured w/copper tacks &
bentwood swing handle, old blue
paint, 10" d., 11½" h. .... 120.00 to 150.00
Swigler (small keg that held a swig
of rum), lathe-turned w/lids fitted
in, dated "1776," 4¼" l. 185.00
Tallow skimmer, hand-hewn,
pierced, 18th c., 18" l. 220.00
Tape loom board, pine, lollipop
back, 22½" l. .... 120.00 to 175.00
Tankard w/hinged lid, stave construction w/wooden banding, old
dark patina, 11" h. 200.00
Trencher plate, turned treenware,
8½" d. (varnished) 80.00
Trencher platter, hand-hewn w/grip
handles on each end, deep dish,
24 x 14" oval, 3" deep 260.00
Washboard, mortised & pinned,
w/soap bucket 55.00
Water keg, stave construction,
finger-lapped bandings w/forged
rosehead nails, large square
wood peg & raised bung hole 285.00
Whetstone holder, hollowed log
w/hand-hewn cone-shaped end to
thrust in ground, w/wrought iron
belt-clip at top, w/whetstone 95.00

Wood Sculpture

THE CAROUSEL

by Tobin Fraley

Along with a multitude of inventions, the Industrial Revolution produced a working middle class with something usually reserved for the elite---recreational time. The 14-hour work day shrunk to ten hours and the weekend came into existence, leaving time for picnics, Sunday strolls through the park and, of course, a ride on the carousel. Thus, a new industry was born. An industry which produced over three-thousand carousels in this country and employed many of the country's most talented woodworkers and artisans.

Although the golden age of the carousel was between 1880 and 1930, the origins of this marvelous machine can be traced to 17th century France where, under the auspices of King Louis XIV, grand tournaments, called Carrousels, were held. At these great gatherings, skilled horsemen would perform astounding feats, including piercing a small stationary ring with their sword while at full gallop. Soon these events became important arenas to display one's talents and prowess and members of the aristocracy began having craftsmen construct practice machines.

These devices were usually round platforms with a few seats and a ring hanging from a pole just in reach of the riders. The platform would be turned by a servant or perhaps by a horse walking in a circular trench beneath the platform. It soon became apparent that this was not only practice for a serious event, it was a lot of fun and other members of the court wanted to give it a try.

Carousels were rather a small, sedate, popular ride until 1870 when Frederick Savage added the power of a steam engine to an English "roundabout." Soon larger and faster machines began to spring up throughout England and subsequently Europe. Savage was also responsible for developing a cranking system which allowed the carousel animals to go up and down.

About the same time Savage was producing his "roundabouts" for the Continent, an enterprising young immigrant, Gustav Dentzel, was deciding that the carousel business seemed like a good idea here in America. He built his first machine in 1867 and then converted his Philadelphia cabinet shop to a full-time carousel manufacturing company.

Several years later he was joined in this young industry, first by Charles Looff in Brooklyn, New York and then by Allan Herschell in North Tonawanda, New York. Each of these manufacturers developed distinct styles which would be mimicked by other companies yet to come.

Gustav Dentzel created elegant and realistic animals. He studied muscle structure and great care was taken to portray each animal accurately. The use of glass jewels as ornaments was almost non-existant for the main emphasis was on the animals themselves. When both Daniel Muller and Henry Auchy's Philadelphia Toboggan Company opened carousel businesses, they closely followed the style set by Dentzel. Today this type of animal is referred to as the Philadelphia style.

The flamboyant, highly ornate Coney Island style animals have their origins in the designs of Charles Looff. Wild manes, flying hooves and colored glass jewel ornaments were not uncommon on these animals. Under the guidance of Looff, carvers such as M.C. Illions, Charles Carmel, Solomon Stein and Harry Goldstein went on to create animals of their own distinct styles.

All of the carousels produced in Brooklyn and Philadelphia were made for permanent locations such as city parks or large amusement parks, so Allan Herschell of the Armitage-Herschell Co. decided to build smaller carousels for traveling carnivals. These animals were generally smaller, lighter and of a more rigid design that could be more readily transported. As traveling shows grew in popularity so did the demand for these smaller carousels. Other companies to produce these "country fair" type animals included C.W. Dare, also of North Tonawanda, and Col. Charles Parker of Abilene, Kansas. Although the Armitage-Herschell Co. was dissolved in 1898, Allan Herschell remained active in the carousel industry, first founding the Herschell-Spillman Co. with his brother-in-law, Edward, and then starting the Allan Herschell Company in 1915.

Carousel animals were usually made of Eastern Yellow Poplar or Basswood, both medium hardwoods, very good for carving and fairly durable. Animals were constructed like a box, hollow in the inside and generally made from about 30 separate pieces of wood. The head, legs and body were carved separately and then joined to form the entire figure.

With the onset of the Depression, the demand for frivolous items like carousels dropped off dramatically. By 1935, only three of the original companies were still in existance. Of these, two were still making carousels but they were the very simple machine-carved variety. By the late 1930's, because of technological advances in the metallurgical fields, all carousels were produced of cast aluminum. The master carvers still active were reduced to repair work or producing an occasional replacement animal. The skill of carving was no longer considered an art but a novelty. Most carvers eventually moved on to other endeavors or retired.

Because of the increasing popularity of movies during the 1940's and the advent of television during the 1950's, many amusement parks saw the public drift away from their traditional entertainments. High insurance costs and constant maintenance made the operation of these parks marginal at best. To draw crowds back, many of the outdated rides were replaced with brand new, more exciting ones. In many cases, the carousel--one of the oldest and most sedate rides--was the first to go.

Appreciation of these wood sculptures began in the late 1960's when people took a look under the dozens of layers of old paint and found, not just an old riding figure from an amusement park, but a work of art. In 1972, The National Carousel Association was formed to protect and preserve the remaining 300 operating carousels and to educate the public about this aspect of our cultural heritage. A few years later the American Carousel Society was created by a group interested in preserving the hundreds of individual figures which had been scattered throughout the country when carousels were dismantled and left to decay in old barns and storage areas.

Today there are thousands of carousel enthusiasts who travel around the country, riding, photographing, collecting and generally just enjoying these masterpieces of the past.

(Editor's Note: *Tobin Fraley's parents, Maurice and Nina, inherited a Dentzel menagerie carousel from his grandfather's amusement park in 1962. After extensive research, the Fraley family opened a restoration and sales gallery devoted exclusively to carousel animals. In 1975, Tobin began working with his parents and by 1979 the business had grown to such an extent that he opened his own restoration business, Tobin Fraley Studios, taking over the general repair work from Maurice and Nina. In 1983, Tobin wrote and published* The Carousel Animal, *a beautifully illustrated book available from Zephyr Press, P.O. Box 3066, Berkely, California 94703.)*

* * * * *

Prices are based on several factors, including the carver, type of animal, ornateness, size and condition. The carver and intricacy of the trappings are the major determining factors. A simple Allan Herschell Co. "jumper" (horse) may be worth about $1,600, while an outside row "armored" horse by the Philadelphia Toboggan Co. may be valued upwards of $30,000.

Over the past fifteen years, values of carousel animals have risen about 1400 per cent and they continue to climb but only buy a carousel animal you really like—not with an eye to investment—for there is no guarantee values will continue to grow.

With the rising prices of the past few years, there has been an ever-increasing number of forgeries sold. Generally speaking, most of these copies are very poor reproductions and are easily spotted by any knowledgeable carousel person. If you have doubts about any piece you consider purchasing, and if you have the time, contact a dealer in your area or send a photograph to one of the carousel organizations and get a second opinion.

Carousel figures listed below are separated into groups by the type of carousel they once adorned and the company that made them.

PERMANENT CAROUSELS

PHILADELPHIA STYLE

Dentzel
Horses:
 Outside row stander, w/figure
  on side, restored,
   ca. 1914 . . . .$22,500.00

Dentzel Outside Row Stander

Outside row stander, excellent
condition, park paint, ca. 1895
(ILLUS.) 13,800.00

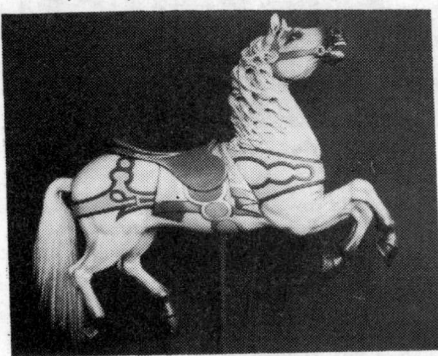

Dentzel Middle Row Jumper

Middle row jumper, restored,
ca. 1910 (ILLUS.) 8,500.00
Middle row jumper, very good
condition, paint removed,
ca. 1890 . . . . .6,900.00
Inside row jumper, good con-
dition, park paint, ca. 1905 . .5,400.00

Dentzel Rabbit

Rabbit, middle row, very good
condition, park paint, ca. 1905
(ILLUS.) 17,200.00
Boar (pig), good condition, paint
removed, ca. 1905 . . . . .7,200.00
Cat, middle row, restored,
ca. 1910 .17,900.00
Lion, w/figure on side, restored,
ca. 1905 .36,000.00

Philadelphia Toboggan Company
Horses:
Outside row stander, w/heavy
armor, very good condition,
park paint, ca. 1924 . . . . . . .32,000.00
Outside row stander, ornate,
very good condition, park
paint, ca. 1914 . . . . .16,350.00

Philadelphia Toboggan Co. Horse

Middle row jumper, good condition, paint removed, ca.
1912 (ILLUS.) 7,400.00
Inside row jumper, very good
condition, original paint,
ca. 1909 . . . . .6,350.00
Inside row jumper, good con-
dition, park paint, ca. 1924 . .4,700.00
Dog, St. Bernard w/cask, excellent
condition, factory paint, ca.
1909. . . . . .30,000.00
Sea horse, very good condition,
park paint, ca. 1911 . . . . .27,500.00

Daniel Muller
Horses:
Outside row stander, w/mili-
tary trappings, excellent condition, paint removed,
ca. 1907 . . . . .24,000.00
Middle row prancer, w/figure,
very good condition, original
paint, ca. 1910 . . . . .11,500.00
Middle row jumper w/flying
mane, good condition, park
paint, ca. 1907 . . . . .9,850.00

Daniel Muller Inside Jumper

Inside row jumper, good condition, park paint, ca. 1920
(ILLUS.) 5,600.00

CONEY ISLAND STYLE

Charles Looff
Horses:
   Outside row jumper, elaborate,
   good condition, park paint,
   ca. 1915 ....19,400.00
   Outside row jumper, w/Indian
   Head, good condition, paint
   removed, ca. 1914 ....16,000.00
   Outside row jumper, w/plaster
   rosettes, good condition,
   park paint, ca. 1887 ....12,500.00

Charles Looff Middle Row Stander

Middle row stander, excellent
   condition, paint removed, ca.
   1914 (ILLUS.) 9,400.00
Middle row jumper, w/glass
   jewels, good condition, park
   paint, ca. 1916 ....8,450.00
Middle row jumper, restored,
   ca. 1890 ....6,200.00
Inside row jumper, w/plaster
   rosettes, fair condition, paint
   removed, ca. 1890 ....3,900.00

Inside row jumper, restored,
   ca. 1916 ....6,750.00
Giraffe jumper, very good condition,
   park paint, ca. 1912 ....17,900.00
Goat, outside row, very good condition, paint removed,
   ca. 1915 ....14,500.00

Charles Carmel

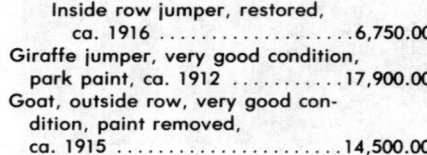

Charles Carmel Stander

Horses:
   Outside row stander, w/angel
   at saddle cantle, very good
   condition, paint removed, ca.
   1915 (ILLUS.) 17,750.00
   Outside row jumper, restored,
   ca. 1914 ....14,700.00

Charles Carmel Jumper

Middle row jumper, restored,
   ca. 1912 (ILLUS.) 8,200.00
Inside row jumper, excellent
   condition, paint removed,
   ca. 1914 ....5,700.00

Stein & Goldstein
Horses:
   Outside row stander, ornate,
   very good condition, paint
   removed, ca. 1916 ....16,600.00

Middle row jumper, very good
condition, original paint,
ca. 1917 . . . . .8,400.00
Inside row jumper w/cropped
mane, good condition, park
paint, ca. 1916 . . . . .3,950.00

M.C. Illions
Horses:
Outside row jumper w/fly-
ing mane, restored,
ca. 1922 . . . . .21,000.00
Middle row jumper, very good
condition, paint removed,
ca. 1922 . . . . .8,700.00
Middle row jumper, very good
condition, paint removed,
ca. 1908 . . . . .5,900.00
Inside row jumper, good
condition, paint removed,
ca. 1912 . . . . .4,770.00

COUNTRY FAIR STYLE

Herschell-Spillman
Horses:
Outside row jumper, very good
condition, park paint,
ca. 1912 . . . . .8,700.00
Outside row stander, armored,
very good condition, park
paint, ca. 1914 . . . . .14,900.00
Middle row jumper, very good
condition, park paint,
ca. 1912 . . . . .3,950.00
Frog, w/bow tie, very good con-
dition, park paint, ca. 1909 . . . . . .9,000.00
Pig, outside row, good condition,
paint removed, ca. 1912 . . . . .4,200.00
Rooster, restored, ca. 1907 . . . . . . .5,800.00

Spillman Engineering Corp.
Horses:
Outside row jumper, good con-
dition, park paint, ca. 1927 . .9,600.00

C.W. Parker
Horses:
Outside row large jumper,
w/flowers, good condition,
park paint, ca. 1920 . . . . . . .8,700.00
Outside row jumper, w/lariat
& gun, restored, ca. 1921 . . . .4,800.00

TRAVELING CAROUSELS

Armitage-Herschell
Horses:
Jumper, fair condition, park
paint, ca. 1894 . . . . .2,400.00
Jumper, restored, ca. 1896 . . . .3,600.00

Charles Dare
Horses:
Jumper, good condition, park
paint, ca. 1890 . . . . .3,100.00
Jumper, restored, ca. 1890 . . . .3,900.00
Jumper, good condition, original
paint, ca. 1895 . . . . .4,300.00

C.W. Parker
Horses:
Outside row jumper, fair condition, paint removed,
ca. 1914 . . . . .3,200.00

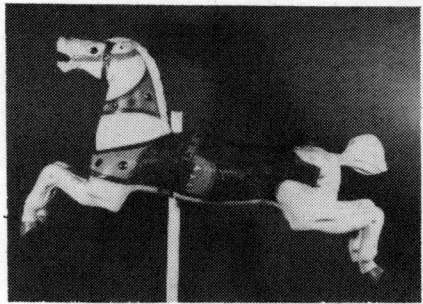

C.W. Parker Inside Row Jumper

Inside row jumper, restored,
ca. 1920 (ILLUS.) 3,450.00

Allan Herschell Co.
Horses:
Outside row jumper, fair condition, park paint, ca. 1928 . .2,100.00
Inside row jumper, fair condition, park paint, ca. 1928 . .1,450.00
Jumper w/metal legs & metal
head, good condition, paint
removed, ca. 1937 . . . . .1,400.00

Herschell-Spillman
Horses:
Jumper, fair condition, park
paint, ca. 1915 . . . . .2,300.00
Zebra, good condition, paint
removed, ca. 1915 . . . . .3,700.00

* * * * *

*The following organizations may be con-
tacted for further information about carousel
animals and carousels in general: National
Carousel Association, Attn: Gail Hall, P.O.
Box 307, Frankfort, IN 46041; American
Carousel Society, Attn: Mary Fritsch, 470
South Pleasant Ave., Ridgewood, NJ 07450;
Carrousel Art Magazine, Attn: Marge Swen-
son, P.O. Box 992, Garden Grove, CA 92642
and The Carousel Company, Attn: Susan Dar-
ran, 295 Fourth St., Oakland, CA 94607.*

(End of Special Focus)

WORLD FAIR COLLECTIBLES

There has been great interest in collecting items produced for the great fairs and expositions held through the years. During the 1970's, there was particular interest in items produced for the 1876 Centennial Exhibition and now interest is focusing on those items associated with the 1893 Columbian Exposition. Listed below is a random sampling of prices asked for items produced for the various fairs. Also see HISTORICAL & COMMEMORATIVE GLASS.

1893 COLUMBIAN EXPOSITION

Libbey Glass Paperweight

Paperweight, "Machinery Hall," scene under glass, olbong	$30.00
Paperweight, "Michigan State Building," scene under glass, signed Libbey Glass Co., 4 x 2" (ILLUS.)	45.00
Pin cushion, pewter model of lady's slipper dated & marked on sole	45.00
Plate, china, "Agricultural Building," blue transfer on white, Wedgwood, 8½" d.	37.50
Plate, china, "Horticultural Building," black transfer on white, Wedgwood, 8½" d.	35.00
Playing cards	50.00
Reverse painting on glass, "Ferris Wheel," pewter frame, oblong	38.00
Ring, sterling silver, description of Exposition in Spanish	65.00
Rose bowl, Amberina glass, crimped rim, etched souvenir, Libbey Glass Co.	345.00
Salt shaker w/original top, lay-down egg shape, white satin glass lettered "1893 World's Fair" in gold, Libbey Glass Co. (single)	90.00
Teaspoon, sterling silver, figural Art Nouveau nude lady handle, "Woman's Building" in bowl	50.00 to 70.00
Teaspoon, sterling silver, figural Indian handle, engraved Government Building in bowl	50.00
Teaspoon, sterling silver, bust of Columbus in relief on handle, ship in bowl	40.00
Thimble, sterling silver, w/history of the fair in Spanish	50.00
Tumbler, clear glass acid-etched w/various fair buildings or inscriptions, each	25.00 to 40.00
Tumbler, ruby-stained glass, etched souvenir	35.00 to 45.00

1901 PAN-AMERICAN EXPOSITION

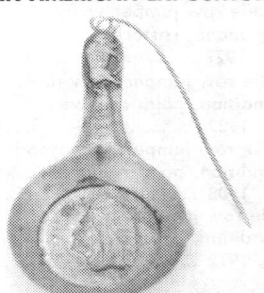

Fry Pan Stickpin

Bandana, silk, 20 different flags	32.50
Bell, brass	22.00
Bookmark, celluloid	15.00
Clock, model of a fry pan, 12" d.	140.00
Mug, china, Columbia Art Pottery Co.	75.00
Paperweight, clear glass, embossed buffalo	20.00
Ring, sterling silver, Gorham mark	45.00
Stickpin, brass, model of a fry pan w/bust of Indian in relief center, 2¾" l. (ILLUS.)	50.00
Teaspoon, sterling silver, Indian & buffalo handle, globe & "Pan-American 1901" engraved in bowl	35.00
Token, "Good Luck," w/Indian Head (1901) penny center, aluminum holder	16.50
Tumbler, clear acid-etched glass w/scene of Manufacturing & Liberal Arts Building	25.00
Watch fob, pot metal, bust of Columbus in relief against "Machinery Hall" background	20.00

1904 ST. LOUIS WORLD FAIR

Change tray, metal, pavilion & inset portraits of Napoleon & Jefferson, American Can Co.	30.00
Change tray, metal, advertising, "Red Raven"	75.00
Corkscrew	7.50
Cup, collapsible-type, nickel-plated brass, "Palace of Mines & Metallurgy"	18.50

Cup & saucer, demitasse, china, "Administration Building" decor, marked "Made in Germany" 60.00

Gyroscope, in original box 27.50

Handkerchief, silk, lithographed picture of Teddy Roosevelt, American Eagle & "Louisiana Purchase," embroidered flowers around edge, 12" sq., framed, overall 16" sq. .. 95.00

Letter opener, brass, figural cupid handle 40.00

Mirror, pocket-type, "Palace of Mines" 16.00

Model of a hatchet, clear glass, embossed "St. Louis World Fair" & engraved name 50.00

Mug, china, 1904 fair scenes decor, marked "Carlsbad, Austria" 38.00

Mug, graniteware, Napoleon, Jefferson, view of St. Louis & U.S. map decor 67.50

Picture, woven silk, portraits of Roosevelt, Jefferson & Napoleon, framed, 13¼ x 12" oval 175.00

Pinback button, multicolored fair scene, 1¼" d. 22.50

Plaque, Weller Art Pottery, portrait of William B. McKinley, 4½" 300.00

Plate, frosted & clear glass, reticulated border, "Festival Hall" & "Cascade Gardens" center, gold trim, 7¼" d. 30.00

Purse, leather w/braided leather handle, "Cascade Gardens" & date on front, 9¼ x 5" 50.00

Stamp box, pocket-type, aluminum 30.00

1904 Sugar Shell

Sugar shell, sterling silver figural mermaid w/shell handle, natural shell bowl w/colorful Indian portrait & inscribed "1904 World's Fair, St. Louis," 5½" l. (ILLUS.)...................... 45.00

Teaspoon, demitasse, silverplate, "Palace of Electricity" in bowl 20.00

1904 Tray

Tray, heavy tin, lithographed scenes of old West w/Indian in canoe & paddle wheeler on Mississippi, some wear, 16½ x 13½" oval (ILLUS.)....................... 75.00

Tumbler, pressed glass, clear 15.00

Vase, Weller Art Pottery, bulbous w/narrow neck & angular handles, lettered "St. Louis World's Fair 1904" one side & w/sport figure decor opposite, miniature size 120.00

Watch fob, advertising, "Dr. Pepper" factory scene 85.00

1933-34 CHICAGO WORLD FAIR

1933 World Fair Sugar & Creamer

Ash tray, brass, "Sky Ride" & "Fort Dearborn," ornate, 3½" sq. 10.00

Ash tray, graniteware, advertising, "Porcelain Enamel Institute," navy & light blue, fair logo, fraternal symbol & visitor's name, original felt label underside ......42.50 to 75.00

Change tray, metal, "Century of Progress - Fort Dearborn"........ 20.00

Creamer & cov. sugar bowl, scene of Carillon Tower, gold-etched ground, pr. (ILLUS.).............. 75.00

Crumb set: tray & blade; silver finish metal w/fair scenes, pr.......................10.00 to 18.00

Pinback button, "I Was There"...... 4.50

Plate, Fort Dearborn decor, marked
"Pickard," 7½" d. . . . . .15.00 to 20.00
Plate, Carillon Tower decor in
green, marked "Pickard". 20.00

World's Fair Playing Cards

Playing cards, galaxy logo, 53 fair
views, original box (ILLUS.) 25.00
Print, bird's eye view of fair,
w/"Goodyear" blimp & large
"U.S.S. Akron" dirigible,
19¾ x 13". 45.00
Tea set, pewter, "World's Smallest
Tea Set," in original box, 20
miniature pcs. 38.00
Teaspoon, silverplate, fair scene in
bowl, 6" l. . . . . .12.00 to 18.00
Teaspoon, silverplate, "Hall of
Science" in bowl 10.00
Thermometer, w/picture of Fort
Dearborn 15.00
Token, brass, "Ford," 1934 . . . .8.00 to 15.00
Token, "Lucky Penny" 12.00
Vase, china, bulbous w/small loop
handles, pale blue glaze, original
paper label, 3" h. 23.00
Water bottle w/metal lid, embossed
& dated clear glass. . . . . . . .15.00 to 22.00

1939 GOLDEN GATE INTERNATIONAL EXPO

Golden Gate Ash Tray

Ash tray, china, "San Francisco Bay
Golden Gate International Exposition," multicolored decor on
white, marked "Homer Laughlin
China," 6½" d. (ILLUS.) 18.00

Banner, felt. 20.00
Booklet, "Golden Gate Guide
Book" 9.00
Booklet, "Japanese Pavilion" 4.00
Ice pick . . . . :   19.00
Plate, china, multicolored decor on
white, marked "Homer Laughlin
China," 10" d. 42.50
Teaspoon, silverplate, Treasure
Island on handle 12.50
Token, aluminum, "Union Pacific". . .   5.00

WRITING ACCESSORIES

*Early writing accessories are popular col-
lectibles and offer a wide variety to select
from. A collection may be formed around any
one segment—pens, letter openers, lap desks
or ink wells—or the collection may revolve
around choice specimens of all types. Material, design and age usually determine the
value. Pen collectors, like the large fountain
pens developed in the 1920's but also look for
pens and mechanical pencils that are solid
gold or gold-plated. Also see ADVERTIS-
ING ITEMS, METALS and WORLD FAIR
COLLECTIBLES.*

FOUNTAIN & DIP PENS
Dip pen, mother-of-pearl handle,
14k gold nib $20.00
Aiken-Lambert fountain pen, silver
filigree, eyedropper fill 165.00
Belmont fountain pen. 5.00
Conklin fountain pen, brown
marbled, 1925 . . . .   30.00
Dunn "Dreadnaught Sea Thru"
fountain pen. 75.00
Holland "Royal Stylographic" foun-
tain pen, eyedropper fill 30.00
Moore "Midget" fountain pen 15.00
Parker "Challenger" fountain pen,
maroon marbled 40.00
Parker "Duofold" fountain pen,
lady's, green. 18.00
Parker "Duofold" fountain pen,
man's, Mandarin yellow, 1927 . . . 225.00
Parker "No. 33" fountain pen, gold
floral overlay, eyedropper fill 525.00
Parker "Parkette" fountain pen,
maroon marbled, 1950 . . . .   15.00
Sheaffer "Lifetime" fountain pen,
green marbled 30.00
Sheaffer "No. 5" fountain pen,
man's, sterling silver, 1916 . . . .   85.00
Swan "Model 44 ETN" fountain pen,
black, England 60.00
Wahl-Eversharp, Art Deco design,
black, 1929 . . . . 185.00

Waterman "Ideal No. 4 Ink-Vue"
  fountain pen, transparent copper
  & black, 1936 .... 18.00
Waterman "Patrician" fountain pen,
  pearl & black, 1929-34 .... 450.00

INK WELLS & STANDS

Swedish Silver Ink Stand

Brass stand, gallery tray holding 2
  cov. wells, w/attached pen tray .. 350.00
Brass well w/hinged lid, 3 agates on
  tray, 6" d. 150.00
Bronze well, model of a bird & egg,
  original porcelain insert, 5½" w.,
  3½" h. 295.00
Cast iron stand, ornate base fitted
  w/two clear pressed glass wells
  w/hinged lids above graduated
  3-slot pen rest, marked Judd,
  w/patent date of 1879,
  8 x 4 x 4" 115.00
Cast iron well, model of a Bulldog
  w/pipe in his mouth, glass eyes .. 175.00
China well, pink florals & green
  leaves & large butterfly on soft
  blue ground w/dark green edging, hinged lid, 3½" d.,
  3 5/8" h. 85.00
Cut glass well, clear w/diamond
  points & fan cutting, multi-rayed
  base, sterling silver dome-shaped
  hinged lid w/repousse, 2" d.,
  1¾" h. 100.00
Fulper pottery well, Art Deco style,
  lavender & blue matte finish 200.00
Glass well, clear, pear-shaped
  w/lift-off top, France 225.00
Pewter well, cylindrical, banded &
  ribbed sides, 5 quill rests 150.00
Pot metal well, model of fox head,
  marked J.B., 5" 85.00
Silver stand, formed as a rocky
  mound w/a swan in a pond in
  front of a tree trunk, rock-form
  waterfall forming inkwell w/lizard
  finial on inner cover, boulder-form
  sander shaking through fissures
  w/toad finial on inner cover, Pehr
  Fredrik Palmgren, Stockholm,
  Sweden, 1851, 11½" l. (ILLUS.)...2,750.00

Silver overlay well, square, clear
  glass w/silver overlay scrolls &
  foliage, figural moose on lid,
  marked Whiting, 4" sq. 495.00
Silverplate well, Bulldog w/glass
  eyes on footed base, framed by
  horseshoe w/figural cherubs,
  Meriden, 7 x 5" 425.00
Staffordshire pottery well, Robert
  Burns & Highland Mary, cobalt
  blue & orange decor, 4¼" 110.00

LAP DESKS

Fruitwood veneer, oblong case
  w/hinged leather-lined slant lid
  opening to fitted interior, patterned tulipwood banding
  throughout, 19th c., 21 x 17½",
  5" h. 440.00
Mahogany, oblong case banded
  w/maple & ebony, hinged lid
  opening to fitted interior
  w/leather-lined slanted writing
  surface, fitted drawer at side,
  George III period, England,
  ca. 1800, 20 x 10", 8" h. 242.00
Painted pine, oblong case w/hinged
  slant lid opening to interior w/sin-
  gle shelf, old dark "alligatored"
  painted finish, America, late
  19th c., 18½ x 17¼", 10" h....... 80.00
Rosewood veneer, oblong case
  w/hinged lid opening to fitted interior, w/single ink bottle marked
  "London Patent" on brass cap (&
  replacement bottle), England, late
  19th c., 16 x 9¾" 85.00
Walnut w/inlaid brass stringing, oblong case w/leather-lined slant lid
  opening to fitted interior, America, 19th c., 19¾" l., 10" deep,
  7" h...................100.00 to 250.00
Yew wood, oblong case opening to
  form writing surface, single drawer at side, inlaid decor, George
  III period, England, late 18th c.,
  13½" w., 6¼" h. 1,430.00

LETTER OPENERS

Advertising, "Yale Locks," metal,
  replica of padlock on handle 65.00
Brass, figural cupid handle,
  Victorian 65.00
Bronze, figural mermaid w/long
  flowing hair, 8¼" l. 58.00
Bronze, model of totem pole, "Seat-
  tle" souvenir, 8" l. 27.50
Bronze, pierced design of deer in
  handle 35.00
Celluloid, pencil replica 22.00
Celluloid, plain................... 2.50
Copper, figural Indian handle, sou-
  venir "Quincy, Massachusetts".... 18.00

Mother-of-pearl blade, sterling silver handle w/florals in relief 28.00

Letter Opener with Gold Fittings

Nephrite shaft fitted w/gold tip &
gold-embellished handle w/six
navette-shaped sections fitted
w/marquise-shaped lapis lazuli &
w/rock crystal cabochon cap,
10½" l. (ILLUS.) 1,980.00

Silver Letter Opener by Georg Jensen

Sterling silver, cylindrical handle
sculpted w/parallel ribbing,
designed by Sigvard Bernadotte,
executed by Georg Jensen,
11¾" l. (ILLUS.) 715.00
Sterling silver, Washington's Sword
patt., by Tiffany Studios, 8" l. 80.00
Wooden, tiger maple, curved blade,
inlaid handle, ca. 1870, 8¼" l. ... 20.00

PAPER CLIPS
Brass, Victorian lady's hand
w/elaborate cuff, hallmarked "Birmingham," England, 19th c. 120.00
Bronze, model of duck's head w/bill
as clip, signed "Hershey" 85.00
Celluloid, w/advertising 8.00

POUNCE SANDERS
Cherrywood, lathe-turned, attributed
to Shakers, Mt. Lebanon, New
York, 3 1/8" h. 65.00
Maple, lathe-turned, incised bands,
18th c., 1-piece w/plug in base ... 50.00
Wooden, lathe-turned, dark blue
painted bands decor, 18th c. 85.00

WAX LETTER SEALS

Musical Seal

Bone seal, carved fist handle
w/twisted stem, "M.C." seal,
2¾" h. 15.00
Brass seal, figural Duke of Wellington handle, 3 1/8" h. 45.00
Cut glass seal, paperweight-type,
multicolored latticino swirl ribbon
encased in clear facet-cut
knobbed stem .... 75.00 to 150.00
Gold & champleve enamel musical
seal, enameled colorful flowering
foliage each side, stem wind set
w/colored pastes, Swiss, early
19th c., 1½" h. (ILLUS.) 1,760.00
Sterling silver seal, plain, w/initial
"M" 28.00
Wooden seal, carved model of
horse's leg w/silver horseshoe &
Gothic letters "I.C.," old darkened
finish, 3 7/8" h. 145.00

YARD LONG PICTURES

*These out of proportion colorful prints were
fashionable wall decorations in the waning
years of the 19th century and early in the 20th
century. They are all 36" wide and between
8" and 10" h. A wide variety of subjects, ranging from florals and fruits to chicks and puppies, is available to collectors. Prices for these
yard-long prints have shown a dramatic increase within the past two years. All included in this list are framed unless otherwise
noted.*

Autumn Leaves $50.00
Battle of the Chicks, signed Ben
Austrian, 1902 .... 80.00 to 115.00
Cats 90.00
Cherries, signed Guy Bedford 55.00
Chickens, signed Van
Vredenburgh 135.00
Chrysanthemums, signed Maude
Stumm 80.00
Dogs, signed Guy Bedford 75.00
Dog Show Prize Winners, signed
Van Vredenburgh 95.00
Easter Greetings, signed Paul de
Longpre 65.00
Kittens, signed Van Vredenburgh ... 125.00
Puppies w/bowl of milk 165.00
Roses, signed Paul de Longpre,
1903 .... 85.00
Roses, signed Ella Barbour 48.00
Roses & snowballs................ 50.00
Shaggy Dogs, signed 105.00

YARN WINDERS

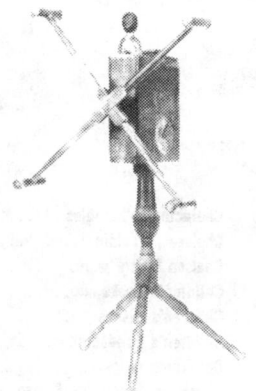

Floor Model Yarn Winder

Floor model yarn winder, wooden, 4-arm reel, rectangular box containing a carved & painted wood figure of a black man which "forces" the hinged door open & drops again when winder turns, on turned standard w/three raking turned legs, American, 3rd quarter 19th c., 35½" h. (ILLUS.) 2,750.00

Floor model yarn winder, wooden, 4-arm reel w/chip-carved arms & original geared clicker mechanism, 2 arms detach for yarn removal, shoe-foot base, Wisconsin, 19th c., 41" h. 250.00

Niddy noddy hand reel, maple, turned center post, mortised arms, 17¾" l................... 85.00

Niddy noddy hand reel, wooden, hand-carved 60.00

Table model yarn "swift," maple, clamp-on type, turned finial, adjustable arms 275.00

ZEPPELIN COLLECTIBLES

Glass Candy Container

Not all airships are zeppelins. Only those lighter-than-aircraft ships that resemble the huge cigar-shaped type designed by Count Ferdinand von Zeppelin of Germany are referred to as zeppelins. The famed "Graf Zeppelin" was the only airship to fly around the world, making this trip in twenty-one days, eight hours, in 1929. Used for commercial flights from 1933 until 1937, its success led to the building of the "Hindenburg," the largest airship ever built. The tragic crash of the "Hindenburg" on May 6, 1937, ended regular airship service.

Badge, "Graf Zeppelin" employee, enameled $140.00

Bank, cast iron, model of "Graf Zeppelin," 6½" l. ....125.00 to 195.00

Book, "The Giant Airships"......... 9.00

Book, "The Nations of Europe - Causes & Issues of the Great War," by Charles Morris, 1914, cover w/dirigible by L.T. Meyers.. 15.00

Candy container, clear glass, replica of U.S. Airship "Los Angeles" (ILLUS.) ....140.00 to 175.00

Chocolate mold, tin, zeppelin-shaped........................ 285.00

Cocktail shaker, chrome-plated, zeppelin-shaped............... 550.00

Flag, silk, small size attached to 2" l. zeppelin replica 48.00

Harmonica, zeppelin decor on top .. 45.00

Letter, mailed via "Graf Zeppelin," United States to Germany, October 28, 1928 .... 25.00

Lunch box, tin, color-printed scene of children waving to zeppelin airship 198.00

Magazine, "Der Wochne," Sonderheft, Berlin, 1908, photographs, large 45.00

Photograph, "U.S.S. Akron" airship, in duralumin frame, ca. 1931 ..... 325.00

Pill box, cov., silverplate, embossed zeppelin decor 32.50

Pin, metal replica of "Graf Zeppelin," lettered "Round the World, 1929, DLZ127," 2" l. 65.00

Poster, chromolithograph of zeppelin flying over castles on the Rhine, E. Montaut, Paris, 35 x 17" 137.50

Poster, "Zeppelin - Fahrten Uber See Und Land," w/scene of zeppelin over water & land, "Hamburg-Amerika Line" 550.00

Propeller, wood & metal, probably from the airship "U.S. Los Angeles" 550.00

Toy, cast iron replica of "Graf Zeppelin," original propellers, 11½" l. 700.00

Toy, sheet metal replica of zeppelin, repainted grey, 24" l............. 145.00

Watch fob, duralumin, replica of airship "Akron" 40.00

INDEX

*Denotes "Special Focus" section

Acanthus, 472; Acorn, 472; Acorn Burrs, 472; Advertising & Souvenir Items, 473; Age Herald, 473; Apple Blossoms, 473; Apple Blossom Twigs, 474; Apple Tree, 474; Australian, 474; Autumn Acorns, 474; Aztec, 474; Basket, 474; Basketweave Variant Candy Dish, 474; Beaded Cable, 474; Beaded Shell, 475; Beads & Bells, 475; Beauty Bud Vase, 475; Big Fish Bowl, 475; Birds & Cherries, 475; Blackberry, 475; Blackberry Block, 475; Blackberry Bramble, 476; Blackberry Spray, 476; Blackberry Wreath, 476; Blossom Time, 476; Blueberry, 476; Bo Peep, 476; Bouquet, 476; Broken Arches, 476; Butterflies, 476; Butterfly & Berry, 476; Butterfly & Fern, 477; Butterfly & Tulip, 477; Captive Rose, 477; Carolina Dogwood, 478; Caroline, 478; Chatelaine, 478; Checkerboard, 478; Cherry (Dugan), 478; Cherry (Fenton), 478; Cherry (Millersburg), 478; Cherry Chain, 479; Christmas Compote, 479; Chrysanthemum,

479; Circled Scroll, 479; Cobblestones Bowl, 479; Coin Dot, 479; Coin Spot, 480; Comet, 480; Cone & Flute, 480; Constellation, 480; Coral, 480; Corn Bottle, 480; Corn Vase, 480; Cornucopia, 480; Cosmos, 480; Cosmos & Cane, 481; Country Kitchen, 481; Crab Claw, 481; Crackle, 481; Crucifix, 481; Cut Arcs, 481; Dahlia, 481; Daisies & Drape Vase, 482; Daisy & Lattice Band, 482; Daisy & Plume, 482; Daisy Block Rowboat, 482; Daisy Wreath, 482; Dandelion, 482; Dandelion, Paneled 482; Diamond, 483; Diamond & Rib Vase, 483; Diamond & Sunburst, 483; Diamond Concave, 483; Diamond Lace, 483; Diamond Point Column, 483; Diamond Ring, 483; Diving Dolphins Footed Bowl, 484; Dogwood Sprays, 484; Dolphins Compote, 484; Double Dutch Bowl, 484; Double Star, 484; Double Stem Rose, 484; Dragon & Lotus, 484; Dragon & Strawberry, 485; Drapery, 485; Embroidered Mums, 485; Estate, 485; Fanciful, 485; Fantail, 485; Farmyard, 485; Fashion, 485; Feather & Heart, 485; Feather Stitch Bowl, 486; Feathered Serpent, 486; Fenton's Basket, 486; Fenton's Flowers, 486; Fentonia, 486; Fern, 486; Field Flower, 486; Field Thistle, 486; File & Fan, 486; Finecut & Roses, 486; Fine Rib, 487; Fisherman's Mug, 487; Fishscale & Beads, 487; Fleur De Lis, 487; Floral & Grape, 487; Floral & Wheat Compote, 487; Flowers & Frames, 487; Flute, 487; Flute & Cane, 488; Four Seventy Four, 488; Frolicking Bears, 488; Frosted Block, 488; Fruit Salad, 489; Fruits & Flowers, 489; Garden Path, 489; Garland Rose Bowl, 489; Gay Nineties, 489; God & Home, 489; Goddess of Harvest, 489; Golden Harvest, 489; Good Luck, 490; Grape & Cable, 490; Grape & Gothic Arches, 492; Grape & Lattice, 493; Grape Arbor, 493; Grape Delight, 493; Grapevine Lattice, 493; Greek Key, 493; Hammered Bell, 493; Harvest Flower, 494; Hattie, 494; Headdress Bowl, 494; Heart & Vine, 494; Hearts & Flowers, 494; Heavy Grape (Dugan), 495; Heavy Grape (Imperial), 495; Hobnail, 495; Hobstar, 495; Hobstar